Birnbaum's Great Britain

A BIRNBAUM TRAVEL GUIDE

Alexandra Mayes Birnbaum
EDITORIAL CONSULTANT

Lois Spritzer
Editorial Director

Laura L. Brengelman
Managing Editor

Mary Callahan
Senior Editor

David Appell
Patricia Canole
Gene Gold
Jill Kadetsky
Susan McClung
Associate Editors

HarperPerennial
A Division of HarperCollins*Publishers*

To Stephen, who merely made *all* this possible.

 For information address HarperCollins*Publishers*, 10 East 53rd Street, New York, NY 10022.

FIRST EDITION

ISSN 0749-2561 (Birnbaum Travel Guides)
ISSN 0896-8683 (Great Britain)
ISBN 0-06-278192-8 (pbk.)

95 96 97 98 ❖/CW 5 4 3 2 1

Cover design © Drenttel Doyle Partners
Cover photograph © Charlie Waite/Tony Stor[illegible]
Cottage, Broadway, Cotswolds, England

Contents

Getting Ready to Go

Practical information for planning your trip.

The Cities

Thorough, qualitative guides to each of the 19 cities most often visited by vacationers and businesspeople. Each section offers a comprehensive report on the city's most compelling attractions and amenities—highlighting our top choices in every category.

Diversions

A selective guide to active and/or cerebral vacation themes, pinpointing the best places to pursue them.

Exceptional Pleasures and Treasures

For the Experience

For the Mind

For the Body

Directions

The most spectacular routes and roads; most arresting natural wonders; and most magnificent castles, manor houses, and gardens—all organized into 16 specific driving tours.

Glossary

Foreword

This guide is dedicated to Grace and Herbert Mayes, my parents. Though this dedication indicates the affection and regard in which my husband, Steve Birnbaum, and I held these two extraordinary people, it is also a recognition of the relationship they had with the British Isles.

My father was an Anglophile of the most fanatic sort. I hardly consider it coincidental that his initials were HRM, my mother's name was Grace, and my sister and I were named Victoria and Alexandra. When my father retired, he and my mother chose to move to London. This provided them with the closest possible proximity to all things English—and Scottish and Welsh.

And so it was no mere coincidence that this guide to Great Britain was the initial volume of a new phase in our travel guide series. Whereas our first half-dozen guides covered rather broad geographic areas, this in-depth examination of Great Britain was our first guide to treat the world's most popular travel destinations in considerably greater detail than is possible in an "area" book. Our guidebooks to France, Italy, Ireland, Spain, and Portugal have continued this direction, and we have also further expanded to include guides to individual cities—including a guide to the city of London.

We have tried to create a guide to Great Britain that's specifically organized, written, and edited for today's demanding traveler, one for whom qualitative information is infinitely more desirable than mere quantities of unappraised data. We realize that it's impossible for any single travel writer to visit thousands of restaurants (and nearly as many hotels) in any given year and provide accurate appraisals of each. And even if it were physically possible for one human being to survive such an itinerary, it would of necessity have to be done at a dead sprint and the perceptions derived therefrom would probably be less valid than those of any other intelligent individual visiting the same establishments. It is, therefore, both impractical and undesirable (especially in a large, annually revised and updated guidebook *series* such as we offer) to have only one person provide all the data on the entire world. Instead, we have chosen what we like to describe as the "thee and me" approach to restaurant and hotel evaluation and, to a somewhat more limited degree, to the sites and sights we have included in the other sections of our text. What this really reflects is personal sampling tempered by intelligent counsel from informed local sources.

This guidebook is directed to the "visitor," and such elements as restaurants have been specifically picked to provide the visitor with a representative, enlightening, and, above all, pleasant experience. Since so many extraneous considerations can affect the reception and service accorded a regular restaurant patron, our choices can in no way be construed as an exhaustive guide to resident dining. We think we've listed all the best places, in various price ranges, but they were chosen with a visitor's enjoyment in mind.

Other evidence of how we've tried to tailor our text to reflect modern travel habits is apparent in the section we call DIVERSIONS. Where once it was common for travelers to spend a foreign visit seeing only the obvious sights, today's traveler is more likely to want to pursue a special interest or to venture off the beaten path. In response to this trend, we have collected a series of special experiences so that it is no longer necessary to wade through a pound or two of superfluous prose just to find exceptional pleasures and treasures.

Finally, I also should point out that every good travel guide is a living enterprise; that is, no part of this text is carved in stone. In our annual revisions, we refine, expand, and further hone all our material to serve your travel needs better. To this end, no contribution is of greater value to us than your personal reaction to what we have written, as well as information reflecting your own experiences while using this book. Please write to us at 10 E. 53rd St., New York, NY 10022.

We sincerely hope to hear from you.

Alexandra Mayes Birnbaum

ALEXANDRA MAYES BIRNBAUM, editorial consultant to the *Birnbaum Travel Guides*, worked with her late husband, Stephen Birnbaum, as co-editor of the series. She has been a world traveler since childhood and is known for her travel reports on radio on what's hot and what's not.

Great Britain

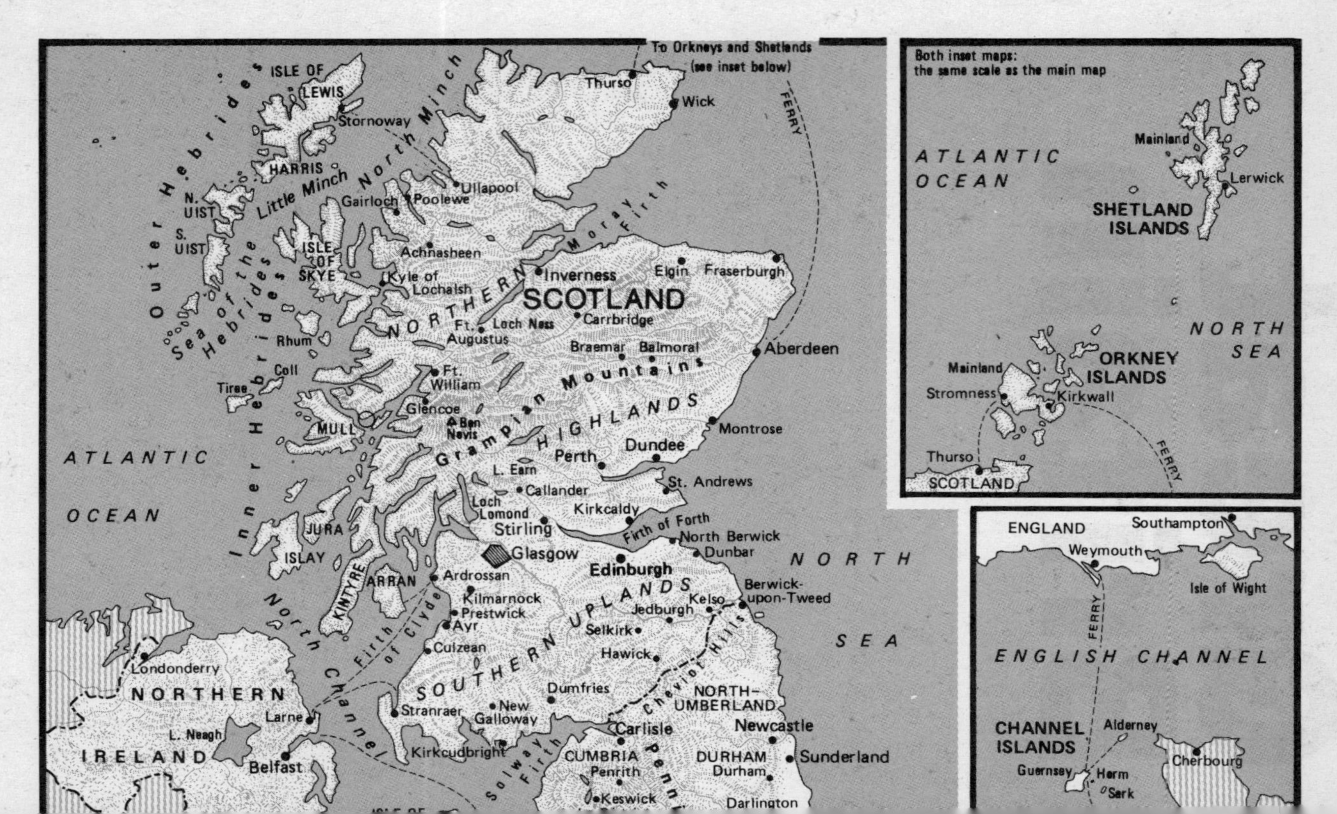

To Orkneys and Shetlands (see inset below)
FERRY
ISLE OF LEWIS
Stornoway
HARRIS
N. UIST
S. UIST
Outer Hebrides
Little Minch
North Minch
Sea of the Hebrides
ISLE OF SKYE
Rhum
Coll
Tiree
Inner Hebrides
MULL
JURA
ISLAY
KINTYRE
ARRAN
North Channel
Firth of Clyde
ATLANTIC
OCEAN
Thurso
Wick
Ullapool
Poolewe
Gairloch
Achnasheen
Kyle of Lochalsh
Moray Firth
Inverness
Elgin
Fraserburgh
SCOTLAND
NORTHERN
Ft. Augustus
Loch Ness
Carrbridge
Braemar
Balmoral
Aberdeen
Ft. William
Glencoe
Ben Nevis
Grampian Mountains
HIGHLANDS
Montrose
Perth
Dundee
L. Earn
Callander
St. Andrews
Loch Lomond
Kirkcaldy
Stirling
Firth of Forth
North Berwick
Dunbar
Glasgow
Edinburgh
Ardrossan
Kilmarnock
Prestwick
Ayr
Culzean
SOUTHERN UPLANDS
Berwick-upon-Tweed
Kelso
Jedburgh
Selkirk
Hawick
Cheviot Hills
Dumfries
New Galloway
Stranraer
Kirkcudbright
Solway Firth
NORTH-UMBERLAND
Carlisle
Newcastle
Sunderland
CUMBRIA
Penrith
Keswick
DURHAM
Durham
Darlington
NORTH
SEA
Londonderry
NORTHERN
IRELAND
L. Neagh
Larne
Belfast
Both inset maps:
the same scale as the main map
ATLANTIC
OCEAN
Mainland
Lerwick
SHETLAND ISLANDS
NORTH
SEA
Mainland
ORKNEY ISLANDS
Stromness
Kirkwall
FERRY
Thurso
SCOTLAND
ENGLAND
Southampton
Weymouth
Isle of Wight
FERRY
ENGLISH CHANNEL
CHANNEL ISLANDS
Alderney
Cherbourg
Guernsey
Herm
Sark

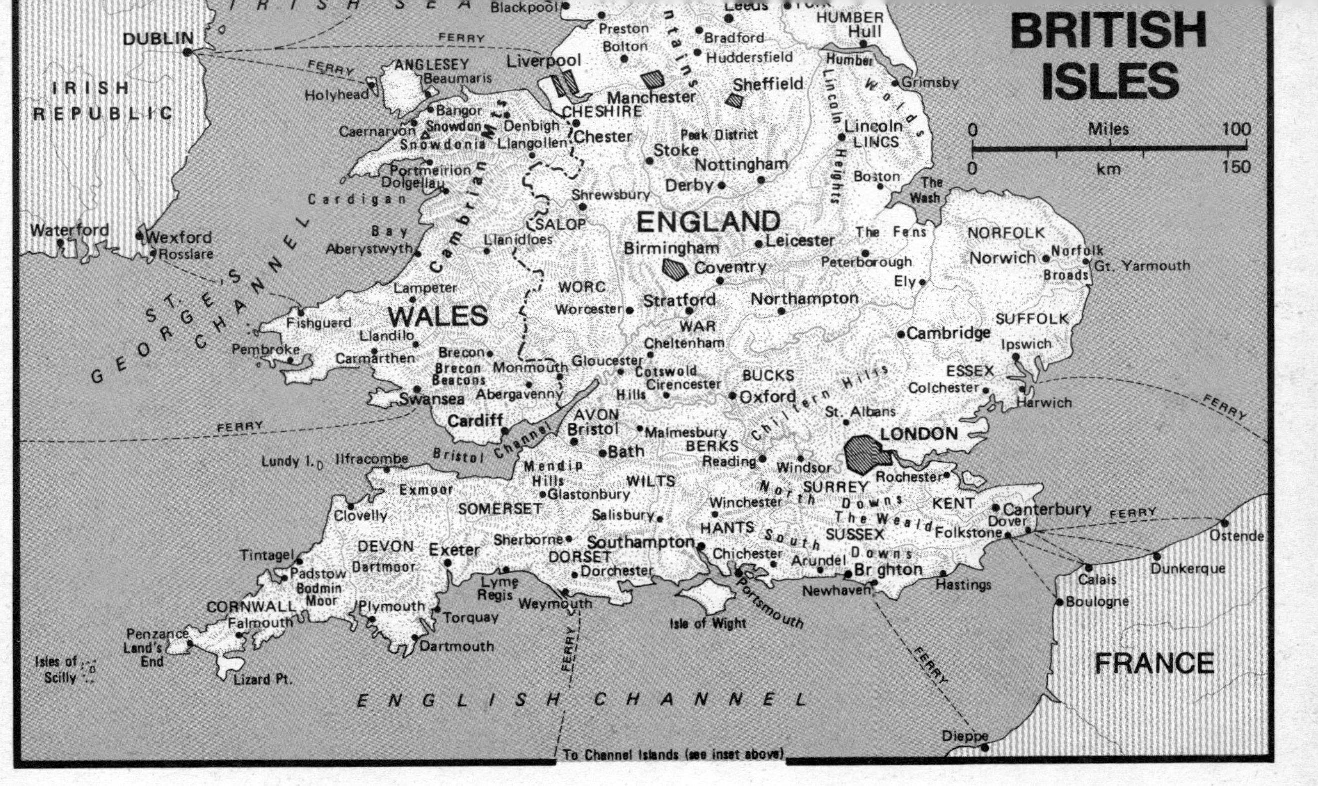

BRITISH ISLES
Miles 0 100
km 0 150
IRISH SEA
DUBLIN
IRISH REPUBLIC
Waterford
Wexford
Rosslare
ST. GEORGE'S CHANNEL
FERRY
ANGLESEY
Beaumaris
Holyhead
Bangor
Caernarvon
Snowdon
Snowdonia
Denbigh
Llangollen
Portmeirion
Dolgellau
Cardigan Bay
Aberystwyth
Cambrian Mts
Llanidloes
Lampeter
WALES
Fishguard
Llandilo
Pembroke
Carmarthen
Brecon
Brecon Beacons
Monmouth
Abergavenny
Swansea
Cardiff
Blackpool
Preston
Bolton
Liverpool
Manchester
CHESHIRE
Chester
Leeds
Bradford
Huddersfield
Sheffield
Peak District
Stoke
Nottingham
Derby
Shrewsbury
SALOP
ENGLAND
Birmingham
Coventry
Leicester
WORC
Worcester
Stratford
WAR
Northampton
Cheltenham
Gloucester
Cotswold Hills
Cirencester
HUMBER
Hull
Humber
Grimsby
Lincoln Wolds
Lincoln Heights
Lincoln
LINCS
Boston
The Wash
The Fens
Peterborough
Ely
NORFOLK
Norwich
Norfolk Broads
Gt. Yarmouth
SUFFOLK
Ipswich
Cambridge
ESSEX
Colchester
Harwich
BUCKS
Oxford
Chiltern Hills
St. Albans
LONDON
AVON
Bristol
Malmesbury
BERKS
Bath
Reading
Windsor
Rochester
Bristol Channel
Lundy I.
Ilfracombe
Mendip Hills
Glastonbury
WILTS
North Downs
SURREY
KENT
Canterbury
Dover
Folkstone
Exmoor
SOMERSET
Salisbury
Winchester
The Weald
Clovelly
HANTS
South Downs
SUSSEX
DEVON
Exeter
Sherborne
Southampton
Chichester
Arundel
Brighton
Hastings
Dartmoor
DORSET
Dorchester
Newhaven
Tintagel
Padstow
Bodmin Moor
Lyme Regis
Weymouth
Portsmouth
Isle of Wight
CORNWALL
Plymouth
Torquay
Falmouth
Penzance
Land's End
Dartmouth
Isles of Scilly
Lizard Pt.
ENGLISH CHANNEL
To Channel Islands (see inset above)
Ostende
Dunkerque
Calais
Boulogne
FRANCE
Dieppe

How to Use This Guide

A great deal of care has gone into the special organization of this guidebook, and we believe it represents a real breakthrough in the presentation of travel material. Our aim is to create a new, more modern generation of travel books, and to make this guide the most useful and practical travel tool available today.

Our text is divided into five basic sections in order to present information in the best way on every possible aspect of a vacation to Great Britain. Our aim is to highlight what's where and to provide basic information—how, when, where, how much, and what's best—to assist you in making the most intelligent choices possible.

Here is a brief summary of the five sections—and what you can expect to find in each. We believe that you will find both your travel planning and en route enjoyment enhanced by having this book at your side.

GETTING READY TO GO

A mini-encyclopedia of practical travel facts with all the precise data necessary to create a successful journey to and through Great Britain. Here you will find how to get where you're going, currency information and exchange rates, plus selected resources—including useful publications, and companies and organizations specializing in discount and special-interest travel—providing a wealth of information and assistance useful both before and during your trip.

THE CITIES

Individual reports on the 19 British cities most visited by travelers and businesspeople offer a short-stay guide, including an essay introducing the city as a historic entity and a contemporary place to visit. *At-a-Glance* contains a site-by-site survey of the most important, interesting, and unique sights to see and things to do. *Sources and Resources* is a concise listing of pertinent tourism information, such as the address of the local tourism office, which sightseeing tours to take, where to find the best nightspot, to play golf, to rent scuba equipment, to find the best beach, or to get a taxi. *Best in Town* lists our cost-and-quality choices of the best places to eat and sleep on a variety of budgets.

DIVERSIONS

This section is designed to help travelers find the best places in which to engage in a variety of exceptional—and unexpected—experiences for the mind and body without having to wade through endless pages of unrelated text. In every case, our particular suggestions are intended to guide you to that special place where the quality of experience is likely to be highest.

DIRECTIONS

Here are 16 itineraries that range all across the British countryside, along the most beautiful routes and roads, past the most spectacular natural wonders, through the most historic cities and most scenic countryside. DIRECTIONS is the only section of this book that is organized geographically, and its itineraries cover the touring highlights of England, Scotland, and Wales in short, independent journeys of three to five days' duration. Itineraries can be "connected" for longer sojourns, or used individually for short, intensive explorations.

GLOSSARY

This compendium of helpful travel information includes a climate chart, a weights and measures table, and *Words to the Wise,* a brief introduction to the way that the English language is spoken in Great Britain. The English, of course, speak English—but their use of words isn't always the same as ours (to us, a boot is something to be worn on the foot; in Great Britain, it's also the trunk of the car). This collection of often-used words and phrases will help you to order a meal or a drink, shop, and get around.

To use this book to full advantage, take a few minutes to read the table of contents and random entries in each section to get a firsthand feel for how it all fits together. You will find that the sections of this book are building blocks designed to help you put together the best possible trip. Use them selectively as a tool, a source of ideas, a reference work for accurate facts, and a guidebook to the best buys, the most exciting sights, the most pleasant accommodations, the tastiest foods—*the best travel experience* you can possibly have.

Getting Ready to Go

Getting Ready to Go

When to Go

Great Britain's temperate climate makes it a multi-seasonal travel destination. Summmers usually are cool and winters are mild—although parts of northern England, Scotland, and Wales may experience occasional bitter cold and heavy snowfall. Throughout the year, skies frequently are overcast and it rains fairly often—especially in the northern and western parts of the country.

The the period from mid-May to mid-September has long been—and remains—the peak travel period, traditionally the most popular vacation time. However, travel during the off-season (roughly November to *Easter*) and shoulder seasons (the months immediately before and after the peak months) also offers relatively fair weather and smaller crowds, and may be less expensive.

If you have a touch-tone phone, you can call *The Weather Channel Connection* (phone: 900-WEATHER) for current worldwide weather forecasts. This service, available from *The Weather Channel* (2600 Cumberland Pkwy., Atlanta, GA 30339; phone: 404-434-6800), costs 95¢ per minute; the charge will appear on your phone bill.

Traveling by Plane

SCHEDULED FLIGHTS

Airlines offering flights between the US and Great Britain include *Aer Lingus, Air India, Air New Zealand International, American, British Airways, Continental, Delta, El Al, Icelandair, Northwest, TWA, United,* and *Virgin Atlantic.*

FARES The great variety of airfares can be reduced to the following basic categories: first class, business class, coach (also called economy or tourist class), excursion or discount, and standby, as well as various promotional fares. For information on applicable fares and restrictions, contact the airlines listed above or ask your travel agent. Most airfares are offered for a limited time. Once you've found the lowest fare for which you can qualify, purchase your ticket as soon as possible.

RESERVATIONS Reconfirmation is strongly recommended for all international flights. It is essential that you confirm your round-trip reservations—*especially the return leg*—as well as any flights within Europe.

SEATING Airline seats usually are assigned on a first-come, first-served basis at check-in, although you may be able to reserve a seat when purchasing your ticket. Seating charts sometimes are available from airlines and also are included in the *Airline Seating Guide* (Carlson Publishing Co., 11132 Los Alamitos Blvd., Los Alamitos, CA 90720; phone: 310-493-4877).

SMOKING US law prohibits smoking on flights scheduled for six hours or less within the US and its territories on both domestic and international carriers. These restrictions do not apply to nonstop flights between the US and international destinations. At press time, most major airlines allowed smoking on flights to Great Britain, although *Delta* had announced plans to ban smoking on all of its transatlantic flights, and other carriers (such as *American* and *United*) were offering nonsmoking flights on a trial basis. A free wallet-size guide that describes the rights of nonsmokers under current regulations is available from *ASH* (*Action on Smoking and Health;* DOT Card, 2013 H St. NW, Washington, DC 20006; phone: 202-659-4310).

SPECIAL MEALS When making your reservation, you can request one of the airline's alternate menu choices for no additional charge. Though not always required, it's a good idea to reconfirm your request the day before departure.

BAGGAGE On major international airlines, passengers usually are allowed to carry on board one bag that will fit under a seat or in an overhead bin and to check two bags in the cargo hold. Specific regulations regarding dimensions and weight restrictions vary among airlines, but a checked bag usually cannot exceed 62 inches in combined dimensions (length, width, and depth), or weigh more than 70 pounds. There may be charges for additional, oversize, or overweight luggage, and for special equipment or sporting gear. Note that baggage allowances may be more limited on domestic routes abroad. Check that the tags the airline attaches are correctly coded for your destination.

CHARTER FLIGHTS

By booking a block of seats on a specially arranged flight, charter operators frequently can offer travelers bargain airfares. If you do fly on a charter, however, read the contract's fine print carefully. Federal regulations permit charter operators to cancel a flight or assess surcharges of as much as 10% of the airfare up to 10 days before departure. You usually must book in advance, and once booked, no changes are permitted, so buy trip cancellation insurance. Also, make your check out to the company's escrow account, which provides some protection for your investment in the event that the charter operator fails. For further information, consult the publication *Jax Fax* (397 Post Rd., Darien, CT 06820; phone: 203-655-8746; fax: 203-655-6257).

DISCOUNTS ON SCHEDULED FLIGHTS

COURIER TRAVEL In return for arranging to accompany some kind of freight, a traveler pays only a portion of the total airfare (and sometimes a small registration fee). One agency that matches up would-be couriers with courier companies is *Now Voyager* (74 Varick St., Suite 307, New York, NY 10013; phone: 212-431-1616; fax: 212-334-5243).

Courier Companies

Discount Travel International (169 W. 81st St., New York, NY 10024; phone: 212-362-3636; fax: 212-362-3236; and 801 Alton Rd., Suite 1, Miami Beach, FL 33139; phone: 305-538-1616; fax: 305-673-9376).

F.B. On Board Courier Club (10225 Ryan Ave., Suite 103, Dorval, Quebec H9P 1A2, Canada; phone: 514-633-0740; fax: 514-633-0735).

Halbart Express (147-05 176th St., Jamaica, NY 11434; phone: 718-656-8279; fax: 718-244-0559).

Midnite Express (925 W. Hyde Park Blvd., Inglewood, CA 90302; phone: 310-672-1100; fax: 310-671-0107).

Way to Go Travel (6679 Sunset Blvd., Hollywood, CA 90028; phone: 213-466-1126; fax: 213-466-8994).

Publications

Insiders Guide to Air Courier Bargains, by Kelly Monaghan (The Intrepid Traveler, PO Box 438, New York, NY 10034; phone: 212-569-1081 for information; 800-356-9315 for orders; fax: 212-942-6687).

Travel Unlimited (PO Box 1058, Allston, MA 02134-1058; no phone).

CONSOLIDATORS AND BUCKET SHOPS These companies buy blocks of tickets from airlines and sell them at a discount to travel agents or directly to consumers. Since many bucket shops operate on a thin margin, be sure to check a company's record with the *Better Business Bureau*—before parting with any money.

Council Charter (205 E. 42nd St., New York, NY 10017; phone: 800-800-8222 or 212-661-0311; fax: 212-972-0194).

International Adventures (60 E. 42nd St., Room 763, New York, NY 10165; phone: 212-599-0577; fax: 212-599-3288).

Travac Tours and Charters (989 Ave. of the Americas, New York, NY 10018; phone: 800-872-8800 or 212-563-3303; fax: 212-563-3631).

Unitravel (1177 N. Warson Rd., St. Louis, MO 63132; phone: 800-325-2222 or 314-569-0900; fax: 314-569-2503).

LAST-MINUTE TRAVEL CLUBS Members of such clubs receive information on imminent trips and other bargain travel opportunities. There usually is an annual fee, although a few clubs offer free membership. Despite the names of some of the clubs listed below, you don't have to wait until literally the last minute to make travel plans.

Discount Travel International (114 Forrest Ave., Suite 203, Narberth, PA 19072; phone: 215-668-7184; fax: 215-668-9182).

FLY ASAP (PO Box 9808, Scottsdale, AZ 85252-3808; phone: 800-FLY-ASAP or 602-956-1987; fax: 602-956-6414).

Last Minute Travel (1249 Boylston St., Boston, MA 02215; phone: 800-LAST-MIN or 617-267-9800; fax: 617-424-1943).

Moment's Notice (425 Madison Ave., New York, NY 10017; phone: 212-486-0500/1/2/3; fax: 212-486-0783).

Spur of the Moment Cruises (411 N. Harbor Blvd., Suite 302, San Pedro, CA 90731; phone: 800-4-CRUISES or 310-521-1070 in California; 800-343-1991 elsewhere in the US; 24-hour hotline: 310-521-1060; fax: 310-521-1061).

Traveler's Advantage (3033 S. Parker Rd., Suite 900, Aurora, CO 80014; phone: 800-548-1116 or 800-835-8747; fax: 303-368-3985).

Vacations to Go (1502 Augusta Dr., Suite 415, Houston, TX 77057; phone: 713-974-2121 in Texas; 800-338-4962 elsewhere in the US; fax: 713-974-0445).

Worldwide Discount Travel Club (1674 Meridian Ave., Miami Beach, FL 33139; phone: 305-534-2082; fax: 305-534-2070).

GENERIC AIR TRAVEL These organizations operate much like an ordinary airline standby service, except that they offer seats on not one but several scheduled and charter airlines. One pioneer of generic flights is *Airhitch* (2790 Broadway, Suite 100, New York, NY 10025; phone: 212-864-2000).

BARTERED TRAVEL SOURCES Barter—the exchange of commodities or services in lieu of cash payment—is a common practice among travel suppliers. Companies that have obtained travel services through barter may sell these services at substantial discounts to travel clubs, who pass along the savings to members. One organization offering bartered travel opportunities is *Travel World Leisure Club* (225 W. 34th St., Suite 909, New York, NY 10122; phone: 800-444-TWLC or 212-239-4855; fax: 212-564-5158).

CONSUMER PROTECTION

Passengers whose complaints have not been satisfactorily addressed by the airline can contact the *US Department of Transportation* (*DOT;* Consumer Affairs Division, 400 Seventh St. SW, Room 10405, Washington, DC 20590; phone: 202-366-2220). Also see *Fly Rights* (Publication #050-000-00513-5; *US Government Printing Office,* PO Box 371954, Pittsburgh, PA 15250-7954; phone: 202-783-3238; fax: 202-512-2250). If you have safety-related questions or concerns, write to the *Federal Aviation Administration* (*FAA;* 800 Independence Ave. SW, Washington, DC 20591) or call the *FAA Consumer Hotline* (phone: 800-322-7873). If you have a complaint against a local travel service in Great Britain, contact the British tourist authorities.

Traveling by Ship

Your cruise fare usually includes all meals, recreational activities, and entertainment. Shore excursions are available at extra cost, and can be booked in advance or once you're on board. An important factor in the price of a cruise is the location (and sometimes the size) of your cabin. Charts issued by the *Cruise Lines International Association* (*CLIA;* 500 Fifth Ave., Suite 1407, New York, NY 10110; phone: 212-921-0066; fax: 212-921-0549) provide information on ship layouts and facilities and are available at some *CLIA*-affiliated travel agencies.

The *US Public Health Service (PHS)* inspects all passenger vessels calling at US ports; for the most recent summary or a particular inspection report, write to Chief, Vessel Sanitation Program, *National Center for Environmental Health* (1015 N. America Way, Room 107, Miami, FL 33132; phone: 305-536-4307). Most cruise ships have a doctor on board, plus medical facilities.

For further information on cruises and cruise lines, consult *Ocean and Cruise News* (PO Box 92, Stamford, CT 06904; phone/fax: 203-329-2787). And for a free list of travel agencies specializing in cruises, contact the *National Association of Cruise Only Agencies* (*NACOA;* 3191 Coral Way, Suite 630, Miami, FL 33145; phone: 305-446-7732; fax: 305-446-9732).

A potentially less expensive alternative to cruise ships is travel by freighter—cargo ships that also transport a limited number of passengers. For information, contact the *Freighter Travel Club of America* (3524 Harts Lake Rd., Roy, WA 98580; no phone), *Freighter World Cruises* (180 S. Lake Ave., Suite 335, Pasadena, CA 91101; phone: 818-449-3106; fax: 818-449-9573), *Pearl's Travel Tips* (9903 Oaks La., Seminole, FL 34642; phone: 813-393-2919; fax: 813-392-2580), and *TravLtips Cruise and Freighter Travel Association* (PO Box 188, 163-07 Depot Rd., Flushing, NY 11358; phone: 800-872-8584 or 718-939-2400; fax: 718-939-2047).

A number of companies, both in the US and Europe, offer cruises on Britain's inland waterways; for further information, see *Wonderful Waterways and Coastal Cruises* in DIVERSIONS. In addition, numerous ferries link mainland Britain with its islands, Ireland, and the rest of Europe; nearly all carry both passengers and cars and most routes are in service year-round.

International Cruise Lines

Cunard (555 Fifth Ave., New York, NY 10017; phone: 800-5-CUNARD or 800-221-4770; fax: 718-786-0038).

Holland America Line (300 Elliot Ave. W., Seattle, WA 98119; phone: 800-426-0327; fax: 800-628-4855).

Marquest (101 Columbia, Suite 165, Aliso Viejo, CA 92656; phone: 800-510-7110 or 714-362-2080; fax: 714-362-2081).

P&O Cruises (c/o *Golden Bear Travel,* 16 Digital Dr., Suite 100, Novato, CA 94948; phone: 800-551-1000 or 415-382-8900; fax: 415-382-9086).

Princess Cruises (10100 Santa Monica Blvd., Los Angeles, CA 90067; phone: 800-421-0522; fax: 310-284-2844).

Raymond & Whitcomb (400 Madison Ave., New York, NY 10017; phone: 212-759-3960 in New York State; 800-245-9005 elsewhere in the US; fax: 212-935-1644).

Royal Cruise Line (1 Maritime Plaza, Suite 1400, San Francisco, CA 94111; phone: 800-792-2992 in California; 800-227-4534 elsewhere in the US; fax: 415-956-1656).

Royal Viking Line (95 Merrick Way, Coral Gables, FL 33134; phone: 800-422-8000; fax: 305-448-1398).

Seabourn Cruise Line (55 Francisco St., Suite 710, San Francisco, CA 94133; phone: 800-929-9595 or 415-391-7444; fax: 415-391-8518).

Special Expeditions (720 Fifth Ave., New York, NY 10019; phone: 800-762-0003 or 212-765-7740; fax: 212-265-3774).

Freighter Companies

Cast (c/o *TravLtips Cruise and Freighter Travel Association;* address above).

Deutsche Seereederei Rostock (c/o *Freighter World Cruises*; address above).

Egon-Oldendorff (c/o *Freighter World Cruises*).

Grimaldi (c/o *Freighter World Cruises*).

Mediterranean Great Lakes Line (c/o *Freighter World Cruises*).

Mediterranean Shipping (c/o *Sea the Difference,* 420 Fifth Ave., Suite 804, New York, NY 10018; phone: 800-666-9333 or 212-354-4409; fax: 212-764-8592).

Inland Waterway Cruise Companies

Abercrombie & Kent (1520 Kensington Rd., Suite 212, Oak Brook, IL 60521; phone: 800-323-7308 or 708-954-2944; fax: 708-954-3324).

Anglo Welsh Waterways Holidays (The Canal Basin, Leicester Rd., Market Harborough, Leicestershire LE16 7BJ, England; phone: 44-1858-466910; fax: 44-1858-434618).

The Barge Lady (225 N. Michigan Ave., Suite 224, Chicago, IL 60601; phone: 800-880-0071 or 312-540-5500; fax: 312-540-5503).

Blakes Holidays (Wroxham, Norwich, Norfolk NR12 8DH, England; phone: 44-1603-782911; in the US, contact *Blakes Vacations,* 1076 Ash St., Winnetka, IL 60093; phone: 800-628-8118 or 708-446-4771; fax: 708-446-4772).

Le Boat (215 Union St., Hackensack, NJ 07601; phone: 800-922-0291 or 201-342-1838; fax 201-342-7498).

Cruise Company of Greenwich (31 Brookside Dr., Greenwich, CT 06830; phone: 800-825-0826 or 203-622-0203; fax: 203-622-4036).

Elegant Cruises and Tours (31 Central Dr., Port Washington, NY 11050; phone: 800-683-6767 or 516-767-9302; fax: 516-767-9303).

EuroCruises (303 W. 13th St., New York, NY 10014; phone: 800-688-3876 or 212-691-2099; fax: 212-366-4747).

European Waterways (140 E. 56th St., Suite 4C, New York, NY 10022; phone: 800-217-4447; fax: 212-296-4554).

Five Star Touring (60 E. 42nd St., Suite 612, New York, NY 10165; phone: 212-818-9140 in New York City; 800-792-7827 elsewhere in the US; fax: 212-818-9142).

Hideaways International (767 Islington St., Portsmouth, NH 03801; phone: 800-843-4433 or 603-430-4433; fax: 603-430-4444).

Hoseasons Holidays Ltd. (Sunway House, Lowestoft, Suffolk NR32 2LW England; phone: 44-1502-500555; fax: 44-1502-500535; in the US, contact *Skipper Travel Services,* address below).

Kemwel's Premier Selections (106 Calvert St., Harrison, NY 10528-3199; phone: 800-234-4000 or 914-835-5555; fax: 914-835-5449).

Skipper Travel Services (9029 Soquel Ave., Suite G, Santa Cruz, CA 95062; phone: 408-462-5333; fax: 408-462-5178).

Ferry Companies

B & I Line Services (in the US, contact *Lynott Tours,* 350 Fifth Ave., Suite 2619, New York, NY 10118; phone: 800-221-2474 or 212-760-0101; fax: 212-695-8347).

Condor Weymouth Ltd. (The Quay, Weymouth, Dorset DT4 8DX, England; phone: 44-1305-761551; fax: 44-1305-760776).

Hoverspeed Ltd. (International Hoverport, Marine Parade, Dover, Kent CT17 9TG, England; phone: 44-1304-240241; fax: 44-1304-240088).

P&O European Ferries (Channel House, Channel View Rd., Dover, Kent CT17 9TJ, England; phone: 44-1304-203388; fax: 44-1304-223464).

Scots-American Travel Advisors (26 Rugen Dr., Harrington Park, NJ 07640; phone: 201-768-1187; fax: 201-768-3825).

Spena Sealink (Charter House, PO Box 121, Park St., Ashford, Kent TN24 8EX, England; phone: 44-1233-647047; fax: 44-1233-623294; in the US, contact *BritRail Travel International,* address below).

Swansea Cork Ferries (Ferry Port, King's Dock, Swansea SA1 8RU, Wales; phone: 44-1792-456116; fax: 44-1792-644356).

UK Waterway Holidays (1 Port Hill, Hertford SG14 1PJ, England; phone: 44-1992-550616; fax: 44-1992-587392; in the US, contact *Alden Yacht Charters,* 1909 Alden Landing, Portsmouth, RI 02871; phone: 401-683-1782; fax: 401-683-4200; or *Skipper Travel Services,* address above).

Weltonfield Narrowboats Ltd. (Weltonfield, Daventry, Northamptonshire NN11 5LG, England; phone: 44-1327-842282; fax: 44-1327-843754).

Traveling by Train

British Rail (or *BritRail,* as it also is known in the US) is Great Britain's national railroad company. It operates some 15,000 trains a day, including *InterCity* trains, which connect cities within Britain, and car-carrying *Motorail* trains. In the US, *British Rail* is represented by *BritRail Travel International* (1500 Broadway, Suite 1000, New York, NY 10036-4015; phone: 800-677-8585 or 212-575-2667; fax: 212-575-2542).

All *InterCity* trains have first class and standard class cars, as well as a dining car. Trains on local routes, especially rural ones, may have one class only, equivalent to standard. Sleeping cars are found on night trains to Scotland and to northern and western England. Both first and standard class seats on *InterCity* trains can be reserved in advance. Sleeper reservations are recommended and should be made as far in advance as possible, as should reservations for travel on *Motorail* trains. *BritRail* offers several types of discounted excursion tickets and rail passes (which must be purchased in the US before going abroad). The *BritRail* Pass is good for unlimited travel throughout Great Britain; the England/Wales Pass covers travel in England and Wales; and the BritFrance Railpass encompasses both Britain and France.

Most trains do not have baggage cars, and luggage may be placed on the overhead racks or at either end of the car. Travel light, since porters often are in short supply, particularly at smaller stations. In the US, reservations can be made through travel agents or *BritRail Travel International* (address above). In Great Britain, there are *British Rail Travel Centres* in train stations that provide information on *BritRail* schedules and services and help with bookings.

BritRail also offers a series of all-inclusive, escorted rail tours (sometimes combined with bus travel), which begin and end in London. A US agency specializing in rail travel, and offering packaged rail tours, as well as *BritRail* passes and individual tickets for British trains, is *Accent on Travel* (112 N. Fifth St., Klamath Falls, OR 97601; phone: 503-885-7330).

FURTHER INFORMATION

The *Thomas Cook European Timetable,* a compendium of European rail services, is available in bookstores and from the *Forsyth Travel Library* (9154 W. 57th St., PO Box 2975, Shawnee Mission, KS 66201-1375; phone: 800-367-7984 or 913-384-3440; fax: 913-384-3553). Other useful resources with information on rail travel in Great Britain include *Britain by BritRail,* by George and LaVerne Ferguson (Globe Pequot Press, PO Box 833, Old Saybrook, CT 06475; phone: 203-395-0440; fax: 203-395-0312) and the *Eurail Guide,* by Kathryn Turpin and Marvin Saltzman (Eurail Guide Annual, 27540 Pacific Coast Hwy., Malibu, CA 90265; no phone).

CONTINENTAL CONNECTION

The recently completed Channel Tunnel (often called the "Chunnel"), an underwater passage between Britain and France through the English Channel, makes it possible for the first time to travel by train, bus, or car between Great Britain and France.

Traveling by Bus

A map of local British bus routes is not much different from a road map. The network of express buses—traveling long distances with few stops en route—is only slightly less extensive.

Express coach service throughout Great Britain is provided by *National Express* (main booking office: Westwood Garage, Margate Rd., Ramsgate, Kent CT12 6SL, England; phone: 44-1843-581333; fax: 44-1843-580675). Service is provided to approximately 1,500 destinations, about 200 of which are served by *Rapide* buses (some of them double-deckers); these provide comfortable seating, plus a host or hostess, refreshments, and toilets on board. Although food is not served on most buses, some of the *National Express* buses making longer trips provide light refreshments, such as sandwiches and soft drinks.

Reservations are not necessary on most local bus routes and tickets usually are purchased on the bus. For long journeys, reservations are advised (though not required) to ensure that you will get a seat. During the busiest seasons and holidays, be sure to reserve and purchase your bus tickets early. Note that buses usually are the main form of transport in rural areas and are often very crowded, and tickets on local buses—as well as some passes for long-distance trips—do not guarantee you a seat.

For long-distance trips, you often can reserve seats and purchase tickets by credit card over the phone, through a travel agent, or at the bus station. If there is no ticket office open at the bus station, you also can purchase your ticket on the bus. *National Express* also offers many types of bus passes at discounted rates.

Traveling by Car

Driving is the most flexible way to explore Great Britain. To drive in Great Britain for a period of up to one year, a US citizen must have a valid US driver's license. Proof of liability insurance also is required and is a standard part of any car rental contract. (To be sure of having the appropriate coverage, let the rental staff know in advance if you plan to cross any national borders.) If buying a car and using it abroad, the driver must carry an International Insurance Certificate, known as a Green Card, which can be obtained from your insurance agent or through branches or the main office of the *American Automobile Association* (*AAA;* 1000 AAA Dr., Heathrow, FL 32746-5080; phone: 407-444-7000; fax: 407-444-7380).

The British drive on the left-hand side of the road and pass on the right. Pictorial direction signs are standardized under the International Roadsign System and their meanings are indicated by their shapes—triangular signs indicate danger, circular signs give instructions, and rectangular signs provide information.

Unlike the rest of Europe, in Great Britain distances usually are measured in miles, and speeds are expressed in miles per hour (mph). British speed limits usually are 70 mph on motorways (expressways) and dual carriageways (four-lane highways), 60 mph on single carriageways (two-lane highways), and 30 mph in towns or built-up areas—unless otherwise indicated. Note that the British are (slowly) moving towards adoption of the metric system. Although there were no imminent plans at the time of this writing to change the style of highway signs, it is possible that you may see signs in miles *and* kilometers (1 mile equals 1.6 kilometers; 1 kilometer equals .62 miles).

In Great Britain, seat belts are compulsory for front- *and* back-seat passengers—provided the car is equipped with seat belts in the back seat. In addition, children too small for seat belts must travel in safety seats. In many British towns and cities, honking is discouraged during the day and forbidden at night; flash your headlights instead. Pay particular attention to parking signs in large cities. If you park in a restricted zone, you may return to find a wheel "clamped," which renders the car inoperable and involves a tedious—and costly—process to get it freed. For more information, consult *Euroad: The Complete Guide to Motoring in Europe* (VLE Ltd., PO Box 444, Ft. Lee, NJ 07024; phone: 201-585-5080; fax: 201-585-5110).

MAPS

The *British Tourist Authority* distributes free countrywide and city center maps. Britain's *Automobile Association* (*AA;* Fanum House, Basing View, Basingstoke, Hampshire RG21 2EA, England; phone: 44-1256-20123; fax: 44-1256-493389) and *Royal Automobile Club* (*RAC;* PO Box 100, RAC House, Bartlett St., South Croydon, Surrey CR2 6XW; phone: 44-181-686-0088; fax: 44-181-681-8710) publish national, regional, and local maps in varying scales; these can be ordered in the US from the *British Travel Bookshop* (551 Fifth Ave., New York, NY 10176; phone: 800-448-3039 or 212-490-6688; fax: 212-490-0219). The *American Automobile Association* (*AAA;* address above) also provides some useful reference sources, including a country map of Great Britain and an overall planning map of Europe, as well as the *Travel Guide to Europe* and *Motoring in Europe.*

Particularly good maps of Britain are published by *Michelin Travel Publications* (PO Box 19008, Greenville, SC 29602-9008; phone: 803-458-5000 in South Carolina; 800-423-0485 elsewhere in the US; fax: 803-458-5665). In addition, *Freytag & Berndt* maps cover most destinations in Europe (including Great Britain), and can be ordered from *Map Link* (25 E. Mason St., Suite 201, Santa Barbara, CA 93101; phone: 805-965-4402; fax: 800-MAP-SPOT or 805-962-0884). Road maps of Great Britain also are published by *Bartholomew* (HarperCollins Cartographic, 77-85 Fulham Palace Rd., Hammersmith, London W6 8JB, England; phone: 44-181-741-7070; fax: 44-181-307-4417; in the US, contact Hammond, 515 Valley St.,

Maplewood, NJ 07040; phone: 201-763-6000; fax: 201-763-7658) and *Hallwag* (Rand McNally, Inside Sales, PO Box 32, Skokie, IL 60076; phone: 800-627-2897; fax: 708-673-0280).

AUTOMOBILE CLUBS AND BREAKDOWNS

To protect yourself in case of breakdowns while driving to and through Great Britain, and for travel information and other benefits, consider joining a reputable automobile club. The largest of these is the *American Automobile Association* (*AAA;* address above). Before joining this or any other automobile club, however, check whether it has reciprocity with British clubs, such as the *Automobile Association* (*AA;* address above) and the *Royal Automobile Club* (*RAC;* address above).

GASOLINE

Gasoline is sold either by the liter (approximately 3.8 liters = 1 US gallon) or by the British, or "imperial," gallon, which is 20% larger than the US gallon (1 imperial gallon = approximately 1.2 US gallons). Leaded, unleaded, and diesel fuel are available.

RENTING A CAR

You can rent a car through a travel agent or international rental firm before leaving home, or from a local company once in Great Britain. Reserve in advance.

Most car rental companies require a credit card, although some will accept a substantial cash deposit. The minimum age to rent a car is set by the company; some also may impose special conditions on drivers above a certain age. Electing to pay for collision damage waiver (CDW) protection will add to the cost of renting a car, but releases you from financial liability for the vehicle. Additional costs include drop-off charges or one-way service fees.

Car Rental Companies

Alamo (phone: 800-522-9696).
Auto Europe (phone: 800-223-5555).
Avis (phone: 800-331-1084).
Budget (phone: 800-472-3325).
Dollar Rent A Car (known in Europe as *EuroDollar Rent A Car;* phone: 800-800-6000).
Europe by Car (phone: 212-581-3040 in New York State; 800-223-1516 elsewhere in the US).
European Car Reservations (phone: 800-535-3303).
Foremost Euro-Car (phone: 800-272-3299).
Hertz (phone: 800-654-3001).
Kemwel Group (phone: 800-678-0678).
Meier's International (phone: 800-937-0700).
National (known in Europe as *Europcar;* phone: 800-CAR-EUROPE).

Payless (phone: 800-PAYLESS).
Thrifty (phone: 800-367-2277).
Town and Country Car Rental/ITS (phone: 800-248-4350 in Florida; 800-521-0643 elsewhere in the US).

Package Tours

A package is a collection of travel services that can be purchased in a single transaction. Its principal advantages are convenience and economy—the cost usually is lower than that of the same services purchased separately. Tour programs generally can be divided into two categories: escorted or locally hosted (with a set itinerary) and independent (usually more flexible).

When considering a package tour, read the brochure *carefully* to determine exactly what is included and any conditions that may apply, and check the company's record with the *Better Business Bureau.* The *United States Tour Operators Association* (*USTOA;* 211 E. 51st St., Suite 12B, New York, NY 10022; phone: 212-750-7371; fax: 212-421-1285) also can be helpful in determining a package tour operator's reliability. As with charter flights, to safeguard your funds, always make your check out to the company's escrow account.

Many tour operators offer packages focused on special interests such as the arts, nature study, sports, and other recreations. *All Adventure Travel* (5589 Arapahoe St., Suite 208, Boulder, CO 80303; phone: 800-537-4025 or 303-440-7924; fax: 303-440-4160) represents such specialized packagers. Many also are listed in the *Specialty Travel Index* (305 San Anselmo Ave., Suite 313, San Anselmo, CA 94960; phone: 415-459-4900 in California; 800-442-4922 elsewhere in the US; fax: 415-459-4974).

Package Tour Operators

Abercrombie & Kent (1520 Kensington Rd., Oak Brook, IL 60521; phone: 800-323-7308 or 708-954-2944; fax: 708-954-3324).
Above the Clouds Trekking (PO Box 398, Worcester, MA 01602; phone: 800-233-4499 or 508-799-4499; fax: 508-797-4779).
Adventure Golf Holidays (815 North Rd., Westfield, MA 01085; phone: 800-628-9655 or 413-568-2855).
Adventure Tours (10612 Beaver Dam Rd., Hunt Valley, MD 21030-2205; phone: 410-785-3500 in the Baltimore area; 800-638-9040 elsewhere in the US; fax: 410-584-2771).
Adventures in Golf (29 Valencia Dr., Nashua, NH 03062; phone: 603-882-8367; fax: 603-595-6514).
AHI International (701 Lee St., Des Plaines, IL 60016; phone: 800-323-7373 or 312-694-9330; fax: 708-699-7108).

Alternative Travel Groups (69-71 Banbury Rd., Oxford 0X2 6PE, England; phone: 800-527-5997 in the US; 44-1865-310255 in Great Britain; fax: 44-1865-310299).

American Airlines FlyAAway Vacations (offices throughout the US; phone: 800-321-2121).

American Express Vacations (offices throughout the US; phone: 800-YES-AMEX).

American Museum of Natural History Discovery Tours (Central Park W. at 79th St., New York, NY 10024; phone: 212-769-5700).

Archaeological Tours (271 Madison Ave., Suite 904, New York, NY 10016; phone: 212-986-3054; fax: 212-370-1561).

AutoVenture (425 Pike St., Suite 502, Seattle, WA 98101; phone: 800-426-7502 or 206-624-6033; fax: 206-340-8891).

Backroads (1516 Fifth St., Berkeley, CA 94710-1740; phone: 800-462-2848 or 510-527-1555; fax: 510-527-1444).

Bentley Tours (1649 Colorado Blvd., Los Angeles, CA 90041-1435; phone: 800-821-9726 or 213-258-8451; fax: 213-255-7204).

Bike Tours/Bike Events (PO Box 75, Bath, Avon BA1 1BX, England; phone: 44-1225-310859 or 44-1225-480130; fax: 44-1225-480132).

Brendan Tours (15137 Califa St., Van Nuys, CA 91411; phone: 800-421-8446 or 818-785-9696; fax: 818-902-9876).

Brian Moore International Tours (116 Main St., Medway, MA 02053; phone: 800-982-2299 or 508-533-6683; fax: 508-533-3812).

British Airways Holidays (75-20 Astoria Blvd., Jackson Heights, NY 11370; phone: 800-AIRWAYS).

British Coastal Trails (California Plaza, 1001 B Ave., Suite 302, Coronado, CA 92118; phone: 800-473-1210 or 619-437-1211; fax: 619-437-8394).

BritRail Travel International (1500 Broadway, New York, NY 10036-4015; phone: 212-575-2667 in New York State; 800-677-8585 elsewhere in the US; fax: 212-575-2542).

Butterfield & Robinson (70 Bond St., Suite 300, Toronto, Ontario M5B 1X3, Canada; phone: 800-387-1147 or 416-864-1354; fax: 416-864-0541).

Caravan Tours (401 N. Michigan Ave., Chicago, IL 60611; phone: 800-CARAVAN or 312-321-9800; fax: 312-321-9810).

Catholic Travel (10018 Cedar La., Kensington, MD 20895; phone: 301-530-8963 or 301-530-7682; fax: 301-530-6614).

Catholic Travel Centre (7301 Sepulveda Blvd., Van Nuys, CA 91405; phone: 800-553-5233 or 818-909-9910; fax: 818-997-8981).

Celtic International Tours (161 Central Ave., Albany, NY 12206; phone: 800-833-4373 or 518-463-5511; fax: 518-463-8461).

Certified Vacations (110 E. Broward Blvd., Ft. Lauderdale, FL 33302; phone: 800-233-7260 or 305-522-1440; fax: 305-468-4781).

CIE Tours International (PO Box 501, Cedar Knolls, NJ 07927-0501; phone: 800-CIE-TOUR or 201-292-3438; fax: 800-338-3964).

Classic Adventures (PO Box 153, Hamlin, NY 14464-0153; phone: 800-777-8090 or 716-964-8488; fax: 716-964-7297).

Collette Tours (162 Middle St., Pawtucket, RI 02860; phone: 800-752-2655 in New England; 800-832-4656 elsewhere in the US; fax: 401-727-4745).

Contiki Holidays (300 Plaza Alicante, Suite 900, Garden Grove, CA 92640; phone: 800-266-8454 or 714-740-0808; fax: 714-740-0818).

Continental Grand Destinations (offices throughout the US; phone: 800-634-5555).

Coopersmith's England (6441 Valley View Rd., Oakland, CA 94611; phone: 510-339-3977; fax: 510-339-7135).

Cross Country International Equestrian Vacations (PO Box 1170, Millbrook, NY 12545; phone: 800-828-TROT or 914-677-6000; fax: 914-677-6077).

Countrywide Holidays Association (Birch Keys, Cromwell Range, Manchester M14 6HU, England; phone: 44-1612-251000; fax: 44-1612-2242566).

Dailey-Thorp (330 W. 58th St., New York, NY 10019-1817; phone: 212-307-1555; fax: 212-974-1420).

Delta's Dream Vacations (PO Box 1525, Ft. Lauderdale, FL 33302; phone: 800-872-7786).

DER Tours (11933 Wilshire Blvd., Los Angeles, CA 90025; phone: 800-782-2424 or 310-479-4411; fax: 310-479-2239; and 9501 W. Devon Ave., Rosemont, IL 60018; phone: 800-782-2424 or 708-692-6300; fax: 708-692-4506).

Destination Ireland/Grimes Travel (250 W. 57th St., Suite 2511, New York, NY 10107; phone: 212-977-9629 in New York State; 800-832-1848 elsewhere in the US; fax: 212-541-6207).

East Anglia/Scottish Cycling Holidays (Ballintuim Post Office, Blairgowrie, Perthshire PH10 7NJ, Scotland; phone: 44-1250-886201).

Educational Adventures (815 North Rd., Westfield, MA 01085; phone: 800-628-9655 or 413-568-2855; fax: 413-562-3621).

Edwards & Edwards (1 Times Square Plaza, 12th Floor, New York, NY 10036-6585; phone: 212-944-0290 in New York State; 800-223-6108 elsewhere in the US; fax: 212-944-7497).

English Lakeland Ramblers/Outdoor Bound (18 Stuyvesant Oval, Suite 1A, New York, NY 10009; phone: 800-724-8801 or 212-505-1020).

English Wanderer (6 George St., Ferryhill, County Durham DL17 0DT, England; phone: 44-1740-653169; fax: 44-1740-657996).

Equitour (PO Box 807, Dubois, WY 82513; phone: 307-455-3363 in Wyoming; 800-545-0019 elsewhere in the US; fax: 307-455-2354).

Escapade Tours (9 West Office Center, 2200 Fletcher Ave., Ft. Lee, NJ 07024; phone: 800-356-2405 or 201-346-9061; fax: 201-346-0511).

EuroConnection (2004 196th St. SW, Suite 4, Lynnwood, WA 98036; phone: 800-645-3876 or 206-670-1140; fax: 206-775-7561).

Europe Through the Back Door (PO Box 2009, Edmonds, WA 98020; phone: 206-771-8303; fax: 206-771-0833).

European Tours Limited (5725 77th St., Lubbock, TX 79424; phone: 800-722-3679 or 806-794-4991; fax: 806-794-8550).

European Travel Management (237 Post Rd. W., Westport, CT 06880; phone: 800-992-7700 or 203-454-0090; fax: 203-454-8840).

Extra Value Travel (683 S. Collier Blvd., Marco Island, FL 33937; phone: 813-394-3384; fax: 813-394-4848).

Far Horizons (PO Box 91900, Albuquerque, NM 87199-1900; phone: 800-552-4575 or 505-822-9100; fax: 505-828-1500).

Fishing International (PO Box 2132, Santa Rosa, CA 95405; phone: 800-950-4242 or 707-539-3366; fax: 707-539-1320).

FITS Equestrian (685 Lateen Rd., Solvang, CA 93463; phone: 800-666-3487 or 805-688-9494; fax: 805-688-2493).

Five Star Touring (60 E. 42nd St., Suite 612, New York, NY 10165; phone: 212-818-9140 in New York City; 800-792-7827 elsewhere in the US; fax: 212-818-9142).

Forum Travel International (91 Gregory La., Suite 21, Pleasant Hill, CA 94523; phone: 510-671-2900; fax: 510-671-2993 or 510-946-1500).

4th Dimension Tours (1150 NW 72nd Ave., Suite 333, Miami, FL 33126; phone: 800-343-0020 or 305-477-1525; fax: 305-477-0731).

Frames Rickards (11 Herbrand St., London WC1N 1EX, England; phone: 44-171-837-3111; fax: 44-171-833-3752; in the US, contact *Trophy Tours,* 1850 Greenville Ave., Suite 146, Richardson, TX 75081; phone: 800-527-2473 or 214-690-3875; or *California Parlor Car Tours,* 1101 Van Ness Ave., San Francisco, CA 94109; phone: 800-331-9259 or 415-474-7500; fax: 415-673-1539).

Frontiers International (PO Box 959, Wexford, PA 15090-0959; phone: 412-935-1577 in Pennsylvania; 800-245-1950 elsewhere in the US; fax: 412-935-5388).

Funway Holidays Funjet (PO Box 1460, Milwaukee, WI 53201-1460; phone: 800-558-3050 for reservations; 800-558-3060 for customer service).

Globus/Cosmos (5301 S. Federal Circle, Littleton, CO 80123; phone: 800-221-0090, 800-556-5454, or 303-797-2800; fax: 303-347-2080).

GOGO Tours (69 Spring St., Ramsey, NJ 07446-0507; phone: 201-934-3759).

Golf International (275 Madison Ave., New York, NY 10016; phone: 800-833-1389 or 212-986-9176; fax: 212-986-3720).

Golfing Holidays (231 E. Millbrae Ave., Millbrae, CA 94030; phone: 800-652-7847 or 415-697-0230; fax: 415-697-8687).

Golfpac (417 Whooping Loop, Suite 1701, Altamonte Springs, FL 32701; phone: 800-327-0878 or 407-260-2288; fax: 407-260-8989).

Grand Slam Tennis Tours (222 Milwaukee St., Suite 407, Denver, CO 80206; phone: 800-289-3333 or 303-321-1760; fax: 303-321-1771).

Grasshopper Golf Tours (403 Hill Ave., Glen Ellyn, IL 60137; phone: 800-654-8712 or 708-858-1660; fax: 708-858-1681).

HF Holidays Ltd. (Imperial House, Edgware Rd., London NW9 5AL, England; phone: 44-181-905-9558; fax: 44-181-905-9558).

Hiking Holidays (PO Box 750, Bristol, VT 05443-0750; phone: 802-453-4816; fax: 802-453-4806).

Himalayan Travel (112 Prospect St., Stamford, CT 06901; phone: 800-225-2380 or 203-359-3711; fax: 203-359-3669).

In Quest of the Classics (PO Box 890745, Temecula, CA 92589-0745; phone: 800-227-1393 or 909-694-5866 in California; 800-221-5246 elsewhere in the US; fax: 909-694-5873).

Insight International Tours (745 Atlantic Ave., Suite 720, Boston, MA 02111; phone: 800-582-8380 or 617-482-2000; fax: 617-482-2425).

InterGolf (PO Box 500608, Atlanta, GA 31150; phone: 800-468-0051 or 404-518-1250; fax: 404-518-1272).

International Golf Vacations (PO Box 1129, Maplewood, NJ 07040; phone: 201-378-9170; fax: 201-378-9193).

INTRAV (7711 Bonhomme Ave., St. Louis, MO 63105-1961; phone: 800-456-8100; fax: 314-727-6198).

ITC Golf Tours (4134 Atlantic Ave., Suite 205, Long Beach, CA 90807; phone: 800-257-4981 or 310-595-6905; fax: 310-424-6683).

Jefferson Tours (1206 Currie Ave., Minneapolis, MN 55403; phone: 800-767-7433 or 612-338-4174; fax: 612-332-5532).

Keith Prowse & Co. (USA) Ltd. (234 W. 44th St., Suite 1000, New York, NY 10036; phone: 800-669-8687 or 212-398-1430; fax: 212-302-4251).

KLM/Northwest Vacations Europe (c/o *MLT,* 5130 Hwy. 101, Minnetonka, MN 55345; phone: 800-727-1111; fax: 800-655-7890).

Liberty Travel (for the nearest location, contact the central office: 69 Spring St., Ramsey, NJ 07446; phone: 201-934-3500; fax: 201-934-3888).

Lismore Tours (106 E. 31st St., New York, NY 10016; phone: 212-685-0100 in New York State; 800-547-6673 elsewhere in the US; fax: 212-685-0614).

Lynott Tours (350 Fifth Ave., Suite 2619, New York, NY 10118; phone: 212-760-0101 in New York State; 800-221-2474 elsewhere in the US; fax: 212-695-8347).

Marathon Tours (108 Main St., Charlestown, MA 02129; phone: 800-444-4097 or 617-242-7845; fax: 617-242-7686).

Marsans International (19 W. 34th St., Suite 302, New York, NY 10001; phone: 800-777-9110 or 212-239-3880; fax: 212-239-4129).

Matterhorn Travel Service (2450 Riva Rd., Annapolis, MD 21401; phone: 410-224-2230 in Maryland; 800-638-9150 elsewhere in the US; fax: 410-266-3868).

Maupintour (PO Box 807, Lawrence, KS 66044; phone: 800-255-4266 or 913-843-1211; fax: 913-843-8351).

Mountain Goat Holidays (Victoria St., Windermere, Cumbria LA23 1AD, England; phone: 44-15394-45161; fax: 44-15394-45164).

Mountain Travel-Sobek (6420 Fairmount Ave., El Cerrito, CA 94530; phone: 510-527-8100 in California; 800-227-2384 elsewhere in the US; fax: 510-525-7710).

Nantahala Outdoor Center Adventure Travel (13077 Hwy. 19 W., Bryson City, NC 28713-9114; phone: 800-232-7238 for reservations; 704-488-2175 for information; fax: 704-488-2498).

New England Hiking Holidays (PO Box 1648, N. Conway, NH 03860; phone: 800-869-0949 or 603-356-9696).

New England Vacation Tours (PO Box 560, West Dover, VT 05356; phone: 800-742-7669 or 802-464-2076; fax: 802-464-2629).

Olson Travelworld (970 W. 190th St., Suite 425, Torrance, CA 90502; phone: 800-421-2255 or 310-354-2600; fax: 310-768-0050).

Owenoak International (3 Parklands Dr., Darien, CT 06820; phone: 800-426-4498 or 203-655-2531; fax: 203-656-1651).

Past Times Tours (800 Larch La., Sacramento, CA 95864-5042; phone: 916-485-8140; fax: 916-488-4804).

PerryGolf (8302 Dunwoody Pl., Suite 305, Atlanta, GA 30350; phone: 800-344-5257 or 404-641-9696; fax: 404-641-9798).

Petrabax Tours (97-45 Queens Blvd., Suite 600, Rego Park, NY 11374; phone: 800-367-6611 or 718-897-7272; fax: 718-275-3943).

Pleasure Break (3701 Algonquin Rd., Suite 900, Rolling Meadows, IL 60008; phone: 708-670-6300 in Illinois; 800-777-1885 elsewhere in the US; fax: 708-670-7689).

Prospect Music and Art Tours (454-458 Chiswick High Rd., London W45TT, England; phone: 44-181-995-2151 or 44-181-995-2163; fax: 44-181-742-1969).

Ramblers Holidays (13 Longcroft House, Fretherne Rd., Welwyn Garden City, Hertfordshire AL8 6PQ, England; phone: 44-170-733-1133; fax: 44-170-733-3276).

Regina Tours (401 South St., Room 4B, Chardon, OH 44024; phone: 800-228-4654 or 216-286-9166; fax: 216-286-4231).

Saga International Holidays (222 Berkeley St., Boston, MA 02116; phone: 800-343-0273 or 617-262-2262).

Scottish Golf Holidays (9403 Kenwood Rd., Cincinnati, OH 45242; phone: 800-284-8884 or 513-984-0414; fax: 513-984-9648).

Sierra Club Outings (730 Polk St., San Francisco, CA 94109; phone: 415-923-5630).

Smithsonian Study Tours and Seminars (1100 Jefferson Dr. SW, Room 3045, Washington, DC 20560; phone: 202-357-4700; fax: 202-786-2315).

Sportsworld Travel (1730 NE Expwy., Suite 100, Atlanta, GA 30329; phone: 800-338-0155 or 404-329-9902; fax: 404-329-9902).

Steve Austin's Great Vacations (4800 SW Griffith, Suite 125, Beaverton, OR 97005; phone: 800-452-8434 or 503-643-8080; fax: 503-643-1302).

Take-A-Guide (main office: 11 Uxbridge St., London W8 7TQ, England; phone: 44-181-960-0459; fax: 44-181-964-0990; US office: 954 Lexington Ave., New York, NY 10021; phone: 800-825-4946; fax: 800-635-7177).

Tauck Tours (PO Box 5027, Westport, CT 06881; phone: 800-468-2825 or 203-226-6911; fax: 203-221-6828).

Thomas Cook (headquarters: 45 Berkeley St., Piccadilly, London W1A 1EB, England; phone: 44-171-499-4000; fax: 44-171-408-4299; main US office: 100 Cambridge Park Dr., Cambridge, MA 02140; phone: 800-846-6272; fax: 617-349-1094).

Trafalgar Tours (11 E. 26th St., Suite 1300, New York, NY 10010-1402; phone: 800-854-0103 or 212-689-8977; fax: 212-725-7776).

TRAVCOA (PO Box 2630, Newport Beach, CA 92658; phone: 800-992-2004 or 714-476-2800 in California; 800-992-2003 elsewhere in the US; fax: 714-476-2538).

Travel Bound (599 Broadway, Penthouse, New York, NY 10012; phone: 212-334-1350 in New York State; 800-456-8656 elsewhere in the US; fax: 800-208-7080).

Travel Concepts (62 Commonwealth Ave., Suite 3, Boston, MA 02116; phone: 617-266-8450; fax: 617-267-2477).

Travelers International (7711 Bonhomme Ave., Suite 210, St. Louis, MO 63105; phone: 800-882-8486 or 314-721-7800; fax: 314-721-5955).

TWA Getaway Vacations (Getaway Vacation Center, 10 E. Stow Rd., Marlton, NJ 08053; phone: 800-GETAWAY; fax: 609-985-4125).

United Airlines Vacations (PO Box 24580, Milwaukee, WI 53224-0580; phone: 800-328-6877).

Value Holidays (10224 N. Port Washington Rd., Mequon, WI 53092; phone: 800-558-6850 or 414-241-6373; fax: 414-241-6379).

Vermont Bicycle Touring (PO Box 711, Bristol, VT 05443-0711; phone: 802-453-4811; fax: 802-453-4806).

Victor Emanuel Nature Tours (PO Box 33008, Austin, TX 78764; phone: 800-328-VENT or 512-328-5221; fax: 512-328-2919).

Wander Tours (PO Box 8607, Somerville, NJ 08876; phone: 800-282-1808 or 908-707-8420).

The Wayfarers (172 Bellevue Ave., Newport, RI 02840; phone: 800-249-4620 or 401-849-5087; fax: 410-849-5878).

Wide World of Golf (PO Box 5217, Carmel, CA 93921; phone: 800-214-4653 or 408-624-6667; fax: 408-625-9671).

Wilderness Travel (801 Allston Way, Berkeley, CA 94710; phone: 800-368-2794 or 510-548-0420; fax: 510-548-0347).

X.O. Travel Consultants (38 W. 32nd St., Suite 1009, New York, NY 10001; phone: 212-947-5530 in New York State; 800-262-9682 elsewhere in the US; fax: 212-971-0924).

Insurance

The first person with whom you should discuss travel insurance is your own insurance broker. You may discover that the insurance you already carry protects you adequately while traveling and that you need little additional coverage. If you charge travel services, the credit card company also may provide some insurance coverage (and other safeguards).

Types of Travel Insurance

Automobile insurance: Provides collision, theft, property damage, and personal liability protection while driving.

Baggage and personal effects insurance: Protects your bags and their contents in case of damage or theft at any point during your travels.

Default and/or bankruptcy insurance: Provides coverage in the event of default and/or bankruptcy on the part of the tour operator, airline, or other travel supplier.

Flight insurance: Covers accidental injury or death while flying.

Personal accident and sickness insurance: Covers cases of illness, injury, or death in an accident while traveling.

Trip cancellation and interruption insurance: Guarantees a refund if you must cancel a trip; may reimburse you for additional travel costs incurred in catching up with a tour or traveling home early.

Combination policies: Include any or all of the above.

Disabled Travelers

Make travel arrangements well in advance. Specify to all services involved the nature of your disability to determine if there are accommodations and facilities that meet your needs. Regularly revised hotel and restaurant guides, such as the *Michelin Red Guide to Great Britain and Ireland* (Michelin Travel Publications, PO Box 19008, Greenville, SC 29602-9008; phone: 803-458-5000 in South Carolina; 800-423-0485 elsewhere in the US; fax: 803-458-5665), use the standard symbol of access (person in a wheelchair) to point out accommodations suitable for wheelchair-bound guests.

For those visiting London, *Artsline* (54 Chalton St., London NW1 1H5, England; phone: 44-171-388-2227; fax: 44-171-383-2653) offers information on accessibility at London theaters and art venues. *Airbus* and *Stationlink* buses (the aboveground components of London's public transportation system) are wheelchair-accessible. The *London Regional Transport Unit for Disabled Passengers* (55 Broadway, London SW1H 0BD, England; phone/TDD: 44-171-918-3312; fax: 44-171-918-3876) publishes *Access to the Underground,* which includes schedule and fare information.

An increasing number of hotels and other facilities are modernizing and adapting facilities to accommodate disabled travelers. Among the hotels in Great Britain that provide accessible accommodations are the *Alison Park* (3 Temple Rd., Buxton, Derbyshire SK17 9BA, England; phone: 44-1298-22473; fax: 44-1298-72709), the *Berners Park Plaza* (10 Berners St., London W1A 3BE, England; phone: 44-171-636-1629; fax: 44-171-580-3972), the *Copthorne Tara* (Scarsdale Pl., Wrights La., Kensington, London W8 5SR, England; phone: 44-171-937-7211; fax: 44-171-937-7100), and properties of the *Swallow* chain (US office: 188 S. Bellevue Ave., Langhorne, PA 19047; phone: 800-444-1545; fax: 215-741-5156). Agencies that rent properties adapted to the needs of the disabled include *Country Holidays* (Spring Mill, Stonybank Rd., Earby, Lancashire BB8 6RN, England; phone: 44-1282-844284; fax: 44-1282-844288), *Cressbrook Hall Cottages* (Cressbrook, Buxton, Derbyshire SK17 8SY, England; phone: 44-1298-871289), and *John Grooms* (10 Gloucester Dr., Finsbury Park, London N4 2LP, England; phone: 44-181-802-7272; fax: 44-181-809-1754).

Organizations

ACCENT on Living (PO Box 700, Bloomington, IL 61702; phone: 800-787-8444 or 309-378-2961; fax: 309-378-4420).

Access: The Foundation for Accessibility by the Disabled (PO Box 356, Malverne, NY 11565; phone/fax: 516-887-5798).

American Foundation for the Blind (15 W. 16th St., New York, NY 10011; phone: 800-232-5463 or 212-620-2147; fax: 212-727-7418).

Holiday Care Service (2 Old Bank Chambers, Station Rd., Horley, Surrey RH6 9HW, England; phone: 44-1293-774535; fax: 44-1293-784647).

Information Center for Individuals with Disabilities (Ft. Point Pl., 27-43 Wormwood St., Boston, MA 02210; phone: 800-462-5015 in Massachusetts; 617-727-5540 elsewhere in the US; TDD: 617-345-9743; fax: 617-345-5318).

Mobility International (main office: 228 Borough High St., London SE1 1JX, England; phone: 44-171-403-5688; fax: 44-171-378-1292; US office: *MIUSA,* PO Box 10767, Eugene, OR 97440; phone/TDD: 503-343-1284; fax: 503-343-6812).

Moss Rehabilitation Hospital Travel Information Service (telephone referrals only; phone: 215-456-9600; TDD: 215-456-9602).

National Rehabilitation Information Center (8455 Colesville Rd., Suite 935, Silver Spring, MD 20910; phone: 301-588-9284; fax: 301-587-1967).

The National Trust (36 Queen Anne's Gate, London SW1H 9AS, England; phone: 44-171-222-9251; fax: 44-171-222-5097).

Paralyzed Veterans of America (*PVA;* PVA/ATTS Program, 801 18th St. NW, Washington, DC 20006; phone: 202-872-1300 in Washington, DC; 800-424-8200 elsewhere in the US; fax: 202-785-4452).

Royal Association for Disability and Rehabilitation (*RADAR;* 12 City Forum, 250 City Rd., London EC1V 8AF, England; phone: 44-171-250-3222; fax: 44-171-250-0212).

Society for the Advancement of Travel for the Handicapped (*SATH;* 347 Fifth Ave., Suite 610, New York, NY 10016; phone: 212-447-7284; fax: 212-725-8253).

Travel Industry and Disabled Exchange (*TIDE;* 5435 Donna Ave., Tarzana, CA 91356; phone: 818-368-5648).

Tripscope (The Courtyard, Evelyn Rd., London W4 5JL, England; phone: 44-181-994-9294; fax: 44-181-994-3618).

Publications

Access Travel: A Guide to the Accessibility of Airport Terminals (Consumer Information Center, Dept. 578Z, Pueblo, CO 81009; phone: 719-948-3334).

Air Transportation of Handicapped Persons (Publication #AC-120-32; *US Department of Transportation,* Distribution Unit, Publications Section, M-443-2, 400 Seventh St. SW, Washington, DC 20590; phone: 202-366-0039).

The Diabetic Traveler (PO Box 8223 RW, Stamford, CT 06905; phone: 203-327-5832; fax: 203-975-1748).

Directory of Travel Agencies for the Disabled *and* ***Travel for the Disabled,*** both by Helen Hecker (Twin Peaks Press, PO Box 129, Vancouver, WA 98666; phone: 800-637-CALM or 206-694-2462; fax: 206-696-3210).

Guide for the Disabled Traveler (*British Automobile Association,* Fanum House, Basing View, Basingstoke, Hampshire RG21 2EA, England; phone: 44-1256-20123; fax: 44-1256-493389; in the US, contact the *British Travel Bookshop,* 551 Fifth Ave., New York, NY 10176; phone: 800-448-3039 or 212-490-6688; fax: 212-490-0219).

Guide to Traveling with Arthritis (Upjohn Company, PO Box 989, Dearborn, MI 48121; phone: 800-253-9860).

The Handicapped Driver's Mobility Guide (*American Automobile Association,* 1000 AAA Dr., Heathrow, FL 32746-5080; phone: 407-444-7000; fax: 407-444-7380).

Handicapped Travel Newsletter (PO Box 269, Athens, TX 75751; phone/fax: 903-677-1260).

Handi-Travel: A Resource Book for Disabled and Elderly Travellers, by Cinnie Noble (*Canadian Rehabilitation Council for the Disabled,* 45 Sheppard Ave. E., Suite 801, Toronto, Ontario M2N 5W9, Canada; phone/TDD: 416-250-7490; fax: 416-229-1371).

Holidays and Travel Abroad, edited by John Stanford (*Royal Association for Disability and Rehabilitation,* address above).

Incapacitated Passengers Air Travel Guide (*International Air Transport Association,* Publications Sales Department, 2000 Peel St., Montreal, Quebec H3A 2R4, Canada; phone: 514-844-6311; fax: 514-844-5286).

On the Move (*Royal Automobile Club,* PO Box 100, RAC House, Bartlett St., South Croydon, Surrey CR2 6XW, England; phone: 44-181-686-

0088; fax: 44-181-681-8710; in the US, contact the *British Travel Bookshop,* 551 Fifth Ave., New York, NY 10176; phone: 800-448-3039 or 212-490-6688; fax: 212-490-0219).

Ticket to Safe Travel (*American Diabetes Association,* 1660 Duke St., Alexandria, VA 22314; phone: 800-232-3472 or 703-549-1500; fax: 703-836-7439).

Travel for the Patient with Chronic Obstructive Pulmonary Disease (Dr. Harold Silver, 1601 18th St. NW, Washington, DC 20009; phone: 202-667-0134; fax: 202-667-0148).

Travel Tips for Hearing-Impaired People (*American Academy of Otolaryngology,* 1 Prince St., Alexandria, VA 22314; phone: 703-836-4444; fax: 703-683-5100).

Travel Tips for People with Arthritis (*Arthritis Foundation,* 1314 Spring St. NW, Atlanta, GA 30309; phone: 800-283-7800 or 404-872-7100; fax: 404-872-0457).

Traveling Like Everybody Else: A Practical Guide for Disabled Travelers, by Jacqueline Freedman and Susan Gersten (Modan Publishing, PO Box 1202, Bellmore, NY 11710; phone: 516-679-1380; fax: 516-679-1448).

Package Tour Operators

Accessible Journeys (35 W. Sellers Ave., Ridley Park, PA 19078; phone: 800-846-4537 or 215-521-0339; fax: 215-521-6959).

Accessible Tours/Directions Unlimited (Attn.: Lois Bonnani, 720 N. Bedford Rd., Bedford Hills, NY 10507; phone: 800-533-5343 or 914-241-1700; fax: 914-241-0243).

Beehive Business and Leisure Travel (1130 W. Center St., N. Salt Lake, UT 84054; phone: 800-777-5727 or 801-292-4445; fax: 801-298-9460).

Classic Travel Service (8 W. 40th St., New York, NY 10018; phone: 212-869-2560 in New York State; 800-247-0909 elsewhere in the US; fax: 212-944-4493).

Dialysis at Sea Cruises (611 Barry Pl., Indian Rocks Beach, FL 34635; phone: 800-775-1333 or 813-596-4614; fax: 813-596-0203).

Evergreen Travel Service (4114 198th St. SW, Suite 13, Lynnwood, WA 98036-6742; phone: 800-435-2288 or 206-776-1184; fax: 206-775-0728).

Flying Wheels Travel (143 W. Bridge St., PO Box 382, Owatonna, MN 55060; phone: 800-535-6790 or 507-451-5005; fax: 507-451-1685).

Good Neighbor Travel Service (124 S. Main St., Viroqua, WI 54665; phone: 800-338-3245 or 608-637-2128; fax: 608-637-3030).

The Guided Tour (7900 Old York Rd., Suite 114B, Elkins Park, PA 19117-2339; phone: 800-783-5841 or 215-782-1370; fax: 215-635-2637).

Hinsdale Travel (201 E. Ogden Ave., Hinsdale, IL 60521; phone: 708-325-1335 or 708-469-7349; fax: 708-325-1342).

MedEscort International (*ABE International Airport,* PO Box 8766, Allentown, PA 18105-8766; phone: 800-255-7182 or 215-791-3111; fax: 215-791-9189).

Prestige World Travel (5710-X High Point Rd., Greensboro, NC 27407; phone: 800-476-7737 or 910-292-6690; fax: 910-632-9404).

Sprout (893 Amsterdam Ave., New York, NY 10025; phone: 212-222-9575; fax: 212-222-9768).

Weston Travel Agency (134 N. Cass Ave., Westmont, IL 60559; phone: 708-968-2513 in Illinois; 800-633-3725 elsewhere in the US; fax: 708-968-2539).

Single Travelers

The travel industry is not very fair to people who vacation by themselves—they often end up paying more than those traveling in pairs. There are services catering to single travelers, however, that match travel companions, offer travel arrangements with shared accommodations, and provide information and discounts. Useful publications include *Going Solo* (Doerfer Communications, PO Box 123, Apalachicola, FL 32329; phone/fax: 904-653-8848) and *Traveling on Your Own,* by Eleanor Berman (Random House, Order Dept., 400 Hahn Rd., Westminster, MD 21157; phone: 800-733-3000; fax: 800-659-2436).

Organizations and Companies

Club Europa (802 W. Oregon St., Urbana, IL 61801; phone: 800-331-1882 or 217-344-5863; fax: 217-344-4072).

Contiki Holidays (300 Plaza Alicante, Suite 900, Garden Grove, CA 92640; phone: 800-466-0610 or 714-740-0808; fax: 714-740-0818).

Gallivanting (515 E. 79th St., Suite 20F, New York, NY 10021; phone: 800-933-9699 or 212-988-0617; fax: 212-988-0144).

Globus/Cosmos (5301 S. Federal Circle, Littleton, CO 80123; phone: 800-221-0090, 800-556-5454, or 303-797-2800; fax: 303-347-2080).

Insight International Tours (745 Atlantic Ave., Boston, MA 02111; phone: 800-582-8380 or 617-482-2000; fax: 617-482-2425).

Jane's International** and **Sophisticated Women Travelers (2603 Bath Ave., Brooklyn, NY 11214; phone: 718-266-2045; fax: 718-266-4062).

Marion Smith Singles (611 Prescott Pl., N. Woodmere, NY 11581; phone: 516-791-4852, 516-791-4865, or 212-944-2112; fax: 516-791-4879).

Partners-in-Travel (11660 Chenault St., Suite 119, Los Angeles, CA 90049; phone: 310-476-4869).

Singles in Motion (545 W. 236th St., Riverdale, NY 10463; phone/fax: 718-884-4464).

Singleworld (401 Theodore Fremd Ave., Rye, NY 10580; phone: 800-223-6490 or 914-967-3334; fax: 914-967-7395).

Solo Flights (63 High Noon Rd., Weston, CT 06883; phone: 800-266-1566 or 203-226-9993).

Suddenly Singles Tours (161 Dreiser Loop, Bronx, NY 10475; phone: 718-379-8800 in New York City; 800-859-8396 elsewhere in the US; fax: 718-379-8858).

Travel Companion Exchange (PO Box 833, Amityville, NY 11701; phonc: 516-454-0880; fax: 516-454-0170).

Travel Companions (Atrium Financial Center, 1515 N. Federal Hwy., Suite 300, Boca Raton, FL 33432; phone: 800-383-7211 or 407-393-6448; fax: 407-451-8560).

Travel in Two's (239 N. Broadway, Suite 3, N. Tarrytown, NY 10591; phone: 914-631-8301 in New York State; 800-692-5252 elsewhere in the US).

Umbrella Singles (PO Box 157, Woodbourne, NY 12788; phone: 800-537-2797 or 914-434-6871; fax: 914-434-3532).

Older Travelers

Special discounts and more free time are just two factors that have given older travelers a chance to see the world at affordable prices. Many travel suppliers offer senior discounts—sometimes only to members of certain senior citizens organizations (which provide benefits of their own). When considering a particular package, make sure the facilities—and the pace of the tour—match your needs and physical condition.

Publications

Going Abroad: 101 Tips for Mature Travelers (*Grand Circle Travel,* 347 Congress St., Boston, MA 02210; phone: 800-221-2610 or 617-350-7500; fax: 617-423-0445).

The Mature Traveler (PO Box 50820, Reno, NV 89513-0820; phone: 702-786-7419).

Take a Camel to Lunch and Other Adventures for Mature Travelers, by Nancy O'Connell (Bristol Publishing Enterprises, PO Box 1737, San Leandro, CA 94577; phone: 510-895-4461 in California; 800-346-4889 elsewhere in the US; fax: 510-895-4459).

Unbelievably Good Deals & Great Adventures That You Absolutely Can't Get Unless You're Over 50, by Joan Rattner Heilman (Contemporary Books, 1200 Stetson Ave., Chicago, IL 60601; phone: 312-782-9181; fax: 312-540-4687).

Organizations

American Association of Retired Persons (*AARP;* 601 E St. NW, Washington, DC 20049; phone: 202-434-2277).

Golden Companions (PO Box 754, Pullman, WA 99163-0754; phone: 208-858-2183).

Mature Outlook (Customer Service Center, 6001 N. Clark St., Chicago, IL 60660; phone: 800-336-6330).

National Council of Senior Citizens (1331 F St. NW, Washington, DC 20004; phone: 202-347-8800; fax: 202-624-9595).

Package Tour Operators

Elderhostel (75 Federal St., Boston, MA 02110-1941; phone: 617-426-7788; fax: 617-426-8351).

Evergreen Travel Service (4114 198th St. SW, Suite 13, Lynnwood, WA 98036-6742; phone: 800-435-2288 or 206-776-1184; fax: 206-775-0728).

Gadabout Tours (700 E. Tahquitz Canyon Way, Palm Springs, CA 92262; phone: 800-952-5068 or 619-325-5556; fax: 619-325-5127).

Grand Circle Travel (347 Congress St., Boston, MA 02210; phone: 800-221-2610 or 617-350-7500; fax: 617-423-0445).

Grandtravel (6900 Wisconsin Ave., Suite 706, Chevy Chase, MD 20815; phone: 800-247-7651 or 301-986-0790; fax: 301-913-0166).

Insight International Tours (745 Atlantic Ave., Suite 720, Boston, MA 02111; phone: 800-582-8380 or 617-482-2000; fax: 617-482-2425).

Interhostel (*University of New Hampshire,* Division of Continuing Education, 6 Garrison Ave., Durham, NH 03824; phone: 800-733-9753 or 603-862-1147; fax: 603-862-1113).

Mature Tours (c/o *Solo Flights,* 63 High Noon Rd., Weston, CT 06883; phone: 800-266-1566 or 203-226-9993).

OmniTours (104 Wilmot Rd., Deerfield, IL 60015; phone: 800-962-0060 or 708-374-0088; fax: 708-374-9515).

Saga International Holidays (222 Berkeley St., Boston, MA 02116; phone: 800-343-0273 or 617-262-2262; fax: 617-375-5950).

Money Matters

The basic unit of currency in Great Britain is the British **pound sterling,** which is divided into 100 **pence.** The pound is distributed in coin denominations of £1, 50p, 20p, 10p, 5p, 2p, and 1p, and in bills of £50, £20, £10, and £5. Although the Bank of England stopped printing £1 notes some years back, banks in Scotland continue to print a version of the £1 note and these continue to circulate. You also still occasionally may find shillings in circulation, remainders of the pre-decimal currency system, but these no longer are legal tender. Note that the Channel Islands and the Isle of Man have some different coins and notes from the mainland, although the monetary system is the same. At the time of this writing, the exchange rate for British currency was £1 to $1.50 US.

Exchange rates are posted in international newspapers such as the *International Herald Tribune.* Foreign currency information and related services are provided by banks and companies such as *Thomas Cook Foreign Exchange* (for the nearest location, call 800-621-0666 or 312-236-0042; fax: 312-807-4895); *Harold Reuter and Company* (200 Park Ave., Suite 332E, New York, NY 10166; phone: 800-258-0456 or 212-661-0826; fax: 212-557-6622); and *Ruesch International* (for the nearest location, call 800-424-2923 or 202-408-1200; fax: 202-408-1211). In Great Britain, you will find the official rate of exchange posted in banks, airports, money exchange houses, hotels, and some shops. Since you will get more pounds for your US dollar at banks and money exchanges, don't change more than $10 for foreign currency at other commercial establishments. Ask how much commission you're being charged and the exchange rate, and don't buy money on the black market (it may be counterfeit). Estimate your needs carefully; if you overbuy, you lose twice—buying and selling back.

CREDIT CARDS AND TRAVELER'S CHECKS

Most major credit cards enjoy wide domestic and international acceptance; however, not every hotel, restaurant, or shop in Great Britain accepts all (or in some cases any) credit cards. (Some cards may be issued under different names in Europe; for example, *MasterCard* may go under the name *Access* or *Eurocard,* and *Visa* sometimes is called *Carte Bleue.*) When making purchases with a credit card, note that the rate of exchange depends on when the charge is processed; most credit card companies charge a 1% fee for converting foreign currency charges.

It's also wise to carry traveler's checks while on the road, since they are widely accepted and replaceable if stolen or lost. You can buy traveler's checks at banks and some are available by mail or phone. Keep a separate list of all traveler's checks (noting those that you have cashed) and the names and numbers of your credit cards. Both traveler's check and credit card companies have international numbers to call for information or in the event of loss or theft.

CASH MACHINES

Automated teller machines (ATMs) are increasingly common worldwide, and most banks participate in international ATM networks such as *CIRRUS* (phone: 800-4-CIRRUS) and *PLUS* (phone: 800-THE-PLUS). Cardholders can withdraw cash from any machine in the same network using either a "bank" card or, in some cases, a credit card. Additional information on ATMs and networks can be obtained from your bank or credit card company.

SENDING MONEY ABROAD

Should the need arise, you can have money sent to you throughout Great Britain via the services provided by *American Express MoneyGram* (phone:

800-926-9400 for information; 800-866-8800 for money transfers) or *Western Union Financial Services* (phone: 800-325-6000 or 800-325-4176). If you are down to your last cent and have no other way to obtain cash, the nearest *US Consulate* will let you call home to set these matters in motion.

Accommodations

For specific information on hotels, inns, and other selected accommodations, see *Best in Town* in THE CITIES, *Best en Route* in DIRECTIONS, and sections throughout DIVERSIONS. Also consult free brochures available from the *British Tourist Authority,* such as *Stay at an Inn, Stay on a Farm,* and *Stay in a British Home.*

BED AND BREAKFAST ESTABLISHMENTS

Bed and breakfasts (commonly known as B&Bs) are a staple of the lodging scene in Great Britain and range from humble country cottages to elegant manor houses. The *British Tourist Authority* publishes a leaflet called *Britain: Bed and Breakfast,* which explains bed and breakfasts, as well as other brochures listing B&Bs. The national tourist boards and other organizations also publish B&B guides. *The Best Bed & Breakfast: England, Scotland, Wales 1995–96,* a guide to more than 800 member establishments throughout Britain, is published by the *Worldwide Bed and Breakfast Association* (PO Box 2070, London W12 8QW, England; phone: 44-181-742-9123; in the US, contact *UK Bed & Breakfast,* PO Box 1070, San Diego, CA 92112-1070; phone: 800-852-2632 or 619-238-5216; fax: 619-238-5246); it also is available from Globe Pequot Press (6 Business Park Rd., PO Box 833, Old Saybrook, CT 06475; phone: 203-395-0440; fax: 203-395-0312).

Among the organizations that can book accommodations at British B&Bs are the following:

At Home in London (70 Black Lion La., London W6 9BE, England; phone: 44-181-748-1943 or 44-181-748-2701; fax: 44-181-748-2701).

Bed and Breakfast GB (c/o *Hometours International,* PO Box 11503, Knoxville, TN 37939; phone: 800-367-4668).

British Travel Associates (PO Box 299, Elkton, VA 22827; phone: 800-327-6097 or 703-298-2232; fax: 703-298-2347).

Leander Travel (6 Aubrey Ct., San Antonio, TX 78216; phone: 210-545-5129; fax: 210-545-5179).

Travellers B&B Reservation Service (PO Box 492, Mercer Island, WA 98040; phone: 206-232-2345; fax: 206-679-4533).

Uptown Reservations (50 Christchurch St., Chelsea, London SW3 4AR, England; phone: 44-171-351-3445; fax: 44-171-351-9383).

Reservations for B&Bs in London also can be made through the *London Tourist Board* (26 Grosvenor Gardens, Victoria, London SW1, England; phone: 44-171-824-8844; fax: 44-171-259-9056). In addition, the *Bulldog*

Club (35 The Chase, London SW4 0NP, England; phone: 44-171-622-6935; fax: 44-171-720-2748; and 6 Kittredge Ct., Richmond Hill, Ontario L4C 7X3, Canada; phone: 905-737-2798; fax: 905-737-3179) arranges upscale bed and breakfast accommodations for members. Once in Great Britain, travelers can make B&B reservations through the *Bed and Breakfast Great Britain Hotline* (phone: 44-1491-578803), which is operated by *Bed and Breakfast GB* (address above).

RELAIS & CHÂTEAUX

Founded in France, the *Relais & Châteaux* association has grown to include establishments in numerous countries. At press time, there were 21 members in Great Britain. All maintain very high standards in order to retain their memberships, as they are reviewed annually. An illustrated catalogue of properties is available from *Relais & Châteaux* (11 E. 44th St., Suite 707, New York, NY 10017; phone: 212-856-0115; fax: 212-856-0193).

RENTAL OPTIONS

An attractive accommodations alternative for the visitor content to stay in one spot is a vacation rental. For a family or group, the per-person cost can be reasonable. To have your pick of the properties available throughout Great Britain, make inquiries at least six months in advance. The *Worldwide Home Rental Guide* (3501 Indian School Rd. NE, Albuquerque, NM 87106; phone/fax: 505-255-4271) lists rental properties and managing agencies.

Rental Property Agents

At Home Abroad (405 E. 56th St., Suite 6H, New York, NY 10022-2466; phone: 212-421-9165; fax: 212-752-1591).

B & V Associates (140 E. 56th St., Suite 4C, New York, NY 10022; phone: 800-546-4777 or 212-688-9538; fax: 212-688-9467).

Barclay International Group (150 E. 52nd St., New York, NY 10022; phone: 212-832-3777 in New York City; 800-U4-LONDON elsewhere in the US; fax: 212-753-1139).

Blakes Vacations (1076 Ash St., Winnetka, IL 60093; phone: 800-628-8118 or 708-446-4771; fax: 708-446-4772).

Blandings (The Barn, Musgrave Farm, Horningsea Rd., Fen Ditton, Cambridge CB5 8SZ, England; phone: 800-854-0637 in the US; 44-1223-293444 in Great Britain; fax: 44-1223-292888).

British Travel Associates (PO Box 299, Elkton, VA 22827; phone: 800-327-6097 or 703-298-2232; fax: 703-298-2347).

Castles, Cottages and Flats (7 Faneuil Hall Marketplace, Boston, MA 02109; phone: 800-742-6030 or 617-742-6030; fax: 617-367-4521).

Country Cottages (1499 W. Palmetto Park Rd., Suite 304, Boca Raton, FL 33486; phone: 800-674-8883 for reservations; 407-395-5618 for information; fax: 407-395-9785).

Country Holidays (Spring Mill, Stonybank Rd., Earby, Lancashire BB8 6RN, England; phone: 44-1282-844284; fax: 44-1282-844288).

Cressbrook Hall Cottages (Cressbrook, Buxton, Derbyshire SK17 8SY, England; phone: 44-1298-871289).

Europa-Let (92 N. Main St., Ashland, OR 97520; phone: 800-462-4486 or 503-482-5806; fax: 503-482-0660).

Heart of England Cottages (PO Box 878, Eufaula, AL 36072-0878; phone: 205-687-9800; fax: 205-687-5324).

Heritage of England (22 Railroad St., Great Barrington, MA 10230; phone: 800-533-5405 or 413-528-6610; fax: 413-528-6222).

Hideaways International (767 Islington St., Portsmouth, NH 03801; phone: 800-843-4433 or 603-430-4433; fax: 603-430-4444).

Hometours International (PO Box 11503, Knoxville, TN 37939; phone: 800-367-4668).

In the English Manner (main office: 515 S. Figueroa, Suite 1000, Los Angeles, CA 90071-3327; phone: 800-422-0799 or 213-629-1811; fax: 213-689-8784; branch office: 4092 N. Ivy Rd., Atlanta, GA 30342; phone: 404-231-5837; fax: 404-231-9610).

The Independent Traveller (Thorverton, Exeter EX5 5NT, England; phone: 44-1392-860807; fax: 44-1392-860552).

Interhome (124 Little Falls Rd., Fairfield, NJ 07004; phone: 201-882-6864; fax: 201-808-1742).

Keith Prowse & Co. (USA) Ltd. (234 W. 44th St., Suite 1000, New York, NY 10036; phone: 800-669-8687 or 212-398-1430; fax: 212-302-4251).

London Lodgings and Travel (3483 Golden Gate Way, Suite 211, Lafayette, CA 94549; phone: 800-366-8748 or 510-283-1142; fax: 510-283-1154).

Orion (c/o *B & V Associates,* 140 E. 56th St., Suite 4C, New York, NY 10022; phone: 800-546-4777 or 212-688-9538; fax: 212-688-9467).

Property Rentals International (1 Park W. Circle, Suite 108, Midlothian, VA 23113; phone: 800-220-3332 or 804-378-6054; fax: 804-379-2073).

Rent a Home International (7200 34th Ave. NW, Seattle, WA 98117; phone: 206-789-9377; fax: 206-789-9379).

Rent a Vacation Everywhere (*RAVE;* 383 Park Ave., Rochester, NY 14607; phone: 716-256-0760; fax: 716-256-2676).

Sterling Tours (2707 Congress St., Suite 2G, San Diego, CA 92110; phone: 800-727-4359 or 619-299-3010; fax: 619-299-5728).

Uptown Reservations (50 Christchurch St., Chelsea, London SW3 4AR, England; phone: 44-171-351-3445; fax: 44-171-351-9383).

VHR Worldwide (235 Kensington Ave., Norwood, NJ 07648; phone: 201-767-9393 in New Jersey; 800-633-3284 elsewhere in the US; fax: 201-767-5510).

Villa Leisure (PO Box 30188, Palm Beach, FL 33420; phone: 800-526-4244 or 407-624-9000; fax: 407-622-9097).

Villas International (605 Market St., Suite 510, San Francisco, CA 94105; phone: 800-221-2260 or 415-281-0910; fax: 415-281-0919).

Your Home in London (PO Box 2277, Annapolis, MD 21404-2277; phone: 410-269-6232; fax: 410-263-4841).

HOME EXCHANGES

For comfortable, reasonable living quarters with amenities that no hotel could possibly offer, consider trading homes with someone abroad. The following companies provide information on exchanges:

Home Base Holidays (7 Park Ave., London N13 5PG, England; phone/fax: 44-181-886-8752).

Intervac US/International Home Exchange (PO Box 590504, San Francisco, CA 94159; phone: 800-756-HOME or 415-435-3497; fax: 415-386-6853).

Loan-A-Home (2 Park La., Apt. 6E, Mt. Vernon, NY 10552-3443; phone: 914-664-7640).

Vacation Exchange Club (PO Box 650, Key West, FL 33041; phone: 800-638-3841 or 305-294-3720; fax: 305-294-1448).

Worldwide Home Exchange Club (main office: 50 Hans Crescent, London SW1X 0NA, England; phone: 44-171-589-6055; US office: 806 Brantford Ave., Silver Spring, MD 20904; phone: 301-680-8950).

HOME STAYS

United States Servas (11 John St., Room 407, New York, NY 10038; phone: 212-267-0252; fax: 212-267-0292) maintains a list of hosts worldwide willing to accommodate visitors free of charge. The aim of this nonprofit cultural program is to promote international understanding and peace, and *Servas* emphasizes that member travelers should be interested mainly in their hosts, not in sightseeing, during their stays.

Other organizations that arrange home stays in Great Britain are *In the English Manner* and *Uptown Reservations* (addresses above). For more information, see the *British Tourist Authority*'s informative booklet, *Stay in a British Home,* which lists agencies that arrange home stays for foreigners in Great Britain, as well as many individual homeowners interested in such arrangements. Another publication that lists home stay opportunities is *Wolsey Lodges: Welcome to an Englishman's Home;* for a copy, contact *Wolsey Lodges* (17 Chapel St., Bildeston, Suffolk 1P7 7EP, England; phone: 44-1449-741771; fax: 44-1449-741590).

Time Zones

Great Britain is in the Greenwich Mean Time zone. The time throughout the country is five hours later than it is in East Coast US cities. The British move their clocks ahead an hour in the spring and back an hour in the fall, corresponding to daylight saving time, although the exact dates of the changes are slightly different from those observed in the US. British timetables use a 24-hour clock to denote arrival and departure times, which means that hours are expressed sequentially from 1 AM—for example, 1:30 PM would be "13:30 hours" (sometimes written as "13.30 hours").

Business and Shopping Hours

Most businesses in Great Britain are open weekdays from 9 AM to 5 or 5:30 PM. Stores usually are open weekdays and Saturdays from 9 or 9:30 AM to 6:30 PM, and some also are open on Sundays (usually from 9 or 9:30 AM to 5:30 or 6 PM). Department stores and malls often stay open until 8 or 9 PM at least one day a week (usually Thursdays), and also may be open from 9 AM to 6:30 PM on Sundays. In small towns and villages, stores may close for an hour at lunchtime, and some establishments may close for the day at 1 PM on Wednesdays or another day of the week.

Banking hours usually are weekdays from 9:30 AM to 3:30 or 4:30 PM; some banks also are open on Saturdays from 9:30 AM to noon. In some Scottish towns, a break for lunch from 12:30 to 1:30 PM is common. Money exchange houses at major airports may be open 24 hours daily.

Holidays

Below is a list of the public holidays in Great Britain and the dates they will be observed this year. (Note that the dates of some holidays vary from year to year; others occur on the same day every year.)

In England and Wales

New Year's Day (January 1; public holiday, January 2)
Good Friday (April 14)
Easter Monday (April 17)
May Day (May 2)
Spring Bank Holiday (May 29)
Summer Bank Holiday (August 28)
Christmas Day (December 25)
Boxing Day (December 26)

In Scotland

New Year's Day (January 1; public holiday, January 2)
Bank Holiday (January 3)
Good Friday (April 14)
May Day (May 1)
Spring Bank Holiday (May 29)
Summer Bank Holiday (August 7)
Christmas Day (December 25)
Boxing Day (December 26)

Mail

Most British post offices are open weekdays from 8:30 AM to 5:30 PM and Saturdays from 9 AM until around noon or 1 PM. Some post offices in London keep longer hours. Stamps also are sold at hotels, shops, and (primarily in the larger cities) kiosks located in airports, train stations, and shopping areas, as well as from public vending machines. British mail boxes are painted red and usually are cylindrical.

Although letters to and from Great Britain have been known to arrive in as short a time as 5 days, allow at least 10 days for delivery in either direction. Note that the inclusion of postal codes in British addresses is very important; prompt delivery of your letter or parcel may depend on it. If your correspondence is especially important, you may want to send it via an international courier service, such as *Federal Express* or *DHL Worldwide Express.*

You can have mail sent to you care of your hotel (marked "Guest Mail, Hold for Arrival") or to a post office (the address should include "c/o *Poste Restante,*" the British equivalent of "General Delivery"). Many *American Express* offices in Great Britain also will hold mail for customers ("c/o Client Letter Service"); information is provided in their pamphlet *Travelers' Companion.* Note that *US Embassies* and *Consulates* abroad will hold mail for US citizens *only* in emergency situations.

Telephone

Direct dialing and other familiar services all are available in Great Britain. Note that London has two city codes—71 for inner London, and 81 for outer London. As of April of this year, all city codes in the United Kingdom will be preceded by the number 1. (For example, the city code for inner London will be changed from 71 to 171.) In the interim, the city code will work either with or without the 1. We have included this digit in the applicable city codes throughout this guide.

To find a British city code, check the front of a telephone book or call directory assistance or an operator (see "Important Phone Numbers" below). British telephone directories and other sources always include the 0 (used for dialing within Britain) as part of the city code; when dialing from the US, follow the procedure described below, *leaving off the 0.*

The procedures for making calls to, from, and within Great Britain are as follows:

To call a number in Great Britain from the US: Dial 011 (the international access code) + 44 (the country code for Great Britain) + the city code + the local number.

To call a number in the US from Great Britain: Dial 010 (the international access code) + 1 (the US country code) + the area code + the local number.

To make a call from one British city code coverage area to another: Dial the city code + the local number.

To call a number within the same British city code coverage area: Dial the local number.

Although many public telephones in Great Britain still take coins, pay phones that accept only special phone debit cards are increasingly common. Available from *British Telecom (BT),* these cards are sold at transportation centers, post offices, some tourist information offices, newsagents, tobacconists, and other commercial establishments.

You can use a telephone company calling card number on any phone, and some pay phones take major credit cards (*American Express, MasterCard, Visa,* and so on). Also available are combined telephone calling/bank credit cards, such as the *AT&T Universal Card* (PO Box 44167, Jacksonville, FL 32231-4167; phone: 800-423-4343). Similarly, *Sprint* (8140 Ward Pkwy., Kansas City, MO 64114; phone: 800-THE-MOST or 800-800-USAA) offers the *VisaPhone* program, through which you can add phone card privileges to your existing *Visa* card. Companies offering long-distance phone cards without additional credit card privileges include *AT&T* (phone: 800-CALL-ATT), *Executive Telecard International* (4260 E. Evans Ave., Suite 6, Denver, CO 80222; phone: 800-950-3800), *MCI* (323 Third St. SE, Cedar Rapids, IA 52401; phone: 800-444-4444; and 12790 Merit Dr., Dallas, TX 75251; phone: 800-444-3333), *Metromedia Communications* (1 International Center, 100 NE Loop 410, San Antonio, TX 78216; phone: 800-275-0200), and *Sprint* (address above).

Hotels routinely add surcharges to the cost of phone calls made from their rooms. Long-distance telephone services that may help you avoid this added expense are provided by a number of companies, including *AT&T* (International Information Service, 635 Grant St., Pittsburgh, PA 15219; phone: 800-874-4000), *MCI* (address above), *Metromedia Communications* (address above), and *Sprint* (address above). Note that even when you use such long-distance services, some hotels still may charge a fee for line usage.

Useful resources for travelers include the *AT&T 800 Travel Directory* (phone: 800-426-8686 for orders), the *Toll-Free Travel & Vacation Information Directory* (Pilot Books, 103 Cooper St., Babylon, NY 11702; phone: 516-422-2225; fax: 516-422-2227), and *The Phone Booklet* (Scott American Corporation, PO Box 88, W. Redding, CT 06896; no phone).

Important Phone Numbers

Emergency assistance: 999
Local and countrywide information: 192
Local operator: 100
International information and operator: 155

Electricity

Great Britain uses 240-volt, 50-cycle alternating current. Travelers from the US will need electrical converters to operate the appliances they use at home, or dual-voltage appliances, which can be switched from one voltage standard to another. (Some large tourist hotels may offer 110-volt current or have converters available.) You also will need a plug adapter set to deal with the different plug configurations in Great Britain.

Staying Healthy

For up-to-date information on current health conditions, call the Centers for Disease Control's *International Travelers' Hotline:* 404-332-4559.

Travelers to Great Britain face few serious health risks. Tap water generally is clean and potable throughout the country, but if you're at all unsure, bottled water is readily available in stores. Milk is pasteurized (although it may not be homogenized), and dairy products are safe to eat, as are fruit, vegetables, meat, poultry, and fish.

When swimming in the ocean, be careful of the undertow (the water running back down the beach after a wave has washed ashore), which can knock you off your feet, and riptides (currents running against the tide), which can pull you out to sea. Sharks are found in coastal waters, but rarely come close to shore. Jellyfish—including the Portuguese man-of-war—are common, as are eels and sea urchins.

Most British towns and cities of any size have a public hospital, and even the tiniest hamlet has a medical clinic or private physician nearby. All hospitals are prepared for emergency cases, and many hospitals also have walk-in clinics. The *National Health Service (NHS)* provides free medical care to British citizens. However, visitors from the US and other countries that are not members of the European Economic Community (which provides reciprocal health coverage), will have to pay for most services.

Night duty rotates among pharmacies (also called "chemists") in Great Britain, and those that are closed display the address of the evening's all-night drugstore in the window. The address of the pharmacy on duty may be published in newspapers; the police (and often your hotel concierge) also should be able to provide this information.

Should you need non-emergency medical attention, ask at your hotel for the house physician or for help in reaching a doctor. Referrals also are available from the *US Embassy* or a *US Consulate.* **In an emergency: Go directly to the emergency room ("casualty department") of the nearest hospital, dial the emergency number given under *Telephone,* above, or call an operator for assistance.**

Additional Resources

InterContinental Medical (2720 Enterprise Pkwy., Suite 106, Richmond, VA 23294; phone: 804-527-1094; fax: 804-527-1941).

International Association for Medical Assistance to Travelers (*IAMAT;* 417 Center St., Lewiston, NY 14092; phone: 716-754-4883; and 40 Regal

Rd., Guelph, Ontario N1K 1B5, Canada; phone: 519-836-0102; fax: 519-836-3412).

International Health Care Service (440 E. 69th St., New York, NY 10021; phone: 212-746-1601).

International SOS Assistance (PO Box 11568, Philadelphia, PA 19116; phone: 800-523-8930 or 215-244-1500; fax: 215-244-2227).

Medic Alert Foundation (2323 Colorado Ave., Turlock, CA 95382; phone: 800-ID-ALERT or 209-668-3333; fax: 209-669-2495).

Travel Care International (*Eagle River Airport,* PO Box 846, Eagle River, WI 54521; phone: 800-5-AIR-MED or 715-479-8881; fax: 715-479-8178).

TravMed (PO Box 10623, Baltimore, MD 21285-0623; phone: 800-732-5309 or 410-296-5225; fax: 410-825-7523).

Consular Services

The American Services section of the *US Consulate* is a vital source of assistance and advice for US citizens abroad. If you are injured or become seriously ill, the consulate can direct you to sources of medical attention and notify your relatives. If you become involved in a dispute that could lead to legal action, the consulate can provide a list of local attorneys. In cases of natural disasters or civil unrest, consulates handle the evacuation of US citizens if necessary.

The *US Embassy* is located at 24-31 Grosvenor Square, London W1A 1AE, England (phone: 44-171-499-9000; fax: 44-171-495-5012). All consular matters are handled by the *Embassy.* There also is a *US Consulate General,* at 3 Regent Terrace, Edinburgh EH7 5BW, Scotland (phone: 44-131-556-8315; fax: 44-131-557-6023).

The *US State Department* operates an automated 24-hour *Citizens' Emergency Center* travel advisory hotline (phone: 202-647-5225). You also can reach a duty officer at this number from 8:15 AM to 10 PM, eastern standard time on weekdays, and from 9 AM to 3 PM on Saturdays. At all other times, call 202-647-4000. For faxed travel warnings and other consular information, call 202-647-3000 using the handset on your fax machine; instructions will be provided. With a PC and a modem, you can access the consular affairs electronic bulletin board (phone: 202-647-9225).

Entry Requirements and Customs Regulations

ENTERING GREAT BRITAIN

A valid US passport generally is the only document a US citizen needs to enter Great Britain, although immigration officers in British airports *may* ask for proof that you have sufficient funds for your trip, or to see a return or ongoing ticket. As a general rule, a passport entitles the bearer to remain in Great Britain for up to six months as a tourist. Although visas are not needed for longer stays, or for study, residency, or work, other documents are required. Students must have a letter of acceptance from the school at which they plan to study, and those who want to live and work in Great Britain must obtain specific permits. Proof of means of independent financial support is pertinent to the acceptance of any long-term–stay application. US citizens should contact the *British Embassy* or the nearest *British Consulate* well in advance of their trip.

You are allowed to enter Great Britain with the following items duty-free: 200 cigarettes or 50 cigars, up to 2 liters of wine or 1 liter of hard liquor, 60 cubic centimeters (2 fluid ounces) of perfume, 250 cubic centimeters (8 ½ fluid ounces) of cologne, and items designated as gifts that are valued at less than £137 per person (about $205 at press time). Note that only those over 18 (the legal drinking age in Great Britain) are permitted to bring alcohol into the country.

DUTY-FREE SHOPS

Located in international airports, duty-free shops provide bargains on the purchase of goods imported to Great Britain from other countries. But beware: Not all foreign goods are automatically less expensive. You *can* get a good deal on some items, but know what they cost elsewhere. Also note that although these goods are free of the duty that *British Customs* normally would assess, they will be subject to US import duty upon your return to the US (see below).

VALUE ADDED TAX (VAT)

This sales tax is applicable to most goods and services. Although everyone must pay the tax, foreigners often can obtain a partial refund.

Many stores participate in the *Europe Tax-Free Shopping (ETFS)* program, which enables visitors to obtain cash refunds at the airport upon departure. The procedure is as follows: Request a tax-free shopping voucher at the store when you make your purchase. At the airport, have this voucher stamped by *British Customs* officials, and then take it to the cash refund desk or agent (customs officials can direct you) for your refund.

If you purchase goods at a store that does not participate in the *ETFS* program, you still may be able to obtain a refund, although the procedure is somewhat more complicated and, unfortunately, subject to long delays. Request special refund forms for this purpose when making your purchase. These must be stamped by *British Customs* officials at the airport upon departure, and then mailed back to the *store,* which processes the refund. The refund will arrive—eventually—in the form of a check (usually in pounds sterling) mailed to your home or, if the purchase was made with a credit card, as a credit to your account.

Note that stores are under no obligation to participate in either of the VAT refund programs, so ask if you will be able to get a refund *before* making any purchases. For additional information, contact the British office of *Europe Tax-Free Shopping* (15 Galena Rd., London W6 0LT, England; phone: 44-181-748-0774; fax: 44-181-741-5520) or the *British Tourist Authority.*

RETURNING TO THE US

You must declare to the *US Customs* official at the point of entry everything you have acquired in Europe. The standard duty-free allowance for US citizens is $400. If your trip is shorter than 48 continuous hours, or if you have been outside the US within 30 days of your current trip, the duty-free allowance is reduced to $25. Families traveling together may make a joint customs declaration. To avoid paying duty unnecessarily on expensive items (such as computer equipment) that you plan to take with you on your trip, register these items with *US Customs* before you depart.

A flat 10% duty is assessed on the next $1,000 worth of merchandise; additional items are taxed at a variety of rates (see *Tariff Schedules of the United States* in a library or any *US Customs Service* office). Some articles are duty-free only up to certain limits. The $400 allowance includes one carton of (200) cigarettes, 100 cigars (not Cuban), and one liter of liquor or wine (for those over 21); the $25 allowance includes 10 cigars, 50 cigarettes, and four ounces of perfume. With the exception of gifts valued at $50 or less sent directly to the recipient, *all* items shipped home are dutiable.

Antiques (at least 100 years old) and paintings or drawings done entirely by hand are duty-free. However, you must obtain a permit from the *Department of National Heritage* (Cultural Property Unit, 2-4 Cockspur St., London SW1Y 5DH, England; phone: 44-171-211-6162; fax: 44-171-211-6170) to take original artifacts out of Great Britain.

FORBIDDEN IMPORTS

Note that US regulations prohibit the import of some goods sold abroad, such as fresh fruits and vegetables, most meat products (except certain canned goods), and dairy products (except for fully cured cheeses). Also prohibited are articles made from plants or animals on the endangered species list.

FOR ADDITIONAL INFORMATION Consult one of the following publications, available from the *US Customs Service* (PO Box 7407, Washington, DC 20044): *Currency Reporting; GSP and the Traveler; Importing a Car; International Mail Imports; Know Before You Go; Pets, Wildlife, US Customs; and Pocket Hints. Travelers' Tips on Bringing Food, Plant, and Animal Products into the United States* is available from the *United States Department of Agriculture, Animal and Plant Health Inspection Service (USDA-APHIS;* 6505 Belcrest Rd., Room 613-FB, Hyattsville, MD 20782; phone: 301-436-7799; fax: 301-436-5221). For tape-recorded information on customs-related topics, call 202-927-2095 from any touch-tone phone.

For Further Information

In the US, the *British Tourist Authority* is the best source of travel information. Offices generally are open on weekdays, during normal business hours. For information on entry requirements and customs regulations, contact the *British Embassy* or a *British Consulate.*

British Tourist Authority

Chicago: 625 N. Michigan Ave., Suite 1510, Chicago, IL 60611 (phone: 312-787-0490; fax: 312-787-7746).

New York: 551 Fifth Ave., Suite 701, New York, NY 10176-0799 (phone: 212-986-2200 in New York City; 800-462-2748 elsewhere in the US; fax: 212-986-1188).

The British Embassy and Consulates in the US

Embassy

Washington, DC: 3100 Massachusetts Ave. NW, Washington, DC 20008 (phone: 202-462-1340; fax: 202-898-4255).

Consulates

California: *Consulate General,* 11766 Wilshire Blvd., Suite 400, Brentwood, CA 90025 (phone: 310-477-3322; fax: 310-575-1450); *Consulate General,* 1 Sansome St., Suite 850, San Francisco, CA 94104 (phone: 415-981-3030; fax: 415-434-2018).

Georgia: *Consulate General,* Marquis I Tower, 245 Peachtree Center Ave., Suite 2700, Atlanta, GA 30303 (phone: 404-524-5856; fax: 404-524-3153).

Illinois: *Consulate General,* 33 N. Dearborn St., Ninth Floor, Chicago, IL 60602 (phone: 312-346-1810; fax: 312-346-7021).

Louisiana: *Consulate,* 321 St. Charles Ave., 10th Floor, New Orleans, LA 70130 (phone: 504-586-8300; fax: 504-525-9537).

Massachusetts: *Consulate General,* Federal Reserve Plaza, 600 Atlantic Ave., 25th Floor, Boston, MA 02210 (phone: 617-248-9555; fax: 617-248-9578).

New York: *Consulate General,* 845 Third Ave., New York, NY 10022 (phone: 212-745-0200; fax: 212-754-3062).

Ohio: *Consulate,* 55 Public Square, Suite 1650, Cleveland, OH 44113-1963 (phone: 216-621-7674; fax: 216-621-2615).

Texas: *Consulate General* 1000 Louisiana St., Suite 1900, Houston, TX 77002 (phone: 713-659-6270; fax: 713-659-7094).

Washington (state): *Consulate,* 820 First Interstate Center, 999 Third Ave., Seattle, WA 98104 (phone: 206-622-9255; fax: 206-622-4728).

Washington, DC: *Consulate General,* 19 Observatory Circle NW, Washington, DC 20008 (phone: 202-986-0205; fax: 202-797-2929).

The Cities

Aberdeen

With a population approaching a quarter of a million, Aberdeen is Scotland's third-largest city and is among the most distinctive in Britain. Always well known among the British for its striking granite architecture, bracing air, and 15th-century university, this North Sea port unexpectedly became familiar to a far wider audience during the 1970s as the oil capital of Europe. Aberdeen's position as the major service and supply base for the oil-drilling industry in the North Sea made it Scotland's most prosperous city in one short decade and allowed it—until the decline of world oil prices—to ride out Britain's economic recession more successfully than most other cities.

Aberdeen's more traditional commercial mainstays include fishing (built around herring—known as "the silver darling"), which is important enough to make the city the third-largest fishing port of the United Kingdom; shipbuilding; textile manufacturing; papermaking; and last, but not least, its enduring role as the market town for agricultural products raised in the surrounding countryside. Also noteworthy is the granite industry. Aberdeen stands on and is built of granite. Until the city is seen firsthand, few travelers realize what that means: Its streets look and are clean; its magnificent granite buildings always appear freshly renovated. The effect is chilling or cheerful, depending on the weather, but always spectacular. Britain's late poet laureate Sir John Betjeman spoke of the city as "a strange textured place . . . so remote, so windswept and of such a solid, grey strangeness." Others have compared it to St. Petersburg—hardly an unreasonable comparison, considering that Aberdeen lies at the same latitude as that most beautiful of Russian cities, and its Georgian and Victorian neo-Gothic architecture has a similar stateliness.

Granite and gray are not all that predominant, however. Beauty of a more natural variety is also rife. As the city's tourist authorities proudly boast, Aberdeen's numerous parks and gardens—with their abundant floral displays, magnificent roses, and heaths and heather—are nine-time winners of the prestigious *Britain in Bloom* competition. Between them, almost every conceivable kind of plant life is represented, from the exotic tropical and desert plants found in the *Winter Gardens* to the alpine flora of the *Johnston Gardens.*

Another feature adding to Aberdeen's special appeal is its unique location astride not one, but two rivers, neatly named Dee and Don. The Dee is the more famous of the two because of its association with *Balmoral,* the Scottish holiday retreat of British royalty, 50 miles away. What's more, the mouth of the Dee contains Aberdeen's harbor and docks. Yet both rivers have contributed substantially to the fortunes of the city. Had Aberdeen been closer to the sea, much of its charm would be wanting. As it is, a spacious esplanade stretches for 2 miles from Don to Dee, with the golden sandy beach on one side and a stretch of golf courses on the other.

Aberdeen's promotional slogan, "The City for Lovers," has an up-to-date ring, but its official motto is "Bon Accord," which dates from the night in 1308 when Aberdonians attacked the English garrison and razed the fortifications, using the French phrase as a password. The origins of the city can't be traced back much earlier than this event—only to the 12th century—but historians generally agree that settlement here goes back to prehistory. By the end of the 13th century, a succession of charters had created and reaffirmed all the trappings of a medieval royal burgh. The 14th century was turbulent—the English, expelled in 1308, returned in 1336 and devastated the town, causing such great damage that widespread reconstruction was required. That the unruly times continued into the 15th century can be seen in buildings such as *St. Machar's Cathedral,* which was resolutely constructed for defense.

Still, it was in the late 15th century, in "Old" Aberdeen—then known as the Kirktoun of Seaton—that the most important single event in Aberdeen's development took place. In 1494, Bishop Elphinstone obtained a papal bull allowing the establishment of a university, the third in Scotland after *St. Andrews* (1411) and *Glasgow* (1450); England, with a much larger population, had only two universities at this time—*Oxford* and *Cambridge.* Within a century, in 1593, George Keith, the Earl Marischal of Scotland, set up a rival, Protestant university on the site of a Greyfriars monastery in "New" Aberdeen. The two institutions, *King's College* and *Marischal College* (pronounced *Mar*-shall), finally merged into the *University of Aberdeen* in 1860.

During the Reformation of the 16th century, *St. Machar's* and other churches fell into decay; the cathedral was again damaged in the 17th century, during Oliver Cromwell's Commonwealth, when stones from its buttresses were used to fortify the city. The Jacobite risings of the first half of the 18th century—when followers of James Stuart, the Old Pretender, sought to restore him to the throne after the Act of Union of 1707 united England and Scotland as one kingdom—also touched Aberdeen. In 1716, defeated Jacobite army chiefs gathered here after the Battle of Sheriffmuir to learn that their "king" had slipped out of the country. In 1745, the drunken followers of James's son, Bonnie Prince Charlie, proclaimed the Old Pretender at the *Mercat Cross* and poured wine down the shirt front of Aberdeen's provost, who, loyal to George II, had refused to drink. The next year, the Duke of Cumberland stayed in Aberdeen with his army for six weeks en route to defeating Bonnie Prince Charlie's Highland army at Culloden Moor. The Act of Union meant the end of Scottish independence, but it also opened up the English market to Scotland and gave a great boost to Aberdeen's docks. This, along with the onset of the Industrial Revolution, encouraged the development of local industries. Woolen mills were established first; the manufacture of linen, cotton, and paper followed in the late

18th century. Granite quarrying emerged in 1741 with the opening of the Rubislaw quarry, which supplied most of the material used to build the city's elegant and austere houses and contributed to Aberdeen's nickname, "Granite City."

From the mid-18th to the mid-19th century, Aberdeen was also Scotland's leading whaling port. Overfishing destroyed the whaling industry, but the city quickly recouped with its herring fleets. By 1900, the introduction of steam trawling made Aberdeen Scotland's leading fishing port (a position it still holds), with whitefish rather than herring the prime catch. Over the years, however, the fishing industry here has declined. But thanks to the oil trade, Aberdeen has continued to prosper.

In the 19th century, Aberdeen's shipbuilding industry reached its zenith. William and James Hall can be credited with launching the world's first clipper schooner, the *Scottish Maid,* in 1839. This milestone ushered in Aberdeen's clipper era, when beautiful, fast, Aberdeen-built sailing ships won the city an international reputation. When, in 1872, the *Thermopylae* proved to be the fastest sailing ship in the world (in a race against the famous Glasgow-built *Cutty Sark*), the end of the era was already at hand, but it had established a shipbuilding tradition that has lasted to the present day.

Aberdeen is hardly the first place that travelers to Scotland consider visiting, but it shouldn't be given short shrift. Not only is it an attractive city, rich in historical and natural interest, it is also a cosmopolitan city possessed of ample restaurants, hotels, shops, sports facilities, pubs, entertainment, and cultural events. Furthermore, its location offers the best of several worlds: Aberdeen has the convenience of a modern city with many tourist attractions, the holiday atmosphere of a seaside resort (although the water is ice cold), and, finally, proximity to the magnificent scenery of the Highlands and "Castle Country."

Aberdeen At-a-Glance

SEEING THE CITY

It is no longer safe to climb the university's *Mitchell Tower* or the tower of *Aberdeen Town House* as parts of them are structurally unsound. However, for a truly panoramic view, the approach to Aberdeen by the main road from the south (A90) is dramatic compensation. As the highway descends to the 16th-century Bridge of Dee, there appears, in the words of Cuthbert Graham in his book *Portrait of Aberdeen and Deeside,* "a wide spreading silver-veined city arising from a river's brim." To the left, fertile fields, wooded slopes, and ever higher hills stretch almost to the Cairngorm mountain range.

SPECIAL PLACES

Many of the city's sights are found in two fairly compact areas. Aberdeen's most famous thoroughfare, Union Street, runs about a mile east and west across the city center, with Telford Bridge (or Union Bridge) midway in its course and *Union Terrace Gardens* just above. At the eastern end of the street is an open space known as the Castlegate or Castle Street, the city's historic marketplace since the 12th century. Another essential area for any visitor is Old Aberdeen (once known as the Kirktoun of Seaton), about 1½ miles north of the city center. Dating from the Middle Ages, Old Aberdeen has architecture that ranges from the 15th century to the present. It is made up of almost a single line of streets, beginning with College Bounds, which runs into High Street, Don Street, and, finally, Chanonry.

CITY CENTER

THE OLD TOLBOOTH AND ABERDEEN TOWN HOUSE The oldest building on the Castlegate is the *Old Tolbooth,* which dates from 1627, although earlier versions of it go back to King Robert III (1390–1406), who gave permission for the erection of a tolbooth, or burgh jail. The *Old Tolbooth,* its tower and steeple rising to a height of 120 feet, has been incorporated into a newer building, the handsome *Aberdeen Town House.* Completed in 1874, this ornate edifice, in Flemish medieval style, has been the home of the *Aberdeen City Council* for over a century; its tower is more than 200 feet tall. A free tour of the combined structures can be arranged by contacting the town sergeant on weekdays. Corner of Broad and Castle Sts. (phone: 276276).

MERCAT CROSS What is considered the finest old burgh cross surviving in Scotland was designed and built by John Montgomery in 1686. The focal point of the city, the cross stands on a hexagonal platform in the center of the Castlegate and is topped by a unicorn. Its charm and interest derive from both its decoration—the medallions adorning it contain portraits of the Stuart kings and Mary, Queen of Scots—and the rich pageant of history associated with the site. Castlegate.

MARISCHAL COLLEGE Part of the *University of Aberdeen* since 1860, it was built on the site of a Greyfriars monastery in the late 16th century as a Protestant rival to the earlier *King's College.* The college itself is a quadrangle, and most of the buildings on the inner courtyard were completed by 1844, but the primarily granite façade that opens onto Broad Street was completed in 1906. This great Broad Street frontage, designed in Perpendicular Gothic by A. Marshall Mackenzie, has been called "a tour de force of the granite carver's art," a remarkable work of architecture that is a must-see. The college also has the *Marischal Museum of Human History,* displaying exhibits of local archaeology and antiquities from Egypt and other African countries, as well as Europe, Asia, and the Americas. The college and museum are closed weekends. No admission charge. Broad St. (phone: 273131).

PROVOST SKENE'S HOUSE This townhouse, built in the mid-16th century, was extensively altered during the 17th century, when it was the residence of Sir George Skene, Provost of Aberdeen. In the 18th century, the Duke of

Cumberland, known as "Butcher" for his ruthless treatment of his enemies, stayed here for six weeks on his way to defeat the army of Bonnie Prince Charlie at Culloden. Now a museum, the house contains furnished period rooms, displays highlighting local history, and a beautiful painted ceiling dating from 1630. Another must-see, it has a kitchen that is open for tea, coffee, and light meals. Closed Sundays. No admission charge. Guestrow, off Broad St. (phone: 641086).

PROVOST ROSS'S HOUSE (ABERDEEN MARITIME MUSEUM) One of the oldest buildings in Aberdeen, *Provost Ross's House* was built in 1593. As the home of the *Aberdeen Maritime Museum,* it contains exhibits that provide an excellent survey of the city's maritime past. Models of famous ships associated with Aberdeen's port, including those of the clipper era, are a major feature. A *National Trust* shop and a visitors' center also are located here. Closed Sundays and October through April. No admission charge. Shiprow, off Castle St. (phone: 585788).

ST. ANDREW'S EPISCOPAL CATHEDRAL This cathedral is of special interest to Americans because it contains the *Seabury Memorial,* a gift of the American Episcopal Bishops in commemoration of Samuel Seabury of Connecticut, who was consecrated the first Bishop of America in Aberdeen in 1784. Although the structure was built between 1816 and 1817, the interior covers several periods. Closed October through April (except for church services). 28 King St. (phone: 640290).

ABERDEEN ART GALLERY The permanent collection contains paintings by Scottish artists from the 16th century to the present, a series of 18th- and 19th-century British portraits, 20th-century British works, and some French Impressionist paintings. Contemporary foreign and British sculpture also is well represented, plus decorative arts, including an interesting collection of silver and glassware from northeastern Scotland. Open daily. No admission charge. Schoolhill (phone: 646333).

UNION TERRACE GARDENS This delightful sunken Victorian garden runs along Union Terrace, right in the city center. It is a very picturesque and convenient place to relax after a hard day of sightseeing or shopping.

OLD ABERDEEN

KING'S COLLEGE This complex of buildings, the older part of the *University of Aberdeen,* was founded by Bishop Elphinstone in 1495, a year after he received the foundation bull from Pope Alexander VI. The most memorable structure is the delightful chapel, begun in 1501, which has a tower and spire topped by a detailed replica of a king's crown. Open weekdays and for services during university terms. A visitors' center with exhibits covering 500 years of university history is open daily. No admission charge. College Bounds, High St. (phone: 272000).

CRUICKSHANK BOTANIC GARDENS Next to the Chanonry in Old Aberdeen are the *University of Aberdeen*'s botanic gardens, begun in the late 19th century. A splendid collection of exotic plants, shrubs, and trees, a rockery, a water garden, and a heather garden make this a perfect spot for a delightful walk. Closed weekends October through April. No admission charge. Off the Chanonry (phone: 272704).

ST. MACHAR'S CATHEDRAL Described as one of the finest examples of a fortified church in Western Europe, it dates from the 14th, 15th, and early 16th centuries. According to legend, the site was consecrated in the 6th century by Machar, a missionary from Iona, instructed by St. Columba to go north through the land of the Picts until he came to a place where a river made a curve similar to that of a bishop's crosier, which is precisely what the Don does here (as can be seen by looking from the cathedral's northeast side). Work on the present building began in 1357 and finally was completed about 1520, when Bishop Dunbar installed the magnificent heraldic ceiling (bring binoculars). Outside, the west front, with its two great towers, is a particularly impressive sight. The Chanonry, off St. Machar Dr.

SEATON PARK North of *St. Machar's Cathedral* and adjacent to Don Street, it has several attractions, including the *Wallace Tower,* or *Benholme's Lodging,* a worthy example of a 16th-century Scottish tower-castle (172 such towers still exist in Scotland), and the *Chapter House,* built between 1653 and 1655 by George Cruickshank of Berriehill. The park itself, with woodland, gardens, an adventure playground, and a picnic area, is well worth a stroll. The grassy knoll at the Motte of Tillydrone affords an especially fine view of the river Don. Entrance at Don St. or at the end of the Chanonry.

BRIG O' BALGOWNIE (OLD BRIDGE OF DON) Across *Seaton Park* and reached via Don Street, the Brig o' Balgownie is one of Aberdeen's most famous relics of the Middle Ages. The brainchild of two early provosts of the city, Richard the Mason and Malcolm de Balgownie, it was begun in 1286 and completed in 1329. The bridge is 72 feet wide and 60 feet tall at the top of its Gothic arch, and it still is used today, although only by pedestrians.

ELSEWHERE

BEACH ESPLANADE With its 2 miles of sandy beach between the estuaries of the Don and the Dee, the *Beach Esplanade* has all the facilities expected of a typical British seaside resort. These include a children's "fishing village" and adventure playground, along with the £6-million *Beach Leisure Centre* (phone: 647647). The complex contains two pools, a flume, a sauna, a multipurpose gym, an ice skating rink, and a lounge bar, all in a tropical setting. The *Beach Esplanade* (phone: 595910) also has an arcade with video and slot machines (open daily June through August and on weekends in May and September), as well as the *Aberdeen Amusement Park* (phone: 581909), with several rides (including a Ferris wheel and a roller coaster), more video and slot machines, bingo, and a snack bar (the rides are closed October through *Easter*). The *Beach Esplanade* is great for kids—but be sure to have plenty of change.

FOOTDEE VILLAGE Known locally as "Fittie," this model village was built between 1808 and 1809 to house fishermen and their families; people still live here today. Designed by John Smith, city architect of Aberdeen, Footdee consists of two squares of single-story cottages, simple but robustly constructed examples of Georgian architecture. The village has become a popular spot with summer visitors, particularly city dwellers attracted by the secluded atmosphere of this traditional Scottish fishing village, just a short bus ride from the city center. Off the southern end of the *Beach Esplanade.*

WALKER PARK AND GIRDLENESS LIGHTHOUSE On the opposite side of the Dee from the village of Footdee is the grassy headland of cliffs and coves called *Walker Park.* Among its attractions are *Balnagask* golf course (see *Golf*) and *Torry Fort,* a military battery of 60 guns built in 1860, which now serves as a pleasant vantage point. *Girdleness Lighthouse,* designed by Robert Stevenson (the grandfather of Robert Louis Stevenson), was built between 1832 and 1833; it's not open to the public. The park and fort are open daily; no admission charge.

LOIRSTON COUNTRY PARK Near the coast, on the same grassy headland as *Walker Park,* this is the place to take children who like animals, because they can see and handle pets and domesticated farm animals at *Doonie's Farm* (phone: 276276). There is also a convenient picnic area. Open daily. No admission charge. Follow Greyhope Rd. south of *Walker Park.*

DUTHIE PARK AND WINTER GARDENS Overlooking the river Dee, this place makes for a splendid family outing and is Scotland's most visited attraction. *Duthie Park* is a large grassy area containing playgrounds, trampolines, flower gardens, exotic plants and birds, an aquarium, a boating pond, and a self-service restaurant, as well as the *Winter Gardens*—lush, tropical gardens inside heated glasshouses, which have just undergone a major extension from three quarters of an acre to one and a quarter acres. The gardens also have a good restaurant, *Ferns* (phone: 585310), which serves Scottish and continental fare (closed for lunch on weekends). Another interesting sight here is the award-winning cactus house, which boasts a talking cactus, among other attractions. *Duthie Park* is the site of the annual *Santa Lucia Festival of Light,* held throughout December, which includes a spectacular laser show. The park is closed October through June; the gardens are open daily. No admission charge. Access from Polmuir Rd. or Riverside Dr.

BRIDGE OF DEE Built between 1520 and 1527 by the enterprising Bishop Dunbar, this formidable piece of 16th-century engineering, which was widened during the 19th century, has seven semicircular arches of identical size. The bridge is famous as the site of the 1639 battle between the Covenanters under the Earl Marischal and the Earl of Montrose on one side and the Royal Army under the Earl of Aboyne on the other. The outcome was a Royalist defeat, leaving Aberdeen open to the Covenanters. On the Dee at the southern tip of Holburn St. and Riverside Dr.

RUTHRIESTON PACK HORSE BRIDGE A short walk north along Riverside Drive from the Bridge of Dee is the picturesque Ruthrieston Pack Horse Bridge, built by the *Aberdeen Town Council* between 1693 and 1694. It's made up of three arches and squat buttresses and was used to extend the old South Road northward into the city center.

OLD DEESIDE LINE WALKWAY This nature walkway along the Dee was created by lifting the track from a disused railway line. It begins at *Duthie Park* and ends about 4 miles away outside the village of Cults, to the west of Aberdeen. For those who are in the city for any length of time, especially during the spring and summer, the walk is a must. A book describing the route and its wildlife is available from the *City of Aberdeen Information Centre* (see *Tourist Information*).

VICTORIA PARK AND WESTBURN PARK These two adjoining parks just north of the city center provide further evidence of Aberdeen's wide open spaces. Features include flower beds, a paddling pool, a picnic area, a playground for disabled children (play leaders organize games during the summer), a garden for the blind, a restaurant, and a bar. Both parks are open daily. No admission charge. Westburn Rd.

HAZLEHEAD PARK About 2½ miles west of the city center, Aberdeen's largest park offers rose and heather gardens, exotic trees and shrubs, extensive woodlands, nature walks, and an unusual collection of rare birds and animals. Other assets include a maze, electric cars, a putting green, trampolines (closed October through June and weekdays in early summer), and a restaurant. In addition to the putting green, the *Hazlehead Park* golf courses are here (see *Golf*). Open daily. No admission charge. Access at the corner of Hazlehead Ave. and Groats Rd.

JOHNSTON GARDENS Another fine example of Aberdeen's numerous parks and gardens is this sweet little green space, known for its alpine plants, with a rustic bridge crossing a stream. Open daily. No admission charge. Viewfield Rd.

Sources and Resources

TOURIST INFORMATION

The friendly, helpful staff of the *City of Aberdeen Information Centre* in *St. Nicholas House* (Broad St.; phone: 632727) offers information, guidebooks, maps, leaflets, and assistance with accommodations. The center is open daily. *Bartholomew's Colour Street Map* (Geographia; £1.99/about $3), a good detailed map of Aberdeen, is available in bookshops.

LOCAL COVERAGE *The Aberdeen Press and Journal* is the morning daily, and arguably Britain's oldest. *The Evening Express* contains concert and "What's On" guides. For a rundown on local events, call the "Aberdeen What's On Line" (phone: 636363).

TELEPHONE The city code for Aberdeen is 1224.

GETTING AROUND

Quite a few of Aberdeen's attractions are well away from the city center, so visitors will most likely need a car or some other form of transportation.

AIRPORT *Aberdeen Airport* (phone: 722331), approximately 6 miles northwest of the city center at Dyce, is served by flights from London and other British and northern European cities. There is a cabstand and regular bus service to the *Guild Street Bus Station* Mondays through Saturdays (Sunday service is more limited).

BUS *Grampian Transport* (headquartered on King St.; phone: 637047) serves most local routes; fares vary from 25p (about 40¢) to £1.05 (about $1.60), depending on the distance. *Bluebird Northern,* the other major company, operates mainly longer-distance coaches from the *Guild Street Bus Station* (phone: 212266), next to the train station.

CAR RENTAL The major local companies include *Budget* (*Aberdeen Airport;* phone: 771777); *Kenning Car and Van Rental* (236 Market St.; phone: 571445); and *Mitchell's Selfdrive* (35 Chapel St.; phone: 642642).

TAXI There is a cabstand at the train station. Otherwise, call *City Taxis* (phone: 494949), *Mair's Taxis* (phone: 724040), or *TODA Taxis* (phone: 633535).

TRAIN The mainline station with connections to London, Glasgow, Edinburgh, and most other British cities is on Guild Street, a five-minute walk from Union Street (phone: 594222 for general information; 141-204-2844 for 24-hour information; 582005 for sleeper and *Motorail* reservations).

SPECIAL EVENTS

In keeping with Aberdeen's horticultural tradition, the *Aberdeen Spring Flower Show* is held every March. The major annual happening is the *Aberdeen Festival,* also called the *Bon Accord Festival,* which lasts for a week in mid-June. The *Aberdeen Highland Games,* in *Hazlehead Park,* are the highlight of the festival, but the activities also include a parade of floats down Union Street; pipe bands at the *St. Nicholas Shopping Centre* off Union Street; and more music, dancing, and shows. Other events include the youth *Football Festival* in July and the *Aberdeen International Youth Festival* in early August. The latter, 10 days long, draws young performers from many countries and ends with a fireworks display in *Hazlehead Park.* Three events in August, each lasting a day, are the *Grampian Seafood Fayre,* with displays on cooking and serving fish; the *Clydesdale Horse Show,* which, in addition to the fine horses, has pony rides for children and demonstrations by blacksmiths; and the *Rose Festival,* during which 250,000 roses are given away. In mid-October there is the week-long *Alternative Festival,* which showcases mostly local jazz and rock performers and comedians, although occasionally a celebrity is featured (James Brown and Van Morrison have appeared in the past). In December, the *Christmas Festival* sets the mood for the season with carolers, bands, chestnut stalls, and a carnival.

MUSEUMS

In addition to those mentioned in *Special Places,* Aberdeen has a number of other museums of interest.

JAMES DUN'S HOUSE An 18th-century townhouse has been renovated and decorated to reflect its period, with permanent displays and special exhibitions. Closed Sundays. No admission charge. 61 Schoolhill (phone: 646333).

PEACOCK ARTSPACE GALLERIES AND PEACOCK PRINTMAKERS Contemporary Scottish art is housed in an early-18th-century building. Major printing processes since the invention of the printing press in the 15th century also are on permanent display. Closed Sundays. No admission charge. 21 Castle St. (phone: 639539).

SATROSPHERE The first permanent interactive science and technology museum in Scotland, it has exhibits on the oil, fishing, papermaking, and farming industries essential to Aberdonians' livelihoods. There are videos, lectures, and an electron microscope, plus hands-on exhibits. Closed Sundays and Tuesdays. Admission charge. 19 Justice Mill La. (phone: 213232).

SHOPPING

Union Street and its connecting thoroughfares constitute the main shopping area, with a broad spectrum of stores represented, including most of the major department stores. There also are small specialty shops, such as antiques dealers and traditional Scottish shops selling woolens and tartans, plus maritime shops on Trinity and Regent Quays. Aberdeen also offers two shopping malls: *St. Nicholas Shopping Centre* (off Union St.) and the *Bon Accord Shopping Centre* (main entrance off Upperkirkgate). Both centers house major department stores. For standard shopping hours, see GETTING READY TO GO.

Be sure to take your passport when you shop, and always inquire about the Value Added Tax (VAT) refund application forms when your total purchases in a store are over £50 (about $75). The VAT is a surcharge payable at the sales counter, but foreign customers usually will be reimbursed for it at home (for more information see GETTING READY TO GO).

Aberdeen Family History Shop For those with Scottish blood, this shop has practically everything needed to discover one's roots. 152 King St. (phone: 646323).

Alex Scott Kiltmakers A wide assortment of kilts, tartans, jewelry, and Scottish gifts. 43 Schoolhill (phone: 643924).

Crombie Woolen Mill Offers a good selection of fine woolens and cashmeres. *Grandholm Mill,* Woodside (phone: 483201).

Ducks and Drakes Fine Scottish clothing for both sexes, including tweed blazers and kilts. 53 Rose St. (phone: 624207).

J. W. Baker Ltd. Northeastern Scotland's specialist in china, crystal, and pottery, with export facilities. 136 Union St. (phone: 640648).

The Still Man Malt whiskies by the score, many of which are unavailable outside Scotland. 54 Holburn (phone: 210323).

SPORTS

For full details on the wide range of local sports facilities, especially for outdoor sports, consult the free guide offered at the *City of Aberdeen Information Centre* (see *Tourist Information*).

GOLF The most prestigious of the several venues in and around Aberdeen is the *Royal Aberdeen* golf course at Balgownie (phone: 702571), which is of championship standard. Others include the *Links* course (phone: 632269), along the *Esplanade;* the *Balnagask* golf course (phone: 871286), in *Walker Park,* south of the Dee; and the three venues at *Hazlehead Park* (phone: 513747 or 317336)—two 18-hole courses and a nine-hole course.

HORSEBACK RIDING The best local place is the *Hayfield Riding School* (*Hazlehead Park;* phone: 315703); closed Mondays.

SKIING This sport is rapidly increasing in popularity in these parts. Skiing on a slope carpeted with slippery, artificial snow is available Saturday afternoons at *Kaimhill Dry Ski Slope* (Garthdee Rd.; phone: 318707). For real snow and hills, the most famous ski resort in the area is *Aviemore Cairngorm* (100 miles west of Aberdeen; phone: 1479-810310). Closer to Aberdeen, though, are the *Glenshee* (67 miles southwest; phone: 13397-41320) and *Lecht* (56 miles northwest; phone: 19756-51440) ski areas.

SOCCER *The Aberdeen Football Club,* nicknamed the *Dons* and based at *Pittodrie Stadium* (phone: 632328), once dominated Scottish soccer, achieving its most important success when it triumphed at the *1983 European Cup Winners Cup Final.* Now, although fans find the games enjoyable to watch, the team generally comes in second or third in national competition. The season runs from September to May.

SWIMMING There is an indoor pool, Turkish baths, a fitness room, and a sauna at *Bon Accord Baths* (Justice Mill La.; phone: 587920). The *Beach Leisure Centre* at the *Beach Esplanade* has two pools (see *Special Places*).

THEATER

The splendid *His Majesty's Theatre* (Rosemount Viaduct; phone: 641122) opened in 1906. It hosts performances by prestigious visiting companies, such as the *National Theatre of London* and the *Scottish Ballet.* Tragedies, farces, plus a variety of other familiar and contemporary productions share the stage at the *Capitol Theatre* (431 Union St.; phone: 583141). The *Lemon Tree* (W. North St.; phone: 642230) features local performers and short plays; it's also the main arena for the *Alternative Festival* (see *Special Events*).

MUSIC

Besides *His Majesty's Theatre* (see *Theater*), where the visiting *Scottish Opera* performs, there is the *Music Hall* (Union St.; phone: 641122), where the fare runs the gamut from performances by the *Scottish National Orchestra* for classical devotees to major rock and pop concerts for fans of contemporary music.

NIGHTCLUBS AND NIGHTLIFE

The oil boom has livened up Aberdeen's nightlife considerably. However, note that, as elsewhere in Britain, nightclub owners tend to spend vast sums of money on sophisticated lighting and sound effects, and then let them deteriorate rapidly. Furthermore, the music selection is usually banal, admission prices are expensive, and so are drinks (beer drinkers will find a much better pint in any pub). Try *Mr. G's* (70-78 Chapel St.; phone: 642112), *The Ministry of Sin* (15 Gordon St., entrance on Dee St.; phone: 211661), or *The Palace* (Bridge Pl.; no phone). Note: None of these establishments permit jeans on weekends, and sneakers never are allowed.

Best in Town

CHECKING IN

The *City of Aberdeen Information Centre* (see *Tourist Information,* above) has a booking service to help anyone who arrives in town without a reservation. Most of Aberdeen's major hotels have complete facilities for the business traveler. Those hotels listed below as having "business services" usually offer such conveniences as a concierge, meeting rooms, photocopiers, computers, translation services, and express checkout, among others. Call the hotel for additional information. Expect to pay $100 or more per night for a double room (with private bath, TV set, phone, and breakfast, unless otherwise noted) in hotels listed below as expensive, from $60 to $90 in those listed as moderate, and less than $60 in the one listed as inexpensive. All telephone numbers are in the 1224 city code unless otherwise indicated.

EXPENSIVE

Aberdeen Marriott Large (154 rooms) and modern, it offers the facilities expected in a first class establishment, including a restaurant, a fitness room, an indoor pool, a Jacuzzi, a sauna, a solarium, and business services. Riverview Dr., Dyce (phone: 770011; 800-228-9290; fax: 722347).

Ardoe House A baronial mansion built in 1878, it has rich wood paneling and a sweeping grand hall. Its 71 rooms feature amenities such as hair dryers and trouser presses; there is also a restaurant. Business services are available. Located just 3 miles southwest of Aberdeen. S. Deeside Rd. (B9077), Blairs (phone: 867355; fax: 861283).

Caledonian Thistle One of the city's premier hotels, this elegantly furnished and centrally located establishment of many years' standing has 80 rooms equipped with every convenience, including a pay-per-view movie channel. Also within the hotel are a sauna and a Taste of Scotland restaurant. Business services are offered. Union Ter. (phone: 640233; fax: 641627).

Copthorne Occupying a converted warehouse, this modern and centrally located hotel has 89 rooms and a restaurant specializing in Scottish fare, including a "Taste of Grampian" platter with local produce, smoked salmon, and mousseline of sole. Business services are available. 122 Huntly St. (phone: 630404; fax: 640573).

Marcliffe at Pitfodels This property combines a country-house feel in its library and lounges and the efficiency and dependable service of a big-city hotel. The 46 rooms have many conveniences, including satellite TV. There are also two restaurants; business services are provided. Located 3 miles west of Aberdeen. N. Deeside Rd. (A93), Pitfodels (phone: 861000; fax: 868860).

Stakis Aberdeen Tree Tops West of the city center, this modern establishment has 110 well-appointed rooms. Among the facilities are a fully equipped leisure center with a pool, a Jacuzzi, a sauna, and tennis courts; a Taste of Scotland restaurant; and business services. 161 Springfield Rd. (phone: 313377; 800-STAKIS-1; fax: 312028).

MODERATE

Craighaar Conveniently situated just a mile from the airport, this hostelry has 53 rooms equipped with a full range of facilities, including hair dryers and trouser presses. Its restaurant also has a reputation among locals for good, fresh food. Sports enthusiasts can partake of nearby golf, hunting, skiing, sailing, horseback riding, and fishing. Business services are available. Waterton Rd., Bucksburn (phone: 712275; fax: 716362).

Douglas Geared toward businesspeople, this modern hotel has 98 rooms, a restaurant, and business services. 43-45 Market St. (phone: 582255; fax: 582966).

Maryculter House This luxurious, peaceful country house is just 8 miles from town on the Dee. It has 24 well-appointed rooms, a restaurant, and magnificent gardens. Hunting, fishing, and water sports are nearby, and business services are available. S. Deeside Rd., Kincardineshire (phone: 732124; fax: 733510).

INEXPENSIVE

Brentwood Here is a convenient city center hotel with 65 smallish but pleasant rooms and *Carriages,* a popular brasserie. 101 Crown St. (phone: 595440; fax: 571593).

EATING OUT

Whether you're looking for Italian, French, Indian, Chinese, Turkish, or even Scottish fare, Aberdeen has a wide range of restaurants, pubs, cafés, and wine bars that offer excellent preparation and friendly service. To guarantee quality, however, a safe bet is to stick to hotel restaurants—or look for the Taste of Scotland sign, awarded to and displayed only in hotels and restaurants where the very best Scottish dishes are served. Most hotel restaurants close around 9:30 or 10 PM. Expect to pay more than $55 for a dinner for two with wine in restaurants listed below as expensive, from $30 to $55 in moderate places, and under $30 for inexpensive. All restaurants listed below serve lunch and dinner unless otherwise noted. All telephone numbers are in the 1224 city code unless otherwise indicated.

EXPENSIVE

Courtyard This small, elegant restaurant on a quiet lane just outside of the city center serves meticulously prepared continental dishes such as honey roasted boneless quail with oyster mushrooms and toasted pine kernels and grilled filet of Aberdeen Angus beef served on sautéed potatoes with caramelized shallots and red wine sauce. Open daily. Reservations necessary. Major credit cards accepted. 1 Alford La. (phone: 213795).

Gerard's A first class French dining spot with an excellent reputation. Closed Sundays. Reservations necessary. Major credit cards accepted. 50 Chapel St. (phone: 639500).

Silver Darling Fish Restaurant Known for its French cooking, this eatery specializes in fish, which is delivered fresh each morning. The chef also prepares delicious barbecue, and the view of the busy pier from the big bay windows provides continuous entertainment. Closed weekend lunch. Reservations advised. Major credit cards accepted. *Pocra Quay,* North Pier, Footdee (phone: 576229).

MODERATE

Ashvale This award-winning establishment offers the finest fish-and-chips in the land (it also offers take-out meals). Open daily. Reservations unnecessary. Major credit cards accepted. Great Western Rd. (phone: 596981).

Café Colmar A bright and airy eatery, it serves soups, salads, and simple bistro dishes. It's under the same ownership as *Gerard's* (see above), which is on the other side of the same building. Closed Sundays. Reservations unnecessary. Major credit cards accepted. 39 Summer St. (phone: 620333).

Marthas Vineyard Bistro The lively restaurant under the same management as *Courtyard* (see above), located just upstairs, features a casual, simple menu of sandwiches and entrées such as grilled rib eye steaks and *moules marinière* (steamed mussels). Open daily. Reservations necessary. Major credit cards accepted. 1 Alford La. (phone: 213795).

SHARING A PINT

Aberdeen's city center and outlying areas support a fair number of pubs, which operate from mid-morning until the early hours of the next morning. For a decent pint, plus some character and atmosphere, the pubs along the harbor front are the best bet. Like most pubs close to docks, however, they have a reputation for being "rough and ready," and would not normally be frequented by "respectable people"—which may well make them even more interesting. Two pubs in the central Union Street area are *Ma Cameron's* (Belmont La.; phone: 644487), which has oak beams and old paintings and is known for lively conversation; and the trendy *Prince of Wales* (St. Nicholas La.; phone: 640597), whose wooden furniture, incredibly long bar, and old-fashioned atmosphere and decor are popular with students. Other low-key spots are *The Grill* (213 Union St.; no phone), an Edwardian haunt that serves wonderful steak and kidney pie; *Cocky Hunter's* (504 Union St.; phone: 626720), which is decorated with junkyard antiques; and *The Bond Bar* (Broad St., next to *St. Nicholas House;* phone: 623123), a jovial, underground pub with tartan walls.

Bath

Bath was meant to be a beautiful city, and it is. Anchored in the valley of the river Avon and reverberating up seven surrounding hills in the southwest corner of the Cotswolds, it would have been attractive for its location alone. But for more than 1,600 years, this ancient city—known as Aquae Sulis to its Roman founders—remained undistinguished except as the site of Britain's only hot springs. It was a remarkable 18th-century urban planning effort that made Bath the splendid Georgian city that it is today. Then the haphazard parts, including the striking abbey, were unified along classical lines in tier upon tier of crescents, terraces, and squares. As a result, Bath calls itself the first planned city in England, and visitors who see its warm, honey-colored stones set against the rich green of lawn, tree, and wooded hillside probably will agree.

Part of Bath's legacy includes the story of Bladud, the father of King Lear (yes, *that* one), who contracted leprosy; in a dramatic downturn of his curriculum vitae, he descended from prince to swineherd. Observing that his leprous pigs appeared to be cured when they wallowed in mud, Bladud hastily followed suit, made a miraculous recovery, and was reinstated at court. But even before this, the city's history begins with the Romans who, in approximately AD 54, established an elaborate system of baths here, along with a temple to Sulis Minerva, a combination of the Celtic deity Sul and the Roman goddess of wisdom, Minerva. The town grew to become a famous health resort, but it declined rapidly after the Romans left Britain in the early 5th century.

In 781, the Saxons built such a fine abbey that it was chosen as the site of the coronation (in 973) of King Edgar (thought to be the first King of England). The ceremony has remained a model for subsequent coronations of English kings and queens. The city's fame was short-lived, though the sick continued to be drawn to baths erected over the salubrious mineral springs by builders unaware of the ancient prototypes buried underground. As visitors soaked in the *Cross Bath* (dating from the 7th century), the *King's Bath,* and others, Bathonians made a better living in the wool trade.

With the patronage of royalty in the late 17th century, Bath began to regain its reputation as a first class spa. The wife of King James II, Mary of Modena, bore a healthy son after a stop at the *Cross Bath.* His daughter, Queen Anne, later made several trips. Once kings and queens with their entourages, members of court, and country gentry began to flock here, Bath was suddenly fashionable among both the healthy and the sick.

Today's city of elegant squares and crescent streets is the labor of love of three 18th-century men. When Richard "Beau" Nash arrived in 1705, he became master of ceremonies in charge of public entertainment. In the course of his duties, he found the money to pave roads, light streets, and endow the *Royal Mineral Water Hospital,* which survives as the *Royal National Hospital for Rheumatic Diseases.* He also laid down unbreakable rules of etiquette; as a result, duels were suppressed, smoking in public prohibited, and improper dress ridiculed. Within a generation, the sheer force of his personality had made Bath the second capital of English society.

Ralph Allen, who eventually became quite rich as the city's postmaster, arrived next. He bought the limestone quarries on Combe Down, the southern hill of the city. Bath's pale stone was as yet untested for building purposes, so Allen engaged John Wood, a Yorkshire architect, as technical adviser. It was a master stroke. Wood imposed architectural order on the city, designing not just single buildings but entire rows, crescents, and squares in accordance with the neoclassical principles of the Palladian style. Queen's Square, North and South Parade, and the *Circus* are all his, and his son, another John Wood, contributed the *Assembly Rooms* and the grandeur of the *Royal Crescent.*

Visitors to Bath today see it much as the Georgians left it, despite bombing damage during World War II, a growing population (now at 84,283), and the development of light industry. Bathonians carefully safeguard their heritage and architecture—to the point where residents whose tree-lined gardens are visible to tourists receive a maintenance grant from the city. (It is the only complete city in the country ranked by UNESCO as a World Heritage Site, and one of only three in the world—the other two are Florence and Rome.) The congenial blend of past and present is one of the marvels of Bath. It still provides the atmosphere of a gentler age, a time immortalized in the novels of Jane Austen. It's hard to shake this feeling—but why try? Instead, reinforce it by walking to the *Royal Crescent* at dusk. As the honey-colored stones darken to gray, the lights of the city twinkle across the shadows of *Royal Victoria Park* as softly as gas lamps. It's easy to imagine you're in an England of another time.

Bath At-a-Glance

SEEING THE CITY

The up-and-down setting of this city on seven hills provides more than one spot for an overall view. If you have a car, drive north up Lansdown Road and see Bath unfold beneath you or, even better, go to the opposite side of town: From Widcombe Hill or North Road you face directly onto *Bath Abbey,* the *Royal Crescent,* and the *Pump Room.* The ultimate view, however, must be from the air. *Heritage Balloons* (phone: 318747) can take you on a hot-air balloon flight, skimming above Bath and the surrounding countryside.

SPECIAL PLACES

Bath's tourism "musts" are conveniently situated in the heart of town. The hot baths of Aquae Sulis may have given the city its start, but the most commanding building is the 16th-century abbey, a massive square-towered edifice that dwarfs its surroundings. Still later came the *Assembly Rooms,* the *Pump Room,* and Bath's architecturally glorious streets, squares, and crescents.

ROMAN BATHS Undiscovered until the 18th century, the baths are Britain's most complete Roman remains, fed by the country's only hot springs. The water gushes to the surface at 110F (43C) at a rate of 250,000 gallons a day. Established by Britain's Roman overlords in AD 54, the whole system created Aquae Sulis, named in honor of the Celtic goddess Sul. Ailing pilgrims came from all over to cure "Pox, Scab, and Great Aches." When the Romans pulled out of Britain, the baths sank beneath the mud, and subsequent residents built right over them. A nearby museum displays interesting discoveries from excavations—coins, gemstones, mosaics, and a gilt-bronze head of Sulis Minerva. Many of these items had been thrown as offerings to the sacred spring—some to call down curses upon enemies. Closed *Christmas Day* and *Boxing Day.* Admission charge to the *Roman Baths* includes the *Pump Room;* a combined ticket covers admission to the *Assembly Rooms* and the *Museum of Costume* on Bennett Street as well (see below for all). *Abbey Churchyard* (phone: 461111).

PUMP ROOM This grand hall above the baths was built at the end of the 18th century. Then it was one of the town's social centers; today it continues as a meeting place for both natives and tourists. Glasses of the tepid, cloudy, mineral-rich waters are available for sampling in the *Pump Room* for 75p (about $1.15). Geologists say it is the very rainwater that fell upon the Mendip Hills some 10,000 years ago, which could explain why it has a strong flavor of rusty nails. Most visitors furtively abandon their glasses in favor of a pot of Earl Grey tea, sipped to the sprightly strings of the *Pump Room Trio,* which plays a daily morning concert. There's also a grand piano recital and tea with Bath buns every afternoon. Open daily. *Abbey Churchyard* (phone: 461111).

SALLY LUNN'S HOUSE When you've partaken of Bath buns in the *Pump Room,* try a Sally Lunn (a pastry not quite as sweet as a Bath bun, eaten toasted with butter or clotted cream). Sally's house, built in 1482, is supposed to be the oldest in Bath. The buns have been served here ever since Sally, a pastry cook herself, first dreamed them up in the 17th century. Open daily. The downstairs museum is closed Sundays. Admission charge. 4 North Parade Passage (phone: 461634).

BATH ABBEY A Saxon abbey and a Norman cathedral occupied this site before the present church was begun in 1499. The cathedral had fallen into ruin when Oliver King, Bishop of Bath and Wells, was inspired by a dream to rebuild the church. Though its predecessor was much larger, *Bath Abbey* is no disappointment. Inside, daylight pours through sparkling panes of glass in the tall clerestory windows, illuminating the famous fan vaulting, a pale and delicate example of English Perpendicular architecture. Adorning its walls are more memorial plaques than any other church in Great Britain except *Westminster Abbey.* The 19th-century east window over the altar, unusual for its square top, was damaged in World War II and restored by the great-grandson of its original designer. Note also the medieval carving of the Prior Birde Chantry next to the sanctuary and, at the northeast corner of the church, the modern Edgar Window, showing the coronation in 973 of the man thought to have been the first king of England. On the south side of the abbey are the recently opened *Heritage Vaults,* with exhibits about the history of the abbey, including its reconstruction, as well as a collection of Saxon and Norman stonework. (Visitors cannot wander around during services.) The *Heritage Vaults* are closed Sundays. Admission charge. *Abbey Churchyard.*

ASSEMBLY ROOMS Designed by John Wood the Younger, these opened in 1771 as a fashionable gathering place where concerts, dancing, card games, and light refreshments could be enjoyed in surroundings of appropriate elegance. Such light-mindedness was scorned in the Victorian age, and from the mid-19th century on, the *Assembly Rooms* fell into disrepair, then were restored to their former splendor in 1938 only to be gutted, except for the shell, by a World War II bombing raid. Nowadays, the rooms look as they did in the 18th century. The ballroom, lit by five crystal chandeliers that were safely packed away at the outbreak of the war, looks like a giant blue and white Wedgwood confection, and the tearoom is no less delectable. Downstairs is the *Museum of Costume,* with an array of 18th-century finery along with exhibitions dating from 1560 to the present, making up one of the largest costume collections in the world. Admission charge to the museum. Bennett St. (phone: 461111).

ROYAL CRESCENT Considered the finest crescent in Europe, the *Royal Crescent* is the supreme achievement of John Wood the Younger. Begun in 1767, it consists of 30 pale amber Georgian stone houses whose 114 Ionic columns support a continuous, curving cornice. Iron fences, the sidewalk, and the cobblestone street repeat the curve, wrapping it around a sweeping segment of *Royal Victoria Park.* The *Bath Preservation Trust* has restored *No. 1 Royal Crescent* as a Georgian residence and museum of 18th-century cooking. Closed Mondays. Admission charge. At the end of Brock St. (phone: 428126).

CIRCUS Another example of Georgian town planning, this is possibly the greatest achievement of John Wood the Elder, who began it in 1754. It is a stately ring of identically faced stone townhouses surrounding a circular green. Each of its three sections is composed of 11 houses fronted by columns in Doric, Ionic, and Corinthian tiers. Wood designed one of the houses—*No. 7*—for William Pitt, MP of Bath and later Prime Minister of England; and other renowned people have lived here over the years, including painter

Thomas Gainsborough (*No. 17*) and explorer David Livingstone (*No. 13*). At the north end of Gay St.

PULTENEY BRIDGE It's a smaller version of the Ponte Vecchio in Florence. Built in 1770 by Robert Adam, this shop-lined structure on three arches connects Grand Parade and Bridge Street to Argyle Street. Below the bridge is the foaming, boomerang-shaped Pulteney Weir, redesigned in 1972 for flood control.

HOLBURNE MUSEUM Built between 1796 and 1797, this former hotel houses a superb collection of silver, glass, porcelain, bronzes, furniture, decorative art, and paintings by such English masters as Sir Joshua Reynolds and Thomas Gainsborough. A wide range of 20th-century textiles, Bernard Leach pottery, furniture, and calligraphy is displayed in a crafts study center. Closed mid-December through mid-February and on Mondays from November to mid-December and from mid-February through *Easter;* afternoon tea is served daily in the garden *Easter* through early November. Admission charge. Great Pulteney St. (phone: 466669).

AMERICAN MUSEUM IN BRITAIN Oddly enough, this very English town is home to the country's best collection of things American—Hopi kachina dolls and Shaker furniture, patchwork quilts and Pueblo pots, and even a tepee and a Conestoga wagon. While British visitors (particularly children) marvel at these oddities, Americans admire the quality of the items and the thoughtful way the several period rooms are put together. Note that it was at *Claverton Manor,* the Greek Revival mansion housing these exhibits, that Sir Winston Churchill delivered his first political speech in 1897. The museum and grounds are closed Mondays (except after a holiday weekend); the grounds also are closed December through February. Admission charge. Located 2½ miles east of town off A36 (phone: 463538).

THE BUILDING OF BATH Housed in the former *Countess of Huntingdon Chapel* (constructed in 1765) is a museum dedicated to Bath's heritage, with exhibits that explain how a muddy backwater was transformed in the 18th century into an architectural masterpiece. Closed mid-December to mid-January. Admission charge. *Countess of Huntingdon Chapel,* The Vineyards, The Paragon (phone: 333895).

BRITISH FOLK ART COLLECTION Those who enjoy the unpretentious honesty of naive art will be delighted by this collection of innocent images of English life from 1750 to 1900 (formerly called the *Museum of English Naive Art*). The paintings, from a boxer caught in a simple, striking pose to images of everyday life, are hung in a charming 18th-century schoolhouse adjacent to the *Countess of Huntingdon Chapel.* Closed Sundays *Boxing Day* through *Easter.* Admission charge. *Countess of Huntingdon Chapel,* The Vineyards, The Paragon (phone: 446020).

EXTRA SPECIAL

Just outside Bath, the Kennet and Avon Canal winds lazily along leafy banks, linking the river Thames at Reading with the docks at Bristol. Opened in 1810, the long-neglected canal now has been redredged, its 106 locks repaired, and damaged banks and bridges restored. All 87 miles are navigable once again, brought back to life for pleasure craft. On weekend afternoons in spring and summer, a waterbus plies between Bath and Folly Swing Bridge, the prettiest section of the canal. You also can enjoy a cruise on the river Avon aboard the *Scenic I,* which runs daily on the hour from 11 AM to 7 PM, upstream from Pulteney Weir opposite the *Parade Gardens.* For details on other boat trips, check with the tourist information center (see *Tourist Information,* below). It's also lovely to walk alongside the canal on the old towpath where horses drew barges long ago. A trip to the attractive village of Bathampton is another worthwhile excursion, a leisurely hour-long walk from Bath (or you can rent rowboats or punts at the *Bath Boating Station,* just a 15-minute walk from the railway station). Moor at the sandy landing area, head up through the parking lot of the *Beefeater* pub and stop in at *The George* (phone: 425079) for delicious food and ale. Visit *St. Nicholas Bathampton Church,* the final resting place of explorer and Bath native Admiral Arthur Phillip, the man who discovered Australia. Rebuilt in the 19th century, much of the church structure dates back to the 14th century.

Sources and Resources

TOURIST INFORMATION

Details about Bath can be obtained from the tourist information center (11-13 Bath St.; phone: 462831) next to the *Cross Bath.* An excellent *Bath Official Guide Book* is available from the information center and most bookstores. Christopher Ansley's *New Bath Guide,* a satirical look at 18th-century Bath society, was an immediate hit when it was published in 1766, and it is still carried in some local bookstores.

City of Bath honorary guides—known as "the mayor's guides"—will take you on a free, approximately two-hour walking tour; they're carefully trained, unpaid volunteers, and they frown on tips. Tours leave the *Abbey Churchyard* (outside the *Pump Room*); for exact times, consult the notice board outside the *Pump Room* entrance or ask at the information center.

Sulis Guides (phone: 429681) provides a private tour service using qualified, registered professional guides for walks in Bath and the surrounding area; special theme tours such as "Jane Austen," "Isambard Kingdom Brunel," and "West Country Gardens"; and car and bus tours.

LOCAL COVERAGE The daily (except Sundays) *Bath & West Evening Chronicle* has details of events taking place in the city.

TELEPHONE The city code for Bath is 1225.

GETTING AROUND

AIRPORT London's *Heathrow* and *Gatwick Airports* have a direct rail link with Bath via Reading. *Bristol Airport,* at Lulsgate, 15 miles west, is the nearest airport (phone: 1275-474444). Other local airports are at Plymouth, Exeter, and Southampton.

BUS *Badgerline/Guide Friday* and *National Express* operate the city buses and long-distance coaches from the bus station on Manvers Street. The fare varies depending on the distance traveled, but several discount passes are available, including a "Day Rambler" ticket (allowing a day's unlimited travel) that costs £4.50 (about $6.75) for adults and £3.30 (about $5) for children under 12. *Badgerline/Guide Friday* also operates hour-long, open-top bus tours of the city every 15 minutes daily during summer. Guided tours leave from beside *Bath Abbey.* For tour and bus information, call the station (phone: 464446).

CAR RENTAL Among Bath's most reputable car rental dealers is *Avis* (Unit 4B, Riverside Rd.; phone: 446680).

TAXI Cabs are available outside the railroad station, or your hotel can arrange for one.

TRAIN High-speed trains destined for London and other major cities leave regularly from *Bath Spa Station* (on Dorchester St. at Manvers St.). Traveling at more than 125 mph, the trains make the trip to London in 70 minutes. For information, call *British Rail* (phone: 117-929-42555 in Bristol).

SPECIAL EVENTS

One of the world's top music events occurs here in summer.

A FAVORITE FETE

Bath International Festival of Music For two weeks in late May and early June, Bath offers a catholic choice of concerts by top musicians of all persuasions, from medieval to jazz; informative tours and lectures in historic buildings and gardens; performances of opera and dance by leading companies; literary events and lectures; films; art exhibitions, including Britain's only contemporary art fair; relaxed late-night musical shows; and a candlelight procession on opening night. What sets this event apart are the concerts' venues. Choral works and organ recitals are presented in *Bath Abbey* or *Wells Cathedral,* and there are also concerts and operas in beautiful halls that date from the late 18th or early 19th century—chamber music or dance, for instance, in the city's *Theatre Royal.* Reservations are required, and bookings can be made by mail beginning the first week in April. For information, contact the *Bath Festival Office, Linley House,* 1 Pierrepont Pl. (phone: 462231).

The schedule of the *Bath Georgian Festival Society,* which holds concerts throughout the year, is available in the *Pump Room. The Royal Bath and West Show,* the biggest agricultural show in the West Country, is held annually at the end of May at Shepton Mallet, 20 miles south of the city. The *County Cricket Festival* is held in June on the *Recreation Ground.* Several annual antiques fairs also are held in Bath, including the *Bath Guildhall Antiques Fair* in August.

MUSEUMS

In addition to those mentioned in *Special Places,* we recommend the following:

HERSCHEL HOUSE AND MUSEUM Former home of Sir William Herschel, who discovered the planet Uranus. Astronomical and musical exhibits. Open daily from 2 to 5 PM March through October; weekends only from 2 to 5 PM the rest of the year. Admission charge. 19 New King St. (phone: 311342).

MR. BOWLER'S BUSINESS Explores the 190-million-year history of Bath stone; features the preserved contents of a Victorian brass foundry and an aerated mineral water factory; also includes exhibits on the history of cabinetmaking, and an engineering works. Closed weekdays November through *Easter.* Admission charge. Julian Rd. (phone: 318348).

POSTAL MUSEUM Inside is a life-size Victorian post office, where the world's first stamp, called the Penny Black, was launched through the mail in 1840. A display shows the history of mail transmittal through the ages. Closed Sundays in winter. Admission charge. 8 Broad St. (phone: 460333).

ROYAL PHOTOGRAPHIC SOCIETY On display are the society's collection of original Victorian photographs, including the very first photograph ever made, as well as early cameras; there are also changing contemporary exhibitions. Open daily. Admission charge. Milsom St. (phone: 462841).

VICTORIA ART GALLERY On view here are European Old Masters and 18th- to 20th-century British works, etchings, prints, porcelain, and Bohemian glass, as well as temporary modern art exhibitions. Open daily. No admission charge. Bridge St. (phone: 461111).

SHOPPING

Bath, quite justifiably, claims to be one of Britain's premier shopping centers. Antiques shops are numerous, particularly in the streets just south of the *Assembly Rooms,* and there also is a market held every Wednesday on

Guinea Lane, where the private shopper may spot something exquisite before the dealer from London or overseas does. *Aldridges Auction Galleries* (130-132 Walcot St.; phone: 462830) offers viewings on Saturday mornings and Mondays and holds sales on Tuesdays. Rummaging around Walcot Street's Saturday morning flea market may not reveal many genuine antiques, but you might just find the item of clothing, bric-a-brac, or furniture you've always wanted. Also, the *Bath Saturday Antiques Market* (Walcot St.; phone: 422510) features more than 50 stalls.

A taste of old Bath can be found at the *Bath Market* (in the *Guildhall* on Bridge St.; no phone). Butchers, fishmongers, secondhand book vendors, and fruit-and-vegetable stalls spill over one another in an atmosphere that reeks of tradition. It's a cheery, bustling place, especially on dark winter evenings (closed Sundays).

Milsom Street is Bath's main shopping artery. Another complex, the elegant *Shires Yard* (also on Milsom St.; no phone), is far more in keeping with the town's Georgian style of the 1740s, as is the *Podium* (on North St.; no phone); both have restaurants, libraries, and shops that are tiny, exclusive, and expensive. *Green Park* (at the bottom of Charles St.; no phone), a converted railway station, is now filled with artisan stalls and upscale craft shops. Most stores keep regular shopping hours (for details, see GETTING READY TO GO), but a few also close on Mondays.

Be sure to take your passport when you shop, and always inquire about the Value Added Tax (VAT) refund application forms when your total purchases in a store are over £50 (about $75). The VAT is a surcharge payable at the sales counter, but foreign customers usually will be reimbursed for it at home (for more information see GETTING READY TO GO).

Bath Stamp & Coin Shop There's much of interest here for both collectors and beginners. 12-13 Pulteney Bridge (phone: 463073).

Beaux Arts Gallery Popular works by contemporary artists and ceramicists are beautifully displayed in the white-painted rooms of an 18th-century house. 13 York St. (phone: 464850).

China Doll Here is the headquarters of Bath's doll kingdom, with impressive displays of miniatures by Kathe Druse and Annette Himstedt, soft toys, and Lynne and Michael Roche collectible porcelain dolls. The dollhouses, some of which are three-story Georgian heirlooms, are all handmade. 31 Walcot St. (phone: 465849).

E. P. Mallory & Son Two shops: Old jewelry and silver are offered at 5 Old Bond St. (phone: 465443); modern jewelry, silver, and china are the specialty at 1-4 Bridge St. (phone: 465885).

General Trading Company A twin of the Sloane Street shop in London, famous for all kinds of gifts, from traditional to modern, it devotes a large portion of space to antiques, kitchenware, and stationery. 10 Argyle St. (phone: 461507).

Global Village Bright handicrafts, kitchenware, folk art, and costumes from near and far can be found here. 4-5 Green St. (phone: 464017).

Graham Watling's Studio It's worth making the journey to Jane, John, and their father Graham Watling's studio in the 16th-century *National Trust* village of Lacock, 10 miles east of Bath. Their combined goldsmith and silversmith skills produce superb jewelry, goblets, candlesticks, cutlery, trays, and napkin rings. Open daily. 15 East St., Lacock, Chippenham (phone: 249-730422).

Jim Garrahy's Fudge Kitchen It's difficult to wait until you're back out on the street before sampling the results of the 1830s recipes for chocolate, mint, walnut, and other mouth-watering fudge flavors. Union Passage (phone: 462277).

Mementos of Bath Stop here for souvenirs of the *Roman Baths* and the rest of Bath—even a recording of the *Pump Room Trio. Roman Baths* (phone: 461111).

Once A Tree Everything is made of wood, including smooth "eggs," children's toys, and musical instruments. 5 Saracen St. (phone: 442680).

Papyrus Fine Paper Here's a good source for stationery, scrolls, handmade books and albums, pens, and inks. 25 Broad St. (phone: 463418).

Penhaligon's Designer eau de toilette, perfume, and sprays can be purchased, plus badger shaving brushes. 12 Northumberland Pl. (phone: 448422).

Poppy at Gloves Chic daywear is arranged around a selection of specialty gloves (such famous labels as Dents), plus leather accessories and scarves. 16 Northgate St. (phone: 465320).

Rossiter's At this row of several shops, lovely housewares and decorative items for the home—kitchenware, china tea services, chintz fabrics, and more—are sold. 40 Broad St. (phone: 462227).

Silver Gift Shop Interesting silver gifts and jewelry are displayed curiously against a background of furry toys. Union Passage (phone: 464781).

Tapestry Studio Patricia Hecquet's unusual designs are featured among the hand-painted needlework and tapestries. 32 Broad St. (phone: 466609).

Timothy Solloway Fine linen for kitchen, bed, and bath are offered, plus merino wool blankets and wool throw rugs. Abbey Green (phone: 466463).

Walcot Reclamation The largest shop of its type in Britain, it's worth a visit just to browse at objects made from brass, iron, and wood, all rescued from demolition sites. 108 Walcot St. (phone: 444404).

Whittard's of Chelsea Here are "purveyors," rather than vendors, of exclusive tea leaves and coffee beans. Try Pelham tea, vaguely perfumed and distinctly unusual. Union Passage (phone: 447787).

SPORTS

The *Sports and Leisure Centre* on the *Recreation Ground* has some indoor sports and swimming as well as a sauna and a solarium. Across the river via North Parade Bridge (phone: 462563).

BICYCLING *Avon Valley Cyclery* (located just behind the railway station; phone: 461880) offers all manner of bicycles, including tandems.

BOATING *Bath Boating Company* (Forester Rd.; phone: 466407) has skiffs and punts for hire. Information about boat trips on the river Avon as well as on the Kennet and Avon Canal is available at the tourist information center (see *Tourist Information,* above).

CRICKET The *Bath Cricket Club* (phone: 425935) plays at the *North Parade Cricket Ground* across the river and just to the south of the *Sports and Leisure Centre.* The *County Cricket Festival* is held in June, when you'll see some even better teams compete on the *Recreation Ground* (see above). Consult the newspaper or the monthly events list issued by the information center.

FISHING For a license to fish in the river Avon and the Kennet and Avon Canal, apply at the *Wessex Water Authority* (Broad Quay; phone: 313500), or at a local fishing tackle dealer.

GOLF *Entry Hill,* just a mile from downtown, is a nine-hole course which is open daily, and membership is not necessary (phone: 834248). Bath's other golf clubs are on the outskirts of town. The *Lansdown Golf Club,* an 18-hole course, accepts visitors (about 2 miles north of town on Lansdown Hill; phone: 422138); the *Kingsdown* course (18 holes) is a century old and overlooks Box Valley (phone: 742530); another 18-holer, the *Bath Golf Club,* is the oldest of them all (North Rd.; phone: 463834).

HORSE RACING The *Bath Races* take place a few times each month May through October at the *Bath Racecourse* on Lansdown Hill, 2 miles north of town (phone: 466375).

RUGBY The *Bath Rugby Football Club* (phone: 425192) plays on the *Recreation Ground* (see above). For dates and times, check the monthly events list.

SOCCER *Twerton Park,* about a mile west of Bath via the Lower Bristol Road, is the scene of the *Bath City Football Club* games (phone: 23087). Consult the events list for more information.

THEATER

Bath's *Theatre Royal* (in The Sawclose at the end of Barton St.; phone: 448844) dates from 1805 and provides an intimate setting for comedy, drama, musicals, opera, ballet, concerts, and a traditional *Christmas* pantomime. The theater also stages pre-London openings and is a regional base for the *National Theatre.* The *Bath Puppet Theatre* (phone: 480532), which overlooks the picturesque Pulteney Weir (beside the famous bridge), holds performances on weekends and school holidays.

MUSIC

Classical music concerts presented in unusual surroundings by leading artists are part of the two-week *Bath International Festival of Music* (see *Special Events*). The rest of the year, music by local and visiting groups can be heard at the *Theatre Royal* (see above) and elsewhere. The *Pump Room Trio* performs light orchestral music in the *Pump Room* mornings throughout the year and on summer afternoons; band concerts are held on Sunday afternoons during the summer in the *Parade Gardens.* Pubs with live jazz nightly or several nights weekly include the *Hat and Feather* (14 London St.; phone: 425672) and *The Bell* (103 Walcot St.; phone: 460426).

NIGHTCLUBS AND NIGHTLIFE

What little nightlife there is in this quiet city can be found in the pubs: *Joe Bananas* (opposite the *Theatre Royal;* phone: 464311), *Cadillacs* (Walcot St.; phone: 464241), and *Moles* (14 George St.; phone: 333448), which features a live band.

Best in Town

CHECKING IN

Bath has a number of memorable hotels and a few truly outstanding ones. It also has a handful of extremely comfortable, upscale bed and breakfast establishments. Summer visitors, particularly in July or August, must book well in advance. The tourist information center (see *Tourist Information,* above) can help make arrangements. Expect to pay $125 or more per night for a double room (with breakfast, private bath, phone, and TV set, unless otherwise noted) at hotels listed in the expensive category; between $70 and $120 at those listed as moderate; and less than $60 at any listed as inexpensive. All telephone numbers are in the 1225 city code unless otherwise indicated.

For an unforgettable experience in Bath, we begin with our favorites (we admit that they're pricey), followed by our cost and quality choices of accommodations, listed by price category.

SPECIAL HAVENS

Lucknam Park A magnificent Georgian country house, only 6 miles northeast of Bath, it offers a thoroughly English experience. A chambermaid dressed in a crisp white apron tends the fire while sprightly young lads stand ready to take your drink order. Every detail seems to have been anticipated—from the fresh, imaginative flower arrangements right down to the leather-bound books in each of the suites. The 42 rooms and 11 suites are furnished with luxurious fabrics and wallpapers and have marble bathrooms. Four suites have fireplaces, which are lit at 5 PM each night, and the Orchid Suite, with its four-poster, canopied bed, overlooks the property's training course for racehorses. Try to book one of the upper suites facing the front of the grounds and the driveway lined with beech trees. The restaurant (which has earned a Michelin star) offers nouvelle English fare prepared with fresh, local produce and served in generous portions: Fish is brought in daily from the southern coast, and Sunday lunch includes the traditional roast sirloin of beef and Yorkshire pudding. There is a spa—with water pumped in from the hotel's own spring—a steamroom, saunas, a small exercise room, a beauty salon, and a pool. Colerne, Wiltshire (phone: 742777; 800-525-4800; fax: 743536).

Priory This handsome Georgian home built of Bath stone in the neo-Gothic style ranks among the best country hotels in England, and it's just a short stroll through *Royal Victoria Park* to town. The grounds and public rooms are elegant and tranquil, the staff excellent, the furnishings antique and well kept, the pool in the two-acre garden heated, and the dining room's fare French and highly praised (see *Eating Out*). Each of the 21 guestrooms is different but charming, including six beautifully appointed deluxe rooms. Weston Rd. (phone: 331922; fax: 448276).

Royal Crescent Forming the impressive center of the famous *Royal Crescent,* this elegant and historic Georgian hotel is part of the city's architectural heritage. With commanding views, it is within walking distance of the *Assembly Rooms,* the *Roman Baths,* the *Pump Room,* and the abbey. It has 28 deluxe rooms and 14 apartments (three with Jacuzzis). The Sir Perry Blakeney Suite, for example, has a 17th-century canopied bed, pale blue sofas, an Oriental carpet, and a white-and-gold ceiling of intricate gesso swirls. There are magnificent Georgian public rooms, a good restaurant, and attractive gardens. 15-16 *Royal Crescent* (phone: 319090; fax: 339401).

Ston Easton Park Apart from the ticking clocks, occasional groans from the floorboards, and the restless hush of the river Somer as it cascades through the surrounding landscape laid out by Humphrey Repton, this Palladian mansion 12 miles from the city trades in the sounds of silence. A Relais & Châteaux member, the property boasts 20 guestrooms (several with four-poster beds), 30 acres of parkland (to which Sorrel, the resident spaniel, likes to act as a guide), and a magnificent, beautifully restored, 17th-century cottage that is also available for rent. The elegant restaurant serves well-prepared English and French dishes. Ston Easton (phone: 761-241631; fax: 761-241377).

EXPENSIVE

Bath Spa This Forte property is set on the edge of town in a classical 19th-century mansion, formerly used for political meetings by, among others, Sir Winston Churchill. The seven acres of gardens are lovely, complete with fountains, a Grecian temple, and a Victorian grotto. There are 100 elegantly furnished rooms (including nine suites), and although there is no spa, facilities include a pool, sauna, solarium, and gym, as well as an outdoor tennis court. There are also supervised nursery facilities. The *Vellore* restaurant offers a classic international menu. A 10-minute walk across Pulteney Bridge from Bath on Sydney Rd. (phone: 444424; 800-225-5843; fax: 444006).

Fountain House A former Georgian mansion dating from 1735, it was Bath's first all-suite hotel. Set in the city's center, it has 14 one-, two- and three-bedroom apartments with spacious kitchens, marble baths, and living rooms with fireplaces; some even have washing machines. In the morning, you'll find a basket with a pint of milk, a loaf of Hovis bread, and the newspaper on your doorstep. 9-11 Fountain Bldgs., Lansdown Rd. (phone: 338622; fax: 445855).

Francis In an entirely different spirit, this 93-room property—built by John Wood the Elder between 1729 and 1736—forms the southern side of Queen Square. Damaged during World War II, the hotel has been rebuilt in its original style, and furnishings reflect the period, although some of the original charm has been replaced by chain-hotel ambience following its acquisition by the Forte group. It has a good dining room. Queen Sq. (phone: 424257; 800-225-5843; fax: 319715).

Hilton National Built over a municipal parking lot on the banks of the Avon overlooking the river and Pulteney Bridge, Bath's most modern hotel has 150 rooms and a restaurant. There is no period charm here; its main lures are efficiency, convenience, and comfort. Walcot St. (phone: 463411; 800-HILTONS; fax: 464393).

Queensberry In the city center, this elegant 22-room hostelry is composed of three Georgian-period houses. Rooms on the first floor are the most historic, replete with 18th-century stucco ceilings and cornices, iron railings, and colorful window boxes. It has an excellent restaurant, the *Olive Tree* (see *Eating Out*). Russell St. (phone: 447928; fax: 446065).

Somerset House A 30-year-old parrot who is fond of making wolf whistles, a 7.25-inch-gauge steam train in the back garden, and a notice in the hall asking that guests not wear Christian Dior's Poison perfume (since the owner, Jean Seymour, is allergic to it) all set a fairly bizarre tone. However, it is a very professionally run establishment. Its 10 rooms are fairly well appointed, and meals here are very good (there's also an intriguingly good wine list). 35 Bathwick Hill (phone: 466451).

Woolley Grange Here is a rarity—a luxury hotel that not only allows children but caters to them as well. Nigel and Heather Chapman, the owners of this grand Jacobean manor house in a quiet little town 8 miles southeast of Bath, have four children of their own, and so they have made a special effort to create a kid-friendly environment. While children cavort to their hearts' content in the *Woolley Bears' Den* playroom under the supervision of a staff of expert nannies, their parents can relax in the house's cozy living room, library, and lounges or roam the 14 acres of gardens. Each of the 18 well-appointed guestrooms and two luxurious suites has plenty of space to set up additional beds or a crib. Other amenities include a fine dining room, a heated outdoor pool, a croquet lawn, and tennis courts. Woolley Green, Bradford-upon-Avon (phone: 864705; fax: 864059).

MODERATE

Bath Only minutes from the city center, this 96-room hotel is in a modern building, unusual for Bath hostelries. It is superbly sited alongside Widcombe Basin and the river. Widcombe Basin (phone: 338855; fax: 428941).

Haydon House An elegantly furnished four-room bed and breakfast establishment, it is located on a quiet residential street and enthusiastically run by Gordon and Magdalene Ashmans. No smoking allowed. 9 Bloomfield Park (phone: 427351; fax: 444919).

Holly Lodge A large Victorian house set on attractive grounds, decorated in pastels and with stucco walls, this cheerful six-room hotel has won awards for its service, atmosphere, and comfort. No restaurant (but breakfast is included). A few minutes from the city center. 8 Upper Oldfield Park (phone: 424042; fax: 481138).

Pratt's As historic as any hotel in Bath, it was designed by John Wood the Elder in the 1740s. There are 47 modern, comfortable rooms and a restaurant. Saturday night dinner dances are held during the winter. South Parade (phone: 460441; fax: 448807).

Redcar Not far from the center of town, near *Henrietta Park,* it's part of a mellowed stone Georgian terrace and has 31 well-equipped rooms and a restaurant. 27 Henrietta St. (phone: 469151; fax: 461424).

Tasburgh Bath Brian and Audrey Archer's upscale, Victorian bed and breakfast establishment feels like a country house, with its seven acres of land and croquet on the lawn; yet it is only a 20-minute walk from the abbey. All 11 rooms have either king-size or four-poster beds; some overlook the Kennet and Avon Canal. Warminster Rd. (phone: 425096; fax: 463842).

EATING OUT

The range of restaurants in Bath is broad: English, French, Italian, Greek, Indian, Chinese, Japanese, and many more. Expect to pay $85 or more for dinner for two with wine at restaurants listed below as expensive; from $55 to $80 at moderate ones; and less than $50 at inexpensive spots. At the numerous wine bars and fast-food establishments, two people can eat simply for less than $35. All restaurants listed below serve lunch and dinner, unless otherwise noted. All telephone numbers are in the 1225 city code unless otherwise indicated.

EXPENSIVE

Garlands This pretty place with window boxes has become a popular venue for business lunches and special dinners. The menu mainly is English, including such dishes as lamb steaks fried in garlic and filet of brill. Closed Sundays. Reservations advised. Major credit cards accepted. George St. (phone: 442283).

Olive Tree Descend a discrete flight of steps to this trendy, relaxed, and airy bistro in the *Queensberry* hotel. Chef and owner Stephen Ross specializes in modern English cooking with a Mediterranean influence. Fish features prominently, particularly on Thursday nights when there is a separate menu devoted solely to seafood. Closed Sundays and Monday lunch. Reservations advised. Major credit cards accepted. Russell St. (phone: 447928).

Pino's Hole in the Wall Although there is a general feeling of disappointment among the locals, many of whom argue that the menu is overpriced, the setting—beams and flagstones in the basement of a Georgian building—is attractive, and the Italian-dominated food is good. There also are eight guestrooms. Closed Sunday lunch and three weeks at *Christmas.* Reservations advised, especially for Saturday nights. Major credit cards accepted. 16 George St. (phone: 425242).

Popjoy's Beau Nash lived with his mistress Juliana Popjoy in this Georgian house, now one of the best dining spots in Bath. High-quality English dishes are made from seasonal produce (the menu changes frequently) both in the dining room and in the less formal brasserie downstairs. Closed Mondays in winter. Reservations necessary. Major credit cards accepted. Sawclose (phone: 460494).

Priory Dinner is a grand occasion here, relished by locals and out-of-towners. Superb French food is served in three separate rooms offering garden views. There is an extensive wine list. Open daily. Reservations necessary. Major credit cards accepted. *Priory Hotel,* Weston Rd. (phone: 331922).

Bella Pasta Formerly *Prima Pasta,* this friendly, boisterous place serves good pasta, pizza, and hamburgers. Open daily. No reservations. No credit cards accepted. 15 Milsom St. (phone: 62368).

Clarets A downstairs wine cellar and restaurant with contemporary styling, this place features light English-style preparations of salmon, chicken, and pork, and a youngish, sophisticated clientele. In summer, dining is alfresco. Closed Sunday lunch. No reservations. Visa accepted. 7 Kingsmead Sq. (phone: 466688).

Clos du Roy One of Bath's most prestigious restaurants has moved back to the center of town, to *Seven Dials,* a small, modern development of apartments, shops, and restaurants. It still serves imaginatively prepared French food. Homegrown asparagus and seasonal wild truffles make regular appearances on the menu. Closed Sunday and Monday evenings. Reservations necessary. Major credit cards accepted. Sawclose (phone: 444450).

Moon and Sixpence Enjoy enticing fish, meat, and salads at this attractive wine bar–restaurant in a restored courtyard (self-service during the day; waiters and waitresses in the evenings). In summer, dine alfresco at tables surrounding a lovely fountain. Open daily. No reservations. No credit cards accepted. 6A Broad St. (phone: 460962).

New Moon Brasserie This high-quality bistro offers a menu that includes sautéed salmon with sun-dried tomatoes and roast chicken with garlic, lemon butter, and white wine; patrons may bring their own wine. Open daily. Reservations advised. Major credit cards accepted. *Seven Dials,* Sawclose (phone: 444407).

La Parisienne Savory light dishes are served at lunch, with more formal fare offered in the evening at this busy eatery. Closed Sunday and Thursday evenings. Reservations unnecessary. Major credit cards accepted. Shire's Yard (phone: 464616).

La Pentola Take the stairs at the river end of North Parade down to the restaurant's dining area, a stone-vaulted room that was once a cellar for the patrician home above. The fare is strictly Italian and rated among the town's better values. Closed Sundays and Mondays. Reservations advised. Major credit cards accepted. 14 North Parade (phone: 424649).

Que Pasa? Decorated with blue and white tiles, this cheerful Spanish *tapas* bar serves authentic appetizers, from marinated sardines to *tartaletas de congrejo* (crab and prawn pastries). Closed Sunday lunch. Reservations unnecessary. No credit cards accepted. *Gascoyne House,* Upper Borough Walls (phone: 464664).

Theatre Vaults In the vaults of the *Theatre Royal,* this place has quickly gained a good reputation for reasonably priced and tasty lunches and suppers. Closed Sundays. Reservations advised. Major credit cards accepted. Barton St. (phone: 465074).

Woods The two dining rooms, basically Georgian including the fireplaces, have been attractively updated with modern cane seating and finished in tones of beige, burnt orange, and dark red. English and French cooking are featured. Closed Sundays and Mondays. Reservations advised. Major credit cards accepted. 9-13 Alfred St. (phone: 314812).

INEXPENSIVE

Bink's Although it calls itself a coffee shop, this place offers remarkably good hot and cold meals in a pleasant atmosphere. Afternoon tea is served in true English style. Lunches to go also are available. Open daily. No reservations. No credit cards accepted. *Abbey Churchyard* (phone: 66563).

Fodders The best deli sandwiches in town are served in a boisterous, distinctly American atmosphere. Locals line up for takeout, but window seats are also available. Closed Sundays October through May. Reservations unnecessary. No credit cards accepted. 9 Cheap St. (phone: 462165).

Laurel and Hardy's This bistro pays tribute to the comic duo with a decor featuring bowler hats and bow ties and a menu offering "Laughing Gravy's Grills," "Laurel's Lunches," and "Stanley's Sweets." Open daily. Reservations unnecessary. Major credit cards accepted. Monmouth St. (phone: 316694).

Pierre Victoire This small, colorful bistro has a beautiful location overlooking the river Avon at Pulteney Bridge. The menu focuses on classic French fare prepared with meat and seafood, but there's always a vegetarian dish available as well. Lunch here is a particularly good value. Closed Sundays. Reservations advised. Major credit cards accepted. River Walk, 16 Argyle St. (phone: 334334).

Sumo Wok Here, you can select an array of fresh raw vegetables, herbs, meat, and seafood and present them to the chef, who will cook them up in a wok at your table. You also can order from a menu of Japanese specialties in the usual way; good choices include pork pancake rolls served with sweet ginger sauce and chicken *satay* with peanut sauce. Closed Sunday lunch. Reservations unnecessary. Major credit cards accepted. 36 Broad St. (phone: 447600).

Walrus and Carpenter Beefburgers, chili con carne, and steaks are the choices in this attractive place on a corner near the *Theatre Royal.* Closed Sundays. Reservations unnecessary. No credit cards accepted. 28 Barton St. (phone: 314864).

SHARING A PINT

Of the many places to enjoy a pint of ale in Bath, one is our particular favorite.

PERFECT PINTS

Saracen's Head The oldest pub in the city, it looks like an ersatz antique at first. The building was completed in 1713, and Charles Dickens stayed here in 1835 when it was still an inn; the display case in the wall has a few items from his time. The beamed ceiling still retains the handsome original plasterwork. 42 Broad St. (phone: 426518).

Around the corner on Green Street, there's the *Old Green Tree* (no phone), and if business is brisk, you'll have to squeeze in. Its tiny bar, smoking lounge, and snug are paneled in dark wood, and all is very friendly, intimate, and cozy. The *Assembly* (Alfred St.; phone: 333639) also serves hot food and is conveniently located next to the *Museum of Costume.* The *Grapes* (Westgate St.; phone: 310235) occupies a lovely old building—white walls, dark beams, etched glass in the doorway—and the mood is lively. The *Huntsman* (North Parade; phone: 428812) manages to be almost all things to all people. The main lounge bar of this establishment is filled at lunch with office workers and with tourists who come for the great variety of fast, honest food. Downstairs, the noisy *Cellar Bar* is frequented by students and other youth, and there's a quiet restaurant upstairs; the place is sprawling and comfortable, and the entrance toward the river is claimed to be the oldest shopfront in Bath.

Birmingham

According to the *Domesday Book,* the historic census of England ordered by William the Conqueror, Birmingham was one of the poorest manors in England in 1085–86. It had a mere ten inhabitants and was valued at only 20 shillings—just £1! About 500 years later, the town's population still was not especially impressive (probably about 1,500), but the onset of the Industrial Revolution in the 18th century brought boom times. Situated at the center of England, with abundant quantities of coal, iron, and wood, a knack for manufacturing, and energetic inhabitants, Birmingham quickly became "the city of 1,001 trades." Today its population numbers just over a million, making this manufacturing metropolis the second-largest city in Britain.

Although Birmingham makes an excellent geographic base for travelers, with attractive countryside all around, it is not an obvious tourist attraction. It has neither a picturesque setting nor famous ancient buildings. Instead, it is simply a bustling industrial city getting on with the serious business of making a living. As visitors rub shoulders with Brummies (as citizens are known), they hear the famous local accent and get a firsthand glimpse of the down-to-earth flavor of real British working people. Indeed, should they get into conversation, they are sure to find themselves being addressed as "mate" or "luv."

Large areas of the city center, built during Victorian times, were destroyed by Hitler's World War II bombs. Now, surrounded by a high-speed ring road, the center is a mixture of styles, and the few remaining Victorian red brick buildings look rather forlorn amid the tall modern blocks and multistory car parks. The site known as the *Bull Ring,* Birmingham's original marketplace (still serving the same purpose after eight centuries), was developed extensively during the early 1960s, becoming the first symbol of the city's postwar modernization. (Ambitious plans are underway to knock down the *Bull Ring* area once again to create a new district of shops and offices, but the current economic recession has delayed progress.) Gone, too, are most of the narrow back streets, having been replaced by wider, straighter ones. Yet while some Brummies regret the enormous changes, there is no denying that a great deal has changed for the better—there is now plenty to see and do.

Scores of familiar British business names have their roots in "Brum" (and have for over a century)—from Cadbury chocolates, HP sauce, and Typhoo tea to Austin Rover cars and Dunlop tires. Indeed, a quarter of Britain's exports originate here, although many of the city's 5,000 factories and workshops have been badly hit by the national recession. The *National Exhibition Centre,* on the eastern edge of town, has taken up some of the slack: The City Council invested millions of pounds to build it in the 1970s, and now 80% of the UK's major exhibitions are held here, bringing crowds and spawning hotels, restaurants, and conference centers. The *International Convention Centre,* which overlooks Centenary Square, sits close to the city center; next door, the huge *National Indoor Arena* hosts all manner of sports events.

Birmingham's fortunes have centered on crafts and trade since 1166, when Henry II granted Peter de Bermingham a charter to hold a regular market in the *Bull Ring.* During the 17th century, the English Civil War enhanced the city's reputation as a manufacturing center. Birmingham supplied swords, pikes, and armor to the Parliamentary forces—enough of them, unfortunately, to anger King Charles and prompt Royalist soldiers to burn down and loot the city. Later, gun making was established as an important trade.

Toward the end of the 18th century, such pioneering scientists as William Murdoch, who invented gas lighting, and James Watt, who developed the double-action steam engine, made Birmingham their home, giving the Industrial Revolution and Birmingham's part in it no small boost. During the late 18th and early 19th centuries, the city became the center of the canal system that revolutionized the transport of heavy goods in England. Even today, Birmingham has more miles of canals than Venice, although they are rather less scenic. When railways superseded the canals, the city became the natural hub of England's rail network, too. Commercial enterprises multiplied; industrial wealth grew; and in the late 19th century, most of the city's municipal buildings took shape. Joseph Chamberlain, lord mayor from 1873 to 1876 (and father of Neville, also lord mayor and, later, Prime Minister of Britain), was a central figure in pushing through ambitious plans for the *Council House* developments at Victoria Square as well as in founding *Birmingham University.*

The small tea and coffee shop on Bull Street, where the Cadburys started their business in 1824, disappeared long before the city's first major redevelopment in the 1960s. However, the unique "garden factory" George Cadbury opened to manufacture chocolate at Bournville in 1879 still thrives today, as does the car factory that Herbert Austin built at Longbridge in 1906—one of the world's first mass-production car factories. Just beyond it is the pastoral countryside of the Lickey Hills.

Indeed, the city is well endowed with green spaces, boasting 6,000 acres of parkland and six million trees. *Cannon Hill Park,* in the suburb of Edgbaston, ablaze with daffodils and tulips in spring, is the largest. The woodland trails and lakeside pathways of *Sutton Park,* constituting 2,400 acres on the northeastern edge of the city, also seem far removed from heavy industry and motor traffic.

Like the canals and railways before them, Britain's main motorways now converge on Birmingham. Appropriately for the home of the nation's automobile industry, the country's most famous road junction is the interweaving mass of motorway overpasses and concrete pillars at Gravelly Hill, nicknamed "Spaghetti Junction." The best view of it is from a narrowboat chugging along the canal underneath—a vivid reminder of Birmingham's much slower, more peaceful era.

Birmingham At-a-Glance

SEEING THE CITY

The city center has no public towers to climb to gain a vantage point for an all-encompassing view, but since the center itself is built on high ground, watch out for views over the industrial suburbs from the top floors of shops and car parks. Guests at the 24-story *Hyatt Regency* hotel on Broad Street can get a good view of the city from its upper floors.

SPECIAL PLACES

The hub of the city (particularly for shopping) is Stephenson Place at the junction of New and Corporation Streets. Shops proceed in all directions, and large sections have been made into pedestrian zones. A five-minute walk to the top of New Street leads to Victoria Square, which has been converted to a piazza and is dominated by the *Council House* and *Town Hall.* In front of the *Town Hall* are modern sculptures of a goddess on a fountain, a man, and two sphinxes next to an older statue of Queen Victoria. The works are meant to symbolize Birmingham's transformation from the hub of the Industrial Revolution to a modern-day business center. Just beyond, in Chamberlain Square, are the *Birmingham Museum and Art Gallery* and the modern *Central Library.* A short stroll through Paradise Forum, a covered courtyard, leads to Broad Street and the *International Convention Centre* at the far side of Centenary Square. Also nearby are the *National Indoor Arena* and other important civic buildings, including the white Anglesey marble *Hall of Memory,* a war memorial to local soldiers who fell during World War I; and *Baskerville House,* a 20th-century neo-Georgian building housing city offices. A ring road encircles the central area, making the drive from one side to the other easy, though parking is very restricted. The road also has transformed parts of Birmingham into a confusing concrete jungle; visitors should have a street map to avoid getting lost.

CITY CENTER

TOWN HALL The city's main concert hall, styled on the model of the *Temple of Castor and Pollux* in Rome, has neoclassical columns and arches on all four sides and is faced with Anglesey marble. Opened in 1834, it was designed by Joseph Hansom, more famous as the inventor of the Hansom cab. Inside, the white and gold Baroque decorations provide a superb setting for musical events. Mendelssohn conducted the first performance of his *Elijah* here in 1847. It's closed to the public except during concerts. Paradise St. (phone: 236-3889).

COUNCIL HOUSE This is the most impressive Victorian building in town, naturally enough, since it's the headquarters of Birmingham's city government. Built in 1879 in an Italian Renaissance style, it has an elaborate portico, Corinthian columns, and a large dome. Inside are elaborately decorated banquet rooms, as well as the *Council Chamber.* Victoria Sq., Colmore Row (phone: 235-2040).

BIRMINGHAM MUSEUM AND ART GALLERY Boasting one of the nation's most important art collections outside London, with fine examples from the 17th through 19th centuries, this museum/gallery is immediately recognizable by the "Big Brum" clock tower on top. It provides an exceptionally good look at the work of the pre-Raphaelites, English watercolorists from the 18th century onward are well represented, and there is a handsome gallery dedicated to jewelry, metalwork, stained glass, costume design, and ceramics. The *Department of Archaeology and Ethnography* presents objects from cultures around the world; the *Department of Local History* exhibits items from the Birmingham of bygone days; and the *Department of Natural History* displays a life-size replica of Tyrannosaurus rex as well as Britain's finest fossilized Triceratops skull. Temporary exhibitions are shown in the recently renovated *Gas Hall.* A variety of shops and an Edwardian tearoom are also available. The associated *Museum of Science and Industry* is nearby (see below). Open daily. Admission charge for special exhibitions. Chamberlain Sq. (phone: 235-2834).

CENTRAL LIBRARY Built in 1974, this imposing, modern, white stone building is one of the largest library complexes in Europe, with 34 miles of bookshelves and one and a half million books. Specialist sections include a large Shakespeare collection and the Samuel Johnson collection. Closed Sundays. Chamberlain Sq. (phone: 235-4511).

INTERNATIONAL CONVENTION CENTRE This modernistic structure houses 11 conference rooms grouped around a central mall and *Symphony Hall,* the 2,200-seat home of the *City of Birmingham Symphony Orchestra.* It faces Centenary Square, a red brick mosaic piazza and gardens, with a dramatic modern sculpture, *Forward.* Broad St. (phone: 200-2000).

NATIONAL INDOOR ARENA Right behind the *International Convention Centre,* this 13,000-seat center has become one of Great Britain's top indoor venues for conventions, concerts, ice shows, and sports events. King Edward's Rd. (phone: 200-2202).

MUSEUM OF SCIENCE AND INDUSTRY Features an impressive collection of scientific and industrial items reflecting the city's achievements since the Industrial Revolution. Exhibits range from steam engines (including the oldest working one in the world, a 1779 Watt beam), machine tools, cars, motorcycles, and bicycles, to firearms and mechanical musical instruments. Many are in working order and can be operated by visitors. Steam engines are run on the first and third Wednesdays of each month, and special events take place regularly (such as *Steam Weekends* in March and October, the *Traction Engine Rally* in May, and the *Stationary Engine Rally* in September). Open daily. No admission charge. Newhall St. (phone: 235-2834).

ST. PHILIP'S CATHEDRAL The city's Anglican cathedral, built in 1715, is a fine example of the Palladian style. It has four magnificent 19th-century stained glass windows by Sir Edward Burne-Jones. Colmore Row (phone: 236-6323).

ST. CHAD'S CATHEDRAL The first Roman Catholic cathedral to be built in England after the Reformation, this was begun in 1839 and dedicated in 1841. It is the work of Augustus Pugin, who pioneered the Victorian Gothic style and also designed the *Houses of Parliament* in London. St. Chad's Queensway (phone: 236-5535).

ST. MARTIN'S-IN-THE-BULL-RING Birmingham's parish church stands on the edge of the city's market area, so shoppers bustle past it all day long. A church has been here for 900 years, though the present one, in Gothic style, dates from only 1873. It has a Burne-Jones stained glass window and the ancient tombs of the de Bermingham family. Bull Ring (phone: 643-5428).

GAS STREET BASIN Built from the mid-18th to the mid-19th century, the 260 miles of the narrow Birmingham Canal Navigation network are the heart of an English waterways system that reaches as far as the Mersey, the Humber, the Severn, and the Thames. Most of the canals are still in good repair, with restored towpaths alongside for walking. A particularly interesting stretch through the center of the city is that from Gas Street Basin (Gas St., off Broad St.) to the restored Cambrian Wharf, which leads to the Farmer's Bridge flight of 13 locks (off Newhall St.). The *Birmingham Canal Trails* leaflet (available free from the *Birmingham Convention and Visitor Bureau;* see *Tourist Information*) is a handy reference. In summer, short excursions from Gas Street Basin are run by *Second City Canal Cruises* (phone: 236-9811).

SUBURBS

ASTON HALL This fine 17th-century Jacobean mansion is in *Aston Park,* about 2½ miles north of the city center. Built by a wealthy squire, it was attacked by Parliamentarians during the English Civil War, and the marks of their cannon shot can still be seen. The grand balustraded staircase, long gallery, and period furniture are notable—as is the resident ghost, presumably that of one of the squire's daughters, who refused to marry the man chosen for her and was locked in a tiny room in the attic, where she went mad and died. Open daily from 2 to 5 PM; closed November through *Easter.* No admission charge. Trinity Rd., Aston (phone: 327-0062).

BARBER INSTITUTE OF FINE ARTS As part of *Birmingham University* (see below), this art gallery houses one of the finest small collections of paintings in

Europe. Masterpieces by English, Dutch, French, and Italian artists are on display, as well as sculptures, rare books, and antique coins. Closed Sundays. No admission charge. Edgbaston Park Rd., Edgbaston (phone: 472-0962).

BIRMINGHAM UNIVERSITY In the pleasant residential suburb of Edgbaston, about 3 miles southwest of Birmingham's center, this institution dates from the turn of the century, though the campus was greatly enlarged during the 1960s. The Byzantine-style buildings in characteristic red brick are the oldest. The clock tower, nicknamed "Joe" after Joseph Chamberlain, the lord mayor responsible for founding the university, is one of the city's most famous landmarks. It also includes the *Barber Institute.* Bristol Rd., Edgbaston (phone: 414-3344).

BOTANICAL GARDENS Here are 15 acres of beautiful ornamental gardens and glasshouses with tropical plants, as well as aviaries with exotic birds. Open daily. Admission charge. Westbourne Rd., Edgbaston (phone: 454-1860).

BOURNVILLE VILLAGE George Cadbury built his famous chocolate factory 4½ miles south of the city center in 1879. It was a pioneering project, since he also built houses there for his workers, surrounding everything with gardens. The latest sociological and scientific development is an area of solar-powered homes designed to maximize the use of the sun's energy. A permanent exhibit, *Cadbury World—The Chocolate Experience,* tells about the history of the Cadbury family and how chocolate is made. *Cadbury World* is closed Fridays November through April and Mondays and Tuesdays September through late July. Admission charge. Linden Rd., Bournville (phone: 451-4159).

BLAKESLEY HALL This typically Elizabethan timber-framed house was built by a rich yeoman farmer during the late 16th century. Period rooms and items of local historic interest are displayed inside. The area around the house, only 4 miles east of the city center, retains its old-time village atmosphere, with quaint cottages clustered around a 15th-century church. Closed Mondays, Tuesdays, and Fridays November through March. Admission charge. Blakesley Hall Rd., Yardley (phone: 783-2193).

NATIONAL EXHIBITION CENTRE (NEC) Built on a 400-acre site, beside the airport, on the outskirts of the city about 8 miles southeast of the center, the *NEC* now hosts 80% of Britain's major exhibitions, attracting over three million visitors a year from all over the world. With 12 exhibit halls and a 12,300-seat arena, the *NEC* also stages conferences and large-scale entertainment such as pop music concerts, ice skating shows, and horse shows. Other facilities include an artificial lake, hotels, and the adjacent *Birmingham International Station.* Bickenhill (phone: 780-4141).

BLACK COUNTRY MUSEUM Located roughly 10 miles west of central Birmingham, in the heart of the Black Country, an ironworking area so covered with the black smoke of its industries during the 18th and 19th centuries that the name has stuck, even though the grime has long since lifted. To illustrate those difficult times, old buildings and industrial objects from throughout the Black Country are being salvaged and reconstructed at this open-air site, and the result is an entire 19th-century village with houses, shops, a chapel, a pub, an old tram, canal boats, and a fairground. Demonstrations of chain making, glass cutting, and baking complete the picture. Closed *Christmas.* Admission charge. Tipton Rd., Dudley (phone: 557-9643).

EXTRA SPECIAL

To sample the flavor of one of the city's oldest industries, walk 15 minutes down Newhall Street from Colmore Row to Birmingham's famous jewelry quarter. The area, centered around Frederick Street, Warstone Lane, and Vyse Street, is a warren of converted houses and small workshops, many dating from Victorian times. Priceless gold and silver items as well as less expensive costume jewelry are manufactured here by several small businesses. Many shops in the area offer jewelry bargains, and artisans can be seen at work in the *Jewellery Quarter Discovery Centre* in the old Smith and Pepper jewelry factory (77-79 Vyse St.; phone: 554-3598), where little has changed since 1914. The center also sells two interesting books on the area: *Birmingham's Jewellery Quarter* and the *Birmingham Jewellery Handbook and Guide;* both are priced at £5.95 (about $8.99). Closed Sundays. Admission charge.

Sources and Resources

TOURIST INFORMATION

The *Birmingham Convention and Visitor Bureau* (*BCVB*) has five information offices. The first is in the city center (2 City Arcade, off Corporation St.; phone: 643-2514); closed Sundays. It not only dispenses tourist information and helps with travel arrangements such as car rentals and restaurant reservations, but also provides a booking service for theaters, concerts, and sports events (phone: 839-333999; costs between 36p/about 55¢ and 48p/about 75¢ per minute). The second office (Victoria Sq.; phone: 236-5622) is closed Sundays, and there are two others at the *National Exhibition Centre*—one at the Piazza entrance (phone: 780-4321), which is closed weekends; and the other in the *Atrium* (phone: 780-4141, ext. 2231), which is open only during exhibitions. The fifth office is in the *International Convention Centre* (phone: 665-6116); closed weekends.

What's On, a biweekly entertainment guide, is available from *BCVB* offices as well as from hotels, theaters, and libraries. The free *Birmingham Guide,* published annually, is another useful magazine available at hotels and other outlets. It contains articles on tourist attractions in the city, along with comprehensive listings of restaurants, nightclubs, and sports and leisure facilities.

LOCAL COVERAGE The *Birmingham Post,* the *Evening Mail* (both published every weekday), and the *Sunday Mercury* are the local newspapers.

TELEPHONE The city code for Birmingham is 121.

GETTING AROUND

Because traffic can be heavy, the best way to explore the city center is on foot.

AIRPORT *Birmingham International Airport* (Coventry Rd.; phone: 767-5511), 9 miles southeast of the city center, serves both domestic and international flights. Departing every two minutes, a free *Maglev* train (the world's first magnetic suspension rapid transport system) links the airport to *Birmingham International Station* and the adjacent *National Exhibition Centre.*

BUS Local service throughout the city and surrounding area is provided by *West Midlands Travel* and other operators. Fares range from 32p (about 50¢) to £1.37 (about $2), depending on the distance; discounts go into effect from 9:30 AM to 3:30 PM and from 6 PM to midnight. Exact change is required. For information on schedules, contact the Centro Hotline (phone: 200-2700). Longer-distance buses are operated by *Midland Red Bus and Coach Services* (phone: 643-5611), with departures from the *Bull Ring. National Express,* a national network of long-distance coaches, runs from the *Digbeth Coach Station* (phone: 622-4373); smoking is not allowed. *Flightlink* airport coaches make numerous trips daily to *Heathrow* and *Gatwick Airports* from various points (phone: 554-5232). There also are *London Liner* buses from Colmore Row to London (phone: 333-3232).

CAR RENTAL The major companies have offices in the city center and at the airport, including *Avis* (phone: 632-4361), *Europcar UK* (phone: 622-5311), and *Hertz* (phone: 782-5158). Arrangements also can be made through the *Birmingham Convention and Visitor Bureau* (see above) or by using the free phone at *Birmingham International Station.*

SIGHTSEEING TOURS Bus tours, run by *Guide Friday, Ltd.* in Stratford, operate daily April through September, leaving from several locations throughout the city. You can stay on for the entire one-and-a-half-hour tour, or get on and off as often as you like during the day. For additional information and tickets, contact the main *BCVB* office (see above).

TAXI There are several taxi ranks in the city center as well as at the airport, the *National Exhibition Centre,* and railway stations. Radio cab companies include *BB's* (phone: 233-3030), *Beaufort Cars* (phone: 784-3166), and *T.O.A.* (phone: 427-8888).

TRAIN The main railway station is *New Street Station,* in the city center. *Birmingham International Station* serves the *National Exhibition Centre. InterCity* trains between Birmingham and London (the trip takes an hour and 40 minutes; service is every half hour) stop at both. For exact times to London, call 643-4466; for information on trains to other places, call 643-2711.

SPECIAL EVENTS

Throughout the year, Birmingham is host to many outstanding festivals and celebrations, including one that is worth planning your itinerary around.

A FAVORITE FETE

CBSO Summer Season In June and July, *City of Birmingham Symphony Orchestra* principal conductor Simon Rattle—one of Britain's most distinguished conductors—assembles a number of other prominent conductors and soloists for a series of concerts with the orchestra, continuing a tradition inaugurated in 1945. *Symphony Hall,* Broad St. (phone: 236-1555 for information; 212-3333 for the box office).

Towards the Millennium, a 10-year-long arts festival that each year celebrates a different decade of the 20th century, is held from February to April, with a series of concerts, exhibitions, and debates. This year's focus will be on the decade from 1941 to 1950. Other events include the *Readers and Writers Festival* in May; the *Birmingham International Jazz Festival,* a week-long series of concerts held in pubs, nightclubs, hotels, and in the open air in July; a Latin-American music festival in August; the *Film and TV Festival* in late September and early October; and the *Comedy Festival* in October. Exhibitions and trade fairs are year-round events at the *National Exhibition Centre*—most are geared to a specific audience, but some, including the *Cruft's Dog Show* (March), the *British International Antiques Fair* (April), and the *International Motor Show* (held in even-numbered years in October), appeal to and are open to the general public.

MUSEUMS

In addition to those mentioned in *Special Places,* there are two others worth noting.

BIRMINGHAM RAILWAY MUSEUM A working museum featuring 11 steam locomotives, historic carriages, and workshops where visitors can watch restoration work in progress. The engines are steamed up every weekend *Easter* through October (unfortunately, no one is allowed to ride on them). Open daily. Admission charge. Warwick Rd., Tyseley (phone: 707-4696).

NATIONAL MOTORCYCLE MUSEUM A unique collection illustrating the development of British motorcycles from 1901, including racing models. Open daily. Admission charge. Bickenhill, adjoining the *National Exhibition Centre* (phone: 704-2784).

SHOPPING

High Street and the lower end of Corporation Street are the main shopping areas, with several traffic-free market squares leading off them, such as *Corporation Market,* with stalls selling inexpensive clothes and household goods. There are also malls of better quality specialty shops, such as the ornate *Great Western Arcade,* built in 1876; the modern *Pavilions* (High St.), which has four floors of stores and a good selection of restaurants serving snacks; and the quieter, glass-roofed *City Plaza* (between Cannon St. and Needless Alley), close to *St. Philip's Cathedral. The Pallasades* is a large, partially carpeted mall over *New Street Station* that leads directly into the *Bull Ring* market complex, a pedestrian zone also approached by underground walkways from New Street and Smallbrook Ringway. It features the *Bull Ring Open Market*—160-odd outdoor stalls selling fruits and vegetables, plants, fabrics, and china—and the *Bull Ring Centre Market Hall,* whose 190 indoor stalls house the best inland fish market in the United Kingdom, together with a wide variety of meat and other foods, garden accessories, crockery, jewelry, and clothing (the complex is closed Sundays). The *Rag Market* (Edgbaston St., opposite the *Bull Ring*), is the largest covered market in the UK. Open on Tuesdays, Fridays, and Saturdays, its 550 stalls offer everything from sheepskin coats to curtains. On Monday mornings it becomes the site of the largest antiques market in the UK, and every two months (Wednesdays from 2:30 to 8 PM), an antiques fair offers a significant selection of antique clothes, lace, pottery, and furniture. (And don't forget the *British International Antiques Fair*—a prime shopping opportunity; see *Special Events.*) Next to the *Rag Market* are the *Row Market,* selling clothing and accessories for teenagers, and the *Flea Market,* the place for secondhand goods and bric-a-brac. Both are in action Tuesdays, Fridays, and Saturdays.

Be sure to take your passport when you shop, and always inquire about the Value Added Tax (VAT) refund application forms when your total purchases in a store are over £50 (about $75). The VAT is a surcharge payable at the sales counter, but foreign customers usually will be reimbursed for it at home (for more information see GETTING READY TO GO).

Below are some individual stores of note. For standard shopping hours, see GETTING READY TO GO.

Anatomical Boot Co. Made-to-order shoes. 25 Colmore Row (phone: 236-7351).

Arts Crafts Antiques Centre In a converted canalside warehouse, there are stalls and workshops where all kinds of crafts and antiques—from windup gramophones to stained glass—are sold. Holliday St. (phone: 643-9900).

Dillons The city's leading bookshop, it is especially good for academic and local books, as well as a variety of paperbacks. 128 New St. (phone: 631-4333); another large branch, specializing in religious tomes, is in the *City Plaza* mall nearby in Needless Alley (phone: 633-3830).

Ian Allan A treasure trove for aviation, military, motoring, railway, or shipping buffs, it is owned by Britain's main publisher of railway books. It also sells posters, records, videos, and a small selection of models. 47 Stephenson St. (phone: 643-2496).

Inti This shop, operated by a young Peruvian woman, sells arts and crafts from South America, including handmade jewelry, clothing, and pottery. *Arcadian Centre,* Hurst St. (phone: 441-3024).

James Antiques Originally a toll office, this canalside antiques shop is still heated by an 18th-century Colebrookdale iron fire grate shaped like a bridge. Gas St. Basin, off Gas St. (phone: 643-3131).

John Hollingsworth A wide variety of fine cigars, pipes, and tobaccos are offered here. Walking sticks also are sold. 5 Temple Row (phone: 236-7768).

Nathan Famed for over 100 years as "the jewelers under the clock," it's the best in town for top-quality watches, clocks, and gems as well as fine antiques and silver. 31 Corporation St. (phone: 643-5225).

Rackhams The city's leading department store, the largest outside London, is part of the *Harrods* group and is famed for its superb window displays. Excellent for clothing, perfume, and fine foods. Corporation St. (phone: 236-3333).

Record Centre A tiny haven for collectors of old jazz and swing records, particularly big bands and vocalists. 45-46 Loveday St. (phone: 359-7399).

Sherwoods Offers an extensive stock of cameras, telescopes, and binoculars. 11-13 *Great Western Arcade* (phone: 236-7211).

Table Top Top-quality silverware and cutlery, including pieces manufactured in Birmingham and Sheffield. 34 *Great Western Arcade* (phone: 236-5501).

Thorntons Mouth-watering selection of exotic chocolates and truffles. Three locations: 9 *North Western Arcade* (phone: 236-4219), 68 *The Pallasades* (phone: 616-1789), and 6 Union St. (phone: 236-8360).

West End Stamp Company A philatelist's heaven, specializing in British Commonwealth, European, and American stamps. Cigarette cards, old postcards, and autographed photographs of film and sports stars also are sold. 23 Needless Alley, off New St. (phone: 643-1364).

William Powell Hand-crafted guns, rifles, and fishing tackle, since 1802, plus shooting accessories and clothes, including tweed jackets, woolens, and leather. 35 Carrs La., off High St. (phone: 643-0689).

SPORTS

Leisure centers throughout the suburbs are equipped with gyms, pools, and squash and badminton courts. In the city center, private health clubs offering aerobics, weight training, and power workouts to visitors include the *Forte Crest Hotel Club* (Smallbrook Queensway; phone: 643-8171); *Curves* (2 locations: 41 Smallbrook Queensway; phone: 643-8712; and *Piccadilly Arcade,* New St.; phone: 643-3399). Major sports events are held in the *National Indoor Arena* (Broad St.; phone: 200-2202) beside the *Convention Centre* and the outdoor *Alexandra Stadium* (Walsall Rd.; phone: 356-8008) in Perry Barr, a suburb about 4 miles northwest of the city.

CRICKET The *Warwickshire County Cricket Club* (phone: 446-4422) plays at the *County Ground* (Edgbaston Rd.) April through early September. Test matches and one-day internationals also take place there.

GOLF Visitors can play (for a small charge) at any one of the city's eight municipal courses. Call the *Birmingham Convention and Visitor Bureau* (see *Tourist Information*) for details. There are also more than 40 private courses in the area, including the two championship courses at the *Belfry* hotel complex (phone: 1675-470333), 9 miles northeast of the city near Sutton Coldfield, headquarters of the *Professional Golfers' Association,* and one at the *Forest of Arden* hotel (see *Checking In*).

GREYHOUND RACING Call *Hall Green Stadium* (York Rd.; phone: 777-1181) or *Perry Barr Stadium* (Aldridge Rd.; phone: 356-2324) for the latest schedules.

ICE SKATING The *Solihull Ice Rink* (Hobs Moat Rd.; phone: 742-5561) is 10 miles south of the city center.

RUGBY Saturday matches take place during the winter at *The Reddings,* Moseley (phone: 449-2149).

SOCCER The *Birmingham City Football Club* plays at *St. Andrews* (Bordesely Green; phone: 772-0101); the *Aston Villa Football Club* at *Villa Park* (Aston; phone: 327-5353); and the *West Bromwich Albion Football Club* at *The Hawthorns* (Birmingham Rd., West Bromwich; phone: 553-5472).

SQUASH Court time can be rented at the *Metropole Hotel Squash Club* at the *National Exhibition Centre* (phone: 780-4242) and at *Fox Hollies Leisure Centre* (Shirley Rd.; phone: 778-4112).

SWIMMING Most of the city's 21 municipal baths are open daily. There are pools, water slides, and wave machines at the *Cocks Moors Woods Leisure Centre* (Alcester Rd. S.; phone: 444-3584) and the *Kingsbury Leisure Centre* (Kingsbury Rd.; phone: 382-0411).

TENNIS Most parks have public courts that can be booked inexpensively by the hour. Private clubs include the *Edgbaston Priory Club* (Sir Harry's Rd., Edgbaston; phone: 440-2492), where international tournaments are held.

THEATER

Though you might not automatically associate the industrial center of Birmingham with great theater, it has an internationally renowned repertory group.

CENTER STAGE

Birmingham Repertory Theatre A list of the past members of the nation's first repertory company reads like a *Who's Who* of British theater. Julie Christie and Albert Finney have played here, as did Laurence Olivier, Paul Scofield, Ralph Richardson, and Edith Evans during the years after Sir Barry Jackson founded the organization in 1913 "to serve an art instead of making that art serve a commercial purpose." In addition to earning fame for its actors, the *Rep* also became known for its modern work, particularly plays by George Bernard Shaw (back when Shaw was considered contemporary); for its successes in London; and for its modern-dress productions of Shakespeare—all of whose works the company has performed. Kenneth Branagh played here in *Hamlet, Much Ado About Nothing,* and *As You Like It* in 1988 and in *Napoleon* in 1989. The *Rep*'s season includes classics, musicals, and premieres, performed in an attractive, modern 900-seat *Main House* cunningly designed so that no one ever sits more than 65 feet from the stage. Assorted new works and innovative restagings of golden oldies are presented by other local companies in the more flexible 140-seat *Studio Theatre.* Broad St. (phone: 236-4455).

In addition, the *Birmingham Hippodrome* (Hurst St.; phone: 622-7486) presents large-scale musicals and variety shows; it is home to the *Birmingham Royal Ballet,* Britain's national ballet company, and visiting ballet companies (such as the *Bolshoi*) also have performed here. Built as a music hall in 1899, its seating capacity was expanded to 1,950 in the 1970s. The *Alexandra Theatre* (Station St.; phone: 633-3325) hosts national touring companies and London West End productions—mostly plays, although it boasts that it presents everything from Shakespeare to revues. The *Midlands Arts Centre* (in *Cannon Hill Park,* Edgbaston; phone: 440-3838) occasionally stages productions for children; the center also has two theaters and a cinema. The *Crescent Theatre* (Cumberland St.; phone: 643-5858) is the city's leading amateur theater, while the *Triangle Media and Arts Centre* at *Aston University* (Gosta Green; phone: 359-3979) has an avant-garde cinema. Tickets for all theaters are available from the *BCVB* (see *Tourist Information,* above).

MUSIC

The *City of Birmingham Symphony Orchestra,* Britain's first municipal orchestra, came into being in 1920 and now enjoys international renown. Under the baton of music director Simon Rattle, it performs regularly in *Symphony Hall* at the *International Convention Centre* (Broad St.; phone: 212-3333) September through May; informal concerts, including programs by visiting orchestras, take place every evening during June and July (see *Special Events*). Visiting opera companies, including the *Welsh National Opera,* appear at the *Birmingham Hippodrome* (see *Theater,* above). The *Alexandra Theatre* (see *Theater,* above) is the home of England's oldest opera company, the *D'Oyly Carte,* renowned for its performances of Gilbert and Sullivan operettas. The *Midland Youth Jazz Orchestra* and the *Maestros Steel Band* perform at the *Midlands Arts Centre* (see *Theater,* above). Live pop concerts and other star attractions generally take place at the *National Exhibition Centre Arena* (phone: 780-4133).

NIGHTCLUBS AND NIGHTLIFE

Birmingham has more than two dozen nightclubs, most of them within walking distance of the city center. In town, *Bobby Brown's, the Club* (48 Gas St.; phone: 643-2573) is an imaginatively converted warehouse overlooking the canal, with various small bars and a discotheque; it's open Wednesdays through Saturdays. *Liberty's* (184 Hagley Rd.; phone: 454-4444) is a large stylish club with the *Piano Bar* restaurant for dinner (French menu), a cocktail bar, a champagne bar, several other bars, and a disco. *Ronnie Scott's* (Broad St.; phone: 643-4525) has live jazz in a relaxed setting.

Birmingham has five casinos; you are required by law to be 18 or older and to obtain membership 48 hours in advance by contacting the casino where you wish to gamble. The best are the *Stakis Regency International* (84 Hill St.; phone; 643-1777) and *Sergeant Yorke* (Gas St.; phone: 631-2414). They're open daily from 2 PM to 4 AM.

Best in Town

CHECKING IN

As a major business and conference center, Birmingham has a wide range of accommodations in all price brackets, from modern luxury hotels to historic inns. The larger hotels are in the city center, while several of the more intimate ones are found in the suburb of Edgbaston. On the outskirts, areas like Solihull, Meriden, and Coleshill, where many hotels have sprung up as a result of the *National Exhibition Centre,* provide a convenient base with the added advantage of rural surroundings. During major exhibitions, it is advisable to book well in advance. The branch of the *Birmingham Convention and Visitor Bureau* in the Piazza entrance of the *NEC* (see *Tourist Information,* above) offers a free booking service. Most of Birmingham's major hotels have complete facilities for the business traveler. Those hotels listed below as having "business services" usually offer such conveniences as a concierge, meeting rooms, photocopiers, computers, translation services, and express checkout, among others. Call the hotel for additional information. Expect to pay more than $165 a night for a double room (including private bath, TV set, phone, and breakfast, unless otherwise noted) in a hotel listed as expensive, between $105 and $160 in a moderately priced one, and less than $100 at an inexpensive hotel. All telephone numbers are in the 121 city code unless otherwise indicated.

EXPENSIVE

Belfry Visitors have only to venture 9 miles northeast of the city center to find a country–manor-house atmosphere, complete with lovely gardens, two 18-hole golf courses, and a leisure club with a pool and squash courts. Some of the 219 bedrooms even sport four-poster beds. Its French restaurant has a very good reputation, and there is also the popular *Bel Air* nightclub and a piano bar. Business services are available. Lichfield Rd., Wishaw, near Sutton Coldfield (phone: 1675-470301; fax: 1675-470178).

Copthorne Though part of the chain named after the quiet English village, this is very much a big, international-style, city center hotel. A huge, ultramodern structure made of black glass, it is regarded by many local people as the least attractive building in the entire city. (It's also rather difficult to find the entrance, whether on foot or by car.) There are 215 rooms, and complete leisure facilities, including an indoor pool, gym, and sauna. Though very close to the *Convention Centre,* it has extensive conference facilities of its own, as well as other business services. Paradise Circus (phone: 200-2727; 800-44-UTELL; fax: 200-1197).

Forest of Arden On the grounds of *Packington Hall* (home of the Earl of Aylesford), this attractive hostelry overlooks a trout lake where guests can fish between March and November. In addition to the 150 rooms, there are two golf courses, squash and tennis courts, an indoor pool, gym, sauna, snooker, and business services. Close to the M6 and M42 motorways, it's a 20-minute drive from the city center; on Maxstoke La., Meriden (phone: 1676-22335; fax: 1676-23711).

Hyatt Regency Silver and gray glass panels cover this 24-story, 319-room establishment just across the street from the *Convention Centre.* (A footbridge links the two.) There's a superb view across the city from the upper floors and from the two glass elevators. There are two restaurants—*282* is fairly informal, and serves fresh fish dishes, while the *Court Café* offers California concoctions for those longing for a taste of the States. Business services are available. 2 Bridge St. (phone: 643-1234; 800-233-1234; fax: 616-2323).

Jonathans' All 29 rooms at this quaint hotel are furnished with Victorian antiques. It has an excellent restaurant (see *Eating Out*), a bistro, and a tavern that is set on a mock Victorian street. Business services are available. It's 4 miles from the city center at 16-20 Wolverhampton Rd. (phone: 429-3757; fax: 434-3107).

New Hall In its own 26-acre park, this hotel is the oldest inhabited house with a moat in England. Built during the 13th century, it has sandstone battlements and a drawbridge and, fortunately, has lost none of its character. There are 12 luxurious suites in the oldest part of the house, and most have a view of the moat; there is also a wing with 50 rooms built around an attractive courtyard. There is a restaurant (see *Eating Out*), a croquet lawn, a lighted tennis court, a putting green, and trout fishing in a lake on the grounds. Riding and clay pigeon shooting also can be arranged, and business services are available. Despite the rural surroundings, it is only 7 miles northeast of the city center, and the M6 and M42 motorways are only a few minutes away. Walmley Rd., Sutton Coldfield (phone: 378-2442; fax: 378-4637).

Swallow Originally a 1930s office building, it is now a luxurious hotel with 98 rooms and suites decorated in Edwardian/Regency style. Bathrooms are of Italian marble, and bathrobes are provided. Facilities include a pool, Jacuzzi, steamroom, and gym with computerized equipment, along with a "bodyshop" offering massages, pedicures, and more. A traditional barbershop is on the premises, as well as a women's hair salon. The *Sir Edward Elgar's* restaurant serves classic French dishes (à la carte), while *Langtry's* offers English fare. Business services are available. 12 Hagley Rd., Edgbaston (phone: 452-1144; fax: 456-3442).

MODERATE

Grand A traditional city center hotel in a splendid Victorian building, the genteel atmosphere is enhanced by long corridors, and each of the 175 bedrooms is attractive and well appointed. There are two dining rooms (a carvery and a French restaurant) and two bars; the ornate Grosvenor suite, which has hosted Lloyd George, Joseph and Neville Chamberlain, and Winston Churchill, has banquet facilities. Business services are available. Colmore Row (phone: 236-7951; fax: 233-1465).

Marston Farm Only 7 miles from town, this 17th-century house is surrounded by quiet farmland, yet is still a short drive from the *National Exhibition Centre* and motorways. Attractively converted, it has a modern 38-guestroom wing, a restaurant, a tennis court, a croquet lawn, and fishing in a lake on the grounds. Business services are available. Bodymoor Heath, Sutton Coldfield (phone: 1827-872133; fax: 1827-875043).

Midland A city center, privately owned hotel, built in 1872 and refurbished, it caters primarily to businesspeople with 112 rooms (including two small suites with Jacuzzis) and full business services. There is a restaurant and several lively bars, including the *Atkinson,* which serves real ale and is well patronized by Brummies. New St. (phone: 643-2601; fax: 643-5075).

Novotel Part of the worldwide French chain, this modern 148-room hotel is just a three-minute walk from the *International Convention Centre* (it also offers full business services). The restaurant serves a sumptuous buffet breakfast and quick lunches for those pressed for time. 70 Broad St. (phone: 643-2000; 800-221-4542; fax: 643-9796).

INEXPENSIVE

Copperfield House This small hotel, owned and operated by the Bodycote family, offers 17 rooms in a mid-Victorian house on a quiet road. Located 2 miles from the city center, it is particularly popular with visitors to the nearby *Birmingham University.* There is a restaurant serving good English fare. 60 Upland Rd. (phone/fax: 472-8344).

Hagley Court Set in a large Victorian house, this friendly place offers 28 rooms and a restaurant serving well-prepared English dishes. It's conveniently located near a main bus route into the city center. 229 Hagley Rd. (phone: 454-6514; fax: 456-2722).

Ibis Part of the international hotel group, this modern 159-room property offers comfortable bed and breakfast accommodations conveniently located a short walk from the city center. Few amenities are offered (there is no restaurant, although bar snacks are available at lunchtime and in the early evening), but there are several good eateries in the vicinity. Ladywell Walk (phone: 622-6010; 800-221-4542; fax: 622-6020).

EATING OUT

The city has come a long way in recent years. Today its restaurants reflect its multi-ethnic population and status as an international business center and offer a variety of fare—particularly European, Indian, and Chinese. The most authentic Indian food is found in the rather run-down suburb of Sparkbrook, particularly in so-called *balti* houses (fast-food eateries that serve northern Indian fare). For good Chinese food, head for the Hurst Street area, just south of the city center. A dinner for two without wine will cost $75 or more in a restaurant listed as expensive, between $45 and $70 in a moderate one, and less than $45 in an inexpensive one. All restaurants listed below serve lunch and dinner, unless otherwise noted. All telephone numbers are in the 121 city code unless otherwise indicated.

EXPENSIVE

Jonathans' The area's most unusual restaurant (in the hotel of the same name) serves traditional English dishes in a setting that re-creates the genteel 1880s. Victorian furniture and objets d'art prevail in several dining rooms, including the secret "Boardroom," hidden behind a book-lined wall, and smaller rooms for private meals. The two owners are both called Jonathan; one does the cooking, the other looks after the guests. Open daily. Reservations necessary. Major credit cards accepted. 16 Wolverhampton Rd., Oldbury (phone: 429-3757).

New Hall Dining in this hotel's 400-year-old oak-paneled restaurant (which doesn't allow smoking) surrounded by a 13th-century moat is a special experience. The food, prepared by chef Glenn Purcell, is classical English and delicious; fish is the specialty, cooked with fresh, homegrown herbs and watercress. Open daily. Reservations necessary. Major credit cards accepted. Walmley Rd., Sutton Coldfield (phone: 378-2442).

Sloans In the *Chad Square Shopping Centre,* this is the place for intimate, sophisticated dining amid attractive decor. It specializes in modern French dishes. Closed Saturday lunch and Sundays. Reservations necessary. Major credit cards accepted. Hawthorne Rd., Edgbaston (phone: 455-6697).

Teppanyaki The city's first Japanese restaurant has acquired a deservedly excellent reputation. Located in the *Arcadian Centre* opposite the *Hippodrome,* it is named after its cooking style (the food is prepared right in front of you). Closed Saturday lunch and Sundays. Reservations necessary for dinner. Major credit cards accepted. Hurst St. (phone: 622-5183).

MODERATE

Bucklemaker Set in the cellars of an old silversmith and buckle maker's workshop, this spot offers a traditional menu featuring beef, veal, lamb, chicken, and salmon. The vegetables are especially fresh and delicious. There is also a long wine list, and if you enjoy what you drink with the meal, you can purchase a case to take home. Closed Sundays. Reservations advised. Major credit cards accepted. 38 Mary Ann St. (phone: 200-2515).

Le Provençal The French and Swiss "bourgeois" fare served here is definitely not for calorie counters. This dining spot is popular with local businesspeople. Closed Saturday lunch and Sundays. Reservations advised. Major credit cards accepted. Albany Rd., Harborne (phone: 426-2444).

The Square Many of the regular customers of this trendy place liken the dining room's vibrant decor and informal but smart atmosphere to that of an ocean liner. It's located in an attractive Georgian building in the Victorian jewelry quarter. The wine bar serves simple snacks at lunch; the restaurant offers a bistro-style menu. Rather loud pop music is played on Saturday evenings. Closed Saturday lunch and Sundays. Reservations advised. Major credit cards accepted. St. Paul's Sq. (phone: 236-3717).

INEXPENSIVE

Los Andes At closely placed tables, guests feast on tasty, peasant-style Latin American fare, prepared with lots of peppers and chilies and served with Mexican beer or Chilean wine. Traditional music plays in the background. Closed Sundays. Reservations advised. Major credit cards accepted. 806 Bristol Rd. (phone: 471-3577).

Chung Ying Considered one of the country's best Cantonese restaurants, it's decorated in exotic Oriental tearoom style, and the menu offers 314 dishes, including dim sum; the special rice and barbecued duck are outstanding. Open daily. Reservations advised. Major credit cards accepted. 16-18 Wrottesley St. (phone: 622-5669).

Days of the Raj Northern Indian fare, including a huge buffet at lunchtime. The furnishings are of delicate bamboo. Closed weekend lunch. Reservations advised. Major credit cards accepted. 51 Dale End (phone: 236-0445).

Maharaja More northern Indian and Punjabi dishes with very spicy sauces are the stock in trade of this excellent restaurant just a few yards from the *Hippodrome.* Closed Sundays. Reservations advised. Major credit cards accepted. 23 Hurst St. (phone: 622-2641).

Punjab Paradise Also known as "Balti Heaven," this simply furnished, northern Indian eatery offers a variety of *baltis* (spicy meat, vegetables, and fish marinated, cooked, and served in a wok-like metal bowl), which are eaten with the fingers along with chunks of *nan* bread (fluffy white bread). The combinations range from chicken and vegetables to a coconut and yogurt mixture. Open for dinner only (except for Sunday lunch). No reservations. Major credit cards accepted. 377 Ladypool Rd. (phone: 449-4110).

San Carlo This elegant Italian restaurant occupies two floors and boasts a wide variety of pasta, pizza, and meat dishes. The decor features cane furniture, white walls and napery, and plants, and the service is friendly and welcoming. Live music plays on Saturday evenings. Open daily. Reservations advised. Major credit cards accepted. 4 Temple St. (phone: 633-0251).

FISH AND CHIPS

There is no better place to sample the traditional, inexpensive British takeout meal than at *Bedder's Fish and Chips* (898 Coventry Rd., Small Heath; phone: 772-1532). Expect to "queue up," since it's patronized by Brummies from all over the city. The fish is delivered fresh, direct from coastal fishing ports, but no longer does it come wrapped in newspaper. Closed Sundays; dinner served only on Fridays.

SHARING A PINT

Such famous breweries as Davenports, Ansells, and Mitchells and Butlers have been brewing in Birmingham for 150 years. Their beers, often including real ale, can be sampled in a wide selection of traditional to trendy pubs throughout the metropolitan area. The *Bartons Arms* (Newtown Rd., Aston, about 2 miles northeast of the city; phone: 359-0853), one of several fine Victorian pubs, has stained glass windows, heavy mahogany woodwork, and a cast-iron staircase from Ironbridge. Charlie Chaplin frequented it when performing at the nearby *Hippodrome.* In the city center, there are several pubs overlooking the canal, among them the *Glassworks,* in a former glass factory beside the *Hyatt Regency* (Broad St.;

phone: 643-1234); the *James Brindley* (on Bridge St; phone: 643-1230); and the *Firkin and Flapper* (at the Cambrian Wharf junction; phone: 236-2431). Sandwiched between the *International Convention Centre* and the *National Indoor Arena* is the tiny *Prince of Wales* (Cambridge St.; no phone), a cozy pub that dates back to 1854.

Bournemouth

By English standards, Bournemouth is an infant, founded less than 200 years ago. Yet until the 1960s, Bournemouth had a reputation for Victorian primness. Unlike Brighton, its good-time sister just down the coast, it became associated with a picture-postcard stereotype of a bluff Colonel Blimp (retired) taking the air in a Bath chair on the promenade, his heavily bandaged, gouty foot protruding stiffly in front of him.

It's still possible to encounter such people here, refugees from the pages of P. G. Wodehouse's Jeeves books, but the only Bath chair you'll see is in a museum. Bournemouth has taken some pains to rid itself of Colonel Blimp, and to a great extent, it has succeeded. It is now something of a pacesetter among English seaside resorts, attracting about four million visitors a year, but it is a year-round town as well. Though it has few monuments of historic interest, it has a wider range of hotels and restaurants than any English city outside London and ample conference and leisure facilities both indoors and out. It still has the mild, yet bracing, climate that made it a resort in the first place—the sort of fresh air that was recommended in the mid-19th century to those "in delicate health." And it still has the beach—7 miles of golden sand that perfectly fulfilled the Victorian concept of the seaside.

Until the early 19th century, Bournemouth was virtually uninhabited. But then, when the threat of invasion by Napoleon was at its height, one Captain Lewis Tregonwell was dispatched with a troop of Dorset yeomanry to patrol the coast between Christchurch and Poole. Captain Tregonwell was destined to become the founder of Bournemouth when, in 1810, he bought eight acres of land to build the mansion that is today the central part of the *Royal Exeter* hotel. The town grew as wealthy Victorians built their villas around this foundation.

It was not until the railway station opened in 1870, however, that Bournemouth became a full-fledged resort. Speculators found the tops of the hundred-foot-high cliffs the perfect place to build hotels. In 1876, the first *Winter Gardens,* a concert hall in imitation of the *Crystal Palace* in London, was built, and four years later the construction of the present *Bournemouth Pier* attracted more entertainment. In the second half of the 19th century Bournemouth's population grew from a few hundred to 59,000. Today it is in excess of 155,000.

Over the years, Bournemouth has been associated with more than a few notable people. The future King Edward VII, when Prince of Wales, built a house for his mistress, Lillie Langtry, on Derby Road (it's now the *Langtry Manor* hotel). Robert Louis Stevenson lived here for several years during the 1880s—on what is now R. L. Stevenson Avenue—and wrote *Kidnapped* and *The Strange Case of Dr. Jekyll and Mr. Hyde.* The heart of the poet Percy Bysshe Shelley is buried here. Disraeli stayed at the *Royal Bath* hotel, while his archrival, Gladstone, made his last communion at *St. Peter's Church.* And Winston Churchill nearly killed himself in a boyhood prank in Alum Chine.

In his novel *Tess of the d'Urbervilles,* Thomas Hardy immortalized the place as "Sandbourne" and wrote of its eastern and western stations, its gaslit piers, promenades, and covered gardens. Thus Bournemouth's reputation spread far and wide, helped by the promotion of the railway companies. Unlike its sister resorts, however, it did not attract the hoi polloi, and it shunned "What the Butler Saw" machines (coin-operated machines which show a short film when the viewer turns a crank) and cotton candy. Instead, it developed a gentility that survived through the Jazz Age.

Modern Bournemouth has expanded to reach the older towns of Christchurch and Poole, but its heart still is the green valley of the Bourne stream, landscaped to form the *Upper, Central,* and *Lower Bourne Gardens.* To the east and west of the pier, the cliffs are lined with grand hotels built by the Victorians and Edwardians. From the cliff tops, winding paths and steps descend through glades and subtropical vegetation to undercliff drives and promenades, giving access to beaches that are protected from offshore winds and exhaust fumes.

Festivals and entertainment featuring top stars are part of the city's calendar. The town center and the suburbs of Westbourne and Boscombe have Victorian shopping arcades festooned with flowers, and in the Bohemian quarter of Pokesdown, antiques and curio shops abound. Clubs and casinos operate from the evening until the wee hours. Bournemouth has competed ably with other British vacation spots, maintaining its popularity: In 1989 and 1992 it was voted the "Best Resort" by the *British Tourist Authority.* The resort has its own international airport at Hurn, 6 miles from the town center, with regular flights to France, so it attracts many continental visitors as well. Indeed, the whole town has a continental air. Bournemouth has come a long way from its stodgy Victorian origins.

Bournemouth At-a-Glance

SEEING THE CITY

The best view is from the heights of either the West Cliff or the East Cliff, from which the 7-mile sweep of sands fringing Poole Bay can be seen to full advantage. To the west the view extends to Sandbanks, a spit of land at the entrance to Poole Harbour, with the limestone hills of the Isle of Purbeck, an island in name only, beyond. To the east, down the shore to Hengistbury Head, the green hills of the Isle of Wight, beyond Christchurch Bay, can be seen on a clear day.

SPECIAL PLACES

Bournemouth is a city of green spaces: There are 2,000 acres of parks and gardens within the city limits. If the weather is favorable, sit among the pines in the *Lower Gardens* in the morning and listen to the birds or to the military band tuning up for the first of the daily concerts at the bandstand, or browse among the portraits and landscapes by local artists on Pine Walk. On the far side of The Square, the azaleas, magnolias, and rhododendrons follow the Bourne through the *Central Gardens* into the willow-shaded *Upper Gardens* to Coy Pond. The best way to take in the sights is from the breezy, open-top deck of one of the yellow buses that ply the coast regularly in summer, aboard a more antique-looking open-top seaside bus, or on foot (see *Getting Around,* below).

CENTRAL BOURNEMOUTH

THE PIER No English seaside resort is complete without a pier, and Bournemouth's is as fine as any. The original iron structure, which was mentioned by Thomas Hardy in *Tess of the d'Urbervilles,* is still part of the framework. The pier has a theater, a restaurant, and bars, as well as all kinds of amusements for children. To the left and right of the pier is sandy beach lapped by warmish waters. The bathing water is of "Blue Flag" quality, meaning that it meets the standards laid down by the European Economic Community for lack of pollution. Acres of new sand have been dredged ashore, and a specially designed filter keeps the sand clean; dog-free zones are enforced between Fisherman's Walk and Durley Chine May through September; and automobile traffic is banned from most of the undercliff drives and promenades during the summer school holidays and peak season. Lifeguards patrol the beach on summer weekends, and there is no shortage of deck-chair attendants, who also serve as lifeguards. There also are showers, plenty of refreshment outlets, boats for hire, and speedboat cruises from the pier. The pier is located in the center of town, between West Promenade and Undercliff Drive.

PAVILION Opened by the Duke of Gloucester in 1929, it has been the pride of Bournemouth ever since, its terraces looking out over the *Lower Gardens.* It has a theater seating 1,600, a large ballroom also used for banquets, and restaurants and bars. Westover Rd. (phone: 297297).

WINTER GARDENS The Victorian "Crystal Palace" on this site was dismantled in 1935 and replaced by a municipal indoor bowling green, the first of its kind in Great Britain. After World War II, during which it was commandeered by the Royal Air Force, it again became a concert hall, seating 1,800. The acoustics turned out to be excellent, and it became the home of the *Bournemouth Symphony Orchestra.* Exeter Rd. (phone: 297297).

BOURNEMOUTH INTERNATIONAL CENTRE (BIC) Rivaling Brighton's conference and exhibition complex, this is Bournemouth's most emphatic statement that it is looking to the future. Apart from major conferences, the *BIC* stages topnotch entertainment in its two auditoriums, *Windsor Hall* and *Tregonwell Hall.* The *BIC* also contains a fitness center, a gymnasium, a solarium, and a sauna, as well as a lagoon-style indoor pool that simulates the waves breaking on the beach. Exeter Rd., West Cliff (phone: 552122).

ENVIRONS

SOUTHBOURNE Three miles east of Bournemouth, this quiet seaside suburb has a good, sandy beach; a shell house plastered with shells, mosaics, and tiles; and bowling greens fringed with pines. Its large Victorian villas now are mostly hotels and guesthouses, but the river Stour still flows beneath the weeping willows in *Tuckton Tea Gardens,* where small boats can be hired.

HENGISTBURY HEAD East of Southbourne, on the 2-mile crooked finger of low hills, mud flats, and beaches that form the southern side of Christchurch Harbour, this was one of England's busiest ports during the Iron Age. The *Noddy Train* (phone: 425517), a mock locomotive hauling rubber-tired carriages, transports visitors around this archaeological, wildlife, and leisure area for a small fee.

COMPTON ACRES These beautiful gardens overlooking Poole Harbour are 3 miles west of the city center. There are seven individual gardens landscaped in different styles, including Japanese, Italian, and Roman; a rock and water garden; and a subtropical woodland glen. Closed November through February. Admission charge. Canford Cliffs (phone: 700778).

POOLE Suburban development virtually has merged this ancient seaport with its younger neighbor, Bournemouth, but Poole jealously retains its antiquities in the Old Town. Once a principal port for trade with Newfoundland and the rest of the New World, the Old Town and harbor are now a conservation area embracing the *Georgian Custom House and Guildhall,* warehouses, and harbor offices. There are two museums: *Scaplen's Court Museum* (High St.; phone: 683138), showing everyday life in Poole throughout history; and the adjacent *Waterfront Museum* (High St.; phone: 683138), housing exhibits of the town's colorful seafaring history. *Natural World* (The Quay; phone: 686712) houses an aquarium and reptile house with piranhas, snakes, spiders, scorpions, and alligators. (All places are closed on some holidays; separate admission charges.) *Poole Pottery* (The Quay; phone: 666200) offers guided tours of its crafts center. Poole's leisure facilities at *Tower Park* (Dorset Way; phone: 715933) near the town center include an ice rink, a water park with flumes and rapids, a movie theater, a bowling alley, video games, shops, and restaurants.

POOLE HARBOUR Within this enormous natural anchorage, as much as 100 miles around, is Brownsea Island, 500 acres of heath and woodland owned and protected by the *National Trust.* In 1907, Lord Baden-Powell instituted a boys' summer camp (which eventually became the *Boy Scouts*) on the island. Brownsea Island is still a nature lovers' delight, reached by ferry from Sandbanks or Poole Quay. Closed October through *Easter.*

Sources and Resources

TOURIST INFORMATION

Bournemouth's main tourist information center, in the middle of town (Westover Rd.; phone: 789789; fax: 294808), is closed Sundays except mid-May through early September. The center provides full details of tours and excursions, transport, shows and special events, as well as free maps and guides, while its Accommodation Desk supplies up-to-the-minute information and can make provisional bookings. Guided walking tours that leave from the visitors' center are offered June through September.

LOCAL COVERAGE The *Bournemouth Evening Echo* is sold in the early afternoon, and there is also a local radio station, 2CR-FM.

TELEPHONE The city code for Bournemouth is 1202.

GETTING AROUND

The best way to negotiate downtown Bournemouth is on foot; use the bus for longer stretches. Besides the numerous footpaths to the seafront, there are also cliff lifts.

AIRPORT *Bournemouth-Hurn Airport* (phone: 593939), about 5 miles from the city by Hurn, handles domestic flights only.

BOAT In September, the *Waverley,* a restored Scottish paddle steamer, operates pleasure cruises that leave from the pier and travel along the Dorset coastline (phone: 789789).

BUS Yellow buses fan out at frequent intervals from stops around the town center. The minimum fare on these buses is 26p (about 40¢), and it increases depending on how far you're going. A "Day Tripper" ticket, allowing a day's unlimited travel, can be bought from the driver for £2.25 (about $3.40); weekly tickets are also available for £14 (about $21). In summer, open-top yellow buses provide a coastal service between Sandbanks and Christchurch or Hengistbury Head, affording marvelous views of the English Channel. The fare is 50p (about 75¢). For more information, call the bus information office (phone: 557272).

CAR RENTAL All the major companies have branches in Bournemouth.

TAXI Metered cabs can be found at taxi stands around the town center and on Westover Road.

TRAIN Bournemouth's train station is *Central Station* (Holdenhurst Rd.; phone: 292474), 2 miles from the town center. The trip from London's *Waterloo Station,* via express services, can take as little as 96 minutes.

SPECIAL EVENTS

The ever-changing calendar of festivals and theme weeks encompasses everything from parasailing to the visual arts, marching bands to laser light shows. Get a leaflet giving dates and details from the tourist information center (see *Tourist Information*). The year's highlight, however, is Bournemouth's candle illuminations, a tradition for almost a century. Every Wednesday in late July and August, children flock to the *Lower Gardens* to light 20,000 candles that, when burning in unison, create a picture—a flower, a ship, a flag, or even a kangaroo, elephant, or maple leaf. On a midsummer night, the overall effect is enchanting. The *Regatta and Carnival,* held the first week in August, marks the high point of Bournemouth's summer season with fireworks, flying displays by the Royal Air Force (RAF) "Red Arrows," and one of the candle illuminations. For most of August, the city also holds its *Kids' Free Fun Festival,* with shows, films, a games club, and visits from cartoon superstars like Tom and Jerry. Bournemouth hosts a number of national and international sports challenges throughout the year, among them powerboating, windsurfing (*World Fun Board Championships*), bowls, tennis, squash, and badminton. The *Leisure Services Division* (Town Hall; phone: 552066) can supply full details.

MUSEUMS

Considering its relative youth, Bournemouth is well endowed with museums, some of which are housed in mobile buses that make stops at local towns and villages. In addition to those mentioned in *Special Places,* the following may be of interest:

BOURNEMOUTH HERITAGE CENTRE FOR AVIATION AND TRANSPORT The resort's famous collection of historic streetcars, trolleys, and motor buses has joined the more recent aircraft of the jet age in this exciting museum housed in a modern building. There is also a display on the history of airplanes, operating models of trolleys and trains, and a ship. Opening times vary each month; call ahead. Admission charge. *Bournemouth International Airport,* Hurn (phone: 557555).

SHELLEY ROOMS Said to be the world's only museum devoted to Percy Bysshe Shelley, it consists of books, furniture, paintings, and personal effects brought from his Italian villa and installed in his son's former home. Closed Mondays. No admission charge. *Shelley Park,* Beechwood Rd., Boscombe (phone: 551009).

SHOPPING

Bournemouth prides itself on its range of shopping opportunities. Indeed, surveys by tourism authorities show that as many people come here for the stores and shops as for the seaside attractions. The main shopping area, with all the major chain stores as well as a local, family-run department store, is gathered around The Square in the city center. Better ladies' boutiques are dotted among the household names (*Marks & Spencer, C & A,* and *British Home Stores*), and there is an ultra-smart complex known as *J. J. Allen Shopping,* which specializes in housewares. The ornate Victorian arcades in the center and also at Boscombe and Westbourne are another feature of Bournemouth shopping. Antiques, curios, and Victoriana should be sought in the Bohemian quarter of Pokesdown, where there are such items as Oriental lacquerwork, Art Deco teapots, stuffed bears, and decorated headboards to bargain over. It could be an indication of the romantic nature of the resort that there seems to be a jewelry shop around every corner. For standard shopping hours, see GETTING READY TO GO.

Be sure to take your passport when you shop, and always inquire about the Value Added Tax (VAT) refund application forms when your total purchases in a store are over £50 (about $75). The VAT is a surcharge payable at the sales counter, but foreign customers usually will be reimbursed for it at home (for more information see GETTING READY TO GO).

Antique Centre With some 20 stalls under one roof, it's a gold mine of antiques, especially the collectible Moorcroft, Clarice Cliff, and majolica pottery; antique pine; and 1920s and 1930s memorabilia. Old Christchurch Rd. in the Pokesdown area on the outskirts of town (phone: 421052).

Beales Owned and operated by the same family since 1881, this independent department store is up to the minute on fashion—if you want an Aquascutum raincoat or Kurt Geiger shoes, look here first. Old Christchurch Rd. (phone: 552022).

Binnucci Exclusive women's clothing from France, Italy, and Spain. can be found at this upscale boutique. 12 Post Office Rd. (phone: 295068).

Boscombe Militaria One of the numerous antiques and curio shops in Boscombe, it specializes in items handed down by members of the armed forces. 86 Palmerston Rd. (phone: 304250).

Charlotte Here's another chic boutique for womenswear, with prices to match. 118 Poole Rd. (phone: 766555).

Petite Lady Smart casualwear especially designed for the petite woman is offered, including cashmere sweaters and blazers; some fancy dresses, too. 126 Poole Rd. (phone: 767230).

SPORTS

Angling, boating, bowls (bowling), cricket, croquet, cycling, football, golf (serious and not so serious), hockey, horseback riding, rugby, running, sailing, shooting, squash, swimming, tennis, table tennis, and windsurfing—all these and more can be enjoyed in Bournemouth. One of the area's most extensive family sports and recreation facilities is the *Littledown Centre,* which has an Olympic-size pool, a large training pool, a fitness studio, sauna, and steamroom, as well as playing areas for most sports. The facility is in Chaseside off the Wessex Way, to the north of the city (phone: 417600).

BOWLING The tenpin variety, not the kind played on outdoor greens, is available at *Wessex Super Bowl* (382 Poole Rd., Branksome; phone: 765489) and at *Bournemouth Super Bowl* (Glen Fern Rd., Dorset; phone: 291717).

FISHING Daily or weekly permits are available for coarse fishing on the river Stour. The pier is a good place to fish for bass, cod, conger, flatfish, garfish, mackerel, mullet, and whiting. Boats can be hired for harbor fishing at *Davis Boatyard* (phone: 708068). No permit is required.

GOLF Bournemouth has two championship courses. Visitors are welcome at the *Meyrick Park Golf Club* (phone: 290871), whose fine 18-hole course sits in open parkland. The municipal *Queens Park Golf Club* (phone: 396198) has 18 holes (par 72) and is open to everyone. Both courses are easily accessible by bus.

SAILING Canoes, small sailing boats, sailboards, and wetsuits can be rented at *Salterns Marina* in Poole Harbour (phone: 700503). The *Royal Motor Yacht Club* (phone: 707227) offers temporary membership to visitors introduced by members.

SOCCER *AFC Bournemouth* (phone: 395381) plays at *Dean Court* mid-August through early May.

SWIMMING After exhausting the beaches and hotel pools, jump the waves in the Leisure Pool at the *Bournemouth International Centre* (see *Special Places*).

TENNIS The *Bournemouth Tennis Centre* (*Central Gardens;* phone: 298570) has plenty of courts (some covered); professional coaching is also available. It is heavily booked in summer. *West Hants Lawn Tennis Club* (Roslin Rd.; phone: 519455) has indoor courts and accepts temporary members.

THEATER

At the *Pavilion* and *Pier* theaters and at the *Bournemouth International Centre,* the names of television and stage stars are up in lights (see *Special Places*).

MUSIC

Bournemouth has wide tastes in music—from jazz and country and western at the pier to the *Bournemouth Symphony Orchestra,* which gives Sunday concerts at the *Winter Gardens* (see *Special Places*) in June and July.

NIGHTCLUBS AND NIGHTLIFE

Three casinos and a score of discos and nightclubs come to life after sundown. Note that many Bournemouth clubs and all the casinos are for members only—for temporary membership, 48 hours' notice is usually required. Dance the night away at *Magnums* at the *Swallow Highcliff* hotel (see *Checking In,* below), a non-membership disco. *Madison Joe and Lucy's* (on The Square; phone: 290427) offers "exciting lighting and super DJs" for the 18- to 35-year-old set. The *Zoo* and the *Cage* (Glen Fern Rd.; phone: 558778) are two discos under one roof. The *Academy* (570 Christchurch Rd., Boscombe; phone: 304535), with high-tech video alongside a Victorian theater, appeals to most age groups. *Alcatraz* (290 Old Christchurch Rd.; phone: 554566) tries for a "continental" atmosphere. The *Tiberius* casino (phone: 555052) is attached to, but separate from, the *Royal Bath* hotel (entrance on Russell-Cotes Rd.). The *Stanley Sporting Club Casino* (9 Yelverton Rd.; phone: 293188) is well appointed and has its own restaurant. Another casino operates at the *Victory Sporting Club* (Terrace Rd.; phone: 558205). You must be 18 or older to play at the casinos; proof of age and identity (such as a passport) is required.

Best in Town

CHECKING IN

Bournemouth has more star-rated or quality hotels than anywhere else in Britain, outside London. Expect to pay $200 or more per night for a double room (with private bath, TV set, phone, and breakfast included, unless otherwise indicated) in the place listed as very expensive; from $120 to $180 in expensive hotels; from $90 to $120 in moderate places; and under $80 in inexpensive ones. Self-catering apartments range from $100 to $850 per week, depending on size, location, and season. For more information on accommodations, contact the visitors' information center (see *Tourist Information,* above); its Accommodation Desk also can make hotel reservations for you. All telephone numbers are in the 1202 city code unless otherwise indicated.

VERY EXPENSIVE

Royal Bath In 1912, Bournemouth's oldest hotel was awarded five stars by the national *Automobile Association,* and it has maintained that high ranking ever since. Disraeli stayed here for three months in 1874 and reported to Queen Victoria that his health had greatly improved. Oscar Wilde and H. G. Wells also were guests. There are 131 rooms, two restaurants, three bars, gamerooms, an indoor heated pool, a sauna and a gymnasium, baby-sitting services, and splendid sea views from the garden. Bath Rd. (phone: 555555; fax: 554158).

EXPENSIVE

Carlton This well-run and friendly 70-room hotel stands on the cliffs with an excellent beach below. You can catch the view over a meal in the restaurant. There is an indoor heated pool, a health club, shops, and a beauty salon. Meyrick Rd., E. Overcliff Dr. (phone: 552011; fax: 299573).

Langtry Manor The house that the future King Edward VII built for his mistress, Lillie Langtry, is now a hotel whose accommodations include Lillie's suite, with a lace-flounced four-poster bed and corner bath, and Edward's suite, with vaulted ceiling and Jacobean four-poster. The Edwardian atmosphere extends to the *Lillie Langtry* dining room, where the menu and wine list are of high quality and where regular six-course Edwardian dinner parties are offered, Edwardian dress optional. In all, there are 27 guestrooms and suites. 26 Derby Rd., East Cliff (phone: 553887; fax: 290115).

Norfolk Royale An Edwardian-style hostelry with a country-house atmosphere, it's conveniently located near shopping, the *Convention Centre,* and the beach. Its 95 rooms are well appointed and attractive, and there are two restaurants, an indoor pool, a steamroom, a sauna, and a Jacuzzi. Richmond Hill (phone: 551521; 800-228-5151; fax: 299729).

Swallow Highcliff This 157-room hotel offers a choice of three restaurants, including the *Plantation Inn and Brasserie,* which serves American fare. Other amenities include a nightclub, a fitness center, an outdoor heated pool (open April through October), a croquet lawn, a snooker room, a putting green, and tennis courts. 105 St. Michael's Rd., West Cliff (phone: 557702; fax: 292734).

MODERATE

Cliff End Modern wings have been added to this 19th-century villa, which has direct access to the beach through pine-filled gardens with nary a road to cross; there are 40 rooms. Amenities include a restaurant, an outdoor heated pool (open April through September), a mini-gym, a baby-sitting service, and tennis on two courts next to the property. 99 Manor Rd., East Cliff (phone: 309711).

Cumberland With its white Art Deco balconies, sunblinds, and the Union Jack, here is a reincarnation of 1930s chic. The lounges overlook the bay, and there is a 60-foot swimming pool, plus a children's pool. All 102 bedrooms are attractively decorated, and there's a restaurant. E. Overcliff Dr. (phone: 290722; fax: 311394).

Durley Grange A favorite among bowls players and golfers, this family-managed, 50-room hotel is set in a trim, modern building with a dormered red roof. Facilities include an indoor heated pool, sauna, solarium, and whirlpool, and several golf courses and bowling greens are nearby. Some packages include traditional English breakfasts, Sunday brunches, and four-course dinners. 6 Durley Rd., West Cliff (phone: 554473; fax: 293774).

Marsham Court In a quiet area with a restaurant overlooking the bay, this 86-room hotel is only a few minutes' walk from the city center. There is an outdoor heated pool (open late May through September); snooker, weekly barbecues, dances, and video shows are among the activities. Children stay free in their parents' room; no age limit. Russell-Cotes Rd., East Cliff (phone: 552111; fax: 294744).

INEXPENSIVE

Westerham House This cozy, family-run hotel with 10 rooms is ideally located near the chines and beaches, the town center, and Westbourne. It won the

"Bournemouth in Bloom" floral frontage award in 1991 and was a runner-up in 1992 and 1993; it's also noted for its home cooking. 38 Alumhurst Rd. (phone: 763905).

EATING OUT

Bournemouth is a cosmopolitan city with restaurants to appeal to every palate—French, Italian, Greek, and, yes, American, plus more than a whiff of real Indian curry to complement the traditional fish-and-chips. A dinner for two, not including wine and tips, will cost $75 or more in the restaurant listed as expensive, from $30 to $70 in moderate places, and less than $30 in inexpensive ones. Many hotels open their restaurants to non-residents. All restaurants listed below serve lunch and dinner, unless otherwise noted. All telephone numbers are in the 1202 city code unless otherwise indicated.

EXPENSIVE

Sophisticats Although rather small and about 3 miles from the city center, this is one of Bournemouth's most stylish restaurants. Menu choices range from fish in delicate sauces to veal Normandy-style and Javanese steaks marinated in soy sauce and wine. Open for dinner only; closed Sundays, Mondays, two weeks in February, one week in July, and two weeks in November. Reservations necessary. Visa accepted. 43 Charminster Rd. (phone: 291019).

MODERATE

Bourne Set in a split-level building decorated with cane furniture and ferns, this eatery is the place for shellfish from local waters; the chef cooks lobster, scallops, mussels, crab, and fresh vegetables to order. Service is sometimes leisurely, but there is a good choice of reasonably priced wines. Open daily. Reservations advised. Major credit cards accepted. Bourne Ave., near The Square (phone: 551430).

Fishnets Scandinavian smorgasbord in a picturesque old mill: One fixed price covers the whole evening. Closed Sundays and Mondays. Reservations necessary. Visa accepted. The Quay, Poole (phone: 670066).

Solent At this eatery at the *Bournemouth International Centre,* diners can watch the waves in Poole Bay and the artificial waves in the center's pool, while tucking into meat and vegetables. Open daily for lunch only. Reservations unnecessary. Major credit cards accepted. Exeter Rd. (phone: 552122).

INEXPENSIVE

Chez Fred This popular, award-winning spot offers great fish-and-chips both in its dining room and for takeout. It serves its own wine label. Open daily. No reservations. No credit cards accepted. 10 Seamoor Rd., Westbourne (phone: 761023).

Flossies This vegetarian eatery offers good, fresh food; also available for takeout. Open daily. Reservations unnecessary. No credit cards accepted. 73 Seamoor Rd., Westbourne (phone: 764459).

Seashells Wonderful fresh seafood is served at this bustling bistro. Closed Mondays. Reservations advised. Visa accepted. 34 Panorama Rd., Sandbanks (phone: 700610).

SHARING A PINT

Bournemouth is not really a "pubby" place, since wine bars such as *Alcatraz* (Post Office Rd.; phone: 558399) and *Chablis* (on The Triangle; phone: 551380) seem to have taken over. The *Old Barn Farm Inn,* 12 miles away (Three Legged Cross, Verwood; phone: 824925), has a skittle (bowling) alley. The *Old Beams* (Salisbury Rd., Ibsley; phone: 425-473387) serves country beers, and the *Royal Oak* (North Gorley, near Fordingbridge; phone: 425-652244) overlooks a duck pond. Another *Royal Oak,* this one 24 miles from Bournemouth through delightful country (at Okeford Fitzpaine, Blandford; phone: 258-860308), serves magnificent pub grub. *Scott Arms,* on a hilltop at Kingston (on the Isle of Purbeck; phone: 929-480270), overlooks Poole Harbour and the ruin of *Corfe Castle.* Back in Bournemouth, the *Inn in the Park* (Pinewood Rd., near Branksome Dene Chine; phone: 761318) is a family-owned house serving real ale. For a family outing, take the A35 out of Bournemouth and head for the *Oak* pub in the *East Close* hotel (Lyndhurst Rd., Hinton St. Michael; phone: 1425-672404), which serves not only real ale but afternoon teas, and has a model railway and a children's room.

Brighton

Brighton straddles 7 miles of breezy English Channel coast, and although it is England's oldest and most famous seaside resort, it is also a colorful cosmopolitan town, with great character, style, and vitality year-round.

This town has never been prim. In less permissive days, when an illicit weekend was still naughty, Brighton was the place for it. Only an hour's train journey from London left the maximum time available for an interlude in one of the numerous discreet (though unromantic) hotels. Famous men kept mistresses here in elegant bay-fronted houses bordering quiet sea-view squares. The city people brought their manners, fashions, and entertainment with them and nicknamed their coastal capital London-on-Sea.

None of this happened by chance, for Brighton was established by one of the greatest eccentrics of all time—the prince regent who eventually became King George IV of England. This spoiled, wayward, and extravagant libertine first visited Brighton in 1783, lured by the new fashion for sea bathing hailed as a cure-all. The prince loved the place and promptly set about building the most exotic palace in Europe, just across the fields from the narrow, cobbled streets that once made up the original medieval fishing town of Brighthelmstone.

Famous worldwide for its bizarre beauty, the *Royal Pavilion* he conjured up sits like a creamy Oriental fantasy in the middle of a formal English garden. Outside, it resembles a Mogul palace; inside, the decor carries lavish chinoiserie to its limit. The *Royal Pavilion* became the hub of the prince regent's glittering social circle, but not everyone thought it beautiful. Wags at the time not only commented on its onion domes but also referred to turnips and a "considerable number of bulbs of the crown-imperial, the narcissus, the hyacinth, the tulip, the crocus, and others." When the prince regent became king in 1820, he lost interest in the palace, but his successor, King William IV, enjoyed summers here; Queen Victoria stayed here, too, though reportedly was not amused.

The *Royal Pavilion* set the tone for the future: Regency Brighton was extravagant and gay. The narrow streets of the fishing village became the home of hostelries, restaurants, and boutiques. Theaters, music halls, parks, and gardens sprouted around the *Pavilion,* and Brighton became the country's most fashionable resort, graced by a splendid pier at each end of the seafront (one of which, sadly, is decaying). And its popularity has continued from those Regency days, as evidenced by its 3.5 million visitors yearly (although most now come only for the day or weekend). An impressive yachting marina (the largest in Europe)—surrounded by shops and restaurants—and a growing convention trade have made the town far more vital than most resorts. Brighton also has a distinct cosmopolitan flavor, thanks to its proximity to the Continent.

Most visitors still head directly for the beaches, but these are only for the hardiest sun worshipers. The shorefront consists of shingle stones rather than soft sand, and the tides can be strong, fueled by bracing breezes. To the west the beaches are quieter. The central beaches are boisterous, friendly, and the first to become crowded; here are the amusement arcades, fish-and-chips cafés, cockles and whelks stalls, miniature golf . . . in short, all the slightly sleazy glories of the traditional English seaside resort. The crowning glory of this candy-floss (cotton candy) mile is the almost-100-year-old *Palace Pier.*

Lining Brighton's main seafront and stretching into spacious garden squares behind it are hundreds of hotels and guesthouses, large and small. Most are in Regency style with bay fronts, balconies, and wrought-iron trimmings, but there are some good modern hotels as well, a result of the thriving conference trade. Beyond the seafront, the heart of the town lies focused on the narrow streets of the original village and the shopping streets that grew up around it and the *Royal Pavilion.* Cosmopolitan Brighton lives in these "Lanes," with art shops, bookstores, boutiques, antiques stalls, and the best restaurants, cafés, pubs, and wine bars. There's something for every taste and pocketbook here. Residents use this part of town as much as visitors, even in high summer, and if prices are a little inflated, perhaps the atmosphere is worth it!

Real local color is still farther afield, however, and is quite easy to miss. It centers on Gloucester Road and *Kensington Gardens,* in the area between Brighton's railway station and the Dome. This whole section was nearly a slum until a timely preservation order made it trendy again. Now the little flat-fronted laborers' houses are snapped up by aspiring executives who commute to London. It is also the main student quarter and the starting point for many of the latest fashions, and it is certainly the best place for spotting the real eccentrics or one of the many famous actors who live or retire here.

Between this highly metropolitan scene and the seaside razzamatazz, Brighton offers a full range of entertainment, sports, and sights. Few visitors have sufficient time to see it all, let alone the beautiful surrounding Sussex countryside. But the beauty of this lovely, liberal place is that you can spend as little as a day or as much as a year here and still come away satisfied.

Brighton At-a-Glance

SEEING THE CITY

The best view is from the end of the *Palace Pier,* which is at the junction of Marine Parade and the Old Steine. On the clearest days you can see the whole sweep of the coast from Worthing to Beachy Head. To the west, the *Peace Statue* marks the boundary of Brighton and the start of Hove Lawns.

To the east is the impressive seawall of the marina with the white cliffs above. In between is the entire Brighton seafront. Don't neglect the pier itself, a splendid Victorian structure of iron and steel, wood and glass, lined with amusement halls, slot machines, sun decks, fishing platforms, and endless cotton candy and hot doughnut stalls. Open daily (phone: 609361).

For a spectacular, if expensive, night view, several hotels along Kings Road, including the *Metropole* and the *Norfolk* (see *Checking In*), have restaurants overlooking the sea. After attending a concert at the *Brighton Centre* (see *Music*), stop in at its less expensive *Skyline* restaurant, which also has a good view.

SPECIAL PLACES

You'll be doing a lot of walking—browsing through the old quarter, ambling along the seafront promenade, visiting the dazzling *Royal Pavilion*—within a fairly centralized area. For sights outside the center, take the bus unless something more characteristic, such as the electric *Volk's Railway* or open-top excursion buses, is indicated.

CENTRAL BRIGHTON

ROYAL PAVILION The creation of Brighton's prime mover and shaker, the prince regent who became King George IV of England, it was begun modestly in 1786 and was rebuilt in its present extravagant form by the English architect John Nash (who also laid out *Regent's Park* and Regent Street in London) from 1815 to 1822. The state and private apartments are arranged with superb Regency and Chinese furniture and works of art, including many original pieces on loan from Queen Elizabeth II.

The showpiece of the Regency Exhibition, now at the *Pavilion* year-round, is the spectacular Banqueting Room, set with silver, porcelain, and glass from the period and containing what is probably the best collection of gold plate in all of England. Other marvelous rooms include the Salon, the North and South Drawing Rooms, the King's Apartments, and the Great Kitchen, which has the original mechanical spits, over 500 pieces of copperware, and tables showing the preparation of a banquet. The magnificent Music Room, tragically destroyed by fire in 1975, has been restored. The *Royal Pavilion Lawns* have deck chairs and regular summer performances by British and European bands. The *Royal Pavilion* is also the scene of some of the musical events of the *Brighton Festival* (see *Special Events,* below). Open daily. Admission charge. Town center, above the Old Steine (phone: 603005).

BRIGHTON MUSEUM AND ART GALLERY Close to the gardens of the *Royal Pavilion* and housed in buildings originally intended as stables for the palace, this center contains fine collections of Old Masters, watercolors, furniture, musical instruments, costumes, and English pottery and porcelain, as well as archaeological and ethnographic items and displays relating to Brighton history. The collections of applied art from the Art Nouveau and Art Deco periods—in which the museum specializes—and the Fashion Gallery are particularly interesting. The *Hove Amber Cup,* found in 1857 in Hove in a Bronze Age barrow carbon-dated to about 1500 BC, is another treasure. Closed Wednesdays. No admission charge (phone: 603005).

THE LANES The roughly square mile of narrow, paved alleys that made up the original village can be visited only on foot. This area is Brighton's Old Town, and it's full of atmosphere and character, with countless shops, including particularly good ones for books or antiques. Shop around to find the best prices, however, especially for antique jewelry. Entrances to the Lanes are all clearly marked, and the easiest to spot are on East Street, North Street, Ship Street, and Middle Street. Look for Duke's Lane, just off Ship Street, cunningly created out of backyards and filled with boutiques. Brighton Square, another of the more modern additions, is the center of the Lanes, with benches, a fountain, and a café-bar ideal for watching the world go by, continental-style. Guided walking tours, which last about an hour, are available April through September. They depart from the tourist information center (see *Tourist Information,* below).

KING'S ROAD This is the main seafront road. Steps and slopes descend from it to the central beaches and the lower promenade with cafés, amusement halls, and all the traditional seaside entertainment. Fish-and-chips, jellied eels, peanuts, ice cream, cotton candy, and Brighton rock candy are the things to eat. It's inexpensive and cheerful, but rent a deck chair rather than sitting directly on the pebbles as they may be stained with tar. The *Palace Pier* end of the King's Road is most rowdy. The Beach Deck near the *Grand* hotel is another entertainment area with outdoor concerts and games for children. Toward Hove, the scene becomes more sedate, with singsong pubs replaced by boating ponds and putting greens. For grass instead of stony beaches, try the Lawns at Hove.

VOLK'S RAILWAY AND PETER PAN'S PLAYGROUND Britain's first public electric railway opened in 1883 and still runs along the edge of Brighton's easterly beaches. The track starts 200 yards east of *Palace Pier* and extends 1½ miles to the western perimeter of the marina. The ride is inexpensive, and passengers travel in little wooden carriages with open sides and yellow roofs. Take it out to the marina, then either stroll back at sea level along Madeira Drive, passing *Peter Pan's Playground and Fun Fair,* or return via the high-level Marine Parade with its ornate Victorian ironwork. *Volk's Railway* runs from late March to late September and during the *Christmas* season. *Peter Pan's Playground* is closed November through *Easter.* No admission charge (no phone).

BRIGHTON MARINA AND MARINA VILLAGE Built against the odds of gale force winds and tumultuous seas, this is the largest yachting marina in Europe, featuring immense breakwaters that protect the inner harbor and have an enviable record for fishing catches. The 127-acre marina has berths for nearly

2,000 yachts, as well as a *Marina Village* development with an eight-screen movie theater, restaurants, bars, and bistros surrounding a pleasant piazza where visitors can sip drinks and watch the world go by. Reach it by *Volk's Railway,* any open-top bus, or by car—there is ample parking. Open daily. No admission charge. Marine Dr., Black Rock, 1½ miles east of the *Palace Pier* (phone: 693636).

ST. NICHOLAS'S CHURCHYARD Brighton is full of quiet green corners out of sight of the main roads. This is one of the prettiest, perfectly placed for a rest after shopping in nearby Western Road. It's a short walk up the steep hill of Dyke Road (which starts just above the *Clock Tower*) to the shallow brick steps that lead into the peaceful grounds surrounded by the gray flint walls characteristic of the area. The church itself is not always open but has a 12th-century Norman font and some excellent stained glass windows. The top end of the churchyard leads into a small park.

ENVIRONS

BLUEBELL RAILWAY Eighteen miles northeast of Brighton, vintage steam trains run for 9 miles through the glorious Sussex countryside between *Sheffield Park,* near Uckfield, and Kingscote. There also is a museum of railway relics at *Sheffield Park.* Open daily; the fare for the train ride includes admission to the museum. The railway runs year-round (phone: 82-572-2370 for recorded timetable; 82-572-3777 for general inquiries).

DRUSILLAS ZOO PARK This superb small zoo features award-winning exhibits of small creatures such as penguins, monkeys, wallabies, and emus. There also is a nearby playland for children. Open daily. Admission charge. 30 minutes from Brighton on A27 between Lewes and Eastbourne (phone: 323-870656).

BOOTH MUSEUM OF NATURAL HISTORY An entirely different kind of museum, it houses a large collection of British birds, stuffed and displayed in their natural habitats; both British and exotic butterflies; an exhibit of skeletons illustrating evolution; and a Geology of Sussex gallery. Closed Thursdays. No admission charge. 194 Dyke Rd., about 1½ miles from the city center, close to the Seven Dials (phone: 552586).

BRITISH ENGINEERIUM Various Victorian steam engines—and the impressive Easton and Anderson steam engines of 1866 and 1875—puff away efficiently every Sunday in the engine houses of this museum. A huge number of Victorian mechanical inventions and other engineering exhibits are displayed in the restored 19th-century water pumping station. Open daily. Admission charge. Nevill Rd., Hove, 3 miles from Brighton city center (phone: 559583).

STANMER PARK A natural park in the downland of Sussex is the setting for a village preserved as it was at the turn of the century. There are farmyards, a duck pond, a woodland park, and a rural museum that's open Sundays and

Thursdays in summer; most other parts are open daily. No admission charge to the museum. Lewes Rd., 4 miles northeast of Brighton center, just before the *University of Sussex* campus.

CHARLESTON FARMHOUSE This 18th-century building was the favorite country retreat of the Bloomsbury group of artists, writers, and intellectuals during the 1920s and 1930s. Regular visitors included Virginia Woolf, John Maynard Keynes, Benjamin Britten, T. S. Eliot, and Bertrand Russell. The house was fully restored by Vanessa Bell (Virginia Woolf's sister) and artist Duncan Grant. Open Wednesdays, Thursdays, Saturdays, and Sundays April through October. The kitchen is open to the public on Thursdays only. Admission charge. Firle, 6 miles east of Lewes (phone: 321-83265).

EXTRA SPECIAL

When the weather allows, open-top excursion buses run along the seafront to Rottingdean, a picturesque Sussex village set on the cliff tops in downland countryside. Steps and slopes lead to the undercliff walk edging narrow rocky beaches. A very pretty High Street has some good pubs and curio shops as well as the general stores typical of a small village. The *Plough Inn* is on the village green, and Rudyard Kipling lived in a house nearby. Rottingdean is 4 miles east of Brighton, easily reached by several buses.

Sources and Resources

TOURIST INFORMATION

The main tourist information center is in The Lanes at Bartholomew Square (phone: 323755). Hove's tourist information centers are at the *Town Hall* (Norton Rd.; phone: 778087) and at *King Alfred Leisure Centre* (Kingsway; phone: 746100). All three are open daily and carry books, maps, guides, and leaflets. The *British Tourist Authority*'s *Guide to Brighton* (costing 20p/about 30¢) gives a brief outline of attractions and lists accommodations. It has an adequate map, but a better one will cost £1 (about $1.50), or there are various street-by-street guides for £1.20 (about $1.80), all available at bookstores and newsstands. *In and Around Sussex* (£1.20/about $1.80) is good for attractions up to 30 miles from Brighton. Brighton's information center distributes all of these.

LOCAL COVERAGE The *Brighton Evening Argus* is on sale daily (except Sundays) from noon on; there's usually a good entertainment section.

TELEPHONE The city code for Brighton is 1273.

GETTING AROUND

Central Brighton is ideal for walking—the best parts are fairly close together. Outside the center, it gets hilly.

AIRPORT *Gatwick Airport* is 24 miles north of Brighton, and trains operate between the two (about a 30-minute journey). There also are buses and express coaches. For information, call 293-535353.

BUS The best way to get around. Three companies (*Brighton Buses, Southeast Buses,* and *Brighton and Hove Bus and Coach Company*) operate from the Brighton station, Churchill Square, or the Old Steine. Regular local fares start at 50p (about 75¢). Some buses require exact change. Several discount bus passes are available, including a Travelcard that allows unlimited weekly travel in Brighton itself (costs £11.40/about $17) and a MasterRider card that allows unlimited weekly travel within a 35-mile radius of the city (costs £16.20/about $24). Passes can be purchased from any post office or from *One Stop Travel* on St. James's Street. For information on local and regional services, contact the *Travel Enquiry Service* (phone: 886200).

CAR RENTAL All the major firms are represented, but unless you're planning an excursion, you're better off without a car. Traffic is congested, and parking is scarce and by voucher in the city center; vouchers may be purchased individually or in books of 10 from local shops.

SIGHTSEEING TOURS Brighton offers a taxi guide service with drivers who take parties of up to four people for tours of the town and surrounding countryside. For details, call Jim Fleet (phone: 304321).

TAXI There are reliable taxi ranks at the railroad station and at the intersection of East and North Streets. You may be able to hail a cab in the street, and they can be ordered by phone; call *Brighton and Hove Radio Cabs* (phone: 324245) or *Brighton Streamline Taxis* (phone: 747474).

SPECIAL EVENTS

Among the several annual events held in Brighton, one is of particular interest.

A FAVORITE FETE

Brighton Festival For three weeks in May, the largest arts festival in England fills the town with music, both classical and popular, in recitals, chamber and orchestral concerts, and operas. There are also jazz and rock concerts, dance and drama programs, art exhibitions, and seminars and workshops, as well as guided walks, children's events, and open houses at local artists' studios. A festival program becomes available in February. For details, call the *Brighton Festival Office* (phone: 676926).

In addition, the *London to Brighton Veteran Car Run* takes place the first Sunday in November. Antique cars—the "Old Crocks"—make their annual pilgrimage from Hyde Park Corner in London to Madeira Drive in Brighton in celebration of the day in 1896 when a law requiring all motor cars to be preceded by a man waving a red flag finally was dropped. A *Historic Commercial Vehicle Rally,* every year in May, is a runner-up to the Old Crocks. Trucks, fire engines, ambulances, and the like take part.

MUSEUMS

In addition to those mentioned in *Special Places,* there are two other museums of interest.

BRIGHTON SEA LIFE CENTRE The mock Gothic underground galleries of Britain's largest aquarium display a variety of freshwater, marine, and tropical fish; stingrays; and small sharks. Other attractions include a 214-foot, walk-through underwater tunnel made of see-through acrylic; as well as an indoor adventure playground for children. Open daily. Admission charge. Marine Parade (phone: 604234).

HOVE MUSEUM AND ART GALLERY Housed in a Victorian villa near the center of Hove, the exhibitions range from 18th- and 20th-century paintings to antique dolls and toys to the South East Arts Collection of Contemporary Craft. Closed Mondays. No admission charge. 19 New Church Rd. (phone: 775400, ext. 2299).

SHOPPING

Churchill Square is at the heart of Brighton's extensive shopping center—a pedestrians-only, modern precinct with all the major chain stores including *Habitat* (called *Conran's* in the US), the furniture and housewares emporium. It's next to the original shopping street off Western Road, near its eastern end. In the vicinity of Churchill Square, Western Road runs into North Street, giving almost 2 miles of prime shopping; the inexpensive and cheerful shops and stalls of Gardner Street, Bond Street, and the Lanes lead off North Street. Best buys are antiques, bric-a-brac, secondhand books, and local paintings and crafts, plus traditional English glass, china, and woolens. For standard shopping hours, see GETTING READY TO GO. The North Laine area offers the widest choice of antiques on Saturdays, when the shops between North Road and Trafalgar Street are augmented by sidewalk stalls. High-fashion clothing, jewelry, artwork, and other gift items can be found in the *Regent Arcade,* located between East Street, Bartholomew Square, and Market Square.

Be sure to take your passport when you shop, and always inquire about the Value Added Tax (VAT) refund application forms when your total purchases in a store are over £50 (about $75). The VAT is a surcharge payable at the sales counter, but foreign customers usually will be reimbursed for it at home (for more information see GETTING READY TO GO).

Bears and Friends of Brighton This teddy bear lair includes such favorites as Paddington and Winnie the Pooh, as well as the fine stuffed animals manufactured by Steiff, Hermann, House of Nisbet, Canterbury, and Deans. Limited editions also are offered. 41 Meeting House La. (phone: 208940).

Christopher Cowen Antiques Housed in a charming building that was restored to uncover the original flint fascia, this shop specializes in 18th- and 19th-century furniture. 60 Middle St. (phone: 205757).

Culpepper Herbs, spices, natural plant oils, bath salts, potpourri, fine English soap, and herbal medicines are sold here. 12D Meeting House La. (phone: 327939).

Le Jazz Hot An excellent selection of Art Deco and Art Nouveau ceramics is offered, including a collection of Deco chrome, Bakelite jewelry, and period furniture. 14 Prince Albert St. (phone: 206091).

Jolly Good Chocolates The morello cherries, hazelnut pralines, and specialty chocolates live up to this shop's name. 49 Gardner St. (phone: 679678).

Liberty's A local branch of the world-famous store established in 1875 by Arthur Lasenby Liberty, who imported exotic artifacts and silks from the Far East, the shop offers beautifully patterned fabric, as well as fine clothing. 16-18 East St. (phone: 822933).

Pecksniff's Bespoke Perfumery The artisans here ensure the preservation of their ancient craft by hand-blending flowers, herbs, and natural oils to create traditional English scents. You also can commission them to create a new fragrance by mixing the essences of your choice. They then keep the formula handy in case you want more. 45-46 Meeting House La. (phone: 328904).

Sweet Williams Fudge Shop Here is a mouth-watering selection of homemade fudge, nougat candy, and other delectable treats. 26A North St., Meeting House La. (phone: 323234).

SPORTS

The *King Alfred Leisure Centre* (Kingsway, Hove; phone: 822228) offers badminton, snooker, table tennis, bowling, swimming, flumes (water slides), and sauna facilities. There's also a café and a bar. Open daily.

CRICKET For a modest entry fee you can watch a match—also called a fixture—between April and September at the *Sussex County Cricket Ground* (Eaton Rd., Hove; phone: 732161). Contact them for a schedule of current fixtures.

FISHING Good catches are sea whiting, mackerel, occasionally plaice, and very occasionally cod. The best place to fish is at the *Brighton Marina* (see *Special Places*). During the summer, only angling club members can fish from the *Palace Pier:* Try your luck at the groynes (breakwaters) instead. Those toward Hove, where there are fewer boats and swimmers, are preferable. No permits needed.

GOLF With 18 challenging holes and magnificent views over downs and marina, the *East Brighton Golf Club* (Roedean Rd.; phone: 603989) has one of the best courses in the area. Several buses from the Old Steine pass it. The municipal *Hollingbury Park Golf Club* (Ditchling Rd.; phone: 552010) has 18 reasonable holes. The No. 26 bus from the Old Steine takes you right there.

GREYHOUND RACING *Coral Stadium* (Nevill Rd., Hove; phone: 204601 or 204605) has races on Tuesdays, Thursdays, and Saturdays beginning at 7:30 PM; there is also racing on either Monday or Wednesday afternoon. Call ahead to reserve a table in the excellent restaurant that overlooks the course.

HORSE RACING The *Brighton Races* meet frequently between April and October at the *Brighton Racecourse,* Race Hill (phone: 603580). Admission charge.

SOCCER There's good support for the *Brighton and Hove Albion*—known locally as the *Seagulls.* Games are played late August through early May at the *Brighton and Hove Albion Ground* (Goldstone Rd., Hove; phone: 739535).

SWIMMING The *Prince Regent Swimming Complex* (Church St.; phone: 685692) offers an indoor pool, water slide, diving pool, learners' pool, and solarium. Open daily.

TENNIS Twelve parks have public courts. *Preston Park* has 10 hard courts, and another 10 courts are on the other (west) side of London Road, away from the main park in a section called the Rockery. There's no racquet rental, nor can you reserve any of the public courts; be prepared to wait during July and August. *Record Tennis Centre* (Kingsway, Hove; phone: 203795) also has three courts; it's open daily during the summer.

THEATER

The *Theatre Royal* (New Rd.; phone: 328488) has pre-London runs and variety, with weekly changes in the program. Other productions are at the *Gardner Arts Centre,* a modern theater-in-the-round at the *University of Sussex* (Falmer; phone: 685861).

MUSIC

Big pop and rock concerts are at the 5,000-seat *Brighton Centre* (Russell Rd.; phone: 202881). The *Dome* (29 New Rd.; phone: 674357), slightly smaller with 2,000 seats, stages classical, pop, rock, and variety events, including some with international celebrities. Both have an Entertainments Line (phone: 891-800-6666), which provides details of forthcoming performances. *St. Peter's Church* (on London Rd.; no phone) has occasional organ concerts, and several pubs have folk, jazz, and rock groups and informal sing-alongs.

NIGHTCLUBS AND NIGHTLIFE

This scene tends to be bright and informal, with the emphasis on the young and noisy. Apart from the pubs, which are crowded in summer, activity centers on *Kingswest,* an entertainment complex on King's Road close to the West Street intersection. It contains a restaurant complex and two nightspots. *Oriana's* (phone: 325899) is for the smartly dressed (no jeans) over-21 crowd. The music is live, usually pop and rock. The *Event* (phone: 732627) varies, sometimes offering live music, sometimes disco. Farther along the King's Road, the *Metropole* hotel's lively club, the *Metro,* is open until 2 AM. The *Paradox* (West St.; phone: 321628) is the South Coast's most exotic discotheque for the 21-plus crowd. Another leading light on the local disco scene is *Monroes* (West St.; phone: 21692). Check the *Argus* for details. Several hotels and restaurants have dinner dances or cabarets. There are three casinos: *Sergeant York's* (88 Queen's Rd., near the station; phone: 26514), the *International Casino Club* (6 Preston St.; phone: 725101), and *Hove Sporting Club* (28 Fourth Ave., Hove; phone: 72026). To play at the casinos, you must be 18 or older and establish membership 48 hours in advance; proof of age and identity (such as a passport) is required.

Best in Town

CHECKING IN

The best hotels offer sea views, and even inexpensive places can be found overlooking the eastern or western ends of the beaches. At a very expensive hotel a double room (with private bath, TV set, phone, and breakfast, unless otherwise indicated) will cost $200 or more per night, including taxes and service. An expensive hotel will cost $100 to $150; a hotel in the moderate category, $50 to $95; and an inexpensive hotel (guesthouse), $40 or less. The better hotels offer reduced weekly rates in late June, July, and August, when there is no convention business, and many also offer year-round holiday (including weekend) bargains. (The *Brighton & Hove Main Resorts* brochure, available at the tourist information center, lists them all—see *Tourist Information,* above.) Do not arrive without a reservation from late August through early June, the prime convention season. There are also holiday flat-lets available for $120 to $400 per flat per week. For information call *Interhome* (phone: 201-882-6864). All telephone numbers are in the 1273 city code unless otherwise indicated.

VERY EXPENSIVE

Grand Right in the center of the seafront, this is the old and very attractive queen of Brighton hotels. Its Victorian architecture is at its best in the lobby and on the landings. The 200-room hotel features a restaurant, an indoor pool, a sauna/solarium, a fitness center, and the *Midnight Blues* nightclub. Traditional afternoon tea is served daily in the *Victoria Lounge.* King's Rd. (phone: 321188; fax: 202694).

Metropole A large (328 rooms), modernized period place, it has extensive facilities, including a restaurant, health club, beauty salon, and garage. White columns and murals surround a beautiful indoor pool. It has an attached exhibition hall, and since it's the main conference hotel in Brighton, it's one of the first to fill up. King's Rd. (phone: 775432; fax: 207764).

EXPENSIVE

Brighton Thistle Formerly the *Hospitality Inn,* this exciting, modern structure on the seafront boasts 204 rooms and an airy, plant-filled atrium lounge. Its Leisure Club features a pool; there are two restaurants—the *Promenade,* for hot buffet lunches, and the more formal *La Noblesse.* King's Rd. (phone: 206700; fax: 820692).

Old Ship On the seafront close to the Lanes, this is the oldest independent hotel in Brighton, dating to 1559. Much of its original style and charm is intact, especially in the banquet room once used by the prince regent. The 149 rooms vary from simple singles to lavish delights with antique four-poster beds. There is a restaurant. King's Rd. (phone: 329001; fax: 830718).

MODERATE

Kempton House Seafront views overlooking the beach and *Palace Pier* make this cozy place a real charmer. The 12 guestrooms come equipped with everything from the usual TV set to an alarm clock and hair dryer; one has a four-poster bed. The dining room is for hotel guests only. 33-34 Marine Parade (phone/fax: 570248).

Norfolk The 121 rooms at this attractive seaside property recently have been refurbished and redecorated. There is a formal restaurant as well as two bars (one with a brasserie-style menu); other amenities include an indoor heated pool, sauna, solarium, Jacuzzi, hair salon, and fitness center. 149 King's Rd. (phone: 738201; fax: 821752).

Oak This 138-room hotel with Art Deco decor and a restaurant is located 100 yards from the seafront in the heart of Brighton's best area for shopping and eating. West St. (phone: 220033; fax: 778000).

Preston Resort Two miles from the city center, close to *Preston Manor and Park,* and a good stop for visitors who are driving, this modern, attractive 34-room hotel has a restaurant and free parking. It's close to the main London—Brighton road. 216 Preston Rd. (phone: 507853; fax: 540039).

Sheridan This Edwardian-style hotel is situated on a noisy corner of the seafront, but its plushness—velvet, brass, and crystal—and atmosphere make up for the shortcoming of its location. Its 57 rooms are popular with regular customers, so book ahead. There is a restaurant. 64 King's Rd. (phone: 323221; fax: 21485).

INEXPENSIVE

Marina House Just a few yards from the seafront, this nicely furnished 10-room hostelry is run by a cheery husband-and-wife team. The dining room serves English, Chinese, and Indian fare. 8 Charlotte St., Marine Parade (phone: 679484; fax: 605349).

EATING OUT

Brighton is fortunate to have a greater variety of restaurants than most cities its size—there are over 400 from which to choose. Just about every style of cooking is available, including Indian, Chinese, Italian, and better than average Greek. Local fish is delicious. There are some good spots with inexpensive fast food, and there's a healthy sprinkling of better restaurants with excellent and imaginative fare. You can expect to get an English three-course dinner for two for $90 to $130, including wine and tips, in expensive restaurants; $45 to $75, including house wine, in moderate places; and less than $40, excluding wine, in inexpensive eateries. All restaurants listed below serve lunch and dinner, unless otherwise noted. All telephone numbers are in the 1273 city code unless otherwise indicated.

EXPENSIVE

English's Oyster Bar If you can treat yourself well only once in Brighton, do it here. The restaurant is more than 150 years old, converted from 400-year-old fishermen's cottages in the Lanes. It has been owned by the same family for almost 50 years and serves some of the best seafood in the area. In the past it has welcomed such celebrities as Charlie Chaplin, Vivien Leigh, and Laurence Olivier. Open daily. Reservations necessary. Major credit cards accepted. 29-31 East St. (phone: 327980).

Langan's Bistro An offshoot of London's famous celebrity eatery (and co-owned by actor Michael Caine), it serves haute dishes at not-so-haute prices. Specialties include fish soup, monkfish with pine nuts, and guinea hen with shallots. Closed Mondays, Saturday lunch, and Sunday evening. Reservations advised. Major credit cards accepted. 1 Paston Pl. (phone: 606933).

Wheeler's One of the oldest (1856) restaurants in the region (and part of the London-based chain), it offers unsurpassed seafood served in Edwardian elegance. This is one of the area's best-known dining spots, so book ahead. Open daily. Reservations necessary. Major credit cards accepted. 17 Market St. (phone: 325135).

MODERATE

Al Forno Operated by two brothers (who also run *Al Duomo,* at 7 Pavilion Building; phone: 26741), this simple and crowded Italian place is great for pizza and pasta. There's outdoor dining in summer. Open daily. Reservations unnecessary. Major credit cards accepted. 36 East St. (phone: 324905).

Black Chapati Here is a rarity: an excellent Indian eatery owned and operated by an Englishman. The food is prepared with zesty spices and features vivid contrasts of flavor and texture; good choices include breast of wood pigeon with Japanese noodles and coriander, homemade pork sausages with lentils and red pepper chutney, and roast filet of haddock marinated in lemon. There is also a modest selection of wines and an array of ciders and beers. The best value is the special two-course dinner menu offered Tuesdays through Thursdays. Open daily. Reservations advised. Major credit cards accepted. 12 Circus Parade, New England Rd. (phone: 699011).

Le Grandgousier Tiny and informal; everyone shares one huge table and tucks into the simple French country food. The choice is limited, but it's great fun and good value. Closed Saturday lunch and Sunday evenings. Reservations necessary. Major credit cards accepted. 15 Western St. (phone: 772005).

INEXPENSIVE

Food for Friends Tulips on the tables, still lifes on the walls, hanging plants, classical music, and delicious casseroles and wholesome salads served by a young, cheerful staff to a fast-moving (but never-ending) queue of students, Brightonites, and visitors. Open daily. No reservations. No credit cards accepted. 17A-18 Prince Albert St. (phone: 736236).

Palm Court Fish-'n'-Chips Café Right in the middle of *Palace Pier* is this elegant Victorian eatery that serves the eponymous fare. The sea views are spectacular. Open daily. No reservations. No credit cards accepted. *Palace Pier,* Madeira Dr. (phone: 609361).

SHARING A PINT

It's difficult to choose from the wide selection of pubs. The *Colonnade Long Bar* (New Rd.; phone: 328728) is next to the *Theatre Royal* and is used during intermissions; it has Victorian decor and a good selection of playbills. Don't miss *Cricketers* (Black Lion St.; phone: 329472 or 324620), the town's oldest pub. The original parts, dating from 1549, include the stables and coachyard, and there are old mirrors and marble and brass tables. The *Bedford Tavern* (30 Western St.; phone: 739495) is simple and unassuming; if you're passing by, pop in to see its collection of heraldry. *Dr. Brighton's* (King's Rd. by Market St.; phone: 328765) is a traditional-looking pub with good, hot food. The *Druid's Head* (Market Pl., The Lanes; phone: 325490) is an Old World place with beams and horse brasses. Once a smugglers' haunt, it now belongs to the fashionable young set. The *King and Queen* (Marlborough Pl.; phone: 607207), an amusing imitation of a Tudor beer garden, overlooks the *Victoria Gardens;* there's also an aviary. The *Royal Pavilion Tavern* (Castle Sq.; phone: 325684) is a popular central pub with old oak panels and beams and extensive hot and cold snacks. In Rottingdean, the *Black Horse* (High St.; phone: 302581) is a genuine village pub, with a comfortable and friendly large bar and the original snug—a tiny bar for women.

Bristol

As described in the pages of Robert Louis Stevenson's *Treasure Island,* a wide-eyed visitor of a century or so ago could wander the docks of Bristol, sniffing the smell of tar in the salt air, marveling at the figureheads of ships and the "many old sailors, with rings in their ears, and whiskers curled in ringlets, and tarry pigtails, and their swaggering, clumsy sea-walk. . . . " It was a scene that any movie mogul would have been proud to capture.

Naturally, Bristol looks like that no more. Now it's a large, modern, lively city with isolated patches of medieval antiquity reaching through the centuries. Walk along the quayside of the harbor today and see characteristic warehouses, once old, deserted, and decaying, now restored as museums and arts and exhibition centers. Pleasure craft, visiting naval warships, and even a few restored traditional sailing boats now grace the harbor, creating a striking image that is further enhanced by the backdrop of Bristol's city center, dominated by the cathedral's towers and, behind them, the university buildings.

Bristol had been an important port since the 11th century. During the Middle Ages, its merchants traded in wines—bordeaux from France, sherry from Spain, and port from Portugal. By the 15th century its enterprising maritime boldness attracted sailors from Europe bent on discovery. John Cabot (born Giovanni Caboto) came from Italy, found backing by a local merchant, and set sail in 1497 to become the first explorer to reach the American mainland.

Cabot was followed by other explorers, then by thousands of early American settlers who sailed to a new life from here. Having played a part in the discovery of America, Bristol did its share in developing it, financing colonization efforts with trading in Virginia tobaçco and West Indian sugar. A less glorious chapter was the city's involvement in the black slave trade; the Bristol merchants grew fat on the proceeds from it, while the Quakers and John Wesley and his Methodists railed against it.

"All shipshape and Bristol fashion" is an English phrase meaning everything methodical and orderly, recalling the days when this city in the west of England was dominated by the masts of tall ships from all corners of the world. In Bristol, unlike most seafaring cities, the docks are in the heart of the town rather than at its edge. That the ships are no longer there is the result of an error of judgment. The city grew at the confluence of the Avon and Frome Rivers, 7 miles inland from where the Avon—which rises and falls with close to the highest tide in the world—flows out into the Severn estuary. Fear of piracy caused the medieval inhabitants to plant themselves far upstream, a less than ideal location that made docking a tricky business of picking the right moment to set out upriver or risk getting stuck in the mud at low tide. Even berthed ships were in danger of breaking up in the tidal sweep.

To remedy this, the city channeled the Avon into a new cut in the early 18th century, creating a "floating harbor" with a constant level of water. But by then, much transatlantic trade had been lost to Liverpool. By the end of the 19th century, new docks had been built at Avonmouth and Portishead, but, alas, too late to prevent the decline in Bristol's maritime fortunes.

The cityscape underwent further change as a result of World War II. The blitz of 1940–41 damaged some 9,000 buildings, including the medieval core. Throughout history the tallest structures in Bristol had been the spires and towers of churches, but with postwar reconstruction came the first tall office blocks. Now it is necessary to walk between walls of concrete and glass for a glimpse of the fine churches and other reminders of Bristol's heritage—remains of early monasteries and Georgian squares and terraces—that survive.

For many devotees, Bristol's most charming part is suburban Clifton, perched on the Clifton and Durdham Downs above the city and the Avon Gorge. Begun as a dormitory in the healthful high air for visitors to the Hot Well spa at the foot of the gorge, Clifton then became a fashionable place to live. The spa had only a brief moment of glory in the early 18th century, but Clifton was left with Georgian crescents to compete with those of Bath, and large, graceful Victorian villas.

Still, Clifton is far from the reality of a commercial, manufacturing city of nearly half a million people. Throughout its history, Bristol's heart has been in its waterways, its most characteristic visual feature. Although life in the harbor is now a shadow of what it once was, the docks remain a museum of Britain's mercantile past.

Bristol At-a-Glance

SEEING THE CITY

From the top of *Cabot Tower* (built on Brandon Hill in 1897 to commemorate the quadricentennial of John Cabot's voyage to the New World), there is a spectacular bird's-eye view of the center of Bristol and much of the surrounding area. It's quite a climb, however, and the view is almost as good from the base of the tower. The panorama is dominated by church spires, venerable stone buildings, and waterways, but you'll also see a surprising amount of greenery and open spaces. The tower is open daily. No admission charge.

SPECIAL PLACES

The best starting point for exploring Bristol is the vast junction known to residents as the Centre. If it's not marked as such on your map, look for its boundaries: St. Augustine's Parade and Broad Quay to the west and east, Colston Avenue to the north, and the Bridgehead (or Quay Head) to the south, at the tip of St. Augustine's Reach. In recent years the Centre has been taken over by cars, but if you can bear the exhaust fumes and the incessant roar of traffic, you are well placed here to reach the older sections of town, the waterfront, the dignified buildings of College Green, and the shops of Park Street and Queens Road. Most buses also stop here, and there are plenty of taxis. A plaque on the Bridgehead commemorates the spot where John Cabot left on his historic voyage, and the benches around the statue of Neptune provide a welcome chance for modern-day explorers to sit and rest.

CENTRAL BRISTOL

BRISTOL CATHEDRAL The *Cathedral Church of the Holy and Undivided Trinity* was founded in the 12th century as an Augustinian monastery. The Norman chapter house, which dates from this earliest period, should not be missed. Other older parts are the 13th-century Elder Lady chapel and the 14th-century choir and Eastern Lady chapel (with the Jesse window), while the nave is the work of a Victorian architect faithful to the original style. Particularly interesting are the 16th-century misericords in the choir on which monks—who were not allowed to sit during services—leaned. They're beautifully carved and all different, some with serious and some with humorous scenes. College Green (phone: 925-0692).

COUNCIL HOUSE This graceful, curved, 20th-century red brick building across the street from the cathedral is the headquarters of Bristol's municipal administration. The golden unicorns on either end of the roof are symbolic of the city; they are also found on its coat of arms. It is closed to the public. College Green.

GEORGIAN HOUSE Once the home of a wealthy merchant, this is now a museum maintained as though the merchant and his family still lived in it. It was built in 1790, and the furnishings, all of local manufacture, are Georgian. The kitchen shows some of the less-than-luxurious side of downstairs life, including cramped surroundings and a cold-water plunge bath. Closed Sundays and Mondays. Admission charge. 7 Great George St. (phone: 921-1362).

CITY MUSEUM AND ART GALLERY The major museum in the area, it has extensive collections in the fine and applied arts, archaeology and history, geology and natural history, but visitors pressed for time will find exhibits of Bristol blue—and green, amethyst, and white—glass not too far beyond the lobby. (The building next door to the museum is the 20th-century neo-Gothic *Wills Memorial Building* of the *University of Bristol.* It houses the 10-ton *Great George* bell, which sounds hourly in E flat.) Open daily. Admission charge. Queens Rd. (phone: 922-3571).

KING STREET This cobbled street was laid out in the 1660s and remains one of the most picturesque in Bristol. The pink buildings at its western end are the

Merchant Venturers' Almshouses, built in the 17th century for retired seamen. Next is the 18th-century *Old Library;* and farther along, the *Palladian Coopers' Hall,* a guildhall built in 1743, has become the entrance to the *Theatre Royal* (see *Theater,* below). Several other 17th-century edifices line the street, which ends with a group of half-timbered and gabled buildings. Built in 1664, these houses eventually became *Ye Llandoger Trow,* an inn where Daniel Defoe is supposed to have met the man he transformed into Robinson Crusoe, and which still operates as a pub and restaurant. King Street stops at an original stretch of Bristol quayside known as the Welsh Back.

CORN STREET The four bronze "nails," or trading tables, on which 16th- and 17th-century merchants counted out their money ("paid on the nail") characterize this section of Bristol. The heart of the medieval city was at the crossing of Corn, Broad, High, and Wine Streets; the area later became Bristol's center of banking and commerce. Corn Street, especially, is an amalgam of worthy and workaday 18th- and 19th-century buildings. Two to compare are the *Exchange* (1743), behind the nails, designed by John Wood the Elder as a market and meeting place for merchants, and the ornately carved palazzo (1854) across from it, now Lloyd's Bank. Behind the *Exchange* is the *St. Nicholas Market,* a warren of stalls covered over in the 18th century and still going strong (closed Sundays). Several interesting churches include *All Saints* (Corn St.), with Norman foundations; and *Christ Church* (Broad St.), an 18th-century replacement of an earlier church. Walk to the end of Broad Street and you'll come to St. John's Gate, the only survivor of Bristol's nine medieval gateways. The gate (Norse for "street") is home to *St. John's Baptist Church* (phone: 974-1759), which is open for viewing on Tuesday and Thursday afternoons.

CHRISTMAS STEPS This steep, cobbled lane off Rupert Street was constructed in 1669, and today is lined with specialty shops. At the top, turn the corner onto Colston Street for a glimpse of John Foster's almshouses; inside is the *Chapel of the Three Kings of Cologne* (10 Colston St.), dating from the 1480s.

JOHN WESLEY'S NEW ROOM In contrast to the other more imposing churches here, the world's first Methodist chapel is spare and simple. John Wesley built it in 1739, and he and his brother preached here for 40 years. Their former living quarters are upstairs. Closed Sundays year-round and Wednesdays in winter. 36 The Horsefair (phone: 926-4740).

THE HARBOR

BRISTOL MARITIME HERITAGE CENTRE This striking building houses displays that tell the city's maritime history and the SS *Great Britain*'s story. Open daily. Admission charge. *Great Western Dock,* Gas Ferry Rd., off Cumberland Rd. (phone: 926-0680).

SS GREAT BRITAIN Following the SS *Great Western,* the SS *Great Britain* was the second nautical accomplishment of British engineer Isambard Kingdom

Brunel. When it floated out from Bristol in 1843, it was not only the first iron-hulled screw steamship in the world, it was also the largest liner on the seas. The *Great Western,* which had been the first transatlantic steam vessel, is no more; the *Great Britain,* fortunately, is. It was shipwrecked and abandoned in the Falkland Islands in 1886, and its return to the city in 1970 was a nostalgic and emotional occasion. It is now undergoing restoration at the *Bristol Maritime Heritage Centre* dock, where it was built. Open daily. Admission charge. *Great Western Dock,* Gas Ferry Rd., off Cumberland Rd. (phone: 926-0680).

ST. MARY REDCLIFFE The church Queen Elizabeth I described as "the fairest, goodliest, and most famous parish church in England" was built mostly during the 14th and 15th centuries, near the city docks. An outstanding example of Perpendicular architecture, it enlivens a rather dull part of the cityscape. Inside, the nave and choir soar to a ceiling ornamented with more than 1,200 carved and gilded bosses. As you enter, note the unusual hexagonal shape and the very pretty stained glass windows of the outer north porch, which dates from 1290, and the black marble pillars of the late-12th-century inner north porch, the oldest part of the church. Redcliffe Way (phone: 929-1487).

CLIFTON

CLIFTON SUSPENSION BRIDGE Bristol's most famous landmark is another of Isambard Kingdom Brunel's achievements. The bridge has a 702-foot span, 245 feet above the high-water level of the limestone Avon Gorge, which is famous for rare trees and plants. Before it opened in 1864, people crossed the river in a basket on a cable. Since then, pilots have flown underneath it and suicides have been attempted (some successfully) from it. The city's favorite story is that of the young woman who jumped after a lovers' quarrel in 1885—she parachuted in her petticoats to a soft landing in the mud and lived to a ripe old age.

CLIFTON CATHEDRAL The *Cathedral Church of Saints Peter and Paul* is the headquarters of the Roman Catholic diocese of Clifton. Completed in 1973, it is considered an important work of contemporary church architecture, designed to reflect the most recent changes in the form of liturgical worship. Visitors are welcome inside to see its modern works of art. Pembroke Rd. (phone: 973-8411).

CLIFTON AND DURDHAM DOWNS Bristol's largest and most popular open space covers more than 400 acres on the north side of the city. Bristolians play football on the Downs in winter, cricket in summer, and walk on the green expanse year-round.

ZOOLOGICAL GARDENS One of the best zoos in Britain, it has more than 1,000 mammals, birds, reptiles, and fish. There also are extensive gardens. Closed *Christmas.* Admission charge. Clifton Down (phone: 973-8951).

BLAISE CASTLE HOUSE MUSEUM *Blaise Castle* itself is nothing but a Gothic folly, a sham structure built in 1766 to decorate the grounds of this estate. But set up in the estate's real 18th-century mansion is a folk museum of costumes, toys, crafts, and other reminders of West Country life in days gone by. The landscaped grounds contain woodlands, walkways, the remains of an Iron Age hill fort, and a number of attractions for children. Closed Mondays. Admission charge. Henbury, 4 miles northwest of Bristol (phone: 950-6789).

EXTRA SPECIAL

You can sample dockside Bristol by walking from the Bridgehead along *Narrow Quay,* over the Prince Street Bridge and onto *Prince's Wharf,* beyond which is *Wapping Wharf.* (A helpful *Maritime Walks* guidebook is available at the tourist information center.) Another choice is the ferrybus, which crosses to and from *Narrow Quay.* During the season it plies the Avon River between *Narrow Quay* and Floating Harbour, making various stops, including one at the SS *Great Britain.* A tour of the dockside pubs also operates during the summer. Contact the tourist board for more information (see *Tourist Information,* below).

Sources and Resources

TOURIST INFORMATION

The tourist information center in *St. Nicholas Church* (St. Nicholas St.; phone: 926-0767) supplies brochures, maps, and general information. Open daily. For £1.60 (about $2.40), you can pick up the *Bristol Official Visitors' Guide,* a comprehensive introduction to all aspects of the city which includes several walking tours (for more information on walking tours, see *Getting Around*).

LOCAL COVERAGE The morning *Western Daily Press* and the *Bristol Evening Post* are the two dailies, while the fortnightly *Venue* magazine covers what's on and where to go in and around the city.

TELEPHONE The city code for Bristol is 117.

GETTING AROUND

You may want to take a bus or taxi to Clifton, but the rest of Bristol is walkable, with one word of warning. Traffic speeds around and out from the Centre in all directions, and little provision seems to have been made for pedestrians. There are a few traffic lights (all pedestrian operated) and a few striped zebra crossings (where the pedestrian has the right of way once he or she steps from the curb), but you'll see many a Bristolian waiting to dash at the sight of any break in the two-way onslaught.

AIRPORT Bristol's *Lulsgate Airport,* 6 miles southwest of the city on A38 (phone: 1275-874441), has flights to Belfast, Cardiff, the Channel Islands, Cork, Dublin, Glasgow, the Isle of Man, and other domestic destinations. In summer, 50 or more flights per week depart *Lulsgate* for the Continent.

BOAT The *Waverley* and the *Balmoral* operate afternoon and evening summer cruises from the harbor to Ilfracombe in Devon and the isles of Lundy and Steep Holm, as well as trips down the river Avon and tours of the harbor (phone: 1446-720656). Several other companies also offer tours of the harbor and the Avon, including *Bristol and Bath Cruisers* (phone: 921-4307), *Bristol Ferry Boat Company* (phone: 927-3416), and the *Bristol Packet* (phone: 926-8157).

BUS The *Bristol City Line* operates buses within the city and throughout the area, including the inexpensive and friendly yellow minibuses that run approximately every 10 minutes. Most city bus routes include a stop in the Centre; long-distance coaches operate out of the bus station on Marlborough Street, north of the *Broadmead Shopping Centre.* Bus fares around Bristol and the surrounding area vary depending on the distance; discount passes include the Rover Card (costing £10.10/about $15), allowing a week's unlimited travel anywhere in Bristol itself; and the Maxi Rover ticket (costing £19.60/about $29.50), allowing a week's unlimited travel in Bristol, Bath, and Weston. Passes can be purchased at the bus station; for schedule and fare information, call 955-3231.

CAR RENTAL The major national and international companies are represented, including *Avis* (phone: 929-2123), *Budget* (phone: 972-0011), *Europcar* (phone: 927-2111), and *Hertz* (phone: 977-9777).

TAXI You'll have no trouble getting a taxi in the city center for the trip out, but for the return, you'll probably have to call one. Numerous cab companies are listed in the local yellow pages.

TRAIN *Temple Meads Railway Station* (phone: 929-4255) is at *Temple Gate* in the city center. (Visitors may want to see the display on the history of Bristol here, as well as take a look around; this is one of the oldest railway terminals in the world, built in 1839 by Isambard Kingdom Brunel.) Frequent trains connect it with London's *Paddington Station* (journey time: 90 minutes), Britain's other major cities, and South Wales. Several services also stop at *Parkway Station,* on Bristol's northern outskirts; travel time is about 10 minutes shorter.

WALKING TOURS Walking tour guides are available, including a "Walkabout" series on individual routes. The Bristol Heritage Walk is a popular historical tour passing by the docks, historic churches and cathedrals, museums, and more. It begins at the statue of Neptune, down by the docks (at Quay Head, St. Augustine's Parade); the *Bristol Heritage Walk* book is available from the tourist information center for £1.95 (about $3). From late April through September, try one of the regular walking tours led by Bristol's *Corps of Guides.* Visit the tourist information center for details (see above). The walks last approximately one and a half hours, and most cost £1 (about $1.50). Exact departure times are posted outside the tourist information center, at the *Exchange,* or near Neptune's statue at the Bridgehead (Quay Head).

SPECIAL EVENTS

More than 100 dealers exhibit their wares at the *Bristol Antiques and Collectors Fair,* which is held annually on *New Year's Day* at the *Bristol Exhibition Centre* (2 Canons Rd.; phone: 926-4222). Exhibitors from all over the world come to the *Bristol Exhibition Complex,* on Floating Harbour just below the Bridgehead; stands are set up for visitors to sample wines not usually available, and fireworks displays light up the city docks. The docks are also the focus of other events, including the *Bristol Harbour Regatta* in July. In September, the sky over *Ashton Court Estate,* 825 acres of park on the other side of the Clifton Suspension Bridge, is full of multicolored hot-air balloons taking part in the *Bristol International Balloon Fiesta.* Also at *Ashton Court Estate,* kite enthusiasts fly high at the annual *Kite Festival,* held in the first week of September.

MUSEUMS

In addition to those discussed in *Special Places,* Bristol has a number of other interesting museums, including the new *Empire and Commonwealth Museum,* an exhibition of memorabilia about the British Empire. Although the collection was still being assembled at press time, at least part of the exhibit is scheduled to open early this year in the *Temple Meads Railway Station*'s engine sheds (for details, call 925-4980). *Note:* The museums run by the *Bristol Council,* including the *Georgian House, Blaise Castle House Museum,* and the *City Museum* (see *Special Places*), and the *Bristol Industrial Museum* and *Red Lodge* (see below) often close without warning. Check with the *City Museum* before visiting any of them.

BRISTOL INDUSTRIAL MUSEUM Machinery, especially that connected with transport—including horse-drawn carriages, a collection of Bristol-made airplanes, and a model of the *Concorde* cockpit—is displayed in a transit shed on the docks. The *Bristol Harbour Railway* links the museum to the *Maritime Heritage Centre.* Other steam engines and rolling stock are on display outside the museum. Closed Mondays. Admission charge. Prince's Wharf (phone: 925-1470).

EXPLORATORY Housed in Brunel's magnificent engine sheds at Temple Meads, this science museum is notable for its "hands-on" experiments. Open daily. Admission charge. Temple Meads (phone: 922-5944).

HARVEY'S WINE MUSEUM Stop here to see an illustration of how wine is made, plus collections of old wine bottles, glasses, decanters, and silver decanter labels. The well-known wine company founded in 1797 (probably best known in America for its Harvey's Bristol Cream sherry) set up the museum. Open daily. Admission charge. 12 Denmark St. (phone: 927-7661).

RED LODGE A 16th-century house preserved with its 18th-century alterations and furnishings of both periods, it includes superb carved paneling and stone fireplaces. Closed Sundays and Mondays. Admission charge. Park Row (phone: 921-1360).

SHOPPING

Bristol's many stores attract shoppers from all over the west of England and from South Wales. You'll find almost anything, though the emphasis is on the needs of the resident rather than the tourist. *Broadmead* is a large, modern shopping center around a pedestrian mall—with department stores, supermarkets, and the trendy *Galleries* complex. Smaller, more expensive shops are found along Park Street, Queens Road, and Whiteladies Road. For local color, browse through the vegetables, crockery, parakeets, and other things in the *St. Nicholas Market* (off Baldwin and Corn Sts.) any day except Sunday. An antiques and crafts market takes place in the nearby *Corn Exchange* (closed Sundays). For more antiques and small boutiques, visit *The Mall* and its environs in Clifton. The *Clifton Antiques Market* (26-28 *The Mall;* phone: 974-1627) is open Tuesdays through Saturdays. For standard shopping hours, see GETTING READY TO GO.

Be sure to take your passport when you shop, and always inquire about the Value Added Tax (VAT) refund application forms when your total purchases in a store are over £50 (about $75). The VAT is a surcharge payable at the sales counter, but foreign customers usually will be reimbursed for it at home (for more information see GETTING READY TO GO).

Bristol Blue Glass You can watch glassblowers in action produce all manner of glass objects in the famous shade of blue. Colston Yd., Colston St. (phone: 929-0863).

Bristol Craft Centre Jewelers, potters, weavers, leatherworkers, an embroiderer, and others market what they make on the same premises at 6 Leonard La., an exceedingly narrow passage from Corn to Small St., entered from the opening beside 31 Corn St. (phone: 929-7890).

Bristol Guild All manner of arts and crafts shops sell their wares here, from kitchenware and decorative furnishings to basketware and pottery. Also for sale are jams and pickles packaged with pretty gingham tops, plus exotic teas, coffees, and cookies. 66-72 Park St. (phone: 926-5548).

Central Stamp Gallery Although stamps are their business, this is also the place to find a sepia print or black and white postcard of Bristol in earlier times. Christmas Steps (phone: 927-7836).

G. Millhouse Attached to the butcher's shop, which has been here for years and years, is this Old World–type delicatessen. Everything from smoked mussels to haggis is made on the premises; the bite-size pork and apple pies are excellent. 14 *The Mall,* Clifton (phone: 973-4440).

George's Three very good bookshops are all on Park Street: No. 89 for general and art books, No. 81 for academic books, and No. 52 for secondhand books and rare editions (phone: 927-6602).

Global Village Unusual pottery, crafts, and wickerwork can be purchased here. Park St. (phone: 929-0963).

Guilberts Beneath the *Craft Centre,* this long-established shop sells delicious handmade chocolates. Try the Old England selection made according to pre–World War II recipes. 6 Leonard La. (phone: 926-8102).

Hamilton Caswell The window displays in this pretty little 18th-century building will immediately catch your eye. All kinds of stringed instruments, from violas to cellos, are attractively arranged to tempt you inside. 10 Perry Rd. (phone: 929-4642).

SPORTS

Five sports centers provide facilities for squash, badminton, bowls, and various team games. The largest of these is the *Whitchurch Sports Centre* (Bamfield, Whitchurch; phone: 983-3911), south of the city. *Whitchurch* is open daily and has four squash courts, an indoor bowling green, a fitness room, a sauna, and a bar. It is also the scene of spectator events such as basketball and hockey games and karate matches.

CRICKET The *Gloucestershire County Cricket Club* (phone: 924-6743) plays at the *County Ground* (Nevil Rd.), from the end of April through early September.

GREYHOUND RACING Call the *Bristol Stadium* (Stapleton Rd.; phone: 951-1919) for the latest racing schedule.

RUGBY The *Bristol Rugby Club* (phone: 951-4448) is based at the *Memorial Ground* (Filton Ave.); the *Clifton Rugby Club* (phone: 950-0445), at Cribb's Causeway.

SOCCER The *Bristol City Football Club* plays at *Ashton Gate* (phone: 963-2812); the *Bristol Rovers Football Club* plays at *Twerton Park* in Bath (phone: 1225-352508). Most games are on Saturdays at 3 PM.

SWIMMING Those in search of aquatic excitement should try the *Easton Leisure Centre* (Thrissel St., Easton; phone: 955-8840), with its massive water slide; open daily. Bristol has 10 indoor pools that are open daily.

THEATER

Bristol has made quite a name for itself in British theatrical history, and one of its venues is among the best in the country.

CENTER STAGE

Theatre Royal This is Britain's oldest working theater, and since it opened in 1766 many well-known actors have appeared here, ranging from 18th-century greats such as Sarah Siddons (whose ghost is sometimes thought to haunt the building) to present-day stars, including Peter O'Toole and Jeremy Irons. The resident company is the respected *Bristol Old Vic,* which also uses the *New Vic Studio* on the same site. The group presents both classic and new plays, but if you have a choice, see Shakespeare or perhaps a Restoration comedy, as these productions are especially suited to the splendor of the Georgian setting. In addition to contemporary and classic theater, there are also art exhibitions, jazz concerts, comedy, cabaret, and dance. The theater's *Siddons Buttery* serves homemade dishes (closed Sundays). Backstage tours led by expert guides depart Fridays and Saturdays at noon. King St. (phone: 925-0250).

In addition, the *Bristol Old Vic Theatre School* (phone: 973-3535) gives several performances yearly at the aforementioned theaters or at the *Wyckham Theatre* (formerly the *Vandyck;* on Park Row), home of the *University of Bristol*'s Drama Department. The *Bristol Hippodrome* (St. Augustine's Parade; phone: 929-9444) seats 2,000 and hosts touring companies such as the *Royal Shakespeare Company* and the *National Theatre Company.* It is also the stage for visiting ballet companies. The *Watershed,* Britain's first media and communications center (at 1 Cannon's Rd.; phone: 927-6444), and the *Arnolfini Arts Centre* (16 *Narrow Quay;* phone: 929-9191) are dockside warehouses that have been converted to contemporary arts centers, with cinemas, galleries, stage facilities, restaurants, and bars.

MUSIC

Colston Hall (Colston St.; phone: 922-3686) is Bristol's main venue for all types of musical performances, from classical to pop. *St. George's,* a refurbished neoclassical church (on Brandon Hill; phone: 923-0359) serves as an important classical music site with a full program of lunchtime concerts. Touring opera companies stage their productions at the *Bristol Hippodrome,* and concerts of 20th-century music are the specialty of the *Arnolfini Arts Centre* (see *Theater,* above, for both addresses), which showcases the contemporary in all the arts. Recitals are held in many of Bristol's churches. *University of Bristol* students put on concerts, often at lunchtime, in the *Wills Memorial Building* (Queens Rd.; phone: 238028).

NIGHTCLUBS AND NIGHTLIFE

There are several nightclubs, including *Lakota,* the best in town, featuring live music (6 Upper York St.; phone: 924-7147); *Odyssey* (15 Nelson St.; phone: 929-2658), another habitat for pop; and *Ritzy's,* an alternative entertainment and music venue (13-21 Baldwin St.; phone: 922-7177). Bristol has an enviable pub music scene: The *Bierkeller* (All Saints St.; phone: 926-8514) has live rock, as well as a lively disco; enthusiasts of traditional jazz frequent the *Old Duke* (the Welsh Back end of King St.; phone: 927-7137), *Fleece and Firkin* (St. Thomas St.; phone: 927-7150), and *Thelka in the Grove* (phone: 929-3301).

Best in Town

CHECKING IN

Bristol is not the prime tourist destination that prestigious Bath is, but as an important commercial center and the object of many an expense-account traveler, it's no less expensive than its neighbor. A wide range of accommodations is available, however, and if you book in advance, you should be able to find a room at the right price almost any time of the year. Look in Clifton for the broadest choice of reasonably priced small hotels and guesthouses. Few of Bristol's hotels are right in the center of town, and the ones that are tend to be expensive. Expect to pay $200 or more a night for a double room at the hotel listed as very expensive, between $140 and $180 at an expensive one, between $80 and $125 at a moderate one, and less than $80 at an inexpensive one. A hearty English breakfast is usually included, but many of the top hotels now offer room only; private baths, phones, and TV sets are featured in all hotel rooms unless otherwise stated. All telephone numbers are in the 117 city code unless otherwise indicated.

VERY EXPENSIVE

Thornbury Castle A 16th-century country house 12 miles out of town, it once played host to King Henry VIII and Anne Boleyn. Originally it was a restaurant that served bacon from its own pig farm and wine from its own vineyard. While the pigs have gone, the highly regarded wine remains, and the castle now offers 18 rooms above the restaurant (some with superb views of the countryside). Castle St., Thornbury (phone: 1454-418511; fax: 1454-416188).

EXPENSIVE

Berkeley Square Here is a charming Georgian house set on a tree-lined square that was seen in "The House of Elliot," a TV miniseries shown recently on the Arts and Entertainment cable network. Located next to the *City Museum and Art Gallery,* it is also conveniently close to the city center and Clifton. The 43 well-appointed, attractive guestrooms are named after famous Bristolians throughout history (such as Isambard Kingdom Brunel and John Cabot). Other amenities include a small French restaurant, a trendy bar in the basement, and conference rooms. 15 Berkeley Sq. (phone: 925-4000; fax: 925-2970).

St. Vincent Rocks This property is a smaller (46 rooms) and more expensive alternative to the *Avon Gorge* down the road. It, too, overlooks the river's chasm, and its front rooms enjoy an enviable view of the Clifton Suspension Bridge. There's also *Manton's* restaurant. Conference facilities for up to 50. Sion Hill, Clifton (phone: 973-9251; fax: 923-8139).

Swallow Royal Luxuriously restored, this fine Victorian hotel has 242 rooms, a leisure club with an indoor pool, and the superb *Palm Court* restaurant (see *Eating Out*). It is conveniently located near the *Bristol Cathedral.* Conference facilities. College Green (phone: 925-5100; fax: 925-1515).

MODERATE

Avon Gorge This solid-white block of Victoriana perches on the edge of Clifton, overlooking the Avon Gorge and the Clifton Suspension Bridge. It has 76 rooms. If you don't get one gorge-side, enjoy the view at tea on the terrace or from the *Rib Room* restaurant. Sion Hill, Clifton (phone: 973-8955; fax: 923-8125).

Brunel's Tunnel House For those with a car who plan to visit both Bristol and Bath, this hotel is ideally located halfway between the two cities in the picturesque village of Saltford. The beautiful Georgian house was once owned by the railway engineer Isambard Kingdom Brunel; it is now an antique-filled inn with seven rooms. Six miles from either Bristol or Bath. High St., Saltford (phone: 987-3873).

Courtlands Over 30 years of expert hotel management is the hallmark of the Richards family, who maintain this 24-room, red brick establishment. Although it is close to the center of town, the atmosphere is utterly peaceful and charming. The restaurant serves traditional English fare and vegetarian dishes. 1 Redland Court Rd. (phone: 942-4432; fax: 923-2432).

Glenroy Set on one of Clifton's attractive 19th-century squares, this small, comfortable place has 50 rooms and a restaurant. 30 Victoria Sq., Clifton (phone and fax: 973-9058).

EATING OUT

As one of the largest cities outside London, you'd expect Bristol to be well endowed with good restaurants, and it is. There are some excellent eating places in the hotels and some equally good ones outside, in central Bristol and Clifton, offering traditional English, Chinese, French, Indian, and Italian fare, among others. In addition, the city has three floating pub-restaurants, including the *Glass Boat* (see below). Local dishes include Severn salmon, cheddar-cooked ham, jugged hare, and pigeon pie. A dinner for two with wine will cost more than $110 at a restaurant listed as expensive, $80 to $105 at one listed as moderate, and less than $75 at one listed as inexpensive. All restaurants listed below serve lunch and dinner, unless otherwise noted. All telephone numbers are in the 117 city code unless otherwise indicated.

EXPENSIVE

Glass Boat Set in a converted coal barge moored on Floating Harbour in the heart of the city, this elegant restaurant offers English and French fare for lunch and dinner, as well as a choice of full or continental breakfast. Menu items include *mille-feuille* of braised leeks, braised partridge in truffle *jus,* and duck *confit.* Closed Sundays and for breakfast and lunch on Saturdays. Reservations advised for lunch and dinner. MasterCard and Visa accepted. Welsh Back, by Bristol Bridge near the tourist information center (phone: 929-0704).

Harveys The wine cellar of the famous vintners is no ordinary place: Chef/manager Raymond Farthing's wine list is reasonably priced, and his menu of classic English fare is bountiful, with such specialties as lightly poached eggs wrapped in salmon among the appetizers. One of the tastiest entrées is the roast filet of turbot served on a bed of fresh crabmeat and leeks. Closed Saturday lunch and Sundays. Reservations advised. Major credit cards accepted. 12 Denmark St. (phone: 927-7665).

Hunt's Chef Andy Hunt's place by *St. John's Gate* is intimate and small and offers French fare made with local ingredients. Early birds can order pastries and coffee from 8:30 AM. Closed Sundays and Mondays. Reservations necessary. Major credit cards accepted. 26 Broad St. (phone: 926-5580).

Lettonie Martin Blunos and his family prepare such tempting dishes as braised oxtail with tomatoes and chicken, and duck livers with shredded endives. Well worth seeking out, although you should call in advance for clear directions. Closed Sundays and Mondays. Reservations necessary. Major credit cards accepted. 9 Druid Hill, Stoke Bishop (phone: 968-6456).

Marwick's Set beneath the grand neoclassical façade of the old *Bristol Commercial Rooms* is this elegant eatery, complete with heavy, Venetian cut glass chandeliers. The menu includes imaginative dishes of fresh local fish, market vegetables, game, and rich desserts. Closed weekends. Reservations necessary. Major credit cards accepted. 43 Corn St. (phone: 926-2658).

Palm Court Although chef Michael Kitts specializes in French fare at his elegant, very formal restaurant, there are some English favorites (albeit given a continental touch), such as steak and kidney pie with truffles. Open daily. Reservations necessary. Major credit cards accepted. *Swallow Royal Hotel,* College Green (phone: 925-5100).

MODERATE

Colley's Supper Rooms Arrive punctually at 7:45 PM for a wonderful six-course supper. Excellent lunches are also served. There is no menu in the conventional sense, but plenty of variety. Judging by the fact that the place is always crowded, people are happy with the arrangement. Closed Sunday lunch. Reservations necessary; book at least eight weeks in advance for Friday or Saturday seatings. Major credit cards accepted. 153 Whiteladies Rd. (phone: 973-0646).

51 Park Street Owner Terry Timmons has created an eclectic, international menu for his busy bistro-style bar, accented by sticky puddings and organic ales. His young staff rush among elegant chairs and tables to serve a never-ending stream of students, Bristolians, and tourists. The paddle fans and soft music add to the atmosphere. Open daily. Reservations unnecessary. Major credit cards accepted. 51 Park St. (phone: 926-8016).

Jameson's At this lively, informal bistro in a Victorian house a daily fish dish is guaranteed, as well as specialties like lamb noisettes with blackberries and pink peppercorns. Closed Sundays. Reservations advised. Major credit cards accepted. 30 Upper Maudlin St. (phone: 927-6565).

Melbourne's It's a split-level, Australian-style eatery where diners can enjoy hearty meat meals, surrounded by Australian prints, at prices that can't be beat—perhaps because of the restaurant's bring-your-own-bottle policy. Closed Sundays. Reservations advised. Major credit cards accepted. 74 Park St. (phone: 922-6996).

Michael's Here you can feast on such delicacies as cream of Stilton soup, fresh salmon trout in a mushroom sauce, and passion-fruit sorbet. The ornate Victorian dining room, converted from an old garage, is filled with flowers, curios, and tables of assorted shapes and sizes; the bar with chaise longues, stuffed birds, and a fireplace. Closed Saturday lunch, Sundays, and Mondays. Reservations advised. Major credit cards accepted. 129 Hotwell Rd. (phone: 927-6190).

Vintner Despite the rather cavernous atmosphere, good wines and delicious hot food are served. Menu items include moussaka, chili con carne, and smoked salmon. Seating is available in the garden during summer. Closed Sundays. Reservations unnecessary. Major credit cards accepted. St. Stephen's St. (phone: 929-1222).

INEXPENSIVE

McCreadies Whole Food Small and friendly, this spot offers some interesting alternatives to standard health food, including nut roast, vegetable Stroganoff, stuffed peppers, and ratatouille. Open daily for breakfast and lunch only. No reservations. No credit cards accepted. 3 Christmas Steps (phone: 929-8387).

Trattoria da Renato Actors and actresses from the *Old Vic* across the street congregate here. The walls are covered with their photos, and the tables are attractively covered with pink napery topped by white lace. The fare is Italian, featuring well-prepared pasta and meat dishes. Closed Saturday lunch and Sundays. Reservations unnecessary. Major credit cards accepted. 19 King St. (phone: 929-8291).

Woodes A bustling coffee shop with a style all its own, it has two big wooden staircases, unique old furniture, and a slightly bohemian atmosphere. It's a good place for breakfast. Closed Sundays. No reservations. No credit cards accepted. Baldwin St. (phone: 922-7177).

SHARING A PINT

Bristol offers many great pubs, but we have a particular favorite.

PERFECT PINTS

Coronation Tap On Friday and Saturday nights, this tiny tavern at the end of a cul-de-sac in the Clifton district bursts at the seams with local students trying to down more than one pint of the pub's famous thick scrumpy, dredged from the bottom of the 22-gallon cider barrels. In addition to cider, there are English beers and ales, wine, and spirits. Food ranges from light sandwiches to a full-blown Sunday lunch. Between Sion Pl. and Portland St. (phone: 973-9617).

The *Full Moon* (1 North St.; phone: 924-5170) purportedly is Bristol's oldest pub—something by that name was marked as "a very ancient hostellerie" on a map of the city in the 13th century. During the summer, sit outside at the tables in the old stableyard. A popular pub left over from the 17th century is *Ye Shakespeare* (78 Victoria St.; phone: 927-6727). Another good pub is the *Bristol Bridge Inn* (St. Nicholas St.; phone: 929-8467), which plays live music at night (it gets quite noisy at times). In the *Brewery Tap* (6-10 Colston St.; phone: 929-7350), visitors can imbibe the products of the next-door Smiles Brewery or order an English breakfast. Or stop in at the *Highbury Vaults* (164 St. Michael's Hill; phone: 973-3203), which is decorated in dark woods and serves delicious food in cozy little alcoves called "snugs." In Clifton, try the tiny but pretty *Portcullis* (Wellington Ter.; phone: 973-2653), a friendly local spot with a seafood bistro; and *The Royal Oak* (50 *The Mall;* phone: 973-8846), the place to go for traditional brews and atmosphere—stone walls, oak beams, and seating at high-backed oak settees. While you're at it, drink a toast of Bristol milk (sherry), so called according to a 17th-century clergyman, author, and wit, because it was the "first moisture" tasted by infants in this wine-importing city.

Cambridge

Cambridge's bold claim to being the most beautiful city in Britain is based on the majestic architecture of the university's many colleges. The distinction is not often disputed (except by its rival, Oxford). Each year, millions of visitors flock to this small city to marvel at its masterpieces of cut stone, stained glass, and carved wood, and to breathe its rarefied and scholarly atmosphere. They also come to Cambridge for an experience Oxford cannot match: a quiet punt ride up the "Backs" on the river Cam, which slides lazily past the colleges' back lawns (hence the name), and is edged by lush green banks and drooping willows.

This city of great tranquillity and beauty has deep historical roots. Cambridge was established in AD 43 as a Roman camp on a hill overlooking a natural ford in the river Cam at its upper navigable limit. The camp blossomed into a trading town, as the Romans built roads connecting Colchester, the garrison town to the southeast, with Lincoln, a settlement in the north. In the 5th century, the area was overrun and conquered by the Saxons. *St. Bene't's* (a contraction for *St. Benedict's*) *Church* dates from this period; its Saxon tower stands today. In the 11th century, the Normans, too, invaded Cambridge, and built a castle to defend the town.

Details about early scholarly stirrings in Cambridge are vague. There was a monastery in the nearby town of Ely, and the monks may have set up a center of learning when students retreating from a hostile townsfolk streamed here from Oxford in 1209. Whatever the case, by the mid-13th century the university was firmly established, and by 1284 the first college was founded, then called *St. Peter's,* later *Peterhouse.* During the 14th and 15th centuries, 11 more colleges were founded.

Today, education is Cambridge's main industry (there are 31 colleges and about 12,000 students), and the university, like *Oxford,* retains its original medieval organization. Each of the colleges is a self-governing entity within a decentralized university system. Each drafts its own rules and holds title to its own property. While the university provides lectures, conducts examinations, and awards degrees, the individual colleges control admissions and determine the subjects an undergraduate should "read."

Strictly speaking, the term "university" refers not to its imposing granite structures but rather to the community of people involved—the chancellor, masters, and fellows and scholars, to be exact. Ever since the Middle Ages the colleges have provided for their members' every need. Each self-sufficient enclave includes a dining room, with an imposing high table where the master and fellows dine apart from (and a bit above) the undergraduates; a chapel; a library; common rooms; and private rooms where students live. More important, many colleges have remained unchanged over the centuries. *Cambridge* has spawned some of the most influential figures in politics, the arts, and the sciences—people like Cromwell, Pepys, Newton, Darwin, Wordsworth, and Byron.

Cambridge, like any institution that reaches so far into the past, is plagued as well as enriched by traditions out of step with the modern world. The university always has disciplined students rather rigorously. For example, until fairly recently, college gates were locked at 11 PM. As each college is surrounded by high walls often crowned with a row of spikes, latecomers would find it hard to get in. This hardly deterred spirited carousers, however, and the famous night climbs of *Cambridge* have spawned many a British mountaineer.

As a result of this and other episodes, the emphasis at *Cambridge* upon dignity and discipline has become legendary. Consider the oft-told tale of the student who tried to turn the ancient rules to his own advantage. In studying the university statutes he discovered that he had the right, while sitting for an examination, to demand a tankard of ale from the proctor. His request was grudgingly granted . . . but not without a price. It seems that the 14th-century statute also made it compulsory to wear a sword after dark. The next evening the student was found and fittingly—if somewhat uncomfortably—attired.

Cambridge At-a-Glance

SEEING THE CITY

For a fine view of the city, climb to the top of *Great St. Mary's* in King's Parade. The tower is open daily; admission charge. For an alternative perspective, stroll up Castle Mound, once the site of Cambridge's castle, whose stonework was gradually removed over the years and used in the construction of the colleges.

SPECIAL PLACES

Every tour of *Cambridge* should begin at its heart—the colleges, all of which are open in part to the public. A word of warning, however: The colleges are not museums but private places where people live and work, and *Cambridge*'s three million yearly visitors create an enormous problem, especially in spring and summer when students are preparing for exams. The situation would not be unlike finding your own backyard on the itinerary of every tour of England. What's more, the colleges have only recently begun receiving any income from tourists (several now charge admission—partly to discourage visitors—and others are considering following suit). When admission is charged, however, the fee is usually nominal, so visiting college courts should still be considered a great privilege and quiet behavior common courtesy.

In general, visitors are allowed to walk around the courts (but not on the grass, which remains the privilege of fellows only); visit the chapels and some gardens; and occasionally go into other designated areas, such as libraries or dining halls. Members of the college live off a "staircase," as the names at the bottom will indicate, but unless you are visiting a friend or relative in residence, you won't be allowed into these private quarters. The colleges also are sometimes closed to visitors—for example, from mid-April to the end of June, when examinations are being taken. Notices to this effect are posted at the gate; if in doubt, check with the porter in the college lodge.

The selection of colleges below, arranged in walking tour order, is by no means exhaustive, but it does include those most interesting architecturally and most centrally located. If you have time to visit only a few, *King's* and *Trinity* should be at the top of the list. Nearby *Queens'* and *St. John's* (and perhaps the entire area between them) would be both worthwhile and easy to reach, and you'd still have time to explore the Backs. Some of the colleges not mentioned below are *Peterhouse* (founded in 1284), *Gonville and Caius,* pronounced *Keys* (1348), *St. Catherine's* (1473), *Sidney Sussex* (1594), and *Downing* (1800). Then there are the three colleges founded for women, namely *Girton* (1869; out of town), *Newnham* (1871), and *New Hall* (1954). Last, the three newest colleges are *Churchill* (1960; out of town, and inspired by Sir Winston's wish to encourage scientific and technological studies), *Fitzwilliam* (1966; affectionately called "Fitzbilly"), and *Robinson* (1981). For information about university and collegiate procedures, plus events and museums, call the general number (phone: 337733).

THE COLLEGES

CORPUS CHRISTI COLLEGE (1352) Because the *Old Court* has changed little since it was built in the 14th century, it provides a glimpse at medieval college organization. Then four students shared a room but each had his own study cubicle. In the 16th century, one of the cubicles would have been used by playwright Christopher Marlowe when he was a student here. The library, containing a priceless collection of Anglo-Saxon manuscripts (nearly 40 of them, saved from the libraries of monasteries dissolved by Henry VIII and including an important copy of the *Anglo-Saxon Chronicle*), is open by appointment only; contact the college. The chapel is open daily. Be warned: The college is said to have a resident ghost. Trumpington St.

PEMBROKE COLLEGE (1347) The college was founded by Marie de Valence, Countess of Pembroke, and some of the buildings of her time survive. The chapel (built between 1663 and 1666) was Sir Christopher Wren's first building, designed while he was a professor at *Oxford.* The college also is known for its gardens. Trumpington St.

QUEENS' COLLEGE (1448) Founded by Margaret of Anjou and Elizabeth Woodville, the respective queens of Henry VI and Edward IV, *Queens'* has a lovely red brick *First Court* built in the 15th century and decorated with a sundial in the 17th century. But its pièce de résistance is the *New Court.* The cloister around it, also 15th century, supports a wonderful example of 16th-century domestic architecture called the *President's Lodge* (*Queens'* does not have a master), an evocative building of timber and plaster that is put to good use in *May Week* as a backdrop for the college's productions of Shakespeare. Also of interest is the Mathematical Bridge, a copy of an original (1749) said to have been built without nails, nuts, or bolts and held together by geometrical principles alone. According to local lore, some curious Victorians took it apart, only to find they couldn't put it back together without fastenings. Sir Basil Spence's *Erasmus Building* (1959) was one of the first modern contributions to college architecture. (Erasmus, the Renaissance theologian, lived at *Queens'* from 1511 through 1514.) The college is open to visitors afternoons only; closed from mid-May to the end of June. Admission charge from mid-March through October. Queens' La.

KING'S COLLEGE (1441) Of the grand design that Henry VI had for the college he founded, only the chapel was ever realized. It was not until 1724, when the *Fellows' Building* was added, that an actual court began to take shape. But the magnificent Gothic chapel, begun in 1446 and completed 90 years later, largely as the founder planned it, is not only *Cambridge*'s best-known building, it is also often acclaimed the finest building in England—and all this majesty had been meant initially for the private worship of only 70 scholars. Edward IV and Richard III financed further work, but it was Henry VII who began the final stage and left money for its completion, which explains the rose of his Tudor father and the portcullis of his Beaufort mother, symbols carved everywhere as decoration. The chapel has the largest fan-vaulted ceiling in existence; original 16th-century stained glass, the gift of Henry VIII, in all but one (and part of another) of its windows; and an intricately carved wood organ screen bearing the initials of Henry VIII and Anne Boleyn, another gift. Behind the altar is Rubens's *Adoration of the Magi.* The chapel is open daily, but be prepared for unpredictable closings because of choir practice or recording sessions. A permanent exhibition, "The Building of a Chapel," is situated on the northern side, with entry from inside the building. (Hours vary; admission charge.) The *King's College Chapel Choir* is very well known, so if you get a chance, go and listen. Notices of concerts usually are posted on the doorway. Evensong is held (during university terms only) Tuesdays through Fridays at 5:30 PM and Sundays at 3:30 PM. Guided tours of the entire college are available; ask at the porter's lodge. Admission charge. King's Parade.

CLARE COLLEGE (1338) Though one of the oldest colleges, its original buildings were destroyed by fire, and the present ones date only from the 17th century. They rank among the university's most handsome, however, and Clare's bridge is the oldest (1640) and one of the prettiest on the Cam. The college also is known for the elegance of its 18th-century wrought-iron gates and for the delightful *Fellows' Garden* on the other side of the river. The garden is open weekdays from 2 to 4 PM. Trinity La.

TRINITY HALL (1350) Originally all the colleges were called halls, and the people who lived in them were the college. Gradually the latter word became more inclusive in meaning, and by the 19th century, most of the halls had changed their names. Because a *Trinity College* already existed (see below), *Trinity Hall,* traditionally the college for lawyers, is the only one to keep its old name. Its *Front Court* dates from the 14th century but was refaced in the 18th century. You'll get a better idea of *Trinity Hall*'s early days by seeing the 16th-century Tudor brick library. Trinity La.

TRINITY COLLEGE (1546) Founded by Henry VIII, *Trinity* is the largest college in *Cambridge* and home to more than 800 students. The school has a distinguished roster of alumni: Francis Bacon, John Dryden, Isaac Newton, Thomas Macaulay, Alfred Lord Tennyson, Bertrand Russell, six British prime ministers, over 20 Nobel Prize winners, and Prince Charles, not to mention Lord Byron, who eventually was "sent down" (expelled) for rooming with a pet bear and bathing naked in the fountain at the center of the *Great Court* that is the source of the college's water supply. The *Great Court,* the largest court or quad in either *Cambridge* or *Oxford,* is the creation of Thomas Nevile, master of the college in the late 16th and early 17th centuries. He also began *Nevile's Court;* the long cloister on the north side is where Newton worked out his theory of sound. *Nevile's Court* became complete only at the end of the 17th century with the addition of Christopher Wren's library—and the sight of the sun on the *Wren Library*'s many windows is still one of the most memorable in *Cambridge.* The library is open to the public on weekdays from noon to 2 PM and on Saturdays during term from 10:30 AM to 12:30 PM. (It's lavish with carved wood inside, and some of its treasured manuscripts are usually on display.) Nevile's dining hall (again, *Cambridge*'s largest) is between the two courts. Trinity St.

ST. JOHN'S COLLEGE (1511) An enormous, rather austere place, this is the second-largest of *Cambridge*'s colleges, with buildings spanning the centuries. The gatehouse, ornate with the arms of the founder, Lady Margaret Beaufort (mother of Henry VII), is in its original state, the *Second* and *Third Courts* date from the late 16th and early 17th centuries respectively, but across the river Cam are the 19th-century neo-Gothic *New Court* and the ultramodern *Cripps Building.* The two parts of the college are connected by the covered Bridge of Sighs (1831). William Wordsworth was a *St. John's* student. Admission charge during *Easter* and summer vacations. St. John's St.

MAGDALENE COLLEGE (1542) Built in the 15th century to house Benedictine monks studying at *Cambridge, Magdalene* (pronounced *Mawd*-lin) was founded as a college in the 16th century, and its *First Court* has buildings of both centuries. It is a favorite of the British aristocracy, but its most famous student was Samuel Pepys, who left his library to his old school, including the manuscript of his famous diary. The library—arranged in presses Pepys provided—is open Mondays through Saturdays from 11:30 AM to 12:30 PM and from 2:30 to 3:30 PM. Magdalene St.

JESUS COLLEGE (1496) Founded on the site of a convent that dates from the 12th century, *Jesus,* too, has parts that are older than it is, including the chapel—though the pre-Raphaelite stained glass (by Edward Burne-Jones and Ford Madox Brown) and ceilings (by William Morris) came about during a 19th-century restoration. The college is approached via a long brick-walled avenue known as the "chimney," but once past the 15th-century gate tower, the grounds are spacious, with gardens and a delightful Tudor cloister court. Journalist Alistair Cooke (best known in America for hosting PBS's "Masterpiece Theatre") was a *Jesus* undergraduate, as was Samuel Taylor Coleridge. Jesus La.

CHRIST'S COLLEGE (1505) The first of the two colleges Lady Margaret Beaufort founded at *Cambridge* (the other was *St. John's*—see above), and her coat of arms above the gate makes a highly ornamental entranceway. John Milton was a student at *Christ's,* as was Charles Darwin. The beautiful *Fellows' Garden* (open weekdays from 10:30 AM to noon and from 2 to 4 PM) contains a mulberry tree, traditionally associated with Milton. St. Andrew's St.

EMMANUEL COLLEGE (1584) Sir Walter Mildmay, Queen Elizabeth I's chancellor of the exchequer, founded this college on the site of a 13th-century Dominican friary. The monastic buildings were converted to college use (the friary church became the dining hall), then other buildings followed, including the chapel and its colonnade (built between 1668 and 1673), designed by Sir Christopher Wren. *Emmanuel* was meant to educate clergymen and it became a center of Protestant theology, but because of their Puritan sympathies, many of its graduates went to America in the early 17th century. Among them was John Harvard, who died at the age of 31, leaving $1,600 and 320 books for the foundation of *Harvard University.* St. Andrew's St.

OTHER CAMBRIDGE SIGHTS

FITZWILLIAM MUSEUM One of the nation's greatest and oldest public museums, it was founded in 1816, when Richard, the seventh Viscount Fitzwilliam of Merrion, left his superb collections, his library, and a good endowment to his alma mater. The collections—not to mention the museum's stature—have been growing ever since. It also is especially charming and a good deal less chilly and solemn than its peers—the galleries are attractively decorated with Oriental rugs, sculpture, period furniture, and even flowers. Visitors can pick up the museum's brochure to lead them through the extensive collections of European applied arts, Islamic and Far Eastern treasures, manuscripts, paintings and drawings, portrait miniatures, prints, European and Oriental fans, and West Asiatic, Egyptian, Greek, and Roman antiquities. Of particular note are the lovely Roman mosaic fountain niche from 1st-century Baiae, the illuminated 13th-century *Peterborough Psalter,* Frans Hals's *Portrait of a Man,* Delacroix's *Odalisque,* Renoir's *Coup de Vent* and *La Plaçe Clichy,* Stubbs's *Gimcrack,* and masterpieces by the greatest Venetian painters of the 16th century—Palma Vecchio, Titian, Tintoretto, Veronese, and Jacopo Bassano. The music collection, which includes autographed scores of Handel, Bach, Chopin, Britten, and Elgar, is one of Britain's finest, and the collection of works by Blake and the members of his circle is the finest anywhere. Closed Mondays (call for special gallery hours on national holidays). No admission charge. Trumpington St. (phone: 332900).

SENATE HOUSE This classical Georgian building of the 1720s was designed by the English architect James Gibbs, and it, too, belongs to the university. When illuminated at night, its Corinthian details make it resemble an edible confection, and each June it becomes the setting for the "Ceremony of General Admission to Degrees"—graduation, that is. King's Parade.

ROUND CHURCH Built in the same distinctive shape as the *Holy Sepulcher Church* in Jerusalem, the Norman *Round Church* dates from about 1130. It is one of only five Round churches still surviving in England. Bridge St.

FOLK MUSEUM Crafts, tools, kitchen and farm equipment, toys, and furniture are among the objects in a series of rooms meant to illustrate life in Cambridge and the surrounding countryside in the last few centuries. The building itself was formerly a pub (*The White Horse Inn*) and in the courtyard is an 18th-century shopfront, one of several large relics of Cambridge's past. Closed Mondays October through March. Admission charge. Corner of Castle and Northampton Sts. (phone: 355159).

BOTANIC GARDENS These are the university's research gardens. You'll find the hothouses very inviting on cold, windy days, or stop in at the café for a pot of tea. Open daily. Admission charge. Entrances on Bateman St., Trumpington Rd., Brooklands Ave., and Hills Rd. (phone: 336265).

AMERICAN MILITARY CEMETERY More than 3,800 American servicemen who fought in World War II from British bases are buried in these beautifully landscaped grounds. The names of another 5,125 who lie in unknown graves are inscribed on the *Memorial Wall.* On the Madingley Rd., 4 miles outside the city (phone: 954-210350).

EXTRA SPECIAL

One of the most stylish ways to enjoy Cambridge is to hire a punt—a long, flat-bottom, square-nosed boat that is both steered and propelled by pushing a long pole into the muddy river bottom. Either explore the Backs or go on a lengthier excursion up the river to Grantchester for tea. *Scudamore's Boatyards* (phone: 359750) offers punts for self-drive hire at two locations: one at Quayside, off Bridge Street (well positioned for touring the

Backs), and another at Mill Lane, near Silver Street (go to the latter if you're aiming for Grantchester). The *Cambridge Punting Company* (phone: 357565) rents punts with or without a poler and offers a guided river ferry tour combined with a walk (picnic hampers are available with 24 hours' notice); tours leave from Mill Lane, near Silver Street. Farther downriver, punts also are available from *Tyrells Marine* (at *Jesus Lock* on *Jesus Green;* phone: 223-352847). A helpful hint: Don't forget to stand at the back of the boat—especially if you recently have been to Oxford, where they stand at the front.

Sources and Resources

TOURIST INFORMATION

The tourist information center (on Wheeler St.; phone: 322640), which is closed Sundays November through *Easter,* offers guided walking tours to the major colleges and through the intricate maze of small streets and alleyways around them. Tours last approximately two hours and depart from the tourist center; make reservations at least a half hour in advance. Evening walking tours of historic *Cambridge,* starting from the tourist center, are conducted daily except Tuesdays and Fridays during July and August. A drama tour, during which scenes from *Cambridge*'s past are acted out by people in period costumes, departs from the center on Tuesdays and Fridays; you can check tour schedules and prices by calling the number above. Open-topped bus tours of the city and out to the *American Military Cemetery* are run by *Guide Friday Ltd.* (phone: 62444) on a step-on/step-off basis. Running every 15 minutes daily, starting from the railway station and the center, the buses stop every few hundred yards. For events information, check with the tourist office.

The center sells a comprehensive selection of guides to Cambridge, including accommodation and eating out guides and maps. Available at a nominal charge are pamphlets on the area's events, campsites, bike rentals, car rentals, bookshops, antiques shops, and sports facilities.

Most of Cambridge's bookstores (see *Shopping*) carry a broad range of guidebooks including many "picture books" filled with lush photographs. *Look at Cambridge* and *Historic Cambridge* by John Brooks, *Cambridge* by Kenneth Holmes, and *Royal Cambridge* by Marion Colthorpe, which describes the many royal visits to the city since Queen Elizabeth I, are excellent sources of information; though they are out of print, you may be able to find them at one of Cambridge's many secondhand bookshops.

LOCAL COVERAGE The *Cambridge Evening News* is published Mondays through Saturdays.

TELEPHONE The city code for Cambridge is 1223.

GETTING AROUND

Most places of interest in town are within walking distance of each other, so you're unlikely to need other forms of transportation except for the trip into town from the train or bus station and visits to places outside the city.

AIRPORT *Cambridge Airport* (phone: 61133), 2 miles east of the city center on A1303, handles domestic flights.

BICYCLING It's a common mode of transportation around Cambridge; you can rent a bike from *University Cycles* (9 Victoria Ave.; phone: 355517); *Geoff's Bike Hire* (65 Devonshire Rd.; phone: 65629); or *H. Drake* (56-60 Hills Rd.; phone: 63486).

BOAT The *Cambridge Punting Company* offers guided ferry tours (see *Extra Special,* above). A sightseeing alternative for enjoying Cambridge and the surrounding countryside during the summer is a three-day or a week-long cruise aboard the *Westover Boat Company*'s converted narrowboats (phone: 860-516343).

BUS For inexpensive links to other towns in East Anglia and London, try the *National Express* coach (phone: 460711) and local *Cambus* (phone: 423554). Both operate out of the *Drummer Street* bus station. The information office is closed Sundays (phone: 423554).

CAR RENTAL Try *Willhire* (Barnwell Rd.; phone: 414600 or 416634) or *Avis* (245 Mill Rd.; phone: 212551).

TAXI Two of the biggest taxi companies are *Camtax* (26 Victoria Rd.; phone: 313131) and *United* (123A Hills Rd.; phone: 352222).

TRAIN Cambridge and London are linked by frequent trains from *Liverpool Street Station* (travel time: about one and a half hours) and *King's Cross Station* (travel time: one to one and a half hours). The *Cambridge* railway station is at the far end of Station Road, a long walk from the center of town, so take the bus that waits in the front of the station or a taxi. For information, call 311999; for a recorded announcement of the London rail timetable, call 359602.

SPECIAL EVENTS

Although many festive events are held here throughout the year, one summer festival stands out.

A FAVORITE FETE

Cambridge Folk Festival Not limiting itself to traditional English folk music, it attracts performers from far afield who show off contemporary rock as well as many other musical styles. Held the last weekend in July. For details, contact the *Cambridge Festival of the Arts, Corn Exchange Box Office,* Wheeler St. (phone: 357851).

Most university events take place during the university terms—there are three a year—and more toward the end of the term than the beginning. The most celebrated is *May Week,* which actually takes place in June and is closer to a fortnight than a week. It is the busiest time on the social calendar, enhanced by a general feeling of relief at the end of the working year. Many college and university societies put on displays of their activities, the most delightful of which are the plays and concerts held on the college lawns (which the public may attend). Each year several colleges hold elaborate balls—the *May Balls*—at which members and their guests party from dusk till dawn, enjoy champagne buffets, and, if still going strong, punt up to Grantchester for breakfast. Outsiders sometimes can get tickets, too; ask at the porter's lodge of each college.

Student rowing races on the Cam are held during *May Week* as well (rowing is a major university spectator sport). Since the Cam is too narrow for two boats to row side by side, the competitors (sometimes as many as 15) race in a line. The object is to catch up with the boat in front of you and overlap the stern—hence the name of the race, "Bumps." The best place to watch is from the towpath at Fen Ditton.

Late in June, the *Midsummer Fair* takes place on *Midsummer Common*—as it has since the Middle Ages. Also in June is the *Footlights Revue,* a series of comedies most famous as the onetime showcase and launching pad for Graham Chapman, John Cleese, and Eric Idle of *Monty Python.* This year, the performances are being held at various locations around town while its normal venue, the *Arts Theatre,* is being refurbished; for an update, consult the tourist office (see *Tourist Information,* above). On two days at the end of June graduates congregate at the *Senate House* for their ceremonial awards. In July, city "Bumps" (similar to the university races) take place on a course between Baitsbite Lock and Stourbridge Common. The most important winter event is the *King's College Festival of Nine Lessons and Carols* on *Christmas Eve,* which is broadcast live worldwide. Advance tickets are unavailable; lining up early in the morning for the 3 PM service is the price music lovers must be prepared to pay. Details and tickets for most *Cambridge* cultural events are available from the *Corn Exchange Box Office* (see above).

MUSEUMS

In addition to those described in *Special Places,* the Cambridge area has several other fine museums, including the following:

KETTLES YARD ART GALLERY Here is a permanent collection of modern art, including works by Henri Gaudier-Brzeska, Ben Nicolson, and Christopher Wood. Changing exhibits of contemporary arts and crafts are housed in a separate building. Closed Mondays. No admission charge. Northampton St. (phone: 352124).

NATIONAL HORSERACING MUSEUM Five galleries house a collection of art, trophies, and horsy objects, many of which have been owned by famous riders. The galleries, the Jockey Club rooms, the stud, and the training yard are featured by *Equine Tours of Newmarket* and can be booked through the museum. Closed Sundays mid-December through mid-April (also Mondays September through June). Admission charge. 99 High St., Newmarket, 12 miles northeast of Cambridge (phone: 638-667333).

SHOPPING

The marketplace in Market Square, on Market Hill (closed Sundays), has been a shopping area since medieval times. At the stalls, sheltered by bright canopies, most vendors sell fruits, vegetables, and plants, but some sell items of particular interest to visitors, including inexpensive clothing, crafts, records, and secondhand books.

Bookstores abound in Cambridge, stocking much more than just academic tomes. *Heffers of Cambridge* has a main store (20 Trinity St.; phone: 358351) and five other branches, including a children's bookshop (30 Trinity St.; phone: 356200), a stationery store (19 Sydney St.; phone: 358241), and a paperback and video shop (31 St. Andrew's St.; phone: 354778). *Dillons* (27 Sydney St.; phone: 351688) is a nationally known, well-regarded general bookstore; *Deighton, Bell & Co.* (13 Trinity St.; phone: 353939), owned by *Heffers,* offers rare and fine volumes; *Quinto* (34 Trinity St.; phone: 358279) specializes in old leatherbound books and ancient prints; and *G. David,* a Cambridge institution for secondhand books, has two shops (Nos. 3 and 16 St. Edwards Passage; phone for both: 354619). Nearby, the tiny *Haunted Bookshop* (St. Edwards Passage; phone: 68169) offers antiquarian and children's books.

The city has five main shopping areas. The first starts at St. John's Street and continues down Trinity Street, along King's Parade (with colleges on one side and old shop buildings, some dating from the 16th century, on the other), and into Trumpington Street. A second begins at Magdalene Bridge and runs down Bridge Street, Sidney Street, St. Andrew's Street, and Regent Street. Chic, expensive shops line the renovated Rose Crescent, a wide alleyway leading from Market Square to Trinity Street. The Lion Yard pedestrian precinct (between Market Sq. and St. Andrew's St.) has mostly chain stores, including *Mothercare* (No. 43; phone: 62001), *W. H. Smith's* (No. 26; phone: 311313), and *The Body Shop* (No. 22-23; phone: 460518), and is served by its own multilevel parking lot. The fifth shopping area is the modern *Grafton Centre,* 10 minutes from downtown, with department stores, small, less upscale boutiques, and a handful of cafés and restaurants. To get there, walk from St. Andrew's Street through Bradwell's Court and across Christ's Piece. Quayside, on the town side of Magdalene Bridge, is gaining in popularity as modern riverfront shops and cafés steadily appear. For standard shopping hours, see GETTING READY TO GO.

Be sure to take your passport when you shop, and always inquire about the Value Added Tax (VAT) refund application forms when your total purchases in a store are over £50 (about $75). The VAT is a surcharge payable at the sales counter, but foreign customers usually will be reimbursed for it at home (for more information see GETTING READY TO GO).

Blarney Woollen Mills Those not inclined to browse through the gorgeous woolens, Fair Isle sweaters, tweeds, and linen skirts and jackets that fill this wooden-floored emporium can relax over a newspaper on the sofa in front of the roaring fire. 13 Trinity St. (phone: 314504).

Brooke's of Cambridge Formerly *Truffles of Cambridge,* this spot is so small that two customers make a crowd, but it's worth the wait; the superb chocolates from around the world are beautifully packaged. 20 Kings Parade (phone: 353970).

Cambridge Music Shop All manner of musical instruments, books, and scores can be found here. All Saints' Passage (phone: 351786).

Culpepper the Herbalists Here is the headquarters of the chain famous for its herbal cosmetics, soaps, teas, honeys, and fresh herb jellies. Gift wrapping is free. 25 Lion Yard (phone: 67370).

English Teddy Bear Company Every size and color you could possibly want of these handmade, essential bedtime companions line the walls and floors and tumble out of baskets. 1 King's Parade (phone: 300908).

Fitzbillies A part of Cambridge since 1924, this bakery sells cakes, pastries, bread, handmade chocolates, mouth-watering fudge, and souvenirs—T-shirts, sweatshirts, aprons, and tea towels. Many of the special recipe cakes can be ordered, and requests are taken for summer picnic hampers. A tiny tearoom upstairs serves the famous sticky buns, and offers some lighter alternatives for breakfast and lunch. 52 Trumpington St. (phone: 352500).

Heffers Sounds This branch of *Heffers* (next to the main bookstore) is lined with classical and popular music cassettes and compact discs, as well as choral college music. 19 Trinity St. (phone: 358351).

Perfect Setting Upstairs, Crabtree & Evelyn toiletries contend for space with potpourri, patchwork pillows, candles, table linen, lace and embroidery bedroom accessories, plus dried flowers and vases; downstairs is a thriving tearoom. All Saints' Passage (phone: 63207).

Primavera A veritable cornucopia of one-of-a-kind, expensive pottery, glass, cards, ceramics, jewelry, ironwork, and other folk art. There are constantly changing exhibitions in the basement. 10 King's Parade (phone: 357708).

Scots Corner Shelves and tables piled high with kilts, tartans, tweeds, and fine Scottish knitwear. 11 Bridge St. (phone: 61534).

Workshop Unique jewelry designs, mostly in gold and silver, are made (to order if required) in the studio adjoining the workshop. High-quality bags and briefcases also are available. 31 Magdalene St. (phone: 354326).

SPORTS

Both the university and town hold regular sporting events throughout the year. During the winter months, soccer and rugby are the most popular, and in the summer, cricket. The college playing fields are dotted around the town; you'll find many of these indicated on the tourist office map. Schedules of events are posted on the notice boards in the porters' lodges of the individual colleges and in the windows of *Ryder and Amies* at 22 King's Parade.

FISHING In the Cam, naturally. A national rod fishing license, which can be used for all National Rivers Authority regions, can be obtained at *CAST* (143 Milton Rd.; phone: 61989).

GOLF Two private clubs that allow visitors to play on their 18-hole golf courses (for a fee) are *Gog Magog Golf Club* (Babraham Rd.; phone: 247626) and *Cambridgeshire Moat House Golf Club* (phone: 1954-780098) at Bar Hill, 5½ miles northwest of the city.

TENNIS Outdoor grass and hard courts are available for public use at *Jesus Green;* hard courts are available at *Lammas Land,* off Fen Causeway.

WALKING Choose from among the area's several enjoyable walking trails—along the Cam towpaths; across the meadows to Grantchester, so beloved by the poet Rupert Brooke; down the *Coe Fen Nature Trail,* which starts at the bridge near the unpaved car park off Barton Road. Other trails are recommended in the county council's free booklet *Enjoy the Cambridgeshire Countryside,* available at the tourist office (see *Tourist Information,* above), which also offers leaflets on a variety of walks in Cambridgeshire for a nominal charge.

THEATER

The *Arts Theatre* (at Peas Hill; phone: 352000) is currently closed for refurbishment, but it is scheduled to reopen late this fall or early next year; call ahead to check on its status. It presents modern and classic plays, ballet, opera, light opera, and other musical productions by local and touring companies. The university's *Amateur Dramatic Club* (*ADC*) *Theatre* (Park St.; phone: 352001) has an excellent reputation and puts on a broad selection of plays during the university term. *The Junction* (Clifton Rd.; phone: 412600 or 352001) is the city's newest venue for the performing arts, especially for productions of fringe theater.

MUSIC

There are many concerts and recitals at *Cambridge* throughout the year, including large choral works by the *Cambridge University Music Society* and the *King's College Chapel Choir,* organ recitals in *Great St. Mary's* and the *King's College Chapel* (both in King's Parade), and many other solo appearances. Details and times are posted on notice boards in the college porters' lodges as well as in several restaurants, cafés, bookstores, and the various faculty buildings. The *Cambridge University Music School* publishes a concert calendar three times a year.

NIGHTCLUBS AND NIGHTLIFE

Despite the city's youthful population, there isn't much taking place in the wee hours, mainly because the undergraduates have to be back in their dorms. The few discos in town include *Fifth Avenue* (in *Heidelberg Gardens,* Lion Yard; phone: 64222), where Thursday night is for the "oldies"—those over 25—and Wednesday is "Ladies' Night"; and *Route 66* (Wheeler St.; phone: 357503), opposite the tourist information center. Both places serve reasonably priced meals and cocktails. Note that no jeans, T-shirts, or sneakers are allowed, and men must wear jackets and ties.

Best in Town

CHECKING IN

Cambridge offers several moderate and expensive hotels, as well as a wide selection of moderate to inexpensive bed and breakfast establishments. During the summer and particularly toward the close of the school year (about mid-May to mid-June), when the influx of tourists is further bolstered by parents and other relatives visiting students, it is difficult to get a room. Reserve at least two months in advance for *May Week.* Although the tourist office (see *Tourist Information,* above) provides a booking service for visitors who arrive without a room reservation, don't expect miracles, especially on short notice. In Cambridge and environs you'll pay $160 or more per night for a double room (with breakfast, private bath, phone, and TV set included, unless otherwise noted) at an expensive hotel; between $80 and $150 at a moderate one; and less than $75 at an inexpensive one. All telephone numbers are in the 1223 city code unless otherwise indicated.

For an unforgettable experience in Cambridge, we begin with our favorite, followed by our cost and quality choices of accommodations, listed by price category.

A SPECIAL HAVEN

Garden House The three acres of gardens at this modern hotel (the town's most luxurious) stretch to the edge of the river, and on summer mornings the waiters put out bread for the duck colony that inhabits the peaceful waters. Most of the 117 rooms have balconies overlooking the riverside. At dusk, sip cocktails on the lawn before tackling the extensive restaurant menu which includes typical English dishes. The conference facilities are excellent. Granta Pl. and Mill La. (phone: 63421; fax: 316605).

EXPENSIVE

Holiday Inn This member of the indomitable chain is built in a neoclassical style that blends surprisingly well with the city's ancient architecture. Aside from the grand atrium, there are 199 guestrooms, an indoor pool, business facilities, complimentary parking, and an outdoor patio. *Kingsley's* restaurant is named after Charles Kingsley, graduate of *Magdalene College* and author of *The Water Babies.* Downing St. (phone: 464466; 800-HOLIDAY; fax: 464440).

Royal Cambridge Spanning several Regency houses, this completely modernized establishment with a restaurant is on the main London—Cambridge road (A10), close to the city center. It has 74 nicely furnished guestrooms. Perfect for those on business. Trumpington St. (phone: 351631; fax: 352972).

University Arms An imposing Edwardian structure on the edge of Parker's Piece, it has belonged to the same family since 1891. The oak-paneled dining room, which overlooks the park and has a grand fireplace, also boasts an impressive wine list that includes several house wines bottled by the proprietor. There are 117 guestrooms, three bars (one with 100 different types of whisky), and extensive conference facilities. Regent St. (phone: 351241; fax: 315256).

MODERATE

Arundel House This converted Victorian terraced building overlooks the river and *Jesus Green* and offers a cozy atmosphere, friendly service, all modern conveniences, 88 rooms, and a restaurant. The guestrooms on the fourth floor have the best views, but keep in mind that there is no elevator. 53 Chesterton Rd. (phone: 67701; fax: 67721).

Helen There is a charming Italian-style garden in front of this 25-room hostelry with a restaurant, a mile from town and a 10-minute walk from the railway station. 167-69 Hills Rd. (phone: 246465; fax: 214406).

INEXPENSIVE

Mrs. Greening An excellent (and cost-saving) accommodation, this delightful home is a short walk from the city center along the river towpath. The three guestrooms overlook the river and Mrs. Greening's charming and colorful flower gardens. There's no restaurant, and the rooms do not have phones. 7 Water St. (phone: 355550).

EATING OUT

Cambridge is generally better served by eateries in the inexpensive and moderate categories, although there are one or two expensive restaurants (usually located in the more expensive hotels) that cater to the more discerning palate. Most places, including several along Magdalene Street, north and south of Magdalene Bridge, offer extremely good value and large helpings—the latter is an especially important consideration in a town where many of the customers are students. All restaurants listed below serve lunch and dinner, unless otherwise noted. Expect to pay $110 or more for dinner for two, including wine, at the restaurant listed as expensive, from $60 to $100 at moderate places, and less than $50 at inexpensive eateries. All telephone numbers are in the 1223 city code unless otherwise indicated.

EXPENSIVE

Midsummer House Cambridge's smartest eatery is owned by TV celebrity Chris Kelly, a host on the BBC's weekly "Food and Drink" program. Tucked into a corner of *Midsummer Common* on the riverside, the restaurant has an enviable location. Dress smartly to eat upstairs or relax downstairs either in the Blue Room, replete with chintz fabrics, or the flower-filled conservatory. Food is imaginative (typical dishes include venison with wild mushrooms), with fresh vegetables and fixed-price menus offering two to six courses. Closed Mondays, Saturday lunch, and Sunday evenings. Reservations necessary. Major credit cards accepted. *Midsummer Common* (phone: 69299).

MODERATE

Browns Nestled behind the colonnaded façade of the city's old hospital, this is Cambridge's version of Oxford's *Browns.* Inside it's bright and airy, with ceiling fans, masses of plants, and a cocktail bar. The menu is eclectic (offering everything from toasted sandwiches to pasta dishes), and the portions gargantuan. Open daily. Reservations unnecessary. Major credit cards accepted. 23 Trumpington St. (phone: 461655).

Michel's Brasserie Warm calf's liver salad and savory vegetable crêpes are just two of the tempting dishes on the prix fixe menu at this popular restaurant. The house wine is delicious and reasonably priced at £8.45 (about $12.75) a bottle. In summer you can partake of a meal at the wooden trestle tables outside; in winter you can snuggle up to the fire indoors. Open daily. Reservations advised. Major credit cards accepted. 21-24 Northampton St. (phone: 353110).

INEXPENSIVE

Belinda's Coffee/Wine Bar and Beer Cellar This self-service eatery is actually a renovated underground maze of spacious passages. Selections are from a freshly prepared hot and cold buffet, and seating is at counters and tables. There's a good wine list. Open daily. No reservations. No credit cards accepted. 14 Trinity St. (phone: 354213).

Boards Bistro Halfway up the stairs leading to the *Arts Theatre,* this trendy spot for the younger set offers lasagna and salads, beers and wines, and a relaxed atmosphere (although nonsmokers be forewarned—there is quite a bit of cigarette smoke). *Note:* The restaurant is closed while the theater is being refurbished, but it is scheduled to reopen late this fall or early next year. Open daily. Reservations necessary for pre-theater dinner. No credit cards accepted. St. Edwards Passage (phone: 355246).

Carrington's Coffee House A popular lunchtime café that serves far more than coffee: hot soups, quiches, meat dishes, cakes, and crêpes. Closed Sundays. No reservations. No credit cards accepted. 23 Market St. (phone: 61792).

Hobbs' Pavilion A converted cricket pavilion, named after famous cricketer Jack Hobbs and overlooking Parker's Piece, is now *the* Cambridge *crêperie.* Crêpes come sweet and savory—you can even get one filled with Mars bars and cream! Many vegetarian dishes are available. Closed Sundays and Mondays. No reservations. No credit cards accepted. Parker's Piece (phone: 67480).

L'Ile de France A tiny bakery with a café upstairs, run by a French *pâtissier* who produces croissants and pastries that taste heavenly with a strong cup of coffee in the morning. Open daily. No reservations. No credit cards accepted. 16 Round Church St. (phone: 301838).

King's Pantry Health-food enthusiasts queue up by the dozens to taste this establishment's homemade soups and granary bread, spinach lasagna, potato and apple casserole, three-bean chili, and cassoulet. Closed Sunday evenings. Reservations advised. No credit cards accepted. 9 King's Parade (phone: 321551).

Pasta Galore An intimate and friendly Italian eatery that serves homemade pasta with unusual and imaginative sauces, including good vegetarian alternatives. A variety of Italian goodies also is available for takeout from the mini-deli behind the counter. Open daily. Reservations advised. Major credit cards accepted. 5 Jordans Yard (phone: 324351).

Roof Garden Set above the *Boards Bistro,* this casual spot is ideal for a pre-theater baked potato, or fish, spinach, and potato bake with hot vegetables. It is a favorite with local teenagers and *Cambridge* students for coffee and cakes, too. In summer, the outside tables are set beside the window boxes. Like the *Boards Bistro,* it is closed until the *Arts Theatre* reopens late this fall or early next year. Open daily. Reservations unnecessary. No credit cards accepted. St. Edwards Passage (phone: 355246).

TAKING TEA

For cream teas, try *Auntie's Tea Shop* (in St. Mary's Passage; phone: 315-6412; open daily) or *La Cafetière* (off King St.; no phone; closed Sundays). For a coffee and pastry break, lunch, or supper, try the café on the first floor of *Eaden Lilley* department store (Market St.; phone: 358822; closed Sundays); be prepared for a wait—the place is usually very crowded. For a substantial treat, even if you've done nothing more demanding than stroll across from the Backs, try the Post-Tutorial tea at the *Little Tearoom* (in All Saints' Passage; phone: 354188; open daily).

SHARING A PINT

Cambridge has many more pubs than colleges, and most of them serve real ale, although you're just as likely to find a bottle of California chardonnay chilling behind the bar. But one of our personal favorites is just a few miles northwest of the city.

PERFECT PINTS

Three Horseshoes Visitors, academics, university students, and families patronize this thatch-roofed, whitewashed country pub in the tiny village of Madingley. They come in winter, when the atmosphere is cozy and warm, and in summer, when dainty elegance prevails among the tables set up on the back lawn. Lunchtime food is a special delight—smoked fish, salads, pâtés, and cold meat. High St. (phone: 954-210221).

The *Eagle* (Bene't St.; phone: 301286) offers traditional bitter; contained within it is a section called the "RAF Bar," whose ceiling bears the signatures of a number of World War II fighter pilots. The *Baron of Beef* (Bridge St.; phone: 63720) is a wood-beamed, Old World–style student haunt. Tucked away at the end of Thompsons Lane, the *Spade and Beckett* (phone: 311701) has a peaceful garden looking onto the river. The *Fort St. George in England* (*Midsummer Common;* phone: 354327) is a gathering spot for rowing enthusiasts; you can sip ale and watch the boats at the same time. The *Free Press* (Prospect Row; phone: 68337) is a cozy little pub with excellent, inexpensive food, and the *Anchor* pub (Silver St.; phone: 353554) is a good place to stop before resuming your afternoon punt.

Canterbury

Despite the vast damage inflicted by World War II bombing raids and the rebuilding and development that followed, there remains enough history in Canterbury to give the impression that time stopped somewhere along the line and only recently started again to admit the automobile, electricity, and indoor plumbing. The cathedral, begun in the 11th century and completed in the 16th, towers moodily over nearby pubs and shops; half-timbered, whitewashed little houses line the narrow streets; and the river Stour drifts slowly past brilliant flower beds and under arching stone bridges.

But Canterbury's history stretches a good deal farther back than the Middle Ages. The first known settlement of any size in the area dates from about 300 BC. In about 75 BC, these poorly organized natives were conquered by the Belgae, a tribe from across the Channel; still later, in 54 BC, Roman troops led by Julius Caesar stormed and took one of the Belgic fortified camps. A full-scale invasion was launched by Emperor Claudius during the next century, and the Romans settled in permanently. They called the place Durovernum Cantiacorum and built roads connecting the city with other settlements to the north and south. Traces of the Roman period still can be seen; for example, the medieval city walls were built upon the original Roman foundations, and the well-preserved underground remains of a Roman townhouse with a fine mosaic floor will be shown in the new *Roman Museum* on Butchery Lane (scheduled to open this spring).

During the 5th century, Britain was conquered by the Saxons; by 560 the city had forsaken its Roman identity to become Canterbury (actually Cantwarabyrig), the capital of the Saxon kingdom of Kent, ruled by Ethelbert. It was with the arrival in 597 of St. Augustine—sent by the pope to convert Ethelbert and his subjects to Christianity—that Canterbury assumed its new and final role of cathedral city. In the years that followed, Augustine became archbishop, founded the *Abbey of Saints Peter and Paul* (now called *St. Augustine's Abbey*), and established the first cathedral. During the ensuing years, the Vikings, Danes, and Normans destroyed much that they found and built anew (including the cathedral). The incident that really put the city on the map, however, was the infamous murder of Archbishop Thomas à Becket in 1170.

Becket, for years a trusted adviser to King Henry II, was named Archbishop of Canterbury in 1162. Thus began a long power struggle between the two over who was the final authority on church matters. Becket was slain in his own cathedral by four of the king's knights. He was soon canonized and his tomb in *Trinity Chapel* was declared a shrine. The tomb was removed from the chapel in 1538 and the shrine was destroyed on the orders of Henry VIII; now only a plaque marks the spot. People from all over the world began to flock to the shrine to honor the martyr. So popular was the pilgrimage to Canterbury that Geoffrey Chaucer chose it as the narrative vehicle for his classic, *The Canterbury Tales,* in which each pilgrim tells his or her story as the group travels to the shrine.

Canterbury can claim many literary connections in addition to this most famous one. The dramatist Christopher Marlowe was born here in 1564 and educated at the *King's School;* you may be able to catch a performance of one of his plays at the *Marlowe Theatre* in The Friars. Some three centuries later, the playwright and novelist W. Somerset Maugham, also a *King's* alumnus, sent the protagonist in *Of Human Bondage* to school here. R. H. Barham, the 19th-century humorist, was born in St. George's Parish and set parts of his series *The Ingoldsby Legends* in Canterbury. Joseph Conrad, although born in Poland, became one of England's great adventure writers and is buried in *Canterbury Cemetery.* St. Dunstan's is the setting for several episodes of Charles Dickens's novel *David Copperfield.*

A day's stroll will take you past most of these landmarks, retracing the footsteps of the city's illustrious natives (real and fictional). If you just let your imagination run a bit as you wander through Canterbury's prim gates and gardens, you'll soon begin to sense its less decorous past—when the pious thronged the city's crowded streets, the taverns roared a welcome, and the scaffold threatened the woebegone wrongdoer.

Canterbury At-a-Glance

SEEING THE CITY

As you approach Canterbury—by car on the A2 from London, from Dover in the southeast, or from Whitstable a few miles to the north—you are immediately aware of the towering hulk of the cathedral, floodlit by night and somberly gray in the daytime. Four viewpoints should not be missed. The first is the high plateau called Eliot Causeway on the campus of the *University of Kent-at-Canterbury,* about 2 miles along the road to Whitstable. No admission charge, but visitors are not particularly encouraged. The second is the summit of the *West Gate Towers,* a massive fortification abutting the *City Wall.* Closed Sundays. Admission charge. The third is the roof of the multistory parking lot on Gravel Walk. From here the town's remaining ancient buildings can be seen. The fourth is Dane John Mound (see *Special Places*).

SPECIAL PLACES

Although you've seen the splendor of the cathedral from a distance, you haven't experienced the vastness of its frontage. Walk along the busy shop-lined stretch of Mercery Lane, leading from the middle of High Street, and into the broad patio called Buttermarket. Immediately opposite is the *Christ Church Gate;* through here you enter another world. A statue titled *Christ Receiving* marks the gate; unveiled in 1990, it replaces a statue destroyed by Cromwell's Puritans in 1643. From west to east ranges the *South West Tower,* built in 1460, and behind it the *North West Tower* of 1840. Then comes the *Nave,* dating from 1400, and east of that the noble *Bell Harry Tower,* raised in 1500. Next are the *South East Transept,* originating in 1126, and the *Choir,* added during the restoration of 1184. The dates given relate only to the superstructure; the main work was started more than 400 years earlier. In the open, away from the clamor of traffic and trade, you can feel the sensation of stepping into medieval history.

CANTERBURY CATHEDRAL

The traceable story goes back to Ethelbert, who in 597 granted the site now occupied by the cathedral to St. Augustine. Building began in 602. Little is known of subsequent events until the disastrous fire of 1067, after which the cathedral was completely rebuilt. The history of the present fabric starts with this reconstruction carried out by the first Norman archbishop, Lanfranc, in 1070. A century later, Thomas à Becket's murder led to continuing pilgrimages and the acceptance of *Canterbury Cathedral* as "Mother Church of the realm." For further information, contact *Cathedral House* (phone: 762862).

THE NAVE Take a good look at this cavernous, majestic, peaceful enclosure. Designed in about 1400 by Henry Yevele, the architect of *Westminster Hall* and the nave of *Westminster Abbey,* it is an example of Perpendicular Gothic and has long been regarded as one of the world's greatest architectural masterpieces. The West Window portrays Adam in the act of digging. Dating from 1178, it is probably the earliest action picture in existence, for until then, all church windows showed only nonsequential, immobile, and flat outlines. Similar illustrated windows appear in all parts of the vast church, forming a rich gallery of medieval artwork. The brilliant jewel-tone windows high in the clerestory look merely decorative from floor level, but with good binoculars you can see more detail of the fascinating and often lighthearted tales depicted. The so-called Poor Man's Bible illustrates scenes from the Old and New Testaments for the illiterate populace, miracles supposedly performed at Becket's shrine, and accounts of 13th-century life.

THE TOMB OF THE BLACK PRINCE Edward of Woodstock, son of King Edward III, became Prince of Wales, but was survived by his father and never succeeded to the throne. He is remembered as a hero of the battles of Crécy and Poitiers and a tireless patron of the cathedral. Under his sponsorship, Henry Yevele carried out major rebuilding in the crypt and also designed the *West Gate* and a considerable portion of the city walls. In 1363 the Black Prince married Joan, the Fair Maid of Kent; this match and the subsequent marriage of their daughters to almost all claimants to the throne resulted in the start of the York and Tudor dynasties. His shrine and tomb, with all his royal knightly regalia displayed nearby, may be seen in the south aisle of *Trinity Chapel.* It is considered among the most splendid memorials in England.

THE CRYPT This is the oldest part of the cathedral, with a low roof and rounded arches in pure Norman style. Its rather frightening severity is relieved by grotesque and deliberately humorous carvings on the pillars.

THE MARTYRDOM The site where Thomas à Becket was slain by four French knights—Fitzurse, de Moreville, de Tracy, and le Breton—on December 29, 1170, is in the northwest transept of the crypt. A shrine to the archbishop was erected after his death and canonization. It rested first in the *East Crypt* and then was moved to *Trinity Chapel,* after which the jewel-encrusted coffin was taken to London by order of Henry VIII (1538) and was never seen again. Henry reputedly denounced Becket in a public ceremony, desecrated his remains, and ordered that the jewels from the coffin be removed to the royal coffers.

THE QUIRE This might be called the jewel of the cathedral, because of the sparkling beauty of its glasswork, the oldest examples of which are the Twelve Miracle Windows.

THE CLOISTERS, CHAPTER HOUSE, GREEN COURT, AND KING'S SCHOOL To see the cathedral's entire interior takes the better part of a day, but be sure to make time for the peripheral buildings that date from when the whole was a Benedictine monastery. The *Cloisters,* leading from the *Chapter House,* are virtually "corridors in the vale of time." If as you stroll through the passageway called the Dark Entry you encounter the ghost of a certain Nell Cook, don't be alarmed—you're not the first. The story of her origin is obscure, and her occasional appearances are rarely sinister. The *Chapter House* was where former Prime Minister Margaret Thatcher and France's President François Mitterrand met in 1986 to sign the treaty that set in motion the Channel Tunnel (which opened last summer). Beyond the *Green Court,* and traditionally associated with the cathedral, is the *King's School,* the oldest public school in the land. ("Public" is the British term for what Americans call a private school.) The *King's School,* notable architecturally for its handsome Norman staircase, stages its own annual *King's Week* (see *Special Events*).

In *St. Margaret's Church* near the cathedral, visitors can experience a re-creation of Chaucer's pilgrims' journey from London to *Canterbury Cathedral.* The 40-minute, walk-through exhibit traces the route described in *The Canterbury Tales,* with visuals, sounds, even smells. Open daily. Admission charge. St. Margaret's St. (phone: 454888).

WITHIN THE OLD CITY WALLS

About half of the initial wall structure still stands; the walkway atop it makes a fascinating hike in good weather.

WEST GATE The next most imposing of Canterbury's historic buildings is at the extreme end of St. Peter's Street, as it joins St. Dunstan's Street, following on from High Street, five minutes' walk west from the cathedral. As a relic and the last of the city's fortified gatehouses, it is magnificent, but it has a grisly history: Construction of the *West Gate* was started at the order of Archbishop Simon of Sudbury about 1380. Soon after, it became the city jail, which it remained until 1829. Today it is a museum exhibiting arms and armor, manacles, fetters, and instruments of torture; and the old prison cells still retain their original doors and fittings. Closed Sundays. Admission charge. St. Peter's St. (phone: 452747).

DANE JOHN MOUND Nothing to do with Danes, but a prominent feature of central Canterbury, this prehistoric rise gives fine views of the red tile Tudor houses in the neighborhood from its highest point (about 57 feet). The name comes from the Norman-French word *donjon,* meaning a castle or keep, or—more chillingly—a dungeon. Dane John Mound lies southwest of the cathedral on Pin Hill, about five minutes' walk from *Christ Church Gate* near *East Station.*

NORMAN CASTLE A vast ruin, it possesses one of the largest Norman keeps in the country. It was built between 1070 and 1094, has been surrounded and captured several times, and was once the royal prison for the County of Kent. When the fanatical Mary I was on the throne, many Protestants were imprisoned here before being burned at the stake for their religious beliefs. The castle is at the junction of Castle Street and Rheims Way.

OUTSIDE THE PERIMETER

ST. DUNSTAN'S This is the section of Old Canterbury beyond the *West Gate* and leading toward the railway crossing on St. Dunstan's Street near *West Station.* A good place of call is the *House of Agnes,* now a hotel on St. Dunstan's Street (see *Checking In*). The interesting old *Falstaff Inn,* dating from at least the 15th century, is nearly opposite.

ST. AUGUSTINE'S ABBEY It was founded by St. Augustine, with the support of King Ethelbert, in AD 602. Though largely a ruin, it is still a beautiful relic of Canterbury's past, particularly the finely restored *Fyndon Gate.* The entrance is on Longport.

ENVIRONS

HOWLETTS AND PORT LYMPNE WILD ANIMAL PARKS The largest breeding colony of gorillas outside the US is contained within these two zoo parks, run by John Aspinall and his family. Also here is a fine collection of other rare, endangered species, including great cats and free-roaming herds of deer and antelope. Closed *Christmas.* Admission charge. *Howletts* is at Bekesbourne, 3 miles southeast of Canterbury (phone: 721286); *Port Lympne* is off A20 between Ashford and Folkestone or at Exit 11 of the M20 highway (phone: 264646).

FORDWICH Drive to Sturry, almost 3 miles northeast of Canterbury on the A28. Turn right at the signpost to Fordwich, and the tiny hamlet on the river

Stour is less than a minute away. It is an exquisite little town of some 300 inhabitants and is remarkable for having the smallest town hall in England, scarcely bigger than a farmworker's cottage. Nobody knows how old the structure is, but records show that extensive repairs were carried out as far back as 1474. Here again, you'll see instruments of torture. The stocks are outside in the courtyard, their oaken clamps worn slim from centuries of use; the small prison is in one corner; and overlooking the river stands the crane that once lowered condemned miscreants into the water for drowning. Beside it is the ducking chair that was used for the correction of shrewish wives. The *George and Dragon* hotel, around the corner from the *Town Hall,* is an excellent place for lunch (see *Checking In*).

Sources and Resources

TOURIST INFORMATION

The tourist information center (closed Sundays October through *Easter*) is close to the cathedral (34 St. Margaret's St.; phone: 766567); many of the staff are French, which hints at the nationality of most of Canterbury's visitors. The center stocks helpful guidebooks, brochures, and maps. Guided tours, including cathedral precincts, leave St. Margaret's Street daily at 11 AM and 2 PM from April through October; there is a fee. To arrange additional or off-season tours, consult the *Guild of Guides* (*Arnett House,* Hawks La.; phone: 459779). Guided tours of the cathedral only are conducted weekdays and Saturdays year-round. Direct general inquiries to *Cathedral House* (see *Special Places,* above). The city also has a *Leisureline Information Service* (phone: 767744).

LOCAL COVERAGE The weekly *Kentish Gazette* is available at *Kent County Newspapers Ltd.* (9 St. George's Pl.; phone: 768181).

TELEPHONE The city code for Canterbury is 1227.

GETTING AROUND

As Canterbury is very small, walking is the best form of transportation within the city. To visit some of the outlying areas, other transportation is necessary.

BUS From the bus station on St. George's Lane (near *Riceman's* department store), you can catch *National Express* coaches to London's *Victoria Station* (about two hours) and buses to Deal, Dover, Folkestone, and Margate (each about an hour's ride). For information, call 1843-581333 in Ramsgate.

CAR RENTAL There are many car rental firms in Canterbury, including *Budget* (phone: 451330 or 470297); *Europcar* (phone: 470864); *Hertz* (phone: 765654); and *U-Drive Rentals* (phone: 463700). There is adequate, inexpensive parking in the city.

TAXI Quick and courteous cab service is available at all times. Try *City Cars* (phone: 454445) or *Lynx* (phone: 464232).

TRAIN *British Rail* trains run frequently from London's *Victoria Station* to *Canterbury East Station* (Station Rd.), continuing on to Dover. London—Canterbury travel time is an hour and 20 minutes. Regular service between London's *Charing Cross Station* and *Canterbury West Station* (Station Rd. W.) takes about an hour and 40 minutes. For information, call 1732-770111 in Tonbridge.

SPECIAL EVENTS

The *King's School* stages a music festival in late June and early July, with excellent performances in glorious surroundings (phone: 455600). During the summer, the *Chaucer Festival* is celebrated with various medieval events, including a costumed procession through the streets; contact the *Chaucer Centre* (see *Shopping*) for more details. In October, the annual *Canterbury Festival* (59 Ivy La.; phone: 452853) takes place, with plays and concerts.

MUSEUMS

Besides those discussed in *Special Places,* consider the following:

HERITAGE MUSEUM Housed in the 13th-century *Poor Priests' Hospital,* it offers a walk through the city's history: The museum contains the 150-year-old *Invicta,* a steam-powered locomotive designed by George Stephenson, and a working remnant of one of the earliest passenger railways in the world. On the more whimsical side, there is also a display about Rupert Bear, a cartoon character created in 1920 (eight years before Mickey Mouse). Closed Sundays except in summer. Admission charge. Stour St. (phone: 452747).

ROMAN MUSEUM Scheduled to open this spring, this museum below street level displays the remains of a Roman townhouse, with beautiful mosaics and other artifacts that tell the earliest known history of Canterbury. Several of the mosaics were reconstructed with the aid of a computer. At press time, the museum's hours were uncertain; call ahead to the *Heritage Museum* (see above) to check. Admission charge. Butchery La.

ROYAL MUSEUM AND ART GALLERY (THE BEANEY INSTITUTE) It incorporates *Buff's Regimental Museum* and chronicles the area's history and archaeology. There also are numerous paintings of cattle and sheep, so beloved by Victorians, by local artist Thomas Sidney Cooper. Closed Sundays. No admission charge. 18 High St. (phone: 452747).

SHOPPING

Wednesday is market day, although Canterbury's compact size makes any day here a shopper's dream. If your hobby is antiques, spend a morning in Palace Street—turn right out of *Christ Church Gate* and then right again. There are many old buildings here that contain treasures, including *Conquest*

House Antiques, housed in an 11th-century building (at No. 17). Another good shop on Palace Street is the small, family-run *Aristocrat* (No. 19; phone: 464035), which specializes in engraved glass and collectors' items. For standard shopping hours, see GETTING READY TO GO.

Be sure to take your passport when you shop, and always inquire about the Value Added Tax (VAT) refund application forms when your total purchases in a store are over £50 (about $75). The VAT is a surcharge payable at the sales counter, but foreign customers usually will be reimbursed for it at home (for more information see GETTING READY TO GO).

Albion Bookshop An interesting place for browsing, it has an excellent section on local maps and guidebooks. 13 Mercery La. (phone: 768631).

Cable and Keane Fine cheeses, English wines, homemade jams, honey, and relishes are among this shop's offerings. 24 Sun St. (phone: 765196).

Canterbury Pottery Pottery is handmade on the premises. On the far side of Buttermarket, just before Mercery La. at 38A Burgate (phone: 452608).

Chaucer Bookshop The place to pick up *The Canterbury Tales* as well as out of print, antiquarian, and general secondhand tomes. 6 Beer Cart La. (phone: 453912).

Chaucer Centre As the name implies, all things Chaucerian may be found here. Books, souvenirs, and gift items are the main draw. 22 St. Peter's St. (phone: 470379).

Deakins Well established and equally well frequented, this men's and boys' outfitter carries the usual classic stock, plus regimental ties and walking sticks. 1-2 Sun St. (phone: 462116).

English Teddy Bear Company Literally hundreds of handmade teddies line the shelves. Among the stuffed animals are many versions of Rupert Bear, a cartoon character similar to Winnie the Pooh that was created by Canterbury resident Mary Tourtel in 1920. If you like, you can relive the tea parties of your youth with your new purchase in the little café upstairs. 4 St. Peter's St. (phone: 784640).

Liberty In a fine old building, this branch of the famous London emporium specializes in high-quality fabrics and clothes; upstairs visitors can enjoy refreshments in the tearoom. Corner of Burgate and Butchery La. (phone: 454244).

Saunders Prints, old postcards, and unusual tin boxes in the shape of old trams and trains are the specialties found here. 12 and 50 St. Peter's St. (phone: 472562).

SPORTS

CRICKET Canterbury is prime cricket territory; to watch this very British game, go to the *Kent Country Cricket Club* (at *St. Lawrence Ground,* off Old Dover Rd.; phone: 763421). Tickets are available at the gate. *Canterbury Cricket*

Week is held every August; details are available from the tourist office (see *Tourist Information*).

GOLF The well-kept 18-hole *Canterbury* golf course (Littlebourne Rd.; phone: 453532) is open to the public; players with established handicaps are preferred. Clubs may be rented.

HORSEBACK RIDING Horses can be hired at two stables nearby: *Bourne Park Stables* (in Bridge; phone: 830245) and *Bursted Manor Riding Centre* (in Pett Bottom; phone: 830568).

SWIMMING The *Kingsmead Leisure Centre* (on Kingsmead; phone: 769817) has an indoor pool that is open to the public; admission charge.

THEATER

Canterbury has only one commercial playhouse, the *Marlowe* (The Friars; phone: 767246), which features weekly plays from Agatha Christie to Shakespeare, classical music concerts, ballet and contemporary dance; comedians also perform here. The *Gulbenkian Theatre* of the *University of Kent* (on Giles La.; phone: 769075) is generally open to the public only during the university terms; its offerings include plays, recitals, concerts, and lectures. Check the newspapers for schedules.

NIGHTCLUBS AND NIGHTLIFE

There's not much after-dark entertainment in Canterbury. However, one possibility is *Alberry's Wine and Food Bar* (38A St. Margaret's St.; phone: 452378) for an enjoyable evening of eating and drinking and, on Monday, Tuesday, and Thursday nights, listening to live music downstairs in its Roman cellar. *Crotchets Wine Bar* (59 Northgate; phone: 458857) has more than 60 wines on its list, a garden, and live music (often jazz) nightly, except Sundays. *The Bizz and the Works* (15 Station Rd. E.; phone: 462520) is the town's classiest disco (you must be 21 or older).

Best in Town

CHECKING IN

Book well in advance, because the city welcomes about two million visitors during the summer (and the numbers are expected to swell with French tourists arriving via the newly opened Channel Tunnel). Most of the hotels listed below are smallish but make up for this shortcoming with their cheerful and attentive service. None, however, is in the true luxury class, except for nearby *Eastwell Manor,* in Ashford. For a double room (including private bath, TV set, phone, and breakfast, unless otherwise indicated), expect to pay $100 to $175 per night in those hotels we list as expensive; $55 to $95, in moderate places; and $30 to $50 in inexpensive ones. All telephone numbers are in the 1227 city code unless otherwise indicated.

EXPENSIVE

Abbots Barton At this large country house (just a half mile from the city center) surrounded by two acres of attractive grounds, guests will find a quiet, old-fashioned ambience, log fires, good food, and solid, comfortable furniture. In short, it's the perfect base for families. Facilities include 48 modern rooms and parking. 37 New Dover Rd. (phone: 760341).

County First licensed in 1629, it is considered the best in Canterbury and is richly decorated and furnished in antiques. *Sully's,* the hotel's excellent restaurant, specializes in continental fare (see *Eating Out*). There are 74 rooms and conference facilities; parking is available. High St. (phone: 766266; fax: 451512).

Eastwell Manor This turreted, rambling country-house hotel offers 23 luxurious, spacious rooms furnished with antiques, a billiards room, and an accomplished kitchen, all set amid extensive gardens. It's about 10 miles southwest of Canterbury, and a first class choice for visitors who long to experience life in an elegant country setting. *Eastwell Park,* Boughton Aloph, near Ashford (phone: 1233-635751; fax: 1233-635530).

MODERATE

George and Dragon This 16th-century inn near the river Stour has 13 comfortable, attractively decorated rooms. Its restaurant, which serves steak dinners, also offers a fine hot and cold buffet lunch. Fordwich, near Sturry (phone: 710661).

House of Agnes A small, cozy Tudor building with nine compact and well-appointed rooms (purportedly used as a model in Dickens's *David Copperfield*); its restaurant serves good, hearty English fare. 71 St. Dunstan's St. (phone: 472185; fax: 464527).

Millers Arms With all the warmth and antiquity you would expect from a former coaching inn, this 13-room hostelry provides appealing rooms overlooking the river Stour. The informal, reputable restaurant serves simple fare such as homemade soup, grilled chicken, sausages, and chips (French fries). Mill La. (phone: 456057).

INEXPENSIVE

The White House There are three beautiful rooms in this pretty guesthouse at the end of a quiet lane. Each has all the Regency trimmings—high ceiling with white coving (stucco) work, chandelier-style lamps, and a mahogany fireplace. There's no restaurant, and the guestrooms do not have phones. 6 St. Peter's La. (phone: 761836).

EATING OUT

Canterbury is not the ideal place for haute cuisine, with only one truly fine restaurant; however, the area does have several cozy little eateries that serve good, basic fare at reasonable prices. A dinner for two, excluding wine, tips, or drinks, will run $70 or more in the place listed as expensive; $40 to $65 at a moderate restaurant; and less than $35 at an inexpensive spot. All restaurants listed below serve lunch and dinner, unless otherwise noted. All telephone numbers are in the 1227 city code unless otherwise indicated.

EXPENSIVE

Sully's Recently arrived chef Eric Marin Gavignet has elevated this formerly standard hotel restaurant to a truly excellent dining room in one short year. The menu offers exquisitely prepared continental specialties including savarin of fish in lobster sauce and noisettes of venison with *poivrade* sauce in polenta. The trendy decor clashes somewhat with the Old English, timber-beamed look of the *County* hotel in which the restaurant is located. Open daily. Reservations necessary. Major credit cards accepted. High St. (phone: 766206).

MODERATE

Cate's Brasserie At this timbered building-turned-restaurant (formerly known as *Reids*), the French chef and his staff prepare predictable yet fine fare, and you'll always find a *plat du jour* on the menu as well as a good selection of wines. Open daily. Reservations necessary. Major credit cards accepted. 4 Church St. in the St. Paul's area (phone: 456655).

Duck Inn This snug little spot, set in a 16th-century cottage in the middle of a farm field, is warmed by a roaring fire in winter and offers alfresco dining in the garden in summer. Its upstairs dining room is noted for fine French cooking, but you also can get a less expensive meal in the bar downstairs. This place may be of special interest to James Bond aficionados, since according to the film *You Only Live Twice,* 007 grew up next door. The pub was featured in several Bond films. It's about 5 miles outside Canterbury, not far from the village of Bridge on the road to Dover. Closed Mondays and Tuesdays. Reservations necessary. Major credit cards accepted. Pett Bottom (phone: 830354).

George's Brasserie French regional fare is well represented here; the chefs use fresh local produce, but also slip in a few European favorites, including swordfish, wild salmon, turbot, Scotch steaks cut from the bones, and breast of chicken in mustard sauce. There's always a dish for vegetarians, such as charcoal-grilled eggplant with pasta. Dine alfresco in the summer in the large garden. Closed Sundays. Reservations advised. Major credit cards accepted. 72 Castle St. (phone: 765658).

Merefield's Hostelry Though the name implies that it is a hotel, this place is actually a converted corner pub offering good basic English dishes such as Pickwick pie (a steak-and-kidney pie that also features mushrooms and oysters) and puddings. Its location near the *Marlowe Theatre* makes it a good place to grab a bite before or after the show. Closed Sundays. No reservations. Major credit cards accepted. 51 King St. (phone: 456209).

River Kwai A highly commendable Thai dining spot that also provides take-out meals. Open daily. Reservations advised. Major credit cards accepted. 49-50 Castle St. (phone: 462090).

Stowaway's Walk through a Gothic archway and down a passage into *Cogan House,* one of Canterbury's oldest buildings. The restaurant upstairs specializes in local Whitstable fish, while tea is served downstairs in the old Tudor dining room. The walled garden is open for alfresco dining in summer. Closed Sundays. No reservations. Major credit cards accepted. 53 St. Peter's St. (phone: 764459).

INEXPENSIVE

Caesars A student haunt, with huge hamburgers and generous portions of ribs and other transatlantic dishes. Open daily. No reservations. Major credit cards accepted. 46 St. Peter's St. (phone: 456833).

Fungus Mungus It's well worth taking a walk up to the end of St. Peter's Street to find this charming tearoom and restaurant; its owners say the name means "a lot of mushrooms." In a cottage-like interior with lacy tablecloths and old wooden chairs, 170 different teas are served, as well as vegetarian meals. Open daily. No reservations. No credit cards accepted. 34 St. Peter's St. (phone: 781922).

SHARING A PINT

For a special experience, stop by the *Millers Arms* (see *Checking In*). Summer lunches outdoors are *the* thing to do in the beautiful garden at the *White Hart* (on Worthgate Pl.; phone: 765091). Possibly the friendliest and most atmospheric pub, which also serves tea and coffee all day, is the *Olive Branch* (39 Burgate; phone: 462170), opposite the cathedral gates. The *City Arms* (Butchery La.; phone: 457900) has good bar lunches, real ale, and live music on Wednesday evenings.

Cardiff

"A proper fine Towne" was how the 17th-century cartographer Christopher Saxton described Cardiff. And today it's a proper fine city: handsome, spacious, and genial, with a definite sense of its own importance. It is, after all, the capital city of Wales. And it has a capital feel about it. A headquarters for commerce, industry, government, the arts, and communications, it has perhaps the most attractive city center in Britain—the Welsh Washington, as it's called.

There is a strong sense of civic pride in this Welsh city; its people have nicknamed Cardiff the "City in Bloom" for its award-winning abundance of flowers. Cardiff also boasts the *Welsh National Opera,* arguably Britain's best opera company outside of London, and a wealth of indoor malls and beautifully restored Victorian shopping arcades. Above all, the city has a special European flavor, best exemplified in its turreted, fairy-tale–like buildings.

From London, Cardiff is two and a half hours away on the M4 (Swansea) motorway, or less than two hours by the 125-mph super-train. And the *Central Station* sign says *Caerdydd*/Cardiff in salute to the two languages of Wales, hinting at the history, pride, and fascination of this singular land. Nationalist pride runs high—woe betide anyone who calls a Welshman an Englishman!

Welsh, spoken by one-fifth of the principality's 2.8 million people, is Wales's distinction among nations. In Cardiff you'll see the language (it dates from the 6th century) written on all manner of signs. You're sure to see the word *croeso*—"welcome"—and the Welsh mean it. You may hear the language spoken in the streets and shops and on radio and television—but not a great deal. Cardiff is in southeast Wales, and the strongly Welsh-speaking areas are in the north and west.

Cardiff has its own distinctive character. It is a multilayered and cosmopolitan place (twinned with Nantes in France, Stuttgart in Germany, Lugansa in Ukraine, and Xiamen in China), an outward-looking, modern European city of warm people, as well as a storehouse of the history of a fascinating area—three of the thirteen Welsh signatories of the Declaration of Independence were sons of Cardiff.

Cardiff was named the Welsh capital by Queen Elizabeth in 1956, at a time when Wales was demanding some recognition of its special identity within the United Kingdom. Other towns applied for the honor, but Cardiff was the home of the Welsh Office, headquarters of all Welsh administration, and the Temple of Peace, which administers all liaison between Wales and the United Nations. With such administrative prowess and a population of about 245,000 (today, it's 280,000), the city had the scale, background, and facilities to make it a realistic contender.

Diligent Romans built a no-nonsense little Cardiff beside the river Taff (the city's name means "castle on the Taff") as part of their network of conquest. The thick-walled stone fortress they constructed around AD 76 served as a defense and trading post. The Roman stones, still visible around the first two feet of the castle walls, were already old when the Normans established their own stronghold on the site of the old Roman fort in the 11th century. On a mound they raised a keep, a noble medieval fist, and it remains intact: one of the finest examples of its kind in Britain. Castle, moat, and green are right in the city center, and Cardiffians like to saunter or doze on the green in summer.

King Edward I of England conquered stubborn Wales in the late 13th century. But 100 years or so later, in 1404, Owain Glyndwr fanned the embers of resistance, started a war of independence, and sacked Cardiff. Eventually he lost his struggle, but five centuries later Cardiff was generous enough to erect a marble statue of the hero in its city hall. Roundheads took the town from Royalists in Britain's 17th-century civil war, but for nearly 200 years after that, life was peaceful enough. Cardiff bloomed quietly, a market town, seaport, and occasional bolt-hole for pirates.

Then came the Industrial Revolution. Up in the winding green valleys, in mines spoking from Cardiff's hub, men tore out coal to fuel factories, furnaces, mills, and ships. The coal was sent to Cardiff, first by mule, then barge, then rail, for shipment to British cities and the rest of the world. A new Cardiff soared on the dizzy spiral of the great coal rush, the central event in post-1800 Welsh history. The riches of the valleys poured in, the river Taff ran black, and Cardiff became the world's greatest coal port. The *Cardiff Coal Exchange,* a stately Victorian edifice, still stands in the dockland, a monument to an age long gone. Cardiff, struggling to forge yet another new identity in the wake of Britain's economic slump, today promotes itself as a center of finance and tourism.

During Cardiff's Victorian and Edwardian expansion, its top citizens consolidated its position as chief city of Wales. Among lawns, shrubs, and boulevards they built their halls of government and culture: city hall, county hall, a museum, law courts, and a university, laid out in a grand, magisterial sweep. Meanwhile, the burgeoning middle classes built lovely villas in places like Cathedral Road.

One of the most pleasant things about Cardiff is that its heart remains village-size. You can traverse the city by way of parks, greens, and footpaths; the stroll across *Llandaff Fields* to Llandaff is a great favorite. One of the famous parks, though, is not a park at all: *Cardiff Arms Park National Rugby Stadium* is a temple of rugby, a game to which Welshmen devote blood, sweat, and tears. On big-match Saturdays, the Red Dragon flag of Wales is hoisted aloft and almost everyone seems to have a leek or a daffodil, the national emblems, pinned to hat or coat. To be in Cardiff on one of these days is to experience a kind of Welshness in the raw, humorous and exuberant.

Cardiff At-a-Glance

SEEING THE CITY

Right in the middle of town is the best place to get a feel for Cardiff: the exhilarating castle (see *Special Places*). Cross the moat bridge, go through the gatehouse, turn left, and make for the clock tower. From here you get a sentry's-eye view of the castle itself, the river Taff, the *Cardiff Arms Park National Rugby Stadium, Sophia Gardens Cricket Ground,* and busy shopping streets. You also can see the famous "animal wall"—a row of sculptures of beasts and birds perched on battlements. You can see *Bute Park,* stretching off in the direction of the cathedral at Llandaff; and the pristine towers, domes, and greenery of *Cathays Park* (pronounced Cat-*hays*). Much the same view can be had from a slightly different vantage point, the roof garden of the castle. On the northwest edge of Cardiff is The Wenallt, an area of rolling woodland that offers a superb view of Cardiff, laid out on its coastal plain, and of the Bristol Channel. For the best view of the bay area, climb the cliff above *Penarth Marina.*

SPECIAL PLACES

Although Cardiff owes much of its importance and growth to coal, there has been over the years a conscious effort to keep its center free of grime. Cardiff is, at its center, a place of gracefulness, greenery, and wide avenues. Its compactness means that, for the most part, you can park the car and walk to the principal sights and that you are never far from a little restaurant, a jolly pub, or a stretch of grass where you might do as the locals do and chat, read, gaze, or snooze.

CITY CENTER

CARDIFF CASTLE Nineteen hundred years of history are stored here. The Roman walls are 10 feet thick, and the Norman stone keep on its *motte,* or mound, was built in the 11th century to show the locals who was boss. In the 19th century, the third Marquess of Bute, one of Wales's great coal moguls, commissioned architect William Burges to design the renovations and extensions that give the castle its unique appearance. The result is the baroque and charming place of today, full of color, exquisite murals, carvings, and painted ceilings and windows. The castle's nursery is decorated with painted tiles that depict fairy tales, and there is even a room based on Topkapi, the sultan's palace in Istanbul. Part of the castle is now used for civic receptions and special events, including Welsh banquets that are held here every evening in summer. Other rooms and towers house the *Museum of the Welsh Regiment.* A visit to the castle includes an excellent conducted tour every 20 minutes in the summer and four times daily in winter, although you also can wander on your own. Open daily. Admission charge. Castle St. (phone: 822083; 372737 for banquet booking and information).

CATHAYS PARK Avenues of a cheery pink stone, blossoms, shrubs, walks, statuary, and buildings of an almost Athenian aspect are some of the reasons the Welsh are rightly proud of this stunning parkland.

NATIONAL MUSEUM OF WALES One of the largest museums in Britain, this institution, opened to the public in 1927, concentrates on things Welsh—plants and animals, history and prehistory, rocks and minerals, and fine and applied arts. Among the archaeological exhibits, the *Caergwrle Bowl,* noteworthy for its gold embellishments, and the collection of stone monuments and casts from the 5th through the 9th centuries are particularly interesting. The building has recently undergone a major renovation. Among the additions are a display called *The Evolution of Wales Since the Big Bang* and six new courtyard galleries housing the museum's fine-arts collection, which includes works by such distinguished Impressionist and post-Impressionist artists as Cézanne, Corot, Degas, Monet, Pissarro, and Renoir. Welsh painting is represented by the 18th-century landscape artist Richard Wilson and several 20th-century painters. Apart from the main building in Cardiff's civic center, the *National Museum of Wales* comprises nine branches scattered throughout the country, including the *Welsh Folk Museum* and the *Welsh Industrial and Maritime Museum* (see below for both). Closed Mondays (except bank holidays). Admission charge. Museum Ave., *Cathays Park* (phone: 397951).

CITY HALL Next to the museum and the first building to go up in *Cathays Park* (1905), it is distinguished by its clock tower and ornate stonework. Inside is the *Marble Hall,* with its statues of the great men of Welsh history. Closed weekends. No admission charge. City Hall Rd., *Cathays Park* (phone: 822000).

BUTETOWN Cardiff's famous and notorious Tiger Bay of bygone days. The seafaring men from many parts of the world who settled this dockland area created a vibrant, tough, and often seamy and squalid community. Things have changed a lot, and though Butetown is still a lively, mixed community, it prides itself on its respectability. The coal trade isn't what it was, but the docks are still very important, and it's interesting to see the imposing shipping and banking offices. The *Coal Exchange,* built in the great days of the coal rush, and the small *Norwegian Church,* built for the benefit of homesick Norwegian sailors, are both now used for cultural performances and art exhibitions (for information, contact *Cardiff Arts Marketing*—see *Theater*). Attractions here include the *Welsh Industrial and Maritime Museum,* the *Cardiff Bay Visitors' Centre,* and *Techniquest* (see below for all). The area is undergoing a major renovation (scheduled to be completed around the turn of the century) as part of the Cardiff Bay regeneration program. Take a bus from *Central Station* or a train from the *Queen Street Station* to the heart of Butetown. The *Cardiff Bay Development Corporation* runs free one-and-a-half-hour coach tours of the area, including a stop at the visitors' center.

Welsh Industrial and Maritime Museum Four acres of Pier Head in Cardiff's dockland are devoted to this museum, which tells the story of Welsh industrial progress. The exhibits include coal mines, iron and steel works, and tinplate mills, plus outdoor displays featuring trains and ships. Closed Mondays. Admission charge. Bute St. (phone: 481919).

Cardiff Bay Visitors' Centre Housed in a viaduct-like, award-winning building next to the *Welsh Industrial and Maritime Museum,* this is the showcase for the *Cardiff Bay Development Corporation,* which is busy transforming Cardiff Bay into the largest inner-city renovation project in Europe. There are exhibits about the history of the region and models of the city center and what the area will look like when the project is completed. Open daily. No admission charge. *Atlantic Wharf* (phone: 463833).

Techniquest Children can learn about computers through hands-on experience at this science center, which recently moved to much larger quarters near the *Welsh Industrial and Maritime Museum.* Closed Mondays (except during school holidays). Admission charge. Bute St. (phone: 460211).

ROATH PARK Here are some 100 acres, with an attractive lake and rose gardens, which include a cornucopia of rare plants nestling under glass. You can rent a rowboat very inexpensively. Admire the geese camped on the island and pause at the miniature lighthouse, a memorial to the Antarctic hero Captain Robert Falcon Scott (1868–1912), who sailed from Cardiff to make his ill-fated expedition to the South Pole.

ENVIRONS

LLANDAFF Two miles from the city center, Llandaff can be reached by bus or by walking across *Llandaff Fields* from the castle. Llandaff is a charming city in its own right: Somehow it has retained a sleepy village air with its neat and solid Victorian houses, inns, whitewashed deanery, and a village green from which a path leads to the cathedral, beautiful and discreet in its hollow. St. Teilo founded a settlement here in the 6th century, which is how Llandaff got its name: *llan* (church) and *taff,* from the river Taff. The cathedral dates from the 12th century. One of its most striking (and controversial) features is Epstein's aluminum figure of Christ, which dominates the nave.

CASTELL COCH (RED CASTLE) With turreted, fairy-tale towers, this castle dominates the northern pass into Cardiff from the South Wales valleys. Built on medieval foundations by William Burges, it was designed as a hunting lodge for the third Marquess of Bute (1846–1900), the romantic model for Disraeli's novel *Lothair* (1820). Its remarkable, fantastic (in the literal sense of the word) interior includes a carved wooden ceiling as well as wooden parrots along the gallery. Open daily. Admission charge. Taffs Well, Tongwynalais (phone: 810101).

DYFFRYN GARDENS These are 3 miles west of the city, on Route A48 at St. Nicholas. On the way down the winding country road, stop at the Tinkinswood long barrow, one of the finest examples of a Neolithic burial chamber to be found in Wales: It has a 40-ton capstone. *Dyffryn House* is a spacious mansion with 70 acres of spacious grounds to match. It has masses of flowers, shrubs, and trees—and a tea house (called the *Garden's Rest*). The house itself is not open to the public, but the gardens can be visited; many special events are held here in summer, including open-air productions of Shakespeare's plays. The gardens are closed November through April. Admission charge. You can reach St. Nicholas by bus from *Central Station* (No. X1 or No. 231), but you will still have a walk of about a mile. St. Nicholas, Cardiff (phone: 593328).

CAERPHILLY CASTLE This masterpiece of medieval military architecture was built in the 13th century by Earl Gilbert de Clare. The concentric rings of walls within a moat would still provide a formidable challenge to a determined foe. It lies largely in ruins, with a leaning tower that lists even farther than the renowned tower in Pisa. Inside, exhibitions tell of the castle's history and give an overview of castles in Wales. Open daily. Admission charge. 7 miles north of Cardiff on the A469 (phone: 883143).

PENARTH Just across the Taff estuary (some 3 miles by bus or train from Cardiff) lies this small Victorian town. A major port once lay at the foot of the cliffs; today, it is the bustling *Portway Marina,* one of the first stages in the overall redevelopment of Cardiff's docklands. On the other side of Penarth Head is the Penarth seafront and pier, a magnificent example of Victorian seaside architecture. From here, you can walk a couple of miles along a well-maintained coastal path, with wonderful sea views all the way.

EXTRA SPECIAL

Out on the edge of the Vale of Glamorgan, 4½ miles from the city center, is one of Cardiff's most pleasant treats, the *Welsh Folk Museum.* Among the buildings in the 100-acre estate around this Tudor mansion are cottages, farmhouses, barns, a smithy, a tollhouse, a chapel, a tannery, a cockpit, a bakery, and a grocer's shop. Each was carefully taken apart where it once stood in some part of rural Wales; its stones, slates, and beams were numbered; then it was reconstructed in the sheep-grazed meadows of St. Fagan's. The furnishings and equipment are authentic, too, and you can wander through the houses to see how Welsh people lived through the centuries. Note the cozy box beds (resembling cupboards) and the love spoons that young men carved for their sweethearts: the more intricate the carving, the deeper the passion! The jolly, helpful attendants speak Welsh as well as English. One of the best exhibits is a series of six terraced cottages furnished in styles ranging from the 16th century to the 1980s, and there is a reconstructed Celtic village (from pre-Roman history) as well. St. Fagan's

also has a large museum, a buttery, and a restaurant. The museum hosts the annual *May Day* and *Christmas* fairs, the *Midsummer Festival,* and the *Harvest Festival* (see *Special Events*); at those times, staff members dress in period costumes. Closed Sundays November through March. Admission charge. St. Fagan's (phone: 569441). Take the No. 32 bus, which leaves from *Central Station* every hour on the hour.

Sources and Resources

TOURIST INFORMATION

In the Welsh language the name of the *Wales Tourist Board* is *Bwrdd Croeso Cymru*—literally translated as "Wales Welcome Board." It indicates how the Welsh feel about showing visitors their land. The board's office in Cardiff is in *Central Station* (off Wood St.; phone: 227281). Here visitors can get maps, guidebooks, leaflets, advice, and directions (closed Sundays). There is also a small office at the airport (no phone), which is open daily.

The *Wales Tourist Board* publishes an excellent, clear, and colorful map of Wales as well as *A Visitor's Guide to South Wales* by Roger Thomas (costing £2.95/about $4.50). Good inexpensive maps and guides to Cardiff are available from newsagents and bookshops like *W. H. Smith* and *Menzies* (both have branches throughout the city). *H. J. Lear Ltd., Dillons, Waterstone's,* and *Oriel* (see *Shopping* for all) carry a wide selection of books about Wales.

LOCAL COVERAGE The city's public relations office publishes brochures, books, and a monthly guide called *Events Sheet.* Two other helpful monthly booklets are *What's Happening* and the *Cardiff Bulletin.* Information about restaurants and entertainment is available from the *Wales Tourist Board.* Daily movie, theater, and concert listings are in the *Western Mail* (published Monday through Saturday mornings), *Wales on Sunday,* and the *South Wales Echo* (Cardiff's afternoon paper). Two free weekly papers are the *Cardiff Post* and the *Cardiff Independent,* which both come out on Thursdays or Fridays. Information on local events also is available on BBC's local radio service and the privately owned Red Dragon radio.

TELEPHONE The city code for Cardiff is 1222.

GETTING AROUND

AIRPORT *Cardiff—Wales Airport* (phone: 1446-711111), 10 miles west of the city center on A4226, has flights to Aberdeen, Belfast, the Channel Islands, Edinburgh, Glasgow, the Isle of Man, and Manchester, as well as international service to Amsterdam, Brussels, Dublin, and Paris.

BOAT From mid-May to October, the *Waverley,* the world's last seagoing paddle steamer, and the *Balmoral* run short sightseeing cruises along the South Wales coast and across to Bristol, north Devon, and Somerset. For information, contact the tourist office (see above) or *Waverley Excursions* (phone: 1446-720656). Cruises depart from the end of *Penarth Pier.*

BUS Cardiff is a walker's city, but there's a bus network that operates until late at night. *Cardiff Buses* (phone: 396521) runs a good variety of tours in summer using open-top double-decker buses, starting from Greyfriars Road. An information kiosk is in the bus station. Coaches traveling to points outside of town are operated by *Red and White Bustler* and *National Welsh Companies* (phone: 371331); *National Express* offers national service (phone: 344751); each line leaves from *Central Station* (off Wood St.).

CAR RENTAL Most major national and international firms have offices in Cardiff: *Hertz* (9 Central Sq.; phone: 224548; and *Cardiff-Wales Airport;* phone: 1446-711722); *Avis* (14-22 Tudor St.; and the airport; phone for both: 342111); and *Europcar* (1-11 Byron St.; phone: 497110; and *Cardiff-Wales Airport;* phone: 1446-711924).

TAXI Cabs (*thacsis*) don't cruise as a rule. The *Wales Tourist Board* (see above) has a good taxi list, and there are plenty of firms listed in the yellow pages. *Amber Cars* (phone: 378111 or 555555), *Castle Cabs* (phone: 394929), *City Centre Cars* (phone: 488888), and *Metro Cabs* (phone: 464646) are among those offering 24-hour service. There are cab ranks at *Central Station* and the Friary.

TRAIN There is good rail service to the suburbs, outlying towns, valleys, and villages, as well as fast *InterCity* service. London is an hour and 50 minutes away. *Valley Line* local trains run from both *Central* and *Queen Street Stations.* A direct line links Cardiff to Bangor in North Wales, which allows speedy access to Snowdonia. For information about *British Rail,* call 228000.

SPECIAL EVENTS

Cardiff's *Welsh Folk Museum* (see *Extra Special*) hosts the annual *May Day Fair,* which includes crafts, folk dancing, a Maypole dance, and farming exhibitions—held 4 miles from the city center. The museum also hosts a *Midsummer Festival* in late June, a *Harvest Festival* in late September, and a *Christmas Fair* in mid-December. The key summer classical events are the *Cardiff Singer of the World Competition,* held in June (odd-numbered years only), the *Lower Machen Festival,* a chamber music festival in late June, and the *Welsh Proms* in late July. The *Cardiff Summer Festival,* held in July and August, is now in its eighth year. Street celebrations, parades, and artistic events mark the event. The *Cardiff Festival of Classical Music and Literature* convenes for three weeks from mid-September into October. The festival now ties in with the *Welsh National Opera* season, which usually starts in October.

SHOPPING

The Welsh capital offers a wide range of goods, expensive and bargain, in big stores, little stores, and friendly boutiques. The main shopping streets are Queen Street, Working Street, the Hayes, and St. Mary Street, nearly all of them pedestrian malls and well signposted. In addition to the standard British shopping hours (see GETTING READY TO GO), some supermarkets stay open weekdays until 9 PM. The three major bookstores are *H. J. Lear Ltd.,* at two locations (13-17 *Royal Arcade* and 37 St. Mary St.; phone for both: 395036), which is particularly good for maps and guidebooks of the area; and *Waterstone's* (the Hayes; phone: 665606) and *Dillons* (in St. David's Link; phone: 222723). *St. David's Centre* and the *Capital Centre* are huge, modern malls with branches of the major chain stores, boutiques, and supermarkets (including *Marks & Spencer* and *Debenham's*). Both are particularly lively at lunchtime. By contrast, the city's famous shopping arcades (Dominion, Queen Street, Castle, Morgan, Royal, and Oxford) contain smaller specialty shops, many selling Welsh craftwork—woolen products, beautiful bedspreads, flannel, pottery, and woodwork. There's a smaller, fast-developing shopping area out near Roath, on Wellfield Road, with a number of specialty shops and health food restaurants.

Be sure to take your passport when you shop, and always inquire about the Value Added Tax (VAT) refund application forms when your total purchases in a store are over £50 (about $75). The VAT is a surcharge payable at the sales counter, but foreign customers usually will be reimbursed for it at home (for more information see GETTING READY TO GO).

Castle Welsh Crafts and Woollens Designer fashions, plus traditional quality woolens. 1 Castle St. (phone: 343038).

Central Market All the bustle, noise, and color of Wales, with a wide range of goods and accents can be found at this excellent indoor market. Welsh lamb is a specialty, as is *bara brith,* a kind of fruit bread. And try some "laverbread," a Welsh delicacy. It's a thick black seaweed, something of an acquired taste, but locals say it's delicious with ham or bacon. Cockles, another Welsh favorite, are available here. Closed Wednesdays and Sundays. Enter from St. Mary St. or the Hayes.

David Morgan Founded by entrepreneur David Morgan, it's the biggest independently owned department store in Wales, and the building is now listed as a historic site. The Hayes (phone: 221011).

Howells of Cardiff One of the city's major department stores, it's got almost everything, including a good range of glassware, china, and gifts. Also a savvy delicatessen and restaurant. St. Mary St. (phone: 231055).

Jacob's Antiques Market Crafts and antiques are sold here Thursdays and Saturdays. W. Canal Wharf (phone: 390939).

Old Library Arts Centre A wonderful collection of ceramics, textiles, and jewelry crowds this shop, owned and operated by the *Makers Guild of Wales.* The Hayes (phone: 342015).

Oriel With a focus on Welsh culture, this shop offers books on Wales (some in Welsh), locally made crafts, and recordings of traditional music; there also are occasional poetry readings. The Friary (phone: 395548).

Things Welsh Quality pottery, crafts, woolens, metalwork—including Welsh gold. 3-7 *Duke St. Arcade* (phone: 233445).

Wally's Delicatessen A well-stocked deli counter at the back (Belgian pâté is a specialty), plus shelves loaded with Oriental delicacies, herbs, whole grains, and wines. 46 *Royal Arcade* (phone: 229265).

SPORTS

Visitors are welcome to use the wide range of sporting facilities at *Blackweir Park* (North Rd.; phone: 226552), *Western Leisure Centre* (Caerau La.; phone: 593592), *Fairwater Leisure Centre* (Waterhall Rd.; phone: 552210), *Llanishen Leisure Centre* (Ty Glas Ave.; phone: 762411), and *Pentwyn Leisure Centre* (Bryn Celyn Rd.; phone: 593592). There are also several good leisure centers in the nearby suburbs; for information, contact the *Cardiff City Council* (phone: 751235).

BOWLING There's a large bowling alley with 40 lanes (featuring computerized scoring) at *Superbowl* (376 Newport Rd.; phone: 461666).

HOCKEY The Cardiff *Devils,* one of the top teams in Britain, takes to the ice at *Wales National Ice Rink* (Hayes Bridge Rd.; phone: 383451).

ICE SKATING Available at *Wales National Ice Rink* (see above).

RUGBY The immensely popular *Cardiff Rugby Club* plays at the *Cardiff Arms Park National Rugby Stadium* (phone: 390111) on the right bank of the Taff River.

SOCCER League and international matches in football (soccer) are held at *Ninian Park* (Slope Rd.; phone: 398636).

SWIMMING Go to the *Wales Empire Pool* (Wood St.; phone: 382296), where you also can have a Turkish bath and sauna.

THEATER

During the last decade, Cardiff has made a name for itself as a leader of avant-garde theater and dance productions that draw considerable talent from elsewhere in Britain, including London.

CENTER STAGE

New Theatre Drama, opera, concerts, and ballet are staged at this large 1,140-seat theater. Major touring companies, including the

Royal Shakespeare Company and the *National Theatre Company,* play here; at *Christmas,* there is also a family pantomime. Park Pl. (phone: 394844).

In addition, the *Sherman* (on Senghennydd Rd.; phone: 230451) is a modern theater with two stages that puts on plays by major professional groups and sometimes by local amateur groups; it is also home to the *Sherman Theatre Company,* Cardiff's excellent repertory group. The *Sherman*'s smaller stage is known for its fringe productions. The *Chapter Arts Centre* (on Market Rd.; phone: 399666) features regular theater productions; there's also a small restaurant and two cinemas on the premises that present a wide range of foreign films. *Moving Being* (phone: 228741), Wales's leading experimental theater group, appears in a variety of venues throughout Cardiff and Wales. Show schedules can be found in the local papers. The *Welsh College of Music and Drama* (*Castle Grounds,* Cathays; phone: 372175) presents some impressive student productions. For recorded information about both theatrical and music events, contact *Cardiff Arts Marketing* (phone: 236244).

MUSIC

"Praise the Lord—we are a musical nation," one of Dylan Thomas's characters said. And Cardiff does its best to live up to that with a regular program of concerts. *St. David's Hall* (Working St.; phone: 371236), a 2,000-seat national concert and conference center, presents a variety of music, including classical, jazz, rock, and folk. Lunchtime concerts can be heard here, in *City Hall,* and at the *BBC Wales* concert hall in Llandaff. The recently opened *Cardiff International Arena* (Mary Ann St.; phone: 224488) seats up to 5,500 and hosts a variety of events, including pop and rock concerts. The *Cardiff Male Choir,* formed in 1898 and an impressive example of Wales's famous singing heritage, can be heard in concert or during rehearsal on Wednesdays and Fridays between 7:30 and 9:30 PM (at the *Conway Road Methodist Church;* Conway Rd.; phone: 625051 or 616617); if you want to sit in on a rehearsal, be sure to call ahead. The *New Theatre* (see *Theater* above) is the home of the *Welsh National Opera* (phone: 464666; 236244 for recorded information), which has earned a high reputation for its quality productions, both around Britain and abroad. Cardiff's *New Arts Consort* (phone: 497157) is a contemporary music group founded by composer Charles Barber.

NIGHTCLUBS AND NIGHTLIFE

Cardiffians take their evening pleasure with some enthusiasm. They enjoy going out to dinner, lingering quite a long time over the meal. And they like propping up a bar, talking, and listening to music. You'll find it easy to join them in any of these activities. Cardiff also has a number of nightclubs; these include *Philharmonic/Lloyd's* (76 St. Mary St.; phone: 230678), with a pub upstairs and a nightclub downstairs; *Coco Savannah's* (Greyfriars Rd.; phone: 377014); and *Jackson's* (Westgate St.; phone: 390851). *Sam's Bar* (63 St. Mary St.; phone: 345189) has live music—mostly rhythm and blues, rock 'n' roll, and heavy metal—every evening except Wednesdays, which is comedy night. The best jazz venue in town is the *Four Bars Inn* (Castle St.; phone: 374962), which features local and international performers in the upstairs room. Welsh bands play most nights at *Club Ifor Bach* (11 Womanby St.; phone: 232199). For the wheelers and dealers, there's gambling at *Les Croupiers* (32 St. Mary St.; phone: 382810). You must be 18 or older to gamble; bring your passport to the casino.

Best in Town

CHECKING IN

Wales always has been popular with travelers, and some of its hotels are justly famous. Moreover, standards have improved considerably in recent years. If you want the tops in comfort and class in Cardiff you'll have to pay a lot, but in the more modest places you will find considerable comfort, excellent home-cooked food, a warm welcome, and a bill that doesn't make you pale. Consult the tourist board (see *Tourist Information,* above), which has lists of recommended and inspected hotels. Most of Cardiff's major hotels have complete facilities for the business traveler. Those hotels listed below as having "business services" usually offer such conveniences as a concierge, meeting rooms, photocopiers, computers, translation services, and express checkout, among others. Call the hotel for additional information. A double room (with private bath, TV set, phone, and breakfast, unless otherwise noted) in a hotel in the expensive category will cost $100 or more per night; in the moderate, $60 to $100; and in the inexpensive, less than $60. All telephone numbers are in the 1222 city code unless otherwise indicated.

EXPENSIVE

Angel Built over 250 years ago, Cardiff's oldest and one of its most attractive hotels offers splendid views of a nearby castle from the third floor guestrooms. There are 91 rooms, a gym with a sauna and a solarium in the basement, and a good restaurant. Business services are available. Castle St. (phone: 232633; fax: 396212).

Cardiff International This neighbor of the *World Trade Centre* treats its guests with a friendly, helpful attitude that makes staying in one of the 143 guestrooms a pleasure. Traditional fare is served in the restaurant. Business services are available. Mary Ann St. (phone: 341441; 800-528-1234; fax: 223742).

Celtic Bay A 19th-century, brick docklands warehouse was carefully restored and converted into this attractive, modern establishment with vaulted ceilings, mahogany furniture, and a handsome display of model sailing ships. In addition to the 64 guestrooms, there is a health club, a restaurant, a cocktail bar, and business services. No credit cards accepted. Schooner Way, Cardiff Bay (phone: 465888; fax: 481491).

Celtic Manor Although this 19th-century manor house, comprised of 17 rooms and a 58-room annex, has a commercial atmosphere, special features are large bedrooms, views over Chepstow, flower-filled gardens, and a wood-paneled restaurant. Facilities also include a sauna, a gym, a solarium, an 18-hole golf course, and business services. 12 miles outside Cardiff, off M4. Coldra Woods, Newport (phone: 633-413000; fax: 633-412910).

Churchill About 2 miles from the city center, this Victorian hotel has lovely views of *Llandaff Fields.* There are 35 rooms and a restaurant, and parking and business services are available. Cardiff Rd., Llandaff (phone: 562372; fax: 568347).

Egerton Grey This small Victorian rectory with 10 guestrooms was restored in a sumptuous fashion, with oak and mahogany paneling, antique furniture, and Oriental rugs. Four-poster beds adorn some of the rooms. The house stands on seven acres, and has fine sea views, tennis courts, and a croquet lawn. Inside, the restaurant serves English dishes, and is considered by many to be the finest in South Wales. Off A4050, 10 miles from Cardiff, near the airport, Porthkerry (phone: 1446-711666; 800-435-4504; fax: 1446-711690).

Marriott This establishment boasts 182 rooms and all the modern conveniences, including a pool, gym, sauna, spa bath, restaurant, piano bar, and business services. Children under 19 can stay without charge in their parents' room. Mill La. (phone: 399944; 800-228-9290; fax: 395578).

Park In the center and considered the best in town, with a gracious, spacious air and attentive staff. There are 119 large, attractively decorated rooms and two good restaurants—the *Caernarfon Room* and the *Theatre Garden.* Parking and business services are available. Park Pl. (phone: 383471; fax: 399309).

MODERATE

Beverley Comfortable and friendly, this recently refurbished property has 18 rooms, a good restaurant, and a popular pub. 75 Cathedral Rd. (phone: 236233; fax: 221432).

Hayes Court Representative of a number of good, clean, comfortable, and rather homey hotels, not far from the city center, this place has 45 guestrooms, a sauna, and a restaurant. 154-164 Cathedral Rd. (phone: 394218; fax: 221790).

Phoenix and Cedars In a pleasant, quiet suburb, this comfortable place has 50 rooms and a restaurant. 199 Fidlas Rd., Llanishen (phone: 764615; fax: 747812).

INEXPENSIVE

Llanerch Vineyard A tiny bed and breakfast place (only three rooms) overlooking Wales's largest vineyard and surrounded by 10 acres of lakes and woodland. There's a coffee shop that serves lunch. A mile from Junction 34 on M4, 15 minutes from Cardiff. Hensol, Pendoylan (phone: 1443-225877; fax: 1443-225546).

Preste Gaarden Once the *Norwegian Consulate,* this finely restored, 10-room Victorian villa is in the conservation district of Pontcanna, a mile from the city center. No restaurant. 181 Cathedral Rd. (phone: 228607).

Town House Here is a bed and breakfast establishment set in a Victorian villa and run by a charming American couple. The six guestrooms are nicely decorated and feature the usual amenities, and the food is good and plentiful (there is no restaurant). 70 Cathedral Rd. (phone: 239399; fax: 223214).

EATING OUT

Cardiff is a cosmopolitan city, and this is reflected in its restaurants. While you're here, though, be sure to try local specialties, such as Welsh lamb. Pluck up courage and taste "laverbread"—remember, it's not bread but seaweed. Also, don't miss fresh Welsh salmon or "sewin," a kind of trout. For starters, you'll find "cawl" (a thick vegetable, leek, and lamb soup) delicious. And to round off a meal, homemade pies and fruit tarts are usually good. Eating out in Cardiff is less expensive than in London. Expect to pay $70 or more for dinner for two, including wine and tips, in places listed as expensive; $45 to $65 in moderate restaurants; and less than $40 in inexpensive ones. All restaurants listed below serve lunch and dinner unless otherwise noted. All telephone numbers are in the 1222 city code unless otherwise indicated.

EXPENSIVE

Blas ar Gymru This cozy eatery, whose name means "Taste of Wales," serves up generous helpings of good, wholesome, traditional Welsh dishes like cawl (a thick vegetable, leek, and lamb soup) and Gower cockle and bacon pie, all washed down with local wine or mead. Closed Saturday lunch and Sundays. Reservations advised. Major credit cards accepted. 48 Crwys Rd. (phone: 382132).

Le Cassoulet As its name suggests, the specialty of the house is cassoulet, a filling casserole of beans, sausage, and pork that is a traditional dish of southwestern France. This small, intimate bistro produces such succulent French fare that you might not notice that you're not sitting near the Left Bank. Closed Sundays and Mondays. Reservations advised. Major credit cards accepted. 5 Romilly Crescent (phone: 221905).

Chikakos Opposite the *Marriott* hotel, Cardiff's first Japanese restaurant opened in response to the growing Japanese community here. Though the entranceway is a bit seedy, don't let that put you off: Inside, the place has a fun atmosphere. One of the dining rooms is decorated in traditional Japanese style, with low tables and cushions for kneeling; the other has Western-style seating. The menu emphasizes fresh seafood, including sushi, and you can prepare your meal yourself at the table if you like. Open daily. Reservations advised. Major credit cards accepted. 10-11 Mill La. (phone: 665279).

Yr Ystafell Gymraeg The name (never mind how to pronounce it) means "the Welsh Room," and not surprisingly, the restaurant is furnished with Welsh antiques. You'll find many enjoyable native dishes here: Choose from cockles, laverbread, and lamb. The steak and kidney pie is lovely, and so is the cawl. Closed Saturday lunch and Sundays. Reservations advised. Major credit cards accepted. 74 Whitchurch Rd., Gabalfa (phone: 342317).

MODERATE

Armless Dragon Bright and cheery, with a number of surprising specialties, including shark curry, laverbread balls, wild rabbit, and rack of Welsh lamb. Closed Saturday lunch, Sundays, and Mondays. Reservations advised. Major credit cards accepted. 99 Wyverne Rd., Cathays (phone: 382357).

Mulligans Everything from hearty fish-and-chips to delicate lobster is prepared with a master hand in this cheerful establishment. Be prepared to join the queue, as this place is a local favorite. Open daily. Reservations advised. Visa accepted. Stalling Down, Cowbridge (phone: 1446-772221).

Porto's This Portuguese establishment serves first-rate dishes and local wines. Open daily. Reservations advised. Major credit cards accepted. St. Mary St. (phone: 220060).

Riverside Cantonese A cut above the average Chinese restaurant, it offers a great variety of dishes, cooked by talented hands. It also serves an interesting Chinese beer. Open daily. Reservations advised. Major credit cards accepted. 44 Tudor St., Riverside (phone: 372163).

Savastano's The reason Jimmy Savastano's place is usually busy, and the customers keep coming back, is because it provides a happy, delicious, and informal eating experience. Italian fare is the specialty; the veal dishes are especially good. Open daily. Reservations advised. Major credit cards accepted. 302 North Rd., Gabalfa (phone: 621018).

Thai House Praised by many locals for serving the best food in town, this is also the only Thai establishment in the area. Dishes such as emperor prawns with spicy pears in a coconut and lime sauce, cod wrapped in a banana leaf soaked in coconut milk, and bananas poached in honey are beautifully prepared. Closed Sundays. Reservations advised. Major credit cards accepted. 23 High St. (phone: 387404).

INEXPENSIVE

Arnolds Americans say that this hamburger joint is as good as the best back home. There's a bright and breezy atmosphere, with desserts like apple pie, colossal ice cream dishes, and cheesecake. Open daily for dinner only. Reservations unnecessary. Visa accepted. 167 Albany Rd. (phone: 499893).

Henry's Café Bar For a pre-theater bite or a filling breakfast, this brash, cheerful place proffers ample, tasty fare. Open daily. Reservations unnecessary. Visa accepted. 8-16 Park Chambers, Park Pl. (phone: 224139).

Louis Just the place for a Welsh afternoon tea, with friendly waitresses and plenty of room. It serves traditional meals from a large menu. Closed Sundays. Reservations advised. No credit cards accepted. 32 St. Mary St. (phone: 225722).

Peppermint Lounge Where you go when you have the munchies, it features homemade burgers and a full range of drinks. Open daily. Reservations advised. No credit cards accepted. 34 Woodville Rd. (phone: 374403).

Tandoori Mahal Typical of the many Indian eateries in Cardiff, it offers authentic tandoori (clay oven) cooking served by a friendly staff. Open daily. Reservations unnecessary. Major credit cards accepted. 98 Albany Rd., Roath Park (phone: 491500).

Truffles Offered here is a conservative menu of steaks, fish, and the like, with a tearoom downstairs. Closed Sundays. Reservations unnecessary. No credit cards accepted. 3 Church St. (phone: 344958).

Zio Pin This lively Italian restaurant serves pizza, homemade pasta, and calzones. Closed Sundays. Reservations advised. Major credit cards accepted. There are several locations throughout the city, including 74 Albany Rd. (phone: 485673), 126a Cowbridge Rd. E. (phone: 220269), 9 Park La. (phone: 340397), and The Esplanade, Penarth (phone: 703428).

SHARING A PINT

Cardiff has pubs for all tastes—quiet, noisy, intimate, brash. And it has its own beer, made at Brain's brewery (that's the malty smell in the air on St. Mary Street!). The *Park Vault,* the club-like back bar in the *Park* hotel (see

Checking In), is busy at lunchtime and in the early evening. The *Market Tavern* (Trinity St.; phone: 224482) and the *Owain Glyndwr* (St. John's Sq.; phone: 221980) are typical, large, friendly Cardiff pubs, as is the *Butcher's Arms* (on High St., Llandaff; phone: 561898). The *Conway* (Conway Rd.; phone: 232797) is a favorite haunt of young Welsh-speaking people. Out at St. Fagan's is the elegant *Plymouth Arms* (phone: 569130), where you can eat well, too. The *Captain's Wife* (Beach Rd., Swanbridge, Sully; phone: 530066) is a popular drinking and eating spot on the coast; it's great for summer evenings.

Chester

The red sandstone walls surrounding the old city of Chester are the only city walls in Britain to have come down to the 20th century very nearly intact. For the last three centuries they have been a pleasant place to walk to get a better view of one of the most medieval-looking British cities. Before that, however, these walls did their share of preserving it. Though it's now been more than 300 years since Chester's streets have seen any fighting, the walls are a reminder that it has been a military city for all its 19 centuries of existence.

The original town—called Deva or Castra Legionis, meaning "fortress of the legions"—was laid out by the battle-tested veterans of the 20th Roman Legion when Britain became the newest province of the empire only decades after the Crucifixion. Centuries after the Romans had abandoned Britain, Hugh Lupus suppressed the local tribes, thus gaining the Earldom of Chester (a title held ever since by the monarch's eldest son). He built the castle at Chester from which Edward I set out to crush the rebellious Welsh, binding them into submission in the 13th century with a chain of coastal fortresses from Flint to Caernarfon. Later still, Chester's position astride the route to Ireland was of strategic importance to Charles I, who expected reinforcements from his armies there during the mid-17th-century Civil War.

Since Roman times, there have been soldiers in Chester. Today it is the home of the First Battalion, the King's Regiment, and the permanent depot of its own Cheshire Regiment, formed three centuries ago. This presence has stamped itself firmly on the city. The four main streets follow the line of the main roadways laid out inside the Roman fort almost 2,000 years ago, and the *Church of St. Peter* is built on the foundations of the Roman headquarters and the residence of the military commander. Even the Rows, Chester's aboveground shopping walkways, may owe their origins to the city's military past. According to one of the more convincing theories, the ruins of the buildings left by the Romans were so massive that their Saxon successors preferred to build on top and in front of them rather than to remove the stonework. The surviving rows follow the four main streets that existed within the Roman fortress, and even the one exception, a now-vanished set of rows down Lower Bridge Street, lies along the road from the fort to the Dee crossing—which also would have been lined with Roman buildings.

Chester's military history has left a practical legacy. Before mechanization, an army marched on its feet—despite what Napoleon might have said—and this is a city designed as much for today's pedestrian as it was for yesterday's infantryman. The almost-complete circuit of the city walls, built on the north and east over the original Roman ramparts but extended to the south and west to take the city's defenses closer to the river, links with the Rows to form a network of walkways completely free from the traffic below. In addition, the four main city streets have been partially turned into a pedestrian area, so that traffic levels within the walls are low enough to give a feeling of the city before the coming of the automobile.

One reason Chester still possesses so many links with the past is that it has been in decline, in a sense, ever since the Middle Ages. Originally a major port, the silting-up of the Dee eventually killed the seaborne trade with Ireland and America. In the end, shipping moved to Liverpool (at the time an obscure fishing village) on the nearby river Mersey, and with it went the industrialization and urbanization that would have obliterated the old Chester.

Instead, the city found a new role as a prosperous market town, a trading center between northwest England and North Wales, and a destination for one and a half million tourists a year who are treated to the sight of as picturesque a town as any in old England. Yet in spite of the abundance of black and white half-timbering, Chester's buildings are largely the work of Victorian restorers and rebuilders. Fortunately, they were enthralled by the traditional Cheshire "magpie" decoration, and their revival designs give the city a remarkable unity of style. Among the Georgian brick and Victorian plaster are genuine ancient houses such as the *Leche House* (now a shop) and *Bishop Lloyd's House,* dating from the 16th and early 17th centuries. It's entirely typical of Chester that the real and the reproduction are intermingled and, sometimes, virtually indistinguishable.

Chester At-a-Glance

SEEING THE CITY

In a city as tightly packed as Chester, there's no single spot for a panoramic vista. The Grosvenor Bridge across the Dee, the longest single masonry arch in the world when it was completed in 1832, gives a good view of the racecourse, the river, and the city skyline behind the western ramparts of the city walls. But for a closer view of the city's bustle, pick a spot on the Rows overlooking Chester Cross, where you can lean on the old balustrades and watch the world go by. Another means of seeing the city is by boat (see *Sightseeing Tours,* below).

SPECIAL PLACES

Chester's compact layout, not to mention its tougher-than-average parking problems, make it an ideal city to explore on foot. Pubs, restaurants, museums, and shops are all within a few minutes' walk of one another. For the more energetic, the two-mile circuit of the city walls (see *Extra Special*) is a useful link to the cathedral and the river, where tree-lined walks and benches make an ideal spot to end a walking tour.

THE ROWS Chester's above-pavement-level pedestrian shopping "streets" were built in the Middle Ages over the main roads of the original Roman fortress.

Bridge Street and Eastgate Street Rows have the most cosmopolitan shops, but Watergate Street Row has the strongest flavor of the past, with its antiques and curio shops and magnificent old houses such as the *Leche House.* It was built in the mid-16th century as the town residence of the Leche family, so called because they were originally leeches (as surgeons were called then) to King Edward III in the 1300s. Another magnificent house on Watergate Street Row is *Bishop Lloyd's House,* built in the late 16th and early 17th centuries for the Bishop of Chester. The house contains elaborate carvings (including the three-legged crest of the Isle of Man) and broad windows, a local fashion that turns up again in the *Falcon Inn* and the *Bear and Billet* pub on Lower Bridge Street, where the original Rows have all but vanished. *Leche House* is now an antiques shop; visits to *Bishop Lloyd's House* must be arranged in advance by contacting the *Tourist Information Centre* (see *Tourist Information*).

CATHEDRAL Not originally a cathedral at all, this was founded in 1093 by Hugh Lupus, the Norman Earl of Chester and alleged nephew of William the Conqueror, as the *Benedictine Abbey of St. Werburgh.* The abbey was broken up in 1540 when Henry VIII dissolved England's monasteries, and the following year the church became the cathedral of the new diocese of Chester. You can still see the monks' dining room, the wonderful choir stalls with their intricate woodcarvings of men and fabulous beasts, the cloisters where they studied, and part of the shrine to St. Werburgh (an Anglo-Saxon abbess who died ca. AD 700). In the cloisters is an audiovisual show that provides a half-hour introduction to the cathedral, plus a bookshop and the original 13th-century refectory, which offers tea, coffee, light refreshments, and lunch. Outside is the bell tower; in 1975, when it was erected, it was the first separate bell tower to be added to an English cathedral in 500 years. The cathedral celebrated its 900th anniversary in 1993. St. Werburgh St. (phone: 324756).

CASTLE These colonnaded buildings at the city end of the Grosvenor Bridge don't look much like a castle today. The original Norman fortress overlooking the river and the Old Dee Bridge was transformed between 1788 and 1822 to house the *Assize Courts.* Behind the Georgian court building (now housing Chester's *Crown Courts*), the 750-year-old *Agricola Tower* is the only part of the medieval castle that survives. It can be viewed on request—ask at the *Cheshire Military Museum* (see *Museums,* below)—and the court buildings can be seen from the *Public Gallery* when the courts are in session. Castle St. (phone: 327617).

ABBEY SQUARE The low arch of the 14th-century *Abbey Gateway,* where the *Chester Miracle Plays* were performed in the Middle Ages, is on the eastern side of Town Hall Square. Through the gateway is Abbey Square, a peaceful oasis of cobblestones and Georgian houses. From the opposite corner of the square, Abbey Street leads to *Kaleyards Gate,* a gap in the city walls that once gave access to the abbot's private garden; just south of the gate are parts of the original Roman wall.

OLD DEE BRIDGE Until the opening of the Grosvenor Bridge 160 years ago, all traffic across the river had to use this narrow medieval bridge, built on the site of the Roman crossing more than seven centuries ago. It leads from the city to the old suburb of Handbridge, called Treboeth, or literally, "Burned Town" by the Welsh, who burned it more than once during cross-border raids before they were subdued in the 13th century.

RIVER DEE AND THE GROVES The name comes from that given by the Romans to both town and river—Deva. Below the city walls is the Groves, Chester's tree-lined riverside promenade, with seats used by fishermen, by audiences for the Sunday brass band concerts (held May through September), and by picnickers watching the boats. (Unfortunately, the charm of this beautiful spot is marred by an amusement/games arcade.) Motorboats, pedal boats, and rowing skiffs can be rented from *Bramston Launches* (11 The Groves; phone: 325294); however, watch out for the weir just above the Old Dee Bridge. Or you can book a trip on one of the sightseeing cruises going upriver to Heronbridge and the tranquil, charming village of Eccleston. Evening musical cruises (featuring discos, live jazz, and parties) are also available. The cruises, which depart from the *Boating Station* (Souters La., The Groves), are operated by *Bithell Boats Ltd.* (phone: 325394). Return by boat, by city bus from Eccleston, or on foot along the riverbank path through the Meadows on the Handbridge side. Another company that offers cruises is *Bramston Launches* (see above).

CHESTER ZOO On the outskirts of Chester is one of Britain's largest and most comprehensive zoos, with guided tours, an overhead railway, restaurants, and a shop. A farm area is available to children for petting animals, and the zoo's newest addition is a free-flight aviary with dozens of bird species on view. Closed *Christmas.* Admission charge. Off A41 (phone: 380280).

AMPHITHEATER On Vicar's Lane, opposite the *Chester Visitor Centre,* stands the northern half of the Roman amphitheater, the largest yet uncovered in Britain, and remarkably well preserved. The oval arena measures approximately 64 by 54 yards and once held about 7,000 people. A complete excavation of the site is being planned for the future. Open daily. No admission charge.

ST. JOHN'S CHURCH AND RUINS To the east of the amphitheater is the *Church of St. John the Baptist.* From 1075 to 1102 it was Chester's cathedral, and in 1975 it celebrated its 900th anniversary. Embedded in its ancient walls is a coffin. The ruins of the 12th-century choir are among the finest examples of Norman architecture in Europe. The church is still used for Anglican services, as well as for concerts. The summer lunchtime programs on Wednesdays at 1 PM are especially popular (light refreshments are available if you don't want to bring your own). Opening times vary. For information, contact Rev. Lunt (phone: 326357 or 323657).

EXTRA SPECIAL

Chester's walls are nearly complete, which makes them unique in Britain, and a first class way to explore the city. Start by climbing to the top of the *Eastgate* arch, crowned by the much-photographed clock commemorating Queen Victoria's *Diamond Jubilee* in 1897 and symbolizing Chester to expatriates all over the world. On a clear day, you can see the brooding Welsh hills on the horizon to the west. Follow the wall southward, and near the modern *Newgate* arch you'll see the foundations of one of the corner towers of the original Roman fort. Across Vicar's Lane is the excavated half of the amphitheater the Romans used for gladiatorial contests. Next to the *Newgate* arch, the old *Wolfe* (or *Wolfeld*) *Gate* gives an idea of just how narrow the Roman and medieval city gates must have been. Across the road are the *Roman Gardens,* where columns and stones discovered nearby have been rebuilt, along with a Roman "central heating system." Beyond the *Newgate* arch are six short flights of steps—the Wishing Steps. According to tradition, if you make a wish, run from the bottom to the top, then down and back again without drawing breath, your wish will come true—if you survive.

As the walls swing west, there's a good view of the river and the old bridge. After crossing the *Bridgegate* arch, rebuilt and widened like the other city gates in the 18th century, you come to the only gap in the walls, beside *County Hall.* Look for the signposts on the other side of the hall and rejoin the ramparts as they turn north beside the *Chester Castle.* You pass the racecourse on the Roodee—a recreation area first used for racing in 1540, making the *Chester Races* the oldest in the country (see *Special Events*)—and the *Watergate* arch before reaching the old *Bonewaldesthorne's Tower* in the northwestern corner of the defenses and the *Water Tower* at the end of a spur wall. The *Water Tower* is closed weekdays and November through March. One admission charge for both the *Water Tower* and *King Charles's Tower* (see below).

The northern face of the walls is the most impressive of all, since the original ditch that ran full circuit was widened and deepened here in the 18th century as part of Chester's canal. You'll pass the *Goblin Tower,* nicknamed "Pemberton's Parlour" after a rope maker who sat in comfort to watch his workers toiling below, then, close to the *Northgate,* a bastion called *Morgan's Mount,* after the commander of a royalist battery placed here in the Civil War siege of 1645. If you look out over the parapet, you'll see the precarious Bridge of Sighs spanning the giddy drop to the canal.

Finally, the northeastern corner of the walls is crowned by *King Charles's Tower,* built on the site of the original Roman tower. Here Charles I is supposed to have stood while his army was crushed on the field of Rowton

Moor in September 1645. He fled afterward, begging the city to hold out for 10 more days. When Chester finally surrendered to Parliament—five months later—its citizens were ill and starving, but its walls still held the enemy at bay. The building now contains displays concerning the English Civil War and the siege of Chester. The tower is closed weekdays and November through March (phone: 318780). Walk around to the back of the cathedral to return to your starting point.

Sources and Resources

TOURIST INFORMATION

Guides, lists of events, maps, and a monthly *What's On* bulletin are available at the *Tourist Information Centre* at the *Town Hall* (Northgate St.; phone: 317962 for general information; 313126 or 318356 for walking tours); it is closed Sundays November through April. The center also provides an accommodations bureau and booking service (phone: 313126). An exchange bureau and booking service are available at the *Chester Visitor Centre* (Vicars La.; phone: 351609; also see *Museums*); open daily. *Chester at Home,* a program where visitors can spend an evening in the home of a local resident, can be arranged by calling Len and Betty Holland (phone: 677644), Margaret Brockley (phone: 380749), or Jim and Rhona Read (phone: 151-339-6615 in Liverpool); these folks organize this friendly service at no charge. For more information write to Len Holland (5 Coopers Croft, *Deva Park,* Chester CH3 5XJ, England).

LOCAL COVERAGE Six newspapers report on town events: the *Chester Chronicle,* whose files include issues that give day-to-day coverage of the American Revolution, appears Fridays; the *Chester Herald and Post* on Tuesdays; and the *Evening Leader* and the *Standard* on weekdays. There also is coverage in the *Liverpool Daily Post* (mornings) and the *Liverpool Echo* (evenings).

In keeping with its old-fashioned medieval nature, Chester also has a town crier, who stands by Chester Cross to bring the citizens up to date on the day's events at noon and 3 PM Tuesdays through Saturdays May through September; it's a more atmospheric (if less practical) way to get the news.

TELEPHONE The city code for Chester is 1244.

GETTING AROUND

AIRPORT The nearest airports are *Manchester International Airport,* 40 minutes by car (phone: 161-489-3000 for general information; 318356 for coach link to Chester); and *Liverpool Airport* (phone: 151-486-8877).

BUS *Chester City Transport Ltd.* (phone: 347452) operates services inside the city area; the fare ranges from 30p (about 45¢) to 75p (about $1.10), depending on how far you're going. Contact one of the city's information centers for details. *Crosville Motor Services,* with an inquiry office (phone: 381515) at the *Delamere Street* bus station, operates services outside the city.

CAR RENTAL A car is unnecessary to explore Chester itself; however, for travel outside the city, it makes sense to have one. There are offices of *Avis* (128 Brook St.; phone: 311463); *Budget* (Lower Bridge St.; phone: 313431); and *Hertz* (Trafford St.; phone: 374705).

SIGHTSEEING TOURS A variety of coach excursions offer sightseeing tours as far as North Wales and throughout the northwest of England. The largest operator is *Lofty's Tours Ltd.* (phone: 300469). Excursions can be booked at the *Tourist Information Centre* and at the *Chester Visitor Centre* (see above). A Pastfinder tour leaves *Town Hall* twice daily (except Sundays January through April); the tour allows visitors to discover where the 20th Roman Legion (which defeated Queen Boadicea) built their fortress and where Hugh Lupus, the bloodthirsty nephew of William the Conqueror, built a stronghold; in the summer, a Ghosthunter Trail and an Ale Trail also can be explored. Another tour puts you on Roman Wall patrol with a Roman legionary, Caius Julius Quartus, whose tombstone can be seen in the local *Grosvenor Museum* (see *Museums*). Full details of walking tours are available from the *Tourist Information Centre* (see above). Canal cruises of various lengths, some including meals, leave daily from the *Mill* hotel (Milton St.; phone: 350035); in the summer, make reservations well in advance.

TAXI Chester's complex parking arrangements make cabs a good idea in the city area. Cab ranks are in front of the *Town Hall* and outside the railway station on City Road. You can flag down the licensed black taxicabs anywhere you see them, or you can book cabs in advance from *Chester Radio Taxis* (phone: 372372) or *Kingkab* (phone: 342248).

TRAIN Chester's station is on the north side of the city on Station Rd. (phone: 151-709-9696). Fast *InterCity* 125 trains connect Chester to London's *Euston Station* (travel time is about two hours and 45 minutes).

SPECIAL EVENTS

A week-long *Film Festival,* featuring both new and old movies, usually is held during March. For horse racing enthusiasts, the *Chester Races* are held May through September. Staged on the Roodee, once the site of a massive Roman harbor, they're the oldest races in the country. For information contact the manager, *Chester Race Co. Ltd.* (phone: 323170). In late May, *Beating Retreat,* a military ceremony with a display of massed bands, takes place on the castle grounds. The *Chester Sports and Leisure Festival,* with concerts, theater, dance, displays, and river and canal trips, takes place in *Grosvenor Park* in late June to early July. The nearby town of Llangollen, Wales, hosts the *International Musical Eisteddfod* (folk festival) early in July, attracting thousands of singers and folk dancers from all over the world (also see *Best Festivals* in DIVERSIONS). The *Chester Summer Music*

Festival, held during the last half of July, features a week of orchestral concerts, recitals, and choral works. The *Chester Fringe* runs for two to three weeks from late July to early August. The dramatic and comic presentations, held in various venues throughout the city, are modeled after the *Edinburgh Festival Fringe* and often feature the same performers. The *Chester Literature Festival,* featuring poetry and prose readings by prominent British writers, goes on for two weeks in late July and early August. For information about these and other events, contact the *Tourist Information Centre* (see *Tourist Information*).

MUSEUMS

Chester has several museums devoted to preserving and presenting its long history. Among them are the following:

BOAT MUSEUM Several miles north of Chester at the junction of the Shropshire Union and Manchester Ship Canals is Britain's largest floating collection of canal and river craft, featuring traditional canal narrowboats and demonstrations of 19th-century living and working conditions on the canals. The museum is easily accessible by train from the railway station or by the No. 3 bus. Closed Fridays November through March. Admission charge. Dockyard Rd., Ellesmere Port (phone: 51-355-5017).

CHESHIRE MILITARY MUSEUM Explore three centuries of the Cheshire Regiment (the Cheshire Yeomanry and others), including their service in America and India and the campaign under General Sir Charles James Napier, who annexed the Indian province of Sind for the British in 1843 and announced his success with the terse Latin *Peccavi,* meaning "I have sinned." Closed *Christmas.* Admission charge, which also includes admission to the *Agricola Tower. Chester Castle* (phone: 347203 or 327617).

CHESTER HERITAGE CENTRE On view here are a video show on the history of Chester, before and after photographs of the restoration of its buildings, and a changing exhibition on the city's heritage. It is also the starting point for a series of self-guided heritage walks around Chester. Open daily. Admission charge. *St. Michael's Church,* Bridge St. Row (phone: 317948).

CHESTER TOY AND DOLL MUSEUM A fascinating collection featuring 5,000 exhibits, including cars, airplanes, boats, games, and dolls. The toys date as far back as 1830. There is also a *Toy Shop* and a *Dolls Hospital* which restores teddy bears and dolls "to full health." Open daily. Admission charge. 13A Lower Bridge St. (phone: 346297).

CHESTER VISITOR CENTRE Here are video presentations of the city's 2,000-year history and a life-size reconstruction of an 1850s street scene, old shop and pub fronts transported from the Rows, and a coffee and lunch bar in an old oak-beamed school. Open daily. No admission charge. Vicar's La. (phone: 318916).

DEVA ROMAN EXPERIENCE Chester's Roman history is explored in a museum housed in a building that also is the site of an ongoing archaeological dig. The archaeologists' findings are exhibited, as well as videos detailing the excavation process. The dig, run by the *Chester City Council,* is continuing indefinitely; if you're lucky, you may see people working in the site when you visit. Open daily. Admission charge. Commonhall St. (phone: 343407).

GROSVENOR MUSEUM The main museum is named after Hugh Lupus Grosvenor, first Duke of Westminster, who donated part of the site on which the museum was built in the 1880s. It contains many relics of Chester's Roman past, natural history exhibits, paintings, and silver. Particularly impressive are the period interiors from Stuart to Victorian times, complete with life-size models, and the *Roman Stones Gallery,* re-creating life in Chester some 1,500 years ago. The museum also has a wide variety of temporary exhibits. Open daily. No admission charge. Grosvenor St. (phone: 321616).

SHOPPING

Most of the best shops are along the elevated, two-tiered walkways of the Rows and the arcades leading off them, above the traffic and covered from the weather. (Godstall Lane, a narrow alley off Eastgate Row, is especially rewarding, with women's clothing shops and *Roberts' Specialty Tea and Coffee Shop,* which serves samples at outside tables.) Antiques shops and silversmiths are especially good. For centuries, Chester's silversmiths were so famous that the city had its own Assay Office on Goss Street where the Chester hallmark was stamped on their handiwork. Today you can buy fine gold, silver, and jewelry from specialists like *Boodle and Dunthorne* (near the *Grosvenor* hotel on Eastgate St.; phone: 326666) and *Lowe & Sons* (11 Bridge St. Row; phone: 325850). For antiques in the wider sense, try the shops down Watergate Row. Among them, *Erica and Hugo Harper* (at No. 27; phone: 323004) and *Chester Antiques* (at No. 49; phone: 316286) sell anything from a silver spoon to a full dinner service, from a delicate miniature to a Georgian table or Welsh dresser. Chester also has a fine variety of clothing shops, from expensive fashion stores to inexpensive boutiques. For standard shopping hours, see GETTING READY TO GO.

Be sure to take your passport when you shop, and always inquire about the Value Added Tax (VAT) refund application forms when your total purchases in a store are over £50 (about $75). The VAT is a surcharge payable at the sales counter, but foreign customers usually will be reimbursed for it at home (for more information see GETTING READY TO GO).

Adams Antiques Unusual cabinets, chandeliers, 18th- and 19th-century furniture, a wide selection of clocks, and objets d'art. 65 Watergate Row (phone: 319421).

Blakes An old family bake house, virtually unchanged since Victorian days. Shop early in the day, as the delicious homemade bread, cakes, and pies tend to sell out by mid-afternoon. Watergate Row (phone: 325933).

Brown's of Chester The city's premier department store, founded during the reign of the same George III who so enraged the American colonies. It's now owned by the Debenham chain, but much of the old ambience survives. Particularly good for women's clothes and perfume. Eastgate St. (phone: 350001).

The Cheese Shop A mouth-watering selection of English, Welsh, and continental cheeses, as well as a variety of locally made wines and preserves. Northgate St. (phone: 346240).

Chester Candle Shop Huge array of candle ware and gifts. Visitors can see carved candles in the making, and children can make candles under supervision. 75 Bridge St. Row (phone: 346011).

Dollectable Tiny, but packed with dollhouses, dolls, their clothes, and teddy bears. Open Saturdays only, although appointments for other times can be made by calling ahead. 53 Lower Bridge St. (phone: 344888).

Three Kings Studios Pottery plus other work from more than 70 local artists and craftsmen. There's also a traditional tearoom in the back of the shop. 90-92 Lower Bridge St. (phone: 317717).

William Jones Three Old Arches Ltd. Specialty foods—coffee, tea, chocolates, sausages and pies, cheeses, bacon. Owen Bridge St. (phone: 321555).

SPORTS

Chester's leisure center, *Northgate Arena* (corner of Victoria Rd. and St. Oswalds Way; phone: 380444), has squash courts, badminton courts, and a pool with palm trees, rocks, a massive slide, a children's paddling area, and training pool.

CRICKET For those who want to watch Britain's national game, *Chester Boughton Hall Cricket Club* has matches every Saturday afternoon and some Sundays from May to late September at the *Filkins Lane* ground (Tarvin Rd.; phone: 326072).

GOLF There are clubs for hire at the nine-hole municipal golf course at *Westminster Park* (phone: 680231). Visitors with a guest membership also have access to the 18-hole courses at the *Chester Golf Club, Curzon Park* (phone: 675130); the suburban *Upton-by-Chester Golf Club* (phone: 381183) and *Vicars Cross Golf Club* (phone: 335174); and the *Eaton Golf Club* at Eccleston (phone: 335885).

HORSEBACK RIDING *Pen-y-Bryn,* in nearby Wales at Pehtre Broughton, near Wrexham (phone: 978-752909), caters to riders of all levels.

SOCCER From August through May, the English league, third-division *Chester Football Club* plays on most Saturday afternoons at *The Stadium* (Bumpers La.; phone: 371376).

THEATER

Local repertory, some touring productions, and one of Britain's last medieval mystery play cycles take place in the *Gateway Theatre* (Hamilton

Pl.; phone: 340393), and in the *Theatre Clwyd* (at Mold, 12 miles away; phone: 352-755114). Alternative productions take place at the *Little Theatre Club* (Gloucester St., Newton; phone: 322674). And Liverpool's wider choice of theaters (see *Liverpool,* THE CITIES) is only 45 minutes away by car.

MUSIC

Occasional concerts are presented in the *Gateway Theatre* or at the *Theatre Clwyd* in Mold (see above for both). The *Chester Symphony Orchestra* or visiting artists and ensembles do the honors. Much more happens during the week-long *Chester Summer Music Festival* (see *Special Events*). The *Town Hall* hosts a variety of free lunchtime concerts; some, featuring classical composers and organ recitals, are heard in the Chester cathedral, as well as in the *Church of St. John's.* For current details about both theater and music, consult *What's On* (see *Tourist Information*).

NIGHTCLUBS AND NIGHTLIFE

Raphael's (Love St.; phone: 340754) is predominantly a disco with occasional live music, as are *Whispers* (Frodsham St.; phone: 348682); *Blimpers* (City Rd.; phone: 314794); and *Rosie's* (Northgate St.; phone: 327141), which has a quieter wine bar downstairs as well. For a more refined atmosphere, the *Plantation Inn* hotel (Liverpool Rd.; phone: 374100) has dinner and dancing on Saturdays. In the city, there are jazz nights on the last Friday of the month at the *Chester Grosvenor* hotel (see *Checking In*). *Alexander's Bar* (Northgate St.; phone: 340005) has a different kind of music (including blues and jazz) every night Sundays through Fridays; stand-up comedians perform here on Saturday nights. There is live cabaret at the *Merseyview Country Club* (Overton Hill, Frodsham; phone: 928-733108), about 30 minutes from the city center.

Best in Town

CHECKING IN

Hotels in Chester generally fall into three categories: old and expensive, new and moderately priced, and small and inexpensive. However, many establishments offer special deals for two or more nights, and it is always worth checking. Most properties in the city include breakfast—which, in Great Britain, is a meal in its own right—in room rates; out-of-town places charge a small additional amount. Expect to pay more than $290 per night for a double room (including private bath, TV set, phone, and breakfast, unless otherwise noted) in hotels listed as very expensive; $210 to $290 for expensive places; $130 to $200 for those listed as moderate; $80 to $130 for inexpensive ones. All telephone numbers are in the 1244 city code unless otherwise indicated.

VERY EXPENSIVE

Chester Grosvenor Built between 1863 and 1866, it has a reputation as the city's best hotel, a luxurious establishment with 87 rooms and suites, superb service, and an excellent restaurant. Sadly, the traditional pianist and tea lounge have been lost to a £12-million face-lift, which included the renovation of the ground-floor *La Brasserie* restaurant and its à la carte counterpart, *Arkle* (see *Eating Out* for both). There is a health club and access to a nearby pool. Eastgate St. (phone: 324024; fax: 313246).

EXPENSIVE

Crabwall Manor This 48-room country-house hotel, set on 11 acres of woodland and landscaped gardens, has an ageless quality. The original hall dates to the 10th century, and the castellated frontage was added in the early 17th century; the architecture, however, looks surprisingly modern. There is a good restaurant open to non-residents. Breakfast is not included. Located in Mollington, 2 miles outside of Chester (phone: 851666; fax: 851400).

Moat House International Tastefully modern, and part of the Queen's Moat House group (it used to be called the *Chester International*), it offers everything from a good restaurant to leisure facilities, including a sauna. There are 152 rooms. Trinity St. (phone: 322330; fax: 316188).

Soughton Hall What used to be a stately home is now a 12-room hotel, complete with luxurious fixtures and fittings, antique furniture, a restaurant serving fine traditional English fare, and aristocratic gardens. At night the front windows glow from the warm light of chandeliers. Breakfast is not included. Northop, 10 miles from Chester (phone: 1352-840811; fax: 1352-86382).

MODERATE

Blossoms Despite its fairly recent exterior face-lift and its refurbished interior, this 16th-century hotel (a member of the Forte group) retains its traditional manner, with sweeping staircases, thick carpeting, and 64 comfortable rooms. There also is a restaurant and two bars. St. John St. (phone: 323186; 800-225-5843; fax: 346433).

Cavendish This is a beautifully restored and elegantly furnished Georgian house with 20 guestrooms, set in its own landscaped gardens on the edge of town. There are tennis, croquet, boating, fishing, and golf nearby. The dining room (for hotel guests only) serves classic French food. 42-44 Hough Green (phone: 675100; fax: 681309).

Chester Town House A friendly, trendy little (four rooms) bed and breakfast establishment in a conservation area of cobbled lamplit streets and alleyways. There's no restaurant, and the guestrooms do not have phones. 23 King St. (phone: 350021).

INEXPENSIVE

Pied Bull Passengers used to board the stage for London at this coaching inn, one of Chester's oldest. It's a really cheerful pub with 12 rooms, and a king-size bedroom still retains its original 18th-century oak paneling. Northgate St. (phone: 325829).

Ye Olde King's Head One of the city's oldest inns (dating to the 16th century), this charming little place has eight guestrooms, half with private baths. Two of the rooms have four-poster beds, and Room No. 4 has an extra added attraction—it's said to be haunted by the ghost of an elderly housekeeper who used to work here. The lovely timbered dining room serves hearty English fare. 48 Lower Bridge St. (phone: 324855).

EATING OUT

Chester's choice of restaurants is surprisingly good. You could eat in a different place every night for a month and still not cover the whole list. Generally prices are lower than in larger British cities: $90 for two, including wine, is the absolute top (expensive). Most restaurants will set you back less than $70 (moderate), and by choosing carefully you can get away with a dinner for two for $50 or less (inexpensive). Some of the ethnic restaurants—French, Italian, Greek, Mexican—offer a lot for the money, and the best value of all must be the hot and substantial Indian curries and the more exotic Chinese specialties. All restaurants listed below serve lunch and dinner, unless otherwise noted. All telephone numbers are in the 1244 city code unless otherwise indicated.

EXPENSIVE

Arkle The main dining room of the *Chester Grosvenor* hotel serves classic French fare using trout, veal, and lamb, and does it impeccably (it has a Michelin star). Closed Sundays, Monday lunch, and *Christmas Eve* through *Boxing Day.* Reservations necessary. Major credit cards accepted. Eastgate St. (phone: 324024).

Boat Inn Every inch of the 15-mile drive to this country pub and restaurant is worth it. The setting above the beautiful upstream reaches of the Dee is incomparable. Pheasant and fresh Dee salmon are on the mostly English menu in season, along with vintage clarets and burgundies. Open daily. Reservations advised. Major credit cards accepted. Follow A483 to Wrexham (12 miles south), then take A539 and look for the sign for Erbistock. Erbistock, Clwyd (phone: 1978-780143).

Craxton Wood Classic French cooking; a current specialty is the *suprême Louise,* chicken with langoustine sauce. Closed Sundays, bank holidays, the last two weeks in August, and one week at *Christmas.* Reservations advised. Major credit cards accepted. Puddington, 5 miles north of the city on the main Parkgate Rd. (A540) (phone: 151-339-4717).

Rossett Hall This Georgian country house offers first class English cooking and top-quality local cheeses. Follow A483 south 5 miles to the village of Rossett, then look for *Rossett Hall* behind the long wall on the right-hand side, in the center of the village. Open daily. Reservations advised. Major credit cards accepted. Chester Rd., Rossett (phone: 570062).

MODERATE

Abbey Green Its setting is a Georgian house, and organically grown vegetables and quiche made with the eggs of free-range chickens are on its inventive vegetarian menu. Closed Sundays. Reservations necessary. Visa accepted. 1 Rufus Ct., Northgate St. (phone: 313251).

Blue Bell In the city's oldest medieval inn (it's even got a resident ghost, that of a Civil War widow), this place offers a traditional menu of English fare, such as halibut with grapes or orange, and lemon pork—but there's not a chip to be seen. Closed Sunday evenings. Reservations necessary. Visa accepted. 65 Northgate St. (phone: 317758).

La Bohème The menu is authentic French, the setting stylish, and the food tasty. Open daily. Reservations necessary. Major credit cards accepted. 58 Watergate St. (phone: 313721).

La Brasserie A casual dining room in the *Chester Grosvenor* hotel, it serves light, elegant fare, such as filet of salmon with sorrel and scallop stew. Open daily. Reservations necessary. Major credit cards accepted. Eastgate St. (phone: 324024).

Jade Cantonese The only place in town with a full Cantonese menu. Behind its rather garish façade are delicious, subtle flavors, crisp vegetables, and a genuine mixture of Chinese diners among the clientele. Closed Sundays. Reservations advised. Visa accepted. 43 Watergate St. Row (phone: 321455).

INEXPENSIVE

Francs Lively and often crowded, this French bistro offers an excellent value, and especially good pastries. Open daily. Reservations advised. Major credit cards accepted. 14 Cuppin St. (phone: 317952).

Watergate Wine Bar Below street level in an oak-filled, 12th-century crypt, this eatery is popular for its atmosphere and tasty menu, featuring leek-and-parsnip soup and Tilly-Ann pie (a specialty prepared with beef and beer). Closed Sunday dinner. Reservations unnecessary. Visa accepted. Watergate St. (phone: 320515).

SHARING A PINT

Pubs are the center of Chester life. In the old days they were simply places to drink and chat, but now most of them serve food, too, and the best of them give even good restaurants a run for their money. The *Boat House* (phone: 328709), at the upstream end of the Groves next to the school and club boathouses, used to be a real rowing man's pub, with faded photographs of long-gone oarsmen and autographed oars on the wall. Full of young people and music, the cheerful, busy river bars are another option; they serve excellent American food and offer unmatchable views of the Dee. The *Albion Inn* (close to the walls on Park St.; phone: 340345) is a real, old-fashioned, cozy, back-street Chester pub with draught beer "from the wood" (beer actually brewed in a wood keg) and the traditional steak and kidney pie, black pudding and mushy peas, bread and cheese, and treacle tart. *Ye Olde Deva* (on Watergate St. Row; no phone) is similarly atmospheric—it even has a gentlemen's powder room (now one of the back rooms) dating to the 18th century. Other drinking haunts favored by locals include the *Pied Bull* (see *Checking In*), *Custom House Inn* (Watergate St.; phone: 324435), *Boot Inn* (Eastgate St.; no phone), and *Falcon* (Lower Bridge St.; no phone).

Edinburgh

Other beautiful and famous urban centers such as Rome or San Francisco may share the distinction of being built on hills, but Edinburgh alone can claim to be built on extinct volcanoes. Astride one of these, high above the houses where the city's 445,020 inhabitants dwell, looms *Edinburgh Castle,* a fairy-tale structure that often makes visitors gasp the first time they see it. It seems almost supernatural, with ancient stonemasonry rising seamlessly out of volcanic rock.

From the 7th century on, there was a fortress where *Edinburgh Castle* now stands, and as the Middle Ages became more civilized, life within the fortress spilled onto the long sloping ridge that runs down from *Edinburgh Castle* to the foot of Arthur's Seat, another extinct volcano, crowning *Holyrood Park,* Edinburgh's central park. The ridge, with its stone and wood tenements, its one snake-like public street, its cathedral, and its tolbooth, remains the knot at the center of Scotland's legal, commercial, and artistic fiber.

Walking around central Edinburgh today is sheer joy. There's little need for a map; it's hard to get lost. Every hilltop commands a glorious vista, and every alley reveals fantastic steeples, jagged, chimney-potted skylines, or beauteous rotund domes. And nature provides incredible sunsets, the product of Scotland's unique slowly fading evening light (the "gloaming") and rapid change in the evening temperature. Legend and romance are at every hand, and somebody famous lived in almost every residence.

The city's most legendary citizens are the arch Presbyterian John Knox and Mary, Queen of Scots, who dominated the Edinburgh of the late 16th century. The political and religious strife attendant upon Mary's reign is notorious, as are her two marriages and the three deaths associated with them, including her own (she was beheaded at *Fotheringay Castle* in 1587 by order of her cousin Queen Elizabeth I). Mary lived in the *Palace of Holyroodhouse,* by the abbey at the base of Arthur's Seat. John Knox lived up the ridge from her near *St. Giles' Cathedral,* within the city gates—according to legend, anyway (historians think otherwise). Both residences still stand, and are open to the public.

The Edinburgh of the late 17th century, however, was far from romantic: Tenements along the ridge had grown 15 (or more) tottering stories high and housed uncounted numbers of people, all of whom threw their garbage into the central street. Buildings frequently collapsed. Water could be had only from one of the city's six wells, called "pennywells," and inhabitants had to line up with buckets as early as 3 AM. These cramped and malodorous conditions no doubt had something to do with the locals' favorite sport—rioting on fete days, parade days, and the king's birthday.

This wizened medieval town had to spread out somehow, and luckily, in the second half of the 18th century, its by now thoroughly Protestant God sent it an increase in trade and prosperity. City fathers erected several buildings on another ridge to the north—known as the New Town—connected to the Old Town by bridges. The classically proportioned beauty of New Town buildings, many of which were designed by the world-renowned British architect Robert Adam, is a testament to Edinburgh's golden age, part of the so-called Scottish Enlightenment. It was a great age not only for architects but for writers, publishers, philosophers, and politicians. Throughout the city, taverns became the sites of ongoing seminars. This was the time of David Hume, Adam Smith, and James Boswell, all Edinburgh men.

Today's Edinburgh has lost some of its traditional vibrancy and color, though it is certainly safer and cleaner. The near stranglehold the Presbyterian Church of Scotland had on social institutions during Queen Victoria's reign meant that industriousness, temperance, and respectability—all the middle class virtues—took supreme command of the city. Even today, as most city residents are white-collar workers, the local flavor is somewhat staid. Nonetheless, things seem to be livening up with the appearance of flashy pubs, restaurants, and nightspots.

Edinburgh always has been favored by geography, situated as it is on the Firth of Forth, an inlet from the North Sea, and surrounded by woods, rolling hills, and lochs (lakes), though even in summer it can be surprisingly cold. It is not only a national capital but a port whose chief exports include whisky, coal, grain, and petrochemicals; there also is a large brewing center, and a center for information technology and electronics research.

The world-renowned *Edinburgh International Festival* (see *Special Events*), despite being threatened by the slashing of arts budgets and charges of elitism, continues to maintain high standards and has reached out to embrace populism, internationalism, and the avant-garde. And the idea of a Scottish Assembly at Edinburgh has grown tremendously as Scots seek greater control of their own affairs. Edinburgh's second golden age may well be at hand. Perhaps not all its volcanoes are extinct.

Edinburgh At-a-Glance

SEEING THE CITY

Edinburgh has many wonderful views; on a clear day, there are striking panoramas from the top of any of its extinct volcanoes. Another option is to climb the 143 steps to the top of the *Nelson Monument* (phone: 556-2716), built in 1815, on Carlton Hill at the east end of Princes Street. It is closed Sundays; admission charge. To the north lies the sparkling Firth of Forth and, beyond it, the ancient Kingdom of Fife. To the south are the lovely Pentland Hills and surrounding plowed farmlands. Look eastward to the giant Bass Rock, off the coast of Berwickshire. Look westward to see Ben Lomond, nearly on the west coast of Scotland! If you have a car, drive up Arthur's Seat (the road begins just by the *Palace of Holyroodhouse*), park at Dunsapie Loch, and walk to the uppermost height (a steep and furzy climb—wear flat shoes and watch out for falling sheep). If you have no car, view the city from *Edinburgh Castle,* or take an open-top tour bus from *Waverley Station* (see *Sightseeing Tours,* below).

SPECIAL PLACES

The "Royal Mile" is the name given to the oldest part of the city, the cobbled road that runs downhill from *Edinburgh Castle* to the *Palace of Holyroodhouse.* It comprises four contiguous streets: Castle Hill, the Lawnmarket, High Street, and the Canongate. Since the entire citizenry of Edinburgh lived and worked for centuries either on or just off these four streets, the Royal Mile is practically groaning with objects and sites of historic fascination.

THE ROYAL MILE

EDINBURGH CASTLE The oldest building in Edinburgh is part of the castle structure, a tiny chapel built in the 12th century by Queen Margaret, wife of the Malcolm who is featured in *Macbeth.* The Scottish Regalia, including sceptre and crown, are on display as part of an exhibition that tells the story of Scotland's turbulent history. The regalia disappeared after the union of Scotland with England and were found, more than a century later, by Sir Walter Scott in an old locked box. Also here are the *United Services Museum,* documenting Scottish participation in the British armed forces; two regimental museums, focusing on the Royal Scots Regiment and the Royal Scots Dragoon Guards; the *Great Hall,* built by King James IV in the 16th century and featuring a lofty wood-beamed ceiling and huge stained glass windows; and the *Scottish National War Memorial,* honoring Scots who died in the two world wars. At 1 PM Mondays through Saturdays, a gun is fired from the ramparts. Open daily. Admission charge (phone: 244-3101).

OUTLOOK TOWER AND CAMERA OBSCURA A short distance east of the castle, climb up 98 steps and find yourself face to face with church spires. Opened in 1853, the camera obscura, actually a periscope, throws a revolving image of nearby streets and buildings onto a circular table, while one of the tower's denizens gives an excellent historical talk. There also are exhibitions of holography and pin-photography—tiny photos taken through matchboxes. Downstairs is a very good bookshop. Open daily. Admission charge. Castle Hill (phone: 226-3709).

SCOTCH WHISKY HERITAGE CENTRE Just next door to the entrance to *Edinburgh Castle,* this attraction features an hour-long tour, in an electric barrel-car, that shows the role of whisky in Scotland's turbulent past. You will emerge knowing exactly how whisky is made. The heritage shop stocks over 60 brands of malt and blended whiskies. Open daily. Admission charge. 354 Castle Hill (phone: 220-0441).

PARLIAMENT HOUSE Built from 1632 to 1640, this historic sanctum once housed Scotland's Parliament and is today the country's supreme court. Its showpiece is the *Great Hall,* with a fine hammer-beam roof and walls laden with portraits by Raeburn and other famous Scottish artists. Closed weekends. Admission charge for library. Upper High St. (phone: 225-2595).

ST. GILES' CATHEDRAL A church of some sort has stood here for over 1,000 years. The 12th-century building here was named for the Athenian saint Egidius (Giles). From 1559 to 1560, during the Reformation, soldiers were stationed at the church and many of its treasures hidden in private homes; Protestant nobles nonetheless ravaged the altars. Later, English troops joined them and stripped *St. Giles'* from top to bottom. It was at this stage that John Knox was made minister of *St. Giles'*. His unmarked grave is believed to be under Parliament Square, just outside the cathedral. Admission charge. Upper High St. (phone: 225-9442).

MERCAT CROSS, OR MARKET CROSS Near the east door of *St. Giles'* stands a monument restored in 1885 by Prime Minister W. E. Gladstone. Proclamations were read out and hangings took place at this site until well into the 19th century (and announcements are still made here on special occasions, such as the accession of a new monarch). It was also the commercial focal point of old Edinburgh, the place being so thick with butchers, bakers, merchants, lawyers, and other shopkeepers and businesspeople that the town council issued ordinances requiring each trade to occupy its own separate neighboring street or close (hence the names on the entrances to the closes: Fleshmarket Close, Advocates' Close, and so on). High St.

ADVOCATES' CLOSE AND ANCHOR CLOSE These are typical of the narrow alleys that gave access to the inns and taverns that were so much a part of Edinburgh's 18th-century cultural life. Doors to these places (taverns no longer) were topped by stone architraves dating from the 16th century and bearing inscriptions like "Blissit Be God of Al His Gifts" or *"Spes Altera Vitae"* (these two examples are still in Advocates' Close today). In Anchor Close was *Douglas's,* where the poet Robert Burns habitually drank. Entrances to both closes are from High Street.

JOHN KNOX'S HOUSE Legend says that Scotland's fieriest preacher lived here; history disagrees. However, legend has won, and this 15th-century dwelling was preserved when most of its neighbors were razed during the widening of High Street in 1849. Closed Sundays. Admission charge. 45 High St. (phone: 556-2647).

SCOTTISH POETRY LIBRARY For anyone who visits Britain to explore America's literary ancestry, an hour or two browsing here is richly rewarding. An extensive collection of books, magazines, and tapes with Scottish works in English,

Scots, and Gaelic is housed in this 18th-century building in a courtyard off the Royal Mile. Closed Sundays. No admission charge. 14 High St. (phone: 557-2876).

ACHESON HOUSE When King Charles I was crowned at Edinburgh in 1633, Sir Archibald Acheson was his secretary of state. Acheson built this small courtyard mansion, the only one of its kind in Edinburgh, in the same year. Although the house is closed to the public, the exterior is well worth seeing. 140 Canongate.

BRASS RUBBING CENTRE Visitors may rub any of the brasses or stones on display. Materials are provided for a small fee. The brass commemorating Robert the Bruce, King of Scotland from 1306 to 1329, is very impressive. Closed Sundays (except during the *Edinburgh International Festival*—see *Special Events*). In Trinity Apse, Chalmers Close, off High St. (phone: 556-4364).

PALACE OF HOLYROODHOUSE A royal retreat since the 16th century, the stone palace is where Queen Elizabeth II stays when she is in residence in Edinburgh. Most of what you see of it now was built by Charles II from 1671, but it is chiefly associated with Mary, Queen of Scots, who lived in it for six years. The old part contains her bedroom and the supper room in which David Riccio, her secretary, was brutally murdered before her eyes by a gang that included her jealous husband, Lord Darnley. By the side of the palace are the picturesque ruins of *Holyrood Abbey* and the lodge known as *Queen Mary's Bath House.* A guide will take you through it all, sparing no gory details. Closed Sundays in February, March, November, and December; also closed January and when the queen is in residence. Admission charge. At the bottom of the Canongate (phone: 556-1096).

BEYOND THE ROYAL MILE

PRINCES STREET GARDENS Princes Street is modern Edinburgh's Main Street, its Broadway, and its Fifth Avenue. The street can be surprisingly cold, in any season—deserving of its nickname, "The Valley of Winds." The gardens, lined with wooden benches, stretch nearly the street's whole length on the south side. The city spends thousands of pounds every year to keep the gardens opulent with flowers. In summer months (June—September) there are concerts, children's shows, variety acts, and do-it-yourself Scottish country dancing (to professional bands). Gates close at dusk. Princes St.

NATIONAL GALLERY OF SCOTLAND One of a trio of *National Galleries of Scotland* within walking distance of each other, this museum stands on a manmade embankment known as the Mound at the center of *Princes Street Gardens.* Opened in 1859, it has a small but vital collection of European paintings, prints, and drawings that includes works by Verrocchio (*Madonna and Child*), Poussin (*Mystic Marriage of St. Catherine*), Gauguin (*Vision After the Sermon*), Andrea del Sarto (*Portrait of Becuccio Bicchieraio*), Velázquez (*Old Woman Cooking Eggs*), Rembrandt (*Woman in Bed*), Vermeer (*Christ *in the House of Martha and Mary*), Watteau (*Fêtes Vénitiennes*), and Degas (*Diego Martelli*), as well as works by van Gogh, Renoir, Cézanne, Monet, Goya, Gainsborough, Reynolds, Constable, Millais, and Turner. The collection of works by Scottish artists is particularly good; visitors should not miss Henry Raeburn's *Rev. Robert Walker.* Open daily. No admission charge except for special exhibits (phone: 556-8921).

SCOTTISH NATIONAL GALLERY OF MODERN ART Scotland's choice collection of painting, sculpture, and graphic art of the 20th century features works of established masters such as Picasso, Matisse, Ernst, Kirchner, Dix, Moore; major Scottish artists; and leading figures of the national contemporary scene. Open daily. No admission charge. Belford Rd. (phone: 556-8921).

SCOTTISH NATIONAL PORTRAIT GALLERY On display are portraits—in all media—of people who have played a significant role in Scottish history from the 16th century to the present, rendered by the most famous artists of the day, as well as the *National Collection of Photography.* The gallery shares a splendid neo-Gothic building with the *Royal Museum of Scotland* (one of the *National Museums of Scotland*), whose collection includes a 14th-century longbow recently found in the Tweedsmuir Hills in southeast Scotland and several exhibits about science, technology, and natural history. Open daily. No admission charge. 1 Queen St. (phone: 556-8921).

SCOTT MONUMENT Sir Walter Scott is certainly one of Edinburgh's favorite sons—his face even decorates all Bank of Scotland notes, even though he was the most famous bankrupt in Scottish history. The elaborate 200-foot Gothic monument helps make Edinburgh's skyline an ornamental marvel. Its 287 steps take you to the top. Plans to clean the monument's grimy stonework have been postponed amid controversy about whether the process will cause damage. Closed Sundays. Admission charge. Princes St. (phone: 225-2424, ext. 6596).

ST. JOHN'S CHURCH At the west end of *Princes Street Gardens* is this stolid Episcopal church, built in 1818, with richly colored stained glass windows that are among the finest in Scotland. From time to time, large murals with a peace theme are painted on the outside walls (the artwork is sponsored by the church), causing a stir among staid passersby. The stone arched terrace on the far side of the church houses several shops, a café, and in August, a lively crafts market. Princes St. (phone: 229-7565).

NEW TOWN To the north of Princes Street lies the largest neo-classical townscape in Europe, built between the 1760s and 1830s. Assiduous conservation means that little has changed externally. Three of the more interesting places are Charlotte Square (designed by Robert Adam), Moray Place, and Ann Street. The *New Town Conservation Centre* (13A Dundas St.; phone: 557-5222) offers exhibitions, a reference library, and various publications; it is closed weekends.

GEORGIAN HOUSE On the most gracious square in the elegant New Town, the *National Trust for Scotland* has furnished a house in period style and opened it to the public. Fascinating audiovisual sessions on the New Town are included. Closed Sundays November through March. Admission charge. 7 Charlotte Sq. (phone: 225-2160).

EDINBURGH ZOO Opposite the Pentland Hills, away from the city center, is a zoo with a view and the world's most famous penguins, the largest colony in captivity. Every afternoon at 2:30, April through September, they perform their delightful Penguin Parade through the park grounds. Open daily. Admission charge. Corstorphine Rd., Murrayfield (phone: 334-9171).

GRASSMARKET This ancient street is flanked by many eateries, elegant shops, and flophouses. The West Bow, off the street's east end, has some intriguing boutiques and antiques shops. Leading from the Grassmarket is Cowgate, with the 16th-century *Magdalen Chapel;* to see it, contact the *Scottish Reformation Society* (phone: 220-1450).

GREYFRIARS KIRK This historic Presbyterian church, dedicated on *Christmas Day* in 1620, was the site of a pre-Reformation Franciscan friary. It is also where Presbyterians declared their opposition to the prescribed Episcopalianism of Charles I by signing the National Covenant in blood in 1638. Sunday services are given in English and in Gaelic. The church is closed (except on Thursdays and for services) October through February; the *Kirkyard* (graveyard) is open daily. George IV Bridge (phone: 225-1900).

EDINBURGH CRYSTAL VISITORS CENTRE Cut-glass items sell like hotcakes in Edinburgh, and here's a chance to see how they are made. Operating in a town about 12 miles south of Edinburgh, the center offers guided tours on weekdays. There is also a factory shop and a restaurant. Children under 10 are not allowed. Open daily. Admission charge. At Eastfield near Penicuik; take Straiton Rd. south out of town (phone: 1968-675128).

ST. MARY'S CATHEDRAL Consecrated in 1879, this Episcopal church has a lofty 270-foot main spire and two smaller ones at the west end which were added between 1913 and 1917 (named Barbara and Mary, after the women who paid for their construction). The rows of modern, light wood chairs brighten up the dark stone interior and the lectern's base is a pelican instead of the usual eagle. Palmerston Pl. (phone: 225-6293).

Sources and Resources

TOURIST INFORMATION

Located next to *Waverley Station,* the *Edinburgh and Scotland Information Centre* (3 Princes St., Edinburgh EH2 2QP; phone: 557-1700) has an accommodations desk, details of guided walking tours, and a ticket center for Edinburgh events. It also offers maps, leaflets, and all City of Edinburgh publications, some at a nominal charge. On sale here is the *Essential Guide to Edinburgh,* updated annually. The center is closed Sundays October through April. There is also a tourist information desk at *Edinburgh Airport* (phone: 333-1000); open daily. For information concerning travel in other parts of Scotland, drop by the *Scottish Tourist Board* (23 Ravelston Ter.; phone: 332-2433).

LOCAL COVERAGE The following publications are available: the *Scotsman,* morning daily; the *Edinburgh Evening News,* evening daily; the information center's free *Day by Day,* published monthly (except during the *Edinburgh International Festival,* when it's published every two weeks), listing forthcoming happenings; and *The List* (phone: 558-1191), a comprehensive biweekly Glasgow and Edinburgh events guide.

TELEPHONE The city code for Edinburgh is 131.

GETTING AROUND

AIRPORT *Edinburgh Airport* is about a half hour from the center of town. An *Airlink* bus (No. 100) travels from the airport to Waverley Bridge, making stops en route at Haymarket and Murrayfield (phone: 226-5087). The *Edinburgh Airbus* (phone: 556-2244), which also connects the airport and the city center, stops at most of the major hotels.

BUS *Lothian Region Transport* bus route maps and information are available from the information desk at the *Ticket Centre* on Waverley Bridge (phone: 220-4111), except for buses that run from St. Andrew Square (phone: 556-8464). Passengers can reach most places from Princes Street. Fares range from 40p (about 60¢) to £1.10 (about $1.65); exact change is required. The information center (see above) can provide information on bus tours of the city and countryside. Longer-distance buses leave from *St. Andrew Square Bus Station* (St. Andrew Sq.). The Edinburgh Touristcard provides unlimited bus travel for two or more days; it may be purchased at either the *Lothian Region Transport* office (14 Queen St.; phone: 554-4494) or the *Ticket Centre* (see above). A two-day pass costs £4.80 (about $7.20); a seven-day pass costs £8 (about $12).

CAR RENTAL Major firms represented include *Avis* (100 Dairy Rd.; phone: 337-6363); *Europcar* (24 E. London St.; phone: 661-1252); and *Hertz* (10 Picardy Pl.; phone: 556-8311).

SIGHTSEEING TOURS *Guide Friday* (Platform 1, *Waverley Station;* phone: 556-2244) and *Lothian Regional Transport* (see above) run hour-long tours of the city that leave every hour (every 15 minutes during peak time). Open-top, double-decker buses depart from various points; tickets are valid all day so you can get on and off as often as you like.

University-trained historians from *Mercat Tours* (14 Redford Ter.; phone: 661-4541) lead guided walks from the *Mercat Cross* next to *St. Giles'* on the

Royal Mile. Guided walks around the Royal Mile also are offered, and ghosts are the subject of an evening walk that ends with a drink in a historic tavern; both tours are given once or twice daily, depending on the season. Another night walk along the "Ghost Hunter Trail" leaves once a day June through September to visit sites of reputed macabre and supernatural events.

Robin's Tours (60 Willowbrae Rd.; phone: 661-0125) leads several excursions, including Grand City, Royal Mile, 18th-century Edinburgh (April through October), and Ghosts and Witches tours. All leave from outside the information center. A Murder & Mystery tour led by a guide dressed as Adam Lyal, a highwayman executed in the city's Grassmarket in 1811, leaves from outside the *Witchery* restaurant in Castle Hill every evening (times vary); book in advance (phone: 225-6745).

TAXI There are cabstands at *St. Andrew Square Bus Station* (see above), *Waverley Station* (see below), opposite the *Caledonian* hotel (west end of Princes St.), and in front of the *Cameron Toll Shopping Centre* (Lady Rd.). To call a taxi, contact *Capital Castle* (phone: 228-2555), *Central Radio Taxis* (phone: 229-2468), or *City Cabs* (phone: 228-1211).

TRAIN The main railway terminal is *Waverley Station* (off Princes St.; phone: 556-2451). Between Edinburgh and London, 17 *InterCity* trains run daily each way; the fastest takes just under four hours. (Somewhat slower, but far more atmospheric, is the *Flying Scotsman,* which has made the trip from *Waverley Station* to London at 10 AM every day since 1862.) A shuttle train to Glasgow runs every half hour; the trip lasts about 50 minutes. There is a 24-hour *British Rail* information service (phone: 556-2451).

SPECIAL EVENTS

There's plenty going on in Edinburgh all year, but several festivals are worth arranging your itinerary around.

FAVORITE FETES

Edinburgh International Festival During its three-week run from mid-August to early September, this world-renowned festival offers a cornucopia of activities. The city's theaters, concert halls, museums, churches, community centers, and some schools are taken over for theater, dance, and opera performances; for lectures, master classes, conferences, exhibits, and other cultural affairs of global significance; and for nearly 1,000 presentations of the *Festival Fringe,* which the *Guinness Book of World Records* lists as the largest arts festival in the world. The *Fringe* nowadays embraces the traditional as well as the experimental and gives particular encouragement to comedians; past performers have included Eric Idle, Michael Palin, and Terry Jones (all later of *Monty Python*), as well as Dudley Moore.

The artists are among the best in the world, and the audiences are big and international. The colorful *Edinburgh Military Tattoo,* a spectacular pageant featuring a performance of the massed pipe bands of Her Majesty's Scottish regiments in full Highland dress, is equally popular; it takes place at the castle every night (except Sundays) for the last three weeks in August.

Coinciding with the first two weeks of the *International Festival* is the *Edinburgh International Film Festival.* Entries are screened at *Filmhouse* (88 Lothian Rd.; phone: 228-4051). The *Edinburgh International Jazz Festival* is held at various sites throughout the city during the first week of the *Tattoo;* for information, contact the festival office (116 Canongate; phone: 557-1642).

It's a good idea to reserve tickets—and hotel space—as far in advance as possible, especially for the most popular attractions; the film and jazz festivals are easier to get into on short notice. For details on events, contact the *Festival Society* (21 Market St., Edinburgh EH1 1BW, Scotland; phone: 226-4001), the *Edinburgh Military Tattoo* (22 Market St., Edinburgh EH1 1QB, Scotland; phone: 225-1188), and the *Festival Fringe Society* (180 High St., Edinburgh EH1 1QS, Scotland; phone: 226-5257).

Edinburgh International Folk Festival Folk music, dance, drama, a crafts fair, children's events, lectures, courses on traditional instruments, *ceilidhs,* workshops, and an Oral History Conference are the heart of this event (not to be confused with the *Edinburgh International Festival*), which takes place over the 10 days that lead up to *Easter* weekend. The *Edinburgh Harp Festival* and the *Festival of European Piping* are an integral part of the event. For details, contact the *Edinburgh International Folk Festival* (PO Box 528, Edinburgh EH10 4DU, Scotland; phone: 556-3181).

Other events include *New Year's Eve,* or "hogmanay," which is celebrated with a three-day festival that includes torchlit processions through the streets, fairs, markets, and a huge party held in one of the major theaters. After midnight on *New Year's Eve,* people visit the homes of friends and acquaintances (it is customary to take a half-bottle of whisky or another favorite tipple to share with your hosts). The world's only international science fair, the *Edinburgh Science Festival,* is held in early April; it includes films, talks, and conferences on such topics as superconductivity, high-tech wine making, and genetic engineering. For more details contact the *Science Festival Box Office* (1 Broughton Market; phone: 556-6446).

MUSEUMS

In addition to those described in *Special Places,* the city runs two museums of local history: *Huntly House* (142 Canongate; phone: 225-2424, ext. 4143) and the *Lady Stair's House* (Lawnmarket; phone: 225-2424, ext. 6901), a

Burns, Scott, and Stevenson museum. Both are closed Sundays (except during the *Festival*). Admission charge. Other museums include the following:

LAURISTON CASTLE A fine enlarged 16th-century tower, the castle overlooks the estuary of the Firth of Forth. The interior is filled with period furniture and collections of Derbyshire Blue Hogn, Crossley wool mosaics, and objets d'art. The castle may be visited on guided tours only. Open daily. Admission charge. Off Cramond Rd. S. (phone: 336-2060).

MUSEUM OF CHILDHOOD A treasure house of historic toys, dolls, and children's clothing, it also features a time tunnel with reconstructions of a schoolroom, a street scene, a fancy dress party, and a late 19th-century nursery. Closed Sundays (except during the *Festival*). No admission charge. 38 High St. (phone: 225-2424, ext. 6645).

THE PEOPLE'S STORY Tells the tale of the working class of Edinburgh through the centuries, including sections on the development of trade unions, health, welfare, and leisure. Operating days are the same as for the *Museum of Childhood* (above). No admission charge. At the *Canongate Tolbooth,* 163 Canongate (phone: 225-2424, ext. 4057).

SHOPPING

Princes Street is Edinburgh's main venue, with some of Scotland's best shops as well as branches of several British department stores, though there are also some interesting shops on George Street, two blocks north, and on the Royal Mile. In addition, at the east end of Princes Street is *Waverley Market,* a large, modern shopping mall with *Waverley Station* at its base. The best buys are Scottish tartans and woolens.

Also worth a look are antiques on Dundas Street, West Bow (off Grassmarket), Randolph Place, Thistle Street, or in the area around St. Stephen's Street in Stockbridge—and three-day antiques fairs are held in January, April, August, and November in the *Roxburghe* hotel (see *Checking In*). Also, *Phillips Scotland* (65 George St.; phone: 225-2266) has monthly sales of paintings, furniture, Oriental rugs, clocks, bronzes, and silver; European ceramics and glass, Orientalia, jewelry, and watercolors are auctioned bimonthly; books, postcards, and maps are offered in five annual sales; and two annual sales are devoted to dolls, costumes, and textiles. Viewing is usually two days prior, on Wednesdays and Thursdays; there's always something to be seen, not least of which is one of the best panoramic views of Edinburgh from the fifth floor. *Lyon and Turnbull* (51 George St.; phone: 225-4627) is another good auction house.

Bone china and Scottish crystal are attractive, and don't miss the shortbread, which is on sale everywhere. St. Mary's Street, leading off the Royal Mile, is rapidly becoming famous for shops selling secondhand clothes, jewelry, and objets d'art. For standard shopping hours, see GETTING READY TO GO.

Be sure to take your passport when you shop, and always inquire about the Value Added Tax (VAT) refund application forms when your total purchases in a store are over £50 (about $75). The VAT is a surcharge payable at the sales counter, but foreign customers usually will be reimbursed for it at home (for more information see GETTING READY TO GO).

We especially recommend the following stores:

Andrew Pringle Old books, maps, and prints. 7 Dundas St. (phone: 556-9698).

Belinda Robertson This shop's a bit hard to find, as it has no window display and is hidden in a cluster of terraced houses that have been converted into offices. But its high-quality cashmere tunics, sweaters, skirts, and other clothing in classic designs make it worth seeking out. 22 Palmerston Pl. (phone: 225-1057).

Blackfriars Music Folk music records, sheet music, and books, as well as all types of instruments from fiddles to bagpipes. 49 Blackfriars St. (phone: 557-3090).

Bruntsfield Clocks A tiny shop filled with old clocks of all shapes, sizes, and decorations. They also repair and restore. 7 Bruntsfield Pl. (phone: 229-4720).

Burberrys Scotch House Men's and women's clothing and accessories including women's kilts and splendid tartan umbrellas. 39-41 Princes St. (phone: 556-1252).

Cashmere Store The best place in town for cashmere sweaters and scarves. 2 St. Giles' St. (phone: 225-5178).

Chit Chat Antique cutlery and china, old prints, and rare books are featured at this small shop. 134 St. Stephen St. (phone: 225-9660).

Cornerstone Bookshop Books on religion, ecology, and women's issues are the main draw here; plus Celtic books and imaginative postcards. Behind *St. John's Church.* Princes St. (phone: 229-3776).

Crabtree & Evelyn Classical music plays quietly in this shop selling toiletries, chocolates, biscuits, and preserves. 4 Hanover St. (phone: 226-2478).

Edinburgh Gallery The best place in the city for contemporary paintings. 18a Dundas St. (phone: 557-5227).

Edinburgh Woollen Mill Good, inexpensive woolens such as kilts, sweaters, tweeds, scarves, shawls, and mohairs. Three locations: 62 Princes St. (phone: 225-4966); 453 Lawnmarket (phone: 225-1525); and 139 Princes St. (phone: 226-3840).

Eric Davidson Antique furniture, ceramics, paintings, and clocks. 183 Causewayside (phone: 662-4221).

Festival Fringe Society The *Fringe*'s headquarters and ticket office includes a small shop that sells colorful T-shirts and postcards. 180 High St. (phone: 226-5257).

Gieves & Hawkes The only branch in Scotland of the famous Savile Row tailors whose customers include the Prince of Wales. 48 George St. (phone: 225-7456).

Hamilton & Inches A grand, but friendly, jewelry shop that was established in 1866; the queen's silversmith and clock specialist. 87 George St. (phone: 225-4898).

Hector Russell Kiltmaker Everything in tartan including deerstalkers and caps and Scottish music in the background. 95 Princes St. (phone: 225-3315).

Hugh Macpherson Ltd. A three-generation family business that sells, in addition to bagpipes, Highland costumes handmade by local women on the premises. To go with the bagpipes, shoppers might buy a pipe band uniform or a custom-made tartan skirt or kilt. 17 W. Maitland St. (phone: 225-4008).

James Pringle Weavers Beautiful knitwear in cashmere, lamb's wool, and classic Shetland, as well as tartans and tweeds. Offering low prices for top-quality goods is the policy of this factory outlet, which also provides free taxi service from hotels in the city to the shop's door. 70-74 Bangor Rd. (phone: 553-5161).

James Thin Books, newspapers, magazines, and stationery since 1848. There is a quiet tearoom upstairs. 57 George St. (phone: 225-4495). There are also branches at *Waverley Market,* Princes St. (phone: 557-1378); and 53-59 S. Bridge (phone: 556-6743); the latter sells mostly textbooks.

Jenner's Sells everything, especially bone china and Scottish crystal. A particularly good selection of fine food items. Don't miss the china and glass shops in the lofty rear hall. The restaurant on the second floor has a good view of Princes Street. Princes and South St. David's Sts. (phone: 225-2442).

John Dickson This gunmaker and fishing tackle shop has been supplying sporting gear to Scotland's gentry since 1820. It also offers a fine selection of outdoor countrywear. 21 Frederick St. (phone: 225-4218).

Joseph H. Bonnar A wide assortment of antique and modern jewelry. 72 Thistle St. (phone: 226-2811).

Justerini & Brooks Established in 1749, these wine merchants are suppliers to the queen, as they also were to seven of her predecessors. 39 George St. (phone: 226-4202).

Kinloch Anderson Serving the royal family, it's the place where Prince Charles, among others, obtains his kilts. Kilts for men and women can be made to order in some 400 of the tartans in existence; some ready-made kilts and accessories are available as well. 4 Dock St. (phone: 555-1371).

Laurence Black Ltd. A wide variety of Victorian Scottish antiques, including napkin rings, furniture, and knickknacks. 45 Cumberland St. (phone: 557-4545).

Margaret Duncan Books Antiquarian and other secondhand books sold by experts. 5 Tanfield (phone: 556-4591).

One World Shop Excellent selection of Third World crafts and small gift items from rugs to soaps. Behind *St. John's Church.* Princes St. (phone: 229-4541).

Pine and Old Lace A tiny shop specializing in antique lace garments, linen, and pine furniture. 46 Victoria St. (phone: 225-3287).

Pitlochry Knitwear Bargains in Scottish products, especially sweaters, kilts, and ladies' suits. 26 N. Bridge (phone: 225-3893).

Ragamuffin Designer knitwear for men and women, including some ladies' jackets commissioned on the Isle of Skye. 276 Canongate (phone: 557-6007).

Robert Cresser This is the brush center of Edinburgh; everything from shaving brushes to brooms is made on the premises and sold here. 40 Victoria St. (phone: 225-2181).

Royal Mile Whiskies Paradise for whisky lovers—a huge selection from the Highlands, Lowlands, and the islands, ranging from miniatures to elaborate presentation bottles. Scottish foodstuffs, such as smoked salmon and haggis, also can be found here. 379 High St. (phone: 225-3383).

Scottish Gems Most of the traditional and modern jewelry in this shop is made in Scotland and depicts Celtic and Nordic influences; also Scottish pottery and glassware. 24 High St. (phone: 557-5731).

Scottish Gifts, Curios, and Crafts This tiny shop is the place to find genuine handmade Scottish goods (most are crafted in nearby workshops). It's stuffed to the rafters with antique jewelry, weapons, badges, kilts, bagpipes, and other items characteristic of Scotland. 499 Lawnmarket (phone: 225-6113).

Second Edition Bookshop Fine arts and literature books. 9 Howard St. (phone: 556-9403).

Top Brass Top-quality antique brass furnishings from candelabras to bedframes. 77 Dundas St. (phone: 557-4293).

Waterstone's The Edinburgh branches of this huge chain of bookstores, whose instant success is due mainly to an enterprising, well-informed staff and late hours (it's open weekdays until 9 PM). Three locations: 83 George St. (phone: 225-3436), 13 Princes St. (phone: 556-3034), and 128 Princes St. (phone: 226-2666).

SPORTS

BICYCLING Rentals are available from *Central Cycle Hire* (13 Lochrin Pl., Tolcross; phone: 228-6363).

FITNESS CENTER *Meadowbank Sports Centre* (139 London Rd.; phone: 661-5351) has a large gym with weights and exercise equipment, a 400-meter track, and classes in archery, boxing, fencing, and judo.

GOLF With more than 20 courses, Edinburgh is a good place to practice Scotland's national mania. One course in the area, however, is merely the greatest.

TOP TEE-OFF SPOT

The Honourable Company of Edinburgh Golfers The single best course in Scotland is in nearby Gullane (pronounced *Gill*-in), and it boasts the golf club with the longest continuous history in the world, one that has grown in status with each decade since its formal beginnings in 1744. Tucked along the south shore of the Firth of Forth, the course—most commonly called *Muirfield*—is totally challenging as well as beautifully simple. (For an idea of just how challenging it can be, know that the House Committee has imposed a maximum handicap of 18 for men and 24 for women because so many visitors, "unable to cope with the difficulty of the championship course," took longer than four and a half hours to get around it.) Note that access is granted to non-members only by advance arrangement, and then only on Tuesday, Thursday, and Friday mornings (Tuesdays and Thursdays only in July and August); when writing, include alternate dates. *Muirfield* last hosted the *British Open* in 1992. For information or reservations, contact *The Honourable Company of Edinburgh Golfers* (Muirfield, Gullane; phone: 1620-842255).

A letter from your home club president or pro should get you into any of the city's courses; other fine venues are *Royal Burgess* and *Bruntsfield,* both in suburban Barnton, *Carrick Knowe* (in Glendevon Park; phone: 337-1096), and *Silverknowes* (Silverknowes Pkwy.; phone: 336-3843). Reserve tee-off times at these clubs ahead of arrival. Golf clubs can be rented. And if you can't get into any of these, the *Braids Hill Golf Centre* (91 Liberton Dr.; phone: 658-1755) has a driving range.

JOGGING A good bet is *Holyrood Park,* near the huge stone palace at the foot of Canongate. An especially popular run is around Arthur's Seat, the extinct volcano in the center of the park.

SWIMMING Have a dip in the luxurious *Royal Commonwealth Pool* (Dalkeith Rd.; phone: 667-7211), which features a water slide, re-created river rapids, a twister, and a stingray. Open daily.

THEATER

Edinburgh's main venues are the *King's* (2 Leven St.; phone: 220-4349), which presents touring productions, including the finest from London's *National Theatre;* the *Playhouse* (20 Greenside Pl.; phone: 557-2590), which features a variety of plays, concerts, and musicals; and the *Royal Lyceum* (Grindlay St.; phone: 229-9697), which has a fine reputation for interesting productions of both classic and contemporary plays. Pop stars and extravaganzas are frequently presented at the *Edinburgh Exhibition Centre* (Ingliston; phone: 333-3036). The *Traverse* (Cambridge St.; phone: 228-

1404) is a small theater which is internationally well known for its avant-garde pieces and for presenting the works of new playwrights from all over the world. The *Netherbow* (43 High St.; phone: 556-9579) and *Theatre Workshop* (34 Hamilton Pl.; phone: 226-5425) mount small-scale, artistic productions. In summer, open-air productions are performed at the *Ross Theatre* (phone: 220-4348) in *Princes Street Gardens.* Schedules are in the dailies, *Day by Day,* and *The List* (see *Local Coverage*), and tickets for most productions can be purchased at *Ticket Centre* (31-33 Waverley Bridge; phone: 225-8616), as well as at individual box offices.

MUSIC

Classical music is the city's overriding passion. Highbrow musical events are held at *Usher Hall* (Lothian Rd.; phone: 228-1155), where the *Royal Scottish Orchestra* holds performances most Friday nights at 7:30. Internationally famous musicians and ensembles (both classical and nonclassical) perform at the *King's* and the *Playhouse* theaters (see above for both). The old *Empire Theatre* (famous for its Art Deco decor) recently reopened as the *Festival Theatre* (13 Nicholson St.; phone: 662-1112); boasting the largest stage in Great Britain (about 9,300 square feet), it hosts performances by the *Scottish Opera,* as well as classical music concerts and a variety of musicals and other plays. Concerts also are held at *Saint Cecilia's Hall* (Canongate; no phone). For chamber music and occasional jazz, try *Queen's Hall* (Clerk St.; phone: 668-2019). *St. Giles' Cathedral* regularly hosts organ recitals, and at *St. Mary's Cathedral,* evensong is sung on weekday afternoons at 5:15 by a trained choir with boy sopranos (see *Special Places* for both). Details on other musical events are available in the dailies, *Day by Day,* and *The List* (see *Local Coverage*).

NIGHTCLUBS AND NIGHTLIFE

Although Edinburgh isn't exactly Las Vegas (or even Philadelphia), a number of nightspots have opened here in recent years. Discos usually are filled with a very young crowd, but you could risk the following if you're under 30: *Century 2000* (1 Lothian Rd.; phone: 229-7670); *Buster Brown's Disco* (25 Market St.; phone: 226-4224); and the *Red Hot Pepper Club* (3 Semple St.; phone: 229-7733). *Minus One,* the nightclub in the *Carlton Highland* hotel (see *Checking In*), attracts a somewhat older crowd (it's open only on Thursday, Friday, and Saturday nights). Jazz and folk music can be heard around the city; check the *Evening News*'s "Nightlife" page, *Day by Day* magazine, or *The List* (see *Local Coverage*).

Edinburgh also has several private casinos: *Berkeley* (2 Rutland Pl.; phone: 228-4446); *Stanley's* (5 York Pl.; phone: 556-1055); and *Stakis Regency* (14 Picardy Pl.; phone: 557-3585). Anyone who's 18 or older can join, but you must apply for membership (free) at least 48 hours before your visit.

Best in Town

CHECKING IN

In Scotland, it is practically impossible to get a room without an accompanying kippers-to-nuts Big Scottish Breakfast (you usually pay for it whether you eat it or not). Most of Edinburgh's major hotels have complete facilities for the business traveler. Those hotels listed below as having "business services" usually offer such conveniences as a concierge, meeting rooms, photocopiers, computers, translation services, and express checkout, among others. Call the hotel for additional information. Expect to pay more than $190 per night for a double room (including private bath, phone, and TV set, unless otherwise indicated) in the hotels listed below as expensive; $115 to $190 for those in the moderate category; and less than $115 for inexpensive places. Lower rates are available on weekends at the larger hotels (except in August). You can make reservations in more than 70 hotels and guesthouses in the city by calling *Dial-a-Bed* (phone: 557-4365; 800-616947 toll-free within Britain). Should you find it impossible to get into any of our selected hotels, the tourist information center (see *Tourist Information,* above) has an accommodations service covering all of Edinburgh and the surrounding district. All telephone numbers are in the 131 city code unless otherwise indicated.

EXPENSIVE

Balmoral Forte Grand At the turn of the century, two rival railway companies raced to be the first to erect its own hotel; the *North British Railway Company* won, and its huge, Scottish baronial-style establishment began receiving guests in 1902. Locals still refer to the property (now part of the Forte chain), with 189 rooms and suites, as the "North British." Its Victorian features have been retained, although it has been revamped for the 21st century. Other amenities include a restaurant, 24-hour room service, foreign currency exchange, and business services. Princes St. (phone: 556-2414; 800-225-5843; fax: 557-3747).

Caledonian The city's other railroad hotel opened next to *Caledonian Station* in 1903 (the station has since closed). The decor is very engaging, and some of the 238 rooms and suites have great views of *Edinburgh Castle.* Celebrities love it. The hotel's first class *Pompadour* dining room (see *Eating Out*) is nearly matched by the *Carriages* restaurant, with the old station clock proudly mounted on the wall. There also are three bars. In addition, the property is conveniently close to Edinburgh's new *International Conference Centre,* which is set to open this fall. Other amenities include 24-hour room service, foreign currency exchange, and business services. Princes St. (phone: 225-2433; 800-641-0300; fax: 225-6632).

Carlton Highland Remarkably transformed from an old department store into a grand and sophisticated Victorian hotel with 207 rooms, two dining rooms, and a bar. Health facilities include a pool, squash courts, a gym, saunas, and a Jacuzzi, and there is dancing at the *Minus One* nightclub (see *Nightlife*). Business services are available. North Bridge, off Princes St. (phone: 556-7277; fax: 556-2691).

Howard This luxurious, 16-room hotel, which deliberately has no reception desk, looks and feels like a splendid, elegantly decorated Georgian townhouse. The fabrics and furnishings are in soft Highland heather tones. Its restaurant serves a mix of continental and Scottish fare. Business services are available. 36 Great King St. (phone: 557-3500; fax: 557-6515).

Prestonfield House One of Scotland's finest historic houses, this lovely 1687 mansion with its original furnishings is a very special place to stay. There are only five guestrooms (two with private baths), but the 13-acre gardens, where peacocks, pheasants, and partridges are familiar sights, make a stop here truly idyllic. The restaurant serves excellent fare (see *Eating Out*). An 18-hole golf course is also on the grounds, and business services are available. Located 2 miles southeast of the city center. Priestfield Rd. (phone: 668-3346; fax: 668-3976).

Royal Terrace A portrait of the Duke of Edinburgh over the open fire near the reception desk sets the tone for this luxurious 97-room hostelry. Occupying a row of beautiful Georgian houses, fully restored to their original grandeur, the establishment offers a lush decor, with marble fireplaces and crystal chandeliers. The *Conservatory* restaurant serves Scottish fare. There is a large landscaped garden, and a health club with a heated pool, gym, sauna, and massage room. Business services are available. 18 Royal Ter. (phone: 557-3222; fax: 557-5334).

Scandic Crown Located halfway between *Edinburgh Castle* and the Royal Mile in Edinburgh's Old Town, this establishment, though modern, has an antiquated air, which goes well with the neighboring architecture. Rooms have heated floors, security safes, satellite TV, free in-house movies, and minibars. The two restaurants serve a combination of Scandinavian and Scottish fare. There's also a health club with Finnish saunas. Other amenities include 24-hour room service, foreign currency exchange, and business services. 80 High St. (phone: 557-9797; 800-44-UTELL; fax: 557-9789).

Sheraton Grand After a complete overhaul that gives it a thoroughly Scottish feel, this comfortable 263-room hotel is now decorated with tartan and tweed fabrics, and the *Grill Room* restaurant serves authentic regional dishes. The airy *Terrace* brasserie overlooks the fountains of Festival Square, and diners might well enjoy their meals to the accompaniment of the pipes and drums of the Scots Guards. There are also lovely views of *Edinburgh Castle*, and many of the city's other attractions are a short walk away. Other amenities include 24-hour room service, a pool, a health club and gym, a sauna and whirlpool, foreign currency exchange, and business services. 1 Festival Sq. (phone: 229-9131; 800-334-8484; fax: 228-4510).

MODERATE

Braid Hills Muriel Spark fans will remember that this is where Miss Jean Brodie, by then past her prime, took tea. An old, established, family-run, 68-room hotel with restaurant in the southern suburbs toward the Pentland Hills. Business services are available. 134 Braid Rd. (phone: 447-8888; fax: 452-8477).

Bruntsfield Set in a Victorian townhouse about a mile south of the city's center is this friendly 54-room hotel. Its *Potting Shed* restaurant specializes in tasty, light dishes, including crêpes, and the large bar attracts a lively crowd in the evenings. Business services are available. 69 Bruntsfield Pl. (phone: 229-1393; fax: 229-5634).

Channings Five fine Georgian townhouses have been joined to create this elegant hostelry on a quiet cobbled lane within walking distance of Princes Street. There are 48 beautifully appointed rooms with modern amenities, and the bar and brasserie offer Scottish and international dishes. Other amenities include 24-hour room service, foreign currency exchange, and business services. S. Learmonth Gardens (phone: 315-2226; fax: 332-9631).

George Inter-Continental Located in the New Town between Charlotte and St. Andrew Squares, this gracious 19th-century establishment—originally apartments for the aristocracy when the New Town of Edinburgh was created by architect Robert Adam and his pupils—retains a luxurious ambience. Now affiliated with the Inter-Continental hotel group, it has 195 bedrooms, two dining rooms, and the *Gathering of the Clans* bar. Other amenities include 24-hour room service, foreign currency exchange, and business services. 19-21 George St. (phone: 225-1251; 800-327-0200; fax: 226-5644).

Holiday Inn Located a mile northwest of the city center, this modern property has 120 comfortable rooms, a restaurant, and a small gym. Its friendly service, reasonable prices, and fine views of the city and the Firth of Forth from some rooms make up for its lack of historical ambience. Business services are available. Queensberry Rd. (phone: 332-2442; 800-HOLIDAY; fax: 332-3408).

Mount Royal Located next to *Jenner's* department store, this 160-room hotel with a restaurant and café has splendid views of the *Scott Monument* right across the street and of *Edinburgh Castle* towering high above it. Be sure to ask for a room in the front. Business services are available. 53 Princes St. (phone: 225-7161; fax: 220-4671).

Norton House Set in a secluded parkland on the edge of Edinburgh, this ornate Victorian mansion with 46 rooms was once the home of the Ushers (they founded the brewing firm). Dine in the lovely conservatory restaurant or the more informal *Norton Tavern,* located in what once was the walled garden. Other amenities include 24-hour room service, foreign currency exchange, and business services. In Ingilston, near *Edinburgh Airport* (phone: 333-1275; fax: 333-5305).

Old Waverley This pleasant 1870s hostelry has 66 rooms (ask for one at the front); *Cranston's,* its charming restaurant decorated in soft pink tones, has wonderful views of the *Scott Monument* and *Edinburgh Castle.* Business services are available. 43 Princes St. (phone: 556-4648; fax: 557-6316).

Roxburghe One of the best examples of Robert Adam's townhouse architecture, this distinguished, tranquil oasis at the west end of Princes Street is where Scottish gentry with no townhouse of their own stay. Scottish seafood and game are the specialties in the *Consort* restaurant. There are 75 well-appointed rooms. Other amenities include 24-hour room service, foreign currency exchange, and business services. 38 Charlotte Sq. (phone: 225-3921; 800-528-1234; fax: 220-2518).

INEXPENSIVE

Albany Three elegant Georgian townhouses make up this comfortable hotel with 22 rooms of varying sizes and shapes. The staff is friendly and there is a restaurant and bar. 39 Albany St. (phone: 556-0397; fax: 557-6633).

Bank As its name implies, this hostelry, conveniently situated on the Royal Mile, used to be a bank. Still corporate-looking on the outside, it has been charmingly redecorated within, and today offers eight simply furnished guestrooms, plus a large, bistro-style café. 1 South Bridge (phone: 556-9043; fax: 558-1362).

Donmaree This establishment has nine rooms in the original 1830s house and eight more in a modern annex with a conservatory overlooking the gardens. The restaurant offers good, traditional dishes. 21 Mayfield Gardens (phone: 667-3641; fax: 667-9130).

Galloway Guest House Just off the panoramic Dean Bridge, this place has 10 rooms (six with private baths), but no restaurant (there's a breakfast lounge). There's also on-street parking. No credit cards accepted. 22 Dean Park Crescent (phone: 332-3672).

EATING OUT

Reports on Scottish food vary, but suffice to say, it cannot lay claim to culinary laurels. Still, visitors might want to try some of the following specialties: cock-a-leekie soup (chicken and leek), salmon, haddock, trout, and Aberdeen Angus beef. Skip haggis (spicy intestines), except on a purely experimental basis. Scones originated in Scotland, and shortbread shouldn't be missed. There are a number of quality dining spots away from the center in the waterfront district of Leith. Restaurants usually keep the city's formal hours (lunch until 2:30, dinner anywhere from 6 on). As the city's restaurants can get very crowded during August, be sure to call ahead. Expect to pay more than $60 for a dinner for two, excluding wine and tips, in establishments listed as expensive; $40 to $60 in moderate establishments; and less than $40 in inexpensive places. All restaurants listed below serve lunch and dinner, unless otherwise noted. All telephone numbers are in the 131 city code unless otherwise indicated.

EXPENSIVE

L'Auberge A discreet, indeed positively diplomatic, dining spot that serves French fare, most notably fish and game. Open daily. Reservations advised. Major credit cards accepted. 58 St. Mary's St. between Cowgate and Canongate (phone: 556-5888).

Pompadour The fascinating lunch menu provides a history of Scottish cooking, while dinner features French dishes (some of the recipes were used in the *Palace of Holyroodhouse* when Mary, Queen of Scots, was married to the heir to the French throne). Closed weekend lunch. Reservations advised. Major credit cards accepted. In the *Caledonian Hotel,* Princes St. (phone: 225-2433).

Prestonfield House A 300-year-old country estate within its own peacock-laden park grounds offers French fare in a candlelit dining room with tapestries, paintings, and an open fireplace. Open daily. Reservations necessary. Major credit cards accepted. Priestfield Rd. (phone: 668-3346).

Stac Polly This restaurant (formerly *Grindlay's*) is named after a Scottish mountain. The menu features well-prepared Scottish fare using fresh local ingredients such as salmon, mussels, and lamb. If you're in the mood to try haggis, this place offers an interesting version of it (wrapped in phyllo pastry). Conveniently located near the *Royal Lyceum Theatre* and *Usher Hall,* it's ideal for either pre- or post-performance dining. Closed Saturday lunch and Sunday evenings. Reservations necessary. Major credit cards accepted. 8-10 Grindlay St. (phone: 229-5405).

MODERATE

Atrium Andrew Radford, formerly the chef on the luxurious *Royal Scotsman* touring train, oversees the kitchen at this elegant dining room in the foyer of the *Traverse Theatre.* The menu presents innovative versions of English and continental dishes, such as game casserole, shellfish bisque, and sticky toffee pudding. Closed Saturday lunch and Sundays. Reservations advised. Major credit cards accepted. Cambridge St. (phone: 228-8882).

Bay of Bengal Excellent tandoori dishes are cooked from scratch with delicate spices; there may be a bit of a wait, but it's well worth it. Closed Sunday evenings. Reservations advised. Major credit cards accepted. 164 High St. (phone: 225-2361).

Merchant's Trendy and French, with white tablecloths, silver, and crystal, this eatery is decorated in a minimalist style, with bare floorboards and white walls. Closed Sundays. Reservations advised. Major credit cards accepted. Off Candlemaker Row, 17 Merchant St. (phone: 225-4009).

Patio A trendy, attractive Italian place just off Princes Street, it serves steaks and seafood specialties along with good pizza and pasta dishes. Closed Sundays. Reservations advised. Major credit cards accepted. 87 Hanover St. (phone: 226-3653).

Skipper's Bistro A jolly waterfront seafood spot in Leith, justly known for its imaginative preparations and fresh ingredients. Closed Sundays and Mondays. Reservations necessary. Major credit cards accepted. 1A Dock Pl., Leith (phone: 554-1018).

INEXPENSIVE

Cornerstone Café This tiny vegetarian restaurant also has tables on its outdoor terrace. Excellent salads, stuffed potatoes, rolls, and homemade cakes. Closed Sundays. No reservations. No credit cards accepted. Behind *St. John's Church,* Princes St. (phone: 229-0212).

Harry Ramsden's A branch of the nationwide chain of fish-and-chips eateries, this place has done a booming business ever since it opened a couple of years ago. Diners are also treated to a great view of Newhaven Harbour. Open daily. Reservations advised for large groups. Major credit cards accepted. *Newhaven Fishmarket* (phone: 551-5566).

Pierre Victoire Excellent fare such as salmon with raspberries and champagne and lobster in a light curry sauce, low prices, and informality have made this French-style bistro quite popular. Closed Sundays. Reservations advised. Major credit cards accepted. Three locations: 38-40 Grassmarket (phone: 226-2442), 8 Union St. (phone: 557-8451), and 10 Victoria St. (phone: 225-1721).

Waterfront Wine Bar A former ticketing office for ships houses this lively wine bar, which features interesting fish dishes such as smoked trout mousse. There are meat and vegetarian fare as well, and a good selection of wine and beer. Open daily. Reservations advised. Major credit cards. 1c Dock Pl., Leith (phone: 554-7426).

SHARING A PINT

Edinburgh has (believe it or not) more than 750 pubs to choose from—which means it has more quaffing places per capita than anywhere else in Britain. The largest concentration of pubs is in the waterfront district of Leith, but the most famous area is the narrow Rose Street, just a block north of Princes Street. Here the tradition of the pre-wedding pub crawl lives on—the bride-to-be and her friends gradually work their way down from the west end of the street, while the groom and his mates start from the east end. Eventually everyone meets in the middle. The *Rose Brewery* (55 Rose St.; phone: 220-1227) serves Auld Reekie (named after the smell of coal smoke that used to cling to the city's buildings) that is brewed on the premises and comes in two strengths. Nearby is the *Café Royal Oyster Bar* (17 W. Register St.; phone: 556-1884), the longest bar in Britain; its stained glass windows and dark paneling were featured in the film *Chariots of Fire.* Also nearby is the *Guildford Arms* (1 W. Register St.; phone: 556-4312), a Victorian-style tavern with mahogany walls, a lovely plasterwork ceiling, and a gallery alcove where you can look down on the action in the main bar. If you enjoy folk music, try the *Fiddler's Arms* (9-11 Grassmarket; phone: 229-2665) or the *Auld Hundred* (100 Rose St.; phone: 225-1809). Another good pub with a turn-of-the-century atmosphere is the *Barony Bar* (81-85 Broughton St.; phone: 557-0546).

The large *Preservation Hall* (9 Victoria St.; phone: 226-3816) is ornamented with fine epigraphs against drink and offers rock and jazz music in the evenings. *Mather's* (25 Broughton St.; phone: 556-6754) is the ecumenical watering hole for left-wing, nationalist, and sexual politicos. Opulent barges sometimes carry licenses in tourist season on the Leith waterfront. Find out at the *Waterfront Wine Bar* (see *Eating Out*). Also try *Leith Oyster Bar* (57 The Shore, Leith; phone: 554-6294). Both offer bar lunches.

Glasgow

"The Second City of the Empire"—this grand sobriquet belonged to Glasgow through the glorious reign of Queen Victoria, when only London surpassed it in size, wealth, and might. From a tiny 7th-century cathedral town on a tributary of the river Clyde, Glasgow grew into an international industrial capital, the world's foremost shipbuilding center, and a pioneer in mining, railroading, canal cutting, ironworking, steam engineering, and scientific invention. From the time of Glaswegian James Watt (1736–1819), the city never looked back.

Today Glasgow is Britain's third-most-visited city (after London and Edinburgh), renowned for its magnificent and extensive Victorian architecture. Greek, Gothic, Venetian, Beaux Arts, Renaissance, Art Nouveau—you name it, Glasgow's effervescent coterie of 19th-century architects copied and improved it. Public buildings the size of a chain of Alps capture the pomp and circumstance of the Victorian Age, while in the west end, private residences from the same period show an unrivaled variety and graceful delicacy of line.

Although Scottish nationalists today bitterly lament the union of the English and Scottish parliaments in 1707, this move actually put Glasgow on the map. Freed from stringent laws prohibiting trade with the American colonies, merchants exploited Glasgow's relative proximity to the open sea. While cargoes from London were attacked by pirates in the English Channel, clippers zoomed along the Clyde, carefree, to Virginia. In exchange for Scottish muslins and linen, merchants acquired tobacco—and got it faster than their English competitors. Soon Glaswegian tobacco merchants were supplying half of Europe.

As the Industrial Revolution gathered momentum, pressure to increase the efficiency of the Clyde, which was too shallow to allow heavy ships, became fierce. Parliament approved a plan to strip away miles of adjacent factories and build in their stead high quaysides acting as dikes. Steam dredgers and the development of underwater blasting did the rest. By 1886, 58 million cubic yards of waste and sludge had been dispatched, and the whole riverbed had been lowered by about 29 feet. "Muddling through" wasn't good enough for Glasgow in those iron-willed days; when Man fought Nature, Nature lost.

Daniel Defoe glowingly described Glasgow's spacious streets and beautifully proportioned houses, and other writers noted how eager the natives were to point these out. Signs of civic pride are everywhere. Glaswegians have long had a penchant for showing off; witness the large number of official and unofficial parades, elaborate *World's Fair*–type exhibitions, and crowded sailings down the Clyde. The city crest, bearing symbols associated with Glasgow's founder and patron saint, St. Mungo, appears on everything, even the sides of city buses. Museums are municipal, free, and very special, especially the *Museum of Transport,* where you can sense how wheels have become an absolute cult for Glaswegians in the climate of nostalgia and waning power that is the aftermath of their enormous share of the Industrial Revolution.

Glaswegians' gargantuan civic pride is nowhere more evident than in the city's famous slum subculture, associated primarily with a southside district called the Gorbals. The virile mix of football, folklore, hard drink, and Red politics was fanned and molded in the 19th century by whole new populations that poured into the Clyde Valley from Catholic Ireland and the Scottish Highlands. Staid old Presbyterian Glasgow hardly knew how to absorb the shock, and this is the origin of much of the city's present orange-green antipathy, exemplified by the rivalry between the *Rangers* and *Celtics* soccer teams.

Glasgow today is a mass of contradictions. It has more high-quality cultural events than Edinburgh (except during the *Edinburgh International Festival*), yet it also has some very rough areas where crime rates are high. Right near its most elegant buildings are shamefully derelict streets. The Gorbals and other tenement areas have been bulldozed and refitted with faceless skyscraper apartments, yet the rambunctiousness and camaraderie lingers.

The Second City, however, is gone. Elevated motorways on concrete slabs crisscross parts of Glasgow's urban scene, and the Clyde's docks are now still. Population has declined from over a million to around 750,000, and Birmingham is now Britain's second-largest city; still, at least half of all Scots live within 20 miles of Glasgow, and engineering, printing, textile, food, drink, tobacco, and chemical industries soldier on despite rising unemployment.

The key to Glasgow's future seems to lie in tourism. This fun-loving city's rebirth of cultural productivity and awareness started in the early 1970s, when street after street began major renovations. Indeed, since then a Glasgow renaissance has captured the attention of the entire country, arising from such fine additions as the *Burrell Collection,* as well as from the European Parliament's selection of Glasgow as the Cultural Capital of Europe for 1990; a permanent legacy of that event is the impressive *Royal Concert Hall,* which opened as part of the festivities. Today a brighter-than-ever spotlight shines on the city.

Glasgow At-a-Glance

SEEING THE CITY

Getting an overhead gander at Glasgow is almost like finding the Holy Grail. The city is devoid of rooftop restaurants and publicly accessible steeples. In spring and summer, you can go to *Glasgow University* (Buses

No. 44 and No. 59 leave frequently from Hope Street), and storm the Gothic vaults of the main building, architect Sir George Gilbert Scott's elephantine monstrosity built on Gilmorehill in 1870. The "Bedellus" (janitor) at the visitors' center can unlock a door that leads up 252 steps to the top of *Glasgow University Tower.* If you can stand the climb, the reward is spectacular: Just below is lovely *Kelvingrove Park,* with the river Kelvin winding through. South of you is the river Clyde, and southeast is downtown Glasgow. The tower is open to visitors on Fridays at 2 PM mid-April through September. *University of Glasgow* (phone: 339-8855, ext. 4252).

SPECIAL PLACES

One way to see Glasgow is to take it period by period. But start in the middle of things, with the grid of streets that makes up Victorian Glasgow, because it is this era that is the essence of the city. The rest of the sights—Medieval Glasgow, the Old Merchants' City, Modern Glasgow, and Clydeside attractions—are not far away, but don't expect to cover everything in a day. If you visit April through October, take a bus tour; you can choose to get on and off to see sights that interest you, or else remain on the bus for the complete 9-mile, one-hour circuit. Tours depart several times daily from the tourist information office at 35 St. Vincent Pl. (phone: 942-6453).

VICTORIAN GLASGOW

GEORGE SQUARE Also called Glasgow's Valhalla, this intriguing mix of statues, flower plots, and pigeons was originally laid out in 1781 and named after King George III. It came into its own in Victorian times, when most of the grandiose buildings now surrounding it were constructed. Since Bloody Friday it has been the undisputed central focal point of the city.

CITY CHAMBERS William Young, a local boy who made good in London, designed Glasgow's Italian Renaissance *City Hall,* and Queen Victoria officially opened it in 1888. Inside, the loggia, staircases, and grand banquet hall, with their sumptuous interplay of granite, mosaics, marble, and stone, make a millionaire's mansion look like a log cabin. Guided tours are given weekdays (except Thursdays and during banquets). No admission charge. George Sq. (phone: 221-9600).

MERCHANTS' HOUSE Opposite George Square's west side is the *Glasgow Chamber of Commerce* building, built in 1877 by native architect John Burnet. Glasgow invented chambers of commerce in 1659 when its *Merchant Guild* erected a house from which to minister to the widowed and orphaned of the collective merchant poor. That building—and that institution—was this one's ancestor. (Glasgow's traders, not to be outdone by their arch rivals—the merchants, followed suit with a similar institution and eventually built the elegant *Trades Hall* of 1794, designed by the renowned Scottish architect Robert Adam; it is well worth a look.) *Trades Hall* (85 Glassford St.; phone:

552-2418) and *Merchant's House* (7 W. George St.; phone: 221-8272) may be visited by prior arrangement only; neither charges admission.

BUCHANAN AND GORDON STREETS For row after nonstop row of massive, public architectural Victoriana, nowhere in the world beats these two thoroughfares!

TENEMENT HOUSE Restored by the *National Trust for Scotland,* this modest flat situated in a 19th-century tenement building is furnished with late-19th-century and early-20th-century relics and provides an interesting look at life in Victorian Britain. The table is still set for tea in front of a glowing coal fire. Open daily from 2 to 5 PM April through October; weekends from 2 to 4 PM the rest of the year. Admission charge. 145 Buccleuch St. (phone: 333-0183).

MUSEUM OF TRANSPORT In 1962, a huge turnout of Glaswegians wept openly as they watched a parade of trams from all eras make a farewell memorial run through the streets. The trams were then lovingly roundhoused and became the nucleus of this museum. Displays include a simulated Glasgow street of 1938 with period shop fronts and appropriate vehicles on the cobbled roadway; there's also a reconstruction of one of the Glasgow underground (subway) stations. An authentic period motor car showroom has displays of historic automobiles. Superb and varied ship models in the *Clyde Room* reflect the significance of Glasgow and the river Clyde as one of the world's foremost areas of shipbuilding. Open daily. No admission charge. *Kelvin Hall,* Bunhouse Rd. (phone: 357-3929).

GLASGOW UNIVERSITY Most of the buildings here are a legacy from the university's rapid growth in Victorian times, although it was founded in 1451. The quadrangles, cloisters, and chapel always are open to visitors, but the best way to see the campus is on a 75-minute guided tour. It leaves from the visitors' center twice daily on Wednesdays, Fridays, and Saturdays April through September; and once on Wednesdays the rest of the year. Admission charge. University Ave. (phone: 330-5511).

ST. MUNGO'S MUSEUM OF RELIGIOUS LIFE AND ART Named after Glasgow's patron saint, it is the only museum in the world that covers the six major religious groups: Christians, Jews, Buddhists, Hindus, Muslims, and Sikhs. Works of art by members of each of these groups give insights into their beliefs and ways of life; there are exhibits about lesser-known religions as well. Open daily. Admission charge. Located next to the university (phone: 553-2557).

MEDIEVAL GLASGOW

GLASGOW CATHEDRAL A perfect specimen of pre-Reformation Gothic architecture, this was the only church on the Scottish mainland to have its inner structure spared during pillaging by 16th-century Protestant zealots bent on destroying "monuments of idolatry." The cathedral was founded by St. Mungo in the 6th century, though much of the building has been rebuilt several times over. Look at the 15th-century carved stone choir screen, the remarkable fan vaulting in the crypt over the tomb of Glasgow's patron saint, St. Mungo, and the chair Oliver Cromwell sat in when he visited Glasgow in 1650. Cathedral Sq. (phone: 552-3205).

PROVAND'S LORDSHIP Just opposite the cathedral is the oldest house in Glasgow, built about 1471. It was the townhouse of the prebend, or provand, of a nearby country see. Imagine a colony of such buildings and you will have an idea of Glasgow at the time of Mary, Queen of Scots. The house is now a period museum with displays of Scottish furniture. Open daily. No admission charge. 3 Castle St. (phone: 552-8819).

THE OLD MERCHANTS' CITY

GLASGOW CROSS This was the heart of the city in the 18th century, before George Square took over. The large reproduction of an etching that hangs on a wall of *Merchants' House* shows what it used to be like looking west down the Trongate. Today the *Tolbooth* steeple (1626) and the *Tron Church* steeple (1636) are all that's left from earlier times. Intersection of Gallowgate, Trongate, Saltmarket, and High St.

STIRLING'S LIBRARY The main part of this structure was the mansion of William Cunningham, the most famous tobacco lord of all. Ask at the front desk for the historical pamphlet. Closed Sundays. No admission charge. Royal Exchange Sq., off Queen St. (phone: 221-1876).

GLASGOW ART GALLERY AND MUSEUM A fine red sandstone building near the banks of the river Kelvin in *Kelvingrove Park* houses one of Britain's finest civic art collections, with a variety of works from many European schools; Corot, Degas, Monet, Millet, Raeburn, Turner, van Gogh, and Whistler are among those represented. Other works include Rubens's *Nature Adorned by the Graces,* Giorgione's *The Woman Taken in Adultery,* Rembrandt's *A Man in Armour,* and Salvador Dalí's *Christ of St. John of the Cross.* The *Glasgow Style Gallery* houses the work of architect and designer Charles Rennie Mackintosh and his contemporaries. In addition, there are galleries devoted to natural history (British birds and geology in particular), Scottish prehistory and history, ethnographical materials from as far away as Africa and Polynesia, and more. The collection of European arms and armor, housed in a striking glass-roofed hall, is especially fine. Open daily. No admission charge. *Kelvingrove Park* (opposite *Kelvin Hall*) on Dumbarton Rd. (phone: 357-3929).

POLLOK HOUSE Works by El Greco, Goya, Murillo, and William Blake, plus antique furniture, silver, porcelain, and glass, all displayed in a house designed by William Adam, the patriarch of the famous family of Scottish architects, and completed in 1752 (later additions by Sir Rowand Anderson were begun in 1890). Surrounded by extensive park grounds, the house also hosts chamber music concerts and other recitals (call the tourist board for details; see *Tourist Information*). Open daily. No admission charge. *Pollok Country Park,* 2060 Pollokshaws Rd. (phone: 632-0274).

MODERN GLASGOW

GLASGOW SCHOOL OF ART This is the most famous building in Glasgow and one of the most famous buildings of its period in the world—Charles Rennie Mackintosh's finest example of the style poet laureate Sir John Betjeman called "Beardsleyesque baronial." Its east wing was completed in 1899, the rest, with additions to the east wing, in 1909. Ironically, Mackintosh, an architect, interior designer, and artist of the avant-avant-garde, won the competition for the design of the school because his plan was the cheapest to build! Today, few dispute his unqualified genius. The school is open to the public on weekdays for tours between 11 AM and 2 PM. Admission charge. 167 Renfrew St. (phone: 353-4500).

ROYAL CONCERT HALL This imposing modern building occupies a commanding position at the end of Sauchiehall Street facing toward the Clyde. The lovely main auditorium (with 2,459 seats) is the home of the *Royal Scottish National Orchestra.* The hall also has a large, marble-paneled foyer, exhibition area, and restaurant. Guided 50-minute tours are given weekdays starting at 2 PM. Admission charge. Sauchiehall St. (phone: 332-6633).

BURRELL COLLECTION Built in 1983 in *Pollok Country Park* to house the collection given to the city by Sir William and Lady Burrell in 1944, this museum's rich and varied assemblage of art and artifacts reflects the wide-ranging tastes of its collectors. Paintings by Cézanne, Rembrandt, and Hals as well as fine examples of the arts of Egypt, Iraq, Iran, Greece, and Rome highlight the 8,000-piece collection. Pieces of medieval stonework are built into the fabric of the building, and three of the rooms from the Burrells' home at *Hutton Castle,* Berwickshire, have been reproduced and are grouped around the courtyard. Open daily. No admission charge. 2060 Pollokshaws Rd. (phone: 649-7151).

BY CLYDESIDE

CUSTOM HOUSE QUAY The *Glasgow City Council* has fitted out some of its disused docksides with flower-decked walkways. Bands play here in summer and discos blare at night; along the waterfront, renovations eventually will produce luxurious apartments and office buildings (however, the project has been delayed by lack of funds). *Custom House Quay* adjoins Clyde St.

GLASGOW GREEN Europe's oldest public park, it has certainly seen a lot of action! The statue at the west entrance was erected in 1881 by temperance reformers, after which public temperance pledgers were a common sight on the green for decades. During World War I, you couldn't see the grass for the sea of tweed caps at Red Clydesiders' rallies, and immediately afterwards, the green was the site of frequent and bloody gang wars. It was on *Glasgow Green* in 1765 that James Watt envisioned the steam condenser that changed the world. The *Hunterian Museum* (see *Museums*) houses a painting of the green by John Knox, one of the "Glasgow boys," a group of local artists that rose to international fame. The west entrance to the green is opposite the *Justiciary Courthouses* in the Saltmarket.

PEOPLE'S PALACE You never know what you'll find at this museum of local history, since the city owns more objects than it can possibly display at once and keeps changing the show. This institution traces the chronological development of trade, industrial unions, labor movements, women's suffrage, entertainment, and sports in the city; there are exhibits from every century. The place is impressionistic and fun, with everything from theatrical bills and political pamphlets to elaborate wrought-iron streetlights and fountains and the ridiculous pouting stone faces that once adorned the façade of the *Tontine* hotel. Open daily. No admission charge. East side of *Glasgow Green* (phone: 554-0223).

EXTRA SPECIAL

For an interesting and unique experience, take a trip aboard the world's last seagoing paddle steamer, the *Waverley.* On Fridays through Sundays from late June to late August, this charming craft has day-long round trips from *Anderston Quay,* Glasgow, to scenic spots beyond the Firth of Clyde. You'll see the cranes and derricks in the dockyards that once supplied over half the world's tonnage of oceangoing ships. Have lunch in the self-service restaurant (with bar) on board, or bring sandwiches. For full details, contact *Waverley Excursions Ltd., Waverley Terminal, Anderston Quay,* Broomielaw (phone: 221-8152).

Sources and Resources

TOURIST INFORMATION

The *Greater Glasgow Tourist Board* (35 St. Vincent Pl.; phone: 204-4400 or 204-4480) has free leaflets recommending things to see and do not only in Glasgow but throughout Scotland. Closed Sundays in winter. Ask at the desk for the official city guidebook, *Greater Glasgow Quick Guide* (costs £1/about $1.50), and for *City Live,* a free monthly booklet published by the *Glasgow Herald* that features a comprehensive diary of local entertainment. *John Smith and Son* (see *Shopping*) carries *Glasgow at a Glance* (Robert Hale; £9.99/about $15), which describes every important building in town. Short historical paperbacks about Glasgow also are sold, plus touring and restaurant guides and maps.

LOCAL COVERAGE The *Glasgow Herald* is the one respectable morning daily; the evening daily is the *Evening Times.* A valuable fortnightly guide to Glasgow events is *The List,* available at newsstands and the tourist office for £1.20 (about $1.80). It also contains excellent features and reviews.

TELEPHONE The city code for Glasgow is 141.

GETTING AROUND

Rule number one is to use your feet in the George Square district—you can't view Victorian architecture properly unless you wallow in it. Parts of Buchanan and Sauchiehall Streets are pedestrian zones.

AIRPORT *Glasgow Airport* (phone: 887-1111), 8 miles west of the city, serves European and transatlantic flights, while *Prestwick Airport* (phone: 1292-79822), 30 miles southwest, handles mostly domestic flights. There's frequent bus service between the city center and *Glasgow Airport,* and trains run from *Prestwick* to *Glasgow Central Station* and between Paisley and both airports.

BOAT For a scenic tour of the Clyde, hop a ride on the *Waverley* paddle steamer (see *Extra Special,* above).

BUS Glasgow's bus service has improved appreciably—both in schedule and equipment—in recent years. The fare ranges from 30p (about 45¢) to £1.05 (about $1.60), depending on the distance; a one-week pass allowing travel on both buses and subways costs £12.30 (about $18.50). For information on bus travel within Glasgow, call *Strathclyde's Buses* (phone: 226-4826); call the *Travel Centre of the Scottish Bus Group* (phone: 332-9191) for information about *Citylink* buses to other parts of Britain. Buses for destinations outside the Strathclyde region depart from the *Anderston* bus station (on Argyle St.; phone: 248-7432) and the *Buchanan* bus station (on Killermont St.; phone: 332-9191).

CAR RENTAL Renting a car is recommended because there is plenty to lure you out of downtown Glasgow. The major firms are *Avis* (161 North St.; phone: 221-2827); *Europcar* (556 Pollokshaws Rd.; phone: 423-5661); and *Hertz* (106 Waterloo St.; phone: 248-7736).

SUBWAY Subway trains, with varnished wooden floors, are known as the "Clockwork Orange," because of their color and circular route; they run every five minutes, Mondays through Saturdays from 6:30 AM to 10:30 PM; check at the tourist office for Sunday times. One ride costs 50p (about 75¢). The system's stops are listed in *Greater Glasgow* or on a city center map. *Hillhead Station* is a good alighting point for West End shops and restaurants.

TAXI They are reasonably priced, but hard to get (especially at night). To visit places such as the *Burrell Collection,* call for a taxi in advance: *Albany Radio Cars* (phone: 778-9999), *Croft Radio Cars* (phone: 633-2222), or *Radio Taxis* (phone: 332-6666) are recommended companies.

TRAIN *Central Station* (on Gordon St.; phone: 204-2844) is the departure and arrival point for trains to England; there are 14 *InterCity* trains daily between Glasgow and London (on the fastest trains, the trip takes less than five hours). *Queen Street Station* (phone: 204-2844) serves Edinburgh and the north of Scotland. A bus connects the two stations.

SPECIAL EVENTS

Parades, concerts, sports competitions, beauty contests, and discoing are what goes on in summertime at community festivals, and every Glasgow district has one. We begin with one of the best in the area—if not the country.

A FAVORITE FETE

Mayfest Now the second-largest arts festival in Britain, this three-week event (held, not surprisingly, in May) offers popular and classical music, drama, art exhibitions, street theater, cabaret, and community-based events throughout the city. 18 Albion St. (phone: 552-8000).

Another popular event is the *Royal Scottish Orchestra (RSO) Proms,* a series of 14 concerts with famous guest soloists and conductors which alternates among Edinburgh, Glasgow, Aberdeen, and Dundee in summer. Contact the *RSO* (73 Claremont St.; phone: 226-3868). The *Glasgow International Folk Festival* (phone: 552-8605) is held in late June, and the *Glasgow International Jazz Festival* (phone: 552-3552) takes place in early July. A complete list of events is available from the *Greater Glasgow Tourist Board* (see *Tourist Information,* above).

MUSEUMS

In addition to those described in *Special Places,* here are two other museums worth a visit.

HUNTERIAN MUSEUM Paintings, drawings, prints, and furniture by Whistler (the largest collection of his works in the world), Charles Rennie Mackintosh, and other artists are displayed. Closed Sundays. No admission charge. Hillhead St. (phone: 330-5431).

SCOTLAND STREET SCHOOL Formerly a turn-of-the-century school designed by Charles Rennie Mackintosh, it is now an education museum. Mackintosh's original designs, including tiled corridors and semicircular windows, were fully restored, and the classrooms set up just as they were in Edwardian and Victorian times. A walk-through exhibit re-creates school days during World War II. Open daily. No admission charge. 225 Scotland St. (phone: 429-1201).

SHOPPING

Local wares include woolens, pottery, crystal, Victorian bric-a-brac, jewelry, shortbread, and whisky. The *Argyle Arcade,* the L-shaped passage between Argyle and Buchanan Streets, is home to Glasgow's famous diamond and jewelry center. The arcade itself is something to see: Built in 1828 by John Reid, it has a magnificent mosaic roof best viewed from the Buchanan Street entrance. Also of interest is the historic *Sloan's Arcade Café. Savoy Centre,* a shopping complex off Sauchiehall Street, is clean and well maintained, with 160 shops selling almost everything you can imagine. *Princes Square* (off Buchanan St.; phone: 221-0324), Glasgow's shopping showpiece, has a glass roof and is equipped with elevators and escalators. The honey-colored sandstone houses, built in 1841, now house specialty shops, cafés, and restaurants. *St. Enoch Centre,* located on the site of the former *St. Enoch* railway station, is an extensive merchandise complex with shops, an indoor skating rink, and the largest glass roof in Europe (designed to withstand winds of up to 110 mph), which utilizes solar heat.

Candleriggs Market (71-73 Albion St.; no phone) is a good place to hobnob with residents and inspect local wares. It was converted from an old fruit market and is open Fridays, Saturdays, and Sundays only. *Paddy's Market,* operating daily by the railway arches in Shipbank Lane, is, however, the place for an authentic taste of old-fashioned Glasgow street vending. And antiques hunters should visit the Scottish branches of London's top two auction houses: *Christie's Scotland* (164 Bath St.; phone: 332-8134) has auctions of jewelry, silver, objets d'art, and furniture, and regular sales of special-interest items—including Scottish silver, collectibles, and paintings; and *Phillips Glasgow* (207 Bath St.; phone: 221-8377) holds auctions of furniture, paintings, ceramics, silver, and jewelry the first Monday of each month; annually they have two special sales of fine jewelry. For standard shopping hours, see GETTING READY TO GO.

Be sure to take your passport when you shop, and always inquire about the Value Added Tax (VAT) refund application forms when your total purchases in a store are over £50 (about $75). The VAT is a surcharge payable at the sales counter, but foreign customers usually will be reimbursed for it at home (for more information see GETTING READY TO GO).

All Our Yesterdays This small shop is filled with a variety of intriguing collectors' items ranging from lampshades to snuffboxes. 6 Park Rd. (phone: 334-7788).

Bath St. Antique Centre Quality antiques from 16 different dealers. Items sold here include jewelry, dolls, porcelain, clocks, prints, and small pieces of furniture. 203 Bath St. (phone: 248-4220).

Catherine Shaw Specialists in Art Deco jewelry and clocks by leading Glasgow designers, including Charles Rennie Mackintosh. In the *Argyle Arcade* (phone: 221-9038) and at 24 Gordon St. (phone: 204-4762).

De Courcy's Antique and Craft Arcade A good place for bargains in pottery, knickknacks, knitwear, and jewelry. Its *Café de Courcy* is famous for coffee and scones. 5-21 Cresswell La. (phone: 334-6673).

Fraser's This four-tiered, balconied, Victorian-vintage department store with a central court, a restored barrel-vaulted ceiling, and several hundred feet of suspended chandelier offers Caithness glass, English bone china, clothes, linen, Edinburgh crystal, or just a beautiful breath of rarified air. 21 Buchanan St. (phone: 221-3880).

Glasgow Print Studio An excellent selection of attractive modern prints, including limited editions. 25 King St. (phone: 552-0704).

Graham's Established in 1874, this is a haven for pipe smokers, with a huge selection of pipes and tobaccos. It sells cigars and lighters as well. 71 St. Vincent St. (phone: 221-6588).

Henry Burton Established in 1847 as hosiers, shirtmakers, and glove makers, this shop is now one of the city's leading menswear stores; there is also a small section of women's clothing. 111 Buchanan St. (phone: 221-7380).

Jean Megahy Elegant antique furniture. 481 Great Western Rd. (phone: 334-1315).

John Smith & Son Scotland's oldest bookshop (established in 1751) has six floors of volumes on every imaginable subject. 57 St. Vincent St. (phone: 221-7472).

Lawrie's Since 1881, it has been *the* place where the landowning milord buys his deerstalking "breeks" (breeches). There are also kilts, skirts, jackets, pure wool plaids, tweeds, mohairs, accessories, and souvenirs. Highland dress made to order and clan tartans traced for visitors unsure of their Scottish connections. 110 Buchanan St. (phone: 221-0217).

Maxwell & Kennedy Fine chocolates and confections. 48 *Princes Sq.* (phone: 221-3848).

Nancy Smillie Attractive modern ceramics and glass, including Saltoun pottery made on the premises. Two locations: 53 Cresswell St. (phone: 334-4240) and 35 *Princes Sq.* (phone: 248-3874).

National Trust for Scotland Glass, pottery, and books about Scotland. *Hutcheson's Hall,* 158 Ingram St. (phone: 552-8391).

Pen Shop High-quality fountain pens and other writing implements, as well as desk accessories. 19 *Princes Sq.* (phone: 226-4193).

Pitlochry Knitwear The best of Scottish woolen clothing for men and women, including tartan skirts and cardigans. 130 Buchanan St. (phone: 221-3434).

Scottish Craft Centre Here's a wide range of fascinating crafts, including jewelry, ornaments, and pottery made by artisans from all over Great Britain, particularly rural areas. The Courtyard, *Princes Sq.* (phone: 248-2885).

Slater Menswear Featured in the *Guinness Book of World Records* as the largest menswear shop in the world, it has a huge range of formal and casual clothing. 165 Howard St. (phone: 552-7171).

Thornton's Here's a mouth-watering selection of exotic chocolates and toffee. Two locations: 97 Buchanan St. (phone: 204-3154) and *Central Station* (phone: 221-1059).

Tim Wright An elegant antiques shop featuring furniture, glass, and ceramics. 147 Bath St. (phone: 221-0364).

Victorian Village Antiques, roomfuls of ornaments and old lace. Beethoven's *Pastoral* wafts through the adjoining corridors while you browse through the 14 tiny shops or dawdle in the charming tearoom. 53-57 W. Regent St. (phone: 332-0808).

Waterstone's Another link in the chain of large, modern bookstores with clearly marked sections and a helpful, knowledgeable staff. Two locations: 132 Union St. (phone: 221-0890) and 45-50 *Princes Sq.* (phone: 221-9650).

SPORTS

FISHING The Firth of Clyde, the ocean, and the upland waterways near Glasgow are all popular. The *Greater Glasgow Tourist Board* has details (see *Tourist Information,* above).

GOLF Get *Scotland: Home of Golf* (costs £3.50/about $5.25) from the *Greater Glasgow Tourist Board* office (see *Tourist Information*). It supplies details of championship courses along the Ayrshire coast, such as *Royal Troon* and *Turnberry* (see *Great Golf* in DIVERSIONS), as well as the Glasgow courses. There are several worthwhile courses in the area, including *Haggs Castle,* a private club with an 18-hole course (phone: 427-1157). There is also *King's Park,* a nine-hole course (phone: 637-1066). To play at either, you'll need an introductory letter from your home club secretary.

SOCCER The sport's called football here, and in Glasgow it is just about synonymous with the two home teams, the *Celtics* and *Rangers.* Kickoff is on Wednesdays at 7:30 PM and on Saturdays at 3 PM from August through May. *Celtic Park* (95 Kerrydale St.; phone: 556-2611) is the *Celtics* home stadium, and *Ibrox Park* (150 Edmiston Dr.; phone: 427-8811) is the home of the rival *Rangers.* Get tickets from the turnstiles prior to the games and take no intoxicating beverages; police may search you. *Firhill Stadium* (80 Firhill Rd.; phone: 945-4811) is used by other local teams, *Patrick Thistle* and *Clyde.* League playoffs and cup finals are at *Hampden Park* (on Somerville Dr.; phone: 632-1275). It's fair to say that football violence is now much less evident in Scotland than in England, but *Rangers* crowds still make anti-Catholic noises.

WALKING Glasgow has 7,000 acres of municipal green space, much of it woodland, in over 70 parks. The *Greater Glasgow Quick Guide* (see *Tourist Information*) describes attractions in the larger parks.

THEATER

The city has a wealth of theatrical riches, including an outstanding repertory company and a first class venue that hosts a wide variety of cultural events.

CENTER STAGE

Citizens' Theatre The accolades for this first-rate regional theater, established in 1942, just don't stop. The *London Times* called it Britain's "most challenging theater," the *Observer* characterized it as "the most cosmopolitan, mischievous, and wilful theatre in Britain," the *Daily Mail* noted that it "puts the West End in the shade," and the US's *After Dark* commented on its "outrageously adventurous nature" and its "perverse and avant-garde flair." The century-old playhouse's exterior has been refurbished with a more modern front and glass roof; the inside, though, continues to be a stunning example of a traditional proscenium-arch Victorian theater. The company has performed nearly 200 British and foreign—especially Italian—classics since its formation, and has earned a worldwide reputation. 119 Gorbals St. (phone: 429-0022).

Theatre Royal Those who think that Edinburgh is home to everything cultural in Scotland are forgetting that Glasgow has the *Scottish Opera,* the *Royal Scottish National Orchestra,* and the *Scottish Ballet.* Built in 1882, the *Theatre Royal*—Scotland's only opera house—is without question one of Britain's most gorgeous Victorian relics. Now owned by the *Scottish Opera,* it has been ingeniously restored so that its modern theatrical equipment is largely hidden, and marvelous plasterwork ornaments the swooping balconies and the domed ceiling. Unlike many refurbished opera houses, this one is not done in red and gold but in various shades of cream and brown, highlighted with blue and orange. The *Scottish Opera* subscription season runs year-round, and the hall also hosts performances by many other British and international companies, including the *Scottish Ballet,* the *Birmingham Royal Ballet,* the *English National Ballet,* the *Dance Theatre of Harlem,* the *Royal Shakespeare Company,* the *National Theatre,* and the *Scottish Theatre Company.* 282 Hope St. (phone: 332-9000).

In addition, the *Pavilion* (121 Renfield St.; phone: 332-1846) is the inheritor of the rich "Scottish comic" music hall tradition—typified by Harry Lauder—that Glasgow has given the world. Pre-London runs and large amateur productions play at the *King's* (335 Bath St.; phone: 227-5511). *The Mitchell Theatre* (Granville St.; phone: 227-5033) has variety acts and light musicals. There also are two locales showcasing the innovative work of young, upcoming artists: the *Glasgow Print Studio and Drama Centre* (22-25 King St.; phone: 552-0704) and the *Royal Scottish Academy of Music and Drama* (100 Renfrew St.; phone: 332-4101). The *Glasgow Film Theatre* (12 Rose St.; phone: 332-6535) is the place for art films. The *Tron Theatre Club* (63 Trongate St.; phone: 552-4267) stages trendy new productions by small theater companies.

MUSIC

The *Scottish National Opera*'s main venue is the *Theatre Royal* (see above). The *Royal Concert Hall* (Sauchiehall St.; phone: 332-3123) hosts performances ranging from the *Royal Scottish Orchestra* and the *City of Glasgow Philharmonic Orchestra* to rock, pop, and jazz artists. The *Henry Wood Hall* (73 Claremont St.; phone: 226-3868) presents orchestral concerts, and *Glasgow Cathedral* often hosts choral and sacred works. The *Scottish Exhibition and Conference Centre* often stages pop music concerts (off Finnieston St., on the banks of the river Clyde; phone: 248-2000). Bagpiping and Highland and Scottish country dancing must be traced to city parks and to small parish halls—consult *The List* (see *Local Coverage*) for details. Several locally popular jazz bands play the pub and restaurant circuit. Check the dailies for locations. The *City of Glasgow Country Music Club* runs a *Grand Ole Opry* house on Friday, Saturday, and Sunday nights (2-4 Govan Rd., Paisley Road Toll; phone: 429-5396).

NIGHTCLUBS AND NIGHTLIFE

The safest course is to chart a theater evening with a restaurant meal afterward. Gambling halls and dance hangouts can have an unadorned and (to a tourist) tawdry air. The best discos in town are *Tuxedo Princess,* on a boat at *Anderston Quay* (phone: 204-1150), which is open Monday, Friday, and Saturday nights; and *Victoria's* (98 Sauchiehall St.; phone: 332-1444), which is open every night except Mondays.

Glasgow also has several private casinos: *Berkeley* (506 Sauchiehall St.; phone: 332-0992); *Stakis Chevalier* (95 Hope St.; phone: 226-3856); and *Stakis Regency* (15 Waterloo St.; phone: 221-4141). Anyone 18 or older can join, but you must apply for membership (free) at least 48 hours before you plan to play.

Best in Town

CHECKING IN

A well-known Scottish television executive once defined a typical Glasgow hotel as a "reasonable, functional, bathroom's-got-a-bath, bedroom's-got-a-bed kind of place." You'll get comfort all right, but don't expect to be overwhelmed by the picturesque. The price of a room usually includes breakfast, and top class establishments will want you to show your mettle by consuming prunes, porridge, herring, eggs, bacon, sausages, tomatoes, baked beans, black pudding, fried bread, coffee, and toast—all in one sitting. Most of Glasgow's major hotels have complete facilities for the business traveler. Those hotels listed below as having "business services" usually offer such conveniences as a concierge, meeting rooms, photocopiers, computers, translation services, and express checkout, among others. Call the hotel for additional information. Hotels in the expensive range will cost $135 or more per night for a double room (including private bath, phone, and TV set, unless otherwise indicated); moderate hotels charge $90 to $130; and inexpensive hotels, less than $90. Guesthouses and bed and breakfast inns are much less expensive, and most hotels have lower rates on weekends. Lists of these for Glasgow, Renfrew, Strathkelvin, and Monklands are available in the *Greater Glasgow Quick Guide* (see *Tourist Information*). All telephone numbers are in the 141 city code unless otherwise indicated.

EXPENSIVE

Copthorne The owners have restored this old railway hotel, formerly the *North British* and one of Scotland's premier railway hostelries, to its original grandeur (although it does have a plain, modern-looking extension). After a few nights here, you'll pretend you own half of Glasgow. Winston Churchill described his January 8, 1941, meeting in an upstairs room with Harry Hopkins, Franklin Delano Roosevelt's personal emissary, as one of the turning points of World War II. Ask for a room in the front overlooking George Square with its fine statues. The hotel has 140 rooms, a restaurant, and a café. Business services are available. On George Sq., perpendicular to the *City Chambers* and adjacent to *Queen St. Station* (phone: 332-6711; 800-44-UTELL; fax: 332-4264).

Devonshire After years of neglect, this large Victorian corner house is now an opulent luxury hotel, restored to its original appearance. The interior includes ornate doorways, pillars, a majestic staircase, and original paintings. Each of the 14 guestrooms has a name (no number); for a very special stay, ask for Dunrobin, which has a four-poster bed, or Craigevar—both are enormous. The dining room serves classic Scottish fare, and business services are available. 5 Devonshire Gardens, Great Western Rd. (phone: 339-7878; fax: 339-3980).

Hilton Scotland's tallest building and the city's largest hotel, this immense glass-and-granite structure is an elegant accent on the skyline. The building rises 20 stories high, with 321 guestrooms, three restaurants, extensive health club facilities (including an indoor pool), business services, a grand ballroom, and ample parking. William St. (phone: 204-5555; 800-HILTONS; fax: 204-5004).

Hospitality Inn This spacious, modern 307-room hotel is ideally located close to Sauchiehall Street, the *Glasgow School of Art,* and the *Royal Concert Hall.*

It has two restaurants—*Prince of Wales,* which serves French food, and *Garden Café,* which has an American-style menu of steaks, burgers, chili, and fried chicken. Business services are available. 36 Cambridge St. (phone: 332-3311; 800-44-UTELL; fax: 332-4050).

Marriott This stylish, red-brick 298-room hotel towering over the M8 highway junction at the edge of the city center has everything from individual mini-bars in the guestrooms to a heated indoor Jacuzzi. Ask for one of the rooms facing south—they have the best views and sunlight. French fare is served at *L'Academie,* and the informal *Terrace* offers traditional food. Business services are available. 500 Argyle St. (phone: 226-5577; 800-831-4004; fax: 221-7676).

Moat House International Sleek and classy, this 19-story establishment looms like a colossus over the river Clyde. It's set in the city's old shipbuilding district near the *Scottish Exhibition and Conference Centre,* and the area's history is re-created with nautical themes throughout the hotel; guests can even arrive by boat (by prior arrangement). All 284 rooms boast a panoramic view of Glasgow, plus mini-bars and trouser presses. Other pluses include two restaurants, business services, and the *Waterside Club,* which offers a swimming pool, whirlpool bath, gym, and health bar. Congress Rd. (phone: 204-0733; fax: 221-2022).

One Devonshire Gardens This award-winning hotel, set in a stately, distinguished row of three townhouses, makes guests feel like 19th-century aristocrats. The decor is luxurious, with such elegant touches as hand-painted French wallpaper and silver sugar tongs in the excellent dining room (see *Eating Out*). There are 27 lavishly furnished guestrooms. If sleeping in a black four-poster bed sounds intriguing, ask for No. 9; Room No. 14 is strikingly decorated with black walls and furniture and a red canopied bed. Business services are available. 1-3 Devonshire Gardens, Great Western Rd. (phone: 339-2001; fax: 337-1663).

MODERATE

Central An architecturally distinguished railway hotel of the 1880s, next to *Central Station,* it's spacious and gracious in the Victorian mode, but it was built right over a streetful of slum houses, so it may be haunted by the home-loving ghosts of the dispossessed. There are 219 rooms, a health club, and business services. Its restaurant offers Scottish food. Gordon St. (phone: 221-9680; 800-44-UTELL; fax: 226-3948).

Sherbrooke Castle The bar here is the neighborhood pub, ideal for helping you forget you're a tourist. This 25-room Scottish baronial mansion-house is on a knolltop on the city's south side; its restaurant serves international fare. Business services are available. 11 Sherbrooke Ave. (phone: 427-4227; fax: 427-5685).

Stakis Grosvenor This lovely 95-room Victorian showpiece opposite the *Botanic Gardens* is elegance incarnate. The *Lafayette* restaurant serves French fare and the *Steakhouse* is a grillroom. Business services are offered. Grosvenor Ter., Great Western Rd. (phone: 339-8811; 800-STAKIS-1; fax: 334-0710).

INEXPENSIVE

Babbity Bowster Fraser Laurie, who owns and runs this French-style pension, named it after a saucy 18th-century dance. It has six simply furnished rooms (no TV sets or phones), a lively café/bar on the first floor, and the excellent *Scottische* restaurant (see *Eating Out*) on the second. 16-18 Blackfriars St. (phone: 552-5055).

Town House This charming, family-run, 10-room guesthouse, built in 1882, still has its original elaborate plasterwork and ornately carved banisters; it's not to be confused with the larger *Town House* hotel in the city center. The restaurant serves dinner. 4 Hughenden Ter. (phone: 357-0862; fax: 339-9605).

Victorian House The decor is crimson and white at this smart guesthouse, which used to be three Victorian houses. Most of the 45 guestrooms have private baths. There's no restaurant. 214 Renfrew St. (phone: 332-0129; fax: 353-3155).

EATING OUT

Native food, too quickly dismissed because of the names of some of its dishes ("haggis," "howtowdie," "cullen skink"), actually can be delicious. Tops in Scottish gastronomy are Aberdeen Angus steaks, lamb with rowanberry jelly, venison, moor grouse, salmon, and trout. For a dinner for two, expect to pay more than $60 at restaurants listed as expensive; $40 to $60 at moderate places; and less than $40 at inexpensive ones. This selection does not include any of Glasgow's numerous pubs with catering facilities, fish-and-chips shops, and plastic-age fried chicken or burger joints. All restaurants listed below serve lunch and dinner unless otherwise noted. All telephone numbers are in the 141 city code unless otherwise indicated.

EXPENSIVE

L'Ariosto High-back pine chairs, tile floor, dim lighting, candles, soft music, and lots of lovers' nooks make this romantically Italian. The bill of fare doesn't stop at spaghetti; there are lots of different varieties of pasta, as well as steaks, chicken, and seafood. There's dancing Tuesday through Saturday nights. Closed Sundays. Reservations advised. Major credit cards accepted. 92-94 Mitchell St. (phone: 221-8543 or 221-0971).

Buttery One of the city's finest dining spots, serving inventive fare. Carrot and orange soup, venison with madeira sauce, and beef with lentils are just some of its offerings. The original Victorian decor has been embellished with a bar made from church pews and a pulpit. Closed Saturday lunch and Sundays. Reservations necessary. Major credit cards accepted. 652 Argyle St. (phone: 221-8188).

Crannog Just across the motorway from the *Marriott* and *Hilton* hotels, this friendly dining place serves superb Highland seafood, freshly caught and smoked at their own facilities in Fort William. Among the offerings are langoustine, salmon, pink mussels, and bouillabaisse. Closed Sundays and Mondays. Reservations necessary. Major credit cards accepted. 28 Cheapside St. (phone: 221-1727).

One Devonshire Gardens Considered by many to be the best in the city, it serves a combination of rich British and French fare. Closed Saturday lunch. Reservations necessary. Major credit cards accepted. *One Devonshire Gardens Hotel,* 1-3 Devonshire Gardens, Great Western Rd. (phone: 339-2001).

Rogano Halibut in champagne and oyster sauce or monkfish and scallops with onions and ginger are typical of the sophisticated seafood dishes here. Media people and talkative about-towners have claimed this place as their own. Its antique fixtures include mirrors and glass paneling adorned with sea themes, all in Art Deco style. A simpler, but also excellent, menu is served downstairs in the inexpensive *Café Rogano.* Closed Sunday lunch. Reservations advised. Major credit cards accepted. 11 Exchange Pl. (phone: 248-4055).

Scottische Some of the best Scottish food in town, including salmon, lamb, and venison, is served at this restaurant at *Babbity Bowster.* The limited wine list is mostly French. The place is a great favorite with actors and journalists, and there's a real peat fire in winter. Closed Saturday lunch and Sunday evenings. Reservations necessary. Major credit cards accepted. 16-18 Blackfriars St. (phone: 552-5055).

Ubiquitous Chip No, this is not a fish and French fries outlet. The menu caters to the discriminating palate, featuring seasonal local delicacies. And the glassed-in courtyard with a fountain and an Art Deco water lily mural pleases the eye, too. Open daily. Reservations advised. Major credit cards accepted. 12 Ashton La. (phone: 334-5007).

MODERATE

L'Arena di Verona Food is Italian plus basic British. Across the street from the *Theatre Royal,* it is popular with actors and theatergoers. An extension to the dining area is a chic pizza parlor. Closed Sundays. Reservations advised. Major credit cards accepted. 311-313 Hope St. (phone: 332-7728).

October Café A bright and airy Art Deco restaurant under the glass roof of *Princes Square,* it is famous for its large portions of Oban mussels and its pastries.

Closed Sunday evenings. Reservations advised. Major credit cards accepted. Top floor, *Princes Sq.* (phone: 221-0303).

Parthenon This smart Greek-Cypriot restaurant is popular with television and radio people from the nearby BBC studios. A good choice for those undecided about what to order is *mezedes*—small portions of a variety of appetizers and main courses. Closed Sundays. Reservations advised. Major credit cards accepted. 725 Great Western Rd. (phone: 334-6265).

INEXPENSIVE

Café Gandolfi Here you'll find genuine 1930s bits and pieces (like the overhead propeller fan), a larger-than-life delicatessen, taped 1930s jazz, and animated intellectual chat. Closed Sundays. Reservations advised on weekends. Major credit cards accepted. 64 Albion St. (phone: 552-6813).

Drum and Monkey This small bistro offers a varied menu. Try the superb paella of squid, mussels, prawns, salmon, and sole. Formerly a bank, it has ornate pillars and a massive fireplace. With its large leather chairs, the place feels more like a gentlemen's club than a restaurant, but everyone seems to love it. Closed Sunday lunch. Reservations advised. Major credit cards accepted. 95 St. Vincent St. (phone: 221-6636).

H. R. Bradford This coffee shop above a large bakery serves delicious scones and cakes. Open for breakfast, lunch, and tea only; closed Sundays. No reservations. No credit cards accepted. 245 Sauchiehall St. (phone: 332-1008).

TAKING TEA

Naturally, Glasgow has plenty of places to get a nice "cuppa"; but one is our particular favorite.

A PERFECT CUP

Willow Tea Room Above *Henderson's* jewelry shop on the city's most famous shopping street is Charles Rennie Mackintosh's masterful Art Nouveau architectural work, which was designed for the legendary Miss Cranston, who opened guestrooms and a tearoom during the town's artistic heyday in the early 1900s. The rooms are closed now, but the tearoom still operates, offering sippers a choice of 28 different brews. Closed Sundays. No reservations. No credit cards accepted. 217 Sauchiehall St. (phone: 332-0521).

SHARING A PINT

O'Henry's (14 Drury St.; phone: 248-3751) is a traditional British pub. The *Babbity Bowster* hotel (see *Checking In*) features a café bar with live music, mainly traditional and classical, in an 18th-century building. Intellectuals make themselves at home in the bar at the *Tron Theatre* (closed Mondays; 63 Trongate; phone: 552-4267). *Bon Accord* (153 North St.; phone: 248-4427) is known for its wide range of traditional beers. *Uisghe Beatha* (232 Woodlands Rd.; phone: 332-0473), colloquially known as "Isky Be," is a real Gaelic pub (its name means "water of life") that is popular with students. Glasgow is crawling with pubs, and if you stay any length of time, you will soon find your own favorites.

Liverpool

Anyone even remotely aware of the sounds of the 1960s knows that Liverpool is synonymous with the *Beatles.* The "Fab Four"—John, Paul, George, and Ringo—turned a provincial, struggling city into a place at the forefront of a decade. "The Pool" was on the map again, and Liverpudlians never again had to explain where in the world they came from.

Prior to the *Beatles,* Liverpool had not enjoyed such a level of international renown since the years between 1830 and 1930, when its preeminence was intimately tied to the growth of the New World. Then the great port city on the river Mersey, from which ships reach the Atlantic by way of the Irish Sea, was the principal European embarkation point for emigrants to the United States, Canada, and Australia, and it forged more links with America than any other British city. More than nine million emigrants passed through Liverpool's docks during this period, driven by poverty, hunger, unemployment, religious persecution, or just plain ambition to find a more comfortable life, a more democratic government, or a new beginning across the water.

The tiny *Ancient Chapel* in the Toxteth Quarter where Richard Mather, a 17th-century Puritan minister and one of the earliest emigrants to New England, preached is still much as it was over 350 years ago, when he sailed across the Atlantic. His son, Increase, became Rector of *Harvard University;* his grandson, Cotton, became President of *Yale* and a key figure in the Salem witch trials. Low-born Robert Morris, another Liverpool emigrant, was the financial genius behind the American Revolution and a signer of the Declaration of Independence. Not all émigrés, however, were so fortunate. Many failed to reach their "Promised Land" because they ran out of money; others chose to stay in Liverpool. Thus, the names of many of the shops and businesses in this city can be traced to Irish, German, Lithuanian, Polish, and Russian founders, and Liverpool still has Norwegian and Swedish churches.

Since the early 20th century, the last view of England for those who sail abroad from Liverpool has been "The Big Three," a trio of famous white stone buildings around Pier Head: the green-domed *Port of Liverpool Building,* the *Cunard Building,* and the *Royal Liver Building.* These landmarks remain the dominant features of the waterfront and are still best seen from the water.

From its humble beginnings as a tiny fishing village on a muddy tidal creek (the pool from which it takes its name) to its current position as a bustling city (pop. 457,500), Liverpool has been closely linked in its fortunes and history to the river that wends its way south of the city. King John, who granted the village a charter in the early 13th century, used it as a jumping-off place for Ireland. Growth was slow, but once trade began with the Americas in the late 17th century, Liverpool eventually became the second most important city in the British Empire. The first dock opened in 1715, and more followed, trading mainly with the American colonies and the West Indies in sugar, spices, and tobacco, as well as supplying slaves from Africa. Slave trading became illegal in the early 19th century, but immigration to the New World and transatlantic steamships filled the gap. Eventually, Liverpool's docks stretched for 7 unbroken miles. During World War II, 1.2 million American GIs landed here to join Britain and the other Allies in the battle against Nazi Germany.

Although changing world economics and the arrival of the jumbo jet put an end to almost all transatlantic passenger service, Liverpool is still one of Britain's principal commercial ports. Most of the port business has shifted to those docks nearest the mouth of the river, however, and developers have been quick to seize the opportunity to develop the original, now superfluous dockside buildings for new uses. Today, the *Albert Dock* area is a "second city center," offering shops, restaurants, museums, boat trips, and other waterside activities.

In addition to the docks, several city streets have managed to retain their distinctive characters. Among the magnificent Victorian buildings on William Brown Street are the *Liverpool Museum,* the *Central Library,* the *Walker Art Gallery,* and the old *County Sessions House.* Rodney Street, named after British naval hero Admiral Rodney, is Georgian, as is Falkner Square. (The birthplace of William Gladstone, four times Britain's prime minister, is at No. 62 Rodney St.) Nelson Street and Great George Square form the center of Liverpool's Chinatown, the oldest such enclave in Europe.

Liverpudlians are known for their quick wit and dry sense of humor (many British comedians have hailed from hereabouts) and for their distinctive nasal "Scouse" accent. Already a highly individualistic city, Liverpool now has shops to match any thriving High Street, trendy wine bars humming alongside well-preserved pubs, and playwrights, artists, and musicians plugging their vibrant hometown.

Liverpool At-a-Glance

SEEING THE CITY

There are spectacular bird's-eye views of the city, the river, and the docks from the top of the *Anglican Cathedral* and the *Royal Liver Building.* For an all-encompassing view of the waterfront, take one of the boat trips offered by *Mersey Ferries* and *Fantasea Cruises* (see *Getting Around*).

SPECIAL PLACES

The historic waterfront, with its trio of signature buildings and the *Albert Dock,* is a suitable place to begin any tour. Then head inland to the city center, most of whose sights, including the city's two cathedrals, are well signposted and reachable on foot.

CITY CENTER

ROYAL LIVER BUILDING Liverpool's most photographed building is easily recognized by its two towers, each with one of the legendary 18-foot-high Liver Birds on top. Built in 1908, it was among the world's first multistory concrete buildings, and those who believe *Big Ben* is Britain's biggest clock discover their mistake when they see the 25-foot-diameter clock faces on each side of the front tower. Other than the free guided tours to the front tower (given April through September), the lobby is the only part of the building open to the public. The ground floor includes a café and a small shop that sells newspapers, magazines, cigarettes, and sweets. Pier Head (phone: 236-2748).

CUNARD BUILDING This magnificent structure dates from 1915. It was built by Nova Scotia–born Samuel Cunard, who came to Liverpool in 1840 to start the first transatlantic liner service between Liverpool, Halifax, and Boston on his famous ship, *Britannia.* The coats of arms of Britain's allies during World War I are carved between the windows on the top floor. (The United States is absent, since work was completed before the US entered the war.) The massive eagles and the company's shield were carved out of a chunk of stone weighing 43 tons. Since the demise of all *Cunard*'s trade in the city, the building now serves as a regular office block. Pier Head.

PORT OF LIVERPOOL BUILDING The blueprint was an unsuccessful contender in the design competition for Liverpool's *Anglican Cathedral,* so don't be surprised by its ecclesiastical elements, including the green copper dome. Built at the turn of the century and now the central office for all port administration, it's worth taking a look at its impressive marble interior and its window emblems depicting all the Commonwealth countries. Pier Head.

ALBERT DOCK The city's showplace attraction on the waterfront, this was the first of Liverpool's old docks to be reclaimed from decay. *Albert Dock* originally opened to shipping traffic in 1845, closed in 1972, and reopened in 1984. It's now a tall ships center, providing a berth for square-rigged vessels; it also features the popular *Beatles Story,* which presents a fairly exhaustive account of the "Fab Four" (see *Extra Special*). The magnificent restored Victorian warehouses constitute the largest group of "Grade 1 Listed" buildings in the country. Only a short walk from the city's main shopping streets, the area that was once the heart of "sailortown" has become a focal point of the city's leisure activities, boasting wine bars, restaurants, small specialty shops, museums, and exhibition areas. One of the warehouses serves as an extension of London's *Tate Gallery;* another houses the *Merseyside Maritime Museum* (see below for both). A major advantage of the *Albert Dock* scheme is the huge, free car park adjacent to it, making Liverpool one of the easiest cities in Britain in which to find a parking place. The shops are open daily; some restaurants are open in the evening (phone: 708-8854).

MERSEYSIDE MARITIME MUSEUM AND MUSEUM OF LIVERPOOL LIFE This cousin to the *National Maritime Museum* in Greenwich emphasizes the history of the nation's merchant marine. Enter the maritime park, which looks just as it did when sailing ships loaded and unloaded here. The restored *Piermaster's House* and other dockside buildings afford an opportunity to see coopering and boatbuilding as it was done a century ago. "Emigrants to a New World," a permanent exhibition, includes a reconstructed dockland street peopled with hawkers and porters such as emigrants would have seen; a section of a packet ship showing the traveling conditions of the day; and an emigration bureau that advises American visitors on how to trace their ancestry. In the *Battle of the Atlantic Gallery,* exhibits tell the history of the convoys deployed during World War II. Outside, in wet and dry dock, is the museum's growing collection of ships and boats rescued from the junkyard, several of which are open to the public *Easter* through September. Also here is the *Museum of Liverpool Life,* with exhibits about the history of Liverpool and Liverpudlians throughout the centuries; and *Anything to Declare,* a museum about the process of customs and excise in Britain. Open daily. Admission charge. *Albert Dock* (phone: 207-0001).

TATE GALLERY An extension of London's famous gallery, it features a permanent display of contemporary painting and sculpture and temporary exhibitions of modern art. Closed Mondays. Admission charge for touring exhibits. *Albert Dock* (phone: 709-3223).

LIVERPOOL TOWN HALL A palatial Georgian building, topped by a golden dome and a statue of Minerva, it is possibly Liverpool's finest building and the second oldest in the city center (dating from 1754). It was the unlikely setting for the last act of the American Civil War—the surrender of the British-built Confederate raider *Shenandoah* to the Mayor of Liverpool. The building is closed to the public, but its exterior is impressive enough to merit a quick look. Water St. (phone: 236-5181).

ST. GEORGE'S HALL This giant Greco-Roman building of the mid-19th century (the first building visible upon exiting the railway station) reflects Liverpool's former prosperity; Queen Victoria once described it as being "worthy of ancient Athens." With the proportions of a mausoleum, the main hall once housed the law courts, but now it is a venue for exhibitions, conferences, and concerts. An extensive refurbishment of the rest of the building has been put on hold for lack of funds; therefore, those parts remain closed. Admission charge. Lime St. (phone: 225-3938).

WALKER ART GALLERY The best of its kind outside London, it is ranked among the top museums in the world. It contains a notable collection of European art dating from the 14th century to the present day and is particularly rich in Flemish and Italian works, as well as those by progressive 19th-century British artists such as Millais, Leighton, and Sickert. In the *Prince Gallery,* an 11-foot-high model of Sir Edwin Landseer Lutyens's design for a Roman

Catholic cathedral currently is being restored. Open daily. No admission charge. William Brown St. (phone: 207-0001).

ANGLICAN CATHEDRAL There are two modern cathedrals in Liverpool (hence the folk song lyric, "If you want a cathedral, we've got one to spare"), but this one, also known as *Liverpool Cathedral,* looks far too Gothic to be such a recent building. (It was actually begun in 1904, though it wasn't completed until 1978.) It was designed by Sir Giles Gilbert Scott, who was responsible for the *Albert Memorial* in London. Built of locally quarried pink sandstone, the cathedral is massive: It is the largest church in Britain and nearly the largest in Europe—only St. Peter's in Rome and the cathedrals of Milan and Seville exceed it—and it contains the largest church organ and the highest and heaviest peal of bells anywhere. There are guided tours Mondays through Saturdays (except in bad weather) up the 331-foot tower, which provides spectacular views; admission charge. Light meals are served in the small restaurant in the refectory. St. James' Rd. (phone: 709-6271).

METROPOLITAN CATHEDRAL OF CHRIST THE KING The Roman Catholic cathedral is more strikingly modern than its Anglican counterpart. Designed by Frederick Gibberd and completed in 1967, it is a circular structure towering up to a spiked crown of brilliant stained glass. At night, when lit from within, the glass glows, adding to the building's space-age appearance. What is seen today is the third attempt at building a Roman Catholic cathedral in Liverpool, and it rests on the foundations of a 1930s' design still visible in the crypt. There is a bookshop and a tearoom on the premises as well. Mount Pleasant (phone: 709-9222).

THE WIRRAL PENINSULA

PORT SUNLIGHT VILLAGE This planned village was built during the 19th century by William Lever, first Viscount Leverhulme and founder of Lever Brothers, to house his employees when he moved the small family soap business from Warrington to larger premises on the marshy Wirral Peninsula. After strolling through the streets of the benevolent industrialist's vision of a utopian town (including the *Lady Lever Art Gallery*—see below), stop at the *Port Sunlight Heritage Centre* (Greendale Rd.; phone: 644-6466) to see a fascinating record of the creation and life of the community. Closed weekends November through April; admission charge. The famous *Olde Bridge Inn,* the village pub, serves coffee and lunches. Port Sunlight Village can be reached by *Merseyrail* from the city center (20 minutes) or by taking the ferry to Birkenhead and then the No. 42 or 51 bus from Hamilton Square. Wirral.

Lady Lever Art Gallery Built by Viscount Leverhulme in memory of his wife, this gallery contains their magnificent private collection of 18th- and 19th-century paintings by British artists—Reynolds, Gainsborough, Turner, Constable—and other works of art, including a superb collection of

Wedgwood china and English furniture. Open daily. Donation suggested. Port Sunlight Village (phone: 645-3623).

WILLIAMSON ART GALLERY Fine collections of 18th- and 19th-century British watercolors, ceramics, glass, furniture, and pottery are contained in this excellent museum. There are also displays of local and maritime history. Open daily. No admission charge. Slatey Rd., Birkenhead (phone: 652-4177).

NESS GARDENS Owned by *Liverpool University,* these 60 acres of botanical gardens afford charming views over the Dee Estuary and house the most comprehensive collection of plants in northwest England. Attractions include a visitors' center, café, and gift shop. Open daily. Admission charge. Near Neston, South Wirral (phone: 336-8733).

ELSEWHERE

KNOWLSLEY SAFARI PARK A large and impressive wildlife park, it is home to all the animals one would expect to see on the prairie or in the jungle, including lions and tigers and bears (oh, my!), as well as zebras, rhinos, elephants, and monkeys. Facilities include a pets' corner, amusement park, café, and souvenir shop. Closed November through February. Admission charge. Prescot, Merseyside (phone: 430-9009).

CROXTETH HALL AND COUNTRY PARK Just 5 miles from the city center, this 500-acre country park is well worth a day's visit. The hall, with its fine 18th- and 19th-century architecture, is the ancestral home of the Earls of Sefton. Other attractions include the *Home Farm,* with its many farm animals; the walled garden; and the parkland, with a miniature railway, picnic area, and footpaths. The park is open daily; the hall is closed October through *Easter.* Admission charge to the hall. Off Muirhead Ave. E. (phone: 228-5311).

EXTRA SPECIAL

Although the old *Cavern Club*—where the *Beatles* played 292 times—has been torn down, Mathew Street is still something of a Liverpudlian tribute to the city's world-famous offspring. In the place of the old club, there is now a shopping development, *Cavern Walks,* whose tiny atrium contains a statue of all four *Beatles* by John Doubleday and a pub fittingly called *Abbey Road.* (A new version of the *Cavern Club* is underground—see *Nightclubs and Nightlife.*) Also on Mathew Street is the *Beatles Shop* (see *Shopping*). The *Beatles Story,* a walk-through tour and presentation that re-creates the sights, sounds, and even smells of the 1960s during the height of Beatlemania, is at *Albert Dock.* It is the finest testament to the "Fab Four" ever produced by the city. Open daily. Admission charge. *Britannia Pavilion, Albert Dock* (phone: 709-1963).

A cadre of "BeatleGuides"—local fans with exhaustive knowledge of all places of interest—lead tours on double-decker buses every afternoon

year-round (they also can be booked for private tours). The itinerary includes *Sefton Park,* Penny Lane, *Strawberry Fields,* the *Beatles'* houses, and the *Blue Angels* pub, where they played their first professional audition. Organized by *Cavern City Tours* (see *Sightseeing Tours,* below), the tour lasts approximately two hours and departs from the *Pump House Pub* at *Albert Dock* and from the *Merseyside Welcome Centre* at *Clayton Square Shopping Centre.*

Sources and Resources

TOURIST INFORMATION

The *Merseyside Welcome Centre,* in the *Clayton Square Shopping Centre* (phone: 709-3631), is closed Sundays. A smaller branch in the *Atlantic Pavilion* at *Albert Dock* (phone: 708-8854) is open daily. Both locations dispense general information, run an accommodations booking service, and sell show and concert tickets, as well as *Beatles* souvenirs. If you want to chat with a local about what to do and where, ask the tourist information center for details of a free service called "Friends of Merseyside" (phone: 336-6699). Qualified Mersey Guides and BeatleGuides for coach, minibus, car, or walking tours also can be contacted here. The monthly magazine *In Touch,* which has listings of what's on and where, is available from the tourist offices and newsstands.

LOCAL COVERAGE *The Liverpool Echo* is the evening daily, and the *Liverpool Daily Post* is the area's morning paper.

TELEPHONE The city code for Liverpool is 151.

GETTING AROUND

Liverpool's public transportation system is good, but you might find having a car handy for trips outside the city limits. Two road tunnels—the Queensway Tunnel to Birkenhead (just over 2 miles) and the Kingsway Tunnel to Wallasey—connect Liverpool to the Wirral Peninsula (a small charge each way).

AIRPORT *Liverpool Airport* (phone: 486-8877), 6 miles southeast of the center, serves both international and domestic flights, with daily departures to London, the Isle of Man, Belfast, Dublin, and, in summer only, the island of Jersey. *Manchester Airport* (phone: 161-489-3000), 30 miles away, handles international flights, as well as some domestic flights. Buses run between Manchester and Liverpool every hour; the trip usually takes about 45 minutes.

BOAT The *Isle of Man Steam Packet Company* (PO Box 5, Imperial Bldg., Douglas, Isle of Man IM99 1AF, England; phone: 1624-661661) operates ferries between Liverpool and Douglas, the island's capital, with return crossings from Pier Head on Saturdays from mid-September through mid-May and on some weekdays and Saturdays the rest of the year (the schedule varies from week to week). For details, contact the company or the tourist information center. There also is a 50-minute sightseeing cruise called "Ferry 'Cross the Mersey," which makes stops at Pier Head, Seacombe (Birkenhead), and Woodside (Wallasey). The trip takes place aboard one of two restored, historic ferries; departures are hourly. *Mersey Ferries* also offers services to Birkenhead and Wallasey from Pier Head, with departures every 30 minutes during rush hour. Information is available from *Mersey Ferries* (Victoria Pl., Seacombe, Wallasey; phone: 630-1030), from the *Merseytravel* office (Williamson Sq.; phone: 236-7676), or at the *Merseyside Welcome Centre* (see above). Also, *Fantasea Cruises* (no phone) runs half-hour boat trips that leave several times daily from *Albert Dock;* in summer, a water taxi connects various points on the dock as well.

BUS Local buses run frequently, from 7 AM until 10:30 PM; fares range from 35p (about 50¢) to 95p (about $1.40), depending on the distance traveled. Most pass through Roe Street, the best place to hop aboard. A city center/*Albert Dock* bus link No. 222, taking in the *Albert Dock* and *Lime Street Stations* on a circular route, runs daily every half hour, from 10 AM to 8 PM. The city and area's main operator, *Merseybus,* offers schedule information by telephone weekdays (phone: 254-1616). The *Merseytravel* and *Mersey Ferries* offices also give information on all local buses (see above). Long-distance buses depart from *London Road* coach station (phone: 709-6481).

CAR RENTAL Most major companies are represented, including *Avis* (113 Mulberry St.; phone: 709-4737; and at *Liverpool Airport;* phone: 486-6686); *Budget* (39 Leece St.; phone: 709-3103); *Europcar* (St. Vincent St.; phone: 708-9150); and *Hertz* (*Mount Pleasant Car Park,* 8 Brownlow Hill; phone: 709-3337; and at *Liverpool Airport;* phone: 486-7111).

SIGHTSEEING TOURS *Cavern City Tours* (phone: 236-9091) runs an hour-long sightseeing bus tour (on an open-top bus in summer) that leaves daily at 12:35 PM from the *Pump House Pub* on the *Albert Dock* and at 12:45 PM from the *Merseyside Welcome Centre* (with more frequent departures April through October). *Liverpool Heritage Walk,* an illustrated guide to a 7-mile walking tour around the city, is available for £1.50 (about $2.25) from both offices of the *Merseyside Welcome Centre* (see above); you also can do the tour on your own, following the metal markers along the path.

TAXI There are several firms that you can call for a cab, including *Britannia Radio Cars* (phone: 480-4800) and *Mersey Cabs* (phone: 298-2222). Cabstands can be found outside *Lime Street Station* and the *Playhouse Theatre.*

TRAIN AND SUBWAY Most mainline trains come into *Lime Street Station* (phone: 709-9696), which connects with a modest subway system stopping at *Moorfields, Central,* and *James Street* underground stations. There are frequent rail links to London (about three hours from Liverpool), Chester,

Manchester, and most other major cities, as well as to the Wirral Peninsula and North Wales. Pick up trains for Birkenhead at *Lime Street, Moorfields, Central,* or *James Street Stations.*

SPECIAL EVENTS

One of the world's premier horse races is held in the Liverpool area; it's one of the year's highlights.

AND THEY'RE OFF!

Grand National Although marred by the events of the race in 1993 (it was never officially completed as a result of confusion caused by two false starts and controversial interference by animal-rights demonstrators), the grand tradition still endures. The grueling steeplechase described in Enid Bagnold's *National Velvet*—the most famous race of its kind and the premier event of the steeplechase season—subjects competitors to 4½ lung-tearing miles over wickedly mischievous obstacles, including fences reputed to be bigger than those of any other steeplechase course; only a small percentage of competitors finish, and only a half-dozen horses have won the competition even twice in more than a century. Fences such as the Chair, grim and formidable, and Becher's (pronounced *Beech*-ers) Brook, named after the brilliant jockey who fell there during the first Liverpool steeplechase in 1839, make for the sort of race that warms even those who don't know a Totalizator from a ticktack man. On the night before, be sure to stop in at the cavernous cocktail lounge of the immense, rococo *Britannia Adelphi* hotel to see the jockeys who will prove the point on the morrow. The *Grand National* takes place annually on a Saturday at the end of March or early in April. For information, contact the *Aintree Racecourse,* Aintree (phone: 523-2600).

The two-week-long *Mersey River Festival* in June is the highlight of the year for the non-horsey crowd: Its activities include a regatta, live music by local bands, and fireworks, all focusing on the river and dockland area. The annual *Mersey Beatles Convention,* held for five days in late August, gives Beatlemaniacs a chance to indulge themselves in singing, dancing, filmgoing, souvenir hunting, and reminiscing at the *Britannia Adelphi* hotel; there are several activities on Mathew Street as well, including performances by street entertainers. For details on this and other *Beatles* weekends, contact *Cavern City Tours* (see *Sightseeing Tours,* above).

MUSEUMS

Liverpool's rich cultural heritage is displayed in numerous museums and galleries, many of which are underrated and underpatronized. In addition to those mentioned in *Special Places,* other institutions of note include the following:

LIVERPOOL MUSEUM One of Britain's finest, this museum displays exhibits covering a variety of subjects, including antiquities, archives, botany, decorative arts, geology, zoology, physical sciences, social and industrial history, and a transport gallery. The transport gallery houses the museum's most celebrated item—*The Lion,* a steam locomotive built in 1838 for the Liverpool and Manchester Railway Company. It is the oldest working steam engine in the world. The aquarium, vivarium, and planetarium appeal particularly to younger visitors. Open daily. Admission charge to the planetarium. William Brown St. (phone: 207-0001).

WESTERN APPROACHES The secret underground headquarters from which the Atlantic convoys of World War II were directed has been restored to its 1940s condition. It displays furnishings, maps, sea charts, photographs, and other historical exhibits. Open daily. Admission charge. 1 Rumford St. (phone: 227-2008).

SHOPPING

Pedestrians-only Church Street, Lord Street, Bold Street, Whitechapel, and Paradise Street are Liverpool's main shopping arteries. Most of the nationwide chain and department stores can be found here. There are more shops in Clayton Square, as well as in the massive *St. John's Shopping Centre,* which also has a bustling fruit, vegetable, fish, and meat market. The modern and luxuriously appointed *Cavern Walks* complex (on Mathew St.) features two floors of small specialty stores and cafés (open daily). *Albert Dock,* worth a separate expedition, contains dozens of specialty stores. For standard shopping hours, see GETTING READY TO GO.

Be sure to take your passport when you shop, and always inquire about the Value Added Tax (VAT) refund application forms when your total purchases in a store are over £50 (about $75). The VAT is a surcharge payable at the sales counter, but foreign customers usually will be reimbursed for it at home (for more information see GETTING READY TO GO).

Beatles Shop Posters, photos, sheet music, records, T-shirts, scarves, blow-up models, and other Beatlemania memorabilia, sold to the tunes of a working jukebox devoted exclusively to the lads. 31 Mathew St. (phone: 236-8066).

Bluecoat Chambers Discounted books, souvenirs, and videos on local history, as well as artists' materials on sale at four separate well-stocked shops in one building. School La. (phone: 709-4014).

Frank Green's Paintings, prints, and cards—the distinguished Liverpudlian artist's impressions of the city's changing scene since the early 1960s. 10 *Britannia Pavilion, Albert Dock* (phone: 709-3330).

G. Rennie Distinguished, tailored clothing for gentlemen; the shop also carries tie pins and cufflinks. 3 *The Arcade,* Covent Garden (phone: 236-5702).

Heritage Shop Gifts and ornaments related to nautical activity and *Albert Dock.* 1 *The Colonnades, Albert Dock* (phone: 709-7474).

Lewis's The city's leading department store. Don't miss Jacob Epstein's statue of a naked man on the prow of a ship over the main entrance (placed there to symbolize Liverpool's resurgence after being bombed in World War II). Ranelagh St. (phone: 709-7000).

Quiggins Centre Trendy clothes and collectibles in a beautiful 1866 building (although it badly needs a coat of paint). 12-16 School La. (phone: 709-2462).

Sawdust Designs Toys, ornaments, knickknacks, and chests, all hand-crafted in wood, are among the items sold here. 128 Bold St. (phone: 707-0806).

Sewill Marine Established in 1800, this is the world's oldest maker of nautical instruments, such as telescopes and barometers; in addition to its own wares, the shop sells carriage clocks and other items for the landlubber. 20 *Britannia Pavilion, Albert Dock* (phone: 708-7444).

Thornton's A mouth-watering selection of chocolates and toffees. 6 Whitechapel (phone: 708-6849).

W. Richards An old-fashioned hunting, shooting, and fishing emporium, in business since the 18th century. It's one of the places British yuppies buy their Barbours—dark green, oiled, waterproof, expensive coats designed for country walking. *India Buildings,* 42 Brunswick St. (phone: 236-2925).

Waterstone's Yet another member of the British chain of large, well-stocked bookstores staffed with knowledgeable, helpful people. A second store, located in the foyer of the *Tate Gallery,* specializes in books on art, cinema, and photography. 52 Bold St. (phone: 709-0866) and the *Tate Gallery, Albert Dock* (phone: 709-0131).

SPORTS

The *Oval Sports Centre* (Old Chester Rd., Bebington, Wirral; phone: 645-0551) has a full range of facilities, from a swimming pool to a dry ski slope. For up-to-the-minute details on Liverpool's sports scene, call the *Liverpool Sports Information Line* (phone: 225-6351).

GOLF At least 35 golf courses dot the map of Liverpool's environs; one of them is among the best in the country.

TOP TEE-OFF SPOT

Royal Liverpool This was the site of the first *British Amateur* championship—which has been held here on 15 occasions since—and the first international golf competition (played between England and Scotland in 1902). In 1921, "Hoylake," as it's generally called, played host to the first international match between Great Britain and the US, which was dubbed the *Walker Cup* the following year. The club has hosted 10 *British Open* championships and is considered by many to be one of the best tests of golf in Britain. Not for the faint of heart. Meols Dr., Hoylake (phone: 632-3101).

Another world-famous course, the *Royal Birkdale* golf club (phone: 1704-567920), is among the six courses at Southport, along the coast about 20 miles north of town. In addition, the *Liverpool Municipal* golf course (Moor La., Kirkby; phone: 546-5435) has 18 holes and is open daily, and most private clubs admit visitors as well. There's a ladies' course within a gentlemen's course at Formby (phone: 17048-72164), between Liverpool and Southport.

RUGBY Fans can watch one of the country's top professional *Rugby League* clubs at St. Helens, 20 miles east of Liverpool, and there are *Rugby Union* clubs at Waterloo, Birkenhead Park, New Brighton, and Liverpool.

SOCCER The two famous home teams are the *Liverpool Football Club* (nicknamed the "Reds," after their red shirts) and the *Everton Football Club* (the "Toffees" or "Blues"). On most Saturdays during the season, one or the other team is playing a home game, either at *Liverpool*'s *Anfield* (phone: 263-2361) or at *Everton*'s *Goodison Park* (phone: 521-2020). Details of "Soccer Weekends," which include a match, a visit to the club's trophy room, and a guided coach tour of Liverpool, are available from the tourist information offices (see *Tourist Information*), or call the reservations hotline (phone: 709-0123).

WALKING The Wirral Peninsula has superb coast walks, including the Wirral Way, 12 miles down the west coast.

THEATER

Many of the country's top playwrights and actors began their careers here, and the city's largest theater, the *Liverpool Empire* (Lime St.; phone: 709-1555), regularly premiers shows that end up in London. It also hosts visiting ballet companies. Britain's oldest repertory theater, the *Liverpool Playhouse* (Williamson Sq.; phone: 709-8363), is the place to see the classics and contemporary plays. Its *Studio Theatre,* connected to the playhouse, stages more avant-garde productions, as does the *Everyman Theatre,* which serves excellent food in its bistro (see *Eating Out*). The *Unity Theatre* (Hope Pl.; phone: 709-4988) and *Neptune Theatre* (Hanover St.; phone: 709-7844) specialize in small-scale innovative shows.

MUSIC

The city that gave rise to the *Beatles* and the Mersey Sound still has a flourishing live music scene, with the *Royal Court Theatre* (Roe St.; phone: 709-4321) being the biggest rock venue. The *Liverpool Empire* (see *Theater,* above) attracts such major touring companies as the *Scottish Opera* and the *Welsh National Opera;* it also hosts pop concerts. The *Royal Liverpool Philharmonic Orchestra* plays in *Philharmonic Hall* (Hope St.; phone: 709-

3789). There's usually live folk and jazz at one of the pubs and clubs, and in summer there are string ensembles that play regularly in *Cavern Walks* and outdoor bands that perform around the *Albert Dock.*

NIGHTCLUBS AND NIGHTLIFE

Liverpool offers a rich variety of nighttime entertainment ranging from discos and live acts to cabarets and casinos. There are dozens of venues in Liverpool city center. Check *In Touch* and at the tourist information offices (see *Tourist Information*). Sadly, the original *Cavern Club* was torn down in order to build a rail tunnel underneath it; but there's plenty of activity in the wee hours in the newer *Cavern Club* (*Cavern Walks,* Mathew St.; phone: 236-9091), on the same site (closed Sundays and Tuesdays). Other discos include *Friday's* at the *Britannia Adelphi* hotel (see *Checking In*); and *The State* (Dale St.; phone: 236-4735), whose remarkable turn-of-the-century interior contrasts vividly with the modern music and clientele. Inveterate gamblers (who are 18 and older) can try their luck at *Stanley's* casino (45 Renshaw St.; phone: 708-8866); you must apply for membership there 48 hours in advance.

Best in Town

CHECKING IN

There are a limited number of hotels in Liverpool with genuine historic atmosphere, but there's no shortage of empty rooms, particularly on weekends. Most of Liverpool's major hotels have complete facilities for the business traveler. Those hotels listed below as having "business services" usually offer such conveniences as a concierge, meeting rooms, photocopiers, computers, translation services, and express checkout, among others. Call the hotel for additional information. Expect to pay $110 or more per night for a double room (with private bath, phone, TV set, and breakfast, unless otherwise indicated) in hotels listed as expensive, $70 to $105 for those classed as moderate, and less than $70 for those listed as inexpensive. All telephone numbers are in the 151 city code unless otherwise indicated.

EXPENSIVE

Atlantic Tower Modern, distinctively shaped like the bow of a ship, and overlooking the water, it has 226 rooms (many with magnificent river views), an elegant foyer, two restaurants, and the *Tradewinds Bar* with a nautical theme. Business services are available. 30 Chapel St. (phone: 227-4444; fax: 236-3973).

Britannia Adelphi Built in 1914, during the heyday of the transatlantic liners, this magnificent 391-room hotel reflects the style of that era: The marble foyer has a mirrored ceiling, and there is a huge lounge (modeled after the one on the *Titanic*), complete with pillars, chandeliers, and palms. Sunday lunch, while inexpensive, can be highly disappointing; when the crowds rush in, the service staff becomes harried. Business services are available. Ranelagh Pl. (phone: 709-7200; fax: 708-8326).

Gladstone Formerly called the *Forte Crest,* this property has been renamed in honor of 19th-century British prime minister William Gladstone, a native Liverpudlian; however, it's still part of the Forte chain. What this hotel lacks in distinctive character is made up for in practical facilities. There are 154 bedrooms, a restaurant, and business services. The building also has a convenient location beside the *Lime Street* railway station. Lord Nelson St. (phone: 709-7050; 800-225-5843; fax: 709-2193).

Liverpool Moat House Only a short walk from *Albert Dock,* this place is less than elegant, but it's the best of the hotels that sprang up throughout the city after World War II. In addition to its 251 well-appointed rooms and suites, there's a restaurant, sauna, solarium, and indoor pool. Business services are available. Paradise St. (phone: 709-0181; fax: 709-2706).

MODERATE

Leasowe Castle On the Wirral Peninsula near Wallasey, just a short drive off the M53 motorway and within easy reach of the city center via the Mersey tunnel, this excellent establishment is situated in a 400-year-old castle offering old charm and character along with modern conveniences. The 40 rooms are comfortable and equipped with all basic facilities. A fine restaurant and the *Castle Bar,* serving a variety of bar lunches, also are on the premises, and business services are offered. Leasowe, Moreton, Merseyside (phone: 606-9191; fax: 678-5551).

Trials Based in an imposing Victorian building that was once a bank, the city's most stylish hotel (and probably the best value for the money) has 20 large, luxuriously appointed rooms with all the expected modern conveniences, and an elegant restaurant serving French and international fare. Business services are available. 56 Castle St. (phone: 227-1021; fax: 236-0110).

INEXPENSIVE

Aachen Tucked into a row of townhouses near *Metropolitan Cathedral* and the university, its 17 rooms are popular with visiting Americans. The dining room serves simple English fare. The owners, Irene Richardson and Maria Wilson, are true jewels of hospitality. 89-91 Mount Pleasant (phone: 709-3477; fax: 709-1126).

Campanile There are 83 pleasant rooms and a restaurant at this hotel housed in a red brick building on the waterfront at *Queens Dock.* Business services are offered. Chaloner St. (phone: 709-8104; fax: 709-8725).

Feathers A friendly, award-winning place with 84 rooms (69 with baths), a restaurant, and business services. 119-125 Mount Pleasant (phone: 709-9655; fax: 709-3838).

EATING OUT

Rumor has it that some 140 nationalities live in the 1 square mile of the Toxteth Quarter alone, spawning the city's wealth of ethnic restaurants. There is a wide choice of Chinese restaurants, particularly in Chinatown, at the top of Bold Street. More traditional English eateries are everywhere, and even the city's hotel restaurants are slowly attracting locals. And don't be surprised to find "scouse" on a menu; it is the traditional dish of stewed lamb, beef, and vegetables that earned Liverpudlians their famous nickname. A dinner for two without wine or tips will cost more than $60 at a restaurant listed as expensive, $30 to $60 at one listed as moderate, and less than $30 at an inexpensive one. All restaurants listed below serve lunch and dinner unless otherwise noted. All telephone numbers are in the 151 city code unless otherwise indicated.

EXPENSIVE

Armadillo In a converted warehouse, it has a self-service, student-like atmosphere by day, but in the evening it becomes a bustling, full-service restaurant. Imaginative vegetarian dishes include a vegetable and cheese pie and "pease" pudding served with cream, dry vermouth, and a julienne of vegetables. This place offers good value. Closed Sundays and Mondays. Reservations necessary. Major credit cards accepted. 20-22 Mathew St. (phone: 236-4123).

Del Secolo This family-run establishment has an Italian name, but its menu also features a large selection of international dishes. Closed Sundays. Reservations advised. Major credit cards accepted. 36-40 Stanley St. (phone: 236-4004).

L'Oriel Housed in the distinctive *Oriel Chambers Building,* the first office block in the country to be constructed with "picture" windows, this dining spot offers French fare. Closed Saturday lunch and Sundays. Reservations advised. Major credit cards accepted. 16 Water St. (phone: 236-5025).

MODERATE

L'Alouette An imaginatively decorative bistro, it serves a wide selection of French foods. Closed Mondays. Reservations necessary. Major credit cards accepted. 2 Lark La. (phone: 727-2142).

Casa Bella Pasta, pizza, and salads are the specialties of this large airy eatery in a former bank, but it also has good meat and fish dishes (the sirloin flambéed in cognac is wonderful). Closed Sundays. Reservations unnecessary. Major credit cards accepted. 25 Victoria St. (phone: 258-1800).

Est! Est! Est! A large trattoria, its name comes from a 12th-century Italian phrase meaning "good wines." Diners can feast on excellent pasta and pizza (as well as wine) as they watch the activity on the docks. Open daily. Reservations unnecessary. Major credit cards accepted. 5 *Edward Pavilion, Albert Dock* (phone: 708-6969).

Jenny's Seafood A modest basement entrance belies the excellent reputation here. Among the best preparers of fish in town, it's housed in an old building where lines for ships used to be stretched. Closed Saturday lunch, Sundays, and Monday evenings. Reservations advised. Major credit cards accepted. 36 Fenwick St. (phone: 236-0332).

Kebab House Taverna Live music on Friday and Saturday evenings and the best Greek food in town are irresistible temptations. Be certain to sit downstairs so you can catch all the action. Open daily. Reservations necessary only for parties of eight or more. Major credit cards accepted. 22 Hardman St. (phone: 709-6210).

El Macho Mexican Village "Don't siesta; come to *El Macho* and fiesta" is the motto of this excellent south-of-the-border restaurant in a converted row house near the university. Closed Sundays. Reservations unnecessary. Major credit cards accepted. 23 Hope St. (phone: 708-6644).

Qué Pasa Wooden floors, bare brick walls, and the occasional sombrero and other evocative decorations distinguish this small, attractive Mexican eatery. Open daily. No reservations. Major credit cards accepted. 94-96 Lark La. (phone: 727-0006).

INEXPENSIVE

Everyman Bistro Popular with university students, this self-serve spot in the same building as the *Everyman Theatre* offers a wide variety of freshly produced meat dishes and vegetarian fare; it's an excellent value. Closed Sundays. No reservations. Major credit cards accepted. 9-11 Hope St. (phone: 708-9545).

Pâtisserie Here's a peaceful retreat from the bustling activity of Liverpool's main shopping streets. The decor, with its plastic furniture, is a bit tacky, but don't let that put you off—the cakes, pastries, and rolls, all fresh-baked daily on the premises, are superb. There's also a good selection of coffees and teas. Open for breakfast, lunch, and afternoon tea; closed Sundays. No reservations. No credit cards accepted. 27 Tarleton St. (phone: 708-5416).

SHARING A PINT

As in most English cities, there are plenty of pubs to choose from; one is our particular favorite.

PERFECT PINTS

Philharmonic Pub Hands down Britain's most ornate pub, it's famous for its men's room—pink marble lavatories so spectacular that women are actually allowed to come in for a look-see when it's unoccupied. The rest of the huge interior consists of several rooms, some divided by carved wooden partitions leading off from a mosaic-decorated central bar, others huge and sumptuous with padded seats, high ceilings, and stained glass windows. And true Yorkshire bitters are on tap along with a wide range of hot food served at lunchtime. 36 Hope St. (phone: 709-1163).

Other interesting old pubs in which to imbibe include sailortown haunts such as the 18th-century *Pig and Whistle* (*Covent Garden;* phone: 236-4760), which served ale to thousands of emigrants on their way to the New World (see the "Emigrants Supplied" sign inside). *The Vines* (81 Lime St.; phone: 709-3977) is a beautiful Edwardian pub that still sports wooden fixtures made by carpenters who worked on the great ocean liners at the turn of the century. Other pubs in this style include the *Central* (36 Ranelagh St.; no phone), a carefully preserved Victorian pub with sumptuous decorations; and the *Lisbon* (attracting a gay clientele), which is fitted with ornate brass and woodwork and is renowned for its spectacular ceiling (35 Victoria St.; phone: 236-1248). Just off Hope Street is the tiny *Ye Cracke* (13 Rice St.; phone: 709-4171), at one time frequented by the *Beatles.* Also formerly patronized by the *Beatles* is the *Grapes* (25 Mathew St.; phone: 236-2961), a cozy little pub. A place that has become a Liverpool institution with its bizarre mixture of poets, punks, trendy models, and yuppies is the famous *Kirklands Café Bar* (13 Hardman St.; phone: 707-0132), which serves sandwiches and light snacks and features good entertainment. The *Pumphouse* (next to *Albert Dock;* phone: 709-2367), attractively converted from its original function of providing steam to the dock's equipment, has a pleasant waterside terrace that's open in good weather.

London

British author and journalist V. S. Pritchett has noted that the essence of London is contained in the very sound of its name: Lon-don, a weighty word, solid, monumental, dignified, even ponderous. London is a shapeless city without a center; it sprawls anarchically over 620 square miles and brims over with a variety of neighborhoods and people. One of its sharpest observers, Daniel Defoe, portrayed London in the 18th century much as it could be described today: "It is . . . stretched out in buildings, straggling, confused . . . out of all shape, uncompact and unequal; neither long nor broad, round nor square."

London can be best understood not as one city but as a conglomeration of villages—Battersea, Chelsea, Hampstead, and Paddington are just a few. Fortunately, its important parks and squares have remained inviolate, but not without a struggle, for London's merchant class often resisted and defeated town planners, ever since Parliament turned down Sir Christopher Wren's splendid plan to rebuild after the Great Fire of 1666. Royalty and aristocracy created and preserved the parks—*Hyde Park, Kensington Gardens, Kew Gardens, Regent's Park,* and *St. James's Park* were all royal parks—and their enthusiasm became contagious. Today's London—though marred by soulless high-rises, particularly in the financial district—boasts more greenery than any metropolis could reasonably hope to retain in these philistine times. Aside from its many garden squares and the meticulously tended plots of many Londoners' homes, the city is punctuated by a series of large parks and commons; besides those already mentioned, there are *Wimbledon Common, Richmond Deer Park, Primrose Hill, Hampstead Heath*—the list goes on and on. And to make even more certain that citification does not intrude too far into London life, a greenbelt, almost 100 square miles of forest and grassland, virtually encircles the city and, to the chagrin of developers, is meticulously preserved by law.

The city follows the serpentine meandering of the Thames, England's principal river, and nearly everything of interest in London is on or near it. The river always has been London's mainstay, for centuries its only east–west road, and it has been said that "every drop of the Thames is liquid history." At the site of the *Royal Naval College* in Greenwich, for example, there once stood a palace where Henry VIII and Elizabeth I were born, and where tournaments and banquets were held.

A great river port and a city of gardens, London is also a city of stately squares and monuments, of royalty (albeit tarnished) with its pomp and ceremony, a cosmopolitan city of the first rank. Until World War II, it was the capital of the British Empire upon which, it was said, the sun never set. For many centuries, a powerful Britannia ruled a considerable section of the globe, and the English language became dominant all over the world, from North America to India.

If the British Empire has contracted drastically, it has done so gracefully. And if once-subject peoples hated their oppressor, they still love London, and many have chosen to live here. London is still the center of the Commonwealth of independent nations that were once British colonies. The influence of these former colonials is felt in the substantial Indian-Pakistani community in the Southall district of West London, in the strong Caribbean flavor in Brixton, in Chinatown in and around Gerrard Street in Soho, in the Cypriot groceries and bakeries of Camden Town, and in the majestic mosque on the fringe of *Regent's Park.* Here, the English language is flavored by accents from Australia and Barbados, Bangladesh and Nigeria, Canada and Malaysia, Kenya and South Africa, Sri Lanka and Ireland, Hong Kong and the US. And the various inflections of Britain itself also are heard—in the lilt and rasp of cockney and in the accents of Oxford, Somerset, Yorkshire, the Scottish Highlands, and Wales.

London's somewhat onomatopoeic name derives from the Celtic term *Llyn-din,* meaning "river place," but little is known of London before the Romans renamed it Londinium in AD 43. Part of the old Roman city wall may be seen near the *Tower of London,* as can some segments beside the *Museum of London* (see *Special Places*). Even in medieval times, London had grandiose notions of its own importance—a pride that has been amply justified by history.

The city was sufficiently prominent for William the Conqueror to make it his capital in 1066. During the Middle Ages, trade expansion, population growth, and the energetic activities of its guilds promoted London's prosperity. Indisputably, London's golden age was the 16th century, the time of Queen Elizabeth I, Shakespeare, and Drake's defeat of the Spanish Armada. Most of London's Tudor buildings were wiped out in the Great Fire of 1666, and Christopher Wren, the great architect, undertook to reconstruct many buildings and churches, the most outstanding of which is *St. Paul's Cathedral.* The 18th century saw the building of noble homes and stately squares, culminating in the grand expansion program developed between 1811 and 1820 by the prince regent's principal architect, John Nash. One of the best examples of his work is the terrace of largely crown-owned Regency houses surrounding *Regent's Park.* During the early 19th century, interest continued in homes and squares; only in the Victorian age, the height of the Empire, were public buildings like the *Houses of Parliament* redesigned, this time in grand and fanciful neo-Gothic style.

London has seen whole catalogues of heroes and villains, crises and conflagrations, come and go. Still on elegant display is stately *Hampton Court Palace,* the most magnificent of England's palaces, where Henry VIII lived now and again with five of his six wives. There is a spot downtown—in front of the *Banqueting House* on Whitehall—where another king, Charles I, was beheaded by his subjects, who were committing regicide 140 years before the presumably more emotional and explosive French even contemplated such a gesture. London has lived through the unbounded permissiveness of the Restoration period (1660–85), when even King Charles II openly frequented brothels, and it has survived the stern moral puritanism of the Victorian era, when it was downright rude to refer to a *breast* of chicken or a piano *leg.* The city stood up with exemplary courage under the devastating effects of Nazi bombings, which destroyed a great many buildings and killed thousands of people. And, however shaken, today's tabloid-rocked throne still stands.

Many of our images of London, taken from old movies, actually mirror its realities: *Big Ben* rises above the *Houses of Parliament,* somberly striking the hour; ramrod-straight, scarlet-uniformed guards half hide their faces in towering black bearskin hats; clerks (pronounced *clarks*) at the Bank of England still sport the kinds of top hats and tailcoats worn by their predecessors centuries ago; barristers (lawyers) still don wigs and black robes in court. A few images, however, are outdated: The bowler hat has slipped out of fashion, and rigidly enforced environmental regulations have made London's once-famous pea soup fog a thing of the past.

The British genius for government—emphasizing democracy and political tolerance—has been demonstrated ever since the *Magna Carta* was signed in 1215, and it creates an easy, relaxed ambience for individualists of all sorts. The eccentric and inveterate Londoner of the city's 18th-century heyday, Dr. Samuel Johnson, once declared, "When a man is tired of London, he is tired of life, for there is in London all that life can afford." Johnson's opinion, though perhaps somewhat overblown, essentially was shared by one of several American writers who chose to live in London. After living in New York, Paris, and Boston, Henry James chose to move to London in 1881. He summed up his impression of the city as follows: "It is not a pleasant place; it is not agreeable, or cheerful, or easy, or exempt from reproach. It is only magnificent. You can draw up a tremendous list of reasons why it should be unsupportable. The fogs, the smoke, the dirt, the darkness, the wet, the distances, the ugliness, the brutal size of the place, the horrible numerosity of society . . . but . . . London is on the whole the most possible form of life."

London At-a-Glance

SEEING THE CITY

London has, for the most part, resisted the temptation to build high. Aside from a handful of modest gestures toward skyscraping, there are few towering structures to obscure panoramic views of the city from its vantage points, which include the following:

LONDON HILTON INTERNATIONAL There were discreet noises of disapproval from *Buckingham Palace* when it was realized that the view from the roof bar of the *Hilton* included not only the palace grounds but, with high-powered binoculars, the inside of some of the royal chambers as well. In fact, the view over Mayfair, *Hyde Park,* and Westminster is breathtaking. 22 Park La., W1 (phone: 171-493-8000). Underground: *Hyde Park Corner.*

WESTMINSTER CATHEDRAL Not to be confused with *Westminster Abbey,* this is London's Roman Catholic cathedral. The top of its bell tower overlooks a broad expanse of the inner city. An elevator takes visitors up for a token charge (April through September only). Off Victoria St. near the station, at Ashley Pl., SW1 (phone: 171-834-7452). Underground: *Victoria.*

HAMPSTEAD HEATH Climb to the top of Parliament Hill, on the southern rim of this "wilderness" in north London. On a clear day, the view south from the *Heath* makes the city look like a vast village. Underground: *Belsize Park* or *Hampstead.*

SOUTH BANK CENTRE On the south bank of Waterloo Bridge is this large, bunker-like complex of cultural buildings, including the *Royal Festival Hall,* the *Royal National Theatre,* the *National Film Theatre,* the *Hayward Gallery,* and other cultural attractions. For a view of London, look across the Thames—upriver to the *Houses of Parliament,* downriver to *St. Paul's Cathedral.* Underground: *Waterloo.*

TOWER BRIDGE WALKWAY The upper part of one of London's most famous landmarks is open to visitors. In addition to the viewing gallery, there is a museum with state-of-the-art animated figures and the bridge's original Victorian steam pumping engines—which still work. Open daily. Admission charge (phone: 171-403-3761 or 171-407-0922). Underground: *Tower Hill.*

ST. PAUL'S CATHEDRAL The reward for climbing the 538 steps to the dome—the largest in the world after St. Peter's in Rome—is a panoramic view of London. Galleries are closed Sundays and for special services. Admission charge to cathedral, except on Sundays; admission charge to galleries. *St. Paul's Churchyard,* EC4 (phone: 171-248-2705). Underground: *St. Paul's* or *Mansion House.*

THE MONUMENT This 202-foot-high obelisk (commemorating the Great Fire of 1666) affords a good view of nearby churches and across to *Canary Wharf* in the Docklands, as well as to *St. Paul's* and the *Telecom Tower.* Note that there is no elevator. Closed Sundays October through March. Admission charge. Monument St., EC3 (phone: 171-626-2717). Underground: *Monument.*

GREENWICH PARK The lone hill in this large expanse across the Thames in Greenwich provides a panorama over the Docklands and the rest of the city in the distance. The best view is from General Wolfe's statue near the *Old Royal Observatory;* on a clear day you can see the dome of *St. Paul's.* Greenwich can be reached by tube (*Greenwich Station*), *British Rail,* or boat from *Charing Cross, Westminster,* or *Tower Piers.*

SPECIAL PLACES

Surveying London from the steps of *St. Paul's Cathedral* at the turn of the 19th century, a visiting Prussian general commented to his English host:

"What a place to plunder!" Even the less rapacious will appreciate London's wealth of sights, most of which are clustered reasonably close together in or near the inner districts of Westminster, the City, and Kensington. Another area worth exploring is the neighborhood of Chelsea, with quiet, pretty side streets and a long, often frenetic shopping thoroughfare called King's Road.

WESTMINSTER

CHANGING OF THE GUARD An American who lived in London once said, "There's just no better way to convince yourself that you're in London!" This famous ceremony, accompanied by band music (which sometimes features bagpipes), takes place daily April through mid-July (every other day the rest of the year) promptly at 11:30 AM in the *Buckingham Palace* forecourt and at 11:15 AM at *St. James's Palace.* (It is usually canceled in inclement weather.) Arrive early, as it can get crowded (for more information, phone: 839-123411; costs between 36p/about 55¢ and 48p/about 75¢ per minute).

HORSE GUARDS If you haven't had enough, you can see a new guard of 12 members of the Household Cavalry troop in with trumpet and standard, Mondays through Saturdays at 11 AM and Sundays at 10 AM, on the west side of Whitehall. Incidentally, they come from stables not far from *Hyde Park* and make a daily parade along the south roadway of *Hyde Park,* past *Buckingham Palace,* and then on to Trafalgar Square to turn into Whitehall. Their progress is as much fun to watch as the actual ceremony.

BUCKINGHAM PALACE The royal standard flies from the roof when the monarch is in residence at her London home. Although George III bought it in 1762, *Buckingham Palace* did not become the principal regal dwelling until 1837, when Queen Victoria moved in. The gate that originally was built for the entrance, too narrow for the coaches of George IV, now marks the *Hyde Park* end of Oxford Street and is known as *Marble Arch.*

Part of the palace is now open to the public—for a price. During August and September (when the royals are vacationing), visitors may view 18 of the state rooms; on display are many of the works in the nonpareil *Royal Collection* (also see the *Queen's Gallery,* below)—including paintings by Rubens and Van Dyck and the greatest collection of porcelain in the world (acquired by George IV). Other highlights are the *Blue Drawing Room,* with its ice-blue color scheme and exquisite chandeliers; the *State Dining Room,* featuring several royal portraits; the *Throne Room;* the *Music Room;* and the majestic, sweeping staircase to the second floor. Open daily. The steep admission charge is going toward the restoration of *Windsor Castle,* damaged by fire in November 1992; time-specific tickets are sold each day (for that day only) at a kiosk in *St. James's Park,* opposite the palace (phone: 171-930-5526). Underground: *St. James's Park* or *Victoria.*

QUEEN'S GALLERY The *British Royal Collection*—one of the world's greatest—was inaccessible to most people until 1962, when this gallery was created at

Buckingham Palace, and even now only a fraction is on view. The exhibitions here never fail to impress, whether they are devoted to a subject such as royal children, animal paintings, or British soldiers; to single artists—Leonardo da Vinci or Gainsborough or Canaletto or Holbein, to name a quartet of past shows; or to groups of painters—the Italians or the Dutch. Exhibitions change about once a year. There's also a gift shop. Closed Mondays. Admission charge. Buckingham Palace Rd., SW1 (phone: 171-799-2331). Underground: *Victoria.*

ROYAL ACADEMY Britain's oldest fine arts institution is housed in the former home of Lord Burlington. Its permanent collection includes works by Turner, Gainsborough, and West. The Summer Exhibition of living painters has been a tradition for over 200 years. Special displays this year include exhibitions of works by French artists Nicolas Poussin (1594–1665) and Odilon Redon (1840–1916). Open daily. Admission charge. *Burlington House,* Piccadilly, W1 (phone: 171-439-7438). Underground: *Green Park* or *Piccadilly Circus.*

ROYAL MEWS The mews is a palace alley where the magnificent bridal coach, other state coaches, and the horses that draw them are stabled. The public is admitted from noon to 4 PM Wednesdays and Thursdays mid-April through mid-July; Wednesdays through Fridays mid-July through September; and Wednesdays only from early October to just before *Christmas.* Admission charge. Buckingham Palace Rd., SW1 (phone: 171-799-2331). Underground: *Victoria.*

ST. JAMES'S PALACE Built originally for Henry VIII, this forbidding brick palace has decorative chimneys and gates; still serving royalty (Prince Charles has an office here), it is the *Court of St. James,* where new monarchs are proclaimed. The entrance under the clock tower, dating from 1832 during William IV's reign, is guarded by two sentries from rotating regiments who wear scarlet uniforms with busbies (black bearskin hats) and chain chin straps. In 1649, Charles I walked from the palace to his execution at Whitehall. The palace is not open to the public. Pall Mall, SW1. Underground: *Green Park.*

ST. JAMES'S PARK Londoners love parks, and this is one of the nicest. At lunch hour on a sunny day you can see impeccably dressed London businesspeople lounging on the grass, their shoes off and their sleeves rolled up. With its sizable lake (designed by John Nash) inhabited by pelicans and other wild fowl, *St. James's* was originally a royal deer park laid out as a pleasure ground for Charles II. Underground: *St. James's Park.*

THE MALL This wide avenue (rhymes with "pal"), parallel to Pall Mall, is lined with lime trees and Regency buildings and leads from Trafalgar Square to *Buckingham Palace.* It is the principal ceremonial route used by Queen Elizabeth and the Household Cavalry for the State Opening of Parliament

(October/November) and the *Trooping the Colour* (see *Special Events*). It is closed to traffic on Sundays. Underground: *Trafalgar Square.*

PICCADILLY CIRCUS Downtown London finds its center here in the heart of the theater district and on the edge of Soho. This is the London equivalent of Times Square, and at the edge of the busy "circus," or traffic circle, is a statue of Eros, which was designed in 1893 as *The Angel of Christian Charity,* a memorial to the charitable Earl of Shaftesbury—the archer and his bow are a pun on his name. The *Criterion* restaurant (see *Eating Out*) and the *Criterion Theatre* are on the south side; opposite is the *Trocadero,* a converted three-story shopping and entertainment complex whose latest addition is *Planet Hollywood* (see *Eating Out*), a link in the famous restaurant chain. At the *Rock Circus* (phone: 171-734-8025), on the top four floors of the *London Pavilion,* rock music's immortals—from the *Beatles* to the *Who*—are brought to life with lighting, narration, and music. The *Rock Circus* also houses Europe's largest revolving auditorium, where "performances" are offered by rather remarkable robotic figures that move in rhythm to the music. Another popular exhibition is the *Guinness World of Records* display. Both are open daily. Separate admission charges (phone: 171-439-7331). Underground: *Piccadilly Circus.*

TRAFALGAR SQUARE One of London's most heavily trafficked squares is built around *Nelson's Column*—a 145-foot-high monument bearing a 17-foot statue that honors Lord Horatio Nelson, who won the Battle of Trafalgar in 1805. At the base are four huge bronze lions and two fountains. Flanked by handsome buildings, including the *National Gallery* and the 18th-century *Church of St. Martin-in-the-Fields* (have lunch or tea in the *Café in the Crypt;* see *Eating Out*), the square is a favorite gathering place for political rallies, tourists, and pigeons. Underground: *Trafalgar Square.*

NATIONAL GALLERY Among the world's greatest art museums, the *National Gallery* was instituted in 1824, when connoisseur Sir George Beaumont persuaded the government to buy the three dozen–plus paintings offered for sale after the death of merchant/collector John Julius Angerstein—among them Rembrandt's *The Woman Taken in Adultery* and *The Adoration of the Shepherds,* Rubens's *The Rape of the Sabine Women,* and Titian's *Venus and Adonis.* Subsequent gifts and acquisitions have endowed it with a collection that represents a balanced cross section of the chief schools of Western European art, from Giotto to Picasso. Jewels such as Leonardo da Vinci's great cartoon *The Virgin and Child with St. Anne and St. John the Baptist,* Botticelli's *Venus and Mars,* Raphael's *Crucifixion,* and Jan van Eyck's *Arnolfini Marriage* glow on the walls. Most of the more than 2,000 works are organized according to nationality and hang in chronological order. Nearly every item is on view at all times; a computer system enables visitors to locate any painting. Guidebooks are available in the shop, including *Twenty Great Paintings,* featuring photographs and descriptions of the gallery's most famous masterpieces. There are free, hour-long guided tours weekdays at 11:30 AM and 2:30 PM and Saturdays at 2 and 3:30 PM. And to give the footsore art lover a break, the *Sainsbury Wing Brasserie* offers light lunches and wine (phone: 171-389-1769). The museum is open daily. Admission charge to special exhibitions. Trafalgar Sq., WC2 (phone: 171-839-3321). Underground: *Trafalgar Square.*

NATIONAL PORTRAIT GALLERY Established in 1856, this museum is devoted to the portraits of the most important figures in British arts, letters, history and politics, military life, science, and various other fields. In all, over 9,000 likenesses, arranged chronologically, stare down from the walls. Elizabeth I is here as a young woman and a dowager, not far from Shakespeare; Mary, Queen of Scots; Thomas More; Cardinal Wolsey; Sir Walter Raleigh; and Robert Devereux, Earl of Essex. The list of authors reads like the table of contents of a literature text—Pepys, Milton, Dryden, Pope, Swift, Boswell, Johnson, Tennyson, Dickens, the Brontë sisters, Wilde, Auden, and Shaw. Also shown here are such well-known contemporary faces as Peter O'Toole and the Prince and Princess of Wales. Special shows on historical themes or individual artists are mounted frequently as well; every summer, the gallery displays a special collection of portraits by up-and-coming international artists. Open daily. Admission charge to special exhibitions only. 2 St. Martin's Pl., WC2 (phone: 171-306-0055). Underground: *Trafalgar Square.*

WHITEHALL A broad boulevard stretching from Trafalgar Square to Parliament Square, lined most of the way by government ministries and such historic buildings as the *Banqueting House* (completed in 1622, with a ceiling painted by Rubens). This is also where the daily changing of the Horse Guards takes place (see above). Underground: *Trafalgar Square* or *Westminster.*

DOWNING STREET Behind an ornate gate off Whitehall lies a street of small, unpretentious Georgian houses that include the official residences of some of the most important figures in British government—in particular the prime minister at No. 10 and the chancellor of the exchequer at No. 11. Underground: *Westminster.*

CABINET WAR ROOMS This underground complex was Winston Churchill's auxiliary command post during World War II, which he used most often during the German Luftwaffe's blitz on London. Most of the rooms contain their original furnishings. Of special note are the *Map Room;* the *Cabinet Room,* where the prime minister met with his staff; and the cramped *Transatlantic Telephone Room* (No. 63) used only by Churchill himself (it was disguised as a lavatory so no one would recognize its actual purpose). Open daily. Admission charge. Clive Steps, King Charles St., SW1 (phone: 171-930-6961). Underground: *Westminster.*

WESTMINSTER ABBEY It's easy to get lost among the endlessly fascinating tombs and plaques and not even notice the abbey's splendid architecture, so do look at the structure itself and don't miss the cloisters, which display its Gothic design to best advantage. Note also the fine Tudor chapel of Henry VII, with its tall windows and lovely fan-tracery vaulting, and the 13th-century chapel of St. Edward the Confessor, containing England's *Coronation Chair* and Scotland's ancient coronation *Stone of Scone* (pronounced *Skoon*).

Ever since William the Conqueror was crowned here in 1066, the abbey has been the traditional place where English monarchs are crowned, married, and buried. You don't have to be an Anglophile to be moved by the numerous tombs and memorials with their fascinating inscriptions—here are honored (though not necessarily buried) kings and queens, soldiers, statesmen, and many other prominent English men and women. *Poets' Corner,* in the south transept, contains the tombs of Chaucer, Tennyson, Browning, and many others—plus memorials to nearly every English poet of note and to some Americans, such as Longfellow and T. S. Eliot.

The abbey is itself a lesson in English history. A church has stood on this site since at least AD 170; in the 8th century, it was a Benedictine monastery. The current Early English—Gothic edifice, begun in the 13th century, took almost 300 years to build.

Guided tours are offered six times every weekday and three times on Saturdays. The nave and cloisters are open daily; the *Royal Chapel* is closed Sundays. Admission charge to the *Royal Chapel,* to *Poets' Corner,* and to some other sections, as well as for tours. Broad Sanctuary, off Parliament Sq., SW1 (phone: 171-222-5152). Underground: *Westminster.*

HOUSES OF PARLIAMENT The imposing neo-Gothic, mid-19th-century buildings of the *Palace of Westminster,* as it is sometimes called, look especially splendid from across the river. There are separate chambers for the *House of Commons* and the *House of Lords,* and visitors are admitted to the *Strangers' Galleries* of both houses by lining up at St. Stephen's Entrance, opposite *Westminster Abbey. Big Ben,* the world-famous 13½-ton bell in the clock tower of the palace, which is illuminated when Parliament is in session, still strikes the hours. Although the buildings are otherwise closed to the public, there are limited tours outside session hours on Friday afternoons. To make tour arrangements, write in advance to *The Public Information Office* (1 Derby Gate, London SW1A 1DG, England). Particularly impressive are *Westminster Hall,* with its magnificent hammer-beam roof, and the gold-and-scarlet *House of Lords.* No admission charge. Parliament Sq., SW1 (phone: 171-219-4272). Underground: *Westminster.*

TATE GALLERY Built in 1897 on the site of Millbank Prison, the gift of the sugar broker and art collector Sir Henry Tate, this national collection of British painting and 20th-century artwork was established less than half a century after the *National Gallery,* when bequests had swelled the size of the latter's collection to an extent that there was no longer room for all the paintings—including 282 oils and 19,000 watercolors by Turner. Tate bequeathed his own collection plus £80,000 to house it, art dealer Sir Joseph Duveen gave additional funds, and the museum was on its way. The works are arranged in chronological order. The magnificent *Clore Gallery*—designed by James Stirling and set in a newer wing—houses the *Turner Collection.* The group of sculptures offers excellent examples of the artistry of Rodin, Maillol, Mestrovic, Moore, and Epstein. The *British Collection* contains the world's most representative collection of works by Blake, as well as works by Hogarth, George Stubbs, John Constable, and the Pre-Raphaelites. The *Modern Collection* includes works of conceptual, minimal, optical, kinetic, British figurative, pop, and abstract art; it incorporates the most extensive survey of British art of its period in any public collection, including selected examples of very recent art. Rothko, Nevelson, Bacon, Ernst, and Picasso are represented. Rex Whistler, the noted trompe l'oeil painter, is responsible for the decor of the gallery's very good restaurant (see *Eating Out*). Mondays through Saturdays, there are free, hour-long guided tours of several of the collections: "The British Collection before 1900," "Early Modern Art," "Later Modern Art," and "Turner." A tour given once on Sundays highlights all the collections. Open daily. No admission charge, except for special exhibitions. Millbank, SW1 (phone: 171-887-8000; 171-887-8008 for recorded information). Underground: *Millbank.*

SOHO This area of London is full of character: lively, bustling, and noisy by day; indiscreetly enticing by night. Its name comes from the ancient hunting cry used centuries ago when the area was parkland. Once infamous for striptease clubs and tawdry sex, Soho has again become one of London's liveliest bohemian areas. It is home to publishing houses, art galleries, and production studios where commercials are filmed. Young people looking for the new and trendy are drawn here to its smart cafés, brasseries, and other eateries. Soho offers diverse entertainment. Shaftesbury Avenue is lined with theaters and movie houses. Gerrard Street abounds with Chinese restaurants (the *Dumpling Inn* remains one of our favorites—see *Eating Out*), and it is the place to go for *Chinese New Year* celebrations. Frith Street is a favorite Italian haunt, the best place for cappuccino and a view of Italian TV at the *Bar Italia.* Old Compton Street has several good delicatessens, as well as cafés and brasseries. Underground: *Leicester Square.*

COVENT GARDEN Tucked away behind The Strand, *Covent Garden* was the site of London's main fruit, vegetable, and flower market for over 300 years. The area was immortalized in Shaw's *Pygmalion* and the musical *My Fair Lady* by the scene in which young Eliza Doolittle sells flowers to the ladies and gents emerging from the *Royal Opera House.* The *Opera House* is still here, but the market moved south of the river in 1974, and the *Garden* has since undergone extensive redevelopment. The central market building has been converted into a Victorian-style shopping center with about 40 of the old *Covent Garden*'s original wrought-iron trading stands, from which the home-produced wares of English craftspeople are sold. In the former flower market is the *London Transport Museum,* whose exhibits include a replica of the first horse-drawn bus and a steam locomotive built in 1866 (phone: 171-379-6344; open daily; admission charge). Boutiques selling quality clothes for men and women have sprung up all over (especially on Neal, Shelton, and Earlham Sts.), along with crafts shops and brasserie-style restaurants. Underground: *Covent Garden.*

BLOOMSBURY Known for its squares—Bloomsbury Square, Bedford Square, Russell Square, and others—this area has long been home to intellectuals. Within its confines are the *British Museum* and the *University of London.* The Bloomsbury group of writers and artists included Virginia Woolf and her husband, Leonard Woolf; her sister Vanessa Bell and her husband, Clive Bell; Lytton Strachey; E. M. Forster; Roger Fry; and John Maynard Keynes. Living nearby and peripheral to this central group were D. H. Lawrence, Bertrand Russell, and others. Unfortunately, only a few of the original buildings have survived, although nearby Bedford Square remains complete. Virginia Woolf lived at 46 Gordon Square before her marriage. Underground: *Russell Square.*

BRITISH MUSEUM Founded in 1753 around the lifetime accumulations of Sir Hans Sloane, a British physician and naturalist, this is Britain's largest and most celebrated institution, consecrated to the whole of human history. Trying to cover it all in a single visit is like trying to master nuclear physics while having a haircut. The crown jewels of the collection are the renowned *Elgin Marbles,* massive sculpture and reliefs from the Parthenon that Lord Elgin brought, in the early 19th century, from the Turkish sultan and carted off to civilized England, where they were purchased by the government for £35,000 and presented to the museum. Other treasures include the *Rosetta Stone,* the black basalt tablet that provided the key to Egyptian hieroglyphs; the deep blue and white cameo-cut *Portland Vase,* a marvel of the glass-maker's art dating from Roman times; the *Tomb of Mausolus* from Halicarnassus, which brought the word "mausoleum" into the English language; the *Temple of Diana* from Ephesus; and many mummies, among them the one that is widely (and erroneously) believed to have occasioned the legends of the curse of the mummy's tomb.

Seven sculpture galleries exhibit some 1,500 Greek and Roman treasures, including two of the seven wonders of the ancient world and representing the bulk of the museum's Greek and Roman collection. The *Departments of Western Asiatic Antiquities and Oriental Antiquities* are magnificent. The *British Library* displays the *Magna Carta* in its manuscript room and a Gutenberg Bible in its *King's Library.* (The library is in the process of moving to new quarters on Euston Road near *St. Pancras Station.*)

The *British Library Reading Room,* where Karl Marx did research for *Das Kapital,* is accessible only to those who come well recommended (preferably by a scholar of some note) and who apply in advance for a ticket. But visitors, accompanied by a warder, may view the *Reading Room* briefly on weekdays at 2:15 and 4:15 PM. Guidebooks to various parts of the collections, for sale in the main lobby, are good investments, as are the one-and-a-half-hour guided tours (offered several times daily). Open daily. Admission charge for tours. Great Russell St., WC1 (phone: 171-636-1555; 171-636-1544 for the *British Library;* 171-323-7766 for information about the library's move). Underground: *Holborn* or *Tottenham Court Road.*

OXFORD, REGENT, BOND, AND KENSINGTON HIGH STREETS London's main shopping streets include large department and specialty stores (*Selfridges, Debenhams, John Lewis, Liberty, D. H. Evans*), chain stores offering good value in clothes (*Marks & Spencer, C & A, British Home Stores*), and scores of popular clothing chains (*The Gap, Laura Ashley, Benetton, Principles*).

BURLINGTON ARCADE A charming covered shopping promenade dating from the Regency period (early 19th century), it contains elegant, expensive shops selling cashmere sweaters, antique jewelry, and other very expensive items. (The gates are down and the arcade is closed off on Sundays.) One entrance is on Piccadilly (the street, not the circus); the other is near Old Bond St., W1. Underground: *Green Park.*

HYDE PARK London's most famous patch of greenery (361 acres) is particularly well known for its Speakers' Corner at *Marble Arch,* where crowds gather each Sunday morning to hear impromptu diatribes and debates. Among the other attractions are sculptures by Henry Moore; an extensive bridle path; a cycle path; Serpentine Lake, where boats can be rented and where there's swimming in the summer; a bird sanctuary; and vast expanses of lawn. Underground: *Hyde Park Corner* or *Marble Arch.*

MADAME TUSSAUD'S The popularity of this wax museum is undiminished by the persistent criticism that its effigies are a little bland; visitors are quite likely to find themselves innocently addressing a waxwork attendant—or murderer. Madame moved to London from Paris in 1802, crossing the Channel with her waxwork portrayals of heads that had rolled during the French Revolution. The museum includes many modern and historical personalities and the gory *Chamber of Horrors,* with its murderers and hangmen. Another fun attraction takes visitors on a "cab ride" through the 400 years of London's history between the reigns of Elizabeth I and the current queen, with sights, sounds, and smells. Open daily. Admission charge. Marylebone Rd., NW1 (phone: 171-935-6861). Underground: *Baker Street.*

LONDON PLANETARIUM During 30-minute shows, visitors travel through space and time under a huge starlit dome. Interesting commentary accompanies the display. As you wait to get into the star shows, you can enjoy the Space Trail, which is a series of video screens showing how the earth is seen from satellites in space. Open daily; call ahead for show times. Admission charge, but guests can save money by purchasing a combination ticket to the planetarium and *Madame Tussaud's*—both at the same address. Note: As at *Madame Tussaud's,* the lines to get into the planetarium can be long. Marylebone Rd., NW1 (phone: 171-486-1121). Underground: *Baker Street.*

THE CITY

The difference between London and the City of London can be confusing to a visitor. They are, in fact, two distinctly different entities, one within the other. The City of London, usually called only the City, covers the original Roman London. It is now the "square mile" financial and commercial center of the great metropolis. With a Lord Mayor (who serves only in a ceremonial capacity), a police force, and many banks, insurance companies, and other office buildings, it is the core of Greater London.

ST. PAUL'S CATHEDRAL The cathedral church of the London Anglican diocese stands atop Ludgate Hill and is the largest church in London. This Renaissance masterpiece by Sir Christopher Wren took 35 years to build (1675–1710). Its domed exterior is majestic, and its sparse decorations are in gold and mosaic. The interior contains particularly splendid choir stalls, screens, and inside the dome, the *Whispering Gallery,* with its strange acoustics. Nelson and Wellington are buried in a crypt beneath the main floor, and there is a fine statue of John Donne, metaphysical poet and dean of *St. Paul's* from 1621 to 1631. Wren himself was buried here in 1723, with his epitaph inscribed beneath the dome in Latin: *"Si monumentum requiris, circumspice"* ("If you seek his monument, look around you").

A gorgeous monument it remains; though damaged by bombs during World War II, it became a rallying point for the flagging spirits of wartime Londoners. More recently, *St. Paul's* was the site for the 1981 wedding of Prince Charles and Lady Diana Spencer. Guided tours are available. The cathedral, the galleries, and the crypt are closed Sundays. Separate admission charges. *St. Paul's Churchyard,* EC4 (phone: 171-248-2705). Underground: *St. Paul's* or *Mansion House.*

OLD BAILEY This is the colloquial name for London's *Central Criminal Court,* on the site of the notorious Newgate prison. Visitors are admitted to the court, on a space-available basis, to watch the proceedings and to see barristers and judges clad in wigs and robes. No children under 14 admitted. Closed weekends. No admission charge. Old Bailey, EC4 (phone: 171-248-3277). Underground: *St. Paul's.*

MUSEUM OF LONDON A fine introduction to London's history. Exhibits include Roman remains, Anglo-Saxon artifacts, Renaissance musical instruments, a cell from old Newgate prison, Victorian shops and offices, an audiovisual re-creation of the Great Fire of 1666, and the Lord Mayor's Golden Coach. Closed Mondays. Admission charge. 150 London Wall, EC2 (phone: 171-600-3699). Underground: *Barbican* or *St. Paul's.*

BARBICAN CENTRE The modern *Barbican Centre* complex includes 6,000 apartments, the *Guildhall School of Music and Drama,* and the restored *St. Giles' Church* (built in 1390). The center also features the 2,026-seat *Barbican Hall,* doubling as conference venue (with simultaneous translation system) and concert hall *(London Symphony Orchestra);* the 1,166-seat *Barbican*

Theatre and a 200-seat studio theater (the *Royal Shakespeare Company*'s London performance venues); a sculpture courtyard; art exhibition galleries; three cinemas; two exhibition halls; restaurants; and bars. Silk St., EC2 (phone: 171-628-4141, ext. 7537 or 7538 for general information; 171-628-2295 for recorded information; 171-638-4141 for guided tours; 171-638-8891 for the box office). Underground: *Barbican, St. Paul's,* or *Moorgate.*

BANK OF ENGLAND Banker to the British government, holder of the country's gold reserves, controller of Britain's monetary affairs, the "Old Lady of Threadneedle Street" is the world's most famous bank. Its clerks and messengers wear traditional livery. The bank is not open to the public, but the *Bank of England Museum* here can be visited. It is closed Saturdays year-round and Sundays October through *Easter.* No admission charge. Threadneedle St., EC2; museum entrance on Bartholomew La. (phone: 171-601-5792). Underground: *Bank.*

MANSION HOUSE Built in the 18th century in Renaissance style, the official residence of the Lord Mayor of London contains his private apartments. It is difficult to gain admission, but you may request permission by writing, well in advance of your visit, to the *Principal Assistant Office* (*Mansion House,* London EC4N 8EH, England). Mansion House St., EC4 (phone: 171-626-2500). Underground: *Mansion House* or *Bank.*

THE MONUMENT This fluted Doric column, topped by a flaming urn, was designed by Sir Christopher Wren to commemorate the Great Fire of London (1666) and stands 202 feet tall. (Its height was determined because it was allegedly 202 feet from the bakery on Pudding Lane where the fire began.) The view from the top is worth the 311-step climb up a narrow staircase—there is *no* elevator. Closed Sundays October through March. Admission charge. Monument St., EC3 (phone: 171-626-2717). Underground: *Monument.*

TOWER OF LONDON Originally William the Conqueror's fortress to keep "fierce" Londoners at bay and to guard the river approaches, this complex of buildings has served as a palace, a prison, a mint, and an observatory. Today, the main points of interest are the *Crown Jewels,* which recently have been moved to the *Jewel House* (in the Waterloo Block), allowing as many as 20,000 visitors daily to view the dazzling gems, as well as displays about the British monarchy and the coronation ceremony; the *White Tower* (the oldest building), with its exhibition of ancient arms, armor, and torture implements; *St. John's Chapel,* the oldest church in London; the *Bloody Tower,* where the two little princes disappeared in 1483 and Sir Walter Raleigh languished from 1603 to 1616; an exhibit of old military weapons; *Tower Green,* where two of Henry VIII's queens, Anne Boleyn and Catherine Howard, as well as Lady Jane Grey, were beheaded; and *Traitors' Gate,* through which boats bearing prisoners entered the castle. During World War I, German spies were executed in the courtyards, and in 1941, Rudolf Hess, Hitler's deputy, was imprisoned here for a few days. The yeoman warders ("Beefeaters"), who live within the *Tower* with their families, still wear historic uniforms. They also give informative, often theatrical recitals of that segment of English history that was played out within the *Tower*'s walls. You can see the wonderful *Ceremony of the Keys* here every night at 9:30 PM; reserve tickets several months ahead. (Send a self-addressed envelope to Resident Governor, *Queen's House, HM Tower of London* EC3N 4AB, England, and enclose the appropriate international postage coupons.) Open daily. Admission charge (phone: 171-709-0765 for general inquiries; 171-488-5718 for recorded information). Underground: *Tower Hill.*

FLEET STREET Most native and foreign newspapers and press associations once had offices here, but none remain because of the exodus to more technologically advanced plants elsewhere. The street also boasts two 17th-century pubs, *Ye Olde Cheshire Cheese* (No. 145), where Dr. Samuel Johnson held court; and the *Cock Tavern* (No. 22).

JOHNSON'S HOUSE In Gough Square is the house where Dr. Johnson wrote his famous *Dictionary;* the house is now a museum of Johnsoniana, including the high desk behind which he stood as he wrote. Closed Sundays. Admission charge. 17 Gough Sq., EC4 (phone: 171-353-3745). Underground: *Blackfriars.*

INNS OF COURT Quaint and quiet precincts house the ancient buildings, grounds, and gardens that mark the traditional center of Britain's legal profession. Only the four *Inns of Court—Gray's, Lincoln's,* and the *Inner* and *Middle Temples*—have the right to call would-be barristers to the bar to practice law. Especially charming is the still-Dickensian *Lincoln's Inn,* where young Dickens worked as an office boy. It was in its great hall that the writer later set parts of his law case of Jarndyce vs. Jarndyce in *Bleak House.* John Donne once preached in the *Lincoln's Inn* chapel, designed by Inigo Jones. The chapel can be seen on weekdays between 12:30 and 2:30 PM; ask at the *Gatehouse* (Chancery La., WC2; phone: 171-405-1393). Also lovely are the gardens of *Lincoln's Inn Fields,* laid out by Inigo Jones in 1618. The neo-Gothic *Royal Courts of Justice* in The Strand, better known as the *Law Courts,* house the *High Court* and the *Court of Appeal of England and Wales,* which pass judgment on Britain's most important civil cases. Sessions are from 10:30 AM to 1 PM and 2 to 4 PM. No admission charge. Underground: *Holborn, Chancery Lane,* or *Temple.*

OTHER LONDON ATTRACTIONS

REGENT'S PARK The sprawling 472 acres just north of the city center include beautiful gardens, vast lawns, a pond with paddleboats, and one of the finest zoos in the world. Until last year, the zoo was in danger of closing because of a lack of funds, but it was rescued by a £21-million donation from a London doctor as a memorial to his daughter, who died as a young girl 25 years ago. Among several new additions is a children's zoo which depicts how people and animals have lived together throughout history. Open daily.

Admission charge to the zoo (phone: 171-722-3333). Underground: *Camden Town.*

CAMDEN PASSAGE This quaint pedestrian alleyway, lined with antiques and specialty shops, has an open-air market—pushcarts selling curios and antiques—on Wednesdays, Thursdays (books), and Saturdays. Just off Upper St. in Islington, north of the city, N1. Underground: *Angel.*

KENWOOD, THE IVEAGH BEQUEST The collection assembled here includes works by Cuyp, Gainsborough, Hals, Rembrandt, Reynolds, Romney, Turner, and Vermeer. What makes this institution particularly interesting is its setting, a late-17th-century house on *Hampstead Heath* remodeled beginning in 1764 by the Scottish architect Robert Adam. The stately neoclassical villa was rescued from demolition in 1925 by the first Earl of Iveagh, who then presented the house and the better part of his collection to the nation. It has the atmosphere of an 18th-century country house, and in summer frequently offers chamber recitals, poetry readings, and open-air concerts. Closed *Christmas Eve* and *Christmas.* No admission charge. Hampstead La., NW3 (phone: 181-348-1286). Underground: *Highgate, Golders Green,* or *Archway* (note, however, that the underground stops are a long walk away).

KEW GARDENS Here are the *Royal Botanic Gardens,* with tens of thousands of trees and other plants. Located by the Thames, the gardens are intended primarily to serve the botanical sciences by researching, cultivating, identifying, and experimenting with plants. There are shaded walks, floral displays, and magnificent Victorian greenhouses—especially the *Temperate House,* with some 3,000 different plants, including a 60-foot Chilean wine palm. Open daily. Admission charge (phone: 181-940-1171). Underground: *Kew Gardens.*

PORTOBELLO ROAD This area is well known for its antiques shops, junk shops, and outdoor stalls; it is one of the largest street markets in the world. The stalls are open only on Saturdays. Underground: *Notting Hill Gate.*

VICTORIA AND ALBERT MUSEUM An offspring of the *Great Exhibition* of 1851, this museum was originally a repository of the world's finest craftsmanship. The collection, dating from ancient times, was intended to lend inspiration to leatherworkers and ceramists, furniture makers and woodcarvers, architects and dressmakers, silversmiths and goldsmiths, and other artisans working in the applied arts in the 19th century. Though the original function has not been abandoned, the collections are a bit broader in scope: In addition to textiles and furniture there are also watercolors and paintings—including Constable's *Salisbury Cathedral from the Bishop's Grounds;* the collections of British art (including the *Constable Collection,* presented to the museum by the artist's daughter) stand out for their scope and comprehensiveness. Of particular interest are the Raphael cartoons (designs for tapestries for the Sistine Chapel); the period rooms; the world's oldest known teapot; and the intricately carved, abundantly graffiti-covered *Great Bed of Ware,* which Shakespeare's Sir Toby Belch mentioned in *Twelfth Night* and which (measuring about 11 feet square) was purportedly big enough to sleep a dozen couples. Other galleries include the *Medieval Treasury* (note the intricately embroidered bishop's cope); the *T. Tsui Gallery of Chinese Art* (you may touch the serpentine head); the *Nehru Gallery of Indian Art* (the finest collection outside the subcontinent); and the *Toshiba Gallery of Japanese Art.* Guided tours are given Mondays through Saturdays. This museum has something to interest everyone. Don't forget to admire the statues outside. There's also a restaurant and two fine museum shops. Open daily. Donation suggested. Cromwell Rd., SW7 (phone: 171-938-8441; 171-938-8349 for information on current exhibits). Underground: *South Kensington.*

IMPERIAL WAR MUSEUM Tanks, planes, cannons, submarines, rockets, artifacts, and war paintings are housed in this four-floor museum, which covers the history of war from Flanders to the Falklands to the Gulf War. Wartime events are brought to life via films, videos, and telephones that visitors can pick up to hear people describing their wartime experiences. The 20-minute-long "Blitz Experience" confines groups of 20 people in a damp, cramped re-creation of a bomb shelter during a World War II air raid, while "Operation Jericho" is a bumpy simulation of a World War II bombing raid; also see the World War I "Trench Experience." A souvenir shop and a café are also on the premises. Open daily. No admission charge on Fridays. Lambeth Rd., SE1 (phone: 171-416-5000; 171-820-1683 for recorded information). Underground: *Lambeth North, Elephant,* or *Castle.*

DOCKLANDS This area has been developed to such an extent that it even includes its own railroad; modern apartment, commercial, and office buildings stretch seemingly without end. The *Docklands Light Railway (DLR),* an overhead train, runs from the *Bank* tube station to *Island Garden,* Greenwich, speeding over the fast-developing and fascinating terrain. The Docklands also is home to the *Design Museum* (Butler's Wharf, 28 Shad Thames, SE1; phone: 171-403-6933; 171-407-6261 for recorded information). Open daily. Admission charge. Fascinating walking tours of the Rotherhithe district, where the *Mayflower* returned from its journey in 1621, are offered by local historian Jim Nash; for details, contact *Karisma Travel* (21 Hayes Wood Ave., Hayes, Bromley, Kent BR2 7BG, England; phone: 181-462-4953; call a week in advance). The new, 800-foot *Canada Tower* at *Canary Wharf,* containing the offices of the *Daily Mirror* and the *Daily Telegraph* as well as many other businesses, is the tallest building in England (it is closed to the public). The *London Docklands Visitor Centre* (3 Limeharbour, E14; phone: 171-512-1111), near the *Crossharbour* stop on the *DLR,* has a model of the area and other useful information; it is open daily. Further development plans for the Docklands, including the addition of several shopping plazas and other businesses, extend to 1998.

GREENWICH This Thameside borough is traditionally associated with British sea power, especially when Britain "ruled the waves." Here, along Romney Road, is the *Royal Naval College* (phone: 181-858-2154); its beautiful painted hall and chapel are closed Thursday afternoons, when the college is in session. No admission charge. Also here are the *National Maritime Museum,* the *Queen's House,* the *Old Royal Observatory,* and the *Cutty Sark* clipper ship (see the *National Maritime Museum* entry below for details on all four). In addition, there's the *Fan Museum* (10-12 Crooms Hill, SE10; phone: 181-858-7879), a collection of 12,000 unusual and beautiful antique fans from all over the world. Closed Mondays. Admission charge. *Greenwich Park* is 200 acres of greenery with splendid views from the hill across to the Docklands and the rest of London. Greenwich can be reached by tube (*Greenwich Station*), *British Rail,* or boat from *Charing Cross, Westminster,* or *Tower Piers.*

NATIONAL MARITIME MUSEUM This institution tells the story of Britain's long involvement with the sea. There are scores of pictures and silver, porcelain and uniforms, swords and medals, ship models and dioramas. Galleries in the West Wing explore "Discovery and Seapower" and the "Development of the Warship," and the world's largest ship in a bottle is on display in *Neptune Hall.* There, too, are the steam paddle tug *Reliant;* the *Donola,* a 60-foot steam launch; and the smaller *Waterlily.* Next door in the *Barge House,* Prince Frederick's barge glitters in golden livery. Another must-see: the uniform that Lord Nelson wore when he was shot at the Battle of Trafalgar in 1805, complete with bullet hole and bloodstains. Nearby are the *Queen's House,* a beautifully proportioned white structure designed in 1618 by Inigo Jones for James I's consort, Anne of Denmark; and the newly refurbished *Old Royal Observatory*—the home of the Greenwich Meridian—which is centered around Sir Christopher Wren's 1675 *Flamsteed House* and has exhibits that illustrate the history of nautical astronomy, time-keeping, and Greenwich mean time, as well as the largest refracting telescope in the United Kingdom; the *Cutty Sark,* a 19th-century ship that was once the fastest clipper in existence (Cutty Sark Gardens, SE10; phone: 181-858-3445); and the *Gipsy Moth IV,* the 53-foot ketch that, between 1966 and 1967, bore Sir Francis Chichester—solo—around the world. Open daily. There's a separate admission charge to each attraction, but a single "Passport" can be bought which includes entry to the museum, *Queen's House,* the *Old Royal Observatory,* and the *Cutty Sark.* Romney Rd., SE10, Greenwich (phone: 181-858-4422). Greenwich can be reached by tube (*Greenwich Station*), *British Rail,* or boat from *Charing Cross, Westminster,* or *Tower Piers.*

RICHMOND PARK The largest urban park in Britain is one of the few with herds of deer roaming free. (Hunting them is illegal, though this was once a royal hunting preserve established by Charles I.) It also has large oaks and rhododendron gardens. From nearby Richmond Hill there is a magnificent view of the Thames Valley. The park can be reached by tube (*Richmond Station*) or *British Rail*.

SPENCER HOUSE This 1756 mansion owned by the Spencer family—the Princess of Wales is the former Lady Diana Spencer—has been restored and opened to the public. There are nine spectacular state rooms filled with artwork and furniture from the family's wide collection. The neoclassical state rooms were among the first to be so designed in Europe. No children under 10 admitted. Open only for guided tours, which are given on Sundays; closed January and August. Admission charge. St. James's Pl., SW1 (phone: 171-499-8620). Underground: *Green Park*.

HAMPTON COURT PALACE Along the Thames, this sumptuous palace and adjoining gardens are in Greater London's southwest corner. Begun by Cardinal Wolsey in 1514, the palace was appropriated by Henry VIII. Its architecture—including Wolsey's constructions, the modifications made by Henry VIII, and additions designed by Christopher Wren for William III in 1689—represents the very best of England's designers of the 16th and 17th centuries. The equally fine gardens, designed for William and Mary by Henry Wise and George London, comprise a maze and vinery (the Great Vine was planted in 1769). Still a royal palace, its attractions include a picture gallery, tapestries, Tudor kitchens—restored to the grandeur of Henry VIII's day, re-creating the *Feast of St. John the Baptist* on a midsummer day in 1542—the original tennis court, and a moat. Henry VIII's *State Apartments* reopened recently after being restored to their original Tudor splendor. Among the rooms that can be visited are the *Great Hall,* the royal chapel, and a gallery that is reportedly haunted by Catherine Howard, the monarch's fifth wife. Tours led by guides in authentic costume are given twice daily. There are even two apartments for overnight stays (see *Checking In*). Open daily. Admission charge. East Molesey, Surrey (phone: 181-977-8441). The quickest way to get here is by *British Rail* (32 minutes from *Waterloo Station*), but you can take a bus or even a boat from *Westminster Pier* during the summer.

FREUD MUSEUM This was the London home of the seminal psychiatrist after he left Vienna in 1938. His antiquities collection, library, desk, and famous couch are all on display. Closed Mondays and Tuesdays. Admission charge. 20 Maresfield Gardens, NW3 (phone: 171-435-2002). Underground: *Finchley Road*.

HIGHGATE CEMETERY The impressive grave of Karl Marx in the eastern cemetery attracts countless visitors, although the Victorian-style western cemetery is older and more historically interesting. Open daily. Entrance to the western cemetery, with its overgrown gravestones and catacombs of the not-so-famous, is by guided tour only. Admission charge to the western cemetery. Highgate Hill, NW3 (phone: 181-340-1834 for times). Underground: *Archway*.

THAMES FLOOD BARRIER This massive defense structure is located across the river at Woolwich Reach near Greenwich. Boats regularly leave *Barrier Gardens Pier* (or the riverside promenade nearby) for visits up close. Visitors are not allowed on the barrier itself, but audiovisual displays at the visitors' center, on the river's south bank, explain its background and illustrate the risk to London of exceptionally high tides (the last major flood was in 1953). Open daily. Admission charge. 1 Unity Way, Woolwich (phone: 181-854-1373). Accessible from London by road, by river (from *Westminster Pier* to *Barrier Gardens Pier*), and by *British Rail* (to *Charlton Station*).

ENVIRONS

WINDSOR CASTLE The largest inhabited castle in the world, *Windsor Castle* is reputed to be the queen's favorite among her five principal residences. It was founded by William the Conqueror in 1066 after his victory at the Battle of Hastings. Among the royal sovereigns buried here are Queen Victoria and Albert, her beloved consort. Despite the ravages of a fire on November 20, 1992 (which, ironically, was also the queen's wedding anniversary), *Windsor*'s exterior still looks like a picturebook fairy-tale castle. The huge Norman edifice looms majestically above the town; visitors feel awed and enchanted as they climb up the curving cobblestone street from the train station, past pubs and shops, toward *Henry VIII's Gateway.* The castle precincts are open daily, and there's a regular changing of the guard. Thirteen of the 15 *State Apartments* were miraculously unharmed by the fire and can be toured daily (unless there is a state visit); they are splendidly decorated with paintings, tapestries, furniture, and rugs. Queen Mary's dollhouse is displayed in another room. In the *Waterloo Chamber,* visitors can look through glass doors into *St. George's Hall* and the *Grand Reception Room,* which were gutted by the fire. There's a small exhibit recounting the damage. Separate admission charges to the castle complex and to see the dollhouse. For information, call 1753-831118.

The castle is bordered by 4,800 acres of parkland on one side and the town on the other. The *Savill Gardens*—35 acres of flowering shrubs, rare flowers, and woodland—make for a lovely summer walk. Open daily. Admission charge (phone: 1784-435544). While the town still has a certain charm, heavy tourism is beginning to have a deleterious effect. Across the river is Eton—considered by some to be the more attractive town—which is the famous home of the exclusive boys' school founded by Henry VI in 1440.

To get here, take the train from *Paddington* which stops right in the center of Windsor (travel time is 39 minutes), or the *Green Line* coach from *Victoria* (one and a half hours).

EXTRA SPECIAL

There is nothing quite like Oxford or Stratford-upon-Avon, Shakespeare's birthplace—both of which can be seen in a day-long organized bus tour

from London. Or you can choose one; the regular bus from *Victoria Coach Station* to Stratford (90 miles) travels via Oxford (65 miles), so you can catch a fleeting glimpse of the university's ancient colleges if you try hard (for information, call *National Express Coach;* phone: 171-730-0202) or take the *Shakespeare Connection* train and bus from March through September (via Coventry; phone: 171-387-7070). Visitors lodging in London who would like to see a performance of the *Royal Shakespeare Company* in Stratford should purchase tickets as far in advance as possible; contact either the US or London office of *Edwards & Edwards* (see *Theater*). Another highly recommended excursion is to Cambridge, England's other great university city; the trip takes only an hour from London by train. For details on sights and accommodations in Oxford, Stratford-upon-Avon, and Cambridge, consult the individual reports in THE CITIES.

Sources and Resources

TOURIST INFORMATION

The *London Tourist Board and Convention Bureau,* with an office in the forecourt of *Victoria Station,* is a good source of information for attractions and events. Other branches are at the tube station at *Heathrow Airport*'s Terminals 1, 2, and 3 and at *Selfridges* department store (see *Shopping*). Many brochures about the city's landmarks and events are available. Staff is also on hand to answer questions; however, the offices do not handle telephone inquiries. All three centers are open daily. Accommodations and tours can be reserved by telephone using credit cards Mondays through Saturdays (phone: 171-824-8844 for reservations only).

LOCAL COVERAGE Of London's several newspapers, the *Times,* the *Guardian,* the *Independent,* and the *Daily Telegraph* (all dailies) and the *Sunday Times* and the *Observer* (Sundays only) are the most useful for visitors. Also helpful are the weekly magazines *What's On* and *Time Out.* The *Evening Standard,* published weekdays, is the only "local" newspaper for London. For business news, read the *Financial Times* (daily) and the *Economist* magazine (weekly).

The *British Travel Centre* (4 Lower Regent St., W1; phone: 171-730-3400) books travel tickets, reserves accommodations and theater tickets, and sells guidebooks. It has numerous free leaflets with information about walking tours, London's lesser-known museums and attractions, and canal tours. It also offers a free information service covering all of Britain. Open daily.

There have been enough books published on London to fill several libraries. For those who want lots of historic detail, the *Blue Guide to London* (A&C Black; £12.99/about $19.50) is ideal. A less dry and stodgy choice is *The Time Out London Guide* (Penguin; £8.99/about $13.50). There are numerous books that focus on exploring London with a special theme in mind—*Walking London* (New Holland; £7.99/about $12) and *Guide to Literary London* (Batford; £11.99/about $18) are two favorites. For foodies, the annual *Good Food Guide 1995* (Hodder & Stoughton; £14.99/about $22.50) is a must; for theater lovers, *The London Theatre Scene* (Frank Cook; £4.95/about $7.50) is the ticket; and for those who want to take the whole of London home with them, *The London Encyclopedia* by Benjamin Weinreb (Papermac; £25/about $37.50) is a good choice. *Permanent Londoners: An Illustrated Guide to the Cemeteries of London* lists the locations of the graves, along with biographical notes, of some of the more famous Londoners buried in the city. The book is available for $16.95 (plus $3 for shipping and handling) from Chelsea Green Publishing Co. (PO Box 130, Post Mills, VT 05058-0130; phone: 802-333-9073). The *Traveller's Bookshop* (25 Cecil Court, WC2; phone: 171-836-9132) has guidebooks, secondhand books, and travel information. We also immodestly suggest that before you leave home, you pick up a copy of *Birnbaum's London 95* (HarperCollins; $12).

London A-Z (Geographers' A-Z Map Co.) and *Nicholson's Street Finder* (Robert Nicholson), pocket-size books of street maps (the cost varies depending on map size), are useful for finding London addresses; they can be purchased in bookstores and from most "newsagents." Also helpful are maps of the subway system and bus routes and the *London Regional Transport Visitors Guide*—all available free from the *London Transport* information centers at several stations, including *Victoria, Piccadilly, Charing Cross, Oxford Circus,* and *Heathrow Central,* and at the ticket booths of many other stations (phone: 171-222-1234 for information).

TELEPHONE London has two city codes: inner London, 171; outer London, 181. All telephone numbers listed in this chapter, therefore, include the appropriate city code.

GETTING AROUND

AIRPORT London has four airports. The two main airports are *Heathrow,* 15 miles and about 50 minutes from downtown, and *Gatwick,* 29 miles and about 1 hour from downtown. The others are *Stansted,* 30 miles northeast of the city, and *London "City" Airport,* 6 miles from downtown. Airport transportation options include taxis, the London underground (subway), trains, and car services.

BOAT For a leisurely view of London from the Thames, tour boats leave roughly every half hour from *Westminster Pier* (near the *Westminster* tube station) and from *Charing Cross Pier* (across from the *Embankment* tube station); they sail (*Easter* through September) upriver to *Kew Gardens* and *Hampton Court Palace* or downriver to the *Tower of London,* Greenwich, and the massive Thames flood barrier. You also can travel by boat to Marlow, Cookham, or Henley (where the first rowing regatta in the world was held in 1839). A journey along Regent's Canal through north London is offered (summers only) by *Jason's Trip* (opposite 60 Blomfield Rd., Little Venice, W9; phone: 171-286-3428). Also, *Bateaux London* (phone: 171-925-2215), a French-based company, runs lunch and dinner cruises on the Thames in wide riverboats similar to those used in Paris; food is included in the price. The evening trip features after-dinner dancing to live music, and the boat illuminates the buildings along the shoreline with floodlights. For further information about these and other boat trips, contact the *London Tourist Board*'s *River Boat Information Service* (phone: 839-123432; costs between 36p/about 55¢ and 48p/about 75¢ per minute).

BUS AND UNDERGROUND The subway, called the underground or tube, and bus lines cover the city pretty well—though buses suffer from traffic congestion, and the underground is lacking south of the Thames (however, aboveground trains partially compensate for this shortcoming). Avoid the hideous rush-hour traffic from 8:30 to 9:30 AM and from 5 to 6 PM. The tops of London's famous red double-decker buses offer delightful views of the city and its people. The underground is easy to understand and to use, with clear directions and poster maps in all stations. Pick up free bus and underground maps from tourist offices or underground ticket booths.

The fares on both trains and buses are set according to length of the journey. On some buses, conductors take payment after you tell them where you're going; others require that you pay as you enter. Underground tickets are bought on entering a station. Retain your ticket; you'll have to surrender it when you get off (or have to pay again), and bus inspectors make spot checks to see that no one's stealing a ride. There are also *Red Arrow* express buses, which link the main-line *British Rail* stations, but you'll have to check stops before you get on. With a few exceptions, public transport comes to a halt around midnight; it varies according to underground line and bus route. If you're going to be traveling late, check available facilities. For 24-hour travel information, call 171-222-1234.

A London Visitor Travelcard is available for travelers to London; it must be purchased in the US from travel agents, at the *British Travel Bookshop* (551 Fifth Ave., Eighth Floor, New York, NY 10016; phone: 212-490-6688 or 800-448-3039), or at the *BritRail Travel International* offices in New York (1500 Broadway, New York, NY 10036; phone: 212-575-2667). The card provides unlimited travel on virtually all of London's bus and underground networks and costs $25 for three days, $32 for four days, and $49 for seven days (lower fares for children under 15). Also included is transportation to and from *Heathrow Airport* on the underground's *Piccadilly* line, a ride on the *Docklands Light Railway,* and a book of discount vouchers for many of the city's sights. In London, daily (costing £2.70/about $4) and weekly (£10.20/about $15.30) passes are available from newsagents, underground ticket offices, and *London Transport* offices for travel on buses and the underground in the central London area after 9:30 AM weekdays and all day on weekends; for the weekly card, a passport-size photo must be provided.

One of the least expensive and most comprehensive ways to tour the city is to take the *Original London Transport Sightseeing Tour* (phone: 171-918-3456), a one-and-a-half-hour unconducted bus tour, which leaves every hour from four sites: *Marble Arch,* Piccadilly Circus, *Baker Street* tube station, and *Victoria Station.* Other guided bus tours are offered by *Frames Rickards* (phone: 171-637-4171), *Harrods* (phone: 171-581-3603), and *Evan Evans* (phone: 181-332-2222).

CAR RENTAL The major international rental agencies have desks at the city's airports as well as at numerous locations in town.

SIGHTSEEING BY PLANE See London from the air. Sightseeing tours by small airplane are available (by advance reservation only) from *Flights Over London, Biggin Hill Aerodrome,* Kent (phone: 959-540079).

TAXI Those fine old London cabs are gradually being supplemented with more "practical" models, many of which have dashboard computers that allow communication between driver and dispatcher. Whether you end up in a computerized or "regular" cab, taxi fares in London are increasingly expensive (and you can find yourself stuck in horrendous traffic jams, with the meter ticking away); there is a surcharge for luggage, and a 15% tip is customary. Be aware that taxi rates are higher after 8 PM (and sometimes even higher after midnight) and on weekends and holidays.

Tell the driver where you're going *before* entering the cab. When it rains or is late at night, an empty cab (identifiable by the glow of the roof light) is often difficult to find, so it is wise to carry the telephone number of one or more of the "minicab" companies that respond to calls by phone. These taxis (which look like regular cars) operate on a fixed-fare basis, which varies from company to company. Hotel porters or reception desks usually can arrange to have such a cab pick you up at a specified time and place.

Several firms and taxi drivers offer guided tours of London; details are available at information centers. You can arrange for the personal services of a member of London's specially trained "Blue Badge Guides" by contacting *GALS* (phone: 171-370-5063) or *Town Guides* (phone: 171-495-5504).

TRAIN London has 11 principal train stations, each the starting point for trains to a particular region, with occasional overlapping of routes. The stations you are most likely to encounter include *King's Cross* (phone: 171-278-2477), the departure point for eastern and northeast England and eastern Scotland, including Edinburgh; *Euston* (phone: 171-387-7070), serving the Midlands and north Wales, with connections to Northern Ireland and the Republic, northwest England, and western Scotland, including Glasgow; *Paddington* (phone: 171-262-6767), for the West Country and south Wales, including Fishguard and ferries to Rosslare, Ireland; *Victoria* (phone: 171-928-5100), for *Gatwick Airport* and, along with *Charing Cross Station* (phone: 171-928-

5100), for departures to southeast England; and *Liverpool St. Station* (phone: 171-928-5100), for departures to East Anglia and to Harwich for ferries to the Continent, including Scandinavia. All of these stations are connected via London's underground.

BritRail's London Extra transportation program is intended for travelers who wish to venture out of London. It includes the London Visitor Travelcard (see *Bus and Underground,* above) and a special rail pass for unlimited train travel within southern England. Passes are available for three days (about $85), four days ($105), and seven days ($155); there are lower fares for children. Maps and suggested itineraries are also included. *BritRail* London Extra packages must be obtained before leaving the US, from a travel agent or *BritRail* (see *Bus and Underground,* above).

For a special (and pricey) treat, take a day trip on the luxurious British Pullman cars of the *Venice Simplon–Orient Express.* You can see the spas, castles, and more in southwest England on trips (including brunch and dinner) to Bath, Bristol, and Salisbury. Or take a trip that winds through the beautiful Kent countryside while you enjoy a sumptuous, five-course luncheon. For additional information contact *Abercrombie & Kent* (1520 Kensington Rd., Oak Brook, IL 60521; phone: 800-524-2420; 171-928-6000 in London).

WALKING TOURS A trained guide can show you Shakespeare's London or that of Dickens or Jack the Ripper, among other themes. These reasonably priced tours last up to two hours, generally in the afternoon or evening. *City Walks* offers several tours, including a Sherlock Holmes, Jack the Ripper, and Legal London (phone: 171-700-6931). *Citisights* (phone: 181-806-4325) tours start from many places, including the *Museum of London* (London Wall). *Streets of London* (phone: 181-346-9255) tours start from various underground stations. *Londoner Pub Walks* (phone: 181-883-2656) start from *Temple* underground station (*District* and *Circle* lines) on Fridays at 7:30 PM. *The Original London Walks* (phone: 171-624-3978) provides more than 50 tours a week on various subjects (including the *Beatles*). A tour of the Docklands' Rotherhithe district is offered by local historian Jim Nash (see *Special Places*). For informative books on London walking tours, see *Tourist Information.*

ESPECIALLY FOR KIDS

If you're traveling *en famille* and have the urge to be alone but don't want to deprive your offspring (all ages) of what London and its immediate countryside have to offer, *Take-a-Guide* may be the answer. They will provide a car with a driver-guide especially knowledgeable in the ways and wiles of young folk for half- or full-day tours. It's costly: in London, $212 for a half day; $350 for a full day; or in the countryside, $250 for a half day; $500 for a full day. Contact them in the US (phone: 800-825-4946; fax: 800-635-7177) or in London (phone: 181-960-0459; fax: 181-964-0990).

SPECIAL EVENTS

Music is just one inspiration for the variety of festivals that take place in London throughout the year, both in the city center and in the suburbs. Listed below are our personal choices.

FAVORITE FETES

City of London Festival Held for two and a half weeks in July within the Old City's square mile, London's own festival takes advantage of the area's many fine halls and churches—including the *Tower of London, Guildhall, Barbican Centre,* and *St. Paul's*—for concerts of serious music, featuring choirs, orchestras, chamber groups, and leading soloists of international repute. A popular program of jazz, dance, street theater, poetry, and a wide range of exhibitions runs concurrent with the festival. Contact: *City of London Festival Box Office, Bishopsgate Hall,* 230 Bishopsgate, EC2 (phone: 171-248-4260 or 171-377-0540).

Dance Umbrella This festival has been an important part of the international contemporary dance scene since it was founded in 1978, and it attracts participants from all over the world. For six weeks in the fall (the exact dates vary from year to year), festival events are held in theaters in London and around the country. Contact: *Dance Umbrella, Riverside Studios,* 20 Chancellor St., Hammersmith, W6 (phone: 181-741-4040).

Henry Wood Promenade Concerts Better known as "the *Proms,*" it has been so named because this festival offers a large number of "promenade" or standing places at very reasonable prices. The *Proms,* held at the *Royal Albert Hall* from mid-July to mid-September, attract crowds from all over the world. In addition, several million others listen to live broadcasts of the concerts on radio and television. Contact: *Royal Albert Hall,* Kensington Gore, SW7 (phone: 171-589-8212).

London Film Festival Every November the best of British and international movies from the latest international film festivals are presented, with lectures and discussions led by participating film directors after many of the screenings. The *National Film Theatre* on the South Bank is the principal location, but other London houses are used as well. Contact: *National Film Theatre,* South Bank, SE1 (phone: 171-928-3232).

Royal Tournament For nearly three weeks every July, Britain's armed forces stage a spectacular military pageant in the huge indoor *Earl's Court* arena. All sorts of skills are displayed, from musicians on horseback and acrobatic gymnasts to police dogs and cavalry chargers. Tanks and planes are often on exhibit, too. The queen and all the leading royals attend each year. Contact: *Royal Tournament, Earl's Court Exhibition Centre,* SW5 (phone: 171-373-8141).

Note that the exact dates for all events vary marginally from year to year and should be checked with the *London Tourist Board and Convention Bureau* (see *Tourist Information*). In late March/early April, there's the *Oxford* and *Cambridge* rowing "eights" race from Putney to Mortlake, an important competition for the two universities. In April, London hosts the annual *London Marathon,* the world's largest; last year, there were 36,500 participants. The world-famous *Chelsea Flower Show* takes place in late May. In early June, enjoy the annual *Trooping the Colour,* England's most elaborate display of pageantry—including a Horse Guards parade with military music and much pomp and circumstance—all in celebration of the queen's official birthday. You can see some of the parade without a ticket, but for the ceremony you must book before February 28 by writing to the Ticket Office (Headquarters, Household Division, Chelsea Barracks, London SW1 H8RF, England); you must include the appropriate international reply coupons—do not send money. The *Lufthansa Festival of Baroque Music* presents classical concerts at *St. James Church* in Piccadilly throughout June, and the *Greenwich Festival,* a two-week event in mid-June, features mime and dance performances, concerts, and poetry readings. Also in June is the *Spitalfields Festival,* a varied program of 15th- to 20th-century classical music held for three and a half weeks in the *Parish Church of Spitalfields* in the East End. Late June heralds the *Wimbledon Lawn Tennis Championship*—the world's most prestigious—complete with the Duke and Duchess of Kent presenting the prizes (for information, see *Tennis,* below).

The *Henley Royal Regatta,* in early July (at Henley-on-Thames, an hour's train ride from London), is an international rowing competition and one of the big social events of the year. Watch from the towpath (free) or from within the *Regatta* enclosure (admission charge). At the *Punch and Judy Festival,* held the first Sunday in October, the 160 members of the *Punch and Judy Fellowship* gather at *St. Paul's Cathedral* to celebrate the traditional puppet show. October or November is the time for the *State Opening of Parliament; Guy Fawkes Day* is on November 5, when fireworks and bonfires mark the anniversary of the plot to blow up both the *Houses of Parliament* and King James I in 1605. On the first Sunday in November, the *London-to-Brighton Veteran Car Run* features shiny antique autos undertaking a 57-mile drive. The second Saturday in November sees the *Lord Mayor's Procession,* in which the new lord mayor rides in a golden carriage, followed by bands and wacky, colorful floats. On *Remembrance Sunday,* the Sunday nearest to November 11 (*Armistice Day*), a moving and solemn parade of veterans passes before the queen after she lays red poppy wreaths at the base of the *Cenotaph,* on Whitehall.

STATE VISITS

If you aren't going to be in London for the queen's official birthday in June, you might want to see her greet a foreign dignitary in full regalia. The event is announced in the royal calendar in the *Times.* The queen meets her guest at *Victoria Station,* and they ride to *Buckingham Palace* in a procession of horse-drawn coaches, followed by the colorful Horse Guards. Meanwhile, at Hyde Park Corner, the cannoneers on horseback perform elaborate maneuvers before their salute thunders through the whole city.

MUSEUMS

In addition to those described in *Special Places,* other museums of note include the following:

BETHNAL GREEN MUSEUM OF CHILDHOOD It's an impressive collection of more than 4,000 items, including dolls and dollhouses, Victorian-era children's clothing, antique nursery toys, games, and puppets. Open daily. No admission charge. Cambridge Heath Rd., E2 (phone: 181-980-3204). Underground: *Bethnal Green.*

COURTAULD INSTITUTE GALLERIES A remarkable collection of French Impressionist and post-Impressionist paintings (artists include van Gogh, Gauguin, Cézanne, Manet, and Seurat), as well as 20th-century British art, is displayed in a lovely and comfortable setting for visitors. Open daily. Admission charge. *Somerset House,* The Strand, WC2 (phone: 171-873-2526). Underground: *Temple.*

DESIGN MUSEUM Examples of everyday items from today's consumer society are on display at this museum in the Docklands. Teakettles, tables and chairs, cars and bikes are all part of the permanent exhibit explaining the development of such items' design. There is also a library, auditorium, and riverside café. Open daily. Admission charge. *Butler's Wharf,* SE1 (phone: 171-403-6933). Underground: *London Bridge.*

DICKENS HOUSE MUSEUM The author's early works and personal memorabilia are displayed. Closed Sundays. Admission charge. 48 Doughty St., WC1 (phone: 171-405-2127). Underground: *Russell Square.*

DULWICH COLLEGE PICTURE GALLERY Works by European masters are exhibited in one of England's most beautiful art galleries. Among others, there are works by Rembrandt, Cuyp, Gainsborough, Rubens, Watteau, and Raphael. The college itself boasts such famous alumni as P. G. Wodehouse and Raymond Chandler. Guided tours are offered on weekends. Closed Mondays. Admission charge. College Rd., SE21 (phone: 181-693-5254; 181-693-8000 for recorded information). Accessible by British Rail (*West Dulwich Station*).

FLORENCE NIGHTINGALE MUSEUM Not for nurses only, this museum offers a fascinating look at the life of the "Lady with the Lamp." Closed Mondays. Admission charge. 2 Lambeth Palace Rd., SE1 (phone: 171-620-0374). Underground: *Westminster* or *Waterloo.*

GUARDS MUSEUM Close to *Buckingham Palace,* this small collection at Wellington Barracks houses exhibits of memorabilia relating to the Brigade of Guards, including uniforms and weapons—even a cat-o'-nine-tails. Closed Fridays. Admission charge. Birdcage Walk, SW1 (phone: 171-930-3271). Underground: *St. James's Park.*

HAYWARD GALLERY Temporary exhibitions of British and international art are shown in a modern building. Open daily. Admission charge. At the *South Bank Centre* on Belvedere Rd., SE1 (phone: 171-928-3144; 171-261-0127 for recorded information). Underground: *Waterloo.*

HORNIMAN MUSEUM In a striking Art Nouveau building, the exhibits illustrate the cultures, traditions, and changing living conditions of the peoples of the world, focusing on current environmental issues. There's also an excellent natural history collection, including an aquarium where endangered species of fish are bred, as well as a 16-acre park. Open daily. No admission charge. London Rd., Forest Hill, SW2 (phone: 181-699-2339). Accessible by *British Rail* (*Forest Hill Station*).

INSTITUTE OF CONTEMPORARY ARTS Exhibitions of the latest art, film, and theater are shown. Open daily. Admission charge. *Nash House,* Duke of York Steps, The Mall, SW1 (phone: 171-930-3647). Underground: *Charing Cross.*

JEWISH MUSEUM Art and antiques illustrate Jewish history. Closed Fridays and Saturdays. No admission charge. *Raymond Burton House,* 129 Albert St., NW1 (phone: 171-388-4525). Underground: *Camden Town.*

KENSINGTON PALACE William and Mary were the first royals to live in the present-day home of Princess Margaret and other members of the royal family. Open to the public are the *Court Dress Collection* on the ground floor, with dresses and uniforms worn by courtiers throughout the centuries; and the *State Apartments,* including the room where an 18-year-old Victoria learned that she was Britain's new monarch in 1837. Scenes from Victoria's life are depicted in tableaus with lifelike mannequins. Open daily. Admission charge. *Kensington Gardens,* W8 (phone: 171-937-9561). Underground: *High Street Kensington.*

LEIGHTON HOUSE Surrounded by a private, peaceful garden, this house was built in the 1860s by Lord Leighton, a painter and President of the *Royal Academy.* In addition to his own paintings, the walls are hung with works by Sir John Millais, Sir Edward Burne-Jones, and other Victorian artists; but don't miss the *Arab Hall,* replete with patterned tiles. Closed Sundays. No admission charge. 12 Holland Park Rd., W14 (phone: 171-602-3316). Underground: *High Street Kensington.*

LINLEY SAMBOURNE HOUSE This terraced house behind Kensington High Street looks the same as when the *Punch* cartoonist Edward Linley Sambourne lived here early this century. It is filled with Victorian pictures and knickknacks. Open Wednesdays and Sundays, March through September. Admission charge. 18 Stafford Ter., W8 (phone: 181-994-1019). Underground: *High Street Kensington.*

MUSEUM OF GARDEN HISTORY Set in tiny *St. Mary-at-Lambeth Church,* the museum houses a collection of antique gardening tools and horticultural exhibits. A 17th-century–style garden (out back) contains a tulip tree and trumpet honeysuckle. Captain Bligh—who lived down the road—is buried right in the garden's center! Closed Saturdays year-round and the second Sunday in December through the first Sunday in March. No admission charge. Lambeth Palace Rd., SE1 (phone: 171-261-1891). Underground: *Waterloo.*

MUSEUM OF MANKIND Ethnographic exhibitions from the *British Museum* are housed in this structure next to the *Burlington Arcade* in Piccadilly, including items such as bronzes from Nigeria, Maori jade ornaments, and a crystal skull probably made by the Aztec. There's also a popular café. Open daily. No admission charge. 6 Burlington Gardens, W1 (phone: 171-323-8043). Underground: *Green Park.*

MUSEUM OF THE MOVING IMAGE The museum has over 50 exhibits and over 1,000 clips from various old and recent films and TV shows. There's also plenty of movie memorabilia, including Charlie Chaplin's hat and cane and fine movies ignored by big distributors. You can take part in the exhibits, too; there's an abundance of hands-on opportunities (which kids particularly like). But arrive early, before it gets too crowded. Open daily. Admission charge. *South Bank Centre,* SE1 (phone: 171-928-3535). Underground: *Waterloo.*

NATIONAL POSTAL MUSEUM A philatelist's dream—the collection of stamps from all over the world runs into the millions and includes a complete sheet of Penny Blacks printed in 1840, examples of forgeries, as well as changing exhibits of stamps with ship, flower, and animal themes. Closed weekends. No admission charge. King Edward St., EC1 (phone: 171-239-5420). Underground: *St. Paul's.*

NATURAL HISTORY MUSEUM Featured here are high-tech, hands-on exhibits, as well as specimens in glass cases for natural historians of all ages. The huge dinosaur skeleton at the entrance is a favorite with children, who also love the *Creepy Crawlie Gallery* and the *Ecology Gallery.* The *Earth Galleries* feature a simulated earthquake, a collection of gemstones, and an explanation of the solar system. Open daily. Admission charge. Cromwell Rd., SW7 (phone: 171-589-6323). Underground: *South Kensington.*

POLLOCK'S TOY MUSEUM Upstairs there's a museum full of miniatures, dolls, dollhouses, and other toys; downstairs is a shop that offers similar items, including models of Victorian theaters, and teddy bears and reproductions of toys from Victorian and Edwardian times. Closed Sundays. No admission charge for children on Saturdays. 1 Scala St., W1 (phone: 171-636-3452). Underground: *Goodge Street.*

ROYAL AIR FORCE MUSEUM A full exhibition of military planes from the time of the Wright brothers to the present. There also is a special "Battle of Britain" display. Open daily. Admission charge. Grahame Park Way, NW9 (phone: 181-205-2266). Underground: *Colindale.*

SCIENCE MUSEUM Worth more than a single visit to see the seven floors of exhibits here. Get a free map to locate your favorites from among such exhibits as "The Exploration of Space," "Land Transport," "Children's Gallery," and "Photography." "Launch Pad," with problems requiring a hands-on solution, is number one with children. Open daily. Admission charge. Exhibition Rd., SW7 (phone: 171-589-3456). Underground: *South Kensington.*

SIR JOHN SOANE'S MUSEUM Its eclectic collection of arts and antiques, occupying two houses designed by the famous architect, includes Hogarth's series *The Rake's Progress,* Flemish woodcarvings, and the world's greatest collection of 17th- and 18th-century architectural drawings—works by Sir Christopher Wren, Robert Adam, George Dance, and Soane himself, among others. Closed Sundays and Mondays. No admission charge. 13 *Lincoln's Inn Fields,* WC2 (phone: 171-405-2107; 171-430-0175 for recorded information). Underground: *Holborn.*

THEATRE MUSEUM Britain's most comprehensive collection of theatrical material has been given its own home. Everything from circus to pop, grand opera to mime, straight theater to Punch and Judy and pantomime is here; exhibits include costumes, props, and playbills from great London productions. Closed Mondays. Admission charge. 1E Tavistock St., WC2 (phone: 171-836-7891). Underground: *Covent Garden.*

WALLACE COLLECTION Sir Richard Wallace's fine collection of European paintings, sculpture, porcelain, and armor is displayed in his former home. Painters whose works are represented include Fragonard, Gainsborough, Rembrandt, Rubens, Titian, Van Dyck, Velázquez, and Watteau. There are also exquisite pieces of French furniture from the 17th and 18th centuries, 18th-century French clocks, gold boxes, and Sèvres porcelain. Open daily. No admission charge. *Hertford House,* Manchester Sq., W1 (phone: 171-935-0687). Underground: *Bond Street.*

WELLINGTON MUSEUM Set in *Apsley House,* home of the first (and current) Duke of Wellington, this recently renovated museum contains many fine paintings, including portraits of the Iron Duke's fellow commanders from the victorious campaign against the French and a nude (!) statue of Napoleon Bonaparte. Closed Mondays. Admission charge. *Apsley House,* 149 Piccadilly, W1 (phone: 171-499-5676). Underground: *Hyde Park Corner.*

WHITECHAPEL ART GALLERY An East End haven for temporary exhibitions featuring the works of 20th-century artists. Closed Mondays. No admission charge. 80 Whitechapel High St., E7 (phone: 171-377-0107). Underground: *Aldgate East.*

SHOPPING

For general shopping hours, see GETTING READY TO GO. In addition, some stores in Chelsea and Knightsbridge stay open until about 8 PM on Wednesdays, and in the West End, evening hours are on Thursdays. Although London is traditionally one of the most expensive cities in the world, savvy shoppers still can find good buys. The current lure, however, is more for fine British workmanship and style than low prices.

Devoted bargain hunters recognize that the best time to buy British is during the semiannual sales that usually occur from *Boxing Day* (December 26) through the early part of the new year and again in early July. The *Christmas/New Year* sales offer by far the best bargains in the city (and attract crowds of shoppers in search of low-priced goods). Many stores remain open on *New Year's Day* to accommodate bargain hunters. The best-publicized single sale is held by *Harrods* for about three weeks beginning the first Wednesday in January; opening day is an event in itself. Also see *Quintessential Great Britain* in DIVERSIONS.

Though scattered about the city, the most appealing shops tend to center in the West End area, particularly along Old and New Bond Streets; Oxford, South Molton, Regent, and Jermyn Streets; St. Christopher's Place; and Piccadilly. Other good shopping areas are King's Road, Kensington High Street, and Kensington Church Street, along with Knightsbridge and *Covent Garden.*

Endowed with special character and verve, some streets invite shoppers to linger and browse. These areas may be brassy, quaint, or even supremely grand, but each offers a real spectacle made up partly of the stores, partly of fellow shoppers. Beauchamp Place (pronounced *Beech*-um), a short walk from *Harrods,* off the Brompton Road, is a boutiques-filled block known for designer clothes and jewelry, trendy shops and shoppers; nearby Walton Street is similarly packed with upscale specialty shops. The pedestrian streets are special fun. Carnaby and Rupert Streets are lively, having discarded much of their decades-old "tacky" image. Brick Lane is the London equivalent of New York City's Lower East Side—a strip of inexpensive ethnic stores, including great bagel shops, Indian restaurants, and a pets market on Sundays.

In addition to the Regency-style *Burlington Arcade,* crammed with shops filled with cashmeres, antiques, and other costly wares (see *Special Places*), the *Princes* and *Piccadilly Arcades* on the other side of Piccadilly are shorter but offer similar stores.

This is a city of markets; Portobello Road and Camden Passage are described in *Special Places.* Also worthy of note is *Camden Lock Market*

(Camden Town, NW1) on weekends for far-out clothes, leather items, antiques, and trinkets. The *Jubilee Market,* on the south side of *Covent Garden*'s square, is one of the largest indoor markets in the country. The stalls, barrows, and small shops sell mainly crafts, clothes, and gifts, while all around the perimeter are cafés, wine bars, and small restaurants. Or get up early on a Sunday morning and head for the East End to *Petticoat Lane* (Middlesex St., E1) for food, inexpensive clothes, crockery, and even the proverbial kitchen sink. *Columbia Road* (Shoreditch, E2) has been London's top flower market for over 50 years; open daily.

Be sure to take your passport when you shop, and always inquire about the Value Added Tax (VAT) refund application forms when your total purchases in a store are over £50 (about $75). The VAT is a surcharge payable at the sales counter, but foreign customers usually will be reimbursed for it at home (for more information see GETTING READY TO GO).

DEPARTMENT AND SPECIALTY STORES

Fortnum & Mason Boasts designer originals (of the rather dowdy variety), a soda fountain–cum–restaurant (plus a second eatery), and one of the most elegantly stocked grocery departments in the world (where the staff wears striped morning trousers and swallowtail coats). The clock outside is a famous London landmark. 181 Piccadilly, W1 (phone: 171-734-8040).

General Trading Company Good for one-stop shopping, it offers everything from a bridal registry (London's social set shops here) to a place to pick up a wooden crocodile or *Christmas* tree toothbrush. There is also a small café in the basement. 144 Sloane St., SW1 (phone: 171-730-0411).

Hamleys The world's largest toy store, with an extensive selection of games, dolls, model cars, teddy bears, and other playthings, it's a must-see even if you don't have kids. 188 Regent St., W1 (phone: 171-734-3161).

Harrods The ultimate department store, although it does tend to be quite expensive and you'll always be jammed elbow-to-elbow with fellow tourists. It has everything, even a bank, and what it doesn't stock it will get for you. The "Food Halls" particularly fascinate visitors. 87-135 Brompton Rd., Knightsbridge, SW1 (phone: 171-730-1234).

Harvey Nichols Princess Di's favorite luxury department store specializes in women's haute couture; its high-tech food halls are a marvel. Knightsbridge, SW1 (phone: 171-235-5000).

Heal's Trendy and modern, this store stocks high-quality furniture (including handmade beds), home decorations, and jewelry. Large purchases can be shipped abroad at an additional charge. 96 Tottenham Court Rd., W1 (phone: 171-636-1666).

Joseph A trendsetting shopping spot, it has several branches around town that sell everything from luggage and housewares to men's and women's clothing. Try the largest branch, 77 Fulham Rd., SW3 (phone: 171-823-9500), or the one at 26 Sloane St., SW1 (phone: 171-235-5470).

Marks & Spencer Locally nicknamed "Marks & Sparks," this chain specializes in clothes for the whole family, made to high standards and sold at very reasonable prices. Its sweaters (especially cashmere and Shetland) are still among the best buys in Britain; plus linen and their own first-rate cosmetics line. Terrific fresh produce and grocery items, too. 458 Oxford St., W1, and many other branches (phone: 171-935-7954).

Peter Jones Another good, well-stocked department store, offering moderately priced, tasteful goods. Sloane Sq., SW1 (phone: 171-730-3434).

Selfridges This well-known emporium offers somewhat less variety than *Harrods,* but it has just about everything, too—only a bit less expensive. The extensive china and crystal department carries most patterns available. 400 Oxford St., W1 (phone: 171-629-1234).

Whiteleys of Bayswater Once a department store rivaling *Harrods,* the original building has undergone a total renovation and is now a beautiful, enclosed Edwardian mall housing branches of shops such as *Marks & Spencer,* as well as designer boutiques. The top tier has cafés, bars, and restaurants. Queensway, W2 (phone: 171-229-8844).

ANTIQUES SHOPS

Alexander Juran While the showrooms are small and shabby, the textiles, rugs, and carpets here can be exceptional. 74 New Bond St., W1 (phone: 171-493-4484 or 171-629-2550).

Alfie's Antique Market Housed in what was once a Victorian department store, this warren of 370 stalls, showrooms, and workshops is the biggest covered antiques market in London—and likely the least expensive, since it is where the dealers come to buy. 13-25 Church St., NW8 (phone: 171-723-6066).

Antiquarius Antique Market Over 60 vendors with specialties ranging from theatrical items and delft to faïence and finds from the 1950s. 135-141 King's Rd., SW3 (phone: 171-351-5353).

Bond Street Antique Centre Finely worked antique jewelry, watches, portrait miniatures, silver, porcelain, and other objets d'art. 124 New Bond St., W1 (phone: 171-351-5353).

Chelsea Antique Market The original indoor antiques market, and still one of the best. 253 King's Rd., SW3 (phone: 171-352-1424).

Chenil Galleries Though widely known as a center for Art Deco and Art Nouveau objects, this gallery also sells Gothic furniture, tapestries, textiles, 18th-century paintings, scientific instruments, and fine porcelain. 181-183 King's Rd., SW3 (phone: 171-351-5353).

Grays Antique Market Here are dozens of stands selling a fine selection of antique jewelry, as well as antiquarian books, maps, prints, arms and armor, lace, scientific instruments, and thimbles (58 Davies St., W1; phone: 171-629-7034). Around the corner, *Grays in the Mews* (1-7 Davies Mews; same phone) has Victorian and Edwardian toys, paintings and prints, and Orientalia.

Grosvenor Prints More than 100,000 prints, on all subjects. In April, the shop holds an annual portrait exhibition of famous social and historic figures, though prints on other topics are also available at that time. 28-32 Shelton St., *Covent Garden,* WC2 (phone: 171-836-1979).

John Keil Offers a large selection of lovely (but expensive) antiques. 154 Brompton Rd., SW3 (phone: 171-589-6454).

London Silver Vaults A maze of antique silver and jewelry shops below ground, housed in what once were real vaults. (A few shops sell new silver or silver plate, too.) Prices range from astronomical to affordable. 53-64 Chancery La., WC2 (phone: 171-242-5506).

Lucy B. Campbell Here are 17th- to 19th-century decorative prints, as well as contemporary watercolors. 123 Kensington Church St., W8 (phone: 171-727-2205).

Mallett and Son A veritable museum in miniature, it specializes in the finest English furniture, choosing every item with consummate taste (141 New Bond St., W1; phone: 171-499-7411). A branch, selling French and continental furniture and a large, eclectic stock artwork and decorative items, is at *Bourdon House,* 2 Davies St., W1 (phone: 171-629-2444).

Milne and Moller Deals in British and continental watercolors by 19th- and 20th-century artists. By appointment only. 35 Colville Ter., W11 (phone: 171-727-1679).

Partridge Ltd. The absolute best in 18th-century French and English furniture, paintings, and objets d'art can be found here. 144-146 New Bond St., W1 (phone: 171-629-0834).

Pickering and Chatto Antiquarian books in English literature of the 17th through 19th centuries, economics, science, and medicine. 17 Pall Mall, SW1 (phone: 171-930-2515).

S. J. Phillips Silver, jewelry, and objets d'art from the 16th to the early 19th centuries. 139 New Bond St., W1 (phone: 171-629-6261).

Temple Gallery Byzantine, Greek, and early Russian icons. By appointment only. 6 Clarendon Cross, W11 (phone: 171-727-3809).

BOOKS, MAPS, AND STATIONERY

Dillon's One of London's most academically oriented bookstores, though it also stocks general-interest books. 82 Gower St., WC1 (phone: 171-636-1577).

Filofax Shop The famous brand-name personal organizers. 21 Conduit St., W1 (phone: 171-499-0457).

Foyle's London's largest bookstore. 119 Charing Cross Rd., WC2 (phone: 171-437-5660).

Hatchard's Founded in 1797, this is London's oldest bookseller—and one of the most civilized. It currently stocks more than 150,000 titles on its four floors. It has several branches, but the main store is at 187 Piccadilly, W1 (phone: 171-439-9921).

Henry Sotheran Ltd. The large stock here includes volumes on voyages and travel, architectural books, finely bound literature, and children's books. 2 Sackville St., W1 (phone: 171-439-6151).

Maggs Bros. Ltd. The friendly staff at this quaint bookshop will help you find your way through three floors of antiquarian books on travel, military and naval history, and 17th-century English literature. 50 Berkeley Sq., W1 (phone: 171-493-7160).

Map House Antique maps (and reproductions), as well as atlases, engravings, prints, and travel books are sold here. 54 Beauchamp Pl., SW3 (phone: 171-589-4325).

Smythson of Bond Street The world's best place to buy leather diaries, notepads, stationery, and calendars also offers esoteric ledgers for recording odd data. 44 New Bond St., W1 (phone: 171-629-8558).

Stanford's The proprietors contend that it's the world's largest map shop, and they just may be right. If you want a topographical map of the mountains you've just walked, a yachting chart for an area you want to cruise, or a road map of the byways you plan to cycle, this is the place. 12 Long Acre, WC2 (phone: 171-836-1321).

W. H. Smith's Newspapers, magazines, and stationery supplies are sold at many branches throughout the city, including 118 Oxford St., W1 (phone: 171-436-6282).

Waterstone's Look for the signature maroon canopy of this huge chain of bookstores, whose instant success is due mainly to an enterprising, well-informed staff and late hours. There are many branches, including: 68-69 Hampstead High St., NW3 (phone: 171-794-1098); 99-101 Old Brompton Rd., SW7 (phone: 171-581-8522); 121-125 Charing Cross Rd., WC2 (phone: 171-434-4291); and 193 Kensington High St., W8 (phone: 171-937-8432).

CHINA

Reject China Shop Here you'll find good buys in name-brand china, including some irregular pieces, as well as glassware, crystal, and flatware. For a fee, the shop will ship your purchases back home. There are several branches throughout the city, including: 134 Regent St., W1 (phone: 171-434-2502);

33-34 Beauchamp Pl., SW3 (phone: 171-581-0737); and 183 Brompton Rd., SW3 (phone: 171-581-0739).

Thomas Goode and Company London's best china and glass shop first opened in 1827. Even if you don't plan to buy anything, you may want to look at their beautiful 1876 showroom. 19 S. Audley St., W1 (phone: 171-499-2823).

Waterford Wedgwood A full selection of Waterford crystal and Wedgwood bone china (what else?). 158 Regent St., W1 (phone: 171-734-7262).

CLOTHING, ACCESSORIES, AND FABRICS

Anderson and Sheppard Reputable "made-to-measure" tailor for men's clothes. 30 Savile Row, W1 (phone: 171-734-1420).

Aquascutum Famous for raincoats and jackets for men and women. 100 Regent St., W1 (phone: 171-734-6090).

Austin Reed Classic English menswear, plus an old-fashioned barbershop in the basement. Some womenswear, too. 103 Regent St., W1 (phone: 171-734-6789).

Bellville Sassoon This boutique's client list reads like a chapter from *Debrett's;* the Princess of Wales, who chose a saucy sailor dress for her first official picture with the queen, is a loyal customer. The specialty is glamorous evening wear specifically designed for the shop. 18 Culford Gardens, SW3 (phone: 171-581-3500).

Browns Designer clothes for men and women in eight shops along a tiny, pedestrians-only street. S. Molton St., W1 (phone: 171-491-7833).

Burberrys Superb, expensive raincoats and traditional clothes for men and women, and home of the now nearly ubiquitous plaid that began life as a raincoat lining. 18-22 Haymarket, SW1 (phone: 171-930-3343).

Caroline Charles Perfect women's styles for *Ascot* and other very social events. 56-57 Beauchamp Pl., SW3 (phone: 171-589-5850).

Cordings Sportswear for the quintessential country squire—plus a branch of *Hackett* (see below), a major source of elegant menswear. 19-20 Piccadilly, W1 (phone: 171-734-0830).

Courtenay House Particularly beautiful Swiss cotton and silky lingerie. 22 Brook St., W1 (phone: 171-629-0542).

Douglas Hayward A reputable made-to-order men's tailor. 95 Mount St., W1 (phone: 171-499-5574).

Farlows Perhaps the best spot in London to buy the completely waterproof and windproof Barbour jackets and hats and other casualwear for a day in the country. 5 Pall Mall, SW1 (phone: 171-839-2423).

Feathers French and Italian designer clothing for women. 40 Hans Crescent, SW1 (phone: 171-589-0356).

Gieves and Hawkes Over 200 years old, this establishment provides traditional English tailoring—from formal dress to the proper attire for hunting and fishing. The queen, Duke of Edinburgh, and Prince Charles are regular patrons. You can get a suit either custom-made or ready-to-wear. 1 Savile Row, W1 (phone: 171-434-2001), and 18 Lime St., EC3 (phone: 171-283-4914).

Gucci Outposts of the famous Italian fashion, leather goods, and shoe manufacturer are found at 32-33 Old Bond St., W1 (phone: 171-629-2716), and at 17-18 Sloane St., SW1 (phone: 171-235-6707).

Hackett Menswear in these elegant but welcoming shops is neither boring nor predictable. There are branches at several locations, including: 137 Sloane St., SW1 (phone: 171-730-3331); *Cordings,* 19-20 Piccadilly, W1 (phone: 171-734-0868); and 65b New King's Rd., SW6 (phone: 171-731-7964).

Harvie and Hudson Custom-made men's shirts, not to mention a selection of color-coordinated silk ties. Three branches: 77 Jermyn St., SW1 (phone: 171-930-3949); 97 Jermyn St., SW1 (phone: 171-839-3578); and 55 Knightsbridge, SW3 (phone: 171-235-2651).

Jaeger Tailored (and expensive) men's and women's clothes. 202-206 Regent St., W1 (phone: 171-734-8211), and 163 Sloane St., SW1 (phone: 171-235-2505).

James Smith and Sons Believed to be the oldest umbrella shop in Europe, it was opened in 1830 by James Smith, and in 1857 it moved to its current address. It also carries walking sticks and whips. A couple of blocks from the *British Museum.* 53 New Oxford St., WC1 (phone: 171-836-4731).

Katharine Hamnett Beautiful—but pricey—womenswear. 20 Sloane St., SW1 (phone: 171-823-1002).

Kent & Curwen The place to buy authentic cricket caps, Henley club ties, and all sorts of similarly preppy raiment. 39 St. James's St., SW1 (phone: 171-409-1955), and 6 *Royal Arcade* (for *Wimbledon* wear), W1 (phone: 171-493-6882).

Laura Ashley Romantically styled skirts, dresses, and blouses, plus a plethora of decorating essentials. 256 Regent St., W1 (phone: 171-437-9760), and other branches including 47-49 Brompton Rd., SW1 (phone: 171-823-9700).

Liberty Famous for print fabrics. Scarves and ties a specialty. 210 Regent St., W1 (phone: 171-734-1234).

Moss Bros. Men's formal attire (including dress tartans) and high-quality riding clothes for sale and hire. 88 Regent St., W1 (phone: 171-494-0666), and 27 King St., WC2 (phone: 171-240-4567).

Mothercare Children's clothes. Many locations, including 461 Oxford St., W1 (phone: 171-629-6621).

Paul Smith Britain's number one men's designer has four adjacent shops (one sells womenswear) in *Covent Garden.* 41-44 Floral St., WC2 (phone: 171-379-7133).

Scotch House Famous for Scottish cashmeres, sweaters, tartans—a wide selection of well-known labels. 2 Brompton Rd., SW1 (phone: 171-581-2151), and several branches.

Shirin The best designer cashmeres in town. 51 Beauchamp Pl., SW3 (phone: 171-581-1936).

Simpson (Piccadilly) Classic and safe English looks for men and women, including their own famous "DAKS" label. 203 Piccadilly, W1 (phone: 171-734-2002).

Turnbull and Asser Famous for their made-to-order shirts, but they also sell ready-made luxury menswear, as well as womenswear next door. 71-72 Jermyn St., SW1 (phone: 171-930-0502).

Vivienne Westwood Innovative women's clothing from one of Britain's most influential designers. 41 Conduit St., W1 (phone: 171-439-1109).

Westaway and Westaway Cashmere and Shetland wool kilts, sweaters (their great doubleknit Shetlands are half the price of *Hackett*'s), scarves, and blankets. Mail order, too. 65 Great Russell St., WC1 (phone: 171-405-4479; 800-345-3219 for inquiries and mail orders).

Zandra Rhodes The designer's ultra-feminine creations are sold here. By appointment only. 87 Richford St., W6 (phone: 181-749-3216).

COSMETICS

Body Shop More than 150 different beauty aids, including perfume, soap, and hair and skin care products (which are famous for not having been tested on animals), from the worldwide chain that started in Brighton. There are several locations throughout the city, including its main branch at 32 Great Marlborough St., W1 (phone: 171-437-5137).

Boots A good place for cosmetics, pharmaceuticals, and sundries. There are several branches throughout the city, including 73 Piccadilly, W1 (phone: 171-409-2982).

Floris Old-fashioned English scents, soaps, potpourri, and more in a charming Victorian shop. 89 Jermyn St., SW1 (phone: 171-930-2885).

Penhaligon's This chain of Victorian shops offers an extensive range of classical scents, toilet water, soaps, and bath oils for ladies and gentlemen—along with antique scent bottles and old English silver for the dressing table. 41 Wellington St., WC2, and four other locations (phone: 171-836-2150).

FOOD AND DRINK

Charbonnel et Walker Sumptuous candies are "enrobed" with dark chocolate (bittersweet plain) and white chocolate. You can get Prince Philip's favorite chocolate here—a Mocha Baton. The packaging is beautiful. 28 Old Bond St., W1 (phone: 171-491-0939).

Ferns The carved mahogany shelves of this old-fashioned store are crammed with teas, tea caddies, and more, and the drawers are packed with beans of all types. You can smell the coffee from several doors down. 27 Rathbone Pl., W1 (phone: 171-636-2237).

Justin De Blank Excellent specialty foods, especially cheese and take-out dishes. 42 Elizabeth St., SW1 (phone: 171-730-0605).

Paxton and Whitfield This establishment shows cheeses the way some shops display jewelry: cones and cubes large and small, cakes with rinds of gray and tan, huge wheels of brie, deep gold derbies, and more—all of it superb. 93 Jermyn St., SW1 (phone: 171-930-0250).

Prestat The best chocolates in all of London. Try the truffles. 14 *Princes Arcade,* SW1 (phone: 171-629-4838).

Rococo Chocolates London's most eccentric candy store: fresh cream truffles, pralines, and Swiss chocolates (made in London); plus chocolate engagement rings. Tea is served in summer by appointment only. 321 King's Rd., SW3 (phone: 171-352-5857).

Twinings London's oldest tea shop (est. 1706) sells tea in bags, balls, and bulk; there's also a large selection of coffee. 216 The Strand, WC2 (phone: 171-353-3511).

FURNITURE, HOUSEWARES, AND BIBELOTS

The Conran Shop Sir Terence Conran has transformed the beautiful *Michelin Building* into a grander, more exclusive and expensive version of his well-known *Habitat* stores. However, the export of larger furniture and furnishings is probably better arranged through a US branch. 81 Fulham Rd., SW3 (phone: 171-589-7401).

Contemporary Ceramics This gallery-style shop sells ceramic statuary, pots, vases, jewelry, mugs, bowls, and other pieces, all made by members of the *Craft Potters' Association.* 7 Marshall St., W1 (phone: 171-437-7605).

Halcyon Days The best place to find authentic enameled Battersea boxes—both antique and new. 14 Brook St., W1 (phone: 171-629-8811).

Irish Linen Co. Plain and fancy bed and table linen and handkerchiefs. 35 *Burlington Arcade,* W1 (phone: 171-493-8949).

Naturally British Visiting this shop will make you feel as if you've traveled all over the country, even if you never leave London. Its stock includes tapestries from Wales, hand-knits from Scotland, and many wooden items such as rocking horses and traditional pub games. 13 New Row, *Covent Garden,* WC2 (phone: 171-240-0551).

GOLD, SILVER, AND JEWELRY

Asprey & Company Fine jewelry and silver (plus luggage and leather accessories). 165-169 New Bond St., W1 (phone: 171-493-6767).

Mappin & Webb Elegant and traditional gold and silver jewelry. 170 Regent St., W1 (phone: 171-734-5842).

GUNS AND SPORTING EQUIPMENT

Gidden's of London Founded in 1806, it sells saddles and other riding equipment to the queen. On three floors, near New Bond St. at 15d Clifford St., W1 (phone: 171-734-2788).

Holland and Holland Here, gunmaking is high art. It's worth a peek, if only to inspect the binoculars, folding earmuffs, and other appurtenances of hunting and shooting. 33 Bruton St., W1 (phone: 171-499-4411).

James Purdey and Sons The place to go for custom-made shotguns and other shooting gear. 57 S. Audley St., W1 (phone: 171-499-1801).

Lillywhites The whole gamut of sporting goods, from cricket bats to shuttlecocks. Piccadilly Circus, SW1 (phone: 171-930-3181).

Swaine Adeney Riding gear and their famous pure silk umbrellas. 185 Piccadilly, W1 (phone: 171-734-4277).

HATS

Bates Our favorite gentlemen's hat shop. Check out the eight-part caps. 21A Jermyn St., SW1 (phone: 171-734-2722).

Hat Shop Berets, cloches, deerstalkers, fedoras, flying caps, panamas, pillboxes, tam-o'-shanters, even baseball caps with earflaps, along with hats made by designers. Two locations: 58 Neal St., *Covent Garden,* WC2 (phone: 171-836-6718), and 18 St. Christopher's Pl., W1 (phone: 171-935-0820).

Herbert Johnson Men's and women's hats. (It's worth a look just to see the shop's vividly expressive mannequins—they're the cleverest in London.) 30 New Bond St., W1 (phone: 171-408-1174).

James Lock and Company, Ltd. The royal hatters. They fitted a crown for the queen's coronation, and they'll happily fit you for your first top hat. Plus headgear for fishermen, hunters, groundskeepers—and, for the first time in 300 years, women. 6 St. James's St., SW1 (phone: 171-930-8874).

MUSIC

Chappell London's largest supplier of sheet music, from Bach to rock. It also sells pianos, electronic keyboards, guitars, and metronomes. 50 New Bond St., W1 (phone: 171-491-2777).

58 Dean Street Records Offers a wide selection of show tunes and movie soundtracks, and the staff is very helpful. 58 Dean St., W1 (phone: 171-734-8777).

SHOES

Church's Superior men's shoes (and some women's shoes) in various locations, including 58-59 *Burlington Arcade,* W1 (phone: 171-493-8307).

John Lobb World-famous for men's made-to-order shoes—at stratospheric prices—that will last 10 years or more, with proper care. 9 St. James's St., SW1 (phone: 171-930-3664).

Shellys Shoes A wide selection of trendy street footwear from thigh-high suede boots to platform shoes. 159 Oxford St., W1 (phone: 171-437-5842).

TOBACCO

Alfred Dunhill Not only does this store offer the best in precision lighters, pipes, tobacco, and cigars, it claims to provide almost anything that a man can carry or wear—including luxury leather accessories, watches, writing instruments, and casual clothes. The Humidor Room features Havana and other cigars for connoisseurs. 30 Duke St. (near Piccadilly), SW1 (phone: 171-499-9566).

James Fox and Robert Lewis Specializes in cigars from around the world, including Havana, and most brands are represented. Another draw for the connoisseur is the use of humidifying rooms, where cigars mature to peak condition. 19 St. James St., W1 (phone: 171-493-9009).

SPORTS

Soccer (called football hereabouts) and cricket are the most popular spectator pastimes, but London offers a wide variety of other sports.

CRICKET The season runs from mid-April to early September. The best places to watch the matches are at *Lord's Cricket Ground* (St. John's Wood Rd., NW8; phone: 171-289-1615) and *The Oval* (Kennington, SE1; phone: 171-582-4911). For more information on the game itself, see *Spectator Sports* in DIVERSIONS.

FITNESS CENTERS *Pineapple Dance Studios* (7 Langley St., WC2; phone: 171-836-4004); the *Albany Health and Fitness Club* (Little Albany St., NW1; phone: 171-383-7131); *Earls Court Gym* (254 Earls Court Rd., SW5; phone: 171-370-1402); and other locations around town. Several hotels have good fitness centers; see *Checking In.*

GOLF These courses, which are among the finest in England, are a short distance from the capital.

TOP TEE-OFF SPOTS

Sunningdale While the *Old Course* is considered the championship layout here, the *New* is probably the more challenging of the two. When you play them, you will discover that the decision on difficulty is an arbitrary one at best. Fairways and greens are meticulously maintained, and this is perhaps the finest single brace of courses in England. Private but approachable for play on weekdays; call well in advance and have a letter from your home club pro or president ready. Ridgemount Rd., Sunningdale (phone: 1344-21681).

Wentworth Generally considered the prettier of the layouts here, the *East* course can do wonders for a shaky backswing. But it's the *West* course, with its relatively narrow tree-lined fairways, that is sometimes not so affectionately called the "Burma Road." For a high-handicap player, the *West* is not unlike putting an innocent's head into a lion's mouth. The *World Match Play Championship* has been held here every year since 1964. Again, it's a private club; access is available to traveling players on weekdays with prior notice—upon presentation of your own club membership card with a handicap certificate and a letter from your club pro or president. Virginia Water, Surrey (phone: 1344-842201).

Aside from these private facilities, there are several municipal courses, some of which rent clubs. Try *Addington Court* (Featherbed La., Addington, Croydon; phone: 181-657-0281); *Beckenham Place Park* (Beckenham, Kent; phone: 181-650-2292); *Bush Hill Park* (Winchmore Hill, Middlesex; phone: 181-360-5738); and *Pickett's Lock Center* (Pickett's Lock La., N9; phone: 181-803-3611).

HORSE RACING Nine major racecourses are within easy reach of London, including *Epsom,* where the *Derby* (pronounced *Dar*-by) is run, and *Ascot,* where the *Royal Ascot* races take place—both in June. The flat racing season is from March to November; steeplechasing, August to June. Check the daily papers for details.

HORSEBACK RIDING Try *Richard Briggs Riding Stables* (63 Bathurst Mews, W2; phone: 171-723-2813) and *Ross Nye's Riding Establishment* (8 Bathurst Mews, W2; phone: 171-262-3791); *Hyde Park* is a fine place to ride.

ICE SKATING There is the *Queen's Ice Skating Club* (17 Queensway, W2; phone: 171-229-0172) and *Streatham Ice Rink* (386 Streatham High Rd., SW16; phone: 181-769-7771).

JOGGING Most pleasant for running are *Hyde Park,* bordered by Kensington Road, Park Lane, and Bayswater Road; *Hampstead Heath,* North London; and

Regent's Park, bordered by Prince Albert Road, Albany Street, Marylebone Road, and Park Road. Do not jog after dark.

RUGBY An autumn-through-spring spectacle at local clubs throughout Greater London. Major international matches are staged at the Rugby Union world headquarters on Whitton Rd., Twickenham (phone: 181-892-8161).

SOCCER *The* big sport in Britain. The season is autumn to spring and the most popular local clubs are *Arsenal* (*Highbury Stadium,* Avenell Rd., N5; phone: 171-226-0304); *Chelsea* (Stamford Bridge, Fulham Rd., SW6; phone: 171-385-5545); and *Tottenham Hotspur* (White Hart La., N17; phone: 181-808-8080).

SWIMMING Excellent indoor public pools include *Swiss Cottage Center* (Adelaide Rd., NW3; phone: 171-413-6490) and *The Oasis* (167 High Holborn, WC1; phone: 171-836-9555). There is outdoor swimming in *Hyde Park*'s Serpentine Lake and at *Hampstead Heath* in the summer.

TENNIS Aside from private clubs, more than 50 London public parks have tennis courts available to all. Get information from the *Lawn Tennis Association* (phone: 171-385-4233) or the *London Tourist Board and Convention Bureau* (see *Tourist Information*).

TENNIS, ANYONE?

Britain practically closes down in late June and early July, the fortnight of the *All England Lawn Tennis Championships*—also known as *Wimbledon.* Ticket scalpers do a brisk trade outside the gate (and even advertise in the personal columns of the newspapers), and those who aren't lucky enough to secure tickets watch the competition on television.

This year, *Wimbledon* will take place from June 26 to July 9 (excluding Sunday, July 2) at the *All England Lawn Tennis and Croquet Club* in Wimbledon. A magnet for the world's best players, who compete for a total of more than £5 million in prize money, this tourney is an experience even for those who have never held a racquet. Grass courts, strawberry teas, and the legendary *Centre Court* make for such a spectacle that visitors may find the world class matches no more than a diversion. Advance seat tickets for *Centre Court, Number One Court,* and *Court 14* are distributed by lottery. Ticket applications, available from September 1 of the previous year, can be obtained by sending a self-addressed, stamped envelope to the *All England Lawn Tennis and Croquet Club* (PO Box 98, Church Rd., Wimbledon SW19 5AE, England; phone: 181-944-1066). The club must receive completed forms by midnight, December 31. For the first nine days of the tournament, some tickets are available on the day of play for *Number One Court;* for *Number Two Court* and the remaining outside courts, tickets are always available on the day of play. For more details, contact the *All England Lawn Tennis and Croquet Club* (address and phone number above); include a self-addressed, stamped envelope or international postage coupons.

By far the most certain and efficient means of seeing the match of your choice is to purchase one of the many packages from *NAA Events International* (1730 NE Expwy., Atlanta, GA 30329; phone: 404-329-9902 or 800-278-6738), which offers a wide range of selections for first-week, second-week, and men's and women's finals play.

THEATER

London remains the theater capital of the world, with about 50 stages regularly presenting plays in and around its West End theater district and at a vigorous collection of "fringe" theaters in various parts of town. Listed below are our favorite venues in this most dramatic of cities.

CENTER STAGE

Barbican Centre An apparent tribute to modern architecture, this 1982 structure looks like a maze of concrete towers and corridors from the outside. Inside, the complex design, the exciting potential of the building, and the breadth of artistic activity generated are overwhelming. This is the London home of the *Royal Shakespeare Company,* along with the *London Symphony Orchestra.* There are two theaters, cinemas, an art gallery, two shops, and a concert hall that hosts regular performances of classical music, opera, and more. The *Waterside Café,* which offers snacks by the fountains in summer, *Café on Six* (the *Barbican*'s wine bar), and the more formal *Searcey's* all make for delightful interludes. Silk St., EC2 (phone: 171-638-4141 for general information; 171-638-8891 for the box office).

London Coliseum There's a sense of occasion surrounding any visit to this floridly Edwardian, 2,358-seat theater, London's largest, at the foot of St. Martin's Lane. The interiors are all alabaster and marble, bronze and splendid gleaming mahogany, as posh as those of the ships that once crisscrossed the Atlantic when the theater was first opened. Diaghilev's *Ballet Russe* performed here, as did Sarah Bernhardt, Mrs. Patrick Campbell, Ellen Terry, and a child star named Noël Coward. The impresario who conceived the place even staged tennis matches and rodeos to keep it filled. The *English National Opera Company,* which performs classic and contemporary operas in English, has been in residence from October to June every year since 1968. St. Martin's La., WC2 (phone: 171-836-3161).

Old Vic Architects, bombs, and ill-advised alterations had left the *Old Vic* nothing short of a mishmash when a Canadian named "Honest" Ed Mirvish bought it sight unseen in 1982 and transformed it into one of the most elegant and comfortable theaters in central London. The façade was returned to its 1818 incarnation, complete with brick arches; and the interior was restored to a semblance of its 1880s self. Boxes, ceiling, proscenium arch, and tier fronts were elaborately painted in shades of ivory, apricot, coral, pewter, gold, and silver. The entire auditorium was bedecked in wallpaper and carpeting with a period flavor. The remarkable restoration alone makes a visit worthwhile. Waterloo Rd., SE1 (phone: 171-928-7616).

Open Air Theatre (Regent's Park) It's hard to find a more pleasant way to spend a summer evening in London than to see a performance of Shakespeare (or a musical) in this lovely amphitheater in the woods near *Queen Mary's Rose Garden.* Established in 1932, it quickly became an institution among London theatergoers, and actors from Vivien Leigh to Jeremy Irons have played here. Since 1962, the *New Shakespeare Company* has made its home here, offering three plays (two by Shakespeare) every season (May through September). The newer auditorium, which opened in 1975, also has a bar that serves such fare as Puck's Fizz and mulled wine, barbecue, and a cold buffet. *Regent's Park,* NW1 (phone: 171-486-2431).

Royal Court Theatre One of the most famous of London's small stages, this one has made theatrical history more than once—first around 1904, with Harley Granville Barker's stagings of Arthur Pinero farces and George Bernard Shaw plays, and again in the late 1950s, when George Devine's *English Stage Company* presented John Osborne's *Look Back in Anger.* Even today, the theater is associated with very modern works, producing the plays of such contemporary writers as Caryl Churchill and Snoo Wilson. And despite the chronic shortage of money, standards are always high. The *Royal Court* is a great place for spotting talent, and the audience is lively. Stephen Daldry, the theater's new artistic director, has shown a marked preference for contemporary American playwrights; recent productions include David Mamet's *Oleanna* and John Guare's *Six Degrees of Separation.* Sloane Sq., SW1 (phone: 171-730-1745).

Royal National Theatre Anyone who visits this trio of houses in a handsome, large, Thameside drama complex is sure to have plenty to talk about—even if the fare is not to his or her taste. That, however, is unlikely, for Maggie Smith, Albert Finney, John Gielgud, Ian McKellen, and Paul Scofield have appeared here. The building itself is wonderful, too, with an interior that feels like a walk-through sculpture, a huge foyer with bars that seems to be London's answer to Paris's sidewalk cafés, and all manner of walks, terraces, and restaurants with fine views of Somerset House and the river curving off toward *St. Paul's.* Guided tours are given several times a day Mondays through Saturdays for a small charge.

Before performances, ensembles and soloists play for free in the foyers, and you can browse through art exhibitions while listening. There are often so-called platform performances—brief plays, readings, poetry, music, and mime—in all three theaters: the 400-seat *Cottesloe,* which is otherwise mainly used for works requiring small-scale staging, the 890-seat proscenium-arch *Lyttelton,* and the 1,160-seat open-stage *Olivier.* The last two feel almost as intimate as the *Cottesloe,* thanks to their excellent design. South Bank, SE1 (phone: 171-928-2252 for the box office; 171-633-0880 for tour information).

Sadler's Wells Theatre Built on the site of two mineral springs discovered in 1683 by Richard Sadler, this theater has seen its share of jugglers and clowns, rope dancers and performing animals, plays and pantomimes, and even roller skaters and boxers. One of London's oldest more or less continuously operating venues, the hall once hosted the world premiere of Benjamin Britten's *Peter Grimes* and, in its time, also has been home to the *Royal Ballet* and the *English National Opera.* Today, it hosts touring opera and dance companies from all over the world. The London seasons of the country's leading dance companies, including the *Rambert Dance Company,* the *London Contemporary Dance Theatre,* and the *National Youth Music Theater,* also take place here. *Sadler's Wells* has a second auditorium, the *Lilian Baylis Theatre,* beside the principal building. This space is small (220 seats) but is fully equipped technically; presentations here are divided between small-scale professional work (music, drama, dance) and community and education projects. Rosebery Ave., EC1 (phone: 171-278-6563 for general information; 171-278-8916 for the box office).

Savoy Theatre Gutted by fire in 1990, this venerable stage—built in 1881 to showcase Gilbert and Sullivan's operettas—rose like the proverbial phoenix two years ago. The theater underwent an Art Deco transformation in 1929, and it is to this era that the architects and designers have returned. The £11 million project restored such opulent details as the ceiling, painted to resemble a bright April sky; Oriental-style panels that flank the proscenium arch; a silk-tasseled, multicolored front curtain; and 1,100 plushly upholstered seats in five alternating colors—the decor is a show in itself. The fine acoustics have been preserved as well. Noël Coward, Ralph Richardson, and Paul Robeson are just a few of the luminaries who performed here in the past; undoubtedly, more will be playing here in the future. The Strand, WC2 (phone: 171-836-8117).

Theatre Royal (Drury Lane) The productions here may not be London's most innovative, but this 2,283-seat theater, with its beautiful symmetrical staircase and domed entranceway, is definitely one of London's most historic. The fourth playhouse on the site, it was preceded by a theater where Charles II met Nell Gwyn, who once sold oranges at the entrance; another predecessor was designed by Christopher Wren, with John Dryden as chief playwright, and David Garrick and Richard Sheridan as managers; in 1777, the latter wrote his *School for Scandal* upstairs while actors rehearsed completed sections below. The present house, designed by Benjamin Wyatt in 1812, has hosted opera and drama, pantomime and film, and even musicals. Edmund Kean, whom many believe to be the greatest tragedian of all time, played here, as have Sir Henry Irving, Ellen Terry, and Sir John Gielgud, among others. The theater has its tradition, the cutting of the so-called Baddeley Cake (named after the actor whose will supplied the funds) in the *Grand Saloon* after the performance every January 6, and its ghost, a gray-cloaked, high-booted, bewigged fellow who haunts the upper circle—in the daytime only. For a splurge, theatergoers can hire the Royal Box or the Prince of Wales Box, both of which come complete with seating for six and tiny Regency or Adamesque retiring rooms. Guided tours of the theater are offered Mondays through Saturdays. Drury La., Catherine St., WC2 (phone: 171-494-5062 for the box office; 171-836-3352 for tours).

Theatre Royal (Haymarket) Architect John Nash, who designed this small, stylish theater, gave it a wonderful Corinthian portico, which looks all the more grand when floodlit, as it often is at night. Henry Fielding managed a predecessor on the site around 1737, and the present hall, built in 1821, has been the setting for plays by everyone from Ibsen to Wilde, T. S. Eliot and Tennessee Williams to Noël Coward, J. M. Barrie, and Terence Rattigan; Sir Beerbohm Tree played here in the late 19th century. The hall itself, renovated at the beginning of this century, is all white, rich blue, and gold leaf; there's a wonderfully crafted royal arms above the stage. Haymarket, SW1 (phone: 171-930-8800).

Young Vic Theatre This theater, founded in the late 1970s, is new by London standards, but the spirit of experimentation and the *joie de jouer* that go into the productions are as much a tradition in the British theater as is the Bard himself. It is particularly renowned for bringing fresh interpretations and contemporary staging to Shakespeare and modern classics; among the theater's most recent successes have been the European premiere of *The Last Yankee* by Arthur Miller, *All My Sons,* also by Miller, and *The Plough and the Stars* by Sean O'Casey. The works of Shakespeare and Ibsen, as well as those of

David Holman and other modern playwrights, are presented, along with a comprehensive program of works for younger audiences. It's lively and quite different architecturally from most theaters. 66 The Cut, SE1 (phone: 171-928-6363).

The long-awaited, much-ballyhooed restoration of the *Globe Theatre,* the oval-shaped stage where many of Shakespeare's works were first performed, has been struggling with financial difficulties but is scheduled to be completed this spring. The open-air theater, on the south bank of the Thames, will be re-created in the Elizabethan style of the original (which was destroyed by fire in 1613) and will hold about 1,500 people; there will be some tiered seating, but most theatergoers will have to stand, as Shakespeare's audiences did in the 16th century. Plans for future development of the complex include the addition of an educational center, an audiovisual archive and library showing Shakespeare's works performed in various media, and a second theater. The project was spearheaded by the late American actor/director Sam Wanamaker, who felt Shakespeare deserved an important memorial in London, where so many of his plays were first produced. For more information, contact the *Shakespeare Globe Trust* (Bear Gardens, SE1; phone: 171-620-0202).

The best known and most accomplished theater groups are the two main repertory companies—the *Royal National Theatre Company* at the *Royal National Theatre* and the *Royal Shakespeare Company (RSC)* at the *Barbican Centre;* from time to time, both present dazzling versions of classics and new plays, although they sometimes trade on their reputations. (For reliable critical reviews, consult *Time Out* magazine and the *Guardian*'s Michael Billington.)

In the West End, presentations include both first class and second-rate drama and comedy, a fair sprinkling of farce (for which the British have a particular fondness), and the best imports from the American stage. Visitors from the US often find attending theater in London easier—and a little less expensive (depending on the exchange rate)—than it is at home. Except for the small handful of runaway box-office successes, tickets usually are available for all performances. In most cases, you can reserve by telephone, but tickets must be picked up well before curtain time. The *Society of London Theatre* operates a half-price ticket kiosk in Leicester Square. It posts a list of shows for which remaining seats (usually in the orchestra) are available at half price on the day of the performance. Ticket agencies that offer tickets to all shows, charging a (sometimes hefty) commission, include *Edwards & Edwards* (*Palace Theatre,* Cambridge Circus, W1; phone: 171-379-1564; or 1 Times Sq. Plaza, New York, NY 10036; phone: 212-944-0290 or 800-223-6108); *Ticketmaster* (phone: 171-379-4444); *London Theatre Bookings* (96 Shaftesbury Ave.; phone: 171-439-3371 or 171-439-4061); and *First Call* (phone: 171-497-9977). Another service, *Theatre Tonight* (phone: 171-753-0333), offers tickets for same-night performances, which can be charged to

MasterCard or Visa; there's no booking fee or ticket surcharge. A phone service, *Theatreline,* offers information on West End performances (phone: 836-430959 for plays; 836-430960 for musicals; 836-430961 for comedies; 836-430962 for thrillers; 836-430963 for children's shows; 836-430964 for opera, ballet, and dance); calls can be placed from anywhere in Great Britain, and there is a charge per call—36p (about 55¢) to 48p (about 75¢), depending on the time of day.

The quality of London's fringe theater varies from accomplished and imaginative to amateurish. Theaters in pubs are at the *King's Head* (115 Upper St., Islington, N1; phone: 171-226-1916), and the *Bush* (in the *Bush Hotel,* Shepherd's Bush Green, W6; phone: 181-743-3388). The *Riverside Studios* (Crisp Rd., Hammersmith, W6; phone: 181-748-3354), the *Tricycle Theatre* (269 Kilburn High Rd., NW6; phone: 171-328-1000), and the *New End Theatre* (27 New End, Hampstead, NW3; phone: 171-794-0022) have established excellent reputations; their productions often move on to the West End and sometimes even directly to Broadway. Also keep an eye on the *Donmar Warehouse* for major transfers from the *Edinburgh Festival Fringe* or for exciting avant-garde companies such as *Cheek by Jowl* (call 171-793-0153 for information).

A visit to *St. Martin's* (West St., Cambridge Circus, WC2; phone: 171-836-1443) is now tantamount to seeing a major London landmark, as it houses Agatha Christie's *The Mousetrap;* there's a fresh cast each year, and it's been running since 1952—the longest run ever in nightly theater.

Musical nostalgia can be found at the *Players Theatre* (The Arches, off Villiers St., WC2; phone: 171-839-1134), just off The Strand at *Charing Cross Station,* which offers old-fashioned Victorian music hall entertainment.

Check *Time Out* to get comprehensive lists of current productions, plot summaries, and theater phone numbers. Daily papers list West End performances.

Show tours to London are popular in season; see your travel agent for package deals. If you want to reserve specific tickets before you arrive in London, there are agencies in the US that keep a listing of what's on in London. For a service charge (again, it may be a bit steep—as much as 30% of the ticket price), they will sell you the best seats. Contact *Edwards & Edwards* (see address and phone number above) or *Keith Prowse & Co., Ltd.* (234 W. 44th St., Suite 1000, New York, NY 10036; phone: 212-398-1430 or 800-669-7469).

The best of London's ballet performances are presented at the *Royal Opera House* (see *Music*), at *Sadler's Wells* (though the original company has moved to Birmingham), and at the *London Coliseum.* Visiting modern dance companies from all over the world regularly perform at *The Place* (17 Duke's Rd., WC1; phone: 171-387-0031), home of the *London Contemporary Dance Theatre* and the *London School of Contemporary Dance.* Details about concert, recital, opera, and ballet performances are listed in the arts sections of *Time Out.* Tickets to London ballet performances can be obtained in the US by contacting *Edwards & Edwards* (see above).

CINEMA

London may not be the equal of Paris as a movie metropolis, but many say it's stronger when it comes to very good, little-known films, often from the US or Commonwealth countries. British film is startling in both similarities and contrasts to that of the US. The *British Film Institute* (21 Stephen St., W1; phone: 171-255-1444) has a large library of excellent British and international films, administers the *National Film and Television Archive,* contains first class documentation and filmographic material, publishes the monthly *Film Bulletin* and the quarterly *Sight and Sound,* and runs the successful *London Film Festival* in November (see *Favorite Fetes*). Membership is required at the *NFT* (40p/about 60¢ a day or £11.95/about $18 for a year), but it's well worth it for its two cinemas; wide variety of old and new British, US, and international movies; good film bookshop; and eating facilities.

As with the theater, there are big divisions between West End and fringe cinema. The West End strives for probable box-office hits, so look for long lines at Friday openings, and head for early showings, some of which begin not long after noon. The admission charge to West End movies is not inexpensive (tickets can cost £9/about $13.50), though prices are lower on Mondays. The widest selection of films under one roof can be found at *Whiteleys of Bayswater* (Queensway, W2; phone: 171-792-3332), an enclosed mall with eight cinemas. For sheer comfort, the *Curzon Mayfair* in the West End (on Mayfair's Curzon St., W1; phone: 171-465-8865) is unbeatable for both low-budget art and commercial films. The most exciting fare usually is found in independents, and sometimes you must travel to remote parts of London to see outstanding work in an almost empty cinema. If independent films interest you, check places like *Everyman* (at Hampstead; phone: 171-435-1525); the luxurious *Barbican Centre Cinemas* (phone: 171-638-8891); *Screen* (Baker St., W1; phone: 171-935-2772); *Screen on the Green* (at Islington; phone: 171-226-3520); and *Screen on the Hill* (in Hampstead; phone: 171-435-3366). All feature late-night showings and children's screenings on Saturdays (as do the *Barbican* and *NFT*). In some cases you may have to pay moderate club fees. Most British cinemas now ban smoking.

The *Museum of London* (see *Special Places*) and the *Museum of the Moving Image* (see *Museums*) also show films. Since show times are irregular, it is best to call ahead or to check *Time Out.*

MUSIC

Few cities offer a greater variety of musical performances. The four venues listed below—our particular favorites—not only present outstanding performances, but also are architecturally handsome inside and out.

HEAVENLY HALLS

Royal Albert Hall Designed in the classical amphitheater style, and opened by Queen Victoria in 1871 as a memorial to her consort, Prince Albert, this almost round house is truly splendid and imposing, with a seating capacity of 5,500. The domed building, a quarter of a mile in circumference, has terra cotta moldings imposed on a red brick exterior, an immense grand organ, and three tiers of boxes. All kinds of concerts, from a Bach "B Minor Mass" to a spine-tingling, cannon-throttled "1812 Overture," will fill it up. The *Henry Wood Promenade Concerts* ("the *Proms*" in local parlance) are particularly special and attract crowds every night from mid-July through mid-September (also see *Special Events,* above). The *BBC Symphony Orchestra* performs here during most of the season, but most of the other major British orchestras also appear, as well as some of the world's most prestigious ensembles. The *Hall* also has hosted such popular artists as Frank Sinatra, Paul Simon, and Eric Clapton, and it's a venue for championship boxing, tennis, and grand balls as well. Most concerts at the *Hall* have remarkably low ticket prices. Kensington Gore, SW7 (phone: 171-589-8212 for the box office; 891-500252 for recorded information).

Royal Festival Hall Opened in 1951, London's premier concert hall seats an audience of 3,000. The permanent home of the renowned *London Philharmonic,* it is part of the *South Bank Centre,* which also includes the nearby *Royal National Theatre,* the *National Film Theatre,* the *Museum of the Moving Image (MOMI), Jubilee Gardens,* the *Hayward Gallery,* and two smaller halls, the 1,065-seat *Queen Elizabeth Hall* and the 370-seat *Purcell Room.* In addition to a program of 1,200 events that feature most major performers on the international music and lyric arts scenes, there are free foyer exhibitions and lunchtime concerts. Shops and dining facilities are open all day. South Bank, SE1 (phone: 171-928-8800).

Royal Opera House More informally known as *Covent Garden,* it's worth a look for its grandeur alone. This jewel of a 2,098-seat opera house, the third on the site, is splendidly Victorian, with red plush, shaded lights, scarlet and gold tiers, domed turquoise ceiling, and sweeping horseshoe-shaped balconies. But the play's the thing, and the best divas in the world have performed here—among them Dames Nellie Melba and Joan Sutherland, Maria Callas, and Dame Kiri Te Kanawa. The tradition of excellence continues today; the hall ranks among the world's half-dozen true greats. The *Royal Opera* shares the house with the *Royal Ballet,* which, under noted choreographers such as Sir Kenneth MacMillan, and featuring dancers such as Darcey

Bussell, Zoltan Solymosi, Viviana Durante, Anthony Dowell, Dame Margot Fonteyn, and Rudolf Nureyev, has become one of the world's most noted companies. *Covent Garden,* WC2 (phone: 171-240-1066 for the box office).

Wigmore Hall One of Europe's most elegant and intimate concert halls, this fine example of the Art Nouveau style—full of alabaster, marble, polished mahogany, and brass—was created in 1901 by Carl Bechstein (of piano fame) and is famous for its nearly perfect acoustics. A delightful hall for recitals and chamber music, it has hosted debuts by Elisabeth Schwarzkopf (in 1948) and Daniel Barenboim (in 1958) and recitals by Julian Bream, Peter Pears, Andrés Segovia, and many others. Arthur Rubinstein made his second appearance in England here (in 1912) and also his last public appearance (in 1976). Nowadays, the hall attracts artists such as Olaf Bär, Shura Cherkasky, and the *Beaux Arts Trio,* and has a regular series of celebrity and early music concerts, as well as a very popular series of *Sunday Morning Coffee Concerts.* 36 Wigmore St., W1 (phone: 171-935-2141).

Another fine venue for classical fare is the *Barbican Centre* (see *Theater*), home of the *London Symphony Orchestra.* Concerts also are often held in the dignified, splendid setting of *St. John's Church* (Smith Sq., SW1; phone: 171-222-1061). During the summer, outdoor concerts are given at *Kenwood, Crystal Palace,* and *Holland Park,* and bands play in many of London's parks.

In addition to the operatic productions at *Covent Garden,* the *English National Opera Company* performs in English at the *London Coliseum* (see *Theater,* above). If you wish to obtain opera tickets before departing from the US, contact *Edwards & Edwards* (see *Theater,* above).

Good live popular music can be heard in London's music pubs. Among the best of them are the *Dublin Castle* (94 Parkway, NW1; phone: 171-485-1773); *King's Head* (4 Fulham High St., SW6; phone: 171-736-1413); *Hare and Hounds* (181 Upper St., N1; phone: 171-226-2992); and *Half Moon* (93 Lower Richmond Rd., SW15; phone: 181-788-2387). If you are interested in purchasing tickets in the US to see pop and rock concerts featuring superstar performers in London, contact *Keith Prowse & Co., Ltd.* (see *Theater*).

NIGHTCLUBS AND NIGHTLIFE

London offers a lively and often wild nightlife, including nightclubs, jazz clubs, historical feasts, comedy clubs, and gambling casinos. Some wind up around midnight; most go on until well into the early morning hours. In *Covent Garden* and still-trendy Chelsea, particularly along King's and Fulham Roads, are fashionable pubs, wine bars, and restaurants. Two nightclubs with cabarets are *The Talk of London* (Drury La., WC2; phone: 171-408-1001) and *L'Hirondelle* (199 Swallow St., W1; phone: 171-734-1511). The best jazz clubs are *Ronnie Scott's* (47 Frith St., W1; phone: 171-439-0747) and *The 100 Club* (100 Oxford St., W1; phone: 171-636-0933). For jazz and a slice, try *Pizza Express* (10 Dean St., W1; phone: 171-437-9595) or *Pizza on the Park* (11 Knightsbridge, SW1; phone: 171-235-5550).

For a special (if touristy) treat, London offers the medieval banquet, with traditional meals served by costumed waiters and waitresses. Menus resemble those of Elizabethan feasts, and there is period music, horseplay, occasional mock sword fights, Shakespearean playlets, and other light entertainment. Try *Beefeater* (St. Katherine's Dock, E1; phone: 181-405-1516) and *The Cockney Cabaret* (161 Tottenham Court Rd., W1; phone: 171-224-9000); the first is a traditional banquet, while the second is a medieval floor show with dinner.

The disco scene is ever-changing, and many places—such as the pricey *Annabel's* (44 Berkeley Sq., W1; phone: 171-629-1096)—are open only to members. Clubs of the moment include the *Hippodrome* (Charing Cross Rd., WC2; phone: 171-437-4311); *Stringfellows* (16-19 Upper St. Martin's La., WC2; phone: 171-240-5534); *Legend's* (29 Old Burlington St., W1; phone: 171-437-9933); *Crazy Larry's* (Lots Rd., SW10; phone: 171-376-5555); and *Limelight* (136 Shaftesbury Ave., W1; phone: 171-434-0572). A smart club in West London is the *Broadway Boulevard* club (in Ealing; phone: 181-840-0616), particularly convenient for guests at the nearby *Heathrow Airport* hotels.

London's comedy scene took root in the early 1980s with the *Comedy Store* (cofounded by Mike Myers, later seen on "Saturday Night Live" and in the movie *Wayne's World*), which featured both stand-up performers and improvisational humor. Over the years, other similar clubs sprang up throughout the city, and nowadays there are more than 50 to choose from. The *Comedy Store* (1 Oxenden St., WC1; phone: 426-914433 for information), which has moved from its original home in Leicester Square into a larger venue, is still one of the best; top stand-up comedians appear here regularly, and the *Comedy Store Players,* the club's resident troupe, perform clever improvised skits based on audience suggestions. Other good venues are the *Canal Café Theatre* (*The Bridge House,* Delamere Ter., W2; phone: 171-289-6054) and *Jongleurs Battersea* (*The Cornet,* 49 Lavender Gardens, SW11; phone: 171-924-2766). *Time Out* has a complete listing of clubs and current performers.

Female impersonators regularly perform at the *Black Cap* (171 Camden High St., NW1; phone: 171-485-1742). For the latest on what's where in the gay scene, consult *Time Out* or call the *Lesbian and Gay Switchboard* (phone: 171-837-7324).

Best in Town

CHECKING IN

Visitors arriving in London between early spring and mid-autumn without hotel reservations are in for an unpleasant experience. For many years now, there has been a glaring shortage of hotel rooms in the British capital during the prime tourist season. (For a small fee, the *London Tourist Board and Convention Bureau* offices at *Victoria Station* and at the underground station in *Heathrow* will try to help you locate a room; see *Tourist Information.*) This fact, plus years of general inflation, is largely responsible for often excessive hotel charges, generally out of keeping with other costs in Britain. (Because of the current recession, however, room rates have stayed at the same level for the past several years. Also, some of the most expensive hotels may be willing to negotiate a lower rate or to include some luxury freebies, particularly in low season; there's no harm in asking.) Most of London's major hotels have complete facilities for the business traveler. Those hotels listed below as having business services usually offer such conveniences as a concierge, meeting rooms, photocopiers, computers, translation services, and express checkout, among others. Call the hotel for additional information. Very expensive and expensive hotels do not include breakfast; moderate, inexpensive, and very inexpensive hotels generally include continental or full English breakfast. In our selections, prices are $375 or more per night for a double room (including private bath, phone, and TV set, unless otherwise noted, and sometimes including VAT and a 10% service charge) in a very expensive hotel; $250 to $350, expensive; $150 to $250, moderate; $100 to $150, inexpensive; and less than $100, very inexpensive.

For an unforgettable experience in London, we begin with our favorite lodging places (they're pricey, but worth it), followed by our cost and quality choices, listed by price category.

GRAND AND BABY GRAND HOTELS

Blake's Popular with visiting Hollywood royalty, this 52-room complex of Victorian townhouses (including nine suites) offers charming accommodations in an Old World setting: Many of the rooms are decorated in shades of gray, with antique furniture, four-poster beds, and marble baths. Also offered is some of the most attentive service in town, as well as features such as laundry service, 24-hour room service, a concierge, foreign currency exchange, and business services. The hotel also boasts a first-rate restaurant. 33 Roland Gardens, SW7 (phone: 171-370-6701; fax: 171-373-0442).

Capital This intimate hostelry, just steps from *Harrods,* has 48 cozy rooms and suites with Ralph Lauren–like decor, a wonderful wood-paneled bar, and one of the finest dining places in London (see *Eating Out*). And it's one of only two London hotels in the prestigious Relais & Châteaux group (*Fortyseven Park Street* is the other—see below). Don't be put off by its ultramodern exterior; once inside, you'll find everything according to British tradition, taste, and tact. Even the single rooms, though quite small, are cozy and inviting. And no matter when you arrive, service is always warm and prompt. The eight suites are like enchanting apartments—homey in the very best sense. Breakfast is served on delightful "basket trays." Long-term visitors (which means a minimum of three *months*) also can choose to stay in one of the hotel's super-luxurious apartments, located just steps away from the main building. These comfortable suites include a choice of one, two, or three bedrooms, living rooms with ample dining tables, and fully equipped kitchens. Residents here may take advantage of all of the hotel's amenities, which include 24-hour room service, foreign currency exchange, and business services. 22 Basil St., SW3 (phone: 171-589-5171; 800-926-3199; fax: 171-225-0011).

Claridge's Here is the final bastion of the British Empire. Despite its sober red brick façade, its supreme, traditional elegance is as much a part of the London experience as the Horse Guards and the *Crown Jewels.* The 136 rooms and 54 suites are beautifully decorated in Art Deco or traditional style; the bathrooms are worth fighting for. When visiting royalty is in residence here—which is often—the flags of their countries are flown outside, beside the Union Jack. The concierge, however, accords the same personalized attention to monarchs and commoners alike: Regulars will find their favorite soaps and shampoos—even their pillow preferences—waiting in their rooms. Female guests are welcome to use the fitness and pool facilities at the *Berkeley* hotel (see below), since only men are granted entry to the *Bath and Racquet Club* located behind *Claridge's.* In winter, try for a suite with a working fireplace. There is also fine dining in two restaurants. Other amenities include 24-hour room service, foreign currency exchange, and business services. Brook St., W1 (phone: 171-629-8860; 212-838-3110 in New York City; 800-223-6800 elsewhere in the US; fax: 171-499-2210).

Connaught Another stronghold of 19th-century Britain, luxurious and intimate, that soon will have you feeling like a distinguished guest at Lord Hyphen's townhouse. Most impressive are the small details—like tea served in a private lounge reserved only for guests, and the white linen mats laid out every night at your bedside (heaven forbid that you should have to step down onto a carpet, or worse yet, a wood floor!). Small (only 90 rooms and suites)—with a tenaciously faithful clientele—it sometimes seems to be booked several generations in advance. Some may be put off by the hauteur. The two dining rooms each have earned a Michelin star (see *Eating Out*). Additional amenities include 24-hour room service, foreign currency exchange, two private dining rooms, and business services. Carlos Pl., W1 (phone: 171-499-7070; 212-838-3110 in New York City; 800-223-6800 elsewhere in the US; fax: 171-495-3262).

Dorchester The grande dame of London hostelries is more elegant than ever. All 252 rooms and 55 suites have beautiful bed linen and superbly designed bathrooms with Italian marble. (If you can, get the Oliver Messel Suite, whose bedroom, bath, and sitting room were decorated by the great theater designer.) Best of all, the service is fit for royalty. Treat yourself to an elegant afternoon tea in the pink marble *Promenade.* Tuxedoed waiters serve a variety of sandwiches, as well as excellent teas, scones with clotted cream, the best strawberry jam in London, and pastries. And dinner at the *Grill* or *Terrace* restaurant is always a treat. The *Oriental* restaurant has earned a Michelin star (see *Eating Out*), and there is an exclusive basement nightspot—the *Dorchester Club.* The *Dorchester Spa,* featuring Elizabeth Arden products, is a luxurious health club. Additional amenities include 24-hour room service, foreign currency exchange, and business services. Park La., W1 (phone: 171-629-8888; 800-727-9820; fax: 171-409-0114).

Dukes Despite its modest size (only 38 rooms and 26 suites), this establishment exudes nobility and prestige. Here are all the comforts of home, coupled with the attentive service that one leaves home to get. The exterior has an elegant Edwardian façade, there's a peaceful flower-filled courtyard, and some suites are named for former dukes. All the guestrooms and public areas are decorated with great taste and warmth, and the snug location, down a quiet cul-de-sac, makes guests feel protected and private. Some of the suites are actually former apartments in the building next to the original hotel, with their own small—but complete—kitchens. Afternoon tea is a formal affair served in the lounge or the elegant dining room. Piccadilly, *Buckingham Palace,* Trafalgar Square, Hyde Park Corner, and the shops of Bond Street and the *Burlington Arcade* are all within walking distance. Additional amenities include 24-hour room service, foreign currency exchange, and business services. 35 St. James's Pl., SW1 (phone: 171-491-4840; 800-222-0939; fax: 171-493-1264).

Fortyseven Park Street Once one of our most cherished secrets, this now very popular hotel (a Relais & Châteaux member) combines English character with French flair. The 52 large, beautifully decorated apartments, featuring full kitchens and marble baths, are ideal for long-term stays. The luxurious furnishings are in the best English taste; after a recent £3-million renovation, the decor now features muted, autumnal colors. Breakfast alone is worth crossing the Atlantic to experience, since "room service" here is provided by the elegant *Le Gavroche* restaurant downstairs (see *Eating Out*). The location, roughly between *Hyde Park* and Grosvenor Square, also is ideal. A drawback is that the lounge has no liquor license. Additional amenities include 24-hour room service, foreign currency exchange, access to a nearby health club, and business services. 47 Park St., W1 (phone: 171-491-7282; 800-451-5536; fax: 171-491-7281).

Ritz One of the city's finest and most elegant hostelries, this property recently came under the management of Mandarin Oriental, a Hong Kong–based hotel group. The 129 luxurious guestrooms and suites are lavishly decorated. Tea here is as vital a British ritual as the coronation: In probably the most formal tearoom in the city, gracious white-tied waiters carrying silver trays serve guests in the lovely Louis XIV–style *Palm Court* (reservations necessary at least two weeks in advance for weekends and a week in advance for weekdays). The dining room is equally splendid, with its lovely interior columns, opulent ceiling frescoes, and a view of *Green Park.* Try to have cocktails on the terrace—if the sun comes out. Additional amenities include 24-hour room service, foreign currency exchange, and business services. Piccadilly, W1 (phone: 171-493-8181; 800-526-6566; fax: 171-493-2687).

Savoy This 200-room hostelry is to theater what the *Sacher* in Vienna is to music. On The Strand, and very near *Covent Garden* and Waterloo Bridge, this grande dame (she's now 106) remains one of *the* places to stay in London; its lobby is often a *Who's Who* of the international entertainment world. The atmosphere is gently Edwardian, but the management is contemporary—and adept at catering to the demands of plutocrats from every part of the planet. The Thames Suites are London's most beautiful digs. A health club is cleverly sited above the famous *Savoy Theatre,* restored to its former grandeur after the damage caused by a 1990 fire. In addition, there's the *River* restaurant, with a splendid view of the Thames and *Big Ben,* and the legendary *Savoy Grill* (see *Eating Out*); hotel guests can have tea in an open foyer off the lobby. Additional amenities include 24-hour room service, foreign currency exchange, and business services. The Strand, WC2 (phone: 171-836-4343; 800-63-SAVOY; fax: 171-240-6040).

22 Jermyn Street Nestled in the heart of the West End, on one of the city's most fashionable streets, this privately owned, club-like hostelry offers intimacy, charm, and attentive service just a stone's throw from London's best shopping, theater, and other attractions. The 18 rooms and suites are decorated with a pleasing combination of modern and antique furniture; amenities include cable TV, two direct-dial phones, fax machines, and luxurious marble bathrooms. There's no restaurant (although a complimentary breakfast and 24-hour room service are provided); owners Henry and Suzanne Togna will gladly steer you to one of the several fine eateries in the neighborhood. Additional amenities include a valet, foreign currency exchange, access to a nearby health club, and business services. 22 Jermyn St., SW1 (phone: 171-734-2353; 800-682-7808; fax: 171-734-0750).

VERY EXPENSIVE

Berkeley Remarkably understated, this 160-room hotel in Knightsbridge manages to preserve its impeccably high standards while keeping a low profile. Soft-spoken service complements the tastefully lavish, traditional English decor. There also is a restaurant featuring classic French fare, a health club and a rooftop gym with pool. Additional amenities include 24-hour room service, foreign currency exchange, and business services. Wilton Pl., SW1 (phone: 171-235-6000; 212-838-3110 in New York City; 800-223-6800 elsewhere in the US; fax: 171-235-4330).

Four Seasons Don't be deceived by the modern exterior; everything is traditional (and wonderful) within. A fine example of the superb service routinely offered by members of the Canadian chain, this hotel offers 228 rooms (including 27 suites) that are comfortable, tastefully furnished, and spacious. The breakfast buffet is delightful, the restaurant is first-rate, and there is a fully equipped fitness center. Additional amenities include 24-hour room service, foreign currency exchange, and business services. Hamilton Pl., off Piccadilly, W1 (phone: 171-499-0888; 800-332-3442; fax: 171-493-1895).

Grosvenor House This elegant 454-room (including 77 suites and 144 apartments with kitchenettes) grande dame facing *Hyde Park* has a health club, a pool, some interesting shops; the much-lauded and Michelin-starred *Nico at 90* restaurant (see *Eating Out*); the *Park Lounge,* which serves traditional afternoon tea; and the exclusive *Crown Club* on the seventh floor for members only—usually businesspeople who require special services. Additional amenities include 24-hour room service, foreign currency exchange, and business services. Park La., W1 (phone: 171-499-6363; 800-225-5843; fax: 171-493-3341).

Inter-Continental Right on Hyde Park Corner, with a view of the Horse Guards as they trot off for the Changing of the Guard, this hotel has just completed a £3.4-million renovation; its 467 well-proportioned rooms (including 38 suites) are equipped with luxurious amenities, including refrigerated bars. Modern and comfortable, *Le Soufflé* restaurant is an added lure. Additional facilities include 24-hour room service, foreign currency exchange, and business services. 1 Hamilton Pl., Hyde Park Corner, W1 (phone: 171-409-3131; 800-327-0200; fax: 171-493-3476).

Lanesborough Just steps from the *Wellington Gate* in the tony Belgravia area, this luxury hotel at Hyde Park Corner is built within the landmark structure that was *St. George's Hospital* from 1734 to 1980. The interior design re-creates the feeling of an elegant 19th-century residence. There are 95 superbly appointed guestrooms, including 46 suites, some with steam showers and Jacuzzis. Dinner dances on Fridays and Saturdays and Sunday brunches with live jazz are held in the somewhat LA-ish *Conservatory,* which also offers light meals and afternoon tea. Both the club-like *Library* and the *Withdrawing Room* have bars. Additional amenities include 24-hour room service, foreign currency exchange, and business services. Knightsbridge and Grosvenor Crescent, SW1 (phone: 171-259-5599; 800-999-1828; fax: 171-259-5606).

Langham Hilton Originally opened in 1865 as "the first grand hotel of London," it was known for its "rising rooms" (elevators) and famous guests, including Mark Twain, Arturo Toscanini, and Oscar Wilde. The property offers 385 well-appointed rooms (including 26 suites), and its several restaurants include the *Palm Court,* serving light meals and snacks around the clock, and *Tsar's,* specializing in vodka and caviar. Additional amenities include 24-hour room service, foreign currency exchange, and business services. 1c Portland Pl., W1 (phone: 171-636-1000; 800-HILTONS; fax: 171-323-2340).

London Hilton International Well situated off Hyde Park Corner, near shopping and West End theaters, this contemporary high-rise offers comfortable accommodations (448 rooms, including 54 suites) and spectacular views of the park and the city. Special attention to executives includes a conference and business floor, multilingual switchboard, and private dining rooms. There's every conceivable service, plus three restaurants—the rooftop *Windows,* with a stunning view of the city; *Trader Vic's* (Polynesian); and the *Brasserie.* Additional amenities include 24-hour room service, foreign currency exchange, and business services. 22 Park La., W1 (phone: 171-493-8000; 800-HILTONS; fax: 171-493-4957).

Le Meridien Located between the *Royal Academy* and Piccadilly Circus, this hotel has a lofty, Edwardian marble entrance hall that leads to the 263 rooms, including 41 suites. Some of the accommodations here are on the smallish, dark side. The one-Michelin-star *Oak Room* restaurant offers fine French fare. The *Terrace* restaurant, on the second floor, has a glass roof, and the space beneath the hotel has been transformed into a very good health club. Afternoon tea in the lounge is accompanied by a harpist. Additional amenities include 24-hour room service, foreign currency exchange, and business services. Piccadilly, W1 (phone: 171-734-8000; 800-543-4300; fax: 171-437-3574).

St. James's Club For $675 for the first year ($450 thereafter) and an introduction by a member, you can join this exclusive residential club in the heart of London (though you don't need to bother for your first stay). Guests have full use of club suites. Good food is served in the downstairs dining room. Additional amenities include 24-hour room service, foreign currency exchange, and business services. 7 Park Pl., SW1 (phone: 171-629-7688; fax: 171-491-0987).

EXPENSIVE

Abbey Court In the Notting Hill Gate area near *Portobello Market,* this elegant hotel has 22 guestrooms of various sizes, all with hair dryers and trouser presses. The flowers in the common areas are especially lovely. Breakfast is served in the room, and 24-hour room service is available. No restaurant. Business services are offered. 20 Pembridge Gardens, W2 (phone: 171-221-7518; fax: 171-792-0858).

Athenaeum Hotel and Apartments Reopened last year after a $12-million renovation, this property is ideally located in the heart of the stylish Mayfair district, overlooking *Green Park* and *Buckingham Palace.* The 111 guestrooms and 12 suites are decorated in traditional English style with antique furnishings and floral fabrics; amenities include marble baths, mini-bars, in-room safes, satellite TV, compact disc players, and VCRs. The luxurious *Athenaeum Apartments,* located in a row of Edwardian townhouses next to the hotel, are also available. The 33 one-, two-, and three-bedroom apartments are equipped with a full kitchen (including a microwave oven), living and sitting rooms, and a washing machine and dryer; in addition, residents have access to all of the hotel's facilities. *Bullochs,* the hotel dining room, serves Mediterranean fare in an informal atmosphere; and the *Windsor Lounge* offers light snacks and teas around the clock. There's also the Scottish-style *Malt Whisky Bar,* which boasts a selection of 56 rare whiskies. Other facilities include 24-hour room service, complimentary transportation from the airport, baby-sitting services, a health club with fitness machines, a sauna, a Jacuzzi, and spa treatments, and business services. 116 Piccadilly, W1 (phone: 171-499-3464; 800-335-3300; fax: 171-493-1860; 800-335-3200).

Basil Street A relic with a reputation for graceful, old-fashioned service and antique furnishings to match. It draws a faithful international clientele who, if they can reserve one of its 94 smallish rooms, prefer staying here to patronizing any of the modern, impersonal, newer hotels. It sits just down the street from *Harrods.* Other amenities include 24-hour room service, foreign currency exchange, and business services. 8 Basil St., SW3 (phone: 171-581-3311; fax: 171-581-3693).

Beaufort Tranquil and elegant, it is composed of two Victorian houses in the heart of fashionable Knightsbridge. It offers 52 comfortable and attractive rooms, each with stereo/cassette player, hair dryer, magazines and books, a decanter of sherry, and even a teddy bear for the youngsters. Breakfast is brought on a tray each morning; there is no restaurant, but there are many in the area. All drinks and snacks are included. Convenient to shopping (*Harrods* is around the corner). Business services are available. 33 Beaufort Gardens, SW3 (phone: 171-584-5252; 800-888-1199; fax: 171-589-2834).

Britannia Mahogany furniture, velvet armchairs, rooms painted in colors you might choose at home—all tasteful and solid, despite the anonymous (but spacious) foyer with the pretentious chandeliers. This is where the nearby *US Embassy* often puts up middle-ranking State Department officials. This link in the Inter-Continental chain has 316 rooms and suites, as well as three restaurants. Additional amenities include 24-hour room service, foreign currency exchange, and business services. Grosvenor Sq., W1 (phone: 171-629-9400; 800-327-0200; fax: 171-629-7736).

Brown's As English as you can get, it's been renovated, yet still retains a pleasing, quaint, Victorian charm, not at all marred by heavy, sturdy furniture or the somewhat hushed atmosphere. With 109 rooms (including six suites), this hotel is strong on service. If it's an English tea you're after, this is the place (casual dress is acceptable, but not shorts). Additional amenities include a restaurant, 24-hour room service, foreign currency exchange, and business services. Dover St., W1 (phone: 171-493-6020; fax: 171-493-9381).

Cadogan A comfortable 75-room place, redolent of Edwardian England. Oscar Wilde was arrested here, and Lillie Langtry, who was having an affair with the Prince of Wales (later Edward VII), lived next door. The furniture and decor are original, but modern conveniences are offered as well. Amenities include a restaurant, 24-hour room service, foreign currency exchange, and business services. 75 Sloane St., SW1 (phone: 171-235-7141; fax: 171-245-0994).

Chesterfield In the heart of Mayfair and near *Hyde Park*, this small, rebuilt Georgian mansion has a certain exclusive elegance. Its 110 bedrooms are thoroughly modernized and well equipped. There's a restaurant, a wood-paneled library, and a small bar that opens onto a flower-filled patio. Additional amenities include 24-hour room service, foreign currency exchange, and business services. 35 Charles St., W1 (phone: 171-491-2622; fax: 171-491-4793).

Churchill Still thought of as an "American"-style hotel, it remains a favorite among travelers headed to London from the US. Inside, a turn-of-the-century mood is reflected in the discreet decor. This is a well-run 448-room place, with a pleasant restaurant and a snack room that serves the best bacon and eggs in London. Additional amenities include 24-hour room service, foreign currency exchange, and business services. Portman Sq., W1 (phone: 171-486-5800; fax: 171-486-1255).

Cranley Sister hotel of *One Cranley Place* (see below), this is larger, with 36 rooms and suites and plusher furnishings. The unusual decor, described by its

American owner as "gutsy," is bolder than that found in most townhouse hotels. With microwave ovens in the kitchenettes, plus showers and firm mattresses straight from the US, the aim is to provide the comforts of home. Business services are available. 10-12 Bina Gardens, SW5 (phone: 171-373-0123; 313-995-4400 in Michigan; 800-553-2582 elsewhere in the US; fax: 171-373-9497; 313-995-1050).

Delmere This lovely, late Georgian hostelry was designed by architect Samuel Pepys Cockerell, a student of Benjamin H. Latrobe, who designed the south wing of the Capitol building in Washington, DC. Its 40 rooms have private showers or baths, hair dryers, and the makings for tea and coffee. There is also a bar and an Italian restaurant, *La Perla.* The staff, mostly from Holland, is very friendly. *Paddington Station,* where trains depart to Bath and south Wales, is a mere five-minute walk away, as is *Hyde Park.* Additional amenities include 24-hour room service, foreign currency exchange, and business services. 130 Sussex Gardens, W2 (phone: 171-706-3344; fax: 171-262-1863).

Draycott The 26 rooms here are each distinctively decorated. While there's no restaurant, there is 24-hour room service, as well as a drawing room. Staying here is like living in a fashionable London townhouse, and guests must register 48 hours before arrival to become members upon their first visit. Business services are available. 24-26 Cadogan Gardens, SW3 (phone: 171-730-6466; fax: 171-730-0236).

Egerton House Overlooking two garden squares, this property in Knightsbridge is set in a fashionable townhouse. The 30 spacious guestrooms are individually decorated with antiques, traditional English floral fabrics, porcelain, and oil paintings; among the amenities are marble baths, mini-bars, and satellite TV. The atmosphere has an old-fashioned tranquillity, and the service is friendly and attentive. Other facilities include a restaurant, 24-hour room service, and business services. 17-19 Egerton Ter., SW3 (phone: 171-589-2412; 800-473-9492; fax: 171-584-6540).

Gatwick Hilton International This 550-room hotel provides much-needed accommodations for the ever-increasing number of visitors using the *Gatwick* gateway. It is connected to the terminal by an enclosed walkway. There are two restaurants, two bars, a health club, and lounge service. Additional amenities include 24-hour room service, foreign currency exchange, and business services. *Gatwick Airport* (phone: 1293-518080; 800-HILTONS; fax: 1293-528980).

Halcyon The two Belle Epoque mansions that are the foundations of this property have been restored to their original glamour. Some of the 44 guestrooms feature four-poster beds and Jacuzzis, plus all modern conveniences. Its restaurant is one of London's best hotel dining spots. Additional amenities include 24-hour room service, foreign currency exchange, and business services. 81 Holland Park, W11 (phone: 171-727-7288; fax: 171-229-8516).

Halkin This intimate property in the Belgravia area, right near *Buckingham Palace* and *Hyde Park,* boasts 41 individually designed rooms and suites, furnished with a mixture of contemporary and antique pieces. The hotel's restaurant, serving fine Italian food, overlooks a pretty garden. Additional amenities include 24-hour room service, foreign currency exchange, and business services. 5-6 Halkin St., SW1 (phone: 171-333-1000; 800-345-3457; fax: 171-333-1100).

Heathrow Hilton A first-rate hotel at *Heathrow Airport,* with its own covered walkway to Terminal 4. Designed by Michael Manser, it is shaped like a parallelogram, with a five-story glass atrium enclosing a waterfall; there also are three restaurants. The 400 rooms are amazingly quiet (given the location) and are decorated in shades of blue and gray; amenities include everything from trouser presses to an in-room review of accounts and express check-out—on your TV screen. The health club has a pool, gym, steamrooms, and saunas. Additional amenities include 24-hour room service, foreign currency exchange, and business services. Terminal 4, *Heathrow Airport,* Hounslow, Middlesex (phone: 181-759-7755; 800-HILTONS; fax: 181-759-7579).

Holiday Inn Mayfair The Regency-style architecture is unusual for this hotel chain. In London's prestigious Mayfair neighborhood, the property has 185 rooms and the à la carte *Nightingale's* restaurant, with a pianist in the cocktail bar in the evenings. Additional amenities include 24-hour room service, foreign currency exchange, and business services. 3 Berkeley St., W1 (phone: 171-493-8282; 800-HOLIDAY; fax: 171-629-2827).

Hyde Park The only hotel in *Hyde Park,* this establishment—formerly apartments during Victorian times—hosted Rudolph Valentino in the 1920s and George VI and Queen Elizabeth in 1948. The 186 spacious bedrooms and suites feature antique furniture and modern baths. Some rooms also have spectacular views of the park. Marble stairs, chandeliers, and plants are part of the hotel's elegant decor. With huge windows providing panoramic views of *Hyde Park,* the *Park Room* restaurant offers delicious meals, including breakfast—but avoid afternoon tea here. A second dining room, *The Restaurant,* is run by renowned chef Marco Pierre White (see *Eating Out*). Additional amenities include 24-hour room service, foreign currency exchange, and business services. 66 Knightsbridge, SW1 (phone: 171-235-2000; 800-225-5843; fax: 171-235-4552).

London Marriott Close to the *US Embassy* and West End shopping, it's bright and busy, with 223 comfortable rooms and a full range of facilities—a restaurant, café-lounge, shops, a fitness center, attentive staff, foreign currency exchange, and business services. Grosvenor Sq., W1 (phone: 171-493-1232; 800-228-9290; fax: 171-491-3201).

Montcalm A mid-size, elegant hostelry that has a lovely Georgian façade, a warm, understated interior, and topnotch service. Its 98 rooms have all the usual comforts, and its 14 suites are especially luxurious. There's a bar and *Les Célébrités* restaurant. Additional amenities include 24-hour room service, foreign currency exchange, and business services. Great Cumberland Pl., W1 (phone: 171-402-4288; fax: 171-724-9180).

Number Sixteen In four adjoining townhouses, this delightfully comfortable 36-room spot has an accent on personal service. Rooms (some of which have terraces overlooking a conservatory and gardens) feature fresh flowers; most have private baths or showers (though a few singles do not). Continental breakfast is served in all rooms. There is a small bar, but no restaurant. Because of its quiet atmosphere, it is not suitable for small children. Business services are available. 16 Sumner Pl., SW7 (phone: 171-589-5232; fax: 171-584-8615).

Park Lane If you don't mind the noise of the city streets, the site of this hotel, in the heart of the West End, is appealing. Some of the 300 rooms (including 56 suites) have views of *Green Park* across the street, and there is a gym. *Bracewell's* restaurant is an elegant dining spot, and *Brasserie on the Park* is a less formal option. Additional amenities include 24-hour room service, foreign currency exchange, and business services. Piccadilly, W1 (phone: 171-499-6321; fax: 171-499-1965).

Pelham Actually two joined mid-Victorian townhouses in South Kensington that offer 34 stylish (though smallish) rooms and three suites, just steps away from the *Victoria and Albert, Natural History,* and *Science Museums.* There is also a restaurant and two lounges. Additional amenities include 24-hour room service, foreign currency exchange, and business services. 15 Cromwell Pl., SW7 (phone: 171-589-8288; 800-553-6671; fax: 171-584-8444).

Radisson Mountbatten The life of Earl Mountbatten of Burma is the theme throughout this hotel's public rooms, all with exhibitions of various mementos from India. Even the restaurant is called *L'Admiral,* since the earl was a navy man. All 127 rooms feature Italian marble bathrooms, satellite TV, and in-house movies; seven suites have Jacuzzis. A vegetarian tea (scones without animal fat) is served in the country-house–style drawing room decorated with oak paneling and a fireplace. Additional amenities include 24-hour room service, foreign currency exchange, and business services. 20 Monmouth St. at Seven Dials, *Covent Garden,* WC2 (phone: 171-836-4300; 800-333-3333; fax: 171-240-3540).

Regent One of London's newest ultra-posh hotels is also one of its oldest. Originally opened in 1899 next to *Marylebone Station,* this hotel had its career cut short by World War II, but it is now restored to its former splendor. The 309 rooms are richly decorated with Victorian-era furnishings, but modern amenities abound (including two-line telephones and fax machines). The dining room serves French and northern Italian dishes; *Cellars* and the glassed-in *Winter Garden* (which incorporates the original courtyard) serve light fare. Additional amenities include 24-hour room service, foreign currency exchange, and business services. 222 Marylebone Rd., NW1 (phone: 171-631-8000; 212-838-3110 in New York City; 800-223-6800 elsewhere in the US; fax: 171-631-8080).

Stafford In a surprisingly quiet side street close to the city center, this property (owned by Cunard) is where many American television and newspaper organizations often lodge visiting correspondents to give them efficient, friendly, British small-hotel management at its best. The main building has 62 rooms; in addition, the 18th-century stables down the alleyway have 12 "Carriage House" rooms which are decorated in smashing style (complete with compact disc and stereo systems and fax lines). Enjoy tea in the cozy drawing room, complete with fireplaces and comfortable furniture. Additional amenities include a restaurant, 24-hour room service, foreign currency exchange, and business services. 16 St. James's Pl., SW1 (phone: 171-493-0111; 800-525-4800; fax: 171-493-7121).

Whites What used to be three 19th-century merchant bankers' private homes now make up one of London's most charming small hostelries, with 54 rooms. This hotel has personality that larger places lack—a cobbled forecourt, a glass-and-iron-covered entryway, even a wood-paneled writing room where afternoon tea is served. Choose a front room overlooking *Hyde Park,* and take breakfast on the balcony. Additional amenities include 24-hour room service, foreign currency exchange, and business services. 90-92 Lancaster Gate, W2 (phone: 171-262-2711; fax: 171-262-2147).

MODERATE

Academy Not far from the *University of London* and the *British Museum,* this 33-room property in three Georgian townhouses scores for its handy location. Colorful modern art and pretty floral curtains and bedspreads make the rooms cheery whether they are on the ground floor or upstairs. Paperbacks can be borrowed from the library, which overlooks a small patio garden at the back. The stylish restaurant and bar are in the basement. Another attraction—there is an "American Friends" discount (about 10%) for travelers from the US. 17-21 Gower St., WC1 (phone: 171-631-4115; 800-678-3096; fax: 171-636-3442).

Claverley A favorite with Americans, this establishment in Knightsbridge has 32 rooms (including five suites), most of which have private baths; some rooms have four-poster beds. All bedrooms have floral decor, and each has a heated towel rack in the bathroom. Guests are invited to help themselves to newspapers, coffee, tea, and cookies in the reading room. A fine British breakfast (including kippers and kedgeree) is served in the morning (however, there is no restaurant). Just a block from *Harrods.* Business services are available. 13 Beaufort Gardens, SW3 (phone: 171-589-8541; fax: 171-584-3410).

Copthorne Tara Situated on a quiet corner of Kensington, this 825-room giant is just minutes from bustling High Street and within walking distance of the *Albert Hall,* the *Victoria and Albert Museum,* and the *Natural History Museum,* and just a short jog from *Kensington Gardens.* The rooms are on the small side, but all have hair dryers. There also are six fully equipped business suites, four restaurants, a nightclub, a baby-sitting service, and a garage. Additional amenities include 24-hour room service, foreign currency exchange, and business services. Wright's La., W8 (phone: 171-937-7211; 800-44-UTELL; fax: 171-937-7100).

Diplomat Small and charming, with an 1882 white façade, it has 27 rooms. It is comfortable, friendly, and affordable. There is a breakfast room, but no restaurant. In Belgravia at 2 Chesham St., SW1 (phone: 171-235-1544; fax: 171-259-6153).

Dorset Square Set on a lovely garden square (formerly Thomas Lord's own private cricket grounds) in the heart of London, this Georgian house is one of the city's more charming hotels. Guests can choose from 37 rooms and suites. There is a restaurant and 24-hour room service. Business services are available. 39-40 Dorset Sq., NW1 (phone: 171-723-7874; fax: 171-724-3328).

Durrants This elegant Regency-style hotel has a splendid location behind the *Wallace Collection,* and is only a few minutes' walk from the Oxford Street shopping district. It has been family-run for over 70 years, and all 95 rooms have retained their character while being kept comfortably up-to-date. Additional amenities include a restaurant, 24-hour room service, foreign currency exchange, and business services. George St., W1 (phone: 171-935-8131; fax: 171-487-3510).

Ebury Court A quaint hotel with smallish but cozy rooms and an intimate atmosphere (the owners dine with guests in the restaurant). Its faithful clientele testifies to its comfort, suitability, and "country-house" touches. Hard to beat—all things considered—in a town where hotel prices tend to be unreasonable. Half of the 42 rooms have private baths or showers. Business services are available. 28 Ebury St., SW1 (phone: 171-730-8147; fax: 171-823-5966).

Forte Crest St. James' This modern 254-room property offers one of the best locations in central London, a block from Piccadilly. There is a restaurant and a pleasant bar. Additional amenities include 24-hour room service, foreign currency exchange, and business services. 81 Jermyn St., SW1 (phone: 171-930-2111; 800-225-5843; fax: 171-839-2125).

Gore Ten-foot-tall potted palms and a collection of 5,000 prints on the walls set the tone in this 54-room hostelry, just five minutes from *Albert Hall* and the shopping on Kensington High Street. Wall safes are an unusual addition to conveniences such as hair dryers and mini-bars in the rooms. If you can't stay in the Judy Garland room, with its carved medieval-style bed, at least ask to see it. The *Bistro 190* is a popular dining spot, and room service delivers from 7:30 AM to 12:30 AM. Additional amenities include 24-hour room service, foreign currency exchange, and business services. 189 Queen's Gate, SW7 (phone: 171-584-6601; fax: 171-589-8127).

Harewood This modern property is well maintained by a pleasant, efficient staff. Some of its 93 rooms have private terraces, and there's a clubhouse-style lounge that serves food. Additional amenities include 24-hour room service and business services. Harewood Row, NW1 (phone: 171-262-2707; fax: 171-262-2975).

Hazlitt's Formerly the nurses' quarters for the *Royal Women's Hospital* during Victorian times, this row of three adjacent Georgian terrace houses now serves as a cozy bed and breakfast establishment. The *National Trust* building has 23 rooms, each individually decorated in Victorian flavor. Hung on the walls are 2,000 prints depicting Victorian London. Business services are available. 6 Frith St., W1 (phone: 171-434-1771; fax: 171-439-1524).

L'Hotel Owned by the same folks as the wonderful *Capital* just a step away, this comfortable—and much less expensive—12-room bed and breakfast place has a New England colonial–style decor, with pine furniture and a huge patchwork quilt hung over the stairs. All rooms have mini-bars and kettles for making tea or coffee; four rooms have fireplaces. Complimentary continental breakfast is served in *Le Metro* bistro next door or in your room, and laundry and dry-cleaning services are available. Business facilities can be arranged through the *Capital.* 28 Basil St., SW3 (phone: 171-589-6286; 800-926-3199; fax: 171-225-0011).

One Cranley Place Set among a row of Regency houses in South Kensington, this charming and personal bed and breakfast establishment is like a private home. Unique antique pieces furnish the 10 individually decorated rooms (from double rooms to luxury double suites), and fireplaces in some rooms and the common areas make for an exceptionally cozy atmosphere. Some rooms overlook the quiet mews at the back, and there is a small garden. Breakfast is served in the dining room or guestrooms; tea and light snacks also are available. Guests have access to the services of its sister property, the *Cranley* (see above). 1 Cranley Pl., SW7 (phone: 171-589-7944; 313-995-4400 in Michigan; 800-553-2582 elsewhere in the US; fax: 171-225-3931; 313-995-1050).

Pastoria In the heart of the West End, near all theaters, this pleasant, comfortable little hotel has 58 rooms, a bar, a restaurant, 24-hour room service, foreign currency exchange, and business services. St. Martin's St., WC2 (phone: 171-930-8641; fax: 171-925-0551).

Pembridge Court Recommended by bed and breakfast aficionados, this cozy Victorian townhouse has a variety of room sizes, from large doubles to tiny singles. The bistro serves English breakfasts and French fare for dinner. Business services are available. 34 Pembridge Gardens, W2 (phone: 171-229-9977; fax: 171-727-4982).

Portobello Antiques are a main feature in this hostelry, converted from two Victorian row houses, located near the *Portobello Market.* The 25 rooms come in all shapes and sizes; the bathrooms tend to be quite small. There is an informal restaurant and bar. Business services are available. 22 Stanley Gardens, W11 (phone: 171-727-2777; fax: 171-792-9641).

INEXPENSIVE

Bickenhall This Georgian townhouse near the *Baker Street* tube station boasts 18 comfortable rooms and bathrooms with showers and hair dryers (three rooms on the top floor share a bath), as well as a quiet location. No restaurant. 119 Gloucester Pl., W1 (phone: 171-935-3401; fax: 171-224-0614).

Blandford Another pleasant bed and breakfast establishment, this one has 33 rooms, decorated in pastel greens and pinks. No restaurant. 80 Chiltern St., W1 (phone: 171-486-3103; fax: 171-487-2786).

Camelot In this quaint townhouse hotel, each of the 44 rooms is a different size and shape, and each features different amenities—for example, one of the guestrooms has a four-poster bed and another a little balcony. In the basement dining room (which serves breakfast only), the wood floor, fireplace, and pine tables lend a rustic look. 45-47 Norfolk Sq., W2 (phone: 171-723-9118; fax: 171-402-3412).

Elizabeth Overlooking a pretty garden square, this family-run hotel offers 40 neat rooms of varying sizes. Though short on fancy amenities (the rooms do not have phones or TV sets, and only 28 have private baths), this place provides good, basic accommodations for a reasonable price. No restaurant. 37 Eccleston Sq., SW1 (phone: 171-628-6812).

Hallam Incorporated into a modern office complex near Oxford Circus, this well-run establishment has 25 guestrooms that are small, but clean and nicely decorated. No restaurant. 12 Hallam St., W1 (phone: 171-580-1166; fax: 171-323-4527).

Hotel la Place This is a fine bed and breakfast place with 24 rooms, each featuring one king-size or two double beds; some rooms also have mini-bars. A full English breakfast is served in the morning; there is also a restaurant. Additional amenities include 24-hour room service and business services. 17 Nottingham Pl., W1 (phone: 171-486-2323; fax: 171-486-4335).

Winchester Near *Victoria Station,* this 18-room bed and breakfast place is in an old townhouse with a Victorian-style façade. Guests are treated to an English breakfast in the morning. No restaurant. 17 Belgrave Rd., SW1 (phone: 171-828-2972; fax: 171-828-5191).

Windermere Here is an attractive hotel with 23 nicely furnished and appointed guestrooms (19 have private baths). Several of the rooms are equipped with small refrigerators in addition to the usual amenities. There's also a good dining room decorated with some surprisingly elegant touches, such as fine china and fresh flowers. 142-144 Warwick Way, SW1 (phone: 171-834-5163; fax: 171-630-8831).

VERY INEXPENSIVE

Alfa Antiques and interesting knickknacks give this small establishment an eclectic charm. The 33 rooms are simply but attractively furnished. No restaurant. 78-82 Warwick Way, SW1 (phone: 171-828-8603; fax: 171-976-6536).

Jenkins A cozy bed and breakfast place conveniently nestled in the heart of London. The 15 small bedrooms are pleasant, with mini-fridges (no TV sets), though only seven have private baths. There is a breakfast room (prettily decked out in blue and white lace tablecloths), but no restaurant. 45 Cartwright Gardens, WC1 (phone: 171-387-2067; fax: 171-383-3139).

Mabledon Court A former college dormitory, this property has 32 comfortable rooms, a breakfast room, and a lounge (but no restaurant). 10 Mabledon Pl., WC1 (phone: 171-388-3866; fax: 171-387-5686).

Sandringham Some of the 15 guestrooms in this Victorian house have a lovely view of the city and adjacent *Hampstead Heath.* The decor is charming and homey, as is the welcome of the American couple who run the place. No restaurant. 3 Holford Rd., NW3 (phone: 171-435-1569; fax: 171-431-5932).

REGAL RENTAL

If you're curious about what it's like to live in a royal palace, here's an opportunity to find out. At *Hampton Court Palace,* two self-catered apartments are available for rent at a moderate price. Each flat sleeps six to eight people and features a full kitchen and living room; guests have complimentary access to the rest of the palace during its normal operating hours. The 16th-century structure's royal residents have included Henry VIII and William and Mary; its extension was designed by Christopher Wren. (For details on the palace, see *Special Places.*) To book accommodations, contact the *Landmark Trust,* Shottesbrooke, Maidenhead, Berkshire SL6 3SW, England (phone: 1628-825925).

EATING OUT

Once upon a time, a scarce few London restaurants were known for their excellent cooking—and some visitors of times past might call that a charitable overstatement. But there's been a notable transformation. While restaurants offering really good English cooking—and not simply "chips with everything"—are still rare (and tend to be upscale and pricey), there has been a veritable explosion of good ethnic dining places.

A dinner for two will cost $200 or more at a restaurant listed as very expensive; $150 to $190, expensive; $90 to $130, moderate; and $80 or less, inexpensive. Prices do not include drinks, wine, or tips. Most London restaurants have developed the continental habit of automatically adding a service charge to the bill, so make certain you're not tipping twice. All restaurants listed below serve lunch and dinner, unless otherwise noted.

VERY EXPENSIVE

Bibendum Located on the second floor of *Michelin House,* it is stylishly decorated by Sir Terence Conran of the *Habitat* chain of stores. Chef Simon Hopkinson's good taste evokes English dreams of France; he serves the best roast beef in town. Open daily. Reservations necessary. Major credit cards accepted. 81 Fulham Rd., SW3 (phone: 171-581-5817).

Chez Nico at 90 Park Lane Popularly known as *Nico at 90,* this *très elegante,* two-Michelin-star dining room at the *Grosvenor House* hotel features the gastronomic talents of temperamental but brilliant Nico Ladenis. The excellent menu includes such French specialties as smoked salmon with trout mousse, quail pie, and langoustines with garlic butter and ginger. The wine list here is among London's best (and most expensive), and the service is excellent. Closed Saturday lunch and Sundays. Reservations necessary. Major credit cards accepted. 90 Park La., W1 (phone: 171-409-1290).

Connaught With one Michelin star apiece, the two dining rooms at the eponymous hotel are as well mannered as you'd expect at a traditional British establishment. The best dishes are those on which the empire was founded: roast beef and Yorkshire pudding, Lancashire hot pot, and gooseberry pie. After dinner, you will feel as if the gentlemen should retire to the library with a glass of port and a cigar; many still do. Closed weekends and holidays. Reservations necessary. Major credit cards accepted. Carlos Pl., W1 (phone: 171-499-7070).

Le Gavroche After over 70 years of rating restaurants, the *Guide Michelin* gave its first three-star rating in Britain to this most French of restaurants; though it has now lost one star, the establishment is still very special. Proprietor Albert Roux, once the chef for the Rothschild family as well as the royal household, has passed the cooking duties to his son Michel. The wine card is exceptionally long and inviting (listing over 400 items, including a 1945 Château Lafite-Rothschild for about $1,000, though many modest vintages are available for less than $25). Closed weekends, and late December to early January. Reservations necessary (well in advance). Major credit cards accepted. 43 Upper Brook St., W1 (phone: 171-408-0881).

The Restaurant The revamped (but rather blandly decorated) dining room of the *Hyde Park* hotel is presided over by renowned chef Marco Pierre White (formerly of *Harvey's*). His previous efforts have been showered with two Michelin stars, and he's still up to his old tricks, presenting high-quality continental fare. Saddle of rabbit with asparagus and leeks, terrine of pork and foie gras, and *mille-feuille* are only a few of the menu's highlights. Closed Saturday lunch, Sundays, the last week in December, and the first week in January. Reservations advised. Major credit cards accepted. 66 Knightsbridge, SW1 (phone: 171-259-5380).

EXPENSIVE

Bice Imaginatively prepared Italian specialties are served in an Art Deco setting at this fashionable restaurant. Outstanding choices from the menu include risotto with saffron and sausage in red wine sauce, linguine with baby clams, and baked bream served with white wine sauce and black olives. Closed Saturday lunch and Sundays. Reservations advised. Major credit cards accepted. 13 Albemarle St., W1 (phone: 171-409-1011).

Capital Serving some of the best French fare this side of the English Channel (it's earned a Michelin star), this small 35-seat hotel dining room specializes in gracious service and first-rate dishes, including grilled beef filet and root vegetables with foie gras and rosemary sauce, honey roasted French Barbary duckling with red wine sauce, and baked filet of sea bass with thyme and orange sauce. Even if you aren't staying at the hotel, try to make this one of your London dinner stops. We guarantee you won't regret it. Open daily. Reservations necessary. Major credit cards accepted. 22-24 Basil St., SW3 (phone: 171-589-5171).

Clarke's It's London's answer to the San Francisco Bay area's *Chez Panisse,* with set menus of California-style cooking from owner/chef Sally Clarke presented in a lovely, light, basement eatery. Closed weekends. Reservations necessary. Major credit cards accepted. 124 Kensington Church St., W8 (phone: 171-221-9225).

L'Escargot A few years ago, this Soho landmark was in danger of closing; however, two award-winning chefs, David Cavalier and Garry Hollihead, have joined together to save it. The restaurant now features a formal dining room upstairs and a brasserie downstairs; both serve tempting menus of French-influenced dishes. Samples of Cavalier's and Hollihead's handiwork include pot-au-feu, *boudin blanc* (chicken and foie gras sausages), and *cassoulet toulousain* (a stew with pork, sausage, mutton, goose, and green beans). Closed Saturday lunch and Sundays; the formal dining room is also closed Mondays. Reservations advised. Major credit cards accepted. 48 Greek St., W1 (phone: 171-437-2679).

Greenhouse At this garden-style eatery tucked away in a Mayfair mews, chef Gary Rhodes (who had earned a Michelin star at Taunton's *Castle* hotel restaurant) delivers traditional flavors with style, from a simple poached egg with black pudding, bacon, and salad greens to *confit* of duck on butter beans. Leave room for the feather-light steamed jam sponge and custard. After the prix fixe Sunday lunch (which we heartily recommend), take a walk in nearby *Hyde Park.* Closed Saturday lunch. Reservations necessary. Major credit cards accepted. 27a Hay's Mews, W1 (phone: 171-499-3331).

Green's Pinstripes rule at this establishment, which serves some of the best oysters in London, and some would say the best English food. Open daily.

Reservations necessary. Major credit cards accepted. 36 Duke St., SW1 (phone: 171-930-4566).

Greig's Grill Superlative steaks—and plenty of them—are the order of the day at this small restaurant, a favorite among Americans. Diners get to choose from a display of raw Scottish beef (you've never tasted anything this good), lamb chops, or smoked salmon, plus artichokes (always) and asparagus (in season), and what just may be the world's biggest and best baked potato. Open late, this is a good place for an after-theater feast. Save room for the Turkish delight. Closed Saturday lunch and Sundays. Reservations necessary. Major credit cards accepted. 26 Bruton Pl., W1 (phone: 171-629-3064).

Hilaire With light and flavorful dishes drawing on the Mediterranean, the Far East, and the chef's native Wales, this place offers a multicultural dining experience. Don't miss the lemon tart with toffee banana. Closed Sundays. Reservations necessary. Major credit cards accepted. 68 Old Brompton Rd., SW7 (phone: 171-584-8993).

Ivy Since 1911, this has been one of *the* restaurants of London's theater elite. Especially interesting are the commissioned works of contemporary art that contrast with the stained glass and oak paneling. International specialties are served along with British classics like grilled Dover sole, Cumberland sausages, and smoked salmon with scrambled eggs. Some dishes border on the just-too-trendy. Open daily. Reservations necessary. Major credit cards accepted. 1 West St., WC2 (phone: 171-836-4751).

Ken Lo's Memories of China The premier Chinese eatery in London, where Ken Lo, well-known Chinese author and tennis player, and his chefs prepare a wide range of fine dishes from all regions of China, from dim sum to Szechuan food. Closed Sundays (though brunch is served on Sundays at the Chelsea restaurant) and bank holidays. Reservations advised. Major credit cards accepted. Two locations: 67 Ebury St., SW1 (phone: 171-730-7734); and Harbour Yard, Chelsea Harbour, SW10 (phone: 171-352-4953).

Langan's Brasserie Still trendy after all these years, this spot is a haunt for celebrities. Ask for a downstairs table and take your time studying the lengthy menu. (For a lighter menu, try *Langan's Bistro;* see below.) Closed Saturday lunch and Sundays. Reservations necessary. Major credit cards accepted. 1 Stratton St., W1 (phone: 171-493-6437).

Leith's For over 20 years, this continental, one-Michelin-star restaurant in an out-of-the-way Victorian building northwest of *Kensington Gardens* has served superb entrées, hors d'oeuvres, and desserts as part of a fine prix fixe dinner. There's also an excellent vegetarian menu and a good wine list. Though its stuffy "dinner party" style is less than trendy, this is still a popular place. Open daily for dinner only. Reservations necessary. Major credit cards accepted. 92 Kensington Park Rd., W11 (phone: 171-229-4481).

Lindsay House For an unforgettable evening, few places can match this combination of plush, 17th-century decor and traditional English dishes with a twist. The Edwardian house has separate dining rooms furnished with huge gilt mirrors, fireplaces, and drapes, and flamboyant fare to match—cold carrot and orange soup, smoked salmon with creamed chives, and Westend lamb with basil sweetbread mousse in madeira sauce. Open daily. Reservations advised. Major credit cards accepted. 21 Romilly St., W1 (phone: 171-439-0450).

One Ninety Queensgate Just a few years old, these two eateries at the *Gore* hotel are crowded with diners eager to try chef Antony Worrall-Thompson's refined fare—including sea bass with fish mousse and hot crab pancakes. His *Bistrot 190* upstairs serves modern French food at very reasonable prices (but to hotel guests only); *Downstairs at 190* specializes in seafood. Restaurant closed Saturday lunch and Sundays; bistro open daily. Reservations necessary in the restaurant; no reservations in the bistro. Major credit cards accepted. 190 Queen's Gate, SW7 (phone: 171-581-5666).

Oriental London's most glamorous Chinese restaurant is a sparkling jewel in the *Dorchester* hotel's crown; its excellent Cantonese cooking has earned it a Michelin star. The menu features sesame prawns with lemon sauce, medallions of beef, and shredded coconut tarts; the house specialty is Chinese mushrooms stuffed with prawn mousse. Closed Saturday lunch and Sundays. Reservations advised. Major credit cards accepted. Park La., W1 (phone: 171-629-8888).

Pied-à-Terre Richard Neat, the young chef of this hip French bistro, has earned a Michelin star for his innovative creations. The country-style fare includes masterfully prepared rabbit, pigeon, filet of turbot, scallops, and lamb chops; there are several prix fixe lunch and dinner selections, and the wine list is extensive, with both pricey and more affordable vintages. The decor is a bit spare except for some fine artwork on the walls (including a few Warhols), but the dining experience itself provides plenty of distraction. Closed Saturday lunch and Sundays. Reservations necessary. Major credit cards accepted. 34 Charlotte St., W1 (phone: 171-636-1178).

Le Pont de la Tour Sir Terence Conran (of *Habitat* store fame and *Quaglino's*—see below) has designed a "gastrodome" complex overlooking the Thames at Tower Bridge that houses a restaurant, bar/grill, oyster bar, food and wine shops, and a bakery. The innovative restaurant features traditional Arbroath smokies au gratin (smoked Scottish haddock) with fresh tomato, lobster pot-au-feu, baked apple, and citrus fruit salad. Open daily. Reservations necessary. Major credit cards accepted. 36 Shad Thames, Butler's Wharf, SE1 (phone: 171-403-8403).

Quaglino's Yet another triumph for style magnate/restaurateur Sir Terence Conran. Named after an eatery that was *the* meeting place for London's high society in the 1930s (Edward VIII had many tête-à-têtes with Wallis Simpson here), it also occupies the same location, off Piccadilly. The decor, however, is more reminiscent of a chic French brasserie: marble, mosaics, mirrors, and gleaming metal. The bistro-style menu includes a generous seafood platter, braised oxtail, and spiced lamb with roasted onions. There's dancing on Fridays and Saturdays until the wee hours. This place is one of the city's hot spots, so plan ahead. Open daily. Reservations necessary. Major credit cards accepted. 16 Bury St., SW1 (phone: 171-930-6767).

St. Quentin The chef at this popular brasserie with mirrored walls and leather banquettes prepares traditional French fare, adapting the menu to make the best use of seasonal fish and produce. But the focus is not solely on fish; the homemade quenelles and *andouillettes* (spicy, smoked sausages) are also delicious. However, service can be erratic. Open daily. Reservations advised. Major credit cards accepted. 243 Brompton Rd., SW3 (phone: 171-589-8005 or 171-581-5131).

Savoy Grill It's renowned as a celebrity watching ground, but this eatery actually is patronized mostly by businesspeople. Although the menu features some classic French dishes, the English grills and roasts are the house specialties. The lovely decor resembles a luxurious ship's dining room of the 1940s. Perfect for before and especially after theater. Closed Saturday lunch and Sundays. Reservations necessary. Major credit cards accepted. At the *Savoy Hotel,* The Strand, WC2 (phone: 171-836-4343).

La Tante Claire Run by chef Pierre Koffman and his wife, Annie, this airy, attractively decorated establishment has been awarded three Michelin stars *and* is a member of Relais & Châteaux—which puts it among very select company indeed in Britain. While fish dishes are the specialty, everything—especially the duck, calf's liver, and *pied de cochon farci aux morilles* (pig's foot stuffed with foie gras and mushrooms)—is excellent. The prix fixe lunch is a remarkably good value at about $45. Closed weekends. Reservations necessary. Major credit cards accepted. 68 Royal Hospital Rd., SW3 (phone: 171-352-6045).

Wilton's Good food is skillfully prepared and elegantly served in a plush, rather formal Victorian setting. Specialties include game, fish, oxtail, steak and kidney pie—what the best English cooking is about. Closed Saturday lunch, Sundays, and three weeks in August. Reservations necessary. Major credit cards accepted. 55 Jermyn St., SW1 (phone: 171-629-9955).

MODERATE

Alastair Little The decor is minimalist but chic, and many find the chef here to be the most natural cook in the city. The eclectic menu changes twice daily and features French, Japanese, and Italian dishes. Closed Saturday lunch and Sundays. Reservations advised. Major credit cards accepted. 49 Frith St., W1 (phone: 171-734-5183).

Bloom's This kosher restaurant has a bright and bustling atmosphere, a bit like the dining room of a large hotel, with waiters who almost—but not quite—throw the food at you. The popular take-out counter serves the best hot salt beef (like corned beef) sandwiches in town. The house wine is Israeli. Closed Friday evenings and Saturdays. Reservations advised. Major credit cards accepted. 90 Whitechapel High St., E1 (phone: 171-247-6001) and 130 Golders Green Rd., NW11 (phone: 181-455-1338).

Bombay Brasserie At lunchtime there is an Indian buffet; at dinner, classic dishes from all over the land of the Moguls, including Goanese fish curry and Kashmiri lamb curry. And the setting is lovely, with lots of banana plants, wicker chairs, and ceiling fans. Popular with both the American and British show-biz colonies. Open daily. Reservations necessary. Major credit cards accepted. Courtfield Close, Courtfield Rd., SW7 (phone: 171-370-4040).

Chiang Mai Thai restaurants used to be a rarity in London. This one always has been easy to spot since it's the only eatery in Soho (and probably the whole of Britain) with a carved wooden elephant poised on the sidewalk. The menu offers such dishes as coconut chicken and *galanga* soup. Those unfamiliar with northern Thai cooking should inquire about the spiciness of individual dishes before ordering. Open daily. Reservations advised. Major credit cards accepted. 48 Frith St., W1 (phone: 171-437-7444).

Chuen Cheng Ku At this huge restaurant in the heart of Chinatown, the overwhelming majority of the clientele is Chinese. The specialty here is Cantonese-style dim sum; also try the pork with chili and salt, duck webs, and steamed lobster with ginger. Open daily. Reservations necessary. Major credit cards accepted. 17 Wardour St., W1 (phone: 171-437-1398).

Chutney Mary This Anglo-Indian eatery offers delicious echoes of the Raj. Just a few years old, its culinary crossovers include tandoori ginger lamb chops and Sindhi-style fried potatoes. Open daily. Reservations necessary. Major credit cards accepted. 535 King's Rd., SW10 (phone: 171-351-3113).

Criterion Considered *the* place to meet for many years (even Sherlock Holmes and Watson rendezvoused here), this eatery has now reopened after a lengthy renovation. Though the long bar still remains, most of the decor has been updated, with mirrors, hand-painted tables, and gilded mosaics. The Italian-American menu offers pizza with caramelized onions and olives, liver and onions with rosemary mashed potatoes, and fried spaghetti; traditional English tea also is served. Open daily. Reservations advised. Major credit cards accepted. Piccadilly Circus, W1 (phone: 171-925-0909).

dell'Ugo Another culinary endeavor of Antony Worrall-Thompson, the man behind *One Ninety Queensgate* (see above), this trendy, three-level Italian eatery in Soho was an overnight success. And no wonder: The adventurous menu (served in the elegant dining rooms on the top two floors) includes roasted bell pepper and anchovy spaghetti, *tagliarini* (long, thin noodles) with grilled squid, and chicken with zucchini and garlic potatoes; a casual café on the ground floor offers fare that is lighter, but no less delicious. Closed Sundays. Reservations advised for the restaurant; no reservations for the café. Major credit cards accepted. 56 Frith St., W1 (phone: 171-734-8300).

Gay Hussar Among the best Hungarian restaurants this side of Budapest, it has a substantial menu with a varied selection: chicken ragout soup, goulash, roast pork, and lots more. The food here is extremely filling as well as delicious. The atmosphere is informal, with a regular clientele drawn from London's political and publishing worlds. Closed Sundays. Reservations necessary. American Express accepted. 2 Greek St., W1 (phone: 171-437-0973).

Kensington Place Here's a good example of the new breed of London restaurants, set behind a huge glass front, so you can see and be seen. A mix of "Californian new English" cookery from partridge and cabbage to foie gras, oysters, and delicious desserts. Frenzied atmosphere, sensible wine list. Open daily. Reservations necessary. Major credit cards accepted. 201 Kensington Church St., W8 (phone: 171-727-3184).

Kettner's As you check your coat, you have to decide—should you have a bottle of champagne at the bar (25 labels in stock), a humble but tasty salad in the brasserie-style café, or a pizza in the beautifully furnished dining room reminiscent of an Edwardian hotel? Whichever you choose, you can't go wrong. Open daily. Reservations unnecessary. Major credit cards accepted. In Soho, 29 Romilly St., W1 (phone: 171-437-6437).

Langan's Bistro Slightly simpler and less expensive dishes are prepared in the same style as *Langan's Brasserie* (above). Closed Saturday lunch and Sundays. Reservations advised. Major credit cards accepted. 26 Devonshire St., W1 (phone: 171-935-4531).

Museum Street Café It's near the *British Museum,* but there's nothing antiquarian about the fare served by American Gail Koerber and her English partner, Mark Nathan. They've cut out the frills (no liquor license; diners may bring their own alcoholic beverages), but left in the inspiration, with dishes such as salmon with lemon sauce, lamb on a skewer with pesto, and zabaglione. The bread is homemade. Closed weekends. Reservations necessary. No credit cards accepted. 47 Museum St., WC1 (phone: 171-405-3211).

Porters A very English eatery in *Covent Garden,* it's famous for home-cooked pies—steak, mushroom, and vegetable are the specialties. Leave room for such sticky British desserts as treacle and syrup sponge. Open daily. Reservations advised, especially for lunch. Major credit cards accepted. 17 Henrietta St., WC2 (phone: 171-836-6466).

River Café The first "new wave" Italian restaurant in London is hidden away (but overlooks the Thames) in Hammersmith, in a high-tech former architect's canteen serving stylish Tuscan peasant dishes. Closed Monday lunch and weekend evenings. Reservations necessary. Major credit cards accepted. *Thames Wharf,* Rainville Rd., W6 (phone: 171-381-8824).

Rules Approaching its bicentennial, this eatery has been at the same site since 1798. The Lillie Langtry Room, where the actress dined with the Prince of Wales (later King Edward VII), is reserved for private parties. The downstairs retains its Victorian atmosphere and decor. Walls are covered with signed photographs and cartoons of actors and authors. Another *must* for visitors to London, with better-than-average British fare. Start with smoked pheasant with spiced apricots, move on to whatever game and fish are in season, and finish with the treacle sponge pudding. Open daily. Reservations necessary. Major credit cards accepted. 35 Maiden La., WC2 (phone: 171-836-5314).

Simply Nico It's Nico Ladenis's not-so-snooty steak-and-chips joint. Closed Saturday lunch, Sundays, *Christmas* through *New Year's Day,* four days at *Easter,* and bank holidays. Reservations necessary. Major credit cards accepted. 48A Rochester Row, SW1 (phone: 171-630-8061).

Smollensky's Balloon A family place, this cocktail bar/restaurant with a 1930s piano-bar atmosphere is guaranteed to make Americans feel homesick. Steaks and fries figure importantly on the menu, offset by some interesting vegetarian dishes. Magicians and clowns entertain the younger set on weekends. You might even see Princess Di and her children here. Open daily. Reservations unnecessary. Major credit cards accepted. 1 Dover St., W1 (phone: 171-491-1199). There is a branch at 105 The Strand, WC2 (phone: 171-497-2101).

Stephen Bull Light in decor and fare, this clean-cut, modern eatery offers creatively prepared dishes, as well as service pared to essentials for true enjoyment and sensible tabs. Closed Saturday lunch and Sundays. Reservations necessary. Major credit cards accepted. 5-7 Blandford St., W1 (phone: 171-486-9696).

Sweetings A special London experience, this fish restaurant is one of the great attractions in the financial district. You may have to sit at a counter with your lobster, brill, or haddock, but it will be fresh and perfectly prepared. Open for lunch only; closed weekends. No reservations, so expect a wait. No credit cards accepted. 39 Queen Victoria St., EC4 (phone: 171-248-3062).

Tate Gallery Restaurant Who would expect one of London's better eateries to be in a fine art museum? But here it is—a genuine culinary outpost (leaning toward French fare), with a good wine list. Enjoy the famous Rex Whistler murals as you dine. Open for lunch only; closed Sundays. Reservations necessary. Visa accepted. *Tate Gallery,* Millbank, SW1 (phone: 171-834-6754).

Upper Street Fish Shop Try this dining spot for decent salmon, as well as traditional fish-and-chips. Expect to share a table. Closed Sundays. Reservations unnecessary. No credit cards accepted. 324 Upper St., N1 (phone: 171-359-1401).

Wheeler's A link in the national chain of seafood restaurants, this is the original—an old-fashioned, narrow (and very friendly and unpretentious) establishment on three floors. One of the best places in the city to enjoy finny fare, it specializes in a variety of ways of preparing real Dover sole and Scotch salmon. The oyster bar is our favorite perch. Closed Sundays. Reservations advised. Major credit cards accepted. Duke of York St. at Apple Tree Yard, SW1 (phone: 171-930-2460).

INEXPENSIVE

Bangkok Known for its *satay*—small tender slices of beef marinated in a curry and soy sauce and served with a palate-destroying hot peanut sauce. From your butcher block table you can watch your meal being prepared in the windowed kitchen. Closed Sundays. Reservations advised. Major credit cards accepted. 9 Bute St., SW7 (phone: 171-584-8529).

Café in the Crypt Perhaps the best food value in central London is at this self-service eatery in the crypt of the *St. Martin-in-the-Fields Church* right on Trafalgar Square. A simple but good buffet offers many hot dishes and salads. Closed Sunday evenings. No reservations. MasterCard and Visa accepted. *St. Martin-in-the-Fields Church,* Trafalgar Sq., WC2 (phone: 171-839-4342).

Calabash West African fare gives this place a unique position on London's restaurant map, especially since it's in the bubbling *Covent Garden* district. The service is accommodating and helpful, and the food is both good and different. Closed Saturday lunch and Sundays. Reservations advised. Major credit cards accepted. Downstairs at London's *Africa Centre,* 38 King St., WC2 (phone: 171-836-1976).

Chicago Pizza Pie Factory In the early 1980s, an American advertising executive turned his back on the US ad world to bring London deep-dish pizza Windy City–style, along with Budweiser beer and chocolate cheesecake. Londoners beat a path to his door and haven't yet stopped clamoring to get in. Open daily. Reservations unnecessary. Major credit cards accepted. 17 Hanover Sq., W1 (phone: 171-629-2669).

Chicago Rib Shack Under the same ownership as *Chicago Pizza Pie Factory* (above), this is a great place for ribs. Open daily. Reservations unnecessary. Major credit cards accepted. Two locations: 1 Rafael St., SW7 (phone: 171-581-5595) and 13-17 Bear St., WC1 (phone: 171-839-4188).

Cranks There are several branches of this self-service vegetarian eatery. All are popular and serve good homemade desserts, as well as salads, quiches, and other hot food. Drop in for coffee or afternoon tea. Reservations advised.

Major credit cards accepted. Some of the more central branches include 8 Marshall St., W1 (phone: 171-437-9431), closed Sundays; 11 The Market, *Covent Garden,* WC2 (phone: 171-379-6508), open daily; Tottenham St., W1 (phone: 171-631-3912), closed Sundays; Unit 11, Adelaide St., WC2 (phone: 171-836-0660), closed Sundays; 23 Barrett St., W1 (phone: 171-495-1340), closed Sundays; and 17-19 Great Newport St., Leicester Sq. (phone: 171-836-5226), open daily.

Dumpling Inn This Peking-style restaurant serves excellent Oriental dumplings, and most of the other dishes are equally good. Try the fried seaweed; it's got lots of vitamins and tastes terrific. The service, though efficient, is a bit brisk. Open daily. Reservations unnecessary. Major credit cards accepted. 15A Gerrard St., W1 (phone: 171-437-2567).

Geales' Truly fresh fish-and-chips are served in a setting that looks like a 1930s tearoom. Expect to wait in line, because this spot is no secret. Closed Sundays, Mondays, and the last three weeks in August. No reservations. Major credit cards accepted. 2 Farmer St., W8 (phone: 171-727-7969).

Hard Rock Café The original. With a loud jukebox and good burgers, this American-style eating emporium is still crowded after 23 years—the lines stretch well out into the street. As much a T-shirt vendor (at the shop around the corner) these days as a restaurant. Open daily. No reservations. Major credit cards accepted. 150 Old Park La., W1 (phone: 171-629-0382).

Planet Hollywood Another branch of the chain of eateries owned by Arnold Schwarzenegger, Sylvester Stallone, and Bruce Willis, it features displays of film memorabilia that are as popular as its down-to-earth menu of burgers, fries, and shakes. Several gadgets from the many James Bond movies can be seen here, including a model of the flying car from *The Man with the Golden Gun.* The atmosphere is boisterous and crowded. Open daily. No reservations. Major credit cards accepted. 13 Coventry St., W1 (phone: 171-287-1000).

Standard Possibly the best Indian restaurant value in London, so it tends to get crowded quickly. Open daily. Reservations advised. Major credit cards accepted. 23 Westbourne Grove, W2 (phone: 171-727-4818).

Tuttons A popular and lively brasserie in a former *Covent Garden* warehouse, this place is a handy snack spot for theatergoers. Open daily. Reservations advised. Major credit cards accepted. 11 Russell St., WC2 (phone: 171-836-4141).

TAKING TEA

The renaissance of afternoon tea in Britain has especially taken hold in its capital. The ritual, which may well take an hour or two in some hotels and tea shops, is described in detail in *Tea Shops and Tea Gardens* in DIVERSIONS. A round of the best London teas would begin at the following hotels:

Brown's, Dorchester, Dukes, Grosvenor House, Le Meridien, the *Regent,* the *Langham Hilton,* the *Ritz* (make reservations at least 10 days in advance), the *Savoy,* and the *Stafford* (see *Checking In,* above, for addresses and phone numbers). Fine tea shops include *Daquise* (20 Thurloe St., SW7; phone: 171-589-6117); *Maison Bertaux* (28 Greek St., W1; phone: 171-437-6007); and *Pâtisserie Valerie* (44 Old Compton St., W1; phone: 171-437-3466). For those who prefer taking tea at home, *Heritage Touring (GB)* offers travelers the opportunity to enjoy the experience of an English cream tea with a London family at their home. For more information, contact *Heritage Touring (GB),* 754 The Square, Cattistock, Dorchester, Dorset DT2 OJD, England (phone: 1300-320671; fax: 1300-321042).

SHARING A PINT

There are several thousand pubs in London, the vast majority of which are owned by the six biggest brewers. Most pubs have two bars: the "public," which is for the working man who wants to get on with the business of drinking, and the "saloon" or "lounge," which makes an attempt at providing comfort and may serve food and wine as well as beer. Liquor at the latter may cost more. All pubs listed below are open daily unless stated otherwise. For more about general operating hours as well as the etiquette and history of pubs, see *Pub Crawling* in DIVERSIONS. Here are our particular favorites.

PERFECT PINTS

Albert Prince Albert stands holding a flower on the sign outside this smart but genuine Victorian pub, which has gas lamps and wrought-iron balconies. Originally one of the street's most distinguished buildings, it now looks rather small and fragile, surrounded by towering modern office blocks. Inside, the walls are decorated with Victorian prints. Office workers crowd in on weekdays at lunchtime, particularly for the interesting bar snacks. There is a small, excellent-value carvery upstairs that's popular with politicians, who are only minutes away from the *Houses of Parliament.* The stairs leading to the carvery are lined with photographs of Britain's prime ministers dating back to the last century, along with a large portrait of Queen Victoria. 52 Victoria St., SW1 (phone: 171-222-5577).

Dirty Dick's When his fiancée was killed on the eve of their wedding day, the "Dirty Dick" in question, one Nathaniel Bentley, lived out his life in isolation and ever-increasing squalor in the apartments that now make up the downstairs section of this pub. The spiders and bats that used to swing from the walls and ceiling in the downstairs bar have been relegated to a small museum area, and the place is a pleasant enough spot to begin an evening. Galleried and spacious, with wood everywhere and sawdust on the floors, it's plain rather than plush (much like the East End surrounding it), and in its dark and clubby way, it is a supremely restful place to quench a thirst after a hectic Sunday morning's bargaining in nearby *Petticoat Lane* (officially known as Middlesex Street). 202 Bishopsgate, EC2 (phone: 171-283-5888).

Grenadier This is a special stopping place in a most unlikely location. To get here, you have to ignore a barrier and watchman, forbidding obstacles whose purpose actually is to keep cars, not pedestrians, out of this narrow residential street just off Wilton Crescent. The military moniker derives from the time when this was the Officers' Mess for the Duke of Wellington's soldiers. The exterior is chauvinistically red, white, and blue, featuring a bright sentry box, and access from the north is via narrow Old Barracks Yard. Since it's an ideal place to stop for lunch after a trip to *Harrods* or a boutique browse up Brompton Road, the clientele is unceasingly posh. A tiny bar at the front has a rare pewter-topped counter. The resident specter (who seems to make his presence known particularly during September) is purported to be a young officer who was caught cheating at cards and was ruthlessly beaten to death by his fellow officers. 18 Wilton Row, SW1 (phone: 171-235-3074).

Sherlock Holmes Forget about Baker Street; this Northumberland Street pub, which Arthur Conan Doyle knew when it was called the *Northumberland Arms* hotel (and in which he set a scene in his *Hound of the Baskervilles*), is the nearest most people will ever come to the great man. Drawings and photographs of actors playing Holmes and of scenes from stories featuring the detective are among the Holmesiana adorning the downstairs bar; upstairs, on the way to a first-floor restaurant, there's a clever replica of Holmes's Baker Street study, walled off by glass. The collection was assembled in 1951 by the *Sherlock Holmes Society of London,* and this smart and congenial pub provides it with an excellent home. 10 Northumberland St., WC2 (phone: 171-930-2644).

Spaniards Inn Perfectly positioned on Spaniards Lane between the east and west sides of *Hampstead Heath,* this establishment attracts Sunday walkers, visitors to nearby *Kenwood House,* wealthy local residents, and casual passersby. The building, with its large outdoor garden dotted with wooden tables and chairs, is quite pretty. The labyrinthine interior has low-ceilinged rooms paneled in oak and warmed by open fires. Bar food consists of unexceptional rolls, meat pies, and hot daily specials. Spaniards La., NW3 (phone: 181-455-3276).

Ye Olde Cheshire Cheese Here's the perfect place to rest during a tour of the nearby *Inns of Court.* In this environment, it's easy to imagine the London of a century or so ago. Dr. Samuel Johnson lived around the corner, and his intimate circle—notably Boswell, Reynolds, and Gibbon—frequented "The Cheese." The pub's character has remained remarkably intact despite its place on many tourist itineraries and a recent renovation that included the addition of a snack bar. The wooden stairs are narrow and the downstairs bar always several drinkers deep, but somehow the bumping and squeezing past are part of the fun. On a very cold winter's afternoon, a bowl of beef barley soup can be a special savior and the warmth of roaring fires upstairs a consummate joy. Wine Office Court, 145 Fleet St., EC4 (phone: 171-353-6170).

Other fine spots include the *Audley* (41 Mount St., W1; phone: 171-499-1843), a favorite luncheon stop in the high-rent district, with fresh sandwiches and salad plates in an atypically hygienic environment; and the elegant *Antelope* (22 Eaton Ter., SW1; phone: 171-730-7781), where the Bellamys (or even Hudson, their butler) might have sipped a lager on the way home to nearby 165 Eaton Place. *Dickens Inn* by the *Tower* (St. Katherine's Way, E1; phone: 171-481-1786) is a converted warehouse overlooking a colorful yacht marina and serving shellfish snacks; *George Inn* (77 Borough High St., SE1; phone: 171-407-2056) dates from 1676 and retains the original gallery for viewing Shakespearean plays in the summer; *The Flask* (77 Highgate West Hill, N6; phone: 181-340-7260) serves drinks at three paneled bars and on its outside patio; *The Lamb* (94 Lambs Conduit St., WC1; phone: 171-405-0713) is also paneled and hung with photos of past music hall performers; *Museum Tavern* (49 Great Russell St., WC1; phone: 171-242-8987) is across from the *British Museum* and decorated with hanging flower baskets; and *Princess Louise* (208 High Holborn, WC1; phone: 171-405-8816) has live music, cabaret, and a good Thai restaurant. *Bull and Bush* (North End Way, NW3; phone: 181-455-3685) owes its fame to the Edwardian music hall song "Down at the Old Bull and Bush"; Former customers include Thomas Gainsborough and Charles Dickens. It has an outdoor bar and barbecue for balmy summer evenings. *Prospect of Whitby* (57 Wapping Wall, E1; phone: 171-481-1095), London's oldest riverside pub, was once the haunt of thieves and smugglers (now it draws jazz lovers); *Anchor* (34 Park St., Bankside, SE1; phone: 171-407-3003) was possibly one of Shakespeare's haunts—the sites of the *Globe* and *Rose* theaters are close by; and *Black Friar* (174 Queen Victoria St., EC4; phone: 171-236-5650) is decorated in Art Nouveau style (closed weekends). On the south bank of the Thames, in the district of the Docklands called Rotherhithe, are two special pubs, the *Mayflower* (117 Rotherhithe St., SE16; phone: 171-237-4088) and the *Angel* (101 Bermondsey Wall E., SE16; phone: 171-237-3608). The former has been around since the 17th century when the *Mayflower* sailed for the New World and returned to Rotherhithe; today, the partially rebuilt Tudor inn is still a good spot to enjoy beer and ale. The *Angel* is set on stone pillars overlooking the Thames, and the cozy, dark interior hasn't changed much since the days when it was patronized by Samuel Pepys and Captain Cook.

WINE BARS

Growing in popularity on the London scene, these bars serve wine by the glass or bottle, accompanied by such light fare as quiche and salad, and occasionally full meals. Prices tend to be lower in wine bars than in restaurants, and tables often can be reserved in advance. Here's a selection of the finest: *Café Suze* (1 Glenworth St., NW1; phone: 171-486-8216) combines rustic decor with good homemade food (closed weekends); *Cork and Bottle* (44-46 Cranbourn St., WC2; phone: 171-734-6592) is patronized by the London wine trade and serves good hot and cold dishes; *Draycott's* (114 Draycott Ave., SW3; phone: 171-584-5359) has tables grouped outside on the pavement and is frequented by the smart London set; *Ebury Wine Bar* (139 Ebury St., SW1; phone: 171-730-5447), in the heart of Belgravia, serves good food (try the English pudding) and offers live music nightly; *Shampers* (4 Kingly St., W1; phone: 171-437-1692), near the famous *Liberty* department store, is popular with the British media and public relations people; *Skinkers* (42 Tooley St., SE1; phone: 171-407-9189) is an atmospheric spot with sawdust on the floor, serving hearty food (closed weekends); *Café des Amis* (11-14 Hanover Pl., WC2; phone: 171-379-3444) is a crowded watering hole in fashionable *Covent Garden* (closed Sundays); *Brahms and Liszt* (19 Russell St., WC2; phone: 171-240-3661) always has good wines, food, and music; *Julie's* (137 Portland Rd., W11; phone: 171-727-4585) has become a landmark for aging hippies; *El Vino* (47 Fleet St., EC4; phone: 171-353-6786), once a journalists' haunt famous for refusing to serve women, is now full of legal eagles and PR folk in a nice Old World atmosphere; *Bubbles* (41 North Audley St., W1; phone: 171-491-3237) near the *US Embassy* serves champagne by the glass; *Dover Street Wine Bar* (8-9 Dover St., W1; phone: 171-629-9813) is a place to party with live music at night (closed Sundays); *Jimmy's Wine Bar* (18 Kensington Church St., W8; phone: 171-937-9988) serves claret and traditional English food and plays live music; *Le Metro* (28 Basil St., SW3; phone: 171-589-6286)—owned by the *Capital* hotel's David Levin—is across from *Harrods* and has a fine range of wines, good food, and reasonable prices; and near *St. Paul's, Balls Brothers* (6-8 Cheapside, EC2; phone: 171-248-2708), one of several around the city, serves over 60 kinds of wine and huge sandwiches stuffed with meat, fish, and cheese (closed weekends).

Norwich

Drive for miles across the empty, pan-flat landscapes of Norfolk, the ever so English county that forms the great eastern belly of Britain, and eventually you arrive at Norwich. No community within a 40-mile radius of the city's commanding cathedral spire comes close to challenging Norwich's scale (the city has a population of around 125,000), and apart from its perch atop one of the few modest hills in East Anglia—which may once have offered some military advantage—the reason for Norwich's very existence is hard to understand.

From its hazy origins as Northwick ("wick" is the old English word for a small settlement), this "Fine City"—as the boundary road signs proclaim—grew to compete with York as the second-largest city in England, after London (today, it's a moot point, as Birmingham outdistances them both). Settled by Saxons and sacked by Danes, Norwich (rhymes with porridge) began to build up some civic momentum in the 11th century. Its position on the river Wensum, which flows to the sea some 20 miles away, was a vital link to the rest of the world. So when William the Conqueror first landed on Britain's southern shores in 1066, Norwich was already a busy town, importing timber, stone, steel, wine, and cloth from the far corners of Europe and exporting Norfolk's agricultural products. The Normans erected the castle in the center of town and then set about building a monastery and church. French stone from Caen was shipped across the Channel to construct the magnificent cathedral that now stands off a street called Tombland, the original Saxon marketplace.

During the 13th century, Norwich surpassed York as a commercial center, although it rapidly lost its place after the Black Death of the 14th century decimated the population. It was not until the wool trade flourished on the surrounding lands during the 15th and 16th centuries, and Norwich became the industry's chief point of export, that the city recuperated and expanded again. Half-timbered inns, ancient squares, countless churches built by wealthy merchants, and street names like Charing (Shearing) Cross recall these prosperous times when Norwich grew rich on thickly coated sheep.

The city's fortunes ebbed again during the Industrial Revolution. With no coal production or fast waterway links, it was unable to compete with the Midlands and the far north, where higher wages and standards of living lured most of its skilled craftsmen. So the city diversified—into brewing, mustard (the *Colman's Mustard Shop and Museum* tells the whole story), banking, insurance, and candy. Today there's even a small Turkish Delight factory run by two Turks called, appropriately enough, the Sultans.

Despite these industrial inroads, a distinctly medieval air still clings to

Norwich, which has more Grade One Listed buildings than any other comparable city in the country, save historic York. Its heart is a labyrinth of ancient alleys. Lined with unspoiled buildings housing interesting shops, the whole area seems to be from another era. There are still four thatch-roofed buildings within the city center, and clustered around Upper St. Giles Street is a "village," its winding lanes lined with antiquarian bookshops, craft shops, tiny candlelit restaurants, and pretty, half-timbered houses. Portions of the old city wall are glimpsed at the ends of alleyways, and the city's street system, which also dates from the Middle Ages, is finding it hard to support modern rush-hour traffic.

But the most ubiquitous examples of medieval life in Norwich are the churches its merchants built to show off the wealth they had accumulated in textile trading. Five hundred years ago, there were over 50 churches here—more than in any other European city. Today, even in the wake of Henry VIII's Reformation (when numerous ecclesiastical buildings in England were demolished), there are still 32, plus several that are no longer places of worship.

Medieval buildings and glorious churches are the prime reason for visiting Norwich, but they are by no means the city's only asset. The hub of the city is the *Market Place,* a sea of striped awnings lined on one side by the 14th-century *Guildhall,* on another by the rather harsh lines of the modern *City Hall,* and on a third by the colossal proportions of *St. Peter Mancroft,* considered one of the finest churches in the country. This harks back to the city's agrarian roots—a far cry from being just a show for tourists.

Norwich At-a-Glance

SEEING THE CITY

The tip of the tower of the neo-Gothic Roman Catholic *St. John's Cathedral* on Earlham Road, on the western edge of the center, is technically the highest point in the city, but those with less energy may drive (or walk) up to *Mousehold Heath,* just northeast of town. The *Heath,* the site of Ketts Rebellion, a 1549 uprising of 20,000 angry peasants that disrupted Norwich and unnerved the monarchy, is to Norwich what *Hampstead Heath* and *Richmond Park* are to Londoners—there still are local inhabitants who have yet to explore all the leafy dells, undulating hills, and coppices of this huge common. From St. James Hill it is possible to see all the old buildings clustered around the cathedral and to put Norwich into proper perspective.

SPECIAL PLACES

The cathedral and its close, the castle, and the market square are the three major focal points of central Norwich, an area defined by the river Wensum and the line of the old city walls.

NORWICH CATHEDRAL This beautiful church was begun in 1096 by Herbert de Losinga, first Bishop of Norwich. According to the old chronicles, the bishop founded the church and the monastery attached to it in atonement for an act of simony—he had bought his bishopric. Unfortunately, Losinga, whose tomb can be seen before the high altar, did not live to see more than the first three bays of the nave, which was finished by his successor during the first half of the 12th century. Measuring only 250 feet long and 95 feet high, it is not the longest nor the loftiest nave in England, but in this instance grandeur has nothing to do with statistics. The huge square pillars, the great semicircular arches, and the splendid proportions of the triple arcade of white stone are a superb example of the talent of Norman builders. Because the early cathedral was repeatedly damaged by fire and storm, the vaulted stone roof dates from the 15th century. The carvings of Old and New Testament scenes on the roof bosses are notable; they can be seen either through binoculars or on video at the visitors' center. The bosses of the adjoining cloisters, the only two-story monastic cloister (built from the late 13th to the early 15th century) in England, are equally remarkable and much more accessible to the naked eye. Exit the south door to *Life's Green* to best appreciate the cathedral's 315-foot stone spire (the second tallest in the country, topped only by that of *Salisbury Cathedral*). The 15th-century builders who erected it pulled off a daring architectural feat, since the 120-foot Norman tower on which it rests was never intended to support such a soaring structure. The visitors' center sells refreshments and houses an exhibition on the cathedral, and there is a gift shop (both closed Sundays).

Two medieval gateways, the *Erpingham,* with its much eroded statue of Sir Thomas Erpingham (he fought at the Battle of Agincourt), and the *Ethelbert,* lead off Tombland to the Cathedral Close, the "home farm" of the former monastery. Filled with Georgian houses, creeper-covered cottages, and converted stable blocks that lead down to the river, this is a world removed from busy crowds, shops, and traffic. The deanery was once the prior's house. Other old houses stand on the site of the monks' granary. Also inside the close are a statue of Nelson, once a pupil at the nearby school, and the grave of Dame Edith Cavell, a nurse shot in Belgium in 1915 for helping British prisoners escape from the Germans.

NORWICH CASTLE AND CASTLE MUSEUM Another focal point of the city stands 500 yards or so from the cathedral on top of manmade Castle Mound, which is particularly beautiful in spring, when it is covered in daffodils. A wooden castle probably was built here by Ralph de Guader, the only Anglo-Saxon traitor at the Battle of Hastings, but the great square stone keep seen today, albeit much restored, dates from the time of Henry I (1120–30). From the 12th through the 19th centuries, part of the castle was used as the official county jail, and since 1894 it has been a museum housing natural history and archaeology exhibits, as well as some of the finest art collections outside London. Of particular interest are the two *Colman Galleries,* which display works by painters of the Norwich school, a 19th-century movement whose major exponents were John Crome and John Sell Cotman. Slightly offbeat is the *Twinings Gallery,* home to over 2,600 teapots, ranging from 18th-century antiques to Art Deco objets d'art. Open daily. Admission charge. Castle Meadow (phone: 223624).

ST. PETER MANCROFT Often mistaken for the cathedral, this church, built between 1430 and 1455, is the largest and grandest in the city. The massive tower, dramatically floodlit at night, houses the famous set of 12 bells that rang the first true "peal" of 5,040 changes in 1715. Inside, look up to the fine hammer-beam roof, with its angels, fan vaulting, and stone corbels, and then look east, to the flowing medieval glass in the great window above the altar. The 15th-century font has a massive wooden canopy topped by a Victorian dome. *Market Place* (phone: 610443).

ST. PETER HUNGATE CHURCH MUSEUM This tiny former church houses a museum of ecclesiastical art, but its beautiful and unusual roof, the Norfolk tiles on the floor, and the Norwich-made 15th- and 16th-century glass in the windows also make it an exhibit in itself. Displays include a collection of rare medieval items, manuscripts, early Anglican communion plates, Russian icons, and musical instruments. There's also a brass-rubbing center. Closed Sundays. No admission charge. Princes St. (phone: 667231).

ROYAL NORFOLK REGIMENT MUSEUM Housed in the 19th-century *Shire Hall* below Castle Mound, this museum offers a fascinating array of regimental memorabilia and weapons, and a realistic reproduction of a World War I trench. Getting there is an experience in itself—you climb a steep spiral staircase and traverse a dark passageway that once was used by convicts standing trial at the courthouse. Open daily. Admission charge; a combined ticket can be purchased that also includes the *Bridewell Museum* and the *Strangers' Hall* (see below). Market Ave. (phone: 223649).

ST. ANDREW'S AND BLACKFRIARS These two civic halls began as the nave and the chancel of a huge 15th-century Dominican church. The most complete friary complex in the country, they survived Henry VIII's Dissolution of the Monasteries because they were given to the city and adapted for municipal purposes. Now they're used for concerts, exhibitions, craft fairs, and an antiques market every Wednesday. St. Andrew's St. (phone: 628477).

BRIDEWELL MUSEUM Before being turned into a museum, this 14th-century merchant's house had quite a checkered history. In the 16th century, it served as a "bridewell" (a prison for tramps and beggars), as evidenced by the initials and dates scratched in the courtyard walls; later, it was a factory. Now it features exhibits on Norwich's textile, shoe, food, and drink industries over the past 200 years. Special displays include a steam fire engine and a

19th-century smithy (blacksmith's forge). Closed Sundays. Admission charge. Bridewell Alley (phone: 667228).

STRANGERS' HALL Another old merchant's house turned museum, this one is dedicated to urban English domestic life. The mansion's stone-vaulted undercroft dates from about 1320, but enlargement over the centuries left it a complex, rambling structure with numerous period rooms, from Tudor to Victorian, open for inspection. Two cellars house permanent exhibitions of inn and tradesmen's signs as well as a motley collection of old vehicles. Protestant Flemish weavers, fleeing religious persecution and taking refuge here during the reign of Queen Elizabeth I, may have been the "Strangers" who gave the house its name. Closed Sundays. Admission charge. Charing Cross (phone: 667229).

AMERICAN (USAAF) MEMORIAL LIBRARY Commemorates more than 6,000 Americans of the Eighth United States Army Air Force who were killed during World War II flying from East Anglian bases. Included is a collection of books donated in their memory and general World War II memorabilia. Closed Sundays. No admission charge. *Norwich Library,* Bethel St. (phone: 611277).

ASSEMBLY HOUSE An 18th-century Georgian building with a fountain in the elegant courtyard, this was once a meeting place for fashionable society, but it also saw duty as a dancing academy and a school. It is now possible to take tea in the restored, elegant ballroom—a must for any visitor (see *Taking Tea,* below). There is also a small gallery displaying the work of local artists, and a music room in which concerts are held. Closed Sundays. Admission charge for concerts. Theatre St. (phone: 626402).

ENVIRONS

BLICKLING HALL The flagship of Britain's *National Trust* properties, this romantic country house with its impressive red-brick façade and magnificent interior was built between 1616 and 1624. The furnishings, paintings, and tapestries in the Georgian state rooms and the ornate Jacobean plaster ceiling in the *Great Gallery* draw crowds daily. There are over 4,000 acres of park, woodland, and gardens with colorful flower beds and borders, 300-year-old hedges, a huge lake, a temple, and even a secret garden. The hall is closed Mondays and Thursdays (except bank holidays); the park is open daily from dawn to dusk. Admission charge to the hall. In Blickling, 12 miles north of Norwich (phone: 263-733984).

SAINSBURY CENTRE FOR VISUAL ARTS A radical and exciting building, designed by Norman Foster, that houses the collection of ethnographic and modern art donated to the *University of East Anglia* by Sir Robert and Lady Sainsbury, founders of one of Britain's principal supermarket chains. About 2 miles west of the town, the building, financed by the Sainsburys' son, has been compared to the Beaubourg in Paris. In addition to the Sainsbury collection (from African and Eskimo art to Picasso and Henry Moore), the exhibits include the university's collection of 20th-century art and Art Nouveau. Buses run to the center of the university campus (see *Getting Around*). Closed Mondays and *Christmas Eve* through January 2. Admission charge. *University of East Anglia* (phone: 56060).

EXTRA SPECIAL

The river Wensum meanders through Norwich before joining the river Yare, a few miles away, for its final journey to the sea at the popular holiday resort of Great Yarmouth. Just 8 miles away is Wroxham, hub of the Norfolk Broads holiday area, where numerous cruisers can be hired. The Riverside Walk follows the Wensum from Carrow Bridge, in the southeast section of Norwich, through the historic heart of town to Hellesdon, 5 miles upstream (there are directional signs in a number of places). *Southern River Steamers* (phone: 624051) runs riverbus cruises (lasting from one to three hours) *Easter* through September. Boats leave either from the end of the quay at the back of Roaches Court, off Elm Hill, or from outside *Thorpe Station.*

Sources and Resources

TOURIST INFORMATION

Norwich's tourist information center (in the 15th-century *Guildhall,* Gaol Hill, opposite the market; phone: 666071 or 761082; fax: 765389) can supply brochures, maps, and general information, as well as help with rooms through its accommodations booking service. It also houses the city's impressive historical regalia. Closed Sundays. The *Norwich Official Guide* (costing £2.95/about $4.40), a comprehensive introduction to all aspects of the city, and a variety of *What's On* leaflets are available here. The tourist information center also supplies *Norwich Discovery* brochures on walking trails with themes (each costing 60p/about 90¢), which include the *Shopping Lanes and Alleys, City Walls* (a 2½-mile circuit), *Elm Hill: The Medieval Heritage,* and *Markets and Inns* (it points out noteworthy coaching houses and pubs). Guided walking tours leave from the tourist center Mondays through Saturdays at 2:30 PM April through October, with additional tours Sundays and bank holidays at 10:30 AM June through September; tours at other times can be arranged through the tourist office. There's also a useful leaflet describing how best to see the city after dusk—Norwich has won many international awards for its nighttime floodlighting of key attractions.

LOCAL COVERAGE The morning *Eastern Daily Press* and the *Eastern Evening News* are the city's two newspapers (published Mondays through Saturdays). The *Norwich Mercury* is published weekly.

TELEPHONE The city code for Norwich is 1603.

GETTING AROUND

It takes only 15 minutes to walk across Norwich, but a vehicle is necessary to visit points farther afield.

AIRPORT *Heathrow* is only a 2½-hour drive away, and London's *Stansted Airport* is even closer (an hour's drive); both offer international and domestic links. *Norwich Airport* (Fifers La.; phone: 411923), 4 miles north of the center via Cromer Road, has become an important international hub, with frequent flights to Amsterdam and several other European cities, as well as connections with the rest of the world.

BUS The local bus company, *Eastern Counties,* operates four *CityLine* minibus services in addition to its other routes (among which Nos. 526 and 527 are especially useful, since they run from the center of town to the university, as do Nos. 4 and 5 of the *CityLine* service). Long-distance (and local) buses use the bus station on Surrey Street. For information, contact the *Norwich Bus Information Centre* (at *Advice Arcade,* Guildhall Hill; phone: 613613); closed weekends.

CAR RENTAL All the usual international firms are represented, including *Avis* (*Terminal Building, Norwich Airport,* Holt Rd.; phone: 416719) and *Budget Rent-A-Car* (Denmark Opening, Sprowston Rd.; phone: 484004). A good local firm is *Kenning* (106-110 Prince of Wales Rd.; phone: 628271).

TAXI There are cabstands on Tombland (night only), on Guildhall Hill, and near Anglia Square; in addition, there are plenty of taxi firms, including *Beeline* (phone: 623333), *Bell* (phone: 622677), *Bestway* (phone: 620260), and *Courtesy* (phone: 620666).

TRAIN Prince of Wales Road links the city center with Norwich's *Thorpe Station* (across the river at the corner of Riverside and Thorpe Rd.; phone: 632055). There are hourly trains to London (travel time: less than two hours), to the coast, and to Peterborough, where connections to several other major destinations in Britain can be made.

SPECIAL EVENTS

The calendar includes the *Royal Norfolk Show,* an agricultural show held the last Wednesday and Thursday in June; the *Lord Mayor's Procession* in July; and the *Norfolk and Norwich Festival,* with concerts given in various venues throughout the city, in mid-October. Giant games of chess and draughts—the pieces are as big as young children—go on every day throughout the summer in *Chapelfields Gardens.*

MUSEUMS

In addition to those discussed in *Special Places,* Norwich has another interesting museum:

COLMAN'S MUSTARD SHOP AND MUSEUM Exhibits illustrate the history of Colman's Mustard, introduced over 150 years ago; *Colman's Mustard Shop* (see

Shopping) is on the same premises. Tastings of the numerous varieties on sale sometimes can be arranged. Closed Sundays. 3 Bridewell Alley (phone: 627889).

SHOPPING

Since it is the largest urban center for miles around, Norwich draws shoppers from all over the surrounding county. The core of the city is the open-air market on the *Market Place,* the largest of its kind in the country; its vendors sell everything from fresh fruit and vegetables to flowers, fresh fish, watches, clothing, books, and basketware (closed Sundays). The big chain stores—including *Boots, Marks & Spencer, Woolworth's,* and *British Home Stores*—are a few minutes' walk away, augmented by five department stores—*Jarrolds, Bonds, Debenham's, Littlewoods,* and *Butcher's.* The *Castle Mall* underground shopping center at the foot of the castle is another option. London Street, the first street in Britain to be given over to pedestrians alone, is lined with jewelers and national chain outlets, whereas the old shops on Elm Hill, Swan Lane, and Bridewell Alley are well stocked with local arts and crafts, jewelry, and souvenir bottles of old Norfolk Punch—a concoction prepared using natural underground waters and dozens of herbs. The most attractive thoroughfare of all is the *Royal Arcade,* a covered walkway between the walk at *Market Place* and Castle Street, designed in beautiful Art Nouveau style. *Bagley's Court* has open-air shops in the town center. There are some interesting antiques and junk shops to browse in on Upper St. Giles Street, including *Peter Crowe's Antiquarian Books and Prints* (No. 77; phone: 624800), and along St. Benedicts Street. Many of Norwich's designer clothing stores have gathered on Bedford Street; British designer names here include Nicole Farhi and Betty Jackson. Norwich also has a weekly antiques market on Wednesdays at *St. Andrew's Hall* (phone: 628477) as well as longer events in early January, at *Easter,* and during July. It also has an antiques center at *The Quayside.* For standard shopping hours, see GETTING READY TO GO.

Be sure to take your passport when you shop, and always inquire about the Value Added Tax (VAT) refund application forms when your total purchases in a store are over £50 (about $75). The VAT is a surcharge payable at the sales counter, but foreign customers usually will be reimbursed for it at home (for more information see GETTING READY TO GO).

The following shops are worth a look:

Colman's Mustard Shop Gift items and 13 different types of mustard are sold in this attractive store. 3 Bridewell Alley (phone: 627889).

Contact Gallery Small, modern, and cheerful, it features only local artists. 56 St. Benedicts St. (phone: 760219).

James and Ann Tillett Here you'll find a reputable stock of pewter, solid antique silver, jewelry, glass decanters, and tiny enamel pieces. Just opposite the cathedral, Tombland House, Tombland (phone: 624914).

Mousetrap A tiny cheese shop, yet it's packed with many varieties—from Shropshire blue to Cornish Yarg. Other goodies include chocolates and homemade ice cream. 2 St. Gregory's Alley, Church Sq., Pottergate (phone: 614083).

Movie Shop It describes itself as "an antiquarian and nostalgic center." There's lots of kitsch, as well as genuine antiques and film books. 11 St. Gregory's Alley (phone: 615239).

National Trust Stop here for wildlife calendars, nature diaries, woolens, and soaps. Information on local *National Trust* properties is available alongside the tearoom upstairs. Dove St. (phone: 610206).

Neal's Yard Remedies This is the Norwich branch of the London company renowned for its natural treats, gifts, and homeopathic cures, sold by a knowledgeable staff. Also here is a clinic offering many types of healing treatments, from color therapy to shiatsu. 26 Lower Goat La. (phone: 766681).

The Stamp Corner Its wares date back as far as Roman times. Old postcards and cigarette cards are offered, too. Elm Hill (phone: 627413).

Thorntons Derbyshire chocolates, gift boxes, full-blown slabs of toffee, and more will tempt your sweet tooth. 1 Orford Pl. (phone: 612576).

Traditional Jewelers A. J. Podolski, the jeweler and silversmith, sells and repairs interesting old baubles. Bedford St. (phone: 622853).

SPORTS

Norwich has several parks with facilities for outdoor sports. For example, *Eaton Park* (on the southeast edge of the city) offers tennis, bowls, football, hockey, and cricket. In addition, there are several leisure centers offering a variety of activities (see below).

CRICKET The Norfolk county cricket team plays from May through the summer at *County Cricket Ground* (Cricket Ground Rd.; phone: 766788) in Trowse, a suburb southeast of the city.

GOLF The *Royal Norwich Golf Club* (Drayton Rd.; phone: 429928), the *Eaton Golf Club* (Newmarket Rd.; phone: 51686), and the *Costessey Park Golf Club* (West End, Old Costessey; phone: 746333) allow visitors to play, but their abilities may be "tested" by the resident professional.

RUGBY The *Norwich Rugby Club* meets September through May at *Beeston Hyrne Stadium* (North Walsham Rd.; phone: 426259).

SOCCER The local team, *Norwich City,* known fondly as the "Canaries," plays at the *Carrow Road Stadium* (phone: 612131) from August through May.

SWIMMING *St. Augustine's Swimming Centre* (Aylsham Rd.; phone: 620164) and *Broadland Aqua Park* in the *Norwich Sport Village and Hotel* (2 miles north of town, Drayton High St., Hellesdon; phone: 788912) have pools and sauna facilities.

TENNIS AND SQUASH The *Norfolk Tennis and Squash Centre* (Lime Tree Rd.; phone: 53532) and the *Crome Leisure Centre* (Telegraph La. East; phone: 36697) offer both, and the *Norwich Sport Village* (see *Swimming*) has tennis, squash, and badminton. For additional squash facilities, try the *Duke Street Leisure Centre* (Duke St.; phone: 623469); *Norman Leisure Centre* (Bignold Rd.; phone: 408140); or *St. Augustine's Swimming Centre* (see *Swimming*).

THEATER

Among Norwich's many dramatic treasures is one of the most successful provincial theaters in Europe.

CENTER STAGE

Theatre Royal This sleek 1992 update of a structure put up in 1935 in the theater and cinema style of the day (the fourth theater on the site) doesn't hold a candle to London's grander halls. But it is that remarkable thing—an arts institution that manages to be totally self-supporting; many of its large-scale productions go on to become major hits in London's West End. Current management keeps things hopping with a continual and very lively procession of circus, grand opera, ice shows, ballet, pantomime, variety shows, vaudeville, classical music concerts, and programs from the touring companies of the *National Theatre Company, Birmingham Royal Ballet, Glyndebourne Opera, London Festival Ballet,* and foreign dance companies. Closed *Christmas.* Theatre St. (phone: 630000).

The latest addition to Norwich's theater scene is the *Norwich Playhouse Theatre* (St. George's St.; phone: 612580), a resident professional company that performs classic and contemporary works in a new, modern building. The amateur *Norwich Players* produce shows at the *Maddermarket Theatre* (St. John's Alley; phone: 620917), while the *Sewell Barn Theatre* (on Constitution Hill; phone: 411721), named for local author Anna Sewell (who wrote *Black Beauty*), is, as its name suggests, a converted barn seating about 100 people.

MUSIC

The superb acoustics of *Norwich Cathedral* make it perfect for choral concerts and organ recitals; the huge medieval *St. Andrew's* and *Blackfriars Halls* on Elm Hill are venues for choral, symphony, band, and pop concerts. Other performances are held in the *Music Room* of the *Assembly House* (see *Special Places*) and on Thursday afternoons and weekends in the medieval-style hall of the *King of Hearts Arts Centre* (13-15 Fye Bridge St.; phone: 766129). The *University of East Anglia* is the most popular place for pop concerts and bands playing the university circuit, though the *Waterfront*

(139-141 King St.; phone: 766266) has become a close rival. A series of brass band concerts takes place in Norwich's parks most Sunday afternoons during the summer.

NIGHTCLUBS AND NIGHTLIFE

Norwich's most popular discotheque is the neon-lit *Ritzy and Central Park* (phone: 621541), set in a handsome, whitewashed, gabled building on Tombland. Other discos are *Hy's* (also on Tombland; phone: 621155) and *Peppermint Park* (Rose La.; phone: 764192). Nightclubs include *Le Valbon* (Prince of Wales Rd.; phone: 630760) and *Springfields* (Oak St.; phone: 660220).

Best in Town

CHECKING IN

While not Britain's most popular tourist destination, Norwich does have a handful of good hotels catering to a regular business clientele. Most of these properties have complete facilities for the business traveler. Those hotels listed below as having "business services" usually offer such conveniences as a concierge, meeting rooms, photocopiers, computers, translation services, and express checkout, among others. Call the hotel for additional information. Norwich also has several comfortable smaller places that may offer fewer modern conveniences than larger hotels—but more character. Earlham Road, leading west out of the center, is lined with guesthouses and bed and breakfast establishments. As a rough guide, expect to pay more than $100 a night for a double room (including private bath, phone, and TV set, unless otherwise noted) at an expensive hotel, between $70 and $90 at a moderate one, and less than $60 at an inexpensive one. A full English breakfast may be included in the rate. All telephone numbers are in the 1603 city code unless otherwise indicated.

EXPENSIVE

Maids Head Opposite the cathedral, it claims to be the oldest continuously inhabited inn in England, with its roots going back seven centuries. Some of the 81 bedrooms have original oak beams, but most are equipped with modern amenities. The *Minstrel Room* restaurant serves a traditional Sunday lunch, and a courtyard bar, converted from the original coach "garage," is popular with locals. Business services are available. Tombland (phone: 761111; fax: 613688).

Nelson Modern and fairly close to the railway station (across a bridge over the river). From the lounge and many of the 121 bedrooms, patrons can watch the boats floating downriver. Most of the accommodations are Executive and Superior Executive Rooms, with refrigerators stocked with milk, soda water, and orange juice; there's also a restaurant. Business services are offered. Prince of Wales Rd. (phone: 760260; fax: 620008).

Norwich Thoroughly modern and primarily a retreat for business travelers, it's on the outer ring road around Norwich, about 3 miles north of the city center. However, thanks to an energetic manager and a friendly staff, it's far from anonymous. The 108 bedrooms are well equipped, from cable TV to trouser presses. The *Rouen* restaurant competes with Norwich's best, and there are excellent de-stressing leisure facilities, including a swimming pool and sauna. Business services are available. 121-131 Boundary Rd. (phone: 787260; 800-528-1234; fax: 400466).

Norwich Sport Village and Hotel Ideal for combining sightseeing and sports, this place has 55 rooms and three restaurants surrounded by a huge sports complex. Facilities include saunas, spa baths, solariums, gyms, and squash courts. Children will enjoy the *Broadland Aqua Park* on site. Business services are available. Drayton High Rd., Hellesdon (phone: 789469; fax: 406845).

Sprowston Manor There has been a manor house on this site—about 3 miles northeast of the city center—since 1559, although most of the present building is 19th-century. Walk through 10 acres of parkland to reach the 18-hole golf course next door; other amenities include a restaurant and a palm-filled leisure club with a pool. The 97 bedrooms ooze character from every timber beam and sloping ceiling, but they have all manner of modern amenities. Business services are available. Wroxham Rd. (phone: 410871; 800-528-1234; fax: 423911).

MODERATE

Arlington A superb Georgian building sitting pretty in a quiet countryside setting only a 15-minute walk from the town center, this hotel has 40 rooms, some with four-poster beds. Two restaurants on the premises mean that guests don't even have to venture out in the evening. Newmarket Rd. (phone: 617841; fax: 663708).

Beeches Keith and Liz Hill's stolid, gray hotel is a homey-looking mansion with 28 guestrooms on busy Earlham Road. Yet inside the traffic seems miles away, and people who stay here have a privileged view over Norwich's "secret garden," a Victorian plantation carefully restored to its original state but rarely open to public view. *Antonio's* restaurant serves Italian and English dishes. 6 Earlham Rd. (phone: 621167; fax: 620151).

Cavalier Margaret and Ken Mortimer, a friendly English couple, run this comfortable, unpretentious property located a mile from the city center. There are 21 guestrooms, furnished in an attractive, homey style; amenities include cable TV. The dining room serves traditional English fare. 244 Thorpe Rd. (phone: 34291; fax: 31744).

INEXPENSIVE

Crofters A welcoming, self-service cold supper buffet is laid out in the kitchen on weekends for late arrivals who haven't the energy to go out to a restaurant. With 15 rooms, this is a pleasant place on private grounds next to *St. John's Cathedral.* 2 Earlham Rd. (phone: 613287).

EATING OUT

By no stretch of the imagination can Norwich be considered a gastronomic center; although there's plenty of interesting produce to be found in the surrounding countryside, only a handful of restaurants use it to best advantage. Look for menus featuring samphire, a salt-marsh plant served with butter or vinegar that is better known as the poor man's asparagus. Look, also, for crabs from Cromer, cockles and mussels from Moreston, Great Yarmouth herring, Lowestoft kippers, Stiffkey (pronounced *Stoo*-kee) Blues or oysters, Norfolk dumplings served sweet or savory, and wild duck and geese from the fens. Don't forget to accompany everything with a generous dollop of mustard—they say Mr. Colman made his fortune from the mustard that people *left* on their plates. A dinner for two with wine will cost more than $75 at a restaurant listed as expensive, $45 to $70 at one listed as moderate, and less than $40 at an inexpensive one. Restaurants listed below serve lunch and dinner, unless otherwise noted. All telephone numbers are in the 1603 city code unless otherwise indicated.

EXPENSIVE

Adlard's This is undoubtedly the best restaurant in Norwich. Chef/owner David Adlard uses local seasonal ingredients in the French and British dishes offered at this dining spot. The prix fixe menu changes daily, but a typical dish worth sampling is the rack of English lamb with ratatouille and *gratin dauphinois.* Lunch here is a particularly good value. Closed Sundays, Mondays, and Saturday lunch. Reservations advised. Major credit cards accepted. 79 Upper St. Giles St. (phone: 633522).

Brasted's Although it looks like a smart private house, there's nothing pretentious about the cozy decor with striped fabrics offset by fresh carnations, or the handwritten menu offering simple yet delicious fare: Grilled lemon sole, *boeuf en croûte,* steak and kidney pie, and the chocolate *marquise* are true standouts. Closed Sundays. Reservations necessary. Major credit cards accepted. 8-10 St. Andrew's Hill (phone: 625949).

By Appointment A small, romantic place decorated something like a Victorian sitting room, with antiques and armchairs. The food is far from old-fashioned, though: Outstanding dishes include panfried medallions of pork, poached Scottish salmon, and fresh mussels. Open for dinner only; closed Sundays. Reservations necessary. Major credit cards accepted. 27 St. George's St. (phone: 630730).

Green's Seafood One of the city's few excellent restaurants, it has a menu devoted to fish (try the sea bass filet with tarragon or scampi tails), with the exception of one vegetarian dish and two meat dishes. It's a good place for pre- or post-theater dining. Closed Sundays. Reservations advised. Major credit cards accepted. 82 Upper St. Giles St. (phone: 623733).

Marco's It's one of Norwich's smartest dining spots. Proprietor/chef Marco Vessalio tops off his provincial Italian specialties with a superb zabaglione; anything from the Tuscan section of the menu is guaranteed to please. Closed Sundays and Mondays. Reservations necessary. Major credit cards accepted. 17 Pottergate (phone: 624044).

MODERATE

Boswell's This lively brasserie and cocktail bar occupies the old creeper-covered pub next to the cathedral. The menu is eclectic, featuring such continental dishes as spinach and mushroom lasagna, steaks, and smoked salmon with gravlax; there's often live music. In summer, enjoy the weekend brunch sitting under umbrellas outside. Open daily. Reservations unnecessary. Major credit cards accepted. 24 Tombland (phone: 626099).

Sasses This lovingly restored 1930s restaurant near the railway station specializes in French and Italian fare. Before dining, have a drink upstairs in the elegant cocktail bar whose furniture has graced many a film set. Open for dinner only; closed Sundays. Reservations advised. Major credit cards accepted. 2-6 Thorpe Rd. (phone: 622424).

Siam Bangkok Dine beneath a ceiling of painted paper parasols in this small Thai restaurant. Hot and sour soup, perfumed rice, and "Bags of Gold" (pork and prawns served in an edible bag) appear on the menu. Closed Sundays. Reservations advised. Major credit cards accepted. 8 Orford Hill (phone: 617817).

Wine Press In a basement down a pretty Georgian alley, this former newspaper press room has been converted into an attractive wine bar serving salads and snacks at lunchtime (weekdays) and light meals in the evening (Wednesdays through Saturdays). Closed Sundays. No reservations. Major credit cards accepted. 8 Woburn Ct., Guildhall Hill (phone: 622134).

INEXPENSIVE

Briton's Arms Morning snacks, light lunches, and tea, all homemade in classic English manner, are served in this 15th-century cottage; in winter, diners can enjoy their food in front of a blazing fireplace. Closed Sundays. No reservations. No credit cards accepted. 9 Elm Hill (phone: 623367).

Crypt Tea Rooms The old crypt walls meet a modern glass roof laced with red framing, the whole creating an attractive, if rather bizarre, setting for hot lunches, snacks, cakes, and coffee. On Saturdays, there's often a crafts fair going on in the same building. Closed Sundays. No reservations. Major credit cards accepted. St. Andrew's and Blackfriars Halls, Elm Hill (phone: 614971 or 623574).

Gedge The full name is *Gedge of Elm Hill,* where it sits perched on the corner at the top. The smell of coffee and home-baked cakes, scones, pastries, and rolls wafts outside the door, a hint of things to come. In warm weather, tables are available outside. Closed Sundays. No reservations. Major credit cards accepted. 2 Elm Hill (phone: 624847).

King of Hearts This restaurant-cum-gallery serves salads, soups, eggplant lasagna, and other light lunch fare, as well as afternoon tea. There are lunchtime concerts upstairs, and the local paintings on display are for sale. Closed Sundays and Mondays. No reservations or credit cards accepted. 13-15 Fye Bridge St. (phone: 766129).

Tree House Next door to the *Rainbow Wholefood Shop* (under the same ownership), this tiny eatery does a roaring business, serving all-natural foods to a health-conscious clientele. It's just the place for a vegetarian meal. The hot, spiced apple juice is a must on chilly days. Closed Sundays. Reservations advised for dinner Thursdays through Saturdays. No credit cards accepted. 14 Dove St. (phone: 763258).

TAKING TEA

Naturally, Norwich has plenty of afternoon tea spots; one, however, is special.

A PERFECT CUP

Assembly House The 18th-century building in whose former banquet hall this tea shop makes its home was once the meeting place for fashionable society, later a dancing academy and a school. With a fountain in the courtyard, it is as elegant as can be. No visitor should miss a tea or lunch in the ballroom, full of fancy plasterwork and ornate lamps. Closed Sundays. Theatre St. (phone: 626402).

SHARING A PINT

In 1892, the local Temperance Society listed more than 800 pubs in the city. Today there are a "mere" 200, many with several centuries of history and resident ghosts. The oldest pub in the city is also one of its most special.

PERFECT PINTS

Adam and Eve Dating from 1249, this pub was first used as a brew house to which artisans laboring on the nearby cathedral would repair. Customers can sit outside on wooden benches or indoors, where low beams and bare tiled floors recall the spit and sawdust of wherryman days. Morning coffee, grills, salads, hot and cold snacks, and a formal Sunday lunch are available. 17 Bishopsgate (phone: 667423).

The *Coach and Horses* (Bethel St.; phone: 631337) is an old coaching inn whose exterior walls still carry the medieval parish boundary marks and whose interior woodwork dates from 1400, while the *Lamb Inn* (off Haymarket; phone: 625365), another old coaching inn down a passageway, was the scene of the infamous murder of one of its landlords in 1787. *Micawbers Tavern* has a cozy, old, dark wooden interior but remains more offbeat, situated at the quiet end of Pottergate on the corner of Cow Hill (phone: 626627). Nearby, the livelier *Ten Bells* (76 St. Benedicts St.; phone: 667833) has real ale, live jazz in the evenings, and tempting Sunday lunches.

Oxford

For 600 years, England had only two universities, and though more than 40 institutions of higher learning have opened their doors since the early 19th century, the two venerable ancients are still so embedded in the British psyche that they often are called by one name, "Oxbridge," and put asunder only by scholars debating questions of academic supremacy or by tourists comparing the universities' visible merits. Although neither issue has a clear-cut conclusion, the casual visitor will notice a difference between Oxford and Cambridge. Whereas Cambridge, often described as a "city within a university," has the atmosphere of a small country town, Oxford is larger and bustling, not quite a metropolis, but transformed by a 20th-century auto industry on its outskirts into a "university within a city."

Though only part of present-day Oxford, *Oxford University* remains the city's historic core; it is one of the world's greatest living architectural treasures, where examples of every building style from the 11th century on are preserved in less than a square mile. *Oxford* is Britain's oldest university, but age coupled with academe has not produced a dark, dreary collection of moss-covered monoliths. A much-quoted line by 19th-century poet Matthew Arnold—"That sweet city with her dreaming spires"—aptly describes the university's towers, domes, and constant repetition of pinnacles when seen from afar or above. Close up, as the visitor stands before a single façade of ribbed golden stone, limpid panes of glass, or alternating panels of the two, any sense of the laborious process of study fades, and *Oxford* becomes the idea of learning incarnate, all light, clarity, and brilliance, even in the most inclement weather.

No one knows why scholars began to gather here. The city was probably in existence on the banks of the river Thames (called, in Oxford, the Isis) and its tributary, the Cherwell, long before the first reference to it appeared in the *Anglo-Saxon Chronicle* in 912. In 1121, the *Priory of St. Frideswide* was founded, and it was possibly the presence of scholarly monks that drew English students to Oxford after a quarrel between Henry II and the French resulted in the closing of the *Sorbonne* to Englishmen in 1167. The university then developed quickly. By 1300, the first colleges had been established (*University, Balliol,* and *Merton*), and there were 1,500 students on hand.

Relations between town and gown were immediately antagonistic. Early students lived in lodging houses at the mercy of price-gouging townspeople; townspeople saw their city taken over by a young and boisterous army. An outbreak of hostilities in 1209 caused some students to flee and set up a university at Cambridge. Even greater trouble in 1355, on *St. Scholastica's Day,* resulted in the deaths of 62 students and in the rest being driven from town. That the dispute was eventually resolved in favor of the university was a measure of its royal protection (because scholars became the basis of a king's loyal civil service, the gown-crown connection was strong). Thereafter, on every *St. Scholastica's Day* from 1357 to 1825, city dignitaries performed the humiliating penance of placing 62 pennies on the altar of the university church of *St. Mary the Virgin.* During that period, the university virtually ruled Oxford.

Rivalry between town and gown is now lighthearted, but the structure of the university has scarcely changed since the Middle Ages. By 1400, every student was required to be listed on the roll (matricula) of a master (or teacher—later to be called a don, from the Latin *dominus* for "master") responsible for him, and all were required to live in colleges or halls rather than in scattered lodging houses. The proliferating colleges (there are 36 today) became self-contained communities—behind the gates of each were living quarters, a chapel, a library, a kitchen, a dining hall, and even a brewery. This collegiate system in its modern guise continues to baffle visitors. Many an undergraduate popping out of *Worcester* or *Wadham* has been accosted by lost tourists looking for "Oxford College," unaware that *Oxford*'s colleges are part of the university as a whole. Young men and women (the first of five women's colleges opened in 1878, and all but one of *Oxford*'s colleges are now open to both sexes) seeking admission to the university have to pass a highly competitive examination given by individual colleges, and to live in them or in lodgings approved by them. But the university arranges academic curricula, administers financial aid from the government, and awards degrees.

Oxford's medieval organization accounts for the type of sightseeing experience it offers. More than 600 buildings in the city are considered to be of outstanding architectural merit, and most belong to the university. Your time in *Oxford* will be spent wandering through gateways into "quadrangles," or courtyards (the students live up numbered staircases around the quads); discovering gardens, cloisters, and chapels; visiting the occasional open library or hall; and following a passageway through still another arch and into one more quadrangle, often a spacious green lawn coaxed to perfection by centuries of loving care and hardly any pounding of feet—the sign will say who's allowed to walk on the grass, and it's usually dons, sometimes postgraduates, occasionally undergraduates, never visitors.

Much of *Oxford*'s history is brought to life by the anecdotes of local guides well versed in the city's folklore: How Samuel Johnson, a poor student at *Pembroke College,* was ashamed to walk into nearby *Christ Church*—always a grand college—because of his run-down shoes, yet threw away a pair of new ones left at his door by a rich scholar. Or how one prospective undergraduate was greeted superciliously by a don who turned away, opened a copy of the *Times,* and said, "Right, impress me"—at which the boy took out a box of matches and set fire to the paper. He won a scholarship.

Oxford's students (comprising more than 10% of the city's total population of 116,000) occasionally use humor to relieve the weight of tradition that is everywhere. Some of the weightier traditions, in fact, seem actually born of silliness: "The Mallard Song," sometimes sung by the fellows of *All Souls,* celebrates a duck that flew out of a drain when the college was built. The *Boar's Head Ceremony,* held at *Queen's College* at *Christmas,* honors a legendary scholar who saved himself from a wild boar's attack by stuffing a Greek book down the animal's throat.

None of this, however, changes the fact that *Oxford*'s stock-in-trade is the pursuit of knowledge, and visitors tiptoeing around quadrangles are constantly reminded of this by the firm signs asking them to be quiet. Such a polite command is not hard to obey, especially if it's all the easier to hear the choristers of *Christ Church* singing in the cathedral. But even without the background sound, the sight of the sun glinting off the exalted architectural complex of Radcliffe Square, or of the progression of college façades on High Street coalescing to a magnificent skyline, is an inspiration.

Oxford At-a-Glance

SEEING THE CITY

An initial bird's-eye view of Oxford is absolutely essential, since it gives a clear idea of the layout of the colleges. Four of the best vantage points for such a perspective are the gallery near the top of the spire of *St. Mary's Church* on High Street (colloquially known as The High), the cupola at the top of Christopher Wren's *Sheldonian Theatre* on Broad Street (better known as The Broad), *Carfax Tower* in the center of town (closed November through February), and the tower of *St. Michael* at the North Gate (admission charge for all). From *St. Mary's* you see much of The High, with its gentle curve that is fancifully said to reflect most people's natural stroll: *All Souls College; University College;* and the *Radcliffe Camera,* a library. From the *Sheldonian* you look onto Broad Street; across to *Balliol* and *Trinity Colleges;* closer by, down at *Exeter College,* the *Bodleian Library,* and the *Clarendon Building*—once the home of the university printers, later to become the *Oxford University Press.* The view from *South Park* (east of Magdalen Bridge) of the "dreaming spires" set amid the trees is lauded in many a guidebook. For another traditional view of Oxford's spires, find the slightly unkempt piece of common land called *Port Meadow,* between the river Thames and the railway line. Or, closer and more congenial, though slightly less panoramic, *Christ Church Meadow,* near the city center to the east of St. Aldate's, part of which is a farm.

SPECIAL PLACES

Ask any but the most disenchanted *Oxford* graduate about special places and he or she will answer "my college." Virtually all 36 of them are worth a visit, but happily the most impressive are the most central. Not one is too distant from *Carfax Tower* (from the French *quatre voies,* "four ways," or from the Latin *quadrifurcus,* "four-forked"), where the four main streets of Oxford met in Saxon times (and still do), to be visited on foot. Most offer a glimpse of inner sanctums: quadrangles, chapels, and dining halls hung with portraits of distinguished former students and benefactors. Opening times vary. Many of the colleges have begun charging admission to their quads in summer (if not year-round).

For an overview of the entire university over the past eight centuries, the *Oxford Story* describes important events and personalities involved with *Oxford.* After a four-minute video on the modern goings-on of the university, small cars shaped like medieval scholars' desks transport visitors on a slow 30-minute ride past life-size tableaux with dramatic sounds, smells, and lighting effects accompanied by commentary, which visitors listen to on headphones. The highlights of the university's history are included, from Archbishop Cranmer being burned at the stake in 1555 to the development of penicillin and a modern undergraduate wondering which clubs and societies to join. There's also an excellent gift shop. Open daily. Admission charge. 6 Broad St. (phone: 728822).

THE HEART OF OXFORD

MAGDALEN COLLEGE *Magdalen Tower* (pronounced *Mawd*-lin), guarding the eastern end of High Street, was called by King James I, "the most absolute building in Oxford." An anthem is sung from the top of the tower at 6 AM every *May Day* morning. The college was established in 1458 by William of Waynflete, a Bishop of Winchester, who was one of the first college founders to emphasize the importance of a chapel. There is a famous deer park (phone: 276000), where the animals are fairly tame. Open daily from 2 to 6:15 PM. Admission charge June through September.

Across the street from *Magdalen* is the *Botanic Garden,* the oldest in Britain. It was laid out in 1621 with approximately £5,000 given by Henry Danvers, Earl of Danby, primarily for the study of medicinal herbs. Open daily. Admission charge in July and August. High St. (phone: 276920).

ALL SOULS COLLEGE Founded 21 years before *Magdalen* by Henry Chichele, Archbishop of Canterbury, *All Souls* does not have undergraduates, only 60 fellows engaged in research and teaching. (A member of the college once remarked that he never needed an encyclopedia; if he wanted to know anything he just had to ask a colleague.) Behind *All Souls*' small 15th-century quadrangle is the 18th-century great quadrangle, with twin towers and the magnificent *Codrington Library,* adorned by a sundial made by Christopher Wren. Open daily from 2 to 4:30 PM. High St. (phone: 279379).

UNIVERSITY COLLEGE Across High Street from *All Souls,* "Univ," as it is known, has the oldest building foundation in *Oxford* (1249). It used to be believed that the college was founded by Alfred the Great, though the most telling comment on that occurred when one don—on being asked to a formal dinner to celebrate the millennium of Alfred's "foundation"—declined to come and sent two burned cakes instead. There's also a memorial to the poet Shelley (although he was expelled from the college). From 1968 to 1970, a young Rhodes Scholar named Bill Clinton studied politics here. (When Clinton was elected president in 1992, *University* flew the Stars and Stripes from its flagpole as a salute.) Open daily. High St. (phone: 276602).

CHURCH OF ST. MARY THE VIRGIN *St. Mary's* 14th-century spire is one of the dominant features of the Oxford skyline (climb to the tower at the top for a magnificent panorama of the city), and the church is a fine example of Perpendicular Gothic. Alongside the church, and sharing the same entrance, stands the old *Congregation House,* built during the 1320s. The university's first building, it housed the original library. There's also a small gift shop, and the atmospheric *Convocation Coffee House* is right behind the church (see *Eating Out*). The tower is open daily. Admission charge. High St. (phone: 794334).

RADCLIFFE CAMERA This building commemorates *Oxford*'s most generous 18th-century benefactor, Dr. John Radcliffe. When seen from afar under the right conditions and from the right viewpoint, it compares as a landmark with *Cambridge*'s *King's College Chapel.* Designed by James Gibbs and completed in 1749, it was originally called the *Radcliffe Library* and is now a reading room for the *Bodleian,* the university library. Closed to the public. Radcliffe Sq., behind *St. Mary's Church.*

BODLEIAN LIBRARY The earth between the *Radcliffe Camera* and the *Bodleian Library* is only a thin crust: Below it are massive stores of books and underground railways that deliver books to readers on request. The creation of the *Bodleian Library* was the outstanding achievement of 17th-century *Oxford.* It was founded by Thomas Bodley, born in 1544 and a fellow of *Merton* at 19, and opened in 1602, using an older library (*Duke Humfrey's Library,* built over the 15th-century *Divinity School*) as a core. It is one of the greatest libraries in the world and has the right, as do the *British Museum Library* and the *Cambridge University Library,* to a copy of every book published in the country. It already has close to six million books and over a million maps, occupying close to 100 miles of shelves (and another one and a half miles of shelves are added each year). Only readers may enter the library, although conducted tours of the *Convocation House* and *Duke Humfrey's Library* are available on weekdays April through October and Wednesdays and Saturdays only the rest of the year. Admission charge. Radcliffe Sq. (phone: 277000).

SHELDONIAN THEATRE The degree-giving ceremony is held in this theater, which was designed in 1669 by Christopher Wren, then professor of astronomy at the university. Based on a classical amphitheater, it is enhanced by its own courtyard, entered from Broad Street, which it shares with the *Clarendon Building.* The 13 stone heads that depict Roman emperors on the railings outside were carved in the early 1970s. They are the second set of replacements for the original group, which was installed in 1669. Its interior, also used for concerts, is magnificent, among the most attractive of its features being a famous ceiling by Robert Streeter, "sergeant-painter" to King Charles II. You can climb a wide wooden stairway to the cupola for a partial view of central Oxford's spires and gargoyles. Closed Sundays and when in use for ceremonies or meetings. Admission charge. Broad St. (phone: 277299).

NEW COLLEGE Founded by William of Wykeham, Bishop of Winchester, this college is officially named *St. Mary College of Winchester in Oxenford;* but ever since it was completed in 1386, it has been known as *New College.* The front quadrangle is the original one (the first quadrangle built as such in *Oxford,* following the example of *Merton*'s *Mob Quad,* which became a quad bit by bit), though the top story on three of its sides was added in the late 17th century. The other side is formed by the chapel, which should be seen inside, too, for various treasures including the bishop's crosier. *New College*'s garden quad, also added in the late 17th century, incorporates a stretch of 13th- and 14th-century city wall. Open daily. Admission charge June through September. New College La. (phone: 279555).

BALLIOL COLLEGE Apart from *All Souls,* which does not admit undergraduates, *Balliol* is academically the most impressive college in the university, with a long list of distinguished graduates, particularly in the field of politics (Lord Curzon, Harold Macmillan, Edward Heath). The college originated in 1255 when the Bishop of Durham levied a fine upon John de Balliol, a powerful landowner. For several years, he was made to pay a sum of money toward the support of poor *Oxford* scholars. After de Balliol's death in 1269, his wife continued the project. *Balliol,* founded in approximately 1263, was actually a living quarters, not a college as we know it today. Outside *Balliol,* in the middle of Broad Street, a cross on the ground marks the spot where three Protestant martyrs, Thomas Cranmer, Nicholas Ridley, and Hugh Latimer, were burned at the stake during the reign of Mary Tudor in 1555. Open daily. Broad St. (phone: 277777).

CHRIST CHURCH Lesson one: If you don't want to be taken for a complete country bumpkin, never say "Christ Church College," but simply "Christ Church." Lesson two (very subtle, this one): Contrary to usage at the other colleges, fellows, or dons, here are known as "students," but undergraduates never are. *Christ Church* was founded on the site of the *Priory of St. Frideswide* by Cardinal Wolsey in 1525, and was refounded by Henry VIII in 1532 and 1546. It includes among its august alumni such names as Sir Philip Sidney, Richard Hakluyt, John Locke, John Wesley, John Ruskin, Lewis Carroll (né Charles Dodgson), and W. H. Auden. Its exquisitely vaulted chapel is also *Oxford*'s cathedral, one of the smallest cathedrals in England, while its 16th-century *Great Quadrangle* (or *Tom Quad*) is *Oxford*'s largest. *Great Tom,* the imperious bell in *Tom Tower,* hangs right above the main *Christ*

Church entrance and resounds 101 times at 9:05 each night, the original curfew time for the 101 undergraduates it summoned by its first peal. See, also, the paneled and gilded medieval dining hall and the 18th-century Palladian *Peckwater Quad,* behind *Tom Quad.* Open daily. Admission charge. St. Aldate's. (phone: 276150).

MERTON COLLEGE *University College* was founded in 1249, *Balliol* in 1263, but if it's a question of official papers, then *Merton* (founded in 1246, with final statutes dated 1274) can claim to be the oldest college in *Oxford.* It has *Oxford*'s oldest quadrangle, *Mob Quad* (begun 1304), whose south and west sides are formed by a curious medieval library—some of the books still are chained to desks as they were for the early scholars. *Merton* also has *Oxford*'s first collegiate chapel, containing original 13th-century stained glass. The street outside is still cobbled. Open daily; the medieval library is open weekdays from 2 to 3:30 PM (to 4 PM during summer). Merton St. (phone: 276310).

ST. EDMUND HALL A few yards off High Street, this college has what may be the prettiest quadrangle in the university. Though quite small, it has a well, a sundial, window boxes, flowers, and wisteria climbing the walls. The college's architecture ranges from the 16th to the 20th centuries. An archway leads to the former *Church of St. Peter in the East,* a beautiful building which is now its library. Open daily. Queen's La. (phone: 279000).

ASHMOLEAN MUSEUM OF ART AND ARCHAEOLOGY Just as the *Bodleian* was Britain's first truly public library, the *Ashmolean*—opened in 1683—was its first public museum (and possibly the first in Europe as well). Even today a visitor will find many of the same scenes that *Oxford* scholars have enjoyed over the years—among them, items from *Tradescant's Ark,* the "closet of rarities" assembled by John Tradescant the Elder (d. 1638), which forms the nucleus of the collection, as well as odd lots such as Guy Fawkes's lantern, Powhatan's mantle, and the armor-plated hat that belonged to William Bradshaw, president of the court that passed sentence on Charles I. Bronzes (Chinese, Indian, Greek, Roman, Etruscan, Italian Renaissance, later European); ceramics (Chinese, Islamic, Japanese, English, and European); clocks and watches, jewelry, glass, coins and medals, and antiquities (Cretan, Cypriot, Egyptian, Etruscan, Greek, Near Eastern, and Tibetan); paintings (Dutch, English, Flemish, French, Italian); other pieces (classical, European, Dark Age, medieval, and Oriental); and weapons are all represented in this *omnium gatherum* of a museum: There's something here for everyone. Closed Mondays. No admission charge. Beaumont St. (phone: 278000).

OFFBEAT OXFORD

COVERED MARKET Built in 1774, this busy and charming if down-to-earth street market was relinked (after 250 years) to the Cornmarket shopping street by a pedestrian route through the courtyard of the old *Golden Cross Inn.* In its maze of tiny lanes crammed with tiny shops, the aroma of just-ground coffee and fresh fish mingles with that of ripe cheese and bloodstained sawdust from the butcher's shops and that of a game dealer's shop half-buried in fur and feathers. Wander among the banks of fresh fruit and vegetables, salami, mussels, carp, and silver sprats. Or browse through hats, sweaters, jeans, jewelry, and souvenirs. There's even an old-fashioned cobbler's shop. After a colorful morning's stroll, drop by at the rough-and-ready but popular *Beaton's Sandwich Café* or *Georgina's Coffee Shop* (both at 77 *The Market;* phone: 249527). Downstairs, the café sells sandwiches and cakes, while the upstairs coffee shop caters to a health-conscious clientele with salads and homemade soups. Both claim a cult following among undergraduates. The tables may be covered in crumbs, the service offhand, the floor unswept, the other customers morose or argumentative, but the place has style.

BLACKWELLS BOOKSHOP One of the world's biggest bookshops, virtually an Aladdin's cave filled with tomes, *Blackwells* is where tourists buying paperback guides to the city rub shoulders with fellows of *All Souls* collecting esoteric tomes ordered on their behalf, and undergraduates dutifully gathering up texts recommended by their tutors. Branches are located at 48-51 Broad St., opposite the *Sheldonian Theatre* (phone: 792792); 23-25 Broad St. (for paperbacks); 27 Broad St. (for art and posters); 38 Holywell St. (for rare books, music books, records, and sheet music); 8 Broad St. (for children's books); and 53 Broad St. (for travel books and maps).

EXTRA SPECIAL

Early summer sees *Oxford* at its best and brightest, and although most undergraduates have exams on their minds, that does not seem to obtrude—perhaps it even helps. *Oxford* has all kinds of activities and fetes during this season; check at the *City of Oxford Information Centre* (see *Tourist Information*) as well as the college notice boards. There are open-air plays in college gardens; "commem" balls—grand, all-night, black-tie affairs to which you may have trouble obtaining tickets, although it is fun to watch the revelers arriving in their finery; picnics and madrigals on the river; garden parties; church festivals; and much more. (*A word of caution:* Because hotel rooms are at a premium at this time, be prepared to accept accommodations some distance from the city center or even in the surrounding countryside. Woodstock, Abingdon, Witney, Great Milton, and Weston-on-the-Green, for example, have good hotels.)

Sources and Resources

TOURIST INFORMATION

The *City of Oxford Information Centre* (phone: 726871) is on St. Aldate's, opposite the *Town Hall,* about 100 yards from *Carfax Tower;* however, it is scheduled to move early this year to new quarters on Gloucester Green, a paved square near the bus station. The center stocks a massive amount of tourist literature, guides, maps, and souvenirs; there is also a 24-hour informational video screen. It is closed Sundays (except in summer). *Guide Friday* (phone: 790522), a company that offers guided bus tours around the city, has an information center in the railway station.

LOCAL COVERAGE The *Oxford Mail* (whose editor, incidentally, is traditionally allowed to dine in *All Souls*) is the evening newspaper. Also available are the monthly magazine *What's On* and the free leaflet *This Month in Oxford. Daily Information,* a city-published sheet, is available for reference from the information center.

TELEPHONE The city code for Oxford is 1865.

GETTING AROUND

Everyone travels around town on foot or by bicycle; you will need a car or taxi only if you're going to the surrounding area. Note: In some of the older streets, the numbers go up one side and then back down the other, rather than even numbers on one side and odd on the other.

BUS The *Oxford Bus Company* (395 Cowley Rd.; phone: 711312) provides good service linking the city center with its outskirts. Local services also are provided by *Thames Transit* (phone: 772250). Fares range from 25p (about 40¢) to 70p (about $1.05) depending on the distance. The air conditioned *CityLink 190* (phone: 248190) and *Oxford Tube* (phone: 772250) nonstop coaches run every 20 minutes from Oxford's Gloucester Green to London's *Victoria Station.* The *X70* bus (phone: 722270) runs several times daily to London's *Heathrow* and *Gatwick Airports.*

CAR RENTAL You can rent a car from *Budget* (Hythe Bridge St.; phone: 724884); *Europcar* (*Seacourt Tower,* Botley Rd.; phone: 246373); *Hertz* (Woodstock Roundabout; phone: 57291); or *Kennington* (Peartree Roundabout, Woodstock Rd.; phone: 511232). Parking in Oxford is difficult to find, although there usually is space in the big, multistory car park at the back of *Westgate Shopping Centre.* Day-trippers can take advantage of the "Park and Ride" scheme. Leave your car free of charge in the parking lots clearly marked as you enter Oxford, then take the buses that run frequently to the city center (daily except Sundays).

TAXI There are cab ranks in several locations, or call *ABC Taxis* (phone: 770077), *City Taxis* (phone: 794000), or *Radio Taxis* (phone: 242424).

TOURS The walking tours run by the *Oxford Guild of Guides,* including "Oxford Past & Present," "Oxford Detectives," and "Ghosts, Grotesques, and Gargoyles," offer excellent introductions to the city and colleges. Before setting off, everyone is reminded that it is a privilege to visit the colleges, where students both study and live, so it is essential to respect the request for quiet. Tours depart twice daily from the *City of Oxford Tourist Information Centre* (see above).

Spires & Shires (phone: 251785) has minibus tours of Oxford (both city and university) and points beyond, including Bath, the Cotswolds, *Stonehenge,* and Stratford. One stop that may be of particular interest to Americans is the ivy-covered Victorian house at 46 Leckford Road, where Bill Clinton lived when he studied at *Oxford* as a Rhodes Scholar. Open-top, double-decker guided bus tours, operated by *Guide Friday* (see above), travel around the city daily every 15 minutes. Stay on board for the full hour-long tour, or get off and rejoin as often as you like. Similar tours are offered during the summer by *Classic Tours* (phone: 1235-819393), although the commentary is recorded, rather than live.

TRAIN London's *Paddington Station* is an hour-long ride from Oxford by train. The Oxford railway station (phone: 722333), a bright, modern building, is west of the city center just off Park End Street.

SPECIAL EVENTS

The annual *May Day Morning* is celebrated on May 1, with traditional morris dancing and madrigal singing beginning at 6 AM. Late May sees one of the biggest events of the *Oxford* calendar—*Eights Week,* when crews from the colleges compete over four days for the coveted title of Head of the River (*Torpids,* a similar but smaller-scale event, is held in February). *Encaenia,* the university's dedication festival, takes place in the *Sheldonian Theatre* several times during the year, but most spectacularly at the end of the summer term, when honorary degrees are awarded to distinguished men and women. Each September, the two-day *St. Giles' Fair* is held on St. Giles, between the *Randolph* hotel and the point at which the Woodstock and the Banbury roads fork off to the north. Traffic has to be diverted to accommodate this centuries-old fun fair.

MUSEUMS

In addition to those mentioned in *Special Places,* other museums of note are the following:

CHRIST CHURCH PICTURE GALLERY Old Masters, glassware, and antiques are displayed. Open daily. Admission charge. In *Canterbury Quad, Christ Church;* enter from Oriel Sq. (phone: 276172).

CURIOXITY This museum with the unusual name has hands-on displays about science and technology, as well as *Oxford*'s outstanding history of the study of these subjects. Open daily. Admission charge. *Old Fire Station,* George St. (phone: 794494).

MUSEUM OF THE HISTORY OF SCIENCE Early scientific instruments and Einstein's blackboard are exhibited in the building that housed the *Ashmolean Museum* from 1683 to 1845. Closed weekends. No admission charge. Broad St. (phone: 277280).

MUSEUM OF MODERN ART Here is a gallery of paintings and sculpture, a cinema, and a bookshop. Closed Mondays. Admission charge. 30 Pembroke St. (phone: 722733).

MUSEUM OF OXFORD The history of the city from Norman times is described by means of photographs and models. Closed Sundays and Mondays. No admission charge. St. Aldate's (phone: 815559).

PITT RIVERS MUSEUM General Pitt-Rivers's renowned 19th-century collection, including ethnological and archaeological items, musical instruments, and weapons. Closed Sundays. No admission charge (Parks Rd.; phone: 270927). The museum's extension (60 Banbury Rd.; phone: 274726) is also closed Sundays; no admission charge.

UNIVERSITY MUSEUM Mainly natural history is explored in what was once Oxford's most architecturally controversial building. Closed Sundays. No admission charge. Parks Rd. (phone: 272950).

SHOPPING

Just off Cornmarket, the 12th-century courtyard of the old *Golden Cross Inn* was converted into a precinct of specialty shops in 1987. Broad Street, Turl Street, High Street opposite *University College* and the *Examination Schools,* and Little Clarendon Street are other good areas for browsing. For antiques, there are several shops on High Street, or visit the two indoor markets on Park End Street: the *Oxford Antiques Centre* (No. 27; phone: 251075) in the former Cooper's jam factory and the *Oxford Antiques Trading Company* (No. 40-41; phone: 793927). You can pick up some interesting comestibles, clothing, and souvenirs at the *Covered Market* (off High St.; see *Special Places*) or the Wednesday morning open market at Gloucester Green, a paved square near the bus station. Gloucester Green is also the site of an antiques market on Thursdays. The *Westgate Shopping Centre* and the *Clarendon Centre,* both near *Carfax Tower,* contain several well-known chain stores. For standard shopping hours, see GETTING READY TO GO.

Be sure to take your passport when you shop, and always inquire about the Value Added Tax (VAT) refund application forms when your total purchases in a store are over £50 (about $75). The VAT is a surcharge payable at the sales counter, but foreign customers usually will be reimbursed for it at home (for more information see GETTING READY TO GO).

Besides the famous *Blackwells Bookshop* (see *Special Places*), here are several other stores worth browsing through:

Alfred Maltby & Son Since 1834, this shop has specialized in bookbinding and restoring antiquarian tomes—and the work is still done by hand. The elegantly bound, blank diaries sold here make unusual souvenirs and gifts. 28 St. Michael's St. (phone: 243413).

Alice's Shop *Alice in Wonderland* memorabilia, from dolls to chess sets. This tiny establishment is located in a 15th-century building that was mentioned by author Lewis Carroll in many of his stories. 83 St. Aldate's (phone: 723793).

Bodleian Library Shop Quality souvenirs and literary items based on the university library's collections—ranging from bookmarks decorated with university gargoyles to catalogs of old academic books and manuscripts. Old Schools Quadrangle, Radcliffe Sq. (phone: 277175).

Castell & Son Established in 1846, this shop carries a large selection of university and college ties and scarves, as well as crested jewelry and souvenirs. 13 Broad St. (phone: 244000).

Dillons One of Oxford's more recent bookstores, it offers a wide variety of tomes. In the *William Baker House* at Broad and Cornmarket Sts. (phone: 790212).

Ducker & Son Top-quality men's shoes, as well as game fishing equipment. 6 Turl St. (phone: 242461).

Laurie Leigh Browse among antique clocks and keyboard instruments; the family who owns this shop also restores the articles for sale. 36 High St. (phone: 244197).

Macs-a-Million Since 1772, this shop has sold quality boots and shoes for gentlemen and ladies. *Covered Market,* off High St. (phone: 249531).

Magna Gallery One of Oxford's best for old maps and prints. 41 High St. (phone: 245805).

Maison Blanc The owner, Mrs. Blanc, imports many ingredients from France to produce mouth-watering cakes, tarts, chocolate animals, and breads. The window display usually makes anyone with a sweet tooth weak at the knees. 3 Woodstock Rd. (phone: 510974).

Niner & Hill Rare old books, especially tomes on history, art, and travel; also old prints. 43 High St. (phone: 726105).

Once a Tree A whimsical place that offers attractive wooden kitchen utensils, toys, and woodcarvings. 99 Gloucester Green (phone: 793558).

Oxford Cobbler Boots and shoes are repaired as customers watch at this old-fashioned cobbler's shop. *Covered Market,* off High St. (no phone).

Oxford Collection Glass tankards and other high-quality souvenirs bear the university's crest, which dates back to 1429. The crest symbol is an open book with seven seals, three crowns, and a Latin inscription that translates as "The Lord is my light." *Golden Cross Courtyard,* off Cornmarket (phone: 247414).

Oxford Gallery Sells as well as exhibits paintings (mostly contemporary), glassware, pottery, and jewelry. 23 High St. (phone: 242731).

Oxford University Press A full range of books published by the *Press* is available, including dictionaries of all sizes—from paperbacks to the definitive 25-volume *Oxford English* edition. 116 High St. (phone: 242913).

Robin Waterfield's It's the city's largest secondhand and antiquarian bookstore. It is particularly good for 17th- and 18th-century English books, and philosophy, classics, and history volumes from all periods. 36 Park End St. (phone: 721809).

Sanders The city's largest collection of old prints resides here, as well as rare theology books. 104 High St. (phone: 242590).

Shepherd and Woodward For *Oxford University* paraphernalia: sweatshirts, scarves, ties, and such. 109-114 High St. (phone: 249491).

Taylors A traditional grocer specializing in teas, jams, and biscuits. Pop in, even if only to savor the rich aromas. 31 St. Giles (phone: 58853).

Thorntons Its four floors are packed with secondhand books—some quite rare. 11 Broad St. (phone: 242939).

Titles Another rare book specialist. 15 Turl St. (phone: 727928).

Tumi A wide range of Latin American craftwork, including jewelry, ceramics, carvings, and knitwear. 1-2 Little Clarendon St. (phone: 512307).

W. P. Hine Men's clothing and accessories for town and country; women's raincoats, too. 52 High St. (phone: 242663).

Walters The official outfitter for *Oxford University* (providing academic robes, gowns, hoods, caps, and other ceremonial trappings), this shop also offers top-quality men's and women's clothing. 10 Turl St. (phone: 241848).

SPORTS

BICYCLING Bicycles can be rented from *Broadrib* (6 *Lincoln House,* Market St.; phone: 242624); *Cycle King* (55 Walton St.; phone: 516122); *Denton's* (294 Banbury Rd.; phone: 53859); or *Penny Farthing* (5 George St.; phone: 249368). (Though biking around Oxford may seem romantic, there are hundreds of cyclists and the traffic is congested, so unless you're very confident on two wheels, skip it.)

BOATING The sport most popularly associated with *Oxford* is rowing, especially in view of the annual *Boat Race* held on the Thames in London against *Cambridge.* At *Oxford,* the river Thames is too narrow to accommodate teams racing side by side (as is the river Cam at *Cambridge*), so the two universities have devised "Bumps," a series of rows in February and May in which 13 crews start together, one behind the other, and each tries to catch up and "bump" the one in front. But the best way for visitors to get properly acquainted with the river is to hire a punt (a flat-bottom boat propelled and steered by a pole) at *Cherwell Boathouse* (Bardwell Rd.; phone: 515978),

C. Howard & Son (Magdalen Bridge; phone: 61586), or *Hubbocks* (Folly Bridge; phone: 244235). Although unlikely, it is possible to fall into the river, and only competent swimmers are advised to venture out. Motorboats also can be rented for longer excursions from *Salters* (Folly Bridge; phone: 243421) or *Boat Enquiries* (Botley Rd.; phone: 727288).

GOLF The *Southfield Golf Club* (on Hilltop Rd., Headington; phone: 242158) and the *North Oxford Golf Club* (on Banbury Rd.; phone: 54415) welcome visitors who are members of other golf clubs (weekdays only).

SWIMMING Take a dip at the *Blackbird Leys Pool* (Blackbird Leys Rd.; phone: 771565) or the *Ferry Pool* (indoor) near Ferry Centre (Summertown; phone: 510330). *Ferry Pool* also has squash courts, and rents racquets. *Temple Cowley Pool* (Cowley Rd.; phone: 716667) has the only chlorine-free, sterilized pool in the area, as well as a sauna/solarium and fitness rooms.

THEATER

The *Apollo* (George St.; phone: 244544) hosts drama, opera, ballet, and popular music shows, while the *Pegasus Theatre* (Magdalen Rd.; phone: 722851) presents "fringe" productions. The *Playhouse* (on Beaumont St.; phone: 798600) presents plays and performance art pieces. The small theater at the *Old Fire Station* (40 George St.; phone: 794494) specializes in new works, particularly musicals, and has a lively café-bar. University drama groups also stage plays regularly in various colleges. Check the *Daily Information* sheet at the *City of Oxford Information Centre,* the *Oxford Mail,* or *This Month in Oxford* magazine (see *Local Coverage*).

MUSIC

Virtually all the colleges have a chapel of considerable architectural interest, and many of these showcase classical concerts and recitals. The best *Oxford* music is church music, however, and visitors are welcome at services in the three college chapels that have choir schools—*Christ Church, Magdalen College,* and *New College.* Several colleges are used for orchestral and choral concerts, as are the *Sheldonian Theatre,* the *Town Hall,* and the *Holywell Music Rooms,* said to be the oldest of their kind in Europe. *Music at Oxford* (phone: 864056) has a regular program of orchestral and choral concerts, and the *City of Oxford Orchestra* (phone: 252365) also performs regularly. For more details, consult the *Daily Information* sheet (see *Local Coverage,* above).

NIGHTCLUBS AND NIGHTLIFE

During the university term, Oxford is a young city, so there's a lot going on. *Fifth Avenue* (34-35 Westgate; phone: 245136; closed Sundays and Mondays) is fairly dressy; many students prefer the more casual *Coven* (Oxpens Rd.; phone: 242770; closed Mondays) or *Downtown Manhattan* (George St.; phone: 721101), underneath the *Apollo Theatre.*

Best in Town

CHECKING IN

Perhaps it is because members of the university (which includes anyone who has graduated from it) always can get a room in their old college, or perhaps it is because during the vacation there are so many university landladies whose merits are passed by word of mouth—whatever the reason, Oxford is short of top-grade hotels, especially in the city center, and for the few that do exist, it's usually necessary to make reservations well ahead. You need never go without a bed, however; if you are having trouble, consult the *City of Oxford Information Centre* (see *Tourist Information*). Expect to pay more than $150 per night for a double room (including private bath, phone, TV set, and breakfast, unless otherwise indicated) in a hotel listed as expensive; $105 to $150 at a moderate one; and less than $105 in an inexpensive establishment. All telephone numbers are in the 1865 city code unless otherwise indicated.

For an unforgettable experience in the Oxford area, we begin with our favorite, followed by our cost and quality choices of accommodations, listed by price category.

A SPECIAL HAVEN

Le Manoir aux Quat' Saisons Twelve miles southeast of Oxford, this establishment still has the two Michelin stars its restaurant earned even before it became a hotel a decade ago; now it's one of the country's most talked about dining and lodging retreats—with deservedly high prices—(see *Eating Out* for details on the restaurant). It's also a member of the prestigious Relais & Châteaux group. Housed in a 15th-century, golden-hued, Cotswold stone structure, it has mullioned windows, thick stone walls, and molded cornices that are Tudor to the core. Yet the decor is relaxed and airy, and the 17th- and 18th-century Tudor furniture adds a note of elegance and grace. There are 19 rooms, including a honeymoon suite nestled in the dovecote. Four of the bedrooms have four-poster beds and most have fine views of the surrounding 27 acres of gardens. After checking in, guests find fresh flowers, decanters of madeira, and bowls of exotic fruit in their quarters. Church Rd., Great Milton (phone: 1844-278881; 800-677-3524; fax: 1844-278847).

EXPENSIVE

Bath Place This nine-room hotel run by Kathleen Fawsitt and her daughter Yolanda occupies a cluster of tiny 17th-century cottages around a cobblestone courtyard. Two of the guestrooms have four-poster beds, and it's just a two-minute walk from the *Sheldonian Theatre.* Oysters, pigeon, and kidneys feature regularly on the restaurant's menu. 4-5 Bath Pl., off Holywell St. (phone: 791812; fax: 791834).

Eastgate Not quite as luxurious as some, this comfortable hotel is ideally located near *Magdalen* and *Queen's Colleges.* Although the 43 rooms here are smallish, the staff is friendly, and there's a restaurant. The High, entrance on Merton St. (phone: 248244; fax: 791681).

Old Parsonage Dating back to 1660, this attractive, creeper-covered Jacobean building was a Royalist stronghold during the Civil War and later Oscar Wilde's home (it's also reputed to be haunted by the ghost of a nun). After many years as a guesthouse, it was bought by Jeremy Mogford, owner of *Browns* restaurant (see *Eating Out*); it has become the city's classiest hotel. There are 30 rooms, all with satellite TV and marble bathrooms; however, only four are in the original part of the building. The airy *Parsonage Bar,* whose walls are covered with paintings, photographs, and prints, doubles as a restaurant. There's also a pleasant garden. 1-3 Banbury Rd. (phone: 310210; fax: 311262).

Randolph This Gothic monument built in 1864 has an efficient staff and a good location, directly opposite the *Ashmolean Museum.* Richly and elegantly furnished throughout, it has 109 spacious rooms; other facilities include eight luxury suites and the lofty *Spires* restaurant, which serves both à la carte and fixed-price dinners, a coffee shop for quick meals, a bar, and a lounge in which cream teas are served every afternoon. Beaumont St. (phone: 247481; 800-225-5843; fax: 726871).

MODERATE

Hawkwell House Formerly the *Priory,* this quiet country-house hotel with 15 rooms is surrounded by three acres of gardens. It's located just 2 miles southeast of the city's center at Iffley village, famous for its Norman church and the pretty Thames lock. Church Way, Iffley (phone: 749988; fax: 748525).

Westwood Country Although its grounds are filled with all kinds of wildlife, like badgers and deer, this is still a peaceful 22-bedroom place just a five-minute drive from the city center. Four of the rooms have four-poster beds. You can tone up in the gym, which has exercise bikes, rowing machines, a sauna, and a Jacuzzi; or wallow in a whirlpool bath before dinner. Hinksey Hill Top (phone: 735408; fax: 736536).

INEXPENSIVE

Cotswold House Comfortable surroundings and hearty breakfasts are the hallmarks of Jim and Anne O'Kane's highly regarded seven-room hostelry in a large modern house on a busy road 2 miles north of the city center. There's no restaurant, and the guestrooms have no phones. No smoking is allowed, and credit cards are not accepted. 363 Banbury Rd. (phone/fax: 310558).

Highfield West Robin and Tina Barrett's comfortable bed and breakfast guesthouse on the western edge of the city has five bedrooms (no phones in rooms) and a heated outdoor pool. No restaurant. 188 Cumnor Hill (phone: 863007).

Isis Within walking distance of the city center (and also on the bus line), this 37-room bed and breakfast place takes in visitors July through September only, as *Oxford* undergraduates live here the rest of the year. The rooms are furnished simply but comfortably (14 have private baths). There's no restaurant. 45-53 Iffley Rd. (phone: 248894).

EATING OUT

Oxford offers more in the way of restaurants than it does hotels. If you cannot secure an invitation to dine at High Table with a don in one of the colleges (gastronomically it may not be tops, but for atmosphere it's unbeatable), you can still eat very well indeed. This is, after all, a sophisticated community, and fine food is much appreciated. On the other hand, it's also a youthful community, so there are lots of cafés, hamburger joints, and pizza parlors. Expect to pay a whopping $225 or more for dinner for two, excluding wine and tips, in the establishment listed as very expensive; more than $70 in an expensive place; $40 to $70 in moderate establishments; and less than $40 in inexpensive places. All restaurants listed below serve lunch and dinner, unless otherwise noted. All telephone numbers are in the 1865 city code unless otherwise indicated.

VERY EXPENSIVE

Le Manoir aux Quat' Saisons In 1984, Oxford's top restaurant moved to Great Milton, where it became a fine hotel. Its two-star Michelin menu is among the best in Britain, featuring skillfully prepared haute cuisine and game in season, and there's an extensive wine list. The best available ingredients go into every dish (the poultry and cheese come from France), and lightness is the operative word. Sample the *trio de chocolates* or try the filet of wild, home-smoked salmon with horseradish soufflé and cucumber butter. For those who want to learn how to prepare such delicacies, four-day cooking courses (including a stay at the hotel) are offered. In summer, coffee can be served on a lovely terrace overlooking a series of gardens. Open daily. Reservations necessary. Major credit cards accepted. Church Rd., Great Milton (phone: 1844-278881).

EXPENSIVE

Elizabeth This chic little place has a good location opposite *Christ Church* and is housed in one of Oxford's finest late-15th-century buildings. The limited but sophisticated menu features French cooking; house specialties include trout stuffed with seafood mousse, *suprême de volaille au vin blanc,* and *caneton aux abricots.* There's also an excellent wine list featuring French and Spanish vintages. Closed Mondays. Reservations necessary. Major credit cards accepted. 82 St. Aldate's (phone: 242230).

MODERATE

Bandung At this Indonesian eatery that's popular with the university staff, ask for the *sotong masak padang,* otherwise known as spiced cuttlefish. Closed Sunday lunch and Mondays. Reservations advised. Major credit cards accepted. 124 Walton St. (phone: 511668).

Browns This sprawling row house restaurant decorated with lots of mirrors and hanging plants is a popular place for students to entertain their parents. It's always crowded, so be prepared to wait in line and share tables. The entrées are wholesome and filling—spaghetti, steak and mushroom pie, hot sandwiches—and the desserts are homemade. Sometimes a pianist plays in the afternoon. Open daily. No reservations, except for guests at the *Old Parsonage* hotel. Major credit cards accepted. 5-9 Woodstock Rd. (phone: 511995).

Cherwell Boathouse Perched on the Cherwell, a tributary of the Thames, it's in a refurbished boathouse that rents punts and a gondola; they put out eight rooftop tables for summer dining. Two imaginative and set three-course menus are offered daily—a recent example included hot vichyssoise, West Indian deep-dish meat pie, and a Caribbean apple and grape dessert. There are also lunchtime buffets. Closed Sundays. Reservations necessary. Major credit cards accepted. Bardwell Rd. off Banbury Rd. (phone: 52746).

Crypt One of a new breed of wine bars in town, this is in the cellars of the *Oxford Union Society.* It has old mahogany furniture and a candlelit atmosphere. Among other dishes, the traditional English menu offers steak and kidney or chicken and chestnut pies. Closed Sundays. No reservations. Major credit cards accepted. Frewin Passage (phone: 251000).

Dome Live jazz on Wednesday evenings keeps this French café jumping. Open daily. No reservations. Major credit cards accepted. 11A Little Clarendon St. (phone: 310194).

15 North Parade Cane chairs and large plants give this small eatery a fresh, cheerful feeling. It is tucked away on a narrow street north of the city center, but the imaginative cooking—with unusual sauces—makes the journey well worthwhile. Closed Sunday evenings. Reservations necessary. Major credit cards accepted. 15 N. Parade (phone: 513773).

Liaison Excellent Cantonese, Pekinese, and Szechuan dishes are served here. Don't be fooled by the outside—it occupies the ground floor of an unattractive old building, which is dwarfed by the modern car park opposite—

since the atmosphere inside is pleasant and intimate. Open daily. Reservations advised. Major credit cards accepted. 29 Castle St. (phone: 242944).

Michel's Brasserie Tucked away from the hustle and bustle, this intimate spot helped many an Oxford romance to bloom. It serves good French fare at reasonable prices. Open daily. Reservations advised. Major credit cards accepted. 10 Little Clarendon St. (phone: 52142).

Whites Owned by the wine merchants who occupy the 13th-century vaulted cellar underneath it, this restaurant has two small dining rooms (one for nonsmokers). Liver with mango and venison with cherries are among its specialties. Superb wine list. Open daily. Reservations necessary. Major credit cards accepted. 16 Turl St. (phone: 793396).

INEXPENSIVE

Beauchamps This cozy café is for nonsmokers only and serves good soups and simple hot dishes, as well as delicious pastries and cheesecakes. Open daily for lunch and early dinner only. No reservations. No credit cards accepted. 93 Gloucester Green (phone: 793037).

Convocation Coffee House The setting is much more than the name suggests. Diners sit under beautiful stone arched ceilings in a 14th-century meeting room at the back of *St. Mary's Church.* Tasty soup, salads, casseroles, and sandwiches comprise the menu. Open daily for lunch only. No reservations. No credit cards accepted. Radcliffe Sq. (phone: 794334).

Mitre Once the city's most famous hotel, this old coaching inn in the center of High Street is now a quick-service restaurant, and some of the inn's charming old atmosphere remains. It specializes in steaks and a variety of fish and chicken dishes. Open daily. No reservations. Major credit cards accepted. 18 High St. at Turl St. (phone: 244563).

Munchy Munchy Padang-style cooking from Sumatra like beef with mango purée or duck with kumquats soaked in port is served in this unpretentious eatery. The surroundings and very reasonable prices are reminiscent of food centers in the owners' home city of Singapore. Closed Sundays and Mondays. Reservations unnecessary. Major credit cards accepted. 6 Park End St. (phone: 245710).

Rosie Lee One of the coziest places to rest weary shopping legs, where an afternoon tea of toasted tea cakes and Earl Grey or *Rosie Lee*'s own blend of tea are served, as are a variety of other snacks. Open daily for lunch and early dinner only. Reservations unnecessary. No credit cards accepted. 51 High St. (phone: 244429).

SHARING A PINT

The *Turl Bar,* centrally located at the back of a small courtyard on the corner of High and Turl Streets (phone: 793396), still has some of the cozy Dickensian atmosphere from when it was part of the old *Mitre* coaching inn. A great favorite is the *Turf Tavern* (St. Helen's Passage; phone: 243235), a narrow, cobblestone alleyway off New College Lane, snuggled close to the walls of *New College,* which serves excellent snacks, and coffee and tea, as well as special drinks, including hot cider punch in winter; the 15th-century *Bear* (Alfred St.; phone: 721783), close to *Christ Church,* was once a coaching inn and is full of atmosphere (hundreds of neckties donated by customers over the years are displayed in glass cases); the *Eagle and Child* (St. Giles; phone: 580085) was frequented by literary lights such as J. R. R. Tolkien; the *White Horse* (Broad St., opposite the *Sheldonian Theatre;* no phone) is handy and historic, despite the addition of electronic games. On the edge of the city are two famous riverside pubs: the *Perch* (Binsey La.; phone: 240386), where Lewis Carroll reputedly gathered his friends together to hear a reading of his new work, a fantastic tale called *Alice's Adventures in Wonderland;* and the *Trout* (at Godstow; phone: 54485). Both places are popular at Sunday lunchtime and on summer evenings.

Perth

The world knows Edinburgh, Glasgow, and Aberdeen; Perth needs a little finding. To be in Perth means to be *inside* Scotland, both physically and spiritually. Stationed at the head of the river Tay estuary, in the east central part of the country, the city calls itself the Heart of Scotland, a distinction with coordinates in time as well as space (it was the country's capital from AD 838 until 1437). Perth is indeed rich in historical associations (if not actual remnants), and geographically, it is one of several gateways to the Highlands. Many travelers stumble upon it for the latter reason only, but those who prolong the encounter discover this city's special, magical charm.

Perth is set in what is perhaps the oldest inhabited part of Scotland. The discovery here of a dugout canoe from over 8,000 years ago suggests that the river Tay (Scotland's longest) was a natural point of entry at this point even during the Stone Age. Today, it's possible to sense the security of a residential, confident, and comfortable city, while seeing in the river the same purity and bewitchment that must have dazzled ancient travelers.

The great Roman general Julius Agricola came here in AD 80 and established at Inchtuthill (just up the river) the biggest legionary fort north of York. And well he might. The Picts, a Celtic tribe of obscure origin, had been driven away by the Romans but were biding their time and would return. The name of the town itself marks their frontier dispute: Possibly it comes from Agricola's fort, "Bertha," or possibly it is a mutation of a word by which the town was previously called in the largely lost Pictish language.

Christian missionaries arrived later, followed by traders and invaders, and the Tay soon ran blood red. *Scone* (pronounced *Skoon*) *Palace,* 2 miles north of the city, is associated with King Kenneth MacAlpin (usually rendered "MacAlpine"), the great 9th-century ruler of the Scots. Prodded by the need to defend against the invading Vikings, he imposed his rule also on the Picts, thus establishing the united Pict-Scot kingdom that is the traditional nucleus of the kingdom of Scotland. *Scone* became the seat of government and the coronation place of Scottish kings from Kenneth I to Charles II in 1651, even though the Stone of Destiny, on which the coronations actually took place, was stolen by Edward I of England in 1296 and made the Coronation Chair in *Westminster Abbey.* (Officially, the stone, said to have religious connotations, is still in *Westminster Abbey,* but Scottish legend maintains that it is not the *real* stone: According to the tale, when the original was stolen in 1950, the thieves returned a substitute.)

A key to the Highlands even in the Middle Ages, Perth was a walled town until it was swept away by storm and flood in 1209. King William the Lion (1165–1214) then extended the town to the west to make a "new burgh." War, trade, and religious devotion characterized the period, and Scotland itself frequently changed hands. Edward I, in his campaign to make the English king also the ruler of Scotland (which included carrying off the Stone of Destiny), fortified Perth in 1298. The city's capture from the English in 1313, along with the defeat of Edward II at Bannockburn a year later, completed the reconquest of Scotland. But then the next English king, Edward III, ousted Robert the Bruce's son, and Perth became the English headquarters from 1333 to 1339, when it was retaken and its walls cast down.

Perth later became the scene of clan warfare. In 1396, 30 men each from the Chattan and Kay clans gathered on the North Inch and fought to the death of almost every man. The thousands of spectators included King Robert III, who watched from *Blackfriars Monastery* nearby. The same monastery was the scene of the murder of Robert's son, James I (1406–37), whose attempts to impose order led to his being hacked to pieces by some militant nobles in a sewer under the monastery, where he had taken refuge. Afterwards, James's widow and her young son fled to Edinburgh and Perth's longtime role as capital of Scotland ended.

Blackfriars, a Dominican friary founded in 1231, was one of Perth's many royal foundations for the clergy. It arose here thanks to *Scone*'s influence and Perth's location at the crossroads of Celtic-Christian missionary routes. There were also monasteries of the Greyfriars and the Whitefriars. No stone of the medieval friaries survived the 16th century, however, because it was in Perth that John Knox preached some of his most incendiary Reformation sermons, rousing the mob to a frenzy of destruction that leveled them all.

On the westerly outskirts of Perth is *Huntingtower Castle* (formerly *Ruthven Castle*), where the Raid of Ruthven took place. A group led by Lord Ruthven, first Earl of Gowrie, invited the 16-year-old James VI (later James I of England) here in 1582, kidnapped him, and held him prisoner for several months. For this, the earl was beheaded a few years later, and James took further revenge in 1600 when another attempt to kidnap him, this time by Lord Ruthven's two sons, ended in their death at the hands of James's attendants. Much of this episode, which went down in history as the Gowrie Conspiracy, remains a mystery, but it did result in the proscription of the very name Ruthven, hence the castle's name change. The 17th century brought more religious wars as Montrose, then Cromwell, occupied the town. The Jacobites also took over Perth during both the 1715 and 1745 attempts to capture the throne.

Perth's docile appearance today belies its bloody history. It is now a culturally refined city, as well as the center of one of Scotland's richest areas, both agriculturally and economically. Perth (pop. 41,916) has retained its strong commercial character; it is known for its insurance, textile, and dyeing industries, as well as for its cattle markets, its fine wine importation, which gave rise to the renowned port of Sandeman's, and its world-famous whisky. During the early 19th century, Arthur Bell turned a small family whisky business into a great export concern; another family distilling business was begun at the same time by John Dewar. The story is told that Bell and Dewar were going to a church meeting one day and decided to stop for a dram beforehand. Bell asked Dewar what he would have, to be told: "A Bell's. It would not do to go into the meeting smelling of whisky." The Bell family claims that it was Bell who made the remark, just after he ordered a Dewar's.

Perth At-a-Glance

SEEING THE CITY

To experience the magic of Perth, climb to the top of 729-foot Kinnoull Hill, east of the river. There is a tower on the edge of the precipice, one of several placed there by the ninth Earl of Kinnoull, who had been impressed by the castles on the Rhine, though he thought the river inferior to his own Tay. He also put a stone table on the top of the hill and dined there frequently because of his love of the view. The hill now belongs to the city, which lies directly below, with the Grampians to the right, the fields and woods to the left, and the river in front. Beyond, on the north bank, is the "Carse of Gowrie," Scotland's berry-growing district, from which came the country's famed jam and marmalade industry.

SPECIAL PLACES

Perth is small enough to be seen on foot. The city lies on the west bank of the river Tay, with two large green "water meadows"—North Inch and South Inch ("inch" is Scottish for "island")—to the north and south. Between these two parks is something of a grid. Tay Street runs along the river, beginning in the south as Shore Road and eventually passing Queen's Bridge (which connects with the Dundee Road, A85, across the river) and then Perth Bridge (cross it to get to Kinnoull Hill). High Street runs westward off Tay Street midway between the two bridges. South Street runs westward from Queen's Bridge, becoming County Place, then York Place, and then turning south for the Glasgow Road (A9).

CITY CENTER

ST. JOHN'S KIRK Perth's oldest building, this church was founded in 1126 and largely rebuilt during the 15th century. In 1559, it suffered badly from the wave of destruction of religious property caused by Calvinist preacher John Knox's fiery rhetoric against church idolatry here. The Royalist general (and poet) James Graham, Marquis of Montrose, used it as a camp in 1645, and during the 1650s the Cromwellians made it into a courthouse. In 1745, it was used as a church by the Young Pretender, Bonnie Prince Charlie. The church was triumphantly restored in the 1920s, and Queen Elizabeth

II (who, by law, becomes Presbyterian when in Scotland) took part in a *Thanksgiving* service here for her *Silver Jubilee* in 1977. Closed to visitors (except for Sunday services) January through mid-March. Enter by the west door. St. John's Pl., off High St.

SALUTATION HOTEL Built in 1699 and still in full commercial use as a hotel, it became famous as the headquarters of Bonnie Prince Charlie during the Jacobite rising of 1745. 34 South St. (phone: 630066).

WATERGATE The Vikings left their imprint on Perth in the name of this street (*gate* means "street"), which lies between High and South Streets and offers fragments of the medieval town. Look at the wall in Fountain Close, off the east end of South Street, where there is a map of the old narrow passages or "vennels," the most interesting of which is Oliphant's Vennel. Then cross High Street to George Street, which contains some interesting early Victorian architecture.

FAIR MAID'S HOUSE This fine stone house near the North Inch dates from the Middle Ages. It was once the *Guildhall of the Glovers,* but ever since Sir Walter Scott depicted it as the home of the heroine of his novel *The Fair Maid of Perth,* it has been known by Scott's appellation rather than its historical one. Inside are a shop where local crafts are exhibited and sold, as well as paintings by Scottish artists. Closed Sundays. North Port, off Charlotte St. (phone: 625976).

OLD ACADEMY The impressive façade is all that remains of the *Old Perth Academy,* built in 1807; the rest of the rebuilt structure currently consists of expensive apartments. Physicist Adam Anderson, a former headmaster of the famous school, designed Perth's first piped-water system, completed in 1832, and was also responsible for the introduction of the city's gas lighting system. The academy building is on Rose Terrace, overlooking the North Inch, and the area contains some fine 18th-century houses, including one (10 Rose Ter.) in which John Ruskin, the great essayist and critic of art and architecture, spent part of his youth. Atholl Street and Barossa Place, at either end of the street, also have architectural charms. Rose Ter., west of North Inch.

BALHOUSIE CASTLE A 15th-century castle, restored during the 17th century, it is the home of the *Black Watch Regimental Museum,* whose collection commemorates many formidable engagements in British imperial and military history over the last two and a half centuries. Colorful uniforms and some interesting silver pieces are displayed. Closed Saturdays year-round, as well as Sundays October through *Easter.* No admission charge. Hay St. (phone: 621281, ext. 8530).

KING JAMES VI HOSPITAL The site of the old Carthusian monastery founded by James I during the 15th century and destroyed in 1559 is now occupied by a hospital originally endowed by James VI in the 16th century; the present structure, however, is from the mid-18th century. Although the building is not a tourist attraction, it is well worth a look from the outside. Hospital and King Sts., off County Pl.

GREYFRIARS' CEMETERY Behind the *Round House* (the old city waterworks) on Marshall Place, this interesting old burial ground occupies the site of another vanished religious house, that of the Franciscans. A visitors' center is in the *Round House,* also designed by Adam Anderson. Canal St.

LOWER CITY MILLS This restored oatmeal mill powered by a massive 15th-century waterwheel is Perth's latest attraction. Tours, led by the miller, demonstrate the process of grinding oats into meal. The fruits (or rather, grains) of this labor can be purchased in a shop in the mill. Closed Sundays and November through March. Admission charge. West Mill St. (phone: 627958).

ENVIRONS

FAIRWAYS HEAVY HORSE CENTRE This delightful little activities center features rides in wagons pulled by Clydesdale horses, video shows, a display of horse-drawn implements, and the opportunity to see newborn foals and to watch a blacksmith at work. Closed October through March. No admission charge for children under five years old. Walnut Grove, 2 miles east of Perth on A85 (phone: 32561).

SCONE PALACE The ancient historic site of Scone, the traditional coronation place of Scottish kings, has been at the center of Scottish history since Pictish times, although what is here today is *Scone Palace,* a castellated mansion built largely during the first decade of the 19th century. The palace is the last of several structures that occupied this spot, beginning with the 12th-century *Bishop's Palace* and an adjoining abbey that were destroyed in 1559—along with the rest of Perth's religious foundations. The Earls of Gowrie, subsequent owners of the property, built a new palace here in the 16th century but were forced to forfeit it after the Gowrie Conspiracy against James VI.

The interior is famous for its rare porcelain, needlework, furniture, clocks, ivories, and the Vernis Martin collection of 18th-century French papier-mâché objets d'art. Outside, daffodils, rhododendrons, bluebells, roses, and rare trees share 100 acres with Highland cattle, birds, agricultural machinery, a park, and an adventure playground. Of particular interest is Moot Hill, opposite the palace, where the Stone of Destiny was kept and where a replica now stands. Beside the imitation stone is a 19th-century chapel that incorporates a 17th-century aisle of the old parish church of Scone Village, which was re-sited (yes, we mean the *village*) when the present palace was built. Also here is the *Old Gateway,* part of the original *Bishop's Palace;* the graveyard, where Robert II (who reigned from 1371 to 1390), first of the Stuart line of Scottish kings, is buried; and the *Pinetum,* a grove with 135-year-old conifers and the original Douglas fir, grown from seeds sent home by botanist David Douglas, who was born on the estate and worked on it as a young gardener. (The town has dedicated the *Douglas Memorial Garden,* near *Balhousie Castle,* to its green-thumbed "son.") Gift shops and a coffee shop complete the enclave. Open daily. Admission charge. Two miles northeast of Perth by A93 (phone: 552300).

HUNTINGTOWER CASTLE Known as *Ruthven Castle* until 1600 (the time of the infamous Gowrie Conspiracy), this splendid 15th- and 16th-century building consists of two towers joined by a later structure; a painted ceiling that dates from 1540 is among its notable features. Before the ill-fated Earl of Gowrie occupied the castle, Patrick Ruthven, third Baron Ruthven, Provost of Perth from 1553 to 1566, lived here. He played a major part in bringing the Reformation to Scotland, assisted in capturing Perth from the French in opposition to the Regency of Queen Mary's mother, and rose from his deathbed to take part in the murder of Mary's favorite, Riccio, in 1566. Open daily. Admission charge. Three miles northwest of Perth by A9 and A85 (phone: 527231).

ELCHO CASTLE Wrought-iron window grills characterize this well-preserved, 16th-century stately home on the south bank of the Tay. *Elcho Castle* was the ancestral seat of the Earls of Wemyss (pronounced *Weems*), a family whose members took up very different political positions over the generations. The castle may be visited only by prior arrangement. Admission charge. In Rhynd, 4½ miles southeast of Perth; for information or to arrange a tour, call the *National Trust* office in Edinburgh (phone: 131-244-3101).

BRANKLYN GARDEN Within walking distance of the city, southward on the Dundee Road (A85), this small, beautiful garden, run by the *National Trust for Scotland,* displays over 3,000 species of rare shrubs and plants. Some plants and seeds also are available for purchase. Closed November through April. Admission charge (phone: 625535).

BELL'S CHERRYBANK GARDENS Trees, heather, shrubs, and an aviary are set on 18 acres. Home to the famous *National Heather Collection,* the gardens also have decorative sculptures, pools, a waterfall, and a children's play area. On the A9, about 3 miles south of the city. Closed mid-October through early May. Admission charge. Near Glasgow Rd. (phone: 627330).

EXTRA SPECIAL

Free tours are offered by three distilleries in the small villages of Pitlochry (about 20 miles north of the city) and Aberfeldy (32 miles northwest); they also have tastings and shops that sell the finished products. Call ahead to make arrangements. *Aberfeldy Malt Whisky* (in Aberfeldy; phone: 1887-820330) is closed weekends year-round, as well as Mondays, Wednesdays, and Fridays November through *Easter. Blair Atholl Distillery* (in Pitlochry; phone: 1796-472234), owned by United Distillers, is closed weekends

October through *Easter.* The tiny, picturesque *Edradour Distillery* (phone: 1796-472095), in the hills overlooking Pitlochry, makes whisky the way it was done before the machine age; it takes a year to produce what a modern distillery can make in only a week. The distillery is closed Sundays and November through February; its gift shop is closed Sundays.

Sources and Resources

TOURIST INFORMATION

Perth's tourist information center (45 High St.; phone: 638353) is two blocks west of Tay Street midway between Perth Bridge and Queen's Bridge. The office is closed Sundays November through March. Another branch is in the car park of *Caithness Glass* (see *Shopping*); it's closed November through March. The tourist office offers an accommodations booking service. Two indispensable annual publications, *Perthshire Guide* and *Explore Perthshire,* are also available.

LOCAL COVERAGE The *Evening Telegraph* and the *Courier,* a morning daily, are the local papers. The *Perthshire Advertiser* comes out on Tuesdays and Fridays.

TELEPHONE The city code for Perth is 1738.

GETTING AROUND

The city itself is easy to see on foot, but wheels are necessary to get to attractions in the environs. Note that Wednesday is early closing day.

BUS There is local bus service, but it's not used much to get around, even by residents. The two main companies are *Strathtay Scottish Omnibuses Ltd.* at the bus station (Leonard St.; phone: 626848) and *Caledonian Express* (phone: 633481). The station, from which longer-distance buses to Edinburgh, Glasgow, Inverness, and other cities also depart, is north of King's Place, the westward continuation of Marshall Place.

CAR RENTAL Major companies in town include *Arnold Clark Hire Drive* (St. Leonard's Bank; phone: 638511); *Europcar* (26 Glasgow Rd.; phone: 636888); *Hertz* (High St.; phone: 624108); and *Thrifty Rent-a-Car* at the *Station* hotel (Leonard St.; phone: 633677).

TAXI Cab ranks are located on Mill Street. Or call *A & B Taxis* (phone: 634567), *Ace Taxi* (phone: 633033), *Fair City Tours* (phone: 636098), or *Perth Radio Taxis* (phone: 628171).

TRAIN Direct trains to Aberdeen, Inverness, Glasgow, Edinburgh, and Dundee (and through Dundee to the *InterCity 125* network) leave from the railroad station at the far end of King's Place (phone: 637117 for information; 637228 or 637229 for reservations).

SPECIAL EVENTS

The *Perth Food Festival,* spotlighting local chefs and food products, is held the last week of April. The *Perth Festival of the Arts* in May includes drama, music, and visual arts at sites all over the city. The first weekend of August sees the *Perth Agricultural Show* at Lesser South Inch, and the *Perth Highland Games* are held in early August at the same location. Check with the tourist information center (see *Tourist Information*) for exact dates.

MUSEUMS

Besides those mentioned in *Special Places,* Perth offers these two places of interest.

FERGUSSON GALLERY The work of J. D. Fergusson, a top Scottish painter, is showcased. Closed Sundays. No admission charge. Marshall Pl. (phone: 441944).

PERTH MUSEUM AND ART GALLERY Local archaeological discoveries, relics of the glovers guild, and a well-regarded exhibit focusing on Perthshire natural history are presented. Closed Sundays. No admission charge. 78 George St. (phone: 632488).

SHOPPING

Leave major shopping for the big cities and coastal towns; local souvenirs are the main interest here. *St. John's Centre* houses 42 shops, mostly branches of chain stores. It has a historical mural inside and a clock that chimes as two figures emerge and dance to celebrate the hour. Two good thoroughfares to browse through are George and St. John Streets, with antiques shops, jewelry stores, and clothing boutiques. For standard shopping hours, see GETTING READY TO GO; Wednesday is early closing day.

Be sure to take your passport when you shop, and always inquire about the Value Added Tax (VAT) refund application forms when your total purchases in a store are over £50 (about $75). The VAT is a surcharge payable at the sales counter, but foreign customers usually will be reimbursed for it at home (for more information see GETTING READY TO GO).

Cairncross Ltd. Perth is the world's outlet for Scotland's finest freshwater pearls; this third-generation shop offers a full range of Scottish pearls and designs jewelry worn by the royal family. On display here is the famous *Abernethy Pearl.* The perfect pink pearl, one of the largest ever found, was named after its discoverer, William Abernethy, the last of the Scottish professional pearl fishers. Special designs are also available (by appointment only). 18 St. John St. (phone: 624367).

Caithness Glass The factory produces glassware and paperweights, and the factory shop offers splendid bargains. In addition, it is possible to watch glassmaking (on weekdays) and view the *Paperweight Collectors Gallery.* In addition to the standard hours, the shop is open Sundays from 1 to 5 PM (from 11 AM *Easter* through September). One mile northwest of Perth (off A9) at Inveralmond (phone: 637373).

Capercaillie Sells a selection of Scottish-style gifts, such as tartan wrapping paper. 1 S. St. John's Pl. (phone: 441521).

Ellery's Delicatessen Despite its commonplace name, this is an upscale emporium of special delicacies, including British cheeses, smoked meat, pâtés, cakes, and condiments. It's the perfect place to stock up for a picnic or pick up an edible souvenir of your visit to Perth. Mill St. (phone: 633362).

House of Gowrie Fine cigars, tobacco, snuff, clay and wooden pipes, and related paraphernalia. 90 South St. (phone: 626919).

Matthew Gloag and Sons Ltd. A wide variety of whiskies, including magnificent single malts from the islands. *Bordeaux House,* Kinnoull St. (phone: 621101).

Whispers of the Past A quaint shop filled with silver jewelry, locally crafted ceramics, potpourri, dried flowers, and hand-carved wooden toys and children's furniture. 15 George St. (phone: 635472).

SPORTS

Facilities for many activities, from archery, badminton, basketball, and gymnastics to table tennis and volleyball, are at the *Gannochy Trust Sports Complex* (Hay St., North Inch; phone: 622301), which offers a full program of events. If your sport is not on the list, check anyway, because new athletic diversions are continually being introduced.

BOATING *Loch Tay Boating Centre* (Pier Rd., Kenmore; phone: 1887-830291), an hour's drive northwest of the city, rents fishing boats, sailboats, and cabin cruisers from late March through October. Call ahead to reserve.

CURLING The ancient Scottish game, in which players twirl polished granite stones over an ice rink, is popular and worth viewing. It's played at *Dewar's Rinks* (Glover St.; phone: 624188).

FISHING The Tay is well known as a superb angling site, especially for salmon, so only 20 daily permits are issued at one time. Apply well in advance (especially August through October) at the *Perth and Kinross District Council* (3 High St.; phone: 639911). The tourist information center (see *Tourist Information*) issues fishing permits on Saturdays and holidays, when the district council is closed. Fishing is also extensive on the Tay's tributary rivers, the Earn and the Almond, and at lochs, rivers, and even Highland streams nearby. For details, consult the tourist information center (see *Tourist Information*). There is fly-fishing for trout in well-stocked ponds at *Sandyknowes Fishery* (Rhynd Rd., Bridge of Earn; phone: 813033), where there are also nearby picnic areas; *Crook of Devon Fish Farm and Restaurant* (near Kinross, 18 miles south of Perth; phone: 1577-840297); and *Drummond Fish Farm* (in Comrie, 20 miles from the city; phone: 1764-670500), where children can try their hand at the sport, too.

GOLF One of Scotland's greatest golfing venues is within a half-hour drive of the city.

TOP TEE-OFF SPOT

Gleneagles Under the single sobriquet of *Gleneagles,* the range of golf facilities at the eponymous hotel (see *Checking In*) is almost unequaled. There are three 18-hole golf courses (including the *Monarch,* Jack Nicklaus's latest creation), a driving range, and a nine-hole pitch-and-putt course. The *Queen's* course has been restored to James Braid's original design, the *King's* course is an absolute joy to play (in 1987 it became home to the *Bell's Scottish Open* tournament), and all the *Gleneagles* links also are consistently in the best condition of any Scottish course. There is also a nine-hole *Wee* course. Auchterarder, 15 miles southwest of Perth (phone: 1764-663543).

The famous *Rosemount* course (in Blairgowrie, 16 miles north of Perth; phone: 1250-872622) is also nearby. In addition, Perth itself is home to several good 18-hole courses. The public *North Inch* golf course may be the granddaddy of all, because the game has been played here since the 16th century. Private clubs encourage visitors. The *King James VI Golf Club* (phone: 625170) is on Moncreiffe Island in mid-Tay; *Craigie Hill Golf Club* (Cherrybank; phone: 624377) involves higher ground with hilly undulations; and there's also the *Murrayshall Golf Club* (phone: 552784) at Scone, just outside Perth. There is also a putting course at South Inch.

HORSE RACING The most northerly horse racing in Britain takes place at the *Perth Hunt Racecourse* (at *Scone Palace;* phone: 551597) on certain dates April through September. Ask at the tourist information center (see *Tourist Information*).

HORSEBACK RIDING *The Perth Equine Centre at Glendevon Farm* (in the Burghmuir district; phone: 440248) has stables and riding facilities and rents horses.

HUNTING The area surrounding Perth is rich in game. Shooting can be arranged privately or for groups on many estates. For more details, including a list of shooting agents, check with the tourist information office (see *Tourist Information*).

ICE SKATING Visit *Dewar's Rinks* (see above).

SWIMMING The *Perth Leisure Pool* (Glasgow Rd.; phone: 630535; open daily) offers a lap pool, teaching pool for beginners, a children's lagoon with giant flumes, slides, and a waterfall, plus an outdoor heated lagoon. There's also a fitness room, a sauna, a steamroom, and Jacuzzis.

THEATER

The *Perth Theatre* (High St.; phone: 621031), many of whose performers and directors have gone on to considerable success in Glasgow, Edinburgh, and London, has a reputation for work that's enjoyable, if not too harrowing or intellectually demanding. Expect to see an Agatha Christie thriller more often than an avant-garde experimental play. The theater is comfortable, with good restaurant facilities. The *Pitlochry Festival Theatre* (on the water in Pitlochry; phone: 1796-472680) has a repertoire of six entertaining plays (usually comedies and mysteries) that are performed weekly May through early October. Call ahead for ticket availability.

MUSIC AND NIGHTLIFE

Nightclubs here can be booked and patronized only by large local parties. However, traditional Scots Gaelic folk music events—*ceilidhs* (pronounced *kay*-leez)—take place in some hotels. They can be pretty upbeat, featuring singers, dancers, pipe bands, and Highland flings. The tourist board (see *Tourist Information*) also organizes participatory Scottish country dancing weekly May through September.

Best in Town

CHECKING IN

In Perth, the accent is on comfort and common sense rather than luxury, even though Scotland's poshest hotel, *Gleneagles,* is nearby. Most of Perth's major hotels have complete facilities for the business traveler. Those hotels listed below as having "business services" usually offer such conveniences as a concierge, meeting rooms, photocopiers, computers, translation services, and express checkout, among others. Call the hotel for additional information. Expect to pay $150 to $300 per night for a double room (including private bath, TV set, phone, and breakfast, unless otherwise indicated) at a hotel in the expensive category, $100 to $140 in a moderate hotel, and $50 to $100 in an inexpensive place. Guesthouses and bed and breakfast establishments are good and less expensive still. The annual *Perthshire Guide* has an excellent accommodations register listing maximum charges. All telephone numbers are in the 1738 city code unless otherwise indicated.

We begin with our favorite area hotel, followed by our recommendations of cost and quality choices of accommodations, listed by price category.

A REGAL RETREAT

Gleneagles *"Heich abune the heich"*—better than the best—might seem a grandiose claim to make about a hotel. But those who have experienced Britain's finest (and perhaps most expensive) luxury resort—the Versailles of Scottish hotels, located about 15 miles southwest of Perth—believe the boast. The property offers 236 rooms (including 20 suites), four restaurants serving excellent Scottish and continental fare, a complete country club, and business services. Most guests rave about the cluster of world-renowned golf courses (see *Top Tee-Off Spot,* above), but non-golfers will never be bored. The *Gleneagles Mark Phillips Equestrian Centre,* run by the former husband of Princess Anne, features two covered arenas and instruction in show, jumping, and dressage (Captain Phillips himself leads clinics several times a year). The 830-acre grounds also offer fishing, clay-pigeon shooting, croquet, lawn bowling, miniature golf, all-weather tennis, squash, dancing, and billiards; plus a spa, a sauna and Turkish baths, a beauty salon, a Jacuzzi, a pool, and a gym. The gardens alone, spotted with bright flowers, are a joy. The high-ceilinged rooms are spacious; the windows provide an eyeful of the lonely Scottish hills beyond the gardens; and the service can't be faulted, thanks to a better than one-to-one staff/guest ratio. When pipe bands set up on the velvety lawns, quite a few guests get goose bumps. Auchterarder (phone: 1764-662231; 212-838-3110 in New York City; 800-223-6800 elsewhere in the US; fax: 1764-662134).

EXPENSIVE

Auchterarder House This grand 19th-century Jacobean mansion, formerly the home of industrialist Sir James Reid, is filled with rich oak paneling, crystal chandeliers, carved marble fireplaces, and antiques. The 15 bedrooms aren't decorated quite as grandly as the public areas, but they are large, comfortable, and well appointed. Chef David Hunt specializes in innovative preparations of Scottish specialties such as cameo of lemon sole with vegetable spaghetti and saffron sauce and loin of venison crowned with a chicken and mushroom parfait and served with a compote of lentils and bacon. Guests can shoot or hike on the property's 17 acres of grounds (also see *Quintessential Great Britain* and *Stalking and Shooting* in DIVERSIONS), and golf and fishing can be arranged nearby. Business services are available. In Auchterarder, about 15 miles southwest of Perth (phone: 1764-663646; 800-525-4800; fax: 1764-662939).

Ballathie House Set amid the green countryside, this charming estate with round towers and a pitched roof is 12 miles north of the city. It offers such recreations as golf, horseback riding, fishing, and tennis. There are 39 well-appointed rooms which are ideal for families: There is no charge for children under 12 who share a room with their parents. The restaurant serves first-rate traditional Scottish fare, as well as such continental dishes as smoked fish mousseline. Business services are offered. Kinclaven by Stanley (phone: 1250-883268; fax: 1250-883396).

Murrayshall Presiding over 300 acres of magnificent parkland, this baronial, 19-room country-house hotel is impressive but neither as grand nor intimidating as *Auchterarder House* and *Ballathie House.* Its amenities include an 18-hole golf course, tennis courts, nature walks, croquet lawn, local fishing rights, and a restaurant serving Tay salmon and vegetables from the estate's garden. Business services are available. At Scone, just north of Perth (phone: 551171; fax: 552595).

MODERATE

Huntingtower About 3 miles west of town off A85, this half-timbered country house is smallish but restful. There are 43 rooms with plenty of amenities, as well as a good restaurant that specializes in Scottish cooking. The hotel can arrange shooting, fishing, and golf; tours of the countryside also are offered, as well as business services. Crieff Rd., Almondbank (phone: 583771; fax: 583777).

Parklands All 14 spacious rooms in this restored classical townhouse have satellite television. Traditional (and enormous) Scottish breakfasts are served, and the freshest ingredients are used for the Scottish fare offered at all meals. There's an excellent wine cellar. St. Leonard's Bank (phone: 622451; fax: 622046).

Salutation Bonnie Prince Charlie stayed here back in the 18th century, but the hotel has since upped the number of bedrooms to 69 and has installed most modern comforts. There is a restaurant, and business services are available. 34 South St. (phone: 630066; fax: 633598).

Stakis City Mills This property, a member of the Stakis chain, has more charm than most modern hotels; it's built around a watermill that dates back to the 15th century—you can watch the waterwheel turning from a glass panel in the lobby floor. There are 76 rooms, all with satellite TV. Other amenities include two restaurants and business services. West Mill St. (phone: 628281; 800-STAKIS-1; fax: 643423).

INEXPENSIVE

Beechgrove Guest House In addition to a peaceful, attractive setting, this six-bedroom former manse is a "listed building," which is equivalent to "landmark status" in the US. No restaurant. Dundee Rd. (phone: 636147).

Sunbank House Bounded by rolling green lawns above the river Tay, this charming Victorian house in gleaming white stone offers nine bedrooms, all with trouser presses and sumptuous views. There's also a restaurant. 50 Dundee Rd. (phone/fax: 624882).

EATING OUT

Although Perth thinks of itself as a city, it can be absolutely rural when it comes to food: The Tay salmon may have been caught that morning, the bread baked last night, the bacon cured locally. Game is particularly reliable, since restaurant and hotel folk have generations of wisdom on which to draw in selecting venison, grouse, pheasant, and partridge. Consequently, meals can be excellent, fresh, and nutritious. Look for the Taste of Scotland sign as a further guarantee of quality. Expect to pay $70 or more for a dinner for two with wine in the establishment listed as expensive, from $50 to $65 in a moderate restaurant, and under $50 at an inexpensive place. All restaurants listed below serve lunch and dinner unless otherwise noted. All telephone numbers are in the 1738 city code unless otherwise indicated.

EXPENSIVE

Tempest This handsome dining room with a red and blue color scheme and a cozy fireplace in the center serves excellent preparations of both seafood and meat dishes, including breast of pheasant in red currant sauce and west coast seafood in garlic butter. Open daily. Reservations advised. Major credit cards accepted. 80 George St. (phone: 440133).

MODERATE

Brambles Coffee Shop This lovely Victorian dining spot serves homemade scones, cakes, and muffins, and wonderful coffee and tea. It's a perfect luncheon respite from sightseeing. Closed Sundays. Reservations unnecessary. No credit cards accepted. 11 Princes St. (phone: 639091).

The Bridges The hearty Scottish menu includes Tay salmon and beef dishes. Closed Mondays and most of January. Reservations advised. Major credit cards accepted. 70 Tay St. (phone: 625484).

Number 33 Seafood Traditional Scottish fish and shellfish dishes are sublimely and subtly prepared. Children under 12 are not permitted. Closed Sundays and Mondays. Reservations advised. Major credit cards accepted. 33 George St. (phone: 633771).

Patrick's Wine Bar & Bistro Brigitte Bardot's former chef runs the kitchen of this eatery set in a brick-ceilinged former whisky warehouse steps below street level. Flambéed dishes are a specialty here, along with continental fare such as escargots and veal cordon bleu. Closed Sundays. Reservations advised. Major credit cards accepted. 1 Speygate (phone: 620539).

SHARING A PINT

The Granary (Canal Crescent; phone: 636705) is in an interesting old building whose historic granary features have been retained. It has a small restaurant, too. *Strangeway's* (George St.; phone: 628866) is a stylish place for drinks and bar meals. Other good choices include *Twa Tams* (79-81 Scott St.; phone: 634500); *Scaramouche* (103 South St.; phone: 637479); and *Greyfriars* (15 South St.; phone: 633036), a tiny pub that looks much as it did when it opened for business in the 1870s. In nearby New Scone on A94, there's the *Scone Arms* (phone: 551341), a charming country inn 2½ miles north of the city.

Stratford-upon-Avon

Even without William Shakespeare's pervasive presence, Stratford-upon-Avon would be a very pleasant stopping point on a tour through the Warwickshire heart of England. It is a charming town, set congenially amid peaceful green countryside on a bend of the gentle river Avon. It is filled with the elegance of lovely, early-16th-century half-timbered buildings. In its picture prettiness, swans glide by the spire of its riverside parish church, and trees, flowers, and gardens further soften its aspect. It is small enough to be seen in a day's stroll but large enough to have all the attributes of a busy market town—which it is and has been since receiving its first royal market charter in 1196, fully 368 years before Shakespeare ensured its enduring fame.

Stratford was first a Celtic settlement, then a small Roman town, its name—a mixture of the old Welsh for river and the Roman for street—meaning "the place where the street (or *straet*) fords the river (*afon*)." In the 13th century, the *Guild of the Holy Cross,* an Augustinian religious fraternity, was formed, and it fostered the development of industries and crafts. It also maintained the grammar school and had almshouses and its own chapel, all of which were built by citizens of the town and still are among Stratford's most interesting buildings today.

The town always has been fortunate in the generosity of its citizens. John de Stratford, an Archbishop of Canterbury in the 14th century, is thought to have rebuilt *Holy Trinity Church* and to have established a college of priests to serve it. Later on, Hugh Clopton, who was to become Lord Mayor of London at the end of the 15th century, built the nave and tower of the *Guild Chapel* and the splendid 14-arch Clopton Bridge, which still takes the heavy traffic of the 20th century into and out of town. More recent benefactors have been Charles Edward Flower, whose patronage made the first *Shakespeare Memorial Theatre* a reality in 1879, and his grandson Sir Archibald Flower, who was the major contributor to the present theater, opened in 1932.

Stratford's most illustrious citizen was undoubtedly William Shakespeare, son of John Shakespeare—"Gulielmus filius Johannes Shakespere," as the parish register puts it. Though he has been dead for almost 380 years, his attraction is as strong as when he was a famous writer of plays in Elizabethan and Jacobean London. England's, and probably the world's, greatest playwright dominates the daily life of Stratford-upon-Avon: His houses and his children's houses are visited by hundreds of thousands of people every year; the big theater on the river, one of the world's most famous, bears his name and its actors perform his works; hotels and restaurants are named after him; and shopkeepers live on the proceeds from the sale of books, prints, portrait busts, trinkets, and souvenirs with a Shakespearean theme. The

Shakespeare connection is a lucrative one, and it is to the credit of Stratford's residents that they have not allowed it to overwhelm and cheapen their delightful town.

The Shakespeare connection in a nutshell? Well, he was born here, on or about April 23, 1564, and he died here on April 23, 1616. In between, he grew up, went to school, moved to London to seek his fortune, and came back wealthy enough at 33 to buy a large house, *New Place,* in 1597, to which he retired in 1610, and where he died six years later of a fever caused, it is said, by too strenuous an evening of eating, drinking, and being merry.

Shakespeare's father was a glove maker, and his mother, Mary Arden, came from a respectable family of small landowners at Wilmcote, 3 miles from Stratford. The family house, from which John Shakespeare conducted his business, was on Henley Street, slightly to the north of the center of the busy little town. Young William went to school at the *King Edward VI Grammar School* on Church Street, and in 1582 married Anne Hathaway, a yeoman farmer's daughter eight years older than himself. They had three children, Susanna and the twins, Judith and Hamnet (the latter died at age 11 in 1596). Then came the years of fame and glory in London, followed by a short period of happy retirement tending his garden in Stratford.

After Shakespeare's death, the town's interest in its brilliant native son subsided somewhat, though there was always a steady trickle of people to see his house and his garden with its famous mulberry tree. The turning point in the town's long-range fortunes came with David Garrick's *Shakespeare Jubilee* in 1769. The event could be called the original *Shakespeare Festival,* and it grew out of Stratford's plans to decorate its rebuilt town hall.

Garrick was then England's foremost Shakespearean actor and as such was offered the honorary "Freedom" of the borough if he would provide a portrait or bust of Shakespeare to be hung in the town hall along with a portrait of himself. To no one's surprise, he accepted this opportunity to appear before an admiring posterity and organized his great jubilee—three days of celebration that, though marred by torrential rain, helped secure the future of Stratford as a great tourist attraction. The two portraits that were the occasion for the jubilee were both destroyed by fire in 1946, but a bust of Shakespeare that Garrick presented to Stratford still can be seen in the *Town Hall.*

The Shakespeare revival in Stratford grew apace during the 19th century, helped by interest from abroad, especially from the US. The first *Shakespeare Memorial Theatre* opened in 1879 to the sneers of the London theater establishment, but it was not long before they had to swallow their pride and take a serious interest in the little provincial theater, especially once the prominent producer Frank Benson began putting on the Bard's works here in 1886. His company remained for 30 years and established a performing tradition that became influential throughout the theater world.

Today Stratford-upon-Avon may be devoted to Shakespeare, but it has not been completely swamped by his cult. Its other side, its ancient existence as a lively market town, continues unabated and almost undisturbed. Every Tuesday, as has happened for centuries, Cotswold farmers bring their produce to the cattle market and on Fridays, people come in from the surrounding villages to shop at the stalls set up for the day on the *Market Place.* Branches of many of the large chain stores and modern shopping malls are close to the Shakespearean sites, hotels, and restaurants. It's a busy mix of commerce and culture, of modern and medieval, that allows life to go on for its inhabitants while preserving for visitors the feel of countless generations that have gone before, and for the pilgrims who seek it, a shrine.

Stratford At-a-Glance

SEEING THE CITY

The towers of *Holy Trinity Church* and the *Guild Chapel* are not open to visitors and there are no tall modern buildings from which to get a bird's-eye view of the town, but the layout of the center of Stratford is simple. It follows a street plan laid down by the Bishop of Worcester (Lord of the Manor) in 1196. Most visitors start their tour at *Shakespeare's Birthplace* on Henley Street, which runs diagonally down to intersect Wood Street (which later becomes Bridge Street), one of the four main thoroughfares that cut east-west across Stratford. The other three are Ely Street/Sheep Street, Scholars Lane/Chapel Lane, and Chestnut Walk/Old Town. Running north to south starting at the river are Waterside/Southern Lane, High Street/Chapel Street/Church Street, and Rother Street/Windsor Street/Shakespeare Street.

SPECIAL PLACES

The *Shakespeare Birthplace Trust* is the official body that, on behalf of the nation, owns the five most important buildings connected with William Shakespeare. These are the *Birthplace* itself, *New Place* (with *Nash's House*), *Hall's Croft, Anne Hathaway's Cottage,* and *Mary Arden's House.* The *Shakespeare Centre* (on Henley St.; phone: 204016), the *Trust*'s headquarters, is also an academic center, opened in 1964, for anyone wishing to study its splendid collection of books and documents relating to Shakespeare, including translations of his plays in 67 languages. There is usually an exhibition in the front hall, where the engraved glass panels by John Hutton (depicting characters from the plays) are well worth a look. The *Shakespeare Centre* is closed Sundays; admission is free to the library and records office, but there is a charge for the exhibitions. There are separate admission charges to each *Birthplace Trust* building, but it's possible to lower the cost by buying an inclusive ticket for entrance to all five.

Most of Stratford's special places, including the ones without Shakespearean connections, are in the center of town within easy walking distance of each other. In the course of a day's stroll, you can see everything listed here (with the exception of *Anne Hathaway's Cottage* and *Mary Arden's House*), as well as experience the everyday workings of a typical English market town. Alternatively, you can take the *Guide Friday Ltd.* open-top, double-decker bus tour (see *Getting Around*), which runs every day and links all the Shakespeare properties, including *Mary Arden's House* and *Anne Hathaway's Cottage.*

THE SHAKESPEARE BIRTHPLACE TRUST

SHAKESPEARE'S BIRTHPLACE The spiritual center of Stratford-upon-Avon lies in this modest, half-timbered and gabled Tudor building where William Shakespeare was born. The house, visited by more than half a million people of all nationalities every year, is beautifully maintained and furnished with objects typical of Shakespeare's period. The bedroom in which the Bard is assumed to have been born is upstairs, its window scratched with the signatures of famous people who have visited it, including those of Sir Walter Scott, Alfred, Lord Tennyson, and actress Ellen Terry. The *Birthplace* also houses a museum of relics and records of Shakespeare's day and a fine library. Don't miss the well-kept garden behind the house; in it grow many of the flowers, herbs, and plants Shakespeare knew. Open daily. Admission charge. Henley St. (phone: 204016).

NEW PLACE Shakespeare's house stood on this site. The building passed out of the family's hands in 1670, and its last owner demolished it in 1702 in order to build a more modern one. All that can be seen today are part of the foundations and the once-extensive gardens. There is a replica of an Elizabethan knot garden—an elaborately laid-out formal garden typical of those times—and the *Great Garden,* which contains topiary work and a mulberry tree said to have been grown from a cutting from Shakespeare's original tree. The young mulberry in the center of the lawn was planted by Dame Peggy Ashcroft to mark the 200th anniversary of David Garrick's jubilee. *Nash's House,* adjoining the gardens, was once owned by Thomas Nash, husband of Shakespeare's granddaughter Elizabeth Hall, and is furnished with items of their period. It also houses *New Place Museum,* devoted mainly to local archaeological material. Open daily. Admission charge. Chapel St. (phone: 292325).

HALL'S CROFT A short walk from *New Place* to Old Town, a quietly elegant residential street, brings you to this lovely house with a gabled front and overhanging upper floor. Shakespeare's elder daughter, Susanna, and her physician husband, Dr. John Hall, lived here from 1607 to 1616. Inside, it is the beautifully furnished house of a well-to-do Jacobean family, immaculately kept, with brass and copper glowing and flowers in the living rooms. Don't miss the bedroom with its four-poster, and Dr. Hall's dispensary, stocked with pottery jars of herbs and potions, mortars and pestles, and surgical instruments. A large walled garden behind the house, again immaculate, provides an oasis of sweet-scented calm. Open daily. Admission charge. Old Town (phone: 292107).

ANNE HATHAWAY'S COTTAGE So many hundreds of drawings, prints, engravings, and plaques portray this pretty, thatched house, that it is something of a surprise to come across the building itself on the outskirts of Stratford. It's about a mile from town to Shottery Village (take the footpath from Evesham Pl.), but it also can be reached by bus from Bridge Street, or even by bicycle. The trip is worth it, because Anne's cottage retains a charming English country air, with roses, jasmine, and other scented flowers in the garden, and Tudor furnishings in the house. Open daily. Admission charge. Shottery Village (phone: 292100).

MARY ARDEN'S HOUSE Shakespeare's mother lived in this lovely gabled farmhouse in Wilmcote Village before her marriage. The house is set in a garden, and the barns behind it house a museum devoted to rural life and farming. About 3 miles from Stratford, Wilmcote can be reached by road, train, or even by boat along the canal. Open daily. Admission charge. Wilmcote Village (phone: 293455).

OTHER STRATFORD ATTRACTIONS

HOLY TRINITY CHURCH On the bank of the river Avon, this stately parish church dates from the 13th century. Shakespeare was baptized and buried here, and photocopies of the church register entries of both events are on display. On the north wall of the chancel is a bust of the poet carved by his contemporary Gerard Jannsen, a memorial erected by the Shakespeare family in 1623. Shakespeare's grave is below the bust, flanked by those of his wife and other members of his family. Open daily. Admission charge to the chancel. Old Town.

GOWER MEMORIAL An imaginative statue of William Shakespeare crowns this impressive memorial, which its creator, Lord Ronald Sutherland Gower, labored over for 12 years. Unveiled in 1888, it stands with its back to the *Royal Shakespeare Theatre* in *Bancroft Gardens* near Clopton Bridge. The four life-size bronzes at its base are of Hamlet, Lady Macbeth, Falstaff, and Prince Hal.

KING EDWARD VI GRAMMAR SCHOOL This half-timbered building on Church Street can trace its origins back to the 13th century, and it was here that Shakespeare learned his Latin and Greek. Since it is still a school, it is not normally open to visitors, but don't walk by without pausing for a glimpse through the gateway or without noticing the ancient almshouses that border it (phone: 293351).

GUILD CHAPEL The beautiful gray stone tower of this chapel is one of the finest landmarks in Stratford. It rises above the austerely elegant chapel, which was rebuilt by Hugh Clopton about 1496, on the site of a building dating from the mid-13th century. Today it is used by the grammar school, which holds a daily service here during the school term. Of the many paintings that once covered the walls, only one remains—*The Day of Judgment,* which hangs over the chancel arch. The chapel adjoins the grammar school and almshouses on Church Street.

HARVARD HOUSE The Stars and Stripes flying from a flagpole above the front door indicates the special importance of this old half-timbered building, dating from 1596. It was the home of a wealthy Stratford alderman, Thomas Rogers, whose daughter Katherine was the mother of John Harvard, the first benefactor of the Ivy League university. The house now belongs to *Harvard* and is furnished in the style of the Elizabethan period. Open irregular hours; call ahead for details. Admission charge. High St. (phone: 204016).

SHRIEVE'S HOUSE Halfway down Sheep Street, stop for a moment outside this imposing late-16th-century private house with its great studded door and gateway. Shakespeare undoubtedly knew the owners of this Stratford townhouse and may well have attended the wedding feast of their daughter here in 1613.

BRASS RUBBING CENTRE Here is an opportunity to make your own souvenir of Stratford. The center has exact replicas of a large number of brasses, many from the Stratford area, and supplies paper and wax as part of the charge for doing a rubbing. Even a first-timer can produce an attractive rubbing in a half hour—though be advised that it's rather hard work. Closed November through February. No admission charge. *Royal Shakespeare Theatre Summer House, Avonbank Gardens* (phone: 297671).

WARWICK CASTLE Situated 8 miles outside of Stratford (take the bus from Wood St.), this is one of England's most visited stately homes. It contains a superb art collection of Old Masters, and there's also an exhibit called "The Kingmaker—A Preparation for Battle," which allows visitors to walk through several rooms that re-create the medieval household of the Earl of Warwick as he gets ready to fight a battle in the Wars of the Roses. The grounds boast a re-created Victorian rose garden with more than 700 rose bushes of at least 70 varieties, as well as a group of peacocks and peahens. On Saturday afternoons *Easter* through August, the *Morris Dancers* perform on the castle grounds. Open daily. Admission charge. Warwick (phone: 1926-495421).

WORLD OF SHAKESPEARE This 25-minute audiovisual show with life-size tableaux tells the colorful story of Elizabeth I's journey from London to Stratford-upon-Avon and on to *Kenilworth Castle* in 1575. Open daily. Admission charge. Waterside (phone: 269190).

Sources and Resources

TOURIST INFORMATION

The tourist information center (at Bridgefoot; phone: 293127) has maps, leaflets, guidebooks, and a list of restaurants; accommodations also can be booked here; closed Sundays November through March. The *Stratford-upon-Avon Leisure Line* (phone: 267522) gives prerecorded information such as opening times, telephone numbers, and other details of places of interest in and around the town. *Guide Friday Ltd.* (*Civic Hall, Market Place,* 14 Rother St.; phone: 294466) has a tourism center that provides visitors with town maps and area brochures.

LOCAL COVERAGE The weekly *Stratford-upon-Avon Herald* is helpful, as is the free weekly publication called *Why?* available at most hotels.

TELEPHONE The city code for Stratford is 1789.

GETTING AROUND

The best way to see central Stratford-upon-Avon is on foot. There are large maps displayed at the intersections of the main streets and most of the city's important streets are laid out in a simple grid pattern, so it's difficult to get lost. In the town center, street numbers often ascend on one side and descend on the other, rather than one side being even-numbered and the other odd.

BOAT One-hour and half-hour cruises along the Avon and the historic early-19th-century Stratford Canal are available from *Rose's Boathouse* (Swan's Nest La.; phone: 267073) and *Stratford Marina Ltd.* (Clopton Bridge; phone: 269669).

BUS *Midland Red and Stratford Blue* (phone: 1788-535555 in Rugby) serves Stratford and the surrounding villages; tickets are sold on board. Fares range from 38p (about 60¢) to 50p (about 75¢), depending on the distance traveled. *National Express Coaches* (phone: 121-622-4373 in Birmingham) operates daily service to London's *Victoria Station* via Banbury and *Heathrow Airport;* tickets are available from *James Travel* (*Bell Court Centre;* phone: 292393) and the tourist information center (see above). The departure point for both bus lines is on Bridge Street near Clopton Bridge.

CAR RENTAL Two local firms are *Arden Garages* (Arden St.; phone: 267446), and *Yarnolds* (Birmingham Rd.; phone: 205990). *Hertz* has an office at the railway station (phone: 298827).

SIGHTSEEING TOURS *Guide Friday Ltd.* (see above) runs tours via open-air, double-decker buses around the town and to the Shakespeare sites outside town. Buses depart every 15 minutes during the summer, every 30 minutes during spring and autumn, and every hour during winter. A 90-minute guided walk starts from the *Shakespeare Centre* (Henley St.) at 10:30 AM every Sunday morning.

TAXI Cabs can be flagged down on the street. Go to the cab rank in Union Street or at Bridgefoot by the *Pen and Parchment* pub, or call *Taxiline* (phone: 266100) or *007 Taxis* (phone: 414007). Your hotel also can get you a taxi.

TRAIN Fast *InterCity 125* trains run from London's *Euston Station* to Coventry and connect with an express motorcoach to Stratford. Called the *Shakespeare*

Connection, the service is coordinated to suit theatergoers. It runs four times a day Mondays through Saturdays during the winter, six times a day during summer, and twice on Sundays year-round (the trip takes about two hours). For details, call 294466. Slower trains run from *Stratford Station* on Station Road to London's *Paddington Station* (phone: 171-262-6767); it is usually necessary to change at *Leamington Station* (phone: 171-387-7070).

SPECIAL EVENTS

Every spring, usually on the Saturday nearest April 23, Stratford and the world unite to honor Shakespeare. A procession that includes ambassadors from many countries walks from his birthplace to *Holy Trinity Church* to lay floral tributes on his grave. Flags of the nations are unfurled in the center of town, and there is a special performance at the *Royal Shakespeare Theatre.* The *Boat Club* holds its *Regatta* in June (heralded by a popular raft race). The *Stratford Festival* of music, plays, and poetry readings takes place during the last two weeks of July; for details contact the festival office (2 Chestnut Walk; phone: 267969). In October (usually on the 12th) there's the *Mop Fair,* when stalls, sideshows, and amusements take over the town center.

SHOPPING

The town's main shopping area, on Bridge, High, and Wood Streets, is small but charming, having maintained a relatively old-fashioned appearance. Look for high-quality handicrafts—including pottery, stained glass, and carved woods—as well as English sheepskins, leather clothing, and china. Sheep and Chapel Streets have several elegant antiques shops, and the *Antique Centre* arcade (off Ely St.; phone: 204180) has nearly 50 dealers' booths. Open daily. There also is a modern, though unattractive, outdoor mall between High and Rother Streets, called *Bell Court.* For standard shopping hours, see GETTING READY TO GO.

Be sure to take your passport when you shop, and always inquire about the Value Added Tax (VAT) refund application forms when your total purchases in a store are over £50 (about $75). The VAT is a surcharge payable at the sales counter, but foreign customers usually will be reimbursed for it at home (for more information see GETTING READY TO GO).

Arbour Antiques Britain's most comprehensive vendor of antique arms and armor is on the *Tower of London*'s list of recommended dealers. The fascinating stock ranges from single arrows to suits of armor and full-size cannon. Poet's Arbour, Tudorgate Alley off Sheep St. (phone: 293453).

Dianthus Ceramics Beautiful creamware, stoneware, and other traditional English earthenware, all hand-crafted on the premises. *Centre Craft Yard,* off Henley St. (phone: 292252).

Dolls & Toys Museum & Antiques This tiny shop sells small antique items, from Egyptology pieces to toy soldiers; at the back, the museum (admission charge) displays china dolls and teddy bears collected by one of the owners. 30 Windsor St. (phone: 292485).

Jean Bateman A specialty antiques shop that carries a wide range of rare tapestries, embroideries, and scent bottles. 41 Sheep St. (phone: 298494).

Lands Pipes, pipe racks, and all brands of tobacco fill the air with a delicious aroma. The ingeniously carved walking sticks are hard to resist. 29 Central Chambers, Henley St. (phone: 292508).

Montpellier Gallery Attractive contemporary paintings, pottery, and jewelry. 8 Chapel St. (phone: 261161).

National Trust Shop This store carries a wide selection of gifts and trinkets related to *National Trust* properties throughout Britain, from books and calendars to stuffed animals and other toys to jams and chocolates. The quality of the merchandise is very high. 45 Wood St. (phone: 262197).

Needlecraft Centre Cottons, silks, threads, and wools in all colors and thicknesses for needlework; also tapestry patterns. 37 Sheep St. (phone: 414388).

Paxton & Whitfield Over 140 farmhouse cheeses, mostly British and French, as well as wine, coffee beans, and French bread. It's worth stopping in just for the aromas. 13 Wood St. (phone: 415544).

Pickwick Gallery An excellent range of antique maps and prints. 32 Henley St. (phone: 294861).

Robert Vaughan Antiquarian bookshop specializing in the theater and English literature, including first editions. 20 Chapel St. (phone: 205312).

Royal Shakespeare Theatre The kiosk in the main foyer sells all things Shakespearean: books, posters, T-shirts. The shop in the *Swan Theatre* entrance carries books and photographs of recent productions. Waterside (phone: 296655).

Shakespeare Bookshop Shakespearean books and videos plus gifts and souvenirs. This is the best place to learn all about the Bard. 39 Henley St. (phone: 204016).

Spinning Wheel Woolen cloaks, scarves, and ties, handwoven on the premises. 10 Chapel St. (phone: 293375).

Teahouse A vast choice of teas and coffees; also teapots and mugs. Shreeve's Walk, off Sheep St. (phone: 414038).

Trading Post A densely stocked gift shop in the house where Shakespeare's daughter Judith lived with her husband, Thomas Quiney. The selection of dollhouses and furniture upstairs includes tiny four-poster beds and antiques. 1 High St. (phone: 267228).

Traditions of Britain British pottery and woolen goods. 22 Henley St. (phone: 268758).

SPORTS

Stratford has facilities for many kinds of sports; ask at the information center (see *Tourist Information*) for a complete list.

BICYCLING Stratford and its surrounding countryside are ideally suited to cycling excursions. You can rent bicycles at *Clarkes* (Bancrofts Esso Station, Guild St.; phone: 205057).

BOATING Both short trips and long-term boating holidays can be arranged from spring through autumn on the Avon and the Stratford Canal, which flows into the Avon through a lock in the gardens beside the *Royal Shakespeare Theatre.* Rowboats, punts (propelled by poles), and canoes can be rented at *Rose's Boathouse* and *Stratford Marina Ltd.* (see *Getting Around* for both).

CRICKET Matches take place at the *Stratford Cricket Club* on the *Recreation Ground* beside the river, off Tramway Walk (phone: 415285).

FISHING Go to *David Jones Angling Centre* (17 Evesham Rd.; phone: 293950) for the necessary daily or season fishing tickets.

GOLF Visitors may play on the 18-hole courses at the *Stratford-upon-Avon Golf Club* (Tiddington Rd.; phone: 297296), and the *Welcombe* hotel (Warwick Rd.; phone: 299012).

HORSE RACING Races are held about twice a month from September through May at the *Stratford Race Course* (Luddington Rd.; phone: 267949).

SWIMMING The *Leisure Centre* (at Bridgefoot; phone: 268826) has two pools as well as squash courts, a sauna, and a solarium. Open daily. Admission charge.

TENNIS The *Leisure Centre* (see above) has lighted tennis courts, along with squash courts, a gym, and swimming pool. Admission charge.

THEATER

Although the work of other playwrights is sometimes performed, for all intents and purposes, the words "theater" and "Shakespeare" are synonymous in Stratford.

CENTER STAGE

Royal Shakespeare Theatre A visit to this venue at its imposing riverside location is a major event for theater and Shakespeare lovers from all over the world. The senior of the United Kingdom's two national theaters, under the patronage of the queen, this 1,500-seat hall opened on April 23, 1932, on the Bard's own birthday—appropriately enough, since Shakespeare is the sole fare on these boards throughout the season, from late March through January. The immense *Royal Shakespeare Company*—the association of actors, directors, and designers who claim the place as one of their principal homes—has numbered almost all the greats of British theater among its members in the course of the past century. The quality of the work is at least professional if not always superb, and often innovative.

Tickets for all performances should be bought as far in advance as possible from the box office or through a ticket agency. Tickets go on sale in early February, though it often is possible to buy them at the last minute. The theater holds back a few medium-price tickets (maximum two per person) and some standing-room tickets for sale on the day of performance starting at 9:30 AM. Bona fide students (with identification to prove it) may chance upon an unsold ticket immediately before the performance. The theater has two restaurants (see *Eating Out*) and a store (see *Shopping*).

The attached *Swan Theatre,* built within the shell of the old *Memorial Theatre,* has a horseshoe-shaped auditorium that closely resembles those of 16th-century playhouses, and has been earmarked for performing works of Shakespeare's contemporaries; the season runs from April through January. The *RSC Collection Exhibition,* in the same building, has interesting photographs, costumes, and props relating to past productions, as well as relics of famous theater personalities. Open daily. Admission charge. Backstage tours of both theaters are also available daily (except Saturdays) for a separate admission charge. Waterside (phone: 295623 for credit-card bookings; 269191 for 24-hour information on seat availability; 296655 for tours).

In addition, *The Other Place,* a two-minute walk away from the more famous theaters in Waterside, is a theater-in-the-round that presents new and experimental productions, as well as the occasional Shakespearean work (phone: 295623).

MUSIC

Stratford's tradition is drama rather than music, but the town plays host to orchestras, bands, and soloists throughout the year, most often at the *Civic Hall* (phone: 414513). In July, in conjunction with the *Stratford Festival,* the *Royal Shakespeare Theatre* presents occasional concerts.

NIGHTCLUBS AND NIGHTLIFE

Evenings are fairly quiet in Stratford; pubs close at 11 PM, and other than spending a night at the theater, there's not much else to do. *Richies* restaurant (Alcester Rd.; phone: 297812) has a disco Tuesdays through Saturdays, and the *Boat House* (see *Eating Out*) sometimes has jazz or dancing; both places are popular with young people and stay open until the early hours. Along with bistro food, *Celebrities* (4-5 Henley St.; phone: 293022) has a large bar and dancing nightly except Sundays.

Best in Town

CHECKING IN

For visitors who intend to stay in a modest bed and breakfast establishment, there is usually no need to make reservations in advance, except during the summer. Many of these worthy British establishments line roads like Shipston Street and Grove Road. Those who want a good hotel, however, should book ahead, especially during spring and autumn when conference bookings cause hotels to fill quickly. The tourist information center supplies copies of the official *Accommodation Register* and can help you find somewhere to stay, as will *Guide Friday Ltd.* for a small fee (see *Tourist Information*, above, for both).

A bed and breakfast establishment offers a comfortable room (some with private baths) and a good breakfast for about $85 for two per night (some of the smaller bed and breakfast establishments don't accept credit cards). For a double room in a large, expensive hotel, expect to pay $150 or more per night; moderately priced hotels run about $95 to $150; and inexpensive accommodations cost about $90. Reduced rates often apply on weekends. All hotels listed below include private bath, TV set, phone, and breakfast unless otherwise noted. Most of Stratford's major hotels have complete facilities for the business traveler. Those hotels listed below as having "business services" usually offer such conveniences as a concierge, meeting rooms, photocopiers, computers, translation services, and express checkout, among others. Call the hotel for additional information. All telephone numbers are in the 1789 city code unless otherwise indicated.

For an unforgettable experience in Stratford-upon-Avon, we begin with our favorite, followed by our cost and quality choices of accommodations, listed by price category.

A SPECIAL HAVEN

Alveston Manor Whether or not *A Midsummer Night's Dream* actually was first performed here, as some longtime Stratford residents like to suggest, this manor fairly oozes the kind of atmosphere most people travel to England to find. From the warm oak-paneled entryway to the fine lounge, it is the sort of place most people feel they could stay in for days. The atmospheric *Manor Bar* is remarkable for its attractive paneling and beamed ceiling, and the dining room serves a wide variety of continental dishes (the menu changes daily). Of the 106 guestrooms, those in the main building are the most interesting; those in the new wing tend toward the standard British modern. Business services are available. Best of all, it is a mere five-minute walk from the theater. Clopton Bridge (phone: 204581; 800-225-5843; fax: 414095).

EXPENSIVE

Ettington Park Though it lies 8 miles outside of town, this converted Victorian Gothic building (listed in the *Domesday Book*) is considered among *the* places to stay; it retains many features reminiscent of 18th- and 19th-century gracious living. The 39 luxurious rooms and nine suites overlook the 40-acre *Ettington Estate.* Fresh herbs and greens from the garden are served at the imposing *Oak Room* restaurant, and leisure activities include archery, clay-pigeon shooting, riding, fishing, tennis, and swimming in the indoor pool. Business services are also offered. Alderminster (phone: 450123; 800-637-7200; fax: 450472).

Shakespeare A Stratford landmark, this gabled, timber-fronted 16th-century building in the center of town is the place to stay if you want a taste of Elizabethan England. David Garrick stayed here in 1769, and since then most of its rooms have been named after Shakespeare's plays: You could find yourself sleeping in the *Midsummer Night's Dream* room and eating in the *David Garrick* restaurant. The 63-room hostelry has been carefully modernized so that the authentic atmosphere endures (and three of the rooms have four-poster beds). Business services are available. Chapel St. (phone: 294771; 800-225-5843; fax: 415411).

Welcombe Once a private Jacobean mansion, this elegant 76-room hostelry set in extensive parkland on the outskirts of Stratford retains the atmosphere of an English country house, including seven rooms with four-poster beds. The menu in its paneled restaurant is classic French. There is an 18-hole golf course and two all-weather, lighted tennis courts, plus a helipad with connections to nearby *Birmingham Airport.* Coarse fishing and croquet also are offered, business services are available, and the hotel's garage has car service facilities and gas. Closed December 29 through January 3. Warwick Rd., 1¼ miles from the town center (phone: 295252; fax: 414666).

White Swan One of the oldest inns in town, it dates from the 15th century—beautifully evident from its medieval, gabled façade to the sturdy wood beams within. One of the 37 rooms has a large four-poster bed. There's a restaurant, and business services are available. Rother St. (phone: 297022; 800-225-5843; fax: 268773).

MODERATE

Falcon One of those stunning, half-timbered buildings that make Stratford so picturesque, this 73-room hostelry overlooks the gardens of *New Place.* Inside, it is less elegant than the *Shakespeare* hotel, and all but 20 of the rooms are in the modern extension. Nevertheless, the old part has a charm of its own, with a log fire blazing during the winter months. There is a restaurant, and business services are offered. Chapel St. (phone: 205777; fax: 414260).

Stratford House Once a private Georgian home, this charming hostelry, a two-minute walk from the *Royal Shakespeare Theatre,* has been modernized in delightful style, including the incorporation of the *Shepherd's Garden* restaurant (see *Eating Out*). The 10 rooms are small but comfortable. 18 Sheep St. (phone: 268288; fax: 295580).

INEXPENSIVE

Caterham House A three-minute walk from the town center, the Maury family's stylish, comfortable hotel has 13 rooms and the *Bonaparte,* a good French restaurant. 58-59 Rother St. (phone: 267309).

Hardwick House This cozy Victorian house (14 rooms) in a quiet area is only a few minutes' walk from the town center and Shakespearean attractions. It's owned and run by the Wootton family. No restaurant. 1 Avenue Rd. (phone: 204307; fax: 296760).

Payton Another well-maintained little hostelry, with five rooms (one with a four-poster) and a home-like atmosphere, it, too, is in a quiet part of town, though only a short walk from the back gate of *Shakespeare's Birthplace.* No restaurant, and the guestrooms do not have phones. 6 John St. (phone: 266442; fax: 414034).

Stretton House Michael and Yvonne Machin's is the best of five small privately run hostelries that are side by side in a terrace of late Victorian houses less than a five-minute walk from the town center. There are six rooms (no phones). No restaurant, but evening meals are available for residents. No credit cards accepted. 38 Grove Rd. (phone: 268647).

EATING OUT

With the help of a range of fast-food and snack restaurants, Stratford manages to feed its hundreds of thousands of visitors pretty well. Those arriving just for the day find that the coffeehouses and tearooms generally are good, and many of them stay open long enough to provide an evening meal. At midday, there is the ploughman's lunch (bread, cheese, and pickle) to be sampled with a pint of beer in one of Stratford's typical pubs, many of which also offer an array of hot and cold food at the bar.

Those staying overnight can expect a full British breakfast—fruit juice, cereal, sausage, bacon and eggs, toast, and tea or coffee—in the morning, though a lighter continental breakfast—usually fruit juice, croissants or toast, and coffee—also is available. Evening meals range from a standard "meat and three vegetables" to international fare. Prices for a three-course dinner for two, without drinks will cost more than $70 in the expensive category, $45 to $70 in the moderate category, and less than $45 in the inexpensive category. All restaurants listed below serve lunch and dinner unless otherwise noted. All telephone numbers are in the 1789 city code unless otherwise indicated.

EXPENSIVE

Box Tree The *Royal Shakespeare Theatre*'s elegant upstairs restaurant offers top-quality, traditional English fare and a superb view of the Avon. Closed Sundays; lunch served on matinee days only. Reservations necessary. Major credit cards accepted. Waterside (phone: 293226).

Giovanni's A discreetly curtained front and restrained gold lettering hide a plush restaurant very much in the Italian grand manner, complete with leather sofas and chairs, flocked wallpaper, and bronze statues. Delicious Italian cooking. Closed Sundays. Reservations advised. Major credit cards accepted. 8 Ely St. (phone: 297999).

Shepherd's Garden Barely noticeable from the street, this small eatery serving superb English and French fare is tucked away in an airy, elegantly furnished conservatory at the back of the tiny *Stratford House* hotel. Widely regarded as the town's most pleasant restaurant, it overlooks a small garden-courtyard where meals are served alfresco in good weather. Closed Sunday evenings and Mondays. Reservations necessary. Major credit cards accepted. 18 Sheep St. (phone: 68288).

MODERATE

Arden Draws theatergoers (the *Royal Shakespeare* is just across the road), and both restaurant and bar are good places to spot celebrities. The food is simple, based on the best available fresh ingredients. Open daily. Reservations advised. Major credit cards accepted. 44 Waterside (phone: 294949).

Black Swan Stratford's most famous pub (see *Sharing a Pint,* below) has a small, first class restaurant, specializing in roast duck and oxtail, that stays open for after-theater supper. The Sunday brunch, featuring the restaurant's own version of bubble and squeak (a refried cheese and cabbage pancake), is sumptuous. Closed Sunday evenings and Monday lunch. Reservations advised. Major credit cards accepted. 55 Waterside (phone: 297312).

Glory Hole A wide variety of dishes—from pasta to roast meat—is served at this informal eatery. There are also some unusual specialties, including prawn, haddock, and bacon stew. It's famous for the walls in the bathrooms—the "ladies" is decorated with seaside postcards; the "gents" with tongue-in-cheek business advice. Open daily. Reservations advised in summer. Major credit cards accepted. 21 Sheep St. (phone: 293546).

Lambs Bistro Snack lunches and à la carte dinners are served in this versatile eatery housed in a 16th-century building with beamed ceilings and mullioned windows. Open daily. No reservations. Major credit cards accepted. 12 Sheep St. (phone: 292554).

The Opposition A bistro-style restaurant that has won a following for its imaginative and regularly changing menu. Open daily. Reservations unnecessary. Major credit cards accepted. 13 Sheep St. (phone: 269980).

Sir Toby's This small dining spot serves grilled fish and meat; try the homemade *bresoala,* thin slices of smoked raw beef marinated with peppercorns, red and white wine, rosemary, sage, garlic, chilies, and cloves. Closed Mondays and Wednesday through Saturday evenings. Reservations necessary. Major credit cards accepted. 8 Church St. (phone: 268822).

INEXPENSIVE

Boat House Set above *Rose's Boathouse,* this attractive wine bar and restaurant offers a limited menu of entrées and salads and has splendid views of the river and theater gardens. The bar stays open late, and there's sometimes jazz music or dancing in the evening. Open daily. Reservations advised. Major credit cards accepted. Swan's Nest La., Bridgefoot (phone: 297733).

Fatty Arbuckle's This excellent bistro features a whimsical menu warning guests that some dishes are disturbingly large (as was the girth of the 1920s film star for whom this place was named). The crusty granary bread is always delicious, and the day's specials are listed on a blackboard. Open daily. Reservations advised for dinner. Major credit cards accepted. 9 Chapel St. (phone: 267069).

Hussains Actors from the *Royal Shakespeare Theatre* regularly frequent this smart, exotically decorated eatery specializing in well-spiced but not over-curried northern Indian fare. Open daily. Reservations advised. Major credit cards accepted. 6A Chapel St. (phone: 267506).

River Terrace This self-service restaurant on the ground floor of the *Royal Shakespeare Theatre* overlooks the riverside gardens. Closed Sunday evenings. No reservations. Major credit cards accepted. Waterside (phone: 293226).

Shakespeare Coffee House At this spotless coffee shop, the salads are fresh and the pâté is homemade. Opposite *Shakespeare's Birthplace.* Closed Mondays in winter. No reservations. No credit cards accepted. 43 Henley St. (phone: 297490).

Vintner Wine Bar A bistro with beamed ceilings, it serves snacks and informal meals; hot dishes include homemade soups and French-style vegetables. Open daily. Reservations advised. Major credit cards accepted. 5 Sheep St. (phone: 297259).

SHARING A PINT

Among Stratford's array of pubs, one is particularly worth raising an elbow in.

PERFECT PINTS

Black Swan Sir Laurence Olivier, Sir John Gielgud, Albert Finney, Peter O'Toole, and Glenda Jackson all have frequented this place, informally known as the "Dirty Duck," at one time or another; more recently John Hurt, Kenneth Branagh and Emma Thompson, Derek Jacobi, and Helen Mirren have popped by. There are two main reasons why this pub is such a popular hangout for actors—its proximity to the *Royal Shakespeare Theatre* and the special attention the management gives thespian patrons. Although less illustrious visitors may have to try a little harder to order some of the pub food, there's always someone interesting to look at while waiting. Waterside (phone: 297312).

The *Garrick Inn* (on High St.; phone: 292186), next to *Harvard House,* dates back to late Elizabethan times, but its ambience is delightfully Dickensian, with several small bars. *Windmill Inn* (Church St.; phone: 297687) is one of Stratford's oldest pubs and serves good food and ale.

York

"The history of York," according to King George VI, "is the history of England." In 1971, York celebrated its 1,900th birthday, and each epoch of Britain's past is legible in its ruins, buildings, and monuments. The Middle Ages are especially well represented, and for many visitors, this aspect of York is the most interesting. Within the 3 miles of ancient defensive wall is perhaps the best-preserved medieval city in Great Britain, containing its largest medieval church, *York Minster,* and its best-preserved medieval street. The quirky, timbered, slightly akimbo buildings in the Shambles may look like a stage set, but they are as authentic as the day they were built.

In AD 71, the Romans chose the meeting point of the rivers Ouse and Foss as the site of Eboracum, at first a temporary camp, then a permanent fort. From that it grew to become a major Roman city that Emperor Hadrian used as a home base and where Constantine the Great was proclaimed emperor. It flourished as a trade center at the hub of a network of roads and as a port for seagoing ships that navigated the 50-mile stretch up the river Ouse. The most inspiring physical legacy of those times is the surviving *Multangular Tower* in the *Yorkshire Museum* gardens.

The Romans left to defend their own country in the early part of the 5th century, and little is known of the city until the Saxons gained control in the 7th century. They built the first *York Minster,* predecessor of the present building. The conquering Danes, arriving in the 9th century, further developed the city as an important port and called it Jorvik. Some of Jorvik's original Viking buildings, superbly preserved, have been excavated. The Normans' 11th-century presence is recorded in today's landscape as two humps of earth on which William the Conqueror raised two wooden castles. One hump remains as Baile Hill; the other supports *Clifford's Tower,* a later structure in stone.

It was in the 13th century, however, that the city began to assume its familiar shape. Though it had earlier been surrounded by an earth mound and a wooden stockade, these were replaced by the actual limestone walls, together with the four principal gateways (called bars, just to confuse matters): *Monk Bar, Micklegate Bar, Walmgate Bar,* and *Bootham Bar.* Within the boundaries, several churches, friaries, nunneries, and an abbey established York as a cradle of European Christianity and as the country's second city. The minster, growing grander over the 250 years of its construction, was finally completed in 1472, and has been York's crowning glory ever since.

Medieval city planners developed their roads along the main Roman streets. The medievals then built connecting alleyways and the characteristic timber-framed buildings that overhang them, each story projecting farther than the one below. The Shambles is one such street, now restored not as a lifeless museum piece but as a busy commercial artery.

During the mid-15th century, the House of York and the House of Lancaster struggled for the English throne. Richard, then Duke of York, opposed Lancaster's King Henry VI; thus began the extended fight known as the Wars of the Roses (the house of Lancaster's emblem was a red rose, and the house of York, white). Since those battles, the dukedom of York has been awarded to the second son of the royal family; Queen Elizabeth conferred the title on Prince Andrew the day he married Sarah Ferguson.

The prosperity of medieval York stemmed from its thriving wool trade. With the slow decline of this industry, and Henry VIII's purge of the church, the city played only a minor role in English history until it became a fashionable social center in 18th-century Georgian Britain. The racecourse, *Assembly Rooms,* and many splendid townhouses were part of this scene. The aristocracy, and others who could afford it, chose to live in York rather than in the more industrialized cities perched on the rich coal deposits found almost everywhere in Yorkshire except York itself.

Because it was widely favored by wealthy northerners as a refuge from the grime of early industrialization, York remained relatively factory-free, with candy works a notable exception. It did, however, spawn George Hudson, a railway inventor and entrepreneur who was largely responsible for making the city a keystone in Britain's expanding railway network.

To absorb York's antiquated atmosphere, simply wander around, particularly in the labyrinth of streets and alleyways in the shadow of the minster. Stroll along the gates—the activities that once took place in them are evident in their names: Colliergate was the street of the charcoal dealers, Spurriergate belonged to the spurmakers, and Stonegate was the route used to carry building materials to the minster. Whip-ma-whop-ma-gate is a short street whose long name derives from a whipping post where criminals were punished. And don't miss walking on one of York's 50 famous "snickelways"—narrow pedestrian passageways that connect streets, walls, or buildings. Unique to York, most of these alleyways played a part in the city's history.

Everywhere are curiosities of the past. In Deangate, for example, there is a working gas lamp in front of the minster's south door. On Stonegate, be sure to look at the sign for the *Ye Olde Starre Inn* pub, stretched across the street—once the city's most popular form of advertising. Above all, be sure to listen as well as look—the Yorkshire accent of the 123,000 city residents is as much a part of the local atmosphere as the historic buildings. There's even a town crier who shouts out the latest news Mondays through Saturdays in Coppergate at 11 AM, King's Square at 11:20 AM, Parliament Street at 11:40 AM, St. Helen's Square at noon, and Swinegate at 12:30 PM.

York certainly has its modern (and sometimes shabby) aspects, but it has managed more successfully than most cities to conserve its age-old character. Yet, it remains to be seen whether York can continue to resist pressures to keep up-to-date by widening streets and building taller buildings. In the meantime, it is not unusual for over 2.5 million visitors a year to step into York's time capsule to enjoy its ancient airs and graces.

York At-a-Glance

SEEING THE CITY

For those who want an aerial perspective, the city walls offer a 2½-mile-long vantage point. The route along the crest of the barricades dates from the 1200s and is still the traditional promenade. The path—three feet wide and often without handrails, so be careful—can be reached from the bars, or gateways, where the walls join the major roads (*Bootham, Monk, Walmgate, Fishergate, Victoria,* and *Micklegate Bars*). The stretch between *Bootham Bar* and *Monk Bar* is particularly attractive and affords a good view of the spires and buttresses of *York Minster.* The walk, which is delightful in springtime, is open daily. The walls of *Clifford's Tower* (see *Special Places*) also offer fine vistas of the city. The *Minster Tower* affords a good panoramic view of the city and the surrounding Yorkshire Dales. Open daily. Admission charge.

SPECIAL PLACES

Nearly everything you'll want to see in York is in the medieval heart of the city. The only exception is the *National Railway Museum* on the west side of the river Ouse near the railway station on Station Road, which is just outside the Old City walls.

YORK MINSTER York without the minster's imposing skyline presence would be like Paris denied its *Eiffel Tower.* This grandiose church—the *Cathedral of St. Peter*—is the largest Gothic cathedral in northern Europe. It was built over a period of about 250 years, from 1220 to 1472, but even before that, there had been several churches on the spot. *York Minster* contains the finest collection of medieval stained glass in England. Of the 130 windows, the 13th-century Five Sisters Window of delicate grisaille glass is the most famous, although the West Window, with its heart-shaped tracery, is perhaps the most beautiful. The Rose Window, commemorating the 15th-century War of the Roses, was badly damaged in a 1984 fire, but it has since been fully restored. The church was in danger of collapsing until desperately needed renovations were begun in 1967. During the course of the repairs, the foundations of an early Norman cathedral were revealed, and it was discovered that the medieval church had been raised right above the city's Roman headquarters. The foundations are open to the public, and visitors can see the massive 20th-century concrete underpinnings as well as an exhibit on the history of the minster and its site. It costs nothing to wander around the minster itself, but there is an admission charge to climb the tower (see *Seeing the City*) and to see the foundations and *Chapter House,* which contains a small collection of medieval stone carvings.

TREASURER'S HOUSE The official residence of the treasurer of the minster (the post was abolished in 1547) is behind the minster on the site of a Roman building. Though it dates from the 13th century, most of what exists today is from the 17th century. The last owner, Frank Green, renovated the building and gave it to the *National Trust* in 1930. Visitors can walk through about 20 rooms furnished with period pieces and see a lively exhibition about some of the personalities associated with the house. Closed November through March. Admission charge. On some summer evenings (call the number below or contact the *York Center* of the *National Trust* at 798110 for dates), you can enjoy "Coffee by Candlelight" in the main hall and music in the garden. Minster Yard (phone: 624247).

ST. WILLIAM'S COLLEGE One of York's many picturesque half-timbered structures, this was built in 1453 to lodge the minster's chantry priests and has been restored as a meeting place for church convocations. The "World of the Minster" exhibit on the upper floor gives amazing insight into the lives of the people connected with the minster for the last 800 years. The exhibition is open daily; the rest of the building is closed during meetings. Admission charge. College St. (phone: 637134).

HOLY TRINITY CHURCH Completed before 1500, this picturesque church contains a split-level pulpit, 18th-century wooden box pews, a sloped floor, and an angled peephole for the priest to look up from the chapel altar to the church's high altar. Goodramgate. Next to the church is Lady Row, a brightly painted group of cottages from the early 14th century that are among the oldest in the country.

SHAMBLES Mentioned in the *Domesday Book,* this narrow cobblestone alley is one of the best-preserved medieval streets in Britain, if not Europe. Originally it was a street of butchers' shops, known as "fleshammels," but it is now lined with antiques, crafts, and gift shops. People living in the upper stories of these typically medieval overhanging buildings can shake hands with their neighbors across the road if they lean out the windows far enough. In the Middle Ages, this construction also made it easier for residents to dump their chamber pots out into the ditch in the street below, accompanied by the cry, "*Gardez-l'eau!*" Legend has it that "loo," a British term for bathroom, came from that medieval warning. The Shambles leads from King's Square (at the foot of Petergate) to The Pavement.

JORVIK VIKING CENTRE At this successful "way of life" museum, small electric "time cars" take visitors underground and back a thousand years to see a busy market and houses—all of which have been reconstructed on the excavation site of an old Viking street beneath the modern Coppergate—populated with wax figures re-creating the Viking lifestyle. The preserved excavation site is also visible from the cars. This amazing and very important find unearthed houses, workshops, kitchenware, tools, fragments of clothing, and other artifacts of 9th-century life that had been untouched since the Vikings lived here. Sounds and smells are used to evoke an even more authentic atmosphere. Open daily. Admission charge. Coppergate (phone: 643211).

MUSEUM OF AUTOMATA Over 2,000 years of automation is chronicled, from simple wind-up toys to complex robots. There are many hands-on displays to experiment with. In the *French Gallery,* Parisian café society is startlingly re-created with video, sound, and light effects. There's also a reconstructed 1950s seaside pier. Open daily. Admission charge. Tower St. (phone: 655550).

ARC At this hands-on attraction run by the *York Archaeological Trust,* visitors can examine pottery shards, bones, soil samples, and other finds from archaeological digs; learn about what it's like to participate in an excavation through interactive videos; and perform ancient crafts, including sewing Roman sandals, and weaving on a Viking loom. Closed December 1 through January 2. Admission charge. St. Saviourgate (phone: 654324).

FAIRFAX HOUSE An 18th-century townhouse displaying the famous *Terry Collection* of furniture and clocks, entitled "Life in Georgian York." Now owned by the *York Civic Trust,* the house was used as a movie theater and dance hall from 1920 to the mid-1960s. Closed January through mid-February. Castlegate (phone: 655543).

CASTLE MUSEUM A private collection, accumulated by a doctor from Pickering (25 miles northeast of York) and donated to the city in 1925, forms the basis of one of the country's most important folk museums. Stars of the show are the reconstructed streets: a Victorian cobbled one complete with Hansom cab (the original taxi, whose inventor, Joseph Hansom, lived in York); candlemaker's, blacksmith's, and other shop fronts; and an Edwardian street with gaslighted pub. Among the diverse displays are a Victorian parlor, a Georgian dining room, snuffboxes, policemen's truncheons, old musical instruments, vintage candy bars that include sugar pigs and spice mice, firearms, and unintelligible tape recordings of the local Yorkshire dialect. All this is housed in an 18th-century women's prison, with various craftsmen's workshops set up in the converted cells. Open daily. Admission charge; you also can buy a combined ticket to the museum and the *York Story* (see below). Tower St. (phone: 653611).

YORK STORY York from pre-Roman times to the present is the subject of exhibits in the city's *Heritage Centre,* housed in the former *St. Mary's Church.* Lots of lavishly constructed models, a slide show, and audio presentations are included. See this before you explore the real thing. Open daily. Admission charge. Castlegate (phone: 628632).

BARLEY HALL For a glimpse of York life in 1480, visit this three-story townhouse, the home of a medieval mayor of York. Buried until 1986 behind a modern plumber's yard, the house is currently undergoing reconstruction and restoration. Several rooms, refurnished in their original style, are open to the public. Knowledgeable volunteers in period clothing conduct tours of the house (prior arrangement necessary). Closed Sundays and from December 20 through *New Year's Day.* Admission charge (payable at the *Barley Hall Collection Shop,* located nearby on Swinegate Court West). Coffee Yard (phone: 635985).

CLIFFORD'S TOWER This remnant of *York Castle* has a checkered past. William the Conqueror erected a wooden fortress on a manmade earth mound here in 1068. In 1190, a rioting anti-Semitic mob burned it down, killing 150 Jewish townsfolk who had taken refuge inside. The existing quatrefoil stone tower was built in the 13th century, gutted by fire in the 17th century, and later restored and named after Roger de Clifford, a leader of the Lancastrians during the Wars of the Roses, who was executed here in 1596. In the 19th century, the tower was used as a prison. Open daily. Admission charge. Tower St. (phone: 646940).

ASSEMBLY ROOMS Built in the 1730s, this was *the* place to go in Georgian times to play cards and dice, drink tea, or attend a grand ball. The design of the building is Italian Palladian, and the colonnaded Egyptian Hall is its chief interior feature. The building has undergone extensive renovation. Open Tuesdays and Thursdays or by appointment. No admission charge. Blake St. (phone: 613161).

YORKSHIRE MUSEUM AND BOTANICAL GARDENS The museum contains exhibits that date back 160 million years, but it is probably best known for its collection of archaeological remains (particularly from Roman York) and for the Middleham Jewel, a Gothic gold and sapphire pendant. Found in 1985 near Richard III's Yorkshire palace, the necklace is estimated to be worth £2.5 million. The museum's galleries outshine even the *York Story* exhibits (see above), with displays including a Roman kitchen, mosaics, and priceless gold and silver jewelry. In the 10-acre botanical gardens, in which the museum stands, are the ruins of *St. Mary's Abbey* (founded ca. 1080), once the most important Benedictine monastery in the north of England. The *Multangular Tower* and a section of the city walls are also in the gardens, and make a good introduction to the museum (to get there, go up Museum Street past the museum entrance to the *York Library* and make a left at the "Pedestrian Access" sign). Open daily. Admission charge to the museum. Museum St. (phone: 629745).

CITY ART GALLERY The collection includes minor Old Masters dating from the 14th century, but works of 19th- and 20th-century European painters dominate. The building itself is Victorian. Open daily. No admission charge. Exhibition Sq. (phone: 623839).

NATIONAL RAILWAY MUSEUM One of the few national museums outside London, it is packed with reminders of the days of steam and appropriately housed in the old depot where the locomotives went for maintenance and repairs. It now houses the largest collection of railway-related material in the world. The most famous items are the *Mallard* locomotive, which still holds the world's steam speed record at 126 mph, and Queen Victoria's luxuriously appointed *Pullman* carriage, complete with mannequins of the queen, her personal Indian manservant Abdul Karim, and her youngest daughter, Princess Beatrice. The "Great Railway Show" has actual railway platforms with trains from different periods in railroading history. The latest additions are a 24-foot-wide, walk-through section of the Chunnel (the under-the-English-Channel tunnel, which opened last summer) and an art gallery. There is a shop and an upstairs restaurant overlooking the main London—Edinburgh line. Open daily. Admission charge. Leeman Rd. (phone: 621261).

EXTRA SPECIAL

The oldest inhabitants of York are its ghosts—the city is widely reckoned to be the most haunted in Europe. Several buildings are steeped in ghostly tales. The modern *Theatre Royal,* for example, stands on the ruins of *St. Leonard's Hospital,* whose medieval crypt is now a theater club room inhabited by the Grey Lady, the ghost of a young nun said to have been buried alive in the walls for having an affair with a monk. You can see for yourself: The "Original Ghost Walk of York" begins nightly at 8 PM, April through October, from the *King's Arms* pub (King's Staith; phone: 646463). Reservations are unnecessary.

Sources and Resources

TOURIST INFORMATION

The tourist information office of the *York Visitor and Conference Bureau* (6 Rougier St.; phone: 620557) has lots of free or nominally priced pamphlets on the city and the surrounding area, including the *Official York Guide,* which is also available from the *British Tourist Authority* (40 W. 57th St., New York, NY 10019; phone: 212-581-4708). Other branches are located in the *De Grey Rooms* (St. Leonard's Pl.; phone: 621756) and at the *York Railway Station* (Station Rd.; phone: 643700). All three offices are closed *Christmas* and *Boxing Day* (December 26); the branch at the *York Railway Station* is also closed *New Year's Day.* Visitors also will find a copy of *York*

Diary (listing the current month's events) and a *York Welcome Folder* in their hotel rooms.

LOCAL COVERAGE The *Yorkshire Evening Press* is the city's daily newspaper, on sale at various newsstands and from street-corner vendors (because of their strong accent, their cry often doesn't sound anything like *"Yorkshire Evening Press"*).

For a European city that is not a capital, York has been the subject of an unusually large number of books and guides. A broad selection is for sale at the *York Minster Bookshop* in the minster (phone: 630391), at *Godfrey's Bookstore* (32 Stonegate; phone: 624531 or 641739), and at the *York Visitor and Conference Bureau*'s main office (see above). Some worth reading are *York, The Official Guide* (£1.95/about $2.90), published by the *York City Council; The City of York and the Minster,* by Amy Oldfield (Maxiprint; £1.50/about $2.25); and for a bit of local flavor, *The Inns and Alehouses of York,* by Alan Johnson (Hutton Press; £2.80/about $4.20). *A Walk Around the Snickleways of York,* by Mark and Ann Jones (Maxiprint; £4.50/about $6.75), offers a unique insight into York's past.

TELEPHONE The city code for York is 1904.

GETTING AROUND

York is meant to be explored on foot, especially since parking is virtually impossible on the street and most of the major car parks are outside the walls, away from where you really want to be. Because it is a compact city, with all places of interest within strolling distance, you won't be logging mammoth mileages.

A computerized service—"Info Point"—is located at various spots around the city. It has a screen similar to an automated teller machine, and when the appropriate button is pushed, information about trains, buses, taxis, tours, and other transportation options appears.

BICYCLE Not at all an unusual mode of transportation in York. Rent one from *Cycle Scene* (2 Ratcliffe St., at Burton Stone La.; phone: 653286), or the *York Cycleworks* (14-16 Lawrence St.; phone: 626664).

BOAT *White Rose Line* (The Boatyard, Lendal Bridge; phone: 628324) arranges daily sightseeing cruises and a variety of evening cruises from King's Staith or Lendal Bridge February through November.

BUS The hub of the bus network is conveniently located at the tourist information office at *York Railway Station* (see above). *Rider York* (Walmgate; phone: 624161) sells a "Minster Card," allowing unlimited travel on any of its city bus routes; a weekly card costs £5.25 (about $8), and a monthly one costs £21 (about $30). These passes can be bought on board any bus, at the tourist information office at *York Railway Station* (see above), or at any large post office.

CAR RENTAL A car isn't necessary (or even desirable) to see the city, but it's essential if you plan an excursion into the countryside. Major firms include *Avis* (3-7 Layerthorpe; phone: 610460); *Budget* (15 Foss Island Rd.; phone: 644919); *Godfrey Davis Europcar, Ltd.* (Foxton's Garage, Leeman Rd.; phone: 620394 or 659790); and *Thrifty* (Auster Rd.; phone: 691509).

SIGHTSEEING TOURS *Guide Friday Ltd.* (8 Tower St.; phone: 640896) offers a variety of tours, including one of the city in open-top, double-decker buses and others of the surrounding countryside in coaches. Tickets for the city tours can be purchased on board or at *Guide Friday*'s office and are valid for the day; you can get on and off the bus at any of 12 sites (buses leave every 12 minutes from various points around the city). There are also half-hour clip-clops around the town in a horse-drawn carriage, with en route commentary by the driver. They leave from opposite the front of the minster.

Yorspeed Walkman Tours offers a unique experience—visitors see York at their own pace, using a personal stereo and audiotapes that have been scripted with period music, sound effects, and a carefully checked historical commentary. There are currently three recorded tours, "The Walls," "The Streets," and "Ghost Tour"; each takes about two hours to complete (longer if you stop in at the places discussed). Tapes can be rented at the tourist information office (see *Tourist Information,* above) and the *Thomas Cook* office at the railroad station (Station Rd.; phone: 643700); if you call 762622 a day in advance, the personal stereo and tapes will be delivered to your hotel.

TAXI Centrally located cab ranks are at the railroad station (Station Rd.). Reliable radio taxi companies include *Fleetways Taxis* (phone: 623332) and *York Station Taxis* (phone: 623332).

TRAIN It takes only two hours to travel from London's *King Cross Station* to the York terminus, which is west of the city on Station Rd. (phone: 642155).

SPECIAL EVENTS

York's calendar offers plenty of festivities, including a must-see event.

A FAVORITE FETE

York Early Music Festival Ancient York is the ideal setting for this annual July event, one of the world's leading festivals devoted to music from medieval to classical. Concert venues are historic—ancient churches, museum gardens, and country houses. Early dance workshops, medieval drama productions, talks, and exhibitions round out the program of concerts. For information, contact the *York Early Music Festival,* PO Box 226, York YO3 6ZU, England (phone: 658338; fax: 612631).

For two weeks in February, join the locals in the increasingly popular *Jorvik Festival,* which celebrates the Viking, medieval, and Georgian history of York. Its events include an ancient ritual boat burning on the Ouse, parades, pageants, and fireworks displays. For more information, contact the *Jorvik Festival Office* (phone: 611944), which is open weekdays. The *York Races,* run a few days each month from May through October (the most important horse race, the *Ebor Handicap,* takes place in August), and are usually the biggest events on the calendar. For details about these and other events, contact the tourist office (see *Tourist Information,* above).

MUSEUMS

In addition to the museums described in *Special Places,* you may want to visit the *York Dungeon* (12 Clifford St.; phone: 632599), a spine-chilling, permanent historical exhibition of "blood, death, and torture." Open daily. Admission charge. *Friargate Wax Museum* (on Friargate, phone: 658777) is another oddity, a mini–Madame Tussaud's with 70 life-size wax models from various periods of English history, particularly the Tudors and Stuarts. Closed December and January. Admission charge.

SHOPPING

York's *Newgate Marketplace* (closed Sundays), the focal point of trading activities since medieval times, sells clothing, bric-a-brac, and food from Yorkshire and beyond. More conventional shop premises range from Georgian frontages in the city's older thoroughfares to modern shopping center facilities. The *Coppergate* pedestrian mall around St. Mary's Square contains shops, restaurants, branches of most chain stores, and exclusive jewelers, as well as the *Jorvik Viking Centre.*

Antiques seekers will find that the curiosities of the past available in York are not restricted to unusual street names like Whip-ma-whop-ma-gate or to the museums. Antiques shops stocking a selection of pieces from all periods are in abundance as well—though the concentration is slowly moving from Goodramgate (and its rising rents) to Micklegate. If you're here in October, don't miss the *York Antiques Fair,* held in the *De Grey Rooms* (St. Leonard's Pl.); for details, contact the tourist office located here (see *Tourist Information*). For standard shopping hours, see GETTING READY TO GO.

Be sure to take your passport when you shop, and always inquire about the Value Added Tax (VAT) refund application forms when your total purchases in a store are over £50 (about $75). The VAT is a surcharge payable at the sales counter, but foreign customers usually will be reimbursed for it at home (for more information see GETTING READY TO GO).

Blake Head Bookshop and Café There are books in the front and a vegetarian café in the back. 104 Micklegate (phone: 623767).

Droopy & Brown's Somewhat pricey, but the original designs of women's daytime and eveningwear—made from such fabrics as velvet, corduroy, and wool—are worth it. 21 Stonegate (phone: 621458 or 637632).

Ellerker's of York Established in 1795, this timbered shop offers an unrivaled selection of riding equipment, saddlery, and country clothing. They have greatly expanded their range of top names to include Barbour, Gieger, and other brands that epitomize the English country look of recent years. 25 Walmgate (phone: 654417).

MacDowell It carries a large stock of antiquarian books. 56 Micklegate (no phone).

Maxwell & Kennedy Delicious chocolates and other confections abound. 79 Low Petergate (phone: 610034).

Mulberry Hall One of the finest medieval homes in York is now one of England's most respected porcelain dealers. Twelve elaborate showrooms sprawl over three floors. 17 Stonegate (phone: 620736).

O'Flynn Antiquarian and used books, as well as manuscripts dating from the 15th century and antique maps and prints of York, Britain, and the world can be found here. 35 Micklegate (phone: 641404).

Paperweight Collection Here is an array of stunning, contemporary glass paperweights available at a variety of prices. Some of the designs are striking enough to belong in a museum or gallery, including a scale replica of the *Domesday Book* (price tag: £650). The owner shows some of the most interesting examples of his wares in a special show around *Easter* time. 19 High Petergate (phone: 631662).

Spelman's A coal fire warms visitors in the chilly season at this antiquarian bookshop, with volumes dating from the 17th century. 70 Micklegate (phone: 624414).

Wooden Horse Don't miss this interesting collection of diverse ethnic items, from African tribal rugs to Nepalese clothing, Chinese kites, and Mexican silver. 9 Goodramgate (phone: 626012).

SPORTS

CRICKET To see a first class match, go to Leeds, 25 miles away. Yorkshiremen always have been fanatical cricketers, and the *Yorkshire County Cricket Club* is based at the *Headingley Cricket Ground* (St. Michael's La., Leeds; phone: 532-787394). When *Yorkshire* meets *Lancashire,* it's the Wars of the Roses all over again—check local papers for the date of the annual "battle."

FISHING Licenses can be bought at *Hookes* (40 Huntington Rd.; phone: 610357) and *G. E. Hill* (40 Clarence St.; phone: 624561).

GOLF There are more than 60 courses within an hour's drive of York, but several are within easy reach of the city center, including one of the best in Britain.

TOP TEE-OFF SPOT

Fulford For an inland course in a county with plenty of ups and downs, it is remarkably flat. Many of the fine copper beech and oak trees that dominate it define the shape of the visitor's shot both from the tee and to the green; the good driver is always rewarded. There are two distinctly different sets of holes, one starting from the first to the sixth on the way out, the other from the 12th homeward to the finishing green near the clubhouse. Heslington La. (phone: 412882 or 413579).

Other good courses are the 11-hole *Heworth Golf Club* (Muncastergate, Malton Rd.; phone: 422389), the 18-hole *Pike Hill Golf Club* (Pike Hills, Tadcaster Rd.; phone: 708756), the 18-hole *York Golf Club* (6 miles out of town at Strensall; phone: 490304), and the nine-hole *York Golf Centre* (1 mile north of the city on A19; phone: 470549). Visitors are granted temporary membership at these clubs (only weekdays at the *York*); call ahead. There is also the *Melodies* driving range (Wiggington Rd.; phone: 690421). Open daily.

HORSE RACING The *York* racecourse (on the Knavesmire; phone: 620911), a mile south of the city, is the most important racetrack in northern England; admission charge. The races are held a few days each month May through October. The season peaks with the running of the *Ebor Handicap* in August.

SWIMMING The *Barbican Centre* (Paragon St.; phone: 630266) houses the city's two most modern pools. Open daily. Admission charge.

TENNIS Outdoor courts are available at *Rowntree Park, Hull Road Park, Glen Gardens,* and the university, as well as on Scarcroft Road. Book at the courts.

THEATER

York's main stage is also one of Great Britain's outstanding theatrical venues.

CENTER STAGE

Theatre Royal Built in 1746, this hall retains its 18th-century appearance in spite of the addition of a café in the 1960s and other modern renovations. Touring companies, Sunday concerts, and an annual yuletide pantomime flesh out a repertory program of modern and classical drama. The box office is open Tuesdays through Saturdays from noon to 3 PM and an hour before showtime (most performances begin at 7:30 or 8 PM). St. Leonard's Pl. (phone: 623568).

The *Arts Centre* (in Micklegate; phone: 627129) has much more varied entertainment—films, exhibitions, music, and other events—in addition to plays. Despite its name, the *Grand Opera House* (Clifford St.; phone: 671818) no longer offers opera; however, it does put on light entertainment such as comedies, musical theater, and revues.

MUSIC

The *University of York Music Department* gives weekly concerts during the school year in *Lyons Concert Hall* (phone: 432447 for inquiries; 432439 for box office). A few pubs and restaurants have live folk or jazz performances, and there are a couple of discos (see *Nightlife,* below). The tourist office (see *Tourist Information*) has information on musical events offered at specific theaters. Also consult the free monthly publication *Your K Music,* available at various outlets, including the tourist information office.

NIGHTCLUBS AND NIGHTLIFE

York is not a night town. If you crave action in the wee hours, your best bet is to drive to Leeds. However, York does have a few discos worth visiting. Some require jackets and ties for men; others allow informal attire (but not jeans). Entrance charges vary according to the DJ and night of the week but generally are inexpensive; membership, if necessary, is nominal for the visitor. *Ziggy's* (55 Micklegate; phone: 620674) has two bars and a disco. *Winning Post* hotel (Bishopthorpe Rd.; phone: 625228) has entertainment Wednesday through Sunday nights, including live bands most Fridays and Saturdays. Another popular nightspot is *Toffs* (3-5 Toft Green; phone: 620203). Since nightclubs are constantly opening and closing in the city, be sure to call before you go.

Best in Town

CHECKING IN

August is a hopeless time to visit York if you want to stay in the city center. Not only is it the peak time for tourists, but their numbers are swelled by racegoers, here for the *Ebor Handicap,* the most important meeting on the calendar (see *Horse Racing*). Rather than try to squeeze into too few city beds, car drivers are advised to travel out and find smaller hotels in the Vale of York, the flat band of land to the north of the city, or even in Harrogate, a half-hour ride to the west, where there's bound to be a room, even at the height of the summer. The tourist office (see *Tourist Information,* above) can give on-the-spot advice about room availability and operates a booking service (for a fee) for those who apply in person or call on the phone. Most of York's major hotels have complete facilities for the business traveler. Those hotels listed below as having "business services" usually offer such conveniences as a concierge, meeting rooms, photocopiers, computers, translation services, and express checkout, among others. Call the hotel for additional information. A double room (with private bath, TV set, phone, and English breakfast included, unless otherwise indicated) costs $200 or more per night at the hotel listed as very expensive; from $130 to $180 at expensive ones; $75 to $125 at moderate places; and less than $60 at inexpensive ones. All telephone numbers are in the 1904 city code unless otherwise indicated.

VERY EXPENSIVE

Middlethorpe Hall Built as a country home in 1699, this nine-year-old hostelry is one of York's finest. The buildings and grounds have been restored to their original state and all the decorations, antiques, and pictures are late 17th century. Some of the 30 guestrooms surround an 18th-century courtyard in what was once the property's stables; but ask for a room in the main house—they are larger, and a few have views of *York Minster.* All have Edwardian-style bathrooms, complete with brass fixtures, and are filled with Crabtree & Evelyn toiletries. The restaurant overlooks the gardens and offers fine continental fare (see *Eating Out*). Business services are available. Breakfast extra. The only drawback for some is its location 2 miles from town. Bishopthorpe Rd. (phone: 641241; fax: 620176).

EXPENSIVE

Abbey Park A vintage Georgian brick building with 84 renovated and updated bedrooms, it's a 20-minute wander away from the city center. The restaurant serves typical Yorkshire fare, including Yorkshire pudding and syllabub. Business services are available. Breakfast extra. The Mount (phone: 658301; fax: 621224).

Grange Set in a 19th-century townhouse restored by a Swiss designer, this elegant hostelry is ideally located just a few minutes' walk from the city walls. All 29 rooms are individually decorated with antique furniture and chintz fabrics. They also have satellite television. The two dining spots—a bistro with a relaxed ambience and the more formal *Ivy* restaurant—are frequented by locals. Business services are available, and there is private parking. Bootham (phone: 644744; fax: 612453).

Mount Royale Two Georgian houses were restored and combined to form this lovely hostelry minutes away from the city walls and the racetrack. The four suites in an annex face an English garden, landscaped with a variety of rare plants and flowers and an outdoor heated swimming pool. Some of the 23 guestrooms are furnished with graceful antique beds and other period pieces. The restaurant overlooks the garden and serves nouvelle English fare (i.e., traditional dishes prepared with a lighter touch). Each of the common rooms is dedicated to a group of celebrities—the bar, to film stars; the drawing room, to jockeys; and the coffee lounge, to golfers. There also is a snooker table, steamroom, and sauna, as well as parking facilities. The Mount (phone: 628856; fax: 611171).

Royal York Victorian charm at its most overwhelming, this magnificent 145-room railway hotel has been in operation just over 100 years. Although necessary steps toward modernization have been taken, its traditional air remains. There is a traditional English restaurant, a wine bar, a coffee lounge, and a putting green in the formal gardens. Business services are available. Naturally, it's convenient to the station. Station Rd. (phone: 653681).

Swallow The 113-room hotel—19th century with later additions—overlooks the *York* racecourse, which encircles the *Knavesmire Green.* Formerly traditional, it underwent extensive refurbishing and is now quite modern. Amenities include a pool, a fitness center, steamrooms, and business services—real draws for business travelers and for those who prefer more exercise than walking around the city. There is also a putting green, a driving range, croquet, two restaurants, and parking. The grounds have been redesigned to restore them to their former state as Victorian gardens. About 1½ miles from the center. 1 Tadcaster Rd. (phone: 701000; fax: 702308).

Viking Large (188 rooms), centrally located, and with excellent service, this hotel is an expanse of Scandinavian modernity right down to the sauna and whirlpool. There's also a fitness center, two driving ranges, business services, and parking. The restaurant specializes in local dishes, including apple pie and wensleydale cheese. North St. (phone: 659822; fax: 641793).

MODERATE

Grasmead House All six rooms in this inn are furnished with antique four-poster beds (the oldest dates back to 1730). The owner will not only give a history of each bed, but can help you plan your stay in York as well. There's no restaurant, and the guestrooms do not have phones. 1 Scarcroft Hill (phone: 629996).

Knavesmire Manor A former home of the local Rowntree chocolatier family, this Georgian establishment is less than a mile from the railway station. The 22 rooms are well appointed, and the Queen's suite has a four-poster bed and sunken bath. A health spa, complete with exercise room, heated pool, sauna, and whirlpool, is situated in a tropical conservatory. The restaurant serves traditional English fare. 302 Tadcaster Rd. (phone: 702941; fax: 709274).

INEXPENSIVE

Bowen House A Victorian townhouse is the setting for a charming five-room family-run guesthouse, just five minutes from the city walls. Two rooms have private baths. No restaurant, but traditional and vegetarian breakfasts are served. No smoking throughout the house; parking is available. 4 Gladstone St. (phone: 636881).

Regency House Located on a quiet, private street just outside the city walls, this seven-room bed and breakfast establishment was built during the Regency period. Two of the guestrooms have private showers; no smoking is allowed in the house. No restaurant, and none of the rooms have phones. Parking is available. 7 South Parade (phone: 633053).

VERY INEXPENSIVE

Youth Catering to the budget traveler, this unassuming place offers meals, bike rentals, and dormitory-style and basically furnished private rooms for as little as $15 per person per night. 11-13 Bishopshill Senior (phone: 625904; fax: 612494).

EATING OUT

Yorkshire's reputation for mountainous portions of everything is as apparent in its major city as anywhere else in the county, although the more cosmopolitan restaurants are less likely to plump you out of all proportion than those that pride themselves on real Yorkshire kitchens. Most also offer light fare such as salads and sandwiches at lunchtime, in addition to heartier main courses. The most renowned local specialty is Yorkshire pudding—a traditional accompaniment to roast beef served at Sunday lunch. And if you thought there was nothing as American as apple pie, be advised that—topped with a slice of wensleydale cheese—it is just as much of an institution here as it is back home. Expect to pay $150 or more for a full three-course dinner for two, including wine, in the restaurant listed below as very expensive, $90 to $130 at an expensive place, $45 to $85 at a moderate establishment, and less than $40 at one in the inexpensive category. All restaurants listed below serve lunch and dinner, unless otherwise noted. In addition to its restaurants, several of York's pubs serve good-quality bar snacks at lunchtime. All telephone numbers are in the 1904 city code unless otherwise indicated.

VERY EXPENSIVE

Middlethorpe Hall The elegant, paneled dining room overlooking the gardens of the eponymous hotel offers continental and English fare. If terrine of sole, salmon, and red mullet, grilled scallops and caviar, and crab ravioli are too rich for your palate, the chef also can prepare steaks or fish and vegetarian dishes. Open daily. Reservations advised. Major credit cards accepted. Bishopthorpe Rd. (phone: 641241).

EXPENSIVE

Melton's Trained by the renowned Roux brothers of London's two-Michelin-star *Le Gavroche,* chef Michael Hjort prepares fine Anglo-French dishes. This informal and unpretentious dining spot offers the freshest vegetables, fish, and game. Specialties include filet of brill with lobster sauce and peppered ribs of beef with pasta and wild mushrooms. Additional seafood dishes grace the menu on Tuesdays, and Thursday is vegetarians' day. Save room for the wonderful desserts (the homemade ice cream is delicious). There also are some excellent, reasonably priced wines. Mineral water and coffee are gratis. Closed Sundays and Mondays. Reservations necessary. Visa accepted. 7 Scarcroft Rd. (phone: 634341).

19 Grape Lane This intimate spot serves some of the best food in York. Chef Michael Fraser uses the freshest ingredients to prepare specialties such as a delicious seafood pâté, lamb's liver with onion marmalade, salmon with salmon mousse in phyllo pastry and a saffron and ginger sauce, delicious salads (only local produce is used), hot Yorkshire treacle (molasses) tart, and homemade ice cream. There also is a good wine list. Closed Sundays, Mondays, three days at *New Year's,* the first two weeks in February, the last two weeks in September, and three days at *Christmas.* Reservations necessary. Visa accepted. 19 Grape La. (phone: 636366).

Partners Wild mushrooms appear in several dishes at this friendly eatery that offers English (and some French) fare. There are several vegetarian dishes and a variety of moderately priced wines. Closed Sundays. Reservations necessary on Saturdays. Major credit cards accepted. 13a High Ousegate (phone: 627929).

MODERATE

Betty's Tea Room There's nothing better than to come in from York's chilling winter air and wallow in the coziness of toasted, home-baked tea cakes and crumpets puddled in butter, Brontë-liqueur–rich fruitcakes, apple strudel, and *Betty's* famous rarebit, made from farmhouse cheddar and Yorkshire ale, grilled on toast, and all according to a secret recipe. Lunch and dinner also are served. Open daily. Reservations unnecessary. Major credit cards accepted. St. Helen's Sq. (phone: 659142).

Kite's The influence of many cultures—especially Asian—is apparent in the fare served at this comfortable and relaxed restaurant on a quiet street. Beef filet with black bean sauce, served with spring rolls stuffed with smoker oysters and onions, is only one of the many delicious offerings. There also are vegetarian dishes and the homemade soups are a perfect choice on a winter night. Open for dinner only (except Saturdays, when lunch is also served); closed Sundays and *Christmas Eve* through January 2. Reservations advised. Major credit cards accepted. 13 Grape La. (phone: 641750).

Old Orleans A rare discovery, this informal spot in old York serves rich and spicy creole and Cajun food, and Mexican fare. Live jazz on Tuesday nights. Open daily. Reservations unnecessary. Major credit cards accepted. 9-11 Low Ousegate (phone: 620158).

Plunkets For those with a hankering for food from the US Southwest and Mexico, this is one of the best places in York. Nachos, quesadillas, *fajitas,* burritos, and *chalupas* are favorites, as well as steaks, Guinness pie, burgers, salmon cakes, salads, and Spanish *tapas.* Open daily. Reservations unnecessary. No credit cards accepted. 9 High Petergate (phone: 637722).

INEXPENSIVE

King's Manor In the historic Tudor setting of the *York University* refectory morning coffee, lunch, and afternoon tea are served. Salads, hot meals, lager, and wine are available at lunchtime. Open daily. No reservations. No credit cards accepted. Exhibition Sq. (phone: 433995).

Lew's This unpretentious little eatery is usually packed with locals, who come here for the simple, reasonably priced English food. Typical dishes include liver and bacon and English lamb with tarragon. Closed Sundays. Reservations advised. No credit cards accepted. King's Staithe (phone: 628167).

St. William's Once a medieval house for chantry priests, the place retains a monastic air, tempered with just a hint of luxe. A very popular luncheon spot for salads, quiche, teatime tea, and cakes. Stop in after visiting the nearby minster. Enjoy a glass of elderberry wine at one of the festive tables outside, during the summer. Lunch and afternoon tea only; open daily. Reservations unnecessary. No credit cards accepted. 3 College St. (phone: 634830).

Thomas Gent's Coffee House Step into the year 1770 and rooms filled with heavy tables, dressers, and candles. The waiters and waitresses dress in period clothing, and the delicious sandwiches, soups, and cakes are prepared from 18th-century recipes. Closed Sundays. Reservations unnecessary. No credit cards accepted. 3 Coffee Yard (phone: 647845).

TAKING TEA

Afternoon tea is particularly popular in York; nearly every other shop is a tearoom. If the line at *Betty's Tea Room* (see above) is too long—a likely event during the peak of summer—try its sister shop, *Taylor's* (Stonegate; phone: 622865). Another good place to enjoy the English tea ritual is the *National Trust* tearoom (30 Goodramgate; phone: 659282), which is set in an elegant, but modern building.

SHARING A PINT

York has an embarrassment of riches when it comes to pubs. There are over 100, quite a few of them crammed with character and characters. The drink is beer, especially beer from the local breweries and especially the famous Theakston's Old Peculier. The *Bay Horse* pub (55 Blossom St.; phone: 654998), where you can try the locally brewed John Smith beer, and the *Bootham Tavern* (29 Bootham; phone: 631093) are good places to imbibe in a Victorian setting. The *King's Arms* (King's Staithe; phone: 659435) serves Sam Smith's Ale, another excellent local brew; the pub is still sometimes flooded in winter with waters from the adjacent embankment—a board records the various flood levels. General Wolfe, who lost his life winning Quebec for the British, spent part of his youth in his mother's home, the *Black Swan Inn* (Peasholme Green; phone: 625236). It was a merchant's house in the 16th century. Two other pubs on nearby Stonegate, the *Punch-bowl* (No. 7; phone: 622305) and *Ye Olde Starre Inn* (No. 40; phone: 623063), claim association with Guy Fawkes, the infamous plotter who tried (unsuccessfully) to blow up the British Parliament in 1605, bequeathing to children all over England an excuse to set off firecrackers every November 5. The *Punch-bowl* also has live music on Monday nights.

Diversions
Unexpected Pleasures and Treasures

For the Experience

Quintessential Great Britain

With a natural ocean-bound border guarded by a battery of quirks and customs, Great Britain enjoys a respectable distinction and distance from the rest of Europe. You need only glance from the edge of a Scottish Highland cliff or the top deck of a London bus, and you're sure to see something for which only the British have a word—a fell, a moor, or a mews. The public image of Britain is one of a nation of discreet aristocrats—stately bagpipers in tartan kilts, barristers with rolled umbrellas—but there is another England behind the dignified façade. When a soldier thinks of home, the memory of a fluffy Yorkshire pudding is enough to make his normally stiff upper lip quiver. The Londoner who sedately states his opinions in the hush of an oak-paneled social club secretly may wish to join the ranks of the shrill-voiced soapbox orators who preach at Hyde Park Corner on Sunday mornings. The Peer of the Realm, sporting a morning coat and sipping champagne at the *Royal Ascot Horse Races,* may have a daughter in studded leather anklets and a spiked Mohawk hairdo, eating fish-and-chips on the Brighton waterfront. So Great Britain is a land of contrasts and contradictions, but fortunately for a visitor, it isn't hard to become immersed in this panoply of paradox.

A PINT AT THE PUB, Anywhere in Britain Creaking over at least one door in every town and neighborhood in Britain is a wooden sign painted with a name suggestive of ancient myths or old mundanities: the *Penny Farthing,* the *Plough and Stars,* the *Tin Kettle,* the *Pale Horseman.* The sound of singing may draw you into a smoky room, where, from behind a scratched and polished wooden counter, tankards and mugs are filled from the ornate taps of a pantheon of beers. There is a measure of pomp in the slow ritual of serving up the ales, stouts, and bitters—tinted a pale barley gold, a rich amber, or a solid Guinness black—then skimming off the thick, creamy foam. Even if you don't believe in drink, a pub is the best place to come for a pork pie, a weather forecast, a game of darts, a family history of the local squire, a colorful commentary on a rival football team, or just a corner booth in which to shake off the perennial British chill.

SHOOTING, Auchterarder House, Auchterarder, Tayside, Scotland Though it has its roots in a time when eating meat meant stalking it first, over the years the privilege of shooting largely became reserved for that creature of both the wilderness and the drawing room—the British sportsman. He has traditionally been portrayed as striding through the marshes of his estate in a tweed coat and thigh-high rubber boots, equipped with a cartridge belt and a flask of vintage port, a shotgun slung over his shoulder and a pipe between his teeth. These days, shooting is popular with women as well as men; should you desire to partake, you may traverse the 4,000 game-stocked acres of *Auchterarder,* where the only noises are the flapping of wings, the distant barking of hounds, the polished banter of sportsmanlike competitiveness, and the occasional gunshot and thud of fallen grouse. After a day of stalking red deer, you can dress for dinner, doze over a book by a crackling fire, then rest your weary legs and battered shoulder in a cozy four-poster bed.

CAERNARFON CASTLE, Caernarfon, Gwynedd, Wales Though little remains of this castle except its walls, it is easy to imagine the grandeur that King Edward I planned when he began construction almost 600 years ago. *Caernarfon* was the strongest link of a chain of castles he built to bind the "troublesome" Welsh to England. This was more than a military fortress; it symbolized his sovereignty over Wales. Accordingly, he had it executed much in the style of the Romans who had ruled Wales centuries earlier from this site on the Menai Strait, with stonework much like that of the 5th-century Roman wall at Constantinople. The cost of building the castle was immense. There were shooting galleries both high and low, courtyards and drawbridges, portcullises, arrow loops and spyholes—many of which, or remnants thereof, still can be seen. Dr. Samuel Johnson, on visiting the castle two centuries ago, remarked that he had not thought such buildings existed, that it surpassed all his ideas.It was here that Edward dubbed his eldest son the Prince of Wales, and it also was here that, seven centuries later, Charles Philip Arthur George Windsor assumed the same title in a ceremony aimed more at a worldwide television audience than at rebels hidden in the mountains of Snowdonia. Today, peaceful activity surrounds the castle—tourists amble along the ramparts, moored pleasure boats bob on the water beyond the floodlit walls—but none of this can surpass the beauty of the castle's massive, battlemented structure, nor can it disguise the castle's martial past. The clank of swords, the clink of mail, the orders barked in guttural Middle English still seem to float across the gray stone courtyard. From here, set out for some of the other castles and towers that guard every hill and port in Wales: *Herlech,* so intimidating that even the sea has retreated from its base; *Carreg Cennen,* where the Black Mountains muse over the castle's scant, romantic remains; *Caerphilly,* with one tower left at a wild tilt by one of Cromwell's cannonballs; and *Powys,* still a pristine one-family home, now guarding only its terraced gardens and antique furniture.

PUNTING ON THE CAM, Cambridge, Cambridgeshire, England Like many quintessentially English expressions, this one requires a translation. It is Cantabrigian shorthand for gliding in a flat-bottom boat, past the swooning willows, reaching spires, graveled walkways, and letter-perfect lawns that line the river Cam. On a late, moonlit evening in June, undergraduates in black tie or long gown, on their way to or from a ball, deftly guide their punts with long poles pushed into the river's shallow bed. You may choose to drift along at lunchtime—splash your feet in the water and unpack a picnic hamper filled from the markets of this greenhouse of the British Empire. Many an English youth lolled here before giving the world the Theory of Evolution, the Law of Gravity, *Harvard University,* the state of India, *Paradise Lost,* and *Winnie the Pooh.*

WALKING THE SOUTHWEST COAST PATH, Cornwall, Devon, and Dorset, England The trail winds along the crags and cliffs for over 500 miles, through crashing waves, lashing storms, and quiet coves where buccaneers and bandits hid from the law. If you don't have time to hike the entire path, stick to the relatively tropical southern end of Cornwall, where the sun is not uncommon, even if you've just squinted at a menacing sky and decided to put on your rain gear. Life here has mellowed in recent centuries; the scenery has not. The *Minack Open Air Theatre* near Porthcurno claims the sea air as its curtain, the Atlantic as backdrop, and the cliffside as orchestra, mezzanine, and balcony. Pirate refuges, like the cobbled fishing villages of Newlyn and Mousehole, are now artists' havens. This finger of Britain points toward Brittany, and Celtic language and history connect Cornwall to Cournouaille; St. Michael's Mount, a castle-topped hillock that juts up and out toward France, bears a striking resemblance to Mont-St-Michel across the Channel.

MOTORING THROUGH THE COTSWOLDS, Gloucestershire, England Nestled between these soft, rain-nurtured hills are the genteel English villages of honey-colored stone cottages, ivy-covered inns, and low walls. From this preserve of courtesy and fastidious pruning, the English once set out to convert aborigines, find the source of the Nile, export the language now spoken in Nome and Nairobi, and fight on the battlefields of France. "Motoring" is driving, without destination, along sunken lanes and over swirling streams, stopping every mile or two for tea, antiques, a particularly exquisite rosebush, or a cricket match on the village green of Chipping Camden, Bourton-on-the-Water, or Upper Slaughter.

THE MALT WHISKY TRAIL, Grampian Highlands, Scotland Since long before the process was legal, Highlanders have been turning water into whisky. Mixed with barley toasted an earthy brown, fermented in copper stills, and aged a dozen years in wooden casks, the river waters of the Livet, the Spey, and the Fiddich take on the golden color and the smoky taste of a Highland single malt. This alchemy is practiced in fog-shrouded mountain hamlets, its mysteries protected by secret formulas and code words like "tun" and "wort." Its success depends on such forces of nature as the pungency of the water, the particular reek of compressed heather decaying into peat, and the dents in the swan-necked pot stills. The spirit that issues from these remote northern keeps like Tamdhu, Tamnavulin (both near Elgin), and Strathisla is so revered that "Scotch" refers not to people or to language, but to whisky. When the Scotsman Bill McCoy smuggled this whisky into Prohibition America, his wares, and everything genuine since, became known as "the real McCoy." Start the trail in Keith or Dufftown (16 miles southeast of Elgin), and follow it among plunging gray rocks and deep green moors to such elite distilleries as Glenfiddich near Dufftown and Glenlivet. Signposts will keep you on the proper path, but it's your responsibility to keep your eyes on the road—if not all the time, at least often enough to keep your car there.

WORDSWORTH'S LAKE DISTRICT, Grasmere, Cumbria, England You may recognize from your mind's eye this romantic landscape that inspired many an ode. William Wordsworth grew up in *Dove Cottage* in Grasmere, and his poetry seems to have grown like moss from the fells, moors, and dales, and revealed itself in the reflections of steel-gray crags and the orange-streaked clouds of sunset in Cumbria's dozen lakes. He sang of this country's seasons, its "splitting fields of ice" and "hazel bowers/With milk-white clusters hung" and made it famous by his lyric love. So wander as he did in the luscious spring, through tilled valleys in the shadow of forbidding peaks, south to the tip of expansive Lake Windermere, and north to the wall that Hadrian built to guard the northern border of the Roman Empire. You may find yourself on a small stone bridge with a flock of Herdwick sheep or in a meadow with a group of morris dancers in white costumes and red vests.

AFTERNOON TEA AND AN EVENING AT THE THEATER, London, England One cannot live by bread alone, so at a full-scale cream tea at the *Savoy* hotel, you may have to eat cake—as well as buttered scones and crumpets, finger sandwiches with watercress, cucumber, and egg salad, clotted cream, strawberry jam, and the ubiquitous English "cuppa." It is symptomatic of the effort to Anglicize the exotic that, just as the British brought sheep to Australia and cricket to India, so, too, did an infusion made from the dried leaves of an East Asian shrub become England's national beverage. Four o'clock tea is England at its Englishest, with courteous gossip, starched white aprons, and polite but firm exclusion of the rain and mist outside. From the trellised summer Art Deco decor and domed gazebo of the *Savoy*'s Thames Foyer, step quickly through the dark London winter to the warm plushness of a West End theater—the glow of chandeliers, and the dazzle of the hottest ticket in town. In the revived *Savoy Theatre,* or the *Theatre Royal* in the Haymarket, or the *Drury Lane,* or the farther-flung *Royal National Theatre,* is kept the flame of the English-speaking stage, a light passed down from Shakespeare to the *Royal Shakespeare Company,* connecting the reign of Elizabeth I with that of Elizabeth II.

CHRISTMAS SHOPPING AND JANUARY SALES, London, England Like the Grand Bazaar of Istanbul, the souks of Marrakesh, and the agora of ancient Athens, the crowded sidewalks of Oxford, Regent, and Bond Streets—and the Brompton Road—provide one of the world's great shopping experiences. They fuse into a shopping mall of fame and frenzy, offering the finest names in everything and an unsurpassed array of specialized retailers of tobaccos and tweeds, silver and salmon, Scottish wool and Irish linen. Try *Liberty* for the perfect paisley to cover your bed, *Hamleys* for a battery-operated model of a 1940s Rolls-Royce, *Fortnum & Mason* for truffled liver pâté, and *Selfridges* for just about anything else. If you can't live without something nobody else could have, tour the galleries and gilded boutiques of Bond Street, and stop in at that ultimate purveyor of the unique—*Sotheby's* auction house. To make the best of *Harrods'* month-long January sale, you'll have to bundle up, join the queue of local housewives and visiting sheiks, and wait for hours for the doors to open on the sale's first day, the first Wednesday in January. But if you sleep through dawn or foolishly stop for breakfast, you'll still find plenty of bargains on everything from china to Chippendale.

ALL ENGLAND LAWN TENNIS CHAMPIONSHIP, Wimbledon (London), England The world's oldest professional tennis tournament, *Wimbledon* is to sports what *Claridge's* hotel is to shelter—the most elegant possible fulfillment of a basic human need. The Duke and Duchess of Kent preside, and total silence reigns as rows of eyes follow the to-and-fro of the little yellow ball. Connoisseurs savor strawberries between serves, and appraise each measured swing. The ball boys and girls move in a fluid dash, and the players, all still dressed in crisp white, scuff, scurry, charge, and leap across the green velvet of lovingly rolled, mowed, and watered grass. To win this tournament, players must be at home with the slick turf and the quick bounce of the ball that can surprise even a master accustomed to gritty clay. Each year's final handshake across the net evokes ghosts of *Wimbledon*'s past—Pat Cash vaulting into the grandstand to kiss his family before accepting the cup; a teenage Bjorn Borg surrendering himself to joy after an icy victory; Martina Navratilova, who won this tournament a record nine times during her illustrious career, retiring gracefully last year (after being defeated by 22-year-old Conchita Martinez—the first Spaniard ever to win *Wimbledon*); and the flawless and freckled Rod Laver, as well as Steffi Graf, Boris Becker, Billie Jean King, Big Bill Tilden, Helen Wills Moody. . . .

Pub Crawling

Everywhere in Britain there are pubs, and in most places, many. London alone has several thousand; in the countryside, there are so many pubs that during World War II, when road signs were removed, people could give directions in terms of the local watering hole: "Turn left at the *Dog and Duck,* go for half a mile as far as the *King's Arms,* then . . . " Those English villages that have lost their last remaining pub have won some degree of celebrity as a result. There are pubs in the city and in the country, pubs in the theater district, pubs patronized heavily by journalists, pubs with gardens, and pubs where you can listen to music or catch a striptease show.

Yet only a fraction of them have the kind of decor and atmosphere that measure up to most Americans' idea of what British pubs are like. Some do have dark paneling, a long mahogany bar, and an abundance of engraved glass mirrors and gleaming brass fittings, but they're the exception rather than the rule.

Though some of the worst abuses of the recent past—the superabundance of Formica and other plastics, loud jukeboxes, the battery of electronic games that bleep and squeal above the noises of good cheer encouraged by a draft from the pressurized aluminum keg—have begun to disappear in pubs in London and the south, the garden variety British pub generally reflects many of the more obnoxious intrusions of 20th-century civilization.

Paradoxically, it doesn't seem to matter. Just as an American neighborhood tavern can be entertaining even when the floor is ugly green tile, the bar stools covered with plastic, and the lighting murky, the pub is a center of British social life. It also is becoming a focus of culinary activity—a decided change over earlier years, when "pub grub" meant a sandwich, cottage pie (ground meat topped with mashed potatoes), or a ploughman's lunch (consisting of a hunk of bread and cheese plus a pickle). Nowadays, with the burgeoning interest in good food and the proliferation of wine bars, many pubs are setting aside rooms especially for more ambitious sit-down meals.

THE PUB CRAWL

Before setting off on this most convivial of pleasures, there are a number of facts a visitor should keep in mind.

Pub crowds vary. British pubs usually attract a mixed crowd of all ages—silver-haired ladies clutching shopping bags and bolting shots of gin; workmen in stained overalls arguing politics side by side with young people in pin-striped suits discussing office gossip over endless rounds of lager; tourists juggling plates of Scotch eggs and pints of real ale (an unfiltered, unpasteurized type of brew).

Pub hours differ from area to area and from pub to pub. Most pubs in England, Scotland, and Wales open in the late morning, do a booming business through the lunch hour, shut down for the afternoon, then start serving again at the end of the workday or around the dinner hour; closing is generally around 10:30 or 11 PM, but local variations are legion. Pubs in Scotland, the Isle of Man, the Channel Isles, and the Scilly Isles are licensed to operate daily from 11 AM to 11 PM, subject only to individual landlord restrictions. Elsewhere in England and Wales, licensing hours are Mondays through Saturdays from 11 AM to 11 PM and Sundays from noon to 3 PM and 7 to 10:30 PM—though a certain amount of flexibility exists in pubs that serve food and/or play live music. In parts of Britain, particularly in the islands and in certain corners of Scotland and Wales, pubs are closed Sundays.

Beer is not the name of the brew. The sheer variety of drafts can perplex newcomers. Britons talk of lagers and ales and their subtypes rather than "beer." Lager is made from a yeast that sinks to the bottom of the brewing tank during fermentation (rather than rising to the top like the yeast used in traditional ales). It also is activated at a lower temperature, so the product stays clear instead of turning cloudy when cooled. Typically, lagers are also lighter in color and body, fizzier, drier, and taste more of malt than of hops. But there are exceptions, because many lagers are made to taste like ales and vice versa.

Ales fall into several distinct categories. Bitter, usually served on draft, has a good strong brown color, a frothy head, and a taste that tends to be sharp or earthy (owing to a large proportion of hops in the brew). The terms "special" and "best," applied to bitter, refer not to quality but to strength. So-called pale and light ales are the bottled versions of bitter; pale is likely to be the stronger. Mild ale, yet a different brew, is made from a recipe that calls for more sugar and less hops. Served on draft, it is usually sweeter and dark brown to black (except in the Midlands, where mild looks almost like bitter). Brown ale is like a bottled version of mild; the most famous brand of this type of ale is a strong brew called Newcastle Brown (also known as "Newkie Brown"). Stouts—brews made from well-roasted, unmalted barley—are all very dark and sometimes sweet; Guinness, Ireland's most famous drink, is thick and rich like all stouts, but not at all sweet.

At one time, pubs in Britain served only keg beers, which have been filtered and pasteurized at the brewery and packed under pressure. Today, most pubs also serve brews that are still fermenting when they are delivered. Unlike keg beers, real ales require careful handling, but the taste warrants the effort. A pint will cost you between £1.50 and £2 ($2.25 to $3), depending on the brew and the type of pub.

The best guide to pubs is the *Good Beer Guide,* published under the aegis of the active Campaign for Real Ale (CAMRA) and available for £8.99 (about $13.50) from its offices (34 Alma Rd., St. Albans, Hertfordshire AL1 3BW, England; phone: 1727-867201). The annually revised *Good Pub Guide* (costing £12.99/about $19.50), published by Consumers' Association and Ebury Press and available at most large bookshops in Britain, also is recommended.

PERFECT PINTS

For information on special pubs in or near major cities, see *Sharing a Pint* in the individual reports in THE CITIES. The following selection describes the very best, most unusual, and most atmospheric pubs that lie off the beaten track in Britain. They are listed alphabetically by location.

MINER'S ARMS INN, Acomb, Hexham, Northumberland, England Only 2 miles from Hexham, a busy market town with a beautiful ancient abbey, this cozy 18th-century coaching inn, comfortable if a bit garish, has thick stone walls, immense and impressive original oak beams, brass ornaments that suggest antiquity, a garden, and—perhaps best of all—a pleasantly mixed clientele that includes not only locals but also bankers and plastics manufacturers who drive out from 20-mile-distant Newcastle, long-distance hikers heading for the *Northumbria National Park,* and campers. Steaks and vegetarian meals are among the moderately priced fare available; real ale and no fewer than eight varieties of imported beers are also on the menu. Main St., Acomb (phone: 1434-603909).

BUCKINGHAMSHIRE ARMS, Blickling, Norfolk, England *Blickling Hall,* the fine, red brick Jacobean house built for Sir Henry Hobart in the early 17th century, is next door to this inn of the same vintage, and two of its three bedrooms have windows looking out on the handsome structure. Each room is attractively decorated and has a four-poster bed. Buffet lunches and dinners are available daily. On the B1354 in Blickling (phone: 1263-732133).

BULL HOTEL, Burford, Oxfordshire, England There's history in every nook and cranny of this 14th-century coaching inn on the doorstep of the Cotswolds on one of England's prettiest and most famous High Streets. A log fire roars in the bar in winter. With its bare stone walls and tapestry-covered chairs, the candlelit restaurant has a more elegant coziness. The name recalls a papal bull of 1397 that authorized the building of a rest house for the *Priory of Burford.* Charles II and Nell Gwyn made the inn their headquarters in 1669, though now it's a bit past its prime. High St., Burford (phone: 1993-822220).

BELL HOTEL, Driffield, Yorkshire, England This white hotel, owned and operated by the Riggs family, was an 18th-century coaching inn popular among wartime officers stationed nearby. The roof of its courtyard has domed windows, and the place is famous for its buffet lunches, served in the adjacent *Oak Lounge,* a venerable environment where the original brickwork coexists happily with baskets of plants and other contemporary decor. Guests line up to have their plates mounded with hot and cold chicken, turkey, or ham, cheeses, and salads. Market Pl., Driffield (phone: 1377-256661; 800-528-1234; fax: 1377-253228).

SPANIARDS INN, Hampstead, North London, England Perfectly positioned on Spaniards Road between the east and west sides of *Hampstead Heath*, this establishment attracts Sunday walkers, visitors to nearby *Kenwood House*, wealthy local residents, and casual passersby. The building, with its large outdoor garden dotted with wooden tables and chairs, is quite pretty. The labyrinthine interior has low-ceilinged rooms paneled in oak and warmed by open fires. Bar food consists of unexceptional rolls, meat pies, and hot daily specials, including two vegetarian meals. The pub is open daily except for Sunday afternoons. Spaniards Rd., Hampstead (phone: 181-455-3276).

EARLE ARMS, Heydon, near Norwich, Norfolk, England Unpretentious and friendly, this 300-year-old pub has so much character that it has been used as a movie set on several occasions. It's especially pleasant in summer, when visitors can emerge from the darkly subdued interior and take their beer or real ale served directly from the barrel on the village green. The village of Heydon lies at the end of a tiny byroad whose natural quiet is broken only by birds twittering, children laughing, and church bells pealing. The Street, Heydon (phone: 1263-87376).

ANGEL, Lavenham, Suffolk, England Even in a superbly preserved medieval town like Lavenham, where scarcely a dwelling seems less than a few centuries old, this inn on the marketplace overlooking the historic gray-and-white half-timbered *Guildhall* is very old. Dating in part from the 15th century, it was built atop the much older remains of a dormitory for a religious order. There are now two bars—one, the public, caters to the needs of locals; the other, oak-beamed and thickly carpeted, is more attuned to the requirements of the many tourists who flock to Lavenham and, after much rubbernecking around the rural corners of Suffolk, want to put up their feet. Excellent home-cooked meals and snacks are available at midday and in the evening. There also are accommodations in seven nicely furnished bedrooms. Market Pl., Lavenham (phone: 1787-247388).

PIKE AND EEL, Needingworth, Cambridgeshire, England Pubs where fishermen congregate tend to be clubby places, however humble, and outsiders may not feel welcome. This establishment, built of brick in the 16th century and much extended during Oliver Cromwell's time, is an exception—yet there's no mistaking where its loyalties lie. In front, a large garden with lawns and umbrella-shaded tables runs down to the river Ouse, where yachts and cabin cruisers are moored in summer. Inside, glass cases show off stuffed pike and eels (not particularly agreeable to look at but a favorite quarry of nighttime fishermen hereabouts). The flat, windswept, and mysterious fens that surround this low-ceilinged, oak-beamed pub make it all the cozier, and it's pleasant to spend the night in one of the six rooms available to overnight lodgers. The restaurant has a fine local reputation, particularly for Dover sole and halibut dishes; bar snacks are also good. There is also a large garden room, seating 85, where bar food and barbecue can be had. Needingworth is not far from St. Ives. Overcoat La., Needingworth (phone: 1480-463336).

PLOUGH AND SAIL, Paglesham, near Rochford, Essex, England This clapboard-walled pub is better known to yachtsmen than to passing motorists. Not far from the town of Rochford, near the Essex marshes and within sniffing distance of the North Sea, it is wonderfully remote. Yet the atmosphere is remarkably lively thanks to the Olivers, the vivacious family of broad-speaking former East Enders who run the place. Summer weekends bring crowds; at other times, things are quieter, and in chilly weather there's always a log fire crackling on the hearth. A wide selection of hot and cold home-cooked food is served for lunch and dinner (the roast meat lunch on Sundays is a particular treat). Paglesham East End (phone: 1702-258242).

THREE HORSESHOES INN, Powerstock, near Bridport, Dorset, England Travelers can squeeze into Pat and Diana Ferguson's "Shoes" (as the locals call it) on a summer's weekend at lunchtime and head straight out through the back door of the structure, which was rebuilt from local stone after a fire in 1906. There, at wooden tables in a garden, they can down award-winning seafood, including crab, lobster, skate, and prawns, along with a salad and a pint of cool scrumpy with the rolling Dorset countryside in full view. Such fare draws crowds from miles around, and four rooms have been converted to guest bedrooms. The view from the front takes in tiny Powerstock's main street, shaded by ancient oaks, where cows walk by at milking time against the backdrop of imposing Eggardon Hill. Powerstock (phone: 1308-485328).

TICKELL ARMS, Whittlesford, Cambridgeshire, England Nothing escapes the eagle eye of this pub's owner, Siegfried Fischer. If your car isn't in line in the parking lot, he will ask you to repark it. No T-shirts are allowed (nor are men with long hair or earrings), and if you make the mistake of lighting a cigarette in the main room, you will be asked to extinguish it. Nonetheless, locals and tourists line up regularly and respectfully for unusual, beautifully presented hot and cold dishes for lunch and dinner, for homemade punch or mulled wine, depending on the season, and for pints of delicious Adnam's Bitter and Greene King Abbot Ale. In summer, the outside lawns are crowded with local university students. North Rd., Whittlesford (phone: 1223-833128; no calls between 2 and 7 PM).

ROYAL OAK, Winsford, Somerset, England There are other pubs that claim to be 300 years older than this pretty West Country village inn, adorned outside by hanging flower baskets. However, the fact that it dates from the 14th century (and some parts of it to the 12th century) still ranks it among the nation's oldest. It is certainly one of the most imposing properties in the area, with its whitewashed stone walls, thick thatch roof, and interesting sign—an oak surrounding the head of Charles I. (In English lore, the tree, which supposedly sheltered the king during his flight from Cromwell's troops, is like the bed in which George Washington slept: Almost every community, in search of a claim to fame, has managed to come up with one.) Popular with passing tourists, it has two heavily beamed bars—a traditional public, with a dart board, and a comfortable lounge. Good snacks are served, including a fine steak-and-kidney pie. Accommodations also are available; there are eight cozy rooms in the main building, plus six more in a modern annex that also houses a restaurant that specializes in English country dishes. Minehead, 10 miles away, is the closest good-size town. Hails La., Winsford (phone: 1643-85455).

GLOBE INN, Dumfries, Dumfries and Galloway, Scotland To Scots, the poet Robert Burns is Shakespeare, Tolstoy, Mozart, and Beethoven all rolled into one; and because this pub on a narrow alley near 56 High Street was his "favourite howff," it is very important indeed—even though it was old before he knew it and though only one room of the building where Burns lodged is really part of today's *Globe.* Certainly, it's an exceptionally charming place—and would be even if it weren't possible to see the verses that the poet inscribed in glass with a diamond stylus, sleep in the room where he slept (albeit on rare occasions), and sit in his favorite chair. Its signpost is not a globe but Burns's head. Meals served at lunchtime—homemade soups, roast beef, fish, and sweets—are good and inexpensive. High St., Dumfries (phone: 1387-52335).

GROES INN, Ty'n-Y-Groes, near Conwy, Gwynedd, Wales This building housing this pub was already old when its license (the first in Wales) was issued in 1573. Whitewashed and pleasantly tree-shaded, with thick walls constructed of locally quarried Conwy stone, the pub boasts a fine collection of photographs of generations of villagers, as well as an inspired collection of antique tins, old hats, and portraits. Here, the wood-burning fireplace conceals a locally famous "priest hole," the hideaway for many devout Roman Catholics during the reign of Elizabeth I. The views—looking out over the Conwy Valley and distant Snowdon, Wales's highest mountain—are outstanding, and the delicious fare includes fresh Conwy salmon and real ale. Rte. B5106, Ty'n-Y-Groes (phone: 1492-650545).

Rural Retreats

To travelers from abroad, the most striking features of the British countryside are the absence of billboards, the scarcity of motels, and the abundance of homey inns, guesthouses, and country manors turned hotels. The tradition of innkeeping, particularly in England, goes back for centuries, and that's easy enough to see: Wooden stair treads are worn down to concavity by the footsteps of travelers over the ages; walls are half-timbered, ceilings beamed. In northern England, the lodging places tend toward the rickety and quaint; in the south, there is an excellent assortment of charming country-house hotels. In addition, a group known as the *Landmark Trust* has purchased and restored about 150 buildings of historical importance that have long outlived their original function (the most eccentric is the *Pineapple,* near Airth, Stirling, in Scotland, built in the 18th century as a fancy summer house for the Earl of Dunmore to celebrate his success in growing hothouse pineapples). These are available for rent to vacationers, complete with basic comforts, at moderate rents; book well in advance, because, despite infrequent advertising, most places fill up early. A fully illustrated booklet on the *Landmark Trust* properties is available for $18.50 from the *Trust*'s US office (28 Birge St., Brattleboro, VT 05301; phone: 802-257-5840 or 800-848-3747).

As for the food, establishments are in varying states of emergence from the age of soggy sprouts, overcooked fish, meat roasted to a fare-thee-well, and vegetables that would make the army's steam-table offerings look crisp. A whole generation of young chefs trained on the Continent has brought a new look to the nation's menus, and such an intense respect for the freshness of ingredients that some masters of the new style of cooking don't just go out and buy the best that the local market has to offer—they also work with local farmers to have vegetables planted and grown to their specifications. The undeniably positive by-products are no longer destroyed through overcooking. And unlike some practitioners of the nouvelle cuisine in France, the new chefs here are delightfully straightforward and unpretentious about their presentations.

Some of these special establishments are more noteworthy than others—whether due to decor, the friendliness of their management (more often than not a whole family), a lovely setting, or their food. The following hostelries are described in their respective chapters in THE CITIES: *Lucknam Park, Priory, Royal Crescent,* and *Ston Easton Park,* in or near Bath; the *Garden House,* in Cambridge; *Le Manoir aux Quat' Saisons,* near Oxford; *Gleneagles,* in Auchterarder (near Perth); and *Alveston Manor,* in Stratford-upon-Avon. Listed below are the best castle-hotels, inns, country houses, and restaurants in truly rural regions. Some warrant a stop when you're in the area; a handful of others, perhaps a shade more wonderful on one or more counts, are worth planning a whole holiday around. The properties are listed alphabetically by location.

WORTH A LONG DETOUR

ELMS, Abberley, Hereford and Worcester, England Built primarily during the early 18th century after designs by a student of Sir Christopher Wren, then added to in a neoclassical style during 1927, this grand country house has a magnificent tree-lined drive and gardens as clipped and formal as they come; the scene suggests morning suits and garden party hats, white gloves and flouncy dresses. The interiors are just as elegant, from the sumptuously carpeted oak staircase to the public rooms full of tufted settees and the fine *Library Bar,* adorned with its original mahogany bookcases; the guestrooms boast interesting knickknacks, spacious bathrooms, antique furnishings (one room is graced by a four-poster bed), and—not the least important—fine views overlooking the surrounding park. Stay in one of the 16 grand rooms of the main building, or relax in the cottage-style atmosphere of the nine guestrooms in the coach house next door. Despite the luxury of the setting, the atmosphere is never stuffy, and it's easy to spend days on end strolling across the grounds, playing croquet, hitting balls on the hotel's tennis courts, and practicing your putting on its green. Information: *Elms Hotel,* Stockton Rd., Abberley, near Worcester, WR6 6AT, England (phone: 1299-896666; fax: 1299-896804).

AMBERLEY CASTLE, Amberley, near Arundel, West Sussex, England The charms of this 12th-century castle, with its oak portcullis, massive battlements, and

14th-century walls are utterly captivating. The interior is replete with fine antiques, suits of armor, and huge wall tapestries, as well as a superb collection of paintings. Each of the 14 exquisitely appointed bedrooms is named after a nearby Sussex castle, and two of the rooms have four-poster beds. The *Arundel Room,* with tapestry-like bed draperies, a 12th-century leaded window, and a lovely view of the garden, recently was voted Britain's best hotel room by readers of the *London Times;* and two other rooms have private access to the battlements which overlook the inspirational beauty of the South Downs. In the *Queen's Room* restaurant, a mural depicts King Charles II's visit to the castle in 1686; the classic continental fare prepared here with incomparable flair is simply superb. Information: *Amberley Castle,* Arundel, West Sussex BN18 9ND, England (phone: 1798-831992; 800-525-4800; fax: 1798-831998).

EASTWELL MANOR, Ashford, Kent, England Set in some 3,000 acres of parkland picturesquely speckled with fluffy white sheep, this elegant, rambling stone country house was opened as a hotel in 1980, and, though the present house was rebuilt in 1926, its history can be traced back to the Norman Conquest. Queen Victoria once visited here. Though the 23 rooms are huge, they are so cleverly decorated with sitting areas, soft colors, and pretty fabrics that they seem positively inviting; all of the bathrooms are vast, and some are sumptuous. Among the public rooms is an oak-paneled bar to lure guests down for drinks before dinner in the baronial dining room. The menu is English but draws on the best concepts of classic French fare. Vegetables are cooked to retain their natural crispness, and meat is left pink as a matter of policy. You'll find such delicacies as caramelized breast of duck served with garlic polenta and braised shallots, or delicious Scotch salmon in a chive-cream sauce. The chef selects game, lamb, and beef from the Eastwell estate and purchases other ingredients from London and Paris markets. A very extensive wine list, which includes English wines, complements the offerings. Information: *Eastwell Manor, Eastwell Park,* Boughton Lees, Ashford, Kent TN25 4HR, England (phone: 1233-635751; 800-525-4800; fax: 1233-635530).

BELL INN, Aston Clinton, Buckinghamshire, England Once a favorite of Evelyn Waugh, this former coaching post (a member of Relais & Châteaux) has been welcoming guests since about 1650. But seldom during the past three centuries has it looked quite as lovely as it does today, with its cozy bar—the ceiling beamed, the floor paved in flagstones, the air warmed by the fire blazing away on the hearth—and its scattering of antiques. Fresh flowers are a common sight, both in the public rooms and in the 21 guestrooms, which are located in former stables and malt houses ranged around a small, cobbled courtyard. Bath salts, bathroom scales, thick terry robes, refrigerators stocked to quench post-midnight thirsts, and other amenities complete the picture. The setting, on the A41 a few miles east of Aylesbury and not far from *Heathrow,* is not the nation's most pastoral, but when one is cosseted in such fashion, it almost doesn't matter. Classical French and traditional English fare is served in the (nonsmoking) dining room, and because the inn is near Aylesbury, home of the famed Aylesbury duck, this fowl is always on the menu. The wine list is especially fine. Information: *Bell Inn,* Aston Clinton, Buckinghamshire HP22 5HP, England (phone: 1296-630252; fax: 1296-631250).

FARLAM HALL, Brampton, Cumbria, England Wild border country, just a few miles from *Hadrian's Wall,* is the setting for this fine 18th-century Victorian house. Each of the 13 bedrooms is a different shape and size and individually decorated, reflecting the Victorian era, but there are late-20th-century conveniences such as Jacuzzis in the bathrooms. The English fare served in the dining room (open to the public) also is a blend of traditional and modern styles; the wine list offers examples from all over the world, including France, Germany, the US, Chile, and Australia, as well as England. Both the guestrooms and the restaurant overlook lovely gardens with an ornamental lake. The surrounding area is renowned for golfing (there are eight courses within a 30-minute drive), walking, horseback riding, and bird watching, and the abundant historical castles, stately homes, and abbeys. A member of the prestigious Relais & Châteaux group. Information: *Farlam Hall Hotel,* Brampton, Cumbria A8 2NG, England (phone: 16977-42634; fax: 16977-46683).

WATERSIDE INN, Bray-on-Thames, Berkshire, England This establishment is one of only two dining places in England with three Michelin stars *and* membership in the prestigious Relais & Châteaux group. But these accolades are just part of the reason to make a detour to the village of Bray, not far from Windsor and 27 miles west of London. Brothers Albert and Michel Roux chose to open their Thameside country restaurant in a setting that provides a feast for the eyes before the feast for the palate begins. In spring, enormous red tulips are in bloom all around, flowering cherry trees line the river, and swans circle past. In summer, the sight of weeping willows and boats on the water may distract a diner—momentarily—from the extraordinary menu. Michel Roux's creations are ceaselessly inventive. Among the specialties are *tronçonnettes de homard* (chunks of lobster in a white port wine sauce); warm oysters served in a puff pastry case, garnished with bean sprouts, raspberry vinegar butter sauce, and fresh raspberries; and a medium-rare roast duckling pierced with cloves and served with a honey-flavored sauce. The wine list, which counts no fewer than 400 bin numbers, is first-rate. A private dining room, serving eight people, can be hired. The cost of all this is "rather dear," as the British would say, but less than its equivalent in Paris and well worth it for a memorable occasion. Six guestrooms have been added for those who wish to spend the night. Closed Mondays and Tuesday lunch, Sunday dinner from October through *Easter* and from *Christmas* through mid-February. Reservations necessary. Major credit cards accepted.

Information: *Waterside Inn,* Ferry Rd., Bray-on-Thames, Berkshire SL6 2AT, England (phone: 1628-20691; fax: 1628-784710).

DORMY HOUSE, Broadway, Worcestershire, England Built on a Cotswolds escarpment above honey-colored Broadway, it began life as a 17th-century farmhouse, and its ancient beams and exposed stone walls confirm the historic pedigree. Open fires, wood paneling, and its 49 comfortable, modern bedrooms add to the charming atmosphere. There also are two bars and a large restaurant serving imaginative light fare with some traditional British specialties. The staff, under Ingrid Philip-Sorensen, is exceptionally cheery. Information: *Dormy House,* Willersey Hill, Broadway, Worcestershire WR12 7LF, England (phone: 1386-852711; 800-323-5463; fax: 1386-858636).

LYGON ARMS, Broadway, Worcestershire, England Though it isn't nearly as old as some buildings in the Cotswolds, 1532 seems a respectable enough birthdate; that makes it old enough to have frequently welcomed Charles I as a guest and to have harbored Oliver Cromwell on the eve of the Battle of Worcester. And there are indications that the building itself is much older. A stone fireplace set into a four-foot-thick wall, for instance, appears to have been crafted in the 14th century; and the rear courtyard door dates from the 15th century, the front door from the early 16th. All of the rooms are furnished with antiques of similar vintage, and a few pieces are of such high quality that they are illustrated in *The Dictionary of English Furniture.* The nine rooms in what is called the Old Wing are a study in Tudor, with beams, charmingly tilted oak floors, and blue Spode dishes on the mantels; the Great Chamber—one of the most famous of the hotel's 65 rooms, for its vaulted timber-crossed ceiling and its massive canopied bed—is number 20. The quality of the service is exemplary. Meals in the main dining room are as elegant as the setting—the Great Hall, with its barrel-vaulted ceiling and great fireplace. After-theater suppers—smoked salmon, cold chicken, roast beef, salad, and fresh strawberries in season—can be a joy. At the *Patio* restaurant, guests can enjoy an alfresco dinner during the summer. Also on the premises are a fitness center with a pool, sauna, gym, and solarium; a beauty salon; and a snooker room. The wide, mile-long street on which the inn fronts is almost as pretty as the cream-colored stone hotel itself, and Stratford-upon-Avon is just 20 miles away. Information: *Lygon Arms,* Broadway, Worcestershire WR12 7DU, England (phone: 1386-852255; 800-63SAVOY; fax: 1386-858611).

GIDLEIGH PARK, Chagford, Devon, England Take over 45 acres of secluded Devon woodlands, add a turn-of-the-century mansion built for consummate comfort and elegance, furnish it in impeccably good taste, and you have *Gidleigh Park.* American owners Paul and Kay Henderson have thought of everything to make guests feel elegantly at home. Each of the 14 rooms is special, but our favorites are Nos. 1, 2, and 3, which overlook the sweeping lawns and rushing brook. Tennis and croquet are popular here, too. For privileged privacy, a three-room thatch cottage has been built beside the croquet lawns, decorated in the same lovely country-English look as the hotel. As if all this weren't enough, there's superb food: Start with perfect pâté de foie gras or salmon tartare, then move on to sea bass with cucumber on a bed of fried noodles. A member of the prestigious Relais & Châteaux group. Information: *Gidleigh Park,* Chagford, Devon TQ13 8HH, England (phone: 1647-432367; fax: 1647-432574).

GREENWAY, Cheltenham, Gloucestershire, England Proprietor Tony Elliott, who has names like *Savoy* and *Claridge's* scattered about his curriculum vitae, runs this refurbished and oft-commended old Elizabethan manor, full of antiques and porcelain, flowers and open fires, on the pastoral fringes of Cheltenham. There are eight rooms in a converted coach house and a dozen more in the main house, where, because Elliott "has a thing about bumping into one's partner in a pokey bathroom," the lavatory facilities are particularly grand. And in the restaurant, candlelit at dinner, the prix fixe menu is lively and imaginative. Standing well back from the busy A46 in formal gardens with a further 37 acres of parkland adjacent, the manor was named for a drovers' road that leads up to the hotel atop the Cotswold escarpment. Information: *Greenway,* Shurdington, Cheltenham, Gloucestershire GL51 5UG, England (phone: 1242-862352; 800-543-4135; fax: 1242-862780).

GRAVETYE MANOR, near East Grinstead, West Sussex, England About halfway between London and Brighton (30 minutes from *Gatwick Airport;* 60 minutes from *Heathrow Airport*) and about 5 miles from East Grinstead, this ivy-covered Elizabethan manor house, built in 1598 and enlarged in the same style over the centuries, not only has become one of rural England's most impressive hostelries, but also has earned an international reputation. In the tranquillity of a thousand-acre forest, the gardens were created by its most famous owner, the great English horticulturist William Robinson, who eschewed the popular formalized style in favor of a more natural look. The rooms are paneled with the estate's oak, bouquets of flowers he planted brighten the corners of all the rooms, and the 18 guestrooms are named for English trees such as bay, holly, beech, and ash. Some of these rooms have fireplaces; all have thick carpets, soothing decor, and such extras as a fruit basket, a thermos filled with *Gravetye*'s own chilled spring water, and books. Touches like these have earned the hotel its membership in Relais & Châteaux. Owner Peter Herbert takes justifiable pride in his wine list, one of the most extensive in the country, and in his menu, which changes seasonally. Among the highlights: a velvety chicken liver pâté, *sole de Douvre Victoria* (grilled Dover sole garnished with langoustine, avocado, and tomato), the tenderest Scottish beef, smoked salmon and venison from the smokehouse on the grounds, and fresh vegetables from the kitchen garden cooked to crisp perfection. A separate dessert menu lists some 20 sweets (including homemade sorbets and ice creams) as well as savories and cheeses.

The steamed rhubarb and ginger pudding served with traditional vanilla custard is outstanding. There are also several activities to keep guests busy, including playing croquet on the lawn, fishing in the well-stocked trout lake, and sightseeing in the neighborhood, where there are several other gardens of note. Information: *Gravetye Manor,* East Grinstead, West Sussex RH19 4LJ, England (phone: 1342-810567; fax: 1342-810080).

FLITWICK MANOR, Flitwick, Bedfordshire, England For most Londoners, who are just a 40-minute car or train ride away from this establishment (whose name is pronounced without the "w"), the meals alone warrant the trip. Chef Duncan Poyser, recently designated a Master Chef of Great Britain (which puts him in a very select group that includes Michel Roux and Raymond Blanc), serves hearty portions of game, fish, and beef. Mahogany paneling and a gallery's worth of portraits make the surroundings as attractive as the food. Guests in the 15 sumptuous bedrooms of this handsome 17th-century structure will find equally noteworthy breakfasts brought to the chamber, complete with newspaper. Honey comes from the manor's beehive, eggs from free-range chickens, and croissants fresh from the oven; muesli and marmalade are made in-house. A pine chest holds an array of green Wellingtons, the only passport necessary to explore the woodlands all around—the 50 acres of parkland adjoining the house, the bordering Woburn estate, or the many other area footpaths. The staff is exceptionally friendly, reflecting the topnotch skills of the family management. Information: *Flitwick Manor,* Church Rd., Flitwick, Bedfordshire MK45 1AE, England (phone/fax: 1525-712242).

COMBE HOUSE, Gittisham, near Honiton, Devon, England It takes a long time to wend one's way up the winding drive to this cream-colored Elizabethan mansion that dates back to the 14th century. But it doesn't particularly matter, because the lush emerald parkland is so lovely. The mansion, owned by a descendant of Dr. Johnson's biographer James Boswell, is roomy, elegant, and furnished throughout with antiques, but not too formal. Most of the 15 rooms have something that catches the eye: for instance, the ornate plaster ceiling and gleaming paneling in the main hall, full of squashy chintz-covered chairs; or the pink dining room's rococo fireplace, attributed to Chippendale; or the bar, hung with old hunting and coaching prints and photographs of the owner's horse-racing triumphs. Most guestrooms are exceptionally large and very quiet. And the food is good, thanks to Cordon Bleu–trained co-owner Therese Boswell. The hotel has fishing rights to 1½ miles of the south bank of the river Otter, which produces some good creels of brown trout, and the establishment makes an excellent base for tours of East Devon and for visits to nearby golf courses or to the ocean only 7 miles away. Restaurant closed Sundays and Mondays in January and February. Information: *Combe House Hotel,* Gittisham, Devon EX14 OAD, England (phone: 1404-42756 or 1404-41938; 800-548-7768; fax: 1404-46004).

HAMBLETON HALL, Hambleton, Leicestershire, England Set on a peninsula jutting into Rutland Water, this Victorian country house offers lovely views over the lake as well as a heated outdoor pool, fishing, tennis, horseback riding, and bicycling. The 15 rooms are a charming, comfortable, eclectic mix—"Fern" is our overwhelming favorite—and the hospitality and service are warm and genuine. The restaurant, under chef Aaron Patterson, has earned a Michelin star. Don't miss the fresh-baked walnut bread and hot passion-fruit soufflé. A Relais & Châteaux establishment. Information: *Hambleton Hall,* Hambleton, Oakham, Leicestershire LE15 8TH, England (phone: 1572-756991; 800-955-6396; fax: 1572-724721).

HINTLESHAM HALL, Ipswich, Suffolk, England In the heart of Suffolk just 5 miles west of Ipswich sits this elegant country-house hotel (a member of Small Luxury Hotels of the World). Though it has an 18th-century façade, the original building dates from the 1570s. Each of the 33 rooms and suites is special: Favorites include the airy and spacious two-story Cherry Orchard suite and the Braganza, with windows on three sides overlooking the front courtyard and woods and a sitting room with a coal fireplace. The dining room offers sophisticated fare; picnic baskets can be prepared. The 170-acre grounds include a tennis court, a heated outdoor pool, an 18-hole golf course, and an orchard. Fishing and clay-pigeon shooting also are available. On the A1071 to Sudbury. Information: *Hintlesham Hall,* Hintlesham, IP8 3N5, England (phone: 1473-652268; 800-525-4800; fax: 1473-652463).

ARUNDELL ARMS, Lifton, Devon, England This former coaching inn, covered with Virginia creeper, would be pleasant enough by anyone's standards: Log fires blaze away on the hearths downstairs; the floors are laid with locally quarried dark blue slate; the 30 guestrooms are decorated in true English country style, with brightly colored floral chintz fabrics reflecting the beauty of the gardens below; and the young French-trained chef Philip Burgess's culinary offerings (which include an excellent Tamar salmon served with a champagne sauce) are of high caliber. But it really stands out for its fishing; for half a century now, it has owned the fishing rights on 20 miles of the Tamar, the stream that forms the boundary with Cornwall and ranks as the best of the West Country salmon streams. There's hunting here as well (for more information see *Gone Fishing* and *Stalking and Shooting* in this section). Information: *Arundell Arms Hotel,* Lifton, Devon PL16 OAA, England (phone: 1566-784666; 800-528-1234; fax: 1566-784494).

COTTAGE IN THE WOOD, Malvern Wells, Malvern, Worcestershire, England Much more than a cottage, this Georgian mansion—rambling but beautifully proportioned—occupies seven acres of woodlands and enjoys wonderful views over the Severn Valley. The style is very English and very traditional; the 20 guestrooms, distributed among the main building, a cottage, and a more modern coach house, are superbly appointed and maintained (three of them have four-posters). The cozy and intimate restaurant is ideal for special meals; English dishes predominate, and the wine list (which includes local English wines) is excellent. Malvern Wells is distinct from Great Malvern, the larger, better-known former spa town to the north, but both places are famous for mineral water; a visitor should be sure to try a bottle of the locally produced Malvern Water—sold in London in the 1780s for a princely shilling, it's considerably more expensive today. Information: *Cottage in the Wood,* Holywell Rd., Malvern Wells, Malvern, Worcestershire WR14 4LG, England (phone: 1684-573487; fax: 1684-560662).

STAPLEFORD PARK, near Melton Mowbray, Leicestershire, England The main claim to fame of this English country retreat (whose name is pronounced *Stapp-ul-fird*), is its 35 guestrooms, each uniquely decorated by one of 20 different designers. You could spend a week in the Crabtree & Evelyn suite, for example, trying all the lotions and potions of that firm's name that line the tub and windowsill; the bed, with huge pillows and crisp linen sheets, is heaven; and botanical prints line the walls. For those who like to shoot, there are gaggles of geese, partridge, woodcock, and pheasant on the estate, set overlooking 500 acres of woods and parklands. There is also a two-acre walled garden, 56 acres of woods and trails, and even a church with an ancient cemetery nearby. Piles of "Wellies" (galoshes) for any size feet are found in the hall, and there are plenty of books in the library. Breakfast is served on Beatrix Potter plates in the *Old Kitchen,* a lovely Gothic-style room; for lunch and dinner, chef Mark Baker presents hearty nouvelle American fare with a northern Italian influence in an elegant, formal dining room (no smoking allowed). Information: *Stapleford Park,* Leicestershire LE14 2EF, England (phone: 157-284522; fax: 157-284651).

MILLER'S HOUSE, Middleham, North Yorkshire, England In 1988, Crossley and Judith Sunderland decided to give up their work as hospital administrators in London and go into the hotel business. After a long search, they found this elegant 18th-century house overlooking the cobbled market square in Middleham in the *Yorkshire Dales.* Several years of effort, plus the Sunderlands' avid interest in cooking and wines, have turned the property into one of the best country-house hotels in Britain. The seven guestrooms are of varying sizes, but all are attractively and individually decorated; one, for example, has windows at both ends and a large roll-top Victorian bath on a pink marble dais at the foot of the four-poster bed. The dining room, run by chef Mark Gatty, offers tasty continental specialties made with the freshest local ingredients, including herbs and vegetables from the hotel garden. Sample dishes include walnut, mushroom, and port soup, pork in puff pastry with apricot sauce, mango mousse, and fine local wensleydale cheese. Afterwards, coffee is served in the lounge, which has a cozy fireplace. Gatty will even prepare a sumptuous picnic lunch for guests going out for the day. Open February through December. Information: *Miller's House,* Market Pl., Middleham, North Yorkshire DL8 4NR, England (phone: 1969-22630; fax: 1969-23570).

CHEWTON GLEN, New Milton, Hampshire, England The New Forest, which William the Conqueror claimed as a royal hunting ground in 1079, was already old when this brick mansion was built on 60 acres of peaceful parkland near its fringes. It must have been an odd contrast at first, but the years have mellowed it, and it now seems almost as old as the forest. This award-winning 58-room property is a Relais & Châteaux member. The guestrooms—named for characters from books by Captain Frederick Marryat, who spent some time in the house during the 19th century—are decorated with pretty, flowered fabrics that are frequently replaced to keep things looking fresh. A decanter of sherry is set out to greet arriving guests, and the bathrooms come furnished with fragrant soaps and bubble bath. The same perfectionism pervades the hotel's restaurant, the *Marryat Room,* from the fresh bouquets of flowers to the Villeroy & Boch dinner plates and the exquisite food produced by French chef Pierre Cheviallard and his staff. Though the raw materials are English, the cooking is nouvelle, with sublime specialties such as *coquilles St-Jacques au gingembre;* fresh salmon marinated in olive oil, coriander, and lemon juice; and *canard aux framboises.* The wine list offers nearly 400 selections, ranging from an inexpensive moselle to a Château Lafite-Rothschild 1952. Sports facilities include an indoor pool, two tennis courts, a state-of-the art health club, and a nine-hole golf course. Travelers who recognize high standards will appreciate all that is here. Information: *Chewton Glen Hotel,* New Milton, Hampshire BH25 6QS, England (phone: 1425-275341; 800-344-5087; fax: 1425-272310).

SHARROW BAY, Pooley Bridge, Cumbria, England For over four decades, this lakeshore establishment (a member of the Relais & Châteaux group) has been cooking up some of Great Britain's best food for its guests. A diner might order avocado mousse topped with tiny cooked prawns and unsweetened whipped cream; roast pork loin with fresh rosemary served with apple sauce and cracklings; followed by an egg custard flan and a coffee soufflé served with petits fours. It's not surprising that some people motor up from London, 300 miles away, just to have lunch. The meticulous care that makes every meal such a treat is also accorded the workings of the hotel. The guestrooms are beautifully decorated with antiques, and books and parlor games are available. Thick carpets ensure a quiet more intense than even the country setting could provide; there is a conservatory for warm weather, as well as an efficient central heating system that keeps the old house comfortable in winter. Proprietors Francis Coulson and Brian Sack (who joined forces in 1952) try to welcome all their guests personally, which gives the feeling of visiting someone's elegant country home. There are 28 rooms and suites (26 with private bathrooms or showers); about half are in the main house, the others scattered among a cottage and a gatehouse on the grounds, and a converted farmhouse a mile away. Open March through November. No credit cards accepted. Information: *Sharrow Bay Hotel,* Lake Ullswater, Pooley Bridge, Cumbria CA10 2LZ, England (phone: 17684-86301 or 17684-86483; fax: 17684-86349).

GEORGE OF STAMFORD, Stamford, Lincolnshire, England It is believed that a hostelry in some form has occupied this site for 900 years, but most of the present building was erected in 1597 by the Lord Burghley who built *Burghley House* (see *Stately Homes and Great Gardens* in this section). The gallows sign originally put up to scare away highwaymen still hangs in front of the inn, and the London and York stagecoaches can almost be heard clattering to a stop in the still-preserved cobbled courtyard behind the hotel. The entranceway has stone floors, the ceiling in the bar is beamed, and paneling and rough stone walls are throughout. There's even a crypt underneath the cocktail bar. Some of the 47 rooms can be a bit noisy because of passing traffic, but many of the windows have been double-glazed and the rooms are quieter than they once were. Good food is available in the *York Bar* restaurant and in the less formal *Garden* lounge. Information: *George of Stamford,* 71 St. Martin's, Stamford, Lincolnshire PE9 2LB, England (phone: 1780-55171; fax: 1780-57070).

CLIVEDEN, Taplow, Berkshire, England One of England's great country estates (and a member of Relais & Châteaux), it stands majestically on 400 wooded acres by the river Thames. Long the property of the legendary Astors—and the meeting place of the fabled "Cliveden Set"—it is now managed by Cliveden Hotels Ltd., who have preserved and redecorated the original rooms of the 17th-century mansion, retaining the works of art that reflect the lives of previous owners. Some of the 31 rooms have terraces with views of the gardens and the Thames River. The *Terrace* dining room serves lunch and dinner, while the *French Room* serves hearty family-style breakfasts; a third dining room, *Waldo's,* with its prestigious Michelin star, serves dinner only. The incomparable grounds include a sweeping pasture, dazzling flower borders, exquisite pavilions, temples, sculptures, 2,000-year-old Roman sarcophagi, and an amphitheater where "Rule Britannia" was first performed in 1740. In addition to beautiful walks, guests can enjoy boat trips on the Thames, tennis (on indoor and outdoor courts), swimming (in indoor and outdoor pools), squash, horse racing, polo, golf, and rowing. A separate building houses a spa with all manner of health and beauty facilities. Information: *Cliveden,* Taplow, Berkshire, SL6 0JF, England (phone: 1628-668561; 800-223-5581; fax: 1628-661837).

HORSTED PLACE, Uckfield, East Sussex, England This stately Victorian mansion, built in 1850, was converted to a luxurious country-house hotel in 1986. It has 14 suites and three double rooms, a heated pool, an all-weather tennis court, a croquet lawn, and 23 acres of magnificent gardens. Right outside the hotel are two 18-hole golf courses (hotel guests pay half the greens fee). Furnished with beautiful antiques, the house is bright and cheery and exudes comfortable country elegance. Afternoon tea is served in the large, multi-windowed drawing room, and there is an impressive library, complete with fireplace, overlooking the garden. As if all this weren't enough to satisfy the most demanding of guests, the dining room serves remarkable food—not what might be expected in an English hotel, but very French and very fine. Only 90 minutes south of London, near Glyndebourne. Information: *Horsted Place,* Little Horsted, Uckfield, East Sussex TN22 5TS, England (phone: 1825-750581; 800-525-4800; fax: 1825-750459).

MILLER HOWE, Windermere, Cumbria, England If you tire of looking at the ever-changing light and shade over Lake Windermere in this lovely Wordsworth country hotel, you can play Scrabble, read a book from your private bookshelf, listen to music on the bedroom's cassette player, or just browse through the knickknacks in the room. There is something very personal about the 13 guestrooms here, which may give occupants the feeling that they have borrowed someone else's private domain for a day or two. The bathrooms are sybaritic: After stepping out of a scented shower, guests will find morning tea in pretty floral pots, along with lemon biscuits to soothe any hunger pangs before the substantial breakfast downstairs. Guests are permitted to watch the cooks prepare roast loin of lamb with five fresh herbs; pea, pear, and watercress soup; or any number of other goodies. These victuals are served in the yellow and brown dining room that looks out on a beautiful flagstone terrace and flower-bordered lawns. Information: *Miller Howe,* Windermere, Cumbria LA23 1EY, England (phone: 15394-42536; fax: 15394-45664).

HOLLINGTON HOUSE, Woolton Hill, near Newbury, Berkshire, England Although only 60 miles west of London, this Elizabethan-style hostelry enjoys the seclusion and gorgeous natural scenery of the Berkshire countryside. Built in 1904 as a private residence, the building served as a nursing home before being converted to a country-house hotel three years ago. Set on 14 acres of woodland, it boasts well-tended gardens with prolific flowers and greenery, including hundreds of rhododendrons. The house itself offers 20 large rooms and one suite, all with separate sitting areas and phones. Each guestroom's decor features individual touches: The Kimono Room, for example, has a canopied bed and a sunken marble bathtub with a double Jacuzzi. Meals in the *Oak Room* restaurant, featuring local game, produce, and seafood, are equally sumptuous (and well worth a visit even if you're not staying here): Cornish mussels in white wine, English lamb, and carrot-and-ginger soup are only a few of the specialties. Sports facilities on the premises include a solar-heated pool, a tennis court, and a croquet lawn; golf, hunting, and riding can be arranged as well, as can excursions to nearby places of interest, such as *Stonehenge, Winchester Cathedral,* and *Highclere Castle* (home of the Earl of Carnarvon). Information: *Hollington House,* Woolton Hill, Berkshire RG15 9XR, England (phone: 1635-255100; fax: 1635-255075).

KINNAIRD, by Dunkeld, Perthshire, Scotland Built in 1770, this sumptuous estate on 9,000 acres (yes, you read that right) overlooking the Tay Valley was previously the home of the aristocratic Ward family. A Relais & Châteaux property, it is the epitome of the luxurious country-house hotel. The public areas and the nine huge bedrooms in the main house are decorated with rich fabrics and Ward family heirlooms, some dating from the late 18th century. Another five cottages on the grounds are much favored by anglers preying on salmon in the Tay; the highly regarded dining room (which has earned a Michelin star) will even prepare your catch for you in superb continental style. The hotel can arrange shooting or stalking as well as fishing; there is also a tennis court and a billiards room. Open March through January. Information: *Kinnaird Estate,* by Dunkeld, Perthshire PH8 0LB, Scotland (phone: 1796-482440; fax: 1796-482289).

INVERLOCHY CASTLE, near Fort William, Highland, Scotland When Queen Victoria visited this baronial granite mansion a decade after Lord Abinger built it in 1873, she noted in her diary that she had never seen "a lovelier or more romantic spot." She wasn't the only visitor to express those sentiments. Outside are the terraced gardens, the rhododendron bushes bigger than a child's playhouse, the emerald lawns, and, beyond them, the great mass of Ben Nevis and the Western Highlands rising in the distance; inside, there are enough antiques to do justice to a museum—carved mahogany sideboards, gleaming oak chests, portraits by Sir Benjamin West, as well as wonderful carved paneling, elaborate moldings, and frescoes. Almost everyone who comes for just a night regrets not having planned to stay longer. The 17 guestrooms (including one suite) are spacious and quiet. Dinner consists of regional game and fish, and the wine list is outstanding. The hostelry is a member of the Relais & Châteaux group. Open April through mid-November; sometimes it reopens for the period between *Christmas* and *New Year's Day* as well. Information: *Inverlochy Castle,* Torlundy, Fort William, Highland PH33 6SN, Scotland (phone: 1397-702177 or 1397-702178; fax: 1397-702953).

RUFFLETS COUNTRY HOUSE, St. Andrews, Fife, Scotland The pursuit of excellence has long been the hallmark of this gracious, 25-room, family-run hotel, as evidenced by the number of awards it has garnered from the *British Tourist Authority,* the *Automobile Association (AA),* the *Scottish Tourist Board,* and Taste of Scotland. Even head gardener Andrew Duncan has earned high praise for the horticultural beauty of the 10-acre grounds and the vegetable garden, whose produce appears regularly on the table of the hotel restaurant, where Scottish cookery and an innovative approach are the features. All public rooms overlook the gardens. Information: *Rufflets Country House,* Strathkinness Low Rd., St. Andrews, Fife KY16 9TX, Scotland (phone: 1334-72594; fax: 1334-78703).

SKEABOST HOUSE, Skeabost Bridge, Isle of Skye, Scotland Built in Victorian times at the southernmost tip of a sea loch, this hostelry—one of the finest on "the islands" (as Scotland's Inner and Outer Hebrides are widely known)—incorporates all the best in Scottish country hotels, without being exorbitantly expensive. Particularly in the old part of the hotel, the ceilings are high, the furniture old-fashioned or antique, and the armchairs and sofas plush and comfortable; when it's cool, log fires blaze on the hearth. One of the 26 rooms has a four-poster bed. There also is a par 29, nine-hole golf course. The restaurant is perhaps more functional than might be expected, but a genuine attempt is made to serve interesting local dishes, and at relatively modest prices. Open April through October. Information: *Skeabost House Hotel,* Skeabost Bridge, Isle of Skye IV51 9NP, Scotland (phone: 147032-202; fax: 147032-454).

PORTMEIRION, Portmeirion, Gwynedd, Wales The only hotel in the bizarre Italianate village created between 1925 and 1975 by the late and celebrated architect Clough Williams-Ellis, this out-of-the-ordinary, exquisite establishment has a superb view over a river estuary and houses a restaurant and a number of public rooms. Guests stay in the house's superbly decorated rooms or in one of the guestrooms and cottages scattered around the ornately decorated and altogether fantastic village. There are 54 units in all, some set in exotic woodland on a promontory overlooking Cardigan Bay, others atop a hill above it all. As close to a fantasy hotel as exists in Wales; perhaps that's why such creative types as Noël Coward, George Bernard Shaw, and Orson Welles spent significant time here. Closed three weeks in January. Information: *Portmeirion Hotel,* PO Box 50, Portmeirion, near Penrhyndeudraeth, Gwynedd LL48 6ER, Wales (phone: 1766-770228; 800-221-1074; fax: 1766-771331).

MAES-Y-NEUADD, Talsarnau, Gwynedd, Wales Pronounced *Mice*-er-*Nay*eth, this establishment (near Harlech) run by two families is one of Wales's most charming country-house hotels. Many of the 16 uniquely decorated rooms are furnished with antiques; some boast hand-hewn beams and dormers, while others have high ceilings and elegant Georgian windows. The front bedrooms have the best views, overlooking Snowdon and the Troeth Bach estuary. Expect superbly cooked Welsh specialties from the kitchen: lamb in honey, cider, and rosemary; herrings with apple and sage; and Welsh amber pudding. Dining reservations necessary for non-resident Sunday lunches. Information: *Maes-y-Neuadd,* Talsarnau, Gwynedd LL47 6YA Wales (phone: 1766-780200; 800-435-4504; fax: 1766-780211).

IF YOU'RE NEARBY

CAVENDISH, Baslow, Derbyshire, England Set on the *Chatsworth* estate (described below in *Stately Homes and Great Gardens*), this 18th-century inn has been restored and added to over the years, but its architecture still retains its original appearance. The Dukes of Devonshire have owned it since 1830, and when it was renamed (Cavendish is the family name of the dukes) and renovated in the 1970s, the duchess herself supervised the decorating—

some of the antique furniture and paintings came from *Chatsworth.* The 23 bedrooms are impeccably elegant and splendidly appointed, with beautiful views over the *Chatsworth* estate. The restaurant's chef, Nick Buckingham, expertly prepares local game such as venison, grouse, pheasant, and hare, all served on Wedgwood china. Information: *Cavendish Hotel,* Baslow, Derbyshire DE4 1SP, England (phone: 1246-582311; 800-235-5845; fax: 1246-582312).

GRAND, Eastbourne, East Sussex, England With its white exterior resembling nothing so much as a cake elaborately covered with royal icing, this Victorian hotel (one of England's most famous), with 149 rooms and 15 suites, is perfectly poised for enjoying the British seaside at its most typical. Outside the hotel are a huge expanse of promenade and shingled beach, quaint shops, and beautifully landscaped gardens; indoors is pure five-star comfort. Guests may book a room with a sea view as far as the eye can see, and when they tire of watching the waves outside, they may make their own in the indoor or outdoor pool. There also is a snooker room, sauna, and gym. On Fridays and Saturdays, there's after-dinner dancing in the two restaurants. Information: *Grand,* King Edward's Parade, Eastbourne, East Sussex BN21 4EQ, England (phone: 1323-412345; 800-463-3750; fax: 1323-412233).

SEAFOOD, Padstow, Cornwall, England Not only one of the best eating places in Cornwall, it has 10 charming rooms (some overlooking the harbor), which make a visit to the Cornwall coast especially memorable. Cotswolds-born owner Richard Stein displays his considerable culinary talent with the sorts of meals found only at the world's finest restaurants (anything and everything from the sea is superb). The fact that the dining room is full summer and winter suggests that people come a very long way to enjoy very good food; sleeping over affords the opportunity to enjoy an extra meal. The restaurant is closed Sundays, but room-service suppers are available; it's also closed *Christmas* through early February. Information: *The Seafood Restaurant,* Riverside, Padstow, Cornwall PL28 8BY, England (phone: 1841-532485; fax: 1841-533344).

CASTLE, Taunton, Somerset, England This erstwhile Norman fortress, now covered with wisteria, has won acclaim from all corners for its peaceful garden and its polished English manner. The 33 bedrooms are especially luxurious; each has its own style (mahogany, walnut, yew, painted bamboo, pickled pine). The fine dining room, with a Michelin star, is the icing on the cake. Information: *Castle Hotel,* Castle Green, Taunton, Somerset TA1 1NF, England (phone: 1823-272671; fax: 1823-336066).

THE CLOSE, Tetbury, Gloucestershire, England This former 16th-century wool merchant's home of Cotswold stone offers 15 guestrooms individually decorated with antiques (three have four-poster beds). The restaurant features well-prepared versions of English dishes, including boiled bacon with mashed potatoes, fish-and-chips, and baked egg custard tart with nutmeg ice cream;

there's also an extensive wine list. On the grounds are a croquet lawn and a walled garden with a lily pond. Information: *The Close,* 8 Long St., Tetbury, Gloucestershire GL8 8AQ, England (phone: 1666-502272; fax: 1666-504401).

IMPERIAL, Torquay, Devon, England Built in 1866 to accommodate the resort's winter visitors, this luxurious haven is set on a sheltered cliff top above Torquay Harbour in five acres of subtropical gardens. Its facilities are so complete that some long-term summer guests never even leave the premises, preferring to lounge around the outdoor pool, pick up barbecue at the grill, and tone up in the health center. Though such behavior may be a shade extreme, it is totally understandable, particularly to those whose visits coincide with one of the hotel's celebrated Gastronomic Weekends, when a continental chef, usually French, takes over the kitchen with a presentation of ambitious native dishes. The hotel also hosts "Murder Mystery" weekends, in which actors perform whodunit plays (audience participation is strictly passive!). Of the 167 rooms, those with the best view look out over Torbay, whose blues and greens, pine-covered cliffs, and Gulf Stream climate have earned it a designation as the English Riviera. Clay-pigeon shooting weekends also can be arranged. Information: *Imperial,* Park Hill Rd., Torquay, Devon TQ1 2DG, England (phone: 1803-294301; fax: 1803-298293).

ISLAND, Tresco, Isles of Scilly, Cornwall, England Old and new architecture keep company in this resort hotel on a secluded, car-free island. It has a tennis court as well as a heated outdoor pool; fishing, sailing, and rowing can be arranged. The 40 rooms are attractively decorated. Visit the *Tresco Abbey Garden,* about 1¼ miles away, which is world famous for its subtropical vegetation. Open March through October. Information: *Island Hotel,* Tresco, Isles of Scilly, Cornwall TR24 0PU, England (phone: 1720-22883; fax: 1720-23008).

BISHOPSTROW HOUSE, Warminster, Wiltshire, England Most guests come here simply to eat and sleep, so the owner provides the wherewithal for pursuing these activities with consummate style. The moment guests roll up in the driveway of this opulent Georgian establishment on 27 acres of river-crossed lawn and orchard, out pops a porter to escort arrivals and baggage through the Georgian portico across a Persian carpet, past log fires, through public rooms scattered with antiques and oil paintings, and, finally, to one of the hotel's 31 calm, elegant rooms (three are deluxe suites with Jacuzzis). Dinners are equally extraordinary, as exceptional for the setting (a candlelit conservatory) as for the menu, which includes light, French-inspired, award-winning fare such as warm salad of pigeon breast in raspberry vinaigrette, as well as a *mille-feuille* of lobster and scallops with a light chervil dressing. Free time can be whiled away on the 25-acre grounds outside, rallying on the indoor and outdoor tennis courts, fishing on the river Wylie, one of England's rare chalk streams perfect for wild brown trout, visiting the temple folly on the river, and making friends with a couple of goats who, bottle-fed at birth, still look upon humans as long-lost mums. There's also an outdoor pool for summer swims and an indoor heated pool. Information: *Bishopstrow House,* Warminster, Wiltshire BA12 9HH, England (phone: 1985-212312; fax: 1985-216769).

Stately Homes and Great Gardens

Many Britons bemoan their nation's penchant for demolition, and there is a great outcry among preservationists each time Britain's death duties, rising maintenance costs, or a personal financial crisis forces an owner of one of the nation's great stately homes (one that may have been in the family for centuries) to sell out. Over 600 of these structures met the wrecker's ball between the end of World War II and the mid-1970s. Fortunately, however, the number of such unhappy events in England, Scotland, and Wales has dwindled to a fraction of what it was then.

The longevity of these stately homes through the centuries also owes something to the fact that England, at least, hasn't been physically invaded since 1066, and its society has remained relatively stable through the years. The system of primogeniture, which allowed the eldest son to inherit the whole of a property, also kept estates together. Since the houses were year-round homes and usually not mere refuges from the hot summers of the city, there developed a devotion for ancestral dwelling places akin to that which citizens of other nations extend only to their children. To see these grand homes, standing regally at the end of tree-lined lanes, surrounded by beautiful parks and gardens full of fountains and miniature temples, enormous trees, and fine hedges, is to understand why.

Many of the finest stately homes date back to the beginning of the great period of English domestic architecture, in the 15th century, when, following the Dissolution of the Monasteries, the estimated one-third of the kingdom that had been cloistral land suddenly became available for purchase by the laity. These homes seldom remained untouched by the fickle hand of fashion, as wealthy landowners strove to keep up with the latest styles. In the 18th century, the symmetrical Palladian style (named for the 16th-century Venetian Andrea Palladio) became the rage, together with the work of designer Robert Adam, who began executing his gracefully articulated designs at *Hatchlands,* now a *National Trust* property in East Clandon, Surrey. In the latter, the ceilings were covered with ornate plasterwork, often painted many colors, and the floors were patterned. But there was a grace and a lightness to it all, and Adam interiors made perfect settings for glittering society in their bright silks and satins. In succeeding years, energetic invention and tireless adaptations of the architectural styles of Italy and France began to appear.

There are so many examples of such houses currently open to the public—sometimes at no charge—in England, Scotland, and Wales, that it would be easy to construct a whole vacation around stately home tours. *Historic Homes of Britain* (21 Pembroke Sq., London W8 6PB, England; phone: 171-937-2402) designs tours for individuals or small groups that may include meals or overnight stays in privately owned historic and stately homes. Tours can be arranged that cater to visitors' special interests—such as gardens, art, or antiques buying—and often feature lectures by specialists in the specific fields.

And lest your spiritual needs be neglected, the annual *Stately Homes Music Festival* series, now in its 12th year, offers musical evenings held in ancestral homes and castles throughout England June through November. This double dose of delight means that you can enjoy a concert of beautiful classical music as you luxuriate in a magnificent setting (for details, see *The Best Festivals*).

For the most extensive listing of country houses that are open to visitors, consult the following publications:

The AA 2,000 Days Out in Britain, available in the US from the *British Travel Bookshop* (551 Fifth Ave., Eighth Floor, New York, NY 10176; phone: 212-490-6688 or 800-448-3039; $9.50, plus shipping). Gives capsule histories, entrance fees, and hours.

Gardens of England and Wales 1995, available in the US from the *British Travel Bookshop* (address above; $7.50, plus shipping). Lists close to 600 private gardens open to visitors.

Historic Houses, Castles, and Gardens 1995 (£7.45/about $11; Reed Information Service, Ltd., *Windsor Court, East Grinstead House,* East Grinstead, Sussex RH19 1XA, England; phone: 1342-326972).

The National Trust Guide to England, Wales and Northern Ireland, 4th edition, edited by Robin Fedden and Rosemary Joekes; available in the US from the *British Travel Bookshop* (address above; $25.50, plus shipping). Interesting discussions of the *National Trust* properties.

Even those who are unimpressed by horticulture are sure to recognize that the English place a high value on their gardens, and not making time for at least one garden stroll during a visit to England is an omission comparable to not partaking of afternoon tea. Generally, English gardens are open several days a week from late March or early April through October. Visitors should check by calling the gardens or inquiring at local tourist offices. A useful folder containing a map and brief descriptions of 150 gardens is available free from the *British Tourist Authority* (551 Fifth Ave., Eighth Floor, New York, NY 10176; phone: 212-986-2200).

Hampton Court Palace, in Greater London, is described in detail in *London,* THE CITIES. A representative selection of other homes and gardens follows, arranged in alphabetical order by location. Note that admission fees can add up for those who want to see many of the homes, so travelers in England should consider purchasing the Great British Heritage

Pass from the *British Travel Bookshop* (see above). These passes allow access to all ancient monuments under the wing of the *Department of the Environment,* every *National Trust* property, and more than four dozen other sites. It's also possible to join the *National Trust* through the *Royal Oak Foundation* (285 W. Broadway, Suite 400, New York, NY 10013; phone: 212-966-6565), and thus be entitled to free admission to all *National Trust* properties. The membership fee (starting at $40 a year), which goes towards financing the upkeep of these sites, is tax deductible. The properties are listed alphabetically by location.

CHATSWORTH, near Bakewell, Derbyshire, England Mary, Queen of Scots, stayed at this home on the banks of the river Derwent (now in the *Peak District National Park*) when she was in the custody of Lord Shrewsbury, the fourth husband of the redoubtable Bess of Hardwick, who began building the place with her second husband, Sir William Cavendish, in 1552. But the quarters in which the unfortunate queen lodged on and off between 1569 and 1584 were rendered unrecognizable in about 1686, when the first Duke of Devonshire spent two decades renovating it into one of the finest houses in the nation and among the most beautiful in Europe. The façade is stately, Corinthian-pilastered and classical, and the interiors are insistently Baroque, with a splendid ornate silver chandelier; wall coverings of oak, silk, and gilt leather (among other resplendent materials); paintings by Laguerre, Verrio, and Thornhill on the walls and ceilings; and elaborate woodcarvings that for many years passed as the work of Grinling Gibbons (they were actually executed by a local artisan).Those, together with the trompe l'oeil violin painted on an inner door of the *State Music Room,* may be the most immediately memorable sights in *Chatsworth.* But the collection of furniture by William Kent, the first English architect to attempt to integrate furniture and architectural ornamentation, is one of the finest that exist. Also on display is a grand collection of works by Hals, Reynolds, Landseer, Lely, Rembrandt, Sargent, and Van Dyck. Travelers have marveled at all of this for centuries, and considering that there are 175 rooms (of which 51 are "very big indeed," according to the Duchess of Devonshire, who lives there), it's not hard to understand the nature of the wonderment, even before a stroll in the 105-acre gardens and the 1,100-acre park, which are no trifles either. A most delightful aspect of a *Chatsworth* visit, the garden was one of several English preserves formally planted in the 17th century by George London and Henry Wise. It was reconstructed a century later, much to the dismay of 20th-century critics, by the ubiquitous Lancelot "Capability" Brown, who, even in a day of formal architectural styles, espoused naturalistic landscape design. (The gentleman's nickname derived from his habit of referring to the "capabilities" of any tract he had been called upon to improve.)

The *Water Garden,* which features a glittering staircase of water called the Grand Cascade, retains most of the original design. The *Emperor*

Fountain, a single jet of water capable of shooting 267 feet into the air, is also worth noting. Its designer, Joseph Paxton, spent 32 years as *Chatsworth*'s chief gardener; he blessed the estate with greenhouses that were the forerunners of the Great Exhibition of 1851's *Crystal Palace,* which earned him not only celebrity but also a knighthood. Sadly, the greenhouses were pulled down long ago, but the garden still illustrates Paxton's imagination and industry.

Chatsworth is, perhaps, the epitome of the "stately home," but for those with children unimpressed by such grandeur, the grounds also contain the *Farmyard* and the *Adventure Playground* (both open daily), with play equipment, barnyard animals, and daily milking demonstrations. The *Carriage House* in the 18th-century stable block serves hearty homemade lunches, and visitors are welcome to picnic in the vast park nearby. Closed November through *Easter.* Admission charge. Information: *Chatsworth House and Gardens,* Bakewell, Derbyshire DE45 1PP, England (phone: 1246-582204).

BOUGHTON HOUSE, near Kettering, Northamptonshire, England In the late 17th century, Englishmen were building grand homes as testimony to their great faith in the future and their increased prosperity—and borrowing architectural styles from the Continent with aplomb. The starting point for the great extension to *Boughton House,* a prime example of French influence, was Ralph, Earl of Montagu, who served Charles II as ambassador to France beginning in 1669 (and made such a favorable impression there that Louis XIV ordered the Versailles fountains to be played on his every visit). Ralph Montagu laid out new gardens with lakes, fountains, and avenues, and added a château-style front wing. Today, several remodelings beyond its 15th-century beginnings as a monastery, *Boughton* (pronounced *Bow*-ton) is an enormous place that boasts a courtyard for every day of the week, a chimney for every week of the year, and a window for every day of the year. The abundance of furniture and porcelain is mostly French, as are the paintings on the ceilings by the Huguenot Louis Cheron, and the floors on a stairway landing and in a state room, made of *parquet de Versailles;* the art collection, which includes paintings by El Greco, Gainsborough, Gheeraerts, Kneller, Lely, and Van Dyck, is particularly impressive.As for the Earl of Montagu, it has been said that he was "too ambitious and in the end too successful to avoid envy, and too overtly pro-French . . . to be trusted in his own time." After returning from the French court, he became embroiled in the intrigues concerning the succession of Charles II and was forced to live in exile from 1679 to 1685. Snubbed by the Catholic James II upon returning, he repaired to *Boughton* and began building the great château-like addition. His marriage to the wealthy widow Elizabeth Wriothesley (you may not believe it, but it's pronounced *Rox*-lee), daughter of the Earl of Southampton, facilitated his patronage of the arts and of the Huguenot craftsmen whose works adorn *Boughton* today. Finally, with Protestants back on the throne, he was made a duke. The property passed through the marriage of his great-granddaughter to the Scottish Duke of Buccleuch (pronounced *Buck*-loo), in whose descendants' care *Boughton House* remains today. The house is open daily from 2 to 4:30 PM in August only; the grounds are open daily in August and Saturdays through Thursdays May through July and during September; separate admission charges. Information: *Boughton House,* Geddington, Kettering, Northamptonshire NN14 1BJ, England (phone: 1536-515731).

HAREWOOD HOUSE AND BIRD GARDEN, near Leeds, West Yorkshire, England Robert Adam was only in his early 30s when he was invited to begin work on the interiors of *Harewood House* (pronounced *Harr*-wood), designed by the York architect John Carr for one Edwin Lascelles. The interiors that resulted, full of delicately fluted Ionic columns, beautifully molded plaster ceilings, and classical fireplaces, confirm his great talent (even though his brother joked that he had only "tickled it up so as to dazzle the eyes of the squire"). And despite exterior renovations since then, this remains a stunning house for its fine Chippendale furniture, made after Adam's designs; its collection of paintings by Bellini, El Greco, Gainsborough, Reynolds, Tintoretto, Titian, Turner, and Veronese; and the collections of Sèvres and Chinese porcelain. The grounds were designed by the prolific Lancelot "Capability" Brown beginning in 1772, a year after the house was finished; the landscape, meant to look as if it were nature's own, was substantially unchanged, except for the 19th-century addition of the terraces near the house, until 1962, when a furious storm smashed some 20,000 trees. There is also a fine *Bird Garden,* where rare and endangered species are bred in cooperation with zoos and gardens around the world. The *Terrace Gallery* is used for a wide variety of art and cultural exhibits that change every season. The estate is currently the home of the seventh Earl of Harewood. The house, gallery, and gardens are closed November through March. Admission charge. Information: *Visitor Information Centre, Harewood House and Bird Garden,* Estate Office, Harewood, Leeds LS17 9LQ, England (phone: 113-288-6225).

BEAULIEU ABBEY AND PALACE HOUSE, near Lyndhurst, Hampshire, England The wars and other extravagances of Henry VIII left the king in less than ideal financial straits, and Parliament was in no hurry to levy new taxes so he could pay his bills. Thus it happened that the Cistercian monastery on the Beaulieu (pronounced *Bew*-lee) River close to the Solent coastline, for which King John had ceded the lands in 1204, came into the hands of Thomas Wriothesley (pronounced *Rox*-lee), who served as secretary of state and lord chancellor to Henry VIII and later became the Earl of Southampton. Working with his minister Thomas Cromwell, the king had cajoled Parliament into dissolving the smaller monasteries and confiscating their lands and their fortunes in plate and jewels, tapestries, statuary, and other portable items. Their sale meant an overflowing treasury for Henry, and for England a legacy not only of stark ruins but also of stately homes built on the grounds of former religious houses. The *Palace House* of *Beaulieu Abbey,* one of a number of lands granted to Wriothesley at the time of the Dissolution, occupies the former 13th-century cloistral gatehouse; the history of how the two-story structure has changed through the years is a topic of great interest. Originally converted after the Dissolution in 1538, it was remodeled beginning around 1870, but many of the original Tudor elements—among them the drawing room, the private dining room, the reception hall, and the gables—still can be seen. Scholarly conjecture maintains that Wriothesley's grandson, known for being Shakespeare's patron, was also the Friend described in the sonnets. *Palace House* is presently the home of Lord Montagu, who in memory of his father, a great pioneer in motoring history, built the world-famous *National Motor Museum* on the property. The museum contains over 250 exhibits portraying the history of motoring from 1895 to the present. Open daily. Admission charge includes entrance to all facilities. Information: *Palace House, John Montagu Building,* Beaulieu, Hampshire S042 7ZN, England (phone: 1590-612345).

CASTLE HOWARD, near Malton, North Yorkshire, England The socialite Sir John Vanbrugh served in the army, spent two years in a French prison on espionage charges, and wrote plays for the theater, such as *The Provoked Wife.* But he is perhaps best known for his work as an architect, and his most famous creation—especially since the television version of Evelyn Waugh's novel *Brideshead Revisited* was filmed here—is the palatial home known as *Castle Howard.* He had met Charles Howard, the third Earl of Carlisle, during his playwriting days, and when the Howard family home was destroyed by fire in 1693, Vanbrugh won the commission. Executed with the help of Nicholas Hawksmoor, who had worked with the great Christopher Wren, it has been earning paeans from travelers ever since. Horace Walpole, after a visit here two centuries ago, noted that he had expected to see one of the finest places in Yorkshire. "But nobody had informed me that I should at one view see a palace, a town, a fortified city, temples on high places, woods worthy of being each a metropolis of the Druids, vales connected to hills by other woods, the noblest lawn in the world, fenced by half the horizon, and a mausoleum that would tempt one to be buried alive. In short, I have seen gigantic places before but never a sublime one."Aside from its lovely site on a plateau north of the river Derwent between York and Malton, its sheer immensity is one of its most overwhelming features. Inside the 323-foot-long, cupola-topped south front and the mammoth wings on either side, there are endless rooms and corridors packed with paintings and porcelains, not to mention bronzes, sculptures, gleaming antique furniture, and impressive architectural features such as the multi-windowed dome that lights the vast marble entrance hall. The grounds consist of 1,000 acres that include a splendid, dramatic fountain and formal gardens surrounding the house, the preserve of the *Castle Howard* peacocks; the broad terrace of grass beyond; and the fine outbuildings meant to add interest to the landscape. Among the latter are the *Temple of the Four Winds,* which Vanbrugh designed, and Hawksmoor's mausoleum for the Howard family, which inspired Walpole's comment about being buried alive. The elegant stables, designed by the same John Carr of York who worked on *Harewood House* (see above), now contain tableaux featuring costumes and accessories from a collection of some 18,000 items that span three centuries; the lavish embroideries in silk thread, silver tinsel, and other rich materials call to mind Beatrix Potter's comment that the stitches "looked as if they had been made by little mice." It is not hard to see why the third earl, whose descendants still own and occupy the place, ran out of money before its completion. Closed November through *Easter.* Separate admission charges to the house and the grounds. Information: *Castle Howard,* York Y06 7BZ, England (phone: 1653-648444).

ALTHORP, near Northampton, Northamptonshire, England This wonderful home had long been known as one of England's greatest country houses at the time the youngest daughter of the then owner Earl Spencer was married to Charles, Prince of Wales. The estate was created by John Spencer, who made a fortune through perseverance, hard work, and good business sense, then cemented his family's place in society by alliances with the wealthy. Almost every successive generation has added to its beauty. Robert Spencer bought pictures when he served three successive kings in Paris and Madrid. The first Earl Spencer commissioned a series of portraits from his friend Sir Joshua Reynolds. The house, an early Tudor structure remodeled in the 17th century, was redone in the classical style beginning around 1790 by the architect Henry Holland, who refinished the walls with a grayish-white tile that was popular at the time and added Ionic decorations to the rooms inside on a commission from the second Earl Spencer, a passionate bibliophile whose collections once filled the *Long Library,* the family's main sitting room. The entire home is filled with great works of art by Gainsborough, Kneller, Lely, Reynolds, Rubens, Sargent, and Van Dyck; fine furniture by Saunier, Vardy, Seddon, and others; china from Sèvres, Chelsea, and Bow; and 18th-century Chinese porcelain. The high-ceilinged entrance hall, one of the rooms open on guided tours, has been characterized as "the noblest Georgian room in the country." Open daily in August and bank holiday weekends and other selected Sundays in April, May, and September. Admission charge. Information: *Althorp House,* Northampton NN7 4HG, England (phone: 1604-770006).

BROADLANDS, Romsey, Hampshire, England A true gem of Palladian architecture, and the former home of such illustrious gentlemen as Victorian Prime Minister Henry Palmerston and Lord Louis Mountbatten. This exquisitely appointed estate is nestled amid a Lancelot "Capability" Brown–landscaped parkland, whose verdant lawns slope down to the river Test—a fine repository of salmon and trout. The manor house itself is dignified by an elegant simplicity, from the creamy white brick and slender exterior columns to the delicate plasterwork and fine antiques that decorate its rooms. Both Queen Elizabeth and Prince Philip and the Prince and Princess of Wales began their honeymoons here.Originally owned by *Romsey Abbey* before the imperious decree of Henry VIII forced all monasteries to relinquish their treasures, *Broadlands* changed hands many times before it was purchased in 1736 by Henry Temple, the first Viscount Palmerston. His grandson, the third Viscount Palmerston, who became prime minister, inherited the manor house when he was only 17. In 1939, *Broadlands* was inherited by Edwina Mountbatten, who had married Lord Louis Mountbatten. Lord Mountbatten, a descendent of Charlemagne and a great-grandson of Queen Victoria, was a brilliant naval tactician who served under Churchill during World War II. He became the youngest admiral to serve in the Royal Navy, and was the youngest Supreme Commander of the Allied Naval Forces. By the end of his career, he had amassed military honors by the dozen. He was assassinated in 1979 in Ireland at the age of 79. After Mountbatten's death, his grandson, Lord Norton Romsey, and his wife opened *Broadlands* to the public. An exhibition on the grounds chronicles Lord Mountbatten's military and personal history.

Splendid ancient Greek and Roman marble sculptures adorn the domed hall, which is painted Wedgwood blue. Be sure to look up at the dome's insets of sculpted snowflakes. Three superb Van Dyck paintings are on display in the dining room. The salon is highlighted by a Sèvres basin and ewer that once belonged to Marie Antoinette, a shimmering crystal chandelier, and white and gold neoclassical designs that cover the walls and the ceiling. Lord and Lady Romsey still entertain in the drawing room; here the walls are graced by a collection of 18th- and 19th-century portraits by Reynolds, Romney, and Lawrence. The *Wedgwood Room* is aptly named, and has immense built-in bookcases. During World War II, the salon and the *Wedgwood Room* were used as a hospital for wounded soldiers. Prime Minister Palmerston's library contains the 18th-century painting *The Iron Forge* by Joseph Wright of Derby, and the *Palmerston Room* displays a collection of walking sticks once used by Lord Mountbatten. Worth noting is the wide, winding, oak ship's passage staircase, which was built in the 17th century and displays historical naval prints. Closed October through March and Fridays *Easter* through September (except in August, when it's open daily). Admission charge. Information: *Estate Marketing Manager, Broadlands,* Romsey, Hampshire SO51 9ZD, England (phone: 1794-516878).

BURGHLEY HOUSE, near Stamford, Lincolnshire, England Queen Elizabeth I last visited this house in the closing years of the 16th century, when its creator and owner, William Cecil Lord Burghley (pronounced *Bur*-lee)—who served her for four decades, first as secretary of state, then as high treasurer—was on his deathbed. Its exterior now exhibits the same Italianate columns and the same bristle of domes and clustered chimneys that it did then. Indeed, the design of this assemblage suffers, said one critic, from the loss of the restraints of medieval architectural rules: "Nothing as yet had appeared to take their place, so that the architects, with a number of new processes at their disposal, were at a complete loss as to how best to apply them." But most other visitors to this splendid place, which was built lavishly enough for entertaining a queen and has served as the home of the Cecils and the Exeters for four centuries since, agree that it is not only the nation's largest Elizabethan home but also one of its grandest and most beautiful. A 17th-century remodeling of the interior eradicated most of the original Tudor design, but the years since William Cecil's day also have been marked by the acquisition of vast art collections. Together with the second Lord Sunderland of Althorp, the fifth Earl of Exeter ranked among the most discriminating collectors of the Restoration era; few besides Charles I himself, who accumulated nearly 1,400 paintings (most returned to the Continent after a Commonwealth sale), owned as many works of art. In the 18 rooms open to the public, the most memorable sights are the magnificent stone staircase and the great hall (both from Tudor days) and the aptly named *Heaven Room,* where Verrio painted the ceiling and walls with his interpretation of the hereafter (there is also a Hell Staircase). As for the huge park, it was landscaped in the 18th century by Lancelot "Capability" Brown. Guided tours are mandatory except on Sunday afternoons. A huge variety of events, including dressage, car rallies, crafts fairs, and gala concerts also take place, mostly in the summer. But the most famous event, the *Burghley Horse Trials,* occurs in September (see *Horsing Around* in this section). Closed October through March. Admission charge. Information: *Burghley House,* Stamford, Lincolnshire PE9 3JY, England (phone: 1780-52451).

BLENHEIM PALACE, near Woodstock, Oxfordshire, England Britons come in droves to see the bedroom where Sir Winston Churchill was born. But that is certainly not all they see in this giant house. Built essentially as a monument to England, with funds supplied by Parliament on direction from Queen Anne in gratitude to the Duke of Marlborough for his 1704 victory over the French at Blenheim (pronounced *Blen*-um), the structure was designed by Sir John Vanbrugh with the assistance of Nicholas Hawksmoor. Sarah, Duchess of Marlborough, never wanted anything more than "a clean sweet house and garden be it ever so small"; the battles she had with the architect—while some 1,500 artisans were laboring on the job and the cost of construction climbed toward the final £250,000—have become legendary. Reportedly, she even refused to let him enter her home after its completion. The structure measures 850 feet from end to end, and there are Tuscan colonnades galore, not to mention a vast Corinthian portico, a balustraded roof bristling with statues and towers, and more. From the great state rooms and the library to the saloon, the rooms dwarf mere mortals. The art collections are every bit as dazzling as their setting. The gardens, laid out in the 1760s by Lancelot "Capability" Brown, were restored and expanded by the ninth duke two centuries later. Visitors also can explore the *Marlborough*

Maze. Closed November through mid-March. Separate admission charges to the house, gardens, and maze. Information: *Administrator's Office, Blenheim Palace,* Woodstock, Oxfordshire OX7 1PX, England (phone: 1993-811325).

CRATHES CASTLE, Banchory, Kincardineshire, Scotland In Scotland, the wealthy built castles—not houses—right up until the time of Cromwell. Nonetheless, through the years, the importance of matters of defense in the layout of domestic structures dwindled considerably, and as part of a growing concern with design, erstwhile defensive features were exaggerated and used as decorative elements. Thus Scotland developed an indigenous domestic architecture unique in all of Europe. Along with *Fyvie* and *Craigievar Castles, Crathes Castle* offers a prime example of this style. Like them, *Crathes* is built of stone—the nation had almost no trees until the mid-18th century—in a configuration that is more vertical than horizontal so as to cram the most living space possible under the smallest amount of roof. And because of the established traffic among Scotland, Scandinavia, and the Benelux countries, the castle exhibits the national taste for brightly colored designs painted on the ceilings. It is not dreary inside, as a reader of *Macbeth* might surmise, but is surprisingly cheerful. The procession of gables and turrets is almost as fascinating as the rumor of appearances by a female ghost with a child in her arms, or the gardens outdoors, a series of small plantings separated by gigantic yew hedges, which rank among the finest in the country. On the 595-acre estate, there are also some fine trees and 15 miles of nature trails. A visitors' center presents exhibitions on the natural history of the area as well as the history of the Burnetts, the family that owned the castle. The restaurant is closed November through March. Information: *The Administrator, Crathes Castle,* Banchory, Kincardineshire AB31 3QJ, Scotland (phone: 1330-844525).

PICTON CASTLE, Haverfordwest, Dyfed, Wales Built ca. 1300 near the site of a Norman fortress 96 miles west of Cardiff, *Picton Castle* survived three sieges: It was taken by the Welsh hero Owain Glyndwr in 1405; by the Royalists during the Civil War in 1643; and two years later by Cromwell's forces. Now the home of the Philips family, descendants of the medieval owners, it is open to the public. The castle is surrounded by gardens, and its courtyard contains the *Graham Sutherland Gallery,* which houses a famous collection of portraits by this renowned English artist. The main apartments are open at *Easter;* on May 4, June 1, and August 28 (bank holiday Mondays); and on Sundays and Thursday afternoons from mid-July to mid-September. The grounds and gallery are closed Mondays and October through May. Information: *Picton Castle,* Haverfordwest, Pembrokeshire, Dyfed SA62 4AS, Wales (phone: 1437-751326).

BODNANT GARDENS, near Llandudno, Clywyd, Wales Although now owned and run by the *National Trust,* these 80 magnificent acres of gardens are very much the creation of two families: the Aberconwys, whose family has lived on the estate since 1874; and the Puddle family, who have maintained the grounds for three generations. The garden is in two sections. The more formally landscaped area is a series of terraces dropping away from the house, with a rose garden, lily pond, flowering borders, lawns, and a croquet pitch. Here, visitors can see a lovely view of the surrounding countryside, including the Snowdon Mountains. The other section is wilder: a rough-and-tumble array of trees and flowering shrubs, with narrow paths leading to a stream. April and May are the best times, when the gardens are resplendent with daffodils, crocuses, camellias, rhododendrons, and magnolias. Located 7 miles south of Llandudno on A470. Closed November through mid-March. Admission charge. Information: *Bodnant Gardens,* Tal-y-Cafn, Colwyn Bay, Clwyd LL28 5RE, Wales (phone: 1492-650460).

ERDDIG HALL, near Wrexham, Clwyd, Wales It's not possible to view these fine old homes without wondering about everyday life—cooking meals, changing sheets, and other such homely chores. Unfortunately, the quarters of the servants to whom these tasks fell are seldom on view. Not so at *Erddig.* In this 17th-century country home occupied by generations of the Yorke family until the 1980s, though there are numerous stately chambers and an abundance of fine furniture (many pieces with original upholstery), the most riveting area is "downstairs," where some 45 staff members labored. This includes the laundry, where clothing was boiled in copper caldrons, wrung out on rollers, dried on racks, and ironed; the joiners' shop (still operational), where furniture, fences, and other wooden items were mended; and the kitchen (detached from the house in the 18th century as a precaution against fire), where three kitchen maids and a cook toiled over the meals. The gallery of staff portraits with clever rhymes penned below and the display of photographs are particularly intriguing. Until 1973, when the *National Trust* acquired and restored it, the house was in sad disrepair: Philip Yorke III lived in two unheated rooms with no electricity, and he often was seen picking up scraps of paper off the floor. "I wish nothing should be parted with," wrote the first Philip Yorke of *Erddig* in 1771. Consequently, every bicycle, every automobile, and reams of receipts and letters have been saved; what the master of it all was salvaging from the floor were bits of priceless hand-painted Chinese wallpaper that had peeled off the walls. Closed Thursdays and Fridays and November through March. Admission charge. Information: *Erddig Hall,* Wrexham, Clwyd, Wales LL13 0YT (phone: 1978-355314).

Tea Shops and Tea Gardens

As an afternoon meal, tea was first served in the late 18th century by the Duchess of Bedford to entertain her guests between the early breakfasts and late dinners at her house parties. It soon became an integral part of everyday life. A whole industry grew up around the manufacture of teacups and saucers, cake stands, tea forks for the cakes, silver teapots, sugar bowls and tiny silver tongs, linen, and the like. “Everything stops for tea” became a popular English saying, and the World War I poet Rupert Brooke wrote about it, referring to a tea garden at Grantchester, near Cambridge. (That tea garden still exists, after all these years, in a sun-dappled meadow close to where the undergraduates leave their punts.)

Honey and country preserves, particularly strawberry jam, show up on tea tables, to be served on biscuit-like scones. At the delicious, calorie-laden “cream teas,” originally a specialty in Devon and Cornwall but now served all over the country, thick clotted cream also accompanies the spread. Other variations include strawberry teas, accompanied by a bowl of the luscious red fruit, and “farm teas,” hearty repasts (often featuring salad, ham, or fish) served in the Midlands and the northern part of England.

In Scotland, fruitcakes, soda bread, and tea breads (a sort of cake and bread hybrid) show up on the tea table. In Wales, you can expect bacon, fish, pancakes, and *bara brith* (currant bread). Many of the food specialties of the south appear most frequently at teatime: brandy snaps doused with fresh cream, custard tarts smoothed with red currant jelly and slathered with more cream, Chelsea buns, and above all, crumpets—wintertime delights that resemble American English muffins but are chewier and more flavorful.

As served in its most elaborate form at some London hotels, afternoon tea may take a couple of hours to come to the end of the procession of comestibles—elegant, tiny sandwiches filled with wafer-thin cucumber slices, watercress, or smoked salmon; warm scones with clotted cream and preserves; and delicate pastries; not to mention the good selections of fine Chinese, Indian, and even herbal brews.

WHERE TO TAKE TEA

The settings for tea are as varied as the food. In Scotland, with rare exceptions, travelers will have to take their chances at big hotels. In Wales, except in a few towns that are more frequented by tourists, cafés offer the best teas. In England, tea lovers may choose to pour their Earl Grey in some unpretentious shop or in the orangery, the dairy, or the stable of a stately home (especially if the house is owned and run by the *National Trust*). They also can munch tea cakes on a battlefield, in a castle, in *Sally Lunn's* original shop or the *Pump Room* in Bath (see *Bath* in THE CITIES for details about both), and in the shop where the lace for Queen Victoria's wedding dress was made (*The Old Lace Shop,* Fore St., Beer, Devon; phone: 1297-22056). On the Isle of Wight, a thatch cottage half covered with creepers and rambling roses (such as *Dunnose Garden Cottage,* see below) is an exceptionally good place for summertime tea seekers. Local tourist offices generally can recommend something good in their area. For information on tea shops in or near major cities, also see *Taking Tea* in the individual reports in THE CITIES.

For those who prefer taking tea in a more home-like atmosphere, *Home Hosting (GB)* offers travelers the opportunity to enjoy the experience of a bona fide cream tea with an English family at their home. Tea is often complemented by the family's best linen and china. Hosts are chosen for their desire to welcome foreign visitors and their interest in sharing an insider's knowledge of Britain's many treasures. For more information, contact *Home Hosting (GB),* 754 The Square, Cattistock, Dorchester, Dorset DT2 OJD, England (phone: 1300-320671; fax: 1300-321042). The entries below are listed alphabetically by location.

WORTH A LONG DETOUR

SHIP'S LIGHTS, near Bridport, Dorset, England Eype (pronounced *Eep*), a pretty hamlet a mile or so southwest of Bridport and only about a five-minute walk from the sea, is so tiny that it may come as a surprise to find anything in the way of a tea shop among its handful of little houses. But there it is, in one of those archetypically whitewashed two-story cottages that are scattered so picturesquely along the winding lanes of this part of England. Inside, there's a little parlor for tea when the weather is poor. But the best thing about this establishment is the garden, a glorious flagstone enclosure that in summer fills up with emerald green and scarlet, brilliant yellow and orange, and, next to an old stone wall, there is an old ship's light. Visitors can take tea here and savor scones slathered with clotted cream and jams as sweet and full of fruit as any they'll ever taste; and those who are really hungry can sample some of the establishment's own pastries or fancy cakes and sandwiches—all the tastier for the fresh sea air that comes with the package. Lunch is available in summer. Closed October through *Easter.* Eype's Mouth, by the sea (phone: 1308-425656).

GATEWAY CAKESHOP, Evesham, Worcestershire, England With the proliferation of uninspiring snack bars and fast-food chains, it's increasingly difficult to find a pleasant spot for tea in a town; most tea shops are such small operations that rising rents have almost abolished them. But every country market town has its cake shop, and many serve tea on the side. The *Gateway,* in a pretty Tudor townhouse in the oldest part of this historic town, is a good example. Dark and cozy, with plain old-fashioned furniture, ancient oak beams overhead, and round panes of Georgian bottle glass in many of the windows, the establishment is perfect for afternoon tea (and it's for this that the place is locally best known, even though morning coffee and cakes and light lunches also are served). John Miller, who does the baking, is famous for his fruit pies and gooey cream-and-liqueur cake. 7 Market Pl. (phone: 1386-442249).

SETTLE, Frome, Somerset, England This small establishment is in the most charming part of the oldest corner of this old town, an area of cobbled streets and half-timbered houses. Even from the outside, it looks invitingly homey, with brick walls and black-and-white paintwork. Inside, vases of flowers brighten the windowsills, and pressed wildflowers decorate the menus. An autumnal color scheme—russets, grays, and golds—makes things even more appealing. Best of all is the variety of imaginative yet inexpensive food and beverages. Earl Grey, Chinese, Indian, and herbal teas are served along with the following savories: homemade scones with clotted cream and assorted jams and jellies; Frome bobbins (sweet pastries made with sultanas, figs, and honey), a local specialty; and a range of British pâtisserie, including a luscious chocolate layer cake and Sunday cake (a fruitcake traditionally made for the vicar's weekly call). The menu also offers English breakfasts, traditional lunches, and, for the oenophile, a selection of renowned English country wines, such as elderberry or elderflower. Cheap St. (phone: 1373-465975).

IF YOU'RE NEARBY

OLD LACE SHOP, Beer, Devon, England The lace for Queen Victoria's wedding dress was made on these fairly unpretentious premises, now a quaint 17th-century village tea shop noted for its old oak tables and its location in a deep, narrow glen on a small creek that runs out to the sea. Lunches are available as well as cream teas that feature homemade tea cakes, *gâteaux,* and plenty of scones still warm from the oven, ready to be slathered with clotted cream and strawberry jam. Fore St. (phone: 1297-22056).

HORSE WITH THE RED UMBRELLA, Dorchester, Dorset, England This establishment, in a former theater, offers a good assortment of cakes, pastries, and savories, not to mention the largest selection of fresh cream cakes for miles around, many of them baked by friends of owner Daphne Kendall. No one knows for sure where its name came from, but it may have been the title of a play that was performed at the theater. It's a great place to stock up for a picnic. Hot meals are also available for breakfast, lunch, and early dinner. 10 High West St. (phone: 1305-262019).

ANGLER'S REST, Fingle Bridge, near Drewsteignton, Devon, England For over 90 years, traditional cream teas—scones, strawberry jam, thick clotted cream, and a pot of perfumed brew—have been served at this delightful family restaurant in the cool green depths of the gorge at Fingle Bridge. Lunch and bar meals are also available, and there's a gift shop for those who'd rather spend than ramble the gorge. Fingle Br. (phone: 1647-21287).

BETTY'S, Harrogate, North Yorkshire, England Those in the know swear by the *Christmas* cakes, which *Betty's* ships all over Europe. The shop—thought by many to be one of the best places for tea in all of England—was founded at the turn of the century by a young Swiss orphan, Frederick Belmont, who arrived in this town by mistake after taking the wrong train. (Still a family business, it's now run by Belmont's nephew, Victor Wild.) Londoners who choose not to hop on a train and make a similar fortuitous mistake use the shop's mail-order service. 1 Parliament St. (phone: 1423-502746; mail-order number: 1423-531211).

DUNNOSE GARDEN COTTAGE, Luccombe Chine, Shanklin, Isle of Wight, England Tucked away in a thatch cottage, this bright and sunny tearoom serves lovely homemade cakes and, on Sundays, a fine hearty roast for lunch and dinner. In fine weather, tea may be taken in the gardens. The Headlams, who run the place, have earned a reputation for serving delicious scones and are said to own the best tea shop on the island. Closed Mondays year-round and weekdays November through March. *Dunnose Cottage* (phone: 1983-862585).

COFFEE SHOP, Yarm, Cleveland, England Quiches, soups, lasagna, cheesey prawns, and mushrooms Provençal are all available here for lunch, and they're all made on the premises, with no unnatural additives of any sort. The sweets served at afternoon tea include Bakewell tart, apple pie so full of apples the proprietors say, "It will never make us rich," homemade ice cream, hazelnut meringue with raspberries, and Yorkshire curd cake. Guests are served inside a family-run gift shop in a Victorian building that most people call genteel and old-fashioned. Old pine church pews and oak chairs provide the seating; high ceilings and big sash windows add another graceful note. 44 High St. (phone: 1642-790011).

Shopping Spree

No matter where the dollar stands relative to the pound, the lure of shopping in Britain is irresistible. Shopping has become such an institution among travelers here that the English word for it has found its way into the other European languages. London in particular seems to awaken the dormant consumer in even the most monastic visitor. Sooner or later, he or she can be spotted walking around with a bulging carrier bag, rummaging feverishly through the sale scarves at *Liberty* on Regent Street, or shuffling past the bric-a-brac stalls on Portobello Road. Oxford Street on a Saturday is the West's most teeming bazaar.

Quality, durability, and what the natives are fond of calling "value for money" are the norm. Britain may be one of the last holdouts against everything synthetic. Some of the products and shops are of superior quality, which puts them on the road to obsolescence. So shoppers should yield to temptation and shop for the classics—the finest china, the softest cashmere, the sturdiest shoes—while they still can get them. The best buys are those articles in which craftsmanship counts: riding equipment, humidors, umbrellas, china, crystal, fireplace tongs, and other items essential to every well-equipped Victorian household. When it comes to clothing, there are many trendy designers in England today.

Never pass up a chance to wander through one of Britain's bustling open markets, a cross section of local life and a glorious experience for all the senses. The stalls are a riot of colors—scarlets and yellows and bright blues. Oranges and tomatoes keep company with spinach and celery and garish crockery. The calls and clatter of startling accents delight the ear. The smells of flowers, cheeses, and fish, one aroma blending with the next, assail the nose.

London is the first place that leaps to mind when the subject is shopping in Great Britain; whether it's designer clothing, rare books, china, silver, crystal, or jewelry, England's capital has at least one shop that carries what you want. Many of Britain's other major cities offer a wide variety of goods as well. If the city you're visiting is covered in THE CITIES, check "Shopping" in the respective chapter for a detailed listing of stores in that area. What follows is an item-by-item guide to what to buy.

BEST BUYS

BAGPIPES It may take a lifetime to learn to play them, but you'll never forget the day you bought them. As you might expect, Scotland is the best place to look, particularly in Edinburgh.

BOOKS Don't leave Britain without buying at least one book. Rare and secondhand volumes are available and well priced. London, Cambridge, Oxford, Stratford-upon-Avon, and Edinburgh have many fine bookstores, but a lesser-known haunt for addicted browsers is Hay-on-Wye in Wales. The town has become almost entirely devoted to secondhand bookstores. *Richard Booth (Bookseller) Ltd.* (Lion St.; phone: 1497-820322), listed in the *Guinness Book of World Records* as the largest secondhand bookshop on earth, displays about a million books on nearly 11 miles of shelves. A dozen more competitors line the streets. It's a must for passionate readers.

CHINA The world's best pottery and porcelain has been produced in England since the 18th century, and many of the factories whose names are synonymous with elegance and quality are in and near the town of Stoke-on-Trent in Staffordshire. Royal Doulton, Spode, Minton, and Wedgwood all originate here. Travelers may visit the factories and the exhibitions; only the most resolute will leave without a souvenir. Contact the *British Tourist Authority* (phone: 171-730-3400 in London; 212-896-2200 in the US) for its booklet *Fine English Glass and China,* which provides complete information about factory visits.

Derby, Derbyshire, England Royal Crown Derby porcelain has been "royal" since the days of Queen Victoria. Factory tours are available by appointment for individuals or groups (children under 10 not admitted). In addition, a museum established by the Duchess of Devonshire in 1969 is on the premises. Contact Sue Morecroft, the tour organizer, at *Royal Crown Derby,* Osmaston Rd., Derby (phone: 1332-712800).

Stoke-on-Trent, Staffordshire, England Most of the following illustrious firms offer tours of their premises. All have good shops or museums on site. Be sure to call ahead (ask for the tour organizer).

Royal Doulton (Nile St., Burslem; phone: 1782-292434). The *Sir Henry Doulton Gallery* tells the story of the Doulton tradition established by its namesake, who did the work that earned the company the right to call itself "royal." The company's historical figure collection is also on display at the gallery. Visitors to the factory can see the production of tableware, giftware, and figurines, from the semi-automatic platemaking to the hand-painting of limited-edition pieces.

Spode Ltd. (Church St., Stoke; phone: 1782-744011). Bone china was developed on this site in the last years of the 18th century and is still made here by the original processes, which visitors can see while touring the factory. The two-hour connoisseurs' tour takes visitors through rooms not normally open to the public, including the superb *Blue Room.* Reservations should be made well in advance.

Wedgwood (Barlaston; phone: 1782-204141). A visitors' center offers a craft manufacturing hall, a film, and a living museum that houses the world's most comprehensive collection of Wedgwood in period settings, such as Josiah Wedgwood's Etruria workshops and the 18th-century London showrooms.

All of the above sell both fine china and seconds (china with slight imperfections, sold at a substantial discount). To facilitate visiting many establishments, there is the *China Service,* a bus operating *Easter* through early November that constantly circulates among all of Stoke's shops. The brochure *The China Experience* has more information, including timetables; to obtain a copy, write the *Stoke-on-Trent Tourist Information Centre, The Potteries Shopping Centre,* Quadrant Rd., Hawley, Stoke-on-Trent ST4 THP, England (phone: 1782-284600).

Just outside Stoke-on-Trent in Longton, tour the *John Beswick Studios* (Gold St.; phone: 1782-313041), where the Royal Doulton Bunnykins and Brambly Hedge collections as well as a variety of toby jugs and animal figurines are made.

CLOTHES AND ACCESSORIES When it comes to clothing, what Paris is to women, London is to men—it has the finest of everything, with designer names galore. And ever since the appearance of a young royal named Diana, the city has become well known for women's designer fashion as well—everything from the traditional to the fantastic can be found here. The best-quality rainwear in the world is available in London as well. The umbrellas ("brollies"), particularly, are durable and distinguished. And the traditional cool, damp weather has led to the evolution of a number of distinctive kinds of headgear here. Again, Great Britain's capital is home to some of the world's finest hat makers.

The tweeds, plaids, and knits of Britain are justly famous, and nearly every shop and department store carries them. Wool is a way of life as well as a tourist attraction. Scotland is best known for its subtly patterned and colored Harris tweeds, woven by hand in the Outer Hebrides. Shetland and

Fair Isle sweaters also are made here, along with most of the world's best lamb's wool and cashmere pullovers and cardigans. And tartans are a Scottish tradition; there are more than 500 patterns, most of which can be purchased by the yard or stitched up into a kilt (or a "kilted skirt" for women). One of the best places for Harris tweed and other hand-crafted items is *Annie Morrison* (*Post Office House,* Drinnishader, Isle of Harris, Scotland PA85 3DX; phone: 1859-511200). A mail-order service is available.

St. Helier, Jersey, Channel Islands, England There used to be plenty of craftswomen on Jersey and the neighboring island of Guernsey who spent their time knitting the islands' distinctive navy blue, oiled wool pullovers. Now they only finish by hand what machines have made, and their products come in all colors and can be bought at shops in town; these sweaters are available in lightweight cotton as well. (The cabbage walking sticks that are made and sold here also make unusual mementos.)

Galashiels and Hawick, Borders, Scotland Both of these towns are well known for knitwear and woolens. The former is the home of the *Peter Anderson* factory (Nether Mill; phone: 1896-2091), which offers 750 different tartans as well as factory tours weekdays at 10:30 and 11:30 AM and at 1:30 and 2:30 PM April through October (closed end of July through the beginning of August). Nearby shops sell tweeds, mohairs, cashmere items, and knitting yarn.

Hawick (pronounced *Hoick*), the largest of the Scottish Border towns, has two major mills, *Teviotex* and *Trowmill,* where visitors can see tweeds being made. Some of the most famous knitwear producers are also here; they do not have mill shops, but a wide range of local shops stock their goods.

There also are factories in Innerleithen and at Walkerburn, the site of the Scottish *Museum of Woollen Textiles* (phone: 1896-87619) and annual ram sales at Kelso. Jedburgh, Kelso, Galashiels, and Selkirk also have a good selection of knitwear and tweed shops. *Scotland: Borders Woollen Trail,* a brochure that gives background on the industry and highlights the area mills, museums, and shops, is available from the *Scottish Borders Tourist Board,* Murray's Green, Jedburgh (phone: 1835-863435).

Outer Hebrides, Western Isles, Scotland The wool cloth bearing the distinctive trademark of Harris tweed, a circle and a Celtic cross, is handwoven by islanders following age-old methods; the yard goods are for sale in shops throughout the islands. Stornoway, the largest town of the Lewis-Harris landmass, has a mill that sells tweeds at competitive prices. Sweaters knit from Harris wool are available at all the local craft shops. On Eriskay, island women produce distinctively patterned fisherman's sweaters.

St. Andrews, Fife, Scotland One of the biggest and best outlets for knitted and woven woolens and cashmeres is the *St. Andrews Woollen Mill.* First-quality goods, as well as seconds, discontinued lines, and remnants, are available at its former golf club factory *The Golf Links,* just beside the 18th green of the *Old Course* (phone: 1334-72366).

CRYSTAL AND GLASS The manufacture of crystal in England is centered in the West Midlands; in Scotland, it's at Penicuik near Edinburgh. But outstanding items can be purchased all over the country, including these spots off the beaten path.

Aylsham, Norfolk, England *Barretts,* established in 1782, stocks Waterford, Stuart, and Edinburgh crystal in addition to David Winter Cottages and a selection of china. 20 Red Lion St. (phone: 1263-735006).

Stourbridge, West Midlands, England Many manufacturers of fine crystal offer tours of their premises (reservations necessary) and sell a good selection of their wares in their factory shops.

Royal Brierley (North St., Brierley Hill; phone: 1384-70161). Tours are given weekdays at 11 AM and 2 PM; there's also a shop around the corner on Moor St.

Royal Doulton Crystal (Coldbourn La., High St., Amblecote; phone: 1384-440442). On weekday mornings, factory tours are available in which all stages of the manufacture of English full lead crystal are shown.

Stuart and Sons Ltd. (the Redhouse Glassworks; phone: 1384-71161). The *Redhouse Cone Museum* (phone: 1384-571161), down the street from the glassworks, is the historic home of Stuart crystal. Tours are no longer offered at the glassworks.

Tudor Crystal (Junction Rd.; phone: 1384-393325). Visitors may purchase fine Tudor crystal at the shop; the factory does not give tours.

Aberbargoed, Mid-Glamorgan, Wales At *Stuart and Sons Ltd.* (see above), visitors can take a self-guided tour and see every aspect of glassmaking and glass cutting—and then purchase the output in the factory shop (closed weekends). Angel La. (phone: 1443-820044).

FABRICS The yard goods available in Britain will bring out the seamstress in even the least handy traveler—from luscious woolens in the colors of an Irish landscape to fine lawn reminiscent of an English meadow in springtime. *Laura Ashley* has cloth steeped in the English country look; there are branches in many locations in England, Scotland, and Wales (where the late designer was born).

FOODSTUFFS AND LIQUOR Jams and marmalades, blended teas, Stilton cheese, shortbreads, and other edibles make wonderful souvenirs and presents. London is a center for upscale foods, including fine teas, cheese, chocolates, and specialty items; and Norwich is famous for its *Colman's* mustard. If you're visiting Scotland, don't fail to bring home a bottle of Scotch whisky. More than 200 brands are produced here, and although it's not inexpensive, you won't find some of them at home. Single malts are the ones to go for, from the better-known names such as Glenfiddich and Glenmorangie to the smoky, mysterious Islay malts (Lagavulin is one of the best). On some airlines, you even can get a duty-free selection of miniature bottles of a variety of whiskies. Bring home a vacuum-sealed side of salmon, too.

GUNS London is the source for precision arms. Many gun owners choose their firearms with more care than they would choose a home. Even if you're not interested in buying, you may want to take a look in a gunmaker's shop just to see the binoculars, folding earmuffs, and other accessories of hunting and shooting that pay tribute to the way England used to be—and may still be for some.

HANDICRAFTS Especially in Scotland and Wales, there are handwovens, handspuns, hand-throwns, and hand-knits galore. The *British Tourist Authority* publishes *See Great Britain at Work,* a useful guide to local crafts.

Herstmonceux, East Sussex Traditional English baskets known as "trugs" are the specialty here. They're shallow and made mainly of bent willow, and they come in seven different styles of varying size at the workshop of *Thomas Smith,* established in 1829. Each one is fully hand-crafted, individually finished, and made from locally grown woods—pliable sweet chestnut for the rims and handles and split-resistant willow for the body—to produce a basket that is lightweight and incredibly durable. The wide, shallow flower trugs and the strong, deep fireside log trugs are particularly handsome. Visitors are welcome to look around the workshops. *Thomas Smith* was the trug manufacturer to Queen Victoria. Hailsham Rd. (phone: 1323-832137).

Scotland Potters, weavers, and knitters predominate among the artisans who run more than 1,000 crafts workshops here. Jewelers make wonderful pieces using Celtic motifs. For a list of those that welcome visitors, order *See Scotland at Work,* available free from the *Scottish Tourist Board,* 23 Ravelston Ter., Edinburgh (phone: 131-332-2433).

Wales The national traditions of weaving, pottery, woodworking, leatherworking, and goldsmithing are still flourishing. The *Wales Tourist Board*, *Brunel House,* 2 Fitzalan Rd., Cardiff (phone: 1222-499909) furnishes information on current goings-on and the whereabouts of craft enterprises open to the public. Cardiff is a good place to begin your hunt.

JEWELRY Beautiful jewelry is available all over Britain. Nearly every antiques shop, for instance, sells jewelry, and more and more artisans are using silver and gold. In Scotland, shoppers will find Luckenbooth brooches representing two entwined hearts surmounted by a crown, as well as clan brooches, kilt pins, and other treasures set with quartz, amethyst, cairngorm stones, and other semi-precious jewels. Distinctive local pieces are often available as well. Outside the major cities, outstanding jewelry can be found in the following places:

Castleton, Derbyshire, England Blue John, the semi-precious yellow and blue decorative stone found in ancient mines of the *Peak District National Park,* is made into jewelry and sold at the entrances to the mines and in local shops.

Southwold, Suffolk, England Amber, a fossilized resin common in Suffolk, is carved or made into jewelry here. The *Amber Shop* has colors that range from pale opaque yellows to honey and prices from £7.20 (about $11) to £900 (about $1,350). Various nuggets are on display in their unworked states, along with other pieces made into jewelry; the rarest is a necklet reportedly found in Tutankhamen's tomb. 15 Market Pl. (phone: 1502-723394).

St. Andrews, Fife, Scotland The *Iona Shop* specializes in Celtic jewelry, including handmade pieces in silver studded with burnished Scottish stones. The shop also carries Scottish crafts in silverplate as well as a line of Art Nouveau–inspired boxes and frames. 7 Bell St. (phone: 1334-73102).

Tregaron, Wales One of only three licensed users of real Welsh gold, the *Craft Design Centre of Wales* produces an exclusive line of Celtic design jewelry. Main Sq. (phone: 19744-415).

MAPS AND PRINTS A map of an area just visited makes a fine and eminently packable souvenir, and antique maps are a specialty at many stores. A beautiful print—especially an old one—can bring many years of enjoyment at home. Again, London offers the widest selection and the highest quality.

SHEEPSKINS Warm and nearly indestructible, sheepskin makes up into a winter coat that is close to ideal, and England and Scotland are among the principal sources.

Bungay, Suffolk, England *Nursey & Sons,* founded in 1790, keeps on making and selling increasingly lighter and more colorful English sheepskin coats, hats, gloves, rugs, and leather jackets. 12 Upper Olland St. (phone: 1986-892821).

Loch Lomond, Strathclyde, Scotland The *Antartex Village,* only about a half-hour's drive from Glasgow, offers top-quality sheepskin jackets at factory prices. The company, which has supplied sheepskins to British Antarctic expeditions since 1955, has broadened its line to include sheepskin accessories, rugs, fashion leathers, and knitwear. Lomond Industrial Estate, Alexandria (phone: 1389-52393).

SHOES In England there are still places to have a pair of shoes made to order, but patience is required, since the labor can take months. People with time to wait can choose from a seemingly unlimited variety of wonderfully high-quality footgear that, with care, may well last longer than the wearer. Outside London, *Clarks* (40 High St., Street, Somerset; phone: 1458-43131) is the name to look for. Founded 150 years ago in the small town of Street, it's still going strong, offering low-price seconds as well as a fascinating museum that displays the queer-looking footgear of ages past.

SPORTING GOODS The great outdoors figures so strongly in leisure activities here that it's not surprising to find an abundance of excellent equipment for the sports enthusiast's pleasure—including some of the best riding equipment on earth. London and York are the best places to look.

Antiques and Auctions

Perhaps no nation takes better care of its past than Britain. From the top of the *Tower of London* to the most remote Scottish crypt, tradition is a cherished possession. So, if you're one of those people who is driven to possess a chunk of history, not simply observe it, and who would rather own a genuine 19th-century coal scuttle than just ogle the *Crown Jewels,* grab your checkbook and head for these isles. You'll have the chance to outbid a London dealer at a rural Ayrshire auction, blow dust off a first edition of Dickens at an Aberdeen antiquarian's, and haggle for a special price at a village flea market—if you decide to take the Georgian silver salver *and* the yeoman's crossbow. There's no time like the past—and no time like the present for enjoying it. For prime antiques shopping in the major British cities (particularly London), consult the respective chapters in THE CITIES. In this section, we concentrate on those little-known, out-of-the-way spots which may well be hiding a special treasure.

At the low end of the scale are the flea markets, where true bargains are often available—to those willing to sift through piles of not always interesting miscellanea. Auction houses frequently yield a find, under the right circumstances, to those able to visit the presale exhibition before bidding. Antiques shops offer convenience; dealers have made the rounds of the markets and purchased the pick of the auction houses for resale—and customers pay the price for the dealers' time and trouble. Fairs often bring many dealers and many wares together in one place. The quality may be high, with prices to match, but the selection can't be beat.

In short, the repertoire of sources for antiques is not so different than that in the US, Canada, and many other countries. What is notable is the selection of these flea markets, auction houses, shops, and fairs. Below we describe a few of the very best.

ANTIQUES DEALERS

Ethical standards are generally high, and dealers usually will spontaneously divulge all the defects of an item a customer is considering buying. A number are members of recognized, reputable national guilds, with clear and rigorous codes in matters of authenticity and quality. But if the caveats aren't offered unsolicited, prospective buyers should be sure to question the dealer about what is original, what has been restored or retouched, and what has simply been replaced. If a purchase involves a significant sum, the buyer also should ask to have the qualifications put in writing.

Note that many genuine antiques taken out of the country are subject to duty. Also, an export license may be required; when you purchase an item, the antiques dealer will help you apply for one. For advice about purchasing and shipping and customs regulations, and for a list of members (who adhere to association standards), contact one of the following dealers' associations:

British Antique Dealers' Association (20 Rutland Gate, London SW7 1BD, England; phone: 171-589-4128). Members of this organization, to which some of the most reputable shops and dealers belong, display a blue-and-gold plaque engraved with the figure of the Renaissance sculptor and goldsmith Benvenuto Cellini.

Cotswold Antique Dealers' Association (Barcheston Manor, Shipston-on-Stour, Warwickshire, CV36 5AY, England; phone: 16086-61268).

London and Provincial Antique Dealers' Association (*LAPADA;* 535 King's Rd., London SW10 0SZ, England; phone: 171-823-3511). This is the world's largest association of antique dealers; it has over 700 members, who follow the strict *LAPADA* code; look for the chandelier sign. The association offers a directory, as well as a computerized information service and can put you in touch with its local members.

ANTIQUES PEAKS ON THE BRITISH LANDSCAPE

FLEA MARKETS AND OTHER WEEKLY SPECTACLES That heady mixture of rubbish and relic known as the flea market is the ultimate paradise for the collector. It offers the chance to find that special, unrecognized rarity, the eye-catching castoff whose true value only a devout aficionado would appreciate—say, a yak saddle from the Indian Mutiny, a left-handed pewter monocle, or a chipped 78 rpm recording of Edward VIII's abdication speech. For those who dream of snapping up a precious item before the professionals send it successively to auction, fair, and trendy shop (at prices that spiral ever upward), the weekly markets are a must, especially those that flourish outside London. One of the best markets in the British countryside is the *Wimborne Market,* which is held Fridays from 7 AM to 2:30 PM, Saturdays from 8 AM to 1 PM, and Sundays from 9 AM to 4 PM. Newborough Rd., Wimborne Minster, Dorset (phone: 1202-841212).

The buyer's best allies in this odyssey are bad weather and early arrival. A serious collector should get to the market before dawn and pray for torrential rain; the casual visitor who just wants to take in the spectacle itself should hope for a sunny morning. Fine days provide such good theater—at such moderate cost—that even the most eager treasure seekers won't be too disappointed at trudging home empty-handed. Though the British have managed to get many of their markets under a roof, thereby sacrificing local color to comforts, the bargains are still there.

AUCTIONS An auction, as any addict knows, is a mixture of stock market, gambling casino, and living theater. It's the perfect answer to rainy day blues provided newcomers pay attention to these notes:

Don't expect to make a killing. Even Chinese peasant children are hip to the art market today, it seems. But the chances of unearthing a real find are better for those who shop at smaller country auctions. Look carefully at mixed lots, and always venture out in inclement weather. Occasionally someone will pick up a golden goblet for 10p at a church rummage sale and then resell it for £9,000. In any event, there is about a 30% saving on the shop price of a comparable item.

Buy the catalogue before bidding. Catalogues often include a list of estimated prices. Those prices are not a contractual commitment, but they do act as a guide for prospective buyers. An elaborate stylistic code hints at the conviction the house may have about the age and authenticity of an item. The use of capital letters, of artists' full names, and of words like "fine," "rare," and "important" all carry positive connotations. The use of a last name only and of words like "style" and "attributed" should serve as warnings.

Visit the presale exhibition carefully, thoroughly, and even repeatedly. There is the pleasure of browsing in a store without a hovering clerk. Even more important is the prospective buyer's chance to examine the offerings. *Caveat emptor* is the prevailing rule at an auction. Serious buyers should have paintings taken down from the wall and ask to handle objects under lock and key. Those who can't be at the sale can leave a commission bid with the auctioneer or even place a bid by telephone—but if they can't be at the exhibition, they should be wary of buying.

Decide on a top bid before the auction begins, and don't go beyond it. The bidding has its own rhythm and tension. The auctioneer becomes a Pied Piper, with the buyers winking, blinking, and nodding in time to his music. This situation arouses unusual behavior in some people. Suddenly their egos are at stake, and they'll bid far beyond what they can afford—or even what the items are worth. A bid may be canceled by promptly calling out "Withdrawn." *Note:* In determining your top price, remember to add the house commission (which is generally 10%, but can be more), and any Value Added Tax (currently 17½%, although visitors can get a rebate—for more information, see GETTING READY TO GO).

Fingers rise and hammers fall all over Britain—particularly London—but the following out-of-the-way spots warrant prime attention:

Aylsham, Norfolk, England *Aylsham Salerooms* has regular sales of furniture, silver, porcelain and glass, collectibles, and books; and bimonthly sales of paintings, watercolors, and prints. *G. A. Key,* 8 Market Pl., Aylsham (phone: 1263-733195).

Penzance, Cornwall, England *W. H. Lane and Son* has about a dozen general sales annually of antiques and objets d'art. In addition, there are a number of special sales devoted to antique books, coins, medals, stamps, and pictures; occasionally there are also treasure trove sales in which pieces of eight and other finds from old shipwrecks are put on the block. 65 Morrab Rd. (phone: 1736-61447).

SHOPS AND ANTIQUES CENTERS From Abbotsbury to Zither-on-Thames, there are some 6,000 "olde curiosity shoppes" dappling the landscape of Britain. Whether the quest be for barometers or bond certificates, tools or toy soldiers, enthusiasts will find a shop catering exclusively to their collecting passions. Over the centuries the antiques trade in Britain has become very sophisticated in many specialties.

Before heading for a small shop in a small town, it's wise for visitors to phone ahead. Most dealers will see prospective buyers by appointment, even outside normal shopping hours.

A recent trend has been the gathering of many small shops into antiques centers—something like tony shopping centers or indoor markets with all the stalls under one roof. These are intriguing places to spend a rainy hour and to get a quick overview of the local market, with no great pressure to buy. There are hundreds of interesting items that rarely make it across the Atlantic.

Great Britain's major cities—particularly London, Bath, Brighton, Bristol, Edinburgh, and Glasgow—are the most obvious places to begin your search (see these chapters in THE CITIES). However, if you find yourself in Bedfordshire, try the *Woburn Abbey Antiques Centre* in Woburn Abbey (phone: 1525-290350). Collectibles are housed in an old stable behind façades that were rescued from demolition, restored, and then re-erected. Items range from furniture to paintings and prints, silver and glassware—most date from before 1870.

FAIRS There are dozens of fairs in all sizes and qualities. Whether they last two days or 10, they attract dealers from all over the region, the country, and Europe. Many dealers make the rounds of these events, beginning in January and continuing throughout the year. The *Antique Dealer and Collectors' Guide* magazine (Status Court Ltd., PO Box 805, Greenwich, London SE10 8TD, England; phone: 181-318-5868) publishes a comprehensive yearly calendar listing antiques fairs throughout the country; the price is £2.75 (about $4) per issue.

The most prestigious fairs by far are the *Burlington House Fair,* held in September in odd-numbered years at the *Royal Academy* in London, and the *Grosvenor House Antiques Fair,* held in June at the *Grosvenor House* hotel on Park Lane. But there are dozens of others, including the following:

Buxton Antiques Fair, *Pavilion Gardens,* Buxton, Derbyshire, England. Early May.

East Anglia Antiques Fair, *Athenaeum,* Bury St. Edmonds, Suffolk, England. September.

Kensington Antiques Fair, New Town Hall, Kensington, London W8, England. Early November.

Warwickshire County Antiques Fair, Cricket Ground, Edgbaston, Birmingham, England. Early March.

THE BEST HUNTING GROUNDS

A handful of cities and towns in Britain stand out for their selection of shops, antiques centers, flea markets, and auction houses. These are the places that savvy antiques dealers from the Continent visit when they're on the prowl for newly fashionable 19th-century English furniture and objets d'art—and they are a must on any antiques lover's tour of Britain. For details on the action in Bath, Bristol, Cambridge, Canterbury, Chester, Edinburgh, Glasgow, London, Oxford, and York, check the respective chapters in THE CITIES; outside these main areas, the following are the places to look.

COTSWOLDS, England The most romantic antiques hunting in Britain is in the Cotswolds, about 100 miles west of London. The area's charming, unspoiled towns, its quaint stone cottages, and its oh-so-English countryside make it very popular with visitors, so bargains are rare. But the antiques shops are so close to one another that visitors can cover quite a few without racking up excessive mileage. An expert shipping service for furniture and other large items is available.The most important towns for antiquing include Stow-on-the-Wold, a hilltop community whose low houses huddle around a handsome market square (its selection of furniture is so enormous that locals joke that an American who'd just finished a spending spree had labeled his purchases for shipping with "Stow in the Hold"). Other good bets are Broadway; Moreton-in-the-Marsh (particularly on High St.); Chipping Norton; Burford (especially on High St. and The Hill); Cirencester, an old market town with a 12th-century church, originally founded by the Romans and second in size to Roman London; and Cheltenham, a genteel spa town with spacious gardens and perfectly preserved Regency buildings.

The *Cotswold Antique Dealers' Association* (*CADA*) members' directory lists information on over 40 reputable dealers and their stock in the Cotswolds. It's available free from *CADA, Barcheston Manor,* Shipston-on-Stour, Warwickshire, CV36 5A4, England (phone: 16086-61268).

Some well-known dealers in these very special towns and others include:

Christopher Clarke Antiques (The Fosse Way, Stow-on-the-Wold GL54 1JS, England; phone: 1451-830476). For furniture, pictures, pottery, and other works of art dating from the 17th to the 19th centuries.

Rankine Taylor Antiques (34 Dollar St., Cirencester GL7 2AN; phone: 1285-652529). For 17th-, 18th-, and early 19th-century furniture and objets d'art from France, Italy, and America as well as England, Scotland, and Wales displayed in room settings that show off the proprietor's eye for the decorative and the unusual. The atmosphere is reminiscent of some 18th-century grande dame's drawing room.

EAST ANGLIA, England This bulge of coastline to the northeast of London is off the beaten track and little frequented by overseas visitors. Nonetheless, it's rich territory for the antiques collector. The Essex towns of Battlesbridge, Coggeshall, Colchester, Stansted Mount Fitchett, and Kelvedon (particularly High St.) make for especially happy hunting.In Ely, the items available at *Waterside Antiques* (The Wharf; phone: 1353-667066) run the gamut from jewelry to art objects to furniture. Open daily.

Antiques Centre in Coggeshall has 10 dealers stocking items both large and small, and several others have shops nearby. *The Market Place* (no phone).

There are also frequent antiques fairs worth attending in Bury St. Edmunds and a well-established fair at Snape in July.

HAY-ON-WYE, Powys, Wales Visitors to this tiny town (pronounced Hay-on-*Way*) in the Wye Valley always are astonished to discover that it is the center of the European antique book trade. Business is concentrated in the lanes of the old town center, and most shops are open on Sundays. It's easy to spend an entire day browsing or even finishing a whole book.

RULES OF THE ROAD FOR AN ODYSSEY OF THE OLD

Buy for sheer pleasure and not for investment. Treasure seekers should forget about the carrot of supposed resale value that dealers habitually dangle in front of amateur clients. If you love an object, you'll never part with it. If you don't love it, let someone else adopt it.

Don't be timid about haggling. That's as true at a Bond Street jeweler's as at the most colorful flea market. It's surprising how much is negotiable—and the higher the price, the farther it has to fall.

Buy the finest affordable example of any item, in as close to mint condition as possible. Chipped or tarnished "bargains" will haunt you later with their shabbiness.

Train your eye in museums. Museums that specialize in items dear to a collector are the best of all, though they may break his or her heart. The coins and medals of the *Fitzwilliam* in Cambridge or the furniture and clocks of London's *Wallace Collection,* for instance, all help to set impeccable standards against which to measure purchases. Special tours of Britain's historic homes are also offered (described in *Stately Homes and Great Gardens,* in this section).

Get advice from a specialist when contemplating a major acquisition. The various dealers' guilds can be helpful. Major auction houses like *Sotheby's* and *Christie's* have fleets of resident specialists who can be consulted. So does the *British Museum.* Those who are interested (and are planning a lengthy stay in Britain) might enroll in a special instructional program to become experts in their own right. *Christie's Education* (63 Old Brompton Rd., London SW7 3JS, England; phone: 171-581-3933) offers several evening courses (lasting about two months) on specialized subjects, including wine. *Sotheby's Educational Studies* (30 Oxford St., London W1R

1RE, England; phone: 171-323-5775) also offers long-term evening lectures on topics such as glass, furniture, and fakes and forgeries. Both companies also sponsor longer courses that last from three months to a year. The *British Tourist Authority* offers a list of special interest holidays that includes several others.

When pricing an object, don't forget to figure the cost of shipping. Shipping home a large piece—furniture, sculpture, antique garden paraphernalia—can be considerable. Be sure to add this into the cost of your purchase.

Peruse British art books and periodicals. Among the best publications are the following:

Antique Collector is available from the National Magazine Company (72 Broadwick St., London W1V 2BP, England; phone: 171-439-5000), and on newsstands.

Antique Dealer and Collector's Guide is available by mail (Status Court Ltd., PO Box 805, London SE10 8TD, England; phone: 181-318-5868), and from *W. H. Smith* (bookstores) and leading newsagents.

Antiques Trade Gazette, a weekly newspaper listing and reporting on auctions and shows in Britain and on the Continent, is available by mail (17 Whitcomb St., London WC2H 7PL, England; phone: 171-930-7192, subscriptions department) and at the newsstands adjoining *Sotheby's* on Bond Street (W1) and other antiques centers.

Apollo, an international magazine of arts and antiques, is available from 29 Chesham Pl., London SW1 X8HB, England (phone: 171-235-1998) and on newsstands.

Burlington Magazine, available by subscription only (14-16 Dukes Rd., London WC1H 9AD, England; phone: 171-430-0481).

Guide to the Antique Shops of Britain (£14.50/about $22), revised annually by the *Antique Collectors Club* (5 Church St., Woodbridge, Suffolk IP12 1DS, England; phone: 1394-385501), reviews over 6,000 antiques dealers, outlining the type of stock, size of showrooms, years in business, hours, and more.

International Herald Tribune features art pages, particularly in the Saturday/Sunday edition.

Miller's Antiques Price Guide (£19.95/about $30), published annually by Miller's Publications (The Cellars, 5 High St., Tenterden, Kent TN30 6BN, England; phone: 1580-766411), provides references with captions and prices for items sold in the previous year.

For the Mind

Marvelous Museums

It often has been said that when King Charles I died in 1649, and Parliament auctioned off his collection of paintings and other treasures, Britain lost its heritage. But the growth of the great national collections has more than compensated, beginning as early as the 17th century with the founding of *Oxford*'s *Ashmolean Museum,* and including the collecting mania of the 18th and 19th centuries—when the rich were really rich and gentlemen made careers of their hobbies, accumulating not only the fine art of Western Europe but also trifles and prizes from the farthest corners of the Empire. Today, Britain is home to a staggering agglomeration of artwork from all over the world. And although some of these treasures are privately owned, the majority are on display in the nation's great museums, not to mention the hundreds of country houses whose fine collections are often as stunning as their architecture. (The estimable *National Portrait Gallery,* for instance, has two collections outside London at Montacute, Somerset, and at Beningbrough, North Yorkshire.) The furnishings in such homes often are in mint condition, and seeing them displayed along with porcelain, silver, and tapestries enhances the experience.

Britain's museums usually are well conceived and designed to provide ideal space and lighting for the works on display. But because of recent cutbacks in government support, more and more museums have introduced admission charges. Even those that still are free hope for generous donations. However, many continue to offer free guided tours and lecture programs designed as much for experts in the fields as for beginners seeking a greater appreciation of what they've seen and admired. Local newspapers and museum calendars are good sources for details.

A museum can be a great deal more pleasurable if a few simple guidelines are kept in mind. Visitors should plan several short visits to a large museum rather than one long one, stay for about an hour, and take in no more than a dozen fine works. There's no fatigue quite like achy, yawny museum fatigue—once described as the dread "museum foot"—and when it has set in, merely sitting for three minutes in front of a Rubens won't cure it. If possible, travelers should know what they want to see before beginning their rounds, so as not to clutter the experience with too many bleeding saints and blustery seascapes. Most museums publish excellent pamphlets and booklets to steer visitors to the more noted works in their collections.

And everyone should visit an art gallery or an auction house occasionally—just as a reminder that once it was all for sale. Besides those museums located in Great Britain's major cities (consult the individual reports in THE CITIES), listed below are a trio of hidden gems—institutions in out-of-the-way locales that are worth seeking out.

BEAMISH, THE NORTH OF ENGLAND OPEN AIR MUSEUM, Beamish, County Durham, England The property aims to give visitors a taste of what life was like in the North of England early in this century. It was founded in 1972 by enthusiast Frank Atkinson, who collected items and buildings connected with the region's social, agricultural, and industrial history. The buildings he acquired have been rebuilt on this 200-acre site and furnished as they would have been around the turn of the century. Visitors can take a tram ride to the reconstructed Old Town, a working farm, Colliery Village, and the railway station. It's easy to spend a day here, but shorter visits also are possible; routes are marked in the museum guidebook. Closed Mondays and Fridays November through March and the week before *Christmas.* Admission charge. Information: *Beamish, The North of England Open Air Museum,* Beamish, County Durham DH9 0RG, England (phone: 1207-231811).

CECIL HIGGINS ART GALLERY AND MUSEUM, Bedford, Bedfordshire, England The museum in this fine old Victorian structure, once the home of a local brewer and art lover named Cecil Higgins, spills over into a modern annex. Lively and hospitable, it boasts a distinguished collection of English and continental porcelain and glass, and watercolors by Constable, Cotman, Gainsborough, and Turner. Prints by Dürer, Picasso, Rembrandt, the Impressionists, and others are displayed in a succession of changing exhibitions in the newer building. The Victorian mansion is set up to show how a family might have kept house about a century ago and has a lived-in look. A fire burns on the hearth, clocks tick, children's toys litter the floor next to a dollhouse, a letter lies half written on the desk, and a white scarf hangs from the hat stand. Closed Mondays except bank holidays. No admission charge. Information: *Cecil Higgins Art Gallery and Museum,* Castle Close, Bedford, Bedfordshire MK40 3NY, England (phone: 1234-211222).

IRONBRIDGE GORGE MUSEUM, Telford, Shropshire, England This is not just "another" museum. Between 1777 and 1779 Abraham Darby built England's first iron bridge, from which the town takes its name. As a result, he ushered in the great era in industrial architecture that culminated with the construction of *Paddington Station* and the *Crystal Palace* in London's *Hyde Park.* Today, not only is the bridge itself a tourist attraction, but the whole area—a wooded stretch of the river Severn, all small hills and secret valleys—has been transformed into a beehive of activities reflecting the days of steam two centuries ago. At Blists Hill, once the site of the most dramatic industrial activity of all, major exhibits focus on relics from the days of coal mines and blast furnaces, plus a re-creation of a 19th-century village that demonstrates the harsh, often drab conditions of many workers' lives. Nearby Coalbrookdale, whose foundry produced the components for the famous bridge, was Britain's first coke-smelting center; early castings, cast-iron rails and wheels, and ironmasters' houses and workers' cottages are on display. And at Coalport, site of the china works, visitors can stroll along a bit of unused canal that once linked the factory to the Severn. The workshops that produced the china are open to visitors, and exhibits recount the day-to-day pleasures and tribulations of the local residents who worked here generation after generation. To encourage visits to all the *Ironbridge Gorge Museum*'s components, a special "Passport to the Gorge" ticket allows one visit to each site and is valid indefinitely until all museums have been seen. A good place to start is at Coalbrookdale or the *Museum of the River.* Most of the museum is open daily; in winter, a few of the smaller sites are closed. Information: *Ironbridge Gorge Museum,* Telford, Shropshire TF8 7AW, England (phone: 1952-433522 on weekdays; 1952-432166 on weekends).

The Performing Arts

When the summer festival season ends, winter's cultural whirlwind begins. London indisputably is a hotbed of the performing arts, with literally hundreds of offerings in hundreds of playhouses, dozens of theaters in the West End, the best of ballet, and music in the air at all times.

But throughout Britain, some theaters reliably turn out productions and concerts that are more interesting or wonderful than others, and some are worth a visit simply because they are particularly beautiful or unusually historic. A few are quite small, so that even the most remote corner (or "gods," as the heights of the balconies in large theaters and opera houses are called) affords a fine view of the activities on stage—and the prices remain relatively low by Broadway standards.

CONCERT HALLS AND THEATERS

In THE CITIES chapters, we've given our choices of exemplary stages in Great Britain's major metropolitan areas. What follows is a sampling of halls that culture buffs will find worth going out of their way to experience. If you still haven't had enough, there are many other theaters and concert halls all over Britain. It's possible to order tickets in advance of arrival in Britain directly through the individual box offices and through *Keith Prowse & Co.* (234 W. 44th St., New York, NY 10036; phone: 212-398-1430; 800-669-7469 outside New York City). This organization, which has been in business for 213 years, is the world's largest entertainment ticket agency and sells some 53,000 tickets a week; its allocations range from one-fifth to nearly one-third of all the seats at London theaters. Tickets to theater and major festival events also can be booked in advance through *Edwards & Edwards* (1 Times Sq. Plaza, New York, NY 10036; phone: 212-944-0290 or 800-223-6108, except in New York City).

GRAND THEATRE & OPERA HOUSE, Leeds, West Yorkshire, England This restoration with its elaborately decorated interior is one of the most impressive Victorian theaters in Britain. It is home to *Opera North* and hosts touring ballet and drama companies when that company is not in residence. Information: *Grand Theatre & Opera House,* New Briggate, Leeds, West Yorkshire LS1 6NZ, England (phone: 113-245-9351).

ROYAL EXCHANGE THEATRE, Manchester, England A futuristic steel-and-glass structure (often referred to as the "National Theatre of the North"), it is housed in Manchester's historic Victorian *Cotton Exchange.* The resident company, whose roots go back to 1959 and a group of actors who had trained at the *Old Vic Theatre School,* performs Shakespeare, Marlowe, Sheridan, Chekhov, Ibsen, Coward, and a variety of other works old and new, including an occasional world premiere. Several productions that started here have gone on to London's West End and New York's Broadway, and audiences pack the unusual theater-in-the-round close to capacity. The company also has a mobile theatre that tours countrywide. Classical, folk music, and jazz concerts also are held here. Information: *Royal Exchange Theatre,* St. Ann's Sq., Manchester M2 7DH, England (phone: 161-833-9333; fax: 161-832-0881).

THEATRE ROYAL, Newcastle upon Tyne, Tyne & Wear, England This superbly appointed theater has extensive conference and catering facilities within the original Victorian building. The theater presents touring performances of drama, ballet, and opera, as well as an annual five- or six-week visit by the *Royal Shakespeare Company.* Information: *Theatre Royal,* Grey St., Newcastle upon Tyne, Tyne & Wear, NE1 6BR England (phone: 191-232-2061).

THE BRITISH FOLK MUSIC SCENE

Folk music is alive and well in England, Scotland, and Wales. There are all manner of outdoor folk music festivals between *Easter* and September. And every week in the British Isles, singers, guitarists, banjo and mandolin players, and other musicians, as well as aficionados of their music, get together at local pubs to play and sing along at the meetings of the nation's some 1,500 folk clubs. The events, which are usually held on weekends, are announced via local papers or radio stations, information bureaus, or postings at libraries. The atmosphere is informal, but a strict etiquette prevails: no talking and no service from the bar during songs.

ENGLAND In addition to folk clubs and festivals, England offers a lively roster of summer folk dance, which derives an additional measure of fascination from its long roots in the past. There are processional dances associated with ancient rituals, such as the famous Furry Dance at Helston in Cornwall on May 8, for instance, which celebrates the passing from the darkness of winter into the light of spring. Morris dancing, the best-known form of English folk dance, probably developed from pagan sacrificial rites.

Traditionally, only men take part; they are decked with ribbons and bells and flourish handkerchiefs and garlands as they tread the age-old measures to the accompaniment of custom-honored pipe and tabor (a drum) and the more contemporary fiddles, melodeons, and concertinas. Particularly numerous in the Cotswolds, they also perform in many other parts of England, usually outside public houses. In London, it is a long-standing tradition for morris dancers to perform outside *Westminster Abbey* early on Wednesday evenings May through July.

For a comprehensive list of festival dates and folk clubs, contact the *English Folk Dance and Song Society* (*Cecil Sharp House,* 2 Regents Park Rd., London NW1 7AY, England; phone: 171-485-2206). They welcome visitors and will let you browse in the library among the specialized books (predominantly British and American); closed weekends. There also are magazines, photographs, tapes, pamphlets advertising events and festivals, and a bookshop (closed Sundays)—and if you peep into the main hall you may even see some dancing!

SCOTLAND With its own Celtic music tradition featuring pipe, fiddle, *clarsach* (harp), music, and song, Scotland's many festivals, often dedicated to preserving the Gaelic language, literature, and culture, frequently include *ceilidhs,* evenings of traditional music, song, and dance. Performances and casual gatherings that take place all over Scotland throughout the year, as well as competitions, festivals, and *Highland Games* events, are good places to hear Scottish bagpipes and fiddles.

The *Traditional Music and Song Association of Scotland* (*TMSA*) is a group of organizers, tradition bearers, singers, musicians, storytellers, collectors, publishers, and others who are actively concerned with fostering interest in the traditional arts in Scotland. There are branches in Aberdeen, Angus, Dundee, Isle of Bute, Perthshire, Fife, Glasgow, and Edinburgh, and festivals are offered in Keith, Newcastleton, Auchtermuchty, and Kirriemuir. At the festivals, competitions are held for singing and storytelling; as well as for playing music with many types of instruments, including the fiddle, accordion, tin whistle, mouth organ, Jew's harp, and the *ceilidh* band. A calendar with a comprehensive list of the year's festivals is available from the *Traditional Music and Song Association of Scotland* (10 Belmont St., Fourth Floor, Aberdeen AB1 1JE, Scotland; phone: 1224-632978); when writing, be sure to include a self-addressed envelope and the appropriate postage coupons.

Scottish country dancing has a worldwide following these days, and many foreign visitors join the *Royal Scottish Country Dance Society*'s annual summer school at St. Andrews from mid-July through August. There are performances and casual gatherings all over Scotland year-round as well as competitions, festivals, and displays at *Highland Games.* During the summer, there even is dancing in the streets of Edinburgh. Information: June Moore, *Royal Scottish Country Dance Society,* 12 Coates Crescent, Edinburgh

EH3 7AF, Scotland (phone: 131-225-3854) or the *Scottish Tourist Board,* 23 Ravelston Ter., Edinburgh EH4 3EU, Scotland (phone: 131-332-2433).

The *Scottish Folk Directory* is also a good resource. It lists folk clubs offering many types of entertainment, from unaccompanied ballads to Cajun music. Also listed is a calendar of festivals, along with artists and what they perform. Information: Willie Haines, *Blackfriars Music,* 49 Blackfriars St., Edinburgh EH1 W1S, Scotland (phone: 131-557-3090).

WALES The Welsh folk tradition, distinct from that of the British, focuses attention on the country's own language. Many nationwide folk festivals and *eisteddfodau* (poetry and song competitions) are held every year, usually in summer. The best-known are the *Royal National Eisteddfod,* held in North Wales and South Wales in alternate years, and the *International Musical Eisteddfod* in July at Llangollen (for details about both, see *Best Festivals,* below). The former offers a particularly good representation of Welsh literature, drama, folk dancing, and music. For more information on the Welsh folk scene, contact David Evans, *Welsh Folk Dance Society,* Flynnonlwyd, Trelech, Camarthen, Dyfed SA33 6QZ, Wales (phone: 1994-484496).

The Best Festivals

With so much talent in so many fields, it's hardly surprising that Britain is blossoming with festivals. It is surprising, however, that they take place virtually year-round and last anywhere from a day or a week to a month or even a whole summer. Some are devoted to Britain's musical goings-on—jazz, rock, symphonic and chamber music, opera, and the like; others are oddball events that focus on snuff taking or pancake racing; and still others are rooted in centuries-old tradition, with plenty of morris dancing, craft displays, and brass band music. The *British Tourist Authority* publishes *Customs and Pageantry,* which describes a number of these more unusual affairs.

At larger festivities of all types, there is also the "fringe"—a group of events that complements the main festival. The one at the *Edinburgh Festival* is world famous (and sometimes more interesting than the main show). Most host towns are often *en fête,* too, with floral displays everywhere.

One of the most eclectic affairs, held May through September, is the *Stately Homes Music Festival,* a series of classical concerts and operas performed at some of the finest historic houses throughout Britain. There are about 18 performances in all, and guests are invited to bring a picnic supper to eat on the stately grounds of these homes in the early evening, or they can purchase a special picnic hamper (prepared at each site). For details, contact *Stately Homes Music Festival* (PO Box 1, St. Albans, Hertfordshire AL1 4ED, England; phone: 1727-841175; fax: 1727-851676). Information about other events may be obtained from the *National Trust,* the various Garden Schemes, and local tourist boards.

Even though festivals may be full of "serious events," they are also, in a word, fun—and the opportunity to meet and talk with local people who are delighted to welcome foreign visitors is part of the experience. Therein lies a good deal of the charm and pleasure of a country festival and the memories that go with it. The various tourist boards can provide listings of festivals of all types. Besides those found in Great Britain's major cities (for details, see the individual reports in THE CITIES), below are some of our favorite fetes that are off the well-trod tourist track. They are listed alphabetically by location.

WORTH A LONG DETOUR

ALDEBURGH FESTIVAL, Aldeburgh, Suffolk, England Beloved by musicians the world over for its warmth, intimacy, and exceptionally fine acoustics, the remarkable concert hall established by composer Benjamin Britten and tenor Peter Pears is the focal point of this quaint little sea town's annual music festival, which has been held since 1948. During the last two weeks of June, it presents a platform for recent developments in British and American music and honors the anniversaries of the classical masters. Most of the events take place in the main concert hall, a converted brewery situated 6 miles from Aldeburgh in Snape; nearby churches and stately homes are used for other events such as lectures and poetry readings. Throughout August each year the *Maltings Proms,* featuring a rich variety of artists and programs, are held at Snape; various other concerts are performed throughout the autumn. The *Britten-Pears School for Advanced Musical Studies,* also at Snape, is where young artists come to study and participate in festival events. Information: *Aldeburgh Foundation,* High St., Aldeburgh, Suffolk IP15 5AX, England (phone: 1728-452935, information; 1728-453543, box office).

ARUNDEL FESTIVAL, Arundel, West Sussex, England Held annually for 10 days from August to early September, this festival takes place in a charming South Downs resort dominated by a Norman castle owned by the Dukes of Norfolk. Performances of Shakespeare take place at the open-air theater built against the castle walls, and each year there is special emphasis on one other aspect of the arts. There are many other events as well, ranging from concerts of classical music to gymkhanas. Information: *Festival Office,* The Mary Gate, Arundel, West Sussex BN18 9AT, England (phone: 1903-883690).

BUXTON FESTIVAL, Buxton, Derbyshire, England This three-week July festival, focusing primarily on opera but supplemented by jazz performances, cabarets, and discussions, usually has a particular theme such as "Love and Marriage." The attractive Georgian spa town possesses a fine concert hall and an elegant Edwardian opera house. In fact, since its beginnings in 1979, this festival's productions of lesser-known operas have put it on the map alongside such events as those in Bayreuth and Glyndebourne. The town nestles amid the rugged hills of central England's Derbyshire *Peak District National*

Park and is easily accessible from Manchester. Information: *Festival Office,* Hall Bank, Buxton, Derbyshire SK17 6EN, England (phone: 1298-70395; fax: 1298-72289).

CHELTENHAM FESTIVAL OF LITERATURE, Cheltenham, Gloucestershire, England For nine days in mid-October some of the world's greatest literary names and curious audiences gather in an enchanting setting to celebrate the written, printed, and spoken word in various venues throughout the region. The breadth of the festival program is an essential part of its wide appeal; it offers conversations, lectures, poetry readings and workshops, theater, children's events, a book fair, and exhibitions. Information: *Town Hall,* Cheltenham, Gloucestershire GL50 1QA, England (phone: 1242-521621, information; 1242-227979, box office).

CHELTENHAM INTERNATIONAL FESTIVAL OF MUSIC, Cheltenham, Gloucestershire, England This event takes place during two weeks in early July and presents a wide program of musical offerings, with an emphasis on the contemporary and the British in a continuing classical tradition. The backbone of the festival includes morning chamber concerts in the glorious setting of the historic *Pittville Pump Room* (the spa waters still are available for tasting), full-scale orchestral concerts in the *Town Hall,* and opera and dance in the splendidly restored *Everyman Theatre.* Other events feature mime, film, master classes, composers- and photographers-in-residence, jazz, ethnic music, talks, tours, fringe performances, and more. Information: *Town Hall,* Cheltenham, Gloucestershire GL50 1QA, England (phone: 1242-521621, information; 1242-227979, box office).

CHICHESTER FESTIVAL THEATRE, Chichester, West Sussex, England The repertory of this extremely popular theater festival, which runs May through October, includes a mixture of the old and the new. The emphasis is on entertaining rather than experimenting, and the most successful plays usually end up in London. During the theater's 33 years of existence, the roster of performers has grown into a veritable *Who's Who* of the English-speaking theater, and the festival has become the most important annual theatrical event outside London, Edinburgh, and Stratford. The theater, opened in 1960, is attractively modern, hexagonally shaped, and set in a lovely parkland; every seat gives a good view of the stage. Other pluses: the alternative productions of the *Studio Company,* and Chichester itself, a magical place in some of the most enchanting country in Sussex, sophisticated enough that restaurants keep late hours and chefs serve lobster thermidor as well as steak and kidney pie. Information: *Chichester Festival Theatre Box Office, Oaklands Park,* Chichester, West Sussex PO19 4AP, England (phone: 1243-781312).

CHICHESTER FESTIVITIES, Chichester, West Sussex, England In celebration of the founding of *Chichester Cathedral*, this event, held for two and a half weeks in July, features artists, musicians, and poets of national and international repute, along with jazz, films, dance, exhibitions, opera, and children's events. Past themes have been "An Anglo-French Affair" and "A Touch of Romance." A program for the festivities is published in mid-April. Information: *Chichester Festivities, Canon Gate House,* South St., Chichester, West Sussex P019 1PU, England (phone: 1243-785718).

THREE CHOIRS FESTIVAL, Gloucester, Gloucestershire; Hereford, Herefordshire; and Worcester, Worcestershire; England This August event, which rotates annually among the three cathedral cities, is a tribute to the great English tradition of choral singing and the oldest music festival in Europe. The three cathedral choirs join forces with one another and with first class artists, orchestras, and ensembles from around the world to provide a week of splendid music that ranges from the 16th century to the present. A few works are commissioned especially for the occasion, and there's a varied fringe program. The surrounding countryside—the Cotswolds and the Malvern Hills—is wonderfully scenic and full of beautiful old buildings. Information: *Festival Office, Community House,* College Green, Gloucester, Gloucestershire GL1 2LX, England (phone: 1452-529819).

GLYNDEBOURNE FESTIVAL OPERA, Glyndebourne, East Sussex, England Founded in 1934 by John Christie and his wife, singer Audrey Mildmay, and held on their ancient Sussex country estate some 50 miles south of London, this opera festival, which runs from the third week in May through late August, is top drawer musically—with artists from all over the world—and socially as well. Now held in the larger *Glyndebourne Opera House* (which opened last year), the splendid program (featuring six productions each summer) has a 75-minute supper interval—perfect for a meal in one of the restaurants or for champagne picnics in the gardens and on the velvety English lawns. *British Rail* has service between London's *Victoria Station* and Lewes. Information: *Glyndebourne Festival Opera,* Lewes, East Sussex BN8 5UU, England (phone: 1273-812321, information; 1273-813813, box office).

HARROGATE INTERNATIONAL FESTIVAL, Harrogate, North Yorkshire, England Elegant buildings stand beside modern facilities in this Victorian spa town, whose two-week festival in early August embraces all the arts. The various halls and churches used for the event, among them the 9th-century *Ripon Cathedral,* host everything from orchestral and chamber music, celebrity recitals, plays, late-night shows, and literary events to opera. Information: *Festival Office, Royal Baths,* Harrogate, North Yorkshire HG1 2RR, England (phone: 1423-562303).

KING'S LYNN FESTIVAL, King's Lynn, Norfolk, England The Queen Mother is the sponsor of this late-July fortnight of art exhibits and classical music, both serious and light, plus jazz, puppetry, children's programs, theater, film, talks, and late-night shows—and she usually attends. Street shows and fireworks are part of a fringe that rounds out the program. The site, an ancient market town with quaint streets, curious churches, and historic buildings, is also a delight. Information: *King's Lynn Festival,* 27-29 King St., King's Lynn, Norfolk PE30 1HA, England (phone: 1553-773578).

MALVERN FESTIVAL, Malvern, Worcestershire, England In 1929, Sir Barry Jackson directed the first *Malvern Festival,* George Bernard Shaw wrote plays especially for it, and Edward Elgar conducted his own compositions. The festival provides an environment in which new works are presented, new composers heard, and new drama productions introduced. The fringe, which offers offbeat theatrical and musical performances, is the largest in Britain outside Edinburgh. And Elgar and Shaw still play a part. The picturesque Malvern Hills are within easy reach of the Cotswolds and Wales. Information: *Malvern Festival Administrator,* Grange Rd., Malvern, Worcestershire WR14 3HB, England (phone: 1684-572725, information; 1684-892277, box office).

HOBBY HORSE CELEBRATIONS, Padstow, Cornwall, England Among Europe's oldest festivals, this annual event held on May 1 (unless it's a Sunday, in which case it is held the next day) brings this sleepy seaport town to life. Caroling and carousing go on all night, but the real highlight is a long parade in which the Hobby Horse—a fabulous creature with a fierce-looking cone-shaped head protruding through a black, sailcloth-covered hoop—acts out a skit in which he dies and is revived over and over, then, at day's end, prances around a Maypole. According to one story, the "'Obby 'Oss," as it is locally known, started when the village women, whose husbands were off fighting the French in one of the numerous wars between the English and their Channel neighbors, fashioned an enormous stallion to scare away enemy raiders. However, most think the raucous celebration has its roots in earlier pagan times. Information: *West Country Tourist Board,* 60 St. David's Hill, Exeter, Devon EX4 4SY, England (phone: 1392-76351).

SALISBURY FESTIVAL, Salisbury, Wiltshire, England This nine-day September event, one of the leading cultural affairs in southern England, includes the performance of major orchestral works in the cathedral and lovely concerts by candlelight in neighboring churches, operas and plays, a variety of late-evening shows, and assorted outdoor events. There are many points of interest in the region—mysterious, prehistoric *Stonehenge* and the charming *Wilton House* among them—and Salisbury itself is a fine ancient town. Information: *Salisbury Festival, The King's House,* 65 The Close, Salisbury, Wiltshire SP1 2EN, England (phone: 1722-323883).

INTERNATIONAL MUSICAL EISTEDDFOD, Llangollen, Clwyd, Wales Music and friendship abound here for a week in July as over 6,000 competitors from 30 countries from Hungary and Bulgaria to Norway, Italy, Japan, the US, and others compete in folk song and dance competitions and choir contests. Evening concerts are given by choirs, dance groups, and renowned singers and instrumentalists. The colors, costumes, and sounds are dazzling, and there's always a special moment—as when an American choir and a Russian chorus got together and sang the Welsh national anthem, in Welsh, or when a group of Zulu dancers swept onstage and interrupted the national anthem to present the festival's music director with their tribe's highest honor. Another part of the festival is the *Choir of the World* competition, in which the title is bestowed on the winning choir. Information: *Eisteddfod Office,* Llangollen, Clwyd LL20 8NG, Wales (phone: 1978-860236).

ROYAL NATIONAL EISTEDDFOD, Wales What other country would celebrate a poet as national hero and king-for-a-day? This is the biggest of the Welsh *eisteddfodau* (competitive festivals of poetry and song); it always attracts huge crowds, and the winning poets are treated like pop stars, feted by crowds, blinking in the TV lights. Traditionally a nomadic festival, it is held alternately in North and South Wales. This year, it is scheduled to take place in Colwyn Bay August 5–13. Information: *Royal National Eisteddfod Office,* 40 Park Ty Glas, Llanishen, Cardiff CF4 58U, Wales (phone: 1222-763777; fax: 1222-763737).

IF YOU'RE NEARBY

WINDSOR FESTIVAL, Windsor Castle, Berkshire, England Concerts, dance programs, readings, lectures, walks, and exhibitions take place at *Windsor Castle* and *Eton College* and occupy this community every year for two weeks in September or October. Information: *Windsor Festival,* 14 North Croft Rd., Englefield Green, Surrey TW20 0DU, England (phone: 1784-432618).

BILLINGHAM INTERNATIONAL FOLKLORE FESTIVAL, Billingham, Cleveland, England This folk festival, whose events take place in four different venues in August, is unusual because it presents traditional music, song, and dance from many countries in a theatrical setting. Open-air concerts are held daily, and package tours of the area are available. Information: *Festival Office, Municipal Buildings,* Town Centre, Billingham, Cleveland TS23 2LW, England (phone: 1642-558212, information; 1642-552663, box office).

HASLEMERE FESTIVAL, Haslemere, Surrey, England At this early-music festival held in July, performances follow original manuscripts in the town's *Dolmetsch Library* and reproduce playing styles of the period in which the various pieces were composed. Arnold Dolmetsch, the library's namesake, founded the event in 1925; Carl Dolmetsch, his son, has been festival director since 1940. Information: *Festival Secretary, Dolmetsch Foundation,* Jesses, Grayswood Rd., Haslemere, Surrey GU27 2BS, England (phone: 1428-642161).

HAXEY HOOD GAME, Haxey, Humberside, England One of dozens of festivals rooted in age-old tradition, this one got started some 600 years ago when Lady Mowbray lost her hood to a sudden gust of wind and thanked the 13 men who strove gallantly to retrieve it by instituting an annual reenactment of the occasion. Believed by some to have been the origin of rugby, the game is played today—on January 6—by the descendants of those men and their neighbors. The contest involves a Lord, 13 Boggins, a Fool, a bonfire, a no-holds-barred free-for-all in which writhing and grunting masses of humanity struggle for long hours over a piece of leather stuffed with straw, coins, and other fillings, and equally drawn-out victory celebrations in the local pubs. Information: *Tourist Information Centre, Doncaster Central Library,* Waterdale, Doncaster, South Yorkshire DN1 3JE, England (phone: 1302-734309).

HENLEY FESTIVAL OF MUSIC AND THE ARTS, Henley-on-Thames, England This event is timed to follow the *Henley Royal Regatta.* In fact, it takes place in the *Stewards' Enclosure* the week immediately after the *Regatta* in July. Concerts, recitals, art displays, and fireworks make up the fare. Information: *Henley Festival of Music and the Arts,* 42 Bell St., Henley-on-Thames, Oxon RG9 2BG, England (phone: 1491-411353).

MINACK THEATRE FESTIVAL, Porthcurno, Cornwall, England The setting of the open-air *Minack Theatre,* on the cliffs 3 miles from Land's End, is as provocative as the 17-week season of productions (from Gilbert and Sullivan to Shakespeare) staged by professional and amateur companies May through September. (Even though it's summer, be sure to wear warm clothes.) Information: *Minack Theatre,* Porthcurno, Penzance, Cornwall TR19 6JU, England (phone: 1736-810696).

SIDMOUTH INTERNATIONAL FESTIVAL OF FOLK ARTS, Sidmouth, Devon, England The largest folk festival in Britain (founded in 1955), this week-long event in early August presents everything from song and dance to crafts, processions, and special children's activities in venues ranging from pubs to huge open-air theaters. Information: *Sidmouth International Festival of Folk Arts,* 6 East St., Sidmouth, Devon EX10 8BL, England (phone: 1395-515134).

TILFORD BACH FESTIVAL, Tilford, Farnham, Surrey, England Devoted mainly to the music of Bach and organized by the *Tilford Bach Society,* this village festival has been in existence since 1953. This three-day event in mid-May features concerts given by the *London Handel Orchestra* in *All Saints' Church,* and the intermissions are long enough to allow the audience to stroll over to the local pub for refreshments. Information: *Helen Malyron, Festival Secretary,* Old Quarry House, Seale, Farnham, Surrey GU10 1LD, England (phone: 1252-782167).

DUMFRIES AND GALLOWAY ARTS FESTIVAL, Dumfries, Scotland This youthful affair, founded in 1980, offers a ten-day program of drama, music, and visual arts in the town's *Theatre Royal* and in various schools, churches, and halls throughout the region late May to early June. Information: *Dumfries and Galloway Arts Festival, Gracefield Arts Centre,* 28 Edinburgh Rd., Dumfries DG1 1JR, Scotland (phone: 1387-620447).

FEIS BHARRAIGH (BARRA FESTIVAL), Isle of Barra, Western Isles, Scotland Devoted to fostering Gaelic language and culture, this event held in July encompasses drama, literature, music, and dance. Traditional instruments like the *clarsach* (a small harp), bagpipe, tin whistle, and fiddle are featured, along with Highland and Hebridean dancing. Information: *Feis Bharraigh,* 9 Ardmhor, Northey, Isle of Barra PA80 5YB, Western Isles, Scotland (phone: 18715-237 or 18715-344).

UP-HELLY-AA, Lerwick, Shetland Islands, Scotland This annual tradition takes place toward the end of January to celebrate the end of the winter solstice. Dating back to times when the islanders were compelled by their rulers to embrace Christian beliefs but were instead holding on to their pagan Norse ways, this celebration marked the ending of the Christian holy days of *Christmas.* Each year a Viking galley is built and transported in torchlight procession by up to 900 Shetlanders dressed in Viking or fancy dress costume to the park where the torches are used to set fire to the ship. After the blaze has reached the skies, the "guizers" visit each of several halls open to invited guests, where they perform a sketch inspired by their garb, then dance the night away. Information: *Shetland Tourist Organisation,* Market Cross, Lerwick, Shetland ZE1 0LU, Scotland (phone: 1595-3434).

PITLOCHRY FESTIVAL, Pitlochry, Tayside, Scotland Plays in repertory, celebrity concerts, and art exhibitions are presented in Scotland's stunning *Theatre in the Hills* May through October. Information: *Pitlochry Festival Theatre,* Pitlochry, Tayside PH16 5DR, Scotland (phone: 1796-472680).

ORKNEY TRADITIONAL FOLK FESTIVAL, Stromness, Orkney, Scotland Based on the main island of Orkney, this event held in May attracts both local amateurs and professional musicians from various parts of Britain and has lately spread to other islands. Many competitions and other activities are organized for young performers and children. Information: *Orkney Traditional Folk Festival,* 12 Guardhouse Park, Stromness, Orkney KW16 3DP, Scotland (phone: 1856-850773).

FISHGUARD MUSIC FESTIVAL, Fishguard, Dyfed, Wales The renowned Welsh choral tradition has generated this week-long July annual. The music is mainly classical, but new works are commissioned for performance by visiting musicians from home and abroad; and there's also jazz, film, and art. The festival often ends with the presentation of a large choral work. Concerts take place in ancient *St. David's Cathedral* in Fishguard. The setting for the 1971 filming of Dylan Thomas's *Under Milk Wood,* starring Richard Burton, this town on the edge of *Pembrokeshire National Park* is beautiful—backed by cliffs and partially edged by a shingled beach. Information: *Fishguard Music Festival Office,* Fishguard, Pembrokeshire, Dyfed SA65 9BJ, Wales (phone: 1348-873612).

HAY-ON-WYE FESTIVAL, Hay-on-Wye, Powys, Wales A small town on the English-Welsh border, Hay-on-Wye has given itself almost entirely over to the selling of secondhand books. This festival, begun in 1988, has rapidly become one of the country's leading celebrations of literature. For a 10-

day period at the end of May, the town is rife with exhibitions, literary workshops, readings, and lectures, including the *Raymond Williams Lecture* (an annual event honoring the great border novelist and critic). Many of Britain's most prestigious authors have taken part over the years—even Salman Rushdie came out of hiding two years ago to make an appearance here. Information: *Peter Florence, Festival Box Office,* Hay-on-Wye, Powys HR3 5BX, Wales (phone: 1497-821299; fax: 1497-821066).

FOR MORE INFORMATION

ENGLAND The following regional arts associations can provide a great deal of additional information about concerts, festivals, and other cultural affairs:

East Midlands Arts Board (*Mountfields House,* Forest Rd., Loughborough, Leicestershire LE11 3HU, England; phone: 1509-218292). Covers Buckinghamshire, Leicestershire, Northamptonshire, Nottinghamshire, and part of Derbyshire.

Eastern Arts Board (*Cherry Hinton Hall,* Cherry Hinton Rd., Cambridge CB1 4DW, England; phone: 1223-215355). Covers Bedfordshire, Cambridgeshire, Essex, Hertfordshire, Norfolk, and Suffolk.

Merseyside Arts, Bluecoat Chambers (12 Harter St., Manchester M1 6HY, England; phone: 161-228-3062). Covers the District of West Lancashire, Ellesmere Port, the Halton Districts of Cheshire, and the Metropolitan County of Merseyside.

North West Arts Board (12 Harter St., Manchester M1 6HY, England; phone: 161-228-3062). Covers Cheshire, Greater Manchester, the High Peak District of Derbyshire, and most of Lancashire.

Northern Arts Board (9-10 Osborne Ter., Jesmond, Newcastle upon Tyne, Tyne & Wear NE2 1NZ, England; phone: 191-281-6334). Covers Cleveland, Cumbria, Durham, the Metropolitan County of Tyne & Wear, and Northumberland.

South East Arts Board (10 Mount Ephraim, Tunbridge Wells, Kent TN4 8AS, England; phone: 1892-515210). Covers East Sussex, Kent, and Surrey.

South West Arts Board (Bradninch Pl., Gandy St., Exeter, Devon EX4 3LS, England; phone: 1392-218188). Covers Avon, Cornwall, Devon, Gloucestershire, Somerset, and part of Dorset.

Southern Arts Board (13 St. Clement St., Winchester, Hampshire SO23 9DQ, England; phone: 1962-855099). Covers Berkshire; the Districts of Bournemouth, Christchurch, and Poole; Hampshire; Isle of Wight; Oxfordshire; West Sussex; and Wiltshire.

West Midlands Arts (82 Granville St., Birmingham B1 2LH, England; phone: 121631-3121). Covers the County of Hereford and Worcester, the Metropolitan County of West Midlands, Shropshire, Staffordshire, and Warwickshire.

Yorkshire and Humberside Arts Board (21 Bond St., Dewsbury WF13 1AX, England; phone: 1924-455555). Covers North, South, and West Yorkshire.

SCOTLAND Information on the festivals and other events taking place all over Scotland is available from the *Scottish Arts Council,* 12 Manor Pl., Edinburgh EH3 7DD, Scotland (phone: 131-226-6051).

WALES Information on festivals and other arts activities in Wales is available from the following sources:

North Wales Arts Board (10 *Wellfield House,* Bangor, Gwynedd LL57 1ER, Wales; phone: 1248-353248; fax: 1248-351077). Covers Clwyd, Gwynedd, and Montgomery.

Southeast Arts Board (Victoria St., Cwmbran, Gwent NP44 3YT, Wales; phone: 1633-875075; fax: 1633-875389). Covers Gwent, Mid-Glamorgan, South Glamorgan, and part of Powys.

Welsh Arts Council (9 Museum Pl., Cardiff, South Glamorgan CF1 3NX, Wales; phone: 1222-394711; fax: 1222-221447). Covers Wales in general.

West Wales Arts (3 Red St., Carmarthen, Dyfed SA31 1QL, Wales; phone: 1267-234248; fax: 1267-233084). Covers Dyfed and West Glamorgan.

Ancient Monuments and Ruins

Britain has been inhabited for thousands of years, and scarcely a single one of the population groups who have settled here has disappeared without leaving a trace. The countryside is littered with their remains: stone walls, tombs and burial chambers, barrows and henges, hilltop forts, castles, abbeys, crosses, churches, and towers. Ruined and crumbling, they stand as reminders of a turbulent and fascinating past.

Many of these ancient sites are looked after by an independent body called the *Historic Buildings and Monuments Commission for England (and Scotland),* more briefly known as *English Heritage.* It was established in 1984 to record and preserve many of these important places. Several now ask for admission charges to cover upkeep. The organization's *Guide to English Heritage Properties* gives information on 350 historic sites throughout England and Scotland. (It is available for £2.25/about $3.40 by writing to D. Gorman, *English Heritage,* Reception, *Fortress House,* 12 Savile Row, London W1X 1AB, England; phone: 171-973-3000). The admission charges to these places can add up, so travelers should consider purchasing the Great British Heritage Pass, available at the *British Travel Bookshop* (551 Fifth Ave., Eighth Floor, New York, NY 10176; phone: 212-490-6688 or 800-448-3039). This pass allows access to all ancient monuments under the wing of the *Department of the Environment,* every *National Trust* property, and more than four dozen other sites. Another option is to join the *National Trust* through the *Royal Oak Foundation* (285 W. Broadway, Suite 400, New York, NY 10013; phone: 212-966-6565), and thus be entitled to free admission to all *National Trust* properties. Memberships start at $40 per year, and the fee (which supports the upkeep of these sites) is tax deductible.

The *Roman Baths* and the *Tower of London* are described in detail in the *Bath* and *London* chapters in THE CITIES. Listed below (in alphabetical order by location) are several other historic sites worth going out of your way to visit.

AVEBURY STONE CIRCLE, Avebury, Wiltshire, England Eighteen miles from *Stonehenge* (see below), the area explodes with prehistory. Not only is it the site of *Silbury Hill* (Europe's most massive artificial earth mound), but there is also an abundance of long barrows, standing stones, and stone circles—among them, just off the A4 between Marlborough and Calne, the *Avebury Stone Circle.* One of the world's largest, and certainly the greatest among Britain's some 900 megalithic rings, it dates several centuries before *Stonehenge,* and encloses approximately 28 acres, at the center of which are traces of two smaller stone circles. The whole is ringed by an earthen bank that stands 20 feet high in spots, and, abutting it, a ditch up to 30 feet deep.About 200,000 tons of earth were moved to create the ditch and bank; some of the heaviest stones weigh over 40 tons and would have required about 200 people to raise. It has been estimated that if 750 people worked here 10 hours a day for two months every year (after the harvest was in), the enclosure would have taken about four years to complete. And this was during the 2nd millennium BC, when the estimated population of the surrounding region was only about 1,500. Why a small society of farmers was prepared to spend the vast amounts of time and effort needed to create such a place in an age when merely subsisting was a struggle is not known; nor is the nature of the ceremonies that took place here, or the beliefs that governed them, or even the ring's exact function. As is the case with most stone circles, there is no evidence of human sacrifice. Yet Christians who sought to eliminate all records of their pagan past attempted in the 14th century to break up and bury many of the stones. Other early efforts to destroy the great stone circle never entirely succeeded. Though it probably ceased to serve its original purpose in the 1st millennium BC, the tradition of its importance persisted, and it was still in use as late as the 19th century.

The stones here are smaller than those at *Stonehenge* and natural rather than hewn; *Avebury* exceeds the more widely known circle, in the words of one 17th-century observer, "as a cathedral doeth a parish church." Today, one of the wide avenues of stones that led to the site is practically obliterated, but much of the one to the south, now West Kennet Avenue, has been restored. *Overton Hill,* a huge cemetery site once reached along this former processional route, is now accessible via A4 at West Kennet. The barrows still can be seen clearly, and the site of the *Sanctuary,* a hilltop late Neolithic religious building of some importance, is now marked with concrete blocks and pillars. For information about the region, contact the *West Country Tourist Board,* 60 St. David's Hill, Exeter, Devon EX4 4SY, England (phone: 1392-76351).

BATTLE ABBEY, Battle, Hastings, East Sussex, England Here, 6 miles northwest of the coastal resort of Hastings, between the South Downs and the Channel, William of Normandy launched the last successful invasion of Britain in September 1066 against Harold of Wessex, who had succeeded Edward the Confessor nine months earlier. Harold, a distant cousin and the son of Edward's adviser, had an equal size army of spear carriers who marched here from the north of England. William, who felt his was the stronger suit, had archers and cavalry, and where his cavalry charges failed against Harold's wall of shields, a rain of Norman arrows succeeded. Harold and his supporters perished, and a new era began for England.Built by William four years after the battle, with its High Altar poised on the spot where Harold was killed, the abbey was colonized by the Benedictine Order until the Dissolution of the Monasteries; it was then granted to a courtier of Henry VIII, who pulled down the church and remodeled the abbey. The oldest remains are the battlemented *Gatehouse,* the monks' dormitory with lancet windows, and the *Undercroft,* with its beautiful English vaults. Surviving parts of the *Abbot House* are now used as a school, but the grounds are open to the public daily, and the building is open during the school's summer holidays. Beyond the dormitory to the right, a broad walk looks out over the battlefield and across the valley to the heights of Telham and Senlac (as the invaders called Battle), where the Normans pitched camp the night before the battle. A 10-minute audiovisual presentation on the Battle of Hastings is shown continually. Information: *Battle Abbey,* Battle, near Hastings, East Sussex TN33 0AD, England (phone: 1424-773792).

GLASTONBURY ABBEY, Glastonbury, Somerset, England Romance and tradition cling to this historic site like ivy to the walls of a *Harvard* dormitory. The site itself was probably sacred in pre-Christian days; later, progressively larger churches were built as the abbey became increasingly wealthier. One of Britain's more irreverent observers once noted that the first son born of a marriage between the Abbot of Glastonbury and the Abbess of Shaftesbury would own more land than the king. Under Dunstan, who introduced the Benedictine Rule after he was chosen as abbot in the year 940, the abbey became a center of learning, producing many great ecclesiastics, and for many years, England's premier abbot was *Glastonbury*'s. The position's importance diminished only with the Dissolution of the Monasteries in 1539 under Henry VIII, when Thomas Cromwell (later executed at the *Tower of London*) ordered the 60th abbot of *Glastonbury* hanged on the Tor. Lead stripped from the roofs was melted down in fires fueled by priceless manuscripts and carved wooden screens that were antique even then.Legend has elaborately embellished the known history of the millennium before this debacle. One story reports that Christ came here as a child with Joseph of Arimathea, the wealthy trader in whose garden tomb Christ's body was placed when it was taken from the cross. Tradition also records that King Arthur was buried at *Glastonbury,* and it is widely told that toward the end of the 12th century, when Henry II ordered excavations here, monks found a stone inlaid with a leaden cross that had been inscribed: "Here lies buried the renowned King Arthur in the isle of Avalon with Guinevere his second wife." There were two skeletons, one of a gigantic man, and one of a woman with a lock of golden hair that crumbled at the touch. The bones were reburied at *Glastonbury*'s high altar, but the tomb was broken up at the Dissolution, and the bones were dispersed; the leaden cross no longer exists, but a drawing made at the beginning of the 17th century does. As to the veracity of the whole story, no one can say, but *Cadbury Castle,* believed to be Arthur's Camelot, is not far away, and roads still can be traced between the two sites.

The impressively large ruins of the abbey, surrounded by manicured lawns ringed by a stone wall, are open to visitors; they can walk down into an ancient crypt, take in a performance of a play or pageant (in summer), climb to the top of a 525-foot rise for a view over Wiltshire Downs and the Mendips all the way to Bristol (on a clear day), poke around at the *Chalice Well* where the Holy Grail is believed to be lost, and see a thorn tree grown from a cutting of the one that sprouted from Joseph of Arimathea's staff. The Glastonbury Thorn still flowers in midwinter. The abbey now belongs to the Church of England, the Tor to the *National Trust.* A visitors' center, which tells the history of the abbey from construction to destruction, recently opened. The *Abbey Barn,* which contains a *Rural Life Museum,* and the historic *George and Pilgrim's Inn,* which opened in 1475, are nearby. Information: *West Country Tourist Board,* 60 St. David's Hill, Exeter, Devon EX4 4SY, England (phone: 1392-76351), or the *Custodian, The Abbey Gatehouse,* Glastonbury, Somerset BA6 9EL, England (phone: 1458-832267).

HADRIAN'S WALL, near Newcastle upon Tyne, Tyne & Wear, England Any road west of this Northumberland shipbuilding city leads to the country of *Hadrian's Wall,* that phenomenal fortification put up by the Emperor Hadrian in AD 122 to mark the northern limit of the Roman Empire and to protect the legions from the northern barbarians. A standout even in an empire full of impressive fortifications, the wall's construction required 16,000 men to quarry and cart to the site over a million cubic yards of stone. The wall stretched over 70 miles across the neck of England, from what is now Bowness-on-Solway, on Solway Firth in the west, to Wallsend, near the mouth of the river Tyne in the east. It consisted of a broad V-shaped ditch (the vallum) and a stone barrier 15 feet high, up to nine feet thick, and punctuated at 3-mile intervals by so many guard towers, massive forts, and "milecastles" that some 5,500 cavalry and over half that many infantry were required to man it.Surprisingly, considering the battles that have taken place on and around it over the centuries, many of these fortifications still are standing. The ditch is almost entirely intact; the wall itself can be seen from the Military Road, and the remains are particularly extensive in the area between Housesteads and Greenhead (where the wall runs alongside *Northumberland National Park* for some 15 miles). There are fine views into the hills, and, at Housesteads, site of the most impressive remains of the 17 forts that once punctuated the wall, there are the remainders of the barracks, the commandant's offices, the granaries, a hospital, and a latrine. Similarly well preserved are the remains west of Housesteads at Peel Crag and Walltown Crags.

At Vindolanda, near Bardon Mill, and farther west near Greenhead, two fine museums depict life on *Hadrian's Wall* during the Roman Army's occupation. Roman artifacts are on display alongside the Roman fort at Corbridge. As an introduction to what visitors will see on the wall itself, the scale models and exhibits at *Newcastle University*'s *Museum of Antiquities* at Newcastle upon Tyne (phone: 191-222-7849) are a must. Closed Sundays. Admission charge. Information: *Northumbria Tourist Board,* Aykley Heads, Durham DH1 5UX, England (phone: 191-384-6905; fax: 191-386-0899).

VERULAMIUM, St. Albans, Hertfordshire, England Built alongside the river Ver to the west of the present St. Albans, the *municipium* of Verulamium was one of the leading cities of Britain during Roman times—its full municipal status confirmed its importance. Britain's first Christian martyr, a pagan Roman soldier named Alban who had given shelter to a Christian and was converted by him, was executed here on a small hill in the year AD 209, 500 paces from Verulamium. A church was built on the site in his honor, and in the 8th century, King Offa II rebuilt this structure to include a special repository for the martyr's bones. Adrian IV, the first English pope, enthroned in 1155, was the son of a tenant of this abbey, which became a cathedral in 1877.While the town of St. Albans grew up around the abbey and shrine, the original Roman town was left to crumble undisturbed in the fields to the southwest. But though sections of walls, gateways, and part of the basilica, grouped near St. Michael village, remained, they generally were ignored until the 1930s, when archaeologists were able to date them to the 1st through 4th centuries. The most impressive of the Verulamium discoveries was the *Roman Theatre;* with a little imagination, the present-day visitor to the ruined walls and now-grassy seating area can envision the spectacle of perhaps 6,000 Roman citizens being entertained with cockfights, pantomime, and an occasional classical drama. Beneath a modern building is preserved, in even better condition, a hypocaust—a Roman underground heating system that used channels of hot air under a mosaic floor. The on-site *Verulamium Museum* is a must; the important material it contains can make the Roman city spring vividly to life. Open daily.

Admission charge to the museum. Information: *Verulamium Museum,* St. Michael's St., St. Albans, Hertfordshire AL3 4SW, England (phone: 1727-866100).

STONEHENGE, Wiltshire, England It's been hard in recent years to appreciate this fantastic monument, surrounded as it is by gates—and all the more so when it's deluged by masses of tourists on day trips from London. *Stonehenge* has earned some criticism over the past few years, at least partly because of its inadequate tourist facilities and the fact that the famous vistas are spoiled by the wire fences. Yet the mysterious pull exerted by England's most famous prehistoric monument—two concentric circles of stones, some over 20 feet high, ringed by a ditch 300 feet in diameter—is so strong that it's hard to ignore the myths that explain its origins in terms of Merlin and magic.Certainly the fiction is only a little stranger than the fact—that its construction began in about 2750 BC, with stones that were rafted and dragged for many miles (some from as far away as southwestern Wales) and then raised with wooden levers and rollers and ropes made of leather thongs. Its function is unknown; some archaeologists—remarking about the way various stones are aligned with midsummer sunrise and midwinter moonrise—hypothesize that it was a sort of vast open-air observatory; another theory is that it was used for worship. Until recently, English druids still came here in midsummer to celebrate their antique rites. Dressed in hooded white robes and carrying mistletoe and holly and banners emblazoned with mystical signs, they sang their hymns and chanted strange runes as they marched in procession among the megaliths, awaiting the dawn. (Modern-day followers, including young and older hippies, still arrive to celebrate the dawn of the longest day.) The decision to close the road leading up to the circle of stones should help restore *Stonehenge*'s mystical tranquillity. Open daily. Admission charge. For details about the region, contact the *West Country Tourist Board* (address above).

GLENELG BROCHS, Glenelg, Highland, Scotland The palindromic name of this hamlet by the sea ranks with the lovely rocky mountain scenery as one of its more fascinating aspects. Archaeologists and lovers of antiquities, however, are most drawn by the presence of two of the best preserved of Scotland's defensive stone towers known as "brochs." Many now are little more than piles of rubble; the ones at Glenelg are not too different than they were when the Picts built them all over the country during the Iron Age, with their 30-foot-high dry stone inner and outer walls, hollow between; their stone lintels; and their center courtyard. Nearby Dun Grugaig, another broch, occupies a lovely site close by a roiling cascade and affords fine views southward toward Ben Sgriol. For local information, contact the *Portree Tourist Office,* Portree, Isle of Skye IV51 9BZ, Scotland (phone: 1478-612137).

ISLE OF IONA, Inner Hebrides, Strathclyde, Scotland The whole island, a place of pilgrimage since the Irish missionary St. Columba came here in AD 563, has become a modern shrine under the protectorship of the *National Trust;* it's popular with crofters, pilgrims, and tourists. It is still a haven of peace, and an aura of the spiritual hangs over the ruined Benedictine nunnery and the fully restored cathedral, also known as the abbey, now the home of the Iona Community. This resulted in large part from the work of St. Columba, who brought Christianity to this island, and who also made it his headquarters during the 34 years that he traveled throughout Scotland converting the nation to Christianity. It was in testament to the impact of his work in the area that almost every Scottish king through the 11th century—some 50 in all, including Duncan (who was slain by Macbeth) and several Norwegians—are buried in the abbey graveyard. St. Columba's cell and the slab of stone on which he slept have been excavated; three magnificent Celtic crosses of the hundreds that once bristled in the abbey cemetery remain. And in the almost deserted southern corner of the island, visitors can see the Bay of the Coracle where St. Columba landed, the marble quarry from which the abbey's communion table was cut, and Martyr's Bay, where the island's monks were slaughtered by the Norsemen who periodically raided and ravaged Iona for centuries. A passenger ferry crosses regularly from Fionnphort on the Isle of Mull, a 10-minute run. Information: *Scottish Tourist Board,* 23 Ravelston Ter., Edinburgh EH4 3EU, Scotland (phone: 131-332-2433).

SKARA BRAE and MAESHOWE, Mainland, Orkney, Scotland This group of about 70 islands across the Pentland Firth from John O'Groats on the Scottish mainland has a dense concentration of prehistoric monuments—an average of about three recorded sites of archaeological note per square mile; those on the large island known as Mainland are particularly notable. Maeshowe (or "greatest mound"), for instance, is Europe's best example of a Stone Age circular chambered cairn, and it has no rival on mainland Britain. Constructed as the tomb of a very important chieftain and measuring over 110 feet across and over 300 feet around, this hollow, 24-foot-high mound of rock and clay is entered through a low stone passageway, which gives access to a vaulted chamber 14 feet square flanked by a trio of burial niches walled and paved in huge single stones embellished in what some authorities believe to be the single richest collection of runic inscriptions in any one place in the world. The carvings, left by Norsemen who raided the grave in the 12th century, describe how the contents were spirited away by night, hint of a hiding place nearby, and tell of the problems that resulted when two members of a band that had sought refuge here during a storm went crazy.The kind of village where Stone Age people lived can be seen at Skara Brae, which was constructed at about the same time as Maeshowe, lived in for perhaps six centuries, and then inexplicably buried with sand for the almost four millennia that followed, until unearthed by another storm around 1850. Most of the pottery, beads, tools, and implements found on the site are now displayed in the *National Museum of Antiquities* in Edinburgh; but the site as it exists today—a group of small, squared, lane-linked huts clustered around a central courtyard in a field just about 20 feet above sea level—is impressive enough. The flagstone blocks with which the structures were built, the slate shale with which they were paved, the shelves and built-in boxes and cubbyholes, stone beds, drains, and other appurtenances are still remarkably well preserved.

Other major sites are nearby: the four remaining *Standing Stones of Stenness,* a henge dating from about 2300 BC; the great *Ring of Brodgar,* where more than two dozen stones can be seen inside a ditch on a two-and-a-half-acre site; the *Broch of Gurness,* Orkney Mainland's best representation of this type of structure, situated amid a group of other stone buildings of assorted ages; the *Onstan Chambered Cairn,* dated about 2500 BC; and many more. Not all archaeological sites can be seen at all times, and some are relatively inaccessible, so it's wise to plan a visit well before arriving. Information: *Orkney Tourist Board,* 6 Broad St., Kirkwall, Orkney Islands KW15 1DH, Scotland (phone: 1856-872856).

MELROSE ABBEY, Melrose, Borders, Scotland "If thou would see fair Melrose aright/Go visit it by the pale moonlight," wrote Sir Walter Scott in his *Lay of the Last Minstrel* about the ruins here. Among the finest and best preserved in Scotland, the abbey ruins move present-day visitors just as they did that celebrated 19th-century Scottish poet, who spent the last two decades of his life at nearby Abbotsford in a turreted, baronial sort of manse that is open for tours. *Melrose Abbey,* one of four Border abbeys founded for a group of Cistercian monks by David I in 1136 just after the return of Roman Christianity to Scotland, was destroyed during English raids in 1322, restored by Robert the Bruce in 1326, battered again in 1385, and ultimately destroyed in invasions in 1543 and 1544—except for the few sections that stand today in mute testimony to its past beauty. The reddish stonework in parts of the nave is particularly lovely: the large five-light window in the south transept, the elaborately carved foliage embellishing the capitals nearby, the flying buttresses, and the porcine gargoyle playing bagpipes on the roof. According to tradition, the heart of Robert the Bruce—which Sir James Douglas was taking to the Holy Land when he was killed—was buried under the east window, and Tom Purdie, the forester for Scott's estate, and Peter Matheson, the writer's coachman, are interred in the abbey cemetery.

The ruins of the abbey's cloister are remarkably preserved—far better than those at the ruins of the remaining pair of David I's Border abbeys, *Kelso* and *Jedburgh.* Both of these are also worth visiting; at *Jedburgh,* the house where Queen Mary stayed for a short while can be toured, as can the imposing, 19th-century museum devoted to the penal system of the period (phone: 1835-863254). Open daily. Admission charge to the museum at *Jedburgh.* Information: *Melrose Tourist Information Center, Abbey House,* Abbey St., Melrose, Roxburghshire TD6 9LG, Scotland (phone: 1896-822555); or call the abbey itself (phone: 1896-822562).

SHETLAND ISLANDS, Scotland Five centuries of Scottish culture have painted little more than a veneer over the deeply rooted Scandinavian character of these hundred-odd islands, which were Danish until they were given away as a dowry to a 15th-century Scottish earl. Their names still read like the pages of a fantasy by Tolkien—Foula, Mousa, Muckle Roe, Noss, and Papa Stour—and their linguistic allegiances are still Nordic. Of a large number of ancient monuments in the Shetlands, perhaps the most important is *Jarlshof,* occupied for some 3,000 years and now layered with the remains of three prehistoric civilizations that lay buried until a ferocious storm unearthed the site in 1905. Now that it has been finely excavated, visitors can view remains in varying states of preservation: an oval hut dating from the Stone and Early Bronze Age, remains of the larger circular huts and earthen houses from the Early Iron Age, stone wheelhouses from the 2nd and 3rd centuries, long houses and a medieval farm complex constructed by two successive groups of Vikings, and a castle built by unpopular 16th-century Stuart earls and sacked a century later. (Sir Walter Scott set his novel *The Pirate* here, and coined its name, Jarlshof.) The magnificently preserved red sandstone Iron Age broch on the grassy, seal-haunted island of Mousa is another must, a striking reminder that once every headland on the northern isles was guarded by such an edifice. Standing 43 feet high, this purest surviving example of broch architecture thickens at the bottom to withstand attacks, incorporates a circular courtyard, and has hollow walls pierced by stairways that bind the outer and inner shells together. In addition, there are some 134 other ruins officially classified as being of archaeological importance on the islands, which are accessible by plane and ferry. Information: *Shetland Tourist Organisation,* Market Cross, Lerwick, Shetland ZE1 0LU, Scotland (phone: 1595-3434).

CAERNARFON CASTLE, Gwynedd, Wales Though little remains of this castle except its walls, it is easy to imagine the grandeur that Edward I planned when he began construction almost 600 years ago. With the many turrets and towers to explore, vaulted chambers to poke around in, walls and lawns to walk upon, a museum to visit, and a film on the castle's history to view, this is understandably a popular destination in Wales. (For more details, see *Quintessential Great Britain.*) Information about the area is available from the *Northern Regional Office, Wales Tourist Board,* 77 Conway Rd., Colwyn Bay, Clwyd LL29 7LN, Wales (phone: 1492-531731).

CONWY CASTLE, Conwy, Gwynedd, Wales Counted among Europe's greatest fortresses, this magnificent piece of medieval architecture built by Edward I must have been all the more striking in its early years when its then-whitewashed walls gleamed brightly from afar. But even now the structure impresses. Built mainly between 1283 and 1287 after designs by the king's castle engineer, James of St. George, it required the work of some 1,500 men and the expenditure of some £15,000 to complete it. The eight towers, each with walls 15 feet thick, rise to a height of 70 feet; they seem perpendicular to the ground, but instead taper gradually toward the top. The *Northwest Tower* has a fine view over the river, and the *Prison Tower* has a concealed dungeon as fearsomely dark and close as the imposing 38-by-125-foot *Great Hall* just above is spacious and airy, with its grand north- and east-facing windows. In the part of the castle known as the *Inner Bailey,* which lies to the east of the *Great Hall,* you can view the elegantly detailed *Queen Eleanor's Chapel,* the best-preserved part of the structure; the name is merely traditional, because the castle wasn't finished during her lifetime. Another exhibit, *Chapels in Castles,* features photographs, models, and panels of castle chapels of Britain since Edward I.The most important battle fought within the castle's walls took place in 1294, during a rebellion led by Prince Madog ap Llywelyn. Edward I took refuge here and, when trapped without proper food and water by the rising tide of the river, was almost beaten. The castle's subsequent history was marked by a visit of Richard II at the end of the 14th century (he was captured by the Duke of Northumberland—and Archbishop Arundel—for Henry Bolingbroke, later Henry IV); by occupation by Royalist forces during the 17th century; and by plundering, dismantling, and damage during the 19th century. A more tranquil attraction is the *Teapot Museum* located in one of the castle's towers. More than 500 teapots from 1740 to the present are on display, including many rare and unusual types, as well as a self-pouring teapot. Open daily. Admission charge. 25 Castle St. (phone: 1492-592358, castle; 1492-593429, museum). Information: *Northern Regional Office, Wales Tourist Board* (address above).

TINTERN ABBEY, Tintern, Gwent, Wales On the Welsh side of the border 5 miles north of Chepstow, this most atmospheric and impressive of the country's ruined abbeys stands in the sheltered lee of wooded hills of a bend in the river Wye. The beauty and peace of the spot, recorded in poetry by Wordsworth and in watercolors by Turner, is overwhelming. The abbey was founded in the 12th century and reached the height of its prosperity in the next 200 years; most of the ruins visible today, including the chapter house, kitchen, refectory, and sacristy, belong to this period. Then, in 1349, the Black Death wiped out most of the monks and lay brothers. The walls of the church still stand, along with four great arches in its center; the windows are huge and exquisitely proportioned, particularly the fine traceried rose window, which takes up most of the supporting east wall and frames the rugged scenery outside. Open daily. Admission charge. Information: *South Wales Regional Office,* Ty Croeso, 6 Gloucester Pl., Swansea, West Glamorgan SA1 1TY, Wales (phone: 1792-468321).

For the Body

Great Golf

True golf devotees contend that many of the finest—and most traditional—golf courses in the world are found in Britain. This is hardly surprising since the game was born on the sandy land along its coasts. It's hard to believe that barely a century ago golf was virtually unknown anywhere outside Scotland, though the Scots proved great apostles, spreading the word from Perth (where the first recognizable six-hole course is thought to have been constructed on the North Inch), St. Andrews, Prestwick, and Dornoch.

These are the icons of a game that has gripped the attention of an entire planet. And even now, the courses found in Scotland and England provide a very different sense of the game than can be acquired anywhere else. But it's more than history that lures generations of modern golfers to the game's breeding grounds. The challenge remains as vital as ever, and the chance to pit one's own skill against the achievements of golf's greatest historic figures is nearly irresistible. Not to play these courses at least once in a lifetime is not to know the real horizons of the game.

The following courses are described in their respective chapters in THE CITIES: *The Honourable Company of Edinburgh Golfers* (familiarly known as *Muirfield*) in Gullane (near Edinburgh); *Sunningdale* and *Wentworth* (both near London); *Gleneagles* (in Auchterarder, near Perth); and *Fulford* (in York). Listed below, in alphabetical order by location, are the other outstanding golfing venues in Great Britain's countryside. Be sure to bring a copy of your handicap certificate and a letter of introduction from your golf club.

ALDEBURGH, Aldeburgh, Suffolk, England Now 1½ miles inland, this immensely popular course, laid out by persons unknown, was undoubtedly once a part of the shore, and for nearly a century the name Aldeburgh has been synonymous with the classic sandy links—sea turf covered by the first markers of heathland, clumps of trees, and bright gorse. The first of *Aldeburgh*'s short holes features a kidney-shape green set right behind a great sleepered bunker that extends to the right. The flag can be set at the back of the green close to still more bunkers. And while the 4th's 140-yard length may not intimidate, finding the green certainly will. Information: *Aldeburgh Golf Course,* Aldeburgh, Suffolk IP15 5PE, England (phone: 1728-452890).

GANTON GOLF CLUB, Ganton, North Yorkshire, England The east coast of England is not well known for its golfing venues, but this Yorkshire course is one of Britain's finest inland layouts. The holes are positioned on open heathland. The prime hazards here are bunkers and gorse, especially those placed alongside and amid fairway landing areas. Straight hitting is a must. Perhaps the greatest lure is the variety of challenge that requires accurate play and consummate concentration. Information: *Ganton Golf Club,* Ganton, North Yorkshire YO12 4PA, England (phone: 1944-710329).

HUNSTANTON GOLF COURSE, Hunstanton, Norfolk, England The town of Hunstanton has two distinctions: First, it is the only east coast resort that faces west (because it is on the cusp of Norfolk as it dips into the Wash); second, it is home to the *Hunstanton* golf course. Shaped by George Fernie in 1891 along the shore north of town, this layout is sure to challenge with its formidable set of bunkers. Information: *Hunstanton Golf Course,* Hunstanton, Norfolk PE36 6JQ, England (phone: 1485-532811).

ROYAL LYTHAM & ST. ANNE'S GOLF CLUB, Lytham St. Anne's, Lancashire, England Possessed of little visual splendor and in an essentially urban setting, this course remains one of the most difficult of all the tracks in Britain, and has maintained a special place on the *British Open* championship rota. Don't be deceived by the apparent tranquillity; the course is a test of golf that's among the finest in Britain, and nerve and subtlety are both required. A special package including accommodations, golf, breakfast, dinner, and Value Added Tax (VAT) is available for male guests only (though women can play at the club, they can't stay at the house where the package accommodations are offered); advance reservations are required. Information: *Royal Lytham & St. Anne's Golf Club,* Links Gate, Lytham St. Anne's, Lancashire FY8 3LQ, England (phone: 1253-724206).

ROYAL ST. GEORGE'S GOLF CLUB, Sandwich, Kent, England This corner of Kent is rich in history, and no course has a more constant involvement with the evolution of English championship golf. Often called "Sandwich," it was the site of the first official *Walker Cup* matches ever held in England. It was also the scene of the first ever American victory in the *British Amateur* championship and in the *British Open* (by Walter Hagen). It was here that Henry Cotton ended American postwar domination of the *Open* by winning the first of his three titles. And it was here in 1949 that the *Open* saw the memorable tie between Henry Bradshaw and the South African Bobby Locke (who won the 36-hole playoff). This is a place where golf history buffs will want to make their mark. Those interested in completing a tour of Kent's triumvirate of *Open* championship courses (or those who cannot be accommodated at the *Royal St. George's*) should try their skills at two other fine layouts nestling cheek by jowl with it on the county's eastern shore, the *Royal Cinque Ports* and the beautiful *Prince's.* Information: *Royal St. George's Golf Club,* Sandwich, Kent CT13 9PB, England (phone: 1304-613090); *Royal Cinque Ports Golf Club,* Golf Rd., Deal, Kent CT14 6RF, England (phone: 1304-374007); and *Prince's Golf Club,* Sandwich Bay, Sandwich, Kent CT13 9QB, England (phone: 1304-611118).

ROYAL BIRKDALE GOLF CLUB, Southport, Merseyside, England This Lancashire coast setting in a stunning expanse of dunes is one of the most popular and demanding championship courses in the country. It has hosted many international competitions, most recently the 1991 *British Open.* In addition, *Formby* and *Hillside,* two other notable layouts, are within 5 miles of here. Information: *Royal Birkdale Golf Club,* Waterloo Rd., Southport, Merseyside PR8 2LX, England (phone: 17045-567920).

CARNOUSTIE, Carnoustie, Tayside, Scotland Just 5 miles from St. Andrews as the crow flies (or 25 miles by road) is this site of five *British Open* tournaments. If the *Championship* course (the best of the trio of tracks here) appears to be least impressive of the championship Scottish courses at first glance, its true value is easily appreciated in a single round. It encompasses the very essence of what's best about playing golf in Scotland, and the back nine in particular—with the famous 14th hole, called "Spectacles" because of two yawning twin bunkers in mid-fairway—as well as the three backbreaking finishing holes leave memories (not necessarily pleasant) that do not soon fade. Information: *Carnoustie Golf Links,* Links Parade, Carnoustie, Tayside DD7 7JE, Scotland (phone: 12418-53789 for reservations).

ROYAL DORNOCH, Dornoch, Sutherland, Scotland No course in the world offers more wild beauty than this northernmost of the globe's great golf layouts. The course sweeps in a great curve along the shores of the Dornoch Firth, a site of splendid isolation that seldom fails to inspire a feeling of singular elation; many players echo the sentiments of Tom Watson, who remarked that the three rounds he played during one 24-hour visit were more fun than any other golfing experience of his life. Information: *Royal Dornoch Golf Club,* Dornoch, Sutherland IV25 3LW, Scotland (phone: 1862-810219).

THE OLD COURSE, St. Andrews, Fife, Scotland Dating at least from the 15th but more likely from the late 14th century, this is the sport's greatest magnet, drawing all of the world's golfers, and its aura is only slightly diminished by the bathers and strollers who frequently cross the first and 18th fairways of the *Old Course*—it's the shortest route to the beach. Once on the course, golfers soon become aware of its extreme difficulty and subtle layout, which was fashioned by nature, with the help of the sheep and rabbits who created bunker locations when burrowing underground to escape the offshore winds that blow year-round. There are four other courses on the same site—the *Balgove, Eden, Jubilee,* and *New* (which was *opened* in 1896). However, the real attraction for the dedicated golfer is the *Old* (the site of no less than two dozen *British Opens*—including this year's tournament—and now the permanent home of the *Dunhill Nations Cup* held each October). Make plans carefully to be here on the right day (the *Old Course* is closed Sundays), and confirm tee-off times well in advance—a year in advance is not too early. The *Strathtyrum,* a sixth (less challenging) course, a nine-hole course, and a driving range make the site more accessible to players at all skill levels. (*Note:* Women are not allowed to play on the *Old Course.*) Information: *Links Management Committee,* Golf Pl., St. Andrews, Fife KY16 9JA, Scotland (phone: 1334-75757).

ROYAL TROON, Troon, Ayrshire, Scotland Laid out along the beach, with the outgoing nine heading virtually straight down the strand and the closing nine paralleling it only a few yards inland, this course offers stunning views of the Firth of Clyde, the Isle of Arran, and the flaming sunsets. There's only one problem: it's also located directly below the flight path into *Prestwick Airport,* so it sometimes seems as though players are about to be sucked up into the jet wash. With its classic *Open* layout, the course is one of the few important private clubs in Scotland open to visitors (in limited numbers). Playing privileges are offered Mondays, Tuesdays, and Thursdays only to members of US clubs who can produce a letter of introduction and a respectable handicap certificate (advance arrangement required). The day-ticket greens fee also covers a round of play on the *Portland,* which some have pronounced even tougher than the *Old Course* (see above). Plan to book well in advance. Information: *Royal Troon Golf Club,* Craigend Rd., Troon, Ayrshire KA10 6EP, Scotland (phone: 1292-311555).

TURNBERRY HOTEL GOLF COURSES, Turnberry, Strathclyde, Scotland The two courses here, the *Ailsa* and the *Arran,* are quite close in quality, but it's the *Ailsa* that has hosted several *British Opens*—in 1977, 1986, and most recently in 1994. A clubhouse that contains a unique collection of golf artifacts and curios opened two years ago. The wind blows in from the sea, and it sometimes takes sheer courage just to stand on the craggy tees and hit into the teeth of what may seem like a major gale. Information: *Turnberry Hotel Golf Courses,* Ayrshire KA26 9LT, Scotland (phone: 1655-31000; 212-838-3110 in New York City; 800-223-6800 elsewhere in the US).

ST. PIERRE GOLF AND COUNTRY CLUB, Chepstow, Gwent, Wales Two fine 18-hole courses are here. The beautiful, *Old* parkland course is laid out within the tree-studded bounds of an old deer preserve, with an 11-acre lake. Its high quality has made it the chosen venue for several tournaments, including the *Dunlop Masters Tournament,* the *Curtis Cup,* the *Silk Cut Masters,* and the *Epson Grand Prix of Europe.* The opening holes are played between daunting ranks of chestnuts, which seem to move, according to many visitors, specifically to block their shots. The *Mathern* course is on a pleasant meadowland with a meandering stream, which comes into play on most of the holes and provides a good challenge. The club is on the A48, the main Chepstow-to-Newport road. Information: *St. Pierre Hotel Golf and Country Club, St. Pierre Park*, Chepstow, Gwent NP6 6YA, Wales (phone: 1291-625261; fax: 1291-629975).

ROMAN ROAD GOLF COURSE, Celtic Manor, Newport, Gwent, Wales Set to open this summer, this course is the first Robert Trent Jones Sr.–designed venue in the entire United Kingdom. It is on the grounds of the *Celtic Manor* hotel, a Victorian manor house on 300 acres of woodland just outside Newport, and the design of the 7,100-yard, par 70 course takes full advantage of the impressive scenery of the surrounding countryside. Many of the holes are laid onto rolling terrain that makes them especially difficult. Another shorter, easier course, also designed by Jones, is scheduled to open on the hotel grounds at the end of the year. There's also a large clubhouse. The manager, Jim Mackenzie, formerly ran the *Wentworth* course in Surrey; the touring professional is Ian Woosnam. Information: *Celtic Manor,* Coldra Woods, Newport, Gwent NP6 2YA, Wales (phone: 1633-413000; fax: 1633-412910).

ROYAL PORTHCAWL, Porthcawl, Mid Glamorgan, Wales Not a links course in the strictest sense, though there are occasional sand hills. The main hazards, however, are gorse, hummocks, heather, and deep bunkers. The good news is that the lay of the land permits players to look across Bristol Channel to the long, dark line of the Somerset coast—and see the sea from any tee or green. Founded in 1891, the course combines links and heathland play, and there's a particularly high premium on a golfer's ability to place shots accurately against often furious natural elements. Just finding the fairway can be a humbling experience. Information: *Royal Porthcawl Golf Club,* Rest Bay, Porthcawl, Mid Glamorgan CF36 3UW, Wales (phone: 1656-771627).

FOR THE ADVENTUROUS

A golfing expedition to the Outer Hebrides, the rugged island chain about 50 miles northwest of mainland Scotland, is bound to be a terrific tee-time experience. No manicured fairways here—and if the roaring Atlantic gales don't faze you, check out the wandering sheep on the nine-hole *Askernish* course on the island of South Uist. Or pit yourself against the notorious par 5, 547-yard 11th hole called "Dardanelles," considered one of the toughest holes in Europe and located at *Stornoway Golf Club* on Lewis, the largest and most northerly of the islands. Rare is the greens fee or starting time, and from March through October the sun is out until midnight, but Sunday golf is strictly prohibited. Information: *Western Isles Tourist Board,* 4 South Beach St., Stornoway PA87 2XY, Scotland (phone: 1851-703088).

Tennis

Britain practically closes down in late June and early July, the fortnight of the *All England Lawn Tennis Championships* (more colloquially known as *Wimbledon*). Ticket scalpers do a brisk trade outside the gate (and even advertise in the personal columns of the newspapers), and those who aren't lucky enough to secure tickets stay home and watch the competition on television (for more information, see *London* in THE CITIES).

This passion has definitely had its effect on the number of participants in the sport. Although tennis still has a long way to go before it becomes the national mania in Britain that it is in the US, there are now hundreds of thousands of players, and courts are seldom hard to find. Tennis buffs should be sure to pack their racquets and tennis whites, since a tennis match is a fine, rapid way to get off the standard tourist circuit and into local upper middle class life. In these circles, playing well is important—but focusing on victory at all costs isn't the style. If you pass muster, you may end the match with at least an invitation to tea.

Municipal courts abound in Britain; tourist literature can provide their locations in the towns you'll be visiting. In addition, many of the more luxurious hotels have their own courts. The best source of information, including lists of affiliated private tennis clubs where visiting players may be able to get a game, is the *Lawn Tennis Association* (*Queens Club,* West Kensington, London W14 9EG, England (phone: 171-385-4233).

Those who want to spend more than just a casual hour a day on the courts may want to plan their trip around stops at a handful of resorts, tennis schools, and other spots at which the game is given more than just a passing nod. The following establishments are listed alphabetically by location.

BEACONSFIELD SCHOOL OF LAWN TENNIS, Beaconsfield, Buckinghamshire, England Established 30 years ago (and pronounced *Beckons*-field), this school is open year-round and offers individual and group courses at modest cost. Principal Godwin Johnson does not push a single style but works to encourage the skills of each individual player, whether beginner or pro. Lodging is in hotels or with local families; the setting is the rolling, wooded Chiltern Hills, only 20 minutes from *Heathrow* and 40 minutes by train or car from central London. Information: *Beaconsfield School of Lawn Tennis,* The Oval, Wilton Crescent, Beaconsfield, Buckinghamshire HP9 2BY, England (phone: 1494-674744).

HOLBROOK HOUSE, Holbrook, Wincanton, Somerset, England Here is your chance to see how it feels to play on grass: This family-run hotel with 18 rooms and a restaurant has a good grass court in addition to its all-weather court. Lodgings are in a former country house dating from 1530 that was extensively rebuilt in 1846. No instruction is available. Information: *Holbrook House,* Holbrook, Wincanton, Somerset BA9 8BS, England (phone: 1963-32377).

WINDMILL HILL PLACE TENNIS RESORT, Windmill Hill, East Sussex, England Modeled after *Windmill House,* a fine Georgian mansion deep in the East Sussex countryside, this elegant center has been instructing all levels of players—from beginners to professionals—since 1976. Its eight grass courts are popular with *Wimbledon* players for pre-championship practice. There also are five synthetic grass, two French clay, and four indoor courts. Accommodations are available in 40 well-appointed rooms, and there is a good restaurant. If you want to take a break from tennis, there are attractive gardens, lakes, an outdoor heated pool, and a nine-hole golf course. Information: *Windmill Hill Place Tennis Resort,* Windmill Hill, East Sussex BN27 4RZ (phone: 1323-832552).

Horsing Around

Britain is among the world's most horse-mad nations—and has been practically ever since the Romans, and later the Normans, brought horses to Britain many centuries ago. There were races as early as the 12th century at London's *Smithfield Market.* Period romances speak of races between knights and noblemen. Later, Henry VIII and James I kept stables (the latter's at *Newmarket*), and from James II on down, English monarchs have been horse fanciers. Elizabeth II, who keeps a stable and rides regularly, can be at her most animated when urging on her horse. Princess Anne, a former European champion in the demanding game of three-day eventing, used to compete in shows all over the country with her ex-husband, Captain Mark Phillips, who also conducts clinics at the *Gleneagles* hotel's equestrian center, which he helped plan.

For travelers, the ubiquity of the mania for horses means that equestrians will never want for a common ground for conversation in village pubs and that horse-oriented vacations abound.

MEETS, SHOWS, AND RACES

You'll be meeting Britons on their favorite turf when you take in one of the dozen international shows and hundreds of national events held in Britain every year. Britain alone has some 59 racecourses—15 devoted solely to flat racing (whose season runs from the third week in March to the first week in November) and 24 solely to *National Hunt* racing (or steeplechasing, whose season runs year-round except for June and most of July), and the rest with facilities for both. Major courses include *Royal Ascot,* near Windsor in Berkshire (see below); *Doncaster's Town Moor* course, in South Yorkshire (the successor to two other courses that flourished in the area as early as 1595), home of the *Racing Post Trophy,* a mile-long contest for two-year-olds, and of the *St. Leger Stakes,* a September race for three-year-old colts and fillies and the last classic of the flat racing season and the third in Britain's *Triple Crown; Epsom,* in Surrey (see below); the lovely *Goodwood,* in Sussex in the *Duke of Richmond's Park,* especially noted for the three-day *Glorious Goodwood* meeting, held in late July; *Newmarket,* the celebrated old course in Cambridgeshire; and *Sandown Park,* founded in 1875, now the home of the *Eclipse Stakes,* a 1¼-miler run every July since 1886 and named to honor the 18th-century nonpareil from whom all of the world's thoroughbred race horses are said to be descended. The *Triple Crown* of the British racing season goes to the horse that wins *Newmarket's Two Thousand Guineas,* the *Epsom Derby,* and Doncaster's *St. Leger.*

Newmarket, the center of flat-track racing in England and the focal point of British training, is also the home of the *National Horseracing Museum,* which traces racing's development in England and shows videos of classic races (for more information, see *Cambridge* in THE CITIES). There are a number of stud farms in the area, including the *National Stud* (phone: 1638-663464), open to the public on special days during August. *Tattersalls,* the celebrated English horse auctioneers founded in London in 1766, conducts a number of sales throughout the year, the most important being the two *Yearling Sales* held in the fall.

Tracks are mostly grass, so meetings last only four or five days at a stretch (just three days in winter) and are spaced far enough apart to give the turf time to recover; the nationwide schedule is arranged so that there's always something going on in each region of the country. For dates and locations of upcoming weeks' "fixtures" (as racing events are called here), consult listings in newspapers such as the *Sporting Life* and the *Racing Post.* Following is a list of major events; a season-long fixtures calendar, which includes smaller events such as the *Great Yarmouth Races* in July, is available from the *Racecourse Association Ltd.* (Winkfield Rd., Ascot, Berkshire SL5 7HX, England; phone: 1344-25912).

For details on the *Grand National,* see *Liverpool* in THE CITIES; the following race meetings are also worth noting. They are listed alphabetically by location.

ROYAL ASCOT, Ascot, Berkshire, England The June meeting at this racecourse on the southern edge of *Windsor Great Park,* 25 miles west of London, has enjoyed royal patronage ever since Queen Anne drove over to watch the first races on the *Ascot Common* in 1711—and it is still considered a high point of the London social season. Ascot is where Eliza Doolittle (of George Bernard Shaw's *Pygmalion* and Lerner and Loewe's *My Fair Lady*) first encountered high society; things are as oh-so-social even today. In the Royal Enclosure—the most exclusive part of the seating area—men wear top hats and morning coats, and women, their smartest dresses and hats. The sovereign and members of the royal family drive in state carriages from *Windsor Castle* on each day of the four-day meeting. The key race in the meeting is the *Ascot Gold Cup*—a 2½-mile race that ranks as one of the most important of Britain's flat racing season. *The King George VI and the Queen Elizabeth Diamond Stakes,* a 1½-miler first run in 1951, takes place each July. Information: *Ascot Racecourse,* Ascot, Berkshire SL5 7JN, England (phone: 1344-22211).

BADMINTON HORSE TRIALS, Badminton, Avon, England Three-day eventing (which is a bit of a misnomer, since the competition actually is spread out over four days) is one of the toughest tests that horse and rider can face; these trials, held annually since 1949 at the Duke of Beaufort's lovely green estate in Badminton, are so important that they're regularly televised—in prime time: Certainly, the trials are the world's longest running and most famous.

Competitors come from all over the world, and over 250,000 spectators attend. The first two days are devoted to dressage and the fourth to the jumping test, both in the main arena. But the main feature is the speed and endurance test, which takes place on Saturday, the third day. The cross-country section takes riders over about 30 terrifying obstacles of every description (which are fixed so they can't be knocked down); and though there are always several new fences to test competitors' courage, hardy annuals like the famous Jump into the Lake and the Quarry reappear frequently in different guises. While competitors are risking their necks, spectators can watch on closed-circuit television sets in several marquees or follow the event's progress, fortified by visits to the several large refreshment tents around the course. It's also fun to see the *Deer Park,* full of red and fallow deer, and to browse through the many shops and exhibits that go up for the duration in *Badminton Park.* The competition takes place in the first half of May. Ticket application forms are available in early January. Information: *Badminton Horse Trials Office,* Badminton, Avon GL9 1DF, England (phone: 1454-218375).

EVER READY DERBY STAKES, Epsom, Surrey, England The race after which the *Kentucky Derby* was named, itself named for one of the men who founded it in 1780, the sporting 12th Earl of Derby, is a carnival as much as a 1½-mile speed trial for three-year-old colts and fillies. All kinds of people turn up: ancient Gypsy families come to settle debts and arrange marriages; the top-hatted and tail-coated with their Rolls-Royces and picnic hampers; families with children; cockneys from the East End just out for a good time; fortune-tellers; gaudy tipsters predicting the winners; and bookies with bulging Gladstones stuffed with fivers quoting the odds, their helpers peering through binoculars to the other side of the course, where white-gloved ticktack men are using age-old hand movements to signal how the money is going. The spectacle of this national festivity—the event that Benjamin Disraeli himself called the Blue Riband of the Turf—has hardly changed a bit since the 18th-century English painter George Stubbs memorialized it on canvas. Ever since Sir Charles Bunbury's horse Diomed won the first race in 1780, the *Derby Stakes* has had a history punctuated with colorful characters, among them Jem Robinson, who in the early 19th century wagered a thousand pounds that, within a single week, he would win the *Oaks* and the *Derby* (the latter for a seventh time) *and* marry (he won the bet); and Emily Davison, a suffragette who died in 1913 after hurling herself under the hooves of King George V's Anmer. The meeting usually takes place during the first week in June; the *Ever Ready Derby* is staged on a Wednesday, and the *Gold Seal Oaks*—Epsom's other major contest, a 1½-miler for fillies which is named after the Earl of Derby's shooting box—three days later. Buy a grandstand ticket if you must, but it's more fun to watch the goings-on from the hill in the middle of the course. Tickets are available from *Keith Prowse & Co.* (234 W. 44th St., Suite 1000, New York,

NY 10036; phone: 800-669-8687). Information: *United Racecourses, Ltd.*, Racecourse Paddock, Epsom, Surrey KT18 5NJ, England (phone: 1372-463072).

ROYAL INTERNATIONAL HORSE SHOW, Hickstead, West Sussex, England Even those who sit in the stands at this course 10 miles north of Brighton and refer to the dressage display as "those circus horses who dance" find that its magic wins their hearts in a twinkling. This immensely popular June annual was first held in 1907; the "Royal" was added to its name in 1911. Among the most prestigious shows in the international equestrian calendar, it features dressage, Arabians, hackney ponies in single harness, pairs of ponies, weight-carrying cobs, heavy horse turnouts, and children's ponies ridden sidesaddle, along with lightweight, middleweight, and heavyweight hunters, small and large hacks, ladies' hacks, and costers' turnouts. Jumping competitions keep spectators on the edge of their seats from start to finish: Sometimes the outcome is in doubt right up until the last animal has taken the last fence. Information: *Royal International Horse Show, All England Jumping Course,* Hickstead, West Sussex RH17 5NU, England (phone: 1273-834315).

SILK CUT DERBY, Hickstead, West Sussex, England This August event at the *All England Jumping Course* ranks as the nation's premier show-jumping event. The fact that only 24 horses have jumped clear rounds on the course since 1961 suggests its difficulty; the Derby Bank, one of several permanent obstacles in the *International Arena* here, is famous among horse folk. Novice jumping, showing classes, and driving take place in other arenas. The whole production is fast and easily understood. Information: *The Secretary, All England Jumping Course,* Hickstead, West Sussex RH17 5NU, England (phone: 1273-834315).

BURGHLEY HORSE TRIALS, near Stamford, Lincolnshire, England The *Burghley Remy Martin* three-day horse trials take place on the grounds of the famous Elizabethan mansion *Burghley* (pronounced *Bur*-lee) *House* at the beginning of September, and attract the top international riders. The cross-country phase includes many new fences, plus old favorites such as Capability's Cutting (named after the celebrated 18th-century landscape architect Lancelot "Capability" Brown, who created the grounds of *Burghley Park* itself). Information: *Burghley Horse Trials,* Stamford, Lincolnshire, PE9 2LH, England (phone: 1780-52131; fax: 1780-66868).

RIDING HOLIDAYS AND PONY TREKKING

The British flock to horse holidays with exactly the same enthusiasm that Americans flock to dude ranches—except that they are more likely to wear jodhpurs than jeans, swing into saddles without horns as well as with, and do their riding at a stable that doesn't always have anything more than a casual arrangement with their lodging place. Topnotch horses, delightful scenery, and the chance to join the natives in one of their favorite pastimes are the main attractions for foreign visitors.

When you do begin to look into an equestrian holiday, you may at first find the lingo bewildering. The term *riding holiday,* for instance, refers not to just any vacation spent on horseback, but specifically to one where you'll trot, canter, occasionally even take small jumps, and get basic instruction, whether from a full-fledged instructor accredited by the *British Horse Society* (*BHS*), from a *British Horse Society*–designated assistant instructor (*BHSAI*), or, in smaller establishments, from horse folk who instruct as a summer job. The organizations that sponsor such activities, called "riding holiday centres," also may arrange for guests to compete in local shows and contests—great fun—where they may find themselves engaging in horse talk with anyone from a local farmer to the squire's lady. Some riding holiday centers—those termed "residential"—have accommodations; some arrange for lodging in nearby guesthouses, old coaching inns, quaint hotels, or with local families. Rank beginners and advanced equestrians alike can sign up for riding holidays, which are available year-round.

Pony trekking, on the other hand, involves a day-long ride on the back of a sturdy native pony or cob (a stocky, short-legged horse); participants travel mainly at a walk—partly because most are inexperienced riders, partly because the riding is on narrow trails across moors, through dense forests, and in steep mountain country mainly in Scotland, the *Lake District,* the north of England's Dales, and sections of Wales. Absolute novices may be given some instruction, but the riding will ordinarily be at a relatively elementary level. The season generally runs from mid-April until late September or early October. Note that *Ponies UK,* a nonprofit organization that inspects both trekking and riding holiday centers in Britain, suggests that children under 12 will get tired and bored while pony trekking and are generally better off at a riding holiday center that specializes in youngsters. The real joy of pony trekking is the scenery en route—forests, fields, and meadows full of ferns or bracken, or spotted here and there with a clump of rosy heather or purplish foxglove and thistle—that may not otherwise be accessible to any but the most intrepid walkers.

The following, listed in alphabetical order by location, include some of the best British centers offering riding holidays and pony trekking. To get other ideas, send a self-addressed, stamped envelope to *Ponies UK* (*Ascot Racecourse,* Ascot, Berkshire SL5 7JN, England; phone: 1487-830278); or send £7.95 (about $12) to the *British Horse Society* (*British Equestrian Centre,* Stoneleigh, Kenilworth, Warwickshire CV8 2LR, England; phone: 1203-696697) to get a list of over 680 inspected centers.

TRIPLE BAR RIDING CENTRE, Broadmoor, Dorking, England This center offers by-the-hour or day-long riding on prize Arabians over the adjacent 6,000 acres of *National Trust* land; riding holidays, including accommodations, also can be arranged. Information: *Triple Bar Riding Centre, Home Farm Cottage,* Broadmoor, Abinger Common, Dorking RH5 6JY, England (phone: 1306-730959).

GOOSEHAM BARTON STABLES, near Bude, Cornwall, England There's lovely riding through quiet, scenic countryside and woods, with a sandy beach nearby. Three cottages with kitchens are available. The name derives from one Sir William de Gooseham, who is said to have owned the farmhouse around 1310. A member of the *British Horse Society* (*BHS*). Information: *Gooseham Barton Stables,* Gooseham, Morwenstow, Cornwall EX23 9PG, England (phone: 1288-331204).

LYNCOMBE LODGE, Churchill, Avon, England Here's the place for a farmhouse holiday and long rides away from towns and traffic in the heart of the Mendip Hills, midway between Bath and the sea. Information: *Lyncombe Lodge,* Churchill, Avon BS19 5PG, England (phone: 1934-852335).

HARROGATE EQUESTRIAN CENTRE, Harrogate, North Yorkshire, England Situated in a pretty area, this *BHS*-affiliated facility is 3 miles from the ancient spa town of Harrogate. Facilities include a large covered school and an outdoor school. All types of instruction are available for adults and children, including dressage, show-jumping, and cross-country riding over the more than 100 fences on 70 acres of grassland, including an official horse trials course. Information: *Harrogate Equestrian Centre,* Brackenthwaite La., Burn Bridge, Harrogate, North Yorkshire HG3 1PW, England (phone: 1423-871894).

PAKEFIELD RIDING SCHOOL, Lowestoft, Suffolk, England This *BHS*-approved school offers week-long holidays with five days' riding at nearby stables, often on beaches, plus videotapes and discussion groups. For a small extra charge, riders can use the indoor and outdoor rings, which are floodlit. Information: *Pakefield Riding School,* Carlton Rd. S., Lowestoft, Suffolk NR33 7RD, England (phone: 1502-572257).

FLANDERS FARM RIDING CENTRE, near Lymington, Hampshire, England Adult riding courses are offered with instruction in show-jumping and cross-country. Beginners and children from age six are welcome. It's *BHS* approved. Information: *Flanders Farm Riding Centre,* Silver St., Hordle, Lymington, Hampshire SO41 6DF, England (phone: 1590-682207).

NORTH WHEDDON FARM, near Minehead, Somerset, England Riding at all paces is provided here on the wild moors of surrounding *Exmoor National Park,* which has been called "the riding playground of England." Lodging is in a fine, attractive, old Georgian farmhouse. Information: *North Wheddon Farm,* Wheddon Cross, Somerset TA24 7EX, England (phone: 1643-841224).

SHILSTONE ROCKS STUD, Newton Abbot, Devon, England A riding and trekking center and stud farm on a Dartmoor farm with a history that goes back to 1244. With its granite tors, deep bogs, and untamed ponies grazing on the open moorland, Dartmoor has a reputation for wicked storms and thick, swirling mists, making it the perfect setting for Sir Arthur Conan Doyle's eerie novel *The Hound of the Baskervilles.* It's one of Britain's greatest authentic wildernesses, a hill range of remarkable beauty. Children over age six are welcome. It's *BHS* approved. Information: *Shilstone Rocks Stud,* Widecombe-in-the-Moor, Newton Abbot, Devon TQ13 7TF, England (phone: 13642-281).

LEA BAILEY RIDING SCHOOL, Ross-on-Wye, Herefordshire, England Riding holidays in the Royal Forest of Dean and lessons in sidesaddle, jumping, driving, and stable management are offered. Information: *Lea Bailey Riding School,* Byeways, Ross-on-Wye, Herefordshire HR9 5TY, England (phone: 1989-750360).

ABERGWYNANT FARM TREKKING CENTRE, Dolgellau, Gwynedd, Wales Take scenic treks over the mountains and foothills of Cader Idris, up valleys, past lakes and derelict gold mines, and through woods and *Forestry Commission* land overlooking the superb Mawddach Estuary. Over 60 horses and ponies are available at this peaceful farm, which has won awards for its location and facilities. Book well in advance. Information: *Abergwynant Farm Trekking Centre,* Penmaenpool, Dolgellau, Gwynedd LL40 1YF, Wales (phone: 1341-422377)

HIGHLAND RIDING CENTRE, Drumnadrochit, Highland, Scotland In one of the loveliest parts of Scotland, overlooking Loch Ness, this *BHS*-affiliated center is especially good for families. There are Shetland ponies for small children and novices and livelier mounts for experienced riders. Instruction, available indoors and out, can be tailored to all levels. And when chore time rolls around—grooming the ponies, cleaning tack, mucking out the stalls, helping the blacksmith, caring for lambs, searching for eggs, even making hay—guests are welcome to lend a hand. It's long established and well run. Information: *Highland Riding Centre, Borlum Farm,* Drumnadrochit, Highland IV3 6XN, Scotland (phone: 1456-450020).

BLAIR CASTLE TREKKING CENTRE, Pitlochry, Tayside, Scotland Experienced guides lead hour-long, half-day, and day-long treks on surefooted Highland ponies. Instruction is available for children. Open from April to mid-August. Information: *Blair Castle Trekking Centre, Blair Castle, Caravan Park,* Blair Atholl, Pitlochry, Tayside, PH18 5SR, Scotland (phone: 1796-481263).

CAE IAGO TREKKING CENTRE, Llanwrda, Dyfed, Wales There's excellent trekking through beautiful wild country for all levels of riders, as well as trail rides for the experienced. Day rides as well as holidays can be arranged. It's *BHS* approved. Information: *Cae Iago Trekking Centre,* Farmers, Llanwrda, Dyfed SA19 8LZ, Wales; phone: 155-85303).Also note that *Hoofbeats International* (162 Cambridge Ave., Englewood, NJ 07631; phone: 201-568-3471 in New Jersey; 800-733-2995 elsewhere in the US) offers seven- to 10-day horseback holidays in England, Scotland, and Wales. For a list of tour packages offering riding and other package tours in Great Britain, see GETTING READY TO GO.

POST TREKKING

There's nothing quite as delightful as seeing the country from the back of a horse or surefooted native pony, heading from inn to inn through narrow trails, along abandoned train beds, and down wide sandy beaches—and staying away from the trekking center for up to a week at a time. *Post trekking,* or *trail riding,* as this activity also is called, is not widely available, and it is not generally recommended for riders without experience, as it usually involves good horses and a fast enough pace to cover about 25 miles a day. Usually a warm camaraderie develops en route, so that you become one of a cohesive band of pilgrims straight out of *The Canterbury Tales* as you traverse the miles. That's one reason for going. Post trekking is also a practically worry-free holiday: There are guides to keep you going at a reasonable pace, to make sure you don't get lost, and to arrange for your luggage to be transported from one hostelry to the next. And at the end of each day, there's always a hot bath, a rustic feast, a good night's sleep in a clean-sheeted bed, and one of those massive breakfasts (the kind that make you feel as if it's going to take an Act of Parliament to get you into the saddle) before you hit the trail once again. For information about post treks other than the one described below, contact *Ponies UK* (see *Riding Holidays and Pony Trekking,* above) or Nigel Boase of the *Scottish Trekking and Riding Association* (*Appaloosa Riding Centre,* Craobh Haven, by Loch Gilphead, Argyllshire, Scotland; phone: 18525-632).

WEST HIGHLANDS, Scotland This is post trekking at its best. The routes follow tracks up lonely glens and through rugged hill passes, providing magnificent panoramas of mountains and lochs. Participants are mounted on Connemara ponies, which combine an inherent surefootedness on hills with a steady ride. A day's ride is between 15 and 20 miles, and riders must be proficient in the basics—walking, trotting, and cantering—and capable of spending more than six hours in the saddle. Accommodations range from hotels, guesthouses, farmhouses, and self-catering cottages. Information: *Equiventure,* Achinrier, Barcaldine, by Oban, Argyllshire, Scotland (phone: 1631-72320).

CARAVANNING

Meandering along a narrow lane flanked by billowing meadows and fields, in a horse-drawn wagon, with grand vistas stretching off toward a purple-hazed horizon, is one of the most relaxed ways to spend a week—especially where the roads are small, traffic-free, and dotted with quaint old pubs, interesting restaurants, and historic sites. Agencies that rent well-equipped caravans, many of them brightly painted, make this possible in a number of areas for about $350 a week; the agent usually can direct you along routes that have the most beautiful scenery and the best overnight spots. Some good ones to try include:

Waveney Valley Horse Holidays (Air Station Farm, Pulham St. Mary, near Diss, Norfolk IP21 4QF, England; phone: 1379-741228).

Welsh Covered Wagon Adventure Holidays (Rhydybont, Talgarth, Powys LDE OEE, Wales; phone: 1874-711346). Offers week-long trips up the Wye Valley and around the Llangorse region.

Welsh Horsedrawn Holidays (Greystone, Bell St., Talgarth, Brecon, Powys LD3 OBP, Wales; phone: 1874-711346). For trips in the Brecon Beacons area of Wales, from the beginning of June to the end of September.

HUNTING

In Britain, hunting has nothing to do with shooting. Here, shooting involves going after game with firearms. Hunting means riding to hounds, and it is extremely popular, with so many meetings scheduled from November until spring that you could hunt every day of the week with a pick of locations.

Quite apart from the quality of the horses, stupendous scenery awaits the visitor; a rider may be forgiven for taking a tumble if distracted by the view—for example, the rolling farmlands of Leicestershire, England's best hunting country.

The pack of hounds—usually 30 to 40 in number and counted in "couples"—are under the control of the huntsman, who may be the master or a professional hunt servant. The huntsman is assisted by his "whippers-in" (usually two in number). The mounted spectators, or "followers," usually are led by the field master, who's responsible for seeing that the hounds are not ridden over and that the farmers' land, used for the hunt, is not abused. Non-riders often follow the action by bicycle, on foot, or in their cars and stand by for the chance to watch the hounds and the horses passing. From the stirrup cup that almost invariably precedes each meet to the rendezvous afterward in some favored hostelry, the atmosphere is at once efficient, orderly, friendly, and convivial; the participants are judged as much by their sportsmanship as by other qualities such as dress and "turnout" for both the rider and the horse, which should be neat, clean, and "workman-like" at all times.

Some hunts exclude all non-members; others accept only local visitors. However, there are many that admit visiting non-members temporarily upon payment of the "cap"—a day's hunting fee. The hunt secretary can advise on horse hire and correct clothing.

Riding to foxhounds is not the only way to follow hunting in England. It also is possible to ride with one of the four packs of staghounds or with one of the 22 packs of harriers. Of the latter, 10 hunt only hares, seven hunt only foxes, and five hunt both. There also are 10 packs of draghounds that follow an artificial trail. Hunters who do not ride can still participate with one of the 80 packs of beagles, nine packs of bassets, or 19 packs of minkhounds, all of which are followed only on foot. The seasons are September through March for hare, summer for mink, and August through April for deer.

The following associations can provide further details on these forms of hunting:

Association of Masters of Harriers and Beagles (*Horn Park,* Beaminster, Dorset DT8 38B, England; phone: 1308-862212).

Masters of Deerhounds Association (c/o Dr. John Peck, *Bilboa House,* Dulveston, Somerset TA22 9DW, England; phone: 1398-22475).

Masters of Foxhounds Association (*Parsloes Cottage,* Bagendon, Cirencester, Gloucestershire GL7 7DU, England; phone: 1285-831470).

Masters of Minkhounds Association (8 Wilson-Valkenburg Ct., Bath Rd. Newbury, Berkshire RG13 1QP, England; phone: 1635-44754).

FOR MORE INFORMATION

Information on these and other field sports is available from *British Field Sports Society,* 59 Kennington Rd., London SE1 7PZ, England (phone: 171-928-4742).

Wonderful Waterways and Coastal Cruises

Whether you're dangling your hand from a dinghy or slicing through the waves underneath a billowing sail, being on a boat is something special. People wave and sing and talk to each other, the winds whip at your hair, the waves rock you like a baby. The pace of your trip slows to a blissful crawl, and when your foot touches the shore again, you can't help but feel supremely relaxed.

Britain's varied and often rugged coastline and its complex weather patterns provide a challenge to even the most experienced sailor, while novice crew members find the sport both invigorating and exciting. Consequently, British vacationers head for the water in droves—and support all manner of boat rental firms, sailing schools, and cruising establishments. Once a sport reserved only for the wealthy, sailing has become so democratized that you no longer have to own your own craft to enjoy the nation's offshore pleasures.

SAILING

Many boaters do sail in the English Channel—and they savor the challenges posed by its changeable winds, fierce tides, heavy shipping traffic, and busy harbors. But Britain offers more forgiving waters that don't require such stout seagoing yachts and solid sailing experience. There are the sheltered bays along the notched Devon, Essex, and western Scotland coasts; the celebrated Solent, the 3-mile-wide arm of water between the north coast of the Isle of Wight and England's southern shore, south of Southampton, known as the cruising ground of the rich ever since the mid-19th century when Queen Victoria started summering there in a palace-size "cottage" designed by her husband, Prince Albert; and the coastal waters of East Anglia, where splendid sprit-rigged sailing barges—once used for cargo and now revamped to accommodate passengers—are common sights. (The sailing barge *Victor,* built in 1895, rerigged in 1974, and refurbished every year, departs for summer cruises from Strood Pier out of the river Medway; for information, call 1634-723272.) Art and birding cruises are other possibilities.

The best sources of suggestions for sailing in any given area are always local yacht clubs and harbor masters. Another is whichever pub is patronized by the local branch of the *Royal National Lifeboat Institution*'s members, who are apt to be experienced watermen whose families have fished in the area for hundreds of years; their advice will come salted with tales of shipwrecks, which can be contemplated over a pint of beer.

SAILBOAT CHARTERS

These are widely available in resort centers of the most popular sailing areas; experienced sailors can charter bareboats for cruises, while novices can hire their craft with a professional crew. Information regarding charters can be obtained from the *Yacht Charter Association* (60 Silverdale, New Milton, Hampshire BH25 7DE, England; phone: 1425-619004; fax: 1425-610967). It gives details on member charter operators throughout Britain that offer insured craft that meet the association's standards. Since no registration exists in the United Kingdom, and charter yachts are not required to carry any specific safety equipment—not even a compass—it is highly advisable to charter only from *YCA* members, who achieve membership by meeting its safety standards.

SAILING SCHOOLS

Week-long sailing courses in dinghies and cruisers, for novices and more advanced sailors, are available at reasonable cost at dozens of sailing schools and clubs. The largest organization setting minimum safety standards and levels of instruction for these is the *Royal Yachting Association* (*RYA House,* Romsey Rd., Eastleigh, Hampshire S05 4YA, England; phone: 1703-629962); upon request, it will send a free complete list of recognized schools. Among the most noteworthy places are the following (listed alphabetically by location).

FOWEY CRUISING SCHOOL, Fowey, Cornwall, England Courses in theory and practice at *Fowey* (pronounced *Foy*) are approved by the *RYA,* and are taught year-round. Skippered cruises are available from April through October; the sailing area includes the coasts of lush South Devon, Cornwall, the Scilly Isles, the Channel Isles, and even such international destinations as Brittany and Portugal. Information: *John Myatt, Fowey Cruising School,* 32 Fore St., Fowey, Cornwall PL23 1AQ, England (phone: 1726-832129).

EMSWORTH SAILING SCHOOL, Portsmouth, Hampshire, England Weekend to multi-week courses using cruising dinghies or yachts. Accommodations are provided. Information: *Emsworth Sailing School, The Port House,* Port Solent, Portsmouth, Hampshire P06 4TH, England (phone: 1705-210510).

JERSEY CRUISING SCHOOL, St. Helier, Jersey, Channel Islands, England Sail an Anglo-French cruising ground with the third-highest tidal range in the world. Bareboat and skippered charters also are available. A full range of *RYA* certificates has been awarded here. Information: *Jersey Cruising School,* St. Helier Marina, St. Helier, Jersey, Channel Islands, England (phone: 1534-888100).

ISLAND CRUISING CLUB, Salcombe, Devon, England The club offers cruising, keelboat, and dinghy sailing to individuals, families, and groups. Accommodations are available on the ship *Egremont.* The season runs from March through October. Information: *Island Cruising Club,* 10 Island St., Salcombe, Devon TQ8 8DR, England (phone: 154-884-3481).

UK SAILING CENTRE, West Cowes, Isle of Wight, England Formerly the *National Sailing Centre,* and still one of the country's best-known sailing schools, it offers five-night and weekend programs in dinghy sailing and canoeing, from March through October. *RYA* certificates at all levels are awarded upon successful completion of the respective course. Accommodations are in waterside premises that include a bar, indoor heated pool, and marina. Information: *UK Sailing Centre,* West Cowes, Isle of Wight PO31 7PQ, England (phone: 1983-294941 or 983-290154).

DOLPHIN SAILING SCHOOL, Wootton Bridge, Isle of Wight, England There's dinghy sailing in the scenic Solent for beginners and more seasoned sailors, with all equipment and training meeting *RYA* standards. Lodging is in the *Foreshore,* a century-old former boathouse between the woods and the water, with lawns running down to the sea. Information: *Dolphin Sailing School, The Foreshore,* Woodside, Wootton Bridge, Isle of Wight PO33 4JR, England (phone: 1983-882246).

TIGHNABRUAICH SAILING SCHOOL, Argyll, Strathclyde, Scotland This large sailing school specializes in dinghy sailing and offers courses for novices and experienced sailors alike. The scenery is nothing short of magnificent. Information: *Tighnabruaich Sailing School,* Tighnabruaich, Argyll, Strathclyde PA21 2BD, Scotland; (phone: 1700-811396).

PLAS MENAI NATIONAL WATERSPORTS CENTRE, Caernarfon, Gwynedd, Wales The only year-round, sea-based center in the country, it offers courses at all levels in dinghy sailing, canoeing, and cruising. Also featured are adventure activity and sailing camps with 24-hour supervision for children ages eight to 18. Information: *Plas Menai National Watersports Centre,* Caernarfon, Gwynedd LL55 1UE, Wales (phone: 1248-670597).

EVENTS

Not only do all the sailing craft look picture-postcard perfect against the blue sky and the blue water on a breezy summer's day, but the well-tanned yachting folk striding around in Topsiders and toasting their victories at local pubs also make for an entertaining spectacle. One of the biggest of the British events is *Cowes Week,* which takes place in the Solent the first week of August. It is run by the Cowes sailing clubs, among them the *Royal Yacht Squadron,* an organization so exclusive that even some members of royalty have been barred from joining. True, you don't see the 300-foot spectator craft—floating hotels, really—that once appeared at Cowes every year in August, or the grandiose racing yachts that used to accompany them; and gone is the era when you might have seen four bearded gentlemen promenading along the waterfront and later learned that all of them were kings, as in Edwardian days. But the event still brings literally millions of pounds' worth of yachts to the area, along with an equally high sum's worth of rich boating enthusiasts. The goings-on are as tony as ever, and the race is remarkably easy to see from shore, especially around the *Royal Yacht Squadron*'s esplanade and Egypt Point, where the racers nearly touch land. The tough *Fastnet Race,* held on the Saturday of *Cowes Week* in odd-numbered years, is another exciting event.

CRUISING THE INLAND WATERWAYS

Salt air isn't the only tonic that will enliven a vacation: While thousands of Britons descend on the coast, just as many head for waters inland to spend their holidays floating down narrow canals or streams, or navigating lakes and broads such as those described below. This extensive system of waterways, some 2,200 miles in England alone, takes in the most wonderful scenery—castles of kings and queens, universities renowned around the globe, exquisite gardens manicured to perfection, nature preserves, and tranquil lakes and fens. While many of the noteworthy streams of other countries carry too much ship traffic to be enjoyable for pleasure boaters, most of Britain's canals are free of commercial craft and ideal for recreation.

There are basically two ways to go—by self-skippered boat or on a fully catered hotel boat cruise. The self-skippered arrangements work like this: You hire a craft with berths for two to 12, either a cabin cruiser or a steel-hulled narrowboat (so-called because they are only about seven feet wide in order to pass through the locks—which you work yourself, please note). Someone shows you how to operate the craft and tells you whom to call if you need any help. You hire a bicycle for countryside explorations, buy a pile of groceries, some fishing tackle, and a few books, then cast off for a floating holiday that will take you along as many miles of waterways as you choose, at the rate of about 15 to 20 miles per day. There are plenty of places to moor, to walk and bicycle in the countryside, and to buy fresh supplies. If you fear you'll feel as if you're driving at *Indy* after only an hour of driver's ed., you sometimes can hire a skipper to do the piloting (a skippered charter). And if you don't feel like cooking, you can stop in restaurants and pubs along the way.

Alternatively, you can join a group on one of the many hotel boats that cruise some of the waterways and let the hotel staff provide your meals (still another option—charter the hotel boat yourself). The cruising life is simple, idyllic, and restorative, and everyone who does it goes home talking about next year. *British Waterways* (*Willow Grange,* Church Rd., Watford, Hertfordshire WD1 3QA, England; phone: 1923-226422) can supply a great deal of general information about the cruising possibilities in Britain as well as maps and charts of the entire system.

Bookings for a variety of types of craft on a wide assortment of British waterways can be arranged through a number of organizations in both Europe and the US. A comprehensive list of such companies can be found in GETTING READY TO GO; some also are mentioned below. When considering your options, be sure to review sales material thoroughly to determine what exactly is included. Some firms offer a discount for two consecutive weekly bookings, and some rates include linen, fuel, car parking, and VAT. Also find out if there is a cancellation penalty.

NORFOLK BROADS, England Described in a Nature Conservancy Report as "an extensive system of marshland, interconnected waterways, and shallow lakes or Broads lying in the valleys of the rivers Bure, Yare, and Waveney and their tributaries," this area—formed as a result of medieval peat digging—was discovered by vacationers at the end of the 19th century, and has been booming as a recreational center ever since. The villages are full of establishments where you can park your car, have a meal and a good night's sleep, and rent or moor a boat. Thousands of British families do just that every summer; along with fishing, boating is the prime recreational activity in the Broads. They are the finest inland sailing waters in Europe, with the exception of Holland, and the rivers and lakes teem with cruisers chugging along at about 5 miles an hour. Certainly, most Broads cruisers don't come here to get away from the crowds but to join them. If you want privacy, the months of April, May, June, September, and October are the best times to go, as the waters are relatively peaceful throughout the area. But even in season (July and August), there are a number of sections in this lacework of dikes and rivers—some 140 miles of navigable waterways in all—where it is possible to get off by yourself for a bit among the reedy swamps, scrubland, and occasional patches of forest. Acle, Potter Heigham, Horning, Stalham, Norwich, and Wroxham are the centers for most commercial facilities. Most boats are floating bungalows, complete with television sets, showers, cooking facilities, and central heating; prices vary according to the time of year and the size of the boat. For more information, contact *Blakes Holidays* (Wroxham, Norwich, Norfolk NR12 8DH, England; phone: 44-1603-782911; in the US, contact *Blakes Vacations,* 1076 Ash St., Winnetka, IL 60093; phone: 800-628-8118 or 708-446-4771; fax: 708-446-4772) or *Hoseasons Holidays Ltd.* (Sunway House, Lowestoft, Suffolk NR32 2LW England; phone: 44-1502-500555; fax: 44-1502-500535;

in the US, contact *Skipper Travel Services* 9029 Soquel Ave., Suite G, Santa Cruz, CA 95062; phone: 408-462-5333; fax: 408-462-5178).

ENGLISH RIVERS Of all the nation's rivers, three warrant special attention because of their navigability and accessibility. The Thames, which stretches across the breadth of the southern part of the country and is navigable for about 125 miles, winds its long way through pastoral green landscapes punctuated by villages so quaint you'll think you've stepped into a photograph from *National Geographic.* Commercial traffic along most of the Thames's navigable length is light, and the current is almost nonexistent in most seasons. A recorded announcement of Thames River cruises can be heard by calling the *River Boat Information Service* of the *London Tourist Board and Convention Bureau* (phone: 839-123432, costing 35p to 48p per minute). Also delightful is the river Avon, between Stratford and Tewkesbury, which meanders through a string of delicious 16th-century villages and towns (including none other than Stratford-upon-Avon, where it's possible to take in performances of the world-renowned *Royal Shakespeare Company*); the river proper is linked to a system of narrow canals that give the option of making loop cruises. The Severn, England's longest river, travels through towns like Worcester, noted for its splendid cathedral and its porcelain manufactory, and Upton-upon-Severn, a market town full of houses dating to the Georgian era and earlier, as it meanders for 42 navigable miles from Stourport to ancient Gloucester. *Blakes Holidays* (address above), *Hoseasons Holidays Ltd.* (address above), and *UK Waterway Holidays* (1 Port Hill, Hertford SG14 1PJ, England; phone: 44-1992-550616; fax: 44-1992-587392; in the US, contact *Alden Yacht Charters,* 1909 Alden Landing, Portsmouth, RI 02871; phone: 401-683-1782; fax: 401-683-4200; or *Skipper Travel Services,* address above) lease craft here. Also consult the *Upper Avon Navigation Trust* (Bridge 63, Harvington, Evesham, Worcestershire WR11 5NR, England; phone: 1386-870526) regarding the river Avon between Stratford-upon-Avon and Evesham; the *Lower Avon Navigation Trust, Ltd.* (*Mill Wharf,* Mill La., Wyre Piddle, Pershore, Worcestershire WR10 2JF, England; phone: 1386-552517) for information about the Avon between Evesham and Tewkesbury; and the *National River Authority, Thames Region* (*Kings Meadow House,* Kings Meadow Rd., Reading, Berkshire RG1 8DQ, England; phone: 1734-535000) regarding the Thames above Teddington.

BRITAIN'S CANALS The Industrial Revolution brought many changes to Britain, not the least of them being the lacing together of the country by hundreds of miles of canals—waterways abandoned not long after the ascendancy of the railroads. Many of the canals continued to be used for freight, but only recently have they seen anything approaching the traffic they used to know. Boats that now thread the waters transport holidaymakers, and their primary function is not commerce but leisurely pleasure in the now-pastoral scene along the route. Some cruisers take bikes along on the cabin tops for cycling into villages along the way for a drink in a pub or a foray to the local greengrocer's. Children work the locks by which the craft journey uphill. All along the route are old buildings whose impressive size or construction testifies to the canals' former importance. Some have been converted to contemporary uses: The canal-side granary on the Grand Union Canal at Stoke Bruerne in Northamptonshire now houses the *Waterways Museum* (phone: 1604-862229) with exhibits relating to the canals' heyday. It is closed Mondays October through March. Admission charge.

The Grand Union Canal, the major transportation artery between London and the Midlands for a century and a half, is the longest canal in England. The main line leaving the Thames at Brentford suffers some urban suffocation but comes into its own about 10 miles out when it starts its long climb through increasingly rich countryside toward a summit in the Chiltern Hills, 55 wide locks up. It continues to the aforementioned Stoke Bruerne, and the Northampton arm joins the river Nene soon after. There are other arms well worth exploring at Aylesbury, Welford, Market Harborough, and Trent Junction; the landscape on the Leicester arm is remarkably beautiful. Also consider the Regent's Canal, which winds past the *London Zoo* in *Regent's Park* on its way to the Thames.

For more information about planning a cruise, contact the *British Waterways* (address above) or write to *UK Waterway Holidays* (address above) for a copy of their brochure.

CALEDONIAN CANAL, Scotland This 60-mile-long waterway, one of the grandest in Britain, joins the east and west coasts of Scotland and links Loch Ness, Loch Lochy, and Loch Oich through the heart of the Great Glen, a valley rich in history and wildlife, once occupied by clans like the MacDonalds, the Camerons, and the Stuarts. In the pretty, loch-side communities, villagers sell crafts; restaurants purvey venison, salmon, pheasant, and other local specialties; and the pubs serve single malt whiskies. It's a beautiful trip, whether you come for the vivid greens and brilliant yellows of spring, the wildflowers and heather purpling the mountainsides in summer, or the splashes of color in autumn, when you'll appreciate the heating in your boat. The cabin cruisers in which most people make the trip can be hired from *Caley Cruises,* Canal Rd., Inverness IV3 6NF, Scotland (phone: 1463-236328; fax: 1463-238323).

Gone Fishing

It's not hard to understand the overwhelming popularity of Izaak Walton's sport given just how much water there is in Britain, how pretty most of the angling hot spots are, and how good the fishing is. Though the day when a monster 50-pound salmon could be caught in the London section of the Thames is long past, most of Britain's streams and lakes are remarkably pollution-free, and conditions in the others are improving. The game fishing—that is, for salmon, sea trout, brown trout, and rainbow trout—is some of the best in the world, and the sea fishing and coarse fishing—for bream, carp, chub, dace, perch, pike, roach, tench, eel, and other species—are excellent.

Each section of Britain offers a different proportion of these three types of angling, and where to go will depend on the objective. In Scotland and Wales, the rivers are thought of entirely as game fishing streams. Scottish rivers are world famous for their salmon (though other game species are taken), particularly because of the consistent excellence of the fisheries; Britain's record salmon, a 64-pounder bagged in 1922, was caught in Scotland's Tay. In Wales, salmon, and to an almost equal extent sea trout (which the Welsh call "sewin"), are the big deal. English streams stand out for the sheer variety of angling offered: Some streams are consecrated primarily to game fishing; some entirely to coarse fishing; and some are mixed fisheries, offering both coarse and game species. There are many reservoirs, and many waters are stocked.

Game fishing is the glamour sport on the local angling scene, and while many vacationers do some coarse fishing or some sea angling as a sidelight to a sightseeing vacation, game fishing is something to plan a trip around. In Britain, that's all the more true because of the existence of many quaint and comfortable old fishing hotels, the perfect answer to one pressing problem encountered by most avid anglers—the fed-up fishing widow (or widower). Attractively situated within a short drive of all the shops, ruins, and cathedrals an inveterate sightseer could desire, the best of these hostelries offer spacious chambers with high ceilings, French doors, balconies entwined with wisteria, or similar delightful features. Cucumber sandwiches and currant scones, fruitcakes and jam tarts may be standard fare at tea; and at dinner, guests discuss not just the best flies of the day but also where to get the best buy on a pair of sheepskin gloves or a handmade tapestry.

For details about fishing in England, Scotland, and Wales, consult the excellent *Where to Fish* (£19.95/about $30), available from Thomas Harmsworth Publishing (*Old Rectory Office,* Stoke Abbott, Beaminster, Dorset DT8 3JT, England; phone: 1308-868118). Published biannually, this 480-page guide contains thousands of entries, with information supplied by hoteliers, tackle dealers, club secretaries, and other on-the-spot sources. A number of publications covering angling in specific regions of England are available, among them *The Northumbrian Water Fishing Handbook* (available free from *Northumbrian Water, Eldon House, Regent Centre,* Gosforth, Newcastle upon Tyne, Tyne & Wear NE3 3UD, England; phone: 191-213-0266).

GAME FISHING

Nearly all game fishing waters in England, Wales, and Scotland are private, with the fishing rights controlled by clubs and associations. Some permit no outsiders at all, and some charge a fee high enough to make them unofficially exclusive; but some sell day tickets, weekly tickets, or short-term memberships at prices rising—usually with the quality of the fishing—from the nominal to the expensive-but-still-not-exorbitant range. These are generally available in advance through the association's office or on the spot through hotels, pubs, and tackle shops.

In addition to permission, game fishers also usually need, for salmon, sea trout, and brown trout, *River Authority*–issued rod licenses, available through fishing hotels, post offices, pubs, and tackle shops. When purchasing a license, be sure to inquire about local rules on season, minimum sizes, permissible bait and tackle, and Sunday fishing.

ENGLAND Hatchery-raised trout can be found almost everywhere in the country in lakes, reservoirs, and a variety of rivers. Native brown trout proliferate in the famous chalk streams of the southeast, which offer some of the world's best dry-fly trout fishing. Fast, clear-flowing, and highly alkaline, these streams are generally ideal for nurturing big ones that rise freely even when they reach four pounds or more.

Because of their popularity among fishermen, it's usually necessary to wait a decade to fish more famous rivers like the Itchen and the Test, which flow practically in the shadow of *Winchester Cathedral,* Izaak Walton's burial place. But *The Orvis Co., Inc.* (The Mill, Nether Wallop, Stockbridge, Hampshire SO20 8ES, England; phone: 1264-781212) offers exceptional, though inevitably expensive, fishing with guides (unusual for trout rivers in England) to an international clientele on private stretches of these two legendary streams. *Orvis*'s waters include a short stretch on the celebrated Itchen, which produces extra-wily wild trout, and several on the Test, including one that ranks among the best free-rising stretches in the country, good for large and exceptionally active trophy fish. *Orvis* also will outfit anglers by mail order or from their shops located in Stockbridge, Hampshire (phone: 1264-810017), and 27 Sackville St., W1 (off Piccadilly; phone: 171-494-2660) in London's West End.

Other well-known area streams include the Derwent, an important and especially scenic tributary of the immense Trent; the Dove, where Walton fished, though it's generally not the stream it once was; the Eden, famous for its January-to-May salmon run; the Kennet; the Lune; the Ribble, especially in the middle reaches; and the Wharfe. The Camel and the Fowey (pronounced *Foy*) are two of Cornwall's important sea trout rivers, and some hotels have good water on the Tamar, among southwest England's most important game fisheries; the Taw, a game river known for a March-to-May salmon run, with good sea trout action beginning in July, with some roach and dace downstream; and the Torridge, where the same salmon-in-spring, sea-trout-in-July patterns prevail. In the northeast, the Coquet and the Tweed are the best-known salmon streams.

In general, closed season in England is from October 1 to March 24 for trout and November 1 to January 31 for salmon. However, dates vary from area to area, so it's always a good idea to check with the local region of the *National Rivers Authority* (*NRA*). The coarse fishing season is closed March 15 through June 15, though this will vary by region.

Whatever the venue, the first thing to do is get a license, available from local fishing tackle suppliers, or from the appropriate *NRA.* Then get permission to fish there from whoever owns the rights, a task that usually involves the purchase of a temporary membership or angling ticket. Regions of the *NRA* in England and Wales include the following:

Anglian Region—NRA (Regional headquarters: *Kingfisher House,* Goldhay Way, Orton Goldhay, Peterborough PE2 OZR, England; phone: 1733-371811). Covers the counties of Bedfordshire, Cambridgeshire, Essex, Lincolnshire, Norfolk, Northamptonshire, Suffolk, and part of Buckinghamshire and Hertfordshire; and controls the Blackwater, Bure, Cam, Chelmer, Colne, Crouch, Great Ouse, Nene, Stour, Waveney, Welland, Witham, Yare, and tributaries; also Kielder Water, northern Europe's biggest manmade lake.

North West Region (*Richard Fairclough House,* Knutsford, Warrington, WA4 1HG, England; phone: 1925-53999). Covers Cheshire, Greater Manchester, Lancashire, Merseyside, and part of Cumbria, Derbyshire, and Staffordshire; and controls the Calder, Derwent, Eden, Esk and Esk (Border), Greta, and Lune, as well as the following lakes: the Bassenthwaite, Brotherswater, Buttermere, Coniston, Crummock Water, Derwentwater, Elterwater, Ennerdale Water, Grasmere, Haweswater, Loweswater, Rydal Water, Thirlmere, and Ullswater.

Northumbrian Region (*Eldon House, Regent Centre,* Gosforth, Newcastle upon Tyne, Tyne & Wear NE3 3UD, England; phone: 191-213-0266). Covers Cleveland, Durham, Northumberland, and part of Cumbria, Tyne & Wear, and North Yorkshire; and controls the Aln, Byth, Coquet, Tees, Tyne, Wansbeck, Wear, and tributaries.

Severn-Trent Region (*Rivers & Regulation Division,* Sapphire East, 550 Streetsbrook Rd., Solihull B91 1QT, England; phone: 121-711-2324). Covers Leicestershire, Nottinghamshire, Shropshire, Warwickshire, the West Midlands, and part of Derbyshire, Gloucestershire, Hereford and Worcester, Powys (Wales), and Staffordshire; and controls the Warwickshire Avon, Churnet, Dove, Derbyshire Derwent, Dove, Manifold, Soar, Teme, Trent, Vrynwy in Wales (excluding Lake Vrynwy and streams running into it), Derbyshire Wye, and their tributaries.

South West NRA (*Manley House,* Kestrel Way, Sowton, Exeter, Devon EX2 7LQ, England; phone: 1392-444000). Covers Cornwall, Devon, and parts of Dorset and Somerset; controls the rivers Camel, Dart, Erme, Exe, Fowey, Lyn, Tamar, Taw, Teign, and Torridge.

Southern Region—NRA (*Guildbourne House,* Chatsworth Rd., Worthing, West Sussex BN11 1LD, England; phone: 1903-820692). Covers Hampshire, East and West Sussex, and parts of Dorset and Kent; and controls the Adur, Arun, Beaulieu, Cuckmere, Hamble, Itchen, Lymington, Medway, Meon, Ouse, Rother, Stour, and Test.

Thames Region (Fisheries Manager, *National Rivers Authority,* Kings Meadow Rd., Reading, Berkshire RG1 8DQ, England; phone: 1734-535000). Covers Berkshire, Greater London, Hertfordshire, Oxfordshire, Surrey, and parts of Buckinghamshire, Essex, Kent, and Wiltshire; and controls the Cherwell, Colne, Kennett, Lea, Mole, Roding, and Wey.

Wessex Region (*Rivers House,* East Quay, Bridgewater, Somerset TA6 4YS, England; phone: 1278-457333). Covers Avon and part of Dorset, Somerset, and Wiltshire; and controls the Bristol and Hampshire Avon, Axe, the Piddle, and the Hampshire Stour.

Yorkshire Region (21 Park Square House, Leeds LS1 2QG, England; phone: 113-244-0191). Covers North (James Herriott country), West, and South Yorkshire, as well as North Humberside; rivers include the Aire, Calder, Derwent, Don, Esk, Hull, Nidd Wharfe, Ouse, Swale, and Ure. Fishing rod licenses are available from the Fisheries Manager (same address as *Yorkshire Region,* above).

SCOTLAND Exclusiveness is the hallmark of the very finest Scottish angling—some streams are so private that even rich folk and VIPs may find the door barred—but it does not prevail along all of the Tay, the king of Scotland's salmon rivers, or along the entire length of its rivals: the Aberdeenshire Dee, noted by some fly-fishermen as Britain's best major salmon stream; the fast-flowing Spey, Scotland's most thrilling fishery; and the prolific Tweed. Also good are the aptly named Awe; the Don, superb for dry-fly trouting; the Northern Esk, which produces abundant numbers of medium-sized salmon; the Findhorn, among the more outstanding of the smaller Scottish salmon streams, with brown trout sport rivaling that of the nearby Spey and good sea trouting in summer; the fairly exclusive, fly-only Helmsdale; the good-quality Naver, especially for salmon and sea trout; and the 30-mile-long Ythan, an excellent sea trout fishery. Many huge fresh-water lochs and reservoirs are also rich in trout.

In Scotland, closed season is October 7 through March 14 for trout and late August through February, depending on the area, for salmon. Also, throughout the year, most localities prohibit Sunday fishing. No rod licenses are required for Scottish angling, but to fish for salmon, trout, or sea trout, written permission from the water's owner is necessary.

Local district fishery boards can spell out the rules on seasons and permissible fishing days, and provide information about who owns fishing rights for a given stretch of water. To locate district fishery offices, see a local tackle shop or contact the area tourist board (the address of which can be obtained from the *Scottish Tourist Board,* 23 Ravelston Ter., Edinburgh EH4 3EU, Scotland; phone: 131-332-2433).

WALES Here, the Wye (pronounced *Way*) is justly famous for salmon, and several hotels have water on the main river and on its tributaries. The Dee, which yields good-size salmon and smaller browns and sea trout, and the swift Usk, which has an average rod catch per season of some 800 salmon, usually averaging 10 pounds, are Wales's other important salmon rivers. The prolific Towy, and the Dovey and the Conwy, both of which hold numerous records, are the counterparts of the Dee and the Usk for sea trout sport. Offering good opportunities for both sea trout and salmon action are the Clwyd; the Glaslyn, which rises in Snowdon; the Mawddach; the Taf, whose source is on Mynydd Prescelly; and the important Teifi, which claims some of the principality's top trout fly-fishing.

On the whole, there are fewer big fish in Welsh reservoirs and lakes than in English and Scottish still waters. Most of the reservoirs and many lakes are in the mountainous districts of Snowdon and the Brecon Beacons, where visitors may well find that fishing is free, the only requirement being the owner's permission to fish.

NRA Welsh Region (*Rivers House, St. Mellons Business Park,* St. Mellons, Cardiff CF3 0LT, Wales; phone: 1222-770088) regulates fishing on Welsh rivers and issues licenses. It controls the Alwen, Alyn, Arrow, Bala Lake, Ceiriog, Ceirw, Clwyd, Conway, Welsh Dee, Dovey, Elwy, Irfon, Ithon, Lliw, Lugg, Neath, Rhymney, Taf, Teifi, Towy, Tryweryn, Twrch, Usk, Wye, and tributaries.

COARSE FISHING

All the fish in freshwater rivers and lakes that are not trout or salmon—bream, carp, chub, dace, perch, pike, roach, rudd, eel, and tench—go by the name of coarse fish, and there are millions of anglers who have made this quarry their specialty, using rods and lines with natural bait such as maggots, worms, or bread. The almost total absence of coarse fish in the streams and still waters of Scotland and Wales is compensated for by their abundance in England, where they often may be fished free of charge, and where the range of possibilities is enormous, particularly in the eastern and central regions: the giant and sluggish Great Ouse, where there is almost every kind of fish (although some stretches boast larger populations of a given species than others), with the town of Huntingdon among the most favored angling centers; the Nene, primarily for bream and roach; the Norfolk Broads and the Broadland rivers, like the Bure, the Waveney, the Yare, and their tributaries (except during the daytime in summer, when boat traffic makes the angling fairly slow), especially for bream and roach; and the Welland, another important coarse fishing stream.

Refer to *Where to Fish* (£19.95/about $30), available from Thomas Harmsworth Publishing (*Old Rectory Office,* Stoke Abbott, Beaminster, Dorset DT8 3JT, England; phone: 1308-868118) for more information.

Fishermen also may take advantage of unused sand and gravel pits, England's foremost fishing grounds. In these still waters, roach and bream, tench, eel, rudd, and some pike are commonly found. Angling also is available in Britain's canals, most of which are controlled by *British Waterways* (see *Wonderful Waterways and Coastal Cruises,* above, for address and phone number). However, canal fishing tends to be more difficult, the fish are smaller, and anglers compete with pleasure boats.

SEA ANGLING

Among all types of fishing in Britain, sea angling has grown most rapidly in the last few years. That's not surprising: Britain has hundreds of miles of ragged coastline, and anglers reel in an abundance of fish in species that come and go throughout the season, from half-pound flounders and sand dabs to giant mako sharks, 200-pound skate, and 300-pound halibut, plus wrasse, pollack, and mackerel, as well as sea bass, common in southern England and a favorite. No license is necessary, and few advance arrangements are required; tackle usually can be hired; and the chefs in most hotels will cook a guest's prize on request. For trips out over the wrecks and sunken reefs where some of the bigger fish lurk, boats and professional skippers are readily available, and a day out with a group in a boat with a local who knows how to rendezvous with fish can be a most rewarding (and reasonably priced) experience. All that's required is a stomach strong enough to hold up through a day on the choppy seas.

Shore fishing with a powerful rod and reel for sea bass or cod, also known as beach casting, requires a little more equipment, namely good oilskins, since these delicious creatures favor "storm beaches," and the best fishing is done when there's a strong onshore wind that will drench an angler to the skin with salt spray.

In the majority of coastal fishing hot spots, experienced anglers man Angling Times Report Stations, which dispense valuable advice on local conditions. Many areas also have sea angling festivals; the *British Tourist Authority* or regional tourist office can provide details.

For more information, consult *Sea Angler* and *Sea Angling Weekly,* available at newsstands. The *National Federation of Sea Anglers* (51A Queen St., Newton Abbot, Devon, England TQ12 2QJ; phone: 1626-331330) organizes over 100 competitions annually through its affiliated clubs, to which visitors are welcome, and will answer questions about the events. For Scottish sea fishing information, contact the *Scottish Federation of Sea Anglers* (*Caledonia House,* South Gyle, Edinburgh EH1 9DQ, Scotland; phone: 131-317-7192). In Wales contact *NRA Welsh Region* (address and phone number above).

ENGLAND In England, the best areas include the Channel ports of Dover and Deal, in Kent; the small resorts of New Haven and Littlehampton, in Sussex; Salcombe, on a many-branched estuary with wooded hills in rolling Devon; Fowey and Looe, among the rocky cliffs of Cornwall; and the mountainous Isle of Man, in the middle of the Irish Sea between England and Ireland. Off the coast of Cornwall alone, there are four species of shark; those interested can arrange to go for them on any number of organized trips.

SCOTLAND The sea angling potential in Scotland is largely unexploited. Shetland and Orkney have Britain's best common skate action, and the Pentland Firth, which separates Orkney and the mainland, produces large halibut. In the southeast, there's plenty of good shore fishing from the rocks and beaches.

WALES In Wales, the best shore fishing is found in the west, and the fishing offshore in the south can be superb. In the north and west, boat fishing is also quite good.

FISHING SCHOOLS

ARUNDELL ARMS, Lifton, Devon, England This traditional West Country hotel, an excellent destination in its own right (see *Rural Retreats*), pioneered fishing courses many years ago and now offers them for beginning, intermediate, and advanced anglers. Courses are taught by a Cornish champion tournament caster who is reckoned to be one of the best fly-fishing instructors in the country and, as lecturer, Conrad Voss-Bark, the *London Times*'s fishing correspondent, who is married to the proprietor (herself a passionate fly-fisher and an author of books on the waters of the area). All of the courses, which are run on the inn's extensive river, mix fly-fishing theory with a great deal of on-the-water experience. In addition, there are always two bailiffs on the property to advise visiting fishermen. Weekend fly-tying courses are available in winter. (Also see *Game Fishing Hotels,* below.) Information: *Arundell Arms Hotel,* Lifton, Devon PL16 0AA, England (phone: 1566-784666; 800-528-1234; fax: 1566-784494).

CHARLES BINGHAM (FISHING), LTD., Tavistock, Devon, England Mr. Bingham, who has landed more than 200 salmon on the fly and thousands of trout from some of England's most famous rivers, has fished on Dartmoor rivers for more than 40 years. He has written many best-selling books on fishing, including *Salmon and Sea Trout Fishing* (Batsford, £19.95/about $30), *The Game Fishing Year* (Batsford, £19.95/about $30), *Fishing on the River Test* (HF&G Withersby, £20/about $30), *Chalk Stream Salmon and Trout Fishing* (Swan Hill, £19.95/about $30), and *Trout, Salmon, and Sea Trout Fishing* (Cassell, £18.99/about $28.50). The school, which emphasizes fly-fishing, teaches beginners the basics, but Charles will also take out experienced anglers. Groups are limited to three or four people, so each participant gets plenty of personal attention. March through October is the season. Lodging is available in hotels or farmhouses on Dartmoor. Information: *Charles Bingham (Fishing), Ltd.,* West Down, Warren's Cross, Tavistock, Devon, England (phone: 1822-613899).

GLEN AFFRIC, Cannich, by Beauly, Highland, Scotland Beginners are welcome at this family-run roadside hotel's summer course, where instruction is given in casting and in trout and salmon fishing. Guests should provide waterproof jackets, hats, Wellingtons, and fishing equipment; the hotel can advise on particulars. For the non-angler, guided walks in the countryside, clay-pigeon shooting, and mountain biking can be arranged. The nearest rail and bus stations are 27 miles away at Inverness; transport to the station may be arranged for a small charge. Reserve well in advance. Information: *Glen Affric Hotel,* Cannich, by Beauly, Highland IV4 7LW, Scotland (phone: 1456-415214).

PEEBLES, Peeblesshire, Scotland This small county town in the beautiful rolling Borders area is just 25 miles from Edinburgh. In April and May this popular center for fishing on the river Tweed offers Friday-through-Sunday trout fishing courses presided over by former *British Open* casting champion Andy Dickison, who is Tweed Valley born and bred. There also are Sunday-to-Sunday salmon week courses in November, when the large salmon, usually weighing in between 10 and 30 pounds, are running. Private instruction in both bait and fly-casting techniques also is available, and nearby sights include *Melrose Abbey* (for more details, see *Ancient Monuments and Ruins*) and *Abbotsford,* the onetime home of novelist Sir Walter Scott. Accommodations are at the *Tontine* hotel, a Forte establishment. Information: *Peebles Angling School,* Craigiedene, 10 Dean Park, Peeblesshire EH45 6DD, Scotland (phone: 1721-720331).

GWYDYR, Betws-y-Coed, Gwynedd, Wales Anglers interested in perfecting their techniques in salmon and sea trout fishing can do so here; tuition covers casting, knots, rod and reel care, and night fishing. The hotel has waters along 8 miles of the rivers Conway and Lledr. Information: *Gwydyr Hotel,* Betws-y-Coed, Gwynedd LL24 0AB, Wales (phone: 1690-710777; fax: 1690-710777).

GAME FISHING HOTELS

Anglers can simplify the complicated process of arranging to fish in areas where the angling rights are privately held by basing themselves at a special fishing hotel, which may either control a stretch of a nearby stream or be able to carry out the necessary negotiations with owners of local estates. Most of the following establishments are country-house hotels in attractive settings; waters to which they control rights are indicated. Hotels mentioned in areas where fishing is free are conveniently located with respect to the best local waters—and, like the rights-owning establishments, are exceptionally hospitable to anglers: Enthusiasts who want to haul out their tales of that day's triumphs will be sure to find a willing ear. The hotels are listed alphabetically by location.

HOLNE CHASE, Ashburton, Devon, England Surrounded by woodlands and by the *Dartmoor National Park,* this singularly secluded and romantic hotel (with

17 rooms and a restaurant) on an 11th-century hunting estate has about a mile of fishing on the river Dart, whose valley the principal rooms overlook. Sea trout in the one-and-a-half to four and a half pound range, as well as salmon weighing from eight to 15 pounds, have been taken in recent years. Although the season is April through September, the hotel is open year-round. Information: *Holne Chase,* Ashburton, Devon TQ13 7NS, England (phone: 1364-3471; fax: 1364-3453).

CAVENDISH, Baslow, Derbyshire, England The fly-fishing available on the rivers Derwent and Wye, by courtesy of the Duke of Devonshire, provides only part of the charm at this 23-room establishment, where diners eat off Wedgwood china with Sheffield silver and rest up from a day on the stream in lounges with open fires, oak beams, fresh flowers, and fine views of the *Chatsworth* estate. Guests may borrow fishing tackle if they forget their own. The setting is *Chatsworth,* described in *Stately Homes and Great Gardens* in this section, and the magnificent Derbyshire *Peak District National Park,* which provides excellent hiking for non-fishing partners. Also see *Rural Retreats* in this section. Information: *Cavendish Hotel,* Baslow, Derbyshire DE45 1SP, England (phone: 1246-582311).

HALF MOON INN, Beaworthy, North Devon, England This quaint, friendly, and comfortable village inn with 14 rooms and a restaurant has been owned by the Inniss family since 1958. It offers 9 miles of privately owned salmon and trout fishing on the river Torridge, a small river renowned for its spring run of salmon, its fly-fishing May through September, and its excellent run of sea trout in July and August. Information: *Half Moon Inn,* Sheepwash, Beaworthy, North Devon EX21 5NE, England (phone: 140923-376).

DEER PARK, Buckerell Village, Honiton, Devon, England This family-run country-house hotel (with 30 rooms and a restaurant) in a 17th-century hillside Georgian manor stands on 40 acres of Devonshire countryside. Overlooking the valley of the river Otter, it offers 5 miles of private fishing for brown trout; additional fishing includes a two-acre lake for rainbow trout and a mile on the river Coly, where sea trout and salmon can be caught. The hotel also can arrange hunting trips (see *Stalking and Shooting*). Information: *Deer Park Hotel,* Buckerell Village, Honiton, Devon EX14 0PG, England (phone: 1404-41266; fax: 1404-46598).

TILLMOUTH PARK, Cornhill-on-Tweed, Northumberland, England This Victorian mansion-turned-inn occupies over 1,000 acres of rolling Northumberland border countryside—and boasts 9 miles of water on the rivers Till and Tweed. Good for salmon, grilse, and sea trout fishing. Spring season is February through mid-May, and following it is the summer season. The inn offers 14 guestrooms and a restaurant. Information: *Tillmouth Park Hotel,* Cornhill-on-Tweed, Northumberland TD12 4UU, England (phone: 1890-882255).

CARNARVON ARMS, Dulverton, Somerset, England This fine English country sporting hotel, built in 1873 by the fourth Earl of Carnarvon at one of the entrances to the *Exmoor National Park,* occupies 50 acres along the banks of the rivers Barle and Exe and offers its guests some 5 miles of fishing along these waters. In the heart of Negley Farson country, these typical moorland rivers run clear, bright, and shallow between pools. Late May, June, and early July are the best months for wild brownies—small but excellent fighters; prime salmon season is July through September. The hotel itself—a warm and friendly 22-room establishment run by Toni Jones for more than three decades—has spacious lounges with open log fires and is furnished with comfortable armchairs and fine antiques. There's also a good restaurant, an outdoor heated pool, a hard tennis court, and a full-size billiard table. Information: *Carnarvon Arms Hotel,* Dulverton, Somerset TA22 9AE, England (phone: 1398-23302; fax: 1398-24022).

ARUNDELL ARMS, Lifton, Devon, England This 30-room inn offers some 20 miles of private salmon, sea trout, and brown trout fishing on the river Tamar and its tributaries, and a three-acre lake stocked with rainbow and brown trout. There's also an excellent restaurant. (Also see *Fishing Schools, Stalking and Shooting,* and *Rural Retreats.*) Information: *Arundell Arms,* Lifton, Devon PL16 0AA, England (phone: 1566-784666; 800-528-1234; fax: 1566-784494).

ANGLERS ARMS, Morpeth, Northumberland, England Guests can fish for trout and salmon on a mile of the river Coquet. The hotel, in a 16th-century building, has five rooms, plus a restaurant that serves traditional Northumbrian and English fare. Half of the restaurant occupies a converted Pullman car reminiscent of the *Orient Express.* Information: *Anglers Arms Hotel,* Weldon Bridge, Morpeth, Northumberland NE65 8AX, England (phone: 1665-570655).

WHITE HART, North Tawton, Devon, England This tiny inn (three rooms), located 100 yards from the river Taw, arranges fishing excursions and lessons in angling for trout and salmon. Duck shooting also is available, as is rough shooting (shooting in rough country rather than on flat land). There's also a restaurant. Information: *White Hart Inn,* Fore St., North Tawton, Devon EX20 2DT, England (phone: 1837-82473).

WHITTON FARM HOUSE, Rothbury, Northumberland, England This charming, 12-room country hotel, which occupies a converted farm built in 1829, has, by special arrangement with the *Northumberland Angler's Federation,* access to some of the river Coquet's lower stretches (described by *Trout and Salmon* magazine as some of the top club-owned waters in Britain). After guests have had their fill of fishing, they can have a drink in the former calf house, eat dinner in the former milking parlor, and then go to bed in a converted stable. There are beamed ceilings, stone walls, and polished pine floors throughout. A stable with 20 horses and ponies for trekking and trail riding is on the premises. Information: *Whitton Farm House,* Rothbury, Northumberland NE65 7RL, England (phone: 1669-20811).

RISING SUN, Umberleigh, Devon, England This 13th-century cottage-style fishing hotel (with 11 rooms and a restaurant) has 3½ miles of salmon, sea trout, and brown trout fishing on the river Taw—the first waters above the tides. The salmon action is liveliest March through May, with the average catch weighing in at 10 to 12 pounds. Large sea trout averaging four or five pounds run in mid-April; small sea trout of one and a half pounds are running the third week in June until late September. Grilse run at the end of July and summer salmon in August and September. Information: *Rising Sun,* Umberleigh, Devon EX37 9DU, England (phone: 1769-60447; fax: 1769-60764).

ALTNAHARRA, Altnaharra, by Lairg, Southerland, Scotland One of the country's most celebrated angling hotels, this 20-room establishment has been welcoming anglers since 1887 to the tiny hamlet of Altnaharra and the superb private fishing on 4 miles of the river Mudale. Salmon and brown trout are the quarry here. There also are private beats on several nearby lochs, where there is also sea trout to be taken. Best times are late June through late September for sea trout, late May into September for brown trout, and April through June and September for salmon. There's also a good restaurant. Information: *Altnaharra Hotel,* Altnaharra, by Lairg, Southerland IV27 4UE, Scotland (phone: 1549-81222).

BANCHORY LODGE, Banchory, Kincardineshire, Scotland At this 22-room country house full of Georgian charm, fishing is on the river Dee, one of the world's most celebrated salmon rivers, and anglers come from the far corners of the earth to experience the salmon season here, February through September (only fly-fishing is permitted after April). The dining room and lounges of the hotel itself are furnished in period style, have open log fireplaces, and overlook the river, as do many of the bedrooms (some of which even have four-poster beds). Information: *Banchory Lodge,* Banchory, Kincardineshire AB31 3HS, Scotland (phone: 1330-822625; fax: 1330-825019).

TULCHAN LODGE, Grantown-on-Spey, Highland, Scotland Edward VII used to come to shoot and fish at this Scottish estate and country house overlooking the Spey Valley. In the midst of Highland malt whisky distilling country, it is as delightful as it was then, with its magnificent paintings, paneled hall and library, and elegant drawing and billiard rooms. There are nine rooms, a restaurant, and 8 miles of private fishing for salmon and sea trout on the river Spey. Fishing season runs mid-February through September, with April through August the best for salmon, June and July for sea trout. Open May through October. Information: *Tulchan Lodge,* Advie, Grantown-on-Spey, Highland PH26 3PW, Scotland (phone: 1807-510200).

EDNAM HOUSE, Kelso, Borders, Scotland This stately 32-room establishment built in 1761 has a high percentage of repeat business, thanks to the excellent sport in the river Tweed, which flows just outside (so that all the bars, the restaurant, and the public rooms have river views, as well as half of the guest quarters). Most anglers come for the salmon fishing in spring and fall; however, rights are privately owned and difficult to negotiate. For trout, 8 miles of the Tweed and the Teviot and numerous other small streams in the district are available to hotel guests at a nominal sum; best sport is in May and June. Information: *Ednam House Hotel,* Kelso, Borders TD5 7HT, Scotland (phone: 1573-224168; fax: 1573-226319).

KENMORE, Kenmore, by Aberfeldy, Tayside, Scotland Handsomely situated in one of Scotland's prettiest villages and surrounded by pristine countryside, this 38-room inn, established in 1572 (Scotland's oldest) on the banks of the river Tay in an area of impressive natural beauty, stands out for more than its setting. It offers 4 miles of private salmon fishing on the river Tay and has rights for salmon and brown and rainbow trout for the entire 16 miles of Loch Tay. Salmon season runs from mid-January through mid-October (and is best April through June and in September and October); brown trout may be taken mid-March through mid-October. Those who tire of aquatic pursuits can enjoy the establishment's 18-hole golf course; there's also a good restaurant. Information: *Kenmore Hotel,* The Square, Kenmore, by Aberfeldy, Tayside PH15 2NU, Scotland (phone: 1887-830205; fax: 1887-830262).

CROOK INN, Tweedsmuir, by Biggar, Borders, Scotland This 16th-century coaching inn, set on five and a half acres of the border hills, was where the Scottish poet Robbie Burns wrote "Willie Wastle." Now it has eight rooms, a restaurant, and 8 miles of private fishing on the river Tweed for trout, with an additional 30 miles of association and club brown trout waters available. April through September is the season for salmon and sea trout; May through July is tops for brown trout. You also can fish for rainbow and brown trout from boats on the nearby reservoirs. Information: *Crook Inn,* Tweedsmuir, by Biggar, Borders ML12 6QN, Scotland (phone: 1899-7272; fax: 1899-7294).

TWEED VALLEY, Walkerburn, Borders, Scotland One of the major attractions of this former Edwardian country house with 15 guestrooms is its traditional Scottish food; another is the area's reputation as a significant Atlantic salmon and sea trout fishing center for the past 30 years. Private salmon beats are also available, and guests may purchase permits to fish for brown trout and grayling on more than 30 miles of the river and its tributaries. Especially convenient is that the hotel has its own smoker, so you don't have to eat your monster catch all at once. Best times are from February through May, with peak runs of sea trout and salmon in late September, October, and November. Guides, lessons in both fly and bait casting, and tackle hire are available to guests. Information: *Tweed Valley Hotel,* Walkerburn, Peeblesshire, Borders EH43 6AA, Scotland (phone: 189-687636; fax: 1896-87639).

GLIFFAES COUNTRY HOUSE, near Crickhowell, Powys, Wales The river Usk, celebrated for its wild brown trout season, is a prime attraction of this stately, late-19th-century private-home-turned-inn, with 22 guestrooms and a restaurant. The average brown trout catch is 10 ounces, but there are three good stretches of salmon water as well, with average annual catches at around 25 to 30 fish. Eight reservoirs stocked by the *Welsh Water Authority* lie within a 15-mile radius. Information: *Gliffaes Country House Hotel,* near Crickhowell, Powys NP8 1RH, Wales (phone: 1874-730371; fax: 1874-730463).

LAKE, Llangammarch Wells, Powys, Wales Besides 50 acres of sweeping lawns and thick woods, this elegant 18-room country house—including nine suites—offers a three-acre trout lake and 4½ miles on the rivers Wye and Irfon, two of the best salmon streams in Wales, with the latter passing through the grounds of the hotel. Salmon fishing comes into its own in the latter part of the season, which runs from late January to late October on both streams. The spring fish are very powerful and can occasionally run over 30 pounds. Trout—mostly wild local fish weighing up to 34 pounds—can also be taken on the Irfon. The smaller Chewfru also offers interesting sport, while the Wye often provides specimens of trout weighing a pound and more. The largest salmon ever caught on hotel waters weighed in at a whopping 28 pounds, 8 ounces. Guests won't lack for good food or wine here either. The wine list offers 300 varieties, and the kitchen serves home-made chocolates, sausages, and bread. Information: *Lake Hotel,* Llangammarch Wells, Powys LD4 4BS, Wales (phone: 1591-2474; fax: 1591-2457).

LAKE VYRNWY, near Oswestry, Shropshire, Wales It is the fishing on Lake Vyrnwy, which is best in May, that brings some guests to this 37-room establishment, whereas others are drawn by the sailing, walking, bird watching, and the like. The atmosphere is old-fashioned and unpretentious; the view of the mountain setting is spectacular. There's also an excellent dining room. One American visitor implored his hosts, "For heaven's sake, don't modernize the place! It's perfect!" Information: *Lake Vyrnwy Hotel,* via Oswestry, Shropshire SY10 0LY, Wales (phone: 1691-73692; fax: 1691-73259).

TYN-Y-CORNEL, Talyllyn Tywyn, Gwynedd, Wales Angling on Talyllyn Lake is the prime attraction of this lakeside property. The private lake contains wild brown trout as well as hatchery-bred fish. The hotel is owned by the *Welsh Water Authority,* and, despite being recently refurbished, retains its quaint country-hotel character. Parts of the building date back to the 1500s, but the plumbing is strictly 20th century. There are 15 guestrooms and a restaurant. Information: *Tyn-y-Cornel,* Talyllyn Tywyn, Gwynedd LL36 9AJ, Wales (phone: 1654-782282; fax: 1654-782679).

Freewheeling by Two-Wheeler

The landscapes seen from the roads of Britain unfold with such endless diversity at every bend and turn that traveling through quickly in a car seems a real shame: The villages full of ancient half-timbered houses, the heather-clad plateau country with its deep valleys and minuscule settlements, the rolling hills, the quaint seacoast towns, and the regions of moors and mountains all beg to be explored at bicycle speed—that is, fast enough to cover a fair amount of terrain, but slow enough to stop to inspect a wildflower or to admire a view.

The fact that Britain offers not only a great variety of scenery in a relatively compact area, but also an abundance of well-surfaced, little-trafficked secondary roads, as well as many facilities for rental and repair and hundreds of small restaurants and informal hotels that are no less than delighted to welcome bedraggled pedalers, makes the country a well-nigh perfect candidate for cycling vacations—for beginning tourers and experts alike. Even those who are not particularly experienced and postpone their planning until the last minute still can enjoy a two-wheeling vacation here: Just travel light, start out slowly, and don't give up just because of saddle-soreness and tender muscles.

Rentals are widely available outside London, though it may not be possible to hire bikes for children. Prices begin at about £15 (about $22.50) a day for basic machines in rural towns, and go up when brand-new bikes, locks, lights, panniers, and insurance are supplied. Costs are also higher in larger cities, where broader selections are usually available. In London, *Yellow Jersey* (phone: 171-485-8090) and *Bell St. Bikes* (phone: 171-724-0456) rent bicycles by the day or week. *London Cycling Campaign* (phone: 171-928-7220) also is a good source.

Since the amount of pleasure at least partially depends on the bike, cyclists may well want to bring their own. Airlines will generally transport bikes as part of passengers' personal baggage, but may insist that the whole machine be crated. At any rate, be sure to check your insurance coverage before leaving home. If you have none, consider joining the *Cyclists' Touring Club* (*Cotterell House,* 69 Meadrow, Godalming, Surrey GU7 3HS, England; phone: 1483-417217), which has a plan for its members. Cyclists also will need to bring a basic set of tools and spares, including tire pump, puncture repair kit, tire levers, wrenches, spoke key, chain rivet extractor, chain links, inner brake cables, pliers, odd nuts and bolts, brake blocks, oil can, batteries and bulbs, freewheel block remover, rag, extra spokes, inner tubes and outer tires, and a small file for honing spokes. British law requires cycles to have two independent brakes and a red rear light and reflector, as well as a white light in the front for night riding; since riding is on the left here, it's a good idea to fix the front light onto the right-hand side. Not required by law—but certainly eminently practical—are a padlock and chain, though theft is not the problem in rural areas that it is in centers such as Birmingham, Glasgow, Liverpool, Manchester, Sheffield, and London.

To get out of these cities without battling the traffic is a relatively simple matter, since bikes are allowed to accompany passengers on trains at no extra charge. The procedure is simple: Buy a ticket, take the bike onto the platform, and ask the guard's permission to put it in the luggage van—a request usually refused only when the car is full of other goods. There are a few exceptions (for example, the fast *Inter-City* trains charge an extra £3/about $4.50), and they change occasionally, so check with *British Rail* for specifics. Always label your bike with your name, address, and the station of origin and destination.

BEST CYCLING AREAS

The touring possibilities are extensive. In England, for instance, any number of "B" and unclassified roads connect nearly every community in the country. In Wales, only the trunk routes in the southeast are too busy for cycling. In Scotland, their counterparts in the south are generally busy. In summer, Scotland's "A" routes in the north can be congested, more because of their narrow and winding nature than because of the quantity of traffic they carry, as can the north and west coast routes and some of the interior highways in Wales. In addition, there are unsurfaced tracks, cattle drovers' routes, bridleways, and woodland paths that lend themselves to two-wheeling (though the going can be a bit rough). Britain has, for instance, hundreds of miles of towpaths along the canals that ribbon the countryside, waterways constructed during the Industrial Revolution and now largely deserted by commercial transport. For information about necessary permits, contact *British Waterways* (*Toll House,* Delamere Ter., London W2 6ND, England; phone: 171-286-6101).

Here are some of the best cycling areas in Britain. Bike rentals, routes, lodgings and camping, and repairs for most of these are covered by the invaluable *Cycling World* magazine (£1.80/about $2.70, from *Andrew House,* 2A Granville Rd., Sidcup, Kent DA14 4BN, England; phone: 181-302-6150).

EAST ANGLIA, England The generally low-lying terrain of Suffolk and Norfolk, which, along with parts of neighboring counties, used to be an old Saxon kingdom, seems custom-made for cycling—though there are enough gentle hills to keep the horizons constantly changing. East Anglia is a land of farms, isolated villages full of thatch houses, grand mansions, and inspiring Gothic churches. Where these flatlands slip gently into the sea, there are salt marshes and sand dunes teeming with birds, deserted beaches, and The Broads. Information: *East Anglia Tourist Board, Toppesfield Hall,* Hadleigh, Suffolk IP7 5DN, England (phone: 1473-822922).

LAKE DISTRICT, England Unquestionably one of England's grandest regions, this mountain mass, its valleys bejeweled with lakes, is a favorite among Britain's national parks—and with reason: The ravines and their sapphire tarns, and the volcanic peaks, stark and jagged, sometimes rising abruptly from just above sea level so that they seem even bigger than they really are, create an effect of striking grandeur. Considering the manmade landscape as well—the velvety pastures laced with lichen-splotched drystone walls, the antique farmhouses, and the lovely villages—it's not hard to see why William Wordsworth, a native son whose various cottages are preserved and open for tours, was so inspired (as were countless other poets and artists down through the years). The hills can be steep—but then, some of those whistle-fast descents from the tops rank among the country's most exhilarating. Despite the area's popularity, there are still plenty of quiet roads. To detour farther from the beaten path, a good bet is the Cumbria Cycle Way, wending along the Smugglers' Coast and through the secluded hamlets of the Eden Valley. There are information offices throughout Cumbria. Information: *Cumbria Tourist Board,* Ashleigh, Windermere, Cumbria LA23 2AQ, England (phone: 15394-44444; fax: 15394-47439).

LAND'S END TO JOHN O'GROATS, England The three-week challenge known as "the End to End" covers approximately 1,000 miles from the southwest to the northeasternmost corners of a country crowded with traffic, towns, estuaries, motorways, and hills. There is no officially designated route, but most cyclists who make this varied trip pedal via Bath, Stratford-upon-Avon, Lincoln, York, Durham, Galashiels, Pitlochry, and Inverness, taking in the Cotswolds, the Yorkshire Moors, the Cheviot Hills, and the Grampian Mountains. Travel from south to north to take advantage of the prevailing wind. Cyclists can expect to average 50 miles a day at first, more as they build strength.

NORTHEAST, England Apart from a few urban areas near the coast, this is a quiet, sparsely populated region that boasts more ancient remains and medieval castles than any other part of Britain: *Hadrian's Wall, Bamburgh Castle, Alnwick Castle, Dunstanburgh Castle, Lindisfarne Priory, Durham Cathedral,* the 8th-century churches at Hexham and Jarrow, and Scotland's *Melrose, Jedburgh,* and *Kelso Abbeys* (described in *Ancient Monuments and Ruins*) are only a few. Roads through the grass-covered Cheviot Hills offer particularly challenging cycling; the rest of the area, mainly given over to forests, farms, and beaches, is more rolling. Information: *Northumbria Tourist Board,* Aykley Heads, Durham City, Durham DH1 5UX, England (phone: 1913-846905).

PEAK DISTRICT, England The Pennine Hills, England's great backbone, begin in this wild upland practically within shouting distance of the great industrial centers of the Midlands. The more southerly area offers steep-sided valleys; in the north, the characteristic formations are the sharp-edged gritstone cliffs that inspired Daniel Defoe to dub them the nation's Andes. Farther north, the Pennines become wilder, more remote, and harder to cycle. Information: *East Midlands Tourist Board,* Exchequergate, Lincoln, Lincolnshire LN2 1PZ, England (phone: 1522-531521; fax: 1522-532501).

SOUTHEAST, England Even as close as this area is to London, the countryside is still given over to orchards and hop fields, woods, and farmlands green and fertile enough to warrant the nickname the "Garden of England." Most cycling is on roads and country lanes through the ranges of low chalk hills known as the North and South Downs, which stretch eastward to the high cliffs on the shores of the English Channel and are separated by The Weald—the farm- and village-dotted remains of a once-large regional forest. Much of the area has been designated an *Area of Outstanding Natural Beauty; Canterbury, Chichester, Guildford,* and *Rochester Cathedrals,* the area associated with the Norman invasion and the Battle of Hastings, and a number of seacoast castles and fortifications are among the points of interest. Information: *Southeast England Tourist Board, The Old Brew House,* 1 Warwick Park, Tunbridge Wells, Kent TN2 5TU, England (phone: 1892-540766).

SOUTHWEST, England From the cathedral cities and *Stonehenge,* on the Salisbury Plain, to the New Forest, through the peaceful towns of Dorset (Thomas Hardy's Wessex), and on to the Somerset and Devon uplands—among them Exmoor and Dartmoor—and rugged Cornwall, the southwest of England will challenge even expert cyclists, though less so along the coast than throughout the hilly inland areas. But toward Land's End the scenery rewards cyclists amply for their efforts. The villages are lovely, the vistas unfailingly grand or pastoral, the traditional cream teas scrumptious, and the seacoast wonderfully varied. There are desolate moors, medieval churches, and the prehistoric ruins described in *Ancient Monuments and Ruins.* Information: *West Country Tourist Board,* 60 St. David's Hill, Exeter, Devon EX4 4SY, England (phone: 1392-76351).

YORKSHIRE DALES, England Rivers flowing down from high in the Pennine Hills have cut out a wondrous landscape of steep mountains and deep valleys whose finer points are not well known even in Britain. Like Teesdale, the northernmost of the dales, most boast impressive waterfalls. Swaledale is generally ranked as one of the lovelier dales, but the others have their particular charms as well: Wensleydale, with its local cheese; austere, lonely-looking Wharfedale; Nidderdale, with its impressive How Stean gorge; Airedale, with its spectacular Craven Country, Malham Cove's gigantic limestone bluffs, and the heavily visited Gordale Scar gorge; and not too well known Ribblesdale, in the center of the Pennines, where there are abundant potholes and waterfalls—to name only a few. Nearly 700 square miles of this water-carved wonderland have been designated as a national park. Information: *Yorkshire & Humberside Tourist Board,* 312 Tadcaster Rd., York, North Yorkshire YO2 2HF, England (phone: 1904-707961).

WELSH MARCHES, England and Wales In this area between Chepstow, on the Bristol Channel to the south, and Liverpool Bay, just north of Chester, the green and gentle hills of the valley of the meandering Wye and the country north of that offer some pleasant cycling. There's the Forest of Dean, the wild woods between the rivers Severn and Wye; Hay-on-Wye, a town full of secondhand bookshops, including "the world's largest"; the Shropshire Hills; and historical towns like the ancient religious center of Hereford, picturesque Ludlow, and Shrewsbury, full of half-timbered houses. Castles and abbeys are abundant. In few places in England will visitors find so little motor traffic. Information: *Heart of England Tourist Board,* PO Box 15, Worcester, Hereford and Worcester WR1 2JT, England (phone: 1905-763436).

HIGHLANDS, Scotland This region of ridges and glens, many loch-filled, is really restricted to cyclists with plenty of pedal power and a love of wilderness wandering: There are few major roads (though hundreds of miles of narrow lanes), particularly in the west, and those that exist get somewhat more crowded during the summer; outside the main towns, there are few bicycle shops, so it's necessary to carry all spares. The rewards are many, however: the northwest coast, looking much like Norway with its fjords; the vistas of snow-capped peaks; the islands, where it is flatter, less crowded, and even wilder; ancestral castles with long histories of the Scottish clans; and vast blue lakes like Loch Ness, Loch Long, and Loch Lochy—to name only a few. Information: *Ross and Cromarty Tourist Office,* North Kessock, Black Isle, Ross-shire IV1 1XB, Scotland (phone: 1463-73505).

MID AND SOUTH WALES Inland, the terrain is peaceful: Farms are interspersed with patches of woods; rolling hills climb out of pastoral valleys; the neat hamlets scattered here and there are woven together by country lanes and "rough stuff" tracks—unsurfaced but bikeable by the adventurous. But in the south, the countryside is dramatic. There are the mountains of the Brecon Beacons, with their thundering cascades, lakes, forests, moorlands, passes, and deeply incised valleys rich in industrial and cultural heritage; and the Pembrokeshire coast, where mountains plunge to the sea and rocky headlands are interspersed with delightful sandy beaches punctuated by ancient towns such as Cardigan, Pembroke and its castle, St. Davids with its historic cathedral, and delightful Terby. For intermediate cyclists, this is Wales's must—and an experience of a lifetime, to boot. Worth a look is the *National Mountain Bike Centre* at Llanwrtyd Wells, which stages a number of "fat tyre" competitions in season. Information: *Mid Wales Regional Office, Wales Tourist Board,* Canolfan Owain Glyndwr, Machynlleth, Powys SY20 8EE, Wales (phone: 1654-702401), and the *South Wales Regional Office, Wales Tourist Board*, Ty Croeso, Gloucester Pl., Swansea, West Glamorgan SA1 1TY, Wales (phone: 1792-781212).

NORTH, Wales Apart from the highway along the north coast, the roads here—as elsewhere in the country—are not at all heavily trafficked as they twist and climb into wild, mysterious mountains that are some of the most beautiful in all of Britain—slate brown and full of foaming rivers, huge smooth lakes, castles, and prehistoric sites. The Isle of Anglesey, across a narrow channel to the north, is more rural than rugged, making for a pleasant contrast. Information: *North Wales Tourism, Wales Tourist Board,* Colwyn Bay, 77 Conway Rd., Colwyn Bay, Clwyd LL29 7LN, Wales (phone: 1492-531731).

PLANNING A BIKING TOUR

After choosing a region to explore, it's a fairly easy matter to sketch out an itinerary. For ideas, review local tourist literature and articles about touring in bicycling magazines such as the following:

Cycle Touring, published bimonthly by the *Cyclists' Touring Club* (*Cotterell House,* 69 Meadrow, Godalming, Surrey GU7 3HS, England; phone: 1483-417217). £1.75 per copy on newsstands or from the club.

Cycling World, published by Stone Industrial Publications, Ltd. (2A Granville Rd., Sidcup, Kent DA14 4BN, England; phone: 181-302-6150 or 181-302-6069). £1.50/about $2.25 per copy on the newsstands, or £1.80/about $2.70, including postage, from the publisher.

Also consult specialized bicyclists' books such as the following:

Cycling in Britain, a publication of the *British Tourist Authority,* provides information on various aspects of biking and also describes several routes.

Cycling World magazine also publishes a ***Cycling Log*** outlining routes and facilities for lodging, camping, and cycle rental. £1.50/about $2.25 each.

Europe by Bike, by Karen and Terry Whitehill (Mountaineers Books; £9.95/about $15), outlines a tour covering the length of England from Canterbury to York.

Weekend Cycling, by Christa Gausden (Oxford Illustrated Press; £6.95/about $10.50).

Once a general itinerary has been sketched, plot out the tour on a small-scale highway map of the country—the sort of map supplied by a national tourist office. Base the daily mileage on the distance usually covered on the road at home, but be sure to allot time for en-route dawdling—chatting with the locals, long stops for admiring the panoramas from a picnic spot, walks through ruined abbeys, and the like.

Then tackle detailed route finding with large-scale topographical maps that will not only display the smallest country lanes, but also indicate the contours of the land and the steepness of the hills throughout the area to be covered. The 1:100,000-scale *Leisure Map* series (£2.50 to £3.50/about $3.75 to $5.25 from John Bartholomew & Son, 12 Duncan St., Edinburgh EH9 1TA, Scotland; phone: 131-667-9341) keys contours to colors and is excellent; maps can be ordered directly from the company or from the

Cyclists' Touring Club (address above). These can be used in conjunction with lodging guides, such as the *British Tourist Authority* publications *Britain: Stay on a Farm; Britain: Stay at an Inn;* and *Cycling;* as well as the *CTC*'s annual handbook for members, which lists not only some 3,000 inexpensive hotels and bed and breakfast establishments that extend particularly warm welcomes to cyclists but also bicycle repair shops throughout the country. The *CTC* touring department also provides its members with excellent help in planning trips.

Several package tour operators in Britain offer inclusive packages that include bed and breakfast accommodations, bikes, itineraries, and niceties such as repair kits; sometimes luggage is transported to the next night's destination as well. These companies are listed in GETTING READY TO GO.

Stalking and Shooting

People have been making sport of their search for game, both large and small, since the time of the pharaohs (who were so enamored of the activity that they looked forward to continuing it in the afterlife)—and devotees in Britain are no less enthusiastic. In fact, the *Glorious Twelfth* (of August), which marks the opening of the shooting season for grouse, is something of a national day of festivity in rural parts of Britain.

But grouse are only one quarry. Also available are species ranging from rabbits and pigeons to wildfowl and pheasants (which were first brought to Britain by the Romans). Scotland and northern England are known all over the world for their red grouse shooting, and sportspeople from the far corners of the globe come here to participate in shoots at which teams of beaters drive the birds over a line of concealed guns, or to flush them out with the aid of dogs—pointers or setters. (This is known as driven shooting and is distinct from rough shooting, which requires that the huntsman seek out the quarry himself.) Woodcock, some of them resident in Britain and others that overfly the islands during their fall migrations, are another favorite target, challenging because of their predilection for flying erratically between trees. Also sought after are capercaillie, which inhabit pine and fir forests, and fast-flying, unpredictable snipe, which favor marshy areas and are numerous in the boggy country of Wales, Norfolk, and Scotland's Western Isles.

Pheasant shooting is of excellent quality and good value, often with the possibility of guaranteed bags. For a party of six to nine guns, 100- to 250-bird days are typical. These are usually driven out of woodland to the standing guns, and bookings are generally made with a bag expectancy in mind.

Shoreline duck and goose hunting is a chancy affair, and access is fairly unrestricted throughout most of Britain. The principal areas are the Solway Firth in southwest Scotland and The Wash on the east coast of England. However, there are good areas for duck and goose hunting inland, particularly in Scotland for geese. In winter, wildfowlers position themselves by rivers and estuaries to catch the birds at dawn as they fly out to rest and at dusk when they fly inland in search of food.

In Scotland, sportspeople enjoy stalking, the taking of deer with a rifle, as well as shooting. Stalking involves the hunter's creeping up on the animal, taking advantage of all available cover—often over a period of several hours and a distance of several miles—until he is within 120 to 180 yards of it. Though this can be a very expensive proposition, it is one of the most exciting sports that the United Kingdom has to offer, and even though the red deer trophies taken here are not generally as large as those on the Continent, many a sportsman prizes his Scottish trophies far more than larger ones taken more easily. Roebuck and Sika stag trophies are often far superior to continental Europe's because of more selective shooting over the years. The most widely available in Britain, roebuck stalking is also the best value. And the delights afforded by the scenery—everything from flat heather moors to mountainous rocky countryside and wooded farmland—may even outweigh the pleasures of the sport.

For hunting in England, Scotland, and Wales, proper firearms certificates or licenses must be obtained by visitors from overseas; arrangements can be made through reputable agents, such as a holiday tour organizer, with a minimum of a month's notice. Game licenses, available from all main and branch post offices, are also required for most quarry, with the major exceptions of duck, wood pigeon, rabbit, and deer, which are not considered "game."

Shooting and stalking are permitted only during certain seasons, mainly in autumn and winter; dates vary with the quarry. Open season is August 12 through December 10 for grouse, October 1 through February 1 for pheasant, and September 1 through February 1 for partridge (an East Anglian specialty). Deer seasons depend on species and sex. In addition, shooting of any kind is forbidden on Sundays in Scotland, and shooting of game is prohibited on Sundays and on *Christmas Day* in the rest of Britain.

BOOKING AGENCIES

These organizations can send the particulars describing several estates, including the details of the shooting and fairly complete descriptions of available accommodations. Most shoots are organized for groups of six to eight, and it's common for friends to get together to form a shoot; if a sportsman can't make up a party on his own, the agents usually can fit him into someone else's (though, quite naturally, most groups are wary of having an inexperienced sportsman in their midst because of the danger of injury). The organizers can advise visitors in advance about open seasons and license requirements.

A & C Sporting Services (*Burnside Lodge,* Port Wenyss, Isle of Islay PA47 7SR, Scotland; phone: 1496-86296).

Major Neil Ramsay (*The Railway Station,* Dunkeld, Perthshire PH8 0DQ, Scotland; phone: 1350-728991; fax: 1350-728800).

Peter Readman Sporting Agent (Hirsel Law, Coldstream, Berwickshire TD12 4HX, Scotland; phone: 1890-882139).

Sport in Scotland, Ltd. (22 Market Brae, Inverness, Highland IV2 3AB, Scotland; phone: 1463-222757).

Strutt & Parker Sporting Agency (13 Hill St., Berkeley Sq., London W1X 8DL, England; phone: 171-629-7282).

Tours and Travel Promotions (25 Brunstane Dr., Edinburgh EH15 2NF, Scotland; phone: 131-669-5344).

HOTELS FOR SHOOTING HOLIDAYS

A number of hotels located in the richest shooting areas also can organize shooting holidays for their guests; among them are the following (listed alphabetically by location):

DEER PARK, Buckerell Village, Weston, Honiton, Devon, England This Georgian manor, set in 40 acres of Devonshire countryside, can arrange all forms of game shooting, from driven duck to clay shooting. There are 30 guestrooms and a restaurant. Private fishing is also available (see *Gone Fishing*). Information: *Deer Park Hotel,* Buckerell Village, Honiton, Devon EX14 0PG, England (phone: 1404-41266; fax: 1404-46598).

ARUNDELL ARMS, Lifton, Devon, England The well-organized program at this sportsman's hotel (with 30 rooms and a fine restaurant) includes four-day shoots for driven snipe, as well as driven pheasant shoots, duck flighting, rough and woodcock shooting, and red and roe deer stalking. (See also *Rural Retreats* and *Gone Fishing.*) Information: *Arundell Arms,* Lifton, Devon PL16 0AA, England (phone: 1566-784666; 800-528-1234; fax: 1566-784494).

AUCHTERARDER HOUSE, Perthshire, Scotland A sportsman's haven, this Victorian Scottish country retreat boasts a baronial, plant-filled, marble entry hall, a fine dining room, a wood-paneled library with a grand piano (the perfect spot for tea), and 15 elegant, antique-furnished rooms. Management can arrange stalking parties (for red deer), and guests can take advantage of the 4,000 game-stocked acres of parkland close by. Information: *Auchterarder House,* Perthshire PHE 1DL, Scotland (phone: 1764-663646; fax: 1764-62939).

TWEED VALLEY, Walkerburn, Borders, Scotland This former Edwardian country house, with beautiful views of the river Tweed and its valley, can arrange for grouse, pheasant, and mixed shooting as well as for roebuck and Sika deer stalking. There are 15 guestrooms and a good restaurant. Information: *Tweed Valley,* Walkerburn, Peeblesshire, Borders EH43 6AA, Scotland (phone: 1896-87636; fax: 1896-87639).

GOLDEN PHEASANT, near Chirk, Llangollen, Clwyd, Wales Perched in the Berwyn Mountains, this 18-room, 18th-century hotel with a restaurant is set in one of the finest areas in Wales for shooting high and fast pheasant as well as blackcock, another area specialty. There is also sport for grouse, partridge, and duck from August to November. Information: *Jenny Gibourg, Golden Pheasant,* Glyn Ceiriog, Llangollen, Clwyd LL20 7BB, Wales (phone: 1691-718281; fax: 1691-718479).

FOR FURTHER INFORMATION

For more details about shooting-oriented holidays, sports-minded visitors should contact the following:

British Field Sports Society (59 Kennington Rd., London SE1 7PZ, England; phone: 171-928-4742). A membership organization devoted to hunting, shooting, and fishing, the society can provide lists of shooting agents in the United Kingdom.

Clay Pigeon Shooting Association (107 Epping New Rd., Buckhurst Hill, Essex IG9 5TQ, England; phone: 181-505-62212). Governs and provides information about the sport in England.

Scottish Clay Target Association (10 Balgibbon Callander, Perthshire FK17 8EU, Scotland; phone: 1877-331323). Scotland's sister organization to the above.

Scottish Sporting Gazette (22 Market Brae, Inverness IV2 3AB, Scotland; phone: 1463-222757). A glossy 150-page annual (£10/about $15, including airmail) filled with articles on all aspects of Scottish hunting and fishing; advertisements for private hunting estates, country hotels, gun shops, and the like complete the coverage.

Great Walks and Mountain Rambles

Almost any walker will say that it is the footpaths of a country—not its roadways—that show off the landscape to best advantage. Closer to earth than when driving or even biking, those on foot notice details that might not otherwise come to their attention: tiny wildflowers blossoming cheerfully in a crack between limestone boulders, or a fox lurking in the shadows of the woods at dawn. Britain offers an enormous range of landscapes, from the subarctic Cairngorms to the tropical gardens at Inverewe, from volcanic forms to dumpling-like Ice Age deposits—and on any given day, the walker may traverse whole geological epochs.

And the scenery moves by at a relatively slow speed: Hedgerows, fences, and green velvet pastures can be contemplated at leisure. Churches and barns, old windmills and lichen-crusted stone walls, and farms and villages are seldom far out of sight when treading in the footsteps of Neolithic people or Bronze Age gold traders, traveling along Roman ways, or following tracks first defined by smugglers, cattle drovers, abbots, or coffin carriers, whose ways would often be marked at the tops of passes by the stone piles where they rested their loads. Many paths were literally walked into existence by generations of country folk traveling to work, market, church, or the ale house, and in all, over 100,000 miles of public footpaths have been recorded and mapped (a number that swells still further when those in Scotland, where the laws do not require that they be mapped and measured, are considered).

In England and Wales, many footpaths are in the 10 national parks and nearly 40 *Areas of Outstanding Natural Beauty* (*AONB*). The national parks, which cover some 5,256 square miles, about 9% of the total acreage of England and Wales, contain some of their most spectacular scenery, a blend of mountain and moor, down and heathland, cliffs and seashore, and all offer plenty of relatively wild mileage for the pedestrian. The land is not owned by the state, as in some countries, but remains in private hands, so that walkers must stick to the public rights-of-way unless a so-called access agreement exists, permitting otherwise (as in over half of Dartmoor and the *Lake District,* for example). *AONB*s enjoy a looser measure of legal protection. The *Countryside Commission,* the body responsible for designating these especially scenic areas, also has created several official long-distance trails by negotiating new rights-of-way and linking them to established footpaths. Each of these trails is highlighted by signposts, which announce its beginning and its direction, and by waymarkings, acorn symbols placed at potentially confusing junctures. (The *Countryside Commission* now advocates a standard system of marking throughout the country, using yellow arrows for footpaths and blue ones for bridleways.)

In Scotland, walkers won't be rambling in national parks as in England, because there are none, despite the fact that the land is some of Britain's loveliest and most varied—mountains and moors, lochs, grassy hills, forests and glens, cliffs and sandy beaches—and also its least populated. The law regarding rights-of-way is complex—and in principle walking just anywhere is not allowed. But in practice, it is possible for walkers to roam more or less freely as long as they respect the obviously off-limits, and keep off the moors during the early August through late October grouse-shooting and deer-stalking season.

The whole experience can be enormously rewarding—even when the weather turns rainy, as it often does at the height of the British summer (which King Charles II once gloomily described as "three fine days followed by a thunderstorm"). But come prepared. Stout walking shoes or boots are essential, as is a good rain parka with leggings. And in addition to the usual walker's gear, a spare sweater is essential, even on a day hike—especially on the British hills, where conditions can turn literally arctic within a matter of hours. Both hiking and backpacking equipment are best bought in the US, where the selection is greater and prices are lower.

WHERE TO WALK

Visitors don't have to dismiss the idea of walking in Britain just because they're not hotshot mountaineers at home. Even novices can share the delights: Just find a hotel in the heart of good walking country, and use it as home base for daily expeditions; at the end of each day, there'll be a hot bath and a hearty meal.

Areas that offer these experiences are delightfully abundant. Among *Areas of Outstanding Natural Beauty,* a number are really good for walking: the path-crossed, beechwoods-dotted chalk uplands known as the Chilterns, which roll through parts of Bedfordshire, Buckinghamshire, Hertfordshire, and Oxfordshire (for details, contact the *Southern Tourist Board,* 40 Chamberlayne Rd., Eastleigh, Hampshire S05 5JH, England; phone: 1703-620006); the 582 square miles of the oh-so-English Cotswolds, full of cozy villages, extending through the counties of Avon, Gloucestershire, Hereford and Worcester, Oxfordshire, and Wiltshire (*Heart of England Tourist Board,* Woodside, Larkhill Rd., Worcester WR5 2EF, England; phone: 1905-763436); rolling Dorset, with the "far from the madding crowd" scenery of novelist Thomas Hardy and its fine seaside vistas (*West Country Tourist Board,* 60 St. David's Hill, Exeter, Devon EX4 4SY, England; phone: 1392-76351); the distinctive Norfolk Coast, a delight to those whose souls resonate to its moody expanses of salt marshes and tidal creeks (*East Anglia Tourist Board,* Toppesfield Hall, Hadleigh, Suffolk IP7 5DN, England; phone: 1473-822922); the meandering Wye Valley and the Forest of Dean, where there are woodlands and lovely cliffs and gorges along the river to be explored (*Heart of England Tourist Board,* above). The Wye Valley continues through Wales, the country that is home to the breezy Gower Peninsula, where it's possible to tramp through the coastal dunes and beach country or head inland up into the hills (*Wales Tourist Board,* 14 Bridge St., Cardiff CF2 1OY, Wales; phone: 1222-499909).

National parks offer still better experiences—and public transportation is good enough that you don't have to plan all your trips to end back at your starting point.

Despite Britain's dense population, it is remarkably easy to get on a train or bus and, in a few hours, be walking alone through as remote a landscape as can be found almost anywhere—no matter where the starting point. Within a morning's ride of London, for example, there are expanses of land unexploited by agriculture, let alone by industry, which appear just as they would have to Stone Age man. (Don't wait too long to enjoy them. Every year more than 100 square miles of countryside disappear under asphalt or concrete, are inundated by manmade reservoirs, or are spiked by chimneys and telecommunications masts.)

Some of the most interesting of Britain's walking country—at the moment—is described below. Places are listed alphabetically by location.

DARTMOOR NATIONAL PARK, Devon, England The "melancholy moor" of Arthur Conan Doyle's *Hound of the Baskervilles,* a granite upland with bare hills sometimes crowned with weather-wrinkled granite tors, is a beautiful yet mostly savage area, intensely lonely. But there are some 500 miles of foot and bridle paths and 180 square miles of open moorland on which walkers may wander freely. Adventurous perambulators beware: Steer clear of the large chunks in the north that form part of military firing ranges (marked on OS maps); avoid the marshes; and never venture onto the moor without a compass, spare clothing, and emergency rations. Information: *Dartmoor National Park,* Haytor Rd., Bovey Tracey, Devon TQ13 9JQ, England (phone: 1626-832093).

EXMOOR NATIONAL PARK, Devon and Somerset, England Bounded on the north by the sea and a spectacular stretch of the South-West Peninsula Coast Path, the sandstone uplands of *Exmoor* are less harsh and more varied than *Dartmoor:* They are covered in grass or heather and bracken; riven by combes, or valleys, dense with scrub oak, birch, ash, elder, holly, and conifers; crisscrossed by lively rivers; patched with farmlands; and scattered with pretty villages. It is a rounded, curvaceous world. "The land lies softly," said Lorna Doone. Red deer, a legacy of the days when central *Exmoor* was a royal hunting forest, still can be seen here, along with herds of wild ponies. Since *Exmoor*'s open moorland is primarily restricted to the west, walkers are more restricted to defined routes than at *Dartmoor,* but there are still 600 miles of way-marked paths and bridleways from which to choose. Information: *Exmoor National Park, Exmoor House,* Dulverton, Somerset TA22 9HL, England (phone: 1398-23665).

LAKE DISTRICT NATIONAL PARK, Cumbria, England This 880-square-mile area is the largest national park in Britain. It is also one of the most beautiful, with jewel-like lakes, steep mountains, and dazzling seasonal color changes. Poets and writers—among them Samuel Taylor Coleridge, John Ruskin, Hugh Walpole, and Beatrix Potter—have been inspired by the landscape; the area's fame has grown to such proportions that walkers can no longer expect to "wander lonely as a cloud" just everywhere—as did the 19th-century romantic poet William Wordsworth. To experience the real, natural beauty of the *Lake District,* steer clear of the larger tourist centers such as Ambleside, Keswick, and Windermere; avoid weekends and public holidays; or go just a bit farther afield than everyone else—something that is not too difficult since there are hundreds of miles of footpaths here, ranging from nature trails along the lakeshore and in the valleys to the strenuous routes that cross the mountains. By tradition, visitors can go almost anywhere on the open Highland, and with care, anyone can reach the summits of 3,206-foot Scafell Pike, 3,054-foot Skiddaw, and 3,116-foot Helvellyn—three of the park's more noteworthy peaks. Leaflets describing various walks are available from the park's information office, and guided walks are also available. The best general guidebook to the area is the *A. A. Ordnance Survey Leisure Guide to the Lake District* (£9.99/about $15; available from the *Park Management and Visitors Services National Park Office,* address below); the best footpath guides are in Alfred Wainwright's seven-volume *A Pictorial Guide to the Lakeland Fells*

(£8.99/about $13.50 per volume; available through the park office). *English Lakeland Ramblers* (18 Stuyvesant Oval, #1A, New York, NY 10009; phone: 212-505-1020 or 800-724-8801; fax: 212-674-5711) offers escorted hiking and walking tours monthly May through October. Visitors also can sightsee by minibus. For general information, contact the *Park Management and Visitors Services National Park Office,* Brockhole, Windermere, Cumbria LA23 1LJ, England (phone: 15394-46601; fax: 15394-45555); and the *Cumbria Tourist Board,* Ashleigh, Windermere, Cumbria LA23 2AQ, England (phone: 15394-46499; fax: 15394-47439).

NORTHUMBERLAND NATIONAL PARK, Northumberland, England This long, narrow 398-square-mile region, one of England's least populated, extends southward from the Scottish border, through the lonely sheep-spotted Cheviot Hills and the heather- and bracken-clad Simonside Hills, to *Hadrian's Wall*—the most spectacular legacy of Britain's 400-year Roman occupation, and one of the world's most important archaeological remains outside Greece and Italy (see *Ancient Monuments and Ruins*). The diversity of landscape results from a lively geological history whose players include the ancient volcano that created the Cheviots, the sea (which subsequently inundated the land), the monumental up-thrusting forces that created the Highlands, and the glaciers that carved the terrain into an approximation of its present shape. The Pennine Way, one of the most difficult of England's long-distance footpaths (described below), is among the especially scenic trails in the park. Information: *National Park Officer, Northumberland National Park,* Eastburn, South Park, Hexham, Northumberland NE46 1BS, England (phone: 1434-605555).

NORTH YORK MOORS NATIONAL PARK, North Yorkshire, England The site of the largest expanse of heather-covered moorland in England and Wales, this 553-square-mile park is a walker's paradise with 1,130 scenic miles of public footpaths. From rolling heather moors, which flower to even higher glory in August, to placid, rich green dales and vale plains full of market towns, villages, neat rows of cottages, and a peppering of distinctive farmhouses looking as solid as fortresses, it offers a naturally beautiful landscape that man's additions have only enhanced. Considering the additional visual rewards offered by the dramatic, cliff-lined coastline that edges the park on the east, it's not hard to understand why, each year, the area attracts some 137,000 visitors on an average summer Sunday. But once on the moors, except at *Easter* and during the summer, only the occasional sheep staring contentedly through the mists is to be seen. The Cleveland Way, a walk that consists of over 100 miles skirting the coast and the park's inland boundaries on its way around most of the circumference of the park, and the Esk Valley Walk, which follows the river Esk for 30 miles from its source on the high moors to the sea at Whitby, are among the longer footpaths, but there are many others. Details about the park and leaflets describing area long-distance walks and accommodations are available from the park's *Information Service, North York Moors National Park, The Old Vicarage,* Bondgate, Helmsley, York YO6 5BP, England (phone: 1439-70657).

PEAK DISTRICT NATIONAL PARK, Derbyshire, England An island of rugged countryside standing close to but aloof from the booming metropolises of Manchester, Sheffield, and Derby, the *Peak District National Park* consists of green and grassy limestone uplands, known as the White Peak, and moorlands that form a horseshoe around it, the sharp-edged gritstone Dark Peak. The aggregation offers walking of every grade, from gentle strolls along the river valleys of, say, the Dove and Derwent, through limestone outcrop country, with its caverns and cliffs, to the bracing treks across the moors and wild peat bog of Kinder Scout, Bleaklow, and Black Hill. The Pennine Way begins at Edale, the southern end of the Pennine chain, and works its way up and over the tough plateau. Information: *Peak District National Park Office, Aldern House,* Baslow Rd., Bakewell, Derbyshire DE45 1AE, England (phone: 1629-814321; fax: 1629-812659).

BRECON BEACONS NATIONAL PARK, Brecon, Powys, Wales The national park is centered in southern Powys and extends into the neighboring counties of Dyfed, Mid-Glamorgan, and Gwent. These 519 square miles of high hills, crags, and bleak moors in mid-Wales, with the lonely Black Mountain on the west and the flat-topped Black Mountains (a different mountain range) on the east, embody the sort of imposing area that most people either love or hate. Apart from summits, ridges, and moorland, it encompasses woodlands, farms, lakes, and the valley of the river Usk. Those who like their strolls low and level may enjoy the 30-mile-long Monmouthshire and Brecon Canal towpath. Offa's Dyke Path passes over the Black Mountains. Information: *Information Officer, Brecon Beacons National Park,* 7 Glamorgan St., Brecon, Powys LD3 7DP, Wales (phone: 1874-624437).

SNOWDONIA NATIONAL PARK, Gwynedd, Wales Bordered on the west by the beaches and sand dunes of Cardigan Bay, this 838-square-mile expanse of mountains, glacier-scoured passes and valleys, lovely lakes, and white-foaming waterfalls is flecked with hill farms, solid little market towns, and sleepy villages. Climbers come here by the score to tackle 3,560-foot Snowdon (the loftiest summit in England and Wales) and the other 14 peaks over 3,000 feet in the challenging Snowdon range. But the area is also a hiker's paradise: there are guided walks, nature trails, and scores of footpaths. Information: *Snowdonia National Park Information Service,* Penrhyndeudraeth, Gwynedd LL48 6LF, Wales (phone: 1766-770274), and, for lodging, the *North Wales Tourism Marketing Bureau,* 77 Conway Rd., Colwyn Bay, Clwyd LL29 7LN, Wales (phone: 1492-531731), and the *Mid Wales Regional Office, Wales Tourist Board,* Canolfan Owain Glyndwr, Machynlleth, Powys SY20 8EE, Wales (phone: 1654-702401).

STAR TREKS

If day-tripping seems a bit tame, consider a walking tour along one of several long-distance footpaths in England and Wales. Fourteen of them already have been created by the *Countryside Commission,* and others are being planned. They are created by establishing new rights-of-way to link previously existing trails to form continuous, multi-mile stretches of public footpath, which are then signposted and, at shifts in directions and other potentially confusing points, way-marked with acorn symbols. In addition, there are over 70 other recreational walks devised by local county councils, rambling groups, and even individual enthusiasts eager to share their love of a particular corner of the English landscape, sometimes their own rural backyard. The number of these long-distance delights, both officially and informally arranged, is steadily increasing all the time.

One of the pleasures of traversing these routes is that, while they cover some of the nation's loveliest countryside, they're close enough to civilization that it's possible to stay overnight en route at small hotels, bed and breakfast establishments, or huts and mountaineering hostels—or to camp out with tent, sleeping bag, and cook stove. The *Ramblers' Association* (1-5 Wandsworth Rd., Vauxhall, London SW8 2XX, England; phone: 171-582-6878) publishes an annually updated *Ramblers' Yearbook* (available for £10/about $15, including postage), which lists 2,500 bed and breakfast houses convenient to long-distance footpaths. Camping is permitted, though it's essential to ask permission of the landowner before pitching a tent for the night, particularly where the surrounding land is cultivated, not only to avoid problems but also to make friends: More than one farmer has been known to show up in the morning bearing a pint of fresh milk for visiting campers to pour over their morning granola. For a free leaflet on long-distance footpaths, *Britain for Walkers,* contact the *British Tourist Authority* or the *Countryside Commission* (Postal Sales, PO Box 124, Walgrave, Northampton NN6 9TL, England; phone: 1604-781848). Also contact the *Ramblers' Association* (address above). A guidebook series on long-distance routes in both England and Scotland, copublished by the *Countryside Commission* and Aurum Press, contains detailed maps and information and is available from the *Countryside Commission* (address above); each book costs £9/about $13.50, including postage.

A number of walking guides, such as *Remote Walks Around Lakeland, Forty-Four Walks on the Island of Arran,* and *Walks on the Isle of Skye,* are available from their publisher, the *Westmorland Gazette* (Attn. Bookshop, 22 Stricklandgate, Kendal, Cumbria LA9 4NE, England; phone: 1539-720555). Each of the guides mentioned above costs £5.95 (about $9), plus shipping and handling.

CLEVELAND WAY, from Helmsley to Filey, North Yorkshire, England This horseshoe-shape, 100-mile footpath bobs along over moors and down dales, then sweeps along the cliff tops of the county's stunning coastline. The going, while not particularly rough, does demand more than either the North and South Downs trails or the Ridgeway (all described below), and, though rain is not a problem in this relatively dry corner of the nation, occasional chilly spells require warm clothing. For details, consult Ian Sampson's *The Cleveland Way* (£8.99/about $13.50), which may be ordered from the *Countryside Commission* (address above).

COTSWOLD WAY, from Chipping Campden, Gloucestershire, to Bath, Avon, England The attractions of this 100-mile route, which runs along the crest of a limestone escarpment—one of those outside the purview of the *Countryside Commission*—include ever-changing skies, panoramic views out over wooded valleys and lush green fields, and frequent calls at the delightfully mellow yellow villages scattered here and there along the way. The pathway ends at the *Roman Baths* themselves. *The Cotswold Way* by Mark B. Richards, describes the route; it's available from Thornhill Press (3 Fountain Way, Park End, Lydney, Gloucestershire GL15 4H, England; phone: 1594-564984) for £1.50/about $2.25 (£2.25/about $3.40 if ordering by mail from the US).

DALES WAY, from Ilkley, West Yorkshire, to Bowness-on-Windermere, Cumbria, England Apart from a climb over the Pennines' watershed (where only fate determines whether a raindrop finds its way to the North Sea instead of the Irish), this 78-mile-long hike involves low-lying country along the banks of lovely clear rivers. For details, see Colin Speakman's *The Dales Way* (£4.95/about $7.50), which can be ordered from Dalesman Publishing, Ltd. (Clapham, Lancaster LA2 8EB, England; phone: 15242-51225) or Terry Marsh's *The Dales Way* (£5.99/about $9), which can be ordered from Cicerone Press (Milnthorpe, Cumbria LA7 7PY, England; phone: 15395-62069).

HADRIAN'S WALL, near Newcastle upon Tyne, Tyne & Wear, England This ancient Roman barrier against barbarians survives only in parts: Some are buried by Newcastle, some have been used as a foundation for a military road, and some can be found embedded in the walls of churches and farmhouses in the vicinity. But forts, castles, turrets, and other features remain, along with parts of the wall itself, and the Pennine Way follows it for 9 of its 73 miles from Wallsend to Bowness, near Carlisle, on the Solway Firth. While there is no continuous right of way along the wall, it can be pursued further on a path that runs for 28 miles from *Sewingshields Farm,* near Hexham, to Wallfoot, near Carlisle; there is a particularly impressive stretch between Chollerford and Gilsand. Accommodations are difficult to find and usually out of the way. A good guidebook is *The Wall Walk,* by Mark Richards (£7.99/about $12), which can be ordered from Cicerone Press (Milnthorpe, Cumbria LA7 7PY, England; phone: 15395-62069). Information: *Northumberland National Park Information Service,* Eastburn, South Park, Hexham, Northumberland NE46 1BS, England (phone: 1434-605555; fax: 1434-600522).

NORTH DOWNS WAY, from Farnham, Surrey, to Dover, Kent, England This 141-mile-long footpath travels through the rolling Surrey Hills and Kent Downs, along the crest of the North Downs, and across several rivers and highways to its end at Shakespeare Cliff, where the panorama is of the celebrated English Channel. In parts, the footpath follows the medieval Pilgrims' Way. The North Downs Way is similar to its cousin, the South Downs Way (described below), but has more nooks and crannies and fewer grand, obstacle-free stretches in which to develop a steady stride. But the going is relatively easy, as is access to London via train and bus. For details, consult Christopher John Wright's *A Guide to the Pilgrims' Way and the North Downs Way* (£10.95/about $16.50) available from Constable & Co. (3 The Lanchesters, 162 Fulham Palace Rd., London W6 9ER, England; phone: 181-741-3663).

PENNINE WAY, from Edale, Derbyshire, England, to Kirk Yetholm, Borders, Scotland The first of the official trails to be designated "expressly for those who seek the call of the hills and the lonely places," this track comprises 250 demanding, often extremely boggy miles, up the backbone of England to a point just north of the Scottish border, traversing the Pennines, the *Peak District National Park,* and the Cheviots en route. It also offers great diversity, traveling through eerie forests and over high peaks, down old pack horse and shepherds' tracks and old Roman roads, across several rivers, and along well-preserved portions of *Hadrian's Wall* to a point not far from the impressive fort at Housesteads. But it's not for everyone: More altitude is gained than climbing Everest, and the weather can be terrible (and dangerous, particularly at this latitude and these altitudes). In addition, although bed and breakfast accommodations can be found along some of the route, along other sections it is essential to plan stops carefully—or to carry camping gear. But for experienced walkers, this famous footpath is a delight.

RIDGEWAY, from Overton Hill, near Avebury, Wiltshire, to Ivinghoe Beacon, Buckinghamshire, England Following the ancient Icknield Way and the Great Ridgeway, first trod by Neolithic man, this 85-mile-long footpath offers an abundance of ancient burial places, religious monuments, Iron Age hill forts, and other evidence of bygone days as it traverses farms, beech woods, and downlands. The section from Overton Hill to Goring has been designated a bridleway, permitting its use by cyclists and horseback riders as well as by hikers, but at no point is the going particularly difficult.

SOUTH DOWNS WAY, from Eastbourne, Sussex, to Harting, near Petersfield, Hampshire, England In his *Natural History of Selbourne,* Gilbert White referred to the South Downs as "majestic mountains"; and, indeed, when standing on high and looking southward toward the sea or in the opposite direction, across the partly wooded Weald (the remains of an ancient forest), toward the North Downs, most hikers do feel themselves at the top of the world. Nonetheless, the 80-mile route through the range of chalk hills known as the South Downs offers relatively gentle walking. And there's no shortage of places to stay along the way. Most of the South Downs Way is also a bridleway, shared with cyclists and horseback riders—in fact, only the segment across the cliff tops of the Seven Sisters near Eastborne is exclusive to walkers. For details, consult the *Society of Sussex Downsmen*'s *Along the South Downs Way to Winchester,* which describes the route in both directions and on to Winchester; it can be ordered for £5.40 (about $8.10) from *Society of Sussex Downsmen* (254 Victoria Dr., Eastbourne, East Sussex BN20 8QT, England; phone: 1323-732227).

SOUTHWEST COAST, from Studland, Dorset, to Minehead, Somerset, England For lovers of hours spent with the sea as a constant companion, this 567-mile track is not only England's longest long-distance footpath but also its best, and, except for its considerable number of ups and downs, the walking is not difficult. There are four sections: The shortest stretch, at 72 miles, is the Dorset Coast Path. Noted for its special, quiet loveliness, it consists essentially of high cliff walking, nearly always in sight of the sea. The South Devon Coast Path passes largely through the *South Devon* and *East Devon Areas of Outstanding Natural Beauty,* which are full of stunning headlands, broad rivers, busy resort towns, quiet bays, and lush greenery. The Cornwall Coast Path leads around Land's End, past spectacular cliffs, lighthouses, stone circles, and more resorts. And the Somerset and North Devon Coast Path travels through 35 miles of *Exmoor National Park,* from Minehead into the *North Devon Area of Outstanding Natural Beauty* as far as Marsland Mouth, bordering Cornwall. The trip is not strenuous, except for the Woody Bay-to-Coombe Martin leg and the last slog before Marsland Mouth. On a clear day, the fortunate can catch a glimpse of Wales from Foreland Point and Selworthy Beacon.Alông the path, accommodations and campsites are easy to find. But since this is a resort area, reserve ahead for visits during school holidays.

For more information, consult the *Sou'West Way Association*'s *Complete Guide to the Coastal Path* (£3.95/about $6), which is available from the *Sou'West Way Association* (1 Orchard Dr., Kingskerswell, Newton Abbot, Devon TQ12 5DG, England; phone: 1803-873061).

WOLDS WAY, from Filey, North Yorkshire, to North Ferriby, Humberside, England This long-distance footpath traverses considerable agricultural land and follows the chalk hills and pretty valleys of the Yorkshire Wolds for 71 miles, from the eastern terminus of the Cleveland Way to the banks of the river Humber to the south. For details, consult Roger Ratcliffe's *Wolds Way* (£8.99/about $13.50), which can be ordered from the *Countryside Commission* (address above).

OFFA'S DYKE PATH, from near Chepstow, Gwent, to Prestatyn, Clwyd, Wales For 60 of its total 168 miles, this Welsh track follows the distinctive earthwork built in the 8th century by King Offa of Mercia as a frontier between England

and Wales. It meanders through the *Shropshire Hills* and *Wye Valley Areas of Outstanding Natural Beauty;* climbs up into the imposing Black Mountains; passes through Hay-on-Wye, the town of books (see *Shopping Spree*); and eventually tracks a high ridge through the Clwydian Hills. The walking can be demanding in spots; the terrain is wonderfully varied, taking in everything from wild hills to wooded valleys and peaceful lowlands. For details, consult Christopher John Wright's *A Guide to Offa's Dyke Path* (£8.95/about $13.50, from Constable, address above); Mark Richard's *Through the Welsh Borders Country Following the Offa's Dyke Path* (£4.50/about $6.75, from Thornhill Press, address above); and the Offa's Dyke Association's *Offa's Dyke Path South* and *Offa's Dyke Path North* (each £8.95/about $13.50, from the *Countryside Commission,* address above). For more information on the South Wales region bordered by the path, contact the *South Wales Regional Office, Wales Tourist Board,* Ty Croeso, 6 Gloucester Pl., Swansea, West Glamorgan SA1 1TY, Wales (phone: 1792-781212).

PEMBROKESHIRE COAST PATH, from St. Dogmaels to Amroth, Dyfed, Wales Despite the beauty of the wild seascapes of this southwestern part of the country, the area has remained unspoiled by visitors, and often it's possible to walk for many hours along this 180-mile-long footpath without meeting a soul. Not the least of its special offerings, it also provides wonderful scenery: limestone and sandstone cliffs, windswept headlands, jagged inlets and coves, splendid beaches, and blue water (warm in summer, icy the rest of the year). The walking varies from easy to the occasionally strenuous. The *Pembrokeshire Coast National Park* (address below) publishes a series of ten Coast Path cards, a mileage chart, and other informational pieces. Information: *Pembrokeshire Coast National Park,* County Offices, Haverfordwest, Dyfed SA61 1QZ, Wales (phone: 1437-764591).

MAPS AND MORE INFORMATION

When Daniel Boone was once asked whether he had ever been lost, he replied, "Nope, but I was a mite confused once for three days." To avoid that fate, and to help plan a trip, it's essential to have the proper maps and guidebooks.

Some of the most beautiful areas of Britain are covered by an-inch-equals-a-mile tourist maps and by 1:25,000-scale outdoor leisure maps. These are the best choices for those regions for which they exist. Elsewhere, consult the relevant 1:50,000 Ordnance Survey maps. Rights-of-way are indicated by red lines (the dotted lines referring to footpaths, the dashes to bridleways). These symbols and the many others are explained in an elaborate key, a brief study of which will have anyone with even a little aptitude reading these British plans as well as, if not better than, the far less colorful US Geological Survey maps.

In addition, virtually every defined trail in Britain is also covered by one or more step-by-step guidebooks. To find out exactly what's available and what you need, contact the *Ramblers' Association* (1-5 Wandsworth Rd.,

Vauxhall, London SW8 2XX, England; phone: 171-582-6878) for copies of county *Path Guides* (£1/about $1.50 each, postpaid), which list relevant guidebooks and maps for the main walking areas of the country and include a practical guide to way-marking—an essential for someone who doesn't know the system. Authoritative general books on walking in Britain provide information for footpaths, *AONB*s, and national parks throughout England, Scotland, and Wales.

A good magazine for the hiking enthusiast is *The Great Outdoors,* published monthly by George Outram Ltd. (*Plaza Tower,* Seventh Floor, The Plaza, East Kilbridge, Glasgow G74 1LW, Scotland; phone: 13552-42464), which is available by direct subscription and from most major newsstands and outdoor equipment shops. In addition to both informative and descriptive articles on hiking, backpacking, and cycling, each issue includes a useful directory that lists stores specializing in outdoor equipment; reviews of equipment, maps, local guidebooks, and other books; and advertisements for equipment rental agencies and organizations that sponsor walking tours.

As background reading, try to locate a copy of John Hillaby's *A Walk Through Britain* (Houghton Mifflin; out of print, but check your library).

Many useful hiking publications and maps can be bought at *Edward Stanford Ltd.* (12 Long Acre, London WC2E 9LP, England; phone: 171-836-1321).

Several firms in Britain coordinate group excursions for people who don't want to go it alone—or do all the requisite planning. For more information, see GETTING READY TO GO.

Spectator Sports

After many a round on any one of Britain's classic golf layouts or multiple tennis matches played on grass, there are those quintessentially British sports that are best enjoyed from the vantage point of a comfortable seat. While many of these national sports are barely known in the US, there are games that are, in fact, the ancestors of our own national pastimes. And for those Americans interested in getting to know football and baseball's British cousins, herewith a spectator's sampling.

CRICKET For many visitors, cricket is idiosyncratically English—and far too slow for most to sit enraptured for hours on end. The game dates from the 12th or 13th century, although the official rules were not established until 1744. Yet, baseball fans will discover that while the two games appear to be different, there are many parallels, especially now that one-day matches are played (usually on Sundays). There was a time when a Test Match—an international competition between Britain and teams from its former colonies, such as Australia, India, Pakistan, New Zealand, or the West Indies—could last a week and still end in a draw. Given the potentially interminable nature of the game, the *Marylebone Cricket Club (MCC)*—the body that controls cricket—has changed the rules to speed things up.

In the center of its large expanse of immaculately mown grass, 15 men dressed in white perform the game's complicated rituals. The two men in coats are the umpires; the two with bats are part of the team that is "in" (up) trying to score "runs"; the other nine members of the team are in the pavilion, or dugout, awaiting their turn at bat. The bowler (pitcher) tries to get the batsmen "out" by hitting the wickets (three wooden sticks behind the batsman) with the bowled ball. For his part, the batsman is trying to hit the ball and prevent it from hitting the wicket. The rest of the men on the field try to catch a hit before it bounces. Everyone cheers when a batsman hits a ball to the boundary (the equivalent of the outfield wall) for four runs, or better still if the ball goes over without bouncing (six runs). After the bowler throws the balls six times from one end (this is called an "over"), the bowling changes ends and all the fielders move around. During this British version of a seventh-inning stretch, spectators also can move around; during play, however, they are expected to remain seated.

If you want to understand the English character—which emphasizes good sportsmanship, team spirit, skill, courage, and endurance—there is no substitute for spending an afternoon sipping beer in the shade with friends on a languid summer day, listening to the *thwack* of leather on willow. Whether it's a local cricket match on the village green, a county match, or the country's best players matching wits and stamina with teams from abroad at *Lord's Cricket Ground* in London, try to watch the game with someone who can explain it. The pace at which cricket is played is slow enough so that there is plenty of time to learn what is happening without missing any of the action—which, at times, can be explosive and spectacular.

The season runs from mid-April to early September, and matches are played by both university teams and professional county teams. International, or Test, matches take place annually. The importance of the game was solidified in 1882 at the *Oval* when the Australians trounced the British; the morning after, London's shocked *Sporting Times* ran an obituary for British cricket, announcing that its remains would be cremated. Since then, any England-Australia Test Match is played for the "Ashes," which repose in an urn that never leaves the *Cricket Memorial Gallery* at *Lord's Cricket Ground*—not even if Australia wins. *Lord's Cricket Ground* (St. John's Wood Rd., London NW8, England; phone: 171-289-1611), home of the *MCC*, is *the* place to see a game. The next best place is the *Oval* (Kennington, London SE11, England; phone: 171-582-6660), home of the *Surrey County Cricket Club* and site of the 1882 humiliation.

CURLING Scotland participates in the *Rugby Union Football* frenzy, but it also has its own pastimes. Assuredly its renown lies in golf, whose origins are firmly ensconced in the country. Yet, Scotland is also responsible for the development, if not the birth, of curling, a major winter sport. Curling is somewhat related to shuffleboard and has been almost as successful an export as golf. There are now many more curlers in Canada than in Scotland, but the Scots have the historical advantage: They have been curling since the 16th century. The *Royal Caledonian Curling Club (RCC),* founded in 1838, is the governing body of the sport. The game is played on a 46-yard-long ice rink with 40-pound stones (also known as "granites"). Two players or "curlers" slide eight stones toward a circular target, while assistants vigorously brush the ice with brooms along the stone's path in an attempt to place a stone nearest the center. For more information: contact the *RCC* at 81 Great King St., Edinburgh EH3 6RN, Scotland (phone: 131-225-7083).

HIGHLAND GAMES You'll see plenty of kilts, not to mention sheer brute strength at these traditional athletic meets, which have taken place since the 11th century. The games are an integral part of the clan gatherings and bagpipe and dance competitions all over the Scottish Highlands during the summer. The calendar is especially busy in August and early September. Even the queen attends the *Braemar Royal Highland Gathering,* the best known of the Highland games, which is held near *Balmoral Castle* on the first Saturday in September. Most of the games are running and throwing events that are venues for professional players. The main event at many a gathering is a sport called "tossing the caber"; actually a tree trunk of considerable weight is "tossed" from a vertical position by a stalwart athlete (if he can manage it). The 19-foot, 120-pound caber employed at the *Braemar* games has rarely been tossed. The rules of the *Scottish Games Association* require that the caber starts out bigger and heavier than any of the athletes can handle, but that it can be cut down if it can't be tossed. Trust us, it takes superhuman strength. Besides those at Braemar, other important games are the *Portree Highland Games* on the Isle of Skye, the *Cowal Highland Gathering* at Dunoon, and the *Aboyne Highland Games.* A detailed list of events is available from the *Inverness, Loch Ness and Nairn Tourist Board, Castle Wynd*, Inverness IV2 3BJ, Scotland (phone: 1463-234353).

POLO No one is sure where this game originated—it's presumed to come from somewhere in central Asia (and according to one tale, in the 12th and early 13th centuries, the Mongols used to play a version of it using the heads of slain enemies as the ball). However, it's known to have arrived in Britain via India, where enthusiastic British Army officers discovered its charms. The first match seems to have been played in 1871 on the outskirts of London. From the beginning, it has been a rich man's sport, since it takes a lot of money to maintain a string of polo ponies—and a string of them is necessary: The game is a fast and punishing one for the horses (they're called ponies, though technically, they're not), and the players change mounts more than once during a game. There are some 1,300 players in Britain, and the fact that Prince Charles is among them helps to keep the game very much alive. The *Hurlingham Polo Association* (Winterlake,

Kirklington, Kidlington, Oxford OX5 3HG, England; phone: 1896-50044) is polo's governing body. To see a match, go to *Smith's Lawn* (*Windsor Great Park,* Windsor) or to *Cowdray Park* (Midhurst, West Sussex) on summer weekends.

RUGBY FOOTBALL The irony of rugby football is best expressed in an old saying that states "Rugby is a game for ruffians played by gentlemen, while soccer is a game for gentlemen played by ruffians." In 1823, a schoolboy at the great English public school of *Rugby* unwittingly invented an entirely new game when, contrary to the rules, he picked up a soccer ball and began running forward with it. This deviation of play, along with direct tackling, became the basis of the new sport, and was formalized in 1871, when the *Rugby Football Union* was established. Once rugby was exported to the US, it developed into American football, which it resembles—somewhat. In Britain, rugby is played from September to April on Saturday afternoons by school and university teams, county teams, hospital teams, and by anyone else who can bring together the requisite 15 players per side. The most memorable maneuver is the "set scrum," one means by which play begins, when the forwards of opposing teams, like two compact and only apparently disorderly phalanxes, push and shove against each other for possession of the ball. The Welsh, once the undisputed champions, have recently been overrun by powerful English teams, but they continue to fight to regain their status.

The rugby season begins slowly in early autumn, picks up momentum after *Christmas* (when tryouts for places on the English, Welsh, and Scottish teams are held), and climaxes in February with the Internationals, which draws huge crowds. These competitions—called the *Triple Crown* (or, more informally, *Five Nations*)—take place on a home and away basis among Scotland, Ireland, England, Wales, and France. There also are occasional visits from teams from New Zealand (the *Allblacks*) and Australia (the *Wallabies*), who play the British team (made up of players from the national teams within Great Britain). The most important matches are played in southwest London at *Twickenham,* headquarters of the *Rugby Football Union*'s controlling body (Whitton Rd., Twickenham; phone: 181-892-8161 for information; 181-571-6880 for tickets). In Wales, the place to see a match is *Cardiff Arms Park National Rugby Stadium* (phone: 1222-390111), on the right bank of the Taff River.

Rugby League—a semi-professional version—is played largely for and in the working class areas of Northern England using only 13 players on a team. The league stronghold is principally in Lancashire and Yorkshire, but the *Rugby League Challenge Cup Final* takes place at London's *Wembley Stadium* in May.

SOCCER The most popularly attended sport in Great Britain, soccer was originally called football long before Americans began to play anything remotely resembling it. After rugby came on the scene, the *London Football*

Association was formed in 1863 to protect the purity of the original football game, which then become known as "association football" and eventually as "soccer"—an abbreviation for the word "association." During the 1970s and 1980s, however, many fans preferred to watch soccer on TV from the comfort of their armchairs, for fear of spectator violence on the grounds. This reputation was earned through a handful of horrific incidents where spectators were trampled by overexcited fans wedged into cramped standing areas. Increased police protection, however, has quelled the aggressive behavior, and it is once again safe to observe from the stands.

Competitions in Britain and on the Continent are exciting, particularly when the *European Cup* and *World Cup* tournaments are in progress or the *Football Association Cup Final* takes place. The tough competition of the *English Premier Division* in particular shows what an entertaining, skillful sport soccer can be when it is played by topnotch athletes.

Almost every medium-size town has a local soccer team of either professional or amateur standing. For instance, stouthearted visitors to London determined to see what it's all about can follow the crowds to the grounds of some of the most popular professional clubs: *Arsenal, Highbury Stadium* (Avenell Rd., N5; phone: 171-226-0304); *Chelsea, Stamford Bridge* grounds (Fulham Rd., SW6; phone: 171-385-5545); *Tottenham Hotspur, White Hart Lane Stadium* (748 High Rd., N17; phone: 181-808-8080); and *West Ham United, Boleyn Park* (Green St., E13; phone: 181-472-2740).

The *Football Association Cup Final,* the equivalent of the *World Series,* takes place at *Wembley Stadium,* London (phone: 181-902-1234), in May, before a crowd of 100,000. Tickets sometimes can be bought at the stadium up to an hour before the match (at a very dear price), but they usually are sold out in advance to club members for the *Cup Final.* Rest assured it will be on the telly. The season runs August through May, and games are played on Saturday afternoons. For a schedule, contact the *Football Association Ltd.* (16 Lancaster Gate, London W2 3LW, England; phone: 171-262-4542), or any *British Tourist Authority* office.

Directions

The Cotswolds

Less than 100 miles west of London is the region known as the Cotswolds. It encompasses about 450 square miles of rolling limestone upland of the Cotswold Hills, punctuated by charming, carefully preserved medieval towns and villages built from the honey-colored stone, quarried from the hills, which gives the region its character. The Cotswolds themselves stretch northeast in a curving 60-mile arc from Bath to the vicinity of Stratford-upon-Avon. Along their western edge they form a steep ridge of solid limestone, and their crest is the Thames-Severn watershed. But the overall character of the countryside is tranquil and picturesque. Much of this land is a great, sweeping pasture for the famous Cotswold sheep, with their heavy ringlets of fleece that once upon a time brought wealth to the area.

This is the England of the imagination: rolling hills covered by copses of ancient oak and surviving elm, a landscape scaled to size for country walks and bird watching. Towns are tied to one another by twisting country lanes that carry a constant commerce of farmers and shepherds, postmen, parsons, and pubgoers. The vista from any hill is as apt to include the square tower of a Norman church as a far field of cropping sheep, and any church is likely to be surrounded by the stone tile or thatch roofs of a tiny village, now no longer populated by farm workers but by retired folk, weekenders, and commuters to the larger towns. Village cemeteries are shaded by yews and village streams are guarded by weeping willows. Nothing is very far from anything else, but privacy and protective isolation are accentuated by the quiet and country peace that settles over all. Village names are remnants of an earlier language and a younger England: Wyck Rissington, Upper and Lower Slaughter, Oddington, Guiting Power, Clapton-on-Hill, Bourton-on-the-Water, Moreton-in-Marsh.

The Cotswolds provided a rich agricultural center for the Romans until the 5th century, and the Roman presence is still visible in many places, such as the roads out of Cirencester and the baths in Bath. The Saxons routed the Romans; the Normans routed the Saxons; and they all left their mark. But when the Cotswold sheep began to pay off, it was the wool merchants of the Middle Ages who built the enduring symbols of the area—magnificent churches such as the 14th-century *St. John the Baptist* at Cirencester and the 15th-century one at Northleach.

Our route through the Cotswolds is long, lazy, and serpentine. We begin in Oxford and end in Bath, both important and fascinating cities that border the Cotswolds area. In between we savor most of those golden towns that are quintessentially Cotswold in flavor: Burford, Bourton-on-the-Water, Stow-on-the-Wold, Moreton-in-Marsh, Chipping Campden, Broadway, Winchcombe, Cheltenham, Cirencester, and Malmesbury.

An eminently English way to see the Cotswolds is to go on shanks' mare and walk all or part of the 100-mile Cotswold Way, a trail that links a series of well-marked and easily negotiated paths that follow the crests of the Cotswold Hills from Bath to Chipping Campden in the north (see *Great Walks and Mountain Rambles* in DIVERSIONS). The area is also a haven for antiques collectors (see *Antiques and Auctions* in DIVERSIONS).

A useful booklet, *Great Escapes,* is available free from the *Heart of England Tourist Board* (Larkhill Rd., Worcester WR5 2EF, England; phone: 1905-763436).

The area is extremely popular with tourists from all over Britain, as well as visitors from abroad, all wanting to immerse themselves amid the picturesque villages and gentle countryside. Many of the shops selling gifts and souvenirs in the places listed below are open Sundays, too. Although the hotels and inns quickly fill up, especially in summer, it is often possible to find last-minute, simple bed and breakfast accommodations at farms or private houses. Expect to pay at least $135 per night for a double room (with private bath, TV set, and breakfast included unless otherwise indicated) in those places listed as expensive; from $90 to $135 in the moderate range; and less than $90 for inexpensive places. A dinner for two, excluding drinks and tips, will cost $70 or more in places listed as expensive; $40 to $70 in those listed as moderate; and less than $40 in the inexpensive category. All restaurants listed serve lunch and dinner unless otherwise noted. For each location, hotels and restaurants are listed alphabetically by price category.

OXFORD A visit to this beautiful city is the perfect start to a tour of the Cotswolds. For a detailed report on the city, its sights, hotels, and restaurants, see *Oxford* in THE CITIES.

To begin the Cotswold tour, take A46 west 16 miles from Oxford to Burford.

BURFORD Although on the edge of the Cotswolds, Burford is a typical Cotswold community of just over 1,300 people—its steep main street, stippled with ancient stone houses and shops, rolls down a hill to meet the river Windrush. In the 18th century, Burford was an important coaching stop. Now, in the 20th century, it's an antiquer's delight; Burford is full of antiques shops—some of the most expensive in the country.

A number of Burford's buildings are antiques themselves, notably the 14th-century *Bull* hotel on High Street; the almshouses built in 1457; the *Grammar School for Boys* founded in 1571; the *Priory,* an Elizabethan house; the *Great House,* built in 1690; and the *Tolsey* (or Toll House), now a town museum. The *Tolsey* is closed November through *Easter;* admission charge (no phone). The spired church, *St. John's,* is Perpendicular in style and has an old Norman tower. One of the houses in Sheep Street is known as "Kit's Quarry," built by Christopher Kempster, who was the master mason commissioned by Christopher Wren to provide stone from local quarries for

St. Paul's Cathedral. Walking tours of Burford, starting from the *Tolsey,* take place every Sunday afternoon May through October, conducted by members of the *Burford and District Society.*

BEST EN ROUTE

Bay Tree This 16th-century mansion down a side street has retained its cozy, antique, and fireplace-lit atmosphere despite recent updating. Sixteen of its 23 rooms are in converted cottages. There is also a restaurant. 11 Sheep St., Burford (phone: 1993-822791; fax: 1993-823008). Expensive.

Andrew's Colorful baskets of flowers adorn the Tudor frontage of this 15th-century building (formerly the *Cornerhouse* hotel) on the town's busy main street. Here are nine guestrooms, three with four-posters. No restaurant, but breakfast is included, and its lounge is a popular local spot for morning coffee and afternoon tea. High St., Burford (phone: 1993-823151; fax: 1993-823240). Moderate.

En Route from Burford Drive from Burford to Great Barrington (approximately 4 miles) by turning left onto an unclassified road just north of the bridge over the Windrush River.

THE BARRINGTONS AND WINDRUSH From the 14th to the 19th century, the quarries of Great Barrington and Little Barrington produced some of the best Cotswold stone. Many of England's more impressive buildings were constructed using the stone, including sections of *St. Paul's Cathedral* in London and several of *Oxford*'s colleges.

Great Barrington consists mainly of a double row of cottages partly surrounded by a country estate called *Barrington Park.* The centerpiece of the estate is a Palladian mansion (not open to the public) which dates from between 1736 and 1738. Close to the house is *St. Mary's,* a mostly Norman church that underwent a complete restoration in 1815.

Little Barrington, just across the river Windrush (which meanders rather than rushes), is the prettier of the two villages; it is centered around a triangular green, which was supposedly built over old quarry workings. The pub now called the *Inn for All Seasons* (phone: 1451-844324) was popular with coachmen and quarrymen, and it is said that its cellars are on the same level and have access to the quarry's underground passages.

The adjacent village of Windrush is also on this side of the river. From the pleasant shaded lane that links it with Little Barrington there are lovely views across to Great Barrington. But the real reason for stopping in Windrush is to visit *St. Peter's Church,* a Norman building decorated with much fine carving, especially around the south doorway.

En Route from Windrush Take the unnumbered road (signposted to Sherbourne) out of the village and continue another 6 miles through Sherbourne to Bourton-on-the-Water; the ride is scenic and pleasant.

BOURTON-ON-THE-WATER This small village, with a population of about 2,900, is very pretty, with the river Windrush running right through it, crossed by unusual and attractive stone bridges that link rows of shops and small hotels set back behind green spaces where people picnic and children play. (Not surprisingly, it has been called "the Venice of the Cotswolds.") Be sure to visit *St. Lawrence Church,* which has a late-18th-century spire and a 14th-century chancel; it was heavily restored in Victorian times—more successfully than many. Next to the *Old New Inn* is a famous small-scale model village of Bourton (High St.; phone: 1451-820467). It is open daily; admission charge. Also in town is the *Cotswold Perfumery,* where visitors can visit a museum with exhibits on the making of perfume and buy sample fragrances manufactured on the premises. The perfumery is open daily; admission charge to the museum (phone: 1451-820698). *Note:* Almost too popular, Bourton has allowed itself to become very commercial and is jammed with tourists in the summer, so it is best to visit early in the day before the crowds arrive.

En Route from Bourton Stow-on-the-Wold is about 5 miles north via A429; a pleasant 2-mile detour would be a left turn on an unnumbered (but signposted) road toward the Slaughters. This lane leads first to Lower Slaughter, named after the Norman De Sclotre family; it's a rather self-consciously pretty village as yet unspoiled by tourist traffic. You may see artists at work on the green banks of the river. Upper Slaughter is on higher ground, as the name suggests, and is reached by winding leafy lanes. This village is more interesting than its sister. The *Lords of the Manor* hotel at Upper Slaughter (see *Best en Route*) was originally the village rectory, and it was enlarged by one incumbent, the Reverend F. E. Witts, also known as the author of the *Diary of a Cotswold Parson.* Upper Slaughter also boasts the oldest and most impressive dovecote in Gloucestershire, dating from the 16th century. Also of note is the *Manor House,* an interesting Elizabethan building that incorporates the remains of a 15th-century priory and has an outstanding Jacobean porch.

From the Slaughters, return to A429 and continue to Stow-on-the-Wold.

BEST EN ROUTE

Lords of the Manor If Upper Slaughter hadn't had a beautifully preserved 17th-century manor house and surrounding grounds as a hostelry for visitors, it would have been necessary to build one. Luckily it was done some 300 years ago, and from 1763 to 1913 four generations of the Witts family lived in it when it was the village rectory. In 1972, it was converted into a hotel with 29 rooms (three with four-poster beds). A restaurant, fishing, horseback riding, golf, and croquet are available. The hotel's pastries, jam, and marmalade are freshly made by the local villagers. Upper Slaughter (phone: 1451-820243; 800-525-4800; fax: 1451-820696). Expensive.

Lower Slaughter Manor For a real taste of genteel English country life, this 17th-century manor house run by the Marks family offers attractive furnishings, fine fireplaces, and displays of fresh flowers. A decanter of sherry awaits guests in each of the 14 rooms, which are divided between the main building and its former coach house. There are immaculate gardens, croquet, tennis, and an indoor pool. The restaurant features such delights as local asparagus and quail, as well as Scottish salmon. Lower Slaughter (phone: 1451-820456; fax: 1451-822150). Expensive.

Broadlands Guest House A comfortable modern building tucked away on a quiet road, yet close to the busy village center. There are 11 guestrooms and a small garden. Evening meals available. No credit cards accepted. Clapton Row, Bourton-on-the-Water (phone: 1451-822002). Inexpensive.

Lamb Inn In a tiny village near Bourton-on-the-Water, this traditional English pub beside the village green offers 13 guestrooms that are comfortably furnished (but without TV sets), and a restaurant that serves good English cooking. The bar is a popular hangout for the area's residents, so you can get a real sense of local life. An unexpected amenity is the indoor pool (open May through September). In the center of Great Rissington (phone: 1451-820388). Inexpensive.

STOW-ON-THE-WOLD This town sits squarely on the Fosse Way, one of the Roman trunk routes that cuts a swath through southern Britain. (The name is not Roman but Saxon; and the road was used later by Normans as well.) Now a well-known antiques center with almost 1,600 residents, Stow was another important wool market town in medieval times; there were two annual fairs, with merchants dickering over the sale of thousands of sheep. Today, large numbers of Gypsies still gather here to hold fairs twice a year—on the Thursdays closest to May 12 and October 24. Many hotels, shops, and restaurants sprang up around the famous Market Square designed by the lord of the manor, the Abbot of Evesham, in the 11th century. The *King's Arms,* an old inn on the square, was once a lodging house for household servants of Edward VI, son of Henry VIII; in late March 1646, after what was to be the last battle of the Civil War, Cromwell incarcerated 1,500 Royalist troops in *St. Edward's,* the church that stands on one corner of the square.

BEST EN ROUTE

Fosse Manor This ivy-covered manor house stands on 10 acres of land a mile south of town on A429. It has 20 spacious rooms and a restaurant. Fosseway, Stow-on-the-Wold (phone: 1451-830354; fax: 1451-832486). Expensive.

Grapevine Comfortable and serene, despite its location in the village center. Named for the large vine that decorates its pretty conservatory restaurant, this 17th-century hotel offers 23 nicely appointed rooms (one has a four-poster bed).

Sheep St., Stow-on-the-Wold (phone: 1451-830344; 800-528-1234; fax: 1451-832278). Expensive.

Fox Inn Nick and Vicky Elliot serve up interesting variations of English cooking (such as mushrooms in Stilton sauce) at this restored village pub. Eating by the log fireplace in winter or on the garden terrace in summer is particularly charming. Open daily. No reservations. Major credit cards accepted. In Lower Oddington, near Stow-on-the-Wold (phone: 1451-870888). Inexpensive.

Royalist The oldest inn in England (built in AD 947), it is a two-story building made of timber and Cotswold stone. Four of the 13 rooms, however, are in a more modern wing. The Fagg family owns and runs this pleasant establishment; the dining room serves traditional English fare. Digbeth St., Stow-on-the-Wold (phone: 1451-830670). Inexpensive.

En Route from Stow-on-the-Wold From here, an interesting detour is to the two Swells. Lower Swell is a mile west of Stow on B4068; Upper Swell is about a mile from Lower Swell on an unnumbered (but well-signposted) road.

A mineral spring was discovered in Lower Swell in 1807, and for a while it was thought that the Swells might develop into another Cheltenham. All that remains of those fine dreams today, however, is a row of curiously decorated and rather exotic houses optimistically known as the "Spa Cottages." Despite this setback, Lower Swell regained its reputation with the success of another kind of watering hole—the *Golden Ball Inn* (on B4068; phone: 1451-830247), which for many years has greeted travelers with food, drink (including Donnington beer, brewed locally), and a warm welcome. Treat yourself to lunch here.

Upper Swell is a charming 18th-century village known for its handsome early-17th-century manor house, arched stone bridge over the river Dikler, and early-19th-century water mill capped with a Welsh slate roof. Stop for a moment at *St. Mary's Church* for a look at its exceptional Perpendicular font.

From the two Swells, take the side roads north to Bourton-on-the-Hill on the way to Moreton-in-Marsh, 7 miles away. Shortly before the village of Sezincote, you will be rewarded with a superb view of miles of glorious English countryside on the right.

Another side trip from Stow-on-the-Wold is in the opposite direction, to Chipping Norton (pop. 4,847), about 9 miles via A436 and A44.

"Chipping" may be a corruption of "cheapening," meaning "market." Chipping Norton, perched high on a hill near the Evenlode, was a busy market town for centuries. Today its wide streets are no longer filled with medieval wool merchants, and its imposing Victorian tweed mill has been closed down. Instead, the market square now bustles with tourists sampling

Chipping Norton's many cafés, pubs, restaurants, and hotels. The parish church, built in the Perpendicular style by wool merchants in the 14th and 15th centuries, is one of the largest in Oxfordshire and is especially noteworthy for its several fine medieval brasses.

Four miles north of Chipping Norton off A3400 are the *Rollright Stones,* a circle of about 70 stones that date from between 1800 and 500 BC. To one side stand five other stones, said to represent a king and his knights. The name of these stones derives, it is believed, from Rollanriht, or "the jurisdiction of Roland the Brave." The name appears in the *Domesday Book* as Rollandri. To get to Moreton-in-Marsh from the *Rollright Stones,* continue another 2 miles on A3400 and a couple of signposted roads.

MORETON-IN-MARSH This town of about 2,900 residents lies on the mainline railway from London, and therefore has a more workaday atmosphere than most other Cotswold communities. It is another old market town that can be fun to explore on foot. Market day is Tuesday. Main Street, which follows the route of the Fosse Way, is unusually wide and contains many antiques shops. On High Street is the *Market Hall,* built in Victorian Tudor style in 1887. Note the *Curfew Tower* on Oxford Street; it dates from the 17th century and its bell was rung daily until the 19th century.

BEST EN ROUTE

Annie's The fine English and French country cooking at this establishment owned by David Ellis (he named it after his wife) has locals placing reservations well in advance. Closed Mondays through Saturdays for lunch and Sundays for dinner. Reservations necessary. Major credit cards accepted. 3 Oxford St., Moreton-in-Marsh (phone: 1608-651981). Expensive.

Manor House Log fires, old beams, and beautiful gardens delight and soothe the spirit, while the excellent French and English cooking in the restaurant stimulates the palate. The rumors of secret passages in the 16th-century manor house might tempt you to rap on the walls once or twice. There are 38 rooms (four with four-poster beds), an indoor pool, and a sauna. High St., Moreton-in-Marsh (phone: 1608-650501; fax: 1608-651481). Moderate.

White Hart Royal If you stay here, you will have shared a place with royalty—Charles I spent the night in this half-timbered posting inn in 1644. Cobbles more than 300 years old have been carefully preserved, and old hunting trophies and weapons adorn the Cotswold stone bar. The hotel has 18 rooms and a small timbered dining room. High St., Moreton-in-Marsh (phone: 1608-650731; fax: 1608-650880). Moderate.

En Route from Moreton-in-Marsh From here, take A44 west for about 6 miles, then turn right onto B4081 for Chipping Campden, about 3 miles farther.

BEST EN ROUTE

Crown Inn In this 16th-century village inn 2 miles east of Moreton-in-Marsh off A44, there are 21 rooms (three have four-poster beds). The owners, the Champion family, are friendly, and the accommodations are modern and comfortable. There also is a small, cheerful dining room that serves good, simple fare. High St., Blockley (phone: 1386-700245; fax: 1386-700247). Moderate.

CHIPPING CAMPDEN This town (pop. 1,936) was restored carefully by the *Campden Trust,* a group of people mindful of the past; as a result, it is remarkably well preserved. If you can ignore the traffic—mostly visitors looking for somewhere to park—the main street looks just as it did hundreds of years ago. And Chipping Campden's many fine old buildings are a delight. The church, though heavily restored by the Victorians, is one of the best in the Cotswolds. Built in the Perpendicular style by the town's wool merchants in the 15th century, it is unusually large and contains several fine brasses. Near the church are almshouses dating to 1612. All along High Street, you'll see many houses built with warm Cotswold stone; stop to look at the handsome bow-windowed *Grevel House* (the former home of a wealthy woolman) on Church Street. Across the way is *Woolstapler's Hall,* a 14th-century house where wool merchants traded. Today, it's a museum of the town's history. It's closed November through March; admission charge (phone: 1386-840289). The *Market Hall,* a solid yet graceful structure composed of 14 stone arches built in 1627, was where the area's farmers sold their dairy products.

BEST EN ROUTE

Charingworth Manor This fine Tudor manor house with lovely views across the Cotswolds has been painstakingly converted into a luxury 24-room hotel, with log fires and fine antiques. There also is a restaurant and a leisure spa with a heated pool, sauna, and steamroom. Service with a personal touch, as befits a member of the Small Luxury Hotels of the World. Ebrington, Chipping Campden (phone: 1386-78555; 800-525-4800; fax: 1386-78353). Expensive.

Noel Arms A pub-like atmosphere prevails at this 14th-century coaching inn—lots of oak beams, armor-hung walls, and a cheering fireplace. Charles II is reputed to have stayed here in 1651, after the Battle of Worcester. Two of the 26 rooms sport four-poster beds, and there is a good English-style dining room. High St., Chipping Campden (phone: 1386-840317; 800-528-1234; fax: 1386-84136). Moderate.

En Route from Chipping Campden Take B4081 north for 3 miles to Mickleton, then follow signs for *Hidcote Manor Gardens,* opposite which are *Kiftsgate Court Gardens. Hidcote Manor Gardens,* which are run by the *National Trust,* are formal, with impressive and varied hedges, rare trees, and shrubs. The gardens were laid out in the first few years of this century by Lawrence Johnston, and it was here that he originated the mixed or "harlequin" hedge. There are small individual gardens with pools, rare plants, and gazebos. *Kiftsgate Court Gardens* are steeper and less formal. *Hidcote Gardens* are closed Tuesdays, Fridays, and November through April (phone: 1386-438333); *Kiftsgate Gardens* are open Wednesdays, Thursdays, and Sundays, April through September; also Saturdays in June and July (phone: 1386-438776). There's an admission charge to both gardens.

From Mickleton, pick up B4632 and proceed 7 miles south to Broadway.

BROADWAY Henry James once described Broadway thus: "The place has so much character that it rubs off on the visitor . . . it is delicious to be at Broadway." Many people would agree with James, judging from the traffic and numbers of tourists who throng here to shop for antiques and to stroll among the 17th- and 18th-century golden Cotswold stone houses. (Partly due to heavy tourism and partly just to preserve the old stone—which is highly vulnerable to even the comparatively mild Cotswold weather—there has been some renovation and rebuilding. But it has been done well, and stone facing rather than complete razing is the general rule.)

The *Lygon Arms* is probably Broadway's main attraction (see *Best en Route*); the hotel's elegance is only exceeded by its history. The main building dates from 1532, though parts of it are more than 600 years old. Nearby is the *Cotswold Teddy Bear Museum,* which displays a large collection of the stuffed toys, as well as antique dolls and other playthings. It's open daily; admission charge (phone: 1386-858323).

Some of Broadway's other notable structures include *Middle Hill,* the estate of Sir Thomas Phillips, the eccentric and wealthy book collector; *St. Eadburgha's,* a Norman church; and *Broadway Beacon,* an 18th-century, 65-foot-high, stern stone "folly" on Broadway Hill, all of which are within *Broadway Tower Country Park.* You can climb the tower for a view of 12 counties, spread your picnic lunch in one of the designated areas, or visit the 150-year-old barn that houses an exhibit on the geology of the hill. The park is closed November through March; admission charge (phone: 1386-852390).

BEST EN ROUTE

Buckland Manor One of the best hostelries in the Cotswolds, this 13th-century structure provides a tranquil retreat. Just 2 miles from the center of Broadway, it has 12 lavishly appointed rooms and suites with lovely views of the Malvern Hills, attentive service, and an elegant, formal dining room (which has received a Michelin star) serving excellent continental fare. A full English breakfast is included. The grounds, adjoining a 13th-century churchyard, feature a small heated pool, flower gardens, a croquet lawn, and a tennis court. Open February 15 through January 15. Buckland (phone: 1386-852626; fax: 1386-853557). Expensive.

Dormy House This 17th-century converted farmhouse has 49 rooms and a restaurant. Visitors will find plenty of historic architecture, friendly service, and fine food. (For more information, see *Rural Retreats* in DIVERSIONS.) Willersey Hill, Broadway (phone: 1386-852711; 800-323-5463; fax: 1386-858636). Expensive.

Lygon Arms A 16th-century, ivy-covered inn of international repute boasting 66 rooms furnished rooms with antiques (five with four-poster beds), sports facilities, and excellent cooking. Both Charles I and Oliver Cromwell slept here. (For more information, see *Rural Retreats* in DIVERSIONS.) High St., Broadway (phone: 1386-852255; 800-63SAVOY; fax: 1386-858611). Expensive.

Hunter's Lodge A walled garden and log fires add to the charm of this elegant restaurant's two dining rooms, one of which seats 20 and the other 40 guests. The food is French influenced. Closed Sundays, Mondays, weekends for dinner, Wednesdays through Saturdays for lunch, the first two weeks of February, and the first two weeks of August. Reservations necessary. Major credit cards accepted. High St., Broadway (phone: 1386-853247). Moderate.

En Route from Broadway Near the western end of Broadway, *before* you reach B4632 to Winchcombe, turn left on a signposted road for *Snowshill Manor*—about 3 miles. The manor house, a fine example of Tudor and Georgian architecture, was part of Catherine Parr's dowry (she was Henry VIII's last wife). The manor is closed November through March, Mondays and Tuesdays May through September, and weekdays in April and October. There's an admission charge (phone: 1386-852410). It contains an eclectic collection of antiques and miscellany accumulated by Charles Wade, who subsidized his mania with an income from West Indian sugar plantations. He was so devoted to his collection that he actually lived in the adjoining cottage in order to give it more space.

Retrace your route to B4632, then head south 7 miles to Winchcombe.

WINCHCOMBE Though it suffers a little from through traffic, not all of Winchcombe is on the main road, and it is a good example of a genuine Cotswold town, going about its business as it has done for several hundred years. Before the Norman Conquest this was the capital of Winchcombeshire, and here you will see half-timbering among the stone houses. For example, the *George Inn,* which once provided lodgings for pilgrims visiting nearby *Hailes Abbey,* has a half-timbered coaching yard. Winchcombe's 19th-century *Town Hall,* which contains the original stocks, now houses the *Folk Museum,* which has exhibits on the history of local industry, notably agriculture; there are also some old police uniforms on display. It is closed Sundays and November through March; admission charge (phone: 1242-602925). The parish church is mainly remarkable for the gargoyles that decorate its exterior—at least 40 of them; inside there is an altar cloth believed to have been woven by Catherine of Aragon, Henry VIII's first queen.

Half a mile southeast of the town center, clearly signed, lies *Sudeley Castle.* Now the private home of Lord and Lady Ashcombe, its interior is quite labyrinthine. The castle has been the home of several of England's queens: Anne Boleyn and Elizabeth I spent time here, and it was the final home and final resting place of Catherine Parr, the only wife to outlive Henry VIII. During the Civil War that affected so much of this now tranquil part of England, *Sudeley Castle* was extensively damaged, and it was virtually abandoned for nearly 200 years. But with the help of Sir George Gilbert Scott, responsible for, among other things, London's *Albert Memorial,* the castle was restored. The restoration work went on until the 1930s; tantalizing traces of the original buildings remain, including a few dating to the 15th century, and some very old stained glass. The castle now houses an important collection of art treasures, including works by Constable, Turner, Rubens, and Van Dyck. The views from the grounds are superb. It is closed November through March; admission charge (phone: 1242-602308).

From Winchcombe follow B4632 another 7 miles to Cheltenham.

CHELTENHAM Largely regarded as a genteel place inhabited mainly by geriatrics, Cheltenham (pop. 85,000) is livelier than many think. For example, it's practically impossible to find accommodations within a 30-mile radius during *Cheltenham Gold Cup Week,* a national horse race meeting held every March. (For information, write to *Racehorse Owners' Association,* 42 Portman Sq., London W1H 9FH, England.) In addition, there is the *International Festival of Music* in July, and the *Festival of Literature* in October (for information, contact *Town Hall Box Office,* Imperial Sq., Cheltenham, Gloucestershire GL50 1QA, England; phone: 1242-227979). (For more details about both, see *Best Festivals* in DIVERSIONS.) While here, try the waters that made Cheltenham famous—either at the *Town Hall* or the *Pittville Pump Room,* named after local MP Joseph Pitt, who served in the *House of Commons* from 1825 to 1830. The *Pump Room* is closed Mondays and October through May; no admission charge (phone: 1242-512740). The medicinal properties of these waters are said to derive from the magnesium and sodium sulphates and the sodium bicarbonate they contain (but the taste is unpleasant, so few people take more than a sip).

Before leaving Cheltenham, be sure to take a stroll along the famous Promenade, made lovely by its rows of great horse chestnut trees. Along one side are first class shops, similar to those found in the town's Montpellier area; along the other side stand beautifully preserved Regency terraced buildings. The town also has many spacious and colorful gardens, the best of which is the *Imperial Gardens,* adjoining the town hall on Imperial Square (open daily; no admission charge).

BEST EN ROUTE

Le Champignon Sauvage "To eat is to fulfill a need; to dine is to indulge the senses" is the motto of chefs David and Helen Everitt-Matthias. The basically French fare is truly excellent. Closed Sundays and Saturday lunch. Reservations advised. Major credit cards accepted. 24-26 Suffolk Rd., Cheltenham (phone: 1242-573449). Expensive.

Greenway An elegant Elizabethan country house with 18 rooms; its restaurant serves well-prepared, imaginative fare. (For more information, see *Rural Retreats* in DIVERSIONS.) Shurdington, Cheltenham (phone: 1242-862352; 800-543-4135; fax: 1242-862780). Expensive.

Queens This colonnaded hotel overlooking the *Imperial Gardens* has graced the Promenade since 1838. It has grand and lofty layouts, with 74 bedrooms, elegantly furnished and beautifully equipped, as well as a restaurant. The Promenade, Cheltenham (phone: 1242-514724; fax: 1242-224145). Expensive.

En Route from Cheltenham From here, pick up A435 and continue 14 miles southeast to Cirencester.

CIRENCESTER Established by the Romans at the junction at which their vital route Fosse Way met five other roads, Cirencester (or Corinium) was a strategic link in their defenses. As a result, Corinium grew to be second in size only to London (now, however, its population has shrunk to under 18,000). In the 6th century it was destroyed by the invading Saxons, so little of the Roman occupation remains in the town itself. However, mosaic floors, sculpture, and pottery recovered from excavations now form the extensive collection of Roman relics in the *Corinium Museum* (Park St.; phone: 1285-655611). It is closed Mondays November through March; admission charge. Cotswold Avenue is the site of the ruins of a Roman amphitheater. Periods of English history seem piled one atop another by a profligate hand in Cirencester. The parish church, *St. John the Baptist,* built by wool merchants in the 14th century, is a fine example of the Perpendicular style. One of the largest churches in England, it is not to be missed for its rich stone carvings, magnificent array of medieval stained glass, and many fine brasses.

BEST EN ROUTE

Fleece Outside is a handsome black and white half-timbered façade; inside are Cotswold stone walls, fine open fireplaces, low-beamed ceilings, 30 comfortable rooms, and a restaurant. Market Pl., Cirencester (phone: 1285-658507; fax: 1285-651017). Moderate.

Shawswell Country Guesthouse Isolated among pastoral fields of sheep, David and Muriel Gomm's 17th-century house offers five comfortable rooms (one with a four-poster), beamed ceilings, inglenook fireplaces, and traditional furnishings. There's no restaurant, but Mrs. Gomm does provide evening meals (for residents only) which feature such tasty dishes as poached chicken with asparagus and prawns. Open February through November. No credit cards accepted. Rendcomb, 5 miles north of Cirencester (phone: 1285-831779). Moderate.

En Route from Cirencester Take A429 southwest from Cirencester to Malmesbury, a distance of 11 miles.

MALMESBURY This pleasant little town (pop. 4,150) high above the Wiltshire Avon is the site of a magnificent Norman abbey with a most unusual history: During the Dissolution under King Henry VIII in the 16th century, the building was sold to a clothier for £1,500. The man promptly brought in his weaving machinery and converted it into a factory. It was not until 1823 that a restoration effort was begun. Despite the many years of decay, the restoration was eminently successful, and today the abbey is considered one of the finest examples of Norman building remaining in Britain. The richly carved south porch and the musicians' gallery are especially impressive. According to another unusual and interesting tale connected with the abbey, in the 11th century, a monk leaped from the abbey's tower wearing a pair of homemade wings in an attempt to fly. He survived the fall but was lame ever after. The abbey is open daily; no admission charge (phone: 1666-824339).

Malmesbury is one of the oldest boroughs in England and a very well planned medieval city; it was already an important town before the Norman invasion. Some medieval remains still are extant, including fragments of walls and ruins of a 12th-century castle that can be seen today at the *Old Bell* hotel. Six bridges lead to the Market Square, at whose center is an impressive octagonal Tudor market cross. There are several lovely 17th- and 18th-century houses built by rich weavers on the adjoining streets. George Washington's ancestors appear to have come from the region, since at least five Washington predecessors are buried in a churchyard in Garsdon, 2 miles east of town.

BEST EN ROUTE

The Close This 400-year-old townhouse in a small town 5 miles northwest of Malmesbury has 15 rooms, a highly acclaimed restaurant, and a croquet lawn. (For more information, see *Rural Retreats* in DIVERSIONS.) 8 Long St., Tetbury (phone: 1666-502272; fax: 1666-504401). Moderate.

Whatley Manor The Avon River runs through the grounds of this 17th-century manor house with a courtyard, so guests can fish to their hearts' content. The 29 rooms are elegantly and comfortably furnished with antiques, as is the rest of the house; there's a good dining room serving English dishes, and other amenities include an outdoor heated pool, a sauna, and a snooker room. Easton Grey, near Malmesbury (phone: 1666-822888; 800-437-2687; 1666-826120). Moderate.

En Route from Malmesbury The next major stop is Bath, which is 24 miles south of Malmesbury on A46. Along the way, there are several noteworthy detours, including *Badminton House,* 10 miles from Malmesbury off B4040, and *Dyrham Park,* 6 miles farther south and off A46.

Badminton House has been in the same family, the Beauforts, for over 300 years, and is the setting each May of the *Badminton Horse Trials,* an international competition (see *Horsing Around* in DIVERSIONS). For information, write: Box Office, *Badminton Horse Trials,* Badminton, Avon, G9 1DF, England. The house itself is not open, though the duchess sometimes shows groups around by prior arrangement (write to Duchess of Beaufort, *Badminton House,* Avon GL9 1DB, England). A note of trivia: The game of badminton was invented here by houseguests in the 1870s.

You may recognize *Dyrham Park* even if you've never been here before, as the exterior of the house and the grounds were featured in the 1993 film *The Remains of the Day,* with Anthony Hopkins and Emma Thompson. Stop for tea in the orangery of the elegant, low-lying mansion. Afterward, stroll around; the house, built between 1692 and 1704, shows considerable Dutch influence, perhaps because its owner, William Blathwayt, was a representative at The Hague. The park is open daily; the house is closed Thursdays, Fridays, and November through *Easter.* There's an admission charge to the mansion (phone: 1272-372501).

BEST EN ROUTE

Lucknam Park A member of Small Luxury Hotels of the World, this magnificent Georgian country house on the southern edge of the Cotswolds offers 11 suites (four with wood-burning fireplaces) and 42 other well-appointed bedrooms. The superb restaurant has been awarded a Michelin star. (For more information, see *Bath* in THE CITIES.) Colerne (phone: 1225-742777; 800-525-4800; fax: 1225-743536). Very expensive.

White Hart Inn Originally constructed in 1553, this village inn adjoins a pretty trout stream on a country lane 8 miles northeast of Bath. There are three bedrooms in the inn itself, and another eight are located in an old stable block just across the road. A small dining room serves traditional fare. Ford, near Chippenham (phone: 1249-782213; fax: 1249-783075). Inexpensive.

BATH This city was once one of Europe's greatest spas. For a detailed report on the city, its sights, hotels, and restaurants, see *Bath* in THE CITIES.

Southwest England

That the legendary Arthur should spring from this distant corner of England isn't surprising. For here, where the island narrows down to a horny point separating the English Channel from the Atlantic, the boundaries between the natural and supernatural are very indistinct. It doesn't take long to notice it—a constant tug on your imagination; the sense that the low green hills and languorous rivers simmer with an animation barely and only intermittently apparent to human senses. This, after all, is a land where walking sticks sprout into flowering hawthorns, where dancing maidens turn to stone, and where a baby delivered to an old magician on the crest of a fiery wave becomes a warrior, a king, a superhuman mortal who unites and gives identity to the English people. Even today, when modern sensibilities are so ruthlessly rational, there are quite sane folk who claim that fairies dance on the Dorset coast and pixies bedevil Dartmoor travelers.

The land itself conspires to enchant. To the east, Dorset's rich dairyland folds and unfolds in a continuous succession of hills and vales, immortalized a century ago in Thomas Hardy's famous novels, while Somerset's miles of meadows and orchards are cradled in a basin protected on all sides by hills and the sea. In the heart of Devon, the county occupying the broad square of the peninsula, is Dartmoor, a solitary and taciturn landscape of bare hills bristling with strange winds. Beyond, and to the end of England, lie the neat, stone-walled fields and lanes of Cornwall. But nowhere does the magic seduce as powerfully as where land meets the sea, and the southwest has more miles of coastline than any other part of England. Here are long strands of beach that disappear with the tide, steep coves nearly obscured by their dense foliage, headlands shrouded in mist, and towering gray cliffs that meet the crashing sea in an Olympian test of wills.

For all its wildness, though, the southwest is essentially a human landscape. Thousands of years of habitation by man have shaped the countryside as surely and as gradually as the elements. The soft, sculpted shape of the hills is the result of centuries of plowing and grazing, and the high-hedged roads that have carried countless generations from village to village are etched deeply on the land.

Everywhere are reminders of the successive occupants of the land, from Paleolithic drawings in the Mendip caves to a deserted World War II air force base near Bodmin Moor. Bronze Age circles, Iron Age villages, Celtic hill towns, Roman roads, Saxon farms, Norman churches and cathedrals, Tudor coastal fortifications, grand Georgian mansions, and Victorian resorts all combine to make this part of the country a visible record of English history. Some sites, like *Stonehenge* or the Normans' magnificent cathedrals, are well known, but others, perhaps the most rewarding, are those you come across yourself—an enigmatic formation of stones in the middle of a sheep pasture, or a fanciful church carving done by a nameless artisan of the Middle Ages. The southwest is hardly an undiscovered paradise. Britons come in droves every summer to enjoy Cornwall's and Devon's fine beaches and warm weather. But apart from tourism, people make their livings much as they have for centuries, by sheepherding, dairy farming, fishing, and sea trading. There is now a good deal of mining for china clay around St. Austell, but tin mining, which for many hundreds of years brought wealth to Cornwall (or at least to some of its families), is almost a thing of the past. Plymouth and Exeter, both ports, are the only cities of any size that Devon and Cornwall can claim, and although the population in resort towns swells with summer visitors, the rest of the year you'd have to search a bit to find a crowd.

The route suggested here begins in Salisbury and heads west to Sherborne—a Saxon town that arrived in the 20th century with its vitality and charm intact—before it continues south to Dorchester and follows the Dorset coast to Exeter, the gateway to Devon and Cornwall. The route then meanders through Dartmoor, visits the south Devon sea resorts of Torbay and Dartmouth, and rounds the South Hams peninsula to Plymouth. Crossing the river Tamar into Cornwall, the itinerary hugs the coast all the way to the Lizard and Land's End and detours to the Isles of Scilly before turning north. From St. Ives, it climbs up the spectacular west coast of Cornwall, makes a loop through Bodmin Moor, and returns to the coast to stop at Tintagel (the legendary birthplace of Arthur) and Boscastle before continuing along the steep and wooded north coast of Devon to visit such towns as Clovelly and Ilfracombe. Then it passes into Exmoor and the county of Somerset, cutting across the Somerset Levels to the historic town of Glastonbury and the *Cheddar Caves.*

Take your time through this country. Much of its beauty and charm is to be found down exasperatingly narrow lanes that can't be taken at more than 20 miles an hour or along public footpaths that link village to village. There is also an extensive system of splendid coastal footpaths that are quiet, private retreats, even at the height of the tourist season. (The *National Trust,* which maintains some of these paths, along with scores of historic sites, isn't supported by government funds, as most people think. So don't pass up its contribution boxes without expressing—in cash, that is—your appreciation for the fine job it does.) One last tip: Most towns and villages with tourist attractions have large parking lots near the center of town. Use them and save yourself the aggravation of trying to park on streets built for foot traffic—and possibly save your car a dented fender as well.

There are so many excellent small hotels in this neck of the woods that you'll be tempted to extend your stay just to sample as many of them as possible. Most are also well known for their food and open their restaurants to non-residents. These hotels aren't cheap (though most offer reduced rates outside the summer holiday season, especially on weekends), but they are good value for the money. For a double room (with private bath, TV set, and breakfast included except where indicated), expect to pay more than $120 per night at places we list as expensive, $75 to $120 for those in the moderate range, and less than $70 for those listed as inexpensive. Restaurants listed as expensive will charge $60 or more for a dinner for two excluding wine, taxes, and tips; moderate ones will cost between $40 and $60; and the inexpensive ones, less than $40. All restaurants listed serve lunch and dinner unless otherwise noted. For each location, hotels and restaurants are listed alphabetically by price category.

SALISBURY Compared to many, Salisbury (pop. 37,000) is a mere pup of a city. It wasn't until the 13th century that the Church, exasperated by constant quarrels with its military neighbors and tired of the harsh weather it suffered from its exposed position on top of the hill at Old Sarum, decided to move the cathedral to the low-lying meadows beside the river Avon. The very elegant cathedral is crowned by England's highest spire (404 feet) and houses the oldest clock (ca. 1386) in the country. Many other buildings in town present fine examples of medieval and Georgian architecture. *Mompesson House,* built in 1701, retains much of its original plasterwork and paneling. It is closed Thursdays, Fridays, and November through March; admission charge (phone: 1722-335659). Another historic building is *Malmesbury House,* part of which dates from the 14th century. The house is closed Sundays, Mondays, and October through *Easter;* admission charge (phone: 1722-327027). A colorful market has been held in Salisbury's Market Square every Tuesday since 1227; these days, it is held on Saturdays as well. The tourist information center in Fish Row (phone: 1722-334956) is closed Sundays October through May.

About 10 miles north, standing silently on the bleak Salisbury Plain, is *Stonehenge,* a wonder of the world that attracts about three-quarters of a million visitors a year. It is open daily; admission charge (phone: 1980-623108). For more information, see *Ancient Monuments and Ruins* in DIVERSIONS.

The broad plain north of Salisbury probably contains more prehistoric monuments per square mile than any other part of England. There literally are dozens of other relics left behind by men and women who worked the plain as early as 6,000 years ago. A guide, *Stonehenge and Neighboring Monuments,* published by English Heritage (£4/about $6), shows the location of many of the barrows and temples near *Stonehenge.*

Salisbury's bustling downtown is full of pubs, and you could hardly go wrong stopping at any for a tasty lunch. If you're not deterred by convivial lunchtime crowds, try the *Haunch of Venison* (Minster St.; phone: 1722-322024), a venerable old pub in the center of things with good food, or the *New Inn* (New St.; phone: 1722-327679), a cozy 15th-century pub near the cathedral.

Harper's *The* place for English fare, with excellent home-cooked dishes (chalked up on a blackboard), including old favorites treated in imaginative ways—lamb with apricot and cider sauce, for example—as well as traditional desserts. Closed Sundays November through March and Sunday lunch April through October. Reservations advised. Major credit cards accepted. 7 Ox Row, The Market Square, Salisbury (phone: 1722-333118). Moderate.

White Hart A city landmark near the cathedral with a Georgian, pillared portico and 68 rooms in traditional style stocked with plenty of comforts. There's also a restaurant. 1 St. John St., Salisbury (phone: 1722-327476; fax: 1722-412761). Moderate.

Scotland Lodge This comfortable 16th-century house with three rooms and a large garden is within easy reach of *Stonehenge* and offers a taste of English village life. The hotel dining room serves magnificent breakfasts featuring owner Jane Armfelt's homemade marmalade. Winterbourne Stoke, Salisbury (phone and fax: 1980-620943). Inexpensive.

En Route from Salisbury A3094 follows the river Avon out of Salisbury and continues 3 miles west to Wilton, passing through the pretty little village of Netherhampton. Wilton was once the capital of King Egbert's Wessex and Kent, and for many years its abbey was Salisbury's ecclesiastical rival. The abbey was dissolved by Henry VIII and the land given to the Earl of Pembroke. The opulent *Wilton House* that now stands on the abbey grounds was designed by Inigo Jones and contains a Tudor-style kitchen, a superb collection of art and furnishings, and enough gilt to blind the eyes. The house is closed mid-October through March; admission charge (phone: 1722-743115).

In this countryside of tidy villages tucked in the folds of green hills it is usually advisable to stick to secondary roads. At this point, however, it's best to take the main road (A30) from Wilton to Sherborne, 32 miles farther. After passing the town of Shaftesbury, one of the wealthiest cities in England until its powerful abbey was destroyed by Henry VIII, there's a stretch of road that affords some of the most scenic driving in the country. To the left, a 15-mile-long escarpment rises dramatically over the gentle rolling pastures of Blackmoor Vale. Objectively, it's not very high, perhaps 400 to 500 feet. But it comes on so suddenly that Thomas Hardy described it as the "green sea of Blackmoor Vale washing up to the foot of the bare chalk uplands." For Hardy enthusiasts, there is an obligatory stop nearby. About 5 miles outside Shaftesbury, turn left onto B3092 for another 5 miles to the pretty, prosperous village of Marnhull, transformed by Hardy into Marlott, the birthplace of the fictional Tess of the d'Urbervilles. *Tess Cottage,* supposedly the cottage Hardy had in mind when creating the Derbyfields, stands about a mile from the village church. It's a private residence, but can be viewed from the road. Head back to A30 via Fifehead Magdalen—its location above the river Stour is as pretty as its name is melodious—and continue to Sherborne.

BEST EN ROUTE

Stock Hill House This late Victorian manor located in a village 4 miles northwest of Shaftesbury stands on 10 acres of grounds. Its seven rooms and one suite are individually furnished with antiques, and the restaurant serves interesting dishes inspired by co-owner Peter Hauser's Austrian heritage. No smoking is allowed. Wyke, Gillingham (phone: 1747-823626; fax: 1747-825628). Expensive.

Coppleridge Inn The 10 rooms of this 18th-century farm (2 miles northwest of Shaftesbury) are housed in what were originally its stables and outbuildings, spread around a pretty courtyard. Meals are available in either the bar or restaurant. Motcombe, Shaftesbury (phone: 1747-51980; fax: 1747-51858). Moderate.

SHERBORNE Even before reaching Sherborne (pop. 7,600), you catch a glimpse of its powerful past. Standing on a knoll to the southeast of town are the ruins of *Sherborne Old Castle,* a magnificent fortified palace built in the early 12th century by Roger de Caen, Bishop of Sarum and, at his height, second in power only to Henry I. Even the remains are impressive: A grassy moat 30 feet deep encircles the site, and the thick walls and gracefully vaulted hallways catch the late-afternoon sun with a special brilliance. It is closed Mondays October through March; admission charge (phone: 1935-812730). The castle passed back and forth between the monarchy and the church, and then to Sir Walter Raleigh. Eventually it was razed by Parliamentarian troops during the Civil War. From the southeast corner of the castle keep you can see "new" *Sherborne Castle,* an Elizabethan house built by Raleigh after he despaired of ever modernizing Bishop Roger's castle. In the Digby family since 1617, the house contains an impressive collection of paintings, furniture, and porcelain. The castle and its grounds, landscaped by Lancelot "Capability" Brown, are open Thursdays and weekends *Easter* through September; admission charge (phone: 1935-813182).

Sherborne has long since passed into graceful old age. It's a charming town, compact and self-possessed, with an attractive high street. Its main industry is education. There are several private schools here, and on weekday afternoons the streets are awash with blue-uniformed schoolchildren.

BEST EN ROUTE

Eastbury For a taste of seclusion in the town center, try this elegant Georgian townhouse hotel sitting on its own acre of walled garden. It has a large library of antiquarian books and a restaurant, and all 15 bedrooms are named after English garden flowers. Long St., Sherborne (phone: 1935-813131; fax: 1935-817296). Expensive.

Plumber Manor A small jewel set in four acres of gardens in the Dorset countryside southeast of Sherborne, this has been the home of the Prideaux-Brunes family for over 300 years. It's best known—and deservedly—for its food, which is elegantly and imaginatively English, but its 16 attractive rooms are equally special. Open March through January. Hazelbury Bryan Rd., Sturminster Newton (phone: 1258-472507; 800-926-3181; fax: 1258-473370). Expensive to moderate.

En Route from Sherborne Quiet, agricultural Dorset is a collection of villages, each prettier than the next, linked together by fields, hills and valleys, rivers, and spring-fed meadows of unparalleled beauty. While you can travel straight down to Dorchester by heading south on A37 (pick it up at Yeovil, 5 miles west of Sherborne off A30), you'd be missing the best of this county. This is a route that will take you through a handful of Dorset villages and some of the loveliest countryside. The roads are sometimes little more than cow paths, so don't expect to make fast time.

Start at Melbury Osmond, about 6 miles south of Yeovil, just off A37, a village of stone houses jumbled together in some of the greenest hills ever seen. From here there's a public footpath (a little over a mile long) through *Melbury Park,* a lovely and peaceful private estate, to Evershot, a perfect gem of a village—one street long, one street wide—that looks the way Melbury Osmond would if its cottages were laid side by side. (Evershot also can be reached from Melbury Osmond by driving 5 miles roughly due east on A37 and a signposted road.) The cottage just beyond Evershot's parish church is presumed to be Hardy's model for the one where Tess rested during her travels.

From Evershot, take an unnumbered road to Minterne Magna, which will follow along the top of Batcombe Hill. It is hard to imagine a more beautiful drive. From the ridge of the escarpment, the land falls away to soft green pastures, hedged fields, and houses and farm buildings built of mellowed Ham Hill stone. It's a short stretch of road—perhaps 5 miles—but you'll be tempted to make it last much longer.

When this road runs into A352, turn south and proceed another 2 miles to Cerne Abbas. Once an abbey and market town, Cerne Abbas is now a pretty triangle of pubs, inns, and handsome merchant houses sitting in a little valley among the rolling upland hills of Dorset. One of Cerne's claims to fame is the Cerne Giant, a 180-foot-tall man with prominently exposed genitalia carved into the chalk hillside overlooking the old abbey. There's some disagreement over the identity of the original sculptors, although it's safe to say the giant dates back to at least the Romans.

Drive east, pick up B3143 at Piddletrenthide, and follow the road through the other Piddle River villages to Puddletown (8 miles from Cerne Abbas), which for many years also took its name from the river until delicate Victorian tastes demanded the name be changed.

You're in the very heart of Thomas Hardy country now. So many of his fictional characters crisscross this corner of Dorset that there is hardly a village, manor house, farm, or hill that doesn't have literary associations. Hardy himself was born a few miles west of Puddletown (Weatherbury in *Far from the Madding Crowd*) at Higher Bockhampton, on the edge of what he called Egdon Heath, the brooding backdrop for *Return of the Native.* His cottage is now in the hands of the *National Trust;* it can be visited (by prior appointment with the custodian) except Thursdays and November through April. The gardens, however, are open daily. There's an admission charge to the cottage (phone: 1305-262366). A mile or so east of Puddletown is *Athelhampton,* which Hardy called "Athel Hall," a 15th-century Tudor manor house with a remarkably well-preserved dovecote from the same period. *Athelhampton* is closed November through *Easter;* Fridays and Saturdays in August; and Mondays, Tuesdays, Fridays, and Saturdays *Easter* through October. There's an admission charge (phone: 1305-848363).

BEST EN ROUTE

Summer Lodge Everything about this Georgian hotel, another small jewel, speaks of care and thoughtfulness: bouquets of flowers everywhere; homemade shortbread on the tea tray; the quiet, good taste of the decor. Its excellence has been recognized by its membership in the prestigious Relais & Châteaux group. The food—traditional English fare cooked with a French feeling for sauces—is excellent. There's an outdoor heated pool and 17 rooms (including six in a modern wing), as well as tennis courts and a croquet lawn. Summer La., Evershot (phone: 1935-83424; fax: 1935-83005). Expensive.

Le Petit Canard Run by Geoff Chapman, a young Canadian chef, and his English wife, Lin, this tiny restaurant in a 200-year-old cottage offers fare with French, Canadian, and Asian influences. The sauces are light, the vegetables crisp, and the meat grilled. Open for dinner only; closed Sundays and Mondays. Reservations necessary. Major credit cards accepted. Dorchester Rd., Maiden Newton, 5½ miles northeast of Cerne Abbas (phone: 1300-20536). Moderate.

DORCHESTER A town of 14,250 residents, Dorchester has an everlasting connection with novelist Thomas Hardy. He lived here, wrote here, and made the town come alive for all the readers who have never set eyes on Dorchester's ancient cobbled streets or dour stone and brick façades. There's an excellent collection of Hardy material at the *Dorset County Museum* (High West St.; phone: 1305-62735) that includes the original manuscript of *The Mayor of Casterbridge* (Hardy's name for Dorchester) and a reconstruction of the author's study. There also are Roman mosaics and other artifacts from when the town was known as Durnovaria. The museum is closed Sundays; admission charge. Although Hardy's ashes are in *Westminister Abbey,* his heart is interred in *Stinsford Church,* located in the village of Stinsford (1 mile northeast of Dorchester on A35).

Dorchester figured in other aspects of England's history besides its Hardy connection. In 1944, in the weeks before *D-Day,* the US army set up 12 camps all around the town. There are also notable reminders of much earlier days. Dorchester's Roman city boundaries are still visible in the Walks that ring the center. And just a mile or so southwest of here is the astounding *Maiden Castle,* an earthen fort believed to be about 4,000 years old. Sprawling over 120 acres, wave after wave of earth ramparts lap up to an elevated enclosure that could hold 5,000 people. The last occupants of *Maiden Castle* were forcibly evicted by the vastly superior army of the Romans, who then abandoned the site for Dorchester. It's open daily; no admission charge.

If you're here for afternoon tea, take it at the excellent *Horse with the Red Umbrella* (10 High West St.; phone: 1305-262019), which offers home-baked pastries and savories. For more information, see *Tea Shops and Tea Gardens* in DIVERSIONS.

BEST EN ROUTE

Casterbridge This beautifully furnished Georgian guesthouse has no restaurant, but it does have a small bar and a lovely conservatory where tea is served on summer afternoons. Some of the 15 bedrooms are on the small side, but this is generously compensated for by immense breakfasts and reasonable rates. 49 High St., Dorchester (phone: 1305-264043; fax: 1305-260884). Inexpensive.

En Route from Dorchester The straightest route from Dorchester to the seaside village of Abbotsbury, 7 miles away, also happens to be the most scenic. Head out of Dorchester west on A35. About a mile from town turn left onto an unnumbered road signposted to Winterborne Martinstowe, then follow the signs through Portesham to Abbotsbury. During the next 6 miles, the green Dorset hills tumbling down to the coast are a grand sight. (The *Hardy Monument,* about midway on the left, commemorates not the novelist but Thomas Masterman Hardy, a captain who served under Admiral Nelson at Trafalgar.)

ABBOTSBURY With a population of only about 400, this is an exquisite little village of thatch and stone cottages lining a single winding street. All that remains of the 11th-century *Benedictine Abbey* is the tithe barn, although the abbey has survived, in a manner of speaking, since much of it was used to build many of the village cottages. The *Abbotsbury Swannery,* a large breeding ground on the edge of the Fleet freshwater lagoon, shelters many species of wildfowl. It's closed weekdays and Saturdays November through March; admission charge (phone: 1305-871684). The *Abbotsbury Subtropical Gardens* flourish in a deep, narrow valley east of the village. They are open daily; admission charge (phone: 1305-871387). Just outside Abbotsbury, southwest on B3157, stop for a lofty look at Chesil Beach, an 18-mile-long, 600-foot-wide stretch of pebble beach that separates the Fleet lagoon from Lyme Bay. The building standing lonely on a hill in the middle distance is *St. Catherine's Church,* the parish church of Abbotsbury.

En Route from Abbotsbury Take B3157 northeast along the coast for 9 miles to Bridport, a small market town that was thriving when the *Domesday Book* was written and that fortunately has taken good care of its heritage of medieval buildings. Probably the town's greatest event happened in 1651 during the Civil War, when Charles II, fleeing Cromwellian troops after the Battle of Worcester, came here in disguise hoping to escape by sea. His true identity was uncovered, however, and he was chased out of town. A must-stop for tea is *Ship's Lights,* in nearby Eype—pronounced *Eep* (phone: 1308-425656; see *Tea Shops and Tea Gardens* in DIVERSIONS).

From Bridport, the A35 winds along the coast another 7 miles west to Lyme Regis.

BEST EN ROUTE

Innsacre Originally a 17th-century farmhouse, this restaurant still has ducks and goats outside. Local lamb, oysters, and asparagus are featured on the menu, as well as such treats as curried banana soup. Open for dinner only; closed Sundays and Mondays. Reservations necessary. Major credit cards accepted. Shipton Gorge, Bridport (phone: 1308-456137; fax: 1308-427277). Moderate.

Manor Here, in a stone manor house 6 miles from Bridport, are 13 comfortable and attractive guestrooms, a restaurant, and a cellar bar. The many antiques, old books, and glorious views of the sea and the surrounding countryside make this place especially charming. Harbor Rd., West Bexington (phone: 1308-897785; fax: 1308-897035). Moderate.

Three Horseshoes Inn This delightful village pub offers excellent food, particularly fish. For more information, see *Pub Crawling* in DIVERSIONS. Open daily. Reservations unnecessary. Major credit cards accepted. Bridport (phone: 1308-485328). Inexpensive.

LYME REGIS Lyme Regis is probably best known for the Cobb, "a long claw of old gray wall that flexes itself against the sea," as the town's most famous citizen, author John Fowles, describes it. (It was from the Cobb that Fowles's heroine, Sarah, the French lieutenant's woman, stared for many sad hours at the sea.) Built over 700 years ago to create an artificial harbor, it has probably cost the good folk of Lyme Regis more to repair than it ever generated in trade. Still, the attachment to it is long and unshakable, and today it harbors scores of pleasure craft and lobster boats. With a population of 3,500, this is the quintessential seaside town—whitewashed and salty, built up the steep hillsides overlooking the harbor. Fossil hunting in the sheer sea cliffs near town is a local sport, but there is also a collection of fossils at the *Lyme Regis Museum* for those who aren't paleontologically prone. The museum is closed November through March; admission charge (phone: 1297-443370).

En Route from Lyme Regis The main road west out of Lyme is A3052. From here, turn left onto B3172 and continue 7 miles to Seaton, a small fishing town by the mouth of the river Axe catering unashamedly to holidaymakers. Its steep shingle beach is almost overpowered by the great cliffs of Thorncombe Beacon and Golden Cap. The latter is the highest on the south coast, and its views over miles of headland have earned it the distinction of being named an *Area of Outstanding Natural Beauty* (along with the stretch of coastline from Lyme Regis to Sidmouth). A marked coastal path passing this way is part of the Southwest Coast Path, one of England's official long-distance footpaths (see *Quintessential Great Britain* in DIVERSIONS).

The fastest and most direct route from Seaton to Sidmouth is to take A3052, bearing left onto B3175 at Sidford (a distance of about 9 miles). Another alternative, however, is to drive on a series of signposted roads through the villages of Vicarage, Branscombe, Weston, and Salcombe Regis; the journey, though a couple of miles longer, is far more rural and scenic.

A quiet and distinctly aristocratic resort town where the tiny river Sid meets the sea, Sidmouth was "discovered" and developed during Georgian times and owes much of its charm to the gracious buildings and crescents of that era. The townspeople have an extraordinary propensity to decorate everything with flowers—even the postboxes. Sidmouth offers a popular sailing center, bracing walks along the cliffs, and the *Sidmouth International Festival of Folk Arts* (see *Best Festivals* in DIVERSIONS), held the first week in August.

Hook up with A3052 in the village of Bowd (about a mile northwest of Sidmouth). After 2 miles, take a left onto A376 at Newton Poppleford. Continue to B3178 and head south and west through Budleigh Salterton, a smart little spa town, to Exmouth (about 3 miles from Sidmouth).

BEST EN ROUTE

Combe House This cream-colored Elizabethan mansion is furnished throughout with antiques. Among its appealing features are 14 guestrooms and one suite, fine cooking, and sports facilities. (For more information, see *Rural Retreats* in DIVERSIONS.) Gittisham, near Honiton, 9 miles from Sidmouth (phone: 1404-42756 or 1404-41938; 800-548-7768; fax: 1404-46004). Expensive.

EXMOUTH Devon's oldest resort, set on the estuary of the river Exe, was popular even before the railway to Exeter began to bring visitors from long distances. The town remains relatively small (with a population of just over 28,000), although its superb sandy beaches buzz throughout the summer season.

Lympstone, 3 miles north of Exmouth, provides good views across the Exe estuary to stately *Powderham Castle,* the seat of the Earls of Devon, reached during summer by a ferry trip (passengers only) from Exmouth to Starcross and a 25-minute walk along A379. The castle is closed Saturdays and October through March; admission charge (phone: 1626-890243). On the Lympstone side of the estuary, however, A376 leads north to the M5 motorway—from where roads are well signposted to Exeter, 11 miles away.

BEST EN ROUTE

Woodhayes An award-winning six-room hotel that's set in a small, peaceful Georgian house on its own secluded grounds 8 miles northeast of Exeter. Owners Frank and Katherine Rendle have decorated the rooms with antiques and oil paintings, and the restaurant is known for fine English cooking. Whimple (phone: 1404-822237). Moderate.

EXETER In 1282, Isabella de Fortibus, Countess of Devon, in a fit of pique, built a weir, or dam, across the river Exe below Exeter in order to deprive the city of access to the sea and the rich trade it brought. The infuriated townsfolk vowed to undo the countess's work, and they did—by building a canal to circumvent the weir (called Countess Wear in its builder's honor); even though it took 300 years to accomplish, it's just one indication of Exeter's determination to remain the preeminent city in the region. Exeter is still a thriving commercial center, but it is also a cathedral and university city, a government center, and the gateway to Devon and Cornwall for thousands of vacationers as well as for its 104,000 residents. The tourist information office in the *Civic Centre* (Paris St.; phone: 1392-265700) is closed Sundays.

At the center of the city sits its grand cathedral, a Norman and Gothic work of great beauty. The cathedral is exceptionally rich in carvings, although you need binoculars to really enjoy the often fanciful creatures carved on the roof bosses. The *Minstrels' Gallery* on the north side shows an entire angel orchestra and is utterly charming.

No boating enthusiast should miss the *Maritime Museum* (on the Quay; phone: 1392-58075). With over 100 vessels from around the world, this is considered to be one of the finest collections extant. The museum is open daily; admission charge.

Five miles north of Exeter on B3181 is *Killerton,* an 18th-century mansion housing a fascinating collection of costumes displayed in rooms decorated in different periods. *Killerton*'s superb garden, with rhododendrons, azaleas, magnolias, and stately oak and beech trees, is a beautiful spot, and near here, at Killerton Clump, herons nest from March to July. *Killerton,* a *National Trust* property, is closed Tuesdays and November through March; the garden is open daily. There's an admission charge (phone: 1392-881345).

BEST EN ROUTE

Nobody Inn A busy 16th-century pub with three rooms; another three are in a separate house two minutes' walk away (these are likely to be quieter). Trout cooked in pastry and roast duck are the restaurant's specialties. Doddiscombsleigh, Exeter (phone: 1647-52394). Inexpensive.

DARTMOOR The name "Dartmoor" alone evokes a vivid description: treeless brown hills covered with heather and gorse and pockmarked with treacherous boggy pits, a place where shaggy ponies run wild and the black hounds of hell collect the souls of the damned, a spot so godforsaken and bleak that even desperate prisoners prefer the dank gloom of their cells to the inhospitable hills. The moors are startlingly severe, especially after the cultivated beauty of most English countryside. The B3212 road that runs southwest from Exeter to Plymouth (46 miles away) speeds through this wild landscape, but haste would be a pity, since Dartmoor is far more than the barren, though incontestably beautiful, surface. More than a dozen rivers rise in the upland moors, and as they make their way to the sea, they carve lush, wooded valleys. Chagford, a picture-perfect village near the river Teign north of B3212 (17 miles from Exeter), has for years attracted artists, writers, and fashionable folk, as has Moretonhampstead, 13 miles from Exeter at the junction of B3212 and A382. *Castle Drogo,* strategically set on a granite bluff above the Teign just northeast of Chagford, may look like a medieval fortress, but it was built between 1910 and 1930 by a wealthy grocer with the means to indulge a romantic fantasy and make his home his castle. It is now a *National Trust* property, and is probably the last private house built on such a scale in Britain. The castle is closed Fridays and November through March; admission charge (phone: 1647-433306).

Scattered throughout Dartmoor are tors, rocky hills as high as 2,000 feet, that offer superb views of the surrounding countryside. One especially accessible tor is Haytor, about 9 miles south of *Castle Drogo* on A382. Not far from Haytor is Widecombe-in-the-Moor, one of the most picturesque villages in England and also, in summer, one of the most crowded. There also are numerous relics from prehistoric times—hill forts, stone circles, and barrows. *Grimspound,* about 3 miles from Manaton (which itself is 4 miles north of Widecombe-in-the-Moor), is a Bronze Age settlement consisting of 24 hut circles and a stone enclosure that was probably used for livestock. And everywhere are the sheep, black-faced and woolly, pursuing scrubby moor grasses up steep hillsides, crowding onto narrow Devon roads through a break in the hedge.

Dartmoor is marvelous hiking country (see *Great Walks and Mountain Rambles* in DIVERSIONS). Much of it is now national parkland, so before setting out, stop for maps and advice at the *National Park Information Center* at Postbridge (phone: 1822-88272), which is on B3212 8 miles southwest of Moretonhampstead. These days, the moors no longer seem to have the mysterious ability to swallow up hapless travelers; however, it would be foolhardy to misjudge them.

BEST EN ROUTE

Gidleigh Park An almost indescribably lovely turn-of-the-century country house, it has 14 rooms on more than 45 acres of secluded Devon woodlands, as well as smashing food. A member of the Relais & Châteaux group. (For more information, see *Rural Retreats* in DIVERSIONS.) Chagford (phone: 1647-432367; fax: 1647-432574). Expensive.

Holne Chase At one time a Victorian hunting lodge, it's now a charming retreat overlooking the valley of the river Dart (where salmon fishing can be arranged; see *Gone Fishing* in DIVERSIONS). There are 12 rooms in the main building and five more in a converted old stable house; there's also a restaurant. Holne Chase, near Ashburton (phone: 1364-3471; fax: 1364-3453). Expensive.

Horn of Plenty An excellent lunch or dinner stop while visiting Dartmoor (there also are seven serviceable rooms), it boasts splendid views of the Tamar Valley—especially at sunset. Awarded an Egon Ronay star, it offers such first-rate fare as Cornwall scallop salad and a caramel parfait with poppy seed topping. Closed Monday lunch. Reservations advised. Major credit cards accepted. Gulworthy, Tavistock, Devon (phone: 1822-832528). Moderate.

En Route from Dartmoor Leave the area by way of B3357 southeast to Buckfastleigh (16 miles from Chagford), the site of *Buckfast Abbey.* Since the abbey was founded in the late 1800s, the Benedictine monks there have prepared Buckfast Tonic Wine (exported all over the world) and also tended one of the largest honey industries in the country. All the products of this hard work are available at the abbey shop, which is open daily (phone: 1364-42519). An exhibition on the site's history is located at the abbey. It's closed November through February; admission charge. From Buckfastleigh, take A384 and continue another 6 miles south to Totnes.

TOTNES With just over 6,000 residents, this tiny town looks every bit as medieval as its name suggests. Its steep, narrow streets curl up and around themselves, and the timbered and slate-shingled buildings that overhang the main street lean and sag like clowns in a Shakespearean comedy. If you climb the narrow passageway to the church and guildhall, a wonderful old building with a columned porch and frightfully low oak doors, you'll peer down onto the roofs of buildings. It's closed weekends and November through *Easter;* no admission charge. The ruins of *Totnes Castle,* one of the first to be erected by the conquering Normans, stand near the center of town. The castle is closed Mondays October through March; admission charge (phone: 1803-864406). *Totnes Museum,* in one of the Elizabethan merchant houses, has an interesting collection of local costumes and household goods; there's also a display about Totnes native Charles Babbage, who built the first computer in 1842. The museum is closed weekends and November through March; admission charge (phone: 1803-863821).

BEST EN ROUTE

Cott Inn "Licensed since 1320" reads a large sign on the white stone wall of this long, low thatch inn. Once a row of cottages, it was converted into an inn for shepherds on their way to Totnes market. Now it offers six comfortable guestrooms, and downstairs, the bars sparkle with copper and brass under beamed ceilings. In winter, log fires blaze in the original inglenook fireplaces. The dining room serves traditional fare. Dartington, Totnes (phone: 1803-863777; fax: 1803-866629). Moderate.

En Route from Totnes From here, take A385 east for 5 miles to Torbay.

TORBAY This community comprises three separate towns: the large family resort of Torquay (pronounced Tor-*key*), to the north; the small fishing port of Brixham, to the south; and the small seaside resort of Paignton, in the middle. The area has a total of 180,000 residents. All three towns are on the shores of Tor Bay, and the 22 miles of coastline that join them, commonly referred to as the "English Riviera," wallow in a Gulf Stream climate, which explains the presence of subtropical vegetation. Many of the palm trees here were imported from Australia over 150 years ago.

Torquay, centered around its harbor and marina against a backdrop of Devon's green and rolling hills, has a distinct international ambience. A hive of sporting activity by day and illuminated by night, it is a long way from the days when its beaches and coves were a haven for pirates and smugglers. Many of the villas in the older part of town date from the Napoleonic Wars of the early 19th century, when they were built for officers and their families. Torquay later developed into a fashionable winter holiday resort—a spacious, elegant town famous for its health-giving sea breezes and colorful parks and gardens. Along with large chain stores, there are prettier specialty shops—for Devon clotted cream, bric-a-brac, and such—lining the narrow streets of the Torre area. The best beaches are

Ansteys Cove, a short walk through woodland, and Babbacombe Beach, which sits below the tiny community of Babbacombe, 1½ miles northeast. (These days, the town is probably most familiar to Americans as the setting of "Fawlty Towers," the popular British situation comedy starring John Cleese as an ill-mannered innkeeper.)

The appeal of Paignton, made popular by the Victorians, always has been its long, safe beaches (Hellicombe is the farthest north). Brixham, which concentrates on commercial fishing, is less concerned with tourists than its two sisters but still manages to attract some. To absorb Brixham's history, roam the narrow, winding streets between its tiers of cottages and thread your way up and down the steep flights of steps connecting them.

BEST EN ROUTE

Imperial One of the "English Riviera's" most luxurious hotels occupies a prestigious position overlooking the harbor. It has 167 rooms, indoor and outdoor pools, tennis, squash, and billiards. The food is so good, special gastronomic weekends frequently are held. For more information, see *Rural Retreats* in DIVERSIONS. Park Hill Rd., Torquay (phone: 1803-294301; fax: 1803-298293). Expensive.

Quayside Six 17th-century cottages have been combined to form this cozy, comfortable, and highly rated hotel with 30 rooms. The front bedrooms have views across the inner and outer harbor, as does the candlelit restaurant, which specializes in local fish. King St., Brixham (phone: 1803-855751; fax: 1803-882733). Moderate to inexpensive.

En Route from Torbay Drive south 9 miles via A379 and B3206 until you reach Kingswear. From here, take the car ferry across the river Dart to Dartmouth.

DARTMOUTH In 1147, 164 ships sailed from Dartmouth on the Second Crusade. Some 800 years later, a fleet of 485 American ships left Dartmouth's snug harbor on another crusade, this time to the beaches of Normandy. Between the two events, the town grew and prospered, first from the wine trade with Burgundy, later from cod fishing off the coast of Newfoundland, and whenever it could, from piracy and privateering. Today, about 5,200 people make their homes here.

It was the Elizabethans who really left their stamp on this thoroughly nautical town on the estuary of the river Dart. The crooked, elaborately decorated half-timbered buildings in the harbor area make Dartmouth look much the way it must have when Sir Walter Raleigh brought his royally sanctioned booty here. The *Cherub Pub,* the oldest building in town, dates back to 1380; it has mullioned windows and low doorways, as well as a large cherub on the façade. Nearby, the Butterwalk is a 17th-century structure which now has apartments on the upper stories and shops on the first floor;

along the front of the top story, a balcony supported by stone pillars overhangs the pavement. According to a plaque near Baynards Quay, the *Mayflower* stopped here for repairs before setting out on her historic voyage to America in 1620. Occupying a commanding position above the harbor is the *Royal Naval College,* Britain's main naval training center since 1905. Just outside town is *Dartmouth Castle*, one of Henry VIII's many coastal fortifications and one of the earliest built specifically for the use of guns. The castle is closed Mondays and Tuesdays from October through *Easter;* admission charge (phone: 1803-833588). Not much is left of its twin across the mouth of the river, *Kingswear Castle* (now a private residence), which was abandoned when guns became powerful enough to defend the river entrance from one side alone.

BEST EN ROUTE

Carved Angel This bright and airy restaurant on the quay specializes in seafood dishes in summer and English fare (especially game) the rest of the year. No matter what's on the menu, though, it's sure to be outstanding. Closed Sunday dinner, Mondays, and January through mid-February. Reservations advised. Major credit cards accepted. 2 South Embankment, Dartmouth (phone: 1803-832465). Expensive.

Fingals This elegant Queen Anne house in a valley has 10 comfortable rooms and colorful gardens. Richard Johnston, the proprietor, invites all the guests to sit together for dinner, but separate tables are available. There's tennis, croquet, an outdoor heated pool. Open April through December. Dittisham, Dartmouth (phone: 1803-722398; fax: 1803-722401). Moderate.

Royal Castle Originally built in 1630 as a pair of merchants's houses overlooking the harbor, this privately owned hotel was a favorite of Edward VII when his sons attended the naval academy. The restaurant specializes in fresh fish, and meals also are served in the large *Galleon Bar,* where a joint is often roasted on a 300-year-old spit. Tudor fireplaces, spiral staircases, and antique furniture in the 25 guestrooms are fine touches. The only drawback is that the seagulls can be a bit noisy. The Quay, Dartmouth (phone: 1803-833033; fax: 1803-835445). Moderate.

En Route from Dartmouth About 5 miles south on A379 is Slapton Sands, a shingle trench where thousands of American troops were stationed before the invasion of Normandy. In the middle of the 5-mile-long stretch of sand is a monument erected by the US government, thanking the local people for leaving their homes to provide a battle practice area. Nearby, a Sherman tank, which was lost at sea but was recovered in 1984, stands as a memorial to the 749 Americans who lost their lives in late April 1944 when German warships attacked a practice landing fleet. The tank, which belonged to the American 70th Tank Battalion, was set up as a memorial by the *Fort Carson*

Foundation of Colorado Springs. From here on, you are on the South Hams Peninsula.

Take A379 west for 6 miles to Kingsbridge. From here, the direct route west to Plymouth is a 21-mile drive along A379. However, if you want to explore the area, you'll find its villages are tiny and linked by high-hedged, single-track roads whose infrequent passing places make them slow going for motorists. A passenger ferry has crossed the Kingsbridge estuary from East Portlemouth to Salcombe for as long as residents can remember, but drivers must take the long way around (from Kingsbridge, drive 6 miles on A381). The most spectacular stretch of coastline, between Bolt Head and Bolt Tail, begins south of Salcombe and is owned by the *National Trust.* From Salcombe to Plymouth, it's a 22-mile drive on A381, B3197, and A379.

BEST EN ROUTE

Alston Hall This large Edwardian manor house originally was built by a local clergyman as a wedding gift for his daughter. Sadly, she was jilted at the altar and consequently never lived here. The magnificent oak-paneled entrance hall has stained glass windows, a grand staircase, and a balustraded minstrels' gallery. There are 20 luxurious guestrooms, a restaurant, indoor and outdoor pools, extensive gardens, and tennis courts. Alston Cross, Holbeton (phone: 1752-830555; fax: 1752-830494). Expensive.

Buckland-Tout-Saints A superb example of Queen Anne architecture dating back to the late 17th century, this country-house hotel stands in secluded parkland about 2½ miles northeast of Kingsbridge. Finely furnished, it has 12 rooms and a restaurant. The Buckland Room has a hand-carved four-poster bed, though some of the other rooms are bigger. Goveton (phone: 1548-853055; 800-435-8281; fax: 1548-856261). Expensive.

Burgh Island A unique sea tractor transports guests to this Art Deco establishment's 26-acre tidal island off the coast at Bigbury-on-Sea. (At low tide, you can walk to it.) Agatha Christie often stayed here and set two of her books on the island: *Evil Under the Sun* (called "Smuggler's Island") and *And Then There Were None* (called "Indian Island"). Noël Coward also was a frequent guest. The 14-suite hotel has retained its 1930s decor and a small shop that sells clothing and jewelry from the Deco decades. There's also a good dining room. Burgh Island, Bigbury-on-Sea (phone: 1548-810514; fax: 1548-810243). Expensive.

Start Bay Inn Situated at one end of Slapton Sands, this thatch pub with log fires and low-beamed ceilings makes a useful lunchtime stopover, specializing in fish (locally caught) and chips. Portions are served medium, large, or jumbo. To end your meal, try the treacle pudding with clotted cream. Open daily. Reservations advised. No credit cards accepted. Torcross (phone: 1548-580553). Inexpensive.

PLYMOUTH Anyone driving into Plymouth from the east comes across a curious sight—the ruins of a church in the middle of a traffic roundabout. *Charles Church* was destroyed in the spring of 1941 during a Nazi raid on the city that left over 1,000 people dead, 70,000 homeless, and most of the city center devastated. The spire and shell of the church were left as a memorial to those who lost their lives, and if at first it seems irreverent to surround a memorial with traffic, on second thought it seems entirely appropriate to see it as part of the daily flow of life.

The raid irrevocably changed the face of this vigorous old port; with 242,000 residents, it's the second-largest city in Britain's southwest (Bristol is first). The postwar center is a busy shopping area that draws people from all over the region, although, unfortunately, it isn't very handsome. A lot of Plymouth, however, miraculously was spared damage. The *Barbican,* on an indent of the sea called Sutton Harbor, is where rich Elizabethan merchants built their houses and is now a lively spot full of antiques shops, art galleries, restaurants, and pubs. Nearby is *Mayflower Steps,* a monument commemorating the sailing of the *Mayflower* in 1620 (it set sail from Southampton, but Plymouth was its last port). At the edge of the *Barbican* is *Prysten House,* a 15th-century priory that survived both Henry VIII's purge of the monasteries and Hitler's terrible assault. It is closed Sundays and November through March except by appointment; admission charge (phone: 1752-661414). The tourist information center is in the *Island House* of the *Barbican* (phone: 1752-264851); it's open daily.

In contrast to the amiable bustle of the *Barbican,* the face Plymouth shows the sea is a formidable one. *The Citadel,* a low gray stone fortress built in the late 1600s by Charles II and still used by the military, sits brooding on the high ground above Plymouth Sound. Sharing the commanding position over the sound is Plymouth's famous Hoe, the broad green where Sir Francis Drake leisurely finished his game of bowls before dealing an ignominious defeat to the Spanish Armada. There's a statue of Sir Francis near the bowling green. At the center of the Hoe is another monument, this one to the thousands of sailors, British and Commonwealth, who were killed in the two world wars. It's a moving tribute, especially apt in this city whose namesakes in the far-flung reaches of the Empire number no fewer than 40. Close by, the city's visitors' center, *Plymouth Dome,* features a dramatic exhibition of the city's history from Elizabethan times to World War II. Through satellite and radar facilities, visitors can observe the ships crossing Plymouth Sound. It is open daily; admission charge (phone: 1752-600608). Before leaving the Hoe, walk to the edge of the seaward side. Built into the rocky cliffs of the headland is a series of steps and platforms that lead down to an open-air bathing pool jutting out into the sound, a surprising retreat hidden away from the city that buzzes above it.

Chez Nous Unobtrusively located in a row of city-center shops, this small French dining spot has earned a Michelin star for its excellent cooking; it is one of the best eating places on this tour. Its owner and chef, Jacques Marchal, creates ever-changing dishes with whatever fresh local produce he finds in the market that morning. Closed Sundays, Mondays, and September. Reservations necessary. Major credit cards accepted. 13 Frankfort Gate, Plymouth (phone: 1752-266793). Expensive.

Grand A handsome, 77-room Victorian establishment on the seafront beside the Hoe has been restored to its original elegance with chandeliers, ornate ceilings, and heavy curtains. The 31 rooms facing the sea have either open balconies or raised seating areas to make the most of the view. The dining room serves fine English fare. Elliot St., the Hoe, Plymouth (phone: 1752-661195; fax: 1752-600653). Moderate.

Moorland Links Though only 4 miles from the center of Plymouth, this hotel in a white 1930s structure enjoys a quiet location on the edge of Dartmoor. The restaurant and most of the 30 guestrooms have wonderful panoramic views. There is a tennis court on the grounds, and guests also can play golf on the adjoining 18-hole *Yelverton* course. In Yelverton, just off A386 (phone: 1822-852245; fax: 1822-855004). Moderate.

Trattoria Pescatore Traditional Italian dishes and wonderful seafood concoctions are the main fare here. During the summer, you can sit outside in the tiny, open courtyard in the back. Closed Sundays. Reservations advised. Major credit cards accepted. Admiralty St., Stonehouse, Plymouth (phone: 1752-600201). Moderate.

En Route from Plymouth About 10 miles north of Plymouth at Yelverton (turn left on a signposted road off A386), with a clear view of distant Plymouth Harbor, is *Buckland Abbey,* originally built as a monastery in the 13th century and later turned into a country house for Sir Francis Drake. It now features an exhibition on its history. The home is closed weekdays November through *Easter;* admission charge (phone: 1822-853607).

At Saltash, across the river Tamar (which forms the border between Cornwall and Devon), about 14 miles from Plymouth on A38 and A388, is *Cotehele* (pronounced Co-*teel*), an especially fine gray granite house that was occupied by the Edgcumbe family until 1535. Built around 1485, this *National Trust* property stands in an exquisite setting of wildflowers and meadows on the riverbank. Inside are beautiful furnishings, tapestries, needlework, and armor, and there's also a working 18th-century water mill on the grounds. The house is closed Fridays and November through March; the gardens are open daily. There's an admission charge (phone: 1579-50434). (As you cross the Tamar on the road bridge to Saltash, look to your left for the Royal Albert Bridge, a railroad bridge completed in 1859 and one of Isambard Kingdom Brunel's engineering masterpieces.)

Leave Saltash on A38, heading west, and hook up with A387 signposted to East and West Looe, two old fishing towns joined by a bridge over the river Looe. Turn left over the bridge, past the 14th-century *St. Nicholas Church,* to the steep road down to Looe Bay. Beyond the rocks lies *St. George's Island,* once a Celtic monastery and now a privately owned bird sanctuary. It is possible to walk along the coast path to Polperro from here (a 4-mile hike), but motorists must either return to the church and turn left past the 500-year-old *Jolly Sailor* inn onto a narrow lane—it's extremely steep, so drive slowly—past Talland Bay to Polperro, or backtrack farther inland and take A387 west. Either way, it's about a 19-mile drive.

Whichever route is chosen, it's wiser in the busy summer period to park outside the village and walk down the hill into town, since Polperro is not much more than a covey of whitewashed cottages spilling down a ravine to the sea, and its streets were made for horse traffic. The tiny harbor, old houses, and narrow alleyways give it the picture-book looks of a quintessential Cornish fishing village. In fact, in the peak season it suffers from an excess of picturesqueness and is overwhelmed by tourists, although it somehow retains its charm.

There are two ways to get to St. Austell from Polperro. One is to drive back along A387, bear left along B3359 and left again to Lostwithiel, and hop onto the fast A390, continuing west into St. Austell (a distance of about 20 miles). The other is to proceed west from Polperro, crossing the estuary of the river Fowey aboard the car ferry from Bodinnick. On the other side, Fowey (pronounced *Foy*) clings to a wooded hillside, descending in a maze of twisting, narrow streets. Details of local history are in the *Town Hall Museum* in Trafalgar Square. The museum is closed weekends and October through April; admission charge (no phone). Nearby *Menabilly,* set in the woods behind Polridmouth Cove, was the home of Daphne du Maurier (closed to the public) and the setting for her novel *Rebecca.* From here, drive west another 7 miles on B3082 and A390 to St. Austell.

ST. AUSTELL Clusters of old buildings, still quietly enjoying the life of a medieval village, are harshly offset by a modern shopping precinct. The traffic-free center has a fine church of Pentewan stone, an Italianate town hall, and a bustling market place. St. Austell, a mile inland from the bay of the same name, has been the headquarters of the English china clay (kaolin) industry since the mid-18th century. *Wheal Martyn Museum,* an open-air museum covering the development of the Cornish china clay industry from 1745, is 4 miles north of St. Austell off A391 at Carthew. Set in a restored clay pit, it houses all kinds of extraction and processing machinery. The museum is closed November through March; admission charge (phone: 1726-850362).

St. Austell Bay was once one of the greatest pilchard fishing areas in the country, but this important industry declined dramatically in the 1890s, when the pilchards simply stopped coming, possibly because they had been overfished. Now only the old pilchard fishing villages—such as Charlestown, with its *Charlestown Shipwreck Centre* (open daily March through October; admission charge; phone: 1726-69897), Porthpean, and Polkerris—remain.

BEST EN ROUTE

Alverton Manor Once an elegant manor house and more recently home to a local order of nuns, this 25-room hostelry offers luxurious surroundings and extreme comfort. The former chapel, now known as the *Great Hall,* serves as a venue for weddings, recitals, and banquets. The restaurant, serving English and continental fare, is among the best in western England. Open daily. Reservations advised. Major credit cards accepted. Tregolls Rd., Truro (phone: 1872-76633; fax: 1872-222989). Expensive.

Marina Several of the 11 rooms in this Georgian building, once the summer residence of the Bishops of Truro, have magnificent sea views. The restaurant specializes in traditional English fare. Open March through October. The Esplanade, Fowey (phone: 1726-833315). Moderate.

Pier House A friendly hostelry whose 12 rooms overlook the harbor front in tiny Charlestown, 2 miles southeast of St. Austell. Its restaurant is the best place for sampling locally caught seafood (closed *Christmas;* reservations advised; Visa accepted). Harbour Front, Charlestown (phone: 1726-67955; fax: 1726-69246). Inexpensive.

En Route from St. Austell A pleasant side trip from St. Austell before continuing to St. Mawes and Falmouth is a visit to Mevagissey. Drive 5 miles south from St. Austell (via B3273) to this tiny fishing village, which once was famous as a smugglers' hideaway. Today, Mevagissey is made up of innocent cottages clinging to a hillside around a pretty little harbor. Commercial fishing is still alive here, but with vacationers in mind, the fishermen also rent boats by the hour. The *Mevagissey Museum* (on East Quay; phone: 1726-843568), with exhibits about the town and its seafaring history, is housed in an old boatbuilders' workshop. It is closed October through *Easter;* admission charge. Return to St. Austell, then take A390 southwest. Just beyond the junction with A39, turn left on A3078 to St. Mawes (a distance of about 20 miles).

ST. MAWES AND FALMOUTH Its mild climate isn't all that prompts comparisons between the tiny St. Mawes and the French Riviera. It has the same easygoing charm and the same air of a perpetual party. Sitting on the tip of a peninsula in a large sheltered bay, St. Mawes is a perfect yachting and fishing town. Add stunning coastal walks, secluded beaches, and subtropical gardens, and you can see why well-to-do Britons with a yen for the sea and soft climate have made St. Mawes a sophisticated outpost.

Falmouth (pop. 18,500), a port and also a resort town, is across the Carrick Roads—as the wide estuary of the river Fal is known—from St. Mawes and linked to it by a pedestrian ferry. Sprawling around attractive, wooded rivers and creeks, secluded coves, and subtropical gardens, it is one of the most popular towns on the Cornish Riviera, "discovered" by Sir Walter Raleigh, who recognized its potential as a harbor. The deep-water anchorage was once the permanent home of many craft, including the post office's sail and steam packet ships, tea clippers, and windjammers; even now, one of the most modern coast guard services, the Maritime Rescue Coordination Centre, supervises rescues across the Atlantic as far south as Spain. In the older part of town is *Custom House Quay,* with the great neoclassical *Custom House* overlooking the King's Pipe, a chimney used to destroy confiscated tobacco, and the *Maritime Museum* (open daily; admission charge; no phone). From Falmouth it is possible to take a steamer up the Fal to the ancient high tide port of Truro, Cornwall's cathedral city, or south, down along the coast, then up the Helford River.

Falmouth and St. Mawes share a pair of castles built by Henry VIII. *St. Mawes Castle,* its central tower surrounded by three battlemented semicircles, sits on a knoll outside the village of St. Mawes. It is closed Mondays November through March; admission charge (phone: 1326-270526). Unlike *Pendennis Castle,* its twin at Falmouth, which resisted Parliamentarian troops for five months, *St. Mawes* was never the site of any battles and thus is in near-perfect repair. The view from *Pendennis* is one of the best—on one side the beaches, on the other, the docks and town. *Pendennis* is open daily; admission charge (phone: 1326-316594).

The gardens that flourish around the Carrick Roads are unusually exotic partly because the climate is mild and partly because Falmouth was the first port of call for English ships returning from long voyages, and for hundreds of years sailors brought back plants from the farthest flung reaches of the world. When the English turned their considerable gardening talents to these rare plants, they developed an extraordinary number of subspecies. The church grounds of *St. Just-in-Roseland* (4 miles outside St. Mawes and linked by coastal and inland footpaths) are a splendid garden where date palms, bamboo, camellias, rhododendrons, azaleas, Chilian fire bushes, and magnolias flourish alongside England's own bluebells, snowdrops, and primroses. North of St. Mawes (4 miles south of Truro at Feock) is *Trelissick Garden,* a beautifully tended woodland on the river Fal. The garden is closed November through February; admission charge (phone: 1872-862090). Four miles southwest of Falmouth is *Glendurgan Garden,* on a narrow creek that flows into the Helford River, with enough varieties of subtropical and indigenous plants to satisfy the most avid gardener. There's also a maze comprised of low laurel hedges. It is closed Sundays, Mondays, and November through February; admission charge (phone: 1326-311300). Another garden in the area is *Trebah Garden,* which is planted on the banks of a creek near *Glendurgan;* along with colorful shrubs and flowers, this garden also has a small memorial honoring 5,000 US Army soldiers who sailed from here during the *D-Day* invasion in 1944. The garden is open daily; admission charge (phone: 1326-250448).

BEST EN ROUTE

Budock Vean Though there have been several modern extensions, this 18th-century country house still retains much of its original grandeur. Located in a tiny village near the Helford River 3 miles southwest of Falmouth, the hotel has 32 guestrooms, an indoor pool, and extensive grounds with gardens, a nine-hole golf course, and tennis. There is also a good restaurant; try to get a table by the window to get the best views of the countryside. Open March through December. Mawnan Smith (phone: 1326-250288; fax: 1326-250892). Expensive.

Rising Sun It's hard to imagine a quainter, cozier, more gracious hostelry than this 11-room gem. The front terrace, which receives the overflow from its congenial pub in warm weather, faces the town quay, and guests who get a room in the front will fall asleep to the sound of the tide slapping against the harbor wall. The restaurant serves traditional English fare. The Square, St. Mawes (phone: 1326-270233). Moderate.

Tresanton This lovably overgrown, white, vine-covered cottage combines the sophistication and the country charm of St. Mawes in one delightful package. On the coastal road, it has subtropical terraced gardens spilling down its hillside toward the bay and a beach. Sailing and water skiing are possible. There are 21 bedrooms; the food, particularly the fresh local fish, is delicious. Open March through October and during *Christmas* week. Lower Castle Rd., St. Mawes (phone: 1326-270544; fax: 1326-270002). Moderate.

En Route from Falmouth Leave Falmouth on A394 and continue south about 19 miles to the Lizard and West Penwith.

THE LIZARD AND WEST PENWITH It would take a jaded traveler indeed to resist the urge to travel to the ends of the earth, and in England the earth ends most spectacularly at the two tips of a broad stirrup of land called the Lizard and West Penwith. The Lizard, as the Cornish peninsula south of the Helford River is known, terminates in England's southernmost point: Lizard Point. It is also the site of the Goonhilly satellite-tracking station, whose huge white dishes can be seen rising above the heathland. West Penwith, the peninsula a few miles farther west, stretches to England's westernmost point: Land's End. Despite the summer crowds that converge on these popular spots, they are impressive examples of nature's handiwork. The Lizard ends in cliffs of brilliant serpentine—olive green rock veined with red and purple and polished by the sea and wind—while Land's End meets the sea with granite cliffs and a wash of shiny black boulders. Go early in the morning or at sunset to avoid the crowds. Better yet, park a mile or so away and approach the spots via one of the coastal footpaths. This coast is a notorious shipwrecker: Ferocious seas have slammed many a vessel onto its rocks, and more than one village pub exhibits disaster photos on its walls.

On A394, between the Lizard and West Penwith, is Helston, a pleasant market town best known for its *Flora Day* celebration, when the whole town turns out, flower bedecked and beribboned, to "flurry" dance through the streets to a 1,500-year-old tune. The date, May 8, is well before the annual influx of vacationers, so the holiday is still mostly an event for townsfolk. On the edge of town, *Flambards Theme Park* includes full-size indoor recreations of a Victorian village with 50 shops, and the World War II blitz on London. The park is closed November through *Easter;* admission charge (phone: 1326-574549). Also, 3 miles north of Helston on B3297 is the *Poldark Mine,* an old tin mine that has been converted into an industrial museum. It is closed November through March; admission charge (phone: 1326-573173).

The castle that seems to rise out of the water like a vision as you approach West Penwith is real. It's *St. Michael's Mount,* once a monastery, later a fortress, and for the last 300 years the home of the St. Aubyn family. Now owned by the *National Trust,* it's accessible either by a causeway that can be walked across at low tide or by ferry. The castle is closed weekends year-round, as well as Tuesdays and Thursdays November through March; admission charge (phone: 1736-710507).

Another 14 miles west of Helston on A394 is Penzance, West Penwith's largest town (pop. 19,500). It is a popular resort, warmer year-round than most places in the country and near a broad swath of beach. For that reason, Penzance is crammed with the less appealing aspects of tourism, such as tedious souvenir stores, but the old part of town is attractive, with elegant Regency and Georgian houses and more modest fishermen's cottages. The *Trinity House National Lighthouse Centre* (Wharf Rd.; phone: 1736-60077) has exhibits on the lighthouses, lightships, and buoys that have been used to help seafarers navigate in foggy weather around Britain's coast for four centuries. The center is closed November through March; admission charge. At the sea end of the street, opposite the *Admiral Benbow* restaurant, is the *Nautical Museum,* which contains several items salvaged from local wreck diving. The museum is closed Sundays and November through *Easter;* admission charge (phone: 1736-68890). The town is laden with memories—Admiral Nelson's victory at the Battle of Trafalgar was first announced at the *Union* hotel as ships were seen racing up the channel, and Gilbert and Sullivan's *The Pirates of Penzance* perpetuates stories of piracy in this area's past.

Penzance is only 10 miles from Land's End, where a visitors' complex houses the 34-room *State House* hotel (phone: 1736-871844); an information center with exhibitions about shipwrecks and Cornwall; and craft workshops and gift shops. The complex is open daily; admission charge to the exhibitions (phone: 1736-871501).

This westernmost tip of England is an open-air museum of ancient Britons. There are dozens of stone circles, hut circles, and burial mounds. Near Lamorna, south of Penzance, is a fascinating formation called the Pipers and the Merry Maidens—two tall upright stones and a circle of 19 stones. Local legend has it that village girls were caught dancing on the Sabbath, and they and their musicians were turned to stone as a punishment.

Take a look at Cornwall's fishing industry 1½ miles south of Penzance at Newlyn (once a Victorian artists' colony and now the largest fishing port in the southwest; much of the delicious fish eaten in this part of the country comes from here) and at Mousehole (rhymes with *tousle*), a fishing village about 5 miles farther down the coast. A memorial near the old lifeboat at Mousehole commemorates eight volunteers who drowned in 1981 while trying to save the crew of a ship during the area's worst storm in 20 years. About 9 miles farther along on B3315 at Porthcurno, built into the granite cliffs overlooking the sea, is the *Minack Theatre,* an amphitheater which hosts the *Minack Theatre Festival* in summer (phone: 1736-810696). Also see *Best Festivals* in DIVERSIONS.

BEST EN ROUTE

Lamorna Cove The name comes from the tranquil wooded cove over which this hostelry perches. Although the modern additions don't do justice to the original granite miners' church or the setting, the 16-room hotel is very comfortable, with a heated outdoor pool. The restaurant serves fresh local produce and seafood (there's an unending supply of fish from nearby Newlyn). Lamorna (phone: 1736-731411). Moderate.

ISLES OF SCILLY The often rough two-and-a-half-hour boat passage from Penzance to St. Mary's, the largest of the Isles of Scilly, prompted one wag to describe the islands as a paradise that can only be reached through purgatory. Now, thanks to the invention of the helicopter, you can take a 20-minute flight straight to heaven—in this case a group of 150-plus islands 30 miles off the Cornish coast. Connected by shallow straits treacherously studded with outcroppings of rock and reef, the islands have a schizophrenic nature. Their northwestern sides are usually bleak, windswept plains of gorse and heather. But the sheltered southern sides support vast fields of flowers—daffodils, jonquils, narcissus, anemones, iris, tulips, and lilies. Flowers are the main business of the 2,500 people who live in the Isles of Scilly: more than 1,000 tons of cut flowers are exported from here every year.

Only five of the islands—St. Mary's, Tresco, St. Martin's, Bryher, and St. Agnes—are inhabited. The rest are home to seals, puffins, gannets, kittiwakes, and other ocean birds. Their quiet sandy beaches are perfect for picnicking or sunbathing.

British International Helicopters (phone: 1736-63871) flies daily (except Sundays) from Penzance to *St. Mary's Airport* and to *Tresco Heliport. Isles of Scilly Skybus Ltd.* (phone: 1736-787017) flies (except Sundays) between *Land's End Aerodrome* and *St. Mary's* (it also goes to Exeter March through October); private charters also are available.

Travel from St. Mary's to Tresco, Bryher, St. Martin's, or St. Agnes is remarkably easy, as are visits to the outlying rocks to watch gulls, cormorants, oyster catchers, curlews, and the occasional grey heron, plus seals and, if lucky, playful dolphins. Every morning during summer, the dozen or so ferrymen gather on *St. Mary's Hugh Town Quay* (known locally as "Rat Island," a reference to its earlier residents) to decide on a range of options (depending on the state of the tide and the weather) and then disperse to call on the hotels and inform visitors where they can go that day. The flotilla of boats leaves at 10 AM and again in the afternoon, carrying anywhere from a dozen to 70 people; most of them are bound for the 20 or more brilliant beaches that could easily have been lifted from the West Indies, yet miraculously manage to remain uncrowded even at the height of summer.

The island of Tresco draws the most visitors. The gardens at *Tresco Abbey* contain a staggering variety of plants—between 3,000 and 4,000—the lifetime achievement of botanical zealot Augustus Smith, whose descendants still hold the lease on the island. Also in the gardens is the *Valhalla Maritime Museum,* which has a fascinating collection of figureheads from shipwrecks, relics of the days when Scilly islanders made their living scavenging from the many ships that went aground on the dangerous reefs in the vicinity. The gardens and museum are open daily; admission charge (phone: 1720-22849). If you stop for a pint of beer at the island's *New Inn* in the town of Tresco (phone: 1720-22844), take a look at the wall chart showing the surrounding savage seas as the graveyard of some 2,000 ships: vessels with salt from Spain, silks from Italy, elephant tusks from Africa, hides from Argentina, cotton from Galveston, and tea from Fuchow.

BEST EN ROUTE

Island Perhaps the most elegant place to stay in Scilly, it has 40 guestrooms and five acres of gardens, a private beach, an outdoor pool, and spectacular sea views. The restaurant is first-rate. Open March through October. For more information, see *Rural Retreats* in DIVERSIONS. Tresco, Isles of Scilly (phone: 1720-22883; fax: 1720-23008). Expensive.

St. Martin's This is the only hotel on St. Martin's (which has just 60 permanent residents). The cottage-style property in a modern building has 22 individually designed rooms and two suites, and the setting in the cove by the sea is superb. There's an indoor pool and subtropical gardens. Its excellent restaurant serves local fare, especially fish dishes. Open mid-December through October. St. Martin's, Isles of Scilly (phone: 1720-22092; 800-323-7308; fax: 1720-22298). Expensive.

ST. IVES Ferry back to Penzance, from where B3311 slices across West Penwith to St. Ives (pop. 11,000), 8 miles north. Formerly a fishing town, it is now a seaside resort that has retained its old-fangled Cornish looks. As its pilchard industry declined, a small army of potters, painters, and sculptors moved in, setting up studios and galleries along the narrow tangle of cobbled streets. The town was already established as an artists' colony in the 19th century, when such painters as James McNeill Whistler and Walter Sickert set the fashion. The sculptor Barbara Hepworth spent most of her working life here until her death in 1975. The *Barbara Hepworth Museum and Sculpture Garden* at her home on Barnoon Hill is well worth a visit. Adjoining it is *Tate in the West,* a branch of London's *Tate Gallery,* which stages exhibitions of contemporary art. Both are closed Mondays; separate admission charges (phone for both: 1736-796226). Potter Bernard Leach established one of the most famous potteries in Europe here—students still flock from all over the world to learn their craft from his successors. For those in search of sun and sand, there are Porthmeor Beach, the smaller Porthgwidden Beach, and the long run of Porthminster Beach.

En Route from St. Ives It's best to meander up the rocky north coast of Cornwall. No single road follows the coastline, but there are secondary roads that loop off the main road (A30, which runs about 5 miles inland) to hug the coast for 5 to 10 miles before rejoining it. Newquay, a popular and congested summer resort some 30 miles up the coast from St. Ives, has a fine stretch of beach; in fact, huge Atlantic rollers guarantee the best surfing in Britain. There are also spectacular cliff walks to be enjoyed, each rocky promontory more interesting than the last. Towan Head, the promontory separating Newquay Bay and Fistral Bay, boasts a small, castellated tower and chapel belonging to a local family, and there are burial mounds at Pentire Point at the other end of Fistral Bay, which prove that prehistoric man thought this a good vantage point, too. *Trerice,* 3 miles southeast of Newquay, is an Elizabethan manor house built in 1571 with superb plasterwork and fireplaces. It's closed Tuesdays November through March; admission charge (phone: 1637-875404).

Just past Newquay, take the coast road (B3276) 6 miles to Bedruthan Steps, near Park Head. Here, the mammoth chunks of the cliff that have tumbled onto the wide strand of beach below are said to be the stepping stones of a Cornish giant, Bedruthan. When the tide is in, Bedruthan Steps jut out from the white agitation of the sea like bits of black coral, but when the tide is out, you can explore the rock pools and caverns around them by descending a dramatic cliff staircase. From here, continue on B3276 another 8 miles northeast to Padstow.

PADSTOW From June to September, Padstow's compact horseshoe of a harbor and pleasant tangle of streets ring with the holiday fun of summer folk who come to fish, swim, and sail in the waters of the north Cornish coast and the river Camel. But on May 1, before the season gets under way, the town holds its own celebration, the *Hobby Horse,* a day when a huge, fierce hobby horse prances through the streets in the midst of the 2,200 singing and dancing villagers (see *Best Festivals* in DIVERSIONS).

BEST EN ROUTE

Seafood Primarily known as a superb seafood restaurant, it also has 10 lovely guestrooms, some overlooking the harbor. Closed from *Christmas* to early February; the restaurant is also closed Sundays (but room-service meals are available with advance notice). Reservations advised. Major credit cards accepted. For more information, see *Rural Retreats* in DIVERSIONS. Riverside, Padstow (phone: 1841-532485; fax: 1841-533344). Expensive to moderate.

Old Custom House Set on the quayside, it has 25 rooms, most of them overlooking the busy harbor or estuary. Facilities include an attractive, candlelit restaurant. South Quay, Padstow (phone: 1841-532359; fax: 1841-533372). Moderate.

Rose-in-Vale The reception desk at this stylish hotel 8 miles southwest of Newquay used to be the pulpit of a Methodist chapel. Most of the building is of Georgian design, but some of the 17 guestrooms are in a modern addition. Amenities include a restaurant, a bar, extensive gardens, a tennis court, a croquet lawn, and an outdoor heated pool (open in summer only). Mithian, near St. Agnes (phone: 1872-552202; fax: 1872-552700). Moderate.

Molesworth Manor This hotel, originally built in 1620 as a rectory, has retained its cobbled courtyard and arched entrance. The 10 rooms and a separate cottage are comfortably furnished, though they do not have TV sets. There is no restaurant; however, breakfast is included, and there is a TV room, a lounge, and a library. No smoking is allowed. No credit cards accepted. Little Petherick, 3 miles south of Padstow (phone: 1841-540292). Inexpensive.

En Route from Padstow About 15 miles southeast of the town of Bodmin on B3269 is *Lanhydrock,* a grandiose Tudor house built in the 17th century but almost entirely destroyed by fire and rebuilt according to its original plan in the 1880s (the long gallery remains from the earlier structure). It is set in meticulously tended grounds and rolling parkland, and never were the fruits of the Empire more impressively displayed. The elaborate kitchens—with numerous larders—and lavish baths are especially fascinating insights into that exceedingly wealthy time. The house is closed Mondays and November through *Easter;* the gardens are open daily. There's an admission charge (phone: 1208-73320). Return to B3269 and continue to Bodmin and Bodmin Moor.

BODMIN MOOR An *Area of Outstanding Natural Beauty* north and east of Bodmin, Bodmin Moor reverberates with almost as many legends as the more famous moor in neighboring Devon. Dozmary Pool, a shallow tarn in the center of the moor, is supposedly the pool (one of three) into which Sir Bedivere threw Excalibur, at King Arthur's request. Nearby at Bolventor is *Jamaica Inn,* the scene of Daphne du Maurier's tale of smugglers and pirates. And there are holy wells—at St. Neot on the southern edge, and, on the northern edge, at St. Clether and Altarnun, whose well is reputed to cure madness by the near drowning of the sufferer.

Driving across the bare brown hills broken only by tors, it is easy to see how legends attach themselves to these spots. A few minor roads penetrate the southeast corner of the moor, but to get to Rough (rhymes with *now*) Tor and Brown Willy, the highest points affording the best views, it is necessary to circle the moor and come up behind it at Camelford, on its northwestern edge. From here you can drive to a car park at the foot of Rough Tor and climb up or hike on to Brown Willy, a mile away. Or take the turnoff to the left just before you get to Rough Tor. It leads to an eerie relic of modern times—the ruins of a World War II Royal Air Force base at Davidstow—and could be a scene out of any number of contemporary doomsday stories: abandoned runways, control towers, all the paraphernalia of modern technology left to decay along with the crude barrows and hut circles of ancient Britons. Then, just to balance the vision of life left by the opulence of Lanhydrock, stop in at the *North Cornwall Museum* (at Camelford; phone: 1840-212954), which has a reconstruction of a Cornish cottage. It's closed Sundays and October through March; admission charge.

NORTH CORNWALL COAST It would be a Herculean task to find any part of the Cornish coast not worth seeing, but there is a 20-mile stretch of coast north of the river Camel that contains dramatic cliffs, surfing beaches, sand dunes, historic spots, and exquisite villages and is particularly worthwhile.

From Wadebridge, at the mouth of the Camel estuary about 8 miles east of Padstow, take B3314 about 2 miles to the turnoff to Rock. Travel another 3 miles along this unnumbered road (past this not terribly attractive resort town) to a car park at Daymer Bay. The dunes here are marvelous, covered with clumps of coarse grass and just the place to find dog walkers and families on weekend outings. There is the *St. Enodoc* golf course along the coast (phone: 1208-863216), and in the middle of one of the fairways stands *St. Enodoc Church,* less curious now, even given its fairly odd surroundings, than it was 100 years ago, when it was half buried in sand and the vicar was forced to crawl in through the roof to deliver the sermon; it is hard to imagine who was there to hear it.

Stick to the unnumbered coast road by following signs to Trebetherick, Polzeath (an excellent surfing beach), Pentireglaze, and Port Quin. According to local lore, all the men of Port Quin were lost at sea in one accident, and shortly thereafter, the women mysteriously disappeared as well. The abandoned village—four stone cottages that sit precariously over the water at the end of a steep cove and an old stone barn next to a tumbling stream—is now in the hands of the *National Trust* and is a lovely, quiet spot.

Just a few miles from Port Quin is Port Isaac, an old corn port and modern-day fishing village that you literally descend into. The streets tumble down to a postage stamp of a beach where visitors pay to leave their cars in summer (the only tidal car park in Britain and hence only for those with an accurate sense of timing). The color-washed houses seem to be piled one on top of the other in the narrow valley—one of the streets is even called Squeezibelly Alley because a mere 18 inches separate one wall from the other. Right on the harbor wall is the *Golden Lion* pub (phone: 1208-880336), a congenial spot from which to watch the tide slowly creep in.

At the end of another steep valley about 10 miles up the coast is Trebarwith Strand, where massive fingers of sculpted black rock, pink-veined and highly polished, lead down to a broad swath of beach that during high tide is completely covered.

From here it is just a mile or so to Tintagel, possibly the most visited spot in Cornwall. The town itself is rather tacky and unattractive; the real drawing card is *Tintagel Castle,* the ruins of a 13th-century dwelling and 6th-century monastery where (legend has it) King Arthur was born. Even if you don't subscribe to the story, *Tintagel* is worth a stop. Right on the edge of a rocky promontory, the castle ruins are dramatically beautiful. They are open daily; admission charge (phone: 1840-770328).

BEST EN ROUTE

Port Gaverne A peaceful restored 17th-century inn tucked into a tiny inlet of the same name, only a few yards from the sea (though only one of its 18 rooms has a sea view). Open mid-February through December. Near Port Isaac (phone: 1208-880244; fax: 1208-880151). Expensive to moderate.

En Route from Tintagel From here, the B3263 from Boscastle leads to the A39 coast road. Continue around Bude Bay and across the Cornwall—Devon border and Hartland Point to Clovelly, 10 miles beyond the border.

CLOVELLY This delightful village is so quaint, charming, and perfectly picturesque—an unbroken line of shuttered and flower-bedecked cottages down a steep, cobbled street to the harbor—you can't quite believe it isn't contrived. But Clovelly isn't, although it is on the map for every tourist bus coming to the North Devon coast. It is probably best to avoid it during the day in July and August, but if you go in the early morning or evening, you'll find a beautiful village going about its business. No cars are allowed; visitors and villagers alike have to leave them at a car park at the top of the hill. You might enjoy a cream tea at the *Red Lion* hotel (phone: 1237-431237) at the bottom of the hill on the quay or at the *New Inn* (phone: 1237-431303) at the top of the hill; the main activity in Clovelly is strolling down to the quay and making the arduous climb back up; it is steep, so be sure to wear flat shoes.

BEST EN ROUTE

Yeoldon House This rambling Georgian house on the edge of Bideford was ably converted to an attractive hotel in the late 1940s. The 10 rooms are bright and comfortable, and the English and continental cooking do justice to local produce and fresh fish. Durrant La., Northam, near Bideford (phone: 1237-474400; fax: 1237-476618). Moderate.

NORTH DEVON COAST AND EXMOOR Continue touring the North Devon coast by following A39 through Bideford to Barnstaple, from where B3230 leads north to Ilfracombe, once a port and shipyard, now a popular resort. With its abundance of small guesthouses and imposing Victorian hotels daringly perched on the city's magnificent cliffs, Ilfracombe has a certain period charm.

Leaving Ilfracombe, take A399 east, a road that for about 8 miles follows a beautiful stretch of coast. Just past Combe Martin, a not very pretty resort town, take an unnumbered road signposted to the villages of Hunter's Inn and Trentishoe. The variety of landscapes this road covers in a few short miles will make your head spin. First it follows a ridge above gentle green downs dotted with prosperous-looking farms. Then, suddenly, you're on the loneliest coast road in the world: wild moorland, raw against the sea wind, stretches on either side. Press on, for within another mile or so the road runs along the top of a deep, wooded combe. At the bottom of this serene valley lies *Hunter's Inn* (in the tiny village of the same name; phone: 15983-230), a gabled and Alpinesque hostelry popular with tourists. The spot is unarguably beautiful and a cool beer on the inn's terrace, in the company of the resident peacocks, is almost mandatory.

Lynmouth, about 5 miles farther, is a pretty resort village encompassed by the sheer cliffs of the Lyn River Valley. Romantic poet Percy Bysshe Shelley lived here for a while, although his cottage no longer exists. It requires steady nerves and reliable brakes to take the direct road from Lynton, a larger town that literally hovers 500 feet above Lynmouth. It is a vertiginous drop, and the three sand-filled offshoots along the road—escape roads for runaway cars—probably see their share of business. An alternative route is to bypass Lynton altogether and take the A39 from Hunter's Inn to Lynmouth; the trip is about 5 miles longer this way, but it's less hair-raising.

There are two spectacular drives out of Lynmouth. One is along B3223 inland, following the high curving ridge of the East Lyn River Valley to Watersmeet, where the East Lyn and the Hoar Oak waters meet. Much of this land is owned by the *National Trust,* which has marked several nature trails through the dense woods of the valleys. The other drive is along the coast on A39, up Countisbury Hill (as demanding of a car's engine as the road into Lynton was of its brakes). Superlatives only suffice to describe the view. Bracken- and gorse-covered hills break suddenly at black cliffs, and in the distance looms Foreland Point, at 900 feet the tallest cliffs in England.

Porlock, about 12 miles east of Lynmouth on A39 and across the Somerset border, is utterly unlike most southwest sea towns that either cling to the edge of cliffs or shelter in narrow coves. Occupying a broad, sea level plain that opens up in the Exmoor Hills, it's a sweet little place with a sleepy, satisfied air. Porlock Weir, about 2½ miles from town, is a long curving beach of white boulders and pebbles.

Stretching south of this area is *Exmoor Forest*, a forest in the ancient English sense (meaning land owned by the king and subject to his hunting laws). Anyone expecting dense woods throughout this parcel of hills in northeast Devon and west Somerset is likely to be disappointed, however. *Exmoor* is still more moor and farmland than forest, full of ancient relics, tors, wild red deer, and its famous ponies. Now a 265-square-mile national park, it includes the length of coast from Ilfracombe all the way to Porlock and beyond, but its heart is at Exford, a pretty spot and a good center for fishing, hiking, or horseback riding (also see *Great Walks and Mountain Rambles* in DIVERSIONS). Oare, near the Somerset—Devon border, is at the head of Doone Valley, the setting for R. D. Blackmore's story *Lorna Doone.* Doone Valley and the surrounding area are lovely but somewhat commercialized.

BEST EN ROUTE

Northcote Manor Tucked away on a hillside at the end of a half-mile private lane off the Barnstaple-Crediton road, this Victorian manor house is a lovely hideaway. The hotel, run by Peter and Glenda Brown, offers 11 comfortable and well-appointed guestrooms, pretty gardens, a tennis court, and a croquet lawn. The dining room serves excellent English fare. Open March through October. Burrington (phone: 1769-60501; 800-528-1234; fax: 1769-60770). Expensive.

Simonsbath House In a sheltered valley in the heart of *Exmoor*, this 17th-century house has seven pretty rooms and a dining room with a well-regarded menu featuring traditional English recipes. Open February through November. Simonsbath (phone: 164383-259). Expensive.

Whitechapel Manor Set on 15 acres in North Devon, this 16th-century manor house boasts 10 good-size rooms, fantastic views of the surrounding countryside, plus a very good restaurant. Owners John and Patricia Shapland grow all their own herbs and some vegetables in a garden near the house. Though the rooms have been completely refurbished, the 400-year-old building has, happily, been left intact. Low doorways (people were shorter back then) and slightly tilted steps and window sills (no, you haven't had too much to drink) add to the charm of the place. South Molton, North Devon (phone: 1769-573377; 800-323-7308; fax: 1769-57379). Expensive to moderate.

Heddon's Gate Perfectly poised close to the sea in the midst of *Exmoor National Park,* this 14-room country house has a well-deserved reputation for good food and lodging and is popular with walkers and wildlife lovers. A charming touch is that all the guestrooms have names and individual decors: for instance, "Grandmama's" has a four-poster bed and a Victorian-style bathroom, and "Nannies" has stained glass windows. Open *Easter* through October. Heddon's Mouth, Parracombe (phone: 15983-313; fax: 15983-363). Moderate.

Rising Sun Originally a terrace of 14th-century cottages, this busy thatch inn on a street sloping down to the harbor is a labyrinth of passages and stairways with uneven floors and sloping ceilings. There are 16 rooms (three with four-posters) and a restaurant serving generous portions of continental fare, including steaks, chicken, and seafood. Salmon fishing is available on the East Lyn River from March through September. Harbourside, Lynmouth (phone: 1598-53223; fax: 1598-53480). Moderate.

En Route from the North Devon Coast and Exmoor Forest Around the Somerset town of Dunster (8 miles east of Porlock on A39), the moors give way to soft green meadows backed by even softer hills where clusters of houses linked by ivy-draped walls smugly sit. Dunster itself is a lovely town in a peerless setting, but it is crowded in summer and is best seen off-season. *Dunster Castle,* occupying a knoll on the edge of town, was the home of the Luttrell family from the late 14th century until the 1970s and was the object of both Royalist and Parliamentarian attacks in the Civil War. The castle is closed Thursdays, Fridays, and November through March; the gardens are closed mid-December through January. There's an admission charge (phone: 1643-821314).

Five miles east of Dunster on A39, in a tranquil setting called Flowery Valley at Washford, is *Cleeve Abbey,* built by Cistercian monks in the 12th century. It was spared the full wrath of Henry VIII's Dissolution of the Monasteries, and although the church no longer exists, the gatehouse, refectory, and dormitory are beautifully intact. The abbey is open daily; admission charge (phone: 1984-40377). From here, continue on A39 another 10 miles or so to Nether Stowey, a village nestling on the eastern slopes of the Quantock Hills, where Samuel Taylor Coleridge wrote *The Rime of the Ancient Mariner.* (For a time William Wordsworth and his sister, Dorothy, lived about 4 miles away at Holford.) Coleridge's cottage, now owned by the *National Trust,* can be visited. It is closed Mondays, Fridays, and October through March; admission charge (phone: 1278-732662).

The A39 cuts across a broad basin of land between the Quantock and Mendip Hills called the Somerset Levels, low marshy land reclaimed from the sea over the centuries. Somerton and Glastonbury, about 15 miles inland, were islands until the 17th century, and the sea, at high wind and high tide, still can flood these towns. Indeed, it's thought that Somerset takes its name (meaning summer settlers or settlers by the sea lakes) from this region, because during the summer the lagoons would dry up, leaving behind fertile tidal land for grazing. Early inhabitants would drive cattle and sheep down to the plain for the season and then return to the hills when winter brought more flooding.

BEST EN ROUTE

Raleigh Manor Chris and Jenny Piper own and manage this spacious late-Victorian house on the Brendon Hills. It has seven rooms (one with a four-poster) and enjoys splendid views of *Exmoor*. The restaurant serves traditional English fare prepared by Jenny. Wheddon Cross, near Dunster (phone: 1643-841484). Moderate.

GLASTONBURY About 20 miles east of Nether Stowey is this small town (pop. 7,500), where the strands of early Christianity and English national identity meet and intertwine. Christ himself is said to have built the church that later became the most powerful abbey in the country, and it was to this sacred spot, the fabled Isle of Avalon, that King Arthur and Queen Guinevere were brought to be buried. The long and rich history of Glastonbury and nearby South Cadbury, thought to be Arthur's Camelot, is discussed in *Ancient Monuments and Ruins* in DIVERSIONS.

BEST EN ROUTE

George and Pilgrims Many a pilgrim has bedded down for the night at this venerable old stone inn with 13 rooms (three with four-posters), and although it retains much of the character it has acquired over 500 years, it has managed to incorporate all the comforts a modern traveler demands, including a restaurant serving fine continental fare. 1 High St., Glastonbury (phone: 1458-831146; fax: 1458-832252). Moderate.

WELLS This little town with about 9,500 residents basks on the sunny side of the Mendip Hills about 6 miles farther along A39 from Glastonbury. What makes it a city is its cathedral, an Early English–style church whose elaborately carved west front has been awing visitors for centuries. Inside, of less divine purpose perhaps but of spirited inspiration, is the Wells Clock, an enchanting timepiece made by a Glastonbury monk, Peter Lightfoot, in the 14th century. A carved figure of a man announces the quarter hour by kicking his heels against two bells, and four mounted knights, who charge out and knock each other off their steeds, bring in the hour.

En Route from Wells Leave Wells on A371 and continue about 8 miles northwest to *Cheddar Caves* and *Wookey Hole.*

CHEDDAR CAVES Under the Mendip Hills that tower over the Somerset Levels is a labyrinth of caves eaten out of the soft limestone hills by constant flooding. For thousands of years, and until as late as the mid-19th century, many of these caves were inhabited by people. Adventurous spelunkers still explore the underground streams and roads, and thousands of tourists visit the larger caves, *Cheddar Caves* (phone: 1934-742343), and *Wookey Hole* (phone: 1749-672243). Both are open daily; admission charge. Cheddar Gorge, a deep limestone cleft through the Mendips, offers a scenic drive, but is terribly congested during July and August. The town of Cheddar, near the *Cheddar Caves,* is home to the most famous English cheese.

En Route from the Cheddar Caves From here, it's a 30-mile ride northeast to Bristol on A38.

BRISTOL For a complete description of the city, its sights, hotels, and restaurants, see *Bristol* in THE CITIES.

Southern England

Visitors prepared for a tight little island of narrow, high-hedged roads threaded through a patchwork of tiny fields, orchards, and woods often are surprised by the part of England that lies between the upper reaches of the Thames and the English Channel. Because here, where a subterranean convulsion millions of years ago threw up folds of chalk, limestone, clay, and sand, are some of England's wide open spaces, often without a building in sight, but always with plenty of trees. There are no mountains or gorges in these lowlands between London and the coasts of West Sussex and Hampshire, yet broad vistas unfold. Expanses of heather sweep the land, purple in late summer, splashed with yellow gorse; plains of grass and corn stretch prairie-like to the horizon, highlighted during spring by fields of brilliant yellow rape; and the great whaleback of the South Downs—the range of chalkland running parallel to the coast—rolls across the two counties, sheep-cropped and sprinkled with wildflowers.

Three times in prehistory this land lay beneath the sea, and today it still propels us irresistibly toward the water. The coast of the English Channel, much wider here than at its bottleneck entering the Straits of Dover, is gentler and less dramatic than it is farther east. The chalk, laid down by the broken and powdered shells of primitive crustacea when the land was submerged, does not fling itself against the waves in the white walls seen at Dover and Beachy Head. Instead it approaches the sea down "chines," or ravines, carved through the soft, low hills by time, and there are more stretches of soft sand at the seaside. The only really challenging obstacle between Brighton and Bournemouth are the Needles, those white pinnacles rearing up like icebergs off the most westerly point of the Isle of Wight, where a red-and-white-striped lighthouse warns mariners not to stray too close.

The rivers of Sussex and Hampshire—among them the Ouse, Adur, and Arun, the Test, Stour, and the Avon—do not rush down to the sea but ripple gently, inviting anglers and others to linger on their banks. Between Southampton Water, a tidal estuary into which the Test, Itchen, and Hamble flow, and the old town of Christchurch, on the estuaries of the Avon and the Stour, 90,000 acres of untamed heath, bog, and woodland stretch back into the hinterland. Known as the New Forest, it has been a wildlife preserve for 900 years.

Later, great oaks from this forest were felled and carted and rolled to the slipways where men o' war were built, the "hearts of oak" that defended England against invaders and enforced her sovereign rule over a worldwide empire on which "the sun never set." After William I, no invader succeeded in overcoming the English, but the French remained a great threat for centuries. Henry VIII was watching his fleet do battle with them off

Southsea when his flagship, the *Mary Rose,* inexplicably went down, and the Martello towers that march along the Hampshire coast from Sussex are visual reminders of the fear of Napoleon's fleets.

In 1940, Hitler threatened but never came. Four years later the whole of the region became one vast military camp, ammunition dump, and aircraft carrier as the Allies, under the supreme command of General Dwight Eisenhower, prepared Operation Overlord, a plan to invade Europe and free it from the Nazi yoke. On June 6, 1944—*D-Day*—British and American forces under the command of General Eisenhower and Field Marshal Montgomery landed on the beaches of Normandy. Operation Overlord has become part of the history and legend of southern England, along with the battles of centuries past. Museums and galleries enshrine it.

Although London's commuter belt extends into Hampshire and West Sussex, the region is less dominated by the capital than is southeast England. Hundreds of thousands of its inhabitants look to their livelihoods in the industries that have grown up around the 20th-century cities of Portsmouth, Southampton, and Bournemouth. Tourism is increasingly important. The ancient cities of Arundel, Winchester, and Chichester are easily reached on day trips from London by car or train, as are the seaside resorts of Worthing, Littlehampton, Bognor Regis, and Bournemouth.

Such is the decline of the British Empire and the navy that once ruled the waves, that today the harbor of Portsmouth is more given over to sailing and windsurfing than warships, and there are more day cruisers and motor yachts than merchantmen on Southampton Water. Splendid natural harbors—Chichester, Christchurch, and Poole—abound on this coast, and they are crammed with small boats. Evidently, John Masefield's words "I must down to the seas again, to the lonely sea and the sky . . . " still strike a chord. It was, after all, in 1851, on the Isle of Wight, a green and pleasant chunk of England adrift a few miles offshore, that the *America's Cup* (then worth a mere hundred guineas) was born.

Until World War II and for a short time thereafter, the gateway through which most overseas visitors reached southern England was Southampton, which saw the regular arrival and departure of ocean liners loaded with film stars and millionaires. Today the only transatlantic tourists who arrive by sea are the minority who choose Cunard's *Queen Elizabeth 2* in preference to a jumbo jet or *Concorde;* the majority arrive by air at one of London's major airports, *Heathrow* or *Gatwick,* both good starting points for a southern England itinerary.

The route outlined here begins at East Grinstead, easily accessible from nearby *Gatwick Airport* or an hour's drive from *Heathrow* via the M25 London Orbital Motorway, and proceeds through pleasant countryside to Brighton, just over the border from West Sussex in East Sussex. It then follows the coast west to Arundel, to Chichester, and, entering Hampshire, to Portsmouth. From Portsmouth, ferries ply regularly to the Isle of Wight, where the route traverses this little bit of England, only 60 miles in circumference, before recrossing the water to Southampton. After Southampton, some travelers may want to abandon the *Southern England* route for the *Southwest England* route, which begins at Salisbury, but others will want to continue, heading north to Winchester. Thereafter, a quick return to London is possible, although this itinerary pushes still farther west into the New Forest—whose glades have witnessed kings and gypsies, smugglers and murderers, heroes and villains for 10 centuries—and on to the Dorset resort of Bournemouth.

Like southeast England, southern England is a magnet for tourists, especially in high summer, so book accommodations well in advance. Expect to pay more than $200 per night for a double room (including private bath, TV set, and breakfast, unless otherwise indicated) in those places listed as very expensive, from $130 to $200 in expensive places, from $85 to $130 in moderate hotels, and less than $85 at inexpensive ones. A dinner for two, excluding wine, tips, or drinks, will cost more than $60 in places listed as expensive, $40 to $60 in moderate spots, and less than $40 in inexpensive places. All restaurants listed serve lunch and dinner unless otherwise noted. For each location, hotels and restaurants are listed alphabetically by price category.

EAST GRINSTEAD This pleasant country town only 8 miles from *Gatwick Airport* has expanded as a dormitory for London commuters, but the old High Street, known locally as "the top of the town," has survived the centuries. At its heart is the parish church of St. Swithin, whose great square Norman tower, with a pinnacle at each corner, can be seen for miles over the surrounding countryside (both church and town were built on an outcrop of sandstone, the highest point of the Weald—a band of farm country that separates the North and South Downs). Among the yew trees in the churchyard (approached through an alleyway from one side and a lych-gate on the other) are ancient tombstones, including that of Anne Tree, who was "burned in the High Street" as a witch or a heretic in the 1550s.

East Grinstead's name derives from "green stede," or clearing in the forest. The town flourished as an iron-making center until that industry died; it then became merely a staging post on the road from London to Lewes and Brighton. The pub among the half-timbered Tudor buildings on High Street began as the *Newe Inn* and was the *Ounce and Ivy Bush* and the *Cat* before gaining its present name, the *Dorset Arms,* nearly 200 years ago. Now restored, this old coaching inn serves inexpensive ales and pub grub (phone: 1342-316370).

BEST EN ROUTE

Alexander House This magnificent 17th-century mansion located in its own parkland has 15 luxurious guestrooms. Tennis, croquet, golf, fishing, and horseback riding all are available. The restaurant offers classic English and French fare and an excellent wine list. Turners Hill, 4 miles southwest of East Grinstead (phone: 1342-714914; fax: 1342-717328). Expensive.

Gravetye Manor A Relais & Châteaux member, this ivy-covered, gabled Elizabethan house has 18 rooms and a sumptuous restaurant. For more information, see *Rural Retreats* in DIVERSIONS. About 5 miles outside East Grinstead (phone: 1342-810567; fax: 1342-810080). Expensive.

Woodlands Park In this Victorian country house with oak-paneled reception rooms, several of the bedrooms open onto the balcony of the grand hall. Of the 58 rooms, 32 are in a modern wing. When he was the Prince of Wales, Edward VII often used one of the rooms to entertain Lillie Langtry. The restaurant is excellent. 15 miles from Gatwick or Heathrow; Woodlands La., Stoke D'Abernon (phone: 1372-843933; fax: 1372-842704). Expensive.

The Old House In a 16th-century cottage on B2037, guests make their selections from a marvelously varied menu amid low, beamed ceilings, log fires, and gleaming brasses. Closed weekend lunch year-round and Sundays *Easter* through September. Reservations necessary. Major credit cards accepted. Effingham Rd., Copthorne, East Grinstead (phone: 1342-712222). Moderate.

En Route from East Grinstead From the top of the town take A22 south through Forest Row and Ashdown Forest, a remnant of a primeval forest and once a thriving center of the iron industry. Picnic places are signposted and offer panoramic views of this hilly, wooded country. Continue on A22 to Uckfield, 12 miles from East Grinstead. From here, you can go directly to Lewes, but a couple of attractions are worth a brief detour.

About 4 miles west of Uckfield via A272 and A275 is *Sheffield Park Garden,* owned by the *National Trust.* The garden's hundred acres, laid out in the 18th century by Lancelot "Capability" Brown, contain rare trees and shrubs as well as specimen water lilies in five lakes. The garden is closed weekdays in March, Mondays April through October, Sundays through Tuesdays November through mid-December, and mid-December through February. There's an admission charge (phone: 1825-790655). A short distance farther west is *Sheffield Park Station,* terminus of the scenic *Bluebell Railway* (phone: 1825-723777), so called because in early summer the woods flanking it are carpeted with these lovely wildflowers. Bought by a preservation society when *British Rail* closed the line in 1959, it runs steam locomotives and lovingly restored Victorian coaches (as much in demand by film companies seeking period locations as by visiting tourists) from here to Kingscote. Trains run daily May through September; Saturdays and Sundays only the rest of the year. A modestly priced 18-mile round trip takes about 80 minutes. Return to Uckfield and then continue on A26 another 9 miles northeast to Lewes.

LEWES This historic East Sussex market town has steep, narrow streets, the ruins of an ancient Norman castle and an equally ancient Cluniac monastery, as well as numerous old houses, including some medieval half-timbered ones, and several interesting museums. (For more information, see our *Southeast England* route.)

BEST EN ROUTE

Horsted Place This lovely Victorian Gothic country house has 17 rooms and an excellent French restaurant. For more information, see *Rural Retreats* in DIVERSIONS. Little Horsted, near Uckfield (phone: 1825-750581; 800-525-4800; fax: 1825-750459). Expensive.

En Route from Lewes Take A27 across the South Downs to Brighton (8 miles southwest of Lewes), passing, at Falmer, the campus of the modern *University of Sussex.*

BRIGHTON The popularity of England's most famous resort began in the late 18th century and developed largely during the early 19th century, leaving a wonderful architectural legacy for the modern visitor. For a full report on the sights, hotels, and restaurants of this seaside resort, see *Brighton* in THE CITIES.

En Route from Brighton From here, A27 hurries west through a not particularly pleasing bit of coast, but the reward for the 20-mile drive is that you finally arrive at the small, charming town of Arundel.

ARUNDEL This medieval-looking town on the river Arun is spectacularly dominated by its massive castle and an equally large cathedral. The castle, family seat of the Dukes of Norfolk (nominally the head of England's Catholic church), dates from the 11th century, though most of what is seen today—except for the Norman "keep"—was rebuilt in the 18th and 19th centuries. The picture gallery contains the dukes' collection, including paintings by Van Dyck, Gainsborough, and Reynolds, and on the grounds is the Roman Catholic *Fitzalan Chapel,* occupying a quarter of the town's 14th-century Anglican parish church of St. Nicholas. The dual allegiance is explained by the fact that the 15th duke had a wall built to divide chapel from church and they still have separate entrances. The same duke had previously built the imposing, Gothic, Roman Catholic *Church of St. Philip Neri.* Around these two monoliths of castle and cathedral are many old houses and small inns, and a cheerful Saturday morning market. The *Arundel Festival* of the arts, which includes performances in an open-air theater on the castle grounds, takes place from late August through early September (also see *Best Festivals* in DIVERSIONS). The castle is closed Saturdays and November through March; admission charge (phone: 1903-883136).

Less than a mile to the north, on a signposted road off A27, is the 55-acre *Wildfowl Trust and Wetlands Centre,* where you can watch a sampling of the world's waterfowl from observation hides. It is open daily; admission charge (phone: 1903-883355). North again, in a 19th-century quarry and limeworks, is the *Chalk Pits Museum* at Amberley. On display at this large outdoor museum of industrial history are the original lime kilns, plus a blacksmith's shop, a locomotive shed, a narrow-gauge railway, and much more. The museum is closed November through March and Mondays and Tuesdays in April, May, June, September, and October; admission charge (phone: 1798-831370).

BEST EN ROUTE

Amberley Castle This 12th-century castle has been converted into a magnificent hotel with 14 bedrooms and a superb restaurant. For more information, see *Rural Retreats* in DIVERSIONS. Amberley, near Arundel (phone: 1798-831992; 800-525-4800; fax: 1798-831998). Expensive.

Bailiffscourt Beams and stones from 13th-century buildings were used to construct this replica of a medieval manor in the 1930s. On 23 acres of grounds, it has 20 rooms (eight with log fires and one with side-by-side twin baths). The restaurant specializes in such rustic fare as rabbit seasoned with cinnamon and served with turnips and onions. There's also an outdoor pool, tennis, and croquet. Climping (phone: 1903-723511; fax: 1903-723107). Expensive.

En Route from Arundel Continue on A27 another 10 miles west to Chichester.

CHICHESTER This cathedral city with a population of 25,300 began as a walled Roman town, and Chichester's Roman origins still can be seen in the two long, straight main streets that intersect at right angles at the 16th-century Market Cross. Portions of the walls, both Roman and medieval ones, remain, but Chichester today is predominantly a Georgian market town with many quiet corners and the lovely cathedral at its heart. The cathedral spire, visible from a distance, is a Victorian replacement of one that collapsed over a century ago, but the rest of the cathedral (phone: 1243-782595), built between 1091 and 1199, is largely Norman. The 15th-century bell tower is the only example of a detached belfry still surviving in England.

The most attractive buildings of Georgian Chichester are close by on North Street and in an area called the Pallant, a city-within-a-city southeast of Market Cross. *Pallant House* (9 N. Pallant; phone: 1243-774557), built in 1713, has a rare collection of early 20th-century paintings, a fine collection of porcelain, and a Georgian-style garden. The property is closed Sundays and Mondays; admission charge. The best of Roman Chichester is just outside of town. In 1960, workmen laying a water pipe at Fishbourne

(1½ miles west of Chichester) discovered the remains of a magnificent Roman palace built in AD 70. When fully excavated, it turned out to be the largest Roman palace yet found in Britain. Twelve of the mosaic floors can be seen and there is a museum reflecting the history of the site up to AD 280. The museum is closed Mondays through Saturdays December through mid-February; admission charge (phone: 1243-785859). In mid-July, Chichester stages the *Chichester Festivities,* a varied festival of the arts that lasts two and a half weeks and includes concerts in the cathedral. Better known is the top-flight *Chichester Festival Theatre* season from May through September (phone: 1243-781312). Also see *Best Festivals* in DIVERSIONS.

The nearby harbor is one of Britain's prettiest—it's a natural center for sailors with small boats. On its far shores, small resorts such as Bosham, West Itchenor, Emsworth, and Hayling Island are all quietly attractive. Three miles north on A286 is *Goodwood House,* the historic home of the Dukes of Richmond, and the park around it is the site of the racecourse where the "glorious" *Goodwood Week* of racing takes place at the end of July. The house is open most Sundays and Mondays from May through September and Tuesdays, Wednesdays, and Thursdays in August; admission charge (phone: 1243-774107). Six miles north of the city, at Singleton, the *Weald and Downland Open Air Museum,* high on the South Downs, is especially worth a visit. Typical old buildings have been saved from destruction elsewhere in southeast England and transferred here, among them a 14th-century Kentish farmhouse, a 15th-century Wealdian hall house, and others. The museum is closed Mondays, Tuesdays, and Thursdays through Saturdays November through February; admission charge (phone: 1243-811348).

BEST EN ROUTE

Goodwood Park In an area not noted for good hotels, the transformation of the old *Richmond Arms* coaching inn on the Goodwood estate has proved a real blessing. A large, modern extension has been added, and it is now a comfortable 89-room hotel with extensive leisure facilities, including golf, tennis, squash, and an indoor pool. 4 miles northeast of Chichester. *Goodwood Park* (phone: 1243-775537; fax: 1243-533802). Expensive.

Ship Originally a private house built in 1790 for George Murray, one of Nelson's admirals, it retains some of its 14th-century sections despite several 1930s-era additions. It is large (36 rooms) and wonderfully old-fashioned in the Georgian manner, with Adam staircases. In April 1944, General Eisenhower stayed here prior to *D-Day.* North St., Chichester (phone: 1243-778000; fax: 1243-788000). Moderate.

Comme Ca Specializing in French food, this eatery uses only fresh ingredients. The wine list also is good. Closed Sunday dinner and Mondays. Reservations necessary. Major credit cards accepted. 67 Broyle Rd., Chichester (phone: 1243-788724). Moderate.

En Route from Chichester The A27 continues west to Portsmouth, 14 miles from Chichester.

PORTSMOUTH With a population of about 181,000, the city is "Pompey" to the British Navy, for whom it has been home and impregnable fortress for centuries. Despite heavy bombing by the Germans in World War II and the commercial and shopping center that arose from the ruins, Old Portsmouth still survives, an interesting quarter of pubs, fortifications, gray-painted warships, and bustling ferries, with the sounds and smells of the sea on its doorstep. It is best toured on foot, so leave your car at *Clarence Pier,* from where a short walk northward along the waterfront leads to the *King's Bastion* and the *Long Curtain Battery*—all that remain of the medieval ramparts and moat that once surrounded the old town. Continue straight into Broad Street, whose buildings exhibit a colorful mixture of architectural styles; they once were filled with sailors' pubs and brothels, earning the neighborhood the nickname "Spice Island." It still is the most interesting area in town. Henry VIII built the *Round Tower* beside Broad Street and today military ceremonies dating from the 1840s are regularly reenacted here.

On board Admiral Nelson's flagship *Victory,* in dry dock a mile away in *Her Majesty's Dockyard* along St. George's Road, you can relive the days of sail and hammocks, rum and the lash, and see the spot on which Nelson fell at the Battle of Trafalgar (1805) to become a hero for all time. Tours are conducted daily by retired members of the Royal Navy or Royal Marines. The ship is open daily; admission charge (phone: 1705-819604). A panoramic display of the famous battle is one exhibit in the *Royal Naval Museum,* which is housed in an 18th-century warehouse next to the dry dock and covers naval history from Nelson's day to the present (it also contains memorabilia of the admiral's beloved Lady Hamilton). The museum is open daily; admission charge (phone: 1705-733060). Near the HMS *Victory* is the *Mary Rose Ship Hall and Exhibition.* In 1545, King Henry VIII stood on the battlements of his castle at nearby Southsea watching his fleet engage the French. To his and everyone else's astonishment, the *Mary Rose,* the pride of his fleet, suddenly keeled over and sank, with almost all hands lost. After more than four centuries on the seafloor, the ship was salvaged in 1982 in a brilliant operation supervised by Prince Charles, himself a naval officer, and the restored hull, plus thousands of items recovered from the ship, are now on view. The hall is open daily; admission charge (phone: 1705-750521).

Another historic ship, the HMS *Warrior,* built in 1860 as the world's first ironclad warship, is on display in the dockyard (open daily; admission charge; phone: 1705-839766), but Portsmouth also has numerous other military and naval attractions elsewhere. Near *Southsea Castle,* on the seafront in the suburb of Southsea, is the *D-Day Museum,* devoted to the Normandy landings of June 6, 1944, which were planned (using the code name

Operation Overlord) at *Southwick House* in the hills overlooking the naval base. The museum contains a reconstruction of the *D-Day* operations room, a re-creation of the beach landing at Normandy, and the *Overlord Embroidery,* commissioned in 1968 and finished after five years of painstaking work by 20 needlewomen. It tells the story of the Allied invasion in 34 panels, each eight feet long, and is 41 feet longer than the *Bayeux Tapestry* recording William the Conqueror's invasion in the opposite direction nine centuries earlier. The museum is open daily; admission charge (phone: 1705-827261).

Charles Dickens was born at Portsmouth in 1812, the son of a dockyard clerk. The modest family home (at 393 Old Commercial Rd.; phone: 1705-827261) on the north side of town (signposted off A3) is furnished as it might have looked at the time of his birth, although, in fact, the family moved only a few months later. It is closed November through February; admission charge.

BEST EN ROUTE

Old House Overlooking Wickham's large village square (3 miles north of the Portsmouth-Southampton road), this handsome Georgian house was built in 1715; the current owners, Richard and Annie Skipwith, converted it into a 12-room hotel. The restaurant, which serves superb French food, is located in the original timber-framed outhouse and stables. Closed late August and at *Christmas* and *Easter.* The Square, Wickham (phone: 1329-833049; fax: 1329-833672). Expensive.

En Route from Portsmouth *Wightlink* (phone: 1705-827744) operates frequent car ferries between Portsmouth and the Isle of Wight. The ferries also connect the island to several other towns in the area, including Lymington (which you'll get to later on in the route). A passenger ferry (no cars allowed) links Portsmouth and Ryde, one of the Isle of Wight's major resort towns. In addition, there is hovercraft service between Southsea and Ryde.

ISLE OF WIGHT Though it was once part of the mainland, it's a mistake to think of the Isle of Wight as a small (23 by 13 miles) piece of England cast adrift in the channel; it has a flavor of its own, at once pastoral and nautical. A total of 118,594 people make their homes here. The island's northern end is flat, but its spectacular steep cliffs to the south draw the majority of visitors. Besides the seaside activity, walking is a major pastime here, and a network of footpaths leads nearly everywhere, including around the circumference of the island. For most visitors, the resort town of Ryde is the gateway to the Isle of Wight. On the southeast coast, Sandown, Shanklin, and Ventnor are strictly resorts, busy and particularly sunny ones, and they clearly reflect the Victorian popularity that established and expanded them. Of the three, Ventnor, terraced up to the highest point of the island, is the oldest and perhaps the most interesting. Inland, there are many small villages, doubly remote for their island setting: Godshill has many thatch cottages; Calbourne, too, has thatch cottages and one of the country's finest examples of an early-17th-century water mill, still in working order. It's closed November through *Easter;* admission charge (phone: 1983-531227).

On the north coast, Cowes, divided in two by the river Medina, is internationally famous as the headquarters of the British yachting community. It was Cowes's yacht club, the *Royal Yacht Squadron,* that in 1851 offered a 100-guinea cup for a race around the island. The trophy, won by the schooner *America* for the *New York City Yacht Club,* has ever after been known as the *America's Cup.* The highlight of the regatta season is *Cowes Week,* the first week in August, when ocean racers from all over the world compete in the blue Solent. Cowes is not all ocean yachting, however—there are plenty of facilities for smaller boats. *Osborne House,* Queen Victoria's palatial Italianate retreat (reputedly her favorite—she used it for over 50 years and died there in 1901), is just outside Cowes. The perfectly preserved state apartments and a museum are closed November through March; admission charge (phone: 1983-200022).

BEST EN ROUTE

Farringford A famous Isle of Wight property that once belonged to Alfred, Lord Tennyson. In addition to 16 bedrooms, the hotel offers 20 apartments, eight cottages with fully equipped kitchens, and a fine dining room. Outdoors you can enjoy croquet, a pool, and a nine-hole golf course, and a nine-hole golf course. Freshwater, Isle of Wight (phone: 1983-752500; fax: 1983-756515). Moderate.

Winterbourne Charles Dickens lived here in 1849 and called it "the prettiest place I ever saw in my life, at home or abroad." The hotel is surrounded by large, beautiful gardens, and many of its 19 rooms have magnificent sea views; there's also a good restaurant and an outdoor pool. Open mid-March through December. Bonchurch, near Ventnor, Isle of Wight (phone: 1983-852535; fax: 1983-853056). Moderate.

En Route from the Isle of Wight Hydrofoils depart daily year-round from Cowes to Southampton.

SOUTHAMPTON A fine natural harbor and a famous double tide, which rolls in first from the Solent and two hours later from Spithead, made this city at the head of Southampton Water a major seaport; there are 196,000 residents. There is a tourist information center on Above Bar St. (phone: 1703-221106). Like Portsmouth, Southampton played an important role in Operation Overlord: The whole area had become one huge tented military camp in the spring of 1944, and the city's main highway, The Avenue, was turned into a camouflaged tunnel down which the invasion force moved to the coast en route to the beaches of Normandy. Because of heavy bombing, Southampton looks largely modern today—the Vickers-Supermarine works at Woolston, which produced the first *Spitfire* in 1936, was blitzed, and much of the city center was flattened. There are some medieval remains, however, including parts of the ancient walls and the Bargate, now isolated in the middle of a traffic island, but once the landward entrance of the old town.

Southampton was already an important seaport in the Middle Ages, trading with Venice until the early 16th century, but a setback in its fortunes came when the port of Bristol captured the tobacco and sugar trade with the New World—as well as the black slave trade. Thousands of early American settlers sailed from Bristol, but Southampton has the honor of having waved good-bye to the *Mayflower* in 1620 (and to the *Speedwell,* too, but that ship proved unseaworthy and had to turn back). The *Pilgrim Fathers Memorial* in the shadow of the old walls near the Royal Pier commemorates the sailing. When the day of the large transatlantic liners dawned, Southampton—its double tide providing round-the-clock access—became Britain's chief port for the Atlantic crossing, bar none. The *Maritime Museum* (Bugle St.; phone: 1703-632493), in a 14th-century wool warehouse overlooking the river Test and Southampton Water, recalls that era with huge models of the steamships *Queen Mary* and *Capetown Castle.* The museum is closed Mondays; admission charge. In *East Park,* a white marble memorial honors the engineers of the ill-fated *Titanic.* Southampton is the *Queen Elizabeth 2*'s home port, as well as an embarkation point for other large cruise ships.

En Route from Southampton Southwest of the city, the road leads through the New Forest and on to Bournemouth, the end of the *Southern England* route. However, since the cathedral city of Winchester is only 12 miles north of Southampton via M3 and A33, don't miss the chance to see it now, returning to the New Forest area after the visit. Another alternative, for those anxious to move in a different direction, would be to join the *Southwest England* route, which begins 22 miles northwest of Southampton (via A36) at Salisbury.

WINCHESTER Here one meets the various people who overran, then settled this part of England: Celts founded the town, Romans took it over, Saxons made it their capital, Danes besieged it, and Normans built the cathedral that majestically presides over it. Although Winchester lost its primacy as the capital of the kingdom when William the Conqueror made it a joint capital with London and had himself crowned in both places, it was not until the 12th century that London began to supersede it.

Sheltered between the green hills of the Hampshire downs and fed by the gentle river Itchen, Winchester (pop. 35,500) takes its physical character primarily from the 18th century—Great Minster Street near the cathedral is a charming example of the graceful architecture of that period. But it is the harmonious mix of buildings from every era (including low brick structures from the last few decades) and the welcome lack of quaint trappings that give it its air of vitality. There is a tourist information center on Broadway at the *Guild Hall* (phone: 1962-840500); closed Sundays October through April.

Adjacent to the modern Crown Court building is the *Great Hall,* all that remains of the Norman castle that was a royal residence—until it was destroyed by Oliver Cromwell's Parliamentarians in 1645—considered to be one of the finest examples of a medieval hall in England. The *Great Hall*'s most famous possession is King Arthur's Round Table—although no one claims that this great oak table is *the* legendary table, since it dates from only the 14th century. But such was the continuing power of Arthur's legend that nearly 1,000 years after his death, King Henry VIII, wanting to strengthen his family's fairly recent claim to the throne, had the table painted with Arthur seated above a Tudor rose. The hall is open daily; no admission charge (phone: 1962-846476).

At the center of Winchester, physically and spiritually, stands its magnificent cathedral (phone: 1962-853137), with a recently opened visitors' center (phone: 1962-840471). The massive transepts are Norman, but the long nave, with its intricate web of fan vaulting, is the work of William of Wykeham, a 14th-century bishop who also founded *Winchester College* (phone: 1962-868778) southeast of the cathedral. This, one of the oldest schools in England, retains most of its original 14th- and 15th-century structure. Guided tours are offered daily April through September. The *Wessex* hotel dining room (phone: 1962-861611), which faces the cathedral across the green expanse of the close, is a perfect place for afternoon tea. If time permits, take a walk along the weirs, which follow the Itchen through town, past lovely gardens and the ruins of the bishop's castle (also a victim of the Civil War).

About 16 miles northeast of Winchester, off A31 in the village of Chawton, is the house where Jane Austen wrote *Mansfield Park, Emma,* and *Persuasion.* The two-story red brick building, originally an inn, is furnished with period pieces and a collection of Austen family memorabilia. The house is closed weekdays in January and February and Mondays and Tuesdays in November, December, and March; admission charge (phone: 1420-83262). The town of Alton, a mile farther along, has some attractive Georgian buildings. It also is the northern terminus of the 10-mile *Watercress Line Railway.* Closed by *British Rail* in 1973, the line is now operated by a preservation society which runs trains pulled by veteran steam locomotives (phone: 1962-733810). The trains run daily June through August and weekends only September, October, and March through May.

BEST EN ROUTE

Lainston House A Georgian mansion surrounded by 60 acres of parkland, the house has 38 rooms which offer an authentic taste of English country living. Its restaurant has an excellent reputation for serving well-prepared French and traditional English fare. Two miles west of Winchester (off A272 to Stockbridge). Sparsholt (phone: 1962-863588; fax: 1962-776672). Expensive.

Grange Though housed in a rather unimpressive building, this hotel offers outstanding hospitality and comfort. The 34 guestrooms are attractively furnished, and there is a lovely garden where hot-air balloon rides are given in summer (the Levenes, who own and run the place, have their own balloon). The restaurant serves tasty French and English fare; there's also a terrace, croquet lawn, and putting green. 17 London Rd., Alton (phone: 1420-86565; fax: 1420-541346). Moderate.

Wykeham Arms A busy pub close to the cathedral with seven pleasantly furnished rooms, it's been an inn and restaurant since 1755. 75 Kingsgate St., Winchester (phone: 1962-853834; fax: 1962-854411). Moderate.

En Route from Winchester Travelers eager to return to London can easily do so from here—it's only 66 miles northeast of Winchester on the M3 motorway. Those not in a hurry can continue the route from Winchester through the New Forest to Bournemouth before going back to the capital. Take A3090 south from Winchester, join A31, then take M27 east to Cadnam (a total distance of 19 miles). Along the way, you'll pass through Romsey, just outside of which is *Broadlands.* "One of the finest houses in all England," according to Lord Palmerston, the great Victorian prime minister who lived here himself, it later became the country home of the late Earl Mountbatten of Burma, great-grandson of Queen Victoria and the last Viceroy of India. The house is closed October through March and Fridays *Easter* through September (except in August, when it's open daily); admission charge (phone: 1794-516878). (For more information, see *Stately Homes and Great Gardens* in DIVERSIONS.)

A sight worth the brief detour from Cadnam (take A31 west for 2 miles) is the Rufus Stone, said to mark the spot where William II (the son of the Conqueror and known as Rufus for his red hair) met his death while hunting in 1100. He was struck in the heart by an arrow shot by Sir Walter Tyrrell, a French nobleman in the hunting party, and to this day the question of whether it was an accident or murder is unresolved.

Return to Cadnam and take A337 south toward Lyndhurst, in the midst of the New Forest, which is neither new nor totally a forest (its name goes back to William the Conqueror, who made the area his hunting ground and decreed that commoners who so much as startled a deer here would have their eyes put out). Much of the 90,000 acres of untamed heath, bog, and woodland is still a wildlife preserve (protected by mounted guards) and two-thirds of it is public domain, its inhabitants enjoying medieval rights such as pannage (the feeding of their pigs on forest acorns), turbary (the right to cut turf), and estover (permission to gather firewood). You are certain to see some of the 2,000 wild horses and ponies that roam the area, and several deer, but less likely to glimpse the badgers and otters who live here. Watch, too, for rare birds and species of wildflowers. This is walking country par excellence, but there are also many stables and riding schools.

On the way to Lyndhurst, stop in the village of Minstead, 2 miles from Cadnam just off A337; it has a 13th-century church with an unusual three-deck pulpit inside, along with "parlour pews" that were reserved for the local gentry (the poor sat under rafters in the "Gypsies gallery"). Sir Arthur Conan Doyle, creator of Sherlock Holmes, is buried in the churchyard. From Minstead, Lyndhurst is another 2 miles farther south on A337.

BEST EN ROUTE

Woods Place This former village butcher's shop still has the original, curly-lettered sign and colored tiles on the front, but plants now decorate the rails inside where carcasses once hung. Eric and Dana Norrgren, its Swedish owners, offer good solid fare, and while the wine list is not long, it's sure to please. Closed Sundays and Mondays. Reservations necessary. Major credit cards accepted. Headley Rd., Grayshott (phone: 1428-605555). Moderate.

LYNDHURST The capital of the New Forest is set amid heath and woods, and until the roadside fence was improved a few years ago, it was not uncommon to see wild ponies wandering through its lanes. With about 3,000 residents, the town is the seat of the *Verderers' Court,* which has administered the forest since 1388. It meets six times a year at *Queen's House* (High St.), whose walls are adorned with stags' heads and whose fireplace has a stirrup iron hanging over it that allegedly belonged to William II. Under Norman law, any dog unable to squeeze through the stirrup was pronounced a danger to the deer in the forest and had its claws cut off. East of *Queen's House* is the 19th-century parish church, with a fresco of the *Ten Virgins* painted by the late Lord Leighton and a beautiful Pre-Raphaelite east window designed by Sir Edward Burne-Jones. Mrs. Hargreaves, née Alice Liddell, the heroine of *Alice in Wonderland,* lies in the churchyard.

The *New Forest Visitor Centre* (phone: 1703-283914; open daily) has interesting displays on the history of the area. Since the town is a major crossroads between Southampton and Lymington (pronounced *Lim*-ington), Christchurch, and Bournemouth, A35 funnels cars and buses into its narrow main street (where a one-way system operates). Fiercely argued plans for a bypass may someday come to fruition and bring relief, but in the meantime, escape from the noise and fumes of the infernal combustion engine is possible in the acres of open heathland and dense forest that surround the town.

BEST EN ROUTE

Parkhill This 18th-century Georgian manor house is now a 20-room hotel with an outdoor pool and croquet grounds set on 12 acres. A walk from the doorstep takes in stretches of heath and forest of bare oak, golden bracken, and beech, with deer grazing on the lawn. It's a peaceful place, barring the occasional bloodcurdling cry of the vixen. The food is English with a French flair. Beaulieu Rd., Lyndhurst (phone: 1703-282944; fax: 1703-283268). Expensive.

Le Poussin Wild mushrooms from the nearby New Forest are featured extensively on the menu of the Aitken family's small restaurant 3 miles south of Lyndhurst. Renowned for its excellent value as well as for fine food, it attracts customers from miles around. No smoking allowed. Closed Sunday dinner, Mondays, and Tuesdays. Reservations necessary. Major credit cards accepted. The Courtyard, 49-55 Brookley Rd., Brockenhurst (phone: 1590-23063). Expensive to moderate.

Lyndhurst Park Whitewashed and hung with creeper, this mansion has somewhat lost its original Georgian architecture in the wake of many face-lifts and additions over the years; however, the overall appearance is quite attractive. The 59 rooms look out on manicured lawns. Besides the landscaped outdoor pool and a tennis court, it offers a warm welcome and a traditional but varied English-style menu. High St., Lyndhurst (phone: 1703-283923; fax: 1703-283019). Moderate.

En Route from Lyndhurst Take B3056 7 miles southeast to the village of Beaulieu, set where the Beaulieu River widens into an estuary; midway between Lyndhurst and the village lies *Beaulieu Road Station,* in reality no more than a halt on the Southampton to Bournemouth railway line. Usually, there are few passengers; however, on five separate days in April, August, September, October, and November, when the *New Forest Pony Sales* are held, this rather isolated place comes alive with people.

BEAULIEU From the 13th century to the early 16th century, the main attraction of this tiny village—pronounced *Bew*-lee (there are barely a thousand residents) was *Beaulieu Abbey,* a Cistercian house founded in 1204 by King John. Now visitors come to see the abbey ruins, which survive today, plus *Palace House,* home of Lord Montagu of Beaulieu and in his family's keeping since 1538, as well as the *National Motor Museum,* on the grounds of the estate. The estate is open daily; admission charge includes entrance to all facilities. For more information, see *Stately Homes and Great Gardens* in DIVERSIONS.

BEST EN ROUTE

Montagu Arms Close to the Beaulieu estate, this 24-room hotel is the sort of place where guests dress up for dinner. Though Tudor in style, the building dates back only to the 1920s. On the grounds are terraced gardens with fountains. There's also a dining room serving good French fare. Palace La., Beaulieu (phone: 1590-612324; fax: 1590-612188). Expensive.

En Route from Beaulieu Continue south on B3056 to the village of Buckler's Hard, just over 2 miles away. (If you've a penchant for walking, a waymarked trail follows the sinuous Beaulieu River from Beaulieu village to Buckler's Hard.) In the early 18th century, the second Duke of Montagu established a town, shipyard, and docks here to receive sugar from his West Indian estates. Although the sugar business fell through, the shipyard's proximity to the great oaks of the New Forest made it an important shipbuilding center, employing 4,000 men who turned out some of the most famous men o' war in British history, including the *Agamemnon,* in which Nelson lost his eye off Corsica, and a good part of the fleet that fought at Trafalgar. The *Buckler's Hard Museum* tells the story of the river, the village, and the Adams family who built many of the "hearts of oak" ships; it also displays charts used by Sir Francis Chichester, who in modern times set out from Buckler's Hard on his epic lone voyages across the Atlantic and around the world in *Gypsy Moth* yachts. The museum is open daily; admission charge (phone: 1590-616203). *Exbury Gardens,* a nearby 200-acre area of woodland, contains a spectacularly colorful display of rhododendrons, azaleas, camellias, and magnolias in the spring, as well as delightful summer and autumn displays. The gardens are closed November through February; admission charge (phone: 1703-891203).

Return to Beaulieu and take B3054 6 miles to Lymington. The road crosses one of the largest open spaces in the New Forest, the 5 square miles of Beaulieu Heath. The tumuli, or burial mounds, dotting the landscape were left by a people who lived here 4,000 years ago in the Bronze Age. During World War II, part of the heath became a military airfield. Today, it is ablaze with purple heather in late summer, ponies and rabbits crop the grass where bombers once landed, and there are clumps of gorse and the occasional willow, birch, and Scots pine. To the northeast, the blazing chimneys of the Fawley petrochemical plant on Southampton Water can be seen, and to the southeast, the green hills of the Isle of Wight.

Lymington became a popular resort with the coming of the railway in the 19th century. Before then some of the local families had become rich from the sale of salt from the salterns along the coast, and the Georgian houses on Lymington's broad main street are their legacy. Today it is a boating town with two large marinas filled with sleek yachts and cruisers, and a pretty little quay beside the river. If you haven't already done so, take the ferry to the Isle of Wight—the crossing from here to Yarmouth is the shortest route to the island. (See *Isle of Wight,* above, for details on the island.) Alternatively, follow A337 west 12 miles to Christchurch.

Chewton Glen This internationally famed country house (a Relais & Châteaux member) has 58 rooms, sports facilities, and a fine restaurant. For more information, see *Rural Retreats* in DIVERSIONS. Christchurch Rd., New Milton (phone: 1425-275341; 800-344-5087; fax: 1425-272310). Very expensive.

Gordleton Mill Prettily situated by a mill pond on the edge of the New Forest, this seven-room hotel has been showered with awards for its comfort and hospitable touches (including welcoming guests with fresh flowers and fruit in their rooms). The *Provence* restaurant offers inventive French and English fare, such as lamb and scallops in a foie gras sauce. Hordle, near Lymington (phone: 1590-682219; fax: 1590-683073). Expensive.

Stanwell House Set in the center of Lymington, close to the picturesque cobbled quay area, this comfortable Georgian house has 35 rooms and a restaurant that offers traditional English food and an excellent wine list. On Saturdays until mid-afternoon, its High Street location is filled by lively market stalls selling everything from fruit to furniture. High St. (phone: 1590-677123; fax: 1590-677756). Moderate.

CHRISTCHURCH Another yachtsmen's and fishermen's haven, this Saxon town with a population of 29,000 was one of Alfred the Great's strongholds against the Danes. It appears as Twynham, "the town between two waters," in the *Domesday Book,* a reference to the fact that the river Stour and the Hampshire Avon entwine here, but its modern name came into being with the town's *Priory Church* (phone: 1202-485804), built from the 12th through the 15th centuries. Originally, the church was to have been built at the top of St. Catherine's Hill. But every night, according to local legend, building materials that had been laboriously carried up the hill during the day were mysteriously transported down again. Eventually, the divine hint was taken and the church built at the foot of the hill. As the work neared completion, an unknown carpenter, who took no pay and ate no food, joined the laborers. Before he disappeared, a roof beam that had been found to be a foot short became a perfect fit overnight. The workmen believed that the stranger was Christ, so the building was called *Christ's Church* and the town renamed in commemoration of the extraordinary events. The largest parish church in England, it has England's two oldest church bells, cast in 1370, ringing out from its square tower and contains a notable reredos carved with the Tree of Jesse.

At the same quay where sailing barges used to unload coal and timber, pleasure boats and fishing boats for day trips now ply for hire. At low tide, *Christchurch Harbour* becomes mud flats, and Stanpit Marsh on its northern shore is a haven for wildfowl, with a nature trail marked across it. While the Stour and Avon Rivers offer peace and tranquillity for anglers, there are flatfish, mullet, and eels to be caught in the harbor (pending permission from the local angling club), and Mudeford on the north side is a favored spot for fishing from the sea wall, where whelk pots are piled high.

BEST EN ROUTE

Splinters A good place to taste the local salmon, served with delicious hollandaise sauce, or free-range chickens cooked with seasonal sauces and peppers. Closed Sunday dinner and Mondays. Reservations necessary. Major credit cards accepted. 12 Church St., Christchurch (phone: 1202-483454). Expensive.

En Route from Christchurch The seaside resort of Bournemouth is only 6 miles west of Christchurch on A337 (or rather, central Bournemouth is 6 miles west—in actual fact, Bournemouth has expanded so far along the coast that it has almost incorporated the older town).

BOURNEMOUTH For a full report on its sights, hotels, and restaurants, see *Bournemouth* in THE CITIES.

En Route from Bournemouth Salisbury, the starting point of our *Southwest England* route, also in this section, is 28 miles north of Bournemouth via A338. But if you won't be visiting Wiltshire, Devon, and Cornwall, take A31 out of Bournemouth to the M27 motorway, which meets the M3 motorway and will speed you back to London. The distance from Bournemouth to London is 114 miles.

Southeast England

For better or worse, geography conspired to make Kent and East Sussex—the broad heel of land that opens out below London to form the cliff-lined and beach-speckled coast of southeast England—the only welcome mat England has ever extended to the Continent. It is country suited to landing parties: Kent's rich orchards, hop fields, thatch barns, and high-hedged roads giving way to Sussex's high South Downs, from which one can see for miles in all directions. To the north is the wide estuary of the Thames; to the south, the English Channel; and to the east, where England and France are only some 20 miles apart, the Straits of Dover.

Such an invitation has been hard for European warlords to resist, and for 2,000 years attempts have been made to enter England through the southeast. Some have been successful. The Romans established an administrative center in London, and the Normans conquered all of England after their decisive victory at the Battle of Hastings in 1066, a date no English schoolchild ever forgets. Other attempts have failed. From August to October 1940, Britain stood virtually alone against the full weight of the Nazi war machine as the Battle of Britain raged over Kent. But each of these efforts has left some mark on this extraordinarily rich part of England. Kent, "the Garden of England," nurtures as much history as fruit and hops in its fertile countryside.

Much of the southeast is dominated and influenced by London. Hundreds of thousands of those who live in this region commute daily to and from the capital. The region, too, is London's principal playground, and on good summer weekends its beaches and country resorts fill with hosts of fugitives from town. But the countryside and the coast have proved surprisingly tenacious despite their proximity to a city of more than seven million inhabitants. Since this area, and especially the northern part of Kent, is Britain's main thoroughfare to Europe and is one of the most densely populated parts of the country, do not expect to find vast tracts of it in virgin condition. But having said that, it is surprising that so much of it is still unspoiled and rarely visited and that it has held on to its history remarkably well.

Along the south shore of the Thames as far as Gravesend, major industries dominate the waterfront before the Kent countryside comes into view and Thameside busyness gives way to the first of several holiday resorts that round the northeast coast of the county. Below the river and the coast, parallel to them, lie the North Downs, a range of low chalkland hills that run east from Surrey to meet the sea spectacularly as the white cliffs of Dover. Impossible to cultivate, they are either forested or left to grazing. Still farther south lies the Weald, the central region of the southeast. The Weald takes its name from the Anglo-Saxon *wold,* meaning "a wood."

Throughout the later Middle Ages, the woods of this region were cleared, and the fertile soil turned to agricultural use. The result was a prosperous area of substantial villages and market towns, and to this day it is quite possible to find them still full of 16th- and 17th-century houses and farms, and to sense in them a strong continuity with their isolated past.

Up and over the South Downs that run through Sussex below the Weald, you come to a coast dedicated largely to pleasure. Like the Kent coast, the East Sussex coast abounds with resorts. They are much less fashionable now than in their Victorian and Edwardian heydays, but perhaps more attractive for that very reason. In the little ones especially, you will find clear signs of the elegance that transformed these watering places from the fishing villages that they once were.

The major sights of England's southeast—Canterbury, Dover, Hastings and Battle, Eastbourne, and Brighton—can all be visited on day trips from London. Travelers with little time should certainly choose the most appealing destinations and make the journey by car or, even more simply, by train. But more rewarding is a perambulation through the countryside, following the coast as a rough guide, and taking in both the large, obviously popular spots along the beaten path and the smaller, quieter places off of it.

The route outlined here begins in Rochester (familiar to readers of Charles Dickens), then takes the less traveled road to Canterbury through hops-growing country and the town of Faversham. From Canterbury the route returns to the coast at Sandwich, one of the Cinque (Five) Ports that banded together in the Middle Ages to furnish ships to a previously nonexistent English Navy. Next along the coast is the historic port of Deal, and Dover and Hythe, two more of the Cinque Ports, are a short drive farther south. Then the route crosses the Romney Marsh—a bleak peninsula once known to smugglers, now livened by a string of tiny, traditional beach towns—on its way to Rye and Winchelsea and to Hastings and Battle, where a new era began for England. Next comes a fork in the road: Either detour into the Kent and Sussex Weald, where the essential character of this part of England can still be felt, or head straight to Eastbourne and the hurly-burly of Brighton. The route then returns to London, taking in the spa town of Royal Tunbridge Wells and several historic houses along the way—such as the jumble of gables and towers that is *Knole,* or Winston Churchill's country home, *Chartwell.*

The southeastern region is a popular destination for businesspeople as well as vacationers, so make hotel reservations far in advance (especially on weekdays). Expect to pay $120 or more per night for a double room (including private bath or shower, TV set, and breakfast, unless otherwise noted) in those places listed as expensive; from $85 to $120 in the moderate range; and less than $85 for spots listed as inexpensive. A dinner for two, excluding wine, tips, or drinks, will cost more than $70 in restaurants listed as expensive; $40 to $70 in those listed as moderate; and less than $40 in inexpensive places. All restaurants listed serve lunch and dinner unless otherwise specified. For each location, hotels and restaurants are listed alphabetically by price category.

ROCHESTER The river Medway forms a natural barrier between London and the channel, neatly dividing Kent in two and making Rochester primarily a bridge town for the river. It can easily be overlooked now that the M2 motorway from London to Dover rushes by it 2 miles upriver, but those who take the turn before the Medway bridge will soon find themselves in the center of the city. The Romans recognized Rochester's strategic importance early and built a bridge (the London to Dover extension of Watling Street, England's ancient Roman highway, crossed the river here), and after they left, a succession of bridges followed. The Normans, too, saw the importance of the crossing and late in the 11th century began a magnificent castle to defend it. The enormous square keep, 120 feet high with 12-foot-thick walls, was built in the 12th century and is still standing. It is open to adventurous visitors prepared to climb its steep spiral staircases and be rewarded by a marvelous view of the Medway estuary, the North Downs, and, best of all, *Rochester Cathedral,* which is next door. The castle is open daily; admission charge (phone: 1634-402276). The cathedral (phone: 1634-843366) is set on a 7th-century foundation, with a plain Norman nave and many features gradually added from the 12th to the 14th century. The Norman doorway at the west entrance, the walled choir, and many of the tombs are noteworthy.

Castle and cathedral share the summit of Boley Hill, the center of the old city and an area that boasts many ancient and interesting buildings. They catch the rare flavor of a Victorian city, a flavor enhanced by their close associations with Charles Dickens, who lived in nearby Chatham as a boy and came back near the end of his life to Gad's Hill, 3 miles west. Many scenes in his novels take place in Rochester and the surrounding countryside, and each year, in late May or early June, the city stages a rich festival in his honor. Dickens's favorite inn, *The Leather Bottle* (in Cobham, 5 miles west on A2; phone: 1474-814327), is portrayed in the *Pickwick Papers* and still offers food, drink, and atmosphere. The *Royal Victoria and Bull* (phone: 1634-846266), on High Street near the bridge and Boley Hill (see *Best en Route*), is both the "Bull Inn" of the same novel and the "Blue Boar Inn" of *Great Expectations,* and many of the shops around it are readily identifiable as Dickensian settings. The 16th-century *Restoration House* on Maidstone Road is Miss Havisham's "Satis House" in *Great Expectations;* unfortunately, it is closed to the public. About 6 miles north of Rochester on B2000, in the village of Cooling, there's the original setting of Joe Gargery's forge and the graveyard where Pip first met Magwitch. Both are on the edge of an alluringly bleak marshland. Thinly disguised, Rochester is also the Cloisterham of Dickens's last, unfinished, work, *The Mystery of Edwin Drood.* This strange novel gives a good picture of Victorian Rochester, but much also can be seen in the marvelous *Dickens Centre* in *Eastgate*

House (High St.; phone: 1634-844176). It's open daily; admission charge. The house itself is Elizabethan and appears in *Edwin Drood* as the "Nuns' House." Dickens's Gad's Hill home is not open to the public, but the Swiss chalet in which he wrote has been moved to the garden of *Eastgate House.*

Just off A229 near Rochester is *Aylesford Friary,* a Carmelite retreat. It is open daily; admission charge (phone: 1622-717272).

BEST EN ROUTE

Royal Victoria and Bull In fact, a 28-room, 400-year-old coach house, and in fiction, the scene of Dickensian revels—the novelist thought it was a "good house" with "nice beds." The food is plain English fare, well cooked and well served. 16-18 High St., Rochester (phone: 1634-846266; fax: 1634-832312). Moderate.

En Route from Rochester Before proceeding to Faversham, you may want to make an 8-mile detour along A229 to Maidstone, the bustling agricultural center of Kent, with a long history in the brewing industry. Many old buildings line its streets, several of which have been closed to traffic to preserve these fine examples of early architecture. *Leeds Castle,* built in the middle of a lake in the 1200s, is 4 miles east of Maidstone on a signposted road off A229. This former residence of Henry VIII and Lord Culpepper (Governor of Virginia, 1680–83) is often the focus of a day trip from London. The castle is open daily; admission charge (phone: 1622-765400).

Return to Rochester and continue toward Faversham, 18 miles away. If time is limited or the weather dull, the M2 motorway will whisk you from Rochester to Faversham in half an hour. The old main road (A2), however, winds through Chatham, where the former Royal Navy dockyard has been preserved as a working museum. Its Wooden Walls exhibit tells about the lives of the dockyard workers and the construction of wooden warships. It is closed weekdays in December and January, as well as Mondays, Tuesdays, Thursdays, and Fridays in November, February, and March. There's an admission charge (phone: 1634-812551). In addition, you can take a cruise along the river Medway on the *Kingswear Castle* paddle steamer (phone: 1634-827648); the two-and-a-half-hour trip departs from the dockyard museum on Wednesdays and Sundays May through September (also Thursdays and Fridays in July and August).

FAVERSHAM This town is at the center of hop-growing country, and the conical structures seen frequently in this region, called oasts, are used to dry the hops. Most people bypass the town, a fact that perhaps adds to its attractions for those who do stop. Another Roman site, it received its first charter in 811 and developed afterward into a fine medieval city, not least because it was once a small port on the quiet river Swale, which divides the Isle of Sheppey from the Kent mainland.

The best place to sample Faversham's past is on Preston Street in the *Fleur de Lis Heritage Centre,* a well-illustrated guide to the town's thousand years of history housed in a converted 15th-century inn. It is closed Sundays November through March; admission charge (phone: 1795-534542). In the marketplace at the center of town, where three of its oldest streets meet, is the *Guildhall,* a 19th-century rebuilding of a 16th-century market hall that is raised on pillars. At the north end of the marketplace is Court Street, with many 17th- and 18th-century houses. Joining it is Market Street where, at No. 12, James II was held prisoner by local fishermen as he tried to escape to the Continent. The many 16th- and 17th-century houses on West Street, however, make it the loveliest thoroughfare of all.

BEST EN ROUTE

Read's Despite its drab exterior (it used to be a supermarket), this small eatery in a quiet village 2 miles south of Faversham is a pleasant, attractive dining choice. David Pitchford, who owns the place with his wife, Rona, does all the cooking; his efforts have been rewarded with a Michelin star. Medallions of roe deer with chestnut purée and Romney Marsh lamb with garlic potatoes are typical of the fine dishes, and the portions are generous. Closed Sundays, Mondays, and the last two weeks of August. Reservations necessary. Major credit cards accepted. Painters Forstal (phone: 1795-535344). Expensive.

En Route from Faversham The quickest way to travel the 10 miles between Canterbury and Faversham is to take the M2 motorway heading east.

CANTERBURY This is the spiritual center of the Anglican faith and Britain's cathedral city par excellence. For a full report on the city's sights, hotels, and restaurants, see *Canterbury* in THE CITIES.

Part of Canterbury's prosperity grew from its role as a market center for the many villages and agricultural communities of East Kent, and it still serves the same purpose for the region. If time allows, these small villages are well worth visiting. Particularly nice ones are Chilham, 10 miles to the southwest via A28, which has the magnificent *Chilham Castle* (phone: 1227-730319). The castle is open to the public only when Elizabethan banquets are held in the *Gothic Hall* (which occurs about once a month), although its gardens are open from April to mid-October, and, at various times of the year, jousting and falconry displays are held. It's a good idea to make reservations for the banquets well in advance. Barham, which nestles below the Downs just off the Dover Road (A2), is 5 miles southeast of Canterbury, and Westbere, tucked away off the Margate Road (A28), is 3 miles northeast of the city. Westbere has kept its almost medieval character intact, and in the middle of the village is the *Yew Tree* (phone: 1227-710501), a delightful inn in a medieval house.

Wife of Bath Five miles south of Chilham is Wye, a village that would escape notice altogether if it weren't for this small but very fine restaurant with English and French fare. Weekly menus change with the season to ensure as much absolutely fresh food as possible. Closed Sundays and Mondays. Reservations advised. Major credit cards accepted. 4 Upper Bridge St., Wye (phone: 1233-812540). Expensive.

Thruxted Oast In the little village of Chartham, 4 miles southwest of Canterbury, this hostelry comprises a cluster of Kent oasthouses (which were used to dry hops for beermaking) dating back to 1792. Tim and Hilary Derouet have a picture-framing business here, but they also offer three bedrooms for guests; there's also a comfortable lounge and pleasant garden. Although there isn't a restaurant, the Derouets serve an excellent breakfast in their farmhouse-style kitchen. Note that this place isn't easy to find, so ask directions when booking. Mystole, Chartham (phone: 1227-730080). Moderate.

En Route from Canterbury The A257 leads due east from Canterbury to the medieval port of Sandwich, 13 miles away.

SANDWICH This town, with a population of about 4,000 is one of the original Cinque Ports (see *En Route from Deal*). As its harbor became clogged with silt in the 16th century, Sandwich lost importance; it is now 2 miles from the sea. The town gained lasting fame, however, when the fourth Earl of Sandwich invented the world's most popular and enduring meal. According to legend, the earl was loath to leave the gaming tables to eat and asked that a concoction of bread and meat be made for him. Two inns, the *Bell* (The Quay; phone: 1304-613388) and the *King's Arms* (Strand St.; phone: 1304-617330), will be glad to provide a sample of this handy snack and something with which to wash it down. The town is a major golf center, with several excellent courses (see *Great Golf* in DIVERSIONS). *Richborough Castle,* just off A257 a mile and a half outside of Sandwich, was established by the Romans in about AD 43 and added to by the Saxons during the 3rd century. The castle is closed Mondays from October through March; admission charge (phone: 1304-612013).

En Route from Sandwich From here, A258 leads to Deal, about 6 miles south along the coast.

DEAL Deal was an important shipping center through the early 19th century. Under Henry VIII, three castles were erected here: *Deal Castle,* designed in the shape of a six-petaled rosette (closed Mondays October through March; admission charge; phone: 1304-372762); *Walmer Castle,* more like a four-leaf clover and a mile south of the town (see below); and *Sandown Castle,* now washed away and nothing more than a pile of stones at the northern end of the seafront. There is a good possibility that Caesar's forces landed along this shore when the Romans invaded Britain, and Henry VIII feared a repeat Roman invasion, this time in the form of a Holy War that the pope might launch against him as the self-proclaimed head of the Church of England. Off the coast of Deal are the Goodwin Sands, a dangerous and complicated series of sandbanks that are exposed at low tide. Lighthouses illuminate the area after dark, but maritime accidents persist even though Deal is no longer the swaggering seaport it once was. The *Time Ball Tower* on the seafront, a late-18th-century structure, used to give the correct Greenwich time to ships offshore (the ball is dropped every hour). Other displays include three-dimensional models about satellites, watches and clocks, and the mechanics of signaling. It is closed Mondays and early September through late May; admission charge (phone: 1304-360897).

BEST EN ROUTE

Royal The best features of this comfortable property are the balconies of the rooms facing the English Channel. The hotel has a few Georgian antiques, and its restaurant serves quite good fresh fish. There are 31 rooms (20 have private baths). Beach St., Deal (phone: 1304-375555). Moderate.

En Route from Deal As you continue south on A258 toward the busy port of Dover, stop at *Walmer Castle,* which is only a mile from Deal. Built as a fortress by Henry VIII, the castle became the official residence of the Lord Warden of the Cinque Ports in the mid-1700s. This association of seaports began in the 11th century, when five principal ports—Hastings, Romney (now New Romney), Hythe, Dover, and Sandwich—banded together to provide England with a makeshift navy. Later this was formalized by a charter that granted certain privileges in exchange for the pledge of supplying ships and men for the country's defense. Following the establishment of the Royal Navy, the importance of the association and the post of its highest officer, the lord warden, declined drastically, and though there is still such a title today, it is largely without power. Two of the most prominent lord wardens have been William Pitt the Younger and the first Duke of Wellington. The castle is closed January, February, and when the present lord warden is in residence, usually a weekend in July; admission charge (phone: 1304-364288). Dover, "the Gateway of England," is only 7 miles farther south on A258.

DOVER The chalky white cliffs of Dover have been a strategic landmark since the early Iron Age, when a settlement was established here. Roman invaders quickly erected a fortress and an octagonal lighthouse, or pharos, and an extension of the ancient Roman roadway called Watling Street ran between Dover and London via Canterbury. The Romans' pharos still stands within the walls of the more recent *Dover Castle,* an imposing Norman stronghold on the eastern cliffs of the city. Its huge, square keep was built by Henry II in the 1180s around a 240-foot-deep well—the keep had a lead-piped water supply, a surprising amenity for so old a structure. It is easy to spend several hours wandering throughout the towers, gateways, and chambers, outer bailey, inner bailey, and keep of the enormous fortification. Until fairly recently, the existence of over 3 miles of tunnels inside the cliffs below was a closely guarded secret. Originally built in the 1800s to house cannons to counter the threat of invasion by Napoleon, they were later used as a military headquarters during World War II (particularly for the British Army's evacuation from Dunkirk). Dubbed "Hellfire's Corner," they were opened to the public five years ago. There are 45-minute guided tours of the tunnels, which are open daily; admission charge (phone: 1304-201628). France, roughly 20 miles away, is easily visible across the Straits of Dover on clear days, and the view from the battlements of *Dover Castle,* atop the 400-foot bluff overlooking the city and sea, is magnificent. The many ferries that link England to France and Belgium from here have begun facing steep competition from the Channel Tunnel (located at nearby Folkestone), which opened last summer.

During both world wars, Dover again rose to prominence as a point of departure for troops bound for the Continent and as the goal of planes straggling back from the fighting. The city was pounded by long-range artillery during World War II, and the thick castle walls sheltered the population through the four-year bombardment.

The *White Cliffs Experience* (Market Sq.; phone: 1304-214566) recounts the history of the town since Roman times, including a life-size re-creation of a local street under shellfire in 1944. Next door, the *Dover Museum* (Market Sq.; phone: 1304-201066) houses displays about the town's history. Both are open daily and charge admission.

BEST EN ROUTE

Wallett's Court Table tennis and snooker in the Norman cellars are among the attractions of this largely 17th-century manor house in the countryside 3 miles northeast of Dover. The three best rooms are in the house itself; four other rooms, in a converted barn, are rather plain. The restaurant serves English fare with French touches. West Cliffe, St. Margaret's-at-Cliffe (phone: 1304-852424; fax: 1304-853430). Moderate.

En Route from Dover The famous cliffs extend southwest toward Folkestone, neatly trimming the coastline with a tall white chalk seawall for almost 7 miles. Beyond this point the cliffs fall away, exposing the shore. Stretching westward is a line of defenses constructed in the early 19th century against the threat of an invasion by Napoleon: a series of 74 small coastal fortresses—circular Martello towers—from Folkestone around Beachy Head to Seaford. The towers were reinforced a short distance inland by the Royal Military Canal, dug in the same period, from Hythe to Rye. Additional defenses were erected in 1940, when Hitler massed his forces along the French coast.

From Dover, take A20 southwest along the coast for 8 miles to Folkestone, where, if you're favored with good weather, a stroll on the Leas—a broad, mile-long, grassy walkway on the crest of the cliffs just west of the harbor—is in order. From here the coast of France unfolds in a beautiful panorama 22 miles distant; this coast has become much more accessible with the recent opening of the Channel Tunnel. On the east side of the harbor is the Warren, where a section of the chalk cliff has crumbled and fallen on the beach—a great hunting ground for fossils. Folkestone has a plentiful supply of good, reasonably priced family hotels, many of them on the seafront. From Folkestone, pick up A259 for the additional 4 miles to Hythe.

BEST EN ROUTE

Eastwell Manor Set on 3,000 acres of parkland in Ashford (located 16 miles from Folkestone on the M20), here are 23 huge bedrooms and a baronial dining room serving excellent meals and afternoon tea. For more information, see *Rural Retreats* in DIVERSIONS. *Eastwell Park,* Ashford (phone: 1233-635751; 800-525-4800; fax: 1233-635530). Expensive.

HYTHE Three Martello towers still guard the former Cinque Port of Hythe, although the harbor has long since silted up and the sea receded. There also are fortifications from other periods, including the ruins of a Roman castrum, *Stutfall Castle,* about 2½ miles west of Hythe along the banks of the Royal Military Canal that bisects the city. Above *Stutfall* is *Lympne Castle* (pronounced *Lim*), a home of the archdeacons of Canterbury until the mid-1800s. It incorporates a square 12th-century Norman tower into its otherwise 14th- and 15th-century construction, and though it is not impressively fortress-like, its sweeping sea views would have satisfied any ancient watchman. The castle is closed mid-October through mid-April; admission charge (phone: 1303-267571). *Port Lympne Mansion and Zoo Park,* with its herds of rare horses, deer, antelope, gazelle, rhinos, and other beasts, is nearby. It is open daily; admission charge (phone: 1303-264646). Hythe itself is a pleasant seaside town, a mixture of old houses, inns, and antiques shops on narrow streets, although the presence of over 2,000 human skulls in the medieval church has never been satisfactorily explained. Hythe is also the place to catch a ride on the *Romney, Hythe, and Dymchurch* narrow-gauge railway (phone: 1797-362353), which operates daily April through September and weekends only in March and October. Miniature engines hauling real passengers for modest fares puff back and forth along the 14-mile sea edge of Romney Marsh, the remote, sparsely populated lowland stretching southwest of Hythe.

BEST EN ROUTE

Imperial On the seafront, it's a grand 100-room hostelry with a split-level restaurant, 2 bars, an indoor pool, and a leisure center. Its extensive grounds also include golf, tennis, croquet, and lawn bowling. Princes Parade, Hythe (phone: 1303-267441; 800-528-1234; fax: 1303-264610). Expensive.

En Route from Hythe The A259 leads into Romney Marsh, first following both the coast and the railway as far as New Romney (like Hythe, also a closed port, having lost its harbor in the 13th century), then bearing inland toward the ancient towns of Rye (21 miles from Hythe) and Winchelsea (3 miles farther). If you stopped for the view from *Lympne Castle,* you will have seen a great deal of this flat, sometimes bleak expanse of low-lying fields and marsh grass, full of grazing Romney Marsh sheep and memories of the old smuggling days when untaxed (and often illegal) cargoes were unloaded here. In deep winter, the marsh can seem utterly detached from the present century. In summer, however, there are many attractions. The coast is flat, sandy, and ideal for swimming. Inland, the hamlets and villages of Romney Marsh proper are less frequented than the coastal towns and well worth seeing. These are quiet spots with ancient and historic churches—some of which, at some period in their past, served as caches for smugglers' contraband. Burmarsh, Newchurch, St. Mary in the Marsh, Ivychurch, Snargate, and Fairfield (all off A259), and Old Romney, Brenzett, and Brookland (on A259), are typical. After Brookland, A259 crosses the border of Kent and heads into Rye in neighboring East Sussex.

RYE Along with Winchelsea, Rye is one of the two "Ancient Towns" added to the original Cinque Ports, though the receding sea and centuries of silt buildup have obstructed its port, limiting traffic to small coastal vessels and fishing boats. Now the harbor is no more than a narrow creek winding its way to town, and Rye, essentially a medieval seaport stranded 2 miles inland, combines the flavor of a large fishing village with that of a remote country settlement. The effect is an alluring one that draws nearly as many visitors as Canterbury. Rye stands on an almost conical sandstone hill, its red roofs piled up to the point of the parish church on top, the whole fairy-tale conception circled by a crumbling 14th-century wall. The town was razed by the French in 1377 and again in 1448, destroying the most historic buildings, but many of the houses erected during the late 15th century still grace the narrow, cobblestone streets. Gabled and half-timbered, Rye is quite simply a lovely town, and it retains the atmosphere of medieval times along with a measure of its former bustling activity. You might want to get acquainted with the town before you explore it by watching the *Rye Model Sound and Light Show* (Strand Quay; phone: 1797-226696). A half-hour presentation about the town's history, the show uses a detailed model, dramatic lighting, and sound effects. It is shown daily April through October and weekends only the rest of the year; admission charge.

Both the *Mermaid Inn* (see *Best en Route*), rebuilt during the 15th century and rumored to have been a smugglers' rendezvous, and the timbered *Flushing Inn,* also 15th century (Market St.; phone: 1797-223292), are excellent haunts for travelers. The works of the great clock (ca. 1560) in the 12th-century *Church of St. Mary* are thought to be among the oldest still functioning in England. *Lamb House,* a Georgian building on West Street, was the residence of novelist Henry James from 1898 until his death in 1916. The house is open Wednesday and Saturday afternoons, April through October; admission charge (no phone). Rye specializes in pottery, and it's easy to pick up some good bargains in the many shops and workshops just off the High Street area.

Winchelsea (3 miles farther along A259), also added to the Cinque Ports alliance before the changing coastline ruined its harbor, was completely relocated to its present site in 1283 by Edward I. The church, begun soon afterward, is dedicated to St. Thomas à Becket. Parts of William Thackeray's *Denis Duval* are set in these two towns.

BEST EN ROUTE

Flackley Ash Just 4 miles from Rye, this cozy, 32-room hotel run by Clive and Jeanie Bennett has a well-deserved reputation for serving high-quality food in its candlelit restaurant. There's also an indoor pool, a sauna, a solarium, a beauty salon, and—an unusual touch—a saltwater floatation tank. London Rd., Peasmarsh (phone: 1797-230651; 800-528-1234; fax: 1797-230510). Expensive.

Mermaid Inn When Queen Elizabeth I visited Rye in 1573, she stayed here. Even older than the *George* (see below), this beautifully preserved inn was rebuilt in 1420 and is one of the most charming old hotels in England, now with 28 rooms (four with four-poster beds) and a restaurant. Its walls still conceal the priest holes (hidden compartments in the walls) and secret staircase used to avoid arrest in the old days of pirates and smugglers. Mermaid St., Rye (phone: 1797-223065; fax: 1797-226995). Expensive.

George The tiled façade is a Georgian addition, but behind that is a 400-year-old Tudor inn, with 22 rooms, oak beams, and fireplaces. Traditional English fare—steak and mushroom pie, lamb, and vegetarian dishes—are served in the dining room. High St., Rye (phone: 1797-222114; fax: 1797-224068). Moderate.

Jeake's House Built by Samuel Jeake in 1869 as a wool store and later the home of American poet and author Conrad Aiken, this labyrinthine hostelry is run by Francis and Jenny Hadfield. Two of the 12 rooms have four-posters; there is a small bar, but no restaurant. The complimentary full breakfast is served in the adjoining galleried chapel, now hung with family portraits. Mermaid St., Rye (phone: 1797-222828; fax: 1797-222623). Inexpensive.

En Route from Rye Nine miles from Rye, A259 meets the coast at Hastings and adjoining St. Leonards. The small town of Battle is 6 miles inland.

HASTINGS (ST. LEONARDS and BATTLE) This area is of immense strategic and psychological importance to England, as becomes clear when its history is reviewed: It was here that the last successful invasion of the British Isles began.

Following the death of Edward the Confessor in January 1066, Harold of Wessex, the son of Edward's adviser, ascended to the throne of England. His claim to the monarchy was weak, however, and Duke William of Normandy felt his own to be more justified, since Edward had been a distant cousin and Harold himself, he said, had previously sworn to support William's right to wear the crown on Edward's death.

It was just a few miles west of Hastings, at Pevensey Bay, that William landed his forces on September 28, 1066.

King Harold and his men were busy fighting his brother Tostig and the invading King of Norway (another claimant to the throne) in the north, and after defeating them at the Battle of Stamford Bridge, Harold and his tired army marched southward. They gathered support en route but it was not until the morning of October 14 that Harold's men, perhaps 10,000 ax- and spear-carrying foot soldiers, formed a shield wall along a ridge just north of Hastings. William's force was composed of a few thousand archers and several thousand mounted knights and armed men. Norman arrows rained on the defenders, and cavalry charges broke on the wall of spears and shields. In the late afternoon William faked a retreat, drawing many of the inexperienced English militiamen from their positions, and decimated them with his cavalry. King Harold and the remainder of his army were soon slaughtered. On the spot where Harold planted the Royal Standard, where he and his closest followers actually died, William the Conqueror erected *Battle Abbey.* By *Christmas,* William was crowned King of England in *Westminster Abbey.*

Hastings today is a popular resort much loved by the British for its wonderful setting between the hilly South Downs and the Channel coast. The original Cinque Port city stagnated after the harbor became clogged with silt during the late 12th century, and the 600-year sleep that followed kept the Old Town reasonably intact. This is at the east end of Hastings, which with a small fishing fleet retains its traditional raison d'être. The ruins of *Hastings Castle,* erected around the time of William's invasion, overlook the 3-mile beach area. An audiovisual presentation on the grounds tells the story of the castle and the famous battle of 1066. It is closed January; admission charge (phone: 1424-717963). The magnificent homes in this section of town reflect the resurgence of Hastings as a resort during the late 18th and 19th centuries when sea bathing became popular among the English. Eventually, the town grew westward to meet St. Leonards, a planned Regency "new" town laid out and developed by architects James and Decimus Burton in the 1830s. By the 1870s, the two had coalesced into one resort, with St. Leonards as its stylish western end. Hastings has all the usual seaside entertainments; and a Victorian amusement pier and pavilions plus a model railway add to the gaiety of its beachfront. The most beautiful aspects of the town, however, are natural—the cliff walks to the east of Hastings and St. Clement's Caves (below the castle) once were used by smugglers. They now house the *Smuggler's Adventure,* featuring dramatic tableaux with special sound and lighting effects that re-create dark deeds of the past. It's open daily; admission charge (phone: 1424-422964).

The nearby small town of Battle, which derives its name from the famous Battle of Hastings, includes the abbey founded by William the Conqueror (phone: 1424-773792; also see *Ancient Monuments and Ruins* in DIVERSIONS). The *Battle Town Model Show* (High St.; phone: 1424-772727) features an 18-minute presentation about the town's history using a scale model with sound and light effects. It is shown daily; admission charge. *Yesterday's World* (89-90 High St.; phone: 1424-774269), is a museum that re-creates Victorian and Edwardian rooms and shops, as well as a country railway station. It is open daily; admission charge.

BEST EN ROUTE

Netherfield Place Thirty acres of parkland, a croquet lawn, and a good restaurant with an extensive wine list all help to ensure a pleasant stay at this comfortable Georgian-style country house. Built in 1924, the hotel has 14 guestrooms of varying shapes and sizes; fresh fruit and flowers in each room provide a welcoming touch. Much of the produce used comes from the hotel's garden. Open early January through mid-December. Netherfield Hill, Battle (phone: 1424-774455; 800-828-5572; fax: 1424-774024). Expensive.

Beauport Park Set in a beautiful 33-acre park area, this stately, 23-room Georgian hostelry has a formal garden, a restaurant, and service reminiscent of another, more genteel age; the outdoor heated pool is a bonus during the summer. Battle Rd., Hastings (phone: 1424-851222; 800-528-1234; fax: 1424-852465). Moderate.

George An old coaching inn, it has 22 rooms (one sports a four-poster bed). There is a restaurant serving English and continental cooking, and when it's cold, a log fire burns in the fireplace at the hotel bar. High St., Battle (phone: 1424-774466; fax: 1424-774853). Moderate.

En Route from Hastings If time permits, you may want to leave the sea and salt air behind temporarily and detour 15 miles inland from Hastings to visit the Weald, the band of fertile farmland that stretches between the North and South Downs as far west as Hampshire.

THE WEALD Hawkhurst, reached from Hastings via A21, then A229, is not only a typical example of the prosperous market towns and large villages of the Weald but also an excellent base from which to explore the countryside.

Hawkhurst grew in association with ancient iron and cloth industries, the wealth of which, together with agriculture, fashioned a village of many substantial, weatherboarded houses. In the early 18th century, the town was also famous as the home of the notorious Hawkhurst Gang of smugglers who terrorized the region—their delinquent faces were well known at the *Mermaid Inn* in Rye.

The countryside around Hawkhurst, spanning the meandering border between East Sussex and Kent, is rich in castles and historic houses. About 9 miles southwest of town (on A265, just outside the town of Burwash) is *Bateman's,* a 17th-century stone ironmaster's house that became the home of Rudyard Kipling; the study where he wrote some of his best-known books is just as he left it, the windows looking out on one of the Weald's most beautiful valleys. It is closed Thursdays, Fridays, and November through March; admission charge (phone: 1435-882302). Heathfield, a small country town just west of Burwash, has an interesting market on Sunday mornings.

About 6 miles northeast of Hawkhurst along A229 is *Sissinghurst Castle.* Don't expect to see a castle, however, because these are actually the fragments of a beautiful Tudor house that was rescued from total dereliction by writer Vita Sackville-West and her husband, Sir Harold Nicolson—friends of Virginia Woolf and members of the "Bloomsbury Group"—who laid out lovely formal gardens within its red brick walls. It's closed Mondays and mid-October through March; admission charge (phone: 1580-712850). Note: In order to reduce the risk of damage, the castle allows only a limited number of visitors into the gardens at a time; it's a good idea to call ahead to check if there will be a long wait. *Bodiam Castle,* 3 miles southeast of Hawkhurst (off A229), is most definitely a castle, and its machicolated towers reflected in the still waters of a wide moat make a dramatic first impression. It was built in 1385 against an invasion by the French that never happened and has been uninhabited for 300 years; in spite of this, it remains a well-preserved and interesting specimen of medieval military architecture. The castle is closed Mondays November through March; admission charge (phone: 1580-830436).

En Route from the Weald From Hawkhurst, take A229 to A21, then return to Hastings; from there, proceed west along the coast 20 miles to Eastbourne. Alternatively, turn off A21 to Battle and then bear west to Herstmonceux, 14 miles from Hastings. On the outskirts of this tiny village is *Herstmonceux Castle,* a moated red brick fortified mansion built in the 1440s but completely rebuilt in the early 20th century. From 1948 to 1989 it was the home of the *Royal Greenwich Observatory,* but today it is a university study center. The building itself is closed to the public, but the gardens may be visited. They are closed November through June; admission charge (phone: 1323-833913). Crusaders' tombs can be seen in the church opposite, and locally made "trugs," curved garden baskets woven from willow fronds, can be bought in the village (also see *Shopping Spree* in DIVERSIONS). From Herstmonceux, continue west to A22, which heads south to Eastbourne, 12 miles away.

BEST EN ROUTE

Cleavers Lyng Converted from a 16th-century cottage, this unpretentious little seven-room hostelry run by Douglas and Sally Simpson offers tasty home cooking—the pies are especially good. In summer, tea is served on the lawn. Church Rd., Herstmonceux (phone: 1323-833131; fax: 1323-833617). Inexpensive.

EASTBOURNE This seaside town was developed in the mid-19th century by William Cavendish, the seventh Duke of Devonshire. It was meant to be elegant and has remained so, with a 3-mile-long seafront (unbesmirched by shops, which are not allowed), a pier with the colorful *Carpet Gardens* beside it, and a bandstand distinctively roofed with turquoise-colored tiles. At both ends of the seafront are reminders of Napoleon's plans to invade England in the early 19th century. At the eastern end is the *Redoubt* (phone: 1323-410300), a circular fort built from 1804 to 1812 which has housed a museum of Sussex military memorabilia since the 18th century. The *Wish Tower* (phone: 1323-410440), at the western end, is the 73rd of the 74 Martello towers that line the coast beginning at Folkestone; it houses a museum of coastal defense from Napoleonic times to World War II. Both museums are closed November through *Easter* and charge admission.

Eastbourne's largely shingle beach (sand is uncovered at low tide) is a relatively sunny one by English standards since Beachy Head, only 3 miles southwest, tends to take the brunt of any bad weather and disperse it. This chalk headland is one of the highest points on the Sussex coast, 575 feet above the channel, and the views out to sea or back over the South Downs make it a favorite lookout point. Between Beachy Head and Seaford, several miles west along the coast, the Downs meet the sea in a scalloped white wall of chalk cliffs known as the Seven Sisters. This wild and windy nature reserve can be explored only on foot.

BEST EN ROUTE

Grand A vast Victorian seaport hotel (one of England's most famous) with 164 rooms, a variety of sports, and a fine restaurant. For more information, see *Rural Retreats* in DIVERSIONS. King Edward's Parade, Eastbourne (phone: 1323-412345; 800-463-3750; fax: 1323-412233). Expensive.

Hydro It's a steep climb from the beach to the hotel, but many of the 100 rooms and the outdoor heated pool overlook the sea. Pluses are attractive gardens with croquet and a putting green; and the restaurant offers traditional English fare. Mount Rd., Eastbourne (phone: 1323-720643; fax: 1323-641167). Moderate.

En Route from Eastbourne The coastal road continues west to the large and busy resort of Brighton, another 20 miles or so away. In summer, however, the coastal road often is clogged with traffic, and to avoid it you may want to take the A27 inland to Brighton, stopping at Lewes (about 15 miles from Eastbourne) and a few notable country houses along the way. Or you can walk toward Brighton along the South Downs Way (see *Great Walks and Mountains Rambles* in DIVERSIONS).

Six miles short of Lewes, down a lane to the left between Firle and Selmeston, deep in the Downs, is *Charleston,* the retreat of that Bloomsbury ménage à trois, Vanessa and Clive Bell and Duncan Grant. This 18th-century farmhouse was discovered in 1916 by Vanessa's sister, Virginia Woolf, who told her, "If you lived there, you could make it absolutely divine." The trio who lived there did so by painting everything—tables, chairs, fireplaces, bookcases, and bedsteads—according to the inspiration of the moment, and the rooms still echo the conversation and laughter of such guests as Lytton Strachey, T. S. Eliot, E. M. Forster, and John Maynard Keynes. The walled English country garden is filled with mosaics, busts, and sculptures as well as with old-fashioned flowers, fruit trees, and shrubs. Since the number of visitors at any one time is limited, be sure to call in advance for an appointment. *Charleston* is closed Mondays and Tuesdays and November through March; admission charge (phone: 1323-811265).

Continuing west on A27, in the shadow of Firle Beacon (at 718 feet the highest point of the Downs east of Lewes), a turn to the left a mile or so beyond *Charleston* leads to the gates of *Firle Place,* home of the Gage family since the 15th century. The present owner is the seventh Viscount Gage; an earlier member of the family was General Thomas Gage, who, as commander in chief of British forces at the outset of the American Revolution, took the blame, unfairly in the view of some historians, for the loss of the colonies. The building underwent alterations around 1730, so although outwardly Georgian, it incorporates a Tudor courtyard house. Great elms and beech trees set off its creamy white stonework and the terraced lawns of its extensive park, while the rooms inside contain a notable collection of European and English Old Master paintings and English and French furniture. The house is closed Mondays, Tuesdays, Fridays, Saturdays, and October through April; admission charge (phone: 1273-858335).

Firle Place is just one of the fine parks taking advantage of the shelter of the steep north-facing slope of the Downs. Still driving westward, a turn to the right off A27 leads to the 16th-century *Glynde Place.* It is open Wednesdays, Thursdays, and some Sundays from April through September; admission charge (phone: 1273-858337). Two miles farther on is the unique *Glyndebourne Opera House,* which presents the *Glyndebourne Festival Opera* from late May to early August (a short but very sweet season). For more information, see *Best Festivals* in DIVERSIONS.

Monk's House, the home of Leonard and Virginia Woolf beginning in 1919, is near the church in the village of Rodmell (a left turn off A27 onto the minor road to Newhaven), 2 miles before Lewes. She drowned herself in the river Ouse here in 1941, and her ashes are buried in the garden; he died in 1969. The house and garden are open Wednesdays and Saturdays April through October; admission charge (phone: 1892-890651). From here, return to A27 and continue to Lewes.

BEST EN ROUTE

Quincy's Owners Ian and Dawn Dowding offer such delicacies as goat's cheese and quail's egg salad or chicken breast stuffed with salmon in watercress sauce. And the experience doesn't have to remain a happy memory; you can reproduce the kitchen's secret recipes if you purchase *Quincy's Cookery Book.* Closed Sunday dinner and Mondays. Reservations advised. Major credit cards accepted. On the A259 Eastbourne—Brighton coast road. 42 High St., Seaford (phone: 1323-895490). Moderate.

Old Parsonage Built by the monks of *Wilmington Priory* in 1280, this stone house in a quiet village 9 miles west of Eastbourne has three guestrooms with sumptuous bathrooms. The biggest, known as the Hall, has a carved four-poster bed, a beamed ceiling, and a stained glass window; the others—the Solar and the Middle Room—are furnished with twin beds. There's no restaurant (though breakfast is included in the rate), but owners Raymond and Angela Woodhams always are ready with suggestions of good local dining places. No smoking allowed in the guestrooms. No credit cards accepted. Westdean, Seaford (phone: 1323-870432). Moderate to inexpensive.

LEWES The steep and narrow streets of this ancient and still old-fashioned town are crowded with historical associations. *Lewes Castle* is in the center of town, its late 11th- to early 12th-century Norman keep in ruins, but its 14th-century barbican, or outer gatehouse, in good condition.

Lewes's most famous resident was probably Thomas Paine, who lived at *Bull House* (now closed to the public) from 1768 to 1774, just before he emigrated to America. The author of *Common Sense,* the influential political pamphlet that pleaded the colonies' case for independence, spent evenings debating at the *White Hart* inn (see *Best en Route*), where he repeatedly won the "Headstrong Book," a copy of Homer so named because it was sent in the morning to the most obstinate debater of the night before. Lewes is also known for its own version of *Guy Fawkes Day* (November 5). While all of Britain celebrates the day with fireworks and the burning of effigies of the man who tried to blow up Parliament in 1605 (an act meant to be the beginning of an uprising of English Catholics), here there are elaborate bonfire ceremonies and a torchlit procession to the bridge over the river Ouse, where a blazing tar barrel is hurled into the water. The rites probably predate Guy Fawkes and go back to the mid-16th-century reign of Queen Mary, when many Protestants were burned at the stake on School Hill, leaving a legacy of anti-Catholic feeling.

BEST EN ROUTE

White Hart It was in the wine cellars of this historic coaching inn that many 16th-century "heretics" were held before being burned. It was here, too, that Thomas Paine participated in the debating club that he later described as the "cradle of American independence." The hotel has 48 comfortable guestrooms (some, furnished in more contemporary style, in an annex), and serves excellent ribs of beef and Harvey's real ale from the local brewery. High St., Lewes (phone: 1273-474676; 800-528-1234; fax: 1273-476695). Moderate.

En Route from Lewes Depart Lewes via the A27 and continue 8 miles southwest to Brighton.

BRIGHTON England's most famous seaside resort. For a full report on the city's sights, hotels, and restaurants, see *Brighton* in THE CITIES.

En Route from Brighton Return in the direction of London by backtracking through Lewes and taking the quiet B2192 and B2102 northeast, turning north onto A267 at Cross-in-Hand, a village situated high on the Weald. After Five Ashes, A267 curves east on its way to Royal Tunbridge Wells (30 miles from Brighton).

ROYAL TUNBRIDGE WELLS This elegant town (pop. 45,000) once rivaled Bath as a health resort. The "healing properties" of its mineral springs were discovered in 1606, and by 1638 the Pantiles, a promenade known for the type of tile originally used to pave it, had been laid out. Now shaded by lime trees, with colonnaded houses and shops to one side, this is just as popular today as it was in the 18th century, when Richard "Beau" Nash arrived to preside over public entertainments as master of ceremonies and, just as he had previously done for Bath, raise Tunbridge Wells to the heights of fashion. There it remained until the late 18th century, until, that is, inhaling sea air and bathing in saltwater became the socially and physiologically proper thing to do and the smart set transferred its allegiance to the upstart Brighton on the coast. Queen Victoria spent time here as a princess and because of this and other royal visits, the town of Tunbridge Wells—a relatively new town for this region—was permitted by Edward VII to add "Royal" to its name in 1909. A look at the 17th-century *Church of King Charles the Martyr,* near the Pantiles and noted for its plaster ceiling, is on most visitors' agendas. The heritage center's permanent exhibit, *A Day at the Wells* (at the Corn Exchange on the Pantiles; phone: 1892-546545), transports visitors back into the 1740s through models and sound effects. It is open daily; admission charge. Then, although it is still possible to sample the mineral water from the springs, most prefer tea for two at *Binn's Corner House* (phone: 1892-527690) or something stronger at the Victorian *Duke of York* pub (phone: 1530482); both are on the Pantiles.

BEST EN ROUTE

Cheevers Despite its plain decor, this is a place where guests can count on eating well. The fare is mostly French, but there are English dishes and home-made bread, too. Closed Sundays and Mondays. Reservations necessary. Major credit cards accepted. 64 High St., Royal Tunbridge Wells (phone: 1892-545524). Moderate.

Spa Set on extensive grounds on a hillside with broad views, this 18th-century mansion has 75 rooms, an indoor pool, putting, tennis, and a restaurant with high standards. Mount Ephraim, Royal Tunbridge Wells (phone: 1892-520331; 800-528-1234; fax: 1892-510575). Moderate.

Swan This comfortable establishment dates back to the 1600s, with an elegant colonnaded frontage that is decorated with window boxes in the summertime. Opposite the heritage center, its 17 rooms (two of which offer four-poster beds) are bright and clean. There is a good restaurant. Pantiles, Royal Tunbridge Wells (phone: 1892-541450; fax: 1892-541465). Moderate.

En Route from Royal Tunbridge Wells A26 north to A21 is the way back to London, 36 miles from here. A few short side trips along the way, however, will enable you to visit at least a few of the fine houses in this part of Kent. *Penshurst Place,* in the village of Penshurst (6 miles west of Royal Tunbridge Wells via A26 and B2176), was the birthplace in 1554 of the poet, soldier, and statesman Sir Philip Sidney, and is still the home of his descendant Viscount de l'Isle. One of the great stately homes of England, it was begun in the 14th century and later enlarged with many additions—which fortunately respect the original Gothic style. The Great Hall of 1340, in its pristine medieval state, is its most famous feature, while outside there is a lovely walled garden. The noble house is closed November through February and weekdays in March; admission charge (phone: 1892-870307).

A few miles farther along (up a small lane off B2027) is *Hever Castle,* partly built in the 13th century and later the home of the Bullen (or Boleyn) family. Anne Boleyn, who paid with her head for her failure to produce a living male heir for her husband, Henry VIII (as well as for her supposed adultery), was born here and wooed by Henry here. The moated castle was bought in 1903 by William Waldorf Astor, an American who became a British subject and was later made the first Viscount Astor of Hever. The mock Tudor village around the castle and the wonderful gardens for which the property is particularly noted are the result of Astor's transformation.

The castle is closed November through mid-March; admission charge (phone: 1732-865224).

Outside the town of Sevenoaks, 12 miles north of Royal Tunbridge Wells on A225, deer roam free in the park of *Knole*—seat of the Sackville family and the largest private house in England. This vast mansion was begun in the mid-15th century by an archbishop of Canterbury, then belonged in turn to Henry VIII and Queen Elizabeth I, who gave it to her courtier, the poet Thomas Sackville, whose descendants, the Sackville-West family, have lived here ever since (although *Knole* has been in the *National Trust*'s keeping since 1946). The writer Vita Sackville-West, member of the Bloomsbury Group and restorer of *Sissinghurst Castle* (see *The Weald,* above), was born and raised at *Knole* and chronicled both it and her family in *Knole and the Sackvilles,* but it was her friend Virginia Woolf who referred to the structure as "a town rather than a house," in her novel *Orlando.* The building sprawls over three acres and includes, according to legend, seven courtyards corresponding to the days of the week, 52 staircases (one for each week in the year), and 365 rooms (one for each day in the year). The state rooms contain a fine collection of portraits, including works by Reynolds and Gainsborough, while the furnishings are virtually as they were in Elizabethan times. The house is closed Mondays, Tuesdays, and November through March; admission charge (phone: 1732-450608).

Six miles east of Sevenoaks, off A25, is *Ightham Mote,* another moated manor bought by an American, Charles Henry Robinson, a businessman from Portland, Maine. He first stumbled upon this 14th-century gem while touring the leafy lanes of Kent, bought it in the 1950s, and left it to the *National Trust* in his will. It is closed Tuesdays and November through March; admission charge (phone: 1732-810378).

Another side trip, this time 6 miles west of Sevenoaks on A25, will lead to Westerham, a pretty little town enjoying something of its original peacefulness since most through traffic now uses the M25 London Orbital Motorway. *Pitt's Cottage* (Limpsfield Rd.; phone: 1959-562125), a timbered house used as a summer cottage by William Pitt the Younger, stands on the outskirts and is now a restaurant. Westerham is best known as the birthplace of General James Wolfe, whose victory over the French at Quebec in 1759 gave England control of Canada. His childhood home, a gabled red brick 17th-century house now called *Quebec House,* contains portraits and prints and, in the stables, an exhibition about the Battle of Quebec. The house is closed Thursdays, Saturdays, and November through March; admission charge (phone: 1959-62206). A statue of Wolfe, who was mortally wounded during the battle, shares the village green with one of Winston Churchill, whose country home is about 2 miles south of Westerham via B2026.

Churchill bought *Chartwell* in 1922, entranced by the setting of this Victorian house and by its stunning views across the Weald. The brick wall he built with his own hands around the kitchen garden during his wilderness years in the 1930s, the rose garden where he loved to walk, and the track worn across the carpet of the book-lined study by his endless pacing while dictating to relays of secretaries are as he left them, and the walls of the garden studio are hung with his paintings. The property now belongs to the *National Trust,* donated by a group of his friends who bought it even before his death so that the home of Britain's foremost 20th-century statesman should belong to the nation. The house, garden, and studio are open Tuesdays, Wednesdays, Thursdays, Saturdays, and Sundays April through October (Tuesday mornings are for pre-booked groups only); the house is also open Wednesdays, Saturdays, and Sundays in March and November. There's an admission charge (phone: 1732-866368).

From here, London, about 15 miles away, is reachable by following A223 north to Bromley and picking up A21.

The Channel Islands

Geographically the Channel Islands, lying as little as 8 miles off the coastline of Normandy and Brittany, are close to France. But historically the islands—Jersey, Guernsey, Alderney, Sark, Herm, Jethou, and a smattering of islets—have been connected with the British Crown for almost a thousand years. They were part of the duchy of Normandy when William the Conqueror invaded England in 1066 and became its king, and they remained part of Britain when Normandy was subsequently reunited with the rest of France.

This heritage has given the Channel Islands a mixed identity—they are a sort of halfway house between England and France, partly self-governing, and with a hodgepodge of English and French laws. English is the official language, but a Norman patois still is spoken by some people. They issue their own bank notes, coinage, and stamps, yet British currency is accepted. The food is continental, but habits and manners are English.

The Channel Islands attract upward of 1.5 million tourists every year (the number of year-round residents is one-tenth of that figure). Their popularity is partly due to the feeling of being "abroad" that the blend of cultures gives to both British and French visitors, partly due to their enviable sunshine record (about 100 miles south of the English mainland, they get the best of the weather), and partly because no two of the islands are the same. Jersey, the most southerly of the islands and also the largest (although it only measures 9 by 5 miles), has a reputation as a "swinging" holiday resort with a wide choice of hotels, restaurants, and entertainments. Quieter, centrally situated Guernsey, the other main island, has turned from agriculture to tourism and offshore finance as its principal livelihoods. And on the smaller islands there is little to do except eat, sleep, walk, and admire some stunning seascapes and cliff scenery.

The islanders have been molded both by history and by their surroundings. Calm, unhurried, contemplative, yet with a sharp sense of humor, they also have remarkably sophisticated tastes when it comes to food and wine—the development of smart restaurants on wealthy Jersey or Guernsey may be due to the proximity of France. Islanders couple this with an enthusiasm for their own dialect and for their ancient traditions, the most famous of which is a legal oddity dating from the Norman period and known as the *Clameur de Haro.* There's no need to call an attorney if you feel that you are being legally wronged in Jersey or Guernsey—you just drop to your knees and shout: *"Haro! Haro! Haro! à l'aide, mon Prince, on me fait tort."* ("Help, my Prince, they are wronging me.") This has the same effect as a court injunction, but nowadays it is only used in cases of interference with property. The penalties for ridiculing or abusing this ancient law are heavy.

Other island oddities include the ormer, a rubbery-fleshed shellfish related to the abalone but unique to the Channel Islands, which has a particularly attractive mother-of-pearl–like shell; and giant cabbages with stalks so long that walking sticks can be made from them. More practical for souvenir hunters are the heavy-knit oiled wool sweaters (also sometimes made of cotton) known as "jerseys" and "guernseys," which have given their names to knitwear all over the world (also see *Shopping Spree* in DIVERSIONS).

Jersey and Guernsey continue to make strenuous attempts to extend their tourist seasons. Both offer discounted, inclusive (air transportation and hotel accommodations) winter holidays at major hotels, and provide lively entertainment. This trend is likely to continue because, as the islanders optimistically point out, the climate is similar to that of Bermuda and thus offers an escape from British winters. Prospective visitors also should note, however, that because the islands are exposed to the Atlantic, the sea is colder than you might expect; swimming is comfortable only between June and late September. The islands also are subject to occasional dense sea mists that can disrupt air traffic. Such disadvantages, however, are easily outweighed by the exceptionally clean air.

Jersey has led the way in introducing attractions such as an *Easter Hockey Festival* and a *Jazz Festival* in April, and the annual *Good Food Festival* in May, which encourages island restaurants to submit their culinary delights to be judged by both French and English gourmets. Highlights of the Guernsey calendar are a food festival in April and the *International Powerboat Week* (the first week in September), when top racers compete. But the most popular carnival on both Jersey and Guernsey dates back to the 1902 coronation, the annual *Battle of Flowers.* This colorful and picturesque event, involving processions of floats decorated with flowers as well as other, less formal, celebrations, takes place in August and is the high spot of any visit.

Hotel prices throughout the Channel Islands run $200 or more per night for a double room (including private bath, TV set, and breakfast, unless otherwise indicated) in places noted as expensive, $100 to $180 for moderate places, and less than $80 for inexpensive lodging. An expensive dinner for two (without wine, drinks, or tips) costs $60 or more, a moderately priced meal will be in the $30 to $50 range, and anything less than $25 is considered inexpensive. Restaurants listed serve lunch and dinner unless otherwise noted. For each location, hotels and restaurants are listed alphabetically by price category.

JERSEY

Jersey, the largest of the Channel Islands, got its name from the Normans, who called it Gersey ("the grassy isle"). Between World War I and World War II it earned the nickname "honeymoon isle" because it had become so popular with newlyweds from the mainland. (Traditionally, March was the most popular time for honeymooning because couples who married at the end of the fiscal year could claim full tax allowances for the preceding year. Now, however, honeymooning is a year-round activity here.)

It was during the interwar period that Jersey became less of an isolated farming community and more of a modern holiday resort. Initially, the main attractions were the big, safe, sandy beaches, and the inexpensive accommodations. Today the beaches are unchanged, but now the island also boasts a sparkling nightlife as well as many fine shops, hotels, and restaurants. The tiny land area also offers some glorious woodland walks, exceedingly narrow but navigable roads bordered by brilliant pink and blue hydrangea, and lots of quiet countryside, particularly in the north, where grazing Jersey cattle and historic castles make interesting sightseeing.

The island's capital is the south coast port of St. Helier, which contains about half of Jersey's population. It is built around a rather ugly harbor, and divided by a massive rock on which stands the Napoleonic *Fort Regent*—now converted into a comprehensive, all-weather entertainment, leisure, and sports complex complemented by a marina frequented by visiting yachts. The town itself is a maze of narrow streets, some of them for pedestrians only and many having French names, with a range of shops specializing in low-tax luxury goods.

Another plus for St. Helier is its location on one of Jersey's best beaches, St. Aubin's Bay. *Elizabeth Castle* is here, too, built on rocks in the 16th century and named after Queen Elizabeth I by Sir Walter Raleigh, Governor of Jersey. On summer nights the castle is dramatically floodlit, and at low tide can be reached on foot by causeway; boats service the area at other times. The castle is closed November through March; admission charge (phone: 1534-23971).

In addition, the south coast has the island's most attractive bay, St. Brelade's, which has good recreational facilities as well as miles of sand. The nearby sheltered Portelet Bay is also popular. Those who tire of the beach will find an interesting little structure hidden beside *St. Brelade's Church* called the *Fishermen's Chapel;* some parts of this ancient monastic chapel date to the 6th century. It also has some 14th-century murals.

Five miles out of St. Helier on the east coast at Gorey there is another fine castle, *Mont Orgueil.* Built to defend against attacks by France during the 13th to the 15th century, it is beautifully preserved and floodlit. The castle is closed November through March; admission charge (phone: 1534-853292). Below the castle is the tiny fishing village of Gorey. It's worth exploring, if for nothing else than the popular, reasonably priced pub lunches.

After exploring the east coast, head for the north coast of the island, which is composed mostly of cliffs, hiding many small, sheltered beaches and tiny harbors. Walking here is a must, since there are fine views of the other islands as well as of France.

In contrast to the east coast, the west coast of the rectangular island consists almost entirely of St. Ouen's Bay, backed by sand dunes. Winter seas here, rolling in from the Atlantic, can be awesome. During the summer St. Ouen's is a popular beach, but it's very large and never crowded.

Jersey's history is colorfully displayed in the *Living Legend* theme park in the parish of St. Peter. This village-style complex has gardens and several walkways (each with a different focus) leading up to a manor. Inside, a 23-minute film is screened, complete with three-dimensional special effects—volcanic eruptions, storms, battle roars—and historical commentary and scenes from Jersey's past. The park also has a restaurant, a café, a souvenir and crafts shop, a children's play area, and live entertainment. It is closed November through March; admission charge (phone: 1534-485496).

Visits are free to the island's chapels, old Norman churches, and more modern churches (the "glass church," at Millbrook, is lavishly decorated by Parisian artist René Lalique). But even the island's organized excursions are relatively inexpensive; *Blue Coach Tours* (phone: 1534-22584) and *Tantivy Holiday Coach Tours* (phone: 1534-38877) are among the companies that arrange them. Four attractions are particularly worthwhile.

The first of these is *St. Peter's Bunker,* in St. Peter Parish in the center of the island. This museum, housed in a seven-room German bunker, provides fascinating insight into the German occupation of the Channel Islands during World War II and shows how both occupiers and occupied lived during the war years. It is closed November through mid-March; admission charge (phone: 1534-481048).

Far more ancient history is found at *La Hougue Bie,* one of Jersey's two best-preserved Neolithic tombs. Visitors to the site, at Grouville, can creep down the 33-foot-long tunnel entrance to the tomb itself, where the temperature remains constant whatever the weather. The tomb is covered by a 40-foot-high mound on which two medieval chapels were constructed under a single roof. There are other historical displays on the grounds as well. It is closed November through March and Fridays and Saturdays April through October; admission charge (phone: 1534-853823).

At the *Jersey Museum* (at The Weighbridge; phone: 1534-30511), the island's history, culture, and traditions are outlined in graphic detail. Opened in 1992 at a cost of £3.8 million, the building houses relics from Jersey's past, including a re-creation of the 250,000-year-old La Cottee archaeological site. Also on the premises is the *Barreau-Le-Maistre Art Gallery,* which displays a large collection of paintings, etchings, and sculpture; a space for temporary exhibitions, and a theater. The museum is open daily; admission charge.

Finally, one of Europe's most interesting zoos is on the grounds of *Les Augrès Manor,* located in Trinity Parish on the northeast coast of the island. Gerald Durrell, its founder and honorary director, and J. J. C. Mallinson, the zoological director, have dedicated the *Jersey Zoo* to the preservation and rearing of some of the world's rarest and endangered species rather than to the display of animals or to entertainment. Watch for the families of lowland gorillas, orangutans, Tibetan white-eared pheasants, and Egyptian bare-faced ibis. The zoo is open daily; admission charge (phone: 1534-864666).

Jersey has direct airline links with most British airports, and there are daily services to and from London's three airports only 45 minutes away. There also is air transportation from France. *Condor* (phone: 1305-761551) operates passenger/car catamaran and ferry services between Weymouth and Jersey (crossing time by catamaran is three and a half hours, by ferry, between eight and 12 hours). Several firms specialize in holidays to the Channel Islands from Britain (including air transportation and hotel accommodations); these include *ABC Channel Islands Travelcentre* (phone: 1481-35551), *Channel Island Travel Service* (phone: 1481-35471), *Island Holidays* (phone: 1481-721897; 800-378777 toll-free in Britain), and *Travelsmith* (phone: 1621-784666).

The tourism office is at Liberation Square, St. Helier (phone: 1534 500700); it is closed Sundays October through mid-April.

BEST EN ROUTE

Atlantic This property adjoins *La Moye* championship golf course and features lovely views over St. Ouen's Bay. There are 50 units, all with balconies that overlook either the sea or the golf course; eight garden studios and two luxury suites are linked to landscaped gardens by terraces. Other amenities include a good restaurant and a fitness center with two pools, exercise equipment, several solariums, and a sauna. Open March through October. La Moye, St. Brelade (phone: 1534-44101; fax: 1534-44102). Expensive.

L'Horizon Nestled in St. Brelade's Bay, considered one of Europe's finest beaches, this 104-room hotel has its own indoor pool, solarium, and sauna. There are two outstanding restaurants, the *Crystal Room* and the *Star Grill,* along with the *Brasserie* for informal dining. *Clipper L'Horizon,* the hotel's 40-foot luxury yacht, complete with a professional skipper, is available for day cruising around the islands or to the French coast. St. Brelade's Bay (phone: 1534-43101; fax: 1534-46269). Expensive.

Longueville Manor A member of the Relais & Châteaux group, this property is a magnificently restored 13th-century manor house set on 15 acres of riverside gardens. Each of its 32 rooms is elegantly furnished; afternoon tea is served in either the drawing room or library, and there is a heated outdoor pool and riding stables. In the excellent dining room, the dedicated team of chefs offers prix fixe and à la carte menus prepared from the finest English meat and Jersey's abundant seafood. Many of the fruits, vegetables, and herbs used are grown in the manor's garden, which dates back to the 13th century. Open daily. Reservations necessary. Major credit cards accepted. St. Saviour (phone: 1534-25501; fax: 1534-31613). Expensive.

Victoria's Located in the *Grand,* one of Jersey's period hotels, this mock-Victorian restaurant overlooks the seafront and serves French food. Closed Sundays. Reservations necessary. Major credit cards accepted. Esplanade, St. Helier (phone: 1534-22301). Expensive.

La Buca This Italian eatery offers traditional preparations such as veal with lemon, avocado stuffed with mozzarella and prawns, and crab; there are also seasonal specials. The blue gingham tablecloths add a nice touch to the decor. Closed Mondays. Reservations advised. Major credit cards accepted. The Parade, St. Helier (phone: 1534-34283). Moderate.

La Capannina Much favored by residents, this place specializes in Italian dishes, including homemade pasta, but traditional English roast meat also is served. Closed Sundays. Reservations advised. Major credit cards accepted. 65-67 Halkett Pl., St. Helier (phone: 1534-34602). Moderate.

Château la Chaire This beautiful country house, which nestles at the foot of the Rozel Valley, once belonged to Samuel Curtis, curator of London's *Kew Gardens.* He not only built the house, but also planted the exotic trees and shrubs that surround it today. Some of the 13 rooms feature Jacuzzis. The exquisitely decorated rococo lounge has been restored to its former grandeur, with gold filigree on the walls and ceiling; and the renowned restaurant serves fresh seafood as well as English and classical French fare. Rozel Bay, St. Martin (phone: 1534-863354; fax: 1534-865137). Moderate.

Old Court House Inn Seafood reigns supreme in this informal, oak-beamed establishment. The menu boasts everything from lobster to scallops meunière, and the selection of smoked fish is truly excellent. Open daily. Reservations advised. Major credit cards accepted. St. Aubin's Harbour (phone: 1534-46466). Moderate.

Sea Crest Those who revel in spectacular sea views and glorious sunsets will admire the charms of this small, intimate hostelry. All seven guestrooms overlook the bay, and the staff is wonderfully attentive and friendly. The small restaurant serves traditional fare. Petit Port, St. Brelade (phone: 1534-46353; fax: 1534-47316). Moderate.

Water's Edge At the bottom of a steep hill, beside the sea on the north coast, this handsome 51-room hotel is well away from the crowds and offers fine views. It has a two-tier swimming pool, attractive gardens, a lounge bar, and a restaurant. Open April through October. Bouley Bay, Trinity (phone: 1534-862777; fax: 1534-863645). Moderate.

GUERNSEY

The second-largest of the Channel Islands, Guernsey is roughly triangular; its 5-mile-long east coast contains its two towns: the industrial port of St. Sampson, and the island's capital of St. Peter Port. The latter is a pretty town, built on a hillside overlooking the harbor and the islands of Sark, Herm, and Jethou. Like the other islands, Guernsey enjoys tax advantages, which makes shopping in St. Peter Port doubly appealing. The tourist office (North Esplanade, St. Peter Port; phone: 1481-723552) is closed Sundays October through March.

St. Peter Port is dominated by the town church, a granite building known as "the Cathedral of the Channel Islands," and by the medieval fortress of *Castle Cornet,* which overlooks the harbor. *Castle Cornet* saw action in the English Civil War, when the Royalist governor held it throughout a nine-year siege against a predominantly Cromwellian populace (the castle finally fell to the Parliamentary forces in 1651). It is open daily year-round, but hours are erratic; call ahead for times. There's an admission charge (phone: 1481-721657 or 1481-726518).

In addition to the castle and the church, St. Peter Port's most interesting building is *Hauteville House* (38 Hauteville; phone: 1481-721911), the 19th-century home of the French writer Victor Hugo, who lived in exile on Guernsey from 1855 to 1870; it now belongs to the City of Paris, and is furnished and maintained just as it was in the eccentric Hugo's day. Hugo chose the house because of its fine views of the French coast. The house is closed Sundays and October through March; admission charge.

With beaches on all three of its coasts, Guernsey can provide a sheltered bay whatever the direction of the wind. In good weather, the big, sandy beaches of the west coast are the best, particularly Cobo and Vazon, although swimmers should beware of the strong currents in places marked with danger flags. Children will like Portelet, a little harbor forming a tiny beach of its own within Rocquaine Bay. Lihou, a tiny islet, is offshore, as are the dangerous rocks of the Hanois, marked with a tall lighthouse.

There are several lovely walks along the picturesque south coast, which has a number of rocky headlands, towering cliffs, and good, pebble beaches—of these, Moulin Huet, Petit Bôt, Petit Port, and Saints Bay are the most popular. Visitors can stroll down to the beach along wooded paths beside streams known as *douits*.

Although it's the beaches and cliffs that draw tourists, this is also a horticultural island, and much of the interior is given over to greenhouses in which early tomatoes and flowers are cultivated.

Some of the parish churches on the island are Norman in origin. The sloping aisle of one of these, *St. Pierre du Bois* (St. Peter in the Wood), has led to a popular local joke that any bridegroom leaving the church after a wedding is already going downhill. Outside *St. Martin's Church* stands Guernsey's most famous resident, a 4,000-year-old stone figure known as *La Grandmère de Chimquière* or, more simply, *La Grandmère.* Locals do not pass *La Grandmère* without saying good morning to her.

Excursions on Guernsey are varied, and a circular coach tour of the island is interesting. You can get anywhere on the bus services radiating from St. Peter Port. But do not miss seeing the grim *German Underground*

Hospital, a relic of the World War II occupation, located at St. Andrew's Parish. Open daily April through October and Sundays and Thursdays in November; admission charge (phone: 1481-39100). Also stop in the shell-dotted *Little Chapel* at Les Vauxbelets, an 18-by-10-foot model of Our Lady of Lourdes shrine in France—big enough only for a priest and a congregation of two.

Guernsey has direct airline links with most British airports, and there are daily services to and from London (*Heathrow, Stansted,* and *Gatwick Airports*) and Southampton. The islands' own *Aurigny Airlines* (phone: 1481-822609), based at *Alderney Airport* on Alderney Island, provides regular inter-island service as well as connections to Southampton and France. *Condor* (phone: 1305-761551) operates passenger/car ferry and catamaran service between Weymouth and Guernsey (two and a half hours by catamaran, five to nine hours by ferry). For package tours to Guernsey, contact the firms listed for Jersey, above.

BEST EN ROUTE

Absolute End English, French, and continental dishes are prepared with equal flair in this converted seafront cottage on the northern outskirts of St. Peter Port. Fish, freshly caught locally and smoked on the premises, is the specialty. Open daily. Reservations necessary. Major credit cards accepted. Longstore St., St. Peter Port (phone: 1481-723822). Expensive.

La Grande Mare This elegant hotel dining room, set on about 100 well-landscaped acres, specializes in classic French fare; its wine list contains more than 100 vintages. A vegetarian menu also is available. Reservations advised. Major credit cards accepted. In *La Grande Mare Hotel,* Vazon Bay, Castel (phone: 1481-56576). Expensive.

St. Pierre Park Considered one of the island's best, this smoothly run modern hotel has 134 rooms, a restaurant, tennis courts, a nine-hole golf course designed by Tony Jacklin, a pool, a sauna, a solarium, and a host of other facilities. It's popular with business travelers as well as tourists. Rohais, St. Peter Port (phone: 1481-728282; 800-373321; fax: 1481-712041). Expensive.

Bella Luce One of the few remaining Norman manor houses, it has been carefully and lovingly restored. All 33 bedrooms are handsomely appointed; facilities include a restaurant, outdoor heated pool (open May through September), sauna, and solarium. Moulin Huet Valley (phone: 1481-38764; fax: 1481-39561). Moderate.

Café du Moulin Romantic and remote, this restaurant is set in a farmhouse in a lush, green valley overlooking a picturesque water mill. The menu offers excellent country-style French fare. Closed Sunday dinner and Mondays. Reservations advised. Major credit cards accepted. Rue de Quanteraine, St. Peter Port (phone: 1481-65944). Moderate.

Da Nello Steeped in Old World charm, this Italian restaurant features shipwreck beams in the main dining room and a light and airy conservatory with white linen, wicker chairs, and a profusion of plants. Pasta is a specialty, followed closely by fish and charcoal-grilled meat. Reservations advised. Major credit cards accepted. 46 Pollet St., St. Peter Port (phone: 1481-721552). Moderate.

La Frégate Set on a hill above the harbor, this restored 18th-century manor house has a good restaurant (French, natch) and 13 modern rooms, most of which overlook the sea and the other Channel Islands. Les Cotils, St. Peter Port (phone: 1481-724624; fax: 1481-720443). Moderate.

Hotel de Havelet This gracious Georgian house, overlooking St. Peter Port Harbour, has been converted into a 34-bedroom hotel. The coach house has become the *Wellington Boot* restaurant. Other facilities include a grillroom for informal dining, two lounges (one reserved for nonsmokers), an indoor pool, a sauna, and a Jacuzzi. Havelet, St. Peter Port (phone: 1481-722199; fax: 1481-714057). Moderate.

Old Government House Here, old-fashioned courtesy is combined with 72 modern rooms, an outdoor heated pool (open May through September), the *Regency* restaurant, and a futuristic nightclub, *Scarletts,* set in a soundproof basement. Once the official residence of the Governor of Guernsey, this hotel has been in operation since 1858. Ann's Pl., St. Peter Port (phone: 1481-724921; fax: 1481-724429). Moderate.

La Michele Located in the picturesque countryside in one of Guernsey's loveliest parishes, this family-run property has 14 guestrooms with telephones and tea- and coffee-making facilities. The bright and cheerful restaurant serves traditional English home cooking, and there's an outdoor heated pool. Conveniently located for south coast beaches and cliff-top walks. St. Martins (phone: 1481-38065; fax: 1481-39492). Inexpensive.

ALDERNEY

The most northerly and the most barren of the Channel Islands, Alderney is often ignored by tourists. It's only about 3½ miles long and 1½ miles wide, and although it has a massive breakwater built as part of a Napoleonic military harbor, the port itself is tiny. Most of the population of only 1,700 live in or around the centrally situated town of St. Anne.

Hotel accommodations are usually available in all but the peak months, but can be expensive for what you get. For diversion there is sailing, windsurfing, tennis, squash, or simply walking alongside or swimming in one of the safe and sandy south coast bays. The island's nine-hole golf course has one of the most beautiful sites in the British Isles—it sits right on top of the island with a full view of the ocean from any point. It's also possible to take a scenic steam locomotive ride on the Channel Islands' only working railway between the two broad beaches of Braye and Longy.

Aurigny Airlines provides several flights a day from and to Southampton, and has frequent inter-island flights from Guernsey and Jersey. There are also flights and a summer hydrofoil service to France. The *Alderney Tourism Office* (phone: 1481-823737), operates a 24-hour "Visitors' Hot-Line" (phone: 1481-822994), a recording that gives information about island activities.

BEST EN ROUTE

Belle Vue and Belle Vue Too Two of the largest hotels on the island, these adjoining, family-owned and -operated properties (with a total of 30 rooms and a restaurant) are located close to St. Anne (phone: 1481-822844; fax: 1481-823601). Moderate.

Sea View Located on Alderney's most popular beach, this former dockside inn built circa 1750 offers 16 rooms with central heating, TV sets, direct-dial telephones, and tea- and coffee-making facilities (most have sea views). *Raymond's Wine Bar/Bistro,* the inn's restaurant, has an extensive menu (featuring local seafood) and wine list. Braye Harbour (phone: 1481-822738; fax: 1481-823572). Moderate.

SARK

An unspoiled atmosphere and an extraordinary individuality are the hallmarks of the feudal island of Sark—a rocky plateau of an island 9 miles off the coast of Guernsey. Its constitution dates back to Elizabethan times, and it still has a hereditary ruler called the Seigneur, who today is Michael Beaumont, son of the famous Dame of Sark and her American husband. Cars, divorce, adoption, and income tax are banned on the island, and the Seigneur retains such ancient feudal rights as that of being the only person on Sark who may keep pigeons (a rule designed to protect seed corn).

Sark is, in fact, the smallest state in Europe, which no doubt adds to its attraction. Several small bays and coves are good for swimming and sunbathing; Grande Grave is one of the most popular. There is no actual town and most tourists travel by horse-drawn carriage (expensive) or hired bicycle (inexpensive) and visit tiny Creux Harbour; the 16th-century *Seigneurie* with its walled gardens (not open to the public); the tiny prison, Sark's only other noteworthy building; and the precipitous path known as La Coupée, where only 10 feet of soft rock and clay stops Sark from dividing itself into two islands.

There is a frequent ferry service from Guernsey (except Sundays), weather permitting, and summer excursions also run from Jersey.

BEST EN ROUTE

Aval du Creux Family-run, it is a favorite rendezvous for islanders and continental yachtsmen. Facilities include 13 rooms, a restaurant, a heated pool, a children's pool, and gardens which are floodlit at night. Open spring through fall (phone: 1481-832036; fax: 1481-832368). Moderate.

Dixcart Sark's oldest hotel is situated high up in a sunny, tree-lined valley. The 19 rooms are spacious and utterly comfortable, and there are three large lounges with log fires where you can read a book selected from the extensive library. Traditional fare is offered in the spacious, candlelit dining room (phone: 1481-832015; fax: 1481-832164). Moderate.

La Sablonnerie Retaining the characteristics of a 16th-century Sark farmhouse, this 22-room hotel is an oasis of good living; the excellent dining room serves fare prepared with fresh butter, cream, meat, and vegetables from the property's farm and gardens. Facilities include a granite-walled bar, a lounge, croquet, fishing, and riding. Open *Easter* to October. Little Sark (phone: 1481-832061; fax: 1481-832408). Moderate.

HERM

The attractive little island of Herm, 3 miles off Guernsey's capital of St. Peter Port, is leased by Major Peter Wood, an ex-army officer whose family farms it. Roughly 1½ miles long and a half mile wide, it is a Channel Island in miniature, with cliffs on its northern tip and long, sandy beaches to the south. It's a very popular destination for day-trippers from Guernsey, but some visitors like to stay overnight because of the island's solitude. A pub, some shops, and the island's only hotel cluster around the harbor, and footpaths lead from there to the common, the beaches (Belvoir Bay, on the east coast, is the best), and the farm. Shell Beach, also on the east coast, is the most famous beach in the Channel Islands: Instead of sand, it is made up of millions of tiny shells washed up by the Gulf Stream—many of them originating in the Gulf of Mexico.

A frequent launch service operates from St. Peter Port, Guernsey, in summer; the launch operates once daily during winter.

BEST EN ROUTE

White House An unpretentious yet comfortable hotel with two restaurants, an outdoor pool, and a tennis court offers an unexpectedly high standard of service for such a small island. The 38 rooms, many with superb views, are distributed between the main building and several surrounding cottages; self-catering cottages and family campsites also are available. Open March through October. Reservations necessary (phone: 1481-722159; 481-722377 for self-catering cottages). Expensive.

JETHOU

Once the home of the English writer Sir Compton Mackenzie, this island is privately owned and cannot be visited.

Eastern Midlands

Only an hour's distance from London, it becomes difficult to believe that there are more than 47.5 million souls crammed into England. Two hours from the capital, and the visitor can get lost in little country lanes, be the only guest at a medieval inn, the only photographer trying to capture the beauty of a 12th-century church. It is necessary to leave the main motorways, descending from A roads to B roads and even unnumbered roads, to experience such tranquillity, but make the effort and you'll find the England of storybooks, where roses *do* grow at cottage doors even though television aerials and even satellite dishes sprout from the 500-year-old rooftops. The five shires visited in this itinerary—Cambridgeshire, Leicestershire, Lincolnshire, Northamptonshire, and Nottinghamshire—indulge the traditional fantasy even further, for this is a land of spires, squires, pubs, and hunting horns.

In central England, halfway between London and the cities of York and Birmingham, these five counties make up the eastern part of the Midlands (coinciding roughly with the area English tourist authorities called the East Midlands, which does not include Cambridgeshire, however, but does include another county, Derbyshire). These shires have provided England with agricultural wealth, and as some landowners became immensely rich in this fertile part of the country, they patronized architects, artists, and craftsmen who produced wonderful structures and artworks to decorate distinguished buildings. Trade always has been important; indeed, some of the main north-south routes passing through here date back to Roman times. The Romans laid Ermine Street (A1) from London to Lincoln, and the Fosse Way (A46), which sweeps diagonally across England from the channel near Axminster and also leads to Lincoln. The Great North Road, the old coaching road from London to York, was itself a remake of a Roman route.

Because many small towns lay on these main north-south thoroughfares, inns became a feature of the region as early as Saxon times. And once an inn was built, it remained an inn forever. In some, like the *Angel and Royal* in Grantham, royalty held court seven centuries ago; others found a humbler niche in history: It was a coaching inn in the very ordinary village of Stilton that made the blue-veined cheese of Leicestershire famous. Without busloads of tourists bombarding them, most of the pubs today are comfortable enough for a drink and a sandwich, though some offer more than others. The *Chequered Skipper* at Ashton, near Oundle, is as covered with nature conservation posters as a kid's bedroom is with photos of rock musicians and movie stars. The ancient *Wig and Mitre* in Lincoln stands between the courts and the cathedral, refreshing the servants of both as it has since medieval days.

While the cathedral in Lincoln is one of the most beautiful in all of England, a masterpiece in the English Gothic style known as Early English, the region can claim many others of architectural interest. The villages of Northamptonshire especially are known for spectacular churches. A band of limestone arching across England from Dorset in the south to the Wash in the east provided a stone that can be golden or, when mixed with iron, a darker, mahogany hue. The necklace of churches from Stamford down to Thrapston, or from Melton Mowbray in neighboring Leicestershire up to Grantham in Lincolnshire, consists of separate gems that together make an entrancing whole. The tall spires, visible for miles, are often "broach spires," which means that they soar straight up out of the tower, their lines unbroken by a parapet. This same stone also was used in houses as well as churches, so the villages are the equal of those in the Cotswolds. In fact, they are even more attractive, because tour buses don't line the High Streets, the pubs are not festooned with postcard racks, and local blacksmiths make useful items that work, rather than paltry souvenirs.

The region also boasts a number of large houses—or are they palaces?—that pull in visitors from all over the world. The popularity of the Princess of Wales (which survives despite her marital troubles) has made her childhood home, *Althorp,* near Northampton, a must on everyone's list. In the shadow of Stamford, a town that is itself a collection of architectural treasures, is *Burghley House,* belonging to the Burghley family, Marquesses of Exeter. Vast, palatial, and impressive, it is one of Britain's greatest country homes. *Boughton House,* home of the Dukes of Buccleuch, and *Belton House,* former home of the Brownlow family and now in the care of the *National Trust,* are equally attractive to art lovers and historians.

This is hunt country, too. Hunting deer, especially stags, always had been a royal pastime, enjoyed by King John, for example, in Rockingham Forest, which once stretched across Leicestershire. After the great forests were axed and more and more pasture was turned by the plow, fox hunting replaced deer hunting. In the 18th century, country gentlemen mixed with tenant farmers and village folk in a ritual that was somehow democratic, even though only the aristocracy could afford the huge packs of hounds, stables of horses, and hunt servants all wearing the traditional hunting "pink" (which is, in fact, scarlet). The fox is still common in England, thriving in country areas and making occasional forays into large towns, so the sport continues, centered in towns such as Melton Mowbray and Market Harborough. The Leicestershire countryside around them, a patchwork of fields bordered by brambly hedgerows and small copses, provides a challenge for horses, riders, and hounds, as well as a protective cover for foxes. But this is a winter sport; summer visitors should not expect to see what Oscar Wilde denounced as "the unspeakable in full pursuit of the uneatable," although old prints and long horns decorate every pub and hotel for miles around.

The area has produced some great names and sad stories. Oliver Cromwell was born and educated in Huntingdon, and Samuel Pepys, the diarist, was also a resident. Farther north, Sir Isaac Newton's fertile brain flourished in the peaceful Lincolnshire countryside, producing mathematical principles that were a gigantic step for mankind 300 years ago. Charles Dickens wrote some of his most popular works while staying with friends at *Rockingham Castle,* and ancestors of George Washington in Thrapston could well have inspired the design of the Stars and Stripes. The less ennobling tales record the execution of Mary, Queen of Scots, at *Fotheringhay Castle* and the slaughter of the Royalist Army by Cromwell at Naseby, though the tall *Eleanor Cross* in Geddington is as poignant a memorial as any of a grief-stricken husband for his dead wife.

Food in the region is straightforward fare, with some traditional goodies such as Melton Mowbray pork pies still surviving. But outstanding food can be found, as in the almost Dickensian *Wig and Mitre* pub in Lincoln, where the chefs are Italian, or at *Hambleton Hall,* on a lake (Rutland Water) outside Oakham, another example of the best of modern British hotel-keeping. Expect to pay more than $250 per night for a double room (including private bath, TV set, and breakfast, unless otherwise indicated) at those places listed as very expensive; from $200 to $250 in the expensive range; $105 to $190 in the moderate range; and less than $105 for places listed as inexpensive. A three-course dinner for two, with coffee, taxes, and service, but no wine, will run $70 or more in places listed as expensive; $30 to $65 in those listed as moderate; and less than $30 in inexpensive spots. All restaurants listed serve lunch and dinner unless otherwise noted. For each location, hotels and restaurants are listed alphabetically by price category.

CAMBRIDGE For a full report on this university city, its sights, restaurants, and hotels, see *Cambridge* in THE CITIES.

En Route from Cambridge Take A604 northwest and drive 12 miles to St. Ives, turning right onto B1096.

ST. IVES This small market town (pop. 9,439) on the Great Ouse River was known as Slepe until it was dedicated to St. Ivo in 1050, but the original name lives on at the *Slepe Hall* hotel (see *Best en Route*). An imposing statue of Oliver Cromwell in the town center is a reminder that we are entering Cromwell country. The man who ruled England after the Civil War was born in nearby Huntingdon and spent time in St. Ives; here, in his stylish riding boots and broad-brimmed hat, he looks more like a Royalist than a Puritan as he points accusingly at visitors and their cameras. Russet tiles, pink brick, and half timbering make it a pleasant town, but its main point of architectural interest is in the middle of the river—the *Chapel of St. Leger,* one of only three medieval bridge chapels still surviving in Britain, sits on the six-arched, 15th-century stone bridge. Built as a place of worship for travelers, it gained some stories in the early 18th century (they were removed in the early 20th century) and was used as a house for a while, as shown in Charles Whynter's painting in St. Ives's *Norris Museum and Library.* The museum displays archaeological and more recent finds from the area. It is closed Sundays October through April; no admission charge (phone: 1480-465101).

BEST EN ROUTE

Slepe Hall Small, old-fashioned, and comfortable, with no pretensions, it has 15 rooms and the *Rugeleys* restaurant, which serves English and French fare. Ramsey Rd., St. Ives (phone: 1480-463122; fax: 1480-300706). Moderate.

Pike and Eel Three miles east of St. Ives, off A1123, this is an attractive local pub dating from the 15th century, when a ferry service operated here. Now lawns run down to a marina and there are six simple but comfortable rooms as well as a restaurant to make it a peaceful overnight stop. Also see *Pub Crawling* in DIVERSIONS. Overcote La., Needingworth (phone: 1480-463336). Inexpensive.

En Route from St. Ives Continue in the direction of Huntingdon—6 miles away whether you follow A1123 west or return to A604—but take the time to explore some of the delightful Cambridgeshire villages in the vicinity, still amazingly tranquil considering the volume of traffic rumbling close by. The Great Ouse River, lined with cruisers and houseboats, links them all together. Hemingford Grey (1 mile along B1040, off A1123) sits on the bank, clustered around *St. James Church* and its stump of a tower. A storm blew the steeple down in 1741, burying bits in the mud below, and eight stone balls make up the tower's substitute decoration. Cows drinking from the stream glance occasionally at a 12th-century manor house that is the oldest continuously inhabited house in England. Once the home of the late author Lucy Boston, it is not open to the public but its moat and thick walls can be appreciated from the outside. Grey—the twin village of Hemingford Abbots, downstream along the riverside footpath—has its own church, *St. Margaret's,* built of brown cobbles in the early 14th century. Houghton (pronounced *How*-ton), 2½ miles from St. Ives via A1123, boasts a restored mill on the site of a 10th-century mill. Now owned by the *National Trust,* the four-story brick and clapboard building holds much of the original milling machinery. It is open weekends and bank holidays March through October, as well as Mondays through Wednesdays July through August; admission charge (phone: 1480-301494). Nearby is the *Three Horseshoes* pub (phone: 1480-462410), with low beams, an inglenook, and a snug bar serving hearty fare.

Huntingdon is surrounded by a frustrating ring-road system that seems determined to keep visitors out. Follow signs for the town center, park, and explore the town on foot.

HUNTINGDON This was once the county town of the tiny county of Huntingdonshire, which was swept away in 1974 by 20th-century bureaucracy (monthly publications such as *What's On in Huntingdonshire* show that the locals care little for decisions made in London, however). Its 14,395 residents are Prime Minister John Major's constituency. Originally, the town of Godmanchester, on the other bank of the Great Ouse, was more important, since it stood at the intersection of Roman roads such as Ermine Street and the Via Devana. Nevertheless, Huntingdon grew more affluent, leaving Godmanchester behind as a quiet, elegant village with a Chinese bridge and timber-framed houses. When a bridge was built between the towns in the 14th century, the construction was noticeably fancier at the wealthier (Huntingdon) end.

The town is famous as the birthplace of Oliver Cromwell, who first "saw the light" in a house on the High Street in 1599 and was baptized in *All Saints' Church,* where his father's tomb still can be seen. Both Cromwell and Samuel Pepys were alumni of the grammar school, which now is the *Cromwell Museum* and contains several good portraits of the Lord Protector. The great man was stocky and rather ugly, with a profusion of facial moles and warts, and he always insisted on being portrayed that way. His walking stick, seal, and powder flask are in the museum, as well as the hat which he is reputed to have worn at the Dissolution of the Long Parliament in 1653. The museum is closed Mondays; no admission charge (phone: 1480-425830). Despite Oliver's puritanical leanings, the Cromwells were wealthy landowners, and *Hinchingbrooke House,* the Tudor house in which they lived from 1538 to 1627, is outside of town on Brampton Road. Cromwell's grandfather, Sir Henry, was important enough to have entertained Queen Elizabeth I here in 1564. The next owners were the Montagu family, Earls of Sandwich—it was the fourth earl who "invented" the world's most famous snack. Now the house that Horace Walpole described as "old, spacious, and irregular" is a school, open for guided afternoon tours on Sundays and bank holiday Mondays May through August; admission charge (phone: 1480-451121).

BEST EN ROUTE

George This 17th-century inn has 24 comfortable rooms. The restaurant offers traditional English cooking. Shakespearean plays are performed in the picturesque old courtyard in summer. George St., Huntingdon (phone: 1480-432444; fax: 1480-453130). Expensive.

Old Bridge Overlooking the river, this Georgian house is the best hotel in town. It maintains tradition by serving English dishes such as roast beef and venison in the large oak-paneled dining room, and tea in the garden in summer. The 26 rooms are well appointed and comfortable. 1 High St., Huntingdon (phone: 1480-52681; fax: 1480-411017). Expensive to moderate.

En Route from Huntingdon Pick up A1126, which joins A604 and then intersects with A1 north. After 8 miles, turn left onto a signposted road and continue a half mile to Stilton, at one time a "pit stop" on the Great North Road.

STILTON Britain's best-known cheese is not, and never was, made in the hamlet that gave it its name. Stop outside the *Bell Inn* (phone: 1733-241066), easily spotted because of the huge sign. The large arch shows that it was once a coaching inn, with as many as 40 coaches a day stopping to change horses and allow the passengers a bite to eat. According to one of several legends, a certain Mrs. Paulet, a farmer's wife in Wymondham (east of Melton Mowbray in nearby Leicestershire), first made the blue-veined "King of Cheeses" and sent some to her brother-in-law, Cooper Thornhill, at the *Bell.* The inn's customers were so enthusiastic about the cheese that they took it with them to London, calling it "Stilton" after the place where they had first tasted it. By the time Daniel Defoe visited in 1727, the town and the product had become synonymous enough for him to note that he had "passed through Stilton, a town famous for cheese." Even then, however, the cheese was only sold here, not made here, and now that Stilton has become a registered trademark, its production is officially limited to the three shires of Leicester, Derby, and Nottingham, all northwest of Cambridgeshire.

En Route from Stilton From here, continue 6 miles north on A1 and A15 to Peterborough.

PETERBOROUGH This is a fast-growing, industrial city (pop. 113,404), but its magnificent cathedral, one of the finest examples of Norman architecture anywhere, more than makes up for a dearth of other attractions. Begun in the 12th century on the foundations of a 7th-century monastery, it has an early Gothic, 13th-century west front that immediately arrests the attention, with its three great pointed arches. Inside, the soaring nave is a classic, and its painted wooden ceiling is unique in England: Bishops, saints, and martyrs have adorned the diamond-shaped scenes since about 1220. Note, too, the fan-vaulted retrochoir, a late 15th- to early 16th-century addition. Catherine of Aragon is buried in this church, and so was Mary, Queen of Scots, until her son, James VI of Scotland and James I of England, transferred her remains to *Westminster Abbey.* Don't miss the painting of the gravedigger who buried them both, one Robert Scarlett, who died in 1594 at the age of 98. It lies to the north of the west door and records the long and worthy duties he had performed: "He had inter'd two queenes within this place and this towne's householders in his live's space. . . ."

About 2 miles west of Peterborough (get off the A15 Peterborough bypass at A47 and go into the village of Longthorpe) is *Longthorpe Tower,* a fortified medieval mansion. That Robert Thorpe, the great-grandson of a serf, should have acquired enough money and prestige to build a mansion is unusual in itself, but the real interest here is the most complete set of medieval (14th-century) wall paintings in England, discovered, plastered over, by a local farmer in 1945. The murals depict allegorical and biblical scenes such as The Wheel of the Five Senses, over the fireplace; the Nativity, on the north wall; and the Allegory of the Three Living and Three Dead, in a window recess. Despite the interior comfort, the mansion's crenellations reflect the constant fear of attack. The mansion is closed weekdays; admission charge (phone: 1733-268482).

BEST EN ROUTE

Orton Hall Located on the southwestern outskirts of Peterborough, this 49-room hotel is surrounded by 20 acres of parkland. The spacious guestrooms are comfortably furnished, and the main building has an elegant drawing room, a conservatory, and an oak-paneled dining room that serves good English fare. The stables have been converted into a second restaurant that offers bar food and real ale. Orton Longueville, Peterborough (phone: 1733-391111; fax: 1733-231912). Expensive.

Peterborough Moat House About 2 miles west of Peterborough's center, off A15, this modern hotel with 125 rooms and a restaurant is convenient, but lacks rural character. Thorpe Wood, Peterborough (phone: 1733-260000; fax: 1733-262737). Moderate.

En Route from Peterborough Take A15 in the direction of Sleaford. After 6 miles, in Glinton, make a sharp left turn onto B1443 and continue 1½ miles to Helpston, a pretty village of gray stone houses and the birthplace of the peasant poet, John Clare. Born next to the *Bluebell Inn* in 1793, he became a ploughboy, herdsman, and rural handyman, otherwise unable to hold down a job. After spending the last 23 years of his life in a lunatic asylum, he died in 1864 and was buried at *St. Botolph's Church* on the village green, leaving some memorable lines including the mournful reflection, "If life had a second edition, how I would correct the proofs!"

Another 4 miles farther is the gray-gold limestone village of Barnack, clustered around the Anglo-Saxon *Church of St. John the Baptist* (to the left of B1443), which has its own claim to fame. The "Barnack Hills and Holes"—which make a nice picnic spot—are the now-extinct quarries that provided the stone for the cathedrals at Peterborough and Ely and some of *Cambridge*'s colleges. Now the church, two old pubs, and a well-preserved 18th-century windmill make it worth stopping for a stretch of the legs. The church's early-11th-century tower and a fine sculpture of Christ of the same period (in the north aisle) are its highlights. *Burghley House* is 2½ miles farther along B1443.

BURGHLEY HOUSE "Too large for a subject" was the verdict of King William III on this 16th-century mansion built by the first Lord Burghley (pronounced *Bur*-lee), who served Queen Elizabeth I in several capacities, including secretary of state and high treasurer. *Burghley House* is closed October through March; the admission charge includes parking and a guided tour (phone: 1780-52451). Each September, the grounds are taken over by the world's leading equestrians participating in the *Burghley Horse Trials* (phone: 1780-52131), a three-day event. Princess Anne (officially, the Princess Royal) won the *European Championship* here in 1971. For more information, see *Stately Homes and Great Gardens* and *Horsing Around* in DIVERSIONS.

En Route from Burghley House Stamford is about a mile northwest of *Burghley House* via B1443.

STAMFORD Once described as "a museum piece from a pre-industrial world," the whole town of Stamford is a conservation area, or landmark district; just over 16,100 people live here year-round. Built in yellow-gray stone and set peacefully astride the river Welland, it has an overall Georgian look, reminiscent of 17th- and 18th-century prosperity, but it is also a rich fund of medieval treasures including five parish churches, a 12th-century priory, and the 15th-century *Browne's Hospital.* With 500 buildings recognized as having architectural or historic significance, it is little wonder that Sir Walter Scott judged it "the finest scene between London and Edinburgh." The BBC miniseries *Middlemarch,* based on George Eliot's novel, was largely filmed here in Stamford; the program was broadcast in America last year on "Masterpiece Theatre."

Brochures describing guided walks through town are distributed by the tourist information center at the *Arts Centre* (27 St. Mary St.; phone: 1780-55611), which is closed Sundays. Stroll through Broad Street's Georgian elegance, then admire the brasses of the Browne family in *All Saints' Church* (13th- to 15th-century Early English with a Perpendicular tower and spire), the painted ceiling and timber roof of *St. John's* (15th-century Perpendicular), the 13th-century Early English tower and 14th-century decorated spire of *St. Mary's,* and the 15th-century glass at *St. George's.* South of the river, view the Cecil family monuments and stained glass in *St. Martin's,* where the tomb of the first Lord Burghley has the great man stretched out in full armor, a lion at his feet. On the same side of the river is the *George of Stamford* hotel (see *Best en Route*). In the 18th and 19th centuries, 20 coaches a day rattled past in each direction from London and York, stopping to change horses in the cobbled courtyard, which still can be seen today.

The *Stamford Museum* (Broad St.; phone: 1780-66317) provides a good rundown on the history of the town and also displays a life-size model of Daniel Lambert, a 739-pound man who died in Stamford in 1809 (at the age of 39) and is buried in the *St. Martin's* churchyard. The model, wearing the only surviving suit of his original clothes, is shown next to the clothing of the American midget Tom Thumb. The museum is closed Sundays

November through March; admission charge. The *Stamford Steam Brewery Museum* (All Saints' St.; phone: 1780-52186) shows how beer was made and what working conditions were like at the turn of the century, with coopers, saddlers, and wheelwrights still displaying their crafts. Visitors to the museum also can have a go at push penny, Stamford's local variation on the British pub game of shove ha'penny. The museum is closed Mondays, Tuesdays, and November through February; admission charge. To rest weary bones after a day of sightseeing, stop in at the *Bull and Swan* (on St. Martin's; phone: 1780-63558), an attractive pub, or try the tiny *Bay Tree* (on St. Paul St.; phone: 1780-51219), which serves traditional afternoon tea.

BEST EN ROUTE

George of Stamford Some call it the finest old coaching inn in England, with 47 extremely comfortable bedrooms, a walled garden, and well-prepared British food in the paneled *York Bar* restaurant and the *Garden* lounge. For more information, see *Rural Retreats* in DIVERSIONS. 71 St. Martin's, Stamford (phone: 1780-55171; fax: 1780-57070). Expensive.

En Route from Stamford The 11 miles south from Stamford to Fotheringhay follow several unnumbered (but clearly signposted) country roads and pass through a chain of pretty Northamptonshire villages that parallel anything in the Cotswolds. Leave Stamford on the A43 Kettering road, go through Easton-on-the-Hill, and at Colleyweston, opposite the church, turn left. After a couple of miles, turn left again onto A47, and make a sharp right turn soon after for King's Cliffe. Go left again at the church in King's Cliffe, toward Apethorpe, where there is a striking church built between the 13th and 17th centuries. The old stocks and whipping post stand opposite. Then drive on to Fotheringhay (about 4 miles from King's Cliffe), passing through Woodnewton, which has a quaint main street of stone cottages.

FOTHERINGHAY On February 8, 1587, a plump, 44-year-old woman wearing a reddish wig to hide her graying hair was beheaded in the black-draped *Banqueting Hall* of *Fotheringhay Castle.* Thus Mary, Queen of Scots, who had lost her Scottish throne because of her Roman Catholicism (among other considerations) and spent 20 years as a prisoner of the English, finally met her end, convicted of conspiring to assassinate and seize the throne of her cousin, Elizabeth I, who reluctantly signed the death warrant. As the axe fell, it not only extinguished the threat of a Catholic uprising but also provided the plot of a host of now-forgotten romantic novels and plays as well as Donizetti's opera *Maria Stuarda.* The castle itself, at the end of the village, is today nothing but a mound and a fragment of wall enclosed in iron railings—Mary's son, James VI of Scotland and James I of England, who united the two thrones, ordered it destroyed (its stones and a staircase went into the remodeling of the *Talbot* hotel in Oundle). However, Scottish thistles abound in the summer and, as legend would have it, they were planted by Mary just before she lost her head.

Much earlier, in 1483, Richard III had been born in *Fotheringhay Castle,* one of the strongholds of the Dukes of York. Their family crest, the golden falcon, is repeated at the local pub and atop the tower of *St. Mary and All Saints',* one of the loveliest Norman churches in England. A cathedral in miniature, it has large but delicate windows that give it an ethereal quality daylight in high summer. Another worthwhile stop is *Fotheringhay Forge* (phone: 18326-323), where proprietor Barry Keightley makes and sells medieval-looking fire baskets and fireside sets with ram- and horse-head handles.

BEST EN ROUTE

Falcon Inn Everything that a good English pub should be. Feast on ham carved off the bone, thick homemade soups, and walnut fudge! Closed Mondays. Reservations advised. Major credit cards accepted. Main St., Fotheringhay (phone: 18326-254). Inexpensive.

En Route from Fotheringhay Drive on through Tansor, noting its impressive riverside manor house, and turn right on a signposted road at the church to reach Cotterstock and Oundle, about 4 miles away. Go into Oundle (the first syllable is pronounced *Ow*—as in *ouch!*) at the roundabout.

OUNDLE The tiny town sits on a hill above a loop in the river Nene, its steep roofs and dormer windows overlooking streets and alleys of local stone. There is a famous private school here (the British call them public schools), and Catherine Parr, Henry VIII's last wife, died here. The 14th-century church tower is visible for miles around, but it is the *Talbot* hotel (see *Best en Route*) that is the main attraction, thanks to William Whitwell's modernization in 1626. He used stones from *Fotheringhay Castle,* where Mary, Queen of Scots, was beheaded. The splendid oak staircase down which the sad Scottish queen walked for the last time also was built into the inn, and the outline of a crown in the balustrade is said to be the mark made by her ring as her hand gripped the rail. Her executioner actually stayed at the hotel before performing his bloody deed. Oundle's tourist information center (14 West St.; phone: 1832-274333) is open daily.

BEST EN ROUTE

Talbot The character of the old inn has not been lost even though some of the 40 comfortable bedrooms are in a newer extension. There is also a good restaurant. The superstitious need not worry: No one has seen Mary's ghost here in recent years. New St., Oundle (phone: 1832-273621; fax: 1832-274545). Moderate.

En Route from Oundle Return to the roundabout and take the exit to Ashton. After a half mile, turn left, following the "Ashton Only" sign. If passing through on a Sunday morning in mid-October, be aware that the curious exercise in progress on the village green in front of the *Chequered Skipper* pub (phone: 1832-273494) is the annual *World Conker Championship,* held here since 1965. Players take turns swinging their conkers—a horse chestnut strung on a string or a leather lace—at those of their opponents, and the loser is the one whose conker shatters first. The game, played for centuries by English schoolboys, can be played well with no previous experience, as a Mexican tourist proved in 1976 when he turned up by chance, took part, and won! The pub is worth a visit, and not only because it has excellent food. It takes its name from a now-extinct butterfly that once inhabited the nearby woods; 300 of the insects are encased in glass inside.

Barnwell, one of the most picturesque villages in England, is only 1½ miles from Ashton (return to the road, turn left, and watch for a sign to Barnwell to the right). Really two communities (St. Andrew's and All Saints'), divided by a tiny stream, its mellow stone cottages are frequently pictured on calendars. Linking the two banks are small humpbacked bridges, the main one, between the welcoming *Montagu Arms* pub (phone: 1832-273726) and the general store, being particularly photogenic. On entering the village, the home of the Duke and Duchess of Gloucester (cousins of the queen), a 16th-century manor house next to the pale gray 13th-century castle, can be seen to the right. Neither the house nor the castle is open to the public, but a good view of them can be had from the rear of *St. Andrew's Church,* up a pretty street past a square surrounded by the almshouses. At the other end of the village are the remains of *All Saints' Church,* which in turn contains the remains of the Montagu family. Borrow the keys from The Limes, the house next door, to visit the chancel with its poignant red-painted statue of a small boy on an obelisk. Three-year-old Henry Montagu drowned in a pond in 1625, causing his grief-stricken father to commission this work, which stands on two large human feet, dripping with ooze and supporting a gilt cup inscribed "Pour on me the joys of this salvation."

Go back to the entrance to Barnwell; turn left and left again onto A605 toward Kettering. Along the next 5 miles lie Wadenhoe, Achurch, Thorpe Waterville, and Titchmarsh—all villages typical of this relatively undiscovered part of Northamptonshire, with typical churches. Thrapston, just beyond, has the added distinction of having Sir John Washington, the uncle of George Washington's great-grandfather, buried in *St. James's Church,* and his coat of arms bears an uncanny resemblance to the Stars and Stripes. To see for yourself, turn right at the traffic light in Thrapston, turn right on Chancery Lane after 100 yards, and right again into a car park behind the church. The heraldic shield with its three stars and three stripes is inside, immediately to the left of the interior doors.

Return to the main street and turn right. A mile out of Thrapston, go right at the roundabout, taking A6116 toward Corby. Note the handsome church of Lowick on the left. Shortly after Sudborough, a large sign indicates a right turn onto a single-lane road to *Lyveden New Bield,* a house begun by Sir Thomas Tresham in 1594, but left an unfinished shell. A brisk walk across a field is needed to reach the house, which Tresham, a faithful Catholic, built according to a floor plan in the shape of a cross and decorated with symbols and texts referring to the Passion. It is open daily; admission charge (phone: 18325-358).

Continuing on A6116, turn left at Stanion onto A43. After 3 miles, turn left into Geddington, going into the village on West Street. The tiny square by the church is surrounded by stone cottages and distinguished by one of the *Eleanor Crosses.* When Queen Eleanor of Castile died of a fever in Harby, Nottinghamshire, in 1290, her embalmed body was taken to London. By order of her heartbroken husband, Edward I, each of the 12 overnight resting places of the coffin was subsequently marked by a cross, and Geddington's is one of only three remaining in England. Follow signs past the cross to *Boughton House,* sheltered behind a high brick wall a bit less than a mile southeast of the village.

BOUGHTON HOUSE This structure was just a monastery in 1540, but by 1700 it was a grandiose mansion the size of a small village; treasures include paintings by Murillo and El Greco, 400-year-old carpets, and a host of family portraits. *Boughton* (pronounced *Bow*-ton) *House* is open daily from 2 to 4:30 PM in August only, but its extensive grounds are more accessible: They are open daily in August, and Saturdays through Thursdays May through July and during September; separate admission charges (phone: 1536-515731). For more information, see *Stately Homes and Great Gardens* in DIVERSIONS.

En Route from Boughton House Backtrack through Geddington to A43 and turn left toward Kettering. After half a mile, turn right and go across country to Rothwell. Turn left onto A6 and right after 200 yards to pick up B576 to Lamport. *Lamport Hall,* 10 miles from *Boughton House,* is a mainly 19th-century building with some worthwhile paintings and furniture. It can be visited Sundays *Easter* through September, as well as a couple of other days (which change each week) June through August; call ahead for exact schedule. There's an admission charge (phone: 1601-28272).

Take A508 to Brixworth, turning right into the village after a couple of miles. *All Saints' Church,* standing proudly on a hill, makes all the fine Norman and medieval churches in the area look modern. Now over 1,300 years old and considered one of the finest 7th-century buildings surviving north of the Alps, it is a peculiar mixture of Roman tiles, rubble, and stone, with a bulging external stair turret clinging to the side of the tower. Inside, the ring crypt around the apse at the east end is one of only four in the whole of Europe. Pilgrims used this to circle past the church's relic, presumably the throat bone of an early Christian martyr, St. Boniface. The annual *Flower Festival* and *Fete Day* celebrations, both held on or near June 5 (the saint's feast day), perpetuate traditions that are centuries old.

Continue south on A508, past a reservoir on the left. Turn right at the brow of the next hill, following the sign to The Bramptons and *Althorp.* The famous stately home is well signposted for the remaining 4 miles through country lanes and entered via a long drive through a park.

ALTHORP The Princess of Wales's family home has one of Europe's finest private collections of paintings, plus enough furniture, china, and porcelain to please the pickiest antiques lover. Althorp is open daily in August, and bank holiday weekends and other selected Sundays in April, May, and September. There's an admission charge (phone: 1604-770006). For more information, see *Stately Homes and Great Gardens* in DIVERSIONS.

BEST EN ROUTE

Northampton Moat House One in a chain of competent modern hotels, about 5 miles from *Althorp.* There are 142 rooms, as well as a restaurant, sauna, beauty salon, and massage room. Silver St., Northampton (phone: 1604-22441; fax: 1604-230614). Expensive to moderate.

En Route from Althorp Exiting by the rear gate, turn right, right again at the church, then left onto A428 to the village of West Haddon. A sharp right turn at the beginning of the village will lead onto B4036 to Market Harborough, 16 miles from *Althorp.* On the way, after the village of Naseby, a tall stone obelisk standing out on the right marks the spot where, on June 14, 1645, some 20,000 men fought the decisive battle of the English Civil War. Here Cromwell tested his theory that well-drilled and well-paid men led by officers of ability rather than social status would always win the day. His New Model Army outnumbered King Charles's Royalists by two to one and in a mere three hours delivered a crushing defeat despite its inexperience. The village's simple *Battle and Farm Museum* shows how 5,000 Royalists were killed or captured, as well as 200 carriages and all the king's guns confiscated. The museum is open Sundays and bank holidays *Easter* through September; admission charge (phone: 1604-740241). On entering Market Harborough, which Charles used as his headquarters before the battle, follow signs to the town center, moving toward the church.

MARKET HARBOROUGH The parish church in the center of this small Leicestershire market town (pop. 15,852) was built in the 14th century and enlarged a century later. Dedicated to St. Dionysius and Perpendicular in style, it has a 161-foot-high decorated broach spire that is visible for miles around. The handsome black-and-white timbered building next to it, dating from 1614, is the *Old Grammar School;* it perches on carved oak pillars and beams with plenty of room underneath for the traditional butter market—an early example of a shopping mall. Not far away, the river Welland cuts the town in two. During the 19th and early 20th centuries, Harborough was at its apogee as a fox-hunting center. In the winter, followers of the Quorn, Pytchley, and Fernie hunts would take over hostelries such as the *Angel,* the *Peacock,* and the *Three Swans* (see *Best en Route*). The last, originally called simply *The Swan,* boasts a fine and rare example of a wrought-iron inn sign hanging over High Street. When the name was changed to the *Three Swans* in 1770, two more birds were welded onto the side. The town's tourist information center, in the *Pen Lloyd Library* on Adam and Eve Street (phone: 1858-462649), can supply information on other sights; it is closed Sundays.

BEST EN ROUTE

Three Swans This 15th-century coaching inn was upgraded in 1989 to include 20th-century comforts. Charles I stopped here to fortify himself with a drink or two on the eve of the Battle of Naseby in 1645. There are 36 rooms (two with four-poster beds) and a good restaurant. 21 High St., Market Harborough (phone: 1858-466644; 800-528-1234; fax: 1858-433101). Moderate.

En Route from Market Harborough Take A427 for Corby and there turn north onto A6003 to Rockingham, 11 miles from Market Harborough. However, on a fine day, or on *Easter Monday,* take a different route to Rockingham—the pretty but complicated one through the little villages northeast of Harborough. In this case, take A6 toward Leicester and after 2 miles turn right onto B6047 toward Melton Mowbray and the Langtons. At the Church Langton village green, turn right for Hallaton (13 miles from Market Harborough). Delightful views open up.

Hallaton and the neighboring village, Medbourne, a few miles south, would be worth visiting for their rural prettiness alone, but it's their quaint annual encounter—a bottle-kicking match—that makes them special. On *Easter Monday* there are three parades, each starting from a different pub and the last ending up at a small hill, the Hare Pie Bank. With the marchers are two locally baked, cut-up hare pies (supposedly a symbolic offering of thanks harking back to a woman saved from a raging bull when a hare popped out of the grass to divert its attention). There is a preliminary hare pie "scrambling" wherein the pie portions are distributed to the crowd, and then the youngsters of the two villages line up for a game much like football, except that two touchdowns win the match, the ball is a "bottle" or rather a small barrel of beer, and the goal lines are the streams outside each village. The *Bewicke Arms,* the *Fox,* and the *Royal Oak* in Hallaton are favored for post-game celebrations, but if you miss the big day, they serve "a good pint" and a snack year-round; and the game is explained in Hallaton's simple, unnamed museum about village life. The museum is open weekend afternoons May through October; no admission charge (phone: 1858-89216).

To go to Rockingham from Medbourne (a distance of about 4 miles), turn right onto B664, then left to Drayton. After Drayton, make a sharp right turn through Bringhurst and on to Cottingham. Turn left onto B670 and then right onto A6003 to Rockingham.

ROCKINGHAM Even before William the Conqueror built *Rockingham Castle* in the 11th century, Romans and Saxons already had recognized the strategic importance of its site, an impressive spur overlooking the river Nene. Subsequent kings were partial to the hunting in nearby Rockingham Forest, and in the early 13th century King John used the castle as a royal hunting lodge. Edward I undertook an extensive rebuilding program in the late 13th century, adding, among other things, the twin drum towers guarding the original Norman gatehouse. By the 15th century, the castle had become derelict, so much so that in the 16th century, Edward Watson, ancestor of the present owners, was able to obtain a lease on the property and turn it into a stately Tudor home. The family bought it the following century, only to see it damaged by Cromwellian forces during the English Civil War. In the 19th century, major renovations took care to emphasize the castle's romantic, medieval appearance. Charles Dickens, a friend of the Watson family, visited often, put on plays here, and used the castle as the model for "Chesney Wold" in *Bleak House,* a large part of which was written at *Rockingham.* More recently it was used in a British television series about the Civil War. Now a fine display of furniture and armor as well as Charles Dickens mementos make it an interesting visit. The castle is open Sundays, Tuesdays after bank holidays, and Thursdays *Easter* through September (every Tuesday in August), and by appointment other times of the year. There's an admission charge (phone: 536-770240).

Not much else remains to be seen in Rockingham, but a walk up the wide main street of the village, past the *Sondes Arms* pub and the slate-and-thatch limestone cottages, is like a trip back in history. The view of Corby, a modern steel city over the brow of the hill, brings you back to reality, however!

En Route from Rockingham Take A6003 north to Oakham, 13 miles away. *Uppingham School,* a famous private school founded in 1584, dominates the somber ironstone town of Uppingham, about halfway to Oakham, and just before entering Oakham, the road passes Rutland Water, a large artificial lake.

BEST EN ROUTE

Lake Isle The small country-house restaurant here, formerly a barber shop, has been expanded to include a reasonably priced hostelry with 10 rooms and two suites. The restaurant's magnificent list of burgundies and bordeaux makes it a pleasure for wine connoisseurs, but the menu is equally good—imaginative soups, roast pork with gooseberry sauce, delicate desserts. The restaurant is closed to non-guests Monday lunch and Sunday evenings. Reservations advised. Major credit cards accepted. 16 High St. E., Uppingham (phone: 1572-822951; fax: 1572-822951). Moderate to inexpensive.

OAKHAM This delightful small town of 7,900 residents once had greater status as the county town (capital) of Rutland, whose own status as the smallest county of England ended in 1974 when it was merged into neighboring Leicestershire. *Oakham Castle,* in the town center, gives an idea of its early importance, even though only the *Great Hall* remains. Unimpressive outside, this is one of the finest domestic buildings of the 12th century remaining in England, and one of the earliest to be built of stone rather than timber. A collection of 220 horseshoes covers the walls: According to an ancient custom, as lord of the manor, the Earl of Ferrers (meaning blacksmith) may demand this unusual tribute from peers of the realm or royalty on their first visit here. The oldest is from Elizabeth I, while Elizabeth II handed over her horseshoe in 1967. The castle is open daily; no admission charge (phone: 1572-723654).

The old *Buttercross,* an octagonal market building housing a set of stocks, is nearby on the Market Place. A street market is still held here on Wednesdays and Saturdays. Another private school, *Oakham School,* founded in 1584, occupies much of the rest of the town center, along with the graceful 14th-century *All Saints' Church.* Not open to the public, but worth a look, are *Flore's House* (a 14th-century stone merchant's house at 34 High Street) and a thatch cottage on Melton Road, which was the birthplace, in 1619, of Jeffrey Hudson, "the least man in the least county in England." This Rutland dwarf reached a mere 18 inches in height by the time he was nine years old and was once served up to Queen Henrietta in a pie! The happy ending is that he became her page and is mentioned in Sir Walter Scott's *Peveril of the Peak.* The *Rutland County Museum* (Catmos St.; phone: 1572-723654) records local history, crafts, and archaeological finds. The museum is open daily; no admission charge. The tourist information center is in the public library (Catmos St.; phone: 1572-724329); it's open daily.

Rutland Water, which claims to be the largest manmade lake in Europe, is just east of Oakham. Created during the 1970s, it is 5 miles long, has 27 miles of shoreline, and covers 31,000 acres. It is a well-organized sailing, windsurfing, and fishing center, whose waters produce 60,000 trout a year, many weighing 10 to 12 pounds. Bicycles can be rented to explore the 15 miles of cycle paths that surround the lake; otherwise, take a pleasure cruise on the *Rutland Belle* (phone: 1572-84630), which operates daily except Mondays, May through September. The spire protruding from the water on the eastern side of the lake belongs to *Normanton Church,* now used as a local museum and accessible by land. It is closed October through March; admission charge (phone: 1780-460321).

Hambleton Hall With only 15 bedrooms, this former Victorian mansion (a Relais & Châteaux member) overlooking Rutland Water retains the feel of a luxurious private house. The restaurant is equally fine and has an outstanding wine list. Open daily. Reservations advised. Major credit cards accepted. For more information, see *Rural Retreats* in DIVERSIONS. Hambleton, 3 miles east of Oakham (phone: 1572-756991; fax: 1572-724721). Very expensive.

Whipper-In This 17th-century coaching inn overlooking the Market Place in Oakham has all the modern comforts, but has retained the oak beams, log fires, and plush red velvet chairs of an authentic old English lodging place. It has 24 well-appointed guestrooms. The char-grilled food is excellent. Open daily. Reservations advised. Major credit cards accepted. Market Pl., Oakham (phone: 1572-756971; fax: 1572-757759). Expensive.

En Route from Oakham Take A606 west out of Oakham and pass through Langham (3 miles away), which real ale fans know as the home of Ruddles Brewery. The cult brew can be sampled at the attractive, old *Noel Arms* pub (Bridge St., Langham; phone: 1572-722931). About 5 miles from Langham (a left turn on a signposted road off A606) is Little Dalby, yet another pretty English village, so small that it has no street names. It's associated with another of the Stilton legends, since local residents claim that it was at *Little Dalby Hall* in 1720 that the housekeeper, Mrs. Orton, first made the famous blue-veined cheese and sold it to the *Bell Inn* at Stilton. Melton Mowbray, next, is only 11 miles from Oakham. Follow signs to the town center.

MELTON MOWBRAY The town's market was chartered in 1077, reflecting its situation in rich farming country on the banks of the river Eye. Part of its name comes from the Mowbray family, to whom King Rufus gave Melton in the 11th century. The family was so powerful that Richard the Lion-Hearted, King John, Edward III, Richard III, and Henry VIII all visited Melton Mowbray at one time or another—the latter to inspect the house on Burton Street, next to the church, that he gave to Anne of Cleves, one of his unfortunate wives. The church, *St. Mary's,* was begun in the 12th century and finished in the 16th century, and the house, now a restaurant, was built in the 14th century as a residence for priests serving there.

In more recent centuries, royalty came to Melton Mowbray to hunt. In fact, the town is the center of the most famous fox-hunting country in England, and the Market Place marks the traditional meeting point of the territories of three notable hunt clubs: the *Belvoir* (pronounced *Bee*-ver), *Quorn*, and *Cottesmore* hunts. George IV, Edward VII, Edward VIII, and George VI have all cantered across the local countryside, and Prince Charles has followed in their hoofprints.

The rich meadows in the vicinity are also famous for their production of Stilton cheese, and Melton Mowbray is considered the center of the industry. The town is also famous for its pork pies and the Melton Hunt Cake, both of which can be bought at *Ye Olde Pork Pie Shoppe* (on Nottingham St.; phone: 1664-62341), where they have been sold for more than a hundred years. First recorded in 1831, the unique Melton Mowbray pork pies are "hand-raised," using hot-water crust pastry and no hoop or tin to support them while baking. The filling is chopped (not ground) lean pork, to which a rich stock is added immediately after baking to "jelly" the pie.

The Melton Hunt Cake, "as supplied to Nobility, Clergy and Gentlemen of the Melton Hunt for over 100 years," is a rich, English-style fruitcake with a liberal measure of Jamaican rum. A solid and portable snack like the pork pie, it has been eaten by huntsmen on horseback—washed down with a glass of sherry or "stirrup cup"—ever since bakers Dickinson and Morris first produced it in 1854. A display of these local delicacies is in the *Melton Carnegie Museum* (Thorpe End; phone: 1664-69946), which also houses the *Melton Mowbray Tourist Information Centre* (phone: 1664-480992). Both the tourist office and the museum are closed Sundays October through *Easter;* no admission charge.

BEST EN ROUTE

Stapleford Park At this country estate with 35 guestrooms, you can enjoy fine dining, activities on the 500-acre grounds, and a friendly welcome. For more information, see *Rural Retreats* in DIVERSIONS. Stapleford (pronounced *Stapp*-ul-fird), 5 miles east of Melton Mowbray (phone: 157284-522; 800-456-2499; fax: 157284-651). Very expensive.

George An old coaching inn in the heart of town, it has 22 guestrooms (four with four-posters), modern bathrooms, and hearty fare. In medieval times, stagecoaches used to drive through the archway that now forms the entrance hall, and the original clock that marked arrivals and departures still hangs here. The place is not fancy, but it has atmosphere. High St., Melton Mowbray (phone: 1664-62112; fax: 1644-410457). Inexpensive.

En Route from Melton Mowbray Take B676 east through rolling, open fields. In winter, the bare thorn hedges are characteristic of hunt country. The road jogs through hamlets like Saxby, Garthorpe, Coston, and Stainby, each with a photogenic church, and enters Lincolnshire along the way. Just before Colsterworth, 12 miles from Melton Mowbray, turn left up a small lane to *Woolsthorpe Manor.* Isaac Newton was born on *Christmas Day,* 1642, in this squat limestone house that is still part of a working farm. He returned in 1665 and 1666 to avoid the Great Plague raging through London and made good use of the surrounding peace and quiet, developing differential calculus and discovering the composition of white light. The gnarled apple tree out front was grown from a shoot from the original tree under which he was sitting when a falling fruit inspired him to "discover" gravity. The house is closed Mondays, Tuesdays, and November through March; admission charge (phone: 1476-860338).

Return to B676 and go into Colsterworth; turn left at the crossroad and continue another 6 miles north to Grantham via A1 and B1174 (the route is well marked).

GRANTHAM Because former Prime Minister Margaret Thatcher (who was awarded the title of baroness in 1992) was born here, Grantham (pop. 30,700) has taken to calling itself "the Premier Town." Although not particularly special at first glance, it does have a good ration of history going back to Saxon days. The 282-foot spire of *St. Wulfram's* parish church is the sixth highest in England and is easily spotted by travelers on the express trains that hurtle up and down the London–Edinburgh line. The 13th-century church dominates the town center and has a 16th-century library of chained books, as well as a bone from St. Wulfram's right arm displayed in a room above the *North Porch.* It is open Mondays, Thursdays, and Fridays *Easter* through September, and by appointment the rest of the year (phone: 1476-61342). Isaac Newton went to the nearby *King's School* and like any normal child carved his initials into the wooden sill of the *Old Schoolroom.* (The room, with its thick, small-paned windows, is now part of the newer *King's School* and can be visited by appointment; call 476-68783). A statue of Newton stands in front of the *Town Hall,* and next to it is the *Grantham Museum* (St. Peter's Hill), with a display of his possessions, as well as a Margaret Thatcher exhibition. It is closed Sundays; admission charge. The *Grantham Tourist Information Centre* (in the *Town Hall;* phone: 1476-66444) is closed Sundays.

Baroness Margaret Thatcher's humble beginnings can be traced to North Parade, where she grew up helping her parents weigh groceries in *Gadsby's,* a corner shop on High Street (it has since closed). The *Beehive* pub (on Castlegate, down Firkin St.; no phone) has a most unusual inn sign. Up in a lime tree outside is a real beehive with live bees, a curiosity noted at least 150 years ago in the rhyme, "Grantham, now two rarities are thine/A lofty steeple and a living sign." Another pub, the *Angel and Royal* (see *Best en Route*), has strong claims to being the oldest inn in the kingdom. Built for the Knights Templar, it was requisitioned in 1213 by King John, who held court in the *Chambre du Roi* (later on, Richard III ordered the death of the treacherous Duke of Buckingham in the same room). The carving of an angel holding a crown set over the 15th-century gateway commemorates the visit of Edward III and Queen Philippa in the 14th century; nevertheless, it was only after a visit by the Prince of Wales in the last century that the title "Royal" was added to the *Angel*'s name. One of the town's local delicacies is Grantham gingerbread, which was invented by mistake in 1740 when William Egglestone stumbled around in the dark on a Sunday morning to bake some cakes for his family and mixed up the wrong ingredients.

BEST EN ROUTE

Angel and Royal An ancient inn soaked in history, it now has 30 comfortable rooms, all well appointed with such modern touches as telephones. The restaurant and bars, however, retain the stone walls and beamed ceilings of bygone days. High St., Grantham (phone: 1476-65816; fax: 1476-67149). Expensive.

Barkston House This elegant Georgian farmhouse about 3 miles north of Grantham via A607 is a stylish bed and breakfast establishment with two rooms. A good evening meal will be prepared for guests on request. Reservations necessary well in advance. Barkston (phone: 1400-50555). Inexpensive.

En Route from Grantham *Belvoir Castle* is only 8 miles west of Grantham, but this route travels due north to Lincoln and visits the castle on the return trip south. Leave Grantham on A607 and continue 2 miles, heading toward Leadenham. After Manthorpe, a stone wall on the right announces *Belton House.* A particularly fine example of late-17th-century architecture, it is considered by some to be the epitome of the Restoration country house. The mansion, constructed of gray-gold Ancaster stone, is beautifully balanced outside, with large windows, a lacy balustrade, and a cupola on top. Furniture and paintings of the 17th and 18th centuries (Reynolds, Lely, Hoppner, and Romney) are matched by Edward Goudge's wonderful plaster ceilings in the *Saloon, Little Marble Hall,* and *Chapel,* with Edward Carpenter, a pupil of Grinling Gibbons, proving he was as adept at woodcarving as was his teacher. Edward VIII, a friend of the former owners (the Broenlow family), came here during the abdication crisis, and some of the Duchess of Windsor's mementos are displayed. A thousand acres of landscaped parkland surround the house. The house and grounds are closed Mondays, Tuesdays, and late October through March; admission charge (phone: 1476-66116).

From *Belton House,* continue 22 miles north to Lincoln via A607 and A15, passing the spires of *Fulbeck, Leadenham,* and *Wellingore.* Over the final 3 miles, *Lincoln Cathedral* is visible in the distance.

LINCOLN Tourists too often overlook this city, yet the richness of its history is obvious from the moment you set eyes on its cathedral. Perched high above the surrounding, flat countryside and especially stunning at night when it's floodlit, it is a gem of 13th-century architecture and considered one of the finest cathedrals in England—if not *the* finest. Like *Salisbury Cathedral, Lincoln Cathedral* (also known as *Lincoln Minster;* phone: 1522-544544) is essentially Early English in design and structure; it was begun in 1185 after an earthquake destroyed an original Norman cathedral on the spot and was largely completed by 1280. The *West Front* consists of an arcaded screen that incorporates the surviving Norman fragments, including an impressive frieze of Old and New Testament scenes. The 271-foot central tower, completed in the 14th century, was once topped with a spire that reached a height of 525 feet (the tallest building in the world at the time), but it was blown down in a gale in 1547. Similarly, the twin spires of the west towers were removed for safety reasons in 1807.

Inside, the nave has few tombs or monuments to detract from the vast, echoing space that is often speckled with color as sunlight streams through the stained glass windows. The 13th-century rose window in the north transept is known as the Dean's Eye, while the Bishop's Eye, from the 14th century, is opposite in the south transept. Notable, too, is the brilliantly sculpted *Angel Choir* at the east end of the church. Take binoculars to appreciate the 28 angels that accompany the statues of Mary and Christ high up in the spandrels; lower down, the town's symbolic imp can be seen at the foot of one vaulting shaft. Off the northeast transept is the 13th-century cloister and above it is the chapter library, designed in the 17th century by Christopher Wren. If possible, try to visit the cathedral on weekdays and Saturdays at 5:15 PM or Sundays at 3:45 PM, when a choir of 30 men and boys sing evensong as they have for centuries.

To see the rest of Lincoln (a large city of 79,980 people) requires a good day's worth of walking, best done after visiting the tourist information center (9 Castle Hill; phone: 1522-529828) for some maps and brochures (or the leaflet detailing the days and hours of walking tours). The center is open daily. The city guards a gap in a line of hills and has been important since prehistoric times, when it was called Lindon (Celtic for "hillfort by a pool"). The Romans built it into a thriving town called Lindum Colonia (from which the present name, Lincoln, was derived), and left the *West Gate,* the remains of the *East Gate,* and some walls, as well as the 2nd-century *Newport Arch,* part of the old *North Gate.* Subsequently, the Anglo-Saxons and Danes maintained its strategic importance: The Danish legacy lingers with street names ending in "gate," and the Saxon heritage includes the churches of *St. Peter-at-Gowts* and *St. Mary-Le-Wigford,* both on High Street.

But it was the Normans who cleared 166 houses to build the mighty castle, one of eight known to have been ordered by William the Conqueror himself. Begun in 1068 inside the walled Roman city, it is now reduced to its walls of herringbone masonry (with a walkway on top); the entrance gateway; several towers, including *Lucy Tower* (actually a shell keep) and the *Observatory Tower* (from which there is a good view of the city); plus several 18th- and 19th-century prison and court buildings, one of which now houses the Lincoln copy of the *Magna Carta.* The castle is open daily; admission charge (phone: 1522-511068).

The Normans then raised the original cathedral next to the castle, as well as other churches and new suburbs, everywhere substituting stone for Saxon timber. They also left the stone *Jews' House* (on Steep Hill) with its fine doorway and chimney stack above.

Allowed to tax all wool exports (the Wool Staple), the city thrived in the 12th and 13th centuries. In the 14th century, the Wool Staple was transferred to nearby Boston, and Lincoln began to decline, although the medieval era produced numerous solid timber-framed buildings. Modern Lincoln residents still make time for a drink at the 14th-century *Wig and Mitre* pub (see *Best en Route*), and they still stop for coffee on the High Bridge where the black and white houses march across the river Witham as they did 400 years ago. The late 15th-, early 16th-century *Stonebow Gate,* with the guildhall above it, is not far from the bridge. The city's recovery began in the 18th century—the *Assembly Rooms* are typically Georgian, while the 20th century's contribution is the *Central Library,* with its collection of works relating to Alfred, Lord Tennyson, a local boy.

There are several US links with Lincoln (although no direct connection has been made with Abraham Lincoln). The Pilgrim Fathers and Captain John Smith are shown in the stained glass window in the cathedral's *Seamen's Chapel.* The formidable Thomas Pownall, born in the *Minster Yard,* went on to become, consecutively, governor of New Jersey, Pennsylvania, and Massachusetts, handing over the reins in New Jersey and Massachusetts to Francis Bernard, who also had lived on the *Minster Green.* When the first shots in the War of Independence were fired, it was unknown soldiers from the Tenth Foot, the Lincolnshire Regiment, who died.

BEST EN ROUTE

D'Isney Place This elegant Georgian townhouse in the shadow of the cathedral is a family-run, 18-room bed and breakfast establishment with luxurious touches, such as four-poster beds and large Jacuzzis. There's also an acre of lovely gardens. Eastgate, Lincoln (phone: 1522-538881; fax: 1522-511321). Moderate.

Wig and Mitre A 14th-century pub halfway down Lincoln's famous medieval street, it has the unusual attribute of all-day service—breakfast, lunch, and dinner. Settle into the club-like atmosphere of the upstairs dining room with its Victorian settees and armchairs and old pictures of lawyers and churchmen, or join in the jollier downstairs bar. On a fine day, eat on the terrace. Closed *Christmas.* Reservations advised on weekends. Major credit cards accepted. 29 Steep Hill, Lincoln (phone: 1522-535190). Moderate to inexpensive.

En Route from Lincoln From Lincoln, take A1434 south in the direction of Newark, 16 miles from Lincoln. While passing through Swallow Beck, watch carefully for a right turn to Doddington on B1190. Follow the straight road for 7 miles. *Doddington Hall* (built in 1600), a magnificent example of a late Elizabethan mansion, sits in the heart of the village near the church, approached through a gabled Tudor gatehouse. The warm red brick building is trimmed with Ancaster stone and shaped like an E, with three domed cupolas standing up from the flat roof. The interior is from a later period, because it was refurbished in the 18th century by a local carpenter, who also put in new plaster ceilings. There are good tapestries and fine furniture, as well as portraits of the four families that have lived here (today it is the private home of the Jarvis family). Exhibitions and concerts are set in the 100-foot-long *Gallery*, while outside, the surrounding walled garden is an explosion of perfumed roses in summer. *Doddington Hall* is open Sundays, Wednesdays, and bank holidays, May through September; admission charge (phone: 1522-694308).

Retrace the route along B1190, but after a half mile turn right at the roundabout for Newark on A46 Lincoln Bypass. You'll soon leave Lincolnshire behind and enter Nottinghamshire. Pass the *Newark Air Museum* at Coddington, which is worth a stop if you're an aircraft aficionado. It's open daily; admission charge (phone: 1636-707170). From there, continue a short distance into Newark.

NEWARK-ON-TRENT Often called the "key to the North" because of its strategic position at the crossing of the Roman Fosse Way, the Great North Road, and the river Trent, Newark (pop. 33,143) at one time had a mighty castle. Built between the 12th and 15th centuries, only the *Main Gate, West Tower,* and a portion of riverside wall still survive. King John died here suddenly in 1216; he was borne through the great gate after falling ill at Sleaford in Lincolnshire. The castle, a Royalist stronghold, withstood three sieges by the Parliamentarians before Charles I surrendered in 1646 to end the first part of the Civil War; then Cromwell ordered its demolition, an act the townspeople fortunately never fully carried out.

Despite Newark's rich history, it is often bypassed by visitors, as most are unaware that it contains no fewer than *half* the county's landmark buildings. The 18th-century cobbled Market Square is one of the best in Europe; in it is the handsome Palladian *Town Hall* (1773), so large that it has a ballroom upstairs and a Butter Market below. Just off the square is *St. Mary Magdalene Parish Church,* Early English to Perpendicular in style, with a soaring spire and an impressive collection of silver in the treasury in the crypt. An annual service with distribution of money to the poor takes place here in March thanks to a bequest by Hercules Clay, a prominent citizen of the Civil War era. He moved his family out of his house after a premonition that it was on fire, and almost at once a cannonball hit and ignited the house. Newark also has a number of interesting old inns. The tourist information center is at the *Gilstrap Centre* (Castlegate; phone: 1636-78962) and is open daily.

BEST EN ROUTE

Grange A 15-room, family-run hostelry in a Victorian house, this home-away-from-home offers a pretty decor and the Edmondson family's cooking. 73 London Rd., Charles St. Corner, Newark (phone: 1636-703399; fax: 1636-702328). Inexpensive.

En Route from Newark-on-Trent Heading south from Newark (in the direction of Grantham), A6065 soon merges with A1. After about 4 miles, turn left into Long Bennington and follow the signs for Bottesford, 7 miles farther. The road winds past abandoned airfields, still marked by huge wartime hangars, through the hamlet of Normanton. Next is Bottesford, whose residents can claim to have the tallest *village* church spire in the country (113 feet) as well as fine monuments to the first eight Earls of Rutland. The wooden stocks and whipping post by the market cross are supposed to date from Norman times. From Bottesford, continue south another 5 miles to *Belvoir Castle,* which soon appears silhouetted against the sky.

BELVOIR CASTLE This stately palace, home of the Dukes of Rutland since the reign of Henry VIII, got its name from the French for "good views" (remember, it's pronounced *Bee*-ver-here). Indeed, this huge brick and stone fortress dominates the Vale of Belvoir as its predecessors have since the days of William the Conqueror. Rebuilt after a fire in 1816, the present building is something of a Gothic fantasy. Several films have been shot here, including *Young Sherlock Holmes,* and the showbiz element is always near. There is a fine collection of paintings and furniture, so a tour is worthwhile. After the guard room, entrance hall, and grand staircase up to the ballroom, visitors go through a chilly hall filled with armor and into the 17th/21st Regiment *Lancers Museum,* which contains Bill Brittain's bugle, blown for the "Charge of the Light Brigade" on October 25, 1854. It's a relief to reach the Chinese-style bedroom and dressing room before entering the richly decorated *Elizabeth Saloon,* the outstanding room in the castle. Matthew Wyatt not only painted the complex mythological ceiling and sculpted his patroness, Elizabeth, fifth Duchess of Rutland, in white marble, but also chose the exquisite carpet and French furniture. After the dining room comes the picture gallery, with a host of great names such as Gainsborough, Poussin, and Holbein. Then there are the libraries—two of them—with wonderful collections of books and furniture. The *King's Room,* the 150-foot *Regent's Gallery,* the chapel, kitchen, and cellars make up the finale, a real test of the culture lover's stamina. *Belvoir Castle* is closed Fridays, Mondays (except bank holidays), and October through March; admission charge (phone: 1476-870262).

En Route from Belvoir Castle Return to Bottesford, turn left onto A52 to Bingham, then left onto A46 for Leicester, 32 miles from Bottesford.

LEICESTER Although it has played as important a role in English history as any other town, as one of England's ten largest cities, Leicester no longer has any one specific area dense with historic interest. Solid and comfortable, with a population of 324,394, it prides itself on its shopping, which is offered in everything from a large open market to tiny, Victorian pedestrian streets. The *Jewry Wall Museum and Site* (St. Nicholas Cir.; phone: 1533-473021) is devoted to archaeology from Roman times to the Middle Ages and is especially notable for its excellent Roman mosaic pavements. Exhibits at the *Newarke Houses Museum* (The Newarke; phone: 1533-473222) deal with the social history of Leicestershire since 1500 and include paneled rooms and collections of toys, clocks, and musical instruments. The excellent collection of German Expressionist paintings at the *Leicestershire Museum and Art Gallery* (New Walk; phone: 1533-5542100) also are worth a visit. All of the above are open daily; none charge admission. Leicester's *Tourist Information Centre* (7-9 Every St., Town Hall Sq.; phone: 1533-650555) can provide further information or reserve a place for you on a guided walk about the city. It is closed Sundays October through March.

BEST EN ROUTE

Grand Although such a forward-looking town has local links of the Holiday Inn and Post House chains, this centrally located hotel, with its chandeliers and pillars, is a reminder of Victorian elegance. The 92 rooms are comfortable and the food acceptable. Granby St., Leicester (phone: 1533-555599; fax: 1533-544736). Moderate.

Water Margin A good Chinese restaurant, it serves Cantonese-style dishes made with fresh seafood. Sunday lunches are excellent. Open daily. Reservations unnecessary. Major credit cards accepted. 76 High St., Leicester (phone: 1533-516422). Moderate.

Welford Place The Hope family (owners of the *Wig and Mitre* in Lincoln) operate this convivial eatery. You can read the morning newspaper over coffee and toasted buns, have a sandwich or three-course meal at lunchtime, settle in with tea, a snack, or dinner—the good English food is popular with both visitors and locals. Open daily for breakfast, lunch, and dinner. Reservations advised. Major credit cards accepted. 9 Welford Pl., Leicester (phone: 1533-470758). Moderate.

En Route from Leicester Leave the city on A46 and pick up M69 to Coventry, 24 miles away and clearly signposted. Coventry is only 18 miles east of Birmingham, starting point of our *Western Midlands* route and discussed fully in THE CITIES. Alternatively, those in a hurry to return to London can forego Coventry and speed down the M1 motorway the 107 miles from Leicester to the capital.

COVENTRY The city of Lady Godiva was dramatically transformed on the night of November 14, 1940, when 500 tons of bombs and 30,000 incendiaries aimed at local munitions factories were dropped in a massive German raid that razed most of it to the ground. By the next day, some 50,000 buildings had been damaged or reduced to rubble, including the 14th-century cathedral. The shell of the old cathedral, its sanctuary altar graced with moving crosses—one made of charred timbers, the other of twisted nails—is now a memorial shrine linked to the present cathedral by a porch. Designed by Sir Basil Spence and consecrated in 1962, the cathedral is theatrical in its use of stained glass windows and lights, but its dominant decoration is the huge *Christ in Glory* tapestry above the altar, designed by painter Graham Sutherland. Jacob Epstein's bronze of *St. Michael Subduing the Devil* is on the church's outer wall, to the right of the porch. The top of the church tower affords fine views of Coventry and the surrounding countryside. The cathedral also has a visitors' center (phone: 1203-227597). It is open daily. There are admission charges to the visitors' center and to climb the tower. The tourist information office (Bayley La.; phone: 1203-832303) is open daily.

Lady Godiva was actually Countess Godfygu, wife of Leofric, Earl of Mercia, who established a monastery at Coventry in the 11th century. The good lady tried time and again to persuade her husband to ease the tax burden on the townspeople, and he finally agreed—saying he would do so the day she mounted her horse naked and rode through the marketplace in full view of all. Having told everyone to stay indoors and close the shutters, the courageous Lady Godiva went ahead, her long hair a convenient cover-up. Much later, in the 17th century, Peeping Tom became part of the legend: He took a peek and was struck blind. To commemorate these events, a canopied equestrian statue of Lady Godiva and a clock tower with moving figures of both the lady and Peeping Tom now stand in the Broadgate in the center of Coventry.

BEST EN ROUTE

De Vere A modern property; it is large (190 rooms), efficient, business oriented, located near the cathedral, and has a carvery. The bar and lounge are decorated with pictures of Daimler cars, which were originally manufactured in Coventry. Cathedral Sq., Coventry (phone: 1203-633733; fax: 1203-225299). Moderate.

Leofric There are no old-fashioned hotels left in the city; this place has 94 rooms and is set in a pedestrian shopping zone—follow the signs to West Orchard car park—and convenient to the cathedral. No pretensions to character! There are two restaurants—one formal and the other a brasserie. Broadgate, Coventry (phone: 1203-221371; fax: 1203-551352). Moderate.

Lino's In a town where choice restaurants are hard to come by, this eatery serves good English and French fare. Closed Saturday lunch and Sunday evenings. Reservations advised. Major credit cards accepted. 5 Brinklow Rd., Coventry (phone: 1203-635760). Moderate.

Western Midlands

The Midlands region of central England is an area of contradiction, its very name evoking images of the "dark satanic mills" of the poet William Blake. Communities like the Black Country and the Potteries spring to mind, industrial zones where blast furnaces once lit the landscape, mining ravaged the hills, and thick grimy coal dust hung in the air, coating houses inside and out. Yet, always just a few miles away is "England's green and pleasant land," in the words of the same poet. Here, too, are the peaceful farmlands eulogized by A. E. Housman in *A Shropshire Lad* and the rugged beauty of the *Peak District,* England's first national park.

Although the *Peak District* of Derbyshire has been attracting holidaymakers for centuries, most of the rest of the ground covered by this itinerary—largely in the western part of the Midlands—is overlooked by the average visitor to Britain. Part of the reason may be the sweet and sour nature of the landscape. Even the British might write off Staffordshire and the county of West Midlands as industrial and ugly, although they contain surprising rural stretches. Nottinghamshire has Robin Hood's Sherwood Forest as well as the coal mining community that so influenced D. H. Lawrence. The birthplace of the Industrial Revolution was in Shropshire. Consider these five counties the *real* Britain, where lovely crystal and china are produced in unlovely places like Stourbridge and Stoke-on-Trent, where market towns bustle with activity, where charming villages lie deep in cozy countryside, and where there is plenty of natural beauty.

And there's history, too. Lovers of "industrial archaeology" will certainly be content here, but so will lovers of more distant ages. There are remains of Iron Age forts and also of the Romans, who enjoyed the thermal springs at Buxton and whose Viriconium, near Shrewsbury, was Britain's fourth-largest city. Christianity arrived in the 7th century with St. Chad, missionary to the Anglo-Saxon kingdom of Mercia, and many of the oldest structures are ecclesiastical—Norman abbeys and churches and the medieval cathedral in Lichfield.

Even more is left from Tudor times. Shrewsbury has more than its fair share of black and white half-timbered buildings. *Haddon Hall,* near Bakewell in Derbyshire, is a fine, well-preserved example of a manor house. Also in Derbyshire is the glorious *Hardwick Hall,* built by one of the great women of the Elizabethan Age, Bess of Hardwick. One of her husbands, the Earl of Shrewsbury, was gaoler to Mary, Queen of Scots, so the two ladies spent many hours together, working a tapestry that is now displayed at *Hardwick Hall.*

During the Civil War of the 17th century, Shropshire and Staffordshire aided the Royalist cause, even providing refuge to the defeated Charles II before he fled to France. Then came the Industrial Revolution, which changed the face of the Midlands and the world forever. Thanks to a revival of interest in Britain's industrial heritage, there are now first-rate museums highlighting the achievements of men like Abraham Darby, who discovered how to smelt iron ore with coal, Josiah Wedgwood, who helped to make English china famous around the world, and Thomas Telford, the 19th-century civil engineer who built roads, bridges, and canals. Important as these men were, however, industry developed through the labor of ordinary people, and the Midlands also offer the opportunity to discover how they lived.

The contrast between industrial and pastoral is only one of the reasons a tour of the Midlands is so fascinating. It is also an area rich in such traditions as the semi-pagan ritual of well dressing, which continues each summer in Derbyshire towns and villages. Flowers and leaves pressed into clay form an elaborate natural picture that is used to decorate or "dress" the well, part of a ceremony giving thanks for water. Another tradition is the brewing of real ale, unfiltered and unpasteurized, so it remains cloudy and tastes distinctly of malt and hops.

Another attraction of the Midlands is that, unlike the Cotswolds, it is not overcrowded with tourists. Shropshire is surprisingly untraveled, yet it has its own brand of beauty in fertile valleys overlooked by geological uprisings such as the limestone escarpment of Wenlock Edge and the hills of Long Mynd. Derbyshire is familiar to walkers but seems able to absorb them all in the Peaks—almost half of the county is in the *Peak District National Park.* The Peaks are not so much mountains as a hilly preamble to the Pennines. The Peaks are of two types: In the north are the Dark Peaks, formed of gritstone—dark rock that juts up from rounded hills covered by gorse and heather. Skylarks sing and goshawks swoop upon their prey—this is open, barren country, with virtually no trees. Just south are the White Peaks, undulating country of limestone cut into gentle valleys by rivers like the Derwent and the Wye. In the White Peak area, also known as the Dales, life suddenly seems easier, less exposed to the harsh wind and weather.

Our tour of the Midlands leaves the *Peak District* for next to last, beginning in Birmingham and heading west into the Black Country, still an industrial zone although no longer black with smoke. After a visit to Stourbridge, Britain's glassmaking center, and to Ironbridge Gorge, where several impressive museums illustrate the birth of the Industrial Revolution, it continues west to Much Wenlock and Shrewsbury before returning due east to Lichfield. Turning northwest, and passing the forest of Cannock Chase, this route includes a stately home, the *Shugborough Estate,* then pushes on to Stoke-on-Trent, also known as the Potteries—Britain's "chinatown." Scenic Derbyshire follows, as the itinerary continues north to the resort town of Buxton and then loops eastward through the *Peak District National Park* to the villages of Edale, Castleton, Hathersage, and Bakewell, the Plague Village of Eyam, plus two more stately homes, *Haddon Hall* and *Chatsworth.* An

Elizabethan mansion, *Hardwick Hall,* is next, after which we speed down the motorway to Nottingham, the last stop on the itinerary.

Throughout the route there are friendly pubs for lunch or a snack, good restaurants, and comfortable hotels ranging from simple to elegant. Expect to pay $250 or more per night for a double room (including private bath, TV set, and breakfast, unless otherwise indicated) at places listed as very expensive; $180 to $250 in the expensive range; $100 to $175 in the moderate range; and less than $100 if listed as inexpensive. A three-course dinner for two, with coffee, taxes, and service, but no wine, will run $50 or more in places listed as expensive; $25 to $45 in the moderate range; and less than $25 in places listed as inexpensive. All restaurants listed serve lunch and dinner unless otherwise noted. For each location, hotels and restaurants are listed alphabetically by price category.

BIRMINGHAM For a detailed report on Britain's second-largest city, its sights, hotels, and restaurants, see *Birmingham* in THE CITIES.

En Route from Birmingham The city is a rabbit warren of roads—residents refer fondly to one notorious interchange as "Spaghetti Junction"—so take care when scanning the numerous route signs. The A456 towards Kidderminster leads out of the inner city and through its unattractive outskirts. Turn right onto A491 for Stourbridge (14 miles southwest of Birmingham), where our itinerary enters the Black Country. Roughly triangular, with apexes at Wolverhampton, Walsall, and Stourbridge, the area takes its name from the black smoke that used to pour from its factory chimneys in the 18th and 19th centuries, when the presence of coal, iron, clay, and limestone made this prime territory for smelting iron into steel and for making everything from locks, keys, and springs to the rolling stock for railways. Today the coal and iron mines are depleted, but the area is still devoted to manufacturing.

STOURBRIDGE Rhyming with "hour-bridge," this fairly unattractive town (pop. 55,136) is of interest as the center of Britain's glassmaking industry, a tradition going back some four centuries. The process was refined by "gentlemen glassmakers" of French Huguenot extraction, who fled to England because of religious persecution and began settling here in the early 17th century. By the late 18th century, the landscape was dotted with "glass cones," bottle-shaped structures housing circular furnaces around which teams of glassmakers worked. Bigger and bigger cones were built, but the shape was not stable enough to prevent collapse, so the industry gradually switched to lower, less distinguished-looking, though safer, buildings in the 19th century. The only glass cone remaining in the area (and one of only four left in Britain) is Stourbridge's *Redhouse Cone,* whose silhouette, rising some 100 feet into the sky, is clearly visible along A491 north of town. Part of the Stuart Crystal manufacturing complex, it is now a museum with displays on the art of engraving, exhibits of old glass, and a shop. It is open daily; no admission charge (phone: 1384-571161).

Some famous Stourbridge glass manufacturers that organize factory tours include Royal Brierley weekdays at 11 AM (phone: 1384-70161) and Royal Doulton weekdays at 10 and 11:15 AM (phone: 1384-552900). (Also see *Shopping Spree* in DIVERSIONS.) Still another attraction in the vicinity is the *Broadfield House Glass Museum,* farther north along A491, at Kingswinford. This tells the whole story of glassmaking, with examples from Roman times right through to contemporary designs, although the focus is on the 19th-century colored glass and the lead crystal for which Stourbridge is famous. There also is a glassblowing studio and gift shop. The museum is closed Mondays; no admission charge (phone: 1384-273011).

En Route from Stourbridge Take A491 out of Stourbridge and continue 3 miles north to Kingswinford; shortly afterward, the road becomes A449. The straggling little town of Ironbridge, nestled in the valley of Ironbridge Gorge, is 18 miles farther. To get there, turn left onto B4176 toward Bridgnorth and follow this to a small roundabout by the *Royal Oak* pub; here take the road to Ackleton and continue until it joins A442. After a few hundred yards turn left onto a minor road signposted to Coalport and Broseley. This narrow lane climbs a little hill, then dips down steeply into a valley, the Ironbridge Gorge. At the bottom, turn right and follow the river Severn along to Ironbridge.

IRONBRIDGE GORGE The sky of this lovely wooded Shropshire valley was once red from blast furnaces, the air grimy from coal smoke, the ground littered with slag. Peaceful now except for birds' songs, it is considered the birthplace of the Industrial Revolution, because it was here, in 1709, that Abraham Darby first discovered the technique of smelting iron ore with coke. To commemorate, document, and demonstrate the crucial changes wrought by that momentous event, an entire 6-square-mile area has been turned into a remarkable cluster of museums—including the *Museum of the River,* the *Coalport China Museum,* and the not-to-be-missed *Blists Hill Open-Air Museum*—collectively known as the *Ironbridge Gorge Museum* (for details, see *Marvelous Museums* in DIVERSIONS).

To begin, pick up a map of the area and walk along the river to the Iron Bridge itself, from which the valley takes its name. When it was cast in 1779 by Darby's grandson, Abraham Darby III, it was the world's first cast-iron bridge, a wondrous object that people from all over Europe came to see. The other sights are best reached by car. Most of the *Ironbridge Gorge Museum* is open daily; a few of the smaller sites are closed in winter. A "passport" ticket allows admission to all sites (phone: 1952-433522, weekdays; 1952-432166, weekends).

BEST EN ROUTE

Old Vicarage This solid, red brick former parsonage, built in 1905, stands in quiet seclusion at one end of the village of Worfield, about 4 miles from Ironbridge (take A442 back toward Bridgnorth, then any of three left turns to the village). Victorian antiques and plush yet cozy bedrooms give a homey feel to the hotel, and Peter and Christine Iles, the hosts, are a fount of knowledge on local places of interest. Modern English cooking in the evening and a proper breakfast are offered. There are 14 rooms (six nonsmoking) and a dining room; the overall decor of the guestrooms and public areas is charming, with antiques, paintings, and plush carpeting. Worfield, off A442 (phone: 17464-497; fax: 17464-552). Expensive.

Park House Two country houses on attractive grounds combine to make a comfortable hotel with 54 guestrooms (10 nonsmoking), a grillroom, and a French restaurant. Many weddings, conferences, and other functions are held here, so the atmosphere may be a bit frenetic for some travelers; but the heated pool, sauna, and Jacuzzi make it attractive in an area where good hotels are a bit scarce. Park St., Shifnal, 3 miles northeast of Ironbridge on A464 (phone: 1952-460128; fax: 1952-461658). Moderate.

Madeley Court This building, which dates to the 13th century, has been restored and converted into a 47-room Elizabethan mansion/hotel. Antique fabrics and furniture complete the Old World atmosphere. There's a newer annex with a banquet room, but it was built in harmony with the traditional look of the rest of the building; there are also two restaurants. Telford (phone: 1952-680068; fax: 1952-684275). Moderate to inexpensive.

En Route from Ironbridge Gorge Continue through Ironbridge, keeping the river and four giant cooling towers to the left. Turn left onto B4378 for Much Wenlock, about 6 miles from Ironbridge. After crossing the Severn, the road climbs a hill; at the brow, a backwards glance over the shoulder to the right reveals the ruins of the 12th-century *Buildwas Abbey.* One of many Norman abbeys in England, only the chapter house and a double row of seven arches remain, all open to the heavens. The country lane goes into a narrow valley with hills close upon one another and soon the village of Much Wenlock appears. Turn left into the town center.

MUCH WENLOCK There is much history in Much Wenlock, a lovely market town (pop. 2,486) where half-timbered houses stand next to Georgian brick. Its charter dates from 1468, although back in the 7th century a nunnery was founded by the King of Mercia for his beloved daughter, Milburga, later recognized as a saint. Destroyed by pillaging Danes, it was refounded in the 11th century by the Earl of Mercia, husband of the famous Lady Godiva. Unfortunately, *Wenlock Priory,* a center of Cluniac activity in England, suffered ruin again, after the Dissolution of the Monasteries by Henry VIII. Now green lawns and topiary in the cloister soften the outlines of the limestone chapter house with its interlacing arches. On the lavatorium (a stone trough for hand washing) carved figures are still visible. The medieval prior's lodge is nearby.

Much Wenlock's 16th-century *Guild Hall* sits above the old Buttermarket. Local activity focuses on the stalls of the antiques market in the lower part of the *Guild Hall* every Thursday and Saturday. Another market, selling homemade goodies such as jams and cakes, plus flowers, fruit, vegetables, knitting, and so on, takes place under the *Corn Exchange* on High Street on Saturday mornings. If you miss this, stop for lunch or a snack in the pubs on High Street, including the traditional 16th-century *George and Dragon* (phone: 1952-727312), which serves excellent real ale; the *Wheatland Fox* (phone: 1952-727292); and the *Talbot* (phone: 1952-727077).

At the end of the village is the *Gaskell Arms* (phone: 1952-727212), a coaching inn where a local pioneer of physical education, Dr. William Brookes, gave speeches about the *Wenlock Games,* which he founded in 1850 to combine the Greek ideal of a healthy mind in a healthy body with the British love of sport. Conditions in places such as Ironbridge obviously colored his view that "if there was any class who deserved recreation it was the working class," an unusually enlightened view in Victorian times! The games began with an old English flavor (tilting and medieval costumes), but because the doctor hoped to revive the ancient *Olympics,* they gradually took on Greek trappings, with laurel wreaths and medals for the winners. At their height, thousands attended, including, in 1890, Baron Pierre de Coubertin, who founded the modern *Olympic Games* in 1896. Whether the *Wenlock Games* added to his zeal or not, they are considered a precursor of the modern *Olympic* movement, and they continue to be held, on a weekend in late July, on *Linden Field.* The little museum across from the Buttermarket has photographs, medals, and other memorabilia from the festivities a hundred years ago. It also houses the *Tourist Information Centre* (phone: 1952-727679). Both the museum and the tourist office are closed November through March; admission charge to the museum. In winter, information on the area is available at Bridgnorth's tourist office (Listley St.; phone: 1746-763358); it's closed Thursdays and Sundays October through *Easter.*

En Route from Much Wenlock Shrewsbury is only 12 miles away by the direct route (A458), but if it's a nice day, take the scenic route, approximately a 25-mile drive. In either case, go back to the little roundabout at the end of Wilmore Street in Much Wenlock, turning left to bypass the village. At the intersection opposite the *Gaskell Arms,* either turn right onto A458 (for the direct route) or left onto B4371 (the scenic route). This little road climbs up to the top of a ridge from which the views are superb, the land dropping away steeply to the right and more gently to the left. In summer, trees may obscure the panorama, so stop at one of the parking areas to enjoy the Shropshire farmland below. After a few miles, Wenlock Edge rises on the left. This escarpment of limestone, covered in a blanket of woods to its green summit, belies its earlier existence, millions of years ago, as a coral reef in a tropical sea. Now it stretches southwest a straight 16 miles, the valley below green with lush meadows.

Cross A49 into Church Stretton, a small town with the Stretton Hills on its eastern side and the Long Mynd (*mynydd* is Welsh for "mountain") running north to south on its western side. Both are very popular areas for walking, and the tourist information center (phone: 1694-723133) in the town library can supply information on specific trails. It is closed Sundays and October through *Easter.* In other seasons, contact the library itself (phone: 1694-722535). One favorite hiking destination is the 1,500-foot summit of Caer Caradoc, the highest of the Stretton Hills, about 2 miles northeast of town (it is visible on the right as the road into Church Stretton dips down to A49). As are many hills in the area, Caer Caradoc is topped with the remains of an ancient hillfort, dating from the Iron Age. The fort's double walls protected some six acres, and the view that provided its tactical advantage extends over the surrounding countryside in all directions. It's best to have hiking boots, however, since the trail to the top often is muddy.

An easier walk out of Church Stretton is up, into, and onto the Long Mynd. The rounded shape of this 6-mile-long line of hills is the result of frosts in the last Ice Age breaking up rocks that are 800 million years old. Above, larks sing, although they now have to share the sky with gliders and hang gliders. Much of Long Mynd is owned by the *National Trust,* so the *National Trust Chalet Pavilion* in nearby Cardingmill Valley has information on the trails. In Church Stretton, take the signposted turn left off B4370. There is a gift shop, a café, and an information center, and from the parking area a walk of about 2 miles leads past Light Spout Waterfall to the top of the Long Mynd. The pavilion is closed November through March (phone: 1694-722631).

From Church Stretton, take A49 north to Shrewsbury, passing Caer Caradoc again on the right.

SHREWSBURY The county town, or capital, of Shropshire (pronounced *Shroze*-bury by the English, and *Shrewz*-bury by the Welsh) is best known for its public (which in Britain means private) school of the same name and for its many half-timbered houses; today it's a bustling city with 57,731 residents. Charles Dickens would still recognize the view he saw from his rooms at the *Lion* hotel (see *Best en Route*) looking "all downhill and slantwise at the crookedest black and white houses, all of many shapes except straight shapes." The dramatic combination of black oak timbers against white plaster left by Tudor times, the more regular lines of Georgian red brick, and later examples of Victorian architecture all contribute immensely to the attractiveness of the town, as does its setting, on a peninsula of rising ground formed by a loop of the river Severn.

No one knows exactly when Shrewsbury was settled first, but it was probably sometime in the 5th century, after the Romans left the nearby settlement of Viriconium (near Wroxeter) and withdrew to Gaul. In Saxon times, the town was already an important outpost against the fierce Celts beyond the Welsh border to the west, and it served the same purpose in Norman times, when William the Conqueror's relative and right-hand man, Roger de Montgomery, built the castle at the neck of the peninsula. The Battle of Shrewsbury, fought in 1403 and described by Shakespeare in *Henry IV: Part I,* underscores the town's continuing strategic importance.

Although some 12th-century portions of the castle survive, what's seen today is mainly the result of a 19th-century rebuilding—the original was demolished after the Civil War for having been a Royalist stronghold. The castle is closed, but the grounds are open to the public daily (no admission charge).

From the castle, Castle Street leads up into the old center of Shrewsbury, past the statue of Charles Darwin, who was born just across the river and was a pupil at *Shrewsbury School.* Turn left into St. Mary's Street to see *St. Mary's Church,* topped by a 222-foot spire (one of the three highest in the country). Inside its 12th-century stone walls are medieval carvings and stained glass windows, including a wonderful 14th-century Jesse window. *St. Chad's Church,* built some 600 years later, with an unusual round nave and an even more unusual tower, is at the far end of town, overlooking *Quarry Park,* where on the middle weekend of August the *Shrewsbury Flower Show* proves that England really is a nation of gardeners. A third important church, the *Abbey Church,* is across the 18th-century English Bridge, at the eastern entrance to the town (the Welsh Bridge, also 18th century, crosses the Severn on the western side). Largely of the 14th century, the church is all that remains of a monastery founded by Roger de Montgomery in 1083 and contains his final resting place. It is a modern pilgrimage spot for readers of Ellis Peters's medieval *Brother Cadfael* thrillers. The other monastic buildings fell victim to Henry VIII's Dissolution of the Monasteries and to progress, when Thomas Telford cut a road straight across the site in 1836.

Shrewsbury's *Tourist Information Centre* (phone: 1743-350761) is in the square, in the center of the peninsula. It is closed Sundays October through May. All around it are narrow streets with such delightful, self-explanatory names as Butcher Row and Fish Street or, less obvious, Dogpole, Wyle Cop, and Grope Lane. Many of the cottages were built in the 15th century; in the 16th century, more impressive houses were built with profits from the wool trade. Among these are the elaborately timbered *Ireland's Mansion* and *Owen's Mansion,* both on High Street, and the *Old Market Hall* (where the coat of arms of Elizabeth I is carved over the doorway) in the square. Slightly later is *Rowley's House* (at the corner of Barker St. and Hill's La.; phone: 1743-361196), surprisingly large for a half-timbered building. Now a museum of local history, with a gallery that interprets medieval life, it also contains Roman relics excavated at Viriconium, including a beautiful silver mirror. It is closed Sundays November through March; admission charge.

Shrewsbury is particularly bustling on market days (Tuesdays, Wednesdays, Fridays, and Saturdays). Among the local delicacies are

Shrewsbury biscuits, a shortbread-type cookie with currants, and fidget (or fitchet) pie, a combination of bacon, onions, and apples rounded off by pastry. Look for simnel cake, a dark, rich, spiced fruitcake originally associated with "Mothering Sunday," the fourth Sunday of *Lent,* when girls who worked away from their families had some rare time off to return home, taking a simnel cake as a gift. It now appears at *Easter* decorated with 11 marzipan balls representing the 12 apostles, Judas excepted.

BEST EN ROUTE

Country Friends This comfortable restaurant is at the end of a 5-mile drive south of Shrewsbury on A49. The building is medieval, with warming fireplaces and sturdy beams, but the food is "New British": Traditional dishes have been rethought for modern tastes, and combinations often include fruit, as in the venison with a sauce highlighted by black currant vinegar. The British *can* prepare vegetables well, as you'll find here, but save room for the desserts (particularly the homemade chocolates served with coffee). There also are three guestrooms (only one has a private bath). No smoking allowed in the restaurant. Closed Sundays and Mondays. Reservations advised. Major credit cards accepted. Dorrington (phone: 1743-718707). Moderate.

Lion Built in 1618, this Tudor structure was "modernized" in the 18th century to become the center of the town's social life. Paganini played his violin in the elegant Adam-style ballroom, Jenny Lind sang here, and Disraeli stayed here while campaigning for votes. A George III staircase and huge stone fireplace add to the traditional atmosphere. Underneath it all is a labyrinth of cellars where Catholic mass was whispered in secret during the Reformation. The 59 bedrooms are comfortable, and the bar is a pleasant place for a simple lunch. Wyle Cop, Shrewsbury (phone: 1743-353107; fax: 1743-352744). Moderate.

Peach Tree Serves good traditional British fare, such as venison stew with Stilton and trout stuffed with prawns and mushrooms. Closed Mondays through Saturdays for lunch and Sundays for dinner November through March. Reservations advised. Major credit cards accepted. 21 Abbey Foregate, Shrewsbury (phone: 1743-355055). Moderate.

Prince Rupert Named for the Bohemian prince who was a nephew to Charles I and commanded Royalist forces during the Civil War, this 65-room hotel incorporates *Jones Mansion,* his headquarters. One of its two restaurants serves continental dishes; the other is an Italian trattoria. Butcher Row, Shrewsbury (phone: 1743-236000; fax: 1743-357306). Moderate.

En Route from Shrewsbury The road to Lichfield, 36 miles away, is the old Roman Watling Street, straight as a ruler and now the A5 roadway. Atcham, a village on the banks of the Severn, is just 4 miles along. Slow down on approaching the bridge in order to appreciate the *second* bridge, a lovely stone structure with five arches built about 200 years ago. On the left is a grand triumphal arch leading to *Attingham Park,* a mansion built for the first Lord Berwick in 1785 and now owned by the *National Trust.* Designed by George Steuart (creator of *St. Chad's* in Shrewsbury), its interior is notable in that two separate suites of rooms, one for the lord and one for his lady, lie on separate sides of the entrance hall. Also of interest are the unusual picture gallery and fine staircase by John Nash, the glittering collection of Regency silver, and, in Lady Berwick's apartments, a very pretty, very feminine, painted boudoir. Lunch and tea are available. The house is closed Thursdays and Fridays, weekdays in October, and November through March; the grounds are open daily. There's an admission charge (phone: 1743-709203).

Soon after Atcham there is a turn on the right signposted "Viriconium" and "Ancient Monument." (Don't worry if you miss it, because there are two other turns, also signposted.) The ruins, known as *Wroxeter Roman City,* are worth a side trip, since Viriconium, founded in the 1st century and abandoned circa AD 400, was the fourth largest Roman town in Britain, with an area over half that of Londinium (which later became London). Picture what it must have been like at its height, when the forum was crowded and the public bathhouse was in use. The museum at the site helps to fill in the details. The ruins are closed Mondays October through March; admission charge (phone: 1743-761330).

Return to A5 and continue in the same direction you were heading before. After a few miles look to the right. The large hump of a hill rising from the surrounding flat farmlands is the Wrekin, a famous landmark. It may not seem impressive compared to the Alps, but in a country where the highest point is just 4,400 feet above sea level, even big hills have significance. During the 4th and 5th centuries BC, the Celts spotted approaching enemies and enjoyed the panoramic view from a fortified settlement on the Wrekin's 1,334-foot summit. After the Wrekin, the A5 soon joins M54, passing through Telford, the well-planned and thriving town named for the civil engineer responsible for so many of Shropshire's bridges, canals, and churches in the early 19th century, as well as for his restoration work on *Shrewsbury Castle.* At Exit 3, take A41 toward Whitchurch, noting signs for *Weston Park.* Across to the right is the pretty hamlet of Tong, where Dickens fans may want to visit the distinctive *Church of St. Bartholomew* (though it is made of red sandstone, it actually looks green) described in *The Old Curiosity Shop* as the church that sheltered poor Little Nell and her grandfather. Inside, the fan-vaulted ceiling of the *Golden Chapel* and the carved alabaster funerary monuments are a reminder of the skills of craftsmen hundreds of years ago. Among Tong's black and white houses is the *Bell* pub (phone: 1952-76210), which makes for a good lunch stop.

Leave Tong on A41 and at the next roundabout take A5 to Weston-under-Lizard. Just before the village is the gatehouse of *Weston Park,* the home of the Earl and Countess of Bradford, set in beautiful grounds laid out by the famous Lancelot "Capability" Brown. Yet this imposing red brick edifice is not the work of a professional architect but of Lady Wilbraham, the wife of the owner, who designed it back in 1671. Inside, the furnishings include works by Van Dyck, Holbein, and Stubbs, as well as tapestries from Aubusson and Gobelins. This is one of an increasing number of stately homes to offer something for children, though what Brown would have thought of the *Woodland Adventure Playground* hidden away in his artfully "natural" park is hard to fathom! *Weston Park* is open on *Easter,* then weekends in May and September, daily except Mondays and Fridays from mid-June through late July, and daily from late July through August. There's an admission charge (phone: 1952-76207).

Continue along A5, and after a few miles turn right for Bishops Wood. The oak-lined lane passes the *Royal Oak* pub and soon there is a sharp right turn signposted for *Boscobel House,* with a car park immediately on the left. The 17th-century manor house has been fully refurbished and restored and is known chiefly as the place where Charles II hid in an oak tree to escape Cromwell's forces after Royalist troops were defeated at the Battle of Worcester in 1651, effectively ending the Civil War. There's also a Victorian farm and working forge where you can roam around. The original tree fell prey to souvenir hunters, but a replacement oak stands a short distance from the farmyard. The house has secret rooms that also sheltered the monarch before he fled abroad, and about three-quarters of a mile farther down the track (muddy in wet weather) are the remains of the *White Ladies Priory* (same phone as *Boscobel House*), still another of Charles's havens. The house is closed January; the priory is closed Mondays November through March. There is a separate admission charge for each (phone: 1902-850244).

Return to A5 and take it straight to Lichfield. (The signs will read: "A5," "Gailey," "Cannock," and eventually "Lichfield.") Just past the Belvide Reservoir the road goes under a canal built by Thomas Telford. Remain on A5 and cross over the M6; eventually, after entering Staffordshire, turn left off A5 onto A461 for Lichfield.

LICHFIELD Besides being Samuel Johnson's birthplace, this town (pop. 25,408) also is known for its cathedral, the only one in England with three spires. Although *Lichfield Cathedral* is small, the three red sandstone spires—known as the Ladies of the Vale—are visible from several miles away. Begun in the late 12th century, but mainly decorated in 13th- and 14th-century style, the cathedral succeeds a previous Norman church on the spot, which in turn followed a church consecrated in AD 700 as a shrine for the bones of St. Chad of Mercia. Nothing now is left of either earlier structure, but one relic of the saint's time—a beautifully illuminated manuscript of the gospels of Matthew and Mark known as the "Gospels of St. Chad"—is on view in the *Chapter House* (phone: 1543-250300). Similarly, much of the present cathedral is the result of loving restoration (three centuries' worth), made necessary not only because sandstone is a perishable material but also because the church was fortified by the Royalists during the Civil War and was twice besieged by Parliamentarians. Outside, the 113 statues on the west front are almost all reproductions.

Take a stroll in nearby Vicar's Close, a small green surrounded by 14th- and 15th-century cottages, then continue along Dam Street and Quonian's Lane before heading for the pedestrians-only Market Square. Just past the *Guild of St. Mary's Centre* (phone: 1543-256611), which presents a lively history of the city, is a statue of Dr. Johnson, wit, writer, and compiler of the *Dictionary of the English Language* (published in 1755), facing the house where his father operated a bookshop and where Johnson was born in 1709. Now the *Samuel Johnson Birthplace Museum,* the house contains letters, early editions of his works (including the *Dictionary*), and various memorabilia. The museum is open daily; admission charge (phone: 1543-264972). Look at the statue of Johnson's friend and biographer, James Boswell, a few steps away in the Market Square, then adjourn to *The Scales* (phone: 1543-410653), an old coaching inn on Market Street. This popular pub offers tasty lunchtime food and real ale, not to mention real pub games like darts, shove-ha'penny, and dominoes. Listen to the conversations around you and see if you agree with Dr. Johnson's opinion that the people of Lichfield were "the most sober, decent people in England . . . and spoke the purest English."

BEST EN ROUTE

Jarvis George The 18th-century Shakespearean actor David Garrick, born a few doors away, would have enjoyed the convivial bar and relaxing lounge of this 38-room hotel. There's also a good restaurant, which offers a carvery at Sunday lunch and à la carte dining all other times. Bird St., Lichfield (phone: 1543-414822; fax: 1543-415817). Moderate to inexpensive.

En Route from Lichfield The next major stop, *Shugborough Estate,* is 14 miles from Lichfield. Return to the ring road and follow A51 through the unattractive town of Rugeley. At the whitewashed *Wolsey Arms* pub, bear left onto A513 toward Stafford. Immediately, all is rural again; up the hill to the left is Cannock Chase. Once the hunting preserve of Danish, Saxon, and even Plantagenet kings until ownership was transferred in 1290 to the Bishops of Lichfield, it is now an *Area of Outstanding Natural Beauty* covering some 26 square miles. The fallow deer that the bishops introduced continue to roam through woodlands of beech, oak, sycamore, and pine. Still on A513, you'll soon reach Milford. Just before the *Barley Mow Inn* is the entrance to *Shugborough Estate,* ancestral home of the Earls of Lichfield.

SHUGBOROUGH ESTATE This historic home is still lived in by the photographer, Patrick, Earl of Lichfield, cousin to the queen, even though the *National Trust* now owns, and *Staffordshire County Council* administers, the estate. Set on 900 acres of park and farmland, *Shugborough* has something of interest for everyone. The house itself dates from 1693, although the graceful colonnaded frontage came about later thanks to the first owner's brother, Admiral George Anson, who sailed around the world in the 1740s and was lucky enough to capture a Spanish galleon full of treasure. For those not keen on architecture, furniture, paintings, silver, or the admiral's naval memorabilia, there are the gorgeous 18-acre formal gardens, with roses and rhododendrons. You can even venture a little farther to find the temples, follies, bridges, and ornamental ponds, some of which were designed by the 18th-century neoclassical revivalist James "Athenian" Stuart.

Also on the grounds—actually in the stable block and domestic buildings—are the *Original Servants' Quarters,* which present a view of more ordinary life 200 years ago with a working laundry, kitchen, and schoolroom, as well as a (nonfunctioning) brew house and a coach house with carriages. Antique toys, costumes, guns, and farm equipment are on display, and even the oatcake, a lowly yet staple element of the Staffordshire diet, is given its due. A quarter of a mile from the house, and particularly good for children, is *Shugborough Park Farm,* a working museum with rare breeds of farm animals, 19th- and early 20th-century farming implements, and demonstrations of traditional farming methods. *Shugborough* also has a café that serves home-cooked food. The mansion, museum, and farm are closed November through *Easter.* There are separate admission charges to all three, but a money-saving, all-inclusive ticket also can be purchased (phone: 1889-881388).

En Route from Shugborough Estate Before going on toward Stafford, 6 miles west of Milford, those who "collect" churches may want to search out the rural masterpiece of Sir Christopher Wren at Ingestre, some 4 miles north. A side road off A513 at the entrance to *Shugborough* leads along the boundary of the estate. Take the right fork at the next junction, go through the hamlet of Tixall, and turn left at a sharp bend in the road, following the sign to Ingestre. The square-towered, 17th-century *Church of St. Mary the Virgin* has all the hallmarks of Wren's style: classical arches, the contrast of plain white pillars, oaken pews, and an ornate ceiling. The beautifully carved pulpit and three-part screen are supposedly the work of Grinling Gibbons. That these two famous men were working in rural Staffordshire is due to Walter Chetwynd, scion of a local landowning family, who built the church (open during daylight hours in summer; otherwise ask for the key next door).

Return to A513 and take the bypass around Stafford. An ancient market town on the river Sow, it dates back to AD 913 but is now a mishmash of old and new. During the Civil War, King Charles and his nephew, Prince

Rupert, stayed at the *Ancient High House* on Greengate Street (now the *Tourist Information Centre and Heritage Centre;* phone: 1785-40204; closed Sundays), and *St. Mary's Church* around the corner suffered the indignity of having its weathercock used as a target by the prince to perfect his shooting. Inside the church is a bust of Izaak Walton, author of *The Compleat Angler* (1653), who was born in Stafford and baptized at the church's Norman stone baptismal font. His restored and rethatched cottage has been made into an angling museum while keen fishermen can fish the nearby Meece Brook (apply for a ticket at the museum). The museum is closed Mondays and November through *Easter;* admission charge (phone: 1785-760278).

Take A34 north another 17 miles to Stoke-on-Trent, otherwise known as the Potteries.

STOKE-ON-TRENT Stoke can be confusing, since what is officially known as Stoke-on-Trent is actually six towns—Tunstall, Burslem, Hanley, Fenton, Longton, and Stoke itself—that have managed to hold on to their individuality despite their federation as one city in 1910; a total of 272,446 people make their homes here today. To complicate matters further, Arnold Bennett, their most famous son, thought of them in terms of only *five* towns. (The reason is unknown, but it has been fancifully suggested that he never mentioned Fenton because of a quarrel with a landlady who was a Fenton native.) Their number notwithstanding, the towns also are known as the Potteries, because most of Britain's pottery, from utilitarian earthenware to fine china, has been manufactured here continuously since the 18th century. Visitors come to tour the Royal Doulton, Spode, Minton, and other factories (tours usually must be arranged in advance) and to browse through china museums and china shops.

Although potting in the area began as far back as the Neolithic period and continued through Roman and Saxon times, the great leap forward came in the mid-17th century, when trade with China introduced tea. The effect on the Potteries was the development of stoneware (harder than porous earthenware) for the pots, caddies, cups, and saucers necessary for the ritual of serving and drinking what would henceforth be the mainstay of British life. The next century saw the rise of the most famous name in English ceramics: Josiah Wedgwood founded his company in 1759 and became synonymous with a particular shade of blue, used as a background to a raised white pattern. Other firms subsequently established themselves. Spode, for instance, has produced its Willow pattern, with only slight variations, since approximately 1780. Although the use of purer clays and the building of canals and later of the railroads allowed an expanding repertoire of elegant tableware to reach growing markets, traditional designs continued. For instance, the Toby jug, a mug in the shape of a well-built gentleman in 18th-century frock coat and cocked hat, still is made.

A sign some 3 miles past Stone (just south of Stoke-on-Trent) and immediately before Tittensor marks the right turn to Barlastan, the site of the

Wedgwood Visitor Centre and Museum, a must-see for pottery aficionados. Located at the modern factory that still produces the famous ceramic dishes, the center features a museum that traces the development of techniques and decorative styles over the two centuries of the Wedgwood company's existence, with a large collection of pieces shown in various period settings. Note the black basalt vase thrown by Josiah Wedgwood himself when he opened his Etruria factory at Stoke in 1769. Another early favorite was the cream-colored Queen's Ware, much favored by Queen Charlotte, wife of George III. The center also contains a demonstration hall where potters and painters show their skills and two shops, one selling first-quality pieces and the other less expensive seconds with slight imperfections. It is closed Sundays November through *Easter;* admission charge (phone: 1782-204141).

For information on other china factories, see *Shopping Spree* in DIVERSIONS. To save time and trouble, take the *China Service,* a bus running from *Easter* through early November that constantly circulates among all the shops, museums, and factories of the potteries. It begins and ends at Stoke's *British Rail* station. For a copy of the brochure *The China Experience,* which lists factories, ceramic museums, and retail shops, as well as a timetable for the *China Service* bus, write to *Stoke-on-Trent Tourist Information Centre, Potteries Shopping Centre,* Quadrant Rd., Hanley, Stoke-on-Trent ST4 1HP, England (phone: 1782-284600). The tourist office is closed Sundays.

Another interesting museum not associated with the factories is the *Gladstone Pottery Museum* (Uttoxeter Rd., Longton; phone: 1782-319232); it features the bottle ovens of a preserved Victorian pottery and also provides demonstrations of pottery making. The museum is closed Sundays and Mondays November through February; admission charge.

BEST EN ROUTE

Moat House *Etruria Hall,* Josiah Wedgwood's family homestead, is incorporated into this recently opened hotel. Although some of the original elements remain, such as the staircase and the oak-paneled study, the overall look of the place is modern. The 143 rooms are well appointed and attractively furnished, and there's a dining room that serves continental fare, as well as a sauna, a solarium, and a gymnasium. Festival Way, Etruria, Stoke-on-Trent (phone: 1782-219000; fax: 1782-284500). Moderate.

En Route from Stoke-on-Trent The itinerary now leaves Staffordshire's industrial areas behind and makes its way north on A520 through glorious countryside toward Buxton, 24 miles away. After Leek, the landscape opens out and the road roller-coasters along up to the *Peak District National Park.* Suddenly stone is everywhere, in walls, on remote farm cottages, and as big, dramatic jagged rocks on hilltops. At a sign proclaiming "Derbyshire" (pronounced *Dar*-bee-sher), the road dips down for the last 3 miles into Buxton.

BUXTON This onetime spa town (pop. 19,502) is a favorite base for touring the *Peak District,* although it is not itself part of the national park. One of the highest towns in England, it is surrounded by protective hills, with the rather cold looking yellow-gray stone of its buildings everywhere softened by trees, bushes, and flowers. The Romans, who discovered the site in AD 79, prized the constant temperature (82F) of the bubbling springs and called their health resort Aquae Arnemetiae, or "The Spa of the Goddess of the Grove." By Tudor times, "taking the cure" was popular, and even Mary, Queen of Scots, who suffered from rheumatism, was allowed occasional visits from 1572 to 1580 while in the custody of the Earl of Shrewsbury. (It might have been self-interest on his part since he suffered from gout.) She stayed at *Buxton Hall,* now the *Old Hall* hotel.

The Buxton of today, however, was created largely in the late 18th century by the fifth Duke of Devonshire, who sought to make it a rival to Bath. The graceful, semicircular *Crescent* (which recently was extensively renovated), the Adams-style *Assembly Rooms* (currently being renovated in their turn), the broad-domed *Great Stables* (now the *Devonshire Royal Hospital*), and the parish *Church of St. John the Baptist* date from this period. Later, the Victorians added the *Pavilion Gardens,* bedecked with flowers and lakes, the *Pump Room,* and the *Octagon* concert hall. By then the railways had shortened the journey from industrial cities such as Stoke and Manchester, so the huge *Palace* hotel (see *Best en Route*) was built above the *Crescent* to accommodate visitors who prized the fresh air as much as the water.

Today, people who want to sample the waters swim in the warm, spring-fed public pool in the *Pavilion Gardens,* since the old thermal baths have been turned into a shopping arcade. Also in the gardens is the *Conservatory,* with several goldfish ponds and greenhouses with flowering plants. The *Crescent* contains the tourist information office (phone: 1298-25106; open daily) and a public drinking fountain, also spring fed; the water is tastier than in most spas, but be careful, it's a bit hot. The *Pump Room* next door houses the *Buxton Micrarium,* a museum where the exhibits—live microscopic specimens—are seen projected onto large TV-style screens. It is closed early November through late March; admission charge (phone: 1298-78662). Otherwise, a popular pastime is simply to linger in the *Pavilion Gardens,* enjoy the blooms in the *Conservatory,* and watch the river Wye rush by—perhaps with something delicious to flavor the view, like the ginger parkin, ginger slab cakes, Ashbourne gingerbread cookies, or gingerbread men from *The Gingerbread Shop* (in Spring Gardens; phone: 1298-23752). The *Buxton Antiques Fair* in May draws a moderate number of devotees, and the three-week *Buxton Festival* of music and the arts, held in July, is well known (see *Best Festivals* in DIVERSIONS).

BEST EN ROUTE

Palace Opened in 1870, this is grand in a truly Victorian manner, with a stately staircase, chandeliers, and lofty ceilings. The 122 bedrooms (33 nonsmoking) are prettily decorated and comfortable, suiting 20th-century tastes. Don't worry about eating too much in the carvery; you can work off the calories in the men's and women's gyms and saunas, as well as in the heated pool. Palace Rd., Buxton (phone: 1298-22001; fax: 1298-72131). Inexpensive.

En Route from Buxton Edale and Castleton, other *Peak District* villages, are only about 10 miles northeast. Take A6, which climbs steeply up behind Buxton and then dips down to Chapel-en-le-Frith, and from there take A625 up Rushup Edge. Little sheep farms shelter in deep valleys and moorlands stretch away, smooth except for rocky crags and perhaps a few trees. After about 4 miles, a sign for Edale indicates a sharp left turn just before a copse of trees and a car park at the base of a steep hill. This is the back of Mam Tor, or "Mother Hill," known to the locals as Shivering Mountain because the combination of sandstone and shale can become unstable when wet, leading to rock slides. Park in the car park and take the path (a 10-minute or so walk) to the summit, where an Iron Age fort once stood. The view suddenly opens out along the circle of hills and down into a patchwork quilt of brown and green seamed by gray drystone walls: the Vale of Edale.

Back in the car, follow the sign to the village of Edale, on the river Noe. There is not much to the village, but since it is the start of the Pennine Way, the long-distance footpath that ends just over the Scottish border, it's known to walkers all over the country. Note that proper gear is necessary for anything longer than an hour's hike in this area, because even on a fine day a squall can blow over, or mists set in.

Beyond Edale, the valley road follows the river Noe and then rejoins A625 at Hope, where a right turn leads to Castleton.

BEST EN ROUTE

Poachers Arms Comfortable and well-tended, it has six large bedrooms and a restaurant serving home cooking. Reservations advised. Castleton Rd., Hope (phone: 1433-620380). Inexpensive.

CASTLETON This small village (only 881 residents) is another popular base for excursions into the *Peak District*—consult the *Peak District National Park Information Centre* (Castle St.; phone: 1433-620679), which is closed weekdays November through March. The town is set in the romantic shadow of the 12th-century *Peveril Castle,* a ruined Norman construction described by Sir Walter Scott in *Peveril of the Peak.* Along the main street are souvenir shops selling jewelry and other items made of "Blue John," a semiprecious stone prized for its striations of brown fading into yellow and pink into a deep purple-blue. Found only in Castleton, the stone was discovered by the Romans, and vases made of it even surfaced in the ruins of Pompeii. The *Blue John Mine and Cavern,* just west of the village, taps eight of the 14 veins in the vicinity. It is open for guided tours daily; admission charge (phone: 1433-620638).

The village is also known for its *Garland Ceremony,* held each year on May 29, *Oak Apple Day.* The celebration is said to commemorate the restoration of Charles II to the throne, but some hold that it goes as far back as pagan times. In any case, a "king" in 17th-century costume is led on horseback along the street to the village church, where the enormous bell-shaped floral arrangement that has virtually covered him is removed and put into position on top of the tower, which is itself covered in oak leaves.

BEST EN ROUTE

Castle A comfortable place just opposite the information center. A modernization performed several years ago may have dislodged the ghost of a jilted bride whose wedding breakfast at the inn was canceled. There are nine rooms (three with four-poster beds and Jacuzzis) and a restaurant. Castle St., Castleton (phone: 1433-620578; fax: 1433-621112). Moderate.

Ye Olde Nags Head This 17th-century coaching inn has eight bedrooms (three with four-poster beds). It's also good for a meal, since it's known for good food and a snug atmosphere, with open fireplaces to relieve chilly weather. Open daily. Reservations unnecessary. Major credit cards accepted. Cross St., Castleton (phone: 1433-620248; fax: 1433-621604). Inexpensive.

En Route from Castleton Leave Castleton the way you came, via A625, and retrace your route through Hope to Hathersage, a distance of about 2 miles.

HATHERSAGE This pretty little village is only 5 miles (as the crow flies) from the outskirts of the major industrial city of Sheffield, but judging by its rural, pastoral quality, it might as well be 50 miles. Situated on the river Derwent, its origins predate the Norman Conquest and even the Romans, and its name could come from "Heather's Edge." The moors certainly spread out in all directions when viewed from the vantage point of *St. Michael's,* the 14th-century church on the hill. A few steps from the porch of the church, between two old yew trees, is the 14-foot-long grave of the "friend and lieutenant" of Robin Hood, Little John. It is said that he grew up here, was apprenticed to a nail maker, and died in a nearby cottage (and the legend continues with a well and cave not far away named for Robin Hood). A tall tale perhaps, but the grave, when opened, was found to contain a thighbone 30 inches long; whoever was buried in it must have been a tall man, particularly for those early times.

St. Michael's is interesting also for the 15th-century brass portraits of the local Eyre family. Charlotte Brontë, who stayed at the vicarage during a visit here in 1845, used that name along with a description of the village and the surrounding countryside in *Jane Eyre,* although the name of the village was changed to Morton. Inquire at the vicarage about rubbing the Eyre brasses.

BEST EN ROUTE

George A 16th-century coaching inn. The 18 bedrooms (one with a four-poster) have up-to-date furnishings and amenities, but the stone walls and beamed ceilings in the bar and restaurant preserve the atmosphere of yore. Main Rd., Hathersage (phone: 1433-650436; fax: 1433-650436). Inexpensive.

Hathersage Inn A small Georgian-period inn, it has 15 rooms. Hearty breakfasts make it popular for visitors, and there is a restaurant, candlelit in the evening. Main Rd., Hathersage (phone: 1433-650259; fax: 1433-651199). Inexpensive.

En Route from Hathersage Take B6001 south through the wooded valley of the river Derwent. The itinerary now heads into the Dales, and even before Grindleford (about a mile from Hathersage) the landscape begins to change, taking on a gentler aspect. In Grindleford, turn right onto B6521 for Eyam, about 2 miles farther.

EYAM Pronounced *Ee*-em, this town was ravaged by the Great Plague of 1665–1666 and has ever since been known as the Plague Village. Two days after the arrival of a shipment of contaminated cloth from London, the local tailor fell ill and died. Soon, the telltale signs of "swellings and rose-red rash" began to spread, creating panic. In a decision of extraordinary self-sacrifice, the villagers, led by their vicar, cut themselves off from the world to contain the disease. People from the surrounding countryside left food for them by a well nearly a mile away; money left in payment was "disinfected" with vinegar. Now, wooden plaques by the door of cottage after cottage around the church in the old village center record the death toll.

Each year, on the last Sunday in August, a special service in remembrance of the plague is held in nearby Cucklet Dell, where the villagers held their own services during the plague year. Not all ceremonies in Eyam are somber, however, because this is one of several towns in Derbyshire where the tradition of well dressing (placing flowers around a well) continues. Here it takes place at the end of August or the beginning of September as part of a week of carnival that's complete with village sports and a whole sheep roasted on a spit set up between the church and manor house.

En Route from Eyam Take B6521 Bakewell road to A623 and turn left, passing the stone quarry and heading for Calver (pronounced *Car*-ver). Just after the traffic lights, slow down. On the left is the *Derbyshire Craft Centre,* a small shop full of well-made and well-priced gifts from woolen scarves and jewelry to children's toys, brass, pottery, and glass. The attractive pale wood "eating house" here is a good place for a simple lunch or coffee and cake—all the food is homemade. Open daily (phone: 1433-631231).

A few miles farther along is Baslow; take A619 for Bakewell around the roundabout and almost immediately turn right again. The next 12 miles of the route—Baslow-to-Baslow via Bakewell and two of England's most fascinating stately homes—trace a loop through typical White Peak countryside, with the rivers Wye and Derwent cutting deep into the grass-covered limestone hills, softening the landscape and adding charm to already picturesque villages.

BAKEWELL The town is a popular base for excursions into the southern *Peak District,* but it is also famous for Bakewell pudding, which dates from 1860 or so when a cook misunderstood a recipe for a jam tart and came up with something that a certain Mrs. Wilson later began selling in a cottage on the square. The *Old Original Bakewell Pudding Shop* (phone: 1629-812193) still draws queues of tourists, and the "secret recipe" produces a tempting combination of puff pastry and raspberry or strawberry jam. If you want to decide for yourself, the shop is just over the bridge past the tourist information center and *Peak District National Park Information Centre* in the *Old Market Hall* (Bridge St.; phone: 1629-813227). Both information centers are open daily. The town's name derives not from these culinary associations but from the Anglo-Saxon terms "bad" for bath or spring and "quell" for well; the warm springs here were known as far back as Roman times.

En Route from Bakewell Take A6 in the direction of Matlock; 2 miles farther along there are signs for *Haddon Hall,* the first of the two stately homes in this loop of the itinerary (the car park is on the right, across from the main gate).

HADDON HALL This stately home is sometimes overlooked in favor of its more famous neighbor, *Chatsworth* (which you'll visit next), but that is a mistake, since *Haddon Hall* is a gem of a medieval house. Set on a hill overlooking the peacefully flowing river Wye, it has all the towers, chimneys, gargoyles, and castellations typical of medieval days. Although its ownership dates back to an illegitimate son of William the Conqueror, most of the house was built from the 14th to the 16th centuries. The 14th-century banqueting hall has a minstrel's gallery and high-beamed ceilings, the chapel boasts delicate 15th-century murals, and the beautiful late-16th-century *Long Gallery* has leaded glass windows staggered along its 110-foot length, creating a surprisingly light room for its time.

One of *Haddon Hall*'s characters was Sir George Vernon, a 16th-century owner whose nickname was "King of the Peak." A dominating personality, he wanted his daughter, Dorothy, to marry the Earl of Leicester, who held the favor of Queen Elizabeth I. Dorothy refused, however, and while friends and relations were in the *Long Gallery* celebrating the wedding of her older sister, she stole away to elope with John Manners, son of the Earl of Rutland. Eventually the couple was forgiven; indeed, when Sir George died in 1567, the estate passed to them and is still owned by the Dukes of Rutland. Stroll through the fragrant rose gardens, take a good look at the medieval kitchen with its log box, huge stone fireplace, and meat-salting trough, and pause as the clock in the courtyard weakly chimes the hours. *Haddon Hall* is closed Mondays, Sundays during July and August, and October through *Easter;* admission charge (phone: 1629-812855).

BEST EN ROUTE

Jarvis Peacock Built as a manor house in the 17th century and at one time used as the dower house for *Haddon Hall,* this is now a small, 14-room hotel with gleaming antiques, warming fireplaces, and quiet gardens stretching to the river Derwent. The hotel has fishing rights on both the Derwent and the Wye, so the hotel is popular with fishermen. The restaurant has a good reputation and a local following, especially for Sunday lunch. Open daily. Reservations advised. Major credit cards accepted. Rowsley, near Matlock (phone: 1629-733518; fax: 1629-732671). Moderate.

En Route from Haddon Hall After visiting *Haddon Hall,* continue to the next stately home on this route, *Chatsworth.* It's reached by taking A6 another 2 miles to the pretty stone village of Rowsley and there turning left onto B6012, which passes through a large white gate and into the *Chatsworth* estate shortly after Beeley.

CHATSWORTH Severely classical on the outside, splendidly Baroque on the inside, the magnificent home of the Duke and Duchess of Devonshire is set in an estate of more than 1,000 acres. *Chatsworth* is closed November through *Easter;* admission charge (phone: 1246-582204). For more information, see *Stately Homes and Great Gardens* in DIVERSIONS. The little walled village of Edensor (pronounced Ed-*den*-za), just before the northern gate of the vast park nearby, is an estate village with its own church and a post office that serves tea, although not year-round.

BEST EN ROUTE

Cavendish Set on the *Chatsworth* estate, this former inn is now a luxurious country-house hotel with 23 bedrooms. There's also fly-fishing on some 10 miles of the Derwent and Wye, and once you've built up an appetite, you can dine in the elegant restaurant. Also see *Rural Retreats* and *Gone Fishing* in DIVERSIONS. Baslow (phone: 1246-582311; 800-235-5845; fax: 1246-582312). Expensive to moderate.

En Route from Chatsworth From Baslow, take A619 to Chesterfield, famous for its crooked spire. Then take A617 southeast to the M1, cross it, and follow signs to *Hardwick Hall,* an elegant *National Trust* property about 15 miles from *Chatsworth.*

HARDWICK HALL Elizabeth, Countess of Shrewsbury, better known as Bess of Hardwick, made a pile of money through four very lucrative marriages, and she poured all of it into this tall, H-shaped manor house, a wonderful, well-preserved remnant of the late Elizabethan era. Hubby number two had been Sir William Cavendish, from whom she inherited the original *Chatsworth;* hubby number four, the Earl of Shrewsbury, threw her out of *Chatsworth,* so at age 70, the legendary Bess engaged Robert Smythson to design what is a surprisingly modern-looking building. Built between 1591 and 1597, it features huge windows and other revolutionary design points (i.e., the positioning of the entrance hall at right angles to the façade; family quarters on the second floor and servants' quarters on the ground floor rather than vice versa).

Hardwick Hall is also famous for its contents: 16th- and 17th-century tapestries hanging in the formal rooms, priceless 16th-century embroideries, excellent examples of Elizabethan furniture, and contemporary portraits of the Cavendish family, who became the Dukes of Devonshire. The fine formal gardens, which include a walled herb garden, and a country park with rare breeds of domestic animals are a further attraction, and there is also a working 18th-century windmill on the grounds. But it is Bess herself who is worth reading about—she took on Elizabeth I and, despite being imprisoned in the *Tower of London* for three months for her cheek, she was one of the most powerful women in the land. *Hardwick Hall* is closed Mondays, Tuesdays, Fridays, and November through March; admission charge (phone: 1246-850430).

BEST EN ROUTE

Chesterfield A good, 73-room, Edwardian-style hotel, opposite the railroad station; its *Bejeranu's* restaurant offers traditional English food, and there's a leisure center. Malkin St., Chesterfield (phone: 1246-271141; fax: 1246-220719). Inexpensive.

En Route from Hardwick Hall Continuing south on M1 en route to Nottingham (20 miles away), fans of D. H. Lawrence may want to stop at Eastwood (off Exit 27), the dreary mining suburb of Nottingham where the writer was born and grew up (it figures prominently as "Bestwood" in *Sons and Lovers*). Lawrence's humble birthplace (8A Victoria St.; phone: 1773-763312) has been restored to its Victorian appearance. It is closed *Christmas Eve* through *New Year's Day;* admission charge. The *Breach House* (28 Garden Rd.; phone: 1773-719786), the family home from 1887 to 1891 (he called it "Bottoms" in the same novel), is now a re-creation of the workman's cottage described in *Sons and Lovers.* It is open by appointment only; no admission charge. A walking tour of Lawrence sites in Eastwood also would include 8 Walker Street, the family home from 1891 to 1904 (he romanticized it as "Bleak House"), and 97 Lynncroft, where his mother died. *Eastwood Library* (Wellington Pl.; 47 Nottingham Rd.; phone: 1773-712209) houses the *Lawrence Study Room,* with a collection of his books and papers; it's closed Sundays and Wednesdays. The *Eastwood Craft Centre,* around the corner from the birthplace, contains several small workshops where potters, sculptors, and others make and sell their wares. The center itself has no phone; for information, contact the *Leisure Services Division* (phone: 1602-254891).

NOTTINGHAM The first name that springs to mind when you think of this place is Robin Hood, battling away against the evil Sheriff of Nottingham. There is still a sheriff, but whether or not there ever was an outlaw who robbed the rich to feed the poor, all that's left of him now is ballad, legend, a statue of Robin just outside the walls of the castle (which stands on a high rock at the edge of the city center), and several attractions in and around Nottingham which celebrate his famous exploits. The *Tales of Robin Hood* theme center on Maid Marian Way, around the corner from the castle, offers an attraction called "a flight to adventure," where visitors ride a chair lift to flee from the Sheriff of Nottingham in the medieval city out to Sherwood Forest. You also can try to shoot a real longbow and arrow at the center. It is open daily; admission charge (phone: 1602-483284). Most of Sherwood Forest, which once stretched from the outskirts of Nottingham north some 19 miles to the village of Edwinstowe and comprised some 100,000 acres, was chopped down for firewood or dug up by coal mining. It's now shrunk to the 450 acres that make up the *Sherwood Forest Country Park,* just north of Edwinstowe. The park's visitors' center (phone: 1623-824490 or 1623-823202) can provide information on special events such as the *Robin Hood Festival,* held during the last two weeks of July and including storytelling, music, dance, and two jousting tournaments; and the *Robin Hood Pageant,* a program that features fencing demonstrations, falconry, jousting, and medieval banquets, held on the castle grounds from the end of October through the beginning of November. The park is open daily; no admission charge.

Besides Robin Hood, Lord Byron, and D. H. Lawrence, Nottingham and its environs have several other famous sons, including George Green, the 19th-century genius who was a pioneer of modern nuclear physics, and William Booth, the founder of the *Salvation Army.*

Most of the main points of interest in Nottingham itself are clustered around the castle. The original fortress on the spot, dating from the time of William the Conqueror, did not survive the English Civil War, but by the late 17th century a new castle had been built to replace it. In the late 19th century, this in turn became the *Nottingham Castle Museum and Art*

Gallery, exhibiting a good collection of silver, ceramics, and art. Videos about royal Nottingham, sports in Nottingham, and more bring the city's history to life, while the Sherwood Foresters (Notts and Derby Regiment) is commemorated with arms, uniforms, and medals. (A special car is available at the *Gatehouse* to transport visitors who cannot manage the steep climb.) Look outside the castle for Mortimer's Hole, one of many subterranean tunnels carved into the soft sandstone on which Nottingham is built. This one, a secret entrance to the castle, is thought to have been used in the 14th century by 18-year-old King Edward III when he and a small armed band sneaked in to grab Roger Mortimer, his mother's lover, and avenge his father's death by having Mortimer hanged, drawn, and quartered in London. The museum is closed *Christmas;* admission charge on weekends and bank holidays only (phone: 1602-483504).

Below the castle, built into the rock, is the famous white-painted *Ye Olde Trip to Jerusalem* pub (phone: 1602-473171), yet another claimant to the title of "oldest pub in Britain." Sand from the rocky ceiling occasionally drops into the beer, but locals and visitors alike enjoy the Old World atmosphere. Next door is the delightful row of 17th-century cottages that makes up the *Brewhouse Yard Museum of Social History,* featuring period rooms and other displays that re-create daily life in Nottingham 300 years ago. It is open daily; admission charge on weekends and bank holidays only (phone: 1602-483504). Across the street in a 15th-century half-timbered building is the *Lace Centre* (Castle Gate; phone: 1602-413539), with a collection of Nottingham's most famous product. It is open daily; demonstrations of lace making take place Thursday afternoons *Easter* through summer. The excellent *Museum of Costumes and Textiles* (51 Castle Gate; phone: 1602-483504) is next door, as is a small display about Robin Hood. Both are open daily; no admission charge. Other attractions include *Lace Hall* (High Pavement; phone: 1602-484221), in a converted church, where lace making on original machinery is demonstrated. It is open daily; admission charge. The *City of Nottingham Information Bureau* (1-4 Smithy Row; phone: 1602-470661) shows the video *Nottingham History* hourly; it's open daily.

Elsewhere in this busy but spacious city, there are many gardens, parks, and squares. *Wollaton Hall,* an awe-inspiring Elizabethan mansion built from 1580 to 1588, is set on the beautiful grounds of *Wollaton Park,* about 4 miles west of the center. The house contains the city's *Natural History Museum,* while the 18th-century stable block has become an industrial museum. The hall and museums are closed Sundays and October through March; no admission charge on weekdays (phone: 1602-281333). *Newstead Abbey,* about 12 miles north of the center, was built as a priory in the 12th century and converted into a mansion in the 16th century by the ancestors of Lord Byron, who inherited it in 1798. It now contains many of the poet's possessions (it has its own ghost, the Black Friar, which Byron claimed to have seen himself!). The house is closed October through March; the gardens are open daily. There's an admission charge (phone: 1623-793557).

There is one vestige of the Middle Ages that has not only survived but thrived in Nottingham. This is the annual *Goose Fair,* which begins at noon on the first Thursday in October and for three days thereafter transforms 18 acres of the city into something like a huge state fair. Named for the geese originally sold here, the fair dates back to the 13th century.

BEST EN ROUTE

Forte Crest Modern, central, and efficient, this 130-room hotel caters to businesspeople and conventioneers as well as to tourists. There are good views from the top floors. The *Carvery,* with its "as much as you want" roast beef, pork, lamb, and gammon (similar to ham), is always popular. St. James's St., Nottingham (phone: 1602-470131; 800-225-5843; fax: 1602-484366). Moderate.

Royal Moat House International Another modern hotel, convenient to the *Royal Centre* (with the *Theatre Royal* and the *Royal Concert Hall*), this place is large (201 rooms) and always bustling. A glass arcade with tropical plants links restaurants and bars attractively, and the cocktail bar on the top floor overlooks the city. Wollaton St., Nottingham (phone: 1602-414444; fax: 1602-475667). Moderate.

Truffles Located on the east side of the city, this informal restaurant specializes in game and fish dishes such as sea bass. There's also a varied wine list. For dessert, try sticky toffee pudding or chocolate terrine with coffee-bean sauce. Dinner only; closed Sundays and Mondays. Reservations advised. Major credit cards accepted. 43 Broad St., Nottingham (phone: 1602-526116). Moderate.

Loch Fyne Oyster Bar Near the *Town Hall,* this purveyor of seafood receives crabs, lobsters, mussels, oysters, and clams fresh overnight from Scotland. Simple cooking with white wine or cream is all these prime ingredients need—and get. A great place to try a real grilled kipper or to have tea and a cake. Closed Sundays. Reservations advised for dinner. Major credit cards accepted. 17 King St., Nottingham (phone: 1602-508481). Moderate to inexpensive.

En Route from Nottingham From here, you can continue to London (135 miles away) via the M1 motorway south.

East Anglia

When asked what Norfolk was like, one of Noël Coward's characters simply replied "flat!" The same charge is often leveled at the entire East Anglian region of Britain, which includes Suffolk, Essex, and Cambridgeshire, as well as Norfolk. While the label certainly applies to areas such as the Fens in the western part of East Anglia, it is far too dismissive a description of the remaining parts. With its subtle range of gradients and variety of landscapes—wild and sandy heaths, woodlands, salt marshes, tidal creeks, waterways, and even hills and valleys—East Anglia is never monotonous.

Despite its proximity to London, this fat belly of land that reaches out into the North Sea is surprisingly remote and rural. Few highways bisect it—they could serve as routes to nowhere "farther on." In fact, the majority of its thoroughfares are narrow back roads overgrown with grass and just barely able to accommodate the width of two vehicles. The area is thinly populated, too, although this wasn't always the case. During the 15th century it was the center of a prosperous wool trade and one of Britain's most highly populated regions. The largest city, Norwich, was at one time second in size only to London. But when the sheep business began to dwindle, shifting farther north to Yorkshire, people began to drift away. East Anglia was largely unaffected by the Industrial Revolution fervor that swept the country in the late-18th to mid-19th centuries and has remained somewhat of an economic backwater.

Today, while driving through the pastoral East Anglian villages, you'll see plenty of testimonials to their former prosperity and importance. Towns that have faded to a fraction of their former size are dominated by churches magnificent both in terms of scale and Gothic richness. It is hard to travel more than a mile or so without seeing at least one looming on the horizon. These churches were built by the wool merchants partly in thanks to God for his help with their commercial success and partly as unholy status symbols. Today, there may be as few as half a dozen red brick cottages in their shadows, and even fewer parishioners for the Sunday morning service.

Most East Anglian villages are found in the classic format of cottages, church, pub, and local manor house, all clustered around a village green where you may see a local cricket or soccer match. Since the cultivation of food crops, particularly potatoes, sugar beets, and other vegetables, is the area's principal industry, the villages are primarily hardworking farm communities. They cannot match the bijou villages of Britain's more southerly and westerly belts of countryside in Kent, Surrey, Sussex, Berkshire, and Hampshire, with their tea shops, posh "horse brass pubs," and generally precious airs and graces. But the area also is endowed with an unlikely number of grand houses, ranging from "modest" manor farmhouses to the stately mansions of the aristocracy, such as the queen's own favorite retreat at

Sandringham. Most estates, especially those with fine period furnishings, impressive art collections, and beautiful gardens, open their doors to the public in summer, and many serve tea in as grand a setting as you could ever hope to find.

Our route spans two of the area's four counties: Norfolk and Suffolk, land of the North Folk and the South Folk. These were once two distinct groups of people; even today county chauvinism remains strong, although both "sides" share a similar dialect and a unique vocabulary that includes words such as *mardle* (to gossip), *rummun* (a peculiar person), and *squit* (nonsense).

Suffolk is the hillier of the two counties, full of tiny, huddled villages and timber-framed farmhouses, with a coastline indented by finger estuaries and dotted with delightfully old-fashioned seaside resorts. Inland is the leafy, peaceful corner of the country that so inspired the great landscape painter, John Constable. Norfolk has broad, plain-like farmlands and thus far grander horizons. Its coastline, one of the most pristine in Europe, is a moody expanse of salt marshes, tidal creeks, shingle spits, and sandy dunes beloved by sailors ever since Admiral Nelson learned to sail here as a boy. If you can't tour with a hired boat, at least bring binoculars, since flocks of seabirds and waterfowl have chosen its vast acreages as their nesting grounds. Norfolk also has the Broads, a sprawling network of manmade waterways dating from the Middle Ages when peat was cut from the bogs to heat homes and the resulting ditches subsequently flooded. The Broads, too, are best seen from a boat—and soon, before they sink or become silted up, polluted, or commercialized.

The drive outlined below begins not far from Cambridge in Newmarket, Suffolk, and moves east to Bury St. Edmunds before dropping south to wind through wool towns such as Sudbury (a good place to pick up the route for those beginning in London) and Lavenham and dip into the Stour Valley on its way to Ipswich. It hits the Suffolk coast at Aldeburgh, then climbs up the coast into Norfolk. After a visit to the large, rather brash resort of Great Yarmouth, the itinerary turns inland to pass through the Broads, skirting Norwich (covered in detail in THE CITIES). The final leg follows the north coast of Norfolk, visiting such spots as Blakeney, Burnham Overy Staithe, and Brancaster, before culminating at the larger town of King's Lynn.

East Anglia's accommodations range from picturesque village pubs to grand executive hotels in a city such as Norwich. Expect to pay more than $120 per night for a double room (including private bath, TV set, and breakfast, unless otherwise indicated) in those hotels listed as expensive, from $85 to $120 in moderate ones, and less than $85 in spots listed as inexpensive. A dinner for two, excluding wine, drinks, and tips, will cost $60 or more in expensive restaurants; $35 to $60 in those listed as moderate; and less than $35 in the inexpensive ones. All restaurants serve lunch and dinner unless otherwise noted. For each location, hotels and restaurants are listed alphabetically by price category.

CAMBRIDGE The beautiful university city on the Cam is a convenient place to begin a tour of East Anglia; for a detailed report, see *Cambridge* in THE CITIES.

En Route from Cambridge Take A45 northeast to Newmarket, 13 miles away.

NEWMARKET This town of nearly 17,000 residents has long been the center of British horse racing. What began as the hobby of King Charles II (his grandfather, James I, built *King's House* here but was more of a hunting fan) became big business with the establishment of the *Royal Stables* and the founding of the *Jockey Club* to set up guidelines for the sport. Now the *National Stud,* where the kingdom's finest horses are bred, is here, too. Races are held at *Newmarket Heath,* 1½ miles southwest of town, in April, May, October, and November—the most famous are the *One Thousand* and *Two Thousand Guineas,* the *Cambridgeshire,* and the *Cesarewitch.* Nearby Devil's Dyke, an enormous 7½-mile embankment built in the 7th century as a boundary marker or a defense wall, is traditionally used by locals for a free "grandstand" view of the races. The *National Stud* (phone: 1638-663464), also near the racecourse, is open to the public April through September by appointment only. The galleries of the *National Horseracing Museum* (High St.; phone: 1638-667333) trace the development of British racing—there are also changing exhibitions. The museum is closed early December through March, Mondays April through June, and September through early December. There's an admission charge.

BEST EN ROUTE

Swynford Paddocks Once the home of Byron's half sister (and lover) Augusta Leigh, it's now a country hotel, 6 miles southwest of Newmarket. The atmosphere is that of a well-appointed private home, with 15 rooms and a good restaurant. It's necessary to reserve rooms well in advance. Six Mile Bottom, Newmarket (phone: 1638-570234; fax: 1638-570283). Expensive.

En Route from Newmarket Continue on A45 another 14 miles east to Bury St. Edmunds.

BURY ST. EDMUNDS The town (pop. 31,000) was named after the last King of East Anglia, who was martyred by Danish invaders around the year 870. His burial site became a shrine, and an abbey founded around it in the 10th century grew to be one of the richest and most powerful in medieval England. It is now a ruin, with only two gate towers—the *Norman Tower* and the magnificent 14th-century *Abbey Gatehouse*—to suggest its former scale. The latter, the town's most distinguished landmark, leads into the attractive *Abbey Gardens,* which include a rose garden. Little remains of the abbey church, famous as the spot where the barons conspired to force King John to ratify the *Magna Carta*.

The *Theatre Royal* (Westgate St.; phone: 1284-755127) is a late-Georgian playhouse designed by William Wilkins, who also did the *National Gallery* in London. It can be toured by visitors Mondays through Saturdays when performances are not underway (admission charge). The *Market Cross Art Gallery* (on Guildhall St., off Cornhill St.; phone: 1284-762081), also originally a theater, was designed by the well-known Scottish architect Robert Adam, and is the only one of his buildings in East Anglia. The gallery is closed Sundays and Mondays; admission charge. On display in *Manor House Museum* (Honey Hill; phone: 1284-757072) is the impressive *Gershom Parkington Collection of Clocks and Watches,* dating from the 16th century onwards. The museum is open daily; admission charge. On Wednesdays and Saturdays, a market is held in the middle of town, spilling over into Buttermarket and Cornwall Streets. The Wednesday market features livestock; on Saturdays, the offerings range from copper and brass items and clothing to farm-fresh fruits and vegetables. Many of the vendors have been selling their wares at this market for years (even for generations).

BEST EN ROUTE

Angel When Charles Dickens stayed at this 15th-century, creeper-covered hotel (which he immortalized in his *Pickwick Papers*), he "had a fine room," now No. 15 and still available but with better plumbing. There's also the Louis Phillipe suite, where the eponymous duke lived for 18 months while in exile from France in the 18th century. Opposite the *Abbey Gatehouse,* owned and run by the warmhearted Gough family, this 41-room establishment (four rooms have four-posters) is the social hub of town, and its lounge is particularly popular for afternoon tea (meals are served as well). Angel Hill, Bury St. Edmunds (phone: 1284-753926; fax: 1284-750092). Expensive.

Ravenwood Hall Dating back to Henry VIII's time, this privately owned hotel with 14 rooms (some located in a separate annex) is set on seven acres of lawns and woodland. The ornately carved oak structure is decorated with 16th-century wall paintings. The restaurant, formerly a Tudor living hall, has beautiful carved timbers and a huge fireplace. Other facilities include a bar, an outdoor pool, tennis, and horseback riding. Rougham, Bury St. Edmunds (phone: 1359-70345; fax: 1359-70788). Expensive to moderate.

Mortimer's A restaurant of excellent value, specializing in fish freshly caught from the nearby coast, followed by refreshing desserts such as sorbet or syllabub. Closed Saturday lunch and Sundays. Reservations advised. Major credit cards accepted. 30 Churchgate St., Bury St. Edmunds (phone: 1284-760623). Moderate.

En Route from Bury St. Edmunds Take A134 15 miles south to Long Melford.

LONG MELFORD The old houses of this beauty of a village stretch for 3 miles along the main road, hence the "long" in its name. At the core, they expand around a huge village green. Like its neighbors, Long Melford was a thriving wool town during the 15th century, a circumstance that generated enough money to build the great *Holy Trinity Church* at the top end of the green. Former prosperity is reflected in its ornate flint "flushwork," exquisite stone and woodcarvings, and the 100 elegant windows (including one of priceless stained glass) that ignite the interior on the gloomiest winter day.

Melford Hall and *Kentwell Hall* are Long Melford's two grandest houses. *Melford Hall,* opposite the church on the other side of the green, was built by William Cordell, a 16th-century statesman important enough to have been visited by Queen Elizabeth I. The house was eventually sold to the Parker family, one of whose descendants still lives here. Elizabethan and highly turreted, this *National Trust* property houses an impressive collection of Chinese porcelain treasures captured from a Spanish galleon by one of the Parker family's famous admirals. Beatrix Potter fans will find a permanent exhibition dedicated to the famous author and her "friends." *Melford Hall* is closed November through March, on weekdays in April and October, and Mondays, Tuesdays, and Fridays May through September. There's an admission charge (phone: 1787-880286).

Kentwell Hall, another red brick Tudor manor surrounded by a broad moat, lies at the end of an avenue of limes north of the village. It combines a mixture of styles as large parts were gutted by fire in the early 19th century and were subsequently remodeled. The gardens are especially worth seeing, particularly the walled garden, moated like the house. Re-creations of Tudor life are staged for schoolchildren. *Kentwell Hall* is open daily late July through September and Sundays only April through late July and in October. There's an admission charge (phone: 1787-310207).

BEST EN ROUTE

Chimneys Sophisticated versions of country fare are the main courses in this beamed village house. For dessert, there are puddings such as vanilla soufflé with a bitter chocolate sauce. Closed Sunday evenings. Reservations necessary. Major credit cards accepted. Hall St., Long Melford (phone: 1787-379806). Expensive.

En Route from Long Melford Sudbury is 3 miles farther south of Long Melford on A134.

SUDBURY Another town that grew prosperous as a center of the wool trade, Sudbury, with a population of 10,000, is far larger than its peers, thanks mainly to its commercial importance on the navigable river Stour. It has three Perpendicular churches—*St. Gregory's, St. Peter's,* and *All Saints'*—as well as a stock of typical medieval houses, but its most attractive buildings are Georgian. These include several three-story weavers' cottages that are recognizable from their wide floor-to-ceiling windows where the looms used to stand. The town's main claim to fame is as the birthplace of one of the greatest British painters, Thomas Gainsborough, whose father, a wool merchant, raised nine children at 46 Sepulchre Street (now Gainsborough Street). Their elegant townhouse still stands as an art gallery and museum of Gainsborough's life and work, much of which featured the local landscape, including the *Auberies,* an estate 2 miles outside of Sudbury used in the background of his *Mr. and Mrs. Andrews,* now hanging in London's *National Gallery.* The gallery and museum are closed Mondays; admission charge (phone: 1787-372958).

En Route from Sudbury B1115 followed by B1071 lead northeast 6 miles from Sudbury to Lavenham. The town announces its presence from some distance away, the finely tapered tower of *St. Peter and St. Paul Church* looming larger than a cathedral above the horizon. If its eight bells happen to peal at the time of your arrival, the impact is overwhelming.

LAVENHAM Of all the old wool towns, this gem, with over 300 listed buildings, is certainly the best preserved—and the most visited by tourists in summer. It is every foreigner's dream of England and the reality of numerous filmmakers, since the main street has starred in many a period production. The town looks today as it has since the 15th and 16th centuries, when most of its buildings were constructed. The single most famous of these is the *Guildhall of Corpus Christi,* a timber-framed Tudor building that is hard to miss in the marketplace. Built in 1529 and owned by the *National Trust,* it is home to a local history museum and a beautiful walled garden. It is closed November through March; admission charge (phone: 1787-247646). The *Angel* hotel (phone: 1787-247388), a very old pub in the marketplace, is popular with locals and visitors alike; also see *Pub Crawling* in DIVERSIONS.

BEST EN ROUTE

Great House This French-owned hotel has four large bedrooms with separate sitting rooms. The 14th-century building is decorated with antiques and tasteful accessories. There is a candlelit French restaurant with a fireplace, as well as a paved courtyard where lunch and dinner are served during good weather. The hotel is open February through December. The restaurant is closed Sunday evenings, Mondays, and January. Reservations advised. MasterCard and Visa accepted. Market Pl., Lavenham (phone: 1787-247431; fax: 1787-248080). Expensive.

Swan A wonderfully preserved 15th-century inn, with most of its timbers twisted and gnarled with age, it has 47 comfortable rooms (two with four-posters). There is also a lovely flower-filled courtyard and a separate, heavily beamed restaurant with a minstrels' gallery. High St., Lavenham (phone: 1787-247477; fax: 1787-248286). Expensive.

En Route from Lavenham The road to Hadleigh (A1141), 8 miles farther, is a hilly, rather twisty route. About halfway, off A1141, stands Chelsworth, often bypassed but an absolute delight of old houses, riverside, and graceful trees. Fifteen of its gardens are open to the public on the last Sunday in June.

HADLEIGH Nestled in the valley of the river Brett, Hadleigh (pop. 5,858) was another important center of the wool and grain trades. The town lies between two bridges—the Iron Bridge, crossed when approaching from the northwest, and the attractive, three-arched Toppesfield Bridge, crossed on the way southeast to Layham. Despite the steady stream of traffic, the town is still fine-looking (although without the timeless air of Lavenham) and has figured in many a painting and photograph of rural Britain. The elegant, lead-covered spire of *St. Mary's Church* is as it was in the 15th century and its peal of bells still rings out across the valley (the 600-year-old *Angelus Bell* is inscribed with a worthy sentiment—unfortunately someone forgot to invert the words and they came out of the mold back to front). Inside, in addition to the "ringers' gotch," a jug reserved for the thirsty bell ringers' ale, there are two beautiful 15th-century screens and a 14th-century octagonal font with a paneled pedestal and rich tapestry on the bowl.

En Route from Hadleigh Head south on B1070. Just beyond Holton St. Mary turn right onto A12 and then left down B1029 to Dedham, a total distance of 7 miles.

DEDHAM AND THE STOUR VALLEY This slice of countryside on the border between Suffolk and Essex Counties is known as Dedham Vale, but it's often simply referred to as "Constable country." Specifically, the term refers to a collection of villages that line the valley of the river Stour, each one either painted by the great British artist or otherwise linked to his life. "I associate my careless boyhood with all that lies on the banks of the Stour; these things made me a painter, and I am grateful," he once remarked. Prepare to do some walking along the riverside to best appreciate Constable country. The swiftly flowing river, fringed with reeds, winds through silent marshes and gentle farmland, while the wide skies overhead reveal ever-changing cloud patterns, illuminating a landscape of serene beauty.

Begin your explorations with Dedham, an elegant town of Tudor and Georgian shops, houses, and inns that appears frequently on Constable's canvases—although the painter often indulged in considerable artistic license, changing the location of landmarks (such as *Dedham Church*) to suit his aesthetic purposes. Dedham's old *Sun* hotel is still in its rightful position on High Street, as are the old shop fronts and color-washed cottages with their overhanging stories. On the other side of the river is East

Bergholt, where the painter was born in 1776. Although it has suffered somewhat as an object of pilgrimage, it is still a pleasant village of Georgian houses, and its church has an unfinished tower whose bells are enthusiastically rung by hand every Sunday. Constable's home no longer survives, but the cottage attached to the post office was his studio, and the graves of his parents and of Willy Lott (see below) are in the churchyard.

Flatford Mill, on the Stour a mile south of East Bergholt, was the subject of a painting of the same name, Constable's first important large canvas (it now hangs in the *Tate Gallery* in London). The mill's quiet pond and, beyond it, *Willy Lott's House* (where the mill hand reputedly lived for 88 years) are instantly recognizable as the setting for *The Hay Wain* (in the *National Gallery*). Neither building is open to the public. Nearby *Bridge Cottage* houses an exhibition of Constable's working methods as seen through his sketches. It is open daily June through September; Wednesdays through Sundays in April, May, and October; only Sundays in November. There's no admission charge (phone: 1202-298260).

BEST EN ROUTE

Maison Talbooth Another Victorian house on the banks of the Stour. To say that each of its 10 bathrooms has its own bedroom is a good indication of the grandeur of this country-house hotel, one of Britain's best. The rooms are named after such authors as Kipling and Shakespeare. Breakfast is served in your room, but dinners are taken at *Le Talbooth* (under the same ownership; see below), a quarter of a mile farther on; a courtesy car will take you there. Stratford Rd., Dedham (phone: 1206-322367; 800-635-3612; fax: 1206-322752). Expensive.

Le Talbooth This 16th-century timber-framed building with picturesque gardens on the riverbank has been, in its time, a tollhouse, a weaver's cottage, and a tea house. It's now a restaurant, one of the culinary centers of the county, with a classic menu. Open daily. Reservations advised. Major credit cards accepted. Gun Hill, Dedham (phone: 1206-323150). Expensive.

En Route from Dedham Pick up A137 and continue 11 miles to Ipswich, passing through Brantham, where the altarpiece in the 14th-century church, depicting Christ blessing children, was painted by Constable.

IPSWICH Its prime location at the head of the river Orwell has made Ipswich, the capital of the county of Suffolk, a busy port since Anglo-Saxon times; its population today is 120,000. The town's history lives in its street names (Westgate and Northgate, for example, are all that remain of the old town wall) and in its medieval churches and merchants' and sea captains' houses. The *Great White Horse* hotel (on Tavern St.), where Charles Dickens stayed, is recognized even today as a setting in his famous novel, *The Pickwick Papers.* The tourist information center (St. Stephen's La.; phone: 1473-

258070) supplies an excellent *Town Trail Guide* describing walking tours of the city's cobbled streets that will take you past rows of interesting houses. It is closed Sundays.

Two of the most notable buildings in Ipswich are *Christchurch Mansion* (at *Christchurch Park,* in the northern part of the city) and the *Ancient House* (in the Butter Market; phone: 1473-257761). *Christchurch Mansion,* a 16th-century Tudor townhouse, has become a museum with a collection of antique furniture; paintings by Constable, Rubens, Reynolds, and Gainsborough; and an outstanding collection of the decorative arts, china, and glass. It's closed Mondays; no admission charge (phone: 1473-253246). The *Ancient House,* now a bookshop, also dates to the 16th century and has an exceptional display of decorative pargeting, or painted plasterwork, on its façade.

BEST EN ROUTE

Hintlesham Hall A luxurious country-house hotel with 33 rooms, it also offers sports facilities and an outstanding restaurant. For more information, see *Rural Retreats* in DIVERSIONS. Hintlesham (phone: 1473-652268; 800-525-4800; fax: 1473-652463). Expensive.

Belstead Brook This creeper covered part-Jacobean manor with extensive gardens is about 2 miles southwest of town. Its 92 rooms (six are garden suites) are distributed between the original part of the building and a modern addition; all are decorated in contemporary style. Belstead Rd., Ipswich (phone: 1473-684241; fax: 1473-681249). Moderate.

Marlborough A red brick, 22-room Victorian townhouse on the far side of *Christchurch Park,* it is noted for its quiet traditional atmosphere and its thoughtful service, particularly in the restaurant. 73 Henley Rd., Ipswich (phone: 1473-257677; fax: 1473-226927). Moderate.

En Route from Ipswich The lovely little town of Woodbridge is 8 miles farther northeast along A12.

WOODBRIDGE This boating town (pop. 7,700) is at the head of the long shallow estuary of the river Deban (pronounced *Deeb*'n). It was once prosperous as a commercial port and shipbuilding center, but its boatyards and moorings are now predominantly occupied by pleasure craft, and the town thrives as a center for holidays afloat. Its maritime past resulted in a wealth of historic buildings, from the *Elizabethan Shire Hall,* now used as a magistrates court, to the *Woodbridge Tide Mill,* an old weatherboarded mill on the waterfront, restored to working order so that visitors can see just how it harnessed the power of the tide to drive its corn-grinding machinery. It's closed November through April and weekdays in October; admission charge (phone: 1743-626618).

Seckford Hall The gabled roof, mullioned windows, beamed ceilings, and huge fireplaces are all authentic—because this country-house hotel about a mile southwest of town is a remarkably well-preserved Tudor mansion. Ten of the 33 bedrooms are in converted stables around a courtyard. Breakfasts are so huge they'll set you up for a day's walking in the 34 acres of woods and gardens. There's also a pool set in a Tudor barn and a gym. Off A12, Woodbridge (phone: 1394-385678; fax: 1394-380610). Expensive.

Old Rectory The English cooking in this rambling 17th-century rectory is both adventurous and delicious. Main courses often are served family style, and the menus are substantial—try Muscovy duck with apricots and ginger, followed by upside-down ginger cake. The house also offers accommodations in nine rooms. The restaurant is closed Sunday evenings and Mondays through Saturdays for lunch. Reservations necessary. Major credit cards accepted. To reach it from Woodbridge, take B1069 to Tunstall and turn left onto B1078. Campsea Ashe (phone: 1728-746524). Inexpensive.

En Route from Woodbridge Follow B1438 a mile north to Melton, turn right, and continue about 12 miles along A1152 and B1069 to Snape; Aldeburgh is 5 miles from Snape on A1094. Along the way, a couple of miles out of Woodbridge, a sign points the way to *Sutton Hoo,* near Rendlesham, where one of the greatest archaeological discoveries in Britain was made in the 1930s. Ancient Saxon kings were buried in ships, surrounded by all their treasures (a ship burial is described in *Beowulf*), and this was the site chosen by the Saxon Kings of East Anglia for their burial ground. One of several mounds excavated here yielded the remains of an approximately 85-foot-long wooden ship stuffed with priceless 7th-century objects in gold, silver, and iron—coins, jewelry, dishes, spears—as well as a jeweled sword, shield, and helmet (no body was found, leading to the conclusion that this particular king, whoever he was, was buried elsewhere). The spectacular loot is now in the *British Museum.* Public access to the site is by guided tours given on weekend afternoons, April through August (admission charge), but you can see quite a lot from the nearby footpath (phone: 1473-265204).

SNAPE AND ALDEBURGH Snape is famous for *Snape Maltings,* a complex of old buildings used to store barley in the 19th century. In the late 1960s, one of the buildings was converted into the magnificent *Maltings Concert Hall,* and every June most of the main events of the *Aldeburgh Music Festival,* one of Britain's best, are held here. (For more information, see *Best Festivals* in DIVERSIONS.) The complex also contains a public house called *The Plough and Sail,* which originally served the maltsters, whose photos decorate the bar; a crafts shop; an art gallery (displaying mainly contemporary works by East Anglian artists); a country store; and a tea shop. All are open daily.

The festival's remaining events take place in the seaside town of Aldeburgh itself (the name is Old English for Old Borough) as well as in churches and stately homes in the vicinity. Until the festival brought it renown, Aldeburgh was a fisherman's preserve—operagoers might recognize it as the setting of Benjamin Britten's *Peter Grimes.* A walk through the town is worthwhile: After centuries of erosion, the wide High Street is only a pebble's throw from the shingle beach. In fact, some of medieval Aldeburgh has fallen into the sea. The 16th-century timber-framed *Moot Hall* (more Old English—*moot* means "meeting") stands only yards from the shore, continually bearing the brunt of winter gales, but consult the two maps inside and you'll see that it used to stand in the center of town.

BEST EN ROUTE

Wentworth With 31 rooms, this highly recommended country-house hotel has been owned by the Pritt family since 1920. The hotel, decorated with antiques, has lovely sea views from 12 of the guestrooms, as well as a sunken terrace and a restaurant. Wentworth Rd., Aldeburgh (phone: 1728-452312; fax: 1728-454343). Expensive to moderate.

Crown Opposite the thatch-roofed church in the beautiful village of Westleton, close to Aldeburgh, it has 19 rooms (one has a four-poster bed) and log fires in the common areas. The renowned restaurant serves a choice of fresh fish caught on a line rather than in a net. Richard Price, the proprietor, says it tastes much better that way. Closed *Christmas* and *Boxing Day.* Reservations advised. Major credit cards accepted. Westleton, Saxmundham (phone: 1728-73777; fax: 1728-73239). Moderate.

En Route from Snape and Aldeburgh Take B1122 and hurry through Leiston, an industrial blot on the rural landscape. Bear left here along B1119 and soon the well-preserved ruin of *Framlingham Castle* will loom unexpectedly into view. Begun in 1190, its construction represented an important advance in castle design for the times, since it was built according to the Saracen method, brought back from the Crusades, employing towers linked by massive curtain walls. The towers carry distinctive dummy chimneys, one of several alterations made in the 16th century by the Howards, then Dukes of Norfolk, who inherited the fortress. It was at *Framlingham Castle* that Mary Tudor organized her army to oust Lady Jane Grey from the throne, and later, having succeeded, proclaimed herself queen. Nothing much remains inside the walls now except for some picturesque 17th-century almshouses incorporating fragments of the former great hall, but climb a spiral staircase leading up to the battlements for superb views of Suffolk farmland. The castle is closed Mondays October through March; admission charge (phone: 1728-724189).

The town of Framlingham, 13 miles northwest of Aldeburgh, begins at the castle walls—the back gardens of houses on Castle Street finish at the moat, in fact—and centers on a triangular market square. Since it is so tiny, its narrow streets are best explored on foot, particularly Castle and Church Streets, and the lovely sequence of Georgian cottages on sweeping Double Street.

Leave Framlingham by heading north to Dennington on B1116. This is the only way you'll be able to look back and see the castle in its full glory: The walls rise high above a 40-foot drop into the valley, a sight to make even the most courageous army pause for thought. Then cut northeast (via A1120, A12, and A1095) to Southwold (a distance of 19 miles from Framlingham). Just before the A1095, the grand yet simple 15th-century flint-stone *Holy Trinity Church* in Blythburgh is worth a brief stop. This impressive landmark has been affectionately dubbed the "Cathedral of the Marshes." It has a ceiling carved with angels and on its painted roof and carved bench ends are representations of the seven deadly sins. On August 12, 1944, Joseph Kennedy Jr., the eldest Kennedy brother, flew over this church bound for Germany to carry out a secret mission in a plane packed with explosives—in effect, a flying bomb. The intended target is unknown to this day (although it was probably Berlin), but the bomb blew up too early, and Kennedy was killed.

SOUTHWOLD Even when it was fashionable as an Edwardian bathing resort, Southwold was discreet, elegant, old-fashioned, and charming. During its years of flourishing trade with the Low Countries, the town absorbed certain foreign characteristics and today English cottages mingle with Dutch-style townhouses along the old streets. Other idiosyncracies include seven greens: They mark the sites of houses that burned down in a great fire in 1659 and were never replaced. Among the sights to see, besides the lighthouse on a bracing cliff top, is *St. Edmund's Church,* a very fine Perpendicular-style church with a high pitched hammer-beam roof. Adnam's "real ale" brewery is also in town, its deliveries still made by horse-drawn drays. Its "extra bitter" brew has been called Britain's champion beer by several organizations, including the *Campaign for Real Ale (CAMRA).*

BEST EN ROUTE

Swan Sir Winston Churchill stayed in this ivy-clad Georgian hotel overlooking the market square—he said he enjoyed its "comfortable tranquillity." There are 45 guestrooms, but ask for one of the 18 garden rooms situated around an old bowling green. The fine restaurant (no smoking allowed) has a creative menu. Market Pl., Southwold (phone: 1502-722186; fax: 1502-724800). Moderate.

Crown The Adnam's people who run this hotel are happy to let you taste all their brews. An 18th-century coaching inn, it retains much of its original character, with 12 bedrooms; only 400 yards from the beach. You can eat in the restaurant or the bar—the breakfast kippers are particularly noteworthy. High St., Southwold (phone: 1502-722275; fax: 1502-724805). Moderate to inexpensive.

En Route from Southwold Take B1127 and turn right onto A12 to Great Yarmouth, 24 miles north of Southwold. If it's lunchtime, it's worth a detour to Blundeston (16 miles from Southwold on B1127), where the *Plough Inn* (on Market La.; phone: 1502-730261) has been brought smartly up to date since Barkis, the carter, was housed here in Dickens's *David Copperfield.*

GREAT YARMOUTH The funfairs, amusement arcades, and the constant stream of holidaymakers have all conspired to take their toll on Norfolk's most popular family resort (50,500 people live here year-round). Nevertheless, it is worth seeing, if only to watch the British at play. There's also an older part of town with relics of Great Yarmouth's heyday as a fishing port. The *Tolhouse Museum* (Tolhouse St.; phone: 1493-858900), in a medieval building that was once the town jail, houses local history exhibits (closed Saturdays and October through May; no admission charge), while the *Elizabethan House Museum* (South Quay; phone: 1493-855746) hides a largely 16th-century interior including period rooms behind a Georgian façade (same closing days; admission charge). To get a good view of the town and surrounding area, you can climb 217 steps to the top of the *Nelson Monument.* Open Sundays through Fridays in July and August; admission charge (phone: 1493-855746). The *Maritime Museum* for East Anglia, on the seafront, harks back to Yarmouth's herring fishing days. The museum is closed Saturdays and October through May; admission charge (phone: 1493-842267). If you still fancy fish after a visit, break new gastronomic ground by sampling a Yarmouth bloater, salted and smoked just enough to retain its plumpness.

Beach lovers can enjoy over 15 unbroken miles of magnificent golden sands backed by waves of grass-covered dunes. Yarmouth is also home to one of the largest open-air marketplaces in England. Traditional seafaring pubs include the *Wrestler's Inn* (Market Pl.; phone: 1493-842915)—they claim Lord Nelson stayed here with Lady Hamilton—and the *Dukes Head* (Hall Quay; phone: 1493-859184). Great Yarmouth's *Tourist Information Centre* (at Hall Quay; phone: 1493-846345) is closed weekends.

BEST EN ROUTE

Seafood What you'll find on the menu in this converted Victorian pub depends on the morning's catch at the Lowestoft fish market. Bloaters are a great favorite, or you can select a lobster from the tank, and even shark may be available. Closed Saturday lunch and Sundays. Reservations advised. Major credit cards accepted. 85 North Quay, Great Yarmouth (phone: 1493-856009). Expensive.

En Route from Great Yarmouth Leave Great Yarmouth on A149 and continue northwest toward North Walsham, 24 miles away. Northwest of Caister-on-Sea (at one time a Roman commercial port), the landscape becomes flat and marshy, dotted with windmills. You are now in the famous Norfolk Broads, an area of interconnecting waterways that are, surprisingly, man-made. During the Middle Ages, this densely populated region exhausted its woodland fuel supply and had to resort to the peat marshes around the rivers Bure, Yare, and Waveney for an alternative. Wide but not necessarily deep pits were dug to remove the peat, and when the sea began to rise, flooding the digs, they became the shallow "broads" that are today one of the most popular destinations in Europe for a holiday afloat. The natural rivers and artificial cuttings (called "dykes" or "fleets") link up and meander across north Norfolk, empty into the mud flats of Breydon Water, and eventually meet the sea at Great Yarmouth. Naturally, the best way to explore the 130-some miles of quiet, lock-free, reedy backwaters is by boat. Sailboats or cruisers can be rented in several Broads towns, such as Acle, Potter Heigham, and Stalham, but particularly in the area's two main boating centers, Wroxham and Horning (also see *Wonderful Waterways and Coastal Cruises* in DIVERSIONS).

About 7 miles northwest from Great Yarmouth on A1064, at Burgh St. Margaret, is the *Bygone Village,* a re-creation of a typical small settlement of the 18th and 19th centuries. There are several houses, a pub, a tearoom, a church, and a school, all built around a charming village green and set on 42 acres of woodland. Several of the staff members wear period clothing. Here, visitors can get a taste of what life was like in those times. The village is closed Fridays and Saturdays November through March; admission charge (phone: 1493-369770).

The A149 to North Walsham (where you'll turn left onto B1145 and continue 7 miles to Aylsham) traverses a representative stretch of the distinctive Broads landscape. En route, at Potter Heigham, look for the old bridge that has been the downfall of many a holiday sailor—a favorite pastime for locals is to stand and watch their frantic maneuvering as they try to sail under a bridge with barely any headroom.

Another option from Great Yarmouth is to visit Norwich, capital of Norfolk (see *Norwich* in THE CITIES, for a full description of its attractions, hotels, and restaurants); the city is only 20 miles away via A47 heading west. Aylsham, then, is only 15 miles north of Norwich on A140.

AYLSHAM Make sure you're here on a Monday to catch its enormous market and auction, the biggest for miles around, just outside town on the Norwich Road. After you're through haggling with the vendors, recover in the Queen Anne–style *Black Boy Inn* (phone: 1263-732122) overlooking the main square, because you'll need every ounce of energy for an afternoon walking around *Blickling Hall,* a mile and a half to the northwest (on the north side of B1354). Built in the early 17th century, this is one of the finest *National Trust* properties in the country. Its red brick façade is Jacobean, but the interior was much altered in the 18th century, although the *Long Gallery* contains a remarkable Jacobean ceiling. The staterooms are full of handsome furnishings, paintings, tapestries, and other works of art of various periods. Outside, the parklands include color-matched herbaceous borders, 300-year-old hedgerows, a mile-long lake, a temple, topiary yews, and even a secret garden. *Blickling Hall* is closed November through March, and Thursdays and Saturdays through Mondays in April, May, June, September, and October. There's an admission charge (phone: 1263-733084). Next door is the 17th-century *Buckinghamshire Arms* pub (phone: 1263-732133), an atmospheric place to stop for a drink and some good food (see *Pub Crawling* in DIVERSIONS); there are three guestrooms as well.

En Route from Aylsham Continue 12 miles along B1354 and B1149 to Holt, a market town whose Georgian houses were built after a fire in 1708 destroyed most of the medieval buildings. Cley-next-the-Sea and Blakeney are 5 miles north of Holt on A149. For an interesting side trip along the way, stop at Glandford (take B1156 off A149 for a short distance) and visit its unique *Shell Museum,* displaying thousands of multicolored specimens in all shapes and sizes from all over the world collected by a local traveler, Sir Alfred Jodrell. The museum is closed November through January, Fridays and weekends in February and October, and Sundays March through September. There's an admission charge (phone: 1263-740081).

CLEY-NEXT-THE-SEA AND BLAKENEY Only a mile or so of coast road separates these two towns with a combined population of about 1,800. Despite its name, Cley (rhymes with *sky*) has not been "next the sea" since the 17th century. Walk along the main street, which winds behind the old quay, for a look at its flint-built houses. The village church, largely of the 14th century, is a grandiose building reflecting Cley's former importance as an exporting port of the wool trade, but the town's real landmark is its windmill, a regularly featured "pinup" in local magazines and picture postcards, now converted into a hotel (see *Best en Route*), but open to visitors daily, *Easter* through September; admission charge. East of town, between Cley and Salthouse, is *Cley Marshes,* a nature reserve for migrant birds accessible by permit from its *Visitor Centre* (phone: 1263-740380). It is closed Mondays and November through March; admission charge.

Still another nature reserve is on Blakeney Point, the spit of land that branches away from the Norfolk coastline at Cley. This consists of 1,400 acres of shingle (pebble) beaches, sand dunes capped by marram grass, and flat expanses of mud vacated by each ebb tide. Thousands of birds nest and rear their young on the point, including colonies of common, sandwich, and little terns, plovers, and oyster catchers. You can walk to the tip of Blakeney Point, a *National Trust* area, from Cley (a tough 3-mile hike), or take one of the intimate ferries that ply to and fro from Blakeney, leaving from the quay in front of the *Blakeney* hotel two or three hours on either side of high tide. Note that some areas are roped off during the seabirds' main breeding season (May through July).

BEST EN ROUTE

Morston Hall Though diners don't have much choice about what they'll eat at this restaurant (only one appetizer and one entrée are offered each day), nobody cares because the food is so good. Chef Galton Blackiston always uses the freshest local ingredients—such as sea trout, rhubarb, and wild game—to prepare tasty English fare. Set in a brick house near miles of glorious *National Trust* coastline, this place also offers four guestrooms. The hotel is open March through December; the restaurant is closed Sunday evenings, weekday lunch, and January through February. Reservations necessary. Major credit cards accepted. Morston, 2 miles west of Blakeney (phone: 1263-741041). Expensive.

Blakeney With 57 rooms, this hostelry offers grand views and the highest standards of food and comfort. Its restaurant serves a variety of fish and game dishes, with Holkham venison and Weybourne crab frequently on the menu. There is also an indoor heated pool. The Quay, Blakeney (phone: 1263-740797; fax: 1263-740795). Expensive to moderate.

Cley Windmill One of the most photographed windmills in the country (it dates back to 1824, and its sails and brakewheel are still standing) was converted into a homey guesthouse in the 1980s, but it is still open to non-guests who can climb to the top of its five floors and view the marshes on summer afternoons. There are six bedrooms, four with private baths. No restaurant, but the kitchen provides breakfast for guests (and dinners, on request). Open March through mid-January. No credit cards accepted. Cley (phone: 1263-740209). Moderate.

En Route from Cley-next-the-Sea and Blakeney Continue on A149 another 8 miles to the resort town of Wells-next-the-Sea, passing through the tiny village of Stiffkey (pronounced *Stew*-key), which is famous for its cockles, known as "Stewkey Blues."

WELLS-NEXT-THE-SEA A smashing place to enjoy fish-and-chips, or whelks, for which the Wells' fishermen supply most of the British demand—ships up to 300 tons can be seen unloading their catch. Much of the waterfront has been crassly commercialized, so your time is best spent wandering around the narrow "inland" streets, visiting the several antique dealers and pausing for a draft of real ale at such pubs as the *Globe* (phone: 1328-710206), *Crown* (phone: 1328-862172), and *Edinburgh* (phone: 1328-710120). Or walk along the footpath (paralleling the road on the west side of the harbor) to the old lifeboat house and the magical beach surrounded by dunes beyond.

An interesting side trip from Wells is to detour inland on B1105 about 4 miles to Little Walsingham, where pilgrims streamed during the Middle Ages to visit the shrine of *Our Lady of Walsingham.* Built in 1061 to honor the Virgin Mary, it was subsequently destroyed—along with much of the 12th-century Augustinian priory beside it—and later reconstructed by the Church of England. The priory grounds and remains (notably the arch of the east window, gatehouse, crypt, wells, and refectory) are open daily; admission charge (phone: 1328-820259). A second shrine, the Roman Catholic *Slipper Chapel,* is a mile south of the village. The *Black Lion* pub (phone: 1328-820235) behind the High Street serves lunch and bar snacks.

Five miles farther south at Fakenham, the *Pensthorpe Waterfowl Park and Nature Reserve* has one of the largest collections of ducks, geese, and swans in the world. A network of attractive paths with several designated vantage points enables visitors to see the birds clearly without disturbing them. It's closed *Boxing Day* through *New Year's Day* and weekdays January through *Easter;* admission charge (phone: 1328-851465).

BEST EN ROUTE

Old Rectory This 16th-century manor house with Victorian additions in a hamlet south of Little Walsingham has been entirely a family affair since 1978—Rosamund Scoles running things, her husband, William, doing the odd jobs. The cooking is conservatively English. With just six traditionally furnished rooms, it's utterly peaceful and quiet (fitting for a village called Great Snoring). Great Snoring, between Little Walsingham and Fakenham (phone: 1328-820597; fax: 1328-820048). Expensive.

En Route from Wells-next-the-Sea Return to the A149 coastal road and continue west 2 miles to Holkham, where the beach, backed by Corsican pines, is a wild expanse of dunes and sand whose strange hills, or "meals," were once spits cut off from the mainland. At Holkham, grandly set in a sprawling park, is *Holkham Hall,* an 18th-century mansion originally built for Thomas Coke, the Earl of Leicester and an agriculturalist (potatoes were his specialty). The mansion is enormous and ornate, its interior containing works by Rubens and Gainsborough, plus tapestries, statues, and period furnishings. The grounds, laid out by Lancelot "Capability" Brown in 1762, include old walled gardens (now a garden center) and an artificial lake inhabited by Canadian geese. *Holkham Hall* also has an exhibit of several thousand "bygones"—old agricultural and craft tools, cars, carriages—set up in the stable buildings. It is closed Fridays, Saturdays, and October through May; admission charge (phone: 1328-710227). The Burnhams are 3 miles farther west on A149.

THE BURNHAMS Burnham Overy Staithe is one of a cluster of several villages here that begin with "Burnham." Britain's seafaring hero, Admiral Horatio

Nelson, was born in the rectory at Burnham Thorpe in 1758. Although the rectory has since been torn down, the restored church has a lectern made of timbers taken from Nelson's flagship, *Victory,* and the *Lord Nelson* pub (phone: 1328-738321) is full of the admiral's memorabilia. Burnham Market has Georgian houses and old-fashioned stores.

En Route from the Burnhams Continue on A149 another 4 miles to Brancaster, which is a delightful sailing center, even though the salt marshes are exposed at low tide and harbor access is therefore restricted to two or three hours before and after high tide. The nature reserve at Scolt Head, a 3½-mile shingle spit, attracts many birds, notably red-beaked oyster catchers and several varieties of tern. You can reach it by ferry May through August (they leave from the far end of the dinghy park—check the board opposite the sailing club for times).

From Brancaster, continue on A149 about 4 miles to King's Lynn. Along the way, at Caley Mill, near Heacham, are the fields of Norfolk Lavender (phone: 1485-70384), the largest growers and distillers of lavender in Britain. The grounds are open daily; admission charge for guided tours only.

Another side trip off A149 is to the queen's country house at Sandringham, 8 miles before King's Lynn (turn onto B1140 at Dersingham and continue about 2 miles). Her Majesty's Norfolk estate has a 19th-century Jacobean-style house of brick and stone set on grounds landscaped with lovely gardens and trees. The house, grounds, and a museum of dolls and cars are closed when the queen or another member of the royal family is in residence; admission charge. Call 553-772675 for details of the summer closing and the date of the *Sandringham Flower Show,* an annual event in late July and a nice time to visit.

Return to A149. After a mile, turn onto an unclassified road and continue another half-mile to *Castle Rising.* Once a port and now deserted by the receding sea, *Castle Rising* is a ruined shell of a 12th-century Norman fortress whose inner keep was at one time the mightiest stronghold in the country. Walk around the grassy ramparts and imagine its proud past. It is open daily; admission charge (phone: 1553-631330). Nearby are nine Jacobean almshouses, with chapel, court, and treasury. Return again to A149 and continue another 7 miles to King's Lynn.

BEST EN ROUTE

Lifeboat Inn This old smugglers' inn with low beams and log fires has 13 rooms, mostly in a modern extension with superb views over salt flats to the sea. The restaurant serves locally caught mussels and other seafood whenever available. On Ship La. in Thornham, about 5 miles from Hunstanton on the A149 (phone: 1485-512236; fax: 1485-512323). Moderate.

Titchwell Manor Ian and Margaret Snaithe's comfortable red brick hotel with a walled garden is ideal for bird watchers, as it overlooks the *Titchwell Nature*

Reserve. The restaurant serves English fare; bar meals also are available. Some of the 15 rooms are in cozy converted outbuildings. In Titchwell, a mile west of Brancaster on A149 (phone: 1485-210221; fax: 1485-210104). Moderate.

KING'S LYNN Lynn, as it's colloquially known, lies on the banks of the river Great Ouse close by the Wash, an arm of the North Sea that reaches deep into the East Anglian coastline. People still search the Wash for King John's treasure, lost in 1215 when his entourage miscalculated the tide. The town preserves many medieval buildings that reflect its importance as an international trading center from the 12th to the 15th centuries. Among these is the *Guildhall of St. George* (built in 1410), the largest surviving medieval guildhall in England and now the theater part of the *King's Lynn Arts Centre,* a venue for regular concerts, plays, and art exhibitions, as well as for the annual *King's Lynn Festival* (see *Best Festivals* in DIVERSIONS). It's closed to visitors Sundays and during performances; admission charge (phone: 1553-773578).

BEST EN ROUTE

Congham Hall This Georgian manor house has only 14 rooms, but it also has tennis courts, an outdoor pool, stabling for visiting horses, and even its own cricket field within its 40 acres. Its renowned restaurant features a marathon eight-course menu (though à la carte dining is available, too). Closed Saturday lunch and Monday holidays. Reservations advised. Major credit cards accepted. Lynn Rd., Grimston, about 6 miles northeast of King's Lynn (phone: 1485-600250; 800-323-7308; fax: 1485-601191). Expensive.

Duke's Head Behind the 17th-century façade of this building—the best hotel in King's Lynn itself—are 71 modern rooms. The restaurant exudes Victorian charm. Tuesday Market Pl., King's Lynn (phone: 1553-774996; fax: 1553-763556). Expensive.

Yorkshire

In the 18th century, on his famous travels around England, Daniel Defoe reported: "From hense we entered the great county of York, uncertain still which way to begin to take full view of it, for 'tis a county of very great extent." Today, with its administrative marriage to Humberside, its extent would root Defoe to the spot. The historical county of Yorkshire is now the three modern counties of North, West, and South Yorkshire, which together with Humberside encompass over 5,000 square miles, including two national parks—the *Yorkshire Dales* and *North York Moors*—and part of a third park, the *Peak District.* They also include the 1,900-year-old city of York, plenty of villages with cobbled streets, a string of seaside resorts, battle-scarred castles, time-worn abbeys, and sumptuous country houses.

The long shoreline of Yorkshire and Humberside exhibits every kind of coastal scenery and seascape, from high cliffs and rocky headlands to sheltered coves and broad scimitars of sandy beach, from rock pools abandoned by the receding tide to sand dunes capped with marram grass that the sea never molests. There are fishing villages and smugglers' dens, yachtsmen's havens and bird sanctuaries, and, for the family on holiday, several busy resorts, such as Scarborough and Bridlington.

From anywhere along the Yorkshire coast, it's only a short, pretty drive to the *North York Moors,* protected as a national park since 1952. This vast, heather-clad wilderness, in full purple bloom in August or cringing beneath heavy, rumbling skies in midwinter, is ribbed by softer interludes of countryside. Most of the moor is a plateau naturally protected from human intrusions by the Hambleton Hills and Cleveland Hills to the west, rocky coasts to the east, and by abrupt ridges dropping to valleys to the north and south. But around the edges are the numerous farms, villages, and market towns of a rich agricultural area, connected by good roads and offering a wide variety of accommodations. Where the roads fail to penetrate, lanes, tracks, and footpaths begin. Here, the pedestrian reigns supreme.

To the west of York are the rich, green patchwork valleys of the *Yorkshire Dales,* another national park. Made famous worldwide by James Herriot's series of books on a local veterinarian's life in the 1930s and 1940s, the dales are peppered with market towns, villages, rows of cottages, and lone farmhouses built of light gray or honey-colored stone, crowned by gray slate roofs and solid as fortresses. This huge upland area covers more than 680 square miles and is incised by rushing rivers, providing a variety of scenery for all kinds of outdoor holiday activities. Bronze Age, Iron Age, and Roman remains abound, including hill forts and "green roads" used by today's hikers en route from dale to dale, while Viking legacies linger in the local dialect and in the names of places—the ending "by" means farm, while the word "dale" comes from "thal," the Viking word for valley.

The whole region is full of historic sights and places of interest as well as scenic beauty. Our route begins in York, heads northeast to Malton, then crosses the Wolds Way, a long-distance footpath, and works its way east via Driffield to the coast at Bridlington. In Humberside, it takes in the "nose" of Flamborough Head before continuing to Filey, the Victorian spa resort of Scarborough, the little fishing town of Robin Hood's Bay, and Whitby, then makes a U-turn to cross the river Esk. From here it's a steady trek southwest across the *North York Moors National Park* and along its southern boundary to the market town of Helmsley. After stopping off at Rievaulx to pay respects to the great abbey ruins and detouring to one or two interesting villages in the vicinity, the route goes to Thirsk, James Herriot's hometown, and *Fountains Abbey.* The picturesque old riverside town of Knaresborough comes next and then Harrogate. After taking in the folkloric *Nidderdale Museum* (one of the best in Britain) at Pateley Bridge, the itinerary enters the *Yorkshire Dales National Park,* where it runs along river valleys, crosses isolated moors, and passes through villages of old stone buildings that seem almost untouched by the 20th century. As the route passes through valleys such as Wharfedale, Coverdale, Wensleydale, and Swaledale, it is easy to see why many people regard this as the loveliest area in all England. For those who want to enjoy still more of this unique countryside, a detour to Bushopdale and Longstrothdale is suggested. The route appropriately ends at the historic, quintessentially English town of Richmond.

Since northerners in England always have liked comfortably plumped beds and heaps of home cooking, be prepared to find lots of cozy inns rather than gracious hotels, and plates of roast beef and Yorkshire pudding, piled high with vegetables and topped with nourishing gravy, rather than delicately presented nouvelle cuisine. It's not the place for picky eaters. Lots of old family-run firms brewing real ale in the traditional manner lie in this neck of the woods, too. One of the strongest of the local brews is Theakston's Old Peculier, a dark, rich beer from Masham, near Ripon, locally nicknamed "lunatic broth." Use it to wash down York ham, Wensleydale cheese, Whitby crabs, Scarborough plaice, Grimsby haddock and kippers, and, of course, the ubiquitous fish cooked in batter with chips.

Expect to pay about $120 or more for a double room (with private bath, TV set, and breakfast) in places listed as expensive, from $85 to $120 at moderate ones, and less than $85 at inexpensive ones. A dinner for two, excluding wine, tips, and drinks, will cost $65 or more in expensive restaurants, from $40 to $60 in those categorized as moderate, and less than $40 in inexpensive places. All restaurants listed serve lunch and dinner unless otherwise noted. For each location, hotels and restaurants are listed alphabetically by price category.

YORK In the heart of northern England, a four-hour drive or a two-and-a-half-hour train trip from London, York is widely considered the best-preserved medieval city in Great Britain. For a full report on the city's sights, hotels, and restaurants, see *York* in THE CITIES.

En Route from York Take A64 northeast toward Malton. After 15 miles, turn left and go about 1½ miles to *Castle Howard,* a stately home that was the setting for the TV miniseries of Evelyn Waugh's novel *Brideshead Revisited.* (For more information, see *Stately Homes and Great Gardens* in DIVERSIONS.) *Castle Howard* is closed November through *Easter;* admission charge (phone: 1653-648444). Return to A64 and continue another 3 miles to Malton.

MALTON A solid, ancient market town with about 4,500 residents (and one of the largest livestock centers in England), it has dozens of prehistoric burial grounds within a few miles' radius and one of the best small-town agricultural shows in the country, held each July. Located on the river Derwent, it was once the Roman station of Derventio, so be sure to see the Roman antiquities in the *Malton Museum,* in the 200-year-old former *Town Hall* in the Market Place. The museum is closed November through March; admission charge (phone: 1653-695136). Travelers also can follow the old Roman road by taking B1257 west for 7 miles to the pretty village of Hovingham. With its immaculate lawns, chunky stone cottages, model village green, pub, and hotel, it almost could be described as the perfect village. A mile northeast of Malton is Old Malton, known for its Early English to Perpendicular parish church, part of a former priory. Just north of the village is *Eden Camp,* a group of huts erected in 1942 to house German and Italian prisoners of war. The camp has been converted into a museum devoted to life in Britain during World War II. It is closed January through mid-February; admission charge (phone: 1653-697777).

BEST EN ROUTE

Talbot Originally a hunting lodge, this stone structure was converted to an inn in the 18th century. There are 28 rooms, and the river Derwent flows past the end of the terraced garden. The dining room serves English fare with occasional continental touches. Yorkersgate, Malton (phone: 1653-694031; fax: 1653-693355). Expensive to moderate.

Ranger's House Built in 1639 as a brew house and stable, this guesthouse stands amid quiet, pretty countryside that is a popular hiking area. The six bedrooms are comfortably furnished, and the public areas have such elegant touches as a stag's head, a grand staircase, and a large fireplace. The restaurant serves traditional English fare. No credit cards accepted. Sheriff Hutton, 4 miles west of *Castle Howard* (phone: 1347-878397; fax: 1347-878666). Moderate.

En Route from Malton Take B1248 southeast about 5 miles. After North Grimston, turn onto B1253 and continue another 8 miles to Sledmere, a one-road village little bigger than *Sledmere House,* the Georgian home of the Sykes family, who have been baronets and landowners on the Wolds since the 17th century. A gray, solid-looking building, it sits on grounds landscaped by the famous English gardener Lancelot "Capability" Brown. It is closed Mondays and Fridays; Mondays through Saturdays in April; and October through March. There's an admission charge (phone: 1377-236208).

Driffield (sometimes called Great Driffield to distinguish it from the nearby Little Driffield) is 8 miles from *Sledmere House.* To get there, continue southeast along B1252, an easy, undulating ribbon of road bordered for the most part by long horizons of grass-backed Wolds and fairly empty of traffic, barring the odd precariously overloaded tractor. The stone spire that comes up on the right—looking much like a space-age rocket—is a memorial to Sir Tatton Sykes, baronet of the area in the 19th century, who thus remains a dominating presence for miles around, just as he was in his life. On a clear day the views toward the coasts from here make you feel on top of the world. A few miles beyond the Sykes memorial, branch left onto A166 to Driffield. A canal built in the late 18th century to link it with Beverley and Kingston upon Hull led to the town's prosperity and unofficial ranking as the Capital of the Wolds in the early 19th century. Its weekly cattle market is still an important event for farmers in the surrounding area. The town has a complicated one-way system that makes driving confusing, but it's small enough to be pretty, with a plethora of pubs. Stay on A166 the remaining 12 miles east to Bridlington.

BEST EN ROUTE

Bell Mr. and Mrs. Riggs's 14-room hotel is a traditional English coaching inn dating from 1742, now with a courtyard, gym, sauna, and indoor pool. It's famous for its buffet lunches served in the *Oak Lounge,* where the original brickwork blends with baskets of plants (also see *Pub Crawling* in DIVERSIONS). Market Pl., Driffield (phone: 1377-256661; 800-528-1234; fax: 1377-253228). Expensive.

BRIDLINGTON Besides a dozen miles of beach and safe, clean bathing, the attractions of this seaside resort (pop. 31,000) include a harbor, busy since Roman times, where you can rent a boat, go fishing with an old salt of a skipper, or just take a trip around the bay with a crew singing sea chanteys to the accompaniment of an old-fashioned squeeze-box. Those with a nostalgic hankering for the seaside of their youth can make a beeline for *Topham's* (on Cross St.; phone: 1262-674175), an ice-cream parlor that still serves a genuine Knickerbocker Glory, a type of sundae (layers of different flavors topped with sauce) rarely found in Britain nowadays.

The Old Town, a mile inland, is the site of a medieval priory church and a 14th-century gatehouse, *Bayle Gate,* also part of the onetime priory and now used as a museum of local history. It's closed Fridays through Mondays and October through April; admission charge (phone: 1262-603170). John Bull's rock factory in Carnaby, about 2 miles inland on A166, offers foot-long sticks of rock candy, once synonymous with the British seaside (and now not so common); these make fine souvenirs since the name of the resort is traditionally written in color on the end of the stick and through it, like the colored ribbons in a tube of toothpaste. The factory is open for visits on weekdays; the best time to go is 11:30 AM when they "boil up" the ingredients (phone: 1262-678525).

Another side trip is to detour along B1255 northeast to *Sewerby Hall* and Flamborough Head. *Sewerby Hall,* an 18th-century mansion, stands bravely weathering the winds on a particularly exposed stretch of coastline 2 miles from Bridlington, its 50 acres of grounds sweeping down to the cliff edge with superb views back over Bridlington Bay. Inside, the Georgian house has an oak staircase leading to an art gallery and a collection of trophies of the pioneering pilot Amy Johnson. The monkey-puzzle trees (Chile pine) in the formal garden next to the car park were planted in 1847, making them some of the oldest in England. The house is closed Wednesdays through Fridays October through April; the park is open daily. There's an admission charge (phone: 1262-673769).

Continue east on B1255. After a couple of miles, you'll come to the village of Flamborough and the chalky white cliffs and chasms of Flamborough Head, which form part of Britain's officially designated Heritage Coast and are home to umpteen squadrons of seabirds. Winter visitors are advised to return in spring along with most of the birds, which spend the coldest months out in the North Sea.

BEST EN ROUTE

Blue Lobster Mickey Barron, local fisherman and owner of the best seafood restaurant in town, prefers to serve fish dishes a good deal fancier than can be found in the several fish-and-chips shops. For a really special meal, he recommends smoked salmon followed by oysters, then lobster—and then more oysters for dessert! Less expensive seafood snacks are available in the bar. Open daily. Reservations necessary. Major credit cards accepted. West Pier, Lower Harbor area, off South Cliff Rd., Bridlington (phone: 1262-674729). Expensive to moderate.

Expanse Up at the northern end of the bay, Bridlington's best hotel (built in 1937) is so close to the waves you almost can hear them crashing on the beach as you eat breakfast. It has 48 unpretentious yet comfortable rooms (most overlooking the bay), a friendly staff, and plenty of fresh seafood on the menu. North Marine Dr., Bridlington (phone: 1262-675347; fax: 1262-604928). Moderate.

Bay Ridge Centrally located close to the harbor, this excellent hotel is run by the Myford family. Twelve of the 14 rooms have private baths. The dining room is open to hotel guests only. 11-13 Summerfield Rd., Bridlington (phone: 1262-673425). Inexpensive.

Royal Dog and Duck A flourishing historic pub with a splendid atmosphere, ideal for chatting up the locals and for excellent, inexpensive meals (the fresh crab salads are especially reasonable). Closed in the evenings October through March. Reservations unnecessary. No credit cards accepted. Tower St., Flamborough (phone: 1262-850206). Inexpensive.

En Route from Bridlington Proceed north up the Yorkshire Coast via A165 to Filey, 11 miles away.

FILEY Like so many other English seaside resorts, this began as a spa town during the 18th century; by the closing decades of the 19th century, attractive crescents of Victorian guesthouses and hotels had become well established alongside quaint fishermen's cottages. Charlotte Brontë stayed at *Cliff House,* now the *Brontë and Vinery Café* (Belle Vue St.; phone: 1723-514805). The 6 miles of golden sand at Filey Bay, widely considered the best stretch on the Yorkshire coast, are so flat that in the past the strip was used as a runway for airplanes. Today, the bay is a haven for windsurfers, swimmers, and sailing dinghies.

BEST EN ROUTE

White Lodge The best in town, situated on the cliff top above the bay and close to the town center. It has 19 rooms and a sun lounge with fine sea views. The restaurant serves lobster, salmon, trout, and other seafood all caught daily in the bay. The Crescent, Filey (phone: 1723-514771). Moderate.

En Route from Filey Continue along A165 another 7 miles to Scarborough.

SCARBOROUGH The most popular summer resort in northeast England, with a year-round population of 53,000, was in the 12th century little more than a castle keep. The ruins of *Scarborough Castle* still dominate the town, but in 1622 a canny Yorkshireman saw a way of promoting the virtues of the clear mineral water emerging in a gush at the foot of the South Cliff. The idea caught on, but Scarborough didn't become really popular until Victorian times.

Its two bays, North Bay and South Bay, are separated by a high headland holding the remains of the Norman castle (closed Mondays from October through *Easter;* admission charge; phone: 1723-372451) and by the fishing harbor nestling below it. The main part of town, which has some excellent shops, stretches inland from the castle headland. The *Scarborough Millennium,* on the seafront opposite the harbor, details the town's history from the arrival of the Vikings through the 1920s; its displays include tableaux depicting a 14th-century fish market and the castle under seige during the Civil War. It is open daily; admission charge (phone: 1723-501000).

Royal The grande dame of Scarborough's hotels is another South Bay structure of the Regency period; a classic of its era, with an amazingly grand foyer, double staircase, chandeliers, columns, and galleries around the upper floors, it has 135 rooms, a restaurant, a snooker room, and, in keeping with the times, a pool and health center. St. Nicholas St., Scarborough (phone: 1723-364333; fax: 1723-500618). Expensive.

Wrea Head A solid Victorian country house with all the trappings of the era—a croquet lawn, comfortable furnishings, a well-stocked library, and hot porridge for breakfast. There are 21 rooms and a restaurant. Scalby, Scarborough (phone: 1723-378211; fax: 1723-371780). Expensive.

Crown An old, white-painted hotel with Regency origins on the cliffs above South Bay. It has 78 rooms, a restaurant, large public rooms, and a snooker table. The Esplanade, Scarborough (phone: 1723-373491; fax: 1723-362271). Expensive to moderate.

Lanterna A modest-looking Italian spot that hides its light under a bushel. Owners Mr. and Mrs. Arecco produce homemade pasta and desserts and plenty of fresh fish. Queenies—small, sweet scallops caught locally—are particularly good. Dinner only; closed Sundays and Mondays. Reservations advised. Major credit cards accepted. 33 Queen St., Scarborough (phone: 1723-363616). Expensive to moderate.

En Route from Scarborough Continue north on A165 and A171 another 21 miles to Whitby, entering the *North York Moors National Park* on the way.

WHITBY The river Esk flows to the sea at Whitby, cutting the resort in two, with steep cliffs rising from both banks. In the 18th century, it was a shipbuilding center and the home port of whaling fleets; a century later it had become an important herring port. Today, fishing vessels still wait cheek by jowl for the turn of the tide in the busy harbor, while fishermen mend their nets outside cottages that ring the hillsides. The town spawned such famous seamen as Captain Cook, who was an apprentice on coal ships here and went on to explore the South Pacific in locally built ships. A statue of him looking out to sea now stands above the harbor.

Two notable landmarks crown the hill on the southern side of the river, the old part of town. *St. Mary's Church,* built in the 12th century but much altered in the 17th, is reached by climbing a flight of 199 steps from Church Street. Nearby is *Whitby Abbey,* founded by St. Hilda in 657 and the scene of an ancient synod in 664 that first set the date for *Easter.* Devastated by Danes in the 9th century and then rebuilt, most of the remains date from the 12th and 13th centuries. Among the monks and nuns cloistered at the abbey was Caedmon, an ignorant 7th-century cowherd who, according to the Venerable Bede, miraculously received poetic powers and became the earliest poet in the English language and the father of English sacred songs. A cross to his memory was placed in *St. Mary's Churchyard* in 1898. The most famous personage connected with Whitby, however, was a vampire from Transylvania—the protagonist of Bram Stoker's gothic thriller *Dracula*—who operated out of one of the graves in the same churchyard and preyed on the citizenry below. Pleasant dreams. The abbey is open daily; admission charge (phone: 1947-603568).

BEST EN ROUTE

Magpie Café Tops for fish-and-chips in Whitby—some even argue in the whole of Yorkshire. Cod, plaice, sole, haddock, crabs, and other local catch are served. Lunch and early dinner only; closed December through mid-February. Reservations advised. Major credit cards accepted. 14 Pier Rd., Whitby (phone: 1947-602058). Moderate to inexpensive.

En Route from Whitby Take A171 in the direction of Guisborough. After about 6 miles, take the small road on your left about 4 miles to Egton and Egton Bridge. About 2 miles east of here, at Grosmont, is the northern terminus of the *North Yorkshire Moors Railway*—the *Moorsrail*—which runs restored steam trains 18 miles over Goathland Moor and down lovely Newtondale to Pickering. The line is one of the world's earliest, built by George Stephenson in 1836 (its carriages were horse-drawn at first), and it provides a superb way to see parts of the *North York Moors National Park* that are inaccessible by road. Trains run on weekends in March and daily from April through the end of September (phone: 1751-473535 for details).

Otherwise, from Egton Bridge, continue south and travel "over the tops" across the moors, past ancient crosses, browsing sheep, pheasant, and the occasional walker. After about 4 miles, you'll reach the village of Rosedale Abbey. A ruined 12th-century Cistercian priory gave its name to this village, which was once the thriving hub of an iron ore industry and home to many miners. Above the village, close to the junction of the Blakey Ridge and Castleton roads, stand two moorland crosses affectionately known as *Fat Betty* and *Ralph's Cross.* Together with *Margery,* a rough-hewn stone a few hundred yards away, they are supposed to commemorate a 13th-century meeting between two nuns—sisters Betty and Margery—and Old Ralph, a faithful servant.

From Rosedale Abbey, follow the road southeast toward Pickering. After about 2 miles, look for a sign to Lastingham (just before a small, humpback bridge) and turn off to your right. Lastingham's old stone houses, stream, and typical village green lie half-hidden in the woods and hollows. The town's beautiful Norman church stands on the site of an older Benedictine monastery whose founding is recorded in the writings of the Venerable Bede; the original crypt survives intact beneath the present church. After Lastingham, the road rises, crosses open moors, and plunges down another 2 miles to Hutton-le-Hole.

Lastingham Grange Dennis Wood's award-winning 12-room hotel occupies a stone farmhouse, mostly of 17th-century vintage. It has a real English feel with traditional furnishings, fresh flowers, and a carefully tended rose garden. The restaurant's well-prepared English fare attracts local people from a wide area. Closed December through February. No credit cards accepted. Lastingham (phone: 1751-417345). Expensive.

Mallyan Spout A creeper-clad stone building on the fringes of the moors offers a warm welcome, 30 rooms (six of which are located in a modern annex), open fires, superb cream teas, and robust English cooking, particularly fish. The spout, by the way, is a waterfall that can be reached by following a three-quarter-mile riverside path. Goathland (phone: 1947-86206; fax: 1947-86327). Moderate.

Milburn Arms A 14th-century gray stone inn run by Terry and Joan Bentley with wooden beams, a fireplace, chintz decor, 11 bedrooms, and a popular bar. Its restaurant serves a large selection of well-chosen, expertly cooked dishes using fresh vegetables and other local produce. Rosedale Abbey (phone/fax: 1751-417312). Moderate.

HUTTON-LE-HOLE If the village had been purposely built for the discerning traveler, it couldn't be more picturesque: Lots of cottages of Yorkshire stone sit perfectly poised on the banks of a babbling brook and around a green kept in constant trim by resident sheep. The equally charming *Ryedale Folk Museum* displays reconstructions of village houses, an Elizabethan glass furnace, a blacksmith's shop, and other buildings. The museum is closed November through March; admission charge (phone: 1751-417367).

En Route from Hutton-le-Hole In springtime, before continuing to Kirbymoorside and Helmsley, walk, or drive if you must, north of Hutton-le-Hole into Farndale to see a most stunning display of wild daffodils, more than Wordsworth could ever have laid eyes on in the *Lake District.* But don't be tempted to pick any, as the area is well patrolled by Daffodil Wardens (a highly seasonal occupation).

To reach Helmsley from Hutton-le-Hole, pick up A170 and proceed west 9 miles, visiting Kirbymoorside and *Nunnington Hall* en route. Kirbymoorside, about a mile from Hutton-le-Hole, always has had a flourishing market; the tolbooth (or market hall) was built in 1710 with stone from the ancient *Neville Castle* and is still used on market days. About 2 miles farther, located south of A170 is *Nunnington Hall,* a *National Trust* property that is also worth a visit. A lovely manor house on the banks of the river Rye, it dates back to the 16th century, although the fine paneled bedrooms and hall, carved chimneypiece, staircase, tapestries, and china are mostly of the late 17th century. The famous *Carlisle Collection of*

Miniature Rooms, furnished and decorated in the styles of different periods, is now on permanent display in the house. Ten thousand items strong, it includes a William and Mary parlor, a Queen Anne drawing room, a Chippendale library, a Palladian hall, and a greenhouse and aviary. The house is closed Mondays, Fridays (except July), and November through March; admission charge (phone: 1439-5283). From *Nunnington Hall,* Helmsley is another 6 miles on A170.

BEST EN ROUTE

Ryedale Lodge This former Victorian railway station on a defunct line is now a quiet seven-room hotel with an excellent restaurant (dinner only), set well back from the nearest road. Proprietor John Laird strives to make guests feel that they've been welcomed into his home, rather than a hotel. Nunnington (phone: 1439-748246; fax: 1653-694633). Moderate.

HELMSLEY Situated at the start of the Cleveland Way, a horseshoe-shaped footpath that extends approximately 100 miles around the rim of the *North York Moors National Park* and down the Yorkshire coast to Filey, this cobbled market town (Friday is market day) is a popular spot with walkers. It stands in the shadow of its now hag-toothed castle, whose oldest stonework dates from the end of the 12th century (although the extensive earthworks date from shortly after the Norman Conquest). As is the case with virtually all the castles around the moors, *Helmsley Castle*'s decay is a result of the English Civil War; in 1644 it withstood a three-month siege by the Parliamentarian forces of Sir Thomas Fairfax, then finally capitulated and was thereafter partially demolished to render it useless. The castle is closed Mondays November through March; admission charge (phone: 1439-70442). The *North York Moors National Park Information Centre* (Market Pl.; phone: 1439-70173) offers maps and other information about the area. It is closed weekdays November through *Easter.*

The ruins of *Rievaulx Abbey,* 3 miles northwest of Helmsley, are reachable either on foot via a signposted footpath that follows a section of the Cleveland Way, or by driving along B1257, then turning down a tiny signposted lane off to the left. Founded in 1131 by monks from Clairvaux in Burgundy, the abbey quickly became the largest and most splendid Cistercian monastery in England. Housing 140 white-robed monks and 500 lay brothers, it prospered mainly because of the monks' success at sheep farming in the dales. Rievaulx's greatest glories are the soaring arches in the church choir and the walls of the adjacent refectory, both masterpieces of Early English architecture. There is also a museum displaying the items that have been unearthed on the site. The museum is open daily; admission charge (phone: 1439-6228).

Beautiful *Rievaulx Terrace,* a half-mile of grassy embankment terminating at each end with a temple in classical style, is above the abbey. Added in the 18th century to provide a romantic view of the ruins, it is an excellent example of landscaping at that time. It is closed November through March; admission charge (phone: 1439-6340).

BEST EN ROUTE

Black Swan Overlooking the main square and the marketplace, this 400-year-old inn is a tasteful blend of Tudor, Georgian, and modern. It's old enough to be entitled to a ghost, and there is one—a beautiful nun who appears at midnight. In addition to its 44 rooms, the inn has a restaurant with wooden beams, chintz-covered furniture, log fires, and a reputation for good English dishes, including rack of lamb. Market Pl., Helmsley (phone: 1439-70466; 800-225-5843; fax: 1439-70174). Expensive.

Feversham Arms Yorkshire's probably the last place you'd expect to enjoy an excellent paella or an exceptional selection of rioja wines, but Gonzalo de Aragues, the Spanish owner here, supplies both. Dine in the *Goya* restaurant—shellfish, including paella, and game often are featured—or stick to the snacks in the bar, where visitors can sample 40 different sherries and 18 malt whiskies (not all at once, please). This old inn has 18 rooms, five with four-poster beds, and there's an outdoor heated pool. The restaurant is open daily. Reservations necessary. Major credit cards accepted. 1 High St., Helmsley (phone: 1439-70766; 800-528-1234; fax: 1439-70346). Moderate.

En Route from Helmsley Take A170 westward 8 miles to Sutton Bank escarpment, crossing the Hambleton Hills. (If coming from *Rievaulx Abbey,* drive through Scawton to join A170 and then follow signs to Sutton Bank; the distance is about 6 miles.) The edge of the escarpment offers a fine panorama of glacier-formed Gormire Lake, the vales of York and Mowbray, and the distant *Yorkshire Dales National Park*—a view James Herriot has called the finest in England.

Before proceeding westward to Thirsk, a detour to two interesting villages south of A170 beckons. Descend Sutton Bank on the narrow, rather daunting road to Kilburn, 2 miles away. You might want to stop in the small car park to see the famous White Horse carved into the hillside above Kilburn by a 19th-century village teacher and his pupils. Kilburn itself is remembered mostly because of a local carpenter whose goal was the "satisfaction of knowing anything I create will outlive me by three hundred years." By the time he died in 1955, Robert Thompson's furniture and carvings in English oak could be seen in *Westminster Abbey* and *York Minster,* as well as many other sites throughout the world. Today his two grandchildren run the furniture business; everything produced in the *Robert Thompson's Craftsmen* workshop (phone: 1347-868218) still bears the famous wooden mouse trademark.

From Kilburn, drive eastward 5 miles to Coxwold, a lovely village of a single street, graced by a 15th-century Perpendicular church with an octagonal tower and box pews. "A delicious retreat" was how Laurence Sterne, its famous onetime vicar, described his home on the west edge of the village. *Shandy Hall,* the old rambling house where he lived and where he wrote *Tristram Shandy* and *A Sentimental Journey,* is open on Wednesdays and Sundays June through September; admission charge (phone: 1347-868465). *Byland Abbey,* another Cistercian house, is a mile northeast of Coxwold, just outside the hamlet of Wass. Founded in the 12th century, it was moved from its previous address at Old Byland north of A170 in part because of its unsheltered position there and in part because the monks could hear the bells at *Rievaulx Abbey*—something the inhabitants of neither establishment could endure. Little remains, but the ruins are impressive, especially when silhouetted against a dramatic sky. The abbey is closed Mondays and Tuesdays October through March; admission charge (phone: 1347-868614).

Thirsk is 8 miles from Coxwold; to get there, drive east on an unnumbered road, and then take A19 into the town.

BEST EN ROUTE

Foresters Arms A comfortable, cozy country inn with 10 bedrooms, this property is next door to Kilburn's "mouseman" furniture makers, *Robert Thompson's Craftsmen.* The restaurant serves good English fare, including steaks and duck. Kilburn (phone: 1347-868386). Inexpensive.

THIRSK Until fairly recently, this market town (pop. 7,400) on the northern flanks of the Vale of York was best known for its Perpendicular parish church. All that changed when a Scottish veterinarian, based in Thirsk but practicing over a very wide area of Yorkshire, wrote *All Creatures Great and Small* and other books describing his lifetime of experience. James Herriot still lives in Thirsk, but the town may not be entirely recognizable as Darrowby, which the author says is a composite made up of Thirsk, Richmond, Leyburn, and Middleham (all west of here), plus "a fair chunk" of imagination (Herriot, too, is a pen name). The town of Thirsk, as it really is, is described in *James Herriot's Yorkshire.*

BEST EN ROUTE

Crab & Lobster Not surprisingly, fish is the order of the day at this thatch-roofed, creeper-covered village pub. The decor has a musical theme, featuring an antique organ, a saxophone, violins, and other instruments. The fresh seafood dishes are served either at the bar or in the dining room. Closed Sunday evenings. Reservations necessary. Major credit cards accepted. Asenby, 5½ miles southwest of Thirsk (phone: 1845-577286). Moderate.

En Route from Thirsk When leaving Thirsk, don't be surprised to see a sailplane swish overhead; they are launched from the nearby airfield of the *Yorkshire Gliding Club* (phone: 1845-597237) and take advantage of the uplift from southwesterly winds blowing against the escarpment. Visitors can book a flight for about $40, including the sailplane, tow, and, of course, an instructor.

Take A61 out of Thirsk southwest for 7 miles and then follow B6265 for 6 miles through Ripon to *Fountains Abbey* (off B6265; phone: 1765-608888). Founded by Cistercian monks beside the river Skell in 1132, the abbey grew in wealth and size as a result of its trade in woolen goods and revenues from the land. In 1539, however, during the Dissolution of the Monasteries, the roofs were removed and its treasures scattered, leaving it as the largest—and many would say the most beautiful—monastic ruin in Britain. The 11-bay nave and *Chapel of Nine Altars* at the end are particularly striking, but the chapter house and double avenue of arches in the cellarium also are impressive. The foundation of the infirmary, which was built partly over the river, is also visible. Now in the care of the *National Trust,* the abbey attracts more visitors each year than any of its other properties.

The best way to approach the abbey is on foot through the magnificent *Studley Royal Gardens.* When these Georgian-style gardens were laid out in the 18th century, the abbey was used as a focal point in their design. Water from the river Skell feeds the falls and fountains, and reflecting pools mirror the classical temples, yew hedges, and plantations of trees and shrubs. The nearby *Fountains Hall* estate was built around 1610 with stones from the abbey. It has an imposing hall and minstrels' gallery, paneled bedrooms, superb furniture, and works of art. The church, *St. Mary's,* was built in the 1870s but designed in 14th-century style—it is decorated with carvings, glass, and ironwork, but with walls of Egyptian alabaster and a painted roof. Nearby at *Robin Hood's Well,* the famous outlaw is said to have been thrown into the brook by the Curtal Friar. The abbey, hall, church, and gardens are open daily; admission charge.

Returning to Ripon, join A61 south and continue another 10 miles to Harrogate.

HARROGATE Fashionable as a spa in the last century, this historic town is regarded as one of the most attractive in England because of its colorful gardens and elegant Victorian buildings. Long renowned for its hotels, restaurants, and shops, it has been developed into a cosmopolitan resort with a population of 69,500, particularly favored for business conferences and events held at its modern exhibition center. Its annual festival held in early August is internationally famous (see *Best Festivals* in DIVERSIONS). The high mineral content of Harrogate's waters was first discovered in 1571, and the story of how it subsequently developed into England's leading inland spa, with 88 sulfur and iron springs, is told in a museum in the *Royal Pump Room* (Royal Parade; phone: 1423-503340), the main spa building. Built in 1842 over the largest sulfur spring, it also houses displays of English pottery and jewelry. Visitors can try the pungent water from the spring itself, reputedly the most potent in Europe, but few have more than a sip as the taste is reminiscent of rotten eggs. The museum is open daily; admission charge. The tea served at *Betty's* tea shop (1 Parliament St.; phone: 1423-502746) is much more pleasant, as are the shop's famous *Christmas* cakes. Also see *Tea Shops and Tea Gardens* in DIVERSIONS.

The town also has authentic Turkish baths in the *Royal Baths Assembly Rooms* (Crescent Rd.; phone: 1423-562498), built in 1897. Ornately decorated in their original style, they are open daily (with separate times for men and women); admission charge. The *Tourist Information Centre* (phone: 1423-525666) is in the same building; it's closed Sundays October through March.

From Harlow Hill (Otley Rd.), the view over the town includes York and Ripon, as well as the Tees and Humber Rivers. (Unfortunately, the observatory tower there is closed to the public.) On Crag Lane the *Northern Horticultural Society* has 68 acres of rose gardens, alpine flowers, rock plants, and heathers. It's open daily; admission charge (phone: 1423-565418).

BEST EN ROUTE

Nidd Hall This Victorian mansion offers 58 well-appointed rooms with fine Georgian furniture and lovely gardens. Sports enthusiasts can choose from an indoor heated pool, squash and tennis courts, croquet, and trout fishing and punting on the lake. The dining fare is marvelous, with an emphasis on fresh fruits and vegetables. Closed Saturday lunch. Reservations advised. Major credit cards accepted. Nidd, Harrogate (phone: 1423-771598; fax: 1423-770931). Expensive.

Wood Hall The river Wharfe flows through the extensive grounds of this 43-room hotel situated 9 miles southeast of Harrogate (14 from York). Opened as a hotel in 1987, the house was built in 1750 after Cromwell's army destroyed the original building and threw the stonework into the river. A modern annex houses 27 of the guestrooms, as well as a leisure center with a pool. Traditional Yorkshire fare is served in the restaurant. Fishing and shooting excursions are available. Trip Lane, Linton (phone: 1937-587271; fax: 1937-584353). Expensive.

Drum and Monkey Upstairs above a large Victorian bar, this busy eatery specializes in fish and has a short, reasonably priced wine list. Closed Sundays. Reservations advised. Major credit cards accepted. 5 Montpellier Gdns., Harrogate (phone: 1423-502650). Moderate.

Old Swan Situated on five acres of gardens, within a short stroll of the town center, this imposing ivy-clad hostelry has been welcoming guests for over 200 years. Agatha Christie chose to "disappear" here for a time in 1926. There are 124 rooms, 11 suites, a croquet lawn, and a putting green. The restaurant serves a combination of English and French food. Swan Road, Harrogate (phone: 1423-500055; fax: 1423-501154). Moderate.

En Route from Harrogate Take A61 north across the river Nidd for 3 miles and then turn left onto B6165. This twisting road runs through hilly countryside for 7 miles to Summerbridge. From here, continue another 2 miles or so to Pateley Bridge, a busy little town with a steep high street. The *Nidderdale Museum* (King St.; phone: 1423-711448) has a wide variety of exhibits on Nidderdale life, including a Victorian living room, cobbler's and chemist's shops, a schoolroom, a pub, and a kitchen. It is closed Mondays through Saturdays October through March; admission charge.

Return to Summerbridge and turn onto B6451. After crossing back over the Nidd, this road leads south over Hardgroves Hill to A59. Turn right here to go over the wild Blubberhouses Moor and enter the *Yorkshire Dales National Park*—one of the loveliest areas of England. The dales are river valleys that extend from picturesque old villages and green hillsides up to wild moors high above. Sparkling rivers and tumbling streams reflect the changing skies, while wildflowers splash their colors over the limestone meadows. Stone walls, stone farmhouses, stone barns, and stone cottages are everywhere, with hardly a modern building in sight.

At Bolton Bridge (16 miles from Pateley Bridge), cross the river Wharfe and turn right onto B6160 to Bolton Abbey. Like Rosedale Abbey, this village is named after its 12th-century Augustinian priory (phone: 1756-710533), now mostly in ruins. The nave of the church, however, survived the Dissolution of the Monasteries and is still used for services.

WHARFEDALE This is the first of the dales on this tour. B6160 follows the Wharfe for 6 miles, alongside it or on the hillsides, to Threshfield (14 miles from Bolton Abbey). Cross the bridge here to visit Grassington, whose cobbled main street has several antique shops. The *Yorkshire Dales National Park Information Centre* (Hebden St., Grassington; phone: 1756-752774) is closed weekdays October through February. In this area, the valley is relatively wide and flat, but it narrows up toward the old village of Kettlewell (3 miles from Grassington)—a spot that attracts walkers from far and wide because of the challenging fells that surround it. Grouse live in the deep purple heather that covers the high moors in late summer. It's a popular place for shooting groups when the hunting season starts on August 12 each year.

BEST EN ROUTE

Devonshire Arms Built as a coaching inn in the 17th century, this rambling stone building on the Duke of Devonshire's estate is noted for its antique furniture, large portraits, and top-quality service. The best of the 40 rooms are in the oldest part. The dining room serves English and continental fare prepared with local game. Fishing, croquet, and clay-pigeon shooting are available on the grounds, and the hotel's most recent amenity is a leisure club with an indoor pool. Bolton Abbey (phone: 1756-710441; 800-525-4800; fax: 1756-710564). Expensive.

Ashfield House Owned and run by Keith and Linda Harrison, this cozy seven-room hostelry occupies an ivy-covered 17th-century stone house close to the village center. The restaurant (for residents only) serves adventurous English fare. Grassington (phone: 1756-752584). Inexpensive.

En Route from Kettlewell At Kettlewell on the east bank of the river, leave B6160 and take the unnumbered road to Coverdale Valley. The road begins with a steep climb away from the river and involves negotiating two sharp hairpin bends and gradients. Eventually, the road reaches over 1,500 feet.

COVERDALE As you enter the valley, the streams in front of you alongside the road are the beginnings of the river Cover. The scenery is wild and remote in the secluded moorland. With no walls or fences to restrict them, sheep wander casually to and fro, and an occasional rabbit can be seen darting in and out of the fields. The road then drops down to the Cover and runs briefly along the valley bottom before climbing back up the hillside.

En Route from Coverdale Continue along the road another 15 miles to Middleham. Just beyond Coverdale, the road leaves the *Yorkshire Dales National Park* (but the tour returns to it shortly), and the landscape becomes greener and softer, with trees accenting the drystone walls.

MIDDLEHAM This attractive little town, where Richard III spent much of his childhood, is known in horse racing circles all over the world as the "Newmarket of the North," as it is surrounded by training stables. The tradition of breeding and training horses in the area was started by the monks of *Jervaulx Abbey,* 3 miles to the southeast. Though now a ruin, the ground plan of this great Cistercian abbey, destroyed at the Dissolution, is still clear enough to give an impression of what day-to-day life must have been like in a great monastic house. It is open daily; admission charge (no phone).

Middleham's castle, strategically sited above the river Ure, was one of the greatest strongholds in the north until it was dismantled in 1646 and the stones were used for building houses in the town. Only the walls of the massive 12th-century keep—one of the largest ever built—still stand almost at their original height, together with the remains of its banqueting hall, the 13th-century chapel, 14th-century gatehouse, and deep moat. A replica of the *Middleham Jewel,* a 15th-century gold pendant discovered in 1985 in a field nearby, is on display; the original was sold for over £1 million. The castle is closed Mondays October through March; admission charge (phone: 1969-23899).

Miller's House This elegant Georgian house overlooking the marketplace offers seven nicely decorated rooms and a restaurant serving first-rate continental fare. For more information, see *Rural Retreats* in DIVERSIONS. Open February through December. Market Pl., Middleham (phone: 1969-22630; fax: 1969-23570). Moderate.

Old Rectory Richard and Olivia Farnell's handsome, award-winning bed and breakfast establishment is set in a gorgeous Georgian house at Thornton Watlass (7 miles east of Middleham). The building faces the village green, where guests can watch cricket being played on summer weekends. There are three guestrooms, a lounge with a wood-burning fireplace, and a flower-filled garden. Though the hotel serves only breakfast, the Farnells always can recommend a good restaurant nearby. Thornton Watlass (phone: 1677-423456). Inexpensive.

En Route from Middleham Take A6108 north 2 miles to Leyburn. On the way, cross the river Ure over an extraordinary bridge that resembles a miniature version of London's Tower Bridge. It has a stone arch over each end and small corner towers. Continue on to Leyburn, listed in the *Domesday Book* of 1086 as "Le borne," meaning stream by a clearing. The market that has been held on its wide square every Friday since 1696 (before then it was on Tuesdays) is a good place to buy some of the famous dale cheeses, traditionally wrapped in cheesecloth. You are now in Wensleydale, the broadest of the Yorkshire dales.

WENSLEYDALE The name of this dale came from the village of Wensley, 1 mile southwest of Leyburn on A684. Wensley's 13th-century church, *Holy Trinity,* was the mother church for the area until 1563 when the plague arrived. The few people who survived fled to other villages and the market moved to Leyburn, where it has remained ever since. The valley has more dairy cattle than the other dales and is the home of the famous wensleydale cheese. This cream-colored, crumbly cheese is based on a recipe brought to England by French monks in the 12th century.

From Wensley, go back into the *Yorkshire Dales National Park* on the unnumbered road past Redmire. About 4 miles from Wensley is the village of Castle Bolton, which enjoys panoramic views of the dale. Mary, Queen of Scots, was imprisoned in its solid-looking 14th-century castle in 1568. The castle is closed December through February; admission charge (phone: 1969-23981). Three miles farther on, past Carperby, is Aysgarth Falls, where the *Yorkshire Museum of Carriages and Horse-Drawn Vehicles* occupies *Yore Mill,* built in 1851 as a textile mill. It is closed November through *Easter;* admission charge (phone: 1748-823275). Beside it, the Ure cascades picturesquely down a series of terraces that form the Upper, Middle, and Lower waterfalls.

From the falls, go 5 more miles up Wensleydale to Askrigg. Along this stretch of the valley, roads run along both sides of the river. Although the southern one (A684) is much busier, it's a better choice on sunny days for its superb views across the valley. Otherwise, the quieter unnumbered road on the north side is preferable. In Askrigg, most of the houses date from the 18th and 19th centuries, but it was a market town long before that, having been given a charter by Queen Elizabeth I in 1587. Even earlier it was mentioned in the *Domesday Book* of 1086 as "Ascric," which probably meant Ash Ridge. At one time it was famous as a clock-making center; more recently it acquired a different kind of fame by being featured as the town of Darrowby, the principal location in the BBC series based on James Herriot's *All Creatures Great and Small.*

Six miles farther west at Hawes, the small *Dales Countryside Museum* (Station Yard; phone: 1969-667450) in the former railway station displays old farm equipment as well as local crafts such as knitting and rug making. Outside, the platform still stands, as does the road bridge and a goods shed. The museum is closed December through February and weekdays in November and March; admission charge.

BEST EN ROUTE

Simonstone Hall This comfortable, award-winning, family-run establishment on the edge of town was built in 1733 as the home of the Earl of Wharncliffe. It has wonderful views across Wensleydale and the residents include a family of tawny owls who have taken over one of the old chimneys. There are 10 rooms (one with a four-poster bed), all with modern facilities. Dinner specialties include pork in a port, mushroom, and cream sauce. Simonstone (phone: 1969-667255; fax: 1969-667741). Moderate.

Cockett's "Our hotel cannot live and grow unless you return, so we pledge to do everything possible to make your stay enjoyable," is the motto of Fred and Mary Bedford, who run this cozy eight-room hostelry located in a 300-year-old stone house. Wensleydale lamb cutlets and wensleydale cheese feature regularly on their tasty dinner menu. Market Pl., Hawes (phone: 1969-667312; fax: 1969-667162). Inexpensive.

En Route from Hawes From Hawes, drive 6 miles on the unnumbered road that crosses the river and then climbs steeply over the moors to Muker in the broad Swaledale Valley. In all directions, there are superb views up to sheep-strewn hillsides where narrow streams wind their way down into the deep ravines far below.

SWALEDALE The number of barns dotted over Swaledale's hillsides is an indication of the area's rough winter weather. The barns provide food and shelter for the valley's own breed of hardy black-faced, curly-horned sheep. With such empty hills and tiny villages, it is hard to believe that this was one of the first industrial areas in Britain. Lead was mined on its moors as far back as Roman times, and the mines—long since abandoned—were once the most productive in the world. In the 18th and 19th centuries, they provided lead for cathedral roofs all over Europe, water pipes in the growing cities, and gunpowder.

From Muker, take B6270 east for 9 miles to Reeth. Along the way, there are superb views across the broad valley that has remained completely unspoiled by any modern buildings—none have been allowed to be built for 150 years. The farmhouses and cottages themselves are worth looking at carefully, as many date from the 17th and 18th centuries. Until that time, most were made from timber and plaster, as stone was reserved for important buildings such as castles and churches. Vast quantities of stone also were used for the walls that crisscross the hillsides, looking like neat pencil lines between the fields.

In Reeth, the area's history is explained in detail in the *Swaledale Folk Museum,* tucked away on a cobbled lane near the flagpole on the village's large sloping green. It explains how and why the mines had to close at the end of the last century when it became cheaper to import lead from abroad. Today, the number of people living in Reeth is only a quarter of what it was when the mines were at their peak. The museum is closed November through *Easter;* admission charge (phone: 1748-884373).

Continue east on B6270 beside the Swale, one of the fastest flowing rivers in England, and then join A6108. Follow it out of the park to Richmond, 12 miles from Reeth.

RICHMOND A busy shopping center, with a wide cobbled market square crowded with stalls every Saturday, Richmond (pop. 7,300) is often described as typically English. It has an 11th-century castle and ancient alleys—known as "wynds"—that connect the square with the "modern" Georgian part. *Holy Trinity Church* beside the square was built in 1150 and adjoins the *Museum of the Green Howards* (Trinity Church Sq.; phone: 1748-822133), named after the famous local regiment. On display are original uniforms, medals, and campaign relics, covering its history from 1688 to the Persian Gulf War. The museum is closed December through January, Sundays in November and March, and weekends in February; admission charge.

The castle, one of the most imposing Norman remains in England, is best viewed from the other side of the river Swale, where it can be seen towering over the town, guarding the entrance to Swaledale. The river made it impregnable on three sides and the fourth was protected by the 100-foot-high rectangular keep added in the 12th century. The great hall has been re-floored and re-roofed, giving a good impression of what it was like in medieval times. From the top, there are splendid views over the town and river. The castle is closed Mondays October through *Easter;* admission charge (phone: 1748-822493).

According to local legend, King Arthur and his Knights of the Round

Table have lain for centuries sleeping in a huge cavern under the castle's walls, waiting for the time when England calls them to her service once more. Another legend says that if you listen carefully beside the river on a quiet night you can hear the steady beating of a drum coming from under the ground; it is the sound of a small drummer boy sent to trace the route of a secret passage from the castle—he was never seen again.

The town's *Tourist Information Centre* (Victoria Rd.; phone: 1748-850222; closed Sundays November through March) is opposite the *Theatre Royal* (Victoria Rd.; phone: 1748-823710), one of the oldest theaters in England. Built in 1788, it was at various times between 1848 and 1963 a wine store, auction house, and corn chandler's. Now fully restored, it is used regularly for dramatic productions; the theater also houses an unusual museum that includes the oldest painted scenery in Britain. It is closed January and Sundays in November, December, February, and March; admission charge.

The *Richmondshire Museum* (Ryders Wynd; phone: 1748-825611), near the Market Place, covers the town's history since 1071, with particular emphasis on its buildings, lead and copper mining, farming, and needlecraft. It also has a model of the town's former railway station, Victorian and Edwardian costumes, toys, and old photographs. The most popular exhibit is the vet's office set from the BBC series *All Creatures Great and Small.* The museum is closed November through *Easter;* admission charge.

A pretty walk of just under a mile beside the Swale leads to the extensive ruins of *Easby Abbey.* Founded in 1155, the ruins include a gatehouse, refectory, and church. The abbey is closed Mondays October through *Easter;* admission charge (phone: 1325-468771).

BEST EN ROUTE

Black Bull One of the dining areas in this large, family-run country inn is a renovated Pullman railway carriage. The English fare is delicious and plentiful; the steaks and seafood are particularly good. Closed Sundays and *Christmas Eve* through *Boxing Day.* Reservations advised. Major credit cards accepted. Moulton, about 1 mile from Richmond (phone: 1325-377289). Moderate.

The Lake District

Only 30 miles across in any direction, the *Lake District* has a special beauty—tarns, meres, becks, and fells, scoured and sculpted during the Ice Age and squeezed into the small county of Cumbria, just an hour or so north of Manchester. It is as though nature were offering a consolation for the sprawling rigors of the industrial belt, much too near-at-hand. No part of England is so universally loved by Britons—for the purity of its clear mountain lakes (meres); its almost vertical fields filled with grazing sheep and surrounded by painstakingly maintained stone walls; its sharp rocky peaks; and the thousands of tiny lakes (tarns) fed by innumerable waterfalls and streams (becks). Its traditional industry always has been hill farming, but increasingly the area's livelihood is tourism. Since 1951 the *Lake District* has been a national park, and visitors—hill walkers, rock climbers, historians, artists, ornithologists, and those seeking simply a bit of peace and quiet—number in the millions annually.

The earth-loving aspect of the English spirit is drawn irresistibly to the *Lake District*'s uncompromising beauty. Small wonder that J. M. W. Turner, the famous English landscape painter, spent time here sketching. The *Lake District* is primarily associated, however, with a group of his contemporaries, writers of the late 18th and early 19th centuries who not only celebrated the beauty of the region in words, but discovered here values to stand against the encroaching horrors of the industrial age. Chief among these figures was the Romantic poet William Wordsworth, who lived here for most of his life, but others associated with the region include Samuel Taylor Coleridge, Robert Southey, John Ruskin, and Thomas De Quincey.

One of the most surprising things about the *Lake District* is how small this famous area really is. You can drive right through it in less than an hour and yet spend a month without seeing even half of what time and nature have created. A map of the area shows that the principal lakes—Derwentwater, Ullswater, Windermere, Wastwater, Buttermere, Crummock Water, Grasmere, and Rydal Water—radiate from the Cumbrian Mountains like the spokes of a wheel. Some, such as Thirlmere and Haweswater, are reservoirs slaking the thirst and industry of northern cities, but the living lakes are busy with sails and stately steamers. The distances between these postcard-perfect bodies of water are short, but each lake provides a good base for exploring the neighboring area. Allowing time for some hiking as well as exploration of towns and villages, you could easily spend two days around each major lake—especially Windermere, Derwentwater, and Ullswater—before moving on.

The route described below begins in the southeastern corner of the *Lake District* at Kendal, takes the back road to Lake Windermere, and crosses the water on the ferry to Near Sawrey, Hawkshead, and Coniston. The next leg of the trip, north from Windermere, crosses the paths of the Lake Poets. Wordsworth lived the last 37 years of his life at *Rydal Mount; Dove Cottage,* the home he had occupied previously, is a few miles farther north, at Grasmere. The route then proceeds north from Grasmere and passes Thirlmere, where there is easy access to the challenging 3,118-foot mountain peak, Helvellyn. At the end of this leg is Derwentwater—perhaps the most beautiful of all the lakes. Robert Southey lived here, in the town of Keswick, where he frequently was joined by Percy Bysshe Shelley and Samuel Taylor Coleridge. Buttermere and Crummock Water are just a short drive southwest of Keswick, and beyond them, in the northwest corner of the *Lake District,* is Cockermouth, where Wordsworth and his sister, Dorothy, were both born and raised. From Cockermouth, travelers have two choices: Follow the western boundary of the *Lake District,* heading south, where numerous small roads lead into the heart of the mountains and the area's best climbing; or return to Keswick, drop south off the main road to the lovely lake of Ullswater, and complete the tour at Penrith, which is conveniently at the northeastern flank of the *Lake District* at the intersection of several main north-south and east-west routes.

The *Lake District* offers a wide range of accommodations—from small, comfortable inns to some of the country's best hotels, as well as guesthouses offering a bed, breakfast, *and* an evening meal for as little as $30 per person per night. Expect to pay between $120 and $240 per night for a double room (including private bath, TV set, and breakfast, unless otherwise indicated) in hotels listed as expensive; from $80 to $110 in moderate ones; and less than $80 in inexpensive places. A dinner for two, excluding wine, tips, or drinks, will run about $45 to $60 in expensive places; $35 to $45 in moderate spots; and less than $35 in inexpensive places. All restaurants listed serve lunch and dinner unless otherwise noted. For each location, hotels and restaurants are listed alphabetically by price category.

KENDAL Holiday traffic threads constantly through the one-way streets of this old market town (pop. 23,710), the gateway to the southern part of the *Lake District.* Because it is engaged in the manufacture of shoes, snuff, and Kendal mint cake, the town pays less attention to visitors than other places in Cumbria. Visitors, in turn, in a headlong dash to begin lakeside vacations, often give short shrift to everything but the large shopping center. But the old part of this town on the river Kent is worth exploring: an attractive huddle of slate-roofed buildings separated by small alleyways, yards, and courts; *Kendal Town Trail* (*Westmorland Gazette;* £3.95/about $6), a guide to the town's sights and history, is available in local bookstores. The ruined *Kendal Castle,* on a hill east of town, dates back to Norman times. Claims that it was the birthplace of Catherine Parr, Henry VIII's last wife, have been disputed by historians, although she probably lived here at some time. The 13th-century parish church near the center of town is unusual for its five aisles and its brasses. *Abbot Hall,* a Georgian house beside the river, houses an art gallery with modern collections and 18th-century period rooms displaying furniture and paintings, including one by Turner and one by the famous portrait artist George Romney, who spent his youth in Kendal. It is open daily; admission charge. The *Abbot Hall Craft Museum* offers one of the *Lake District*'s best collections of porcelain, jewelry, carved wood, toys, rugs, and leather items. It is open daily; admission charge (phone: 1539-722464). The *Museum of Lakeland Life and Industry,* installed in what were once the stables of *Abbot Hall,* gives an interesting look at the area's social and economic history. It is open daily; admission charge (phone: 1539-722464).

In the middle of Kendal is the *Brewery Arts Centre,* housed in a splendid 19th-century brewery. A major arts venue, the center presents exhibitions, films, theater, folk music, jazz, and mime. The restaurant and bar are popular. The center is open daily (phone: 1539-725133). The *Kendal Museum of Natural History and Archaeology* (on Station Rd.; phone: 1539-721374) is one of Britain's oldest museums, dating back to 1796. With its exhibits covering local history from Roman times, Lakeland wildlife, and the *World Wildlife Gallery,* it is a must, especially on a rainy day. It's open daily; admission charge. The tourist information center in Kendal's *Town Hall* (Highgate; phone: 1539-725758) has leaflets and hotel lists for the southern *Lake District.* It is closed Sundays October through March.

BEST EN ROUTE

Woolpack Situated in Kendal's town center, this converted 16th-century inn with 53 rooms and a restaurant has immense character and charm, successfully retaining its Old World atmosphere. Stricklandgate, Kendal (phone: 1539-723852; fax: 1539-728608). Expensive.

Natland Mill Beck Farm An extremely warm atmosphere pervades this 17th-century farmhouse with three guestrooms, sturdy beams, pine doors, ancient oak cupboards, and four-foot-thick walls. There's no restaurant, although a full English breakfast is included in the rate. Kendal (phone: 1539-721122). Inexpensive.

En Route from Kendal The main road west out of town climbs a long hill and, after about 2 miles, comes to a large traffic circle. Turn off A591 here and head down B5284 through countryside typical of the edge of the *Lake District:* neat fields, thick woodland, and a landscape that is all mounds and hummocks building up to larger hills. Pass through the village of Crook (2 miles away), and after another 5 miles the route crosses two roads skirting the eastern side of Lake Windermere and comes to a stop at the terminal of the car ferry. Bowness-on-Windermere and Windermere itself are a mile or so before the terminal.

WINDERMERE AND BOWNESS These adjoining resort areas on Lake Windermere make up one town that is a focal point of *Lake District* tourism. Bowness (also known as Bowness-on-Windermere) is the actual port on the water; Windermere is just above Bowness, inland from the lake. Between the two, virtually every recreational activity is available.

It is difficult to actually see Lake Windermere or the surrounding mountains from the town, but a 20-minute walk up Orrest Head hill (to the north of the railroad station) reveals all in a good view of the lake and the hills beyond. Scenic outlooks are a particular attraction of the Windermere countryside and some other notable ones include Queen Adelaide's Hill, an ideal picnic spot between Bowness and the main Ambleside Road; Miller Ground, a little farther along the same footpath; Biskey Howe, reached from Helm Road, Bowness; and School Knott, which has an easy, winding path to its summit east of Windermere. The information centers at Windermere (Victoria St.; phone: 15394-46499; fax: 15394-47439) and Bowness (Glebe Rd.; phone: 15394-42895) have details of these and other walks. The Windermere center is open daily; the office at Bowness is closed during winter.

Lake Windermere, the largest in England (10½ miles long), has a much softer aspect than most, with luxuriantly wooded banks filled with rhododendrons that burst into flaming color each June. The waterfront of Bowness has been attractively developed with restaurants overlooking the lake, chandleries, and shops. Visitors who fancy a pint should try the *Hole Int Wall* (phone: 15394-43488) on Lowside Street in Bowness—a 16th-century pub whose name comes from the hole in the wall that was forged to allow the blacksmith working next door to easily get his ale. Throughout the year pleasure cruises operate from the pier nearby along the length of Windermere between Lakeside at its southern end, Bowness, and Waterhead at its northern end. There are several small islands in the lake; on one of them, Belle Isle, stands an 18th-century mansion that was the first completely round house built in England. It is one of the more unusual stately homes in the *Lake District;* unfortunately it is closed to the public. The *Windermere Steamboat Museum* just north of Bowness has a wonderful collection of Victorian and Edwardian steam launches, including *Dolly,* the oldest mechanically propelled boat in the world, built in 1850. The museum pieces are afloat and you occasionally may see them steaming about on the lake. Weather permitting, you can take a trip on the 1902 *Osprey* steam launch. Contact the museum for information. The museum is closed November through *Easter;* admission charge (phone: 15394-45565). In late summer there is the *Windermere Swim,* when well-greased long-distance swimmers brave the chilly length of the lake. Just outside Windermere in Clearrow is the *Windermere Golf Club* (phone: 15394-43123), where a visitor with a membership card from another club can tee off on its 18 holes.

Just outside Bowness on the way to Windermere is *Old Laundry,* a permanent exhibition of the World of Beatrix Potter, whose *Peter Rabbit* classics, illustrated with drawings and watercolors of the local hills and lakes, have delighted children for generations. The latest lighting, video, and audio techniques bring the books' characters to life. The visitors' center has a souvenir shop and a tearoom. The exhibit is open daily; admission charge (phone: 15394-88444).

About 3 miles from Windermere, on the way to Ambleside off A591, is the *Brockhole National Park Centre,* a country house set in beautiful gardens and grounds that reach down to the lake. The center offers a program of lectures, films, and exhibitions covering crafts, natural history, farming, industrial archaeology, the ubiquitous Wordsworths, and other aspects of past and present life in the *Lake District,* as well as guided walks on the nature trail, and an adventure park for children. It is closed November through late March; no admission charge (phone: 15394-46601).

BEST EN ROUTE

Belmont Manor Located between Ambleside and Windermere, this luxury country-house hotel has 14 rooms, each with a whirlpool. There are also beautiful grounds, a pool, and a restaurant that serves traditional French and English fare. Advance hotel reservations necessary. Windermere (phone: 15394-33316; fax: 15394-33316). Expensive.

Belsfield This magnificent, 66-room Georgian house overlooking Lake Windermere is decorated with an interesting blend of period pieces and modern furnishings. There's a restaurant and a ready-made jogging track that winds through its six acres. Bowness (phone: 15394-42448; 800-225-5843; fax: 15394-46397). Expensive.

Burn How Located in secluded gardens in the center of Bowness, this elegant and comfortable restaurant offers first class service and exciting English and French food using only fresh produce. Open daily. Reservations necessary. Major credit cards accepted. Bowness (phone: 15394-46226). Expensive.

Gilpin Lodge A peaceful nine-room country-house hotel and restaurant, set in 20 acres of woodlands and gardens, it serves beautifully prepared meals with splendid wines. Open daily for dinner only. Reservations necessary. Major credit cards accepted. Crook Rd., Bowness (phone: 15394-88818; fax: 15394-88058). Expensive.

Low Wood Yet another hostelry overlooking Lake Windermere, this one was built around an old stable that dates back to 1600. The hostelry has 98 well-appointed rooms; it also boasts an international restaurant and a leisure center with a pool, a gym, squash courts, a solarium, and a Jacuzzi. Ambleside Rd., Windermere (phone: 15394-33338; fax: 15394-34072). Expensive.

Miller Howe Is it the beautiful view of the placid, tree-lined lake that makes this 13-room hotel seem such a bastion of calm, or is it the impeccable service? In either case, there is hardly a better headquarters for touring the area, and the restaurant is excellent, too. Closed mid-December through February. The restaurant is open for dinner only. Reservations necessary. Major credit cards accepted. Also see *Rural Retreats* in DIVERSIONS. Rayrigg Rd., Windermere (phone: 15394-42536; fax: 15394-45664). Expensive.

Old England Set in a fine old Georgian house in large gardens overlooking Lake Windermere, this luxurious 82-room property is a good base for enjoying Windermere and other local attractions. There is an outdoor pool and a first class restaurant. Closed Sunday lunch. Reservations advised. Major credit cards accepted. Bowness (phone: 15394-42444; 800-225-5843; fax: 15394-43432). Expensive.

Quarry Garth Built with stone quarried from its beautifully landscaped grounds, this mansion is typical of scores of private summer retreats built in the lakes by wealthy industrialists. Although small (there are just 11 guestrooms and a restaurant), the place is run with great professionalism. Ambleside Rd., Windermere (phone: 15394-43761; fax: 15394-46584). Expensive to moderate.

Cedar Manor The name of this small, charming 1860 inn comes from a 200-year-old Indian cedar tree that grows in the private gardens on the grounds. Each of the 12 guestrooms is comfortably furnished with either twin beds or a four-poster. The highly acclaimed dining room serves excellent food, including Herdwick lamb, sugar-baked Cumberland lamb, trout from the lakes, and a variety of local puddings. Open daily for dinner only. Reservations advised. Major credit cards accepted. Ambleside Rd., Windermere (phone: 15394-43192; fax: 15394-45970). Moderate.

Masons' Arms This nationally acclaimed pub offers a wide range of beers from all over the world, including its own brand, which is brewed on the premises. The menu features hearty English fare. In summer, diners can sit at outdoor tables and enjoy lovely views of the lake and countryside. Open daily. No reservations. Major credit cards accepted. Strawberry Bank, Cartmel Fell, 5 miles south of Bowness (phone: 15395-68486). Inexpensive.

NEAR SAWREY Cross to the west bank of Lake Windermere on the car ferry, which runs several times daily. When you disembark, drive about 1½ miles on B5285 to the village of Near Sawrey, the home of a Mrs. Heelis, better known as Beatrix Potter. *Hill Top Farm,* the quaint 17th-century farmhouse she lived in, can be visited by the public. The small building, an extremely popular attraction, can accommodate only a restricted number of visitors at a time, so it's a good idea to call before you come. It is closed Thursdays, Fridays (except *Good Friday*), and November through March; admission charge. When Mrs. Heelis died in 1943, she left all her property, including 4,000 acres of land, to Britain's *National Trust,* which has done much to preserve the surrounding countryside.

En Route from Near Sawrey Stay on B5285; the quiet little village of Hawkshead is another 2½ miles farther.

HAWKSHEAD Just beyond the head of Esthwaite Water, a small lake about 2 miles long, the road threads its way through a picturesque row of buildings. This is Hawkshead (pop. 660), a pleasant place with some interesting literary associations. Start your tour at the *Hawkshead Grammar School* (open daily), founded in 1585 by native son Edwin Sandys, Archbishop of York, and attended by Wordsworth between 1779 and 1783. The poet left a lasting impression by carving his name in one of the original desks. While a student, Wordsworth may have lodged at *Ann Tyson's Cottage,* on a lane off Red Lion Square, before moving to *Green End Cottage* in the hamlet of Colthouse, east of Hawkshead. Years later, he recalled the Esthwaite area where he spent his schooldays as "that belovèd Vale." Friends of Peter Rabbit should visit the *Beatrix Potter Gallery* (Main St.; phone: 15394-36355), which contains a large selection of Beatrix Potter's original watercolor drawings and illustrations. The building in which the collection is housed once was a legal office, where Potter met her future husband, attorney William Heelis. The gallery is closed November through March; admission charge.

BEST EN ROUTE

Grizedale Lodge Tucked away in another elegant former shooting lodge in the magnificent Grizedale Forest, this fine restaurant serves traditional Lakeland and English fare in lovely surroundings. The five-course dinners are particularly memorable. Open daily. Reservations necessary. Major credit cards accepted. Grizedale (phone: 15394-36532). Expensive.

En Route from Hawkshead If you like, you can choose to take B5285 directly to Coniston (a distance of about 3 miles). However, one of the most spectacular vistas on this drive can be seen by taking a short detour. A steep byroad off B5285 leads to Tarn Hows (2 miles from Hawkshead), a small fir-fringed lake high in the hills that has the best views of the surrounding countryside, especially of Coniston Water to the south and of the mountain called the "Old Man of Coniston." The village of Coniston is another 2½ miles from Tarn Hows on another unnumbered road.

CONISTON This small, charming village, which also has strong artistic associations, is about half a mile around the northwest tip of Coniston Water. A Turner masterpiece, now hanging in the *Tate Gallery* in London, was based on studies done at dawn from the crags above the village. Wordsworth wrote lovingly of the place and Alfred, Lord Tennyson spent his honeymoon at *Tent Lodge* at the head of the lake. John Ruskin, the writer, painter, critic, social reformer, and scientist, moved here in 1871, producing some of his finest work at his home, *Brantwood,* on the lake's eastern shore. *Brantwood* is closed Mondays and Tuesdays November through March; admission charge.

Ruskin is buried in the Coniston churchyard. Sir Malcolm Campbell set a world water-speed record of 141 mph in 1939 on Coniston Water, and his son, Donald, later set four world records here. The local history section of the *Ruskin Museum* has photographs of the younger Campbell's last (and fatal) attempt, in 1967, to set a new speedboat record on Coniston Water. The museum is closed November through March; admission charge (phone: 15394-41387). To explore in less hair-raising style, take the renovated Victorian steam yacht *Gondola* (phone: 15394-41288), which tours the lake several times a day March through October.

En Route from Coniston A593 winds north into the junction of the Great Langdale and Little Langdale Valleys. A side trip due west from this point follows a narrow road over two high passes in the mountains. The first, Wrynose Pass, is a long but straightforward climb. The second, Hardknott Pass (at the top of which stands a Roman fort), is reckoned to be the toughest in Britain, a tortuous road climbing the fellside by hairpin curves and descending in the same style into Eskdale, the valley of the river Esk. The reward is a series of wonderful views, but be prepared for some rigorous, adventurous driving. (In winter, it's worth checking with area police to see if the passes are open.)

A less stressful alternative is to ignore the turnoff and follow A593 about 7 miles to Ambleside. Another choice, bypassing Ambleside and nearby Rydal altogether, is to take B5343 to Elterwater, which has an excellent hotel, the *Britannia Inn* (phone: 1966-7210), then proceed directly and spectacularly into Grasmere via the narrow road over High Close, which leads north about 5 miles down a hill called Red Bank.

AMBLESIDE Just under a mile from the north end of Lake Windermere, Ambleside is an excellent touring base for climbers eager to explore Lakeland's hills and crags. Scafell Pike (3,210 feet, the highest peak in England) is a considerable hike from Ambleside, but other peaks are more accessible. Be sure to obtain detailed maps of trails and to make proper arrangements before starting. The local information center is in Ambleside's old *Court House* (Market Sq.; phone: 15394-32582); it's closed November through March. A short distance away, up the lane past the *Salutation* hotel (see *Best en Route*), is Stockghyll Force, a beautiful waterfall cascading 70 feet to rocks below. *St. Mary's Church,* erected in 1854 by Sir Gilbert Scott, has a memorial to Wordsworth and a mural of the village's rush-bearing festival, when flowers and rushes are carried through the streets to the church. The festival, thought to descend from a Roman harvest ceremony, is still held yearly on the first Saturday in July. The *Zefferellis* complex, off Compston Road, has an excellent selection of specialty boutiques, along with a cinema, a pizzeria, and an arcade. Visitors should also stop at *Adrian Sankey's Workshops* (Rydal Rd.; phone: 15394-33039), behind the *Little Bridge House,* where guests can watch lead crystal being made into bowls, vases, and other collectibles. Waterhead, the northern terminus of the Lake

Windermere pleasure cruises (they also can be boarded at Bowness and at Lakeside) is a mile south of Ambleside on A591. At Waterhead is *Haye's Garden World* (phone: 15394-33434), whose plant center is housed in an ornate crystal palace. There is also a café, a patio lounge, and an adventure playground. It's a great place to visit, whatever the weather.

BEST EN ROUTE

Rothay Manor Near Ambleside at the head of Lake Windermere, this elegant, 15-room hotel with its own croquet lawn has a country-house feeling that extends to the restaurant, where traditional fare is served. Open mid-February through December (phone: 15394-33607). Expensive.

Salutation This refurbished 32-room hotel is based in an old 16th-century coaching inn. The restaurant serves traditional fare. Lake Rd., Ambleside (phone: 15394-32244; fax: 15394-34157). Moderate.

Stampers A small cellar restaurant in an old stamp house, it used to be the workplace of William Wordsworth. A wide range of local homemade dishes is served. Fine food and good service support the restaurant's excellent reputation. Open daily. Reservations advised. Major credit cards accepted. Church St., Ambleside (phone: 15394-32775). Moderate.

Sheila's Cottage Country Restaurant and Tea Shop Ideally located in the center of town is this delightful cottage serving a variety of local meat and seafood specialties, as well as an excellent afternoon tea. Closed Sundays and Monday evenings. Reservations necessary at peak times. Major credit cards accepted. The Slack, Ambleside (phone: 15394-33079). Inexpensive.

En Route from Ambleside Rydal is 2 miles north of Ambleside on A591.

RYDAL William Wordsworth, with his wife, three children, sister, and sister-in-law, moved to this village in 1813 and lived here until his death 37 years later. His home, *Rydal Mount,* is an interesting, rambling old house. It contains a large collection of memorabilia, including several portraits of his family and friends, and his personal library. His love of nature is reflected in the four-and-a-half-acre garden he grew around *Rydal Mount.* Wordsworth drew heavily on the surrounding countryside for inspiration and poetic images, and the mute crags and flowered hillsides around his home appear repeatedly in his work. The house is closed Tuesdays November through March; admission charge (phone: 15394-33002).

Set in 30 acres of gardens is *Rydal Hall.* Owned by the Diocese of Carlisle, this Georgian hall is closed to the public, but its lovely gardens are open daily; no admission charge (phone: 15394-32050).

Just a short distance up the road is *Nab Cottage,* occupied briefly by Thomas De Quincey (1806) and later by Samuel Taylor Coleridge's eldest son, Hartley. The cottage is privately owned and closed to the public.

En Route from Rydal From Rydal, continue north on A591 and an unnumbered (but signposted) road about 2½ miles to the village of Grasmere along the north bank of Rydal Water, which is one of the smallest lakes in the district and which, together with the river Rothay, links Lake Windermere to Grasmere Lake. The route skirts Grasmere Lake, just a mile long and half as wide, with an emerald green island in its center. Beyond the lake, off A591 to the right at the edge of Grasmere, is *Dove Cottage,* another of Wordsworth's homes; information and tours are offered by the *Wordsworth Trust* (phone: 15394-35544), a nonprofit organization which runs it.

Wordsworth and his sister, Dorothy, lived at *Dove Cottage* from 1799 until 1808. Before their arrival, the house had been a small inn called the *Dove and Olive Branch.* While they lived there, it became a frequent stop for a stream of eminent literary figures such as Coleridge, William Hazlitt, Charles Lamb, and Sir Walter Scott. After Wordsworth married, he and his family turned the cottage over to their friends Thomas De Quincey and his wife. A Wordsworth exhibition building, including a fine restaurant, is situated in the *Dove Cottage* complex. It contains manuscripts of letters and poems and a remarkable collection of portraits on loan from the *National Portrait Gallery* in London. Both the museum and the cottage are closed January through mid-February; admission charge. Grasmere is just beyond *Dove Cottage* on A591. The road winds through town, its path dictated by the haphazard scattering of houses of somber, blue-green Lakeland stone.

GRASMERE This beautiful village, set against a backdrop of high hills, lies at the heart of the *Lake District.* Before moving to *Rydal Mount,* Wordsworth lived in two other houses in Grasmere besides *Dove Cottage:* first at *Allan Bank* (still a private home), then at an old rectory (which has since been destroyed). Now the squat, foursquare walls of the *Church of St. Oswald* (parts of which may be 13th century) preside over his grave and those of his wife, his sister, and Hartley Coleridge, buried in a corner of the churchyard.

Although August is the most crowded month in which to visit the *Lake District*, it is also the month of the *Grasmere Sports,* usually held on the third Thursday of the month. Begun in the mid-1800s to encourage Cumberland and Westmorland wrestling, the event now includes other traditional Lakeland sports such as fell running and hound trailing. (Cumberland and Westmorland always have been fierce rivals.) The wrestling, especially, is a curious sport to watch. Competitors stand chest to chest and grasp one another by locking arms behind each other's back. The goal is to throw the opponent to the ground; the weighty and well-balanced wrestlers may struggle all day while other events take place elsewhere. Fell running, an all-out dash to the top of the nearest mountain and back, is another spectacle at the Grasmere games. The *Guides' Race* directly up the steep sides of Butter Crags is undertaken by lean athletes who move with astonishing speed up the fell to the turning point and then bound back down with the agility of mountain goats. Other events are the hound trail competitions, which reflect the *Lake District*'s importance as a center for fox hunting, done here on foot with packs of hardy hounds.

Grasmere, like Ambleside, also has an annual rush-bearing ceremony, held on *St. Oswald's Day* (the Saturday nearest August 5). If you want to sample the tasty gingerbread that is distributed to the bearers, stop by *Sarah Nelson's Original Gingerbread Shop* (phone: 15394-35428) in the center of town. There are some other distinctive shops in town, among them *English Lakes Perfumes* (phone: 15394-35444), offering such fragrances as Grasmere Rose and Keswick Gardenia, and the *Heaton Cooper Studio* (phone: 15394-35280), with the work of W. Heaton Cooper, the best known of the *Lake District* watercolor artists. The sound of clattering comes from *Chris Reekie, Weaver* (phone: 15394-35586), a weaving mill and shop with a nice display of woolen wear. All are in the center of town.

BEST EN ROUTE

Michaels Nook A charming Victorian country home containing 12 guestrooms, furnished by the proprietor, Reginald Gifford, with many beautiful antiques. There is also an excellent restaurant offering English fare. Guests may use the pool, sauna, and solarium at the nearby *Wordsworth* hotel, also owned by Gifford. The restaurant is open daily. Reservations necessary. Major credit cards accepted. Grasmere (phone: 15394-35496; fax: 15394-35765). Expensive.

Rothay Garden Overlooking the *Riverside Gardens,* this internationally renowned restaurant offers an interesting choice of entrées using local meat, fish, and game, as well as seasonal vegetables. Closed Sunday lunch. Reservations advised. Major credit cards accepted. Broadgate, Grasmere (phone: 15394-35334; fax: 15394-35723). Expensive.

White Moss House Originally three separate cottages, owned by Wordsworth's family until the 1930s, this property has been converted by its current owners into a pleasant seven-room hotel. It overlooks Rydal Water, and there's usually a welcoming fire blazing in the fireplace. The dining room serves English fare. Open mid-March through early November. The restaurant serves dinner only and is closed Sundays (except to hotel guests). Reservations necessary. MasterCard and Visa accepted. Rydal Water (phone: 15394-35295). Expensive.

Swan Over a century ago, Wordsworth brought Sir Walter Scott and other friends to enjoy a dram or two at this old coaching inn. Today it's a friendly 36-room hotel with a good dining room that features vegetarian dishes. Grasmere (phone: 15394-35551; 800-225-5843; fax: 15394-35741). Moderate.

En Route from Grasmere Continuing north on A591, the road climbs Dunmail Raise. After about 10 miles, Thirlmere comes into view, a long, lifeless-looking lake from which water runs (helped only by gravity) to Manchester, 100 miles south. In 1876, the lake level was raised artificially by the construction of a 100-foot-high dam intended to meet the needs of the Industrial Revolution in urban Lancashire. The unintended flood that was created sparked one of the earliest environmental battles in Britain, which led to the creation of the *National Trust* and, ultimately, the national parks. The village of Wythburn, at the foot of the lake, was lost in the flood, but its tiny 17th-century chapel was on high enough ground to survive. It's worth a visit, and its parking lot is the starting point of a climbing trail to the peak of Helvellyn, the 3,118-foot mountain that rises to the right of A591. Helvellyn offers spectacular views and can be climbed easily from the Thirlmere side. But the climb is more interesting from the east side, where long, lateral ridges fall into Patterdale, near Ullswater. There are few more exhilarating scrambles in the whole of Britain than along Striding Edge to Helvellyn summit and back to Patterdale via Swirral Edge.

Keswick, is about 3 miles north of Thirlmere. You'll get an excellent view of the area from the crest of Castlerigg, and a road on the right leads to the prehistoric *Castlerigg Stone Circle.*

KESWICK Sheltered by the towering Skiddaw (3,053 feet), this ancient and prosperous market town with a population of 4,777 sits close to the north shore of Derwentwater, 3 miles long and a mile wide, surrounded by a mixture of rock, grassy banks, and glens. It is one of the loveliest (some say *the* loveliest) of the area's lakes, and rowboats and cruising craft can be rented to explore, fish, or visit some of its many tiny islands. The remains of a 7th-century retreat are on the island of St. Herbert.

Many poets, including Shelley, Southey, Wordsworth, and Coleridge, were drawn to this area, and the *Keswick Museum and Art Gallery* (Station Rd.; phone: 17687-73263) displays some of their manuscripts, letters, and personal effects. Hugh Walpole, who lived on the shore of Derwentwater and set his powerful "Herries" series of novels in this valley, is also represented in the collection. The museum is closed November through *Easter;* admission charge.

A number of buildings in the area have literary associations. Southey, Wordsworth, and Coleridge patronized the bar at the 16th-century *George* hotel (3 St. John's St.), which claims to be the oldest structure in town; and Southey's home, *Greta Hall* (which Coleridge lived in for three years before the Southey family took over), has become part of *Keswick School* on Main Street. Also, Southey's body lies in the *Crosthwaite Churchyard* (Church La.), and Walpole is buried in *St. John's Churchyard* (Ambleside Rd.).

The *Cumberland Pencil Museum* (Southey Hill Works; phone: 17687-73626) is a unique attraction that illustrates pencil making and displays pencil drawings and the world's largest pencil (7 feet tall!). It is open daily; admission charge.

Keswick earns its living from visitors and caters to them with a long list of hotels, boardinghouses, and bed and breakfast establishments. The information center is in *Moot Hall* (Market Sq.; phone: 17687-72645); it's open daily.

Two of the best points for viewing Derwentwater and its environs are at Castle Head (529 feet), just south of Keswick, and at Friar's Crag, a rocky headland on the lake. John Ruskin was particularly enamored of the latter, and there is a memorial to him here.

BEST EN ROUTE

Grange Country House Set in an elegant 10-room hotel, this cozy restaurant serves fine, traditional English fare. Open daily. Reservations advised. MasterCard and Visa accepted. Manor Brow, Keswick (phone: 17687-72500). Expensive.

Stakis Lodore Swiss Located 3 miles south of Keswick, this property has glorious views of Derwentwater and Lodore Falls. The 70-room hotel is grand in appearance. The restaurant features international dishes, including Swiss specialties. Facilities include indoor and outdoor pools, a sauna, a massage room, tennis, squash, and boat trips on Derwentwater. There is also a beauty shop and a nursery. Open April through December. Borrowdale (phone: 17687-77285; 800-STAKIS-1; fax: 17687-77343). Expensive.

Coledale Inn With lovely mountain views, this friendly family-run inn is located at Braithwaite, just 2 miles from Keswick. Light snacks and full meals of local dishes are served daily. Open daily. No reservations. Major credit cards accepted. Braithwaite, near Keswick (phone: 17687-78272). Inexpensive.

En Route from Keswick Drive south on B5289 to the quite beautiful Borrowdale Valley. The road runs between the east shore of Derwentwater and the high cliffs that are immensely popular with climbers. Before Rosthwaite (6 miles from Keswick), the huge Bowder Stone stands precariously on edge. Across the vale is Castle Crag, a 900-foot-high rock cone that can be climbed without too much effort in under half an hour. Great Gable, a little farther along, is more challenging—2,949 feet of tough climbing. It takes about three hours to ascend this monster, but the view is well worth the effort: The entire area from Skiddaw to Windermere, and even the Isle of Man are visible from the crest.

Continue on B5289, crossing Honister Pass, which rises well over 1,000 feet. From the summit there is an impressive view toward Buttermere Lake, with Fleetwith Pike and the steep face of Honister Crag dominating the road. Beyond the pass, the road drops through rough territory before reaching *Gatesgarth Farm* at the foot of the long, winding descent. The farm specializes in raising Herdwick sheep, a tough breed that is able to survive the often harsh conditions of the *Lake District* fells. (At the well-known *Lakeland* stores in Bowness, Ambleside, Kendal, and Keswick, you can buy clothing made from Herdwick wool.)

About 6 miles from Rosthwaite, the placid waters of Buttermere come into view. Buttermere's twin, Crummock Water, lies just beyond to the northwest. The flat mile of valley floor separating these two lakes suggests that they were once one. Tucked between the lakes are two villages: Loweswater (off the north end of Crummock Water), once the metropolis of these parts; and Buttermere, nothing more than a pretty huddle of houses and a small click-mill to grind rye and oats. The local balance shifted with the coming of the road across Honister Pass. The Lake Poets discovered and wrote about Buttermere and its charms, Turner painted the lake and Honister Crag, and gradually the number of visitors increased. Today the village is a popular destination for trout fishermen (particularly in April, May, and September) and climbers. Not far from Buttermere is Scale Force, a lively waterfall with a drop of over 120 feet. It's a short excursion; the easiest access is by crossing the stream between the two lakes and following the path on the far side, but wear boots or hiking shoes—the trail is muddy.

A few miles north of Buttermere, B5289 intersects B5292; from here, you have two choices: take B5292 east over Whinlatter Pass (not as steep as Honister Pass) toward A66, Keswick, and Penrith, or extend your trip by heading northwest about 10 miles to Cockermouth.

COCKERMOUTH An attractive market town with a number of good antique shops, Cockermouth is famous as Wordsworth's birthplace (1770). It is strategically located at the junction of the Cocker and Derwent Rivers, and though its origins date to pre-Roman times, little remains from its earliest period. Even its 12th-century castle was largely destroyed during the Civil War violence of the mid-1600s. *Wordsworth House* (on Main St.; no phone), built in 1745, is a fairly simple, countrified example of Georgian architecture that has survived intact (though the original furnishings are long gone). The house is closed Thursdays and November through March; admission charge. William's father is buried in the churchyard. Fletcher Christian, leader of the mutiny on the *Bounty,* was born in 1764 at *Moorland Close,* a nearby farmhouse (closed to the public). A special place to take children is the *Cumberland Toy and Model Museum* (Banks Ct., Market Pl.; phone: 1900-827606), where they can play with a huge variety of toys, including dolls, model railways, and remote-control racing cars. It is closed December through January, except by appointment; admission charge.

BEST EN ROUTE

Armathwaite Hall This vast ancestral home, which was remodeled in the 19th century, gleams with wood paneling and is adorned with hunting trophies. Facilities include a restaurant, leisure center, and outdoor equestrian arena. Bassenthwaite (phone: 17687-76551; fax: 17687-76220). Expensive.

Pheasant Inn This 16th-century coaching inn with 20 rooms and huge fireplaces is on Bassenthwaite Lake near Thornthwaite Forest. Views of the lake are, unfortunately, blocked by a hill. The pub restaurant serves simple English fare. Bassenthwaite Lake, off A66, near Cockermouth (phone: 17687-76234; fax: 17687-76002). Moderate.

En Route from Cockermouth Here again, you have two choices. You can take A5086 south, explore the western fringe of the *Lake District,* and leave the area the same way you came, via Kendal. The second option is to return east through Keswick, detour from the main road onto A5091 to the shore of Ullswater, and leave via Penrith to the north.

If you choose A5086 south, Ennerdale Water, perhaps the least visited of the larger lakes, lies about 10 miles away, on a secondary roadway to the east. A similar turnoff about 10 miles beyond leads to Wastwater, the deepest of the lakes, set among stern and savage-faced mountains in marked contrast to the gentle placement of Windermere. The village of Wasdale Head, a mile beyond the lake, is an excellent climbing center (and has been since rock climbing became a popular sport in the 19th century), but these mountains are strictly for experts. Return to A5086 (which becomes A595 near Ennerdale Water) and drive to Ravenglass, at the mouth of the river Esk about 15 miles beyond Ennerdale Water. The Eskdale Valley can be explored either by road or on the narrow-gauge, steam-powered *Ravenglass and Eskdale Railway* (narrow is an understatement—it's 15 inches across), which runs between Ravenglass and *Dalegarth Station* near Boot year-round, although service is only on weekends November through March (phone: 1229-717171). Just beyond Ravenglass, *Muncaster Castle,* the seat of the Pennington family for 700 years, overlooks the Esk. It is closed Mondays (except bank holidays) and November through *Easter;* admission charge. Farther on, at Broughton (12 miles from Ravenglass), another secondary road (A593) leads up another 9 miles to Coniston. Just east of Broughton, A595 bears south along the coast, and A5092 continues east toward A590, A6, the market town of Kendal, and the M6 motorway.

If you choose to visit Ullswater, return to Keswick (either on the main A66 road or on B5292 across Whinlatter Pass). Follow the main road east out of town for 9 miles, turn south onto A5091, and continue another 13 miles to Ullswater, the second largest of the region's lakes. The best way to explore this lovely winding stretch of water, cradled by high fells, is to set out on it. Boats can be hired and cruises start at Glenridding at the head of the lake; at its northern end, the town of Pooley Bridge is another place to arrange an outing. A major attraction near Pooley Bridge is the 18th-century *Dalemain,* an Elizabethan house with a Georgian façade and delightful gardens. There also are three museums and splendid public rooms, as well as a gift shop, restaurant, and adventure playground. It is closed November through March; admission charge (phone: 17684-86450).

The lake is only 7½ miles long (and an average half-mile wide), but the distance between Glenridding and Penrith by road is 13 miles, along a stretch of A592 that skirts the northern bank of Ullswater. This grassy fell comes alive with daffodils each year, and traveling poets can, as Wordsworth did, pause beneath the trees to write about the yellow blooms. On the lake's western shore, the pretty Aira Force waterfall is a pleasant place to stop. A worthwhile diversion off A592 near Pooley Bridge is the secondary road along the southern shore of the lake past the *Sharrow Bay* hotel (see *Best en Route*), which surveys the most scenic views in the district; the road leads ultimately to the peaceful valley of Martindale, 4½ miles from Pooley Bridge.

Return to A592, which continues northeast of Ullswater toward Penrith.

BEST EN ROUTE

Leeming House Commanding fine views over Ullswater, this gracious, porticoed Georgian country house sits on 20 acres of landscaped gardens on the northern shore of the lake. The 40 rooms are comfortable and attractively furnished, and the restaurant is rather grand. There's fishing during the summer. Watermillock (phone: 17684-86622; fax: 17684-86443). Expensive.

Sharrow Bay Partners Francis Coulson and Brian Sack have made this spot one of the most respected and attractive hotels in the area. This stone country house is on the southern shore of Ullswater, and 28 rooms and suites (26 with private baths) are located in the main house, a cottage on the grounds, and a farmhouse 1 mile down the road. Dining on the restaurant's continental fare is a pleasure. A Relais & Châteaux member. Also see *Rural Retreats* in DIVERSIONS. Open March through November. Reservations necessary. No credit cards accepted. Pooley Bridge (phone: 17684-86301 or 17684-86483; fax: 17684-86349). Expensive.

Old Church About 400 yards of Ullswater lap the front lawn of this 18th-century Georgian country house, with 10 rooms and a restaurant serving good English fare. Watermillock (phone: 17684-86204; fax: 17684-86368). Moderate.

PENRITH This charming town was burned twice during the 14th century by bands of marauding Scots, but since then it has withstood time and the onslaught of travelers comfortably; 12,086 people live here today. Its oldest section grew up around the 13th-century *Church of St. Andrew* (rebuilt in the 1700s) and the nearby 16th-century schoolhouse. Several conflicting legends surround the presence of the two stone formations on the church grounds, known as Giant's Grave and Giant's Thumb, but one holds that this is the burial place of an ancient king. The ruins of *Penrith Castle* are now a town park, but two fine 16th-century inns, both on Great Dockray Square, the *Gloucester Arms* (phone: 1768-62150) and the *Two Lions* (phone: 1768-64446), still thrive. Close to the town center, near the main railway station, is the *Penrith Steam Museum,* which displays steam traction engines (in steam most days), steam models, and working blacksmith's and engineer's shops. It's closed weekends and October through *Easter;* admission charge (phone: 1768-62154).

North Lakes Conveniently located off junction 40 of the M6 (though not near enough to hear traffic noise), this 85-room hotel offers a sauna, a pool, a Jacuzzi, a snooker room, squash courts, and a mini-gym. The restaurant serves a wide range of traditional fare. Ullswater Rd., Penrith (phone: 1768-68111; fax: 1768-68291). Expensive.

En Route from Penrith From here you can take the M6 just west of town, pick up A74, and follow A75 into Dumfries (a 53-mile drive) to connect with the *Southwest Scotland* route, also in this section.

Wales

It doesn't take long to understand why Wales is to many Welshmen a song and an inspiration. It has been so for many centuries. From the earliest times—and Welsh has been written since the 7th century—bards have expressed their love of this enchanting land.

Wales is small, so you can get to know quite a lot of it even in a short time. It is just over 8,000 square miles, about half the size of Switzerland, has about 2.8 million people—and about 10 million sheep. Around 160 miles in length, it takes only five hours or so to drive from north to south in normal conditions. But don't: It would be like bolting down an ambrosial meal.

Wales is special. From its seabird-haunted islets and seal-sentried rocks reaching out into the Irish Sea, to its mountains where Everest teams train, Wales mixes sudden drama with soft stillness. There is a grandeur about it, a sense of stubbornness. It is brightly pastoral, offset here and there with dark smudges of industry.

While Cardiff, the capital, can be reached by the 125-mph super-trains in less than two hours from London, there is a sense in which Wales remains England's unknown neighbor. It is, as it always has been, a mountainous stronghold in the west. The land and the original Celtic people somehow keep their separate character. And about one-sixth of the people still use the Welsh language, rich in literature and color, older than English, the tongue of the original Britons. Indeed, the Saxons gave Wales its name, calling the fiercely defiant people who lived there the *wealas,* meaning "foreigners." The Welsh, however, gave their land a different name: Cymru (pronounced *Kum*-ree), "the land of brothers." You'll see the word on the signs as you cross the border: "Croeso i Gymru—Welcome to Wales." (Don't be worried that Cymru changes to Gymru. Welsh is a language in which certain initial letters change, depending on the words preceding them.)

Bear in mind, as you travel around, that the story of the language is a considerable part of the story of Wales. It is one of the oldest languages and literatures in Europe. It is flowing and musical. And lovely Welsh first (given) names remain very popular. Women have names like Lowri, Menna, Megan, and Rhiannon. Men are called Idris, Owen, and Rhys. Language does not present a problem for the visitor, however—everyone speaks English. The chief problem visitors face is some of the jaw-breaking place-names, such as Llanfairpwlgwyngyllgogerychwyrndrobwll Lantisiliogogoch (known for short—thank God—as Llanfair P. G.), the longest place-name in Britain.

During the 6th and 7th centuries Wales became a largely Christian country through the work of St. David and his followers. And St. David, the patron saint of Wales, is one of the prime figures of Welsh history. Between the 6th and 13th centuries Wales was divided into kingdoms and princedoms. The rulers fought among themselves in addition to battling the English. But there were exceptions, like the early-10th-century King Hywel Dda (Hywel the Good), who framed laws for an orderly way of life. A pioneer supporter of women's equality, Hywel decreed that a woman could divorce her husband if he were impotent and had halitosis! Under men like Hywel, culture flourished and the *eisteddfod* (pronounced *eye*-steth-vod), a competitive festival of poetry and song, became part of the Welsh tradition. There are numerous *eisteddfodau* in Wales today, the biggest being the *Royal National Eisteddfod* and the *International Musical Eisteddfod* (see *Best Festivals* in DIVERSIONS).

During the 12th and 13th centuries the rulers of England sought to bring the troublesome Welsh under their control. The most striking reminders of this period are the great castles that dot the land. There are scores of them, many of them the finest in Europe, majestic residue of war and conquest. They look splendid against their backdrops of coast or mountains and reflect the wild land they were built to defend and subdue. Among the best are the eight built by King Edward I of England to complete and sustain his conquest. Warrior Edward was determined to defeat Llywelyn, the last native Prince of Wales, and bring the country to heel. In 1282 Llywelyn's head ended up on a pike in London, and Wales came under English control. When the Welsh demanded a new non–English-speaking prince, the king gave the title to his infant son, who was still too young to speak any language. Thus began the tradition that the male heir to the throne is always invested as the Prince of Wales.

In 1536, during the reign of King Henry VIII, Wales and England were formally joined together and made equal under the law. In 1588 the Bible was officially published in Welsh, the single most important influence on the language's survival. It made the Welsh literate in their own language. And in the 19th century, when Wales embraced the non-Episcopalian form of worship, the Welsh Bible was a keystone of education. During this century use of the Welsh language has declined. Some fear that it eventually will die out, and there have been many campaigns to promote it. It remains the domestic language of many people (there are about a half million who speak it) and it survives in books, songs, comics, radio, and television.

Much of Wales is rural farm country. In the mountains you can see the tough little hill farms and hear shepherds whistling for their scruffy, intelligent, black and white dogs (a good sheepdog is worth hundreds of pounds). The southeast of the country is heavily industrial (coal mining, steelmaking, and manufacturing), and this is where most people live. The narrow and tortuous valleys from Ebbw Vale in the east to Ammanford in the west, an area known as The Valleys, were once peaceful and wooded gorges, but the coal age changed everything. South Wales became an industrial powerhouse, one of the keys to British economic expansion. A century ago this part of Wales was the most intensively mined area of the world, and during the coal rush workers poured in from rural Wales, England, Ireland, Italy, Greece, and Spain. They made an exciting mixture, creating a varied and fascinating community, renowned for its spirit, its politics, and its culture. Coal's heyday has passed, and the towns, with their neat rows of houses slotted into the steep hillsides and the huge chapels, are boarded up. Efforts are currently being made to entice foreign investment in the area to revive the economy.

While Welsh coal was warming the world, Welsh slate was roofing it. The great slate quarries and caverns of north Wales were the heart of a big industry. But that industry has shrunk dramatically and vast heaps of slate waste are monuments to an epoch.

Our route gives travelers the essential flavor of Wales, starting in the southeast and traversing the Brecon Beacons across to lovely Carmarthen. It is all dramatic hills, soft pools, rushing waterfalls, and stately rivers. The route heads northwest across old Cardiganshire to pleasant Mid-Wales. Farther on it forges into sublime Snowdonia with its handsome peaks and robust and defiant cottages and farms. It will be hard to resist the temptation to take diversions from the route—so don't try. Off the beaten track are many small pubs, guesthouses, farmhouses, and restaurants where you can get a night's stay and a decent meal for a very reasonable price. While many Welsh towns adhere to strict religious observance on Sundays, the laws forbidding pubs to remain open on Sundays have been lifted in most towns. When making your travel plans, remember that many of the roads in Wales are unpaved and rather serpentine and that the terrain in general is rather mountainous, so factor in plenty of time to get from place to place.

For additional information on most of the Welsh castles and other historic monuments listed below, contact either *CADW* (Welsh Historic Monuments, *Brunel House,* Cardiff CF2 1UY, Wales; phone: 1222-465511) or the *National Trust* (Trinity Sq., Llandudno, Gwynedd Ll3 02DE, Wales; phone: 1558-822800). For further information on travel in Wales, contact the *Wales Tourist Board* (*Brunel House,* Cardiff CF2 1UY, Wales; phone: 1222-499909).

Expect to pay $110 or more per night for a double room (including private bath, TV set, and breakfast, unless otherwise indicated) in those places we've listed as expensive; $60 to $100 in the moderate category; and less than $60 in the inexpensive range. You'll find that a good majority of the hotels we list in the Welsh countryside are in the moderate range—usually small inns with few rooms and delightful surroundings. But even expensive Welsh hotels aren't *too* expensive considering the experience that awaits, and almost all have lower prices on weekends. Useful to the visitor is *Welsh Rarebits,* a brochure listing many of Wales's most enchanting hotels, and *Welsh Rarebits: Great Little Places,* listing inns, guesthouses, and farmhouses. Both are available at any tourist office, or from *EuroWales* (PentreBach, Montgomery Powys SY15 6HR, Wales; phone: 1686-668030; fax: 1686-

668029). Another excellent source is the *Logis of Great Britain* guide to high-quality, small hotels throughout Great Britain. The guide is not available in bookstores; to order it, write to *Logis of Great Britain* (20 Church Rd., Horspath, Oxford 0X9 1RU, England). The price is £8.95 (about $9), including postage and handling; the publishers will accept payment only in pounds, so it's best to order with a credit card. No matter where you stay, and even if it's off-season, book your room in advance. This is especially crucial in summer, when the national music festivals are held.

Over the last few years, the number and quality of restaurants in Wales have increased. The best (outside Cardiff) are still found in the better hotels; the remainder tend to be small, inexpensive cafés that seem to be caught in a time warp. When choosing a restaurant, look for the Taste of Wales logo, a Welsh Dragon with a plate, knife, and fork. The logo means that the establishment uses Welsh products or provides Welsh specialty meals. For a listing of Taste of Wales members, consult *Wales: A Good Eating Guide* (costing £5.95/about $8.95), published by the Taste of Wales organization and available in many major bookstores. Expect to pay $70 or more for dinner for two, including wine, at restaurants we list as expensive; $45 to $65 in the moderate category; and less than $45 at inexpensive places. All restaurants listed serve lunch and dinner unless otherwise noted. For each location, hotels and restaurants are listed alphabetically by price category.

MONMOUTH The Romans saw at once that this site had an important strategic position at the junction of the rivers Monnow and Wye and built a fort here that they called Blestium. There is not much left of the later Norman fortifications except the remarkable bridge and gatehouse over the Monnow, dating from the 13th century. And almost nothing remains of the castle where King Henry V was born, probably in 1387. Today, Monmouth is an easygoing market town content with its role, and 7,379 people make their homes here. There is an 18th-century shire hall in Agincourt Square with statues of Henry V and Charles Rolls (1877–1910), founder of Rolls-Royce, who grew up nearby. Behind the hall is the *Monmouth Museum,* with exhibits on the town's history. Included among the museum's displays is the Rolls family's private collection of memorabilia about Admiral Horatio Nelson's life. The museum is open daily; admission charge (phone: 1600-713519).

The countryside surrounding Monmouth is delightful, particularly the Wye Valley. And you can take a meandering side trip to Tintern by driving 7 miles south on A466. Here is *Tintern Abbey,* a lovely 13th- and 14th-century ruin in a tranquil setting beside the river Wye. Founded by Baron Walter de Clare in 1131, the abbey fell victim to Henry VIII's Dissolution of the Monasteries in 1539. But though roofless and ruined, it's still romantic and inspiring. William Wordsworth, who wrote the famous poem about the abbey, commented, "No poem of mine was composed under circumstances more pleasant than this."

The Crown at Whitebrook At this 17th-century coaching inn with 12 rooms and a superb restaurant dishes are prepared with local ingredients such as lamb, game, and salmon, and served with French flair. The inn and restaurant are closed *Christmas* and *Boxing Day;* the restaurant is closed to non-guests Monday lunch and Sunday evenings. Reservations advised. Major credit cards accepted. Whitebrook, 5 miles south of Monmouth between the A466 and B4293 (phone: 1600-860254; 800-435-4504; fax: 1600-860607). Expensive.

Riverside Another coaching inn, this time from the 18th century, it overlooks the Monnow Bridge and offers 17 comfortable rooms, as well as a good restaurant and bar. Cinderhill St., Monmouth (phone: 1600-715577). Moderate.

En Route from Monmouth In Gwent, about 8 miles from Monmouth on the main A40, is *Raglan Castle,* built in the 1430s. It's the central feature of the little town and one of the best examples of late medieval castles. One of its oldest sections is the moated, partly destroyed *Great Yellow Tower of Gwent.* Henry VII lived here as a boy, and Charles I stayed at the castle after his army lost the battle of Naseby in the Civil War. Note especially the large hall, the six-sided keep, and the long, surrounding wall. Also see the exhibition on the castle's history. The castle is open daily; admission charge (phone: 1291-690228).

Six miles south of *Raglan,* off the A449 road to Newport, is the meadowy little borough of Usk built on the bank of the river from which it derives its name. Be sure to taste the justly famous Usk salmon. The history-minded will enjoy the 13th-century *Church of St. Mary's* and the ruins of the castle dating from the days when barons ruled the border country in the 12th century.

From *Raglan,* it's another 9 miles west on A40 to Abergavenny.

ABERGAVENNY Gateway to the *Brecon Beacons National Park,* this bustling market town, soaked in history, stands beside the river Usk guarded by four mountains: Sugar Loaf, Blorenge, Skirrid, and Little Skirrid. The streets of Abergavenny are lined with Tudor, Georgian, and Victorian buildings, and canny trading takes place in the marketplace, where weatherbeaten farmers sell their sheep, pigs, cattle, and horses. Romans and Normans occupied the site of the town because of its strategic location, and the frontier Braose family made it their base in the battles against the Welsh. Tough William Braose invited Welsh chiefs to a *Christmas* dinner at *Abergavenny Castle* in 1175 and had them murdered while they supped. The treacherous baron had his comeuppance years later: King John stripped his lands from him in 1207 and William died a beggar in 1211. The castle ruins are worth exploring and from here you can get a great view over the rolling hills. With a population of 9,427, Abergavenny is a good center for tourists: Hill walking, fishing, and pony trekking are excellent and you can rent canal cruisers and other boats from several firms on the west side of town. There is a tourist information center (Cross St.; phone: 1873-857588) with an exhibition on *Brecon Beacons National Park;* it is closed October through April.

BEST EN ROUTE

Allt-Yr-Ynys Set on 16 acres bordering the national park, this Elizabethan farmhouse has been converted into a hostelry with 11 luxurious guestrooms (two with four-poster beds), a Jacuzzi, a sauna, and a heated indoor pool. Clay-pigeon shooting is available on the grounds. There's also a good restaurant that serves hearty fare, as well as vegetarian meals. Walterstone, Herefordshire (phone: 1873-890307; fax: 1873-890539). Expensive.

Llansantffraed Court An imposing red brick, neo-Georgian manor set on 19 acres, with 21 rooms—many with open beams and fine tiled fireplaces. The small restaurant serves Welsh and continental fare. Llanvihangel Gobion, near Abergavenny, Gwent (phone: 1873-840678; 800-435-4504; fax: 1873-840674). Expensive.

Walnut Tree Inn This restaurant's menu, based on local, seasonal produce, changes daily and features game in winter and fish in summer. The wine list is excellent and interesting. There also is a less formal bistro that offers the same food. Closed Sundays and Mondays. Reservations necessary (as far in advance as possible) for the restaurant; reservations unnecessary for the bistro. No credit cards accepted. Three miles north of Abergavenny on B4521 (phone: 1873-852797). Expensive.

En Route from Abergavenny From Abergavenny, it's a straight, 21-mile drive on A40 to Brecon, but if you have time, there are several pleasant detours along the way. On A40 heading toward Brecon is a delightful stretch of driving through the Usk Valley, with the Black Mountains to the right and the outriders of the Brecon Beacons to the left. On the way there are many pubs and small cottages, and little towns like Crickhowell (6 miles from Abergavenny) that welcome fisherfolk and pony trekkers. Many travelers speak highly of the food served at *Nant-y-ffin Cider Mill Inn* in Crickhowell (see *Best en Route*). All along this road are interesting narrow lanes turning off into the hills and anyone with the time and inclination is advised to do just that: Turn off and explore. For example, at Llansantffraid you can turn left on a road signposted for Talybont and drive for 9 miles through forest and hills to Talybont and Taf Fechan reservoirs: This is lovely walking and picnicking country.

Another pleasant diversion on the road from Abergavenny to Brecon is to Hay-on-Wye—although you will need the best part of a day to enjoy it. Turn right onto A479 just after Crickhowell, coast through the hills for about 20 miles to Talgarth, and continue for 6 miles on A438 and B4350 to Hay-on-Wye. Hay (pop. 1,578) is a picturesque little border town whose main industry is secondhand books. In 1977, Richard Booth, the inspiration behind Hay's revival as a book center, became irritated by the local bureaucracy, declared Hay-on-Wye independent, and crowned himself King Richard the Bookhearted! The *Hay-on-Wye Festival* (to be held this year from May 26 through June 4) had its first highly successful run in 1988 (see *Best Festivals* in DIVERSIONS). From here, get back on A438 and continue southwest to Brecon.

Yet another option is to take the southern loop, which leaves Abergavenny by A4077 (signposted to Gilwern). After 3 miles, turn south on B4246 and continue 4 miles to Blaenafon. On the outskirts of town is the *Big Pit Mining Museum,* a colliery until 1980. Exhibits include a blacksmith's shop and baths, and there are also hour-long tours 300 feet underground into the mine. Be sure to wear sturdy shoes. Children under five years are not allowed. It is closed January (and the opening schedule is erratic in February, so call ahead to check hours); admission charge (phone: 1495-790311).

From Blaenafon, head west on B4246 and A465 toward Merthyr Tydfil. About 11 miles along, you'll find the starting point for the *Brecon Mountain Railway,* a vintage steam train that takes passengers on a four-mile ride through the stunning scenery of the Brecon Beacons. It runs daily from the end of May to the end of September and on most weekends in April, May, and October (call ahead to check the off-season schedule). Information on this train, the other nine mountain railways in Wales, and the four- or eight-day *Wanderer* rail pass that allows unlimited travel on them all is available from *GLTW (Great Little Trains of Wales), The Station,* Llanfair Caereinion, Powys SY21 0SF, Wales (phone: 1938-810441).

From the rail station, continue west another 21 miles on A465 and A470 to Brecon. Along the way, stop at *Cyfarthfa Castle,* a mansion built by ironmaster William Crawshay in 1825. It's open daily; admission charge (phone: 1685-723112). The road leads right over the top of the Brecon Beacons.

BEST EN ROUTE

Llangoed Hall This gem of a country home is a member of Small Luxury Hotels of the World and has been hailed as one of the finest establishments in Wales. Sir Bernard Ashley, husband of the late designer Laura Ashley, has transformed this house with antiques, 19th- and 20th-century art, and, of course, the wallpaper and fabrics for which his wife became famous. The building dates from pre-Norman and Jacobean times, and is located in the heart of the Wye Valley and looks out at the Black Mountains beyond. The rooms are painstakingly appointed. Active visitors can pursue tennis or play croquet, and the classic fare served in the dining room is enough to make anyone want to work up an enormous appetite. Llyswen (phone: 1874-754525; 800-525-4800; fax: 1874-754545). Expensive.

The Bear This former 15th-century coaching inn is furnished in a comfortable, traditional fashion, with Welsh antiques and log fires. There are 24 guestrooms. The restaurant serves food with a Welsh flair, using local salmon and game, as well as vegetarian fare, and there is good pub food in its award-winning bar. Crickhowell (phone: 1873-810408; 800-435-4504; fax: 1873-811696). Moderate.

Griffin Inn Another 15th-century inn, this small, ivy-covered hostelry with eight rooms is aimed at the sporting enthusiast. It offers river and lake fishing, shooting, horseback riding, and walking. Only local produce is used at the restaurant. Llyswen (phone: 1874-754241; 800-435-4504; fax: 1874-754592). Moderate.

Nant-y-ffin Cider Mill Inn This excellent restaurant, consisting of a dining room and a separate pub, serves hearty homemade food—terrines, pies, cheesecake, and (in season) local salmon. Open daily. Reservations advised for restaurant. Major credit cards accepted. Brecon Rd., Crickhowell (phone: 1873-810775). Moderate.

Old Black Lion The building dates back to the 13th century, and has been an inn since the 17th century—Oliver Cromwell is said to have stayed here. Although its 10 rooms (nine with private baths) are furnished with modern conveniences, they haven't lost their charm. The restaurant serves excellent preparations of simple Welsh dishes and continental fare. Lion St., Hay-on-Wye (phone: 1497-820841). Moderate.

BRECON The district is still called by the old name of Brecknock, as you will see on some maps, while the town of Brecon (pop. 7,166) is known in the Welsh language as *Aberhonddu.* Its English name is derived from Brychan, the vigorous Irish chieftain who ruled this region in the 5th century. The Welsh name is taken from the river Honddu, which runs into the Usk. Nestled inside the northern boundary of *Brecon Beacons National Park,* Brecon has narrow streets, a cathedral, a busy livestock market, good shops and pubs, and a peaceful air. The 13th-century cathedral, originally a fortified priory, overlooks the Honddu. The town's castle, built by the half-brother of William the Conqueror, was dismantled during the 17th-century Civil War in an attempt to avoid the bloodshed necessary to defend it. The remaining parts of the castle are now in the garden of the *Castle of Brecon* hotel (see *Best en Route*).

The *Brecknock Museum,* in the old *County Hall* on Glamorgan Street, displays interesting examples of Welsh folk art and local crafts, such as the hand-carved wooden "love spoons" young Welshmen used in bygone days to plight their troth. It is open daily (but it's a good idea to call ahead in winter, as hours vary); admission charge (phone: 1874-624121). The *South Wales Borderers Museum* covers the regiment's history over nearly 300 years, including its defense of Rorke's Drift during the Zulu wars. The museum is closed Sundays year-round and Saturdays October through March; no admission charge (phone: 1874-623111). In mid-August every year, the well-known *Brecon Jazz Festival* takes over the town. For information, call 1874-625557.

BEST EN ROUTE

Miskin Manor A stone manor house with 32 guestrooms and a restaurant set on 20 acres of Wye Valley parkland, this hotel was glorious in its 1920s heyday (when the then Prince of Wales paid a visit). It deteriorated over the years, but now it has been restored to its former glory. Miskin, Mid Glamorgan (phone: 1443-224204; fax: 1443-237606). Expensive.

Bishops Meadow Most people stay here for the great views of the Beacons. It's a modern motel with 22 rooms, a bar, a restaurant, and a pool. On B438 (also called Hay Rd.), Brecon (phone: 1874-622392). Moderate.

Castle of Brecon Built of stone and overlooking the river Usk, this hotel adjoins castle ruins. There are 49 bedrooms (including some in a converted coach house) and a restaurant. Castle Sq., Brecon (phone: 1874-624611; fax: 1874-623737). Moderate.

Wellington An old, established hotel in the center of Brecon with 21 comfortable, refurbished rooms; a restaurant; a coffee shop; and a wine bar that serves a good variety of beers. The Bulwark (phone: 1874-625225; fax: 1874-623223). Moderate.

Coach Guest House A small (six rooms), 17th-century inn in the center of Brecon; it has a restaurant. No smoking is allowed. Orchard St. (phone: 1874-623803). Inexpensive.

En Route from Brecon Head back toward Merthyr Tydfil on A470 south for grand views of the Beacons' red sandstone peaks. After Libanus, turn right on A4215 toward Defynnog and you will soon pick up signs directing you to the *Mountain Centre* of *Brecon Beacons National Park* (phone: 1874-623366). The park covers 519 square miles, running east to west. Located in the wilds, the center is a friendly, informal place where the park's staff is keen to help in your exploration of the mountains. You can use the center as a base for walking, for picnicking, for light meals, or for just sitting and staring (highly recommended). Also see *Great Walks and Mountain Rambles* in DIVERSIONS.

Pick up the A40 trunk road on the northern edge of the park. For an interesting side trip, head 10 miles south along A4067 to the *Dan-yr-Ogof Showcaves,* the largest underground cave complex in Western Europe, with wonderful limestone formations. It is closed November through *Easter;* admission charge (phone: 1639-730284). Return to A40 and drive west about 4 miles to Trecastle, with its engaging landscape. It used to be an important stop in the old coaching days, and its coaching inns deserve a visit. To get from here to Llandeilo (20 miles away), you can continue on the A40 road through Llandovery—in Welsh *Llanymddyfri* ("the church among the waters"). Llandovery is a pleasant town where you can eat well and stay comfortably. It stands by the Tywi (Towy) River, the longest of Welsh rivers and famous for its salmon. The alternative route to Llandeilo is more scenic, but it's a bit longer and needs more careful navigation. Turn left along a little-used country road toward Llanddeusant and thread your way through Twynllanan and up A4069 to Llangadog, a quiet market town about 14 miles from Trecastle. The attractive, quiet village of Bethlehem, on an unnumbered road off A4069 4 miles from Llangadog, is also worth a visit. From Bethlehem, it's a 4½-mile drive to Llandeilo on A4069.

LLANDEILO Near this small riverside town (pop. 1,598) are several interesting castles—two of which are named *Dinefwr Castle.* The first *Dinefwr Castle,* described by writer Jan Morris as "the most haunting castle in Wales," is a medieval ruin built in AD 876 by Rhodri the Great, who divided the kingdom of Wales among his three sons. *Dinefwr*—given to son Cadell—was the stronghold of South Wales. The castle also featured in the wars between the Welsh and the English in medieval times, and was improved by members of the great Rhys family. It is now closed for renovation. The other *Dinefwr Castle,* located nearby, is a Victorian mansion set on a lovely patch of ground that was landscaped in the 18th century by Lancelot "Capability" Brown. There are extensive gardens and a park with a herd of fallow deer and other wildlife. Guided tours are available, or there are footpaths for those wanting to strike out on their own. Advance reservations are necessary to visit the house, but the park is open daily; admission charge (phone: 1558-823902). Also in the area is the *Royal Society for the Protection of Birds Reserve at Dinas,* the winter nesting ground for Siberian geese, wild swans, and many other species. The bird reserve has a 2½-mile nature trail and an information center (usually open in high season and on bank holidays; phone: 15506-276). Guided tours are also available (book in advance). The reserve is open daily; no admission charge.

After the English conquest, *Dryslwyn Castle* (no phone), located 5 miles west of Llandeilo, was the center of a Welsh uprising led by Lord Rhys in 1287. It failed, and Rhys was beheaded. *Carreg Cennen Castle* (phone: 1558-822291) stands atop a cliff about 6 miles southeast of Llandeilo, a hard nut for those warring medieval chiefs to crack. Dating from about the 13th century, it commands a marvelous view of the Black Mountain. Both castles are open daily; no admission charge.

BEST EN ROUTE

Cawdor Arms In the center of town with 17 rooms and a restaurant, it's a convenient base for touring West Wales. Rhosmaen St., Llandeilo (phone: 1558-823500). Moderate.

Plough Inn Originally a farmhouse, this establishment has 12 rooms with marvelous views that overlook the Towy Valley. There's also a restaurant. One mile from Llandeilo on A470 toward Llandovery (phone: 1558-823431; fax: 1558-823969). Moderate.

En Route from Llandeilo Carmarthen is 15 miles west of Llandeilo via A40.

CARMARTHEN In one version of the King Arthur legend, Merlin (Myrddin) was born hereabouts and that's how this most pleasant of towns got its name. In Welsh it is called *Caerfyrddin,* or "Merlin's City." In ancient times, as now, "Merlin's City" occupied an important and strategic position above the Tywi (Towy) River. The Romans had a base here, as the deteriorated amphitheater testifies, and the ruins of the Norman castle still can be seen. During the early part of the 12th century, monks collected and wrote poems in the *Black Book of Carmarthen,* the oldest known Welsh manuscript; it can be seen in the *National Library of Wales* in Aberystwyth on the west coast, which we'll visit later in this route.

Carmarthen (pop. 13,860) is also the administrative hub of the southwestern corner of Wales. Its large covered market draws crowds every Wednesday and Saturday, and behind it the cattle market is held each Monday, Wednesday, and Thursday.

In Nott Square stands a monument to Dr. Robert Ferrar, Bishop of *St. David's Church,* who was burned at the stake on this site in 1555. Also of interest is the museum housed in what was the *Bishop's Palace* at Abergwili, on the outskirts of town. It contains a small collection of Roman and Egyptian antiquities and local memorabilia. *Merlin's Oak,* which originally stood on Priory Street, was moved to the entrance to the *City Hall* several years ago. Legend says that when the oak falls, so will the town; to ensure that it won't topple, the townspeople have propped it up with concrete.

An interesting 13-mile side trip from Carmarthen is to Laugharne (pronounced *Larn*), where the Welsh poet Dylan Thomas (1914–53) lived and wrote many of his famous works. This little town is reached by driving along A48 to St. Clear's and turning left on A4066. Thomas's home, called the *Boathouse,* is now a museum devoted to his life and work (open daily; admission charge; phone: 1994-427420). You also can see *Brown's* hotel, where the poet drank; and the churchyard where he is buried. Six miles farther on A4066 is Pendine, with its romantic stretch of sands on which 1930s heroes smashed world speed records in their roaring cars.

BEST EN ROUTE

Ivy Bush Royal With 79 rooms and a sauna, this is certainly one of the best hotels in rural west Wales in terms of atmosphere, design, service, and cuisine. Spilman St., Carmarthen (phone: 1267-235111; fax: 1267-234914). Moderate.

Cwtwrch This converted farmhouse, nestled in 30 acres that overlook the countryside, is a charming retreat with an indoor heated pool and a Jacuzzi. The six rooms are traditionally furnished, and the *Four Seasons* restaurant (in the barn) serves home-cooked local produce as well as salmon and sewin (sea trout). Five miles from Carmarthen off B4310 (phone: 1267-290238). Moderate to inexpensive.

Ty Mawr A tiny 16th-century stone building set in a lush valley near Carmarthen, this property offers five charmingly furnished guestrooms. Both the hotel and its fine restaurant are highly acclaimed. Brechfa, Dyfed (phone: 1267-202332 or 1267-202330; fax: 1267-202437). Moderate to inexpensive.

En Route from Carmarthen Leave Carmarthen via A484, which winds through pleasant wooded country to little Cynwyl Elfed (5 miles away) with its white- and color-washed cottages, a genuine piece of old Carmarthenshire calm and beauty. Seven miles farther north, the road branches northwest to Henllan, where a small road on the left leads to the *Museum of the Welsh Woolen Industry* in Drefach Velindre. The museum has a collection of machinery and memorabilia, and an exhibit on the history of the wool industry. It is closed Saturdays year-round and Sundays October through March; admission charge (phone: 1559-370929).

Return to Henllan, and travel on A484 another 7 miles, where an unnumbered road on the left leads to Cenarth, noted for its waterfalls and the last of the coracle men on this stretch of river Teifi. A coracle is a little basket-shaped boat made from tarred cloth stretched over a frail wooden frame, and it's been used in Wales for 2,000 years. Coracle fishermen work in pairs, drifting down the river with a net suspended between their boats to catch salmon and sewin, a delicious sea trout. During the 19th century, there were thousands of coracles on Welsh rivers, but laws framed to conserve fish and protect the sport of salmon fishing steadily squeezed the coracle men out. Today there are only about a dozen left, mostly on the rivers Teifi and Tywi.

A right turn on A486 from Cenarth leads to the charming town of Llandysul (12 miles away), with its late Norman church and bridge spanning the river rapids. From here, you can take A475 another 15 miles directly to Lampeter. If you have time, though, there's a more roundabout—and more scenic—alternative. About 7 miles from Llandysul on A475, turn right onto B4338 and continue another 2 miles to Llanybydder. This charming, Teifi-side market town has a long-standing tradition of weaving. Try to be here on the last Thursday of any month for the horse fairs. Leave Llanybydder via A485 and continue another 5 miles into Lampeter.

LAMPETER Lampeter in Welsh is *Llanbedr Pont Steffan.* It's a busy place with a farming community of 1,976 people, set in the lush land of the upper Teifi Valley. The most famous landmark is *St. David's College,* part of the *University of Wales* since 1972. Founded in 1822, it had been a college that trained students for ordination in the Episcopalian state church, continued after disestablishment, and was incorporated into the university when it became a liberal arts college. Its buildings are open to visitors.

BEST EN ROUTE

Black Lion Royal This hostelry has 15 comfortable rooms and a restaurant. High St., Lampeter (phone: 1570-422172; fax: 1570-423630). Moderate.

Falcondale Set in its own 14-acre parkland grounds, this historic Victorian country house has 20 bedrooms, a restaurant, two bars, and banquet and conference facilities. Activities include fishing, golf, pony trekking, tennis, and clay-pigeon shooting (phone: 1570-422910; fax: 1570-423559). Moderate.

En Route from Lampeter You have a choice of roads to Tregaron (11 miles away): The main A485 is quicker, but B4343 on the eastern side of the Teifi is more beautiful. The latter passes through Llanfair Clydogau, where the Romans mined silver (or, more accurately, their Welsh slaves did). The lure of Welsh gold and silver was one reason why the Romans conquered Britain. The 2,000-year-old gold mines in the hills at Dolaucothi (5 miles from Lampeter) are open for guided tours April through October; admission charge (phone: 15585-359). Four miles farther along is Llanddewi Brefi, where St. David, patron saint of Wales, preached in 519. Look at the 13th-century church, supposedly built where David delivered an inspirational sermon. Tregaron is 3 miles from Llanddewi Brefi on B4343.

TREGARON A friendly market town with craft workshops and welcoming inns, Tregaron has a statue of its most famous son, Henry Richard (1812–88) in the square. A member of Parliament for Merthyr Tydfil, Richard was dubbed the Apostle of Peace for his espousal of international arbitration and founding of the Peace Union, a forerunner of the *United Nations*. Twm Shon Catti (Thomas Jones), a 16th-century rogue and poet, was born (1530?–1609) and roamed near here. *Canolfan Cynllyn Crefft Cymru* (in The Square; phone: 1974-298415) is an excellent shopping stop, with a wide range of crafts available, including woolen textiles and Celtic jewelry fashioned on the premises. Just north of the town is the 4-mile-long Bog of Tregaron, said to be the largest peat bog in Britain and now the *Cors Goch Caron Nature Reserve.* Tregaron earns part of its living as a summer holiday center for pony trekking, and the land here is just right for riding: wild and remote. The *Wales Tourist Office* (phone: 1222-499909) has a variety of brochures on horseback riding and other sports holidays.

BEST EN ROUTE

Talbot A small, friendly 13th-century coaching inn, it has 14 bedrooms (some suitable for families), a cozy oak bar, and a dining room (with an open log fireplace) serving excellent ales and home cooking. Open daily. Reservations necessary. Major credit cards accepted. The Square, Tregaron (phone: 1974-298208). Moderate to inexpensive.

Neuaddlas Guest House Here is a friendly and informal guesthouse overlooking the *Cors Goch Caron Nature Reserve* and Cambrian Mountains. There are four rooms (three with private baths). The restaurant has no liquor license but serves delicious Welsh home cooking in generous portions. 1½ miles north of Tregaron on A485 (phone: 1974-298905). Inexpensive.

En Route from Tregaron A side trip from Tregaron to Llanwrtyd Wells (20 miles east on B4343) is a thrilling journey over the narrow and winding Abergwesyn Pass. In Llanwrtyd Wells, you can visit the Cambrian Woollen Mill, where an exhibit called *The Wonderful World of Wool* takes you through the history of wool production, complete with audiovisuals and authentic smells, before a factory tour where you can see the way wool is processed into cloth nowadays. The mill is open daily; admission charge (phone: 15913-211). Fabric, spun from locally made wool, is sold in the factory shop. If you visit Llanwrtyd Wells, return to Tregaron before continuing.

Head up B4343 6 miles to Pontrhydfendigaid and the abbey at Strata Florida, known in Welsh as *Ystrad Fflur,* or "Valley of the Flowers." The abbey, built by Cistercian monks in the 12th and 13th centuries, suffered in the fighting between the Welsh and English in medieval days, and received a final blow when Henry VIII ordered the destruction of monasteries. Although crumbled, it's worth a look. Legend has it that beneath a yew is the grave of Dafydd ap Gwilym, one of the leading medieval poets, who divided his time between making verse and love. From the abbey, it's a 15-mile drive northwest to Aberystwyth via B4340.

BEST EN ROUTE

Lake This luxurious country-house hotel on 50 acres, with its own woods and lake, has 18 bedrooms, as well as one of Wales's best dining rooms (the wine list offers over 300 vintages). Activities include tennis, golf on a six-hole course, croquet, clay-pigeon shooting, and fishing. Llangammarch Wells (phone: 15912-474; 800-435-4504; fax: 15912-457). Expensive.

ABERYSTWYTH A popular seaside resort with both sand and pebble bathing beaches, Aberystwyth (pop. 8,636) is also the seat of the major college for Welsh speakers through the *University of Wales* and the administrative center for Cardigan Bay. Its lively seafront promenade is lined with hotels and has a bandstand and the ruins of a castle. History is carefully preserved at the *National Library of Wales* (Penglais Hill; phone: 1970-623816), which houses some of the earliest Welsh manuscripts; and the past still lives at the main train station, where the *Vale of Rheidol Railway,*

British Rail's last steam-powered narrow-gauge railroad, connects Aberystwyth with the spectacular falls at Devil's Bridge—according to legend built by the devil himself—high in the Vale of Rheidol. In this district of old Cardiganshire there were once many lead mines, and the railway started life as an ore-carrying line. It's a romantic ride today. The trains run *Good Friday* through October, but the schedule varies; call for details (phone: 1970-625819 or 1970-615993).

Closer to home, the town's cliff railway carries visitors to the peak of Constitution Hill, where they have a splendid view of the bay and town. It operates daily *Easter* through October (phone: 1970-617642). *Aberystwyth Yesterday* in the *Station Buildings* (Alexandra Rd.; phone: 1970-617119) is a privately owned collection of assorted memorabilia from the mid-19th century to the present, with fashions, furniture, photographs, and even some decorative paper bags. It is closed November through April; no admission charge. A restored theater houses the *Ceredigion Museum* (Terrace Rd.; phone: 1970-617911), which shows exhibits on local crafts and history. It is closed Sundays; no admission charge. Concerts and evening shows are regular features along the promenade. The nearby *Arts Centre* (phone: 1970-623232) holds frequent exhibitions and a summer season of plays.

BEST EN ROUTE

Conrah Country House Here's a special blend of historic Welsh country mansion (the original foundation dates from 1753, the present building was rebuilt in 1870) and the comforts of a modern hostelry. There are 20 rooms set on a secluded site atop a wooded hillside, a wonderful restaurant, plus a small heated indoor pool and sauna. Rhydgaled, Chancery, 3 miles south of Aberystwyth on A487 (phone: 1970-617941; 800-435-4504; fax: 1970-624546). Expensive.

Belle Vue Royal This seafront spot overlooking Cardigan Bay has a large restaurant, 38 comfortable rooms, and an 18-hole golf course nearby where guests can play without charge on weekdays. Marine Ter., Aberystwyth (phone: 1970-617558; fax: 1976-612190). Moderate.

Gannets Everything on the very reasonable menu is homemade, from the quiche and casseroles to the treacle tart. Open daily. Reservations necessary. Major credit cards accepted. 7 St. James Sq., Aberystwyth (phone: 1970-617164). Moderate to inexpensive.

Nanteos Mansion An elegant Georgian mansion with an imposing oak staircase, Italian marble, 30 acres of gardens, and its own lake. According to local legend, it once housed the Holy Grail. There are eight bedrooms and a restaurant serving Welsh food. Four miles east of Aberystwyth, off A4120 (phone: 1970-624363, 1432-342388 in Hereford, for reservations) Moderate to inexpensive.

University College of Wales For something different, stay in one of the more than 1,200 guestrooms and apartments when students are away. Write to the *Conference Office,* Penbryn, Penglais, Aberystwyth SY23 3BY, Wales (phone: 1970-623757; fax: 1970-622899). Inexpensive.

En Route from Aberystwyth Leave Aberystwyth on A44, heading inland through Ponterwyd. On the right you'll see the sweep of the Ystwyth forest and on the left the rolling hills of the Plynlimon range, where the Wye and Severn rivers rise. It is worth penetrating this area on foot if you can. It's wild and haunting, with rushing streams, old caved-in farmhouses, and a few birds circling overhead. The A44 meets A470 at Llangurig, which has a handful of inns and shops. Take A470 and continue to Llanidloes (a total distance of 30 miles from Aberystwyth).

LLANIDLOES The central feature of the town—and you have to drive slowly to negotiate it—is the half-timbered *Market Hall* built in 1609. Llanidloes has a long tradition of wool weaving and trade. During the 1830s, the Chartist workmen's reform movement (a political organization popular in Britain then) began to have some impact on Llanidloes's discontented weavers. The Chartists captured and held the town briefly in 1839. The *Llanidloes Museum* has exhibits about this episode. It was in the process of moving from its home in the *Market Hall* to the *Town Hall,* so its operating schedule was uncertain at press time; for more information, contact the local tourist office (phone: 1686-412605). There's no admission charge.

From Llanidloes, you can take several pleasant side trips into the country lanes of the district. One in particular starts on the eastern edge of the town, on B4518, and leads out to Staylittle and Llanbrynmair. Six miles from Llanidloes you'll come upon a lovely view over Llyn Clywedog reservoir.

BEST EN ROUTE

Trewythen Arms An attractive Georgian house with 12 rooms, it also has two bars and a dining room that offers good country cooking. Great Oak St., Llanidloes (phone: 1686-412214; fax: 1686-413848). Moderate to inexpensive.

Old Vicarage Guest House A converted Victorian vicarage, this hostelry boasts four bedrooms and excellent Welsh food. In Llangurig, about 5 miles southeast of Llanidloes (phone: 15515-280). Inexpensive.

En Route from Llanidloes Follow A470 along the Severn River northeast and pass through Llandinam. Near the bridge you'll see a statue of the village's most famous son, David Davies, the civil engineer, railroad builder, and developer of coal mining in the Rhondda valleys of South Wales. The town of Caersws, slightly northwest of Llandinam and 9 miles from Llanidloes, is typical of the small settlements in this area, planted in the green and open land. From Caersws, it is worth making an 8-mile diversion along A492 east to Newtown. Industrial development here is designed to keep young people from drifting out of the countryside into the bigger towns of England. Newtown's history as a weaving industry giant is chronicled at the *Textile Museum,* which recently reopened after an extensive renovation. At press time, the museum's operating hours were uncertain; call ahead to check. There's an admission charge (phone: 1938-554656). Also here is the *Robert Owen Memorial Museum,* an institution devoted to social philosopher Robert Owen (1771–1858), who was born and buried in Newtown. Owen's theories resulted in an experiment in communal living at New Harmony, Indiana. The museum is closed Sundays; no admission charge (phone: 1686-625544).

The route from Caersws is an 18-mile drive on A470 via Clatter and Carno (headquarters of the Laura Ashley textile manufacturing empire), Commins Coch, and Cemmas Road. From here you can take a 6-mile side trip down A489 to Machynlleth, a market town with a tall clock tower as its signature, standing on the Dovey (Dyfi) River. The Welsh hero Owain Glyndwr chose Machynlleth to convene a Parliament in 1404. The town is also home to the *Museum of Modern Art, Wales,* with a small but impressive permanent collection of works by 20th-century artists, such as Augustus John, Stanley Spencer, and Kyffin Williams, as well as temporary exhibitions. It is open daily; no admission charge (phone: 1654-703353). Three miles north of Machynlleth on A487 is the *Centre for Alternative Technology,* which offers promotional and educational displays devoted to various forms of energy technology and their development. It is open daily; admission charge (phone: 1654-702400).

From Machynlleth, take A470 through the Dovey Valley 3 miles to Mallwyd and Dinas Mawddwy, set in alpine countryside.

BEST EN ROUTE

Court Yard Set in a cozy 19th-century building with pine tables, wood floors, and plenty of plants, this spot serves fresh homemade savories and sweets, vegetarian dishes (at lunch), and typical bistro specialties such as beef goulash, chicken dishes, steaks, and Wiener schnitzel. Closed Saturday lunch, Sundays, and Mondays. Reservations necessary for dinner. Major credit cards accepted. 7th St., Newtown (phone: 1686-624944). Moderate.

Edderton Hall Each of the eight rooms in this country-house hotel has a unique Georgian flavor, reflecting the period during which the house was built. A log fireplace in the lounge makes for a cozy atmosphere. The restaurant decor is quite romantic, and the food—a combination of modern English with a French influence—is prepared with fresh vegetables, many of them grown on the premises. There's a prix fixe menu as well as à la carte dining. Forden, near Welshpool, Powys; on A490 toward Montgomery (phone: 1938-76339; fax: 1938-76452). Moderate.

DINAS MAWDDWY It looks hard to say, but pluck up some courage and say *Deen-ass* Mouth-*oo-ee.* It's a rather special place. The landscape is singular, with steeply sloped hills, and the soaring peaks of the Arans close by, to the north. The people here were once known for their red hair and independent nature. And 400-odd years ago travelers feared a gang of them known as the Red Brigands; these outlaws ambushed and killed a judge in 1555, and for that crime they were finally hunted down and dispersed. But visitors need not worry: Today, Dinas people are perfectly friendly. The town is a restful place, with good fishing for salmon and trout or just for walking. The weaving industry has been revived with some success; the Meirion Mill (phone: 16504-531311) is open to visitors (in summer only), and wools are available for purchase. You also can take a most enjoyable side trip for 15 miles or so along the narrow road to Llanymawddwy and up to Llanuwchllyn, an off-the-beaten-track ride leading to Bala Lake. The largest natural lake in Wales—almost 4 miles long—Bala is the home of the little gwyniad, a fish found nowhere in the world but here. The lake also is a center for sailing, canoeing, and swimming, and the *Bala Lake* narrow-gauge railway (phone: 1678-4666) runs alongside it *Easter* through September. The town, at the lake's eastern end, has plenty of places to eat, drink, and stay.

BEST EN ROUTE

Palé Hall Originally built in 1874 for a Scottish railway engineer, this country house with its own park was visited by Queen Victoria in 1889. Its present incarnation is a sumptuous hostelry, carefully restored and refurbished to the highest standards. No two of the 17 rooms are alike, and several guest accommodations include a private Jacuzzi and a four-poster bed (if you like, you can sleep in the actual bed that Queen Victoria slept in). The restaurant serves Welsh food prepared with fresh local produce and game. The hotel also has its own clay-pigeon–shooting facilities (and pheasant shooting, in season) on the grounds. Sailing, whitewater canoeing, and fishing in nearby Bala Lake are also available, as well as pony trekking and golfing. Llandderfel, Bala (phone: 1678-3285; fax: 1678-3220). Expensive.

Lake Vyrnwy Perched on the edge of *Snowdonia National Park,* offering magnificent views over Lake Vyrnwy, this Victorian-style hotel in the foothills of the Berwyn Mountains has 37 wonderfully furnished rooms and a restaurant. The hotel has exclusive sporting rights to the 24,000 surrounding acres, so guests can enjoy shooting, tennis, sailing, hiking, ballooning, and bird watching. The fly-fishing is especially good (also see *Gone Fishing* in DIVERSIONS). Llanwddyn, via Oswestry, Shropshire (phone: 1691-73692; fax: 1691-73259). Expensive to moderate.

Plas Coch Comfortable and centrally located, this 18th-century hostelry has a restaurant and 10 rooms. High St., Bala (phone: 1678-520309; fax: 1678-521135). Moderate.

White Lion Royal A large and charming old post house, it's right in the center of town with a good restaurant and 26 rooms. 61 High St., Bala (phone: 1678-520314). Moderate.

Buckley Pines Inside *Snowdonia National Park,* this place offers 12 comfortable rooms (five with private baths), a restaurant, and parking facilities. There's a magnificent view over the Dovey, and fishing. Dinas Mawddwy (phone: 1650-531261). Inexpensive.

En Route from Dinas Mawddwy Continue on A470 9 miles to Dolgellau.

DOLGELLAU Pronounced *Doll*-geth-lay, this is the chief town of the old shire of Merioneth, now incorporated into the county of Gwynedd, which also includes Caernarfonshire and the island of Anglesey. Dolgellau (pop. 2,261) is solidly built in dark, local stone and is a sturdy, foursquare town perfectly in tune with its surroundings. It lies under Cader Idris Mountain (the name means "Idris's Chair") and is an important marketplace. It has ancient origins: The Romans were here, as were Cistercian monks who left *Cymer Abbey,* founded in 1199. The church, built in 1726, has an interesting barrel roof, and its graveyard has a fascinating mixture of tombstones with Welsh and English inscriptions. The Welsh *er cof* means "in memory." Dolgellau's bridge, built in 1638, is protected as a historical structure and an old tollhouse also remains. The *Interpretive Centre* in the main square celebrates the town's link with the Quaker movement.

In the midst of *Snowdonia National Park,* Dolgellau is naturally an excellent place for touring on foot. Several paths, ranging from easy walks to hard climbs, lead up the slopes of Cader Idris. Two miles out of town, on the A494 Bala road, there is a turnoff to the left clearly signposted Precipice Walk. This is a scenic walk, not difficult, and takes about two hours. Information on all trails winding up to the summit of Cader Idris is available from the park information office at Maentwrog (phone: 1766-770274). The *Coed y Brenin Forest Park* at Ganllwyd, about 5 miles north off A470, offers some less exhausting walking as well as a children's adventure playground, wildlife observation hides, and an information center (phone: 1341-40666 or 1341-422289).

The *Snowdon Sherpa* bus service is an efficient way to get to and around *Snowdonia National Park.* You catch the bus at designated pick-up points in the area and it drops you off at major walking and hiking paths and trails leading to Mt. Snowdon. A brochure with a map of the bus route is available from the *British Tourist Authority* or the national park office in Betws-y-Coed. For more information about the park, see *Great Walks and Mountain Rambles* in DIVERSIONS.

Gold found at Llanelltyd and nearby Bontddu transformed Dolgellau into a gold rush town for the last part of the 19th century. Traditionally, Welsh gold has been used for royal wedding rings. Although the gold rush days are gone, mining the precious metal again is becoming a lucrative local industry.

BEST EN ROUTE

Dolserau Hall A warm welcome, 14 lovely rooms, and a good restaurant await you at this Victorian manor, set on five acres of gardens. Outside Dolgellau on the Bala road (phone: 1341-422522; fax: 1341-422400). Expensive.

George III Gerard Manley Hopkins once wrote a poem telling those "who pine for peace or pleasure" to "taste the treats of Penmaen Pool." And many say he was referring to this 300-year-old hotel and restaurant delightfully situated at the head of the Mawddach estuary. Freshly caught fish is the specialty in summer, and in winter the menu turns to local game. Six of the 12 guestrooms are in a lodge on the grounds, and all have views of the Mawddach estuary and the mountains. Just out of town on A493 in Penmaenpool (phone: 1341-422525; fax: 1341-423565). Expensive to moderate.

Minfford At the foot of Cader Idris Mountain, this former coaching inn, built in the 16th or 17th century, now is a cozy six-room hostelry with a restaurant, owned and run by Jonathan Pickles and his family. It has a friendly, cozy atmosphere with open fireplaces, beamed ceilings, and uniquely decorated rooms. Tallyllyn, Tywyn, Gwynedd (phone: 1654-761665; fax: 1654-761517). Moderate.

Ty Isaf Here's the opportunity to live in a traditional Welsh "longhouse" with a long (dating back to at least 1624) and romantic history. With only three bedrooms, this old drover's cottage and shoeing station has been lovingly restored and converted into a small, very special house where a maximum of three couples can be accommodated in surprising comfort. The walls are almost three feet thick, massive wooden beams cross the ceiling, and, when necessary, a cheerful blaze fills the inglenook fireplace. No credit cards accepted. Llanfachreth, Gwynedd (phone: 1341-423261). Moderate.

Borthwnog Hall Old deeds reveal that this building was rented by the shoemaker of Dolgellau in 1670 for the sum of one peppercorn, and the present small country-house hotel, with three guestrooms and a restaurant, has operated since before the 18th century. Most rooms offer a spectacular panoramic view that reaches from Cardigan Bay to the Arran Mountains. The hotel also features a gallery with watercolors, oils, sculpture, and pottery. Bontddu (phone: 1341-49271; fax: 1341-49682). Moderate to inexpensive.

En Route from Dolgellau An English poet once mused that there was only one thing better than going from Dolgellau to Barmouth, and that was going from Barmouth to Dolgellau. This route follows the estuary of the river Mawddach, with its fine scenery. You can go direct by A496 (a 10-mile drive), or detour along A493 for 3 miles to Penmaenpool, crossing the river by the narrow wooden toll bridges. There is a *Royal Society for the Protection of Birds Observatory* in Penmaenpool. It is closed mid-September through *Easter;* no admission charge (phone: 1341-422071).

About 8 miles farther along A493 is jolly little Barmouth, a resort tucked in under the mountainside and edging the waters of the Mawddach estuary. It is a good stopping place with beaches and a variety of sports and entertainment. For a few pence, you can walk across the rail and footbridge that spans the Mawddach. The view is sublime: sands, sea, and mountains. For more active outings, Barmouth has swimming, golf, climbing, fishing, and rough shooting. And, like most seaside towns, Barmouth has numerous hotels, inns, and restaurants. It's ideal for those on modest budgets. The *Publicity Association* (Station Rd.; phone: 1341-280787) has a full listing; it's closed October through *Easter. Ty Gwyn,* a medieval tower house in town, has an exhibition of Tudor history. It is closed late September through late May; no admission charge (no phone). At Tel-y-bont, a few miles north of the town, the *Old Country Life Centre* has a collection of vintage cars. The center is closed October through *Easter;* no admission charge (phone: 1766-780785).

The A496 road runs northward another 30 miles or so to Llanbedr. On the left is the haunting stretch of dunes and marsh known as Morfa Dyffryn and to the right are the rather fearsome mountains called the Rhinogs. Llanbedr is a quiet village and nearby is Mochras Island (also known as Shell Island), a peninsula famed for the variety of shells on its shores. Just south of Llanbedr is the *Maes Artro Craft Village,* a converted wartime RAF camp. It has exhibitions on the camp's history, displays of farm equipment, a sound-and-light show, crafts shops, and an aquarium. It is closed November through March; admission charge (phone: 1341-23467). If you continue inland from Llanbedr you will see signs to Cwm Bychan, a remote and peaceful valley.

A few miles north of Llanbedr on A496 is Harlech, one of the romantic names of Wales. Still a small village (only 1,292 residents), Harlech's historic heart and motif is the castle, standing high upon the rocks and defying all who come. It's one of the most photogenic of Welsh castles, and provided the inspiration for "Men of Harlech," one of the best-known traditional Welsh songs. Completed in 1289, the castle was one of the many fortifications built by King Edward I during his campaign to subdue the Welsh in the 13th century. The rebel Owain Glyndwr (freedom fighter for the Welsh) captured it in 1404, but his war of independence came to an end shortly after the castle was stormed and taken by Henry of Monmouth. In 1468, Harlech's was the last castle to fall to the Yorkists in the Wars of the Roses. It was also the last castle to hold out on the Royalist side in the 17th-century Civil War. Thus, the building has its battle scars. Those with no fear of heights can walk all around the castle on its unfenced, 10-foot-thick walls and climb the 143 steps to the top of its gatehouse. *Coleg Harlech,* an independent residential college for adult students founded in 1927 by Lloyd George's adviser Thomas Jones (1870–1955), became a great nursery for writers as staff and students. With many of its graduates going on to university, it is popularly known as "the College of the Second Chance." It makes for an inspirational visit, especially if you attend a dramatic production or contemporary art exhibition at the *Theatre Ardudwy* (phone: 1766-780667) on the college grounds.

From here take A487 toward Talsarnau. On your left there is a good view of Tremadog Bay and the glistening Glaslyn estuary. Follow the signs to Penrhyndeudraeth and cross the river by toll bridge. The town's name is a mouthful; it's actually Welsh shorthand for "peninsula with two stretches of sand." A solid and amiable village, it has lots of ships and pubs. But no doubt it is rather overshadowed by its neighbor, Portmeirion (located about 3 miles from Harlech).

BEST EN ROUTE

Maes-y-Neuadd Whether or not you say the name right (*Mice*-in-Nayeth), you are certain to enjoy a stay in one of Wales's loveliest country-house hotels, which was built between 1350 and 1720. There are 16 bedrooms in this rugged granite and slate building, all decorated uniquely. Very good traditional Welsh dishes are served in the airy dining room; reservations for Sunday lunch are necessary. Major credit cards accepted. For more information, see *Rural Retreats* in DIVERSIONS. Talsarnau, Gwynedd (phone: 1766-780200; 800-435-4504; fax: 1766-780211). Expensive.

PORTMEIRION This is an enchanting corner of Wales, a planned village and hotel created by the distinguished architect Sir Clough Williams-Ellis (1883–1978), who dreamed of a village of "beauty without solemnity." Begun in the 1920s, today it is an established, picturesque, and rather Italianate waterside village with views of the mountains, the sea, and the river and accents of rhododendron, shrubs, trees, and flowers. Home of the lovely (and increasingly popular) Portmeirion pottery, it has been called the Welsh Xanadu. There is a campanile, a dome, a town hall, pools, and statuary. Its character and vistas have made it ideal for film settings. There is an entrance fee for day visitors.

BEST EN ROUTE

Portmeirion The site of this magical place overlooks Cardigan Bay, and each of the 14 bedrooms in the hotel and the 20 self-catering cottages and 20 guestrooms in the village is distinctly decorated. This is ornate Victoriana at its best, including a restaurant and spacious lawns. For more information, see *Rural Retreats* in DIVERSIONS. Portmeirion, Gwynedd (phone: 1766-770228; fax: 1766-771331). Expensive.

En Route from Portmeirion Just outside town, on the main road, is the hamlet of Minffordd, where the philosopher Bertrand Russell (1872–1970) lived for some years and where he organized his worldwide campaign against nuclear stockpiles. He loved this part of Wales, and one of his pleasures in his declining years was to lie in bed and watch the sun go down over Tremadog Bay. From Minffordd, take A487 2 miles west into Porthmadog (which often also appears as Portmadoc), reached by crossing a causeway for a small toll. The causeway is part of the harbor construction planned by William Madocks in the 1820s, which led to the town's economic success as a port. Madocks also built the town of Tremadog (*tre* means town) nearby, one of the first planned towns in Britain and the birthplace of T. E. Lawrence (1888–1935), aka Lawrence of Arabia.

Incidentally, an interesting and rather spectacular side trip from Porthmadog (for train buffs, especially) is to take the narrow-gauge railway to Blaenau Ffestiniog, which runs daily April through September; for more information, call 1766-512340. A former slate railroad that used to bring the stone down from Blaenau Ffestiniog for shipping from Porthmadog quay, it fell into disrepair but has been successfully restored. You will be visiting Blaenau Ffestiniog later in the route, but this train's gleaming steam engines are an impressive sight as they wind through the gorges of Snowdonia.

Another interesting detour is to take A497 5 miles west to the small town of Criccieth. Its small, but dramatic, castle with a high, twin-towered gatehouse, stands on a rocky promontory overlooking the town. Built in 1230 by the Welsh prince, Llywellyn the Great, most of it has been in ruins since 1404, when it was sacked by Owain Glyndwr. In two of the remaining rooms, there are exhibitions on the Welsh princes and the great medieval chronicler Gerald of Wales. It is open daily; admission charge (phone: 1766-522227). A couple of miles farther down A497 is the village of Llanystumdwy, home of the great Edwardian politician David Lloyd George (1863–1945), whose grave is beside the river Dwyfor. His boyhood home, *Highgate,* and its adjacent *Memorial Museum,* filled with his memorabilia, are open daily; admission charge (phone: 1766-522071).

Return to Porthmadog and take the main road (A487) 5 miles to Tremadog. Then turn right onto the Beddgelert road (A498) and continue for 3 miles. Near the village of Beddgelert, at Sygun, is an old copper mine that was abandoned in the 19th century; now imaginatively restored, the mine has tours of the workings and rock formations. It is open daily; admission charge (phone: 1766-86595).

Return to A487. From here go another 2 miles through Ffestiniog, pick up A470 north, and continue 3 miles farther to Blaenau Ffestiniog. Blaenau, one of the great old slate towns, seems to be entirely grayish blue, since buildings, roofs, garden fences, and other items are made from the slate that made Blaenau. The vast slate mines are today a kind of monument to the heyday that straddled the 19th and 20th centuries. Slate is still worked on a smaller scale, and you can visit the enormous caverns hollowed out of the mountains at the *Llechwedd Slate Cavern and Deep Mine* here. It is worth doing, for slate has a fascinating history, which is related as you explore the underground maze of mines. The caverns are open daily (phone: 1766-830306). There are attractions aboveground as well: the *Slate Heritage Theatre,* which presents a short narrative on slate's importance to Wales; the craft shop where workers carve souvenirs from slate and a gift shop where you can buy them; and a tramway exhibit of the old carriers that transported the slate from the mines. *Llechwedd Slate Cavern and Deep Mine* is popular so it's a good idea to reserve tickets at least a day ahead. You also can stop at the *Gloddfa Ganol Slate Mine,* the world's largest, which is open daily; there's an admission charge.

The landscape is dramatic in this area and remains so all along A470 north to Betws-y-Coed (10 miles from Blaenau Ffestiniog). It is a noted beauty spot, resting in a narrow valley, and its famous Swallow Falls are close by, to the north, and worth seeing.

BEST EN ROUTE

Plas Bodegroes This charming hotel and restaurant in a 1780 Georgian building has an appropriate name (it means "place where the rosehips grow"); it is set among five acres of grounds with wonderful rose gardens and ancient beech trees. All eight rooms are furnished with antiques and some have Jacuzzis. The food is superb, imaginatively created from local products; the vegetables come from the hotel's own gardens. One mile west of Pwllheli on A497 (phone: 1758-612363; 800-435-4504; fax: 1758-701247). Expensive.

BETWS-Y-COED The name (pronounced Bet-*too*-see-Coyd) means "chapel in the woods." Because the town is at a major crossroads with easy access to *Snowdonia National Park* and Gwydir Forest, there are crowds here during the height of summer, especially on weekends, so a midweek visit then would be more enjoyable. Betws has ancient origins and a church with parts dating from the 12th to 16th centuries. Its gray stone buildings are typical of this region. Also here is *Conway Castle,* one of the finest medieval fortresses in Europe. It was begun in 1283, soon after Edward I's crushing victory over Llywelyn, Prince of Wales. The construction work took 40 years to complete and cost £2.5 million (a staggering sum in those days). The castle features eight massive round towers and walls that are 15 feet thick in some places. Though the castle is impressive-looking from the outside, its interior is largely a ruin. The castle is open daily; admission charge (phone: 1492-592358). Betws also has a large number of craft shops selling high-quality Welsh woolens, such as the *Anna Davies Welsh Wool Shop* (phone: 1690-710292; open daily), which offers wools, tweeds, quilts, rugs, pottery, sheepskin, perfume, and knitwear.

BEST EN ROUTE

Bodysgallen Hall Over 200 acres of parklands, plus tantalizing views of *Snowdonia National Park* and *Conway Castle,* make this guesthouse an ideal stopping place. The 17th-century building's architectural beauty is breathtaking, from the stone-mullioned windows to the oak-paneled entrance. Its 19 rooms and nine suites have been decorated with great care, and many have lofty four-poster beds with canopies. Superb traditional dishes are prepared in the restaurant, and the menu changes seasonally. Llandudno, Gwynedd (phone: 1492-584466; 800-435-4504; fax: 1492-582519). Expensive.

Royal Oak In *Snowdonia National Park* beside the river Llugwy, this 27-room place has been completely refurbished but still retains its country charm. Six rooms in the back, however, have modern furniture and built-in stereo equipment. The food is good and the service dependable. Holyhead Rd., Betws-y-Coed (phone: 1690-710219; fax: 1690-710603). Expensive.

Craig-y-Dderwen Snuggled in a cluster of trees right on the banks of the river Conwy, this country-house hotel has 19 rooms and a fine restaurant. There's a golf driving range on its 16-acre grounds. Betws-y-Coed (phone: 1690-710293; fax: 1690-710362). Moderate.

Waterloo More modern in design than the other hotels mentioned, with three bars, 39 rooms, and a couple of self-catering apartments. There's also a restaurant for leisurely meals, plus a coffee shop and a fitness center. Betws-y-Coed (phone: 1690-710411; fax: 1690-710666). Moderate.

Fairy Glen This 17th-century white stone house is near the entrance of *Snowdonia National Park* and the Lledr Valley and also overlooks the river Conwy. There are 10 guestrooms (seven with private baths). A bar is available to guests; the restaurant serves home-cooked local food, including Conwy trout and Welsh lamb. Dolwyddelan Rd., Betws-y-Coed (phone: 1690-710269). Inexpensive.

En Route from Betws-y-Coed At this point you may choose either of two side trips depending on how much time you have. First, you can make an expedition into deeper Snowdonia (known in Welsh as *Eryri,* "the land of eagles"). The *National Mountain Centre* (Plas y Brenin, Capel Curig; phone: 1690-4214) runs mountaineering and rock climbing courses. *Snowdonia Guides* (phone: 1690-6554) offers courses in hill walking and mountain climbing; it also provides reliable guided tours through the Snowdonia area.

Or head westward to Capel Curig, Llanberis, Caernarfon, and the Isle of Anglesey.

It is a nice 5-mile drive west along A5 from Betws-y-Coed to Capel Curig. From here, turn left onto A4086 and head for Pen-y-Gwryd, 4 miles farther. Turn right (remaining on A4086) and continue 6 miles to Llanberis, a Snowdonia town of mountains and quarries, passing Llyn Peris and Llyn Padarn (two pretty lakes) along the way. The *Welsh Slate Museum,* near Llanberis, is worth seeing and gives a good insight into the slate industry. It is closed October through March; admission charge (phone: 1286-870630). In the center of town is the *Museum of the North,* part of the *National Museum of Wales.* It has a sophisticated audiovisual display of the history of Wales, as well as a number of smaller, temporary exhibits on traditional folklore. The museum is open daily; admission charge (phone: 1286-870636). The steam trains of the *Snowdon Mountain Railway* (phone: 1286-870549) head up to the dramatic summit of Wales's highest mountain, and the *Llanberis Lake Railway* (phone: 1286-870549), which is 23½ inches in gauge, runs alongside Lake Padarn for 2 miles from *Padarn Park* to Penllyn. Both trains operate daily, April through October.

From Llanberis, it's a short trip to Caernarfon and the Isle of Anglesey—a trip worth considering. Take A4086 7 miles to Caernarfon.

CAERNARFON Rendered in English as Caernarvon (there's no *v* in the Welsh language and *f* is pronounced like *v*), the town is noted for its magnificent castle and setting. *Caernarfon Castle* is one of Europe's greatest; built in 1283, it was the birthplace in 1284 of the first English-designated Prince of Wales (the future Edward II). Like some other grand castles in Wales, it was constructed on the orders of Edward I of England as part of his successful effort to keep the rebellious Welsh under control. From this strategic site on the Menai Strait, the English could command a huge stretch of the Snowdonia wilds.

Although the castle's interior was never fully completed, there are still many turreted towers and narrow passageways to explore. The *Queens Tower* holds the *Museum of the Royal Welsh Fusiliers,* with a collection of regimental memorabilia; the *Northeast Tower* has an exhibit on the investiture ceremony for the Prince of Wales (Prince Charles was invested here in 1969); and the *Eagle Tower* has a display of medieval armor. The last gets its name from three statuettes of eagles that once perched on the tower's turrets; today, only one is left. *Caernarfon Castle* is open daily; admission charge (phone: 1286-676621). Also see *Quintessential Great Britain* in DIVERSIONS.

From the castle's ramparts, you can see the town walls. Built at the same time as the castle, the walls still surround the oldest section of the city. Inside the walls are fascinating narrow streets with little pubs and shops. In the main square (Castle Square) there is a statue of David Lloyd George, former Prime Minister of Britain.

Also in town is the Roman fort of Segontium, a military center founded in AD 78. Although there aren't a great many ruins left to explore, the museum here has interesting exhibits on the history of the Roman takeover of Wales, archaeological finds from the period, and displays on the Roman military system and culture. It is open daily; admission charge.

The shopping in Caernarfon, a small town with a population of 9,271, includes crafts, and there is a branch of the *Craftcentre Cymru* group that sells tweeds, woolens, pottery, and items made from metal and wood. In addition, there's a market on Saturdays in Castle Square. Caernarfon also boasts two yacht clubs, tennis, and golf facilities, and good fishing.

About 6 miles from town off A499 is the *Caernarfon Air Museum* at *Caernarfon Airport,* with hands-on exhibits of old planes and helicopters, a flight simulator, and audiovisual presentations. It's closed December through February; admission charge (phone: 1286-830800). Also operating from here is *Snowdown Pleasure Flights* (phone: 1286-830800), a company that offers thrilling rides over *Snowdonia National Park* by small plane.

En Route from Caernarfon From Caernarfon, it's about 10 miles along the A487 road to Bangor, where you can take one of two bridges across the swirling Menai Strait over to the Isle of Anglesey. One is a lovely stone suspension bridge built in 1826 by Thomas Telford (a Scottish engineer). This bridge is not only handsome, but a tribute to its designer's skill, since it has no problem coping with the traffic loads of the present century. To help alleviate traffic congestion, there is now a second span—the modern Brittania Road Bridge.

BEST EN ROUTE

Seiont Manor Set in 150 acres of parkland, this renovated Georgian manor house is luxuriously furnished with treasures collected from as far away as China and the Philippines. There are 28 comfortable rooms (some with Jacuzzis), as well as a pool, a sauna, a solarium, and gym facilities. The dining room combines classic French fare with Welsh specialties. In Llanrug, about 4 miles from Caernarfon on A4086 (phone: 1286-673366; fax: 1286-2840). Expensive.

Royal A modernized coaching inn with 58 rooms and a well-regarded restaurant that uses fresh local produce. North Rd., Caernarfon (phone: 1286-673184; fax: 1286-671073). Moderate.

Black Boy Inn Dating from the 14th century and inside the old walled section of Caernarfon, this 12-room hostelry has charming wood beams, crooked floors, and low ceilings. Good, hearty meals are served in the attractive restaurant, and colorful locals frequent the bar. North Gate St., Caernarfon (phone: 1286-673604). Inexpensive.

Hafoty Here is a charming 18th-century farmhouse with three guestrooms and superb views of the Menai Strait, the Isle of Anglesey, and *Caernarfon*

Castle. The delicious home-cooked Welsh food is another plus. Rhostyfam, 5 miles from Caernarfon (phone: 1286-830144). Inexpensive.

ISLE OF ANGLESEY This tiny island is a corner of Wales that doesn't see many overseas travelers because it's so far off the beaten track. Anglesey is a place for personal discoveries: a place to wander down narrow side roads and find charming, unspoiled hamlets and pubs.

You can cut diagonally across the island on A5 to Holyhead, a distance of about 20 miles; or northeast to Beaumaris, a 9-mile drive; or, if you have the time, it's very rewarding to drive all the way around the island via A5025 and A4080.

Holyhead and nearby Trearddur Bay bustle with a number of hotels, small restaurants, and pubs. Most likely, the reason for the bustle is the ferry service between here and Dun Laoghaire, Ireland, 3¼ hours away.

The cliff scenery around Holyhead is striking. South Stack, a tiny, rocky island brightened by a lighthouse, is justly famous for its pounding surf, shrieking seabirds, and strong sea breezes.

If you decide to cover the entire coast of Anglesey, there are all sorts of delightful, relaxing places with good beaches: Red Wharf Bay, Moelfre, Amlwch, Bull Bay, Cemaes Bay, and Rhosneigr. Sailing, fishing, walking, swimming, and sunbathing are the order of the day, and you can surf at Rhosneigr.

If you can't travel all the way to Holyhead, take the A545 from the bridge out to Beaumaris (a 4-mile drive).

BEAUMARIS The town of Beaumaris (pronounced *Bow*-marris) proudly harbors the last (and some say the best) castle Edward I built in Wales. Erected at the end of the 13th century, the moated castle guards the entrance to the Menai Strait, and looks particularly fine against a backdrop of sea and mountains. Its beauty, however, is secondary to its impenetrable fortifications: The castle was a milestone in medieval fortress building. The ingenious design includes two defense walls encircling the castle. The inner wall is square, while the outer wall seems square but actually has bowed sides. This roundedness permitted virtually no corner to go unseen by the castle's keepers. The castle is open daily; admission charge. The nearby *Beaumaris Gaol* is also an interesting stop. It has remained virtually unaltered since it was built in 1829. The prison cells, a unique treadwheel, and the condemned prisoner's walk to the scaffold all serve as grim reminders of harsh times. It is closed October through May; admission charge.

BEST EN ROUTE

Llwydiarth Fawr Set in a beautifully decorated Georgian farmhouse, this hotel is small and intimate (only three guestrooms). On the 850-acre grounds is a working sheep and cattle farm; some of the ingredients used to prepare the excellent home-cooked meals are grown on the premises. Llanerchynedd, Isle of Anglesey (phone: 1248-470321 or 1248-470540). Inexpensive.

En Route from Beaumaris Return to Betws-y-Coed and take A470 north. The road winds attractively through the Conwy Valley to Llanrwst (about 5 miles away) This picturesque little market town beside the river boasts an interesting church and a most striking bridge across the Conwy, built in 1636, thought to have been the work of the noted architect Inigo Jones. Seven miles farther north of Llanrwst stand the superb 80-acre *Bodnant Gardens* (on A470; phone: 1492-650460), a beautiful array of bright flowers and trees overlooking the Snowdon range. They are closed November through mid-March; admission charge. Also see *Stately Homes and Great Gardens* in DIVERSIONS.

From the gardens, return to Llanrwst and take A548 for 8 miles. At Llangernyw, turn right onto B5382 and continue 5 miles to Llansannan. The road winds through wild hills, moors, and river valleys. From Llansannan, turn southeast onto A544 (toward Bylchau) and look for signs for A543 to Denbigh (10 miles away). It's a lovely run over the moors.

BEST EN ROUTE

Bulkeley Overlooking Menai Strait, this fine Victorian establishment offers traditional comforts, including 35 large rooms with high beds, a restaurant, and a popular bar. *Christmas* and *New Year's* packages are available. Castle St., Beaumaris (phone: 1248-810415; fax: 1248-810146). Expensive.

Henllys Hall Set on 40 forested acres with superb Snowdonian views, this 15th-century mansion, a former Franciscan monastery site, has tennis facilities, an outdoor heated pool, a sauna, a solarium, a Jacuzzi, a good restaurant, and 24 rooms. It also has two cottages, seven apartments, two bungalows, and a farmhouse under separate management. Beaumaris (phone: 1248-810412 for recreation facilities, restaurant, and rooms, or 1248-811303 for cottages, apartments, and bungalows; ask for Mr. Miners; fax: 1248-811511). Expensive to moderate.

Ye Olde Bulls Head This establishment has been around since 1472, which makes it something of a historical landmark. Copper ornaments dangling from ceiling beams and snapping fires in the hearths warm up the place and the mood quite a bit. There are 11 pleasant rooms and an award-winning restaurant. Castle St., Beaumaris (phone: 1248-810329; 800-435-4504; fax: 1248-811294). Moderate.

DENBIGH Pronounced *Din*-bych, this town looks out over the Vale of Clwyd, the river that gives the county its name. This is true border country, so it has seen its share of battle-axing and swordplay. The castle, which stands on a hill, was first built by William the Conqueror as part of his effort to annex this region. It was greatly extended and improved during Edward I's reign, and along with Edward's other castles, it played a large part in bringing the Welsh under the king's rule in the 12th and 13th centuries. Later, the castle was sold by Queen Elizabeth I to Robert Dudley, her favorite courtier, and it was a focal point of the great Civil War in the following century. Action against King Charles's supporters was directed from Denbigh, and Sir John Owen, leader of a determined Royalist army, was captured and held prisoner in the castle. Note its unusual octagonal towers. The Elizabethan town hall on High Street is just one of many interesting corners of Denbigh. The steep streets make for some memorable snapshots. Perhaps Denbigh's most famous son was H. M. Stanley (born John Rowlands); he emigrated to the US, became a journalist, explored Africa, and found Dr. Livingstone, he presumed.

BEST EN ROUTE

Bryn Morfydd Set on 40 acres, it has 30 comfortable rooms with great views, a restaurant, a tennis court, two golf courses, and an outdoor heated pool. Located 3 miles south of Denbigh on A525 in Llanrhaeadr (phone: 1745-78280; fax: 1745-78488). Moderate.

En Route from Denbigh Eight miles south on A525 lies Ruthin (pronounced *Rith*-in), a handsome town whose market square is fringed by 16th- and 17th-century houses. It was once a wool trade center, but its history goes much farther back. It was here that Owain Glyndwr started his uprising against English rule in 1400. Glyndwr and his men burned the town but failed to capture the castle. The medieval castle is now a ruin, but the big mansion on the site is a fine 58-room hotel, expensive as Welsh hostelries go, but with good facilities and fine dining. It is called, naturally enough, *Ruthin Castle* (phone: 1824-702664; fax: 1824-705978). The hotel offers banquets with ale, mead, roasts, and the like done in what is thought to be a medieval style. It makes for a jolly evening; go with an empty stomach.

The route from Ruthin winds across the Vale of Clwyd and across the Clwydian range of mountains by way of A494. But a side trip 15 miles along A525 to A542 to Llangollen is well worth any effort. The town stands beside the rushing river Dee, and words simply cannot do it justice. The four-arched bridge across the Dee, built in the 12th century and widened later, is traditionally one of the seven wonders of Wales. Llangollen is deeply embedded in Welsh history, and the town is featured in many legends of love, jealousy, rivalry, and blood. It takes its name from Collen, a saint of the ancient Celtic church. The *Valle Crucis Abbey,* 2 miles from Llangollen along the canal, was ruined on Henry VIII's orders, but it is still imposing. Any visit to this town must include *Plas Newydd.* This stately mansion was the home of the "Ladies of Llangollen," two aristocratic Irishwomen, Eleanor

Butler (1739–1829) and Sarah Ponsonby (1755–1831), who settled here in protest against the stifling conformity of the Irish Protestant ascendancy. From 1780 they dominated the life of their haven and shared their happiness with many eminent visitors, including Wellington, Burke, Byron, Shelley, Scott, and Wordsworth. The house is closed November through *Easter;* admission charge (phone: 1978-861314).

Nearby, on the Corwen road, are the remains of *Plas-yn-Ial.* This is the ancient seat of the Ial family, one of whose sons founded the American university (their family name, pronounced *Yal,* was corrupted to *Yale*). Llangollen is abundantly endowed with pubs, hotels, and cafés, and every July it rings to the sound of music during the *International Musical Eisteddfod* (see *Best Festivals* in DIVERSIONS).

Southeast Scotland

No traveler should tread the hallowed ground of southeast Scotland without first learning a few rudiments of the history of Presbyterianism. Here's an emergency grab bag of key religious events in Scotland from the 16th century to the present as well as brief profiles of the two major players.

John Knox, a brilliant and incendiary preacher inspired by the theology of John Calvin, came to *St. Giles' Cathedral,* Edinburgh, in 1559. Many of the Norman-blooded Scottish nobility, looking to aggrandize themselves, hopped on Knox's bandwagon to campaign against a corrupt Catholic church and the Catholic Royal House of Stuart. Thus began the Protestant Reformation in Scotland. With 15 four-hour sermons a week on the democratization of Christian worship, Knox soon gathered the common people to his bosom. His reforms were implemented in every corner of southern Scotland amid the wrecking of church interiors and ravaging of altars. Yet, contrary to generations of popular opinion, Knox was no Puritan; he openly urged his fellow citizens to drink, dance, and be merry. Social restraints closed in on the Presbyterian faith much later, in the wake of royal persecution from London.

Charles II, successor in 1660 to a disagreeable Cromwellian interlude (which had, however, allowed Presbyterianism to flourish), continued his executed father's bad habit of ramming Episcopacy down Scotland's throat, backed by an obsequious and dissolute Scottish Parliament. Groups of worshipers called Covenanters (because of two written oaths they had signed, some in blood, proclaiming their inalienable anti-Episcopal beliefs) gathered away from the churches, flouting a parliamentary act. Charles's troops zeroed in for a series of massacres, accounting in part for the numerous Covenanters martyrs' graves found in this part of the country.

In 1712 England's and Scotland's now unified parliaments passed a new act instituting lay patronage. This system revoked the right of congregations to choose their own ministers and granted the task to each parish's local "laird" (lord or resident aristocrat). The handpicked, often tyrannical ministers tightly controlled life in the southern towns and villages, banning music, dancing, theatrical performances, and country walks on Sundays. Scotland's national bard, Robert Burns, was one of many people who were forced to appease God's wrath by standing publicly in a dock confessing to fornication.

With the coming of the Industrial Revolution, economic and social conditions in southern Scotland became appalling. In comparison to their working class congregations, men of the cloth were fat cats. In 1843, 450 ministers with sorely tried consciences walked bravely out of their manses, their ministries, and the annual General Assembly of the Church of Scotland to form a new movement, the Free Presbyterian Church. This breach was not healed until 1929, after lay patronage had been abolished within the Kirk (as the established Presbyterian Church was—and still is—called). Attendant upon the tireless and dedicated slum-based social work of the new Free Church was a harsh list of "don'ts" for its followers: no uncleanliness; no laziness; no bankruptcy; no "Sabbath breaking"; no drinking and gambling; no loud, indelicate behavior. Today, these cast-iron virtues are woven less tightly into the fabric of Scottish life: Most pubs and bars now are open on the Sabbath. Another indication of the gradual slackening of old ways in the last decade has been the Scots' increasing willingness to admit that *Christmas* is not simply an unnecessarily flamboyant papist holiday, to be eschewed in favor of *New Year's.* Both holidays now are celebrated with two-day breaks.

Apart from the wide east coastal plain and the rich farmlands of East Lothian and the east of Berwickshire, southeast Scotland is hilly country, particularly in the Borders. There are no dramatic peaks such as those in the Highlands; the hills have rounded green tops and steep slopes where the burns (streams) rush down to form waterfalls and pools. The valleys are the home of rivers that flow tranquilly in their deeper reaches and at other times rush wildly over stony beds.

The language spoken by Lowlanders derives from "La'lands," an old form of Norman-infused Anglo-Saxon once known as "Inglis." It's full of dialect words, rolled r's, and unexpected pronunciations: *guid* for "good," *doon* for "down," *fitba* for "football." La'lands is sometimes droll, often pithy, and—with the help of great poets like William Dunbar, Robert Burns, and Hugh MacDiarmid—majestic. It's worth reading a bit of Burns or MacDiarmid to get a sense of southern Scotland's people, speech, and concept of nationhood.

Look also at the English-language poetry of Sir Walter Scott, who set *Marmion* and *The Lay of the Last Minstrel* among the Border country's rolling, brackeny hills. The Borders, Scott's home for many years, are southeast Scotland's most intriguing district: It's a moorish land interspersed with lush farms and prosperous mill-spangled towns. Ruined abbeys sit like sad marooned kings above gladed loops in the river Tweed. Picturesque villages dot its valleys. Its folklore is widely known, especially its ballads, from *Thomas the Rhymer and the Queen of Elfland* to narrative poetry that recounts the dramatic cattle-rustling Border raids of the 14th, 15th, and 16th centuries. As Scots and English clashed for control of the troubled border, known as the "Debateable Land," the landowning families, called "riding families" or "reivers" (raiders), gathered their tenants and their "moss-troopers" (knights) and forayed into each other's territory, burying their differences only when English marauders posed a greater threat. Onetime British Prime Minister Sir Alec Douglas-Home is descended from at least two of these families. The "Riding of the Marches," a way of delineating boundaries by tracing them in assembled companies on horseback, is practiced on a festival day every summer by each of the main Border towns—catch the ritual at least once if you can.

Yet literature, high political drama, and ecclesiastical turmoil are not the only features of southeast Scotland's fascinating history. The area has an enormous concentration of castles, both ruined and intact; aristocratic mansions from every century, with lavish, extensive gardens; harbor towns that have changed very little in a hundred years; and the fresh-air-and-countryside, rich Victorian holiday atmosphere of Peeblesshire. And then there is golf—the mainstay of the seaside towns of East Lothian. Eleven magnificent courses dot the land from Edinburgh to Dunbar, a great challenge to any duffer used to manicured parklands. Dune-shaped terrain and changeable winds will affect the game, and golfers may be advised to use a wedge-shaped club. But take heart—some Scottish king probably once played golf in the same place, with a crabbit wooden stick and a ball stuffed with feathers!

The route begins at Edinburgh and runs east along the Firth of Forth to Dunbar, continuing to Berwick-upon-Tweed, where it veers inland through the Border hill country to Coldstream and Kelso, and on south to Langholm. From Langholm it circles to Scott country, and from there to Moffat, sheltered in the Tweedsmuir hills. From Moffat the route leads north again to Peebles, Galashiels, and back to Edinburgh. The entire distance is about 350 miles. It should take between one and two weeks, depending on how many castles, museums, markets, and festivals you stop to see. It's a good idea to keep scones or sandwiches in the car in case you're still in the wilds when lunchtime rolls around. Don't pass a gas station assuming that there will be another one soon. If traveling from May through September, be sure to book hotels in advance.

The *Tourist Information Centre* in Jedburgh (Murray's Green; phone: 1835-863435; fax: 1835-864099) or its counterpart in Selkirk (*Halliwell's House;* phone: 1750-20054) are the main sources of information and publications about the area; both are open daily. Tourist offices along the route provide information and publish booklets such as *Scotland: Hillwalking* (costing £4/about $6). Ask in the tourist offices about the *Borders Craft Association* and opportunities to tour workshops of various Border crafts such as pottery, candlemaking, woodcarving, and the like; "Scottish Explorer" tickets, giving access to ancient monuments at a fraction of the price it would cost if they were visited individually; and the Borders Woollen Trail of mill factories and shops. Also, be sure to buy the *Scottish Tourist Board*'s kit *Enjoy Scotland* (£7/about $10.50), which includes a detailed touring map and a booklet of 1,001 things to see. A Borders *What's On* guide is published monthly. *Taste of Scotland Scheme, Ltd.* (33 Melville St., Edinburgh; phone: 131-220-1900) publishes a guide to dining on native fare that costs £9 (about $13.50). Border towns are famous for amusing, individually created types of hard candy. The *Royal Commission on the Ancient and Historical Monuments of Scotland* has published a very attractive paperback, with photographs, entitled *Exploring Scotland's Heritage, Lothian and the Borders,* by John R. Baldwin (£9.95/about $15). This is an ideal companion for many of the sights included in this route. Copies are generally available at Edinburgh bookshops, as well as from the publisher, *Her Majesty's Stationery Office* (71 Lothian Rd.; phone: 131-228-4181).

The price categories for the hotels listed in this route are $200 or more per night for two for bed and breakfast at a very expensive place; $100 to $180 at an expensive one; $70 to $95 in the moderate category; and less than $70 at an inexpensive spot. Unless stated otherwise, hotels feature private baths and TV sets. Dinner for two (not including drinks or tip) in a restaurant rated as very expensive will run $80 or more; in an expensive one, $45 to $75; in the moderate category, $25 to $40; and at an inexpensive spot, less than $25. All restaurants listed serve lunch and dinner unless otherwise indicated. For each location, hotels and restaurants are listed alphabetically be price category.

EDINBURGH For a detailed report on the city, its sights, hotels, and restaurants, see *Edinburgh* in THE CITIES.

En Route from Edinburgh Take A1 east from Edinburgh for 2 miles to Portobello; from here, take A198 east for 3 miles along the Firth of Forth. Along the way, you might want to stop in the suburb of Musselburgh; its tourist office (*Brunton Hall;* phone: 131-665-3711; fax: 131-665-7495) has a wealth of information on the entire coastal area. The office is closed October through May. From here, pick up B1348 and travel north 8 miles to Morrison's Haven, site of the 800-year-old Prestongrange coal mine, one of only two former mines open to the public. Operated by the *Scottish Mining Museum Trust,* the site features a visitors' center with exhibitions and an audiovisual display, a massive five-story beam pump dating from 1874, three steam locomotives, a steam navvy (shovel), and a winding engine. (Any of the tour guides can give driving instructions to nearby Lady Victoria Colliery, a mine founded in 1890 and still in operation.) April through October, the locomotives operate on the first Sunday of the month, known as "Steam Day." The mine is open daily; admission charge (phone: 131-663-7519).

About 6½ miles farther along A198, just before the town of Gullane, are several noteworthy attractions. *Gosford House,* signposted off A198, is a seat of the Earls of Wemyss, built by Robert Adam in 1800. It is open Wednesdays, Saturdays, and Sundays from 2 to 5 PM in June and July; admission charge (phone: 1875-870201). *Aberlady Church,* in the village of Aberlady, has part of an 8th-century Celtic cross in the chancel and a fortified 15th-century tower. From Aberlady, you can take a short side trip to Athelstaneford, the birthplace of Scotland's national flag, the Saltire; the banner, designed with a white cross on a blue background, flies continuously from the top of the little kirk in the village. To get there, turn right on A6137 in Aberlady Village, go 2 miles, and then take a left on B1343. (On the way, you also may want to take a quick look at the chimney-like monument on A6137 just beyond the turnoff to Athelstaneford. It was erected to John Hope, the fourth Earl of Hopetoun, 1756–1832, by his admiring tenants. A splendid panorama can be viewed from the top of the tower (open daily; no admission charge). Automobile aficionados will want to visit the *Myreton Motor Museum,* which displays vintage cars and cycles. It is open daily; admission charge (phone: 1875-870288). To get there, return to Aberlady; the museum is signposted for its turnoff from A198 just beyond the village.

GULLANE Despite strong winds in winter, rich Edinburghers maintain a posh suburban existence here. Gullane (pop. 2,124) gets more sun than anywhere else in Scotland, and it has wide, luxurious sandy beaches. Tourists throng here in late spring and summer because of its four incomparable golf courses. *Muirfield,* the finest (a frequent site of the *Opens*), is the home of the *Honourable Company of Edinburgh Golfers;* to play, have your home club secretary send a letter of introduction (include alternate dates) to *Muirfield* (Gullane, East Lothian EH31 2EG, Scotland; phone: 1620-842123). Play at *Muirfield* for guests is on Tuesdays, Thursdays, and Friday mornings only; an 18 or under handicap is required. (For more information, see *Edinburgh* in THE CITIES.) The *Heritage of Golf Museum* (West Links Rd., Gullane; phone: 1875-870277 early mornings or evenings) shows the game's development from the 15th century to the present and sells antique golf clubs, golf balls, and collectible souvenirs related to the game. Open by appointment only; no admission charge.

BEST EN ROUTE

Greywalls Gullane's most exclusive place to stay is this lavishly appointed, 23-room golfers' retreat that was designed by Sir Edwin Lutyens, the eminent English architect. Two comfortable, bright dining rooms serve intriguing dishes (try the smoked trout and prawn terrine) and have an excellent wine list. Next to *Muirfield* golf course, the hotel can arrange specific starting times for guests. Open April through November. Gullane (phone: 1620-842144; fax: 1620-842241). Expensive.

La Potinière The French cooking at this small, unassuming place has earned a Michelin star (there is even a house recipe book, *La Potinière and Friends,* for sale), and it has an award-winning wine cellar. The menu changes every day. Closed October; no lunch on Wednesdays, Fridays and Saturdays, except for private parties. Reservations necessary. No credit cards accepted. On the main route through Gullane (phone: 1620-843214). Expensive.

Mallard A large old house overlooking Gullane's three 18-hole golf courses, it has 18 comfortable rooms and a restaurant. East Links Rd., Gullane (phone: 1620-843288). Moderate.

En Route from Gullane Continue 3 miles northeast on A198 to Dirleton.

DIRLETON With its spectacular castle and busy yew-encircled bowling green, Dirleton is reputedly the prettiest village in Scotland. The castle, entered dramatically by a long ramp leading sharply upward to a gate in its stark and stony heights, was built in 1225. Additions were made in the 15th and 17th centuries, but the whole was sacked by Oliver Cromwell's troops in 1650. It is open daily; admission charge (phone: 1620-85330). The castle shares the borders of the village common with clusters of 17th- and 18th-century cottages. If you feel like taking a walk, trees and springy turf line the lovely Yellowcraig Nature Trail for 2 miles from Dirleton to the sea. The trail is accessible from B1345 down Old Ware Road to the beach.

BEST EN ROUTE

Open Arms A country-style, seven-room hostelry famed for its Taste of Scotland restaurant. Decorated in soft pink and lilac, its candlelit tables are graced by such delicacies as salmon, venison, and cranachan pudding—cream, toasted oatmeal, and rum, topped with fresh berries! Open daily. Reservations advised. Major credit cards accepted. On the main route through Dirleton (phone: 1620-85241; fax: 1620-85570). Expensive.

En Route from Dirleton Continue on A198 another 2½ miles to North Berwick.

NORTH BERWICK Farmers who inhabit the countryside, as well as weekenders from Edinburgh, habitually converge on this holiday spot, making the most of its sands, shops, and two fine golf courses. North Berwick has the kind of natural topography that proves God must be British: The visitors' beach is separated from the town beach by the harbor; its rocky peninsula is well-protected from the east coast breezes.

A mile or so south of the center of town is North Berwick Law, a grassy once-volcanic rise decked with a whalebone arch, from which to enjoy a magnificent view. The *North Berwick Environment Trust* has published a leaflet of six good walking tours in and around the town, available for 60p (about 90¢) at the tourist office (Quality St.; phone: 1620-2197; fax: 1620-4480). The tourist office is open daily. Motorboat tours from North Berwick go in summer to the nearby island of Fidra and also to the fascinating Bass Rock. The rock's steep, straight sides make it look much higher than its 350 feet. It's part of a chain of volcanic masses, made of especially hard stone, that withstood glacial pressure in the last Ice Age. The Bass Rock is inaccessible except at one point, which made it irresistible to hermits in early Christian times; to prison wardens detaining Covenanting ministers at the time of Charles II; and to four Jacobite prisoners who, rallying round the flag of the exiled Stuarts, overcame the garrison to capture and hold the fortress for three years, until they surrendered it and departed as free men in 1694. Today the Bass Rock is "held," as is Fidra, by the keepers of its lighthouse and scores of gannets.

A variety of activities are possible in North Berwick: For boat trips, contact Fred Marr (24 Victoria Rd.; phone: 1620-2838) or check the time schedule posted at the harbor. There is a heated open-air pool on the sea front (phone: 1620-2083). Donald and Fiona Fraser operate a weaving studio (51-53 Forth St.; phone: 1620-894220) where visitors can buy fabrics and designer clothes. Handmade objects are sold at *Shape Scrape Ceramics* (The Pottery, Station Hill; phone: 1620-893157). The *North Berwick Museum* (School Rd.; phone: 1620-893470) has a local history and wildlife exhibition. It's closed late September through March; no admission charge.

BEST EN ROUTE

Nether Abbey Situated in the middle of town, this 17-room hotel in an 18th-century house offers a comfortable, friendly atmosphere—like a Scottish house party. Its restaurant serves excellent venison, game, and wine. Just outside North Berwick (phone: 1620-892802; fax: 1620-895298). Expensive to moderate.

En Route from North Berwick About 3 miles farther on A198 is *Tantallon Castle,* on a cliff overlooking the North Sea. An extensive rose-colored ruin that once was a stronghold of the famous Border family named Douglas, it captured the Scottish popular imagination: An impossible feat is said to be as hard as to "ding doon" (knock down) *Tantallon Castle.* The castle is open daily; admission charge (phone: 1620-892727).

The village of Whitekirk, also on A198 (3 miles south of *Tantallon Castle*), is worth exploring. In the 15th century, pilgrims from all over Europe drank at Whitekirk's Holy Well. The kirk was rebuilt in its original Gothic style after suffragettes burned it down in 1914, presumably because of its association with rack-renting monks (who charged excessive fees to store grain in the tithe barn across the road, also of historic interest).

A 2-mile detour east from Tyninghame along the East Linton road (B1407) leads to *Preston Mill* and *Phantassie Doocot.* The 18th-century mill, with a waterwheel, is still in operation. The "doocot" (dovecote) holds 500 birds and is believed to date from the 16th century, when local lairds kept pigeons to be fattened for their tables, at the expense of their tenants' crops. It's closed weekdays in October and November through March; admission charge (phone: 1620-860426).

Just south of the mill and the town of East Linton, pick up the A1 roadway (also known as the Great North Road) and head toward Dunbar. If you do not detour to the *Preston Mill,* continue south on A198 from Tyninghame and pick up A1 there. Dunbar is about 1 mile farther east.

DUNBAR This quiet town, in sailing ship days the only safe port between Edinburgh and Berwick, England, is now a golfing and sailing haven for vacationers—

a family resort with a year-round population of around 5,000. Here, tomorrow seems to be two weeks away. But it wasn't always restful. The Earl of Hertford attacked it by land in 1544, during the so-called Rough Wooing by which King Henry VIII tried to force the young Mary, Queen of Scots, to marry his son, Edward. Years later, Mary stayed in *Dunbar Castle* (today a mere vestige) with her husband and cousin, Lord Darnley, and again with her lover Lord Bothwell, who carried her off there after the murder of Lord Darnley. The castle was partly destroyed in 1567, after Mary and Bothwell had fled for their lives, and Cromwell finished the job when he laid waste to the town in 1650. Today's harbor—still the home of a small herring fleet—is the more picturesque for the castle ruin. This whole section of Dunbar was part of the original royal burgh of 1369.

A man whose work touched the lives of many Americans had his roots in Dunbar. The building at the north end of High Street is the birthplace of John Muir, the man responsible for the US National Park system. A pioneering geologist, explorer, and naturalist, Muir spent the first 11 years of his life in the top apartment of this building with his family until emigrating to the US in 1849. The Muir flat is appropriately furnished in 19th-century style, and one room is reserved for audiovisual presentations of his life and work. It is closed Wednesdays year-round and Sundays mid-September through May; no admission charge. For more details contact the tourist information center, in the *Town House* (High St.; phone: 1368-63353), where you can purchase a helpful booklet, *A Walk Round the Old Burgh of Dunbar,* by Stephen A. Bunyan, for £2.95 (about $4.50). The center is open daily. The *Town House,* a fascinating 17th-century building with a hexagonal tower, contains Jacobean and Georgian Royal Armorial exhibits and a 16th-century jail; it is the oldest civic building still in continuous use in Scotland.

Other attractions in Dunbar include the *Lifeboat Museum* (call the tourist office for hours; no admission charge), in a harborside shed, staffed by volunteers from the townswomen's *Lifeboat Committee* (who also organize *Lifeboat Day* in July, with stalls, bands, and the crowning of a Lifeboat Queen); *Lauderdale House,* an impressive Georgian building designed by Robert Adam for the Earls of Lauderdale (which can be viewed from the outside only); *Lauderdale Park,* with skittles, tetherball, trampolines, and other family-style activities; a small miniature-golf park; a small amusement park; tennis courts; and two golf links. The *Dunbar Flower Show* is held in early September. The 1,667-acre *John Muir Country Park* provides a field day for naturalists; the park ranger (phone: 1620-842637) and the tourist information office have special guidebooks for the park's Cliff-Top Trail. The park is open daily; no admission charge.

BEST EN ROUTE

Bayswell With excellent sea views, this 14-room, family-run hostelry offers access to many local golf courses. The restaurant specializes in vegetarian dishes and is licensed to serve alcohol. *Bayswell Park,* Dunbar (phone: 1368-62225). Moderate.

Courtyard These converted cottages were once inhabited by fishing families. The seven guestrooms are graced by sea views, and the dining room serves homemade pâtés and chicken breast with wild mushroom sauce. Woodbrush Brae, Dunbar (phone: 1368-64169). Moderate to inexpensive.

Battleblent Sitting atop a hill and resembling a small castle with a turreted roof, this modernized, family-run place has seven guestrooms, a dining room specializing in seafood, and 2 bars. One mile east of Dunbar, in West Barns (phone: 1368-62234). Inexpensive.

En Route from Dunbar Take A1 south out of Dunbar. About 8 miles farther, before crossing from the East Lothian region into the Borders, a mile north of Cockburnspath, you will pass the entrance to *Dunglass Collegiate Church* (follow the turnoff sign for Bilsdean), founded in 1450. The nave, choir, transepts, sacristy, and central tower are still intact. The church (now empty) was used as a barn after extensive plundering during the Reformation; the interior stonework is especially arresting.

A half mile south of Cockburnspath, bear east off A1 onto A1107. Four miles along A1107 is the signposted approach to the ruins of *Fast Castle,* an ancient Home family stronghold spectacularly poised on a cliff. From the castle, return to A1107 and head south toward Coldingham. At Coldingham is a small 13th-century Benedictine priory. Reformation zealots wrecked most of it, but the choir and sanctuary, with later additions, are now the Coldingham parish church.

Just beyond Coldingham, take a detour on the B6438 northeast, which dead-ends after a mile at St. Abbs, a tiny storybook fishing village, where strings of whitewashed cottages uncurl down crags to the sea, flanked by clusters of colored boats. If you paint, bring your palette! A small crab and lobster industry survives here, but somehow the setting doesn't seem quite real. You can visit the nearby nature reserve on St. Abbs Head to behold seabirds, wildflowers, and sweeping views. It's open daily; admission charge. Return to A1107 and continue another 3½ miles south to Eyemouth.

BEST EN ROUTE

St. Abbs Haven This well-known establishment has modernized its 13 rooms while preserving its charm (one guestroom has a four-poster bed). Ideally located on Coldingham Bay, with great sea panoramas and a sheltered beach, there's also a restaurant and two bars. Located off B6438 above St. Abbs Harbour (phone: 1890-771491). Moderate.

EYEMOUTH Don't be misled by the quaint, old-time atmosphere of the harbor into thinking it's a film set or a ghost town tarted up for tourists: Large trawlers dock here, jammed with fish. Among the clients in the cozy pubs along the quay are packers, truckers, rosy-cheeked fishermen, and a three-legged marmalade cat called "Tripod," who prowls ye olde *Ship Inn* (Harbour Rd.; phone: 1890-750678). The trawlers put out to sea on Sunday and come back Thursday, so Thursday is the town's big night!

The *Eyemouth Museum* in the lovely *Auld Kirk* on Manse Road is an award-winning memorial to local fishermen lost in the Great Fishing Disaster of 1881. It is closed November through March; admission charge (phone: 1890-750678). Ochre-bright *Gunsgreen House,* overlooking the harbor pubs, has a romantic, smuggling-related history, which the *Eyemouth Museum* colorfully elucidates.

The chief attraction of Eyemouth for tourists is sea angling. Check for details at the tourist office (in the *Auld Kirk,* Manse Rd.; phone: 1890-750678), which is closed November through March. There's a *Herring Queen Festival* in mid-July and *Eyemouth Lifeboat Week* in early August. The western promontory of the bay has vestiges of various forts, from prehistoric days to the 20th century.

En Route from Eyemouth A short detour (2 miles) from the Berwick-bound A1107 to B6355 out of Eyemouth leads to *Ayton Castle,* where you rejoin A1. The castle, designed in 1846 for a governor of the Bank of Scotland, is a huge, flamboyant Scottish baronial type, built of red sandstone and now a family home. The castle is open Sunday afternoons or by appointment; admission charge (phone: 1890-781212). From here, take A1 another 6 miles south to the city of Berwick-upon-Tweed; at this point, you've crossed the border into England.

BERWICK-UPON-TWEED A medieval walled burgh constructed to withstand invaders' onslaughts, Berwick (pop. 12,772) nonetheless frequently changed hands between warring English and Scots, until it finally became English in 1482. It was in the *Berwick Castle Great Hall*—now the Berwick railway station—that King Edward I of England announced, in 1292, his choice for King of Scots: the limpid John Balliol, known subsequently to his subjects as "Toom Tabard" ("Empty Coat"). John Balliol's maladministrations cost the two nations the truce that should have left Berwick unharmed. The town is still almost wholly surrounded by the impressive walls and towers of the 16th-century defenses. Today the town, despite high unemployment, keeps going, thanks to its small industries, including a woodyard and a Pringle knitwear depot.

Park in the Castlegate car park, close to the *Berwick Tourist Information Office* (phone: 1289-330733; closed November through March). Berwick's streets are so ancient—and jammed with traffic—that a car can hardly move, but the town is so full of intriguing nooks and crannies that it's much more fun to walk anyway. Begin by descending from the railway station (near the car park) to the river Tweed through a delightful small wooded garden. A riverside walk affords a splendid view of three bridges of which Berwick's inhabitants are very proud: the old bridge of 1634, with arches decreasing in height from north to south; the Royal Tweed Bridge of 1928, in a modern mode; and the breathtaking Royal Border Bridge, which carries trains between London and Edinburgh. The Royal Border Bridge has 28 celestial arches and was opened in 1850; on a gray day, the view upriver beyond this bridge can give an ethereal feeling.

Around the mouth of the Tweed are ducks, swans, wheeling gulls, and clusters of red-roofed buildings, some renovated, others with that rare dereliction that transmits ramshackle charm. Restoration work on houses along the quay walls has drawn artists and craftspeople from other parts of Britain as buyers. All periods of history are represented in old Berwick, in an architectural jumble that is deliciously quaint.

Uphill from all this is Marygate, less Old World and more like a typical present-day county town. It's Berwick's main shopping street and houses the old-fashioned-looking offices of the Tweeddale Press Group of local newspapers, as well as the *Town Hall,* a striking example of a Georgian public building. The hall has a local history museum, a jail, and a belfry. Visitors are welcome to look around the building either on their own or on a guided tour (given at 11:30 AM and 2 PM from June through September). The hall is closed weekends; admission charge to the museum. Open-air market days in Marygate are Wednesdays and Saturdays.

The main tourist sights of Berwick are the remains of *Berwick Castle,* on the Tweed at the base of the Royal Border Bridge; the bastioned walls, built by Elizabeth I, which can be walked along from rampart to rampart looking down onto the city; the severely Puritan *Parish Church* of 1652, one of only two churches in Britain built under Cromwell; and the Vanbrugh-style barracks, now a museum, where troops have been garrisoned since 1721. The barracks hold the *Regimental Museum of the King's Own Scottish Borderers* (phone: 1289-307426 or 1289-307427) and the *Borough Museum and Art Gallery* (phone: 1289-330933), including treasures from the collection of Sir William Burrell, the early-20th-century Glaswegian magnate known as "The Magpie Millionaire" because of his compulsion for collecting beautiful things. Both the museum and the art gallery are closed Mondays October through March and charge admission. There also is a magnificent gatehouse and an old barracks block. On Palace Green is the *Wine and Spirit Museum* of the Lindisfarne Liqueur Co. Ltd. where you can purchase the company's products, as well as perfume and Lindisfarne pottery. It's closed weekends and in winter; no admission charge (phone: 1289-305153).

If you're touring with children or need presents for the kids back home, *Border Series* (9 Hide Hill; phone: 1289-305657) has a large toy department with outsized electric model trains that chug around a ledge near the ceiling. *Martin's Border Bakery,* in *The Food Shop* (7 Marygate; phone: 1289-307904), sells tasty buns, or try the home baking in the *Scotsgate Tea Room,* also on Marygate (phone: 1289-308028).

Four miles west of Berwick on the B6461, be sure to stop at *Paxton House.* The 18th-century pink sandstone mansion was built by Patrick of Billy for the daughter of Frederick the Great of Prussia whom he had hoped to marry (but never did), and was designed by the illustrious Adam family of architects. During the 19th century, the mansion was renowned for housing one of the country's largest private picture collections; the original paintings are now supplemented by works on loan from the *National Gallery of Scotland* in Edinburgh. Guests may stroll the (privately owned) estate's extensive gardens and tranquil riverside walks. It is closed November through *Good Friday;* admission charge (phone: 1289-86291).

BEST EN ROUTE

King's Arms The tiny lobby of this restored Georgian coaching inn fans out into two attractive restaurants, a spacious buffet bar, a walled garden café, a gameroom with tables for snooker (a game similar to billiards), and 36 Cinderella-like bedrooms with frilly decor, telephones, and tea- and coffee-making facilities. Three of the guestrooms have four-poster beds. Hide Hill, Berwick-upon-Tweed (phone: 1289-307454; fax: 1289-308867). Expensive to moderate.

Rob Roy Berwick specialties such as fresh lobster, crab, and oysters are offered; there's also a cozy bar that serves snacks. Closed Tuesdays. Reservations advised. Major credit cards accepted. Dock Rd., Berwick-upon-Tweed (phone: 1289-306428). Moderate.

En Route from Berwick Follow the river Tweed 15 miles southwest to Coldstream on A698, re-entering Scotland. Halfway along is the ruin of *Norham Castle,* an ancient stronghold of the Bishops of Durham that reinforced the fort at Coldstream against Scottish invaders and was of major strategic importance under Edward I and Henry II and III. "The loop-holed walls where captives weep" described by Sir Walter Scott in *Marmion* are extant.

COLDSTREAM The Tweed Bridge was built in 1776, after which it became notorious for a heavy traffic in eloping couples heading for the *Old Marriage House.* (Scotland has relatively lax marriage laws.) The town is famous, too, as the starting point of the 1660 march of the Coldstream Guards to London, where they effected the restoration of Charles II. Their original headquarters is on the north side of the main square. The tourist office (Henderson Park; phone: 1890-882607) is closed November through March.

En Route from Coldstream About 2 miles northwest of Coldstream, on A697, is *Hirsel,* the late Sir Alec Douglas-Home's ancestral home. The house itself is closed to the public, but the magnificent gardens are open and include rhododendrons, woodlands, and a small lake chockablock with wildfowl. A museum on the grounds has exhibits highlighting the estate's history. It is open daily; admission charge (phone: 1890-882834). Also here is a crafts center, which holds demonstrations throughout the year, including a *Living Crafts* weekend in May and a *Country Fair* on the first weekend of June. Return to A698 and continue 10 miles southwest to Kelso.

KELSO Site of one of the four Border abbeys of the incomparable Scott country, this small bastion of what could almost be French civilization (its center looks like an enormous *grande place*) is nonetheless the first taste of the netherworld between past and present, legend and reality, which suffuses this part of Scotland. The town, like the abbey, is situated on the rivers Tweed and Teviot. Its five-arched bridge, begun in 1800, was an exact model for the later Waterloo Bridge across the Thames, demolished in 1934. The lamp standards, visible at the bridge's south end, were salvaged and brought here from London after the demolition.

Founded in 1128 by David I (son of the King Malcolm who succeeded Macbeth and who was an ancestor of King Robert the Bruce), *Kelso Abbey* was destroyed by the Earl of Hertford in 1545. What remains of it shows a Norman transitional style unique in Scotland. In the largest Kelso car park behind the abbey is *Kelso Pottery* (phone: 1573-224027), where you can watch the making and glazing of stoneware and buy some of the products. In late May, gaily costumed rafters compete in the *Great Tweed Raft Race.* In June, the town's showground hosts Scotland's largest (and Britain's second-largest) dog show. *Civic Week,* the third week in July, is full of colorful equestrian pageants; and the Borders' major farming event, the *Border Union Agricultural Show,* is held in late July at *Springwood Park.* The mid-September *Kelso Ram Sales,* also in *Springwood Park,* provides a fascinating glimpse of Border life (during the rest of the year, the park is the site of equally colorful horse sales). Kelso also has a steeplechase racecourse, and, at Friarshaugh, hosts the *Berwickshire,* the *Buccleuch,* and the *Jed Forest* hunts in "point-to-point" (a horse race with an undefined course—only a start and finish point). *Turret House* (Abbey Ct.; phone: 1573-223464) is a museum of local history. It is closed November through March; admission charge. The tourist board office (The Square; phone: 1573-223464) can provide plenty of information on local attractions; it's closed November through March.

The *Inspiration Gift Shop* (Bridge St.; phone: 1573-224699) is a good place for clothes and Liberty scarves; they also have a good selection of cushions. The fishing tackle shops sell visitors' tickets for fishing on the popular river Tweed. If you catch a salmon, local hotels will buy it from you for about £2.50 ($4) per pound.

En Route from Kelso Some 2 miles northwest of Kelso, on A6089, is *Floors Castle,* seat of the Dukes of Roxburghe, said to be the largest inhabited mansion in Britain. It has 365 windows, one for every day of the year. Built by William Adam in 1721, it underwent various additions and remodelings and now is spectacularly grandiose, with battlements, water spouts, pepper-pot towers, an amphitheater, and golden gates. The furniture, porcelain, tapestries, and paintings are all superb. The fine grounds include a holly tree supposedly marking the spot where King James II (of Scotland) was killed in 1460 by one of his own cannon. An adjoining verandah restaurant serves food from the castle kitchen. The castle is closed Fridays and Saturdays November through June and Thursdays through Saturdays in October; admission charge (phone: 1573-223333). Pipe bands perform on certain days in the summer.

A 20-mile detour north from here on A6089 to *Hume Castle, Mellerstain House,* and *Smailholm Tower* is a must (the route between them from Kelso and back—B6404, some unnumbered roads, and B6397—forms the shape of a fan). Thirteenth-century *Hume Castle* preceded *Hirsel* (see *En Route from Coldstream,* above) as seat of the Earls of Home, but Cromwell destroyed it in 1651. The view from its parapets (which were reconstructed in the 18th century) is glorious. Consult local tourist offices for details on obtaining the key to the castle.

One of the great Georgian houses of Scotland, *Mellerstain House* is, architecturally, an Adam "pie"—begun in 1725 by William and finished in 1778 by Robert. It is proportionally perfect, and no finer craftsmanship exists anywhere than the plasterwork ceilings inside. There are also outstanding collections of 18th-century furniture and paintings by Old Masters. The house is closed Saturdays and October through *Easter;* admission charge (phone: 1573-281225). *Mellerstain House* takes part in an annual Borders springtime rally by presenting an exhibition of its vintage car collection.

As a young boy, Sir Walter Scott used to climb to the top of *Smailholm Tower,* when he stayed at nearby *Sandyknowe Farm.* The best extant example of a 16th-century Border keep, it has a 57-foot summit overlooking vast expanses of country. Strategically placed stone fortresses like *Smailholm* had roofs fitted with pans of pitch and peat for kindling; on a clear night it was said to take only two minutes for a chain of danger signals to reach *Edinburgh Castle* from the English border. It is closed October through March; admission charge. For more information about the tower, contact *Historic Scotland* in Edinburgh (phone: 131-244-3101), an organization that maintains it and many other attractions in Scotland.

Return to Kelso and continue south 9 miles on A698 to the turnoff for A68. Then continue another 2½ miles south to Jedburgh.

BEST EN ROUTE

Sunlaws House This appealing Georgian hotel is owned by the Duke of Roxburghe and draws guests who enjoy fishing and shooting. Its 21 rooms contain modern amenities, and its restaurant specializes in local game and in salmon pulled from the river Tweed. Heiton (phone: 1573-450331; fax: 1573-450611). Very expensive.

Ednam House Built in 1761 as the abode of a prominent Kelso merchant, this historic 32-room hotel has an arresting façade as well as its original Italian ceilings. The dining room specializes in French food. Also see *Gone Fishing* in DIVERSIONS. Bridge St., Kelso (phone: 1573-224168 or 1573-224169). Expensive.

Cross Keys This coaching inn has 25 rooms, a restaurant, and a charming bar decorated with horse-and-wagon motifs. The Square, Kelso (phone: 1573-223303; fax: 1573-225792). Moderate.

JEDBURGH Although the priory section of *Jedburgh Abbey* was leveled during the Rough Wooing, the church is amazingly well preserved (phone: 1835-863925). The elegant rose window is nicknamed St. Catherine's Wheel. There was a church here as early as the 9th century, but the abbey dates from 1138. It enjoys a lovely setting above the Jed Water, a tributary of the river Teviot. Closed Sunday mornings.

The great and wise Alexander III, the first king of a truly unified Scotland, was married in Jedburgh in 1285 to his young and beautiful second wife. His passionate love for her seems to have spurred him to foolish action: It is said that the spectral figure of Death was seen among the guests at the wedding reception in *Jedburgh Castle*—now the site of the *Jail Museum*—and sure enough, Alexander was killed six months later when he and his horse fell over a cliff as he, against the counsel of his aides, rode out on a stormy night from *Edinburgh Castle* to join his bride in Dunfermline. The museum, in the Castlegate, is as it was in 1823 when erected as an experimental "modern" jail. It is open daily; admission charge (phone: 1835-863254).

Jedburgh was once surrounded (for protection) by a series of "bastel houses," one of which, on Queen Street, was a residence of Mary, Queen of Scots. The house is especially fascinating for the number of portraits it contains of that enigmatic woman, each one looking less like the last. It is closed mid-November through *Easter;* admission charge (phone: 1835-63331). If you are here in mid-February, you can enter the spirit of Mary's troubled times by watching the *Ba' Game,* originally played in the 16th century with the heads of Jedburgh's slain enemies. The "Uppies" (those born above the mercat cross) and the "Doonies" (those born below) have two hours to get a ball into their goal—whether by fair means or foul.

About 1½ miles south of Jedburgh on A68 is *Ferniehirst Castle;* dating from the 16th-century, it is the ancestral home of the Kerr family and was restored by the Marquis of Lothian, the chief of the Kerrs. The castle's museum (with Kerr family memorabilia), small chapel, and gift shop are open Wednesday afternoons May through October; the main building, which houses a notable collection of 17th-century paintings, is open only by prior arrangement; admission charge (phone: 1835-862201).

The end of the first week in July sees the start of the three-day *Jethart Callants' Festival,* in which the *Riding of the Marches* takes the form of mounted ceremonial dashes to historically important places, the Jedburgh flag to the fore. A "callant" is a gallant, or youngblood. Also part of the festival are the *Jedburgh Border Games* held a week later in *Riverside Park* from 10 AM to teatime.

At the north entrance to Jedburgh is a complex of mill outlet shops (with a cafeteria). Stores here include the *Jedburgh Woollen Mill* (phone: 1835-243901), which carries kilts from its own factory, and the *Edinburgh Woollen Mill* (phone: 1835-863773). *First Impressions* (phone: 1835-862973), in Veitch's Close in the Castlegate, has exceptional designer sweaters. These places are open even on Thursday afternoons, when everything else in town closes. The tourist office (at Murray's Green; phone: 1835-863435 or 1835-863688) offers a pamphlet describing a self-guided "Town Trail" tour of streets of historic interest. The office is open daily.

About 3 miles north of Jedburgh is the *Woodland Centre* (at Harestane's Mill; phone: 1835-3306), which has displays about the area, as well as a wildlife garden. It's closed November through March and Mondays, Tuesdays, Thursdays, Fridays, and Saturdays in April, May, and October; admission charge. The town has few restaurants and hotels, but coffee, home-baked goodies, and light meals are available at the *Mercat Café* (in Market Sq.; phone: 1835-862255); the *Castlegate* (in Abbey Cl.; phone: 1835-862552), formerly known as the *Copperkettle;* and the *Chef's Grill* (3½ miles south on A68; phone: 1835-4269). On sale at *Miller's* (10 High St.; phone: 1835-862252) are "Jethart snails," a traditional Jedburgh mint-flavored hard candy the color and shape of escargots.

BEST EN ROUTE

Glenbank Country House A five-minute walk up the Castlegate, this pretty seven-bedroom Georgian house has home cooking served indoors, with tea service on the lawn. Castlegate, Jedburgh (phone: 1835-62258). Moderate.

Jedforest Some 6 miles south of Jedburgh, near the Jed Water, this family-run old house offers 11 quaint rooms that overlook the surrounding parkland. There's also a good restaurant (phone: 1835-4274). Moderate.

Ferniehirst Mill This quiet hotel is ideally situated overlooking the Jed Water. Most of the 11 rooms have private baths, and its restaurant specializes in fresh local ingredients and game. Just off A68, 3 miles south of Jedburgh (phone: 1835-63279). Inexpensive.

En Route from Jedburgh Retrace your path on A68 north for 2½ miles and then head southwest on A698. It's another 7 miles to Hawick; along the way, stop at charming Denholm, with its 18th-century cottages and expansive village green. A friend of Sir Walter Scott's, poet John Leyden, was born here in 1775; Leyden eventually left Scotland to become Commissioner of the Calcutta Mint. A few miles beyond Denholm is *Trow Mill,* an 18th-century grain mill that became a woolen mill around 1800 and today is completely modernized. The mill has factory tours, its own shop, and free coffee for visitors. It is open daily; no admission charge and no advance notice necessary (phone: 1450-72555).

HAWICK Pronounced *Hoyk,* this largest of the Border burghs (pop. 16,213) is best known for its knitwear and electronics. The city stands at the junction of the Teviot and Slitrig Rivers. Its citizens are avid rugby fans, and it has contributed many a famous player to internationally known rugby teams. Its home team, the *Greens,* plays Saturdays at *Mansfield Park.*

In the leafy shades of the 107-acre municipal *Wilton Lodge Park* is the *Hawick Museum and Art Gallery,* bursting with Border relics. It's closed Saturdays October through *Easter;* admission charge (phone: 1450-73457). The *Riding of the Marches* (the Borderers call them *Common Ridings*) takes place during the first full week in June. Hawick's version of the festival is one of the oldest, distinguished by its refusal to allow female riders to participate (though at least one woman is known to have dressed up as a boy and ridden with the pack). Three days of festivities culminate at 6 AM on a Friday with the consumption of a whisky-spiked celebration breakfast and the cutting of a boundary sod (turf) by the "Cornet," or designated unmarried "callant." Then, with their colors aloft, the riders set off on a wild chase up Nipknowes Hill on their way to Hawick Moor, where a hectic program of races awaits them. In the afternoon there are athletic matches between top British professionals in *Volunteer Park;* all-night dinners and dances; and the singing, on the town heights at dawn, of the Hawick battle song "Teribus," which begins in Latin, lurches into Old Norse, and then plunges into Scots. The *Hawick Summer Festival,* held in mid-August, features a range of community arts and local police and high school bands.

Hawick is picturesque because its rivers meet in a basin that holds the town center. It's almost possible to swim to the shops adjoining Tower Mill (*Murray Brothers;* phone: 1450-78958) and Teviotdale Mills (*Charles Whillans;* phone: 1450-73128), which sell Hawick knitwear from well-known Border mills, as do *Angus Knitwear* (phone: 1450-73427) in Wilton Dean and *White of Hawick* (phone: 1450-73206) in Victoria Road (part of the Scottish Borders Woollen Trail). For designer cashmeres, try *Valerie Louthan Ltd.* (at 2 Kirk Wynd; phone: 1450-78000). Hand-crafted gifts are sold at *Arista Designs* (Victoria Works, Victoria Rd.; phone: 1450-75272) and at the *Teviotdale Design Company* (14 Buccleuch St.; phone: 1450-75199). Hawick balls, the local hard candy, are sold at *R. T. Smith* (16 Commercial Rd.; phone: 1450-72142). *James Ingles* (57 High St.; phone: 1450-72574) is an excellent source of good quality jewelry—especially beautiful estate pieces—and Border Fine Arts figurines.

The *Hawick Railway Society* sometimes exhibits its model trains; for information, contact the tourist information office in Common Haugh car park (phone: 1450-72547), which is closed November through March. Nature lovers might like to explore the nearby Craik Forest Walk (take B711, off A7 south of Hawick, to *Robertson Church,* then follow the side road along the Borthwick Water for 7 miles). Hawick Motte is archaeologically interesting; "mottes" are high cones of earth, artificial in construction, on which sat the timber houses that predated the great stone castles of Norman aristocrats. In the 12th century King William the Lion of Scotland granted Hawick to the Somersetshire Lovels, whose seat is thought to have been Hawick Motte. It's down a side road off A7, inside the town boundaries, on the west side of the river Slitrig.

BEST EN ROUTE

Mansfield House Views of lush private grounds make this 12-bedroom Italian villa–like hostelry an excellent retreat. A restaurant is on the premises. Weensland Rd., Hawick (phone: 1450-73988; fax: 1450-72007). Expensive to moderate.

Kirklands This Victorian country house has a striking view across Hawick and the surrounding hills and a reputation for friendliness and elegance. There are 10 rooms and a restaurant. W. Stewart Pl., Hawick (phone: 1450-372263; fax: 1450-370404). Moderate.

Hopehill A big Victorian house and garden offering five rooms with lovely views. There also is a dining room that serves traditional Scottish specialties. Near the town center, Hawick (phone: 1450-75042). Inexpensive.

En Route from Hawick The *Johnnie Armstrong Gallery and Museum,* 8 miles south of Hawick on A7, is immediately identifiable by its intricately carved wooden "totem pole," about 10 feet high and crowned by a figure of a 12th-century Norman knight. The place was named after a robust Border reiver who was hanged by James IV after being convicted of treachery. On the premises is a fascinating collection of old guns and armor, plus a gift shop. It is open daily; hours vary in the winter; admission charge (phone: 1450-85237). There's a memorial to Armstrong on a hill on the right-hand side of the road just before the museum. At Fiddleton, about 5 miles farther south, take a left onto the road indicating *Hermitage Castle* and continue another 8 miles. This castle is where Mary, Queen of Scots, dashed on horseback from Jedburgh for a tryst with Bothwell. Its four towers and connecting walls are in almost perfect condition, powerfully invoking the grim grandeur of 14th-century baronial halls. Like *Smailholm Tower,* this castle is under the administration of *Heritage Scotland* (phone: 131-244-3101). It is closed weekdays October through March; admission charge. Return by the same road along the Hermitage Water to Fiddleton, then rejoin A7 and continue south for 9 miles to Langholm.

LANGHOLM There is an Old and a New Town here, the latter begun in 1778. Langholm was the birthplace in 1892 of Christopher Murray Grieve, a Scottish Nationalist and Marxist poet better known as Hugh MacDiarmid. It is in Langholm also that MacDiarmid is buried, despite the furious opposition of the local inhabitants, who were the raw material for some of the poet's most iconoclastic works. His funeral in 1978 was attended by the great bulk of the Scottish literary and left-wing political worlds. Langholm's colorful *Common Ridings* ceremony takes place at the end of July.

En Route from Langholm Follow B709 and B7009 (two rather rough roads) north toward Selkirk, 34 miles away. Just outside Langholm is the *Craigcleuch Scottish Explorers' Museum,* which houses objects from African, Asian, and Latin American tribal cultures. It is closed October through April; admission charge (phone: 1387-380137). You can make a literary pilgrimage to the birthplace and grave of James Hogg, "The Ettrick Shepherd." The grave is in *Ettrick Kirkyard,* a deserted place a mile down the Ettrick Water west of B709; a monument marks the spot.

SELKIRK *Halliwell's House,* in the main square, is the site of the town's tourist office (open daily; phone: 1750-20054). Also on the premises is an interesting museum of local history. The museum is closed November through March; no admission charge (phone: 1750-20096). Sir Walter Scott was sheriff of Selkirkshire from 1799 to 1832; the courthouse on Market Place has a few portraits of him, plus some of his letters.

The town of Selkirk has an exciting setting, on a high ridge overlooking the Ettrick and Yarrow River Valleys. The mills below the town are architecturally attractive, with clock towers rising symmetrically from their centers and colorful names in bold letters on their sides like "Ettrick and Yarrow Spinners." The weaving process can be observed weekdays at *Andrew Elliott's,* Forest Mill, just north of town on A707; visitors must call in advance (phone: 1750-20412). Selkirk's *Common Riding* ceremony, held in the first week of June, is the Borders' most famous, and, at 400-plus years, its oldest. It's a difficult, nearly five-hour-long ride for the more than 500 participants. Led by the Standard Bearer, they return in a wild gallop along the main A7 (closed to traffic for the occasion). The ceremonies in Selkirk commemorate the Battle of Flodden (1513), when the Scots and their king, James IV, were trounced by the English. Legend has it that of the 80 Souters (the name for a Selkirk man) at Flodden, only one—named Fletcher—returned, bearing a captured English flag. He cast the flag around his head once before he fell dead—the origin of this *Common Riding*'s tradition of "casting the colours." During this part of the ceremony, the Standard Bearer performs a graceful swinging of the town flag around his head as a band plays. Dozens of "exiles" return from England, North America, and Australia to participate in the great festival.

The *Selkirk Glass* factory and showroom, in Linglie Mill, allows visitors to watch the making of designer paperweights (closed weekends; phone:

1750-20954). The *Wellwood Weavers Shop* (phone: 1750-21201) on the Galashiels road sells hand-crafted goods, including sweaters, toys, and jewelry. The *Courthouse Coffee Shop* (Market Pl.; phone: 1750-22058) is a good place to sit down for a piece of Selkirk bannock, the richest raisin bread in the world. Or buy one whole at *Houston Bakers* (who claim to have invented it) across the square (phone: 1750-20244).

There are two Scottish Borders Woollen Trail shops in Selkirk: *John Tulloch,* which specializes in Shetland knitwear (Whitefield Rd.; phone: 1750-20586), and *Brenire Crafts,* with heavy knits (Linglie Mill; phone: 1750-21836).

BEST EN ROUTE

Ettrickshaws The sylvan seclusion and exceptional food at this six-bedroom Victorian mansion by Ettrick Water make this accommodation a top choice. Guests have automatic fishing rights. Open February through November. In Ettrickbridge, 10 miles south of Selkirk on B7009 (phone: 1750-52229). Expensive.

Philipburn House Set in five acres of exquisite gardens, this superb 17th-century Georgian hotel boasts 16 rooms with wood-burning fireplaces. There's also horseback riding, fishing, and a heated swimming pool. The dining room is renowned for its excellent Taste of Scotland fare; try the saddle of roe deer cassis. Selkirk (phone: 1750-20747; fax: 1750-21690). Expensive.

Glen A family-run turreted house, overlooking the river Ettrick. Seven of the nine rooms have private baths. There's good home cooking. 1 Yarrow Ter., Selkirk (phone: 1750-20259). Inexpensive.

Queenshead During a stint as an exciseman, Robert Burns once slept at this former coaching inn. Today, the building houses a restaurant with a friendly atmosphere, a wonderful open fireplace, and tasty homemade soups. Closed Sunday evenings. Reservations unnecessary. No credit cards accepted. West Port St., Selkirk (phone: 1750-21782). Inexpensive.

En Route from Selkirk From here, the most direct route to Galashiels is to drive along A7 north for 6½ miles. However, a 40-mile detour via several smaller roads takes in several interesting places, including *Dryburgh Abbey, Thirlestane Castle,* the historic small town of Lauder, *Melrose Abbey,* and *Abbotsford House.*

On the Tweed near the village of St. Boswell's (head 8 miles east of Selkirk on A699, then continue a few miles north on A68) is majestic *Dryburgh Abbey*—considered by many to have the most beautiful setting of any in Great Britain. It, too, was founded during the reign of David I and later ravaged by English raiders. Only the church's transepts remain, but the cloister is nearly complete. Sir Walter Scott is buried here, as is Earl

Haig, Britain's chief World War I general. It is open daily; admission charge (phone: 1835-22381).

Not far beyond the abbey on A68, is Newtown St. Boswells, which boasts the Borders' largest livestock market, generally held on Mondays and Thursdays. From here, continue on A68 north for about 10 miles; on the left are the distinctive stone eagles indicating the gates of *Thirlestane Castle.* Erected as a *pele* (defensive tower) to guard the southern approach to Edinburgh, it was rebuilt in the 17th century by the Duke of Lauderdale. The architect, Sir William Bruce, also designed the royal *Palace of Holyroodhouse* in Edinburgh. *Thirlestane*'s exquisitely crafted plasterwork ceilings rival those of *Mellerstain House,* near Kelso. In 1745, Bonnie Prince Charlie stayed at *Thirlestane;* his room is on view. For children, there's a huge collection of historic toys and dolls, plus a dressing-up chest. The castle is closed October through April; Mondays, Tuesdays, Fridays, and Saturdays in May, June, and September; and Saturdays only in July and August. There's an admission charge (phone: 1578-722430).

The small 14th-century town of Lauder, another half mile north on A68, was one of Scotland's rare walled villages, and the narrow road between the high walls on either side from East Port to West Port still follows the route travelers had to take when the town gates were closed. The *Golden Bannock* pub (on Market Place; phone: 1578-722324) is a convivial spot to share a pint or have a bite to eat.

From Lauder, turn around and head south along A68 for about 13 miles. At Earlstun, turn off to the right onto Newstead Road. Melrose is 2 miles farther along that road.

MELROSE Another of David I's now ruined monasteries, *Melrose Abbey* graces the central square of the lovely little town of Melrose (pop. 2,143). Notice that the abbey's exquisite 15th-century traceried stonework features a pig on the roof playing bagpipes. (Also see *Ancient Monuments and Ruins* in DIVERSIONS.) According to legend, the Eildon Hills, which loom to the southeast, are shaped as they are (two pointed, one shorter and flat-topped) because the devil was so piqued by the dawn chanting of the abbey monks that he thrust three mountains between them and the rising sun, but dropped and broke one mountain in transit. Sir Walter Scott used to gaze across the Tweed at the Eildon Hills from a point above St. Boswell's now known as Scott's View. (It's on B6356 a couple of miles east of Melrose; see the *Enjoy Scotland* touring map.) There's an admission charge (phone: 189682-2562).

Hikers can take the Eildon Walk with the aid of nature trail leaflets available (free) at the tourist information bureau next to *Melrose Abbey;* the office is closed November through March (phone: 189682-2555). *Priorwood Gardens,* beside the abbey, are pleasant—their specialty is flowers suitable for drying. They are closed January through March and Sundays May through October; no admission charge. The old railway station at Melrose, just off Market Square, is now a crafts center, shop, and venue for fairs and exhibitions.

Dryburgh Abbey This 19th-century red sandstone house offers 26 superb rooms, and fishing, shooting, golf, and horseback riding are all nearby. The *Tweed* restaurant overlooks the river and is the place for traditional Scottish food with an individual touch—try Tweed salmon poached in court bouillon with lobster sauce. The grounds are lovely, and there's a footbridge over the river. St. Boswells, on the banks of the Tweed (phone: 1835-22261; fax: 1835-23945). Very expensive to expensive.

Burt's In addition to full-fledged meals, this bustling 21-room hostelry provides substantial and delicious bar snacks. Gleaming everywhere under its wooden roof beams are pieces of copper and brass. Market Sq., Melrose (phone: 189682-2285; fax: 189682-2870). Expensive to moderate.

George and Abbotsford Conveniently located on the main street, this 18th-century building was the site of many of Sir Walter Scott's convivial evenings. There are 30 modernized rooms, plus excellent British fare. High St., Melrose (phone: 189682-2308; fax: 189682-3363). Expensive to moderate.

Buccleuch Arms Overlooking the village green of St. Boswells, this hospitable old staging post offers 20 bedrooms featuring the usual amenities. There's also a restaurant. On A68 (phone: 1835-22243; fax: 1835-23965). Moderate.

Marmion's The closest thing in town to a French bistro, this oak-paneled eatery attracts diners from all over the area. Try the honey and orange lamb or the delicious kidneys with mustard and lemon. Closed Sundays. Reservations advised. Major credit cards accepted. Buccleuch St., Melrose (phone: 189682-2245). Moderate.

En Route from Melrose Three miles west of Melrose, fascinating *Abbotsford House* broods by the Tweed. Sir Walter Scott custom-built it between 1812 and 1824 as his country home, and a trip here certainly gives a vivid picture of his personality. He tended to carry his starry-eyed antiquarianism to laughable lengths, as when he made off with the door to Edinburgh's just-razed, 15th-century "Heart of Midlothian" (the county jail) and had it installed in a wall at *Abbotsford.* There are historic relics, impressive armories, a 9,000-volume library, and the study in which he wrote the Waverley novels in an attempt to reduce a £117,000 debt. The effort eventually killed him; he died here at the age of 61. There is also a tea shop on the grounds. The house is closed November through late March; the tea shop is also closed in October. There's an admission charge (phone: 1896-2043) .

Retrace your path to Selkirk (this detour's point of origin) and proceed 3 miles to the west on A708 to find Philiphaugh, the field where the army of the noble Scottish cavalier and poet-soldier, the Marquis of Montrose, lost a key battle to Puritan forces in 1645. Near the Yarrow Water is *Bowhill,* home of the Dukes of Buccleuch and Queensberry (one dukedom), another of the Borders' ancestral stately homes. *Bowhill* has early 19th-century silk brocades and hand-painted Chinese wallpapers, art treasures, a tiny theater used by local and visiting theater companies, lush woods and gardens, an inventive jungle-playground–type Tarzan complex for kids, and pony trekking. The house is open afternoons during July only; the grounds are closed Fridays and September through April; the pony-trekking center is open daily. There's an admission charge (phone: 1750-20732). Nearby is the ruin of *Newark Castle,* a five-story tower house where the "Last Minstrel" recited his "Lay" to the Duchess of Buccleuch. It was a royal hunting seat for the Forest of Ettrick in the Middle Ages. Another 4 miles west along A708 is picturesque *Yarrow Kirk,* dating from 1640.

Continuing along the Yarrow Water another 12 miles or so, you reach the wild, godforsaken country over which the merlins fly. These small, ferocious birds are said to embody the spirit of Merlin the wizard. Near remote St. Mary's Loch and its sister lake, the Loch of the Lowes, are two historic inns—the *Gordon Arms* and *Tibbie Shiels* (phone: 1750-42231)—where Sir Walter Scott met literary friends. Across the main road from St. Mary's Loch are the remains of *Dryhope Tower,* which, like *Smailholm,* is a medieval watchtower.

Stay on A708. On the right, about 8 miles before Moffat, is the Grey Mare's Tail, a magnificent 200-foot waterfall formed as the Tail Burn gorge drops from Loch Skeen to meet the Moffat Water. The whole area is resplendent with wildflowers. Covenanters used to hide out here. The hollow below the falls is the "Giant's Grave," which figures in Scott's poem *Marmion.* The *Scotland: Hillwalking* booklet gives instructions for climbing to the top of either side of the Tail Burn gorge.

MOFFAT The pride of this small town (with fewer than 2,000 residents) is *Colvin Fountain,* erected in 1875; the huge bronze ram on top symbolizes the importance of sheep farming in the surrounding districts. For two centuries Moffat was a fashionable resort, and among the 18th-century greats who frequented its spa were James Boswell, Robert Burns, and the "fake" folklorist James Macpherson of the Ossianic ballads. Today it's a touring base full of hotels and Italian cafés, but it retains the atmosphere of a bygone era. The Blacklock family, who have made their now famous Moffat Toffee for generations, maintain a candy shop on High Street (phone: 1683-20032). A good pottery with a retail showroom is the *Moffat Pottery,* Ladyknowe (in the town center beside the telephone exchange; phone: 1683-20793). Also at Ladyknowe are the *Moffat Weavers* (phone: 1683-20134), who display antique looms and demonstrate the art of skirt making. They keep a shop with a wide choice of Scottish products, including their own. Moffat's tourist office, which is closed November through *Easter,* is at Church Gate (phone: 1683-20620).

BEST EN ROUTE

Beechwood Country House A comfortable haven on a Moffat hill, this 14-room home-away-from-home sets a tempting table, including beetroot soup, venison casserole, and the best Orkney cheeses. Restaurant reservations necessary. Harthope Pl., Moffat (phone: 1683-20210). Expensive.

Auchen Castle This 19th-century greathouse-turned-hotel is just south of Moffat. It has 25 bedrooms and is situated in 50 acres of private grounds with a trout loch. The restaurant features a Taste of Scotland menu. A mile north of Beattock on A74 (phone: 1683-3407; fax: 1683-3667). Moderate.

En Route from Moffat Six miles north of Moffat on A701 is the Devil's Beef Tub, famous in literature and lore. An astonishing feature of Dumfriesshire's natural geography, the Tub's vast, smooth, basin-like recess has a rotund regularity more believable in classical art than in nature. As its name suggests, Border reivers herded pilfered steers into the Devil's Beef Tub to conceal them. If your family name is Armstrong or Douglas, your ancestors were the scourge of this part of Scotland.

Continue north on A701 another 14 miles to Tweedshaws. Along the way, the road passes the almost imperceptible source of the river Tweed (identified by a signpost). The route now parallels the Tweed almost all the way to Galashiels, the last stop before the conclusion of this driving tour. The Tweed River valley boasts some of the finest scenery in the world, especially in early spring, when snow remains on the hills.

At Tweedshaws, continue about 7 miles on A701 and turn onto B712 (east) to visit *Dawyck House Gardens* and *Stobo Kirk. Dawyck House Gardens,* located at the intersection of A701 and B712, feature rare trees forming a wood in which a pleasant little chapel sits. The gardens, administered by the *Royal Botanic Gardens* at Edinburgh, are closed mid-October through February; admission charge (phone: 1721-6254). *Stobo Kirk,* a 12th-century building with additions made over the next four centuries, has some particularly fascinating carved tombstones. It's on the west side of the B712 road about a mile beyond *Dawyck House Gardens;* call the tourist office in Peebles (see below) for more information.

From B712 (now heading north), take A72 east for 1 mile to *Neidpath Castle,* which looms above the Tweed in a spectacular fashion. Of 14th-century construction, the castle has walls 12 feet thick and is five stories high; its Great Hall once occupied the entire second floor. It's an interesting example of how such fortresses were adapted to the more civilized lifestyles of the 17th century. After inspecting the pit-prison in its bottom, climb to its parapet. The castle is closed October through *Easter* (except for Tuesdays in October); admission charge (phone: 1721-720333).

From *Neidpath Castle,* continue east on A72 for a half mile to Peebles.

BEST EN ROUTE

Crook Inn The panoramic sweep of the moors at this 18th-century coaching inn defies description! There are seven bedrooms and a restaurant. Also see

Gone Fishing in DIVERSIONS. On A701 about 14 miles north of Moffat, Tweedsmuir (phone: 1899-7272; fax: 1899-7294). Moderate.

PEEBLES Set on a sharp slope beside the meeting of the Eddleston Water with the Tweed, Peebles is the chief town of Tweeddale (formerly known as Peeblesshire); 6,404 people make their homes here. It is laid out like a Highlands town, with one long, wide street around which everything is focused (though there are more recent buildings that stretch behind either side of it). A fortified settlement itself in the 16th century, it is an ideal center from which to explore other, much older fortified settlements in the same area. These date from the 1st century and are accessible by traipsing deep into the local hinterlands along old cattle-droving trails. A copy of *Exploring Scotland's Heritage, Lothian and the Borders* will be invaluable here.

The novelist John Buchan, Governor General of Canada from 1935 to 1940, is a sort of "cottage industry" of Tweeddale. He was particularly fond of the area and took as his title Lord Tweedsmuir. Literary tourists use Peebles as a base for visiting sites mentioned in his novels.

The *Tweeddale Museum* (High St.; phone: 1721-20123) is in the *Chambers Institution* (donated in 1859 by William Chambers, the Edinburgh publisher). It displays objects from Tweeddale's industrial, religious, and domestic heritages. The museum is open daily; no admission charge. The tourist office, closed November through March, is also here (phone: 1721-20138). The *Cornice* (31 High St.; phone: 1721-20212) is a museum of ornamental plasterwork, such as is found on the ceilings of greathouses. The hours can vary greatly; call ahead. There's an admission charge. *Cross Kirk* is the remains of a 15th-century Trinitarian priory that enshrined an earlier sacred cross and a sculpted stone inscribed to St. Nicholas. The walls still stand.

In *Hay Lodge Park* there are tennis courts, a bowling green, a trim track (for jogging), and boating facilities. There is also a municipal golf course, off Kirkland Street (phone: 1721-20197). *Glentress Mountain Bike Centre* (Glentress Forest, 2 miles west on A72; phone: 1721-22934) rents special bicycles on which to explore the local Glentress and Cardrona Forest Trails.

Newby Court Centre, down School Brae off High Street, is a delight; it's a cluster of shops around a small close that leads downhill to a park by the Tweed. The shops sell Highland wear, jewelry, woodwork, and pottery. *Robert Noble* (March St.; phone: 1721-20146) keeps one of the last mill shops in the Borders specializing in fabrics rather than ready-to-wear. Plain old lovable Scottish home baking can be taken with tea at the *Sunflower Coffee Shop* (4 The Bridgegate; phone: 1721-22420).

BEST EN ROUTE

Park A pleasingly peaceful black-and-white house, with extensions and a turret, 24 rooms, a dining room, and stunning views of the Cademuir Hills. Innerleithen Rd., Peebles (phone: 1721-720451; fax: 1721-723510). Expensive.

Peebles Hydro A playground of Victorian captains of industry and still famous today, this grand 136-room hotel exudes an air of wealth and celebration. On 30 acres of grounds; there's also a restaurant. Innerleithen Rd., Peebles (phone: 1721-720602; fax: 1721-722999). Expensive.

Cringletie House Also famous, this private mansion with 13 rooms is open to guests by the resident owner (a talented interior decorator and cook) from March through December. A two-acre kitchen garden supplies the highly regarded dining room with fresh vegetables. On A703, 2 miles north of Peebles at Eddleston (phone: 1721-730233; fax: 1721-730244). Moderate.

Kingsmuir A captivating hotel on a large green lawn, in the style of a family home of the 1850s, with 10 bedrooms and traditional Scottish cooking. Ask for *cullen skink,* a delicious fish soup. Springhill Rd., Peebles (phone: 1721-720151; fax: 1721-721795). Moderate.

En Route from Peebles Two miles east of Peebles on B7062 is *Kailzie Gardens,* on 17 acres of woodland full of small streams and wild daffodils. There are greenhouses, shrub borders, and a laburnum alley, as well as a gift shop, art gallery, and tearoom. The gardens are closed November through mid-March; admission charge (phone: 1721-20007).

At Traquair, where B7062 meets B709 (about 7½ miles southeast of Peebles), is *Traquair House,* Scotland's oldest continuously inhabited mansion. Constructed of whitewashed stone during the 10th century, it is four stories high with round turrets. The expansiveness of *Traquair House* and its slight asymmetry derive from extensions built in the 16th and 17th centuries (to build the latter, the then laird rerouted the Tweed!). The *Bear Gates* at the former main entrance, as guidebooks never tire of telling you, were closed when Bonnie Prince Charlie was defeated at Culloden, and are never to be opened again until a Stuart monarch ascends to the Scottish throne. Free literature about the history of *Traquair House* is available. Also on-site are a working 18th-century brew house (sample its ale), four crafts workshops, and a tearoom and gift shop. Open daily from 1:30 to 5:30 PM during *Holy Week* (*Easter*) and May through September; also mornings in July, August, and the first two weeks of September; admission charge (phone: 1896-830323). Now you also can stay overnight here (see *Best en Route*).

A half mile north of Traquair on B709 is the village of Innerleithen, once a popular spa and now the home of *Robert Smail's Printing Works.* It is a remarkable old printing plant bought in 1986 by the *National Trust for Scotland,* complete with vintage printing machinery, including a 19th-century press originally driven by water, plus a Victorian office. It is closed November through March; admission charge (phone: 1896-830206). From here, pick up A72 and head 1½ miles east to Walkerburn, location of *Tweeddale Mills,* makers of Clan Royal woolens. The facilities include a mill shop, a café, and the interesting *Scottish Museum of Woollen Textiles.* The mill is closed Sundays and November through March; no admission charge (phone: 1896-87619). The name "Walkerburn" (and the surname "Walker") can be traced to "waulking," an early practice during the production of saleable cloth. Young men, and sometimes women, would lay out the wet cloth in the weaving shed and then take off their shoes and trample it vigorously to flatten and stretch it.

From Walkerburn, continue another 10 miles on A72 to Galashiels.

BEST EN ROUTE

Traquair House This fascinating historic house, a tourist attraction for years, now offers overnight bed and breakfast accommodations. The two rooms are well appointed, and guests have access to a tennis court and a croquet lawn; they also will be given personal tours of the property. Pub grub–style fare is offered in the bar. Reservations are necessary. In Traquair (phone: 1896-830323). Expensive.

Tweed Valley This Edwardian country house with fishing, riding, gardens, shops, a sauna, and a solarium has 16 bedrooms. The dining room features local game, and fresh salmon is smoked on the premises. Also see *Gone Fishing* in DIVERSIONS. Off A72 at Walkerburn (phone: 1896-87636; fax: 1896-87639). Expensive to moderate.

Clovenfords Log fires and home cooking provide a comfortable, friendly atmosphere at this five-room coaching inn. Shooting and fishing can be arranged. Clovenfords (phone: 1896-85203). Inexpensive.

GALASHIELS This venerable town's charter was granted in 1599. Situated on the Gala Water, which flows into the Tweed, Galashiels resembles Selkirk and Hawick with its Victorian-era mills along the riverbank, though the number of mills has declined since their early-20th-century heyday. A mill here was the first in Scotland, in 1791, to become a "manufactry," with mechanical spinning jennies turning out yarn.

At the town center is the 17th-century mercat (market) cross and the impressive *Town Hall,* built in 1868, which is guarded by the giant bronze statue of a medieval moss-trooper in full armor on horseback—an imaginative memorial to soldiers killed in World Wars I and II. In the *Peter Anderson* cashmere and woolen mill is the *Peter Anderson Museum* (Huddersfield St.; phone: 1896-2091), with artifacts related to the textile industry, a working waterwheel that runs a loom, and early photographs of old Galashiels and its millworkers. Tours of the still-operating factory are offered as well. The museum is closed Sundays October through May; admission charge. Also on the Scottish Borders Woollen Trail is the *Borders Wool Centre* (Wheatlands Rd.; phone: 1896-4293 or 1896-4774), with a herd of British sheep and spinning and crafts demonstrations. Both the *Borders*

Wool Centre and *Peter Anderson* have good shops on their premises, with discounts on tweeds, knitwear, and other woolens. The *Scottish College of Textiles* (phone: 1896-3351) offers visitors a chance to view the entire wool process under one roof (visits by prior arrangement; no admission charge). The Galashiels tourist office (3 St. John's St.; phone: 1896-55551) is closed November through March.

Old Gala House (Scott Crescent; phone: 1896-2611 or 1750-20096) is the traditional home of two prominent Galashiels families, the Pringles and the Scotts. The building, which dates from 1583, now houses the *Christopher Boyd Gallery,* featuring modern art exhibitions. There's also a display that traces the history of the house. It is closed October through February; no admission charge.

Shops to check out in town include *Jackie Lunn* (Channel St.; phone: 1896-3877), an excellent bakery; *Anne Ruddiman's* (Market St.; phone: 1896-2974), which sells such interesting native candies as "soor plooms," rose- or violet-flavored chocolate creams that commemorate a surprise attack of Galashiels reivers on English soldiers eating sour plums; and *Border Golf* (High St.; phone: 1896-4575), which sells everything a golfer needs, from clubs to sweaters.

BEST EN ROUTE

King's Right in the center of Market Street, this family-run hotel has seven guestrooms. There's good bar fare, plus a restaurant specializing in local recipes. 56 Market St., Galashiels (phone: 1896-55497). Moderate.

Kingsknowes A Victorian family house with a view of Scott's *Abbotsford House,* this 10-bedroom hotel with a restaurant is just south of Galashiels, overlooking the Tweed. Selkirk Rd., Galashiels (phone: 1896-58375). Moderate.

En Route from Galashiels The A7 north leads back to Edinburgh. On the way, you might want to stop at the *Manor Head House* hotel (168 Galashiels Rd.; phone: 15783-201), 6 miles north of Galashiels. It's a great place to share a pint; its bar has won three awards, including a Top 20 UK Pub Caterers plaque. From there, continue north on A7 for 28 miles to Edinburgh.

Southwest Scotland

Southwest Scotland has vastly differing locations and traditions: from proud, modern, urban Glasgow to the isolated but quietly confident Ayrshire towns; from Clydeside ports mourning their former prosperity to remote country towns; from coastline visions of Ireland, only a few miles away, to the supreme natural beauty of the Firth of Clyde and the warmer coastal waters of the Solway Firth, which forms the boundary between Scotland and England.

It was here, in the 18th century, that triumphant Calvinism muted but could not muzzle the genius of Ayrshire's ploughman poet and Scotland's national bard, Robert Burns (1759–96). From obscure origins among the rocky farmlands on the west coast, Burns had a meteoric rise to literary fame. At 25, he was taken into and lionized by the most learned and genteel circles in Edinburgh—at that time the seat of the Scottish Enlightenment. Proficient in Ayrshire dialect and the English versifying conventions of his day, and equally at home writing love poetry or political satire, Burns awed audiences across the nation. The elders of his church at Ayr, however, were unawed when his mistress bore him two sets of twins: He was publicly arraigned before the presbytery and constrained to confess his sins to God and the whole parish congregation. Literary critics see him as a precursor of the romantic movement exemplified by the works of Coleridge and Byron, while the general populace remembers him affectionately for his predisposition for wine, women, and song.

Robert Burns died and was buried in Dumfries in 1796. While you will get your fill of "Burns suppers" elsewhere in the country in the last days of January, southwest Scotland is the place to find them at their most enthusiastic. You will hear some admirable Burns poems and songs, as well as extraordinary Victorian sentimentality; however, by the time the village music teacher sings "The Star of Rabbie Burns," you will probably be past caring.

Though Burns always will be considered first and foremost a progressive, he was also a great folklorist, preserving—through adaptation into verse—much that would otherwise have been lost. Two hundred years after his death there is still a great concentration of folk memories in southwest Scotland, whether in old people's stories of Covenanter and Jacobite times or in artifacts from the past, such as the memorabilia at *Culzean Castle.*

Another great folklorist was Sir Walter Scott. While Scott's career and greathouse lay in the east, his novel, *Redgauntlet,* was set largely between Dumfries and points west. Unlike much of his other work, it moves at a cracking pace, culminating in a last, hopeless return of Bonnie Prince Charlie; the book is notable for including a splendid piece of Covenanter mythology about the Devil and the Covenanters' enemies. Reading it is a great way to discover the hidden folk traditions of the region.

If you are a thriller enthusiast, remember that the area from Dumfries to *Galloway Forest Park* is the location of one of the greatest modern thrillers, *The Thirty-Nine Steps* by John Buchan (1875–1940). Those who have seen the Alfred Hitchcock movie will think of Forth Rail Bridge and a reluctant heroine, but as Buchan wrote it, Richard Hannay was alone here. You may enjoy following the real locations in the book and working out the antecedents of the imaginary ones; and you may still find equivalents of the literary innkeeper, the radical candidate, and the spectacled roadman.

Southwest Scotland is a grand place to visit. It has proved a paradise to many a freshwater fisherman, and it is ideal walking and driving country for people who like to lose themselves in the best of surroundings. (The usual weather warnings apply—a light raincoat is indispensable even on seemingly cloudless days.) Be aware of what may lie hidden from view; the more effort you make to understand what you find, the more rewarding will be your discovery of the country's character.

The driving tour outlined here covers the 210 miles from Glasgow south to Dumfries and back to Paisley; it should be easy to handle in a maximum of four days. But take the same precautions as Richard Hannay about carrying sandwiches; and, while cars are more numerous and roads more accustomed to them than he found in 1914, gas stations still can be scarce, so stock up on fuel. If you run out, you may find yourself having to walk considerably more than 39 steps!

Some tourist offices are open seasonally, but at least one in each area is open year-round. The *Ayrshire Tourist Board* (39 Sandgate, Ayr; phone: 1292-284196 or 1292-79000) and the *Dumfries and Galloway Tourist Board* (Whitesands, Dumfries; phone: 1387-50434; fax: 1387-50462) can assist you with regional information and arrange accommodations; both are open daily. Be sure to buy the *Scottish Tourist Board*'s *Enjoy Scotland* (available for £7.20/about $11 at tourist offices and kiosks), which includes a detailed touring map and a booklet of 1,001 things to see and do. Also ask about "Scottish Explorer" tickets, which grant holders access to ancient monuments at a fraction of the rate they would pay were they charged sight by sight. The *Taste of Scotland* guide recommends places in which to sample both traditional and modern Scottish fare (£3.30/about $5 in bookstores, or available by mail for $15, including postage, from *Taste of Scotland Scheme, Ltd.,* 33 Melville St., Edinburgh EH3 7JF, Scotland; phone: 131-220-1900; fax: 131-220-6102). The *Royal Commission on the Ancient and Historical Monuments of Scotland* has published an attractive paperback entitled *Exploring Scotland's Heritage: Dumfries and Galloway* (£9.95/about $15), an ideal companion for many of the sights included along this route. It can be purchased at specialty bookstores or directly from *Her Majesty's Stationery Office* (71 Lothian Rd., Edinburgh EH3 9A0, Scotland; phone: 131-228-4181).

Hotels categorized as very expensive cost $120 or more per night for a double room (including breakfast, private bath, and TV set, unless otherwise noted); those categorized as expensive, $95 to $110; moderate, $70 to $90; and inexpensive, less than $70. Dinner for two, not including wine, in a restaurant listed as very expensive will cost $70 or more; in an expensive spot it will run $50 to $65; in the moderate category, $30 to $45; and in inexpensive places, less than $30. All restaurants listed serve lunch and dinner unless otherwise indicated. For each location, hotels and restaurants are listed alphabetically by price category.

GLASGOW For a detailed report on the city, its sights, hotels, and restaurants, see *Glasgow* in THE CITIES.

En Route from Glasgow Take A77 southwest for 35 miles to Ayr.

AYR Situated at the confluence of the river Ayr and the Firth of Clyde, this quiet, respectable city (pop. 48,493) derives much of its current prosperity from the worship and study of its most distinguished reprobate, Robert Burns.

Burns was born in 1759 in the "auld clay biggin" built by his father, now the *Burns Cottage Museum* at Alloway, 2 miles south of Ayr on B7024. It's closed Sundays in winter; admission charge (phone: 1292-441215). Nearby is the *Land O' Burns* visitors' center, with its audiovisual program, book and crafts shop, cafeteria, and picnic tables (open daily; no admission charge); the Burns monument, an 1832 neo-Grecian stone folly on a leafy hill; and the 700-year-old Brig O'Doon, the site where the witch in Burns's famous narrative poem, "Tam o' Shanter," caught hold of Tam's mare's tail. Spooky-looking *Auld Alloway Kirk,* a ruin even in Burns's day, has an empty window through which Tam saw the Devil. Burns's father lies in *Auld Alloway Kirkyard.* A week-long *Robert Burns Festival* held every June in the Ayrshire district is administered from Alloway and includes music, poetry, exhibitions, dinners, and dances (phone: 1292-43700).

Back in Ayr, the *Tam o' Shanter Museum* (High St.; phone: 1292-269794) was once a brewery to which Douglas Graham of Shanter (the real-life Tam) supplied the malted grain. It's closed Sundays in April, May, and September; admission charge. Other sights in this busy dairy farmers' town are its large harbor; the 13th-century *Tower of St. John* at Citadel Place; the 15th-century auld brig over the river Ayr; the 15th-century *Loudon Hall,* the house of the hereditary Sheriffs of Ayrshire, in Boat Vennel (open daily; no admission charge; phone: 1292-282109); and the 17th-century auld kirk where Burns was baptized, just off High Street. Ayr is celebrated, too, for its racetrack on Whitletts Road, where the *Scottish Grand National* is held in April or May, and for its panoramic beach looking toward the Isle of Arran. *Belleisle Park* on the south side has a deer park, nature trail, lush gardens, and the championship *Belle Isle* golf course. The park is open daily; no admission charge (phone: 1292-282842). Ayr is one of the few smaller Scottish towns with a theater—the *Gaiety* (Carrick St.; phone: 1292-264639), which offers light entertainment year-round and a special variety show in the summer. The tourist office (39 Sandgate; phone: 1292-284196 or 1292-79000) is open daily.

Belleisle House Once the property of the Magistrates of Ayr, this delightful 18-room hostelry retains such personal embellishments as engraved fireplaces. Elegant traditional dishes are served in one of two dining rooms, one decorated in imitation of Marie Antoinette's music room, the other modeled after her bedroom. The restaurant is open daily. Reservations advised. Major credit cards accepted. Inside *Belleisle Park* on Doonfoot Rd., Ayr (phone: 1292-442331). Expensive.

Pickwick One of the best of a seafront string of Victorian villas; like most of the others, this 15-room property's restaurant specializes in pure malt whiskies and Scottish foods. Restaurant open daily; reservations advised; major credit cards accepted. 19 Racecourse Rd., Ayr (phone: 1292-260111). Expensive.

Northpark House Once the main house of an estate, this attractive building dating from 1720 now has five guestrooms. Every effort has been made to retain the original ambience; the inn's restaurant (good but rather expensive) is housed in four small rooms that the owner left intact, rather than knocking down walls to make one large space. The food is prepared with great care—and mostly seasonal produce is used. 2 Alloway, Ayr (phone: 1292-442336; fax: 1292-445572). Moderate.

Stables Located just behind the tourist information center in the Sandgate, in a tiny Georgian courtyard with a tea garden, this 18th-century restaurant serves wonderful Scottish fare. No smoking is allowed. Closed Sundays and Mondays. Reservations advised. Major credit cards accepted. Queensgate, Ayr (phone: 1292-283704). Moderate.

En Route from Ayr Leave Ayr by the coast road (A719). The shoreline here gleams with watery inlets and, in spring, with wild red poppies. South of the cliffs called the Heads of Ayr is the ghostly shell of *Dunure Castle.* Along this route are some of the most beautiful views imaginable, often augmented by extraordinary climatic effects creating ethereal lights. One peculiar phenomenon is the Croy Brae, also called "Electric Brae" because when its fantastic properties first became apparent, Ayrshiremen thought the cause could only be electricity. Now they think it's an optical illusion: Switch off the motor and you'll seem to coast uphill. (That, however, is nothing compared with the descent from the brae's other side, where you seem to coast uphill backward!) About 12 miles south of Ayr (on a signposted road off A719) is *Culzean Castle.*

CULZEAN CASTLE *Culzean* (pronounced *Ku*-lane), situated within a remarkable 560-acre country park, is one of Scotland's most visited castles. It was designed around an ancient tower of the Kennedy family (the Earls of Cassilis) by Robert Adam in 1777, and its turrets flank the Atlantic. General

Eisenhower became its chief denizen in 1946, using it later as a European White House. The Eisenhower Room is devoted to highlights of the general's career; note the Oval Staircase and the Round Drawing Room, in which even the fireplaces are curved. Ask for the head guide, Isabel Keir, a foremost authority on *Culzean*'s contents and history.

The castle grounds include a walled garden, aviary, swan pond, camellia house, and orangery. There are palm trees everywhere, picnic tables, a seashore trail, and a tearoom. Farm buildings also designed by Robert Adam are now a lecture and exhibition theater and are (in summer) the starting point for conducted nature walks. The park grounds always are open; the castle, exhibition theater, and tearoom are closed November through March; admission charge (phone: 1655-6274). Go in the morning to avoid the tourist buses that pour in after lunch.

En Route from Culzean Castle Return to A719. Another 5½ miles south of *Culzean Castle* is *Turnberry Lighthouse,* which is situated on the spot said to be the birthplace of King Robert the Bruce in 1274. The lighthouse is also near the ninth hole (nicknamed "Bruce's Castle") of the *Ailsa* championship golf course at the *Turnberry* hotel (see *Best en Route*). It's best to get there between 2 PM and about an hour before sunset if you plan to go inside; call in advance. There's an admission charge (phone: 1655-31225). From Turnberry, head north on A77 for the 2-mile drive to Kirkoswald and *Souter Johnnie's Cottage.* This was the home of the village cobbler (Souter) John Davidson, immortalized by Burns in "Tam o' Shanter." Open daily from noon to 5 PM April through October, or by arrangement; admission charge (phone: 1655-6603). Return to Turnberry via A77 and head south for a view of 1,114-foot Ailsa Craig, an island refuge for Catholics during the Reformation and now a bird sanctuary. This great triangular rock also holds an empty castle and chapel and the remains of the quarry once used to fashion stones used in curling (a sport much like bowling on ice). Some remarkable visitors, including poets John Keats and William Wordsworth, have been tempted to swim the sometimes stormy seas to reach it. Pick up B734 just north of Girvan (5 miles south of Turnberry) and follow it another 7½ miles to Barr. At Barr, take an unnumbered side road (following the still-narrow river Stinchar) through Glengennet and South Balloch at the northwest tip of *Galloway Forest Park,* a distance of about 4 miles.

BEST EN ROUTE

Turnberry This lavish, 132-room, Edwardian resort looks like a landlocked ocean liner. It has a tennis court and full health club and offers reduced rates for guests playing on its two 18-hole golf courses: the *Ailsa* and the *Arran* (also see *Great Golf* in DIVERSIONS). The *Ailsa*'s acclaimed restaurant specializes in continental fare; try the roast lamb, venison in game sauce, or duckling pie. Off A719, Turnberry (phone: 1655-31000; 212-838-3110 in New York City; 800-223-6800 elsewhere in the US; fax: 1655-31706). Very expensive.

Malin Court A challenge to the former hegemony of the *Turnberry* resort—it overlooks *Turnberry*'s *Ailsa* golf course and has 17 rooms and a patio garden, plus a restaurant specializing in traditional fare. Off A719, Turnberry (phone: 1655-31457; fax: 1655-31072). Expensive to moderate.

GALLOWAY FOREST PARK A glorious, gargantuan green space, this majestic wilderness has many fascinations; the chief ones are indicated on the *Enjoy Scotland* touring map (see above). Rocky glens and mountain lakes have won it the title "The Highlands of the Lowlands." *Galloway Forest Park* is open daily; no admission charge (phone: 1671-2420). Our route of entry heads into rough moorland country via *Palgowan Open Farm,* which lies beyond the Merrick, southern Scotland's highest peak. *Palgowan* has Highland and Galloway cattle, sheep, working sheepdogs, and demonstrations in drystane dyking (building drystone walls) and other traditional skills. It is closed November through April and Mondays and Fridays in May, June, September, and October; no admission charge (phone: 1236-720047). Detour left along the Water of Trool for Loch Trool. The Bruce's Stone marks the spot where Robert the Bruce and his Scottish forces dropped massive rocks on a band of English soldiers.

From this western side of *Galloway Forest Park,* it is not easy to reach the *Galloway Deer Museum* by car without going almost as far south as Newton Stewart, but it is a beautiful drive. Turn left onto the small road that rejoins A712 east. Queen's Way, which extends 19 miles to the *Deer Museum,* is a lovely road which sometimes runs through narrow cuttings between trees. A few miles along on the left is a goat park, full of Scotland's feral species—they are not averse to descending for a bite of your lunch—and there are lovely spots to picnic or paddle beside the Palnure Burn. On the left, Clatteringshaws Loch has another Bruce's Stone marking a *Red Deer Range* that allows you to photograph magnificent Galloway stags, hinds, and calves at close range. Ranger-guided tours are conducted on Tuesdays and Thursdays at 11 AM and 2 PM in July and August (phone: 1556-3626). You also can see the dam that holds back the loch close to the road just past the *Deer Museum.*

The *Galloway Deer Museum* has exhibitions about indigenous Galloway species. Closed October through March; no admission charge (phone: 1644-2285). But visitors don't need a museum to take in native wildlife: red deer, roe deer, fox, otters, red squirrels, and wild goats abound on the park's secluded footpaths, and the wild geese and ducks, pheasants and grouse, falcons, owls, ravens, and golden eagles make it a bird watcher's paradise.

En Route from Galloway Forest Park Exit the park via A712 near the museum. Heading west past Cairnsmore of Fleet, the highest peak along the road, turn left on A75 for the *Forestry Enterprise Kirroughtree Forest Visitor Centre* (phone: 1671-2420) just 1½ miles down the road. The center has displays on what the commission grows and why; there also is a tree nursery, which shows most of the species that grow in Scotland. It's closed November through *Easter* except by appointment with the *Forestry Enterprise* office near the River Cree Bridge. Return to A712 and continue another 1½ miles to Newton Stewart.

NEWTON STEWART Founded by William Stewart, third son of the Earl of Galloway, the town (pop. 3,212) obtained its charter from Charles II in 1677. Smuggling was an early and profitable activity; handloom weaving, however, has been a successful (and legal) local industry. The *Creetown Gold & Silversmith Workshop* (see "En Route from Newton Stewart," below) has a retail outlet here (27 Albert St.; phone: 1671-82357). The *Newton Stewart Museum* (York Rd.; phone: 1671-2106) has a natural history and social history exhibition. It is closed November through *Easter* and Sundays *Easter* through July and in October; admission charge. Visitors to Newton Stewart also can see mohair in production at the *Creebridge Mohair Mill,* just over the Cree River Bridge from town; tours are held on weekdays; there is also a mill shop (phone for mill and shop: 671-82868). The tourist office (Dashwood Sq.; phone: 1671-82431) is closed November through *Easter.* A useful pamphlet, *The Galloway Craft Guild's Craft Trail Map of Locations,* lists many interesting workshops in this area; it's available at most tourist offices and at many of the workshops.

BEST EN ROUTE

Kirroughtree A much-awarded hotel with a well-known, excellent restaurant. This luxurious country house has 22 bedrooms, spacious grounds, and lovely gardens. Elegant meals are prepared by two nationally acclaimed chefs, Ian Bennett and Walter Walker. There's a good wine cellar, and a nonsmoking dining room. Open daily. Reservations advised. Major credit cards accepted. Newton Stewart (phone: 1671-2141; fax: 1671-2425). Very expensive.

Creebridge House This white-chimneyed, gabled stone house overlooking its own private lawns and gardens has the romance of a country squire's abode. There are 17 elegant bedrooms, open fires in the public rooms, private salmon and trout fishing for guests, and Taste of Scotland home cooking. Restaurant open daily; reservations advised; major credit cards accepted. On the north edge of Newton Stewart (phone: 1671-2121; fax: 1671-3258). Expensive.

Bruce This family-run hotel with 17 guestrooms prides itself on its superb hill views. Guests are offered personal attention and interesting local cooking. Open February through November. Newton Stewart (phone: 1671-2294). Moderate.

WORTH A DETOUR Directly south of Newton Stewart are the hammerhead-shaped peninsulas that form Scotland's southwestern extremity. The Machars

Peninsula is due south, and the narrow strip of land to the southwest is the Rhinns Peninsula. This side trip will add some 100 miles (and at least one extra day) to your tour, but for those who can spare the time, it is well worth exploring a unique area where Christianity first began in Scotland. The detour begins on A714 south from Newton Stewart.

Galloway was a Covenanting stronghold during the "Killing Times," when Charles II ruthlessly tried to impose his own bishops on the Church of Scotland. Some 7 miles south on A714, the *Martyrs' Monument* on the hill and a pillar on the western shore of Wigtown Bay commemorate two women, aged 63 and 18, who were condemned for their faith; they were tied to stakes and left to drown as the tide came in. Stalwart to the end, they met their deaths singing hymns. Their graves are in the Wigtown churchyard.

One mile south of Wigtown is the Bladnoch Distillery; in use since 1814, it produces a distinctive malt whisky. The distillery is closed weekends and October through February; admission charge (phone: 19884-2235). Below Bladnoch, the road divides; take A746 south 9 miles to the village of Whithorn, which sprang into prominence in 1986, when archaeologists began to excavate the site of a 1,000-year-old abandoned town beside the ruins of a priory. Even earlier, a church built by St. Ninian, Scotland's first saint, who brought Christianity to Scotland in the 5th century, once stood here. Visitors can watch archaeologists at the early Christian and Norse excavations, and take an informal tour of the dig. The *Priory Museum* has a superb display of early Christian crosses. It is closed weekends and November through March; admission charge (phone: 1988-500508).

Continue on A476 through Whithorn; bear left on A750 and continue 3 miles to *St. Ninian's Chapel* at the Isle of Whithorn. The chapel where St. Ninian is said to have built his first church can be reached on foot. Two miles west on the shore off Kidsdale is a cave where he sometimes retired to meditate. Each September, a pilgrimage is conducted to the cave, where you can see the early Christian crosses carved into the rock.

Head west, and take A747 along the coast to Monreith (about 9 miles from the Isle of Whithorn). Along the way, stop for a moment at the *Otter Monument,* which commemorates Gavin Maxwell, author of *Ring of Bright Water,* a book about his tame otters. Just before Monreith on A747 is the unusual *Low Knock Open Farm,* which rears exotic ducks as well as otters. It's closed November through March; admission charge (phone: 198-87217). Farther up the coast is the harbor town of Port William. Past the town, look out on the right for *Finian Chapel,* a small structure that dates back to the 11th century, and then proceed to the town of Glenluce at the head of Luce Bay, where the road rejoins A75 (15 miles north of Monreith).

The Rhinns Peninsula contains the Mull of Galloway, the most southerly point in Scotland. To reach it, continue 4 miles out of Glenluce heading west and turn onto A715, which skirts the Royal Air Force Engineering Establishment at West Freuch, hugging the long, winding coast and cutting through the village of Sandhead, 6½ miles farther along A715. If you're in the mood to linger, stop in at *Tigh-Na-Mara,* a whitewashed building on Sandhead's main street. Once an old coaching inn, it has a classic farmers' bar, a restaurant, and seats outdoors in the summer. About 3 miles past Sandhead are the gates of *Ardwell House Gardens,* where formal beds are planted around an 18th-century house set amid acres of woods. They are closed November through February; no admission charge (phone: 1776-87664).

There are more gardens past *Ardwell:* Take B7065 a half mile to *Logan Botanic Gardens,* where palms and other semitropical plants indicate the mildness of the climate. These gardens are closed November through March; admission charge. A few hundred yards farther along B7065, at the start of Logan Bay, is *Logan Fish Pond.* This large, natural, tidal rock pool holds cod that are so tame they come up to take food from your hands. It is closed October through *Easter;* admission charge (phone: 1292-268181).

Follow the route around Port Logan's picturesque old harbor, with its (now abandoned) *Thomas Telford Lighthouse,* built in 1818 to cater to the cattle trade from Northern Ireland; then take the road out of the village over the hill to Drummore, a hamlet that overlooks the Machars Peninsula.

From Port Logan, continue another 8 miles on B7065 for the Mull of Galloway, a magnificent rocky head with 250-foot cliffs, seabirds, the remains of prehistoric fortifications, and a splendid lighthouse. Ireland, the Isle of Man, Wales, and England can be seen from its tower.

The return trip back north to Newton Stewart (via the B7065, A716, and A77) runs via Stranraer (about 19 miles from the Mull of Galloway), which dominates the circular shape of Loch Ryan and is the ferry terminal to Ireland. Every August, this bustling farming community hosts a renowned agricultural show. Catamaran service is available between Stranraer and Belfast, Northern Ireland. The one-way trip takes about 50 minutes, and there are five daily sailings in July and August; four the rest of the year (boats leave from *West Pier;* phone: 1776-2262). From Stranraer, take A75 east toward Newton Stewart. Five miles farther on are the *Castle Kennedy Gardens,* known countrywide for their rhododendrons and azaleas (the best time to see them is in late May and early June); they also feature magnolias. These beautiful gardens are on a peninsula between two lochs. The gardens are closed October through March; admission charge (phone: 1776-2024). To return to Newton Stewart, take the A75 east for another 20 miles.

BEST EN ROUTE

Knockinaam Lodge It's well worth the side trip to find this remote 10-room, 19th-century house, at this tranquil spot right on the west coast of the peninsula. The French fare has earned several awards. Open mid-March through December. Fifteen miles southwest of Stranraer in Portpatrick (phone: 1776-81471; fax: 1776-81435). Very expensive.

North West Castle The former home of Arctic explorer Sir John Ross, this award-winning seafront hotel has huge windows from which you can watch the ferries pass through Loch Ryan. All 28 rooms are comfortably furnished, and facilities include an outdoor pool and curling rink, a Jacuzzi, a gym, and a solarium. In the dining room, try the poached escallop of Cree salmon hollandaise or the superb beef Wellington. Port Roadie, Stranraer (phone: 1776-4413; fax: 1776-2646). Expensive to moderate.

Corsemalzie House This country house 7 miles west of Port William features a first class Taste of Scotland dining room (serving salmon, trout, and roast beef), plus good bar lunches and suppers. There also are 15 guestrooms. Open daily. Reservations advised. MasterCard and Visa accepted. On B7005, just off A747 (phone: 1988-86254). Moderate.

Queen's Arms This small country hotel, with five rooms, serves first class food, including lobster, fish, and Galloway steak dishes. 22 Main St., Isle of Whithorn (phone: 19885-369). Moderate to inexpensive.

En Route from Newton Stewart Take A75 southeast from Newton Stewart 5 miles to the village of Creetown, with its distinctive clock tower. The *Gem Rock Museum* on the main road offers a fine collection of rocks, minerals, and semi-precious stones from all over the world, a testament to Galloway's preeminence in stone-building. A special feature is the *Crystal Cave,* a state-of-the-art grotto where backlighting displays the crystals and a waterfall in iridescent splendor. There also are workshops on cutting and polishing gemstones and gold- and silversmithing, and a shop. The museum is open daily; admission charge (phone: 167182-357). The *Mersey Docks* and part of the Thames Embankment are made of Creetown granite. Well worth a visit is the *Creetown Gold & Silversmith Workshop* (93 St. John St.; phone: 167182-396); its proprietor, John Prince, also teaches jewelry and silversmith courses.

From Creetown to Gatehouse-of-Fleet (8 miles farther), A75 has delightful views and picnic places. The route follows the eastern shore of Wigtown Bay from the Cree River estuary, looking across to the Wigtown Peninsula. You will pass *Carsluith Castle,* a roofless, L-shaped, 16th-century tower house. Nearby is the *Galloway Smokehouse* (phone: 167182-354), where you can sample (and purchase) the excellent local smoked products. Dirk Hatternick's Cave is a voracious crevice in the rocks where pigeonholes were cut to hide the dashing bandit's smuggled brandy. *Cardoness Castle* (6 miles from *Carsluith Castle*), a well-preserved 15th-century stronghold with its original staircase, is run by *Historic Scotland* (phone: 131-244-3101), a historic preservation organization based in Edinburgh. The castle is closed weekdays October through March; admission charge. The route has now moved out of Wigtownshire into the Stewartry of Kirkcudbright, from which the name of the royal house of Scotland, the Stewarts (or Stuarts), originally derived.

Scenic Gatehouse-of-Fleet is renowned for its archaeological remains and its forest trails leading to lovely little Fleet Bay. Among the ancient sites in the district are *Anworth Church,* on the northwest outskirts of town, containing a Dark Ages cross; *Palace Yard at Enrick,* a medieval moated manor with the foundations of a palace of the Bishops of Galloway destroyed during the Reformation; and a 1st-century Roman fort beside the Water-of-Fleet. A more recent relic is the disused early 19th-century, ivy-covered cotton mill above Fleet Bridge. Stop by the *Mill-on-the-Fleet* (High St.; phone: 1557-814009) and trace the town's long history. It is closed November through February; admission charge. The tourist office, which is closed November through *Easter,* is in the main car park on High Street (phone: 1557-814212). Artists of all kinds live in Gatehouse-of-Fleet, as is also true of Kirkcudbright (7 miles farther), reached by taking the A755 south from A75.

BEST EN ROUTE

Murray Arms Well patronized by locals, this small, 13-room hotel in the center of Gatehouse-of-Fleet offers a warm welcome and good food. Robert Burns wrote "Scots Wha Hae" here. Guests can golf, fish, or play tennis, and the delicious fare in the dining room can satisfy even the most finicky palate. Try the locally caught salmon (broiled or smoked) or the Galloway beef. High St. (phone: 1557-814207; fax: 1557-814370). Expensive.

KIRKCUDBRIGHT Kirkcudbright (pronounced Ker-*coo*-bree) was used by members of the late-19th- and early-20th-century Glasgow School of artists—such as James Guthrie and George Henry—as a base from which to create their characteristic "kailyard" (farmyard) scenes. Its flowery lanes, elm-lined streets, and enchanting knots of whitewashed 18th-century cottages still attract a steady stream of painters, pupils, and patrons throughout the summer; 3,352 people live here today. *Hornel Art Gallery* (High St.; phone: 1557-30437) was once the home of E. A. Hornel and contains several of his early post-Impressionist works, as well as paintings from his later Far Eastern journeys. It is closed Tuesdays and mid-October through *Easter;* admission charge. Adjacent to the much-photographed harbor is an exhibition gallery. Dominating the harbor is jagged *MacLellan's Castle,* built in 1582. The town's impressive mercat (market) cross dates from 1610, and the late-16th- or early-17th-century tolbooth once imprisoned the US naval hero John Paul Jones on a charge of manslaughter. Jones's birthplace, near Dumfries, recently was turned into a museum about his life (see below). The *Stewartry Museum* (St. Mary St.; phone: 1557-31643) houses a John Paul Jones display, among other exhibits about Kirkcudbright's history. It is closed Sundays year-round and weekdays November through *Easter;* admission charge. The tourist office is at Harbour Square (phone: 1557-30494); it's closed November through March.

Auld Alliance This cheerful, bow-windowed snuggery across from the castle caters to everybody from snackers to three-course gorgers with its Scots-French fare. Closed *Halloween* through *Easter.* Reservations advised. No credit cards accepted. 5 Castle St., Kirkcudbright (phone: 1557-30569). Moderate.

Ingle The old station building, converted into a family restaurant seating 70, specializes in local seafood—Dover sole, monkfish, queenies (small scallops), and plaice—all caught in the harbor. Open daily for dinner only. Reservations advised. Major credit cards accepted. St. Mary's St., Kirkcudbright (phone: 1557-30606). Moderate.

Selkirk Arms A charming, historic, 15-room, 18th-century coaching inn where Robert Burns wrote the popular "Selkirk Grace." Some of its walls are inscribed with Burns's verses. There is also a Taste of Scotland restaurant. Old High St., Kirkcudbright (phone: 1557-30402; fax: 1557-31639). Moderate.

En Route from Kirkcudbright Take A711 north from Kirkcudbright 5 miles to rejoin A75. Just before the town of Castle Douglas, on the left, is *Threave Castle,* a 14th-century Douglas family stronghold on Threave Island on the river Dee. It is closed October through March; no admission charge. The area's slopes attract thousands of wintering geese (and almost as many bird watchers!). Also here, on the right, is the well-marked *Threave House and Garden,* the *National Trust for Scotland*'s *School of Horticulture.* The best time to visit is in the spring, when some 200 varieties of daffodils are in bloom. There is also a walled garden and fine greenhouses. The gardens are open daily; the visitors' center, exhibitions, and a souvenir shop are closed November through February. There's an admission charge (phone: 1556-2575). Castle Douglas is the commercial capital of the Stewartry; the wide main street has a well-known shopping center, and there is a livestock market nearby. The town is situated on idyllic Carlingwark Loch, asprinkle with brightly painted rowboats (available for rent in the summer at the loch). The tourist office is in the *Town Hall* (phone: 1556-2611).

Take A75 north out of Castle Douglas 18 miles to the quaint town of Dumfries. On the way, a half-mile from Castle Douglas, opposite the *Ernespie* hotel, is the workshop of Hugh Crawford, a specialist in fine gemstones who sells gems and repairs damaged stones; he's a friendly man who enjoys discussing his craft with visitors. The workshop is open daily (phone: 1556-2604).

DUMFRIES Although its written history began in 1186, with its legal recognition by King William the Lion, Dumfries is in fact much older: Excavations have yielded Bronze Age relics. Here, in the gentle dale of the river Nith, visitors will find hilly meadows flecked with buttercups, grazing cattle, and grass as green as any in Ireland. Spring comes earlier to Dumfries and

Galloway than elsewhere in Scotland and the climate is warmer. Dumfries, dubbed "Queen of the South," is the seat of the local government; its current population is 31,307.

In summer Dumfries is populated with students of literature visiting *Burns House* (Burns St.; phone: 1387-55297), where the poet spent his last years. It is closed Sundays and Mondays October through *Easter;* admission charge. His tomb in nearby *St. Michael's Churchyard* is augmented by an unintentionally humorous sculpture showing him at his plough (Scotland knows him as "the Ploughman Poet") somewhat hampered by Coila, the muse of Scottish poetry, who flings a cumbersome mantle o'er his shoulders. The *Globe Inn* (in a narrow alley off High St.; phone: 1387-52335), Burns's "favorite howss," is exactly as it was in his day and is still in the bartending business. The *Robert Burns Heritage Centre* (Mill Rd.; phone: 1387-64808) has an audiovisual show about Burns and the Dumfries he knew. It is open daily; admission charge. The *Robert Burns Associations* have formed a Burns Heritage trail, which indicates locations throughout Dumfries, Galloway, and Ayrshire where the poet lived and worked. Consult the nearest visitors' center for more information.

A saunter through Dumfries will lead to some other not-to-be-missed high spots: *Greyfriars Church* (High St.), whose monastery (now a supermarket) was the scene in 1306 of the murder by Robert the Bruce of John "the Red" Comyn, his cousin and heir to the Scottish throne; the Burns statue opposite this church; the *Mid Steeple* of 1707, which is the remains of the central square's old town hall; and *Dumfries Academy* (Academy St.), where a pupil named J. M. Barrie first conceived the characters Peter Pan and Wendy while exploring the garden of the Moat Brae Nursing Home in the lane behind. The river Nith is spanned by the six-arched Devorgilla's Bridge, a 13th-century gift from Devorgilla Balliol, founder of *Balliol College* at *Oxford.* Don't miss the great gathering of swans in the river; the birds seem completely oblivious to the throng of onlookers. The expansive "caul," or weir, by the bridge is a salmon leap and was originally the power supply for the town's grain mills. The path through the 2-mile wood along the Nith bank is Burns's Walk.

T. C. Farries (Irongray Rd., *Lochside Industrial Estate;* phone: 1387-720755) is considered by many to be the best bookseller north of Oxford (it's off A76 by New Bridge). The *Burgh Museum* (Observatory Rd.; phone: 1387-533741), housed in an 18th-century windmill, has local archaeological and other exhibits and a camera obscura. The museum is closed Sundays and Mondays October through March; admission charge to the camera obscura. There's also a folk museum in *Old Bridge House* (Mill Rd.; phone: 1387-56904) adjacent to Devorgilla's Bridge. It is closed October through March; no admission charge.

October through April, the *Theatre Royal* (Shakespeare St.; phone: 1387-54209), home of the amateur *Dumfries Guild of Players,* produces a variety of shows, from light fare—a *Christmas* pantomime and plays by the likes of Ira Levin—to heavyweight works such as Ibsen dramas. (The theater's phone is answered only sporadically.) *Gracefield Arts Centre* (28 Edinburgh Rd.; phone: 1387-62084) is a showcase for works by Scottish artists; it also takes part in the annual *Dumfries and Galloway Arts Festival* around the last week in May, providing military, rock, and folk bands, a guest orchestra, puppet shows, and exhibitions. *Guid Nychburris* (Good Neighbors) *Week,* in late June, offers concerts, parades, the crowning of a "Queen of the South," the cavalcaded "stobbing and nogging" (tracing out and marking) of Dumfries's boundaries, and the "kirking" (public promenading to church) of a newly elected Cornet, or chief eligible bachelor. The *Dumfries Jazz Festival* takes place in the late summer or early autumn. The local tourist office (on Whitesands; phone: 1387-53862) is open daily.

Several sights near Dumfries are worth a jaunt into the countryside. Located 9 miles south of Dumfries on B725 is the 12th-century *Caerlaverock Castle,* a striking triangular ruin with round turrets and a real moat (especially spectacular at sunset). The castle was a prime target in the 14th century during Edward I's wars against Scotland and its weak king, John Balliol (Devorgilla's son, known to his subjects as Toom Tabard, which means "empty coat"). Next door is the *Caerlaverock National Nature Reserve,* on the river Nith estuary and the Solway Firth: Here you can enjoy the exhilarating spectacle of 9,000 barnacle geese in open flight (observation towers are open mid-September through April).

About 6 miles south of Dumfries on A710 is the *New Abbey Corn Mill;* the former waterpowered mill is now a museum offering demonstrations of how grain was ground in the 18th century. It is closed Thursdays October through March; admission charge (phone: 1387-85260). In the village of New Abbey, another mile farther south on A710, is *Shambellie House.* Approached through an avenue of tall gracious pines, this building houses Scotland's foremost costume museum. It is closed November through late April; admission charge (phone: 1387-85375). Also in New Abbey, near *Shambellie House,* is *Sweetheart Abbey.* Built in 1273, the abbey is the last pre-Reformation Cistercian foundation in Scotland and one of the nation's most beautiful. Devorgilla, who established it, is buried here; her husband's heart, encased in an ivory casket, sits in the tomb upon her bosom—hence the abbey's name. Next to the abbey is *Abbey Cottage Coffee and Crafts,* a good rest stop for light meals, fine home baking, and interesting gifts. It is closed weekdays from October through *Christmas* (phone: 1387-85377).

On A710, about 7 miles farther south of New Abbey, is the village of Kirkbean, the birthplace of John Paul Jones (1747–92), who distinguished himself as a naval officer fighting against the British during the American Revolution. The cottage where Jones was born, located just outside the village, has been restored with period furnishings and turned into the *John Paul Jones Birthplace Museum.* Among its exhibits are a replica of Jones's cabin on the *Bonhomme Richard* flagship, which he commanded in 1779 during the battle when he made his famous declaration, "I have not yet begun to fight!"; a cannon he used; and an audiovisual display about his life. There are also lovely gardens on the grounds. The museum is closed October through March; admission charge (phone: 1387-88613).

BEST EN ROUTE

Casa Toscana Highly acclaimed, this place features both French and Italian dishes, and is particularly distinguished for its fresh seafood and homemade pasta. Its decor is dominated by a gigantic barrel (which once stored wine but is now empty), and lining the walls are 2,000 wine bottles and a display of terra cotta pipes. Open for dinner only; closed Mondays. Reservations advised. Visa accepted. Nunbank, Nunholm Rd., Dumfries (phone: 1387-69619). Very expensive.

Bruno's Thoughts of salmon and haggis vanish at the flick of a cannelloni in this snazzy Italian sanctum. Open for dinner only; closed Tuesdays. Reservations advised. Visa accepted. 3 Balmoral Rd., Dumfries (phone: 1387-55757). Expensive.

Station Owned by one of Dumfriesshire's dairy magnates, this red sandstone, Victorian building with Hansel-and-Gretel portals has 32 rooms, a hearty array of Taste of Scotland delights in its restaurant, and two bars. Lovers Walk, Dumfries (phone: 1387-54316; fax: 1387-50388). Expensive to moderate.

Cairndale Constructed of red sandstone, this 75-room inn counts among its amenities the *Barracuda* spa, a pool, and a sauna. In the summer, Taste of Scotland dinners are the focus, accompanied by Cairndale *ceilidh* (Scottish entertainment); other menu items include scampi and smoked salmon mousse with tayberry sauce. Its 60-car parking lot is handy. English St., Dumfries (phone: 1387-54111; fax: 1387-50555). Moderate.

Hetland Hall Situated on a hill overlooking the Solway coast, this impressive, gleaming-white, 29-room country house with many chimneys will allow you to play the "local laird" in style, with lawn bowling, badminton, a gameroom, and 45 acres of grounds. There is also a restaurant. At Carrutherstown, just outside Dumfries (phone: 1387-84201). Moderate.

En Route from Dumfries Take A76 north toward Sanquhar, following the river Nith into upper Nithsdale. This is spectacular high country, where the hills crowd close and dramatic upland passes cut their way through the Lowther Hills. The Nith is the only river in Britain open for salmon fishing in November. *Lincluden Abbey*—1½ miles outside of Dumfries—was founded by 12th-century Benedictine nuns. It survives chiefly in the choir and south transept of its 15th-century church. The stone screen at the choir entry has carvings from the life of Christ, and there is a fine tomb (1430) for Princess Margaret, daughter of King Robert III and wife of Archibald the Loser, the son of

Archibald the Grim ("the Loser" appears in Shakespeare's *Henry IV, Part I*). The carved doorway has the Douglas insignia of the heart and chalices. Garden terraces are about all that remain of the monastic buildings, hardly surprising in an area where patron and predator often were indistinguishable. The abbey is closed October through March.

From the abbey, continue north on A76 another 4½ miles to Ellisland, where Burns wrote "Tam o' Shanter" and "Auld Lang Syne." Five miles west is Dunscore, and 6 miles west of that is Craigenputtock, where Thomas and Jane Welsh Carlyle lived in poverty from 1828 to 1834 (he wrote *Sartor Resartus* here); both towns are on unnumbered, signposted roads off A76. Dalswinton Loch, east of Ellisland, is where William Symington (1763–1831) made the first ever successful attempt at steam navigation in October 1788, but he could not maintain financial backing and died in poverty.

Closeburn Castle is 4 miles north of Ellisland off A76. It's closed to the public, but you will see its 14th-century tower from the road. About 3 miles west is Keir, where native son Kirkpatrick Macmillan made the first modern bicycle in a smithy in 1839. The machine is now in the *Science Museum* in London. Thornhill (2 miles north of *Closeburn*) is a captivating town with trees lining its broad street. A column was erected here in 1714 to honor the Douglas Dukes of Queensberry, the second of whom, James (1662–1711), maneuvered in 1707 the extinction of the Scottish Parliament in the union with England and Wales. Since the late 1980s, an active Scottish Constitutional Convention, backed by the Labour and Liberal Democrat political parties, has been trying to resurrect it. The success of the ruling British Conservatives in the 1992 elections threw the project into turmoil, but most Scots want some form of devolved Scottish parliament.

Six miles north of Thornhill, take the left fork at Carronbridge to stay on A76. Sanquhar is another 8 miles north. On the left, *Drumlanrig Castle* is another seat of the Dukes of Buccleuch and Queensberry. It was built in the 17th century for William Douglas, first Duke of Queensberry (1637–95), who is reputed to have spent only one night in it on learning its cost. (The ruin of the 15th-century castle William Douglas occupied instead is just outside Sanquhar, north on A76.) The castle's art collection includes works by Rembrandt, Leonardo da Vinci, and Gainsborough, and there is also a crafts center and acres of hills and woods. It is closed Thursdays and mid-August through April; admission charge (phone: 1848-30248).

If you have time, some 8 miles farther north of Drumlanrig, take B797 up over the Mennock Pass, a ruggedly beautiful mountain pass where little grows, except to feed the flocks of black-faced mountain sheep grazing on the hillside. Villages such as Wanlockhead (Scotland's highest, at 1,400 feet), at the head of the pass, were once the center of the old lead mining industry. The *Museum of Scottish Lead Mining* has a mine which can be visited, as well as many mining relics, engines, a smelt mill, and cottages. It is closed November through *Easter;* admission charge (phone: 1659-74387). Then return to A76 and continue to Sanquhar.

BEST EN ROUTE

Trigony House Located on four acres of gardens and woodlands, this sweet country-house hotel has nine well-appointed rooms. In the dining room, a Taste of Scotland menu offers pheasant and venison in season, as well as Nith salmon. Closeburn, by Thornhill (phone: 1848-31211). Moderate.

George A friendly former inn on the long stagecoach route north, this place has eight rooms and serves good family fare in its dining room. Drumlanrig St., Thornhill (phone: 1848-30326). Inexpensive.

SANQUHAR The local post office is Britain's oldest (in use since 1763), but the chief historical interest in Sanquhar lies with the extreme Protestant Covenanters (read Sir Walter Scott's *Old Mortality*). An obelisk denotes the site of the mercat (market) cross, where in 1680 and 1685 leaders affixed declarations abjuring allegiance to Charles II and James VI (II of England), respectively: The declarations meant war, and the first leader, Richard Cameron, fell in an engagement near Cumnock within a few weeks. His admirers were thenceforth known as the Cameronian sect. In 1688 the second declarant, James Renwick, was executed in Edinburgh, becoming the last martyr of the Covenanters. The *Sanquhar Tourist Office* (Tolbooth High St.; phone: 1659-50185) is housed in the *Old Tolbooth,* which was built in 1735; it is closed November through *Easter.* Their publication entitled *Nithsdale Covenanters Trail* gives information about local sites associated with Covenanting; it costs £1 (about $1.50). Also in the *Old Tolbooth* is the *Sanquhar Museum,* with exhibits about local history. It is closed Mondays and October through March; admission charge (phone: 1659-50185).

One of the town's most prominent historical figures is James Crichton, who was born in 1560 in *Eliock Castle,* 2 miles south of Sanquhar. Crichton debated on scientific questions in 12 languages, disputed theology, and served in the French army. He might have accomplished a great deal more had he not been killed in a duel in Italy at the age of 22. This genius became known posthumously as "the Admirable Crichton" (and J. M. Barrie borrowed the title for his play of that name). Unfortunately, *Eliock Castle* is privately owned and closed to the public.

BEST EN ROUTE

Blackaddie House On the banks of the river Nith, this charming, family-operated 16th-century farmhouse provides nine rooms, a children's playground, an adjacent golf course, trout and salmon fishing, and three meals a day. Blackaddie Rd., Sanquhar (phone: 1659-50270). Inexpensive.

En Route from Sanquhar A76 wanders pleasantly northwest, beside the Nith through Kirkconnel and over the Ayrshire border into New Cumnock,

7 miles from Sanquhar. The town is in two parts (separated by 400 yards): "Bank" on the river Nith, and "Path Head" on the river Afton, which descends from the 2,000-foot Blacklorg Hill. The tourist office in the *Town Hall* (phone: 1290-38581) is closed November through March.

Five miles north is Cumnock, whose spirit is realized in the statue by Scottish sculptor Benno Schotz at the Council Chamber commemorating native son James Keir Hardie (1856–1915), the great socialist and labor leader. This is very much a miners' town. Also in the center is the *Baird Institute Museum,* which was endowed in 1891 by a local grocer. This Gothic-style, red sandstone building exhibits Cumnock Victorian pottery and Ayrshire embroidery. Open Fridays and Saturdays year-round; no admission charge (phone: 1290-22111). The tourist office (Glaisnock St.; phone: 1290-23058) is closed November through March.

Another 3 miles north of Cumnock is Auchinleck (pronounced Aw-kun-*lek*), where in 1773 the proprietor of the greathouse (3 miles west), the Scottish judge Alexander Boswell, Lord Auchinleck (1706–82), found himself in heated argument with a difficult English guest introduced by his son and heir, James Boswell (1740–95). Dr. Samuel Johnson (1709–84) is said to have founded this terrible dispute on a disagreement about King Charles (specifically, the retention or removal of his head), but for once it seems to have been a subject James found too embarrassing to record. Boswell is buried here in the *Boswell Mausoleum* (built by the same Lord Auchinleck), which holds five generations of Boswells. In the *Boswell Museum,* there is a memorial to William Murdoch, a 19th-century pioneer in using gas for lighting and heating. If you want to visit, call the curator in advance (phone: 290-20931); there's no admission charge. The parish church originated in a cell maintained by a holy man of the Celtic church; it was enlarged in the 12th and 17th centuries.

The road (A76) leads next to Mauchline (6 miles from Auchinleck), which is said to embody the quintessence of Robert Burns. Here, the poet made a bitter enemy of a kirk elder, against whom he wrote "Holy Willie's Prayer." The *Poosie Nansie* ale house still stands, and you may commune with Holy Willie's ghost in the churchyard, where he is buried. Burns also married his mistress, Jean Armour, in Mauchline in 1788. *Burns House* (Castle St.; phone: 1290-50045) is where the poet lived before moving to Ellisland. It is closed October through *Easter;* admission charge. His former residence at Mossgiel is 1½ miles to the west. *Burns Memorial Tower* (pick up the key at the cottage), which contains relics, stands on the north of Mauchline; there's an admission charge. The tourist office (Kilmarnock Rd.; phone: 1292-51916) is open daily. From Mauchline, continue along A76 another 9 miles north to Kilmarnock.

KILMARNOCK This is the town where publisher John Wilson made Burns famous in 1786. The event is commemorated in the 80-foot sandstone tower in *Kay Park.* The tourist office (62 Bank St.; phone: 1563-39090) is open daily.

Kilmarnock has grown enormously in recent years, though it has retained its old central core. Outside of the city center is *Dean Castle and Country Park* (Dean Rd.; phone: 1563-22702), a 14th-century fortified keep (complete with dungeon) that contains a display of Burns's manuscripts, as well as a fine collection of European arms and armor and early musical instruments. It is open daily; admission charge. The *Palace Theatre* (Green St.; phone: 1563-23590) features light, traditional Scottish entertainment; it also has a pleasant café for snacks and quick meals. The *Galleon Centre* (phone: 1563-24014), a leisure and sports complex in Titchfield, features a pool, an ice rink, and a bowling alley; open daily. The *John Walker & Sons* whisky-blending and -bottling plant (Hill St.; phone: 1563-23401) offers two-hour guided tours Fridays at 9:45 AM; there also is a souvenir shop. The minimum age for visitors is 14.

A detour out of Kilmarnock on A71 eastward to Strathaven (17 miles) and Hamilton (another 6½ miles) passes Loudon Hill, site of Wallace and Bruce victories, and then Drumclog, where there was a Covenanter victory in 1679 over the Royal General Graham of Claverhouse ("Bonnie Dundee"). The discoverer of penicillin, Sir Alexander Fleming (1881–1955), born in nearby Darvel, was educated in Kilmarnock.

BEST EN ROUTE

Chapeltoun House Small and comfortable, this early-20th-century country house was originally built for a wealthy industrialist. There are eight rooms, and the service is attentive. The chefs produce wonderful French and traditional Scottish fare. On B769 near Stewarton, 8 miles north of Kilmarnock (phone: 1560-82696). Expensive.

Coffee Club Located in one of Kilmarnock's oldest streets, opposite the Laigh Kirk, this Taste of Scotland member has hearty, tasty fare. No liquor license, but guests are welcome to bring their own wine. Closed Sundays. Reservations unnecessary. Major credit cards accepted. 30 Bank St., Kilmarnock (phone: 1563-22048). Inexpensive.

Foxbar Family-owned, this modern, spacious 18-bedroom establishment has a restaurant and bar. 62 London Rd., Kilmarnock (phone: 1563-25701). Inexpensive.

En Route from Kilmarnock Take A735 out of Kilmarnock north another 8 miles to Dunlop, famous for its cheese and for first breeding Ayrshire cows under the auspices of the Dunlop family, magnates from the 13th century until 1858. At Lugton, 2 miles farther, A735 joins A736; take A736 northeast and proceed 9 miles farther through Barrhead to Paisley.

PAISLEY Known worldwide for the famous Paisley pattern, the city (pop. 84,330) is also justly famous for *Paisley Abbey,* with its beautiful stained glass windows. Founded in 1163 as part of the European Cluniac Reform movement, the abbey was destroyed at the orders of Edward I of England (1307), and rebuilt after Bannockburn. The tower collapsed in 1553, wrecking the transept and choir and leaving only the nave. Early in this century the abbey was restored. The choir now has a fine stone-vaulted roof. Inside are the tombs of King Robert III and Princess Marjory, daughter of King Robert the Bruce and—by her marriage into the great Stuart family at Paisley—the mother of a great deal of British history. Her effigy supposedly adorns the *St. Mirin Chapel.* An 11-foot-high ("Barochan") Celtic Cross, also here, is said to date from the 10th century. The abbey is closed Sundays (phone: 141-889-7654).

The late-19th-century *Paisley Museum and Art Gallery* (High St.; phone: 141-889-3151) has a world-famous collection of Paisley shawls, as well as displays on the history of the pattern, the development of weaving techniques, and the social history of a formerly "tight-knit" community. The museum also has exhibits on local and natural history, ceramics, and Scottish painting. It is closed Sundays; no admission charge.

The legacy of such great textile families as the Coats and Clarks is evident in Paisley's architecture. The Renaissance-style *Town Hall* (Abbey Close and High St.) was constructed by the Clarks, and across High Street, the tapering spire of the *Thomas Coats Memorial Church* sits atop one of Europe's best-known Baptist churches. *Coats Observatory* (Oak Shaw St.; phone: 141-889-2013) has been the site of astronomical studies since 1883. You can stargaze using a telescope on Thursday nights from 7 to 9:30 (weather permitting) from October through March. It is closed Sundays; no admission charge.

Today, it's nearly impossible to distinguish where Paisley ends and Glasgow begins. Despite this, Paisley has retained its individual character: After all, it is the former seat of kings. In 1888 a memorial was placed in the abbey choir "to the members of the Royal House of Stuart who are buried in *Paisley Abbey,* by their descendant, Queen Victoria." The tourist office is in the *Town Hall* (phone: 141-889-0711) and is open daily.

BEST EN ROUTE

Gleddoch House Beautifully situated on 360 acres overlooking the river Clyde and Loch Lomond Hills, this 33-room property offers gracious living and distinctive fare. Amenities include an 18-hole golf course, a sauna, and horseback riding on the grounds. Formerly the residence of a local shipping magnate, it retains the air of a well-kept private estate. Located in Langbank, 6 miles south of Paisley, on B789 off M8 (phone: 1475-54711; fax: 1475-54201). Very expensive.

En Route from Paisley From Paisley, any of several major roads run east into downtown Glasgow, about 7 miles away. Or take M8 to A82 north to Inverness (for details on this city, see the *Northwest Scottish Highlands* route, also in this section).

Northeast Scottish Highlands

Here at the World's End, on its last inch of liberty, we have lived unmolested to this day, defended by our remoteness and obscurity . . . there are no other tribes to come; nothing but sea and cliffs and these more deadly Romans, whose arrogance you cannot escape by obedience and self-restraint. Robbers of the world . . . if their enemy have wealth, they have greed, if he be poor, they are ambitious . . . To plunder, butcher, steal, these things they misname empire; where they make a desert, they call it peace (*ubi solitudinem faciunt, pacem appellant!*).

These famous words were attributed by the Roman historian Tacitus to Scottish history's first identifiable figure, the Pictish chieftain Calgacus, on the eve of his defeat at the hands of Governor Gnaeus Julius Agricola at Mons Graupius, AD 83. Calgacus's speech could hardly have been a more appropriate curtain-raiser for his country's history. Internecine warfare, endurance, heroism, treachery, lawlessness, and a fierce spirit of independence are the words that come to mind when contemplating the Scottish past, especially the region encompassed by this northeastern tour route.

The exact location of Calgacus's heroic stand at Mons Graupius is still unidentified, but historians believe it to have been somewhere in the present-day Grampian region. It was from here that the Picts, at the end of the 2nd century, swept through the Scottish Lowlands and over *Hadrian's Wall* to wreak havoc and destruction throughout the Roman province of Britain. This only served to bring vicious retaliation from the formidable emperor, Septimus Severus, in AD 209, and the Picts were saved from extermination only by Severus's timely death at York in AD 211.

Of the peoples inhabiting Scotland during the Roman occupation of Britain and the subsequent Dark Ages, none retain more interest and mystery than the Picts. The Latin word *picti,* meaning "painted men," was first used in AD 267 to describe the tribes of the north. In actuality, the word was an adaptation of the name by which these tribes already called themselves. They were of Celtic origin but had different roots from the Britons and the Irish. Their language seems to have been closer in form to that of the Gauls than to the Britons' Brythonic; it differed greatly from Gaelic. The mystery and fascination of the Picts' origins and language remain today. Northeastern Scotland is strewn with examples of Pictish art, chief of which are stone sculptures of a fine, mature character. The symbols that decorate these fascinating archaeological relics represent status, badges, ownership, religion, hunting, and famous battles.

Perthshire, Angus, and Aberdeenshire are modern names for the area that encompassed the Scottish kingdom of Alban in the 9th, 10th, and 11th centuries. The Kings of Alban merit the same credit as Alfred the Great of England for saving their country from 9th-century Viking invaders. But the greater reason this area and period of Scottish history is of interest to the tourist is that it was the scene for one of William Shakespeare's greatest tragedies—*Macbeth.*

Historically, the play derives from events in the time of Malcolm II (1005–29), whose reign was rife with internal feuds. After the death of Malcolm, Macbeth the Mormaer (Earl) of Moray became king by marrying Malcolm's widow, Gruoch, and killing his successor, Duncan, in battle in 1040. Macbeth's reign was one of remarkable contrasts: He and Gruoch were generous benefactors to the shrine of St. Andrew; he went to Rome to see the pope and is said to have scattered "money like seed" there; he was uniquely pious and much more cosmopolitan than any of his predecessors. Nevertheless, his reign also was very violent, marked by continuous struggle to retain the Scottish crown. He was finally defeated and killed at Lumphanan, just west of Aberdeen, in 1057. His successor, Malcolm III, was then uncontested ruler of Scotland and founder of a long dynasty of Scottish kings. Significantly, however, they all ruled in the shadow of the English—a shadow from which Scotland never fully emerged. Shakespeare based his version of events on English stories, and his blatant (if ignorant) sacrifice of historical truth is said by superstitious actors to be the origin of the many disasters in productions of *Macbeth;* because of this "curse," some actors will not even mention the play's name, alluding to it only as "the Scottish play."

The depths of chaos and lawlessness in northeast Scotland were reached during the reign of Robert III (1390–1406). In the last days of the aged and incompetent Robert II, Forres and Elgin were burned by "wyld wykkyd Heland-men." The wild wicked Highland men were in fact led by Alexander Stewart, Earl of Buchan, who came to be known as the "Wolf of Badenoch." Son of the dying Robert II and younger brother of the future Robert III, the Wolf demanded what we now would call protection money, then simply termed "black mail." Perhaps if he had been the first-born son, he might have been the strong king that neither his father nor his brother was able to be (but he also might have been a ruthless tyrant).

Sir James Graham (1612–50), fifth Earl and later first Marquis of Montrose, is one of the most gallant figures of turbulent Scottish history, admired for his sensationally brilliant military campaign of 1644. The year-long campaign had all the ingredients of historical romance and legend and often has been re-created in fiction, most notably by Sir Walter Scott in *A Legend of Montrose.* Although initially with the Covenanter rebels against Charles I, Montrose later joined the king's side. His first victory in 1644 was scored at Tippermuir near Perth. His ragged band of Royalists went on to capture and pillage the city of Aberdeen, after which his reputation for gallantry was deservedly stained, comparing uncomfortably with that of the Wolf of Badenoch. After Aberdeen, Montrose led a campaign unmatched in brilliance since the days of William Wallace and Robert the Bruce (for more information, see the entry for *Stirling,* below). He defeated the Covenanters at Fyvie (about 30 miles northeast of Aberdeen), looted and pillaged Stonehaven, and won further victories at Auldearn (a few miles east of Nairn) and Alford (30 miles west of Aberdeen). Despite these and other victories, Montrose's military genius proved irrelevant to the outcome of the war, which in fact had been decided almost a year earlier when Charles was defeated by Cromwell at Naseby, England. Futile or not, it was one of the most remarkable campaigns in military history. Montrose went into exile, but on his return to Scotland was hanged, on May 21, 1650, in Edinburgh.

Problems with neighbors to the south have dominated Scottish politics and kept the country on tenterhooks for many centuries: through James VI's inheritance of the English throne from Elizabeth I in 1603; through the Act of Union (uniting the Parliaments) in 1707; through the several rebellions for the exiled Stuart Pretenders; and finally through the modern and still continuing crisis of Scottish identity. This intermittent struggle has helped form the Scottish character. In the 14th century, it served to produce history's first nationalist document embodying the wishes of a country and its people. The Declaration of Arbroath, written in 1320 (an original copy of which is on display in *West Register House,* Edinburgh), has been compared by historians and commentators with the American Declaration of Independence and has been ranked one of the world's great assertions in the cause of human freedom.

Northeast Scotland today combines powerful but depopulated landscape with charming seaside resorts and depressed, declining fishing villages. The Highlanders evicted from their crofts in the 18th century were replaced by sheep and their vacant farmland by deer forests for the sport of London-based lairds and their guests. Most recently there has been organized afforestation of the entire region. The oil industry helped some coastal towns to boom, notably Aberdeen, but injured many others. There is evidence of wealth—as at *Gordonstoun School* near Elgin, where the royal family sent their sons, and at *Balmoral,* the royal family's Scottish country residence, west of Aberdeen—but there is also grinding poverty. The region is at times almost incomprehensibly Scottish in manners and mores and particularly in language. (In Aberdeen, for instance, the word *what* is often pronounced "fit.") The alienation of the people and their sense of having been written off by the British government is reflected by the majority voting Scottish Nationalist.

You could spend an entire summer in northeast Scotland and not cover it adequately, for there are literally scores of castles, monuments and ruins, and parks in this area. *Scotland's North-East—What to See and Where to Go,* a free leaflet available at any local tourist information office, provides a comprehensive list of attractions.

This tour route covers 250 miles; allow about a week to cover it comfortably. It begins at Stirling, "the Gateway to the Highlands," and follows northwest through Doune, where it turns eastward to Perth. From Perth it cuts through Braemar, Ballater, and Banchory in Royal Deeside and Stonehaven on the coast on its way to the regional capital city of Aberdeen. From Aberdeen, it cuts inland through Alford and the Malt Whisky Trail center of Dufftown, continues to Nairn, and winds up in Inverness.

A few points to keep in mind: Because most of the drive is along "trunk," or main, roads, there should be no difficulty getting petrol (gasoline) or refreshments. However, for overnight accommodations, book well in advance. Take along a copy of the tourist board's *Scotland for the Motorist* (£3.50/about $5.25) and the annually updated *AA Big Road Atlas of Britain* (£8.99/about $13.50). Another useful source is *The Taste of Scotland* (£3.99/about $6); it lists good hotels and restaurants and is available at branches of the *Scottish Tourist Board* or from the *Taste of Scotland Scheme Ltd.* (33 Melville St., Edinburgh EH3 7JF; phone: 131-220-1900; fax: 131-220-6102).

Hotels listed as expensive will cost $95 or more per night for a double room (with private bath, TV set, and breakfast unless otherwise indicated); moderate ones will cost $65 to $95; and inexpensive places less than $65. Dinner for two, including drinks and tip, will cost $50 or more if listed as expensive, $30 to $50 if moderate, and $30 or less if inexpensive. If you intend to treat yourself to a full-scale restaurant dinner or even lunch, book in advance. All restaurants listed serve lunch and dinner unless otherwise indicated. For each location, hotels and restaurants are listed alphabetically by price category.

En Route from Glasgow or Edinburgh Stirling is a short drive north of Scotland's two largest cities. From Glasgow, take A80 to Dennyloanhead, and from there M80 to Stirling (a distance of 28 miles). From Edinburgh, take A8 to the junction with M9, which heads northwest to Stirling, 37 miles away.

STIRLING Like Edinburgh, Stirling (pop. 36,640) began on an exalted crag and spread downward; unlike Edinburgh, it failed to develop points of interest outside its historic zones. Visitors will spend most of their time in Old Town, the site of *Stirling Castle,* flanked by a handful of aged subsidiary buildings and intriguing ruins. The castle is the most famous in Scottish history, not only for its dramatic 250-foot drop to Stirling Plain and its eye-boggling view, but also for its strategic position, from which it controlled lands to the north during the Middle Ages; for its associations with Robert the Bruce and his predecessor, William Wallace; and for its magnificent Renaissance architecture, lavishly elaborated during its heyday as one of the four royal residences of the Stuart kings. Representations of characters such as Love and Lust on the façade, the work of stonemasons from France employed by Mary of Guise, wife of James V, have been eroded over the centuries but not obliterated. A guidebook available at the castle entrance will increase your knowledge and heighten your enjoyment of the towers built by James III, the fine 15th-century hall, the palace of James V, the parliament hall, and the chapel royal of 1594.

Another attraction of the castle is the *Argyll and Sutherland Highlanders Regimental Museum* (phone: 1786-475165). The castle is headquarters of this regiment—one of the most famous in the British Army. The visitors' center inside the castle (phone: 1786-450000) revives Stirling's past through an imaginative picture gallery and multiscreen show; it also has a restaurant. The castle and center are open daily; admission charge.

Mar's Wark, near the castle, was built in about 1570 by the first Earl of Mar, Regent of Scotland, but was abandoned when the sixth earl had to flee the country after leading a major, but unsuccessful, Jacobite rebellion. The building became a barracks, then a workhouse (hence its name). Bonnie Prince Charlie's army sacked and ruined it in 1746, but some of its exquisite embellishments remain. Also by the castle are the still-used *Church of the Holy Rude,* dating from 1414, where John Knox preached the sermon when James VI, aged 13 months, was crowned (closed October through April except for Sunday services); the *Guildhall,* south of the church, founded in 1649 by the then dean of the guild for the support of 12 "decayed Guild Breithers"; and an impressive 17th-century townhouse, *Argyll's Lodging,* once the residence of Sir William Alexander of Menstrie, founder of Nova Scotia. An exhibition displaying the coats of arms of 107 Nova Scotian baronetcies is at 16th-century *Menstrie Castle,* Sir William's birthplace 5 miles east of Stirling on A91. Open daily by arrangement with the *National Trust for Scotland* (phone: 1738-631296 in Perth); admission charge. *Cambuskenneth Abbey,* on the river Forth a mile northeast of Stirling, was founded in the 12th century by the Scottish King David I, and was the scene in 1326 of King Robert the Bruce's first formal parliament. The church and conventual buildings are rubble, but a detached 67-foot, 13th-century bell tower survives intact.

The Scottish Wars of Independence, which took place around the turn of the 13th century, were distinguished for the valor not only of the aristocrat King Robert the Bruce ("Robert de Brus" in his native Norman tongue) but also of William Wallace, the People's Hero, who drove back an English army in 1297 at the Battle of Stirling Bridge, half a mile northeast of the castle. Wallace's triumph was short-lived—he was defeated at Falkirk in 1298 by a massive avenging force, imprisoned in London, and hacked limb from limb in 1305—but his memory is sacred in Scottish hearts. The grandly towering *Wallace Monument,* near the site of his triumph (off Hillfoots Rd., a mile north-northeast of town), is a famous landmark, erected in 1861. Inside, the *Stirling District Council* offers an audiovisual historical crash course. Views are heavenly from its 220-foot top. The monument is closed November through March; admission charge (phone: 1786-472140).

Bannockburn, off M80 just south of Stirling, is a must. Beside the battlefield is the *Bannockburn Heritage Centre,* which includes a film theater where the full story of the Wars of Independence can be viewed and a *Heritage Exhibition* detailing the fascinating history of Scottish kings, called "Kingdom of the Scots." The center is closed November through March; admission charge (phone: 1786-812664). Robert the Bruce was not eager to fight the English at the time and place now so famous for his victory, but his hand had been forced by his brother, who made a deal in 1313 with the Governor of *Stirling Castle*—in English hands since soon after the defeat of Wallace—securing the castle's return to Scotland if the English did not relieve it by *St. John the Baptist's Day* (*Midsummer Day*) of the following year (the Bruces had the castle under siege). On *Midsummer Day,* 1314, 20,000 English troops, commanded by King Edward II himself, marched on the castle. The Bruce's tactics were brilliant: He let the English come within 2 hair-raising miles of the target and then attacked—on the only piece of ground on Edward's route north where his mere 5,500 spearmen could hope to hold out—at first light, before the king's cavalry could see to charge. Finding themselves cut off to the left and right by unexpected and treacherous marshes, Edward's stalwarts fell back in confusion and flight. A magnificent 20-foot equestrian statue of Robert the Bruce in shining armor, unveiled by Queen Elizabeth on the battle's 650th anniversary, stands today on the spot reputed to have been the Scottish royal headquarters during the fighting. *Midsummer Day* is still celebrated every year in June.

Also to be seen in Stirling are its old mercat (market) cross and its 18th-century tolbooth on Broad Street; the bastion, or jail, within the original fortified town wall, just inside the Port Street entrance to the *Thistle Shopping Centre;* the 15th-century Auld Brig still used by pedestrians at Stirling Bridge (north of the city center off A9); and the *Smith Art Gallery and Museum* (Dumbarton Rd.; phone: 1786-471917), housing, among other treasures, objects from early local history. The museum is open year-round, but its schedule varies; call for hours. There is an admission charge. The *MacRobert Arts Centre* (phone: 1786-461081), one of Scotland's foremost music, film, and theater venues, is on the grounds of *Stirling University* off A9, 2 miles north of town. An important event is the *Stirling Tartan Festival,* held the second and third weeks of July. It includes tartan exhibitions, pipeband championships, *ceilidhs,* dancing, tartan banquets, and beating of the retreat from the *Castle Esplanade.* Throughout the summer, there are medieval plays and historical reenactments. The *Stirling Tourist Office* (Dumbarton Rd.; phone: 1786-475019) is open daily.

BEST EN ROUTE

Cromlix House This grand house, built in 1874 and situated about 9 miles north of Stirling, had fallen into disrepair before being completely and faithfully renovated and opened as a hotel a few years ago. The 14 spacious rooms and large public areas have been decorated with fine antiques and country floral fabrics, and the restaurant features updated versions of classic dishes such as supreme of chicken layered with rosemary and apricot stuffing, and a combination of various types of seafood with a cucumber and dill yogurt cream. Tennis courts, clay shooting, and off-road driving are available on the 3,000-acre grounds; fishing and golf are arranged nearby. There's also a small private chapel attached to the house. On B8033 in Kinbuck, north of Dunblane (phone: 1786-822125; fax: 1786-825450). Expensive.

Gean House This former mill owner's mansion has been exquisitely decorated with French antiques, chandeliers from *Wilkinson of London* (makers of chandeliers for the royal family, including the queen), and lots of overstuffed couches in fine fabrics. The seven bedrooms are also luxuriously appointed, and the dining room is a local favorite because of sumptuous specialties such as duck magret with an orange and Grand Marnier sauce and a super rich bread and butter pudding. Tullibody Rd. in Alloa, 7 miles east of Stirling (phone: 1259-219275; fax: 1259-213827). Expensive.

Royal As a boy, Robert Louis Stevenson stayed in this impressive mansion (now a 32-guestroom hotel), when his family visited the nearby spa. There is a good restaurant. Henderson St., in Bridge of Allan, 4 miles north of Stirling (phone: 1786-832284; fax: 1786-834377). Expensive.

Stakis Dunblane Hydro Set in a 60-acre park, this is the largest hotel in the area and a holiday center in itself. Along with 215 well-equipped rooms and a restaurant serving traditional Scottish fare, amenities include a heated indoor pool, a sauna, tennis courts, a sports hall, and a Jacuzzi. Located in Dunblane, 7 miles north of Stirling (phone: 1786-822551; 800-STAKIS-1; fax: 1786-825403). Expensive.

Stirling Highland A modern property with 76 rooms and four suites located in the grand building that formerly housed the town's high school. There are six meeting rooms; a leisure center with pool, steamroom, and sauna; a snooker room; two restaurants; and a bar in what was once the headmaster's study. Spittal St., Stirling (phone: 1786-475444; fax: 1786-462929). Expensive.

Golden Lion This modest but historic 71-room hotel is the best of Stirling's center-city choices. Robert Burns, the royal family, and a host of film stars have all been guests. The dining room offers topnotch continental fare, and there's a fast-food restaurant serving fish-and-chips and sandwiches as well. 8 King St., Stirling (phone: 1786-475351; fax: 1786-472755). Moderate.

Heritage Beauty and charm abound in this lovely candelit restaurant in a modest 18th-century house that also has four moderately priced bedrooms. Superbly prepared (and presented) Scottish and French dishes are the highlights here. Open daily. Reservations advised. MasterCard and Visa accepted. 16 Allan Park, Stirling (phone: 1786-473660). Moderate.

Number 39 This unpretentious restaurant in Old Town specializes in fresh seafood dishes, such as wild salmon and Hebridean fish soup. Closed Sundays and Mondays. Reservations advised. Major credit cards accepted. 39 Broad St., Stirling (phone: 1786-473929). Moderate to inexpensive.

Cross Keys Inn Dinner at this little Scottish pub with a restaurant and three guestrooms is worth the 10-mile run from town. Steaks are the specialty. Open daily for dinner only. Reservations necessary. Major credit cards accepted. In Kippen Village, via A811 west of Stirling (phone: 1786-870293). Inexpensive.

Garfield One of this Victorian townhouse's finer points is its convenient location near Old Stirling and the castle. Its eight guestrooms are spacious, airy, and altogether charming. Tasty regional fare is served in the small, intimate dining room, and if you like whisky, make a beeline for the bar—the selection is excellent. 12 Victoria Sq., Stirling (phone/fax: 1786-473730). Inexpensive.

En Route from Stirling Take A84 north about 8 miles to Doune.

DOUNE The dark fastnesses of 14th-century *Doune Castle,* ancestral seat of the Earls of Moray, have lasted unscathed. Not so some of its owners: the "Bonnie Earl" of Moray, who was the "Queen's love" in the famous murder ballad (actually he was her nephew; the queen was Mary, Queen of Scots), was killed by the Earl of Huntly in a clan feud in 1592. *Doune Castle* is beautifully set in a wooden clearing at the junction of the Teith and Ardoch Rivers, reached just before Doune Village by taking a side road off A84. The castle is open daily; no admission charge (phone: 1786-841742). In the mid-1970s, the comedy troupe *Monty Python* filmed *Monty Python and the Holy Grail* in the town and surrounding area, including the castle.

Doune Village has a 16th-century bridge, built by James IV's tailor to spite a ferryman who had refused him passage. A mile north of the village is the *Doune Motor Museum,* exhibiting the present Earl of Moray's collection of 50 vintage cars, including the second-oldest Rolls-Royce in the world. The museum is closed November through March; admission charge (phone: 1786-841203). Nearby on the A84 is the magnificent *Blair Drummond Safari and Leisure Park.* Attractions include a comprehensive selection of animals, picnic sites, boat trips, a petting zoo, an adventure playground, shops, and a restaurant. It makes for an ideal family outing. The park is closed early October through early April; admission charge (phone: 1786-841456).

En Route from Doune Take A820 east to A9 north. In Dunblane (4½ miles from Doune), you'll pass *Dunblane Cathedral,* a 13th-century building that was a victim of the Reformation but was restored in 1892. About 10 miles farther, near Auchterarder, are the signs for *Gleneagles,* the distinguished resort and golfer's paradise (for details, see *Perth* in THE CITIES). There are also several antiques shops in Auchterarder, perfect for an afternoon's browsing. Continue on A9 for 15 miles to Perth.

PERTH For a detailed report on the city, its sights, hotels, and restaurants, see *Perth* in THE CITIES.

En Route from Perth Leave Perth via A9 and head north; Dunkeld is about 14 miles farther.

DUNKELD A quaint little town on the river Tay with only a few hundred residents, this was once the home of Pictish kings and later, around AD 729, the site of an abbey founded by Columban monks—St. Columba is purported to have come to the town a century earlier. The most famous landmark in Dunkeld is the impressive cathedral (phone: 1350-244-3101), which was begun in 1318 and completed nearly two centuries later. During the Reformation, however, it was reduced to a roofless ruin; the restored choir is used as the parish church. The cathedral contains the elaborate tomb of church destroyer Wolf of Badenoch.

Dunkeld Cathedral may be the most visible evidence of destruction in town, but it's far from the only site that was damaged. Following the defeat of King William III's army by the Jacobite Highlanders at Killiecrankie, the town was ravaged heavily when the Highlanders stormed it during the Battle of Dunkeld in 1689; what visitors see today is a town rebuilt during the 18th and 19th centuries. The *National Trust* has restored the town's charming black and white cottages called "The Little Houses"; they line the street leading to the cathedral.

While in town, visitors can browse in the antiques shops, pick up some smoked Tay salmon or smoked salmon pâté at *Dunkeld Smoked Salmon* (Brae St.; phone: 1350-727639) or have a cup of tea and some fresh-baked cake at *Tappit Hen* (7 Atholl St.; phone: 1350-727472).

BEST EN ROUTE

Kinnaird A stunningly decorated country house with nine bedrooms on a huge 9,000-acre estate overlooking the river Tay. There are also sports facilities and a fine restaurant. For more information, see *Rural Retreats* in DIVERSIONS. Open March through January. Kinnaird Estate by Dunkeld (phone: 1796-482440; fax: 1796-482289). Very expensive.

Stakis Dunkeld House Built around the original country house of the Earls of Atholl, this 92-room hotel has a spectacular location—directly on the river Tay on 280 acres—and many modern conveniences such as 24-hour room service, laundry service, and a leisure club with pool, sauna, and gym. There's also a restaurant. Other sporting facilities include tennis courts, two private fishing boats, off-road driving, rafting, golf, and a shooting academy. On A923 near Dunkeld (phone: 1350-727771; fax: 1350-728924). Expensive to moderate.

En Route from Dunkeld Take A923 east, a winding road that passes through 12 miles of scenic farming country before reaching Blairgowrie. While the town itself isn't worthy of a stop, nearby is *Kinloch House,* a notable inn for an overnight stay or a meal (see *Best en Route*). For an interesting afternoon's detour from the main route, leave Blairgowrie by A923 south to A94 east, which leads to Glamis (pronounced *Gloms;* the *i* is silent), about 10 miles away.

BEST EN ROUTE

Kinloch House This 19th-century country house set on 25 acres has 21 bedrooms furnished in upscale country decor—rich floral prints, four-poster beds, and period antiques. Fishing, golf, and shooting are easily arranged; and there is a very good restaurant, known for its Highland salmon marinated in honey and whisky. Closed two weeks at *Christmas.* Reservations advised for restaurant. No credit cards accepted. About 3 miles west of Blairgowrie (phone: 1250-884237; fax: 1250-884333). Expensive.

GLAMIS Fairy-tale *Glamis Castle* was the towering, turreted, historic home of the Lyon family, Earls of Strathmore and Kinghorne (the present queen mother, the former Elizabeth Bowes Lyon, was born here). It claims association with the Macbeth story and also has its own legend of a monster. The castle and grounds offer many attractions, including a tearoom, shops, a formal garden, a nature trail, and a picnic area. The castle is closed November through March; admission charge (phone: 1307-840242). In Glamis Village is the *Angus Folk Museum,* a treasure for folklore enthusiasts. It is closed October through April; admission charge (phone: 1307-840288). The museum staff will direct you to the garden of the nearby manse, where there is a sculpted Pictish stone.

En Route from Glamis An interesting side trip from Glamis is to take A928 north about 5 miles to Kirriemuir, the birthplace of Sir James Matthew Barrie (1860–1937)—author of *Peter Pan*—where there is a museum of his memorabilia. The museum is closed October through April; admission charge (phone: 1575-572646).

From Kirriemuir, return to the main route by taking A926 west for 12 miles to Blairgowrie, and then take A93 north 33 miles to Braemar, the entry point to the area of the Grampian Highlands known as Royal Deeside. Queen Victoria and Prince Albert established the royal presence here in 1852 by buying the estate at *Balmoral,* 9 miles east of Braemar, to which the queen and other members of the royal family repair every summer. While staying at *Balmoral* in 1848, Victoria and Albert rode on ponies up Lochnagar, the towering 3,738-foot mountain nearby. Not many people have that kind of stamina today.

Note: If you plan to drive A93 in this area, keep an eye on the weather.

At an elevation of 2,199 feet at the Cairnwell Pass north of Spittal of Glenshee, A93 is often closed if it snows—which it's been known to do into May. If in doubt, have your hotel check with the area police; they keep tabs on when the road will reopen.

BRAEMAR As the road approaches Braemar, the scenery softens, with trees replacing the jagged mountains. As the midpoint of this picturesque scenery, Braemar is a popular base for hikers and mountain climbers. For information on walking tours, including ranger-led walks in summer, contact the tourist information center on Mar Road (phone: 13397-41600); it's open daily.

Braemar may be the busiest town in Scotland on the first Saturday in September, when at least 50,000 people flood into *Princess Royal and Duke of Fife Memorial Park* to watch the *Braemar Royal Highland Gathering* and to catch a glimpse of the royal family, who usually attend. This full-scale gathering of the clans dates back to the 11th century, when King Malcolm III staged a contest so he could conscript the victors into his army. Now, the competitions are more likely to include piping, Highland dancing, and tossing the caber. (To reserve seats, write to The Bookings Secretary, *Braemar Royal Highland Society,* Coilacriech, Ballater, Aberdeenshire AB35 5UH, Scotland; phone: 13397-55377).

The rest of the year, visitors can trace their own clan heritage at the *Braemar Highland Heritage Centre* (Mar Rd., Braemar; phone: 13397-41944; fax: 13397-41405). Scottish descendants can type one of 17,000 names into a computer and get either their clan's history and an illustration of its tartan or (if they aren't affiliated with a clan) information on their family history and original home turf. The center also features a photo exhibition on the *Gathering* and a video on the area's royal connections. It is open daily; admission charge for the video presentation.

Braemar's other main attraction is *Braemar Castle,* a half-mile out of town on A93. A fortress built in 1628 by the Earl of Mar, it was burned by the Farquharson clan in 1689, then repaired and used by the English to garrison troops after the Jacobite uprisings in 1715 and 1745. The Farquharsons later came into the picture again, buying the castle and transforming it into one of the area's most charming, with rounded towers and vaulted ceilings. The castle is closed Fridays and November through April; admission charge (phone: 13397-41219).

BEST EN ROUTE

Braemar Lodge This Victorian house, a former shooting lodge, is just a few minutes' walk from the center of town. There are five pretty bedrooms and a housekeeping cottage, all with views of the mountains; the Taste of Scotland restaurant offers dishes such as breast of duck with green peppercorns and apples flambéed in brandy and cream. Fishing and shooting excursions can be arranged. On A93 just south of Braemar (phone/fax: 13397-41627). Expensive to moderate.

Fife Arms Conveniently located in the center of town, this rather plain-looking 84-room hotel has plenty of modern conveniences, including a sauna. The restaurant serves good, basic British dishes such as roast beef and Yorkshire pudding. Mar Rd., Braemar (phone: 13397-41644; fax: 13397-41545). Expensive to moderate.

Cranford Guest House Not far from the center of town, this bright, cheerful house has six tastefully decorated bedrooms, some with mountain views. There is also a restaurant. 15 Glenshee Rd., Braemar (phone: 13397-41675). Inexpensive.

En Route from Braemar Take A93 out of Braemar and continue northeast about 17 miles to Ballater. Along the way, the route gets even more scenic, with the river Dee threading through velvety green hills flanked by purplish blue mountains. It also gets progressively more royal. Nine miles east of Braemar is *Balmoral,* the country house on 24,000 acres that Victoria and Albert bought for £31,500 and transformed into a baronial palace. The grounds, gardens, and an exhibition in the ballroom are closed to the public Sundays and when the royals are in residence (phone: 13397-42334). Just north of *Balmoral* is *Crathie Church,* which the royals attend, and where Princess Anne held her second wedding. It's closed to the public November through March (except for Sunday services). In contrast to this spiritual place is an earthier one which was also patronized by royalty: Royal Lochnagar Distillery (phone: 13397-42273), a mile east of *Balmoral.* It opened its doors in 1845 and was soon visited by Queen Victoria and Prince Albert. It's been offering tours and tastings ever since. It's closed weekends (except by appointment) November through February.

BALLATER This pretty town came into existence in 1760 when an old woman claimed she had cured herself of a skin disease by immersing herself in a bog here. Inspired by the tale, a local laird, Colonel Francis Farquharson, built a spa that immediately became fashionable. The arrival of Queen Victoria and Prince Albert at *Balmoral* spurred still more growth. Now with 1,051 residents, the town is an upscale resort notable for the number of "By appointment to the Queen" designations displayed on the shops. Those with a sweet tooth should try the shortbread at *G. Leith & Son* (8 Golf Rd.; phone: 13397-55474; closed Sundays); this tiny shop furnishes pastries to the queen and the queen mother. Ballater also has several good hotels; when a royal scandal is brewing (a more frequent occurrence in recent years), the town becomes the base for inquiring journalists. Book ahead to be sure of accommodations.

BEST EN ROUTE

Balgonie Country House A beautifully decorated turn-of-the-century country house on four acres, with nine bedrooms, most offering views of the *Ballater* golf course and the Glen Muick hills. Fishing and hiking are nearby, as well as golf. Dinner, featuring such specialties as roast wild duck with honey-braised red cabbage and filet of Scotch salmon with a fricassee of monkfish and shrimp, is a special occasion; lunch is also available to guests by prior arrangement. Braemar Pl., Ballater (phone/fax: 13397-55482). Expensive.

Tullich Lodge A pink granite baronial mansion with views over the Dee Valley, this country hotel has 10 individually decorated bedrooms and a good restaurant serving a small (but ever-changing) menu each night. Golf, fishing, and trails for hiking are nearby. Open April through November. On A93 one mile east of Ballater (phone: 13397-55406; fax: 13397-55397). Expensive.

Darroch Learg A former shooting lodge built in the late 19th century, this 20-room hotel stands on a hill with wondrous views over the Dee Valley. The Taste of Scotland restaurant features inventive dishes such as *gâteau* of woodland mushrooms, tomatoes, and polenta; and roast stuffed boneless quail with parsnip *confit.* Clay-pigeon shooting, golf, gliding, pony trekking, fishing, and mountain biking can be arranged. Open February through December. On A93 just before Ballater (phone/fax: 13397-55443). Moderate.

Coach House This small, comfortable hotel with six rooms lies just off Ballater's town square. (Ask for No. 5, which is the largest and has the best view of the town.) There is also a Taste of Scotland restaurant. Netherley Pl., Ballater (phone/fax: 13397-55462). Inexpensive.

Green Inn There are just three bedrooms in this charming, tiny inn just off the town square; if you can't stay here, at least come for dinner. Offerings change daily but can include Aberdeen Angus stuffed with smoked oysters, *suprême* of salmon, and sticky toffee pudding with date and armagnac ice cream. The hotel is closed a week in January and two weeks in October; the restaurant is also closed weekday lunch. Reservations advised. MasterCard and Visa accepted. 9 Victoria Rd., Ballater (phone: 13397-55701). Inexpensive.

En Route from Ballater The A93 continues east another 25 miles, passing through the villages of Aboyne (site of the *Aboyne Games* in August, a smaller version of the *Braemar Royal Highland Gathering*), and Kincardine O'Neil before reaching Banchory, a town that these days is mainly a community of oil executives who work in Aberdeen. Its location next to the river Dee, however, does provide excellent opportunities for fishing. As a result, there are two highly regarded hotels in the area.

BEST EN ROUTE

Banchory Lodge A cozy 22-room coaching inn from the 16th century, this is such a prime angling spot that you may well see that day's salmon catch displayed as you check in. There is a restaurant and a beautiful lounge where you can sip afternoon tea and enjoy excellent views of the river. For more information, see *Gone Fishing* in DIVERSIONS. Open February through December. In Banchory, just off A93 (phone: 1330-822625; fax: 1330-825019). Expensive.

Raemoir House The 28 bedrooms in this 18th-century mansion and its 16th-century annex are filled with unusual antiques, such as a 400-year-old Norse four-poster bed with intricate carving. The property sits on a 3,500-acre estate with a tennis court, a croquet lawn, a nine-hole pitch-and-putt golf course, and an exercise room. Fishing and shooting excursions can be arranged. There's also a good restaurant. On A980 about 2 miles north of Banchory (phone: 1330-824884; fax: 1330-822171). Expensive.

En Route from Banchory About 3 miles east of Banchory on A93 is one of the most impressive castles in the region, *Crathes Castle,* the turreted 16th-century domain of the Burnett family of Leys (for more information, see *Stately Homes and Great Gardens* in DIVERSIONS). The castle is closed November through March, but the grounds are open daily; admission charge (phone: 1330-844525). From *Crathes Castle,* pick up A957 and continue 12 miles until you reach Stonehaven.

STONEHAVEN An ideal seaside resort, with sea fishing, sailing, golf, and other family attractions, Stonehaven is also a good place to be when it rains because of its leisure center (phone: 1569-763162), which features an indoor pool and a variety of other activities. Among the town's other attractions is the *Fowlsheugh RSPB (Royal Society for the Protection of Birds) Seabird Colony,* which is open daily (phone: 624824). The Stonehaven harbor, which used to be important as a fishing center, is now host to pleasure yachts, for which it is ideally suited. The oldest building in town—the tolbooth at the harbor—houses the *Tolbooth Museum* and its collection of local artifacts. Closed Tuesdays and October through May; admission charge (phone: 779-477778). A good place for local crafts such as Highland stoneware and hand-knit sweaters is *Just Scottish* (33 Allardice St., phone: 1569-767225).

Just south of Stonehaven on the A92 is *Dunnotar Castle.* This dramatic fortified ruin, with its crumbling walls dashed by violent waves, is the stuff of which poetry is made—indeed, Franco Zefferelli used it as the main locale for his 1990 film version of *Hamlet.* Once the home of the fervid Covenanter, Earl of Marischal, the castle was considered the strongest fortress in the land. The Scottish crown jewels were brought here for protection in 1651 during the Civil War; they were then smuggled out under the eyes of the besieging Cromwellian forces and buried under the floor of the nearby *Kinneff Church* until the restoration of Charles II in 1660. It is said that 167 Covenanters were imprisoned in a single dungeon here in 1685; the stone recording the names of those who died may be found in the Dunnotar churchyard. The castle is closed weekends November through February; admission charge (phone: 1569-762173).

Muchalls Castle This baronial mansion, built in 1619 by the Burnett family, is now a charming hotel. Owner Glenda Cormack has filled the eight bedrooms with antiques she has discovered in the area, such as the gold and crimson canopy under which James VI slept. Especially noteworthy are the ornate sculpted plaster ceilings dating from 1624. The dining room serves simple British fare. No credit cards accepted. To get here, travel a mile north of Stonehaven on the road signposted to Netherley, turn right onto a badly paved road, and continue a mile to the castle (phone: 1569-731170; fax: 1569-731480). Expensive to moderate.

Heugh Small (six rooms) but highly regarded, this establishment in a granite baronial mansion boasts oak paneling and turrets. Horseback riding and golf are among the sports offered, and there is a fine restaurant. Westfield Rd., Stonehaven (phone: 1569-762379; fax: 1569-766637). Moderate.

Marine The main attraction of this six-room hostelry (no private baths) is its unique location overlooking the harbor. There is a restaurant. Shorehead, Stonehaven (phone: 1569-762155; fax: 1569-766691). Moderate to inexpensive.

Royal Set in Stonehaven's former *Town Hall,* this hotel offers fine service and traditional Scottish food. You also can fish, water-ski, and ride horses; and there's a nearby golf course. Eight of the 18 rooms have spectacular sea views (No. 14 also has a four-poster bed), and 14 have private baths. Market Sq., Stonehaven (phone: 1569-762979; fax: 1569-763122). Inexpensive.

En Route from Stonehaven Continue north on A90, a pleasant drive along the Aberdeenshire coastline that often parallels the sea. Approaching Aberdeen, about 14 miles up the coast from Stonehaven, A90 bears left and A956 forks right. Both roads lead into Aberdeen.

ABERDEEN For a detailed report on the city, its sights, hotels, and restaurants, see *Aberdeen* in THE CITIES.

En Route from Aberdeen Take A93 southwest from Aberdeen and continue about 10 miles to *Drum Castle,* a beautifully preserved and furnished 17th-century castle and 13th-century tower (one of the three oldest towers in Scotland). Featured on the landscaped grounds is the *Historic Rose Garden,* a two-acre walled garden showcasing rosebushes planted from the 18th century to the present. The castle and gardens are closed November through March; the castle is also closed weekdays in April and October; the grounds are open daily. There is an admission charge (phone: 1330-811204).

At Banchory, about 7 miles from *Drum Castle,* pick up A980 heading north. About 15 miles farther is the castle many think is the prettiest in

Scotland and the one said to have inspired *Disneyland*'s "Sleeping Beauty Castle": *Craigievar Castle.* The fairy-tale pink structure was built in 1626 for William Forbes, a Baltic merchant known as "Danzig Willie" and brother of the Bishop of Aberdeen. Today, it's perfectly preserved and filled with Forbes family treasures. Although the castle remains open to the public, the *National Trust* prefers that visitors only view it from outside; too many feet pounding through have started to endanger its foundations and ceilings. The castle is closed October through April, but the grounds are open daily; admission charge (phone: 1467-622988).

En Route from Craigievar Castle Continue on A980. About 6 miles farther, at Bridge of Alford, pick up A944 west heading towards Mossat. Another 10 miles along, just south of A944 on A97, is *Kildrummy Castle,* another impressive sight. Though now a ruin, it is the best example of a 13th-century stone castle in Scotland. It was built by St. Gilbert, Bishop Gilbert de Moravia, but just before completion, the area was taken over by Edward I of England and an English-style gatehouse was added. In 1306, a battle raged there between the armies of the future Edward II and Scottish leader Sir Nigel Bruce; *Kildrummy* fell after a blacksmith, bribed with the promise of gold, set fire to it. Over the next century, it was again besieged, and finally much of it was dismantled. Still, it's been described as the noblest of "Northern" castles. For more information, contact the *National Trust* office in Edinburgh (phone: 131-244-3101). The castle is closed weekdays October through March; admission charge.

BEST EN ROUTE

Kildrummy Castle Hotel Proving once again that location is everything, this turn-of-the-century baronial mansion with 16 bedrooms on a five-acre patch of ground has a view overlooking the castle. The Honeybarrel Room even has a stone terrace looking directly down on the ruin; when the night turns misty, the effect is magical. The hotel's decor is sumptuous, from the intricate wood paneling of the main lobby to the antiques and four-poster beds in the guestrooms. Its Taste of Scotland restaurant is also noteworthy, with home-baked breads, pies, and pastries. Golf, fishing, and clay-pigeon shooting can be arranged. Open February through December. On A97, Kildrummy by Alford (phone: 19755-71288; fax: 19755-71345). Expensive to moderate.

En Route from Kildrummy The most direct route from *Kildrummy Castle* follows A97 north 5 miles to A941, a narrow, winding road that continues another 18 miles through the gentle hills of the Spey Valley to Dufftown, the center of the Malt Whisky Trail.

DUFFTOWN Founded in 1817 by James Duff, the fourth Earl of Fife, Dufftown (pronounced *Duff*-ton) is an orderly town. All of its roads converge on the ornate *Clock Tower,* which houses a museum that exhibits photographs and other displays about the town's history (open summer only; no admission charge). The tourist office (phone: 1340-820501), also in the tower, is open daily in summer only; in winter, you can get information by calling 1343-542666 in nearby Elgin. There is an impressive ruin, *Balvenie Castle,* just north of town; the pre-Norman *Mortlach Church* is in Dufftown itself; and nearby Ballindalloch has *Ballindalloch Castle,* a majestic structure built by the Macpherson-Grant clan and still occupied today by Claire Russell, a descendant of the clan, and her husband, Oliver. The castle, built in the 16th century, houses an impressive collection of antique furniture, fine china, and gilt mirrors. *Ballindalloch Castle* is closed November through March; admission charge (phone: 1807-500206). Without a doubt, however, the area's main draw is the Malt Whisky Trail, a collection of distilleries spanning 70 miles, including the following: Cardhu (phone: 1340-810204; admission charge) and Tamdhu (phone: 1340-810486; admission charge), both in Knockando; Glen Grant (phone: 1340-831413; no admission charge) in Rothes; Glenlivet (phone: 1807-590427; no admission charge) in Glenlivet; and Strathisla (phone: 1542-887471; no admission charge) in Keith. Directions are available in a leaflet provided at the tourist office, and signs also are posted on the roads.

Deciding which distillery to visit primarily depends on which is nearest to you at the moment, but Glenfiddich (on A941 just north of Dufftown; phone: 1340-820373) is usually singled out as the most sophisticated. It has an impressive audiovisual show before the tour and tasting. It's closed weekends mid-October through *Easter.* Another fine distillery, Glenfarclas, is in nearby Ballindalloch. Tours of the facility, established in 1836, are offered weekdays year-round and on Saturdays June through September. There is an admission charge (phone: 1807-500245). Also see *Quintessential Great Britain* in DIVERSIONS.

BEST EN ROUTE

The Cross Several miles south of the Malt Whisky Trail but worth the trip, this nine-room hotel occupies a former 19th-century tweed mill. The rooms are light and airy, and some feature skylights; No. 3 has a balcony overlooking a rushing stream. The fine fare includes such specialties as roast Gressingham duck with a sauce of cranberries and ginger and goat cheese soufflé. Open March through November; restaurant closed Tuesdays and Wednesday lunch. Reservations necessary. MasterCard and Visa accepted. Tweed Mill Brae, Kingussie (phone: 1540-661166; fax: 1540-661080). Expensive.

Delnashaugh Inn A cozy whitewashed spot overlooking the Spey Valley and the river Avon, it has nine cheerful, colorful rooms, all with hair dryers. As part of the *Ballindalloch Estate,* which also contains *Ballindalloch Castle* (see above), the inn has access to the river for salmon and trout fishing and the estate's 25,000 acres for hiking. Golf and shooting also can be arranged.

The dining room serves simple Scottish food. Open March through November. On A95 in Ballindalloch (phone: 1807-500255; fax: 1807-500389). Expensive to moderate.

Minmore House This pretty Victorian house, which formerly belonged to George Smith, founder of Glenlivet distillery, is on five acres of grounds next to the distillery. There are 10 beautifully decorated rooms. Meals are sophisticated and excellent, including a lavish complimentary afternoon tea. Fishing and golf can be arranged, and there's a pool and tennis court on the property. Open May through mid-October. On B9008 in Glenlivet (phone: 1807-590378; fax: 1807-590472). Moderate.

A Taste of Speyside Here is a small café showcasing local fare, such as roast loin of Scottish lamb and heather honey and malt whisky cheesecake. Try the Speyside platter, a selection of whiskied chicken liver pâté, smoked salmon, smoked venison, herring, and farmhouse cheese. Closed November through February. Reservations unnecessary. Major credit cards accepted. 10 Balvenie St. (phone: 1340-820860). Moderate to inexpensive.

En Route from Dufftown Follow A941 northwest about 4 miles to Craigellachie, then take A95 south 24 miles through Ballindalloch and the rolling, misty hills of the Spey Valley to Grantown-on-Spey. At Grantown-on-Spey, take A939 north another 24 miles to Nairn.

NAIRN An attractive holiday resort on the coast overlooking the Moray Firth, Nairn has a year-round population of 7,366. The English call this town "Brighton of the North," and it's a Shangri-la for golfers, with two excellent courses, *Nairn* (phone: 1667-452787) to the west and *Nairn Dunbar* (phone: 1667-452741) to the east. The Brighton comparison stems from the Victorian urban planning, particularly on the west side of town. The *Nairn Museum* at the *Viewfield House* (on King St.; no phone) is a 150-year-old institution admired for its varied ethnographic, folk life, and natural history exhibits. It's open June through September, but on an erratic schedule; call ahead for hours. There's no admission charge. The *Highland Railway Museum* (Station Platform, phone: 1456-450527) has a sizable collection of railroad memorabilia such as maps, plaques, and photographs. Call for operating schedule; admission charge. There also is a tourist information office (62 King St.; phone: 1667-452753), which is closed November through *Easter.*

Just 5 miles south of town on B9090 is *Cawdor Castle,* which Shakespeare depicted as the place where Macbeth stabbed King Duncan (although, if true, Lady Macbeth moved faster than anyone else in literary history: She had barely received the news of Macbeth's being made Thane of Cawdor before being discovered at home in their castle). It's been the seat of Thanes of Cawdor for 600 years (which rules it out as a home for the "real" Macbeths). This place truly has everything: a drawbridge, a tower built around a tree, a freshwater well inside the house, gardens, nature trails, a pitch-and-putt golf course, a picnic area, snack bar, licensed restaurant, and gift shop. It's closed early October through April; admission charge (phone: 1667-404615).

BEST EN ROUTE

Clifton House This huge Victorian house is a fun place to stay due to the friendly, exuberant personality of owner Gordon Macintyre (a major theater buff, he has lots of scrapbooks and other mementos of British theater). The decor throughout the house is in bright colors, with paintings and other artwork. There are 12 rooms, some with four-posters and some with views of the Moray Firth. Excellent Scottish cooking. Open March through October. Viewfield St. (phone: 1667-453119; fax: 1667-452836). Moderate.

Longhouse In a former fisherman's cottage, this charming restaurant specializes in seafood such as monkfish in a red pepper cream. Closed Mondays; no dinner on Sundays. Reservations advised. Major credit cards accepted. 8 Harbour St. (phone: 1667-455532). Moderate.

Sunny Brae A real charmer, this lovely little white cottage has 10 rooms with unparalleled views of the sea. Each guestroom is prettily appointed, and the extensive gardens are breathtaking. Fine Scottish fare is served nightly in the dining room. And for absolute privacy, there is a cozy chalet with two bedrooms in the back garden. Open April through October. Marine Rd., Nairn (phone: 1667-452309). Inexpensive.

En Route from Nairn Take A96 another 16 miles to Inverness. For information on this city, see *Northwest Scottish Highlands* in this section.

Northwest Scottish Highlands

The northwest Highlands of Scotland: The very words evoke romantic visions of hill and glen, bagpipe and drum, purple heather and curling mist. But behind the picture-postcard Highlands seen by every visitor from Queen Victoria to Pope John Paul II is a real Highlands that, though scenically among the most glorious places on earth, was for centuries a land of harsh living conditions, brutal internecine clan warfare, and rank exploitation by aristocratic power. It is a kind of divine wilderness suffering from depopulation even today.

That, however, only makes it more attractive to travelers, who can still escape to paradise for two or three weeks in the Highlands, away from the grime and confusion of modern city life. Just driving through the mountains, with their ancient Gaelic names (Beinn Eildeach, Beinn Eighe, Sgurr Dubh) and their plethora of interlinking waterways, is a soul-stirring experience. Even better is getting out and walking—hill-walking, as it's called (it's really mountain climbing), is one of the great Scots pastimes—or just stroll down the glens and look up! Climbers should have a compass, warm clothes, and the right sort of boots, since the hills have everything underfoot from bogs to "scree" (loose slate rubble). And beware of hidden treacheries: A hike to a seemingly low peak from a warm sunlit valley could lead into snow, thick fog, and a loss of direction. Every year people die on Scottish mountains from lack of knowledge, equipment, and good judgment.

Historically, where the Lowlands came under English, French, Norman, and Scandinavian influence, the west Highlands were dominated by the Irish, so that truc Highlanders, those with Celtic blood, are very like their cousins in the Emerald Isle (always excepting Dublin). They are socially conservative, community conscious, and hostile to cosmopolitan ideas; they are courteously hospitable and as a rule no longer speak Gaelic, but an old-fashioned English. While Lowlanders got on with the business of urbanization, farming, trading, and general money making in the 17th and 18th centuries, Highlanders remained nomadic, warlike, and steadfastly loyal to clan chiefs. A Highlander's home, a thatch-roofed stone cottage called a "black house," contained only one room—with a fire in the middle of the earthen floor and wooden shelves for beds—and one stable, joined to family quarters by a large and gaping doorway.

Religion in the Highlands was, as the historian and essayist Thomas Babington Macaulay put it, "a rude mixture of Popery and paganism." But after the Glorious Revolution of 1688–89 (by which the Roman Catholic James II was deposed from the British throne in favor of Protestants William and Mary), Episcopalianism and Presbyterianism both began to penetrate behind the Plaid Curtain. The powerful clan Campbell, Dukes of Argyll, became Presbyterians, and others followed, especially during the late 18th century, when Episcopalianism in its turn declined. Since 1700, a series of schisms have rocked Presbyterian Highland Scotland, throwing up movements faster than people could count them and leaving large parts of the west Highlands today under the rod of the archaic sect, the "Wee Frees." A Wee Free Sabbath makes an ordinary Lowland Sunday look like a chapter in the life of Sodom and Gomorrah, so if you're anywhere west of Inverness on the Day of Rest, don't try to buy anything, including gasoline. Nor is it a bad idea to walk funereally, wear black, and make sure the proprietor of your hotel sees you in church.

Not only religious but social shake-ups in the Highlands occurred on a massive scale. The late 18th and early 19th centuries saw the Clearances, the cruelly inhuman spectacle of landowners driving tenants from their homes in order to replace them with sheep, financially a more profitable venture. Thousands of Highlanders teemed south into Glasgow's slums (and points more distant), never to return. Next came the era of the deer park, when a coterie of London-based aristocrats, the 7% of the Scottish population who owned 84% of the land, evicted another wave of Highlanders in order to create holiday playgrounds in the shape of private shooting and fishing preserves. Queen Victoria's love affair with *Balmoral,* her Highland castle, inadvertently provided these plunderers with a fashionable impetus. These days, the Highlands are undergoing another change: The *Highlands and Islands Development Board,* seeking to lure tourists and to take advantage of the North Sea oil boom that began in the early 1970s, has added new wealth in parts of the Highlands but has increased the isolation of other parts, especially where fishing has suffered from oil operations or railway lines have been cut.

Customs and preoccupations that would long ago have vanished in less remote districts continue here. Apart from obvious examples such as kilt wearing, bagpiping, and the drinking of pure malt whiskies (*never* water them!), there are Highland games (contests of strength featuring such marathon events as "tossing the caber"—a full-grown debranched tree); the *National Mod* (Scotland's peripatetic annual orgy of Gaeldom in which Gaelic singers and reciters compete—the Scottish *Eisteddfod*) and other folk and musical happenings; and "Nessie-Watching" (a sport begun by St. Columba of Iona, the 6th-century Christianizer of Scotland, who reportedly sighted a prehistoric monster in Loch Ness's mysterious deep).

Battlefields, too, are a big draw, not only for tourists but for a number of Scots. Culloden Moor, near Inverness, is thus a focal point. Here Jacobitism, primarily a Highland movement seeking to restore the Stuart descendants of King James VI and I to the British throne, met a dire end in 1746 at the hands of the Duke of Cumberland, second son of the Hanoverian King George II. Whole clans were wiped out under the inadequate generalship of "Bonnie" Prince Charles Edward Stuart, the Jacobite royal heir, who fled in defeat to France from whence he had come. All signs of Highland culture, including the kilt and the Gaelic language, were proscribed for a long time afterward, and the Culloden legend swelled the characteristic ethereal glooms of Celtic composers and poets in both Scotland and Ireland for generations.

The northwest Highlands route begins at Inverness, crosses west to Ullapool, heads south along the rugged west coast through Gruinard Bay, Gairloch, Torridon, and Shiel Bridge, and then continues east through Fort William and takes in Glencoe and several charming seaside villages before ending up in Glasgow. The route isn't crammed with activities; the western Highlands aren't about that. They're about scenery, pure and simple, probably the most beautiful you'll see anywhere. Don't be deceived by what look like short distances on the map. It always seems to take longer to get down the road than you think; plan hotel stops accordingly. The full distance is approximately 365 miles: Allow at least a week.

A knowledge of Scottish driving etiquette will be an enormous advantage along this route, as parts of it will take you along the infamous single-track road—a road with only one lane to accommodate drivers coming from both directions. The etiquette of such matters is simple enough, though. From time to time, there are passing bays on both sides of the road. When two drivers approach one another, whoever gets to one first pulls over to let the other pass—and usually the drivers exchange a small wave of acknowledgement.

As with the other Scottish tour routes, book hotels in advance from May through September; keep sandwiches in your car and be opportunistic about petrol pumps (gas stations), which are harder to find than Brigadoon! An alternative to traveling by car is a Scotrail Pass, which, for a flat fee, provides 8, 15, or 21 days of unlimited travel through the Highlands and Scottish islands by train, bus, and ferry. (A particularly spectacular route is the train from Inverness to Kyle of Lochalsh.) For more information, contact the *Ross and Cromarty Tourist Office* (North Kessock, Black Isle, Ross-shire IVI 1XB; phone: 463-73505) or *BritRail Travel International* (1500 Broadway, New York, NY 10036; phone: 212-575-2667). Be sure to carry the *Scottish Tourist Board*'s *Scotland for the Motorist* book (£3.50/about $5.25), which shows interesting sites along the way. Be warned that, starting in late May or June, the midges come out—these tiny, practically invisible insects are the bane of Highlanders. Bring or buy plenty of bug repellent.

Expect to pay $85 or more per night for a double room (including private bath, TV set, and breakfast, unless otherwise specified) in a hotel listed as expensive; $45 to $85 in a moderate place; and less than $45 in an inexpensive one. A dinner for two, excluding wine and tip, in an expensive restaurant will cost $40 or more; in a moderate one, $25 to $40; in an inexpensive one, less than $25. All restaurants listed serve lunch and dinner unless otherwise indicated. For each location, hotels and restaurants are listed alphabetically by price category.

Many Highland hotels have reduced-rate three-, five-, or seven-day package deals, offering dinner as well as bed and breakfast, plus advice on and/or access to local sports facilities.

INVERNESS You wouldn't realize it to look at Inverness today, but this city, northern Scotland's commercial and administrative center, dates from at least the 4th century BC, when the entire Highland region was ruled from here. In the 12th century, Inverness became a royal burgh under the patronage of King David I, son of King Malcolm III (Macbeth's successor) and the Normanized English St. Margaret. This Norman—Scot influence over Gaelic tradition caused trouble for centuries; the peaceful patterns of Invernessian country life often were disrupted by yet another Highland chieftain or Norman—Scot adventurer sacking the town. The king's keeper of law and order at Inverness, the "Justiciar of the North," lived at *Inverness Castle.* However, these justiciars often were more loyal to local forces than to the crown. One, a follower of the fourth Earl of Huntly, was put to death by Mary, Queen of Scots, in 1562 when he closed his portals against her. About 400 years later, during the North Sea oil boom of the 1960s and early 1970s, Inverness was "sacked" again, this time by government officials, who, in the interest of short-term profit, razed massive portions of the town to make way for concrete office blocks.

Luckily, a few structures have survived the city's rampant modernization, and restoration work in the past several years has begun to turn the tide of officially sanctioned vandalism that had wiped out so many historic buildings. A block from the river is High Street, the town center since medieval times, which is lined with a townhouse, a destiny stone, and a steeple. The small but ornately Gothic townhouse, built in 1882, contains paintings, portraits, and busts of former dignitaries, as well as a collection of heraldic paraphernalia that features an array of former coats-of-arms of the burgh of Inverness. Inside, the council chamber contains a document bearing the signatures of members of David Lloyd George's cabinet (including Winston Churchill). In front of the townhouse is the Clach na Cuddain, or "Stone of the Tubs," where women used to stop to gossip on their way home with tubs of water from nearby wells. The old mercat (market) cross, restored in 1900, stands atop the stone. Opposite, the town steeple of 1791 (originally built as a jail) has a 150-foot spire of particularly arresting Georgian elegance. And *Inverness Castle,* a lovely pink chess piece standing majestically on Castle Hill a few yards from the High Street, still dominates the town; it was constructed during the 19th century on the site of David I's medieval castle, which had been blasted by Jacobites in 1745. Today the building is the *Inverness Sheriff Court;* in summer, people picnic on its lawns, untroubled by its violent history or the proximity of Her Majesty's prison. (The top of Castle Hill affords a bird's-eye view of a good part of the city, including two of Inverness's 22 churches—*St. Andrew's*

Cathedral and *Ness Bank Church*—on opposite sides of the Ness; beyond them, across Moray Firth, looms the 3,429-foot peak of Ben Wyvis.)

Other noteworthy structures in town include *Dunbar's Hospital* (Church St.), a 17th-century grammar school and weighhouse whose façade is ornamented with mythical beasts, fleurs-de-lis, and thistles; and just down the street, the *Parish Church of Old High Church,* built in the 18th century, which is attached to a medieval tower with a 17th-century balustraded spire. The church's graveyard is also interesting, with its mausoleums of some of the hoariest Invernessian clans.

In addition to those sights, Inverness offers some good shopping at the *James Pringle Woolen Mill* (on B862, also called Dores Rd.; phone: 1463-223311), an 18th-century wool factory on the Ness that allows visitors to tour its mills and then browse through a gift shop full of the cashmeres, lamb's wools, and Shetlands produced here (closed Sundays November through March); *Hector Russell Kiltmaker* (4-9 Huntly St.; phone: 1463-222781), which sells fine Scottish wools, crystal, china, perfume from Highland flowers, and handicrafts; and *Bow Court* (on Church St. near *Dunbar's Hospital*), a complex of stores and apartments. While you're here, don't miss the opportunity to stop at *Girvans* (2 Stephens Brae; phone: 1463-711900), a bakery/café that offers a heavenly concoction called "millionaire's shortbread"—shortbread topped with caramel and chocolate.

The *Inverness, Loch Ness, and Nairn Tourist Board* (Castle Wynd; phone: 1463-234353) offers plenty of leaflets, maps, and other information about the city and the surrounding area. It's closed Sundays November through mid-April, but outside the office is an automated information machine for restaurant and hotel referrals. On the whole, a visitor need spend only a half-day or so to see most of the attractions in Inverness itself. Nearby, however, are several points of interest, most of which are linked to the legendary creature known as the Loch Ness Monster.

The first known tale of "Nessie" comes from St. Adamnan, Abbot of Iona in the 7th century; according to his report, St. Columba of Iona was en route to Inverness to convert King Brudei to Christianity in AD 565 when his boat nearly was capsized by the monster. St. Columba managed to fight it off (or so the story goes), and the legend has endured ever since, providing the livelihood for generations of scientists trying to get documented proof of the monster, as well as spawning an entire industry designed to help curious thrill-seekers catch a glimpse of Nessie for themselves.

Scientific evidence of the creature's existence has been sketchy at best, and the few sightings over the years have been revealed to be hoaxes (including the famous 1934 photograph, which was finally exposed as a fake last year when the man who "took" it made a dramatic deathbed confession). Lack of proof, however, has hardly dented the legend's popularity as a tourist attraction.

The point where Nessie has most often been glimpsed (or at least, where most of the sightings have been reported) is *Urquhart Castle,* located by the village of Drumnadrochit, 15 miles south of Inverness on A82. Take binoculars to the top of the castle shell (the castle itself was blown up in 1692). This stretch of Loch Ness is deeper than the North Sea and perfect for prehistoric inhabitants—but thus far, hunts by midget submarine, radar, tungsten TV lamp, strobe light, time-lapse camera, and Spectra Polaroid systems have discovered nothing. The castle is open daily; admission charge (phone: 1463-232034). In the village of Drumnadrochit, also on A82, is the *Loch Ness Monster Exhibition,* with photographs and videos about the various searches that have gone on throughout the years; there's even a fake stuffed plesiosaurus anchored in a nearby pond. It can be found among a welter of shops, eateries, hotels, a visitors' center, and sideshow displays about other topics. The exhibition is open daily; admission charge (phone: 1456-450573). If you want to try to get a look at Nessie, take the *Loch Ness Submarine* (phone: 1285-760762) on an hour-long ride in the murky depths of Loch Ness. It leaves several times daily from the *Clansman Hotel Marina,* near Drumnadrochit.

Even if you couldn't care less about Loch Ness, there are still several attractions in the area worth visiting. About 5 miles east of Inverness on B9006 is the *Culloden Battlefield and Visitor Centre* (phone: 1463-790607), the site of the last pitched battle fought in Britain. On April 16, 1746, a day of infamy that will live forever in Scots' memories, a ragged band of supporters of Bonnie Prince Charlie (heir to the Royal Scots House of Stuart, the Young Pretender to the British throne) were butchered while Prince Charlie himself barely managed to escape to the European mainland via Skye. The full, harrowing story is told at the visitors' center in a multimedia show produced by the *National Trust for Scotland.* Also here are several clan graves, the *Well of the Dead,* the *Memorial Cairn,* and *Old Leanach Cottage* (a small war museum). The battlefield is open daily; the museum and the visitors' center are closed *Christmas, Boxing Day,* and during January. There's an admission charge to the visitors' center and museum.

After the Battle of Culloden, *Fort George* was erected nearby in order to enforce proscriptions against the Highlanders. This 12-acre, polygon-shape garrison, designed by the famous architect Robert Adam, cost £160,000 (a whopping sum in its day) to build. It sits on the Moray Firth with a fine sea view and contains a regimental museum. Visitors can sally around the tops of the defenses. The fort is open daily; admission charge (phone: 1667-462777). It's located on B9006; turn off A96 at Gollanfield. Near the fort, located off B9006, are the *Clava Cairns,* an impressive group of Bronze Age standing stones and burial chambers.

Castle Stuart (on B9039; phone: 1463-790745), 7 miles east of Inverness, is also worth a look. It was the ancestral home of the Earls of Moray, who were relatives of the Scottish Stuart kings, and the house contains several magnificent oil paintings of Bonnie Prince Charlie. Some rooms are available for an overnight stay. The castle is open daily; admission charge.

Craigmonie Adjacent to the *Inverness* golf course, this delightful turn-of-the-century townhouse, owned and run by a friendly family, has 35 bedrooms (three with four-poster beds), a patio overlooking the tree-lined grounds, and a leisure complex with a pool, sauna, and Jacuzzi. The *Chardonnay* restaurant serves mostly seafood dishes. Fishing and shooting excursions can be arranged. Annfield Rd., Inverness (phone: 1463-231649; fax: 1463-233720). Expensive.

Dower House In nearby Muir of Ord, this doll's house of an inn is surrounded by three acres of lovely gardens. The five guestrooms are exquisitely decorated with antiques and country prints, and the restaurant serves excellent continental fare. Closed *Christmas,* two weeks in March, and a week in October. Reservations necessary. MasterCard and Visa accepted. On Rte. 862, 11 miles northwest of town (phone/fax: 1463-870090). Expensive.

Kingsmills Only a 10-minute drive from downtown, this modern hotel, a small part of which is 18th-century, has 84 rooms, four acres of gardens, and a health club with pool, gym, and Jacuzzi. Lunch, afternoon tea, and snacks are served in the conservatory, and the restaurant offers well-prepared local fare. Culcabock Rd., Inverness (phone: 1463-237166; fax: 1463-225208). Expensive.

Bunchrew House The atmosphere of this turreted 17th century mansion (located on 20 acres next to the Beauly Firth) has been revitalized by energetic new owners. The 11 rooms are decorated in grand country-house fashion, and the restaurant serves Scottish fare with international influences. Fishing is available on the property, and golf is nearby. On A862, 1 mile from Inverness (phone: 1463-234917; fax: 1463-710620). Expensive to moderate.

Polmaily House This casual country house hotel on 18 acres has 11 rooms (No. 3, with a four-poster bed and a view of the gardens, is our favorite). The restaurant has an ambitious menu, but the simpler items are the most successful. Facilities include a tennis court, pool, sauna, and gym; golf and fishing are available nearby. On A831, about 1½ miles from Drumnadrochit (phone: 1456-450343; fax: 1456-450813). Moderate to inexpensive.

En Route from Inverness Take A9 north about 7 miles and then head west on A835, cutting through the kind of rugged scenery that leaps to mind when you think of Scotland—hilltops covered with purple mists of heather, glassy lochs fringed by soaring mountaintops. Another 21 miles down the road nature throws in something extra, the Falls of Rogie. In Norse *rogie* means "splashing foaming river." Visitors have seen salmon leap from the suspension bridge that spans the falls.

After passing dramatic Loch Garve on the right, A835 heads north. Over the next 16 miles, the scenery is especially eye-catching. As you drive, you'll see Ben Wyvis on the right and the dense foliage of Corriemoille Forest on the left. Farther up the road, two other lakes sparkle—Loch Glascarnoch and Loch Droma—and there is another splashing waterfall, the Falls of Measach at Braemore. Corrieshalloch Gorge, which contains the waterfall, is a mile long and 200 feet deep; there's a viewing platform (open year-round) for observing the falls.

Just after the falls, Loch Broom comes into sight, and 12 miles farther northwest is the charming town of Ullapool.

ULLAPOOL Sweeping into town from the east, visitors may think they have stumbled into a waterside Brigadoon. Here is a model 18th-century fishing village in a sheltered inlet, on the shores of mountain-hemmed Loch Broom. Designed and built by the *British Fishery Society* in 1788, and with barely a thousand residents today, Ullapool has a colorful pier, where the *Stornoway Ferry* docks, oilskin-clad fishermen arrive with their catch, and boatloads of vacationers depart for a day at sea. The air is kept soft by the neighboring Gulf Stream; the prevailing wind is westerly, bathing the area with passing gentle rains and filling the air with the smell of salt and fish. The townspeople here are generally friendly and helpful.

There are opportunities in Ullapool for sailing, canoeing, sea angling, deep-sea diving, and loch and river fishing. Cruises to the nearby Summer Isles and to the bird-haunted islands of Loch Broom are run Mondays through Saturdays by *Islander Cruisers* (33 Morefield Pl.; phone: 1854-612200) and by *Mackenzie Marine* (*The Pier,* Shore St.; phone: 1854-612008). The tourist office (Shore St.; phone: 1854-612135) is closed November through *Easter.*

The *Ullapool Museum* (W. Argyle St.; no phone) focuses on local history. It is closed Sundays and November through March; admission charge. Good shopping can be had at the *West Highland Woolen Company* (Shore St.; phone: 1854-612134).

A pleasant but rigorous excursion from Ullapool is a trip to Achiltibuie, on the southern shore of *Inverpolly Nature Reserve.* The 25-mile journey includes driving about 15 miles on a winding single-track road off the A835. The *Summer Isles* hotel in Achiltibuie (see *Best en Route*) runs much shorter boat trips to the Summer Isles than those from Ullapool. In the village of Altandhu, a mile or two beyond the hotel, is *Summer Isles Foods* (locally known as the *Achiltibuie Smokehouse;* phone: 1854-82353). From *Easter* through mid-October (daily except Sundays), visitors can watch the curing of meat, fish, and game, and buy the resulting products. *Northwest Frontiers* (19 W. Ter., Ullapool; phone: 1854-612571) offers extended walking tours through the mountains and coasts of the northwestern area. Walking packages range from a weekend of easy mountain trails to a week's worth of taxing mountain hikes.

BEST EN ROUTE

Altnaharrie Inn Access to this luxurious, small (eight bedrooms), lakeside hotel is via its own private boat. The excellent restaurant serves a set, limited menu (for guests only) that changes nightly—but the owners keep records of what their regular guests have eaten so dishes aren't repeated on their next visit. Open April through mid-October. No credit cards accepted. On the south shore of Loch Broom, Ullapool (phone: 1854-83230; fax: 1854-83303). Very expensive.

Summer Isles As the name suggests, this old-fashioned seaside property with 11 guestrooms and one cottage has a timeless view of the isles. Its distinguished dining room is famous for five-course dinners of locally caught seafood and fresh-picked vegetables. Guests are supplied permits to fish among the hill lochs. Open April through October. In Achiltibule, 25 miles north of Ullapool on A835 and a winding single-lane road (phone: 1854-82282; fax: 1854-82251). Expensive to moderate.

Ceilidh Place Here is a lovely row of whitewashed cottages with 13 rooms (10 with private baths) and an adjacent bunkhouse with 10 additional rooms (all with shared baths). *Ceilidhs* (Scottish jam sessions) are held every other night during summer (except Sundays). The two restaurants (a bistro and a more formal dining room) are known for their seafood dishes and home-made desserts, especially banoffee pie, a house specialty featuring banana slices and layers of toffee. 14 W. Argyle St., Ullapool (phone: 1854-612103; fax: 1854-612886). Moderate.

Tigh-Na-Mara Owner Tony Weston has transformed a large, charming apartment in the old lochside shop and a boat shed by Loch Broom into a guest-house with three comfortable bedrooms, complete with beautiful views and a spiral staircase. Guests can try for a hole in one on the nearby golf course or fish in the nearby loch. Seasonal game is served in the dining room. The Shore, Ardindream, Loch Broom (phone/fax: 1854-85282). Moderate.

Morefield Motel Although we don't recommend staying here, this hotel's dining room is definitely worth a stop for its excellent seafood. The owners of this establishment are members of the *Shellfish Wholesalers of Great Britain.* Patrons can eat at the bar or in the candlelit restaurant. Hours vary, but the eatery is usually open daily during peak season (call ahead). Reservations advised. Major credit cards accepted. On A835 just north of Ullapool (phone: 1854-612161). Moderate to inexpensive.

West House Bed and Breakfast This quaint little property, not far from the Ullapool waterfront, has four bedrooms furnished with antiques from the owner's shop next door. A bright, pretty place with a restaurant that serves break-fast to guests only. W. Argyle St. (phone: 1854-612734). Inexpensive.

En Route from Ullapool Take A835 south and turn onto A832 toward Poolewe. After passing through the town of Dundonnell, as you approach Ardessie with Little Loch Broom on the right, the scenery becomes staggeringly beautiful. (Looking down on the sharply carved loch from this high road holds a hidden danger: The view may distract you from your driving!) About 24 miles from Ullapool, rounding the coast around Gruinard Bay, drivers might think they've found a fusion of Scotland and Bermuda—between the jagged coast and the gentle bay are several pristine pink sand beaches. Gruinard Island, out in the bay, looks peaceful today, but it has had a troubled history. During World War II, biological warfare experiments were conducted there and the island's soil was contaminated with anthrax. It remained so until early in this decade, when a massive campaign by the British Army restored it to a safe state. Nearby, the Isle of Ewe, a pretty island with a less disturbing past, sits in the middle of shimmering Loch Ewe.

At Poolewe, another 15 miles on A832 beyond Gruinard Bay, is a natural phenomenon that even non-gardeners should stop to admire. Due to the Gulf Stream bringing warm currents to this coast, tropical flowers flourish here; they have grown in *Inverewe Gardens* since 1862. Throughout the year, there's an explosion of color over the 50 acres from 2,500 species, including Himalayan lilies, South Pacific forget-me-nots, and many others from South America and Africa. Guided walks with the head gardener are given on weekdays April through mid-October. There's also a visitors' center. The garden is open daily; the visitors' center is closed mid-October through March. There is an admission charge (phone: 144586-200). From Poolewe, continue another 6 miles southwest on A832 to Gairloch.

GAIRLOCH This seacoast town is a popular center for water sports. Those who want to brave the chilly water can try windsurfing at the *Gairloch Watersports Centre* (phone: 1445-712131); closed October through April. Bird watching and sightseeing cruises are run May through September from the Gairloch pier by *Gairloch Cruises* (phone: 1445-712175). For landlubbers, the *Gairloch Heritage Museum* (just off A832 in Gairloch; phone: 1445-712287) presents exhibitions of West Highland life from prehistoric times to the present, including Pictish stones and reconstructed rooms from a croft house. It is closed Sundays and October through March; admission charge.

BEST EN ROUTE

Shieldaig Lodge A former Victorian shooting lodge with 13 bedrooms, most of them with private bathrooms, and two cottages overlooking Shieldaig Loch, this is a friendly, rustic place, popular with hikers. Trout and salmon fishing can be arranged, along with stalking and golf. There's also a tennis court on the grounds and a good, basic restaurant. Open March through October. Off A832, just outside Gairloch (phone: 144-583250; fax: 144-583305). Moderate.

En Route from Gairloch Continue on A832 another 12 miles until you reach Loch Maree.

LOCH MAREE This lake, one of Scotland's loveliest, was named after St. Maree, who founded a monastery in the nearby town of Applecross in the 7th century. Ringed with Scottish pines, Loch Maree is a well-known haven for fisherfolk; record-setting trout have been caught here. But there are other activities besides fishing. Hillwalking affords views of some of the wildest and most varied scenery in the West Highlands, including the 2,943-foot peak of Mt. Slioch; and exploring the islands in the loch could yield relics from the Celts, Picts, Gaels, and Vikings.

BEST EN ROUTE

Old Mill This small modern lodge on the site of a former grain store and mill has five comfortable rooms with gorgeous views of the mountains and the pleasant sound of a stream running alongside. There are gardens for walking and a lounge filled with books, as well as a restaurant serving basic Scottish fare. No smoking is allowed. On A832 (phone: 144-584271) Moderate.

Loch Maree Once visited by the peripatetic Queen Victoria, this lakeside lodge with 30 basic rooms is a perfect spot for anglers during fishing season (April through October). Along with fishing, there are nature walks and golf at the nine-hole *Gairloch* course. There's also a restaurant serving basic Scottish food. On A832 (phone: 144-584288; fax: 144-584241). Moderate to inexpensive.

En Route from Loch Maree About 5 miles south of Loch Maree is the *Beinn Eighe National Nature Reserve.* The park has 11,757 acres devoted to the preservation and study of the Caledonian pine forest; animals that may be glimpsed here include white-tailed deer, mountain goats, wildcats, and eagles. There are also several nature trails. The park is open daily; a visitors' center (phone: 144-584258) is closed mid-September through mid-May.

Another 5 miles farther south, turn right on A896, a single-track road. About 9 miles farther is another dazzling stretch of nature: *Torridon,* a 16,100-acre park with some of Scotland's most scenic wilderness, including the 3,456-foot Liathach Mountain (composed of Torridonian sandstone thought to be 750 million years old) and the 3,232-foot peak of Beinn Alligin. Within this nature preserve are the *Trust Countryside Centre* (just off A896; phone: 1445-791221), featuring an audiovisual presentation on wildlife, and the *Deer Museum,* with displays relating to the various stages of a deer's life. The museum and the center are closed October through April. There's an admission charge to the audiovisual show at the center; a donation is suggested to the museum. A few miles farther west on A896 is the village of Shieldaig in the inlet of the loch of the same name.

BEST EN ROUTE

Loch Torridon Formerly a grand shooting lodge built for the Earl of Lovelace in 1887, this property has 20 large, antique-filled rooms and is surrounded by 58 acres of grounds bordering the loch. Of special note is the restaurant, serving dishes such as lamb on a bed of sweetbreads with coriander and madeira, and homemade walnut ice cream with poached pears. Stalking and fishing excursions can be arranged. Open March through January. Reservations advised. Major credit cards accepted. On A896, a mile or so beyond the signposted road to the village of Torridon (phone: 1445-791242; fax: 1445-791296). Expensive.

SHIELDAIG While this village offers nothing specifically of interest to tourists—just a neat line of early 19th-century houses fronting the loch—it's a good place for weary travelers to take a rest stop. Shieldaig is the very image of an unspoiled, peaceful coastal town, and it's friendly as well. A local woman, M. C. Calcott, sells fine hand-crocheted and hand-knitted sweaters, christening gowns, scarves, and shawls. She runs her business, *Angora Ecosse,* out of a shed next to the family farm, located about 1½ miles south of town off A896. It's a good idea to call in advance (phone: 1520-755248). To get there, take the road signposted "Scenic Route to Applecross" and watch for signs pointing toward "Angora Ecosse."

BEST EN ROUTE

Tigh an Eilean This pretty whitewashed cottage facing the loch has 11 bedrooms decorated with charming country fabrics and an ambitious restaurant serving specialties such as local lobster and avocado, and roast wild duck with orange sauce. Everyone in town hangs out at the bar. Fishing and golf can be arranged. Just off A896 in Shieldaig (phone: 1520-755251; fax: 1520-755321). Moderate.

En Route from Shieldaig Continue down A896 through Glenshieldaig Forest, a favorite of hillwalkers. Pick up A890 just after Lochcarron (about 14 miles from Shieldaig) and follow it south toward Stromeferry. For an interesting diversion, take the road signposted to Plockton, a tiny artists' colony on the coast 7 miles off A890. Like Poolewe, this town is a recipient of warm Gulf Stream air currents, as evidenced by the palm trees along the waterfront—certainly a rare sight in Scotland. This is a good place for crafts, such as the jewelry designed by Lindsay Rooney at *The Jewellery Workshop* (9 Cooper St., phone: 159-984408), and *Lochcarron Weavers* (Innes St.; phone: 159-984331), which produce knitwear, tartans, ties, and scarves. There are also sailboats for rent, and seal watching expeditions on picturesque Loch Carron are run by *Leisure Marine* on Shore Front (phone: 159-984306).

BEST EN ROUTE

Haven This charming inn located in what was a 19th-century merchant's house has 13 small but quaintly decorated bedrooms and a Taste of Scotland restaurant. Open February through mid-December. Innes St., Plockton (phone: 159-984223). Moderate.

En Route from Plockton Returning to the main route, continue on A890 and turn left on A87. About 3 miles after the intersection is *Eilean Donan,* a castle that may well look familiar—its picturesque image has adorned cookie tins throughout Britain, and it is purportedly the most photographed castle in Scotland. *Eilean Donan* dates back to 1220 and was the property of the Mackenzies of Kintail. In 1719 it was garrisoned by Spanish Jacobite troops and blown up by an English man o' war. It was completely restored earlier this century; its romantic location on an islet and its background of beautiful Loch Duich draw visitors like a magnet. The castle is closed October through *Easter;* admission charge (phone 1599-85202).

About 7 miles farther southeast on A87 at Shiel Bridge, you'll see a sign-posted road that leads to the tiny village of Glenelg; intrepid drivers who don't mind traveling along an elevated single lane road with no guardrails can take it for about a mile, park, and walk to one of the most awe-inspiring vantage points in the region—affording a panorama of Loch Duich, Glen Shiel, and in the distance, the dramatic, usually snow-covered mountain peaks called the Five Sisters of Kintail. Glenelg is also the site of the *Glenelg Brochs,* two stone towers used for defense against the Romans when the Picts inhabited the area (for more information, see *Ancient Monuments and Ruins* in DIVERSIONS). More cautious travelers can get a closer (but less panoramic and impressive) view of the Five Sisters and Glen Shiel by continuing along A87. In 1773, Dr. Samuel Johnson took a horseback journey through the area with his biographer, James Boswell, and the scenery of Glen Shiel so impressed him that he decided to write *Journey,* a diary of travels around the country. A boulder in the glen known as "Clach Johnson" was supposedly a resting place for Johnson during this trip.

BEST EN ROUTE

Cluanie Inn Here is a late-19th-century house that has been turned into a modern-looking hotel with 13 guestrooms. Among its amenities are a restaurant, a gym, a sauna, and above all, a warm and hospitable welcome. On A87 just past Glen Shiel (phone: 1320-40257). Expensive to moderate.

En Route from Glen Shiel Return to A87 and head south. At Invergarry, about 44 miles farther along the road, turn right on A82 and continue south toward Fort William. Just before Fort William, you'll see not one, but two *Inverlochy Castles:* The ruin of the 13th-century *Inverlochy Castle,* and a more recent (it's only a century old) luxury hotel of the same name. Legend says that on the site of the real castle's ruin, there once was a Pictish settlement where Charlemagne signed a treaty with King Archaius in 790.

BEST EN ROUTE

Inverlochy Castle An opulent estate with 17 bedrooms, it offers fabulous views of Ben Nevis, Britain's highest mountain, and fine regional cooking. A Relais & Châteaux member. Open April through mid-November; sometimes it reopens for the period between *Christmas* and *New Year's* as well. For more information, see *Rural Retreats* in DIVERSIONS. (phone: 1397-702177 or 1397-702178; fax: 1397-702953). Very expensive.

Factor's House Owned by the son of the family that owns the *Inverlochy Castle,* this gatehouse to the estate is a much more relaxed and inexpensive alternative. The public rooms and six bedrooms are cozy and have views of Ben Nevis and the surrounding hills. There is a casual restaurant serving Scottish fare; guests here also get to use *Inverlochy*'s facilities. Open mid-February through October. Off A82 (phone: 1397-705767; fax: 1397-702953). Expensive to moderate.

En Route from Inverlochy Castle From here, travelers have several options. Before reaching Fort William (an uninteresting commercial town with nothing to offer but the fine hotels listed above), drivers pressed for time can turn north on A82 and drive the 65 miles back to Inverness. Or they can choose to take A86 about 50 miles to the Malt Whisky Trail area (see *Northeast Scottish Highlands,* in this section). Those who have a few more days for the West Highlands, however, should continue from *Inverlochy Castle* along A82 to Glencoe, a journey of about 24 miles.

GLENCOE One of Scotland's most dramatic glens with its triangular twin peaks, this is also one of its most sinister looking in bad weather. *Glencoe* means "glen of weeping"; it earned that name in 1692, when it was the site of the horrific massacre of most of the Macdonald clan. Their leader had failed to pledge allegiance to England's King William III in a timely fashion, so 40 of the Macdonalds were killed as they slept by members of the Campbell clan acting on behalf of the king. The act raised a groundswell of fury that spread quickly through the people of Scotland and still permeates the atmosphere. On sunny days some of the gloom lifts, but strangely, the clouds that hug the tops of the hills rarely do.

En Route from Glencoe For more beautiful scenery, follow A828 west and then south alongside Loch Linnhe through the charmingly picturesque villages of Kentallen (10 miles away) and Appin (6 miles farther). In both tiny villages, you'll see a cluster of small, whitewashed cottages framing the dark, blue-gray waters of the loch.

BEST EN ROUTE

Airds A member of Relais & Châteaux, this luxurious former ferry inn boasts one of the most romantic views in all of Scotland, taking in Loch Linnhe, several whitewashed cottages, and a lighthouse in the distance. The main rooms and 12 bedrooms (six with waterfront views) are luxuriously decorated, and the food is regarded as among the best in the country (the dining room has earned a Michelin star). Open mid-March through early January. Reservations advised. Major credit cards accepted. Two miles off A828, just beyond Appin (phone: 163-173236; fax: 163-173535). Very expensive.

Ardsheal House This rambling 18th-century property has 13 modest but comfortable bedrooms; the restaurant is exceptional, as is the view over Loch Linnhe, the Morven mountains, and a sheep pasture. Closed for three weeks in January. Reservations advised. Major credit cards accepted. On A828 in Kentallen (phone: 163-174227; fax: 163-174342). Expensive to moderate.

Kilcamb Lodge Across Loch Linnhe (the easiest way to cross is via the *Corran Ferry,* about 18 miles from Kentallen, which runs about every half hour year-round), this former shooting lodge on 30 acres is a very serene place. The 10 bedrooms, decorated with fabrics in country-style florals and stripes, are cozy and charming, and there are lovely views of the Morven Hills. The restaurant offers ambitious, well-prepared continental specialties such as ravioli of wild mushrooms and *confit* of Barbary duck; fresh-squeezed orange juice (a rarity in this country) is served at breakfast. Fishing and mountain biking can be arranged. Open April through October. Reservations advised. MasterCard and Visa accepted. On A861 in Strontian (phone: 1967-2257; fax: 1967-2041). Expensive to moderate.

Ballachulish House This whitewashed 18th-century house, one of the most historic in Scotland, is furnished with exquisite fabrics and antiques. It was the former home of the Stewart clan, and the murderous decree of Glencoe was signed here. That may be the reason why this is also reputedly one of Scotland's most haunted houses; the ghost of one of the Stewarts, a soldier in full uniform, has been sighted in the past—but not recently. The six rooms vary in size (the two in front are particularly large), but most have views of Loch Linnhe and the Morven Hills. Eating in the lovely dining room is a grand occasion, with exceptionally fresh shellfish often on the menu. Fishing, climbing, and skiing can be arranged nearby. Closed *Christmas.* Reservations advised. MasterCard and Visa accepted. On A82, just south of the Ballachulish Bridge, about 6 miles east of Kentallen (phone: 18552-266). Inexpensive.

En Route from Kentallen and Appin For the most scenic drive south to Glasgow (an 80-mile drive from Kentallen), take A828 and turn left on A85. Continue through the Pass of Brander and Lochawe until you reach A819; turn right towards Inverary. At Inverary, turn left on A83 to Cairndow. On the way, stop at the *Loch Fyne Oyster Bar* (on A83; phone: 14996-264) for fantastic fresh oysters, mussels, herring, and other seafood; open daily. At Cairndow, turn right on A815 to Dunoon. A car ferry leaves Dunoon every hour on the half hour for the town of Gourock, near Glasgow; the trip takes a half hour. When disembarking at Gourock, turn left on an unmarked road and follow it to A8. Continue on A8 a few miles to the M8, which takes you into Glasgow.

Another route from Cairndow, which takes in a view of Loch Lomond, is to continue on A83 10 miles to A82, turn right, and follow it 30 miles to Glasgow. Those in more of a hurry can follow A82 about 80 miles straight from Glencoe to Glasgow; the scenery is still beautiful, but the journey is via a faster road.

GLASGOW For a complete report on the city, its sights, hotels, and restaurants, see *Glasgow* in THE CITIES.

Scottish Islands

Scotland has 787 islands, including uninhabited stone dollops like Bass Rock and Ailsa Craig (see the *Southeast Scotland* and *Southwest Scotland* routes, also in this section). These vary in size, topography, history, climate, ethnic mix, and ethos. The islands included here, however—Orkney and Shetland plus the Hebridean Arran, Skye, Harris, Lewis, Mull, and Iona—share some common denominators. All have a remote otherworldliness, a sense of infinite time; all but Arran reflect antiquity both in archaeological riches and in the natives' ardent tribalism; all have vivid, unusual flora and fauna, colonies of seals, seabirds, and wildlife; all possess multicolored skies and magic. All are sparsely populated (there are 28,508 year-round residents, most of whom live on Orkney). Winds can be incredible (a gale is recorded at the Butt of Lewis one day in every six) and on Shetland, Orkney, Harris, and Lewis there are almost no trees. Skye, Orkney, Arran, and Harris have fantastic gnomic rock formations. All but Arran and Orkney live by fishing and crofting, and all but Orkney and Shetland show a dangerous dependence on *Highlands and Islands Development Board* projects, and on tourism. But so far tourists continue to roll in.

And not just tourists! Drawn to the islands are artists, craftspeople, poets, scholars, and dreamers, who set up shop in deserted thatch-roofed cottages and hag peat, write books, throw pots, and weave caftans. You'll have access to the wares of this entrepreneurial yeomanry as well as to Shetland sweaters and Harris tweeds. Hugh MacDiarmid, the greatest Scottish poet of the 20th century, lived for a time in Shetland; the composer Peter Maxwell Davies finds inspiration in the sounds around his Orkney home; Sorley Maclean, chief among contemporary bards of the Gaelic tongue, dwells in Skye. In addition to works by these giants, try a page or two by Orkney's George Mackay Brown and Eric Linklater, and the Outer Hebrides's Compton Mackenzie (his novel *Whisky Galore* is especially delicious).

Two centuries of Viking invasions, from 800 to 1000, left the islands under Norse control. Scottish Gaelic leadership gradually reemerged in the Hebrides, though the Gaelic Lordship of the Isles was not absorbed into the Scottish crown until the reign of James IV. But Orkney and Shetland continued under Scandinavian occupation through the Middle Ages. Their inhabitants are still primarily Nordic; they keep up special friendship societies with Iceland and the Faroes, and surnames—a break from Scandinavian custom—have existed in Shetland only for the last 100 years. Orcadians and Shetlanders are a down-to-earth, straightforward people—Celtic Twilights and such mystiques have no place among them. Until fairly recently they spoke Norn, a Viking dialect that has fostered a pleasing singsong quality in their English. Shetland fisherfolk employ many "haaf" words from Norn even now (there are 10 different nouns for "wind" and 19 for "sea").

The Western Isles preserve both the Highland culture lost on the mainland (Gaelic still is spoken in parts of Harris, Lewis, and Skye) and the old Presbyterianism gone from the southern part of the country. Many guest-house owners eschew cooking, watching TV, and even their beloved fishing on the Sabbath, so mind when you wash your socks. A duality of the public and private person exists in the Hebrides, epitomized by areas that vote themselves dry before dotting the moors with illegal makeshift drinking *bothans* ("cabins"). The satiric tradition of the ancient Gaelic bards—in which verses were thought to wield witch-doctor-style curses—may have reinforced in Hebrideans their unquenchable love of invective; their mellifluous lilts promise Paradise but shoot wide of the mark, delivering the sentiments of hexmen in accents of angels.

Despite drawbacks like frequent wet weather, summer midges (tiny insects), and occasional roadside views of gargantuan rubbish dumps, the Scottish Islands are unsurpassed as holiday spots. It's said there are peat fires in Hebridean houses that have been alight continuously for over a century, and that there are faeries in Skye's unearthly kaleidoscopes of sunbeams, mists, and rainbows. In Orkney and Shetland, where the land is so flat it scarcely breaks the sky's endless embrace, the moon, stars, and aurora borealis are dazzling. Fiddling and dancing swell all the village halls. Even the food tastes different; for example "bere bannocks" are made from a grain grown only in Orkney, and lamb in Harris and Lewis has a sweetness caused by the heather in the sheepfeed. Best of all are the island people, who welcome you unquestioningly.

Airports in Lewis, Skye, Orkney, and Shetland are a thrill to set down at because of the comprehensive overviews of famous landscapes. Rentable cars get snapped up fast, so make sure you book yours before touchdown. Sea and air links are detailed below for each island individually, as are addresses of the main tourist offices for additional sightseeing advice. Hotels listed as expensive will charge $75 or more for a double room (including breakfast); moderate ones, from $45 to $70; and inexpensive ones, less than $45. Unless otherwise stated, all hotels listed feature private baths. A dinner for two in an expensive restaurant will cost $35 or more; in a moderate one, $20 to $30; in an inexpensive one, less than $20. All restaurants listed serve lunch and dinner, unless otherwise specified. For each location, hotels and restaurants are listed alphabetically by price category.

ARRAN

Just 14 miles off Ayrshire's shore, Arran has nine villages, no towns, and only three roads, one of which skirts a ravishing 60-mile coastline. A schizophrenic terrain, full of craggy Highland hills in the north but lush lowland farms and winsome little resorts in the south, makes the island a miniature

Scotland. Arran's climate is comparatively dry and warm (with palm trees here and there), and every summer families arrive for idyllic low-key holidays. Jukeboxes, casinos, and chromium-fronted fish-and-chips shops are rare to nonexistent; two-year-olds on the beach digging with pails and shovels are prolific.

The chief villages, all by the sea, are Whiting Bay, Lamlash, Corrie, Lochranza, and Brodick. From Whiting Bay you can walk inland to the beautiful 140-foot Glenashdale Falls. Lamlash was a naval base till World War I and is now an educational and administrative center. Corrie with its adorably tiny harbor is the prettiest hamlet on Arran, while northerly Lochranza, dwarfed by Arran's spectacular over-2,000-foot peaks, is dramatically stark. Brodick is the island's main port and biggest tourist haunt; it's guarded by the soaring presence of Mt. Goatfell and has an entrancing *cladach* (old fishing wharf).

Brodick Castle and Gardens (1½ miles north of *Brodick Pier*) are owned by the *National Trust for Scotland,* which also owns 7,000 acres nearby, including the lovely Glen Rosa. The castle is an ancestral seat of the Dukes of Hamilton and contains fine silver, porcelain, pictures, and trophies. The Duchess of Montrose founded its opulent rhododendron garden in 1923 and its formal garden dates from 1710. The castle and gardens are closed mid-October through March and Sundays, Tuesdays, Thursdays, and Fridays in April and the first half of October. There's an admission charge. *Lochranza Castle* in Lochranza is a picturesque 16th-century ruin with two square towers (the key is with the custodian at his house on Croft Bank; no admission charge). *Lochranza* is only one of three places on Arran visited by Robert the Bruce—the others are King's Cross by Whiting Bay, where he embarked for the mainland in 1307, and King's Cave, 2 miles north of Blackwaterfoot on the west coast (you have to walk it), a possible site of the legendary incident when King Robert took refuge in a cave during a battle, saw a spider spinning a web, and took the insect's persistence as a sign to return to the fight.

Isle of Arran Heritage Museum, in an 18th-century croft on Brodick's northern edge, includes a smithy who occasionally demonstrates the art of horseshoeing. The museum is closed Sundays and October through April; admission charge (phone: 1770-2636). Near Kilmory Village on the south coast are the Neolithic Kilmory Cairns, while the Standing Stones of Machrie Moor, a complex of six 15-foot Bronze Age Megalithic circles, rise skyward on Moss Farm Road just south of westerly Machrie Bay; try to see them at sunset.

Details of fishing, sailing, deep-sea diving, golf, swimming, pony trekking, hiking, and hill-walking are available from the tourist information center on *Brodick Pier* (phone: 1770-2401; open daily). The center also issues a comprehensive guide to Arran's crafts shops. Boat trips to Holy Island across Lamlash Bay have become rather difficult to arrange, but there still are a few trips available in summer (call the tourist information center for details). A 12th-century fort, *St. Molios's Well* (St. Molios was an Irish missionary), and a pleasant nature reserve are on Holy Island. You can buy locally produced mustard at the *Arran Mustard Factory Shop* in Lamlash (phone: 1770-6606) and homemade cheeses and other foods at the *Arran Visitors Centre* (phone: 1770-2831). The center (closed November through *Easter*) is located about a mile from Brodick on the road heading north from Lochranza.

Festivals are Arran's long suit: There's a *Music Festival* (February/March), a *Sea Angling Festival* (May), the *Goatfell Race* (May), and *Fiddlers' Rally* (June), a steady stream of assorted small festivals at *Brodick Castle* all summer long, the *Brodick Sheepdog Trials* (June), the *Isle of Arran Folk Festival* (June), the *Heather Queen Gala* (July), *Lamlash Laughabout Week* (July), *Whiting Bay Fun Week* (July), the *Lamlash Horticultural and Agricultural Shows* (August), the *Arran Riding Club Horse Show* (July or August), the *Corrie Capers,* with family events like puppet and dog shows (August), and the *Brodick Highland Games* (August).

Several car ferries go daily from Ardrossan on the Scottish mainland to Brodick; space should be reserved on summer weekends. During the tourist season, there's a route (about ten sailings a day) from Claonaig on Kintyre to Lochranza. For further information, contact *Caledonian MacBrayne Ltd.* (Ferry Terminal, Gourock, Scotland; phone: 1475-33755; fax: 1475-37607). Ask about their special deals called Hebridean Drive-Away, Island Hopscotch, and Car Rover Tickets; these could save you money. Arran is a difficult island to explore without transportation, and mountain or touring bicycles are a popular way to traverse long distances more quickly. *Mini-Golf Cycles* (along Shore Rd.; phone: 1770-2272) offers a wide selection of day and weekly rentals.

BEST EN ROUTE

Anchrannie Country House Set in its own country park, this secluded, sumptuously elegant hotel has an undeniably holiday flair, with 28 bedrooms, antique-style furniture, and a bistro in a conservatory that has wonderful baked goods and meals. Brodick (phone: 1770-302234; fax: 1770-302812). Expensive.

Carraig Mhor Eating House A popular bayside spot with a homey air, it serves seafood at lunch and full dinners, including traditional Gaelic Scottish fare, at night. It also offers catering facilities. Lunch served April through October only. Reservations advised. Major credit cards accepted. Lamlash (phone: 1770-600453). Expensive to moderate.

Glenisle The motto of this 13-room, family-run establishment is, "We treat people as we would expect to be treated ourselves." A wide choice of Scottish/European–style food is served in a traditional dining room (with open hearth fire). Lamlash (phone: 1770-600258). Moderate to inexpensive.

Kingsley Real beer in the bar makes this modest 27-room seafront property with a restaurant a worthy bet. Open March through September. Brodick (phone: 1770-302226). Inexpensive.

SKYE

More Scottish music, poetry, and art have been inspired by Skye than could be contained in any volume. This magical island is the home of hundreds of legends and mysteries—and a few people. The air is wrapped in mist and often touched with a light moving veil of rain. Skye is a large island with six peninsulas, a coastline of sea lochs, and fabulous panoramas. Traditionally it has belonged to the clans Macdonald and Macleod. Set close to the most isolated parts of the West Highlands, it has a population of only 7,000.

On Skye's south shore are the legendary, oft-climbed Cuillins, a high mountain range whose tops bard Sorley Maclean described rhapsodically as "exact and serrated blue ramparts." In some lights they look like the teeth of a black saw blade. Their strange shape is the result of basalt dykes seeping into a hard underlayer of gabbro. Don't be deceived by their innocent appearance, and be sure to consult a local expert or the tourist office (see below) before trying a climb. These very old mountains can be treacherous. Just west of the Cuillins is the lovely lochside campsite Glen Brittle. Bonnie Prince Charlie had popularized Skye by fleeing to it after Culloden with Flora Macdonald, a brave Skye native, disguised as Flora's maid; Boswell and Johnson met Flora 27 years later and wrote a tribute to her, enshrined today on a Celtic cross in *Kilmuir Churchyard* near the island's north tip.

Oak, birch, willow, and hazel grace most of Sleat, Skye's southernmost peninsula. The Aird of Sleat, below the village of Ardvasar, is barren, but its view across Sleat Sound to Mallaig will astonish you! Lava flows and landslips have created the phantasmagoric moss-dappled marvels on the basaltic northern peninsula of Trotternish, including the Old Man of Storr, a 160-foot obelisk well over 2,000 feet above the sea (a three- to four-hour climb from your car); the Kilt Rock; and the weird, pinnacled Quirang. Don't miss traveling the small corkscrew road from the Quirang to the Trotternish west coast.

Give equal time to castles and villages: *Knock Castle* on Sleat, with a vista across Knock Bay to the mainland territory of Knoydart, is a ruined Macdonald stronghold; so is *Dunscaith Castle* at blissful Tokavaig on Sleat's opposite side, and *Duntulm Castle* near the tip of Trotternish. *Castle Moil* ("The Roofless Castle"), a welcoming beacon for voyagers by ferry to the Skye pier at Kyleakin, was a keep of the Mackinnon clan. *Armadale Castle,* on the grounds of the *Clan Donald Centre* north of Ardvasar, was a 19th-century Gothic mansion and family seat of the Macdonald chiefs, Lords of the Isles; nowadays, in summer it's a clan Donald museum with audiovisual presentations, a congenial tearoom, and a bookshop loaded with stuff about Skye. The castle is closed November through March; admission charge (phone: 14716-305). *Dunvegan Castle,* on northwesterly Loch Dunvegan, is the 700-year-old abode of the Macleods, where chamber music is performed on summer evenings. It is closed Sundays and mid-October through *Easter;* admission charge (phone: 14714-305). Villages to see are Portree, Skye's harbor and capital, where you can shop and mail postcards (have a bun from *Mackenzie's Bakery* in the main square, too); Stein, a dreamy shell of an 18th-century fishing settlement on the Vaternish Peninsula beside lavish fields of sweet wild orchids; Carbost, fermenting ground of the incomparable Talisker whisky, on the Minginish peninsula; and Broadford and Elgol, at opposite ends of the majestic A881 past the Red Hills and Mt. Blaven on the island's lower wing. Beautiful Elgol, from which Bonnie Prince Charlie left Scotland forever, has boat trips across Loch Scavaig into Loch Coruisk, a favorite subject of Romantic painters. For more information contact the boatman, Mr. MacKinnon (1 Glasnakille; phone: 14716-242).

The *Skye Museum of Island Life* (near *Kilmuir Churchyard;* phone: 147052-279) is one of two noteworthy folk museums on Skye; the other is the *Black House Museum* (phone: 147022-206) on Loch Dunvegan. Both are closed October through *Easter* and charge admission. Glendale, not far from the *Black House,* has a tempting lineup of crafts shops. There's a permanent display on the history of the bagpipes at *Boreraig,* also on Loch Dunvegan (closed October through *Easter;* admission charge). Two of the finer shops are *Ragamuffin* (phone: 14714-217), located at *Armadale Pier,* which has exquisite designer knitwear and clothing for adults and children, and the *Marble Craft Shop* (phone: 14712-500), 2 miles north of Broadford in Portree, which carries sculptures made from beautiful white Skye marble, shot with colored veins.

Tourist board offices at *Meall House,* Portree (phone: 1478-2137; open daily), and in Broadford (phone: 14712-361; closed November through March) have information about climbing and hiking, swimming, fishing, golf, pony trekking, bird watching, sailing, cruising, and dinghy excursions. En route to the neighboring island of Raasay you can see seals, porpoises, and (with luck) bottle-nosed whales. The *Portree Highland Games* and *Dunvegan Piping Competition* both take place in August. The tourist board also has information about *ceilidhs,* traditional Scottish parties with dancing, drinking, singing, and storytelling, held year-round at *Dunvegan Hall.*

Ferries leave the mainland for Skye from Mallaig (no cars during winter), from near Glenelg (in summer), and from Kyle of Lochalsh. Details are available from *Caledonian MacBrayne, Ltd.* (see *Arran,* above), except for the Glenelg run, which is owned by M. A. Mackenzie (phone: 159-982224). Bike rentals are available in Kyle of Lochalsh at *Hebridean Pedal Highways* (phone: 1599-4842) to take across on the ferry. Those who wish to rent a car in Skye can contact Ewan MacRae in Portree (phone: 1478-2554).

Glenview Inn This traditional Scottish-French restaurant has won awards for its Taste of Scotland cooking. Among its most distinguished visitors were James Boswell and Samuel Johnson, who stayed here in 1773 when this place was a pub that took in overnight guests. Closed November through March. Reservations advised. Major credit cards accepted. On the Staffin road (A855), 13 miles north of Portree (phone: 147062-248). Expensive.

Kinloch Lodge The lovely home of Lord and Lady Macdonald (who will immediately insist that you call them Godfrey and Claire). From the 10 cheery, individually decorated guestrooms to the excellent home cooking to the relaxed conversation with other guests before a crackling fire, a stay here is supremely pleasant. Open April through November. Sleat, Isle Ornsay (phone: 14713-333). Expensive.

Three Chimneys Scallops, crab, salmon, and trout are specialties at this award-winning restaurant set in a whitewashed cottage decorated with propped-up wagon wheels. Closed October through March. Reservations advised. Major credit cards accepted. Colbost, beside the *Black House Museum* (phone: 147081-258). Expensive to moderate.

Broadford In business for over 200 years, this serviceable old hotel with 28 rooms exhibits a four-foot Drambuie bottle in its dining room, honoring a past chef who invented the stuff for Bonnie Prince Charlie. Broadford (phone: 14712-205). Moderate.

Coolin Cuillin Hills Situated on its own grounds and overlooking Portree Bay, this old Victorian mansion used to be a hunting lodge of the Macdonald clan. Its 26 rooms have the facilities of a first class hotel; there also is a good restaurant that serves fresh seafood, and a friendly bar that is popular with the locals. Portree (phone: 1478-2003). Moderate.

Eilean Iarmain Unique in its Gaelicness—there's a Gaelic-speaking staff and Gaelic menus—this 19th-century 12-room hotel, owned and run by an Edinburgh banker who also has established a thriving Gaelic college on the island, proffers the local whisky, Té Bheag. The comfortable bar, complete with an open fire, offers views of the magnificent harbor. The food is excellent, and includes many traditional Scottish dishes. Isle Ornsay (phone: 14713-332; fax: 14713-275). Moderate.

Skeabost House Built in Victorian times, and beautifully set at the southernmost tip of a sea loch, this 26-room hostelry is one of the finest on Scotland's islands. The furniture is antique, log fires blaze on the hearth, and the restaurant serves interesting local dishes. A golf course and salmon fishing also are available. Open mid-April through mid-October. Also see *Rural Retreats* in DIVERSIONS. Skeabost Bridge (phone: 147032-202; fax: 147032-454). Moderate.

Ben Tianavaig Bistro The seafood is unsurpassed, and the vegetarian fare makes you want to swear off filet mignon forever. Beautiful views of the harbor are another plus. Open daily. Reservations advised in July and August. Major credit cards accepted. 5 Boswell Ter., Portree (phone: 1478-2152). Moderate to inexpensive.

Fish and Chips Although the surroundings are unassuming, the food is a standout. Gigantic prawns in garlic butter is one of the tastiest dishes at this low-key dining establishment. Closed Sundays. No reservations. No credit cards accepted. Quay St., Portree (no phone). Inexpensive.

MULL AND IONA

MULL The Isle of Mull, the largest of the Inner Hebrides, is pure Brigadoon. The dramatic, deep glens and wooded mountains are magnificent, and the powdery sand beaches are sheltering havens for swimmers. There even is a sunken Spanish galleon in the bay of Tobermory, Mull's main town (its gold doubloons have been the object of many a diving operation). Great waterfalls and ancient hill forts dot the shores, and there are ruined prehistoric towers, called "brochs," one of which is believed to be cursed. Not that the island is unaccustomed to having an eerie reputation—legend has it that when St. Columba drove all the ancient spirits out of Iona, they moved to Mull.

Mull's wild, magical atmosphere has attracted artists from far and wide; painters take to the soil like mushrooms, and craftspeople, including ceramicists, leatherworkers, papermakers, and weavers, produce the finest traditional goods in Scotland. Mull also is an ideal center for touring the surrounding islands, especially Iona and Staffa, site of Fingal's Cave.

To reach Mull from Skye, take the *Caledonian MacBrayne* ferry (see *Arran,* above) to Mallaig. Then take A830 down to Fort William and proceed along the west coast on A82 to Ballachulish. Continue on A828 to Cornwall, and then take A85, which leads directly into Oban. Mull is a 40-minute ferry ride from Oban (the boat departs from Oban's single pier), and stops at Craignure or Tobermory. From either town you can board a bus for any point on the island. We recommend strongly, however, that you rent a car to tour this breathtaking isle, but remember that the roads are very windy and that sheep frequently lie down for a nap in the middle of your path. In Tobermory, *MacKay Garage* (phone: 1688-2103) rents cars, and *Bayview Garage* (phone: 16802-444) and *Mull Travel and Crafts* (phone: 16802-487) in Craignure also have driving vehicles for adventuresome folk. Don't be surprised if road directions seem vague; there are few streets here, and the locals are intimately familiar with the terrain. The tourist office in Tobermory (Main St.; phone: 1688-2182) is open daily; a second office in Craignure (phone: 16802-377) is closed November through March. Both have plenty of helpful information about Mull and Iona.

Among Mull's highlights is the *Old Byre Heritage Centre* (Torlask Rd., Dervaig; phone: 16884-229); there you can get a sense of the oral history of the island, which has passed from generation to generation for literally thousands of years. The center is closed October through *Easter;* admission charge. At the Isle of Mull Wine Company in the Old Towne Smokehouse in Bunessan (phone: 16817-403), visitors can tour the facilities where dry, medium, and sweet vermouths are produced, and taste and purchase the final products. Another must-see is *Duart Castle,* located off A849, which overlooks the Sound of Mull. For centuries, it was the seat of Clan MacLean (it is still the home of the clan chief), and it contains displays of clan memorabilia. The castle is closed October through April; admission charge (phone: 16802-309). *Torosay Castle,* a mile and a half south of Craignure on A849, is a Victorian baronial mansion, with 11 acres that include rock and Japanese gardens and lovely walks. It's closed November through mid-April; admission charge (phone: 16802-421).

BEST EN ROUTE

Western Isles Overlooking Tobermory's colorful harbor, this beauty of a hotel has 28 charmingly appointed guestrooms, and there are golf and fishing facilities practically on the doorstep. Its dining rooms offer good Scottish dishes, as well as a wide selection of rare island whiskies. Open March through December. Tobermory (phone: 1688-2012; fax: 1688-2297). Expensive to moderate.

Back Brae Located just off the main path, right before a hill called the Back Brae, this establishment is known throughout the island for its wonderful, fresh seafood and venison in season. Open daily; no lunch on Sundays. Reservations advised. Major credit cards accepted. Tobermory (phone: 1688-2422). Moderate.

Ceilidhar Local produce is cooked to a delicious turn here, and this is definitely the place to slake a mighty thirst. Open daily. Reservations advised for dinner. Major credit cards accepted. Craignure (phone: 16802-471). Moderate.

Calgary Farmhouse All nine rooms at this cozy inn are well appointed, and the staff is engaging and inordinately helpful. A good restaurant graces the premises. Open March through October. Dervaig, Calgary (phone: 16884-256). Inexpensive.

Tobermory With 17 comfortable rooms (some with harbor views), this hostelry is well known for its good service. Locals love to gather around the pleasant bar for a bit of gossip or amble into the dining rooms for a filling meal. 53 Main St., Tobermory (phone: 1688-2091; fax: 1688-2140). Inexpensive.

IONA Known as the Isle of the Blest, Iona has been considered sacred since before the days of the druids. Scotland's "holy" island is the legendary home of the mystic cauldron of the Celtic world, the forerunner of the Holy Grail, whose magical brew represented the essence of purity in the ancient world. A drink from it was reputed to heal all wounds, revive the dying, and ensure immortality. The island also is sacred to St. Columba, an Irish monk of royal blood who brought Christianity to Scotland in the 5th century, along with quite a bit of political savvy.

If all this isn't enough to intrigue visitors, the Stone of Scone (pronounced *Skoon*), also called the Stone of Destiny, came from Ireland to Iona. The island was the coronation site of Scottish kings for over 300 years; it also was their burial place, along with kings from Ireland, Scandinavia, and France; theory had it that to be buried on Iona guaranteed resurrection when *Judgment Day* arrived. Eventually, Edward I brought the sacred stone to England in an attempt to consolidate his power, and today it rests in *Westminster Abbey* (Scottish legend, however, maintains that it's not the real stone, but only a replica).

In 1979 Scotland was rocked when the Duke of Argyll, longtime owner of the island, decided to put it up for sale; it was as if Lourdes had suddenly appeared in real estate ads in France. After televised debates and a great deal of heated controversy, the *National Trust* acquired Iona and saved it from becoming a center of commercialization; Iona's intoxicating serenity has been largely preserved.

Perhaps the most peculiar aspect of the island is that apart from the well-marked abbey, the cathedral, the ruins of the 13th-century Augustinian nunnery, and the *Bishop's House,* many sites are difficult to find, even with a map. In fact, there are no roads over the northwest or southern third of the island, just springy turf. If you persist in asking directions, however, you should eventually be able to find your way around. Though there is no tourist office on Iona, the Mull tourist offices (see *Mull*) have information on the island. Physically, Iona is unassuming and nearly flat, with a single village that is simply called "the Village." Certainly its power and attraction as a spiritual center belies its gentle, pastoral appearance.

To reach Iona from Mull, take the ferry which travels back and forth (daily) from *Fionnphort Harbour* to the Village port in Iona. If you are particularly inclined to delve into Iona's magical history, visit *St. Oran's Chapel,* located near the abbey and Augustinian nunnery. Not long after the chapel was built, Danes brutally raided the islands and Viking hellion Magnus Barefoot led his forces to Iona with plans to kill the population and plunder its goods. He intended to begin with *St. Oran's,* but when he opened the door of the chapel, he saw something that left him white and shaken. No one knows what it was, but he left the island with little delay and never returned.

BEST EN ROUTE

Argyll This cozy, 19-room hotel overlooks the Iona Sound. The accommodations are extremely comfortable, and the food is hearty, sustaining Scottish fare.

Open April through October. Located near the Village (phone: 168-17334). Moderate to inexpensive.

St. Columba The 23 beautiful rooms of this property overlook serene, verdant lawns with grazing sheep. Traditional Scottish food is offered in the dining room. Located near the cathedral and the abbey (phone: 168-17304). Moderate to inexpensive.

HARRIS

So unspoiled and deserted is Harris, 40 miles off Scotland's northwest coast, that the *Scottish Tourist Board* lists only one Harris entry in its booklet *1001 Things to See in Scotland: St. Clement's Church,* a cruciform building dating from about 1500 (restored in 1873) at Rodel on the island's southern tip. The exquisite carved stonework behind a Macleod chief's tomb shows the Twelve Apostles, a stag hunt, and an angel and devil weighing souls of the dead. Rodel itself is a tiny hamlet with clean-looking cottages and a pond ringed by slopes of mushrooms and wild blue irises. The key to *St. Clement's Church* is at the *Rodel* hotel in the village of Leverburgh.

The lunar landscape of Harris makes it truly different from Lewis, which it adjoins, and the Forest of Harris, which divides the two parts of the island, is a bare mountain range. North Harris is full of mountains, eight of which exceed 2,000 feet; according to geologists these peaks are so old they antedate the separation of the continental landmass from Britain and Ireland and make parvenus of the Alps. Also on Harris are gleaming beaches, green seas, and, on lucky days, a still, clear air bright with the songs of birds. The ranging moors have no roads, and the whole atmosphere is primitive. The only real village—a one-streeter—is Tarbert. On the east coast are rocky shores verdant with "lazy beds," thin half-arable plots once tilled by crofters. The west coast has the almost Mediterranean sands of Luskentyre and Hushinish.

Your Harris survival kit should contain ordnance maps (the best are *Ordnance Survey* maps Nos. 13 and 18, available for £6/about $9 each), a compass, sandwiches, dubbined (oiled) boots, midge repellent, whisky, binoculars, and angling equipment if you fish (tackle is hard to come by on Harris). Bathing suits will be useful only if you like swimming in temperatures that usually don't rise above 55F.

Tarbert is a picture-book townlet with general stores, a harbor, and a vast public vegetable patch, as well as the *Harris Tourist Office* (phone: 1859-2011), which is closed November through *Easter.* Harris tweed jackets for sale dangle from hangers on the outer walls of brightly painted corrugated-iron Tarbert sheds. You also can buy Harris tweed clothing in Stornoway, or the material itself (for £4.80/about $7.20 per yard) from the weavers themselves in Drinishader on the coast farther south. Hard-wearing, made from the wool of Harris sheep, this world-famous fabric was, until recently, hand-spun, hand-dyed, and handwoven on antiquated looms producing only an old-fashioned, narrow cloth length. Today, a Miss Campbell of Plockropool (the village above Drinishader) is the only Harris native who still spins and dyes by hand, though handweaving continues apace.

Toe Head, the outermost point of the small peninsula northwest of Rodel (served by a sand track), is a wilderness full of golden eagles, sheep, and the distinctive and beautiful *machair,* a beach grass vibrant with a species of pale wildflower found only on Hebridean dunes. The trail from B887 past Mt. Uisgnaval More to Loch Voshimid, about 12 miles round trip on foot, is in some weathers very eerie: It's the setting for J. M. Barrie's mystery *Mary Rose. An Clachan* (phone: 185982-370), at Leverburgh on A859, northwest of Rodel, is Harris's main center for local crafts.

Ferries dock at Tarbert from Skye's port of Uig. Details from *Caledonian MacBrayne Ltd.* (see *Arran,* above).

BEST EN ROUTE

Scarista House Once a manse, this delightful eight-room hotel, near Scarista Beach, still has a fine library that's open to residents. Although there's no bar, liquor is served at the restaurant. Open April through October. No credit cards accepted. 15 miles southwest of Tarbert on A859 (phone: 1859-550238; fax: 1859-550277). Expensive.

Harris This faithful 24-room standby lacks the refinement of *Scarista House,* but it provides reasonable (and more accessible) accommodations. It has its own pretty garden and a cozy bar. No credit cards accepted. Tarbert (phone: 1859-502154). Moderate to inexpensive.

Ardvourlie Castle This indescribably romantic, four-room Victorian hunting lodge is set on a deserted moor with portentous mountains looming over it. Only one of the rooms has a private bath (book early to avoid disappointment); there is also a bar, a library, and a restaurant serving innovative Scottish cooking. No credit cards accepted. At Ardvourlie, north of Tarbert on Loch Seaforth (phone: 1859-502307). Inexpensive.

LEWIS

Lewis adjoins Harris, making the combined island 95 miles in length. Lewis, the upper partner, consists of marshy peat bogs and a coastline with 25 beaches. Again, *Ordnance Survey* maps Nos. 13 and 18 will come in handy.

Its center is Stornoway, the only actual town in the Outer Isles. Stornoway has a charming landlocked harbor with a large, tame colony of inquisitive gray seals—you can watch them from the pier. Churches are everywhere, as befits a locale so Sabbath-conscious you can't even buy cigarettes from a machine on Sundays; neither shall ye drink in hotels ye aren't staying at. There's a pleasant square with an attractive *Town Hall* and a huddle of gracious houses on a hill. The *Stornoway Gazette,* with news of local events, comes out on Thursdays. Key shops are *Loch Erisort Woollens* (on Cromwell

St.; phone: 1851-702372) and *Lewis Crofters* (on Island Rd.; phone: 1851-702350), which sells outdoor gear.

The A858 west from Stornoway has Lewis's main attractions, including the *Standing Stones of Callanish,* an elaborate setting of megaliths, unique in Scotland, running *Stonehenge* a close second; *Dun Carloway Broch,* a well-preserved 30-foot Iron Age tower; the *Shawbost Museum and Mill,* illustrating old Lewis folkways (closed Sundays and December through March; no admission charge; phone: 1851-71213); and the *Black House Village,* a clachan, or adjoining series of traditional thatch-roofed huts, that were inhabited till 1960! The village is closed Sundays and October through *Easter;* admission charge. *Lews Castle Gardens* on the west side of *Stornoway Harbour* are worth a visit (open daily; no admission charge); so is *St. Moluag's,* a restored 12th-century Episcopal church with regular Sunday services at the village of Eoropie, near the Butt of Lewis, the island's north tip (ask at the general store in the village for the key). On the Eye Peninsula to Stornoway's east is *Ui Chapel,* a picturesque ruin of a former priory. *An Lanntair* (phone: 1851-703307), the Western Isles' first permanent art gallery, is on the second floor of *Stornoway Town Hall.* It has changing exhibitions in both English and Gaelic, along with theater productions and musical presentations emphasizing Gaelic culture. The gallery is closed Sundays; no admission charge.

The *Western Isles Tourist Board* (4 S. Beach St., Stornoway; phone: 1851-703088; fax: 1851-705244) offers advice on sailing, fishing, hiking (Uig, in the west, is a good place), and bird watching (Tiumpan Head on the Eye Peninsula has plenty of petrels and kittiwakes); it is open daily. Most of Lewis can be explored by bus, although schedules are extremely erratic. Contact the tourist board for information on bus routes. It also has a leaflet detailing Hebridean crafts and crafts shops: consider buying a handmade set of Lewis Chessmen, modeled on four ancient sets discovered under Uig sands in 1831. Scandinavian in design, carved from walrus tusks and stained red on one side, the originals are thought to have been buried in the 12th century by a shepherd after he murdered a sailor whose ship, carrying the chessmen, ran aground. The *British Museum* in London has the originals today. A book on Lewis Chessmen is available at the *Western Isles Tourist Office.*

Lewis has pretty much taken over the Harris tweed industry; the trade was revived in the crofts a few years back when many farmers found that the profits on their crops were insufficient to keep body and soul together, and set up makeshift looms to work the hand-spun cloth. You can purchase the beautifully wrought cloth at bargain prices all over the island.

Sea-angling competitions are a summer highlight here, with the Western Isles and the Highlands and Islands *Open Boat Championships* in July or August.

Ferries to Stornoway leave from Ullapool on the northwest Scottish mainland: for further information contact *Caledonian MacBrayne, Ltd.* in

Gourock (see *Arran,* above); or you can drive right into Lewis from Harris. *British Airways* and *Loganair* fly to Stornoway from Glasgow and Inverness. The *Western Isles Tourist Board* (see above) is helpful in arranging accommodations (including renting apartments for stays of a week or more) and booking bus tours.

BEST EN ROUTE

Seaforth Here's a 56-room downtown establishment with a nightly movie, disco, restaurant, and cabaret. James St., Stornoway (phone: 1851-702740; fax: 1851-703900). Expensive.

Crown Hospitality is an important feature of this fine 15-room hotel overlooking the harbor and the pier. There's a good restaurant, too. Castle St., Stornoway (phone: 1851-703734). Moderate.

Cabarfeidh This outstanding property (whose name is pronounced Cab-er-*fay*) is the island's best—and its prices are reasonable. Nestled on its own grounds on the outskirts of Stornoway, near the ferry terminal and airport, it boasts 45 well-appointed guestrooms, a good restaurant serving roast meat and seafood, and a cheerful bar that is a center of social activity. *Manor Park,* Stornoway (phone: 1851-702604; fax: 1851-705572). Moderate.

Raebhat House While the vegetarian dishes served at this genteel establishment are quite good, the real draw is the fine wine list and the local whisky. Many of the brews offered here are only found in Scotland. An antique fireplace and wood paneling create an inviting atmosphere. Open daily. Reservations advised. Major credit cards accepted. Shawbost (phone: 1851-71588). Moderate.

Tigh Mealvos This beautiful traditional home with antique furnishings has a welcoming atmosphere, and guests even have access to a working croft. All five guestrooms are nicely decorated, and there's a communal children's play area. Nearby trout and sea angling jaunts also can be arranged. Na H-Aabhine, Callanish (phone: 1851-72333). Inexpensive.

ORKNEY

Orkney comprises about 70 islands, some 29 of which are inhabited. Throughout the whole cluster lie chambered cairns, traces of 78 brochs, rings of standing stones, and vestiges of prehistoric villages. Many are extensive survivals, making Orkney the archaeological treasure house of Great Britain.

Several pre-Pictish peoples lived on Orkney, then Picts, then Vikings. Strangely none of the races they conquered are mentioned by the Vikings in their remarkable medieval epic and folk history, the *Orkneyinga Saga,* a product of Orkney's Golden Age. Washington Irving's father was an Orkney sailor and James Russell Lowell's forebears included two Orcadian clans.

More sunshine bathes Orkney (and Shetland, farther north) than almost anywhere else in Britain, and there are bright-hued farmhouses, green fields, primroses, violets, golden sands, and cliff-top sea-pinks. Fulmars, cormorants, Manx shearwaters, petrels, gulls, kittiwakes, guillemots, puffins, and gannets abound. On country strolls watch out for bulls. Hotels should be booked several months in advance, as there are few of them.

Orkney's two centers of civilization are Stromness and Kirkwall on the largest island, the so-called Mainland. Stromness, in the west, is a small 18th-century port that hasn't changed since its founding; it's full of charm and its main street snakes along the sea. The *Pier Arts Centre* (on Victoria St.; phone: 1856-850209) contains an internationally famous display of works by Ben Nicolson and Barbara Hepworth. It is closed Sundays and Mondays; no admission charge. The *Stromness Museum* (52 Alfred St.; phone: 1856-850025) has a curio collection that derives from local history. It is closed Sundays and during February; admission charge. *Stromness Books and Prints* (on Graham Pl.; phone: 1856-850565) is well worth a browse (limited hours).

Kirkwall, in the east, is the island capital and site of *St. Magnus Cathedral,* Orkney's pride. The cathedral is an impressive 12th-century pink sandstone Norman building still in use, the burial place of St. Magnus, Orkney's patron saint. Take care in Kirkwall's ancient streets, which wind narrowly and seem like pedestrian precincts—till cars belt down them at full throttle! A thriving stone-built town with crow-stepped gabled houses and old-fashioned shops painted berry and peach, Kirkwall also has *Earl Patrick's Palace,* the imposing remains of an accomplished piece of Renaissance architecture belonging originally to a wicked Stuart earl, a nephew of Mary, Queen of Scots; the *Bishop's Palace,* a 13th-century ruin with an ascendable 16th-century round tower (no admission charge); *Tankerness House,* a 16th-century merchant-laird's mansion and museum of 4,000 years of Orkney life (open daily; admission charge); the Highland Park Distillery, which has opened a visitors' center and gives tours of its nearly 200-year-old special processes (and free sips of its whisky), weekdays *Easter* through September, and Tuesdays through Thursdays in March and October (admission charge); and *Robert Towers's Workshop* (at Rosegarth, St. Ola; phone: 1856-853521), a manufacturer of traditional Orcadian tall-backed, straw-weave chairs, which also are sold here. Behind Kirkwall on Wideford Hill the view is a superb pastiche of bays and islets.

In a knot in mid-Mainland near the Harray and Stenness lochs are three venerable marvels: *Maeshowe,* the *Standing Stones of Stenness,* and the *Ring of Brodgar. Maeshowe,* the finest chambered cairn in Western Europe, was constructed around 1800 BC, and is entered by crawling through a narrow downward-sloping tunnel. Viking marauders wrote the runic inscriptions in the cells. In midwinter, dusk's last shaft of sunlight strikes one of the dark entombing walls, a deeply moving sight. The *Standing Stones of Stenness*—four are still upright—are part of a circle dating from 3000 BC;

the *Ring of Brodgar,* 340 feet in diameter, boasts 36 stones of its original 60. Also on the Mainland are *Skara Brae,* a Neolithic complex with a paved courtyard, covered passages, and 10 one-room houses full of "built-in" stone furniture; *Gurness Broch,* over 10 feet high, surrounded by stone huts and inhabited well into Viking times; *Click Mill,* the only operative example of old-style horizontal-wheeled Orkney water power (wear rubber boots, it's in a bog); *Corrigall Farm Museum,* showing old Orkney folkways (closed October through March; admission charge; phone: 1856-771411); and Birsay, a quaint village with another ruined palace of the Stuart earls. Opposite Birsay is the Brough of Birsay, an adorable island and beachcombers' delight (accessible only at low tide), where you'll find the remains of a Romanesque church and of Pictish and Nordic settlements.

Hoy, Orkney's most romantic island, is famous for its strange offshore rock formation, the Old Man of Hoy, a supreme test for rock climbers. Hoy has hills, gaunt high cliffs, and wild unpopulated valleys. There's only one road, along the east coast, passing the Martello towers built in 1812 to protect against attack by American ships. Attainable by tramping inland is panoramic Ward Hill, Orkney's highest point at 1,565 feet, near the site of a supposedly haunted Neolithic sepulcher called the *Dwarfie Stone*—this overlooks the beautiful half-deserted hamlet of Rackwick, Peter Maxwell Davies's home. If you go to Hoy, bring a picnic; there's almost nowhere to buy food.

The island of South Ronaldsay, completely different from Hoy, is another good place to go; you can drive to it from near Kirkwall via the island-hopping Churchill Causeway, erected in 1939-40 to protect the adjacent waterway of Scapa Flow, then a naval base. En route at the island of Lamb Holm is the ornate *Italian Chapel,* built from a mere Nissen hut by Italian World War II prisoners and affectionately preserved to this day by admiring Orcadians. It was near Scapa Flow in 1916 that Lord Kitchener's ship, the *Hampshire,* was blown up by a German mine with him on board, and there three years later that the German fleet heroically scuttled itself in World War I. Hoxa Head, the entrance to Scapa Flow, is a fascinating surreal jumble of half-sunk hulks and wartime concrete barriers. A brisk trade in boat hire and deep-sea-diving equipment rental has sprung up around this maritime graveyard; ask at the tourist offices (see below) for more information. Also on South Ronaldsay is St. Margaret's Hope, an idyllic coastal settlement popular with artists and craftsmen, an excellent place to shop for handmade goods. The *Wireless Museum* offers displays relating to wartime communications. It is closed October through March; admission charge. The museum has no phone of its own; for more information, contact the curator, Mr. MacDonald (phone: 1856-873146).

Two tourist board offices (Broad St., Kirkwall; phone: 1856-872856; and the *Ferry Terminal Building,* Stromness; phone: 1856-850716) have data on the rest of Orkney's islands and archaeology and on interesting natural features you can explore. Both are open daily. Also available are tips on fishing, golf, deep-sea diving, crafts (potters are plentiful), walks, sailing, swimming, bird watching, and island-to-island travel. Many British seafowl nest in Orkney May through July; their favorite places include the deserted islands of Copinsay and Eynhallow, the Mainland cliffs at Marwick, and the bird reserve on Westray at Noup Head. Local events are published Thursdays in the *Orcadian,* available at newsstands.

Twice each winter, on *Christmas Day* and *New Year's Day,* Kirkwall's annual *Ba' Games* are played (they're just like the Jedburgh ones—see the *Southeast Scotland* route, also in this section). The *Orkney Traditional Folk Festival* in late May is another major event (see *Best Festivals* in DIVERSIONS). Other fetes include the internationally important *St. Magnus Festival of the Arts* in June; the *Stromness Shopping Week* in late July, when all Orkney comes to Stromness for seven days of fetes, dances, and general merriment; and Kirkwall's *County Show,* a major agricultural fair in August.

A two-hour car-ferry route links Stromness with Scrabster, near Thurso on the Scottish mainland. For details contact *P&O Ferries Terminal* (*Pierhead,* Stromness; phone: 1856-850655) or *Jamieson's Quay* (Aberdeen; phone: 1224-572615). Besides regular services, including an eight-hour Aberdeen-to-Stromness crossing every Saturday, *P&O* offers special motorists' package tours. *Thomas and Bews Ferries* (phone: 1955-81353) offers service from John O'Groats to Burwick, where buses meet the ferry. They provide a free bus from the Thurso train and offer reduced rates for the afternoon ferry. *British Airways* flies every day but Sunday out of London, Glasgow, Edinburgh, and Inverness to connect in Aberdeen for *Kirkwall Airport,* and *Loganair* (phone: 1856-872421) has connecting flights out of London, Edinburgh, and Wick to *Kirkwall* (weekdays only). Summer coach tours of major Orkney sights are organized by *James Peace* (Junction Rd., Kirkwall; phone: 1856-872866). *Go Orkney* (6 Old Scapa Rd. Kirkwall; phone: 1856-874260), a tour company headed by David Lea, an expert on the archaeology and wildlife of the area, runs coach tours through the Orkney mainland from mid-March through late October. *Maui Diving Center* runs fully equipped diving trips to the sunken German fleet in Scapa Flow and to the Northern Isles (phone: 1856-850434). Trout fishing packages can be arranged through *Orkney Trout Holidays* (phone: 1856-850077), and the *Orkney Sea Angling Association* (phone: 1856-821311) provides listings for sea angling trips. Horesback riding and trekking to ancient monuments can be arranged with the *Cruesday Trekking Centre* (phone: 1856-82236).

For the dedicated shopper, Orkney offers a spectacular array of crafts, from hand-blown glass to knitted woolens to gold and silver jewelry fashioned in Nordic designs. *Eday Spinners* (Blett Studio, Calf Sound; phone: 18572-248) uses select local fleeces and combines them with silk, mohair, and alpaca. Ceramics designed in the Viking tradition are offered at *Fursbreck Pottery* (on Harray; phone: 1856-877419). *Orcadian Crafts* (8 Bridge St., Rousey; phone: 1856-828461) is another good bet for ceramics, as is *The Quernstone* (38 Victoria St., Stronmess; phone: 1856-851010). A gold (and silver) mine of jewelry is at *The Longship* (7-9 Broad St., Kirkwall; phone: 1856-872846), and a whole range of crafts can be found at the *Shapinsay Community Enterprise Group* (Smithy on Shapinsay; phone: 1856-71389).

BEST EN ROUTE

Hamnavoe With an extensive variety of international dishes, this spot already has found its way into various good food guides. Closed Thursdays and during January. Reservations necessary. Major credit cards accepted. 35 Graham Pl., Stromness (phone: 1856-850606). Expensive to moderate.

Ayre This beautiful 200-year-old establishment provides 26 pleasantly furnished rooms, some with romantic views of the sea. Its fine restaurant makes the most of the rich Orkney harvest, producing dishes such as sweet island lamb with giant vegetables. Nightly entertainment in the bar livens the atmosphere considerably. 100 Ayre Rd., Kirkwall (phone: 1856-873001; fax: 1856-876289). Moderate.

Creel This award-winning dining room overlooks the harbor; the open coal fire provides a cozy, intimate atmosphere. A wide choice of local seafood and roasts is on the menu. Open for dinner only; closed Mondays and Tuesdays year-round, Sundays through Thursdays in November and February, and during January. Reservations unnecessary. Major credit cards accepted. St. Margaret's Hope, south of Kirkwall (phone: 1856-83311). Moderate.

Merkister Here is an exceptionally serene 15-room hotel on Loch Harray that caters to trout fishermen, bird watchers, and those who appreciate a great meal (the restaurant and wine cellar are both exceptional). Open April through October. Harray (phone: 1856-877366). Moderate.

Towiston Mill Another award winner; fine fare, huge portions, and sumptuous high teas are offered. Closed Mondays and Tuesdays and October through March. Reservations unnecessary. Major credit cards accepted. Stenness (phone: 1856-76372). Moderate.

Binnacle You guessed it, the theme is nautical. In the *Commodore* motel, it serves a good selection of locally caught seafood and produce; its steaks are notable, too. Open daily. Reservations necessary. Major credit cards accepted. St. Mary's on Holm, south of Kirkwall (phone: 1856-78319). Moderate to inexpensive.

St. Ola This charming, brick, harbor-front hotel has six cozy rooms, a restaurant, and a bar that is the local watering hole. Harbour St., Kirkwall (phone: 1856-5090). Moderate to inexpensive.

Foveran Near Kirkwall, this comfortable, modern, eight-room place has a restaurant that's famous for its local seafood—particularly smoked salmon—as well as its candied pears with Stilton sauce. Closed *Christmas* and January. St. Ola, overlooking Scapa Flow (phone: 1856-872389; fax: 1856-876430). Inexpensive.

SHETLAND

"Ultima Thule" sounds like the name of a "Star Trek" character, but in fact it's what the Romans called Shetland. Nothing lies between Shetland and the Arctic Circle. Lerwick, Shetland's capital, is much farther from Edinburgh than Edinburgh is from London; it's over 60 miles from Kirkwall. The famous north Shetland outpost, the *Muckle Flugga Lighthouse,* poised on faces of sheer, almost vertical rock, is Britain's last window on the world (alas, it's closed to the public).

Shetland's 100 islands (only three are of any size) are chilly even in summer. Winters are very dark but May, June, and July nights are aglow with the "simmer dim," a beautiful horizontal twilight lasting several hours, the nearest thing to a midnight sun—everything under its luminous rays looks phosphorescent. Although the dark winters are known for producing an inordinate amount of stress and depression in Scandinavia, ask about winter in Shetland and everybody gets excited. That's when festivities are at a high point, and locals consider anyone who can't stay up all night drinking and dancing and then work the next day a terrible wet blanket. There are no rivers on Shetland, but there are sparkling streamlets, lily-bright lochans (small lakes), and bays jeweled with waving sea pinks. The sea is inescapable, for you always can see or hear it; Lerwick rises right out of it as if in a fairy tale—houses, stone steps, ramp-shaped flagstone alleys, and all; nets and fishing boats are everywhere and the raucous cry of seabirds splits the air (300 bird species nest in Shetland, lining up colony by colony on rock cliff shelves). Fortunately, the oil spill created by the 1993 wreck of the tanker *Braer* off Shetland's coast so far appears to have had only a minimal impact on this island's precious ecosystem; only 20 miles of the islands' huge coastline were affected. Life on the islands continues largely as it has for generations, with great tracts of land given over to grazing Shetland ponies and the special small sheep that provide the wool for the famous sweaters.

Vikings dominated Shetland as long as 13 centuries ago, though other settlers were on the scene 1,000 years before that, as you'll see on the Mainland's south tip at Jarlshof, a fascinating sunken city with overlayers from three prehistoric civilizations. Orkney's archaeological treasures are older, but it's Shetland that clings to primitive forms: Shetland ponies are still reared on common landholdings, and Lerwick is in a way another Jarlshof with its arrow-thin streets, wharves, and clusters of stone homes and warehouses. Commercial Street, Lerwick's main thoroughfare, is anything but a boulevard—yet it has its own glamour.

In pre-Victorian days when half the fishing fleet of Holland put in at Shetland after sailing the North Sea, Lerwick was a smugglers' nest and an almost European city. Explore Shetland's history at the *Shetland Museum* (Lower Hillhead; phone: 1595-5057; closed Sundays; no admission charge); and the *Lerwick Harbor Trust* (in the Albert Building on the Esplanade;

phone: 1595-2991), which focuses on the seafaring aspects of the island. It is open daily; no admission charge. Other Lerwick attractions are *Fort Charlotte,* built in 1665 to protect the Sound of Bressay from the Dutch; *Lerwick Town Hall,* a Scots-baronial building with stained glass windows and a climbable tower; and Clickhimin Broch, an ancient 17-foot stronghold within the remains of an Iron Age stone fort. The *Shetland Workshop Gallery* (4-6 Burns La.; phone: 1595-3343) has native crafts for sale: sealskin handbags, silver and polished stone jewelry, sweaters, and Shetland shawls.

Yell and Unst are the largest islands after Shetland's biggest, Mainland; they continue north from Mainland in that order and are easily accessible. On Unst is *Mu Ness Castle,* constructed from rubble in the 16th century with an amazing eye for architectural detail. The prettiest Shetland islands are Bressay, Whalsay, Noss, Fetlar, Foula, the Out Skerries and Muckle Roe. Foula, 30 miles west of Mainland, is the most isolated and therefore perhaps most exciting—it's served twice a week by a regular passenger line (no cars) and by *Loganair* (ask at the airstrip at Tingwall; phone: 1595-84246). But close your eyes, touch your map, and go where your finger falls! The islands are *all* pretty and there's no place you can't get by hiring a boatman, unless the weather's too rough—ask at the *Lerwick Tourist Office* (Market Cross; phone: 1595-3434; fax: 1595-5807; open daily), or at outlying coastal pubs.

The tiny seal-haunted island of Mousa opposite Sandwick on the east Mainland (7 miles south of Lerwick) holds *Mousa Broch,* at a princely 40 feet high; some say it's the best broch in Britain. To get ferried across (a 15-minute ride), call Tom Jamieson at 1950-5367. St. Ninian's Isle, not an island but a small south Mainland peninsula, is famous for white sands and the priceless 5th-century silver plate unearthed there on a Dark Age church site in 1958. Other Mainland must-sees are the *Croft Museum* of 19th-century Shetland life on A970 at South Voe (phone: 1595-5057; closed October through April; admission charge); the *Ness of Burgi,* an Iron Age defensive stone structure near the southern town of Sumburgh; and *Stanleydale,* a Neolithic heel-shaped edifice containing an oval chamber, at the western hamlet of Walls. The ruins of *Scalloway Castle,* dating from 1600 and featuring a flamboyant corbel-turreted medieval style, overlook Scalloway, the unbelievably picturesque west coast Mainland fishing village that once was Shetland's capital.

Geological wonders of Shetland, reachable by boat, include "Orkneymen's caves," with narrow entrances but grand as cathedrals inside (the best is the stalactite-filled Cave of Bressay, and there are lots along the coast of the island of Papa Stour); the sea-filled, once natural-bridged Holes of Scrada on the Mainland's northwesterly Esha Ness peninsula (you view these on foot); the Grind of the Navir, also at Esha Ness, where waves have ripped off huge cubic rock hunks and carried them 180 feet; and the Bressay Giant's Leg.

For ornithologists and simple bird fanciers, a visit to Fair Isle is a must. About 750,000 birds make their homes here, and there is an observatory where you can get a good vantage point. The small *Fair Isle Lodge* (see *Best en Route*) provides comfortable accommodations. *Loganair* flies to Fair Isle twice daily from Shetland's *Tingwall Airport.*

The *Lerwick Tourist Office* (see above) has information on fishing, deep-sea diving, crafts, and bird watching. Unst is a good place to see Icelandic owls. Fetlar is now a 1,400-acre statutory bird reserve; other ornithological havens are the islands of Foula, Noss, and Haaf Gruney, the Pool of Virkie on Mainland's south tip, and Hermaness on Unst opposite the *Muckle Flugga Lighthouse.*

"Up-Helly-Aa," a dramatic boat-burning ceremony celebrating the return of the sun, dates from pagan times and is still performed in Shetland on the last Tuesday in January using traditional Viking costumes and boats (also see *Best Festivals* in DIVERSIONS). In addition, a *Shetland Folk Festival* in late April or early May gives full rein to Shetland fiddlers, admired by all of Scotland; the *Lerwick Midsummer Carnival* in mid-June features a parade of floats and dancing in the streets; the *Viking International Festival* at Lerwick in September is a major sea-angling competition. The *Shetland Times,* published Fridays, has news of other events.

Two of the finest shops in the area are *J. G. Rae* (92 Commercial St., Lerwick; phone: 1595-3686), for exquisite gold and silver jewelry in Celtic and Norse designs, and *The Spider's Web* (41 Commercial St., Lerwick; phone: 1595-3299), which offers delicately hand-knit sweaters as well as spinning and knitting lessons.

P&O Ferries (phone: 1595-4848 or 595-5252) runs an overnight route from Aberdeen directly to Lerwick, weekdays; on weekends it makes a stop at Orkney. Flights into Shetland are frequent; *British Airways* has flights from the major Scottish airports (at least four every weekday from Aberdeen alone) and from *Kirkwall Airport,* and *Loganair* zooms direct daily from Edinburgh to a small landing strip at *Tingwall.*

BEST EN ROUTE

Shetland Situated directly opposite the ferry docks is Shetland's largest hotel, with 66 rooms. It contains all the facilities of a modern hotel, including an indoor pool, a fitness center, a solarium, a sauna, a bar, and a restaurant. Lerwick (phone: 1595-5515; fax: 1595-5828). Expensive.

Busta House Though its specialty is traditional Scottish food, its location—in a splendid 400-year-old country house overlooking the picturesque Busta Voe fjord and harbor 23 miles north of Lerwick—also is special. It has the full range of amenities in its 21 rooms; you can even light a peat fire in your room. Brae (phone: 1806-22506; fax: 1806-22588). Expensive to moderate.

Burrastow House In a renovated building dating back to 1759, this excellent two-room inn has a distinguished reputation for its eclectic fare: game, roasts, seafood, and vegetarian dishes. There's also a lovely view of nearby Vaila

Sound. Closed Tuesdays, mid-October through mid-November, January, and February. Reservations necessary. Major credit cards accepted. Walls (phone: 159571-307). Moderate.

Da Peerie Fisk Prime Angus beef, grilled Shetland lamb, and roasted chicken are the delicious mainstays of the menu at this friendly dining spot. An extensive wine list is the pride of the establishment, and a special children's menu is also available. Closed November through March. Reservations advised. No credit cards accepted. Busta Brae (phone: 180622-679). Moderate.

Fair Isle Lodge The only overnight lodgings on Fair Isle, this place offers six single rooms, six doubles, and two family-size suites. While the accommodations are short on amenities (no private baths or TV sets), they are comfortable and clean. All meals at the good Scottish restaurant are included in the rate. On Fair Isle (phone: 1595-84246). Moderate.

St. Magnus Another fine example of Shetland's many picturesque places. Built of pine and spruce in a traditional Scandinavian clapboard style, the 26-room hotel overlooks St. Magnus Bay on one side and West Beach Bay on the other. The restaurant has won several awards for its outstanding Scottish food. Open daily. Reservations necessary. Major credit cards accepted. Hillswick (phone: 1806-23372; fax: 1806-23373). Moderate.

Baltasound This 10-room hybrid is, on the whole, more modern extension than grand old Victorian abode. There's a restaurant and a big bar with attractive local posters. Baltasound, Unst (phone: 195781-334). Inexpensive.

Westings Another contemporary hostelry based in an old building but with a distinctly Scandinavian appeal, it has six rooms and a large bar. Views of the fjords and islands are panoramic, and the peaks of Foula are visible to the west. The service is friendly and the food is good. Wormadale, near Whiteness, Mainland (phone: 159584-242). Inexpensive.

Glossary

Words to the Wise

"Two people divided by the same language" is how Oscar Wilde described the transatlantic relationship between Britain and the US. He had a point. Below are some common British terms followed by their standard American translations. For definitions of terms that do not necessarily have American equivalents—such as "bubble and squeak" (a dish of cold meat fried with chopped vegetables) and "royal duke" (a duke who, as a member of the royal family, is also a prince)—consult *An A to Z of British Life: Dictionary of Britain,* by Adrian Room (Oxford University Press, Customer Service, 2001 Evans Rd., Cary, NC 27513; phone: 800-451-7556; fax: 919-677-1303). It can also take the mystery out of the local newspapers by supplying the meanings of all sorts of British acronyms, from *CAMRA* (Campaign for Real Ale) to *USDAW* (Union of Shop, Distributive, and Allied Workers).

The following words and phrases should help you:

anorak	parka
aubergine	eggplant
bank holiday	any legal holiday
basin	any bowl
bathroom	for baths, not a toilet
beer	Always order a type of beer, never just "beer."
bitter	a dark, dry beer
lager	American-style beer
light ale	sweet lager
pale ale	light-colored ale
shandy	beer mixed with lemonade or a soft drink
stout	a dark, sweetish beer
bespoke	custom-tailored
bill	restaurant check; also can refer to the police
Biro	ballpoint pen
biscuit	cookie or cracker
block (of flats)	apartment house
bonnet (car)	hood
boot (car)	trunk
braces	suspenders
brolly	umbrella
Brummie	person from Birmingham
busker	street musician
café (often pronounced "caff")	cheap restaurant, greasy spoon

candy floss	cotton candy
car park	parking lot
caravan	RV, mobile home
carriage	rail car
chemist's	pharmacy
cheers	to your health
chips	French fries
Christian name	first name
City, the (in London)	equivalent to American Wall Street
clotted cream	very thick sweet cream
coach	long-distance bus
cold (drinks)	cool, not iced
corn	any edible grain
cot	baby's crib
cotton	thread
cotton wool	absorbent cotton
crisps	potato chips
crumpet	English muffin
cul-de-sac	dead end
cupboard	closet
double cream	very heavy sweet cream
dual carriageway	divided highway
dynamo (car)	generator
egg flip	eggnog
first floor	second floor
flannel	washcloth
flat	apartment
flyover	overpass
fortnight	two weeks
gallon (British)	about 1.2 US gallons
galoshes	short rubber boots
garden	yard
gear lever	gearshift
grammar school	selective middle school
guinea	one pound plus five pence
hat trick	three successive wins
high tea	tea plus light supper
hire purchase	installment plan
hoarding	billboard
hogmanay	Scottish *New Year*
hood (car)	soft top of a convertible
hoot	a laugh, a riot
Hoover	vacuum cleaner
hump	carry something heavy

ice	ice cream
ironmonger	hardware store
jelly	gelatin dessert (Jell-O)
joint (meat)	roast
jumper (or jersey)	sweater
kettle	teakettle
knickers	panties
ladder	a run in pantyhose
left luggage office	baggage room
lemon squash	lemon-flavored drink diluted with water
lift	elevator
Liverpudlian	person from Liverpool
loo, lavatory, WC	toilet
lorry	truck
mackintosh, mac	raincoat
Mancunian	person from Manchester
marrow	an oversize zucchini
mince, minced meat	ground meat (usually beef)
mod cons	modern conveniences
nappy	diaper
newsagents	newspaper store
nipple	*not* of a baby's bottle (anatomical meaning only); see *teat*
nosh	food; can also mean to eat
off licence/wine merchant	liquor store
on special offer	on sale
overtake	pass while driving
panto	*Christmas* song-and-dance show
pants	underpants (never use to refer to trousers)
petrol	gasoline
plimsolls	sneakers
pram	baby carriage
pub grub	traditional English pub fare
public school	private school
queue	line of people
queue up	to stand in line
quid	pound (currency)
rasher	slice of bacon
reception	front desk
return ticket	round-trip ticket
ring	to telephone
roundabout	traffic circle
rubber	eraser

saloon bar	more comfortable room in pub
schooner	large sherry glass
Scouser	person from Liverpool
serviette	napkin
shepherd's pie	mashed potato and ground meat pie
shop	small store
sick	nauseous (not ill in general)
silencer (car)	muffler
single ticket	one-way ticket
spanner	wrench
stalls (theater)	orchestra seats
starkers	naked
starters	hors d'oeuvres
stone	measure of weight equal to 14 pounds
store	department store
surgery	doctor's or dentist's office
sweet	candy and/or dessert
ta	thanks
ta-ta	good-bye
take-away	take-out
teat	baby-bottle nipple
telly	television
tights	pantyhose
to let	to rent
trainers	sneakers
trousers	never called pants
trunk call	long distance call
underground, tube	subway
VAT	Value Added Tax (sales tax)
vest	man's undershirt
wally	a fool
wellingtons or wellies	rubber boots
whisky	Scotch whisky only
windscreen	windshield
wireless	radio
yard	paved area
zebra crossing	pedestrian crosswalk
Z	pronounced "zed"

Climate Chart

AVERAGE TEMPERATURES (IN °F)

	January	*April*	*July*	*October*
Aberdeen, Scotland	36–43	40–49	52–63	43–54
Bath, England	38–49	40–54	54–67	41–52
Birmingham, England	36–41	41–54	54–68	45–56
Bournemouth, England	36–45	41–56	56–70	47–59
Brighton, England	43–49	43–56	58–65	47–52
Bristol, England	40–47	38–56	54–67	45–58
Cambridge, England	36–45	40–56	54–72	43–58
Canterbury, England	38–49	41–54	58–68	43–54
Cardiff, Wales	36–45	41–56	54–68	47–58
Chester, England	38–45	40–54	54–68	45–58
Edinburgh, Scotland	34–43	40–52	52–65	45–54
Glasgow, Scotland	34–41	40–54	52–67	43–56
Liverpool, England	36–45	41–52	56–67	47–56
London, England	36–45	40–56	56–72	45–58
Norwich, England	37–47	41–54	56–70	43–54
Oxford, England	34–45	41–58	54–72	45–58
Perth, Scotland	31–43	38–54	52–68	41–56
Stratford-upon-Avon, England	36–47	41–56	52–76	43–59
York, England	36–47	41–54	58–72	43–56

Weights and Measures

APPROXIMATE EQUIVALENTS

	Metric Unit	Abbreviation	US Equivalent
Length	1 millimeter	mm	.04 inch
	1 meter	m	39.37 inches
	1 kilometer	km	.62 mile
Capacity	1 liter	l	1.057 quarts
Weight	1 gram	g	.035 ounce
	1 kilogram	kg	2.2 pounds
	1 metric ton	MT	1.1 tons
Temperature	0° Celsius	C	32° Fahrenheit

CONVERSION TABLES

METRIC TO US MEASUREMENTS

	Multiply:	by:	to convert to:
Length	millimeters	.04	inches
	meters	3.3	feet
	meters	1.1	yards
	kilometers	.6	miles
Capacity (liquid)	liters	2.11	pints
	liters	1.06	quarts
	liters	.26	gallons
Weight	grams	.04	ounces
	kilograms	2.2	pounds

US TO METRIC MEASUREMENTS

	Multiply:	by:	to convert to:
Length	inches	25.0	millimeters
	feet	.3	meters
	yards	.9	meters
	miles	1.6	kilometers
Capacity	pints	.47	liters
	quarts	.95	liters
	gallons	3.8	liters
Weight	ounces	28.0	grams
	pounds	.45	kilograms

SPECIAL MEASUREMENTS

	British	US
Weight	stone	14 pounds
Capacity	Imperial gallon	1.2 US gallons

TEMPERATURE

Celsius to Fahrenheit	(°C x 9/5) + 32 = °F
Fahrenheit to Celsius	(°F - 32) x 5/9 = °C

Index